A CRITICAL EDITION OF ANTHONY MUNDAY'S

Palmerin d'Oliva

Medieval and Renaissance
Texts and Studies

Volume 534

A CRITICAL EDITION OF ANTHONY MUNDAY'S

Palmerin d'Oliva

*Edited with
An introduction, critical apparatus,
Notes, and glossary by*

Jordi Sánchez-Martí

Arizona Center
for Medieval &
Renaissance Studies

Tempe, Arizona
2020

 Arizona Center for Medieval & Renaissance Studies

Published by ACMRS (Arizona Center for Medieval and Renaissance Studies)
Tempe, Arizona
© 2020 Arizona Board of Regents for Arizona State University.
All Rights Reserved.

Library of Congress Cataloging-in-Publication Data

Names: Munday, Anthony, 1553-1633. | Sánchez-Martí, Jordi, editor.
Title: A critical edition of Anthony Munday's Palmerin d'Oliva / edited with an introduction, critical apparatus, notes and glossary by Jordi Sánchez-Martí.
Other titles: Palmerin de Oliva (Romance). English.
Description: Tempe : Arizona Center for Medieval and Renaissance Studies, 2020. | Series: Medieval and Renaissance texts and studies; 534 | Includes bibliographical references and index. | Summary: "This is an accurate and fully annotated text of the first romance in the Palmerin cycle, which was translated into English (from a French version) by Anthony Munday, who has also been the focus of much critical interest recently"-- Provided by publisher.
Identifiers: LCCN 2020002406 | ISBN 9780866985918 (hardcover)
Classification: LCC PQ6419 .P6 2020 | DDC 863/.2--dc23
LC record available at https://lccn.loc.gov/2020002406

Cover Illustration:
The exposure of Palmerin d'Oliva.
Le premier livre du Palmerin d'Olive (Paris, 1546), sig. C1r.
London, BL, shelfmark 12403.i.16.
© The British Library.

∞
This book is made to last. It is set in Adobe Caslon Pro,
smyth-sewn and printed on acid-free paper to library specifications.
Printed in the United States of America

A mon pare,

*José Nicanor Sánchez Blanco
(1929–2015)*

In Memoriam

Contents

List of Illustrations	*xix*
Preface	*xxi*
Abbreviations	*xxv*
Introduction	1
The Iberian romances of chivalry	1
The Spanish *Palmerín de Olivia*	19
The European distribution of *Palmerin d'Oliva*	28
The publication of the English *Palmerin d'Oliva*	41
Anthony Munday: A literary biography of *Palmerin d'Oliva*'s translator	52
Munday's translation of *Palmerin d'Oliva*	77

Palmerin d'Oliva

Part One

The Epistle Dedicatorie	102
To the corteous Readers	103
I. *Of the secrete loue which the Prince Tarisius bare to the yong Princesse Griana: and the arriuall of the Prince Florendos at Constantinople.*	104
II. *Howe the Empresse conferred with the Emperour, as concerning the mariage of theyr Daughter Griana wyth Tarisius, Sonne to the King of Hungaria, whereof they both determined, and of that which happened in the meane time.*	108
III. *Of the battayle fought before the Cittie of Constantinople, betweene the Emperours power, and the Armie of Gamezio.*	112
IV. *Howe Florendos intreated the Emperour, to giue him in mariage his Daughter Griana, and what answere the Emperour made him.*	115

V. *Howe Griana sent a Ring to the Prince Florendos by Cardina her Mayde, desiring him (as he loued her) to comfort himselfe, and of the aunswere he sent her.*   119

VI. *Howe Cardina recited to the Princesse Griana, what speeches had past betweene her and Florendos, and of the counsell shee gaue her Mistresse, to conferre with him in the Garden so soone as he was recouered.*   121

VII. *How Florendos came that night to the Garden, to conclude what he and Griana had intended, and what happened to them.*   125

VIII. *Howe Florendos arriuing on the frontiers of Macedon, made manie sorrowfull complaints, for not bringing Griana away, according to his enterprise.*   129

IX. *Howe the Emperour promised Tarisius, that hee shoulde marrie Griana, whether she woulde or no: and howe she was deliuered of a fayre Sonne, without the knowledge of anie, but olde Tolomestra who had her in guarde.*   131

X. *Howe Gerrard passing where Cardina hadde left the Childe, heard it crye, and so brought it home with him to his wyfe to nourish it.*   135

XI. *Howe Florendos vnderstoode by the Esquire hee sent to Constantinople, the marriage of Griana and Tarisius: whereat he conceiued such inward greefe, as hee would haue died with extreame sorrow.*   138

XII. *How yong Palmerin sleeping, had a strange vision, which prouoked him to know whose Son he was, and of the talk which passed between him and Dyofena, the daughter of Gerrard.*   140

XIII. *How Palmerin went with this Merchant named Estebon to the Cittie of Hermida, who afterwarde gaue him Horse and Armour to be made Knight.*   144

XIV. *How Palmerin arriued at the Court of Macedon, hoping to receiue the order of knighthood at the hande of the Prince Florendos, Sonne to the aged King Primaleon, by the fauoure of the Ladie Arismena.*   145

XV. *Howe Florendos gaue to Palmerin the Armour and Sword of Gamezio, whom hee slewe before Constantinople, and afterwarde Knighted him: and howe a Damosell came to the Court, who presented him with a Helmet and a rich Sheelde.*   149

XVI. *Howe Palmerin fought with the horrible Serpent on the Mountaine Artifaeria, and slewe him, bringing the glasse filled with the water of the Fountaine, whereby King Primaleon of Macedon recouered his health.*   151

XVII. *Howe Palmerin discended from the Mountaine, wyth his Glasse full of the water of the enchaunted Fountaine, and how ioyfull Vrbanillo and the other Esquires were, seeing their Maister returne with so good fortune.*   153

XVIII. *How foure Knights would haue taken the Glasse of fatall water from Vrbanillo, before Palmerin arriued at Macedon, and of the Combat betweene them.*   154

XIX. *How Duke Astor of Durace sent to the King of Macedon, desiring him to sende him the Knight, that had slaine the Serpent on the Mountain Artifaeria, to ayde him against the Countie Passaco of Mecaena, who laide straight siedge to one of his Cities.* — 156

XX. *Howe Palmerin became highlie enamoured with the beautie of the Princesse Laurana, thinking her to bee the Lady that sollicited him in his visions.* — 161

XXI. *Howe Palmerin and Ptolome met with a Damosell, who made great mone for a Casket which two Knights had forcibly taken from her, and what happened to them.* — 165

XXII. *How the Lady of the Castell declared to Palmerin, what mooued the Gyant Darmaco to take from her her Daughter and her goods, whereupon Palmerin promised to enter Combat with the Gyant: as much for pittie, as to acquite his promise made to the Damosell, that brought the Casket, and the enchaunted Sword.* — 168

XXIII. *Howe Palmerin returning with his company to the Ladies Castell, happened to meete with the Giant Darmaco, who lost his life in Combat with Palmerin.* — 172

XXIV. *Howe Palmerin and Ptolome arriued at the Courte of the King of Bohemia, where they entred Combat against the Countie of Ormeque and his two Cozins, who accused the Knight and his Son of treason, that sent to seeke Palmerin.* — 175

XXV. *Howe Palmerin, Adrian and Ptolome entered the Combat, against the Countie of Ormeque and his Cozins, whom they honorably vanquished.* — 180

XXVI. *Howe Palmerin and Ptolome arriued at the Cittie of Gaunt, where the Emperour of Allemaigne kept his Courte, and of the Combat betweene Palmerin and the enchaunted Knight.* — 183

XXVII. *Howe the Empresse came to visite Palmerin, who kept his Chamber, because he had receiued such daungerous woundes, in the Combat with the enchaunted Knight, and of the speech he had with the fayre Princesse Polinarda.* — 185

XXVIII. *Howe Polinarda desired Palmerin to giue her his Dwarffe, and of the speeche which she and Vrbanillo had afterward togeather.* — 189

XXIX. *Howe Palmerin gained the honour of the Tourney, and of that which happened afterward.* — 195

XXX. *Howe Polinarda disclosed her secrets to Brionella, and of the talke she had with Palmerin.* — 198

XXXI. *Howe the King of Fraunce kept a royall and magnificent Courte, and howe his Sonne Lewes became enamored of the Duchesse of Burgundie.* — 202

XXXII. *Of the enterprise of Lewes the Prince of Fraunce, for the loue of the Duchesse of Burgundie.* — 205

XXXIII. *Howe the Prince Lewes and the Duke of Sauoye, sent theyr Heraldes and Horsemen into all parts, to make knowne to all Knights their enterprises, and the conditions of theyr Combats.*   210

XXXIV. *How the Prince Lewes came to see the Duchesse of Burgundie, and what happened.*   214

XXXV. *Of the Combat betweene Prince Lewes of Fraunce, and Crenus the Duke of Gaule.*   218

XXXVI. *Of the Combatte betweene Palmerin, and the Duke of Gaule, with the successe thereof.*   221

XXXVII. *Of the Combat which the Dukes of Sauoye and Lorrayne had togeather, for the beauty of their Ladies, and what was the issue thereof.*   223

XXXVIII. *Howe the Duke of Sauoye entered the Combatte against Ptolome, and howe he sped.*   225

XXXIX. *Of the perillous Combat between Palmerin and the Duke of Sauoye, and the issue thereof.*   229

XL. *Who the Knight of the Sunne was, and of his strange aduentures.*   234

XLI. *Howe Frisol persecuted with his disease, and the mockery of his Bretheren, determined to goe seeke strange aduentures.*   239

XLII. *Of the great courtesie the King of Fraunce vsed to Trineus and Palmerin: and of their returne into Allemaigne.*   244

XLIII. *How Palmerin went in the night to the appointed place, to conferre with his Lady Polinarda, and the amorous communication they had togeather.*   249

XLIV. *Howe Trineus was knighted, and what happened to him afterward.*   253

XLV. *Howe the Armie of the Emperour of Allemaigne arriued in England, vnder the conducte of the Countie Tolano: and howe they were discomfited.*   256

XLVI. *Howe after the Prince Trineus, Palmerin and Ptolome, were arriued in England, they went to the Court, and what torments the Prince endured for his looue to the fayre Lady Agriola.*   259

XLVII. *Of the cruell battayle, betweene the King of Englande and the King of Scots.*   262

XLVIII. *Of the retrait of the King of Englands Armie, and the honor he did to the three strange Knights.*   265

XLIX. *How the Queene of England was aduertised of the victorie against the King of Scots, and the ouerthrowe of his whole Armie.*   267

L. *Howe the King of Englande went to the Castell to the Queene and her Ladies, and of the honourable entertainment made to the three strange Knights.*   270

LI. *How the Queene of England and Agriola her daughter, were in danger to be rauished by the Giant Franarco, and of the succour they had by Trineus, Palmerin and Ptolome.*	277
LII. *Of the conference Palmerin had with the Princesse Agriola after he had slaine the Giant Franarco.*	281
LIII. *Howe in the time of this pleasant and great assembly, there came a Damosell to London, who desired the King to doo her iustice, against a Knight of his owne Court.*	286
LIV. *Howe after the death of Myseres, Palmerin followed Frysol, whome hee had slayne, but that a Damosell intreated his life.*	291
LV. *Howe Palmerin went with the Damosell to accomplishe the promise he made her, and what befell him.*	294
LVI. *Howe Palmerin trauayling through a great Forrest, espyed a Dwarffe enter into a Caue, whom he folowed, and founde there a Knight, with whom he had much conference.*	302
LVII. *Howe Palmerin hauing thus brought away Valerica, conducted her to the Caue to her beloued Varnan, and there confirmed the agreement of theyr loue.*	308
LVIII. *How Palmerin, after he departed from Varnan and Valerica, met with two Ladies in chase, one of them giuing him a Faulcon. And what happened to him against the Duke of Gaule his twelue Knightes, out of whose handes he deliuered Hermes.*	311
LIX. *Howe Frisol was deliuered out of Palmerins handes, by the meanes of Colmelio his Squire.*	314
LX. *Howe Palmerin, Hermes and Colmelio returned to London, and the good entertainement the King of England made them.*	317
LXI. *How Palmerin promised the Princesse Agriola, to conuaie her out of England, with his freend, which he perfourmed, to the speciall content of the Prince Trineus.*	320
LXII. *Howe the King of England and the Queene were aduertysed, how their daughter Agriola was conuayed away, and of their sorrowe for her departure.*	324
LXIII. *Howe Vrbanillo and the Prince Trineus Esquier, arriued at the Emperours Court, and what great ioye their comming procured.*	326
LXIV. *Howe Palmerin beeing thus on the Sea, caused Trineus there to marie the Princesse Agriola.*	330
LXV. *How Trineus, Agriola, Ptolome and al their Mariners, were taken by the Turkes, after that Palmerin was gone to viewe the Island.*	332
Postscript	335

Part Two

The Epistle   339

To the Freendlie Readers   340

I. *How Olimael presented the Princesse Agriola to the great Turke, who immediately became amorous of her: and what rewardes and preferment the Pyrate receiued, for his gift.*   341

II. *How the great Turke summoned all the Kings and Princes his Subiects, because hee minded to hold open Court: and howe he married with the Princesse Agriola his prisoner.*   345

III. *How Palmerin after his recreation, returned to the sea side, and seeing the Ship and his companie gone, made great lamentation, and what after followed.*   349

IV. *How Palmerin counterfeiting himselfe dumbe in the Isle of Calpha, was found by certaine Turkes, as he lay a sleepe by the Fountaine: and howe hee was receiued into the seruice of Alchidiana, Daughter to the Soldane of Babilon.*   351

V. *How Palmerin was put into the Denne among the Lions and Leopards, and hauing killed three of them, escaped valiantly.*   355

VI. *How the Prince Maurice sent his Ambassadors to the Soldane, to desire safe conduct for his comming to the Court: to trie if he could find any Knight there, able to deliuer him of an extreame trouble that hee dured by enchauntment.*   357

VII. *How the Prince Maurice came to the Court of the Soldane of Babilon, where he was deliuered of his burning Crowne that tormented him, by the loyaltie of Palmerin.*   360

VIII. *How the fayre Princesse Ardemia, enduring extreame passions and torments in loue, made offer of her affections to Palmerin, which he refused: wherewith the Princesse (through extreame conceit of greefe and despight) suddainly died.*   364

IX. *How Amarano of Nigrea, eldest son to the king of Phrygia, vnderstanding the death of the faire Princesse Ardemia, who was newly promised him in mariage: made many greeuous lamentations for her losse. And how Alchidiana discouered her amorous affections to Palmerin.*   370

X. *How Amarano Prince of Nigrea, came to the Soldans court, to accuse Alchidiana, as causer of the death of the fayre Princesse Ardemia her Cozin.*   373

XI. *Howe Palmerin seeing that none of the Soldans Knights would aduenture for Alchidiana against Amarano, enterprised himself her cause in combat. And how the Queene of Tharsus sent him a sumptuous helmet.*   376

XII. *How Palmerin entred the Combat with the Prince Amarano of Nigrea, whom he slew, and the great honors the Soldane and his Daughter did him.*   381

XIII. *How the brethren of Amarano, would haue buried his bodie in the Tombe with Ardemia, which Alchidiana would not suffer, but constrained them to carrie him home againe into his Countrey.* 384

XIV. *Howe Alchidiana ouercome by vehemencie of her loue, offered her selfe to Palmerin as his wife, and of the aunswere he made her.* 386

XV. *Howe the Soldane hauing determined to send his armie to Constantinople, would elect Palmerin his Lieutenant generall: which he refused, intreating him to giue the charge to the olde King of Balisarca.* 389

XVI. *How the Prince Olorico, sonne to the King of Arabia, came and offered his seruice to the Soldane, bringing with him fiue hundred armed Knights, and of his entertainment.* 391

XVII. *How the prince Olorico being with Palmerin in his Tent, demaunded of him if hee loued the princesse Alchidiana, and of the answere he made him.* 394

XVIII. *Of the Combat betweene Palmerin, and two of Amaranoes Brethren, whom he valiantly ouercame, and killed.* 396

XIX. *How the Brethren of Gramiell, with all their traine, tooke themselues to flight, and how Palmerin suddainly pursued them with his power, and tooke them prisoners.* 400

XX. *How the Queene of Tharsus came to see Palmerin, in the Citie belonging to Alfarano her Admiral, where by the meane of an enchaunted drinke, shee accomplished her pleasure with him.* 403

XXI. *Howe Palmerin, to colour his intended and desirous voyage into Christendome, perswaded the Soldane to sende his Armie to Constantinople, and what followed thereon.* 408

XXII. *How Palmerin sailing with the Soldanes armie, was brought by tempest into the Sea of Allemaigne, where hee tooke landing with the prince Olorico.* 412

XXIII. *How Palmerin by the meanes of Vrbanillo his Dwarfe, spake with his Lady Polynarda, with whom he stayed fiue daies, to recompence some part of his long absence, and to the great contentment of them both.* 416

XXIV. *How after the tempest was past, the soldans Armie assembled togither, and came against Constantinople, where by the Emperours power they were discomfited: and the King of Balisarca, his sonne Gueresin, and diuers other great Lords of Turkie slaine.* 421

XXV. *How the Prince Florendos of Macedon, accompanied with none but his Cozin Frenato, departed from his Co°untrey in a Pilgrims habit, iourneying in Hungaria, where he killed the King Tarisius: and how he and the Queene Griana were taken prisoners.* 424

XXVI. *The sorowfull complaints made by the Queene Griana, seeing her Husband dead, and her friend taken. And howe the Duke of Pera conueyed her to Constantinople, causing Florendos and Frenato to be brought thither by fiue hundred armed Knights.* 429

XXVII. *How Florendos and Griana were brought to Constantinople, and there were appointed by the Emperours Councell, to purge themselues of their accusation, by the combate of two knights, against their accusers Promptaleon and Oudin.* 432

XXVIII. *How Palmerin hauing staid with his Ladie fiue dayes, in so great pleasure as his heart could desire, fearing to be discouered to the Emperour, tooke his leaue of her, promising to begin the search of Trineus and Ptolome.* 436

XXIX. *Howe after Palmerin was departed from his Ladie, there appeared to him one of the Fayries of the Mountaine Artefaeria, who declared to him part of his fortunes following. And of a Combat which he and Olorico had against ten Knights.* 440

XXX. *How Palmerin, the prince Olorico, and Frysoll, went to Buda, thinking to finde the Court there, where beeing arriued, they heard newes howe the prince Florendos was taken, whom they went to succour with all diligence at Constantinople.* 446

XXXI. *Of the noble Combat in the Cittie of Constantinople, by Palmerin and Frysoll, against the two Nephewes of the deceased King of Hungaria, whome they vanquished, by which meane the Prince Florendos and Queene Griana were deliuered.* 451

XXXII. *How the Queene Griana with the yong Princesse Armida, went to visit Palmerin and Frysoll, and howe the Queene knew Palmerin to be her sonne, to the no litle ioy of the Emperour and the Prince Florendos.* 455

XXXIII. *How Frysoll declared to the Empresse, that he was sonne to her Nephew Netrides.* 462

XXXIV. *How Cardyna the Gentlewoman attending on the Queene, accompanied with her Brother and diuers other Squires, brought Gerrard, his wife and daughter to the Court, and what entertainment Palmerin made them.* 466

XXXV. *Howe the Knight that Florendos sent to Macedon, rehearsed to the King Primaleon the effect of his charge: and how Palmerin entertained his fathers Princes and Knights.* 469

XXXVI. *Howe the Duke of Mecaena, and the Counte of Reifort, arriued at Allemaigne, at the Emperours Court, and after theyr Ambassage dispatched, the Emperour sent backe with them to Constantinople, the Duke of Lorraine, and the Marquesse of Licena, as his Ambassadours.* 472

XXXVII. *Howe after the Prince Florendos and Queene Griana, were espoused togither, Palmerin was sworne Prince and heire of Greece and Macedon, by the consent of the Lords of the Empire and the Realme.* — 477

XXXVIII. *How the aged Knight Apolonio, found Netrydes, father to Frysol, and brought him to Constantinople, where hee was made Gouernour generall of Hungaria: and how Frysol espoused the Princesse Armida.* — 481

XXXIX. *How Palmerin tooke his leaue of the Emperor, his father and mother, to follow the search of the Prince Trineus.* — 484

XL. *How the aged King Primaleon of Macedon, graundfather to Palmerin, dyed, and how the King of Sparta espoused the faire Princesse Arismena, Sister to the prince Florendos.* — 488

XLI. *Howe Palmerin and his companions sayling on the Mediterranean Sea, were taken by Olimaell, Admirall to the great Turke: and of their fortunes in Greece, where Palmerin saued Laurana the princesse of Durace.* — 490

XLII. *How Trineus beeing enchaunted into the shape of a Dogge in the Isle of Malfada, there came a Princesse of the Moores, who requested him of the aged Enchauntresse, to whom he was giuen, and what happened to him afterward.* — 499

XLIII. *Howe the great Turke became enamoured with the Princesse Laurana, by means wherof he was slaine, and Agriola deliuered.* — 501

XLIV. *How Palmerin and his companions mette two Turkish Ships, from whom they deliuered Estebon the Merchant and his Sonnes: and came to the Isle of Malfada, where Palmerin lost them all, and of the sorrow hee made for his mishap.* — 506

XLV. *How Palmerin departing from the Isle of Malfada, came to the Court of the Princesse Zephira, shee that kept Tryneus transformed: where he was entertained, to ayde her against her eldest brother, who vexed her with dayly troubles.* — 511

XLVI. *Howe one of the Nephewes to the King of Balisarca, brought newes to the Soldane of his vncles death, the foyle of his Armie, the losse of Palmerin and Olorico. And how the Princesse Alchidiana bought Ptolome, whom she greatly honored for Palmerins sake.* — 514

XLVII. *How Palmerin and the princesse Zephira, departed from Elain towards Romata, to seeke Muzabelino, and what happened by the way in their iourney.* — 517

XLVIII. *How Palmerin Iousted against Tomano, Drumino and their knights, whome he all dismounted, and what entertainment the king Abimar, and the wise Nigromancer Muzabelino made them.* — 519

XLIX. *The talke that the princesse Zephira and Palmerin had with the wise Muzabelino: and how Palmerin departed from Romata to the Castell of the ten Rocks.* 521

L. *Howe Palmerin passed the tenne Rockes, vanquished the tenne enchaunted Knightes, and entered the Castell, where hee finished all the enchauntments: Trineus returning to his former shape, and what happened to them afterward.* 523

LI. *How the Princesse Zephira was cured of her disease, and Trineus ended the aduenture of the enchaunted sword in the Rocke.* 528

LII. *How Muzabelino gaue Palmerin his Sonne Bellechino, entertaining the King and all his companie royally at his Castle, and how the two Armies of the King Abimar and the Soldane of Persia encountred, with the successe therof.* 531

LIII. *The conference that the Soldane of Persia had with his Sisters, thinking by theyr meanes to stay Palmerin, and Tryneus in his Court, and the honourable entertainement hee made them at the arriuall of the Princesse Zephira. And how by good fortune Palmerin recouered his Squire Colmelio, from the Ambassadour Maucetto.* 534

LIV. *How Maucetto the Ambassadour to the Monarch Misos of Babylon, declared his message before the Soldane and all the princes of Persia. And of the Combate betweene Trineus, and the King Orzodine of Galappa.* 539

LV. *How Aurecinda Sister to the Soldane of Persia, pursued the Prince Tryneus so neere, as in the end, she had her desire, and what followed thereon.* 543

LVI. *Howe the Soldan seeing hee coulde not perswade Trineus to marrie his sister, condemned him to death, and what followed afterward.* 551

LVII. *Howe Palmerin and Trineus hauing soiourned a while at Grisca with the king Abimar, departed to the Isle of Malfada, where by the meanes of Dulacco and Palmerin, all the enchauntments were finished.* 556

LVIII. *How Palmerin and his companions sayling on the Sea, met with Ptolome: and of the honourable entertainment the Emperour Florendos, and the Ladies made them, when they arriued at Constantinople.* 561

LIX. *How the Duke of Mensa, and the Countie of Redona, conducted the prince Olorico into Assiria, where hee was espoused to the princesse Alchidiana.* 565

LX. *How Palmerin, Trineus, and Agriola, accompanied with many great Lords and princes, went to the Emperor of Allemaigne at Vienna, where great triumphs were made at the celebrating of the marriage between Trineus and the princesse Agriola.* 570

LXI. *Howe Palmerin sent Ptolome Duke of Saxon (as his Ambassador) to the King of France, and the Duke Eustace of Mecaena, to the King of England, to treate of the peace betweene them.* 573

Contents xvii

LXII. *How Palmerin and Polinarda, departed from Vienna toward Constantinople, where after the decease of the aged Emperour Remicius, Palmerin was crowned Emperour of Greece, and what ioy was made at the byrth of Polinarda her first sonne.* 576

LXIII. *How the Prince Olorico and Alchidiana, thinking to trauaile to Constantinople to see the Emperour Palmerin and the Empresse Polinarda, strayed on the Sea. And what sorrowful mone she made, and how she was found by Palmerin.* 578

LXIV. *Howe the Prince Olorico was reskewed from the Moores, by the yong Knights that the Emperour Palmerin sent in his search: and what ioy was made at Constantinople at his arriuall.* 583

LXV. *Howe the great Turke refused to assist Lycado, Nephewe to the Admiral Olimaell, against the Emperor Palmerin: and what trouble happened to Constantinople by the Traitor Nardides, Nephew to the King Tarisius, Lycado, Menadeno, and their father.* 586

LXVI. *How the wise Muzabelino knowing by his arte, the cruell treason doone to the Emperour, came to succour him, and of that which followed.* 590

LXVII. *How the Soldane of Babylon sent for the Prince Olorico, and his Daughter Alchidiana, and of the sorrow the Emperour and Empresse made for their departure.* 593

Postscript 596
Notes to the Text
    Part I 597
    Part II 675
Appendix: Alternative Dedicatory Epistles 749
Editorial Principles 753
Textual Notes 759
List of Emendations 765
Historical Collation 777
Word-Division 827
Bibliographical Descriptions 829
Glossary 841
Index of Personal Names 879
Addendum 885

Illustrations

Figure 1: The exposure of Palmerin d'Oliva. *Le premier livre de Palmerin d'Olive* (Paris, 1546), sig. C1^r. — 37

Figure 2: Title Page of *Palmerin d'Oliva*, First Edition (London, 1588), Part 1. — 100

Figure 3: Coat of Arms of Edward de Vere, 17th Earl of Oxford. — 101

Figure 4: Title Page of *Palmerin d'Oliva*, Second Edition (London, 1597), Part 2. — 338

Figure 5: *Palmerin d'Oliva* (London, 1597), Part 2, sig. V5^v, Huntington Library copy. Annotation in contemporary hand. — 546

Preface

This is an original-spelling, critical edition of Anthony Munday's *Palmerin d'Oliva* (printed in 1588), a chivalric romance composed originally in Spanish (printed in 1511) that Anthony Munday translated into English using primarily Jean Maugin's French version (printed in 1546) of the Spanish original. The editorial method followed aims to present the English text in a form as close as possible to its authorial inscription as can be recovered from the extant printed editions and other textual witnesses. I have limited my editorial intervention to correcting cases of textual corruption, while all my departures from the copytext are recorded in the textual apparatus for the benefit of scholars and readers. One scholarly article in particular has been critical in defining my editorial approach and the structure of the apparatus: G. Thomas Tanselle, "Some Principles for Editorial Apparatus," *SB* 25 (1972): 41–88. My adherence to the editorial principles formulated by Tanselle, alongside other influential textual scholars, comes from the conviction that they represent the most reliable instrument to restore authorial intentions, eliminate textual corruption, and present authoritative texts. Thus, the critical text is accompanied by a comprehensive textual apparatus that guarantees the traceability of my editorial decisions and provides readers with all the evidence needed for accessing the printed tradition of this romance. As Tanselle remarks, "the kind of apparatus presented is an indication less of the nature of the text than of the type of audience for which this edition is intended" (42). To be sure, although this work is associated with a literary genre that lacks the scholarly prestige accorded to the written production of other contemporary authors, I have treated it with the utmost textual rigor, as expected by a scholarly audience. With this kind of readership in mind, I settled on an original-spelling edition. But there is one additional reason that compelled me to guarantee that the highest editorial standards are applied to this work, namely that this is the first time that the English *Palmerin d'Oliva* is made available to modern-day readers since it was printed for the last time in 1637.

This last circumstance also demands a greater effort on the editor's part to elucidate the text for the benefit of first-time readers, who thus can more easily understand it and have a more enjoyable reading experience. I have devised the literary annotation to satisfy at least one of three objectives. First, the explanatory notes supply essential information to clarify the text's meaning, mainly by identifying places, persons, literary references and motifs, and by explaining obscure terms, though less frequently so, since lexicological information is provided in the glossary at the back of the book. Additionally, I have also wanted to analyze some textual references from the standpoint of its contemporary audience, especially when they concern the English corpus of chivalric literature that may have been known to the readers of Munday's translation, or at least was available in print at that time. Therefore, I occasionally make allusion to the printed Middle English romances and Malory's *Morte Darthur* in particular, not because they provided Munday with inspiration, but because they represent a literary antecedent that must have resonated with familiarity to some of Munday's readers. Secondly, the notes also contain information about the relation of Munday's text to his French source and record significant passages when the English translator departs from or modifies the French text. This kind of notes can help readers discern Munday's engagement with his source and identify some of the priorities and expectations he brought to his translation. The third objective I established for the explanatory notes is unusual for a critical edition. Aware of the text's length, its convoluted episodic structure, and proliferation of characters, I have elucidated cross-references, both explicit and implicit, in order to facilitate the readers' comprehension, and even navigation through the text. I hope this information will be useful to readers when approaching the work for the first time, or when they want to focus on a section of the romance rather than reading it in its entirety. An index of personal names has been compiled too, so that possible confusion about the identity of any give character can be avoided.

It has taken me a long time to fix and annotate the text. The idea of preparing this edition emerged in 2005, when I was a Postdoctoral Research Fellow in the English Department at the University of Bristol. I was encouraged to embark on this project by the publication of Helen Moore's edition of Anthony Munday's *Amadis de Gaule* (2004), while the monographs by Tracey Hill (2004) and Donna B. Hamilton (2005) awakened my interest in Munday's literary career and his production as a translator. Thereafter Munday's contribution to the literary culture in early modern England has attracted greater scholary attention and more publications have been devoted to his oeuvre. This edition is part of a collective effort to improve our understanding of Munday, in this case by making his literary output accessible. Other relevant examples include a new edition of *Sir Thomas More*, composed in part by Munday, which has appeared recently in the Shakespeare Arden series, and the edition of two of Munday's translations of chivalric romances, which were in preparation at the time of writing: his *Palmendos* was being edited by Leticia Álvarez-Recio, and the first part of his *Palmerin of England* by Louise Wilson.

Many people have been generous in sharing their knowlege and expertise with me. Without their help I couldn't have completed the daunting task of preparing this edition in its current form. Alice Colby-Hall (Cornell) was extremely helpful in revising my translations from the French and saved me from serious misunderstandings. Andrew Galloway (Cornell) and Winthrop

Wetherbee (Cornell) assisted me with difficult readings and editorial choices, as well as with some of the explanatory notes. Helen Cooper (Cambridge), Alex Davis (St Andrews), A. S. G. Edwards (Kent), and Ursula Rautenberg (Erlangen) answered several queries and encouraged me at various moments. Mª José Mora (Seville), Alastair Henderson (Stellenbosch), and Ad Putter (Bristol) read drafts of various sections of the edition and annotation, giving me insightful feedback and also saving me from several errors. W. T. J. M. Kuiper (Amsterdam) answered questions about the Dutch version of *Palmerijn van Olijve*. At the University of Alicante many colleagues and friends have been supportive, in particular José Antonio Álvarez, Silvia Caporale, Lourdes López, Sara Prieto, and Teresa Gómez Reus (I still remember her delicious meals and conversations when they were most needed). Special thanks are also due to my former dean, Jorge Olcina, and the staff at the library's acquisitions and interlibrary loan departments of Alicante. My niece Sirio Canós (UCL) has provided assistance with some bibliographical searches. In the early stages of this project I enlisted the help of two research assistants, Francisco J. Flores and Ángela López, who helped me with the collation of the text. They were supported by grants from the Spanish Ministry of Education. My work on Munday has also benefitted from discussions with members of my research team between 2012 and 2016: Leticia Álvarez-Recio (Seville), José Manuel González (Alicante), and Mercedes Salvador-Bello (Seville). Alejandra Ortiz-Salamovich (Santiago, Chile) took part in some of these discussions and shared with me chapters from her PhD dissertation, although it was too late for me to make full use of it. Agustín López-Avilés (Alicante) has given me access to his PhD dissertation on *Palladine of England*, which was under preparation at the time of writing. The editorial staff at the Arizona Center for Medieval and Renaissance Studies, in particular Roy Rukkila and Todd Halvorsen, have been extremely professional in the way they have handled this editorially challenging publication. To all of them I want to express my most sincere gratitude. All remaining errors are the sole responsibility of the editor.

I also wish to show my appreciation to the various libraries which permitted the use of their books, including the British Library, Cambridge University Library, Cornell University Library, Folger Shakespeare Library, Huntington Library, Lambeth Palace Library, Library of Congress, University Library of Erlangen-Nürnberg, University of Alicante Library, University of Seville Library, and the Lee Library of Wolfson College, Cambridge.

The research for this book was supported in its early stages by grants from the University of Alicante, the Valencian Research Council, and the Folger Shakespeare Library. Yet, this edition would not have been completed in its current form without the generous funding of the Spanish Ministry for Science and Innovation (ref. FFI2011–22811), for which I am most grateful. I wish to thank as well the publishers of *Gutenberg Jahrbuch* for permission to reprint material previously published in this journal.

My family deserves a special mention. This book is dedicated to my late father, who always encouraged me to be a better person and a better scholar. My mother, Palmira Martí Gascó, and my brothers Carlos, Miquel, and Javi have all been very supportive and understanding, and for that I will remain ever so grateful. My wife, Lucía Vegas Moya, deserves credit for having patiently collated the four editions of *Palmerin d'Oliva*, and for enlightening my understanding of some episodes with her passionately creative readings and suggestions. My son Daniel, who came into my life as I was busy with this book, has taught me to be resilient while he brightens every day of my life with his laughter and joviality. I am aware that to finish this project I've had to rob both Daniel and Lucía of family time. This owes much of its existence to their patience, help, and love.

J.S.M.
Moncofa, Spain
1st November 2016

Abbreviations

Abbott, *Grammar* — E. A. Abbott. *A Shakespearian Grammar: An Attempt to Illustrate Some of the Differences between Elizabethan and Modern English*. 2nd ed. London: Macmillan, 1894.

Amadís: Quinientos años — *Amadís de Gaula 1508: Quinientos años de libros de caballerías*. Madrid: Biblioteca Nacional de España, Sociedad Estatal de Conmemoraciones Culturales, 2008.

Apollodorus — Apollodorus. *The Library of Greek Mythology*. Translated by Robin Hard. Oxford: Oxford University Press, 1997.

Arber — Edward Arber. *A Transcript of the Registers of the Company of Stationers of London, 1554–1640 A.D.* 5 vols. London, 1875–1894.

Ascham, *Scholemaster* — Roger Ascham. *The Scholemaster*, in *English Works*. Edited by William Aldis Wright. Cambridge English Classics. Cambridge: Cambridge University Press, 1904.

Barber — Charles Barber. *Early Modern English*. London: A. Deutsch, 1976.

Bergeron — David M. Bergeron. "Munday, Anthony (bap. 1560, d. 1633)." *ODNB*, 39: 739–46.

Bettoni — Anna Bettoni. "Il *Palmerín de Olivia* tradotto da Maugin: editori, storie e mode letterarie nella Francia del Cinquecento." In *"Il n'est nul si beau passe temps Que se jouer à sa Pensee": Studi di filologia e letteratura francese in onore di Anna Maria Finoli*, 173–201. Pisa: ETS, 1995.

BL — London, British Library

Bordman — Gerald Bordman. *Motif-index of the English Metrical Romances*. Folklore Fellows Communications 190. Helsinki: Academia Scientiarum Fennica, 1963.

British Bibliographer — Sir Egert Brydges, ed. *The British Bibliographer* 1 (1810): 135–48.

Bueno Serrano, "Índice"	Ana Carmen Bueno Serrano. "Índice y estudio de motivos en los libros de caballerías castellanos (1508–1516)." PhD diss., Universidad de Zaragoza, 2007.
Bueno Serrano, "Las tres *fadas*"	Ana Carmen Bueno Serrano. "Las tres *fadas* de la montaña Artifaria a la luz del folclore (*Palmerín de Olivia*, caps. xv–xviii)." *Boletín de la Biblioteca de Menéndez Pelayo* 84 (2008): 135–57.
Byrne, "Books"	M. St. Clare Byrne. "Anthony Munday and His Books." *The Library*, 4th ser., 1 (1920): 225–56.
Byrne, "Clue"	M. St. Clare Byrne. "Anthony Munday's Spelling as a Literary Clue." *The Library*, 4th ser., 4 (1923): 9–24.
Campos	Axayácatl Campos García Rojas. "Domesticación y mascotas en los libros de caballerías hispánicos: *Palmerín de Olivia*." *eHumanista* 16 (2010): 268–89.
Cervantes	Miguel de Cervantes. *Don Quijote de La Mancha*. Edited by Francisco Rico with the assistance of Joaquín Forradellas. Barcelona: Crítica, 2001.
Chaucer	*The Riverside Chaucer*. Edited by Larry D. Benson. Boston: Houghton Mifflin, 1987.
CHEL	*The Cambridge History of the English Language, vol. 3: 1476–1776*. Edited by Roger Lass. Cambridge: Cambridge University Press, 1999.
Crane	Ronald S. Crane. *The Vogue of Medieval Chivalric Romance During the English Renaissance*. Menasha, WI: Banta, 1919.
Daniels	Marie Cort Daniels. *The Function of Humor in the Spanish Romances of Chivalry*. New York: Garland, 1992.
DBE	*Diccionario biográfico español*. Edited by Gonzalo Anes y Álvarez de Castrillón. 50 vols. Madrid: Real Academia de la Historia, 2009–2013.
Dini	Encarnación García Dini, "Per una bibliografia dei romanzi di cavalleria: Edizioni del ciclo dei 'Palmerines'," in *Studi sul "Palmerín,"* 3:5–44.
Di Stefano	Giuseppe di Stefano, ed. *El libro del famoso e muy esforçado cavallero Palmerín de Olivia*, in *Studi sul "Palmerin,"* vol. 1.
Edit16	*Censimento nazionale delle edizioni italiane del XVI seocolo*. Istituto Centrale per il Catalogo Unico, Roma. http://edit16.iccu.sbn.it/.
EETS os	Early English Text Society, original series.

EETS es	Early English Text Society, extra series.
Eisenberg	Daniel Eisenberg. *Romances of Chivalry in the Spanish Golden Age*. 1982. Reprint, Newark, DE: Juan de la Cuesta, 2006.
EV	Steven W. May and William A. Ringler, Jr. *Elizabethan Poetry: A Bibliography and First-line Index of English Verse, 1559–1603*. 3 vols. London: Thoemmes Continuum, 2004.
FB	Andrew Pettegree, Malcolm Walsby, and Alexander S. Wilkinson. *French Vernacular Books: Books Published in the French Language before 1601*. 2 vols. Leiden: Brill, 2007.
FQ	Edmund Spenser. *The Faerie Queene*. Edited by A. C. Hamilton. 2nd ed. rev. Text edited by Hiroshi Yamashita and Toshiyuki Suzuki. Harlow: Longman, 2007.
Fr.	French
Freer	Alan Freer. "*Palmerín de Olivia* in Francia." In *Studi sul "Palmerín."* 3:177–237.
Galigani	Giuseppe Galigani. "La versione inglese del *Palmerín de Olivia*." In *Studi sul "Palmerín."* 3:239–88.
Gayangos	Pascual de Gayangos. *Catálogo razonado de los libros de caballerías que hay en lengua castellana o portuguesa, hasta el año de 1800*. Madrid: Rivadeneyra, 1874.
Golding	*Ovid's Metamorphoses: The Arthur Golding Translation, 1567*. Edited by John Frederick Nims. New York: Macmillan, 1965.
González, "Ideología"	Javier Roberto González. "La ideología profética del *Palmerín de Olivia*." *Letras: Revista de la Facultad de Filosofía y Letras de la Pontificia Universidad Católica Argentina Santa María de los Buenos Aires* 37 (1998): 53–81.
González, "Sistema"	Javier Roberto González. "El sistema profético en la determinación del *Palmerín-Primaleón* como unidad textual (primera parte)." *Incipit* 19 (1999): 35–76.
González, "Sueños"	Javier Roberto González. "Los sueños proféticos del *Palmerín de Olivia* a la luz de los *Commentarii in somnium Scipionis* de Macrobio." *Stylos* 7 (1998): 205–64.
Görlach	Manfred Görlach. *Introduction to Early Modern English*. Cambridge: Cambridge University Press, 1991.

Hamilton	Donna B. Hamilton. *Anthony Munday and the Catholics, 1560–1633.* Burlington, VT: Ashgate, 2005.
Hayes, "Romances"	Gerald R. Hayes. "Anthony Munday's Romances of Chivalry." *The Library*, 4th ser., 6 (1925): 57–81.
Hayes, "Postscript"	Gerald R. Hayes. "Anthony Munday's Romances: A Postscript." *The Library*, 4th ser., 7 (1926): 31–38.
Hill	Tracey Hill. *Anthony Munday and Civic Culture: Theatre, History and Power in Early Modern London 1580–1633.* Manchester: Manchester University Press, 2004.
Huguet	Edmond Huguet. *Dictionnaire de la langue française du seizième siècle.* 7 vols. Paris: Champion, 1925–1973.
Huon of Burdeux	*The Boke of Duke Huon of Burdeux.* Edited by S. L. Lee. EETS es 40, 41. London: Trübner, 1882–1883.
IB	Alexander S. Wilkinson. *Iberian Books: Books Published in Spanish or Portuguese or in the Iberian Peninsula before 1601.* Leiden: Brill, 2010.
Keen	Maurice Keen. *Chivalry.* New Haven, CT: Yale University Press, 1984.
Lancelot-Grail	*Lancelot-Grail: The Old French Arthurian Vulgate and Post-Vulgate in Translation.* Edited by Norris J. Lacy. 10 vols. Cambridge: D. S. Brewer, 2010. First published 1993–1996 by Garland Publishing.
Lucía, *Cat.*	José Manuel Lucía Megías. *Libros de caballerías castellanos en las Bibliotecas Públicas de París: Catálogo descriptivo.* Biblioteca di Studi Ispanici 2. Alcalá de Henares: Universidad, Servicio de Publicaciones; Pisa: Università degli Studi, 1999.
Lucía, *Imprenta*	José Manuel Lucía Megías, *Imprenta y libros de caballerías.* Madrid: Ollero & Ramos, 2000.
Lyly, *England*	John Lyly, *Euphues and his England*, in *The Complete Works of John Lyly.* Edited by R. Warwick Bond. Oxford: Clarendon Press, 1902; repr. 1973, vol. 2.
Lyly, *Euphues*	John Lyly, *Euphues: The Anatomy of Wyt*, in *The Complete Works of John Lyly.* Edited by R. Warwick Bond. Oxford: Clarendon Press, 1902; repr. 1973, vol. 1.
Malory	*Caxton's Malory: A New Edition of Sir Thomas Malory's "Le Morte Darthur" Based on the Pierpont Morgan Copy of William Caxton's Edition of 1485.* Edited by James W. Spisak. Berkeley: University of California Press, 1983. 2 vol.

Mancini	Guido Mancini. "Introducción al *Palmerín de Olivia*." In *Dos estudios de Literatura Española*. Barcelona: Planeta, 1970.
Mansel	Philip Mansel. *Constantinople: City of the World's Desire, 1453–1924*. London: John Murray, 1995; repr. 2006.
Marín Pina, "Edición"	Mª Carmen Marín Pina. "Edición y estudio del ciclo español de los Palmerines." PhD diss., Universidad de Zaragoza, 1988.
Marín Pina, "Maga"	Mª Carmen Marín Pina. "La maga enamorada: tras las huellas de Circe en la narrativa caballeresca española." In *Les literatures antigues a les literatures medievals*. Edited by L. Pomer et al., 67–93. Classical and Byzantine Monographs 68. Amsterdam: Hakkert, 2009.
Martín Abad	Julián Martín Abad. *Post-incunables ibéricos*. Madrid: Ollero & Ramos, 2001.
McKerrow, *Introduction*	Ronald B. McKerrow. *An Introduction to Bibliography for Literary Students*. Oxford: Clarendon Press, 1928.
Menéndez Pelayo	Marcelino Menéndez Pelayo. *Orígenes de la novela*. 2nd ed. 4 vols. Madrid: Consejo Superior de Investigaciones Científicas, 1961.
MP	*Modern Philology*
Munday, *Amadis*	*Amadis de Gaule: Translated by Anthony Munday*. Edited by Helen Moore. Non-Canonical Early Modern Popular Texts. Burlington, VT: Ashgate, 2004.
Munday, *Mirrour*	Anthony Munday. *A Mirrour of Mutabilitie*. Edited by Hans Peter Heinrich. Bibliotheca Humanistica 3. Frankfurt: Peter Lang, 1990.
Munday, *Palladine*	Anthony Munday. *Palladine of England*. London: E. Allde, 1588. (STC 5541).
Munday, *Palmendos*	Anthony Munday. *Palmendos*. London: J. Charlewood, 1589. (STC 18064).
Munday, *Palmerin of England*	Anthony Munday. *Palmerin of England*. London: T. Creede, 1596. 2 parts (STC 19161).
Munday, *Primaleon*	Anthony Munday. *Primaleon of Greece*. London: T. Snodham, 1619. 3 parts (STC 20367).
Munday, *Roman Life*	Anthony Munday. *The English Roman Life*. Edited by Philip J. Ayres. Studies in Tudor & Stuart Literature. Oxford: Clarendon Press, 1980.

Munday, *Zelauto*	Anthony Munday. *Zelatuo: The Fountaine of Fame.* Edited by Jack Stillinger. Carbondale, IL: Southern Illinois University Press, 1963.
Mustanoja	Tauno F. Mustanoja. *A Middle English Syntax, Part I: Parts of Speech.* Mémoires de la Société Néophilologique de Helsinki 23. Helsinki: Société Néophilologique, 1960.
NB	Andrew Pettegree and Malcolm Walsby. *Netherlandish Books: Books Published in the Low Countries and Dutch Books Printed Abroad before 1601.* 2 vols. Leiden: Brill, 2011.
Nelson	Alan H. Nelson. *Monstrous Adversary: The Life of Edward de Vere, 17th Earl of Oxford.* Liverpool: Liverpool University Press, 2003.
Norton, *Catalogue*	F. J. Norton. *A Descriptive Catalogue of Printing in Spain and Portugal.* Cambridge: Cambridge University Press, 1978.
Norton, *Printing*	F. J. Norton. *Printing in Spain, 1501–1520.* Sandars Lectures in Bibliography, 1963. Cambridge: Cambridge University Press, 1966.
O'Connor	John J. O'Connor. "Physical Deformity and Chivalric Laughter in Renaissance England." In "Comedy: New Perspectives," edited by Maurice Charney, special issue, *New York Literary Forum* 1 (1978): 59–71.
ODNB	*Oxford Dictionary of National Biography.* Edited by H. C. G. Matthew and Brian Harrison. 61 vols. Oxford: Oxford University Press, 2004.
OED	*The Oxford English Dictionary.* 2nd ed. Prepared by J. A. Simpson and E. S. C. Weiner. 20 vols. Oxford: Clarendon Press, 1989.
OHLTE	*The Oxford History of Literary Translation in English, vol. 2: 1550–1660*, edited by Gordon Braden, Robert Cummings, and Stuart Gillespie. Oxford: Oxford University Press, 2010.
Ovid, *Met.*	Ovid. *Metamorphoses.* Translated by Frank Justus Miller, 3rd ed. rev. by G. P. Goold. The Loeb Classical Library. 2 vols. Cambridge, MA: Harvard University Press, 1977.
Palmerín de Olivia	*Palmerín de Olivia*, edited by Giuseppe di Stefano, in collaboration with Daniela Pierucci and with an introduction by Mª Carmen Marín Pina. Los Libros de Rocinante 18. Alcalá de Henares: Centro de Estudios Cervantinos, 2004.

Palmerín: 500 años	*Palmerín y sus libros: 500 años*. Edited by Aurelio González et al. Mexico, D. F.: El Colegio de México, 2013.
Paris and Vienne	*Paris and Vienne: Translated from the French and Printed by William Caxton*. Edited by MacEdward Leach. EETS os 234. London: Oxford University Press, 1957.
Patchell	Mary Patchell. *The "Palmerin" Romances in Elizabethan Prose Fiction*. Columbia University Studies in English and Comparative Literature 166. New York: Columbia University Press, 1947.
Petruccelli	Mª Rosa Petruccelli. "Personajes femeninos y voluntad de protagonismo en el *Palmerín de Olivia*." In *Actas de la V Jornadas Internacionales de Literatura Española Medieval*. Edited by Azucena Adelina Fraboschi, Clara I. Stramiello de Bocchio, and Alejandra Rosarossa, 302–13. Studia Hispanica Medievalia 4. Buenos Aires: Universidad Católica Argentina, 1999.
Phillips	Joshua Phillips. *English Fictions of Communal Identity, 1485–1603*. Burlington, VT: Ashgate, 2010.
Plutarch	*Plutarch's Lives of the Noble Grecians and Romanes*. Translated by Sir Thomas North. 1579. 8 vols. Boston: Houghton Mifflin, 1928.
PMLA	*Publications of the Modern Language Association*
Purser	William Edward Purser. *Palmerin of England: Some Remarks on this Romance and on the Controversy concerning its Authorship*. Dublin: Browne and Nolan, 1904.
Rawles	Stephen Rawles. "The Earliest Editions of Nicolas de Herberay's Translations of *Amadis de Gaule*." *The Library*, 6th ser., 3 (1981): 91–108.
Ruiz Fidalgo	Lorenzo Ruiz Fidalgo. *La imprenta en Salamanca (1501–1600)*. 3 vols. Madrid: Arco Libros, 1994.
SB	*Studies in Bibliography*
Shakespeare	*The Arden Shakespeare: Complete Works*. Edited by Richard Proudfoot, Ann Thompson, and David Scott Kastan. London: Arden Shakespeare, 2001.
Sir Thomas More	*Sir Thomas More: Original Text by Anthony Munday and Henry Chettle*. Edited by John Jowett. London: Arden Shakespeare, 2011.
Sp.	Spanish

STC	*A Short-Title Catalogue of Books Printed in England, Scotland and Ireland, and of English Books Printed Abroad, 1475–1640*, first compiled by A. W. Pollard and G. R. Redgrave, 2nd ed. rev. and enlarged, begun by W. A. Jackson and F. S. Ferguson, completed by Katharine F. Pantzer, with a chronological index by Philip R. Rider. 3 vols. London: The Bibliographical Society, 1976–1991.
STCN	*Short Title Catalogue Netherlands*. http://www.stcn.nl.
Studi sul *"Palmerín"*	*Studi sul "Palmerín de Olivia,"* 3 vols. Istituto di Letteratura Spagnola e Ispano-Americana 11–13. Pisa: Università di Pisa, 1966.
Thomas	Henry Thomas. *Spanish and Portuguese Romances of Chivalry: The Revival of the Romance of Chivalry in the Spanish Peninsula, and Its Extension and Influence Abroad.* Cambridge: Cambridge University Press, 1920.
Tilley	Morris Palmer Tilley. *A Dictionary of the Proverbs in England in the Sixteenth and Seventeenth Centuries: A Collection of the Proverbs Found in English Literature and the Dictionaries of the Period.* Ann Arbor, MI: University of Michigan Press, 1966.
Toda	Eduart Toda y Güell. *Bibliografia espanyola d'Itàlia: dels origens de la imprempta fins a l'any 1900*. 5 vols. Castell de Sant Miquel d'Escornalbou, 1927–1931.
Turner	Celeste Turner. *Anthony Mundy: An Elizabethan Man of Letters.* University of California Publications in English, vol. 2, no. 1. Berkeley: University of California Press, 1928.
Tyler, *Mirror*	Margaret Tyler. *Mirror of Princely Deeds and Knighthood.* Edited by Joyce Boro. MHRA Tudor & Stuart Translations 11. London: Modern Humanities Research Association, 2014.
Valerius	Valerius Maximus. *Memorable Doings and Sayings*, edited and translated by D. R. Shackleton Bailey. The Loeb Classical Library. 2 vols. Cambridge, MA: Harvard University Press, 2000.
Weddige	*Die "Historien vom Amadis auss Franckreich": dokumentarische Grundlegung zur Entstehung und Rezeption.* Wiesbaden: Steiner, 1975.

Wilson, "Paratexts"	Louise Wilson. "Playful Paratexts: The Front Matter of Anthony Munday's Iberian Romance Translations." In *Renaissance Paratexts*, edited by Helen Smith and Louis Wilson, 121–32. Cambridge: Cambridge University Press, 2011.
Wing	Donald G. Wing. *Short-Title Catalogue of Books Printed in England, Scotland, Ireland, Wales, and British America and of English Books Printed in Other Countries, 1641–1700*. 2nd ed. rev. and enl. by John J. Morrison and Carolyn W. Nelson. New York: Modern Language Association of America, 1994–1998.
Yamada	Akihiro Yamada. *Thomas Creede: Printer to Shakespeare and His Contemporaries*. Tokyo: Meisei University Press, 1994.
Ywain and Gawain	*Ywain and Gawain*. Edited by Albert B. Friedman and Norman T. Harrington. EETS os 254. London: Oxford University Press, 1964.

Introduction

The Iberian romances of chivalry

The Iberian literature of chivalry that circulated in the Middle Ages was directly connected with the Europe-wide dissemination of the Arthurian tradition. Arthurian legends, adventures, and motifs entered the Iberian Peninsula mainly through the Pyrenees, as attests the early allusion to some Arthurian themes in the *sirventes-ensenhamen de joglar* "Cabra juglar," composed in Old Occitan by Guerau de Cabrera in the second half of the twelfth century.[1] In this poem Guerau, a Catalan nobleman of the Cabrera household, reprimands his jongleur Cabra for failing to have built an extensive repertoire that included the following Arthurian stories:

> Ni sabs d'Erec
> com conquistec
> l'esparvier for de sa reion. . . .
> ni de Tristan
> c'amava Yceut a lairon.
> Ni de Gualvaing
> qui, ses compaing,
> fazia tanta venaizon.
> (ll. 73–74, 185–89).[2]

[nor do you know about Erec how he beat the sparrowhawk out of her territory (. . .), nor about Tristram who loved Iseult in secret, or about Gawain who, companionless, made such a great hunt]

---

[1] For a discussion on the date of this poem, see I. Cluzel, "À propos de l'"ensenhamen' du troubadour catalan Guerau de Cabrera," *Boletín de la Real Academia de Buenas Letras de Barcelona* 26 (1954–56): 87–93. On the identity of Guerau, see L. Nicolau d'Olwer, "Clarícies per la història dels vescomtes de Girona-Cabrera," *Anuari Heràldic* 1 (1917): 99–107. Note that both the date of composition and the author's identity are revised in Stefano M. Cingolani, "The *Sirventes-ensenhamen* of Guerau de Cabrera: A Proposal for a New Interpretation," *Journal of Hispanic Research* 1 (1992–93): 191–200.

[2] Edited by François Pirot, *Recherches sur les connaissances littéraires des troubadours occitans et catalans des XIIe et XIIIe siècles*, Memorias de la Real Academia de Buenas Letras de Barcelona 14 (Barcelona: Real Academia de Buenas Letras, 1972), 545–62. All translations are my own unless otherwise stated.

In order for the fictional reprimand to be effective, Guerau had to count on the complicity of his audience. Hence, it seems reasonable to assume that those very stories that Guerau expected his jongleur to know were somewhat familiar, or at least recognizable, in courtly milieux of northern Catalonia.

In the centuries that followed, this literary traffic across the Pyrenees intensified and the rich Arthurian tradition produced in Old French continued spreading across the Christian kingdoms of the Iberian Peninsula in the form of translations and adaptations, thus contributing to shape the Iberian tradition of chivalric literature in the late Middle Ages.[3] The first specifically Spanish chivalric romance, namely the *Libro del cavallero Zifar*, was not composed until the fourteenth century. It contains marvelous episodes that owe much to the Arthurian tradition, without putting the emphasis on martial and amorous action that became typical of the *libros de caballerías*, but instead developing a moral and didactic dimension to its narrative plot.[4] Daniel Eisenberg argues that this work had no "discernible influence on the romances which were to follow it" (28), although somehow it must have contributed to shape the emerging national romance narratives.[5] Still, the one determining influence on the development of the Spanish chivalric romances was French Arthurian literature, which provided inspiration for the author of the primitive, fourteenth-century *Amadís de Gaula*. Similar in structure and narrative style to the French prose *Lancelot* and *Tristan*, and sharing names and literary motifs with other Arthurian works,[6] *Amadís* remained popular in late-medieval Castile, while its text was in a state of flux

---

[3] For a recent overview of the transmission of Arthurian literature in the Iberian peninsula, see Rafael M. Mérida Jiménez, *Trasmisión y difusión de la literatura caballeresca: Doce estudios de recepción cultural hispánica (siglos XIII–XVII)* (Lleida: Edicions de la Universitat de Lleida, 2013), 13–33, esp. 22. See also Sylvia Roubaud-Bénichou, *Le roman de chevalerie en Espagne: entre Arthur et Don Quichotte* (Paris: Champion, 2000), 73–84, and Carlos Alvar, "La Materia de Bretaña," in *Amadís: Quinientos años*, 20–46. For the development of chivalric literature in the kingdoms of Spain, see Marina S. Brownlee, "Romance at the Crossroads: Medieval Spanish Paradigms and Cervantine Revisions," in *The Cambridge Companion to Medieval Romance*, ed. Roberta L. Krueger (Cambridge: Cambridge University Press, 2000), 253–66.

[4] Cf. Thomas, 19–20. See also Fernando Gómez Redondo, *Historia de la prosa medieval castellana, vol. 2: El desarrollo de los géneros. La ficción caballeresca y el orden religioso* (Madrid: Cátedra, 1999), 1371–1459, and José Manuel Lucía Megías, "*Libro del cavallero Zifar*," in *Diccionario filológico de literatura medieval española: textos y transmisión*, ed. by Carlos Alvar and José Manuel Lucía Megías (Madrid: Castalia, 2002), 773–76.

[5] Cf. Thomas, 19, and Fernando Gómez Redondo, "La literatura caballeresca castellana medieval: el *Amadís de Gaula* primitivo," in *Amadís: Quinientos años*, 60. Note that an edition of *Cavallero Zifar* was printed in 1512 (IB 16521–22), thus suggesting that from early on this work could be associated with the corpus of the printed *libros de caballerías*.

[6] Gómez Redondo, *Historia de la prosa medieval castellana*, 1542–47.

and continuously revised in various redactions prior to its first print publication. At the end of the fifteenth century this romance was perceived as old-fashioned, from both a linguistic and a literary point of view, and a revision was in order if it had to be transferred into print for commercial profit. Approximately between 1492 and 1497 Garci Rodríguez de Montalvo (ca. 1440–ca. 1505), a noble alderman from Medina del Campo, was engaged in revising, correcting and expanding the *Amadís* materials that were available to him. The originals he used were organized in three books, to which Montalvo added another two, namely the fourth book and its sequel or fifth book, better known by its title *Las Sergas de Esplandián*.[7]

In the following years the first edition of Montalvo's *Amadís* appeared in print. Although the earliest extant edition was not published until 1508 in Saragossa (IB 16414), it is believed that the *editio princeps* was printed earlier, probably in 1496.[8] The publication of this medieval romance marks the beginning of the production of Castilian chivalric romances, a literary phenomenon that extended over the entire sixteenth century. As Cervantes's curate remarks in *Don Quijote*, printed in 1605, "este libro [i.e., Montalvo's *Amadís*] fue el primero de caballerías que se imprimió en España, y todos los demás han tomado principio y origen déste" (I.vi.77).[9] This statement, however, is in need of some qualification. *Amadís* is indeed the first romance of chivalry printed in Spanish, but not the first printed in the Iberian Peninsula, since *Tirant lo Blanc* (IB 12586), written in

---

[7] For biographical information, see Cristina Moya García, "Rodríguez de Montalvo, Garci," in *DBE*, 44:45–47, and Emilio J. Sales Dasí, "Garci-Rodríguez de Montalvo, regidor de la noble villa de Medina del Campo," *Revista de Filología Española* 79 (1999): 123–58. For more information about the originals and their relation to Montalvo's work, see Juan Bautista Avalle-Arce, *'Amadís de Gaula': el primitivo y el de Montalvo* (Mexico: Fondo de Cultura Económica, 1990). The only existing manuscript witnesses of the primitive *Amadís* are reproduced in facsimile and transcribed in José Manuel Lucía Megías, "Edición de los fragmentos conservados del *Amadís de Gaula* medieval," in *Amadís: Quinientos años*, 80–91.

[8] For a note with illustrations of the only copy of the 1508 edition, see Geofrey West, "La historia de un ejemplar único: British Library: C.20.e.6.," *Amadís: Quinientos años*, 159–61. For a bibliographical description, see Norton, *Catalogue*, no. 625; see also Martín Abad, no. 42. A facsimile edition with introduction by Víctor Infantes is also available (Madrid: Instituto de España, 1999–2000).

[9] "this is the first book of knighthood that ever was printed in Spain, and all the others have had their beginning and original from this," translated by Thomas Shelton (1612). My quotations are taken from *The History of the Valorous & Witty Knight-Errant Don Quixote of the Manxa*, translated by Thomas Shelton (London: Macmillan, 1900), 3 vol., to which I refer by volume and page number. The quotation in this note appears in 1:34.

Catalan by Joanot Martorell, was issued in 1490.[10] Moreover, as soon as this new literary mode became fashionable in Castile, *Tirant* was translated into Spanish and an edition published in Valladolid in 1511 (IB 12588), though apparently with limited success, since it was never reprinted. The second part of the curate's statement, that the publication of *Amadís* set an example for others to follow, is correct, since printers and writers hoped to replicate the commercial success of Montalvo's output by producing continuations and imitations of his original work.[11] From 1508 until the middle of the sixteenth century new romance titles were published at a rate of about one every year, but the pace slowed down in the second half of the century. The entire catalogue of the Spanish chivalric romances totals about sixty separate works, most of which were reprinted repeatedly throughout the century.[12] As the century advanced, the romance genre gradually degenerated, showing a taste for the baroque in style and a liking for the fabulous and unrealistic in content. This literary decay is accurately captured at the turn of the seventeenth century by Cervantes's canon from Toledo: "son en el estilo duros; en las hazañas, increíbles; en los amores, lascivos; en las cortesías, malmirados; largos en las batallas, necios en las razones, disparatados en los viajes, y, finalmente, ajenos de todo discreto artificio" (Cervantes, I.xlvii.549).[13] This unifying description of the contents typical of the romances of chivalry is matched by their physical presentation, for instance making possible their rapid identification in the scrutiny of Don Quixote's library, which contains "más de

---

[10] Note that Martín de Riquer, *Caballeros andantes españoles* (Madrid: Espasa-Calpe, 1967), 11, draws a distinction between *libros de caballerías*, characterized by the marvelous nature of their adventures as in the case of *Amadís*, and what he calls "novelas caballerescas," which deal with the same themes but in a realistic manner, as happens in *Tirant*. This distinction, as Riquer admits, is a methodological one and does not necessarily describe a historical perception.

[11] Cf. Eisenberg, 31.

[12] Cf. Thomas, 147. For a complete list of all the Castilian books of chivalry, see Lucía Megías, *Imprenta*, 609–18. For statistics of the editions published in the sixteenth century, see Maxime Chevalier, *Lectura y lectores en la España de los siglos XVI y XVII* (Madrid: Turner, 1976), tables I and II, between 64–65.

[13] "most harsh in their style, incredible in exploits, impudent in love matters, absurd in compliments, prolix in battles, fond in discourses, uncertain and senseless in voyages; and finally, devoid of all discretion" (Shelton, 2:138). A useful scholarly description of the genre is provided by Helen Moore: "The 'libros de caballería[s]' are . . . amplifications and extensions of the Arthurian literary tradition. They borrow the British and French settings of the original romances, but also extend their geographical scope by including adventures set in exotic locations such as Greece and Constantinople. The knight errant continues to be the main protagonist, and the narrative is structured around his quests, but his amorous adventures are just as important as his chivalric enterprises" (Munday, *Amadis*, xiii). For other definitions, see Martí de Riquer, "Pórtico. Una mirada sobre los libros de caballerías," in *Amadís: Quinientos años*, 15, and Eisenberg, 1–9.

cien cuerpos de libros grandes" (Cervantes, i.vi.76), meaning more than one hundred folio-sized romance volumes. Once again, Cervantes's description is true to life, since the Iberian romances of chivalry, printed in gothic rotunda type, were normally published in folio, a clear indication that they were marketed as an upscale product aimed primarily at the upper classes.[14]

Thomas argues that during the latter half of the fifteenth century a series of historical conditions combined to favor the development of chivalric literature in Spain (28–31). First, chivalry continued to be practiced and to perform a social function in contemporary Spain. A case in point is Joanot Martorell, author of *Tirant*, himself an active knight.[15] A second significant event was the capture of Constantinople by the Turks in 1453, which represented an all too real proof of the threat posed by Muslim and Ottoman expansionism to the West at a moment when the Islamic presence was still a constituent part of Spain's political makeup. A third momentous event was the conquest of America, which opened the eyes of the Spaniards to the existence of a previously unknown mass of land. Such geographical discovery no doubt excited the creative imagination of writers, who were more inclined to conjure up images of fabulous creatures populating fantastic territories. In sum, despite their supposed literary escapism, the Iberian romances of chivalry emerged and developed, in part, as a response to a socio-historical context exploited with public success by authors in their seemingly endless narratives. Yet, there is one further historical circumstance that contributed to transform these romances into a literary phenomenon of unprecedented proportions. I am talking about the introduction of the printing press, which noticeably found an ally in the romance genre for its own economic survival in Spain. The development and expansion of both the romance genre and the printing press went hand in hand in Spain, to the extent that Marín Pina adroitly argues that the *libros de caballerías* must be considered historically as a

---

[14] For a bibliographical discussion of the genre, see Lucía Megías, *Imprenta*. See also Mª Carmen Marín Pina, "Los libros de caballerías castellanos," in *Amadís: Quinientos años*, 166–67. For a discussion of how the bibliographical record does indicate that these books were bought and read by the upper or noble class and those members of the middle class who could pay the high price commanded by these books, see Daniel Eisenberg, "Who Read the Romances of Chivalry?," *Kentucky Romance Quarterly* 20 (1973): 209–33; see also Chevalier, *Lectura y lectores*, 65–103. For the popular appeal of the genre, see Jordi Sánchez-Martí, "The Printed Popularization of the Iberian Broks of Chivalry across Sixteenth-Century Europe," in *Crossing Borders, Crossing Cultures: Popular Print in Europe, 1450–1900*, ed. Massimo Rospocher, Jeroen Salman, and Hannu Salmi (Berlin: De Gruyter, 2019), 159–80.

[15] For the reality of chivalry in fifteenth-century Spain, see Martín de Riquer, *Caballeros andantes españoles*. See also Noel Fallows, *Jousting in Medieval and Renaissance Iberia* (Woodbridge: Boydell, 2010). For biographical information on Martorell and his chivalric endevors, see Jaume Torró Torrent, "Martorell, Joanot," in *DBE*, 33:628–34.

publishing genre.[16] In other words, the literary impulse of the genre is to a certain extent driven by the desires of printers and booksellers alike, that had found in the romance form a wellspring of profitable creativity that matched the public's appetite for chivalric literature. By 1625, when the genre was going out of fashion, a total of 230 editions of romances had been published in Spain, a clear indication that the printers' investment in the genre must have yielded excellent returns.[17]

The genre's profit-making potential did not go unnoticed to foreign printers, who very soon started producing editions of various Iberian romances in Castilian, not in translation. Editions of *Amadís de Gaula* were printed in Spanish outside of Spain in 1519 in Rome,[18] in 1533 in Venice,[19] and in 1551 in Louvain.[20] The original version of *Las Sergas de Esplandián*, the fifth book of the *Amadís* series, was also printed in Rome in 1525.[21] Two editions in Spanish of *Palmerín*

---

[16] See "Los libros de caballerías castellanos," in *Amadís: Quinientos años*, 170.

[17] For a list of all known editions of these texts, see Lucía Megías, *Imprenta*, 597–608.

[18] IB 16421; Toda 180; Lucía, *Cat.*, no. 1. See also F. J. Norton, *Italian Printers, 1501–1520: An Annotated List, with an Introduction* (London: Bowes and Bowes, 1958), 101–2; see also M. C. Misiti, "Alcune rare edizioni spagnole pubblicate a Roma da Antonio Martínez de Salamanca," in *El libro antiguo español. Actas del segundo Coloquio Internacional (Madrid)*, ed. María Luisa López-Vidriero and Pedro M. Cátedra (Salamanca: Universidad de Salamanca, Biblioteca Nacional de Madrid, 1992), 307–23, esp. 310–14, and Stefano Neri, "Il romanzo cavalleresco spagnolo in Italia," in *Repertorio delle continuazioni italiane ai romanzi cavallereschi spagnoli: Ciclo di "Amadis di Gaula"*, ed. Anna Bognolo, Giovanni Cara, and Stefano Neri (Rome: Bulzoni, 2013), 91–93, with facsimile reproduction of the title page on 92, fig. 5.

[19] IB 16436; Toda 182; Lucía, *Cat.*, no. 3. See also Neri "Il romanzo cavalleresco spagnolo in Italia," 94–96, with facsimile reproduction of the title page on 95, fig. 8 (also in Toda, 1:81). A bibliographical description is also included in *Harvard College Library Department of Printing and Graphic Arts Catalogue of Books and Manuscripts, Part II: Italian 16th-Century Books*, compiled by Ruth Mortimer (Cambridge, MA: Belknap Press for Harvard University Press, 1974), no. 19.

[20] IB 16467; NB 802–3; Lucía, *Cat.*, nos 6–7. See also Jean Peeters-Fontainas, *Bibliographie des impressions espagnoles des Pays-Bas méridionaux* (Niewkoop: B. de Graaf, 1965), no. 45, with facsimile reproduction of the title pages to the two volumes. A bibliographical description is also available in *Cristóbal Plantino: un siglo de intercambios culturales entre Amberes y Madrid* (Madrid: Fundación Carlos de Amberes, 1995), 110–11.

[21] IB 16427; Toda 181. For a bibliographical description, see *Harvard College Library Catalogue, Part II*, no. 172. The title page is reproduced in Neri, "Il romanzo cavalleresco spagnolo in Italia," 92, fig. 6.

de Olivia were issued in Venice, one in 1526,[22] the other in 1534.[23] *Primaleón*, the second book in the *Palmerín* cycle, was also published in Venice in 1534.[24] These editions were intended for Spaniards living in Italy, yet they also anticipated an Italian readership with some knowledge of Spanish, as is implied in the didactic paratexts of the 1534 edition of *Primaleón*, prepared by Francisco Delicado for non-Spanish speakers.[25] In addition, the Venice editions printed in Spanish must have also contributed to the continental circulation of this literary corpus.[26] The publication of Italian reprints of original language editions, as in the case of *Amadís* and *Palmerín*, indicates that the first print run was sold out, confirming that the printers' choice was commercially sound. The profits earned with this editorial venture could have only been modest, because the potential market for these texts was limited to the Europeans with reading competence in Spanish.

The process of continental circulation of the genre gained considerable momentum when the Iberian romance corpus was translated into the main European vernaculars and penetrated national book markets abroad, thus making these texts accessible to growing segments of the European population. This international expansion started in France when *Amadís de Gaula* was translated

---

[22] IB 9799; Toda 3715; Lucía, *Cat.*, nos 30–31. A bibliographical description and location of extant copies is also provided by Dini, 10–12, with a facsimile reproduction of the title-page on table II. See also Neri, "Il romanzo cavalleresco spagnolo in Italia," 93, with facsimile of the title page on 94, fig. 7.

[23] IB 16744; Toda 3716; Lucía, *Cat.*, no. 32. See also Dini, 12–14. Neri, "Il romanzo cavalleresco spagnolo in Italia," 97, with facsimile of title page on 98, fig. 10, and Dini, table IV.

[24] IB 16780; Toda 3721; Lucía, *Cat.*, no. 35. See Neri, "Il romanzo cavalleresco spagnolo in Italia," 96, with facsimile of title page on 97, fig. 9, and Dini, table XI, fig. 20 and table XII, fig. 20.

[25] For a transcription of Delicado's brief treatise, see Lilia Ferrario de Orduna, "Hallazgo de un ejemplar más de *Amadís de Gaula* (Venecia, Juan Antonio de Sabia, 1533): Biblioteca Jorge Furt. 'Los talas', Luján (Buenos Aires), Argentina," in *Diálogo: Studi in onore di Lore Terracini*, ed. I. Pepe Sarno (Rome: Bulzoni, 1990), 451–69, at 466–69. Franco Bacchelli, "Il *Palmerín de Olivia* nel rifacimento di Lodovico Dolce," in *Studi sul "Palmerín,"* 3:159, argues that these Italian editions were aimed "non soltanto a un pubblico spagnolo (residente in Italia o in Spagna), ma anche a un pubblico italiano colto, che in quella epoca di normale diffusione della lingua castigliana poteva facilmente leggere l'opera nel testo originale."

[26] Because in the first quarter of the sixteenth century Venice was one of the most influential publishing centers in Europe, it is not unlikely that these editions were also meant for distribution in the rest of the Continent. The presence of numerous Italian editions of *Amadís* in German libraries is an indication that Italian printers put their wares on the international market, as suggests Weddige, 41–42. And the presence of Venetian editions of *Palmerin* romances in Parisian libraries may also indicate the foreign market reached by those printing houses; see Lucía Megías, *Cat.*, 141–53.

by Nicolas de Herberay des Essarts under the auspices of King Francis I.[27] Herberay's translation of the first eight books of the *Amadis* cycle was published between 1540 and 1548 and was an immediate success, in view of the number of reprints that appeared in the following years and of the continuations translated from, and added to, the original *Amadis* series.[28] Herberay handled Montalvo's version creatively, improving the original's style and adding interpolations, most notably of erotically charged scenes. Through Herberay's agency the medieval Spanish *Amadís* was modernized and transformed into a model of French Renaissance prose style, characterized by its elegance and rhetorical finesse.[29] Herberay's translations were initially published in expensive folio-sized volumes, with an accomplished *mise-en-page* that combined the modern-looking roman typeface with elaborate illustrations. The elevated style of the translations in addition to the impressive physical presentation of text displays a desire to invest this work with the qualities more commonly associated with the great humanist works of the period.[30] The final product was a textual object that conquered the high-end commercial market, thus enhancing the prestige of the *Amadis* romances among the French reading public and paving the way for the favorable reception enjoyed by the sixteenth-century translations of other Iberian romances, in particular those in the *Palmerin* series.

---

[27] For biographical information, see Jean-Pierre and Luce Guillerm, "Vestiges d'Herberay des Essarts Acuerdo olvido," *Studi Francesi* 51 (2007): 3–31. Cf. the dedication in Herberay's translation of the *Premier livre de la chronique de dom Flores de Grece* (1552; FB 19974), quoted in Rawles, 94 n. 14.

[28] For a list of all the French editions of the books in the *Amadis* series, see Michel Bideaux, "Bibliographie," in *Les "Amadis" en France au XVIe siècle*, Cahiers V. L. Saulnier 17 (Paris: Éditions Rue d'Ulm, 2000), 209–11, and Stefano Neri, "Cuadro de la difusión europea del ciclo del *Amadís de Gaula* (siglos XVI-XVII)," in *Amadís: Quinientos años después. Estudios en homenaje a Juan Manuel Cacho Blecua*, ed. José Manuel Lucía Megías and Mª Carmen Marín Pina (Alcalá de Henares: Centro de Estudios Cervantinos, 2008), 569–73. A detailed bibliography of all editions printed up to 1544 appears in Rawles, 104–8. For the French continuations, see Thomas, 199–203. As Sylvia Roubaud points out, "Los ocho *Amadises* del señor des Essarts lograron suplantar rápidamente a las viejas narraciones artúricas que, remozadas y reeditadas a menudo durante los primeros decenios del siglo XVI, habían mantenido viva la curiosidad de los lectores franceses por la literatura caballeresca nacional" ("Libros de caballerías en Francia," in *Amadís: Quinientos años*, 321).

[29] See Mireille Huchon, "Amadis, parfaicte idée de nostre langue françoise," in *Les "Amadis" en France au XVIe siècle*, 183–200; and the discussion in Jane H. M. Taylor, *Rewriting Arthurian Romance in Renaissance France: From Manuscript to Printed Book* (Cambridge: D. S. Brewer, 2014), 147–81. Cf. Rawles, 94.

[30] For a discussion of the innovative character of this edition's typographical and iconographic presentation, see Jean-Marc Chatelain, "L'illustration d'*Amadis de Gaule* dans les éditions françaises du XVIe siècle," *Les "Amadis" en France au XVIe siècle*, 41–52.

The publication of French translations of the Iberian romances ran parallel to the appearance of the same corpus in Italian. The first Italian translations of Iberian romances appeared in 1544 and included the *Historia del valorosissimo cavalliere Palmerino d'Oliva* (1544; *Edit16* 55981), translated by Mambrino Roseo da Fabriano and printed in Venice by Michele Tramezzino. The *Palmerino d'Oliva* was soon followed by Roseo's translation of almost the entire cycle of *Amadis*. Between 1546 and 1551 Tramezzino published books I–VII, IX–XII of *Amadis*,[31] and in 1554 Roseo also completed the translation into Italian of the *Palmerin* cycle with the appearance in 1548 of *Primaleone* (Toda 3722)[32] and *Platir* (*Edit16* 55995; Toda 3725), and *Palmerino d'Inghilterra* in 1553–54.[33] The Venetian printers wanted to capitalize on the public's fascination with this genre and, once the two cycles became available in their entirety in Italian translations, they prompted the composition of original continuations. To the twelve Spanish books of *Amadis*, thirteen new books were added, and to the four Iberian titles in the *Palmerin* cycle an additional seven were newly composed in Italian.[34] Unlike the publication of these texts in France, where they were aimed at the more affluent readers, in Italy their target market was more ample and popular. The

---

[31] Roseo failed to translate bk. VIII, Juan Díaz's *Lisuarte de Grecia* (1526; IB 16428) and bk. XI part 2, Feliciano de Silva's *Florisel de Niquea*, part 4 (1551; IB 16466). See Stefano Neri, "Cuadro de la difusión europea del ciclo de *Amadís*," in *Amadís: Quinientos años después*, 566–69.

[32] Not in *Edit16*. See *Short-title Catalogue of Books Printed in Italy and of Italian Books Printed in Other Countries from 1465 to 1600 now in the British Museum* (London: British Museum, 1958), 539. For a bibliographical description of this and the other works that form the *Palmerin* cycle in Italian, see Stefano Neri, "Cuadro de la difusión europea del ciclo palmeriniano (siglos XVI–XVII)," in *Palmerín: 500 años*, 287–94.

[33] Not in *Edit16*. See *Short-title Catalogue of Books Printed in Italy*, 486.

[34] For a description of the Italian circulation of the Iberian chivalric romances with lists of the Italian translations and continuations, see Anna Bognolo, "Il 'Progetto Mambrino.' Per una esplorazione delle traduzioni e continuazioni italiane dei libros de caballerías," *Rivista di Filologia e Letterature Ispaniche* 6 (2003): 190–202; Bognolo, "Libros de caballerías en Italia," in *Amadís: Quinientos años*, 332–41; and Toda, 1:79–88. For the continuations to the *Palmerin* cycle, see Bognolo, "Los palmerines italianos: una primera aproximación," in *Palmerín: 500 años*, 255–84; and for the continuations to the *Amadis* series, see Stefano Neri, "Il ciclo italiano di *Amadis di Gaula*," and "Censimiento bibliografico del ciclo italiano di *Amadis de* Gaula," both in *Repertorio delle continuazioni italiane ai romanzi cavallereschi spagnoli*, 149–61 and 199–257, respectively. See also Thomas, 180–99. For the Italian translation of Iberian books of chivalry other than those belonging to the cycles of *Amadis* and *Palmerin*, see Neri, "Il romanzo cavalleresco spagnolo in Italia," 106–9.

Italian translations were published in affordable, handy pocket-size, octavo editions printed in italic typeface on low-quality paper and with poor-quality ink.[35]

These chivalric texts also attracted the attention of readers in northern Europe. In the Low Countries the dissemination of the Spanish books of chivalry in translation started in the same decade as in France and Italy with the publication in 1546 of the first two books in the *Amadis* series. This is a folio edition, printed in Antwerp by Marten Nuyts, that has remained elusive to scholars, since only one battered and imperfect copy exists, now the property of a private collector.[36] Owing to the relatively early date of this edition, its very existence had been questioned. Thomas declares, "Responsible Dutch writers still quote the *absurdly early* date 1546 . . . The date is no doubt a misprint."[37] This categorical statement rests, however, on rather shaky foundations, since Thomas was unaware not only of the existence of this edition, but also of the relation the Dutch translation had to the other versions of this romance. Thomas erroneously assumes that "The Dutch *Amadis* series was translated from the French" (235), in which case it would not be completely impossible that a Dutch translation could be produced in 1546, only six years after the first appearance of Herberay's translation. Conversely, books I and II were rendered into Dutch directly from the Spanish, and thus it is an inexact overstatement to describe it as *absurdly early* when it appeared some fifty years after the publication of the Spanish *editio princeps*. Although the Dutch edition contains no reference identifying the author of

---

[35] See Augustus Pallotta, "Venetian Printers and Spanish Literature," *Comparative Literature* 43 (1991), 33–34, who argues that the romances were read by "the nobility, by literati, and by the merchants" as well as by members of "the lower urban classes of small merchants, skilled workers, craftsmen, laborers, and the like." For an analysis of the reception of this literary corpus, see Neri, "Il romanzo cavalleresco spagnolo in Italia," 113–39. According to Paul F. Grendler, "Form and Function in Italian Renaissance Popular Books," *Renaissance Quarterly* 46 (1993): 451–83, italic types were adopted for popular texts by Venetian printers in the 1530s.

[36] Only book one of this edition has survived; for a bibliographical description, see Bert van Selm, *De "Amadis van Gaule"-romans: Productie, verspreiding en receptie van een bestseller in de vroegmoderne tijd in de Nederlanden, met een bibliografie van de Nederlandse vertalingen* (Leiden: SNL, 2001), 103–4, with a facsimile reproduction of the title page on 15 and another woodcut on 105; see 14, 28–30 for evidence attributing the edition of book II to the same printer. See also Neri, "Cuadro de la difusión europea del ciclo de *Amadís*," 578–81; Tineke Groot, "Libros de caballerías en los Países Bajos (Flandes y Holanda)," in *Amadís: Quinientos años*, 356–59; Thomas, 234–41.

[37] Thomas, 235 n. 2; my emphasis. For an early reference to the 1546 Dutch edition, see C. J. N[uyts], *Essai sur l'imprimerie des Nutius*, 2nd ed. (Brussels: Vandereyt, 1858), 130.

the translation, it seems probable that it was translated by the printer himself, who before settling in Antwerp had lived in Spain for quite some time.[38]

The Iberian romances were not again reproduced in the Low Countries until 1561, when the prestigious and influential Antwerp printing house of Christopher Plantin put on the market all the first twelve books of the *Amadis* series in French translation.[39] Though intended primarily for an audience assumed not to be native francophones, this massive and unprecedented output of chivalric romances must have opened the door for further developing the Dutch-speaking market.[40] In 1568 Daniel Vervliet in association with Guillam van Parijs reissued Nuyts's translations of books I and II and next printed a translation of books III and IV.[41] Following Plantin's example, the quarto editions produced by Van Parijs and Vervliet were less ambitious than the 1546 edition and aimed at a wider book-buying public. Yet, just as in the 1546 edition, the translation of

---

[38] For information on the printer, see J. F. Peeters-Fontainas, *L'officine espagnole de Martin Nutius à Anvers* (Antwerp: Société des Bibliophiles Anversois, 1956), who comments, "Le jeune Martin a voyagé plusieurs années en Espagne, (c'est sans doute sous le nom de *Martin de Mera* qu'il faudrait y rechercher ses traces) et il s'est assimilé ainsi la langue du pays" (12); see also Anne Rouzet, *Dictionnaire des imprimeurs, libraires et éditeurs des XVe et XVIe siècles dans les limites géographiques de la Belgique actuelle* (Nieuwkoop: De Graaf, 1975), 161–62. For clear proof that the Dutch originated directly from the Spanish, see William Davis, *Verslag van een onderzoek betreffende de betrekkingen tusschen de Nederlandsche en de Spaansche letterkunde in de 16e–18e eeuw* ('s-Gravenhage: Martinus Nijhoff, 1918), 10, and the comparison of the Spanish, French, and Dutch translations included in 15–22.

[39] For bibliographical descriptions of the Plantin editions, see Leon Voet, *The Plantin Press (1555–1589): A Bibliography of the Works Printed and Published by Christopher Plantin at Antwerp and Leiden* (Amsterdam: Van Hoeve, 1980), 1:58–71. See Elly Cockx-Indestege, Geneviève Glorieux, and Bart Op de Beeck, *Belgica Typographica, 1541–1600* (Nieuwkoop: B. de Graaf, 1968–1994), nos 87–91, 5035–53, 7768; see also NB 805, 807, 810, 813–14, 816, 818, 820, 822, 824, 826, 829; and see no. 23506 for an edition of *Palmerin d'Olive* published in 1572.

[40] A new preface was added to the first book of *Amadis* recommending this work "A tous ceus qui font profession d'enseigner la langue françoise en la Ville d'Anvers" [*to all those who teach the French language in the city of Antwerp*]. The preface is edited by Michel Bideaux, *Amadis de Gaule, Livre I*, trans. N. Herberay des Essarts (Paris: Champion, 2006), 681–83. For a discussion of the influence the Plantin's French, quarto editions of *Amadis* had on the Dutch editions, see Sylvia van Zanen, "'Overghezet wt het Fransoys in onse Duytsche tale': De invloed van Franstalige Antwerpse edities van de *Amadis van Gaule* op de Nederlandstalige uitgaven," in Van Selm, *De "Amadis van Gaule"-romans*, 183–97.

[41] Note that there is no surviving copy of Vervliet's edition of bks 1–3; see Van Selm, *De "Amadis van Gaule"-romans*, 104, 110, and 113. For a description of the edition of book IV, published in 1574 (NB 864), see Van Selm, 117–18. For descriptions of all Dutch editions, see also STCN.

books III and IV printed by Vervliet and Van Parijs was made directly from the Spanish, most likely by Vervliet himself, who had lived in Spain for six years.[42] In the following years and up until 1624 new translations of books V to XXI of the *Amadis* cycle, made from French into Dutch, were published, while editions of previous translations were continuously reissued, thus showing how successful this literary corpus proved in the Low Countries.[43]

The *Palmerin* cycle was also represented in Dutch translation, although editions started to appear relatively late. In 1602/3 the inaugural work of the cycle, translated from French, was printed in Arnhem under the title *Een seer schoone en genoechelicke historie, vanden [. . .] ridder, Palmerijn van Olijve*.[44] In the following years editions of *Primalion van Grieken* were published in Rotterdam. The first three parts of *Primalion*, corresponding to the Spanish *Primaleón*, appeared between 1613 and 1621. The final part, based on Roseo's continuation of 1560, was published in 1619.[45]

Next, the Spanish romances of chivalry were translated into German, mostly through French, but also from Italian. Aware of how profitable the publication of this literary corpus had been in other European countries, the influential German publisher Sigmund Feyerabend also wanted to share in these texts' profitability and from 1569 until 1575 he published books I-XIII of the *Amadis* series, all printed in octavo-sized volumes.[46] In the years that followed German printers

---

[42] For biographical information on Vervliet, see Rouzet, *Dictionnaire des imprimeurs de la Belgique actuelle*, 235–36. See Van Zanen, "'Overghezet wt het Fransoys in onse Duytsche tale,'" 198–206, esp. 206. Note that Davids, *Betrekkingen tusschen de Nederlandsche en de Spaansche letterkunde*, 10, considers that the translation of books III and IV was not made from Spanish, a position also adopted by Van Selm, De *"Amadis van Gaule"-romans*: "Alle andere delen [i.e., other than bks I and II] zijn uit het Frans vertaald" (14).

[43] For a detailed list of all these editions with their bibliographic description, see Van Selm, De *"Amadis van Gaule"-romans*, 104–71. For the sixteenth-century extant editions (Bks 1–7, 9–12), see NB 874–78, 880–84, 886.

[44] For a list of all the editions in the Dutch *Palmerin* series, see Neri, "Cuadro de la difusión europea del ciclo palmeriniano," 307–9.

[45] For an analysis of the plot of Roseo's sequel, see Bognolo, "Los palmerines italianos," 271–73.

[46] See Thomas, 221–34; and Weddige, 36–49. For bibliographical descriptions of the *editiones principes* of these works, see Weddige, 346–64, nos 1, 6, 10, 14, 20, 28, 32, 35, 38, 41, 44, 47, 50. Note that in 1583 Feyerabend also produced a folio edition of bks I–XIII; see Weddige, 346–65, nos 3, 7, 12, 16, 22, 30, 33, 36, 39, 42, 45, 48, 51. For an assessment of the German translation of the first book of *Amadís*, see Sigmund J. Barber, "*Amadis de Gaule* in Germany: Translation or Adaptation?," *Daphnis* 21 (1992): 109–28. For biographical information about Feyerabend, see Josef Benzing, "Feyerabend, Sigismund (1527/28–1590)," in *Neue Deutsche Biographie* (Berlin: Duncker & Humbolt, 1961), 5:119. The first book in the *Amadis* series is edited by Adelbert von Keller, *Amadis: Erstes buch. Nach der ältester deutschen bearbeitung* (Stuttgart: Litterarischer verein, 1857). See

published translations of book XIV–XXI as well as the Italian continuations,[47] and in 1594–1595 three original German continuations were added to the cycle (bks. XXII–XXIV).[48] However, none of the other Castilian books of chivalry, including the *Palmerin* series, was made available to German-speaking audiences.

The Iberian romances arrived relatively late to England, owing in part to the successful transition of the Middle English metrical romances to the medium of print. Initiallly published at the end of the fifteenth century by Wynkyn de Worde and Richard Pynson, the English verse romances continued to appear in print in the 1560s, when William Copland was still reprinting texts such as *Bevis of Hampton* and *Sir Degare*, among others.[49] Copland, however, was unable to diversify the catalogue of chivalric romances he inherited from De Worde, and when he died in 1569 the genre's market worth was virtually exhausted. It seems reasonable that the English printers were then prepared to consider alternative sources of chivalric literature to replace the medieval English texts and thus continue exploiting commercially the English audience's fondness for chivalric romance. Joshua Phillips has argued that the resurgence of chivalric romance in the last quarter of the sixteenth century is to a large extent attributable to the patent system established by the Stationers' Company, since many publishers were hard-pressed "to find publishable texts that were both unpatented (perhaps even unpatentable) and, at least potentially profitable" (128–29). One solution, Phillips suggests, was provided by "editing, translating, and printing romances in numbers never before seen in England"(129). There is no denying that the institutionalization of the patent system may have been an incentive to print romances. Yet, it is also true that with the publication of the Iberian chivalric romances printers and publishers stumbled on a seeming goldmine, which had gone unnoticed to previous printers because of their focus on reprinting native

---

also Henrike Schaffert, *Der Amadisroman: Serielles Erzählen in der frühen Neuzeit* (Berlin: De Gruyter, 2015).

[47] See Weddige, 352–70, nos 18, 25, 27, 53, 55, 57–58, 60, 62–64.

[48] See Weddige, 370–71, nos 65–67.

[49] For more information, see Jordi Sánchez-Martí, "The Printed History of the Middle English Verse Romances," *MP* 107 (2009): 1–31. The latest new chivalric romance to appear in print was the *Knight of Curtesy* (STC 24223), printed by Copland around 1556. The prose romances, however, did not prove as profitable to printers as the metrical ones; see Sánchez-Martí, "The Printed Transmission of Medieval Romance from William Caxton to Wynkyn de Worde, 1473–1535," in *The Transmission of Medieval Romance: Metres, Manuscripts and Early Prints*, ed. Ad Putter and Judith Jefferson (Cambridge: D. S. Brewer, 2018), 170–90. For Copland's publication of romance texts, see A. S. G. Edwards, "William Copland and the Identity of Printed Middle English Romance," in *The Matter of Identity in Medieval Romance*, ed. Phillipa Hardman (Cambridge: D. S. Brewer, 2002), 139–47. For biographical information about Copland, see H. R. Tedder, rev. by Mary C. Erler, "Copland, William (d. 1569)," in *ODNB*, 13:336.

romance texts. This new generation of Elizabethan printers and publishers maintained a commitment to the romance genre because these texts elicited a positive response from readers and, potentially, could bring substantial gains. In other words, in the final decades of the sixteenth century, English printers and publishers enlisted the collaboration of a handful of translators to capitalize on the readerly interest in chivalric romance, which had remained more or less unflagging since the introduction of the printing press in England a century before.[50]

Even so, *The Mirror of Princely Deeds and Knighthood* (STC 18859), namely the first English translation of an Iberian romance to appear in print, was not published until approximately 1578. A translation of book I of Diego Ortúñez de Calahorra's *Espejo de Príncipes y Cavalleros* (1555), *Mirror* is also remarkable for having been produced by a woman—Margaret Tyler—, for being a direct translation from Spanish, and for preceding all other European translations of Calahorra's original.[51] In her recent edition of Tyler's *Mirror*, Joyce Boro suggests that this translation "initiated a craze for Spanish chivalric romance."[52] I will argue that this statement is in need of some qualification. To begin with, as early as 1571, the fifteen-year-old Charles Stewart started to translate *Amadis de Gaule* from French, although he left it unfinished before completing the second chapter.[53] The existence of this textual witness is an indication that the adventures of the heroes of the Spanish romances were circulating in England prior to the publication of English translations. In addition, about 1572 Thomas Paynell's translation of the French *Thresor des douze livres d'Amadis de Gaule* was published with the title *The Treasurie of Amadis of Fraunce* (STC 545). This work contains selections from the romance, but does not serve the conventional purposes of a

---

[50] Phillips contends, "that it was not the market (or the "demand" side of the economy) that called for romances, but rather the institutions of production (or the "supply" side) which brought them forth in such great numbers in the last third of the sixteenth century" (129). Still, without the enthusiastic public response received by the romances, their publication would have been discontinued.

[51] Calahorra's *Espejo* was translated into Italian in 1601, into French in 1617, and into German in 1781–83; see Tyler, *Mirror*, 3. Not only is the female agency of the translation remarkable, but also, as pointed out by Helen Moore, Tyler's is "the first English translation of a secular work to be made by a woman," "Ancient and Modern Romance," in *OHLTE*, 337. For biographical information, see Louise Schleiner, "Tyler, Margaret (fl. 1558–1578)," in *ODNB*, 55:769.

[52] Tyler, *Mirror*, 3; cf. a similar statement on 5.

[53] The manuscript version of Stewart's translation is preserved in BL, Lansdowne MS 766, fol. 1–20; for a description, see *Catalogue of the Lansdowne Manuscripts in the British Museum* (London, 1819), 171; H. L. D. Ward, *Catalogue of Romances in the Department of Manuscripts in the British Museum* (London: British Museum, 1883), 1:787–88. For further information, see Thomas, 253 n. 2.

work of chivalric fiction, but instead of a conduct book.[54] Yet, the decision to print a book with such a title very likely implies that some English readers were acquainted with the hero of the Spanish romance and with the immense prestige Herberay's translation enjoyed in France, and thus inclined to purchase this Amadisian spin-off.

Charles Stewart's exercise in translation and the publication of Paynell's *Treasurie*, together with other such like circumstantial testimonies,[55] provide evidence that there existed increasing awareness of the Iberian romances in Britain prior to the publication of Tyler's *Mirror*. Still, in order to judge whether the appearance of Tyler's translation was the starting point for the "craze" for the Iberian romances—as Boro suggests—or not, we need to ascertain if Tyler's example could have directly influenced Anthony Munday's decision to English the Iberian literary corpus. To do so I propose to consider some essential dates in the literary careers of both Tyler and Munday. The license for the first edition of Tyler's *Mirror* was entered in the Stationer's Register on August 4, 1578 (Arber, 2:334), and thereafter printed by Thomas East without date. According to the STC, the text was printed before the end of 1578, while Joseph de Perott thinks possible that the book appeared in 1579,[56] and Thomas believes 1580 to

---

[54] For more information on the French work, see Véronique Benhaïm, "Les *Thresors d'Amadis*," in *Les "Amadis" en France au XVIe siècle*, 157–81. For more on Paynell's translation, see Helen Moore, "Ancient and Modern Romance," 337. Moore considers that with the publication of Paynell's *Treasurie*, "the Spanish books of chivalry, the *libros de caballería*[s], made their first appearance in English"; the same consideration is expressed by Helen Hackett, *Women and Romance Fiction in the English Renaissance* (Cambridge: Cambridge University Press, 2000), 57. Strictly speaking, however, the credit should be given to Charles Stewart. For the French version used by Paynell for his translation, see Alejandra Ortiz-Salamovich, "Establishing the Edition of Thomas Paynell's Source-Text for *The Treasurie of Amadis of Fraunce* (c. 1572)," *Notes and Queries*, n.s., 63 (2016): 379–81.

[55] Cf. Thomas Underdowne's comments in the prefatory address to the reader to the second edition of his translation of Heliodorus's *Aethiopian History* (1577), where he states, "*Mort Darthure, Arthur* of litle *Britaine*, yea, and *Amadis* of *Gaule*, &c. accompt violente murder, or murder for no cause, manhoode; and fornication and all vnlawful luste, friendely loue" (sig. ¶3r; STC 13042). An inventory of Mary Queen of Scots' books dated March 26, 1578, mentions "The first buik of Amades de Gaule," "The nynte buk of Amades de Gaule," "The levint buik of the Amades de Gaule"; see George F. Barwick, *A Book Bound for Mary Queen of Scots* (London: The Bibliographical Society, 1901), 23, 25. Previously, William Cecil, Lord Burghley, bought a copy of the French *Amadis* sometime between January 1554 and December 1555, according to a running account with the London bookseller William Seres; see Conyers Read, *Mr Secretary Cecil and Queen Elizabeth* (London: Jonathan Cape, 1955), 114; on Seres, see Elizabeth Evenden, "Seres, William (d. 1578×80)," in *ODNB*, 49:773–74. See also Julian Sharman, *The Library of Mary Queen of Scots* (London: E. Stock, 1889).

[56] See Perott, "The Mirrour of Knighthood," *Romanic Review* 4 (1913): 397–402.

be more likely (p. 243 n. 1). If the book was printed in the last quarter of 1578 or during the first half of 1579, the publication of Tyler's *Mirror* would have had no direct bearing on the literary activities of Munday, since during that period he was out of the country. As Munday recounts in his *English Romayne Life*, published in 1582, in the fall of 1578 he traveled to the Continent and spent some months in Rome before returning to England in July of 1579. While on the Continent, Munday was cutoff from new English publications, whereas it is quite likely that he became acquainted with the Iberian books of chivalry, as I have discussed elsewhere.[57] In the prefatory epistle to his *Zelauto*, printed in 1580, Munday announces the forthcoming publication of his translation of *Palmerin of England*,[58] whose license was secured by John Charlewood on February 13, 1581 (Arber, 2:388). Irrespective of the date of publication of Tyler's *Mirror*, all the evidence seems to suggest that Munday's interest in and enthusiasm for the Iberian romances emerged independently of Tyler's translation, since it goes back to his time on the Continent, where he traveled before *Mirror* was printed. Still, Tyler does deserve credit for making the commercial possibilities of the corpus of Iberian romances visible to English printers. Having said that, it probably took Munday some convincing to gain Charlewood's commitment to print the Iberian romances, since the printer exercised caution in his actions. First, Charlewood did not rash to apply for a licence, but probably waited until he could read some of Munday's translation of *Palmerin of England*. Second, the decision to alter the narrative order of the *Palmerin* series and start printing not the inaugural work —i.e., *Palmerin d'Oliva*— but a sequel is attributable to Charlewood, who probably wanted to exploit the hero's Englishness and attract the attention of prospective buyers. All in all, it is safe to argue that Thomas East's publication of Tyler's *Mirror* did not trigger Munday's decision to read and translate the Iberian chivalric romances, whereas it probably tipped the balance in favor of convincing Charlewood to print them.

No copy of the first edition of *Palmerin of England* has been preserved, although it must have been favorably received, in view of the publication of other translations of Iberian romances that followed. The next romance to be printed was Munday's *Palmerin d'Oliva* (STC 19157) in 1588, and the entire, original cycle of *Palmerin* was soon completed with the publication of *Palmendos* (1589; STC 18064) and *Primaleon of Greece* (1595–96, [1597], 1619; STC 20366, 20366a, 20367). Additionally, Munday also contrived to translate the four books of *Amadis de Gaule* (1590, 1595, 1618; STC 541, 542, 543), their continuation (1598; STC 542.5), the Italian continuation to *Palmerin of England* (1602; STC 19165),

---

[57] See Jordi Sánchez-Martí, "*Zelauto*'s Polinarda and the *Palmerin* Romances," *Cahiers Élisabéthains* 89 (2016): 74–82.

[58] See Munday, *Zelauto*, 6.

and the non-cyclical *Palladine of England* (1588; STC 5541).[59] Throughout the seventeenth century, most of Munday's translations were reprinted several times: *Amadis de Gaule* (1664; Wing L2731), *Palladine of England* (1664, Wing C5090; 1700, Wing C5090A–AB), *Palmendos* (1653, Wing F377; 1663, Wing F378), and *Palmerin of England* (1609, STC 19162; 1616, STC 19163; 1639, STC 19164; 1664, Wing M2613A, M2613B; 1685, Wing M2613C).[60]

Besides Munday and Tyler, other contemporary translators also contributed to the dissemination of the Iberian romances in England. A translator signing himself "R.P." completed the translation of book I of Ortúñez de Calahorra's *Espejo* (1585–86; STC 18862.5, 18864). Another unknown translator that identified himself as "L.A." translated other parts of *Espejo* (1598–99; STC 18869–70) and was probably responsible for rendering into English the first fifty chapters of the first part of Jerónimo Fernández's *Don Belianís de Grecia* (1547; IB 8699), published in English as *The Honour of Chivalrie set down in the History of Prince Don Belianis* (1598; STC 1804).[61] William Barley produced a translation of *Palmendos* alternative to Munday's and published it under the title *The Delightful History of Celestina the Faire* (1596; STC 4910), in which the names of the protagonists have also been changed.[62] Finally, more continuations to the *Amadis* series were translated during the seventeenth century by Francis Kirkman (1652;

---

[59] For a list of Munday's translations of romances, see Hayes, "Romances" and "Postscript"; Turner, 181–83. Updated bibliographical information is provided in an appendix by Hamilton, 199–206. *Palmendos* corresponds to the first thirty-two chapters in the French version of *Primaleón*; see Leticia Álvarez-Recio, "Chapters Translated by Anthony Munday in *The History of Palmendos* (1589): A Long-Standing Error," *Notes and Queries*, n.s., 62 (2015): 549–51. *Palladine of England* is a translation of the first part of the Spanish romance *Florando de Inglaterra* (1545; IB 16605) based on the intermediary French translation by Claude Colet (1555; FB 40370).

[60] For *Palmerin d'Oliva*, see below.

[61] For more information, see María J. Sánchez de Nieva, "*The Honour of Chivalrie* (1598): The Englishing of the Castilian Chivalric Romance *Don Belianís de Grecia*," *English Studies* 95 (2014): 860–77. The second part to this translation was "newly written in English" by Francis Kirkman in 1664 (Nieva, 866; Wing K633) and a new continuation was added by Kirkman himself in 1673 (Wing K634). As Thomas states, "the *Honour of Chivalry* provides the unique instance of an English continuation of one of the Spanish romances" (257–58). For bibliographical information, see L. H. Newcomb, "Kirkman, Francis (b. 1632, d. in or after 1680)," in *ODNB*, 31:802–3.

[62] For more information on Barley, see Gerald D. Johnson, "William Barley, 'Publisher & Seller of Bookes,' 1591–1614," *The Library*, 6th ser., 11 (1989): 10–46. For Barley's version of *Palmendos*, see Leticia Álvarez Recio, "Anthony Munday's *Palmendos* (1589) in the Early Modern English Book Trade: Print and Reception," *Atlantis* 38.1 (2016): 58.

Wing L2731A), a translator known as "W. P." (1664; Wing H1493), and an anonymous translator (1693; Wing M2877).[63]

The publication of the Iberian chivalric romances in Portugal deserves separate treatment. Owing to the country's linguistic, geographical, and cultural proximity, there was no need to translate Castilian books of chivalry into Portuguese.[64] Editions in Spanish were printed in Portugal and, in addition, original romances were also composed in Portuguese. The most significant Portuguese contribution to the corpus of chivalric romances is undoubtedly *Palmeirim de Inglaterra*, a work composed by Francisco de Moraes (ca. 1543–44) using characters and narrative elements derived from *Palmerín de Olivia*. This connection was seized right away by Spanish printers who published a Castilian translation in 1547–48 (IB 16732–33) that predates the publication of *Palmeirim de Inglaterra* in Portuguese. In fact, the Spanish edition, praised by Cervantes "porque él [i.e., *Palmerín de Inglaterra*] por sí es muy bueno" (1.vi.82; "as a thing rarely delectable"; Shelton, 1:37), put this text on the map and made possible the printing of translations into French, Italian, and English. The Portuguese original was not printed until 1564–1567 (IB 16734/13401). A first continuation was added in 1587 (parts 3 and 4; IB 16735) and a second one in 1602 (parts 5 and 6; IB B22345).[65] Apart from these Portuguese additions to the *Palmerin* series, there

---

[63] For Kirkman's translation of *Amadis*, see Helen Moore, "Admirable Inventions: Francis Kirkman and the Translation of Romance in the 1650s," in *Seventeenth-Century Fiction: Text and Transmission*, ed. Jacqueline Glomski and Isabelle Moreau (Oxford: Oxford University Press, 2016), 143–58. For an overview of the circulation of the Iberian romances in England, see Patchell, 12–22; Helen Moore, "Ancient and Modern Romance," 337–40; Stefano Neri, "Libros de caballerías en Inglaterra," in *Amadís: Quinientos años*, 360–63; Neri, "Cuadro de la difusión europea de *Amadís*," 581–83; Neri, "Cuadro de la difusión europea del ciclo palmeriniano," 300–307; and Thomas, 242–301.

[64] The single one exception is a manuscript translation of the third part of *Florisel de Niquea* in Coimbra, Biblioteca da Universidade, MS 123.

[65] For the *Palmeirim de Inglaterra*, see Purser; Thomas, 103–15; and *Bibliografia Geral Portuguesa*, Academia das Ciências de Lisboa (Lisbon: Imprensa Nacional–Casa de Moeda, 1983), 3:423–26. See also, more recently, Carlos Rubio Pacho, "En torno a la *editio princeps* del *Palmerín de Inglaterra*," in *Amadís de Gaula: quinientos años después*, 711–29, where he argues that Moraes's work was printed in its Spanish translation earlier than in the Portuguese original. For a bibliographical description of the earliest Portuguese edition of *Palmeirim*, see Antonio Joaquim Anselmo, *Bibliografia das obras impressas em Portugal no século XVI* (Lisbon: Biblioteca Nacional, 1926), no. 397; see also Clara Louisa Penney, *Printed Books, 1468–1700, in the Hispanic Society of America* (New York: Hispanic Society of America, 1965), 405. For a brief discussion of the printed dissemination of the Portuguese books of chivalry, see Aurelio Vargas Díaz-Toledo, "Os livros de cavalarias em Castela e Portugal. Um caso particular: a *Selva de Cavalarias Famozas*, de António de Brito de Fonseca," in *Portugal und Spanien: Probleme (k)einer Beziehung*, ed. Tobias Brandenberger and Henry Thorau (Frankfurt: Peter Lang, 2005), 67–68.

is a further series of continuations to the *Palmeirim de Inglaterra* that were composed in the late sixteenth century but are preserved only in manuscript form. These continuations, in three parts, known with the title *Crónica do invicto D. Duardos de Bretanha, príncipe de Inglaterra, filho de Palmeirim e da princesa Polinarda*, are independent from the versions printed in 1587 and 1602, and are attributed to Gonçalo Coutinho.[66] Note, however, that none of the continuations to *Palmeirim de Inglaterra*, either in print or in manuscript, was ever translated into any other language.

The Spanish *Palmerín de Olivia*

The *Libro del famoso e muy esforçado cavallero Palmerín de Olivia* was first published in Salamanca on December 22, 1511, most probably by the printer Juan de Porras.[67] It appeared in the wake of the successful publication of Rodríguez de Montalvo's *Amadís de Gaula* of ca. 1496, reprinted in 1508 (IB 16414), and one year after *Las sergas de Esplandián* (Seville, 1510; IB 16416) and *Florisando* (Salamanca, 1510; IB 16415), respectively the fifth and sixth books of the *Amadís* series. The author of *Palmerín* was hoping to replicate the same commercial

---

[66] See Aurelio Vargas Díaz-Toledo, "Los libros de caballerías portugueses," in *Actas del XIII congreso de la Asociación Hispánica de Literatura Medieval (Valladolid, 15 a 19 de septiembre de 2009). In memoriam Alan Deyermond*, ed. José Manuel Fradejas Rueda et al. (Valladolid: Ayuntamiento de Valladolid; Universidad de Valladolid; Asociación Hispánica de Literatura Medieval, 2010), 2:1755–65. The existing manuscripts are listed in *Palmerín de Ingalaterra (Libro I)*, ed. Aurelio Vargas Díaz-Toledo, Los Libros de Rocinante 23 (Alcalá de Henares: Centro de Estudios Cervantinos, 2006), 239.

[67] IB 16737; Dini, no. 1. The date is included in the colophon to the *editio princeps*: "Acabóse esta presente obra en la muy noble ciudad de Salmantia a xxij días del mes de Deciembre del año del Nascimiento de Nuestro Señor Iesu Cristo del mil e quinientos e onze años" (*Palmerín de Olivia*, 384). The edition was issued with no indication of printer, but Norton, *Printing*, 26, attributes it to Juan de Porras. For a bibliographical description of the only extant copy, see Norton, *Catalogue*, no. 496; Ruiz Fidalgo, no. 88; Dini, 5–8, and table I for a facsimile reproduction of the title page; see also Luisa Cuesta Gutiérrez, *La imprenta en Salamanca. Avance al estudio de la tipografía salmantina (1480–1944)* (Salamanca: Diputación Provincial de Salamanca, 1960), 129. For biographical information about the printer, see Juan Delgado Casado, *Diccionario de impresores españoles (Siglos XV–XVII)* (Madrid: Arco/Libros, 1996), 2:547–49, and Fernando de la Fuente Arranz, "Porras, Juan de. ?, c. 1450–c. 1520," in *DBE*, 42:35–36. According to Thomas, "on the title-page of this edition the hero's name is misprinted Palmerin de Olivia" (85 n. 2). The etymology of the hero's name, however, confirms that the spelling on the title page of the *editio princeps* is accurate: "Aquella montaña adonde Cardín dexó al fijo de Griana [i.e., Palmerín] se llamava en aquella tierra Olivia" (*Palmerín de Olivia*, 27); see further Di Stefano, 630–31. All later editions give the title as *Palmerín de Oliva*.

success of *Amadís* and its sequels, though not by producing yet another continuation, but instead by constructing an original narrative that followed the biographical development of a new hero and all the attendant adventures. Notwithstanding *Palmerín*'s narrative independence from the Amadisian cycle, the author of the new romance took Montalvo's work as his or her model and found inspiration in this text's episodes and motifs (cf. Thomas, 89–90; Patchell, 8). What *Palmerín*'s author was hoping to do was to benefit from the vogue for chivalric literature initiated by Montalvo, but by cloning the formula of *Amadís* s/he also expanded the creative possibilities of the genre. From then on writers could produce continuations to both *Amadís* and *Palmerín*, as we have seen in the previous section of this introduction, and thus multiply the presence of chivalric literature in bookstalls.

Palmerín de Olivia was reprinted in 1516 and published at least thirteen times throughout the century, a figure surpassed only by the twenty editions of books I–IV of *Amadís de Gaula* issued in the sixteenth century.[68] Just six months after the publication of the *edito princeps* of *Palmerín de Olivia*, on July 3, 1512, its first continuation was printed in Salamanca in all likelihood by the same printer,

---

[68] *Palmerín de Olivia* was printed in 1525 (Seville; IB 16741; Dini, no. 4), 1526 (Venice; IB 9799; Dini, no. 5), 1534 (Venice; IB 16744; Dini, no. 6), 1536 (Seville; IB 16745; Dini, no. 7), 1540 (Seville; IB 16746; Dini, no. 8), 1547 (Seville; IB 16747; Dini, no. 9), 1553 (Seville; IB 16748), 1555 (Toledo; IB 16749; Dini, no. 10), 1562 (Medina del Campo; IB 16750; Dini, no. 11), 1580 (Toledo; IB 16751; Dini, no. 14), and 1581 (Évora; not in IB). An entry in the *Catalogue of the Library of Ferdinand Columbus*, no. 4124, reproduced in facsimile by Archer M. Huntington (New York, 1905), mentions an edition printed in 1516 (Salamanca; IB 16738) that has not been preserved; for more information, see Di Stefano, xiv; Martín Abad, no. 1179; Norton, *Catalogue*, no. 596; and Ruiz Fidalgo, no. 110. For facsimile reproductions of most title pages, see Dini, tables I–VIII; see also Di Stefano, xiii–xvii; for a description of the 1511 edition, see also Ferdinand Wolf, *Studien zur Geschichte der spanischen und portugiesischen Nationalliteratur* (Berlin: Asher, 1859), note on 185–86; for the 1525 edition, see Anne Anninger, *Spanish and Portuguese 16th Century Books in the Department of Printing and Graphic Arts: A Description of an Exhibition and a Bibliographical Catalogue of the Collection* (Cambridge, MA: The Houghton Library, 1985), no. 69. A detailed description of the Parisian copies of the editions printed in Venice (1526 and 1534) is provided by Lucía, *Cat.*, nos 30–32. For a bibliographical description with a facsimile of the title page of the 1547 Seville edition, see Clive Griffin, "More Books Printed in Seville by the Cromberger Dynasty," *Bulletin of Spanish Studies* 90 (2013), 710–11; see also José Manuel Lucía Megías, "Un *Palmerín de Olivia* recuperado: Sevilla, Jácome Cromberger, 1547," *Pliegos de Bibliografía* 14 (2001): 69–74. The title page of the 1562 edition is reproduced in Lucía, *Imprenta*, 42. For the location of copies of these editions, see Daniel Eisenberg and Mª Carmen Marín Pina, *Bibliografía de los libros de caballerías castellanos* (Saragossa: Prensas Universitarias de Zaragoza, 2000), 395–99. For the textual relation among the editions of *Palmerín de Olivia*, see the stemma and discussion in Di Stefano, xviii–xxvi.

Juan de Porras.[69] This sequel, titled *Primaleón: Libro segundo del emperador*, went through at least eleven editions during the sixteenth century, one more than the editions of *Las sergas de Esplandián*, the first continuation to *Amadís*.[70]

There is general agreement among scholars that both *Palmerín* and *Primaleón* were written by the same author, yet there is no comparable consensus over the author's identity.[71] At the end of the *editio princeps* we can read a Latin commendatory poem, written by Juan Augur de Trasmiera, in which the authorship of *Palmerín* is attributed to a woman, probably assisted by her son in the composition of violent episodes involving military action: "Quanto sol lunam superat Nebrissaque doctos, / tanto ista hispanos femina docta viros. / [. . .] Femina composuit; generosos atque labores / filius altisonans scripsit et arma libro" (ll. 41–42, 45–46).[72] These lines unambiguously assign the authorship of the romance to a

---

[69] IB 19157. See Dini, no. 15; Martín Abad, no. 1259; Ruiz Fidalgo, no. 93. Note that Frederick J. Norton, "The First Edition of *Primaleón*, Salamanca 1512," *Bulletin of Hispanic Studies* 37 (1960): 29–31, had initially attributed this edition to the printer from Pesaro Lorenzo de Liomdededi, but later changed his mind and assigned it to Juan de Porras; see Norton, *Printing*, 27; cf. Norton, *Catalogue*, no. 500.

[70] The known, sixteenth-century editions of *Primaleón*, apart from that of 1512, are the following: 1516 (Salamanca; IB 19158; Dini, no. 16; and Martín Abad, no. 1260), 1524 (Seville; IB 16740; Dini, no. 17; Lucía, *Cat.*, no. 33), 1528 (Toledo; IB 16743; Dini, no. 19; Lucía, *Cat.*, no. 34), 1530 (s.n.; not in IB), 1534 (Venice; IB 16780; Dini, no. 20; Lucía, *Cat.*, no. 35), 1540 (Seville, not in IB; Dini, no. 21), 1563 (Medina del Campo; IB 16781; Dini, no. 22), 1566 (Lisboa; IB 16782; Dini, no. 23), 1585 (Bilbao; not in IB; Dini, no. 24), and 1598 (Lisboa; IB 16784; Dini, no. 26). For facsimile reproductions of most title pages, see Dini, tables IX–XVI; . For more information about the early editions, see Daniel Eisenberg, "Inexactitudes y misterios bibliográficos: las primeras ediciones de *Primaleón*," *Scriptura* 13 (1997): 173–78, and to locate copies, see Eisenberg and Marín Pina, *Bibliografía de los libros castellanos*, 409–11.

[71] For an overview of the various authorship hypotheses, see María Carmen Marín Pina, "Nuevos datos sobre Francisco Vázquez y Feliciano de Silva, autores de libros de caballerías," *Journal of Hispanic Philology* 15 (1991): 117–30 (esp. 117–24); Mancini, 11–16; Lilia E. F. de Orduna, ed. *Libro segundo de Palmerín que trata de los grandes fechos de Primaleón y Polendos sus fijos* (Kassel: Reichenberger, 2004), 1:3–6.

[72] *Palmerín de Olivia*, 386; "As the sun outshines the moon, and Nebrija the scholars, so this learned woman outshines the men of Spain . . . The woman composed it; in a highflown style the son wrote the noble acts and feats of arms in the book" (ll. 41–42 trans. by Thomas, 97). See also Di Stefano, xxxi–xxxii, 629–30, and 766–67. Di Stefano considers it not unlikely that Trasmiera performed "un ruolo di consulente o piú ancora di revisore assunto dal baccelliere nei confronti di tutto il testo o di parti di esso" (630). Mancini does not consider it unlikely that Trasmiera could have been the author of *Palmerín*, a hypothesis that "tiene al menos la ventaja de no presentar a un autor completamente fantástico, sino a un bachiller existido en realidad" (14). For biographical information regarding Juan Augur de Trasmiera, see Di Stefano, 624–30. For the interpretation of the second distich in the quotation, see Gayangos, xxxix, n. 2.

woman. Accordingly when the book was first published no reader could doubt that it was really composed by a woman. Besides, the 1512 *Primaleón* contains additional evidence pointing to the same conclusion as its predecessor. A poem printed in the book's post-script restates the romance's female authorship and provides further information: "por mano de dueña prudente labrado; / [. . .] es de Augustobrica aquesta lavor / que en Salamanca se ha agora stampado."[73] While the exact identity of this lady remains unknown to us, this poem reveals that she was from Ciudad Rodrigo, a town located between Salamanca and Portugal, here referred to by the learned form of its inhabitant's name, i.e., *Augustobrica*.[74] This edition of *Primaleón*, however, provides information in its colophon that has been interpreted in ways that appear to deny the female attribution of the two-part romance: "Fue trasladado este segundo libro de pal / merin llamado Primaleon τ ansimesmo el pri / mero llamado Palmerin de griego en nue / stro lenguaje castellano τ corregido τ emen / dado en la muy noble ciudad de Ciudaro / drigo por francisco vasquez vecino de la dicha / ciudad."[75] Literary critics have tended to read this passage as a clear indication that the author of both *Palmerín* and *Primaleón* was indeed Francisco Vázquez, and seem also to have adopted this as a preferable, tentative attribution. For instance, the two modern editions of *Palmerín*, on the sole evidence of the colophon, agree in considering that Vázquez was "traduttore dal greco e revisore del testo di entrambi romanzi."[76]

---

[73] *Primaleón*, edited by Mª Carmen Marín Pina, Los Libros de Rocinante 3 (Alcalá de Henares: Centro de Estudios Cervantinos, 1998), 538: "by the hand of a prudent lady worked; . . . by a lady from Augustobriga is this work, which is now printed in Salamanca."

[74] Cf. Menéndez Pealyo, 1:420–21. See also Ramón Menéndez Pidal, *Toponimia prerrománica hispana* (Madrid: Gredos, 1952), 181–82 and 219. Note that the form *Augustobrica* may be better construed as an adjective, referring to a person from Ciudad Rodrigo, whereas the form *Augustobriga*, a noun, corresponds to the place name *Ciudad Rodrigo*.

[75] Dini, 20: "This second book of Palmerín, called Primaleón, as well as the first, called Palmerín, was translated from Greek into our Castilian language, and corrected and emended in the most noble city of Ciudad Rodrigo by Francisco Vázquez." Note that Dini's transcription reads "traslado" instead of "trasladado." For the presence of the false translation topos in chivalric romances, see María Carmen Marín Pina, "El tópico de la falsa traducción en los libros de caballerías españoles," in *Actas del III Congreso de la Asociación Hispánica de Literatura Medieval (Salamanca, 3 al 6 de octubre de 1989)*, ed. María Isabel Toro Pascua (Salamanca: Biblioteca Española del Siglo XV, Departamento de Literatura Española e Hispanoamericana, 1994), 1:541–48. For more information about Francisco Vázquez, see Marín Pina, "Nuevos datos sobre Francisco Vázquez," 120–30.

[76] Di Stefano, 766; Mª Carmen Marín Pina remarks, "por el colofón del *Primaleón* los lectores descubren entonces que los dos libros fueron traducidos del griego al castellano por Francisco Vázquez" (*Palmerín de Olivia*, x). Cf. Marín Pina, "Nuevos datos sobre Francisco Vázquez," 124; Eisenberg and Marín Pina, *Bibliografía de los libros castellanos*,

Proper names doubtless exert a fascination among literary scholars and historians, if only because they allow us to replace the elusiveness of an anonymous author with the concreteness of a named individual. Assigning the composition of the first two instalments of the *Palmerín* series to Vázquez is both legitimate and plausible, but the convenience of a proper name should not blind us to the significant weaknesses of this identification. If we conclude that the author is indeed Vázquez, we are assuming that the information in the 1511 edition of *Palmerín* is spurious and lacking in historical accuracy. Thus, before we can accept the hypothesis of Vázquez's authorship, the following questions need answering: why does the 1511 edition of *Palmerín* assigns the work to a lady?; why does the printer of *Primaleón* include two contradictory attributions, one apparently crediting the work to Vázquez, the other to a "dueña prudente"?; and, finally, why should the information in the colophon to the 1512 edition of *Primaleón*, supposedly pointing to Vázquez's authorship, be more reliable than the evidence pointing to an anonymous female author? I want to propose a solution to this seeming conundrum, since to the best of my knowledge, no convincing answer to these questions has been provided.

If we read the 1512 colophon closely we can recognize that it has a bipartite structure, as it describes two separate sets of actions: first, the act of translating the romance into Spanish ("Fue trasladado . . . en nuestro lenguaje castellano"), and next the act of correcting and emending it ("corregido e emendado").[77] If Francisco Vázquez was indeed the author of the two-part romance or, in the words of the colophon, if he did *translate* the Greek originals, why would the colophon distinguish that action from the one of correcting the text? The process of writing, or for that matter of translating, involves constant revision or editing before the final product is ready for submission to a printer, a reader or an assistant. It makes sense to distinguish the action of composition/translation from that of correction/edition, only if the latter has a significant effect on the former and if it is performed by a different person. But the syntactic organization of the sentence also wants to distinguish between the two sets of actions, since "fue trasladado" appears at the beginning of the colophon, and "corregido e emendado" almost at the end of the sentence. All seems to suggest that these two literary activities need to be distinguished, thus implying that two people participated in the process of composition of the romance, in agreement with the information in the poem by Juan Augur de Trasmiera in *Palmerín*: the lady ("Femina"), who composed the text, and the son ("filius"), who collaborated in the description of battles and tournaments by correcting any factual errors

---

395; Lucía, *Cat.*, nos 30–35; Roubaud-Bénichou, *Le roman de chevalerie en Espagne*, 19. Still Mancini argues that this possibility "es la menos documentada" (11).

[77] This bipartite syntactic structure I propose would be more apparent had the printer placed a comma after "castellano" as I do in my translation (see note above), but the rules of punctuation were rather lax at the time.

and by imbuing those actions with the appropriate *altisonans* prose style.[78] This information in Trasmiera's poem agrees with my reading of the colophon: the *femina* is the one who has *translated* the text of the two-part romance and handed it to her *filius*, i.e., Francisco Vázquez, who *corrected and emended* the texts, in particular those sections dealing with chivalric action.

The colophon to the 1524 edition of *Primaleón* reproduces the exact same wording and information of that in the *editio princeps*.[79] But, when this romance was printed again in Toledo in 1528 there is a change: "Fue trasladado este segundo libro / de Palmerin llamado Primaleon y assi mesmo el primero / llamado Palmerin: de griego en nuestro lenguje [*sic*] cas / tellano e corregido y emendado."[80] No personal name is included and it seems unlikely that the printers would have deleted the name of Francisco Vázquez, had they thought that he was the author. In other words, the printers understood from the colophon of the previous editions that Vázquez had indeed corrected the original, but because they introduced no further editorial alteration, they decided not to name the initial editor since this information was irrelevant to their potential customers. I want to add one further piece of evidence to support my reading of the colophon to the 1512 edition of *Primaleón*. When the Venetian printers Juan Paduan and Venturin de Rufinelli printed an edition of *Palmerín de Olivia* in 1534, they included the following colophon: "Fue corregido y emendado este libro del famo / so cauallero palmerin de oliua: por Juan ma /theo da [*sic*] villa español [*sic*]."[81] The wording is now familiar to us and we can all agree that it means that the text printed had been edited by Juan Mateo for this edition.

---

[78] The 1534 edition of *Primaleón* printed in Venice (IB 16780) contains further evidence of the romance's female authorship. In the introduction to the second part, Francisco Delicado states, "la que lo compuso era muger y filando el torno se pensaua cosas mas fermosas" (Di Stefano, 784: "the composer was a woman and while spinning at the wheel she thought of very beautiful things; trans. by Thomas, 99). Next Delicado adds, "Y es opinion de personas que fue muger la que lo compuso fija de un carpintero [. . .] El defecto esta en los impresores y en los mercaderes que han desdorado la obra de la señora Augustobrica con el ansia del ganar" (Di Stefano, 784; "and people are of opinion that the composer was a woman and daughter of a carpenter . . . but the fault lies in the printers and publishers who, for the sake of filthy lucre, have taken all the shine out of the work of the lady from Ciudad Rodrigo"; this translation is based on that of Thomas, 99). Cf. Purser, 429. For biographical information about Francisco Delicado and description of his editorial activities, see Francisco Delicado, *La lozana andaluza*, ed. Folke Gernert and Jacques Joset, Biblioteca Clásica de la Real Academia Española 22 (Madrid: Real Academia Española, 2013), 371–81; and Carla Perugini, "Delicado, Francisco," in *DBE*, 15:762–65.

[79] The 1524 colophon is transcribed in Dini, 23, and Lucía, *Cat.*, 145.

[80] Dini, 25. Note that her transcription reads "traslado" instead of "trasladado."

[81] Dini, 12: "This book of the famous knight Palmerin de Oliva was corrected and emended by Juan Mateo, of Spanish extraction."

Therefore, my interpretation of the 1512 colophon assigning to Francisco Vázquez the role of *editor* and to his mother that of *author* satisfactorily answers all the questions I raise above and reconciles the apparently contradictory information provided in the first editions of *Palmerín* and *Primaleón*. One may be reluctant to lend credence to the notion that a chivalric text could be penned by a woman at this point in history. It is reassuring, however, to find that other women also participated in the process of creation and distribution of the Iberian romances of chivalry, as for instance Beatriz Bernal, who wrote *Cristalián de España* (Valladolid, 1545; IB 1786), and later Margaret Tyler, in England.[82] Our *femina* would have been the pioneer, making a bold move for a woman by producing the first chivalric text right after the publication of the initial six books in the Amadisian series. It seems natural that she should be hesitant about revealing her literary endeavors and chose to conceal her identity. Even so, we know that she comes from Ciudad Rodrigo, where there is sufficient historical evidence to locate a contemporaneous Francisco Vázquez. If the two of them were mother and son, as Trasmiera suggests, it is possible that we could tentatively name the author of *Palmerín* and *Primaleón* as Catalina Arias.[83] All in all, it seems reasonable that the female authorship, regardless of her actual identity, should be favored unless compelling evidence to the contrary is presented.[84]

While the work produced most probably by this female author was published as two separate books, their narrative development reveals an underlying unified structure organized around the biography of the hero, Palmerín de Olivia. The first book, *Palmerín de Olivia*, narrates Palmerín's conception, birth, and exposure. Next we learn about his childhood with his foster family, whom he leaves when dubbed a knight, and departs to pursue his chivalric vocation. In so doing, Palmerín finds love, comes to discover his identity, reunites with his

---

[82] Mancini uses this argument against the hypothesis of attributing the authorship to a woman: "ni se comprenden los motivos que tuvo la dama para ocultarse tan cuidadosamente, cuando otras mujeres se enorgullecían de componer libros de caballerías" (12). Although Mancini refers to Beatriz Bernal, he does not take into consideration that the author of *Palmerín* predates Bernal's *Cristalián* in more than thirty years. In addition, Mancini also alludes to stylistic features to shed doubts unconvincingly on the possibility of a female author.

[83] The attribution of these romance texts to Catalina Arias has been suggested by some local historians, as cited in Marín Pina, "Nuevos datos sobre Francisco Vázquez," 127, n 25. Cf. Gayangos, xl, and Menéndez Pelayo, 1:421.

[84] We should also take into account that all attributions to Vázquez are erased after the 1525 Seville edition of *Palmerín*; see Marín Pina, "Nuevos datos sobre Francisco Vázquez," 122 n. 15. I am unconvinced by the opinion expressed by Marín Pina in her doctoral dissertation saying that "Madre . . . e hijo son en nuestra opinión una creación literaria, forman parte de una ficción literaria tramada por Trasmiera, es posible que a petición del propio editor o incluso del autor, para hacer más apetecibles las obras" ("Edición," 54).

biological family, marries Polinarda, and becomes emperor of Constantinople.[85] In the second book, *Primaleón*, Palmerín settles in the throne of Constatinople and eventually dies, but during the intervening years the narrative focus moves away from him and centers on his progeny: Polendos (known as Palmendos in the English tradition), Palmerín's illegitame son with the queen of Tharsus; Primaleón, born from the marriage between Palmerín and Polinarda; Don Duardos, Palmerín's son-in-law, married to his daughter Flérida; and Platir, Primaleón's fourth son with his wife Gridonia. The author planned to close her *Palmerín de Olivia* with a prophecy that is fulfilled in *Primaleón*, whereas the latter closes without opening new avenues for the story's narrative continuation. By bringing such a sense of narrative closure to her work, the author of *Palmerín* was indirectly thwarting other romancers' attempts to provide continuity to the adventures of the Palmerinian heroes. At last, more than twenty years after the publication of the two-part romance, a continuation was published under the title *Platir* (1533 Valladolid; IB 16777), but it disregards the narrative events in the final chapters of *Primaleón*.[86] As Marín Pina argues, "la decisión adoptada [of altering *Platir*'s narrative antecedent] es la propia de un lector insatisfecho que, no contento con la materia heredada, se propone él mismo readaptarla."[87] This decision was not well received by the Spanish public, since *Platir* was never reprinted. By contrast, the Italian translation of this romance was much more successful, with nine editions printed from 1548 until 1611, and a continuation produced by Mambrino Roseo in 1560.[88] The last addition to the *Palmerín* series was *Palmerín de Inglaterra* (Toledo, 1547–1548), a translation from a chivalric text originally written in Portuguese by Francisco de Moraes, that describes the chivalric exploits of the twin sons of Flérida and Don Duardos. As happened with *Platir*, *Palmerín de Inglaterra* failed to attract sufficient interest from Spanish readers and was not reprinted.

The inaugural work of the *Palmerín* cycle remained in print from 1511 to 1581. This commercial longevity must have percolated down to and affected popular culture, as signals the transfer of the storyline from the romance to a play in the seventeenth century. Juan Pérez de Montalbán (d. 1638) found inspiration in the first book of *Palmerín* for his comedy *Palmerín de Oliva o la encantadora*

---

[85] For a summary of the romance, see Patchell, 129–30. A more detailed summary is provided by John Dunlop, *The History of Fiction: Being a Critical Account of the most Celebrated Prose Works of Fiction* (Edinburgh: Longman, 1816), 2:51–58.

[86] For a bibliographical description, see Dini, 37–39, where this edition's title page is reproduced in table XVIII. For a genealogical tree of the Palmerinian family, see Gayangos, xlv. Note that Dini, 35–37, includes a bibliographical description of *Polindo*, as if it were an integral part of the *Palmerín* series, but it isn't. See Marín Pina, "Edición", 8–13.

[87] "Edición," 20.

[88] See Neri, "Cuadro de la difusión del ciclo palmeriniano," 291–92.

Lucelinda, which parodies the original romance and transforms it into a baroque *comedia de enredo*.[89] Later on the teacher José Blas Moreno combined this comedy with the opening chapters of the romance to compose a ballad published in the form of a *pliego suelto* or chapbook with the title *Nueva relación y famoso romance en que se refieren los trágicos sucesos, encantos, valentías y venturoso fin de Palmerín de Olivia, príncipe de Macedonia* (Seville, 1755).[90] From this moment onward, knowledge of *Palmerín* seems to have disappeared from popular culture and entered the sole domain of scholars, antiquaries and bibliophiles, who for the most have made deprecating remarks about the romance's literary merits. An influential opinion was that of the Spanish philologist Menéndez Pelayo, who considers that *Palmerín de Olivia* "carece de originalidad . . . el estilo es pobre, el sentimiento ninguno. En las descripciones de batallas y desafíos es pesadísimo" (1:426; cf. Thomas, 90). Yet, some scholars have been more approving in their opinion, as in the case of Purser, who states, "I much prefer *Palmerin de Oliva* to *Primaleon*, and am not sure that it is not the most amusing of all the romances of chivalry I have read" (431).

---

[89] This text is edited by Claudia Demattè, *Palmerín De Oliva* (Viareggio-Lucca: Mauro Baroni Editore, 2006). For a bibliographical note, see Germán Vega García-Luengos, Rosa Fernández Lera, and Andrés del Rey Sayagués, *Ediciones de teatro español en la Biblioteca de Menéndez Pelayo (hasta 1833)* (Kassel: Edition Reichenberger, 2001), no. 3253. Initially it was included in the compilation *Comedias de diferentes autores* (Saragossa, 1650) as part XLIII; for a description of this part with facsimile reproductions, see Maria Grazia Profeti, *La collezione "Diferentes autores"* (Kassel: Edition Reichenberger, 1988), 138–42. For a summary, see George William Bacon, "The Life and Dramatic Works of Doctor Juan Pérez de Montalván (1602–1638)," *Revue Hispanique* 26 (1912), 152–55. Bacon comments, "although the *comedia* is poetical and enjoyable, it is marred by *culteranismo*" (351). For biographical information, see José Enrique Laplana Gil, "Pérez de Montalbán, Juan," in *DBE*, 41:196–98. See also Mancini, 99–100. For the conversion of *Primaleón* into a play, see Marín Pina, "Edición," 25–27 and Demattè's edition, 14–36.

[90] For the identification of this chapbook and its relation to the book of chivalry, see María Carmen Marín Pina, "Romancero y libros de caballerías más allá de la Edad Media," *Actas del VI Congreso Internacional de la Asociación Hispánica de Literatura Medieval*, ed. José Manuel Lucía Megías (Alcalá de Henares: Universidad de Alcalá, 1997), 2: 982–85. The MS 17556 in the Biblioteca Nacional de Madrid, produced c. 1595, contains a collection of popular ballads, one of them starting with the line "El gallardo Palmerin" (fol. 87r–88r). As Marín Pina points out, op. cit., 983, the plot of this ballad is not derived from the romance, its only connection being the name of the hero. For an edition of the ballad, see *Poesias Barias y Recreacion de Buenos Ingenios*, ed. Rita Goldberg (Madrid: Porrúa, 1984), 1:277–80.

The European distribution of *Palmerin d'Oliva*

As part of the chivalric literature that the Iberian Peninsula exported to the rest of Europe, *Palmerín de Oliva* occupied a prominent place. As early as 1526 an edition in Spanish was printed in Venice and reprinted eight years later (cf. n. 22). Moreover, the first romance in our corpus to be translated into Italian was *Palmerín*, published in 1544 with the title *Historia del valorosissimo cavalliere Palmerino d'Oliva* (Venice; *Edit16* 55981, Toda 3717). The translation was made by the prolific writer and translator Mambrino Roseo da Fabriano (ca. 1500–ca. 1580), who also translated *Amadís*, *Esplandián*, and *Primaleón*. While living in Rome during the 1540s, Roseo embarked on a new literary career based on the translation and adaptation of Spanish texts. Roseo's *Vita di Marco Aurelio* (1542) derives from Antonio de Guevara's *Libro áureo*.[91] Similarly his *Instituzione del prencipe cristiano* (1543) is based on Guevara's *Relox de príncipes*. Next Roseo began both his translation of *Palmerín de Olivia* and his long-lasting collaboration with the printing house of Michele Tramezzino, who became Roseo's printer for the rest of his life.[92]

Roseo's translations, and his *Palmerino d'Oliva* is no exception, were published as a bibliographic product that also determined the nature and scope of his work. Just as Tramezzino wanted to make his chivalric books affordable to wide segments of the population by printing them in a cheap octavo format, Roseo chose to make his translations of chivalric romances more accessible to less educated readers even at the expense of compressing or altering the original. Actually Roseo presented his readers not with a word-for-word translation of the Spanish original, but instead with a comprehensive summary focused on the main narrative events written in a rather simple prose style. Passages he considered repetitive or irrelevant were left out from his translation, which was hastily executed. Owing to Roseo's interventions, the narrative becomes more lively and produces a text that is at times more readable, if less ambitious, than the original,

---

[91] For information on Guevara, see Francisco Vázquez Villanueva, "Guevara, Antonio de," in *DBE*, 25:82–87.

[92] Thomas describes Roseo as Tramezzino's hack (184). For the information on Roseo I follow Anna Bognolo, "Vida y obra de Mambrino Roseo da Fabriano, autor de libros de caballerías," *eHumanista* 16 (2010): 77–98, and Bognolo's "Mambrino Roseo da Fabriano: vita provvisoria di uno scrittore," in *Repertorio delle continuazioni italiane ai romanzi cavallereschi spagnoli*, 25–75. On November 20, 1543, Michele Tramezzino obtained from the Venetian Senate a ten-year privilege to print *Palmerino* among others; the text of the privilege is given in Bognolo "Mambrino Roseo: vita provvisoria," 43, n. 45. For the production of Tramezzino's printing house, see Alberto Tinto, *Annali tipografici dei Tramezzino* (Florence: Olschki, 1968) and Pier Silverio Leicht, "L'editore veneziano Michele Tramezzino ed i suoi privilegi," in *Miscellanea di scritti di bibliografia ed erudizione in memoria di Luigi Ferrari* (Florence: Olschki, 1952), 357–67.

instead characterized by the slow development of the plot and the use of parataxis.[93]

The accessible and readable style of Roseo's translation combined with Tramezzino's cheap publication to popularize the genre in contemporary Italy. The case of *Palmerino d'Oliva* is illustrative of the success achieved by this commercial strategy. Tramezzino reprinted this romance on three occassions: 1547 (*Edit16* 55994), 1552 (*Edit16* 56103), and 1558 (*Edit16* 56198).[94] The frequency of the publication of reprint editions is indicative of high public demand for this kind of literary products that needed to be satisfied not just by continually releasing the same works, but also by increasing the supply of romance materials. Tramezzino in tandem with Roseo had the initiative of producing a continuation to the adventures of the hero, not of his progeny. On November 29, 1559, the printer requested privilege to publish such continuation,[95] which was printed in 1560 with the title *Il secondo libro di Palmerino d'Oliva* (*Edit16* 56200; Toda 3718). Other Venetian printers followed suit and started churning out reprint editions of the first and second book of Palmerino: 1559 (Girolamo Giglio), 1560 (Francesco Lorenzini), 1570 (Domenico Farri), 1573 (Domenico Farri; Toda 3719), 1575 (Enea de Alaris; Toda 3720), 1581 (s.n.), 1585 (Pietro Marinelli), 1591 (Giacomo Cornetti), 1592 (Simone Cornetti), 1597 (Marcantonio Bonibelli), 1598 (Marcantonio Bonibelli), 1603 (Lucio Spineda), 1611 (Lucio Spineda),

---

[93] For these considerations I follow the only study, though partial, comparing the Spanish text and Roseo's translation: Bacchelli, "Il *Palmerín de Olivia* nel Rifacimiento di Lodovico Dolce," 160–65. For the methodology Roseo uses in his translations of *Amadís*, see Stefano Neri, "Il ciclo italiano di *Amadis di Gaula*," in *Repertorio delle continuazioni italiane ai romanzi cavallereschi spagnoli*, 146–47. See also Bognolo, "Libros de caballerías en Italia," 335–36. It is remarkable how prolific Roseo's production of translations is: from 1542 to 1571 he translated thirteen Iberian chivalric texts and composed nineteen original romances, in addition to fifteen other unrelated works. For a complete list of works, both original and translations, attributed to Roseo, see Bognolo, "Mambrino Roseo: vita provvisoria," 69–75; cf. Stefano Neri, "El *Progetto Mambrino*. Estado de la cuestión," in *Tus obras los rincones de la tierra descubren. Actas del VI Congreso Internacional de la Asociación de Cervantistas*, ed. Alexia Dotras Bravo et al. (Alcalá de Henares: Centro de Estudios Cervantinos, 2008), 577. The collaboration with other hack writers might account for this prolificness, although there is no supporting evidence for suggesting that he enlisted the collaboration of other translators. Cf. Bognolo, op. cit., 340.

[94] For a bibliographical description of all the editions of the *Palmerín* cycle in Italian, see Anna Bognolo and Stefano Neri, "Ciclo italiano di Palmerin," Progetto Mambrino–Università degli studi di Verona, accessed August 14, 2015, http://www.mambrino.it/spagnole/palmerin.php. See also Neri, "Cuadro de la difusión europea del ciclo palmeriniano," 288–89.

[95] See Thomas, 186 n. 4, and Toda, 3:265.

and 1620 (Lucio Spineda).[96] Counting the two parts of *Palmerino* there is evidence that at least nineteen separate editions were published in Italy until 1620, twenty-one if we include the Italian editions in Spanish, a figure that doubles the ten editions published in Spain. This level of publication of the adventures of Palmerino speaks volumes about the popularity this romance achieved in Italy.

The fame of Palmerino spread beyond popular pulp fiction and provided Lodovico Dolce (1508–1568) with inspiration for his *Il Palmerino* (1561; *Edit16* 17370), a composition in *ottava rima* intended to heighten the aesthetic quailities of this hero's adventures.[97] Dolce's interest in making a versification of the *Palmerín* story emerges from the desire to emulate his contemporary Bernardo Tasso (d. 1569), who the year before had published *L'Amadigi* (1560; *Edit16* 26310) in imitation of Ariosto's *Orlando Furioso*. As Bacchielli (167) affirms, Dolce's *Palmerino* comes halfway between Ariosto's creativity and Roseo's derivative compositions. In this verse composition Dolce reshuffles the storyline of the romance, organizes it in cantos and excludes sub-plots, thus endowing it with greater internal coherence and, according to Bacchielli, Italianizing it.[98]

In France the first translation of *Palmerín de Olivia*, made by Jean Maugin, was not published until 1546, although it is not unlikely that a different translation could have been started even before *Amadis de Gaule* was published in 1540. According to the information Maugin provides in the title page and the preface to the first edition of *Palmerin d'Olive*, it had been "traduite iadis par vn auteur incertain de Castillan en Françoys, lourd & inusité, sans art, ou disposicion quelconque. Maintenant reueuë, & mise en son entier selon nostre vulgaire, par Iean Maugin natif d'Angiers."[99] This textual witness, allegedly revised by Maugin,

---

[96] For information on the printing activities of Alaris, Bonibelli, Farri and the Cornetti brothers, see *Dizionario dei tipografi e degli editori italiani: Il Cinquecento*, ed. Marco Menato, Ennio Sandal, and Giuseppina Zappella (Milan: Editrice Bibliografica, 1997). For basic information about the activity of the other printers, see Ester Pastorello, *Tipografi, editori, librai a Venezia nel secolo XVI* (Florence: Leo S. Olschki, 1924). For Spineda's three editions, see *Le edizioni veneziane del Seicento: Censimento*, comp. by Caterina Griffante with the assistance of Alessia Giachery and Sabrina Minuzzi (Milan: Bibliografica, 2003–2006), nos 235–37.

[97] For biographical information, see Giovanna Romei, "Dolce, Lodovico," in *Dizionario Biografico degli Italiani* (Roma: Istituto dell'Enciclopedia Italiana, 1991), 40: 399–405. For a discussion of his entire literary career, see Ronnie H. Terpening, *Lodovico Dolce: Renaissance Man of Letters* (Toronto: University of Toronto Press, 1997).

[98] For a discussion of *Il Palmerino*, see Bacchielli, "Il *Palmerín de Olivia* nel Rifacimiento di Lodovico Dolce," 167–76; see also Neri, "Il romanzo cavalleresco spagnolo in Italia," 111–12. For a critical appraisal of Tasso's *Amadis* and Dolce's *Palmerino*, see Benedetto Croce, "Gli 'Amadigi' e i 'Palmerini'," in B. Croce, *Poeti e scrittori del pieno e del tardo Rinascimento* (Bari: Laterza, 1945), 1:310–25.

[99] I quote the title and the preface from the edition in Bernard Weinberg, *Critical Prefaces of the French Renaissance* (Evanston, IL: Northwestern University Press, 1950),

has not survived. Yet, in 1584 the bibliographer François Grudé, sieur de La Croix du Maine, contends that a nobleman, Jean de Voyer, Seigneur de Paulmy, (d. 1571), "a traduit d'Espagnol en François, le Roman de Palmerin d'Oliue ou d'Oluide. Ie ne sçay si sa traduction a esté imprimee."[100] The direct relationship of La Croix du Maine to the Voyer de Paulmy's family enhances the credibility of this statement, which confirms that Jean de Voyer's translation was never printed. It is nonetheless a testimony that a translation of the Spanish text previous to Maugin's did exist and, therefore, provides evidence to conjecturally identify the "auteur incertain" of the title page with Jean de Voyer, as other scholars have also argued.[101]

131–34, here 131: "already translated from Castilian into French unskillfully and clumsily by an unknown author, witless and inexperienced. Now revised and completed appropriately in our vernacular by Jean Maugin, native of Angers." Henceforward all references to Maugin's preface refer to this edition and appear in the text identified by page number. See also Bettoni, 193, and Freer, 197–201. Hughes Vaganay, "Les Romans de chevalerie italiens d'inspiration espagnole," *La Bibliofilia*, 9 (1907): 121, states, "*Palmerin d'Olive* . . . fut du reste traduit avant *Amadis*"; cf. Freer, 181. A critical edition of the French *Palmerin d'Olive* for the series "Romans de chevalerie de la Renaissance" was announced in *Amadis de Gaule, Livre I*, ed. Bideaux, 9. The appointed editors were Anibal Pinto de Castro and Isabel Almeida. Sadly Prof. Pinto de Castro passed away in 2010 and the edition has not been completed.

[100] *La bibliothèque du sieur de La Croix-du-Maine* (Paris: Abel l'Angelier, 1584; FB 31761), 273: "He has translated into French the Spanish romance *Palmerin d'Olive* –or *Oblivion*. I don't know whether his translation has been printed or not." Marc Antoine René de Voyer, marquis de Paulmy d'Argenson, *Mélanges tirés d'une grande bibliothèque* (Paris: Moutard, 1781), 16:1–2, used the previous information to dismiss the possibility that Maugin made the translation, and attributed it to Jean de Voyer, considering Maugin simply "l'Éditeur de cette Traduction" (2); cf. Purser, 431. Paul Belleuvre, "Jean Maugin. Deuxième partie," *Revue de l'Anjou et de Maine et Loire* 4.1 (1855), 97–98, provides arguments supporting Maugin's authorship of the translation, although he doesn't rule out the possibility that "ces deux écrivains eussent traduit le même roman" (97). For more information on Jean de Voyer (d. February 10, 1571), see Pierre de Guibours Anselme de Sainte-Marie and Honoré Caille du Fourny, *Histoire généalogique et chronologique de la maison royale de France: des pairs, grands officers de la couronne et de la maison du roy, et des anciens barons du royaume*, 3rd rev. ed. (1730; repr. New York: Johnson Reprint Corporation, 1967), 6:596–97.

[101] See Thomas, 203 n. 2; cf. Freer, 198–99 n. 71, and 203. This reference to the "auteur incertain" is erased from the title in the 1549 and following editions; cf. Bettoni, 193 n. 52. On the contrary, Annie Parent, *Les métiers du livre à Paris au XVIe siècle (1535–1560)* (Geneva: Droz, 1974), 109 n. 2, argues that "cette traduction attribuée habituellement à Jean Le Voyer, soit l'œuvre de N. de Herberay"; see further below. Later on in the preface Maugin refers to the "traducteur antique" (134), which I interpret as referring to the author of the "vieille traduction." On the contrary, Marian Rothstein, *Reading in the Renaissance: "Amadis de Gaule" and the Lessons of Memory* (Newark, DE: University of

In addition to consulting this "vieille traduction," Maugin also states in the preface that "Herberay (traducteur de nostre fleurissant *Amadis*) en avoit mis au net aucuns des premiers cayers" of *Palmerin d'Olive* (133).[102] Thus, according to Maugin, Herberay also had access to that same careless anonymous translation, which Herberay edited supposedly to correct translation mistakes and improve the style, as would be expected of such a renowned prose writer. But Herberay also left his translation unfinished, Maugin supposes because of "la lourderie de la vieille traduction ou la commission ordinaire qu'il a du Roy" (133).[103] Although the reasons Maugin cites for Herberay's giving up the translation are but mere suppositions, his assertion that Herberay was once involved in translating *Palmerin d'Olive* seems more authentic. In 1966 Freer suspected that Maugin simply provided a factual description of what he knew happened, and was proved true in 1974 when the publishing contract for *Palmerin d'Olive* was unearthed and printed by Annie Parent.[104] This contract was signed on April 19, 1543, between Herberay and the publishing consortium formed by the three Parisian *libraires* who had previously published Herberay's *Amadis*, namely Jean Longis, Denis Janot, and Vincent Sertenas. According to the terms of the contract, Herberay undertook to translate *Palmerín de Olivia* and its sequel, *Primaleón*, from the Spanish, and to deliver twenty quires of three sheets by "le jour Jehan Baptiste, prochain venant"—i.e., June 24, 1543—in order that the printers start preparing the text for publication, the rest being expected for August of the same year. Herberay's emoluments include a down payment of 40 pounds due on May 10, 1543, and a promise of 30 solz for each printed quire due on delivery of the manuscript.[105]

It is obvious that the publishers had arranged a very tight schedule for Herberay, who would have to work round the clock to meet the deadline. But there is a clause in the *Palmerin* contract of April 1543 showing that they were aware that maybe their estimates for the delivery of the translation were too optimistic:

Delaware Press, 1999), 48, argues that Maugin refers to the author of the Spanish original, "who is here reduced to the status of translator."

[102] "Herberay, translator of our flourishing *Amadis*, had tidied up the text in some of the front quires of the old translation."

[103] "the rudeness of the old translation or his ordinary commission from the King." Cf. Beittoni, 175, no. 8; Thomas, 204. Herberay was commissary of ordnance to King Francis I, meaning that he was in charge of overseeing the ordnance in a given province; for this explanation I follow Taylor, *Rewriting Arthurian Romance*, 150 n. 14.

[104] The contract is reproduced in Parent, *Les métiers du livre*, 303–4; all my references to the agreement are to Parent's edition, which I cite in the text by page number.

[105] The contract literally reads, "trente solz tournois pour chacun cayer imprimé dudit livre de Palmerin, contenant troys feulles" (303; thirty solz for each quire of three sheets of the said book of Palmerin). Note that the *editio princeps* is made up mainly of gatherings of three sheets.

"A esté accordé, que ou ledict sieur des Essars sera deffaillant de leur délivrer ledict premier livre de Palmerin, mynute, dedans ledict temps, en ce cas qu'il sera tenu, promect et gaige rendre et restituer à chacun desdictz libraires, par esgalle portion, ce qu'il aura recu d'eulx, de ladicte somme de XL l[ivres] t[ournois]."[106]

[It has been agreed that if the said Mr. des Essarts fails to deliver the said first book of Palmerin, in draft, within the said period of time, in this case he will be required, bound, and gaged to render and restitute in equal proportions each one of the said booksellers the amount of the said forty pounds that he will have received from them.]

I want to highlight two details from the clause. First, the publishers foresee the eventuality of Herberay's breaking the terms of the contract, as we know happened. His breach of contract, however, is attributable neither to his royal commission nor to the crudeness of the "vieille traduction," as Maugin adduced, but more likely to work overload: in a previous contract, dated March 2, 1542, Herberay undertook to deliver his translation of the fifth and sixth books of *Amadis* by March 25, 1543. This latter commission was naturally to receive priority over the translation of *Palmerin*, which should be performed "sans toutes voyes déroger ne préjudicier à aucune obligation, que ledict sieur des Essars leur a par cy-devant faite, pour raison de la traduction d'espaignol en francoys des cinq et sixiesme livres d'Amadis de Gaule."[107] Herberay must have failed to deliver his *Amadis* translations before the deadline of March 25, 1543, since these two books were printed respectively in May 1544 (FB 677–81) and July 1545 (FB 686–89).[108] In sum, his commitment to the *Amadis* series prevented Herberay from entirely translating *Palmerin d'Olive*, an eventuality anticipated in the original agreement.

The second feature from the above quotation I want to highlight concerns the state of the copy in which Herberay had to present his translation to the printers, namely, "mynute," meaning a rough draft.[109] The booksellers would have to cover the costs of preparing the copy-text, a process that involved the following actions: "laquelle mynute, lesdictz libraires seront tenuz faire escripre et

---

[106] Parent, *Les métiers du livre*, 304.

[107] Parent, *Les métiers du livre*, 304: "without deviating from or prejudicing any obligation that the said Mr. des Essarts has assumed with them [i.e., the booksellers] regarding the translation from Spanish into French of the fifth and sixth books of Amadis de Gaule."

[108] Cf. Rawles, 95–97.

[109] See Huguet, s.v. *minute*, "brouillon" (rough draft). As explains Philip Gaskell, *A New Introduction to Bibliography* (Oxford: Clarendon Press, 1972), 40, the following description would be applicable to *minute*: a "manuscript copy . . . might be an ill-written author's draft much blotted and corrected."

mectre au net, à leurs despens, tant de foys qu'il en sera besoing, pour la corection et impression d'iceulx [cahiers]."[110] All in all, the terms of the contract were extremely favorable to Herberay, a clear indication that, after the profits gained with his translation of *Amadis,* the publishers considered him a precious asset.

Maugin's preface also mentions a further texual witness: "je [i.e., Maugin] trouvay derechef aucun nombre de chapitres corrigez par un que je n'ay sceu cognoistre; pour lesquelz lier, unir, et rendre conformes au principe, je n'ay eu moindre peine qu'à une invencion, et m'a falu entierement les reffaire" (134).[111] Here Maugin alludes to a text corresponding to various chapters of *Palmerin d'Olive* that had been edited by an unidentified corrector, whose work was of such poor quality that Maugin found it of little use.[112] A corrector was a person whose services were normally hired by printers to revise, correct, and edit texts before they were printed. It seems to me that the only ones that would have any use for an edited copy of the French *Palmerin* in manuscript form were the same publishing consortium that had signed the contract with Herberay in 1543, namely, Janot, Longis, and Sertenas.[113] In view of Herberay's incapacity to deliver his translation of *Palmerin* in a timely manner, this consortium offered the same job to Maugin and it seems reasonable that they should have made Herberay's materials available to him. As we know, Herberay was not expected to provide the publishers with a fair copy of his translation, but with a fairly unprepared draft. In his description Maugin is probably referring to this draft, which would have extended to less than the first twenty quires. The document is described as "corrigez," for which two interpretations seem possible. One possibility is that, since Herberay was not required to produce a fair copy, this document contains the corrections and revisions that he produced as part of the translation process (cf. n. 109). Alternatively, it could be that Herberay did not go beyond correcting and tidying up the old version by Jean de Voyer, a more likely possibility since Maugin admits in the preface that Herberay had edited the "vieille traduction." Despite Herberay's intervention, these "chapitres corrigez" did not represent a

---

[110] Parent, *Les métiers du livre,* 303: "which rough draft, the said booksellers will be required to copy and tidy up, as many times as needed, for correcting and printing those quires." This description appears in the same contract, although it applies to *Primaleon.*

[111] "I have once again found a number of chapters corrected by I know not who. To link, unite and render them according to principle has been no less painful than inventing, and I have had to redo them entirely."

[112] Weinberg, *Critical Prefaces,* 134 n. (e), thinks it possible to identify this person with Jean de Voyer.

[113] In 1544 Janot's place is taken by his widow, Jeanne de Marnef; cf. Bettoni, 173. Note that Janot was the only printer in the consortium, the other two being booksellers; cf. Rawles, 93 n. 13. For information on Janot, see Georges Lepreux, *Gallia Typographica ou répertoire biographique et chronologique de tous les imprimeurs de France,* série Parisienne 1 (Paris: Champion, 1911), 278; and Stephen Rawles, *Denis Janot (fl. 1529–1544), Parisian Printer and Bookseller: A Bibliography* (Leiden: Brill, 2018).

specimen of the much-praised "Essardine" prose, but at most Herberay's engagement with a defective, amateur translation.[114]

In sum, it seems that Maugin could have known the "vieille translation" attributable to Jean de Voyer, but thought that it was "confuz, mal ordonnez, et indisposez," as he explains in the preface (133). This old translation, in turn, was revised and edited by Herberay. When Maugin accepted the commission to translate *Palmerin* he was provided with Herberay's materials, although they appear to have had little bearing on Maugin's final translation. Thus, we can safely attribute the authorship of the French *Palmerin d'Olive* to Maugin, whose role was not that of a mere corrector or reviser, but of a translator.[115] On April 17, 1545, Vincent Sertenas obtained the privilege for publishing Maugin's translation, which was finally printed by Jeanne de Marnef on July 8, 1546 (FB 40395–97; Freer A).[116] Maugin must have completed his translation in little more than two years, if we consider that he was offered to translate the romance soon after August 1543, and deducting the time necessary for printing the edition. Or perhaps he had to finish his translation in less than two years if we assume that when Herberay finished the translation of the fifth book of *Amadis*, printed in May 1544, the publishers realized that they needed another translator to continue reaping the profits of the fashion for the corpus of Iberian romances and having a stranglehold on it.[117] When his translation was finished and delivered,

---

[114] Freer expresses a contrasting viewpoint: "Per quanto concerne i capitoli riguardati da Herberay des Essarts, niente nella prefazione ci permette di affermare che Maugin ebbe occasione di valersene durante la sua revisione" (205). Taylor, *Rewriting Arthurian Romance*, 192, wonders, "is this actually Herberay?" For the use of the adjective "Essardine," see Beittoni, 173–74, n. 2.

[115] Buenaventura Carlos Aribau, "Libros de caballerías: serie de los Palmerines," *Revista Crítica de Historia y Literatura Españolas, Portuguesas e Hispano-Americanas* 4 (1899): 328, argues that Maugin was "únicamente el editor ó revisor, suponiendo algunos que el verdadero intérprete fué *Juan de Voyer*, señor de Argenson." In Menéndez Pelayo's opinion, "Juan Maugin no fué el autor, sino el corrector de esta versión" (1:429). In addition, Paul Belleuvre, "Jean Maugin. Première partie," *Revue de l'Anjou et de Maine et Loire* 3.2 (1854): 374, erroneously states that the French *Palmerin d'Olive* was "traduite de l'italien." For a brief summary of the translation's authorship with attribution to Maugin, see Jean Maugin (?), *Le premier livre de l'histoire et ancienne cronique de Gérard d'Euphrate, duc de Bourgogne*, ed. by Richard Cooper (Paris: Classiques Garnier, 2012), 39–40.

[116] The date of the privilege is mentioned in the *editio princeps* (sig. *a*1v), the publication date in the colophon. See also Bettoni, 175–76. In addition to the FB no., I also include the sigla in Freer (183–84) when there is one.

[117] Unlike Maugin, François de Vernassal complains in *L'Histoire de Primaleon de Grece* (1550; FB 44732) about the "peu de temps que j'ay eu, pour le [i.e., the first book of *Primaleon*] vous donner tel que le voyez: qui n'est que seulement que de huit mois tant à le traduire, revoir, mettre au net, que le faire imprimer"; quoted in Bettoni, 182 n. 34: "I have had little time to give you the book as you see it: which is eight months not only to

however, Maugin was not allowed much time for revising the text of the *editio princeps*, as he declared in 1549: "ie fuz precipité à la premiere fois, tant qu'à grand' peine pouuois lire vn cayer de copie."[118] That is, Maugin complained not about the time he had for translating the romance, but about the little time he had for correcting the proofs of the edition.

The *editio princeps* was printed by Jeanne de Marnef for the publishing consortium and exists in three variant states: one for Jean Longis (FB 40395), one "de l'imprimerie de Jeanne de Marnef, vefve de Denis Janot" (FB 40396), and the other for Vincent Sertenas (FB 40397).[119] *Le premier livre de Palmerin d'Olive* was published in folio and printed in roman type across the full page, all of which combined with an accomplished visual program to confer an air of modernness on the book. This new form of textual presentation had already been tried out with good results by the same group of publishers for the first edition of *Amadis*, setting the Iberian literary corpus visually apart from the Arthurian prose romances, printed in two columns using gothic types.[120] The new *mise en page* feels more spacious, visually cleaner and appealing, an effect to which the small-size vignette woodcuts illustrating the text contributed notably. The *Palmerin* edition contains thirty-five such woodcuts, all of which excepting one had been previously used in the 1540 Janot's edition of *Amadis*, a common and acceptable practice among early printers, who could generically illustrate typical episodes with their stock of images, thus bringing down production costs. The one image not borrowed from *Amadis* was tailor-made to illustrate a significant and distinctive episode in *Palmerin*: the hero's birth, exposure, and discovery among olive and palm trees (see fig. 1).[121]

---

translate, revise and tidy it up, but also to have it printed." Since Maugin makes no similar complaint, we may assume that he was given a more reasonable time limit.

[118] "I was so much pressed the first time that I could barely read one quire of copy." Quoted in Weinberg, *Critical Prefaces*, 134 n. 23. Though Weinberg states that this text was added in 1553, it already appeared in 1549; cf. Beittoni, 175 n. 10. This remark is part of an interpolation added at the end of the preface to the 1549 edition.

[119] For the quotation, see Freer, 183 n. 23. Freer suggests the existence of another edition held in Paris at the Bibliothèque de l'Arsenal. This copy is catalogued as FB 40395, although the change in wording in the title page could actually indicate a further variant state rather than a different edition.

[120] The roman type was first used in a French edition in 1519, in Platina's *Les Généalogies, faitz et gests des sainctz Pères Papes, empereurs et rois de France* (Paris: Vincent Vidoué pour Galliot du Pré, 1519; FB 43936). See Henri-Jean Martin, *La Naissance du livre moderne (XIVe–XVIIe siècles): Mise en page et mise en texte du livre français* (Paris: Cercle de la Librairie, 2000), 193 and fig. 289–290. For the significance of adopting roman types for literary texts, see Harry Carter, *A View of Early Typography* (Oxford: Clarendon Press, 1969), 89. See also Taylor, *Rewriting Arthurian Romance*, 149.

[121] For this episode, see Part I, chap. 9 below. Note, however, that the woodcut as printed depicts the narrative events in a right-to-left order. For a bibliographical

DE PALMERIN D'OLIVE. Fueillet XIII.

Comme l'Empereur promist à

*Tarisius de luy faire espouser Griane, encores qu'elle ne le
vousist : & comme elle acoucha d'vn filz, sans
qu'autre s'en aperceust, que la vieille
qui l'auoit en garde.*

Chapitre IX.

Vand l'Empereur eut leu la lettre de sa fille, que Tolomestre luy presenta, encores qu'elle ne contint chose qui le deust prouoquer à courroux, ains le suplioit tres-humblement auoir pitié d'elle, qui estoit innocente de ce qu'on luy auoit mis sus, si se monstra il plus mal content qu'il ne souloit : & en sorte qu'il fist telle responseà la vieille : Dites à Griane que ie luy máde, puys qu'elle a eu la hardiesse de me desobeïr, qu'elle cognoistra combien ie puis en son endroit : & qu'elle s'asseure que iour de ma vie ie ne la voiray, si elle n'espouse Tarisius, à qui ie l'ay donnée. Ce que la vieille luy recita, mais plustost elle eust fait sacrifice de soymesmes : parquoy si auparauant ses ennuyz la solicitoient, encores luy faisoient ilz alors trop meilleure compaignie qu'au precedent : &
neantmoins

Figure 1: The exposure of Palmerin d'Oliva. *Le premier livre de Palmerin d'Olive* (Paris, 1546), sig. C1r. © The British Library, 12403.i.16.

The ornate and attractive illustration together with Maugin's high-flown translation, modeled on Herberay's *Amadis* —on "cest heureux langaige Essardin" (133) as Maugin describes its style[122]— transforms the medieval Castilian romance into a proto-novel imbued with a Renaissance aesthetic. Maugin fiddles with the text in ways that leave the narrative unchanged. His emphasis is mostly on the expression, and the techniques he deploys include *amplificatio*, recapitulation, cross-referencing, antithesis, periphrasis, explicitation, comparison, and hyperbole. Apart from condensing passages in which the original is perceived as prolix—mainly descriptions of action—Maugin also interferes with dialogues, especially those revolving around love, making them more rhetorical and pompous than the rather jejune original. The question of love receives a sophisticated treatment that is lacking in the Spanish text, but more attuned to the tastes of the Parisian upper classes, including women. Contributing also to increase the refinement and elegance of the text is the interpolation of references to classical literature and mythology, which Maugin uses to suggest analogical relations between the romance narrative and ancient civilization. The classical backdrop added by Maugin infuses greater seriousness and respectability into the romance's narrative events, which in the French translation more easily compel the admiration of a reading public for whom the classical world exuded an aura of dignity and morality.

Maugin's translation methodology results in a lengthier text, of more narrative density than the original, a text in which the plot unfolds more smoothly, the connection among the romance's integral parts becomes more visible, and the causal relationship between events is made explicit. Of greater readability, Maugin's version replicates the same effect of clarity created by the new *mise-en-page* and typography. Through his interventions the French translator replaced the original's plainness of expression with a more refined prose, created a classical background to redeem the old-fashioned medieval ambiance, and made "la versione francese prende una forma notevolmente più letteraria dell'originale."[123]

The essential characteristics of Maugin's text become visible when we compare it with the original Spanish, although he also spells out his approach to

---

description of the Sertenas issue of the first edition with discussion of the illustrations program, see *Harvard College Library Department of Printing and Graphic Arts Catalogue of Books and Manuscripts, Part I: French 16th Century Books*, compiled by Ruth Mortimer (Cambridge, MA: Belknap Press, 1964), no. 408; see also Rawles, *Denis Janot*, 377–79, nos. 109–10. For the illustrations in *Amadis*, see Jean-Marc Chatelain, "L'illustration d'*Amadis de Gaule* dans les éditions françaises du XVIe siècle," in *Les "Amadis" en France au XVIe siècle*, 41–52, esp. 42–44. See also Rothstein, *Reading in the Renaissance*, 85–93.

[122] Cf. Bettoni, 174 n. 2: "this felicitous Essardin language."

[123] Freer, 214. My remarks about the French translation are owing much to the direct comparison in Freer, 206–37. See also Taylor, *Rewriting Arthurian Romance*, 192–96.

the source text and his translation methodology in a preface to the first French edition. There we learn that Maugin's version presents "les amours à la moderne" and also how, in the process of rendering the work in French, he had "usé de metaphores, similitudes, et comparaisons, allegué fables, poësies, histoires, et inventé vers."[124] In addition, the preface also lays bear that Maugin's translation is informed by a nationalist interest in showing how French is stylistically superior to Spanish. Maugin has no qualms in admitting that, in the process of translation, he was moved by "le desir que j'ay eu de monstrer qu'en cest endroit [i.e., in the use of figures of speech] le François y est plus propre que l'Espaignol" (134).[125] Ultimately he was resolved to produce a better text than the Spanish original, and there is little doubt that he succeeded. This same nationalist rivalry with Spanish—or rather the use of a nationalist discourse for commercial purposes—was previously put forward by Herberay in the preface to *Amadis*. Herberay professes to have restored the narrative to the splendour it had prior to its current Spanish instantiation, which seems not to do justice to the eponymous hero, "car ilz [i.e., the Spaniards] en ont omis en d'aulcuns endroictz" from the supposedly original French composition.[126]

Maugin's choice not to translate his original faithfully was sanctioned by the stance previously adopted by Herberay, who advocates to become free from "la commune superstition des translateurs" (168; *the superstition common among translators*) about reproducing the *intentio auctoris*. On the contrary, Herberay proposes to impose the translator's own *intentio* on the original text and adapt it to the "meurs et façons du jourd'huy" (168; *habits and customs of today*). Interfering with the original *materia* was not felt to be reprehensible in this case, since "ce n'est matiere où soit requise si scrupuleuse observance" (168; *this is not a matter requiring such fastidiousness*). That is to say, because the *materia* of chivalric romance was not supposed to contain fact-based stories, it could be freely reworked and altered as part of the translator's creative engagement with the text.

---

[124] "love according to modern fashion"; "used metaphors, similes, and comparison, and cited as examples fables, poems, histories, and composed verses." Freer seems to have misunderstood this passage when he states,"abbiamo invano cercato le 'fables' e les 'histoires' che Maugin affermò di aver inserito nel testo" (208). Maugin explains that he has added allusions to stories in other texts, mostly of a mythological kind, and there are lots of such allusions in the translation; cf. Taylor, *Rewriting Arthurian Romance*, 193–94.

[125] "the desire I have to show that in this place French is more appropriate than Spanish." See also Elsa Neuville, "L'espace paratextuel à la Renaissance: Jean Maugin et ses contemporains," diss. (Lyon: École Nationale Supérieure des Sciences de l'Information et des Bibliothèques, 2010), 43; Neuville (63) considers that Maugin's explicit description of his translation strategies should be interpreted as a vindication of his text's modernity and tastefulness.

[126] *Amadis de Gaule*, ed. Bideaux, 166: "since they have omitted some details from the original." Further references in the main body of the text. See also Rothstein, *Reading in the Renaissance*, 42–45.

Premised on these same principles, Maugin's translation received the recognition of his contemporaries, as exemplifies the poet Jean-Pierre in a prefatory sonnet to *L'Histoire Palladienne* (1555; FB 40371) in which he describes Maugin as "De Palmerin [le] grand reformateur."[127] If above I state that Maugin was not a mere corrector or editor, and we now see that he was not a translator *stricto sensu* either, we can agree that the most accurate description of Maugin in his engagement with *Palmerin* is provided by Jean-Pierre, namely a *reformer* or *adapter* of the original text for a new public of a different sociocultural make-up.

The elegance of the bibliographic product and the style of the romance combined to capture the high-end segment of customers who were prepared to pay a higher price.[128] It seems that the commercial strategy was appropriate, since reprints of the romance appeared in 1549 (FB 40398–99) and in 1553.[129] All the editions printed between 1546 and 1553 were in folio and aimed at customers from well-to-do backgrounds. From then onward, however, printers chose other, smaller formats that were more affordable and contributed to popularize this romance among middle-class readers. In 1563 Galliot de Prés published an octavo edition (FB 40406) and reprinted it in 1573 (FB 40408; Freer D). This kind of dual publishing program, similar to our hardback and paperback editions, had already been applied to *Amadis* as early as 1548, when Groulleau printed it in octavo for Longis (FB 715). Interestingly, this octavo edition contains a prefatory, ten-line poem composed by Maugin, who comments on the advantages of the smaller size: "Or avez vous, Dames de cueur humain, / Vostre Amadis en si petit volume, / Que le pourrez porter dedans la main / Plus aysement beaucoup que de coustume."[130] Maugin explains that the alternative format may be convenient for women, since it allows for a more private and personal reading experience, safe from prying eyes that might disapprove of their choice of reading matter. The popularization of this romance intended with its publication in smaller formats was further increased by the editions printed in Lyon in

---

[127] "Of Palmerin the great reformer." Quoted in Bettoni, 178 n. 18; the sonnet is signed with the motto "Coelum Solum," which reminds us of the same author's more usual motto, "Coelum non solum." See also Rothstein, *Reading in the Renaissance*, 48–51.

[128] For the price of romances in contemporary France, see Rawles, 96–97; we read in the inventory of Herberay's books made at his death that he owned two copies of *Palmerin d'Olive* valued at 15 and 12 solz respectively.

[129] The 1553 edition exists in three variant states printed by Étienne Groulleau: one for Groulleau himself (FB40403), another for Longis (FB 40404; cf. Freer, 183 n. 24), and another for Sertenas (FB 40405; Freer B). Note that in 1546 Étienne Groulleau married Jeanne de Marnef, who was widowed in 1544; for this information, see Bettoni, 173.

[130] *Amadis de Gaule*, ed. Bideaux, 163: "Ladies of human heart, now you have your Amadis in such a small volume that you can hold it in your hand with much more comfort than normal." See also Hugues Vaganay, "Les éditions in-octavo de l'*Amadis* en français," *Revue hispanique* 85 (1929): 1–53.

16° by Benoît Rigaud after 1576 (FB 40413; 1592, FB 40415; 1593, 40416) and by Pierre Rigaud in 1605 and 1619.[131]

Finally, as discussed above, the circulation of the story of *Palmerin* in the Low Countries started later than that of the *Amadis* series. Its first appearance in print happened in 1572, when the Antwerp printer Jan Waesberghe published the French *Palmerin d'Olive* in quarto.[132] This edition follows the pattern began by Plantin with his *Amadis* editions of 1561, which had also been printed by Waesberghe himself. At the turn of the seventeenth century the Dutch *Palmerijn* was printed (1602/3; STCN 160204) and seems to have been commercially more successful than the French, since a reprint was issued in 1613 (STCN 161304).[133] The first edition captivated the imagination of a Dutch playwright, Gerbrand Bredero (1585–1618), who found inspiration in the Dutch version of the romance to construct the plot for the stage in two plays, namely, *Rodd'rick ende Alphonsus* and *Griane*, first performed in 1611 and 1612 respectively.[134]

The publication of the English *Palmerin d'Oliva*

The *editio princeps* of the English *Palmerin d'Oliva* went on sale in 1588. Anthony Munday's epistle to the reader in the first part (STC 19157) reads, "with the new yeere I send him [i.e., the book] abroad" (103.4–5), enabling us to establish the publication date as January 1, 1588.[135] On the same page Munday announces

---

[131] For the editions of 1605 and 1619 respectively, see Roméo Arbour, *L'ère baroque en France: Répertoire chronologique des éditions de textes littéraires* (Geneva: Droz, 1977–1985), nos 4342 and 9344.

[132] FB 40407; see Elly Cocks-Indestege, Geneviève Glorieux, and Bart Op de Beeck, *Belgica Typographica, 1541–1600* (Nieuwkoop: B. de Graaf, 1968–1994), no. 3922. For information on Waesberghe, see Rouzet, *Dictionnaire des imprimeurs de la Belgique actuelle*, 243–44.

[133] A diplomatic edition of the 1613 text is currently being produced and electronically published by Willem Kuiper; see http://cf.hum.uva.nl/dsp/scriptamanent/bml/Palmerijn_van_Olijve/Palmerijn_1613_cumulatief.pdf (accessed 16 September 2015). This edition also provides a transcription of the 1553 French edition at the bottom of the page. At the time of writing 41 chapters, of a total 139, had been transcribed.

[134] For critical editions, see Gerbrand Adriaensz. Bredero, *Rodd'rick ende Alphonsus*, ed. C. Kruyskamp (Zwolle: W. E. J. Tjeenk Willink, 1968); and *Griane*, ed. Foke Veenstra (Culemborg: Tjeenk Willink-Noorduijn, 1973). The relevant sections from the Dutch *Palmerijn van Olijve* are also provided as part of these editions. Kruyskamp edits chapter 105 from the Dutch *Palmerijn* as an appendix to *Rodd'rick*, 209–37; chaps. 1–11, 89–91, 94–96, 98 are edited by Veenstra in an appendix to *Griane*, 271–333. The title page of the 1613 edition is reproduced in Kruyskamp's *Rodd'rick*, 207.

[135] Note that initially Hayes, "Romances," 75, vacillates between 1588 and 1589. In a later article, Hayes admits, "a number of small points seem to suggest that the year-

that "The second parte goes forward on the Printers presse, and I hope shalbe with you sooner than you expect" (103.36–37). Unfortunately no copy of the first edition of the second part, i.e., *Palmerin d'Oliva II*, has survived. It seems, however, that the preface to the readers of the 1616 third edition of *Palmerin d'Oliva II* (STC 19159a) duplicates that of the *editio princeps* and includes the original date of composition: "From my house at Cripple-gate this ninth of March. 1588." (340.19–20).[136] Therefore, between the publication of the first and second part of the first edition there was approximately a two-month interval, just about the time required to complete the impression of a text of this length.[137]

The division of the text of *Palmerin d'Oliva* into two separate volumes was adopted for the English market, since this work had been published on the Continent as a single volume ever since its first appearance in Spain in 1511.[138] Instead of hiding this new bibliographic arrangement, Munday devotes the greater part of the prefatory epistle to the readers to explain the advantages in bringing out the romance in two volumes. The main benefit of this textual segmentation to Munday's readers derives from the fragmentation of payments, since "a man grutcheth not so much at a little mony, payd at seuerall times, as he doth at once" (103.15–16). Munday admits that there is also one advantage to him, namely, "that a little pause dooth well in so long a labour" (103.22), probably an allusion to the over two months required for the printing of the second part, suggesting that the first part was printed before he had completely finished translating the second part.

Some modern scholars, however, have reacted with unwarranted hostility to Munday on account of the division of this romance. Patchell comments,

---

dating should be considered from 1 January, not from 25 March" ("Postscript," 35), thus accepting that the text appeared in 1588. Only two copies of the 1588 edition of *Palmerin d'Oliva I* have come down to us: BL C.56.d.6 and Folger Shakespeare Library, STC 19157.

[136] Additionally, note that in the postface to *Palladine of England* (STC 5541), published on April 23, 1588, Munday refers to the two parts of *Palmerin d'Oliva* as already in print.

[137] The second part, started after January 1, 1588, would have been completed in approximately fifty-one working days according to the standard rate of production of one sheet per day; see H. S. Bennett, *English Books and Readers, vol. 2: 1558–1603, Being a Study in the History of the Book Trade in the Reign of Elizabeth I* (Cambridge: Cambridge University Press, 1965), 290.

[138] Cf. IB 16737–16751. Note, however, that the editions of 1555 (Toledo; IB 16749) and 1562 (Medina del Campo; IB 16750) of *Palmerín de Olivia* were published as four separate volumes; see José Manuel Lucía Megías, "Catálogo descriptivo de libros de caballerías hispánicos. VII. Un *Palmerín de Olivia* recuperado: Toledo, ¿Juan Ferrer?, 1555 (Biblioteca del Palacio Real: I.C.91)," *Voz y Letra* 6 (1995): 41–57, and also Lucía, *Imprenta*, 41–43. And, maybe more significantly, Francisco Delicado had already decided to divide *Primaleón* in three parts.

"Although the original . . . from which he translated had been in one volume, *his mercenary instincts* led him to publish it in two parts several months apart" (19, emphasis mine).[139] In this criticism not only does Patchell show prejudice against Munday, but together with other scholars fails to consider the two-volume publication of this text within the wider context of chivalric romance printing in Elizabethan England. In fact, the textual segmentation of this work is just one of the bibliographical choices made as part of the process of adapting a foreign text to England's print culture and its sociocultural milieu. While *Palmerin d'Oliva* appeared in England as two quarto volumes printed in black letter, the French translation was initially published not only as a single volume, but also in folio size and using roman type. Obviously publishing books in quarto reduced production costs, thus allowing wider distribution among the middle classes, the cornerstone of the romance book trade in early modern England.[140] Aware of the need to market his translation inclusively to middle-class readers, Munday wanted to engage them from the very title-page, in which he addressed "*the inferiour sorte*" (99.9).[141] As regards the choice of font, even though after 1580 roman type was increasingly adopted in England for certain literary modes, black letter remained the preferred option for popular genres including romance.[142] As a matter of fact, these same bibliographical features apply to the English metrical romances—i.e., more or less slender quarto-sized volumes in black letter—published throughout the better part of the sixteenth century and catering to a similar readership. It seems reasonable, therefore, to consider the

---

[139] Munday's "mercenary instincts" had been previously adduced by Thomas, 249. Hill, in a discussion of Munday's epistle to the reader, argues that Munday "makes no pretence that his aim is not to offer his readers one text for the price of two, as it were" (46; cf. Turner, 78), although we have no evidence that this was the case, and Munday states that "the cost [of the book in two parts] is as great, as though it had come altogether" (103.14–15). On the contrary, I don't think he was trying to deceive his customers but was being honest in explaining the rationale behind the publisher's decision of segmenting the work in two parts. To think otherwise and believe that Munday was being deceitful would suggest that he was convinced his potential clientele could be easily misled and that, if exposed, their subterfuge would have no negative commercial consequences.

[140] Cf. Lori Humphrey Newcomb, "Romance," in *The Oxford History of Popular Print Culture, vol. 1: Cheap Print in Britain and Ireland to 1660*, ed. Joad Raymond (Oxford: Oxford University Press, 2011), 363–76.

[141] Cf. Bennett, *English Books and Readers*, 2:253. See also Louise Wilson, "Writing Romance Readers in Early Modern Paratexts," *SPELL: Swiss Papers in English Language and Literature* 22 (2009): 111–23, at 120.

[142] Cf. McKerrow, *Introduction*, 297. For a recent and illuminating discussion of the rationale for choosing black letter, see Zachary Lesser, "Typographic Nostalgia: Play-Reading, Popularity, and the Meanings of Black Letter," in *The Book of the Play: Playwrights, Stationers, and Readers in Early Modern England*, ed. Marta Straznicky (Amherst, MA: University of Massachusetts Press, 2006), 99–126.

textual division of *Palmerin d'Oliva* as part of a marketing strategy to package a foreign product—the Iberian prose romances—with features associated with an already existing product—the native metrical romances—that were recognizable by the same target audience. Although Munday claims responsibility for the decision of dividing the text of *Palmerin d'Oliva* into two parts ("I now deuide it twaine," 103.8), the choices affecting the format, font and segmentation of the work would have been made systematically by printers and publishers, since they were adopted in England for the entire corpus of Iberian romances.[143] But there is yet another issue to be taken into account. The publication of this long work in smaller bibliographic units reduced the potential financial risks incurred by the publisher, since he could start recouping part of the initial investment while the second part was still in production. Additionally, the market demand for this kind of narrative could also be assessed and, in a worst-case scenario, they could have decided to interrupt or postpone the printing of the second half.

The publication of *Palmerin d'Oliva*, as the title page suggests (see fig. 2), was initiated by the publisher and bookseller William Wright (active 1579–1603).[144] Although there is no entry in the register of the Stationers' Company stating the exact date when Wright obtained the licence to print *Palmerin d'Oliva*, we learn from a 1596 entry (see p. 45) that he was the legal licence holder. Sometime in 1587 Wright must have commissioned John Charlewood (d. 1593) to print Munday's translation.[145] Charlewood had an early association with Munday, as he had already printed the latter's first publication in 1577 (STC 18269.5). Furthermore, the geographical proximity of Charlewood's premises and Munday's home, both located in Cripplegate, must have facilitated their long-lived professional relationship.[146] Such physical proximity was particularly convenient for Munday, who could that way more easily see his book through the press, not an unlikely possibility considering the small number of errors of wording and misprints and the existence of stop-press corrections in Charlewood's edition.[147] Note, additionally, that Munday expressed elsewhere his concern with

---

[143] I agree with Phillips when he states, "Munday and his stationers planned and instituted these breaks as part of a publication strategy" (147). Publication decisions belong not to authors but to printers/publishers, a clear example being Munday's *Zelauto*, which he was prevailed upon to publish in its unfinished state as Munday explains in the prefatory epistle: "*The last part of this woorke remaineth vnfinished, the which for breuity of time, and speedines in the Imprinting: I was constrained to permit*" (6).

[144] For more information on Wright, see R. B. McKerrow, *A Dictionary of Printers and Booksellers in England, Scotland and Ireland, and of Foreign Printers of English Books 1557–1640* (London: The Bibliographical Society, 1910), 303–4.

[145] For more biographical information on Charlewood, see H. R. Tedder, "Charlewood, John (d. 1593)," rev. Robert Faber, *ODNB*, 11:176–77.

[146] See William E. Miller, "Printers and Stationers in the Parish of St. Giles Cripplegate 1561–1640," *SB* 19 (1966): 15–38, at 23; and Hill, 32.

[147] See the list of emendations and the historical collation below.

the texual accuracy of his works and his will to erase all errors from them. For instance, in the postscript to *Palladine of England* Munday regrets that "Diuers foule faultes are escaped in the imprinting, in some places words mistaken . . . and diuers other by mishap left out, and partly by want of my attendance to read the proues."[148] While acknowledging the textual deterioration of his work, Munday accepts partial responsibility for it, since he failed to detect and emend all corrupt readings at the proofreading stage. Considering that *Palladine of England* was published on April 23, 1588, just a few weeks after the appearance of *Palmerin d'Oliva II*, the absence of a note of this kind in our romance is all the more telling. This absence together with Charlewood's careful printing suggests that Munday may have corrected the proofs of *Palmerin d'Oliva*, a practice not at all unusual in this period.[149] Once printed, the book could be purchased at Wright's shop "adioyning to S. Mildreds Church in the Poultrie, the middle Shoppe in the rowe," (99.21–24).[150]

On August 9, 1596, the Stationers' Register records that *Palmerin d'Oliva I* and *II* "were assigned from William wright to Thomas Scarlet and from Thomas Scarlet to . . . Thomas Crede" (Arber, 3:68).[151] Therefore, the copyright of *Palmerin d'Oliva* was transferred not to a bookseller but a printer, thus suggesting that Creede, despite not being necessarily as cognizant of the literary preferences of contemporary readers as booksellers, was confident in the market value and financial possibilities of the *Palmerin* romances.[152] Creede, whose printing house was located at the sign of the Catherine Wheel near the Old Swan in Thames Street,[153] printed the second edition of *Palmerin d'Oliva* (STC 19158) in 1597, the second part appearing on August 1, 1597, as Munday states in the dedication: "I humbly take my leaue, this first of August."[154] Creede was fortunate to enlist

---

[148] Cf. also Munday's remarks in the prefatory epistle to his *Gerileon of England* of 1592 (STC 17206), quoted in Byrne, "Books," 244.

[149] Cf. Percy Simpson, *Proof-Reading in the Sixteenth, Seventeenth and Eighteenth Centuries*, (London: Oxford University Press, 1935), 1–45. This edition also retains to a significant extent some of the spelling features identified with Munday, thus suggesting his personal involvement in the preparation of this edition; see Byrne, "Clue."

[150] To locate the exact whereabouts of Wright's shop, see STC, 3:252 (O.1).

[151] Thomas Scarlet was printer and publisher between 1590–96 (Arber, 5:263).

[152] In 1596 Creede printed *Palmerin of England I–II* (STC 19161). Note that during the period 1593–1602 "he printed twice as many books for himself as for others," as stated by Yamada, who prefers to describe Creede as "a printer-bookseller" (Yamada, 41) for this period.

[153] For biographical information, see David L. Gants, "Creede, Thomas (b. in or before 1554, d. 1616)," *ODNB*, 14:128–29; see also Yamada, 3–12. In order to locate his premises on a London map, see Yamada, 16, and STC, 3:255 (T.5).

[154] See the appendix below, 750.15–16. The second edition survives in two imperfect copies: BL C.56.d.7 and Henry E. Huntington Library, 330331. Neri, "Cuadro de la difusión europea del ciclo palmeriniano," 302, locates a copy of the 1597 edition in

the help of Munday in producing the reprint of our romance, though the latter failed to take the opportunity to thoroughly revise the text or make any significant improvement to it. All substantive variants are of no narrative import and thus equally attributable either to Munday or to the compositors and correctors. Instead, Munday is certainly responsible for making changes to the prefatory material. While he had dedicated the first edition of *Palmerin d'Oliva I* and *II* to Edward de Vere, seventeenth earl of Oxford, for the second edition Munday found new patrons, namely, Francis Young of Brent-Pelham, Hertford, and his wife Susan.[155] Except for the prefatory material, Creede's 1597 edition presents a line by line reprint of the 1588 edition,[156] with minimal compositorial interventions correcting obvious mistakes in the printer's copy and introducing minor textual variants.[157]

---

the University of Liverpool Library. Katy Hooper, Special Collections Librarian of the University of Liverpool, has confirmed to me in a personal communication that the item Neri refers to "was a photostat obtained from the (then) British Museum copy C.56.d.7 and not an original text" (email of August 20, 2015). Neri, *loc. cit.*, also indicates that hypothetical editions of *Palmerin d'Oliva I* were printed in 1594 and 1596, although no supporting evidence is provided.

[155] Although the prefatory material pertaining to the second edition of *Palmerin d'Oliva I* has not survived, the 1615 edition preserves the dedication that presumably appeared in 1597; I have included this prefatory material in an appendix. We have no historical information about the identity of the Youngs, but Wilson, "Paratexts," 126, states that Francis Young was a merchant (126). Note that the change of patron was also recorded in other romance translations by Munday published in 1596 and 1597: *Palmerin of England I* and *II* (1596), and *Primaleon II* (1596; STC 20366a); and possibly the nonexistent *Palmerin of England III* (1597) and *Primaleon III* (1597); cf. Turner, 182.

[156] As regards the second edition of *Palmerin d'Oliva I* in the BL, Hayes erroneously conjectures that "this copy appears more probably the original edition of 1588" ("Romances," 66). Later Hayes himself corrects this error of judgment ("Postcript," 35).

[157] The dedication in the 1597 edition of *Palmerin d'Oliva II* contains the following remark: "hauing sent ye the first [part of *Palmerin d'Oliva*], so likewise doe I now the seconde [part], and will make what speede I can in translating *the third and last*" (750.12–14; emphasis added); and in the epistle to the readers Munday again promises a third part. The dedication to the 1615 *Palmerin d'Oliva I*, probably the same that appeared in the 1597 edition, confirms that Munday had obtained a copy of the text supposedly corresponding to the third part: "*the third and last* [part] *that I am now in hand*" (749.13–14). The preface to the 1673 reprint of *Don Bellianis of Greece* (Wing K632A) mentions the existence of "*Palmerin D'Oliva*, in three Parts"; for a partial transcription of this preface, see Thomas, 258–61. There is, however, no bibliographical evidence that this third part was ever published as such. In any event, the continuation to the Spanish *Palmerín de Olivia* is *Primaleón*, with the title *Libro segundo del emperador Palmerín*. But it is unlikely that Munday was referring to this last work, since he had already translated the first thirty-two chapters of the French *Primaleon* and published them as *Palmendos* in 1589 (STC 18064), and the rest in 1595 (*Primaleon I*; STC 20366) and 1596 (*Primaleon II*;

On December 4, 1615, we learn from the Stationers' Register that Richard Heggenbotham "Entred for his Copie by order of a Court, and Consent of Thomas Creed *The first and second partes of* PALMERYN D'OLIVA" (Arber, 3: 579). *Palmerin d'Oliva* is only the second book whose copyright was obtained by Richard Higgenbotham (also spelt Heggenbotham, Higenbotham, and Higginbottam), a London bookseller that had taken his liberty of the Stationers' Company only on April 3, 1615.[158] And before 1615 expired, Thomas Creede printed the third edition of *Palmerin d'Oliva I* (STC 19159), but with no reference to Higgenbotham on the title-page or elsewhere.[159]

It seems that with the new year the third edition was reissued (STC 19159a) with a cancel title page containing more information about this romance's publication: "Printed by *T. C.* [i.e., Thomas Creede] and *B. A.* [Bernard Alsop] for *Richard* Higgenbotham, and are to be sold at his shop at the signe of the Cardinals Hat without Newgate."[160] The change in wording of the cancel title page is attributable to Higgenbotham, who exercised his power as licence holder and financier of this printing project. While no reference to him appeared in the *cancelland*, now the *cancellans* gives prominence to the publisher, whose name is spelled out in full, and describes as was customary the location of his premises,

---

STC 20366a). There is one other alternative continuation to *Palmerin d'Oliva*, composed in Italy and published in 1560 as *Il secondo libro di Palmerino di Oliva*; cf. pp. 29–30 above. See Bognolo, "Los palmerines italianos," 270–71; and Neri, "Cuadro de la difusión europea del ciclo palmeriniano," 289. Nothing prevents the assumption that Munday, who had lived in Rome during a few months in 1579, could translate directly from Italian as he did in the case of *Palmerin of England III*; cf. Hayes, "Romances," 67. Nonetheless, in the absence of any corroborating evidence I agree with Hayes ("Postscript," 35) in considering the identification of this Italian continuation with Munday's third part only a conjectural possibility. There is yet one further possibility. It can be that as part of the serialization strategy used for publishing the Iberian romances it was considered paramount to create the expectation of a forthcoming third part even if in the end this could not be delivered. Failing to fulfil such a promise would have no serious literary consequence, since it was not unusual in contemporary England to publish unfinished texts, as for example Spenser's *The Faerie Queene*, Sidney's *New Arcadia*, and Munday's *Zelauto*; cf. Phillips, 139–47, and Wilson, "Paratexts." For a detailed discussion of *Palmerin d'Oliva III*, see Hayes, "Romances," 63–67.

[158] See McKerrow, *Dictionary of Printers*, 136.

[159] The only existing copy of this issue of the third edition of *Palmerin d'Oliva I* is Lambeth Palace Library, ARC K73.3b P18. For a facsimile reproduction of the title page, see Jordi Sánchez-Martí, "The Publication History of Anthony Munday's *Palmerin d'Oliva*," *Gutenberg-Jahrbuch* 89 (2014), 198, fig. 2.

[160] In order to locate Higgenbotham's shop, see STC, 3:248 (D.9). Of this issue of the third edition the following copies have survived: BL C.56.d.8 (2 parts), Lambeth Palace Library (part 2 only, ARC K73.3b P18), and Henry E. Huntington Library 330330 (2 parts). For a facsimile of the BL copy's title page, see Sánchez-Martí, "Publication of *Palmerin*," 200, fig. 3.

probably not yet well-known due to his recent establishment as a bookseller. By contrast, those responsible for the actual printing of the text receive unequal treatment, as the new title page gives not the full name of the printers, but their initials instead.

The cancel title page of this reissue has been instrumental in revealing that the third edition of *Palmerin d'Oliva I* had been produced not exclusively by Creede and his employees, as the original title page states, but was a joint venture between Creede and his associate Bernard Alsop, a fact that the former wanted to hide.[161] The collaboration Creede-Alsop, which lasted a few more months until Creede's death in 1616, was necessary if the printing of *Palmerin d'Oliva I* started around December 4, 1615, and was finished before the year was over.[162] Considering that one printing press, at a standard rate of production, would have needed forty-seven working days to complete the first part approximately, it was feasible to do the job in twenty-four days when two printers were engaged.[163] In any event, the 1615 edition of the first part was printed on two presses and the text portioned out between the two print shops is still recoverable from the use of two distinguishable sets of black-letter type: the part going from the beginning through signature F was printed using a battered set of type, whereas for the remainder of the book a newly cast set of type was used. Bearing in mind that printing this section of *Palmerin d'Oliva* was in all likelihood Alsop's first commission, it seems reasonable to assign the newer type to him and thus attribute signatures G to Z to Alsop's printing press.[164] Equally, after a twenty-two-year professional career and only months before his death, Creede was more likely than the young Alsop to be using a worn-out font of type. Printing the initial portion of the book, Creede would have also been responsible for designing the cancelled title page on which he appears as the sole creator of this edition.

From all these bits of information we can infer that Higgenbotham commissioned Creede to print the third edition of *Palmerin d'Oliva*, and then Creede contracted out part of the printing work to Alsop, possibly to meet some deadline. The agreement with the subcontractor did not stipulate that Alsop's name should appear on the title-page, nor did it require an equal division of the workload, as the amount of text presumably printed by Alsop nearly trebles that printed by Creede. On account of his well-established position in the London book trade,

---

[161] For more information about Alsop, see Henry R. Plomer, *A Dictionary of the Booksellers and Printers who were at Work in England, Scotland and Ireland from 1641 to 1667* (London: The Bibliographical Society, 1907), 3–4.

[162] For a list of the books published by Creede in collaboration with Alsop, see Yamada, 139–40, and cf. 10–11.

[163] In 1615 Creede was allowed to have one printing press only; cf. Arber, 3:699.

[164] For a facsimile illustrating the final page printed by Creede (sig. F8v) and the first printed by Alsop (sig. G1r), see Sánchez-Martí, "Publication of *Palmerin*," 203, fig. 4.

Introduction 49

Creede seems to have taken advantage of Alsop, who was still in need of making headway in the printing business. Once the job was finished, Creede handed over the sheets of the third edition of *Palmerin d'Oliva I* to Higgenbotham, who appears to have been disappointed with the final product. He could not have been pleased, first, with the title-page originally produced by Creede, and second, with the obvious visual differences caused by the two sets of type used to print this edition. Consequently, Higgenbotham must have required Creede to replace the original title-page with one adapted to the publisher's needs, as has been discussed, and decided that only Alsop's font of type should be used to print *Palmerin d'Oliva II*.[165]

The 1615 edition of *Palmerin d'Oliva I* derives from the second edition, which was printed also by Creede in 1597. The genetic relation of the three editions of *Palmerin d'Oliva I*, therefore, corresponds to their chronological order and can be represented as 1588 > 1597 > 1615 (= 1616). Nevertheless, as McKerrow warns, "the genetic descent of editions . . . is not necessarily the same as the relationship of the texts which they exhibit."[166] While historical collation shows that most of the readings in the 1597 edition agree with those in the 1615 edition, there is one particular case involving greater complexity. At the end of signature G2v the first edition reads, "as well might" (140.8), and the same words appear in the third edition (sig. D6v), but are omitted in the second edition (sig. D6v). One could argue that the compositors were working from different copies belonging to different editions of the same text,[167] but this possibility seems unlikely since the same signature contains variant readings in which the second and third editions agree against the first. I suggest instead that the textual omission was detected and stop-press corrected while the second edition was being produced, and then the compositors of the 1615 edition worked from a copy of the second edition with a corrected signature D6v, although no copy representing the corrected state of the forme survives.[168] Yet this is not all. The compositors

---

[165] Maybe even the substitution of "1616" for "1615" on the new title page was caused not only by the actual change of year, but also to be coherent with the information included in the epistle to the reader, which still states that "with the new yeere I send him abroad" (sig. A3v). Thus the third edition would have gone on sale at the beginning of 1616. Notwithstanding all Higgenbotham's efforts to downplay the printers' role, the title page of the 1616 *Palmerin d'Oliva II* contains one of the devices Creede used in his books that would later be adopted by Alsop. See Ronald B. McKerrow, *Printers' & Publishers' Devices in England & Scotland 1485–1640* (London: The Bibliographical Society, 1913), no. 339: "Device of a griffin seated on a stone (or a book?), under which is a ball with wings" (132).

[166] Ronald B. McKerrow, *Prolegomena of the Oxford Shakespeare: A Study in Editorial Method* (Oxford: Clarendon Press, 1939), 105.

[167] McKerrow, *Prolegomena*, 107 n. 1.

[168] Cf. Fredson Bowers, *Principles of Bibliographical Description* (Princeton, NJ: Princeton University Press, 1949), 46.

of the third edition reproduced the text of 1597 with just minor adjustments, except that from signature I5r a more interventionist compositor got involved at intervals. The first intervention of this compositor, working under Alsop, may be illustrative of his practice of making changes of expression with no narrative consequence: the phrase in his copy-text "make me[e] hide what you please" (190.7) becomes "*compell* mee *to* hide what*soeuer* you *shall* please" (sig. I5r; my italics). This compositor made his presence felt by adding new words, thus stopping the line-for-line correspondence with the previous edition, although he was very careful to bring the text into agreement at the end of each page to prevent any disruption with the work of his fellow compositors. As a result, the third edition of *Palmerin d'Oliva I* presents a page-by-page reproduction of the 1597 edition with the kind of changes already mentioned.

Hayes ("Romances," 76) states that the 1616 edition of *Palmerin d'Oliva II* is based not on Creede's 1597 edition, as one would expect, but on the *editio princeps* of 1588. Unfortunately no copy of the first edition of *Palmerin d'Oliva II* is extant to corroborate Hayes's statement and he provides no evidence to support his position other than the fact that Munday's epistle to the friendly readers is dated March 9, 1588. Of course, this plausible date would not appear in the third edition without the compositors having consulted a copy of the *editio princeps*, since the date is not included in the 1597 edition. But one could still argue that the coincidence of the 1616 edition with that of 1588 as regards the date in the prefatory material represents only circumstantial evidence that does not suffice to prove the textual descent of the 1616 edition from the *editio princeps*. Consequently, we need to substantiate Hayes's position by producing further proof of the third edition's textual derivation from the first. In chapter II.vi, after Maurice, Prince of Pasmeria, marries King Lycomedes's daughter, thus betraying the queen of Tharsus, the latter decides to take vengeance. With the help of a magician, she sends Maurice an enchanted crown that bursts into flames the moment he places it on his head (see the explanatory notes, 683–84). When Maurice's envoys meet the queen asking her to be merciful and free the prince of the enchantment, she declines. These were the Queen's words to the envoys in Jean Maugin's French version from which Munday translated: "Allez, & vuidez incontinent de mes terres: car vostre maistre est tant indigne de faueur, que ses gens en sont tous à haïr."[169] It seems reasonable to expect that the *editio princeps* contained a correct translation of this French quotation. The second edition, however, presents a corrupt reading caused inadvertently by the compositors: "depart my Countrey, for your Maister is so *worthie* of fauour, as for his sake I hate his people" (sig. B6v; my italics; cf. 359.2–3). By contrast, this error

---

[169] "Go and leave my lands immediately, for your master is so unworthy of favour that, on account of him, his people are all to be hated." I quote from Jan Waesberghe's edition of *L'histoire de Palmerin d'Olive* (Antwerp 1572; FB 40407), sig. P7r. For my choice of this edition, see "Editorial Principles" below.

is emended in the third edition, which instead of "worthie" reads "vnwoorthie" (sig. C2v). The reading in the 1616 edition reproduces the one most probably contained in the 1588 (see emendation to 359.3 on p. 768). Even though the narrative context allows for the possibility of emending the text without necessarily consulting the first edition, the compositorial practices in the third edition show consistency in not altering the meaning of the source. Moreover, the use of a doubled *o* in the word "vnwoorthie" represents Munday's preferred spelling, which was already perceived as old-fashioned in 1588 and therefore abandoned in 1597.[170] If the compositors of the 1616 edition had been working from a copy of the 1597 and decided to emend their source, they would not have decided to impose an old-fashioned spelling but would have most probably written "vnworthie". So, in view of all this evidence, the compositors seem not to be emending the 1597 edition, but rather copying from the original version of 1588. In other words, this case of substantive textual variation demonstrates the second and third editions' independent derivation from the *editio princeps*.

In 1637, four years after Munday's death, the fourth edition (STC 19160) was printed "for [i.e., by] B. ALSOP and T. FAVVCET, dwelling in *Grub-street* neere the lower Pumpe", as the title page reads.[171] When Thomas Creede died in 1616 Alsop inherited his business and later formed partnership with Thomas Fawcet, who took up his freedom on May 7, 1621 (Arber, 3:685, 701).[172] This edition retains in the two parts the substantive variant readings of the third edition and

---

[170] Cf. Byrne, "Clue." See below how the spelling of this word is modernized in the 1637 edition.

[171] The following copies of the fourth edition are known to exist in public repositories: University of Alicante Library, FA/012; BL G. 10484; Bodleian Library, Douce PP 241 and Wood 346; Bristol University Library, Restricted M; Dulwich College, accession no. 1673–1674; Cambridge University Library, SSS.26.8; Folger Shakespeare Library, STC 19160 copy 1 and 2; Harvard University Library, STC 19160; Henry E. Huntington Library, 62839; John Rylands University Library of Manchester, R14154; King's College, Cambridge, A.7.19; Library of Congress PQ 6419 .P4 1637 English Print; Mitchell Library, 781140; Newberry Library, Case Y 1565 .P166 and Case Y 7265 .P18 (part 1 only); University Library of Illinois at Urbana-Champaign, IUA09456; Stanford University Library, Rare Books KC1637 .P3; Yale University Library, Ig M922 588g. The copy in the John Rylands Library presents a variant imprint to the title-page of part 1 and replaces *for* with *by*; cf. STC, 2:211. The staff of the New York Public Library inform me that they hold no copy of this book, contrary to the information in the STC. For a facsimile of the title page, see Jordi Sánchez-Martí, "The University of Alicante Copy of *Palmerin d'Oliva* (London, 1637): A Bibliographical Description," *Sederi: Yearbook of the Spanish and Portuguese Society for English Renaissance Studies* 23 (2013): 127, fig. 1.

[172] For more information about Fawcet, see Plomer, *A Dictionary of the Booksellers and Printers*, 72.

agrees with it in departing from the 1588 and 1597 editions accordingly.[173] This edition's textual derivation is best illustrated by the same examples used previously in the case of the third edition: in part I, sig. I5r, the fourth edition agrees substantively with the third in reading, "compell me to hide whatsoeuer you shall please"; the same happens in part II, sig. C1v, which also agrees with the previous edition and reads, "depart my Country: for your Master is so unworthy of favour, as for his sake I hate his people". Note, however, that the compositors make no attempt to follow their copy-text page by page.

In his 1925 article Hayes ("Romances," 75–76) included a table summarizing the publication history of Munday's *Palmerin d'Oliva*. I here follow his example avoiding the ambiguities and inaccuracies in Hayes's original table:

Part I
January 1, 1588 (A) 1st ed.   dedicated to Earl of Oxford.
1597   (B) 2nd ed.; a reprint of (A).   dedicated to the Youngs.
1615   (C) 3rd ed.; a reprint of (B).   dedicated to the Youngs.
1637   a reprint of (C).   dedicated to the Youngs.

Part II
March 9, 1588   (A) 1st ed.; not extant   dedicated to Earl of Oxford.
August 1, 1597   (B) 2nd ed.; a reprint of (A).   dedicated to the Youngs.
1616   (C) 3rd ed.; a reprint of (A).   dedicated to Earl of Oxford.
1637   a reprint of (C).   dedicated to Earl of Oxford.

Anthony Munday:
A literary biography of *Palmerin d'Oliva*'s translator

Anthony Munday was baptized in St. Gregory's by St. Paul's, London, on October 13, 1560, and it is generally assumed that he was born only a few days before.[174] The son of Christopher and Jane Munday, Anthony was left an orphan

---

[173] Cf. Hayes, "Romances," 70. The information Hayes presents in tabular form ("Romances," 75–76) is confusing, since it seems to suggest that the fourth edition of *Palmerin d'Oliva I* is a reprint of the second edition, and the fourth edition of *Palmerin d'Oliva II* is a reprint of the first edition. It seems more accurate to state that the 1637 edition is a reprint of the third edition.

[174] Note that in this section of the introduction I focus on events in Munday's life that have influenced his literary career up until 1588, the year when his translation of *Palmerin d'Oliva* was published. More complete biographical accounts are provided by Turner and Hamilton. For an overview of his output as a translator, see Helen Moore, "Anthony Munday," in *OHLTE*, 74–77. For the date of his birth, see Leslie Hotson, "Anthony Mundy's Birth-Date," *Notes and Queries* 204 (1959): 2–4. The 1633 edition of John Stow's *Survey of London* (STC 23345) contains a misleading inscription: "*Obiit Anno*

before January 9, 1570/1, when a bond was entered stating that four citizens undertook to pay £16 15*s*. 2*d*. "pro Antonio Monday filio et orphano Monday stacyoner ex legacione Jane Monday matris orphani."[175] Although his father Christopher had been a member of the Drapers' Company, the trade he was really engaged in was that of a stationer or bookseller. Christopher was first an apprentice to the printer and bookseller Thomas Petyt (d. 1565/6), himself a member of the Drapers' Company, and later transferred to Anthony Kitson on August 7, 1554, being finally admitted to the freedom on January 13, 1557.[176] Thus, Anthony Munday grew up in a household whose main source of income came from the trade in books.

Despite having been orphaned at such an early age, Munday gives testimony of the central role he attributes to his parents in the formation of his character. In the dedication of his *Mirrour of Mutabilitie*, composed and published at the end of 1579, Munday remembers his parents and "their liberall expences bestowed on vs in our youth, in trayning vs vp in verteous educations."[177] Munday thus constructed a positive memory of his parents and gave them credit for providing him with an education. The exact nature of this education, however, is unknown to us. *Axiochus*, a text attributed to Munday, contains a dedication to Benedict Barnham (bap. 1559–d. 1598) with reminiscences of their youth: "My familiarity with yee in your younger yeeres, when sometimes wee were Schollers together."[178] We know that Barnham, who would become alderman and sheriff

---

Ætatis suæ 80. Domini 1633. Augusti 10." (869; *Died at the age of 80 on August 10, 1633*); quoted in Mark Eccles, "Anthony Munday," in *Studies in the English Renaissance: in Memory of Karl Julius Holzknecht*, ed. Josephine W. Bennett, Oscar Cargill, and Vernon Hall, Jr. (London: Peter Owen & Vision, 1961), 95. This inscription suggests that Munday was born in 1553, seven years before he was baptized.

[175] Eccles, "Munday," 98; "in favor of Anthony Monday, son and orphan of Monday, stationer, from the legacy of Jane Monday, the orphan's mother."

[176] See Eccles, "Munday," 97, and Peter W. M. Blayney, *The Stationers' Company and the Printers of London, 1501–1557* (Cambridge: Cambridge University Press, 2013), 2:816. For Petyt, see Alexandra Gillespie, "Petyt, Thomas (b. in or before 1494, d. 1565/6)," in *ODNB*, 43:962–63. For Kitson, see E. Gordon Duff, *A Century of the English Book Trade* (London: The Bibliographical Society, 1905), 86.

[177] The quotation is taken from Heinrich's edition of *Mirrour*, 9.63–64.

[178] *The Axiochus of Plato*, ed. Frederick Morgan Padelford (Baltimore, MD: The Johns Hopkins Press, 1934), 36. Initially this work was ascribed to Edmund Spenser; see the introduction to Padelford's edition. For its attribution to Munday, see Marshall W. S. Swan, "The *Sweet Speech* and Spenser's (?) *Axiochus*," *ELH* 11 (1944): 161–81. See also Joseph L. Black and Lisa Celovsky, "'Lost Works', Suppositious Pieces, and Continuations," in *The Oxford Handbook of Edmund Spenser*, ed. Richard A. McCabe (Oxford: Oxford University Press, 2010), 349–64. The authorship of *Axiochus*, however, remains contentious; see Kirk Melnikoff, *Elizabethan Publishing and the Makings of Literary Culture* (Toronto: University of Toronto Press: 2018), 3–5.

of London, continued his studies in St. Alban Hall, Oxford, in or before 1572.[179] Considering that Munday and Barnham were not only contemporaries, but lived in close proximity, and their fathers were members of the Drapers' Company, it seems likely that Anthony's parents intended for him an educational path not much unlike Barnham's. These aspirational plans, designed to rise Munday up the social scale, foundered when his progenitors died.

Through force of circumstance Munday chose to channel his energy into more practical affairs and used his father's connections to follow in his steps. On August 24, 1576, Anthony Munday became apprentice to the printer and bookseller John Allde (d. 1584), to whom he was bound for eight years.[180] It is quite probable that the encouragement for Munday to make translations of French texts came from Allde, as Celeste Turner Wright has suggested.[181] The first work Munday translated is *Histoire des nobles prouesses et vaillances de Galien restauré*, to which he refers as *Galien of Fraunce*.[182] While there is no extant copy of this translation, Munday mentions his "book intituled *Galien of Fraunce*, vvherein, hauing not so fully comprised such pithines of stile, as one of a more riper Inuention could cunningly haue carued" (*Mirrour*, 6.9–7.11). That is, Munday acknowledges having attempted to translate *Galien*, but is well aware that his translation left a lot to be desired. In particular, he admits that it failed to reproduce the pithy style of the original owing to his inability to grasp its sense fully.[183]

If Munday decided to undertake the translation, he must have felt confident that he had the necessary skills. Even if he underestimated the difficulties of the task ahead, how did he acquire a knowledge of French? What kind of opportunities did he have to learn the language? In 1575 the French Huguenot refugee Claudius Hollyband (d. 1597) founded a private school in St. Paul's Churchyard, in the area where Munday lived.[184] What is more, we have evidence that Hol-

---

[179] See Sarah Bendall, "Barnham, Benedict (1558/9–1598)," in *ODNB*, 4:2; and Joseph Foster, *Alumni Oxonienses: The Members of the University of Oxford, 1500–1714* (Oxford: James Parker, 1891), 1:76.

[180] On John Allde, see H. R. Tedder, rev. I. Gadd, "Allde, John (b. in or before 1531, d. 1584)," in *ODNB*, 1:768. For Munday's apprenticeship, see Arber, 2:69.

[181] "Young Anthony Mundy Again," *SP* 56 (1959): 151.

[182] First published in 1500 with the title *Galien rethore* (FB 22238), this work was reprinted in 1575 with the title *Histoire des nobles* . . . as mentioned above (FB 22244). Francis Meres, in his *Palladis Tamia* (1598) includes "*Gallian of France*" among the list of books "to be censured of"; see *Elizabethan Critical Essays*, ed. G. Gregory Smith (London: Oxford University Press, 1904), 2:308–9.

[183] See *OED*, s.v. *comprise*, v. 2a. As he explains in *Mirrour* (6.8–9), Munday handed his translation of *Galien* to Edward de Vere. Nelson has suggested that Munday's version "may not have been printed. (Did Oxford bother to return the manuscript?)" (238).

[184] For more information on Hollyband, see Laurent Berec, *Claude de Sainliens: un huguenot bourbonnais au temps de Shakespeare* (Paris: Orizons, 2012); for the establishment of his school in St. Paul's Churchyard, see 135–37.

lyband tutored Munday: the latter's *Mirrour* contains prefatory verses by Hollyband "in the Commendation of his Schollers [i.e., Munday's] exercise" (14). Like other tutors of French, Hollyband used double translation as one of the central activities for the instruction of this foreign language.[185] Such training in written translation from French into English may not be the most appropriate method for the acquisition of a foreign language, but must have provided Munday with the necessary tools and experience to be confident he could render *Galien* into English. The result, however, was felt to be amateurish, probably because he approached the task as another class assignment.[186] Notwithstanding the deficiencies of his *Galein*, Munday must have acquired a taste for translating, especially when he realized that it could help him gain some money and the favor of some noble patron, since he managed to show it to the Earl of Oxford. But if he wanted to earn an income from his translations, it was essential that he acquired greater linguistic competence in French and improved the literary style of his

---

[185] See Berec, *Claude de Sainliens*, 142. For the practical way of using double translation for language teaching purposes, see Douglas A. Kibbee, *For to Speke Frenche Trewely. The French Language in England, 1000–1600: Its Status, Description and Instruction* (Amsterdam: John Benjamins, 1991), 183–85. The same method was espoused by Ascham for learning foreign languages: "duble translation out of one tong into an other, in either onelie, or at least chiefly, [is] to be exercised, speciallie of youth, for the ready and sure obteining of any tong," *Scholemaster*, 242.

[186] Heinrich (Munday, *Mirrour*, 14 n. 1) and Berec (*Claude de Sainliens*, 209–12) argue that Munday started to take lessons from Hollyband after his return from his trip to France and Italy in 1579. There is little doubt that Munday was Hollyband's pupil when *Mirrour* was published at the end of 1579, as the tutor's verses confirm by describing Munday as his "Scholler" (*Mirrour*, 14.2). At the end of his address to the reader, Munday himself remarks, "I leaue thee [i.e., reader], listning to the clock, to take vp my books and hye me to Schoole" (*Mirrour*, 13.17–18). By contrast, Byrne, "Books," 227, suggests that it was in St. Paul's Churchyard "presumably that some time between 1576 and 1578 (i.e., most probably before Munday's journey to Rome in 1578) he [i.e., Hollyband] was Munday's instructor in one or both of these languages [i.e., French and Italian]." Cf. Turner, 29; and Turner Wright, "Young Munday," 152. Could have Munday translated *Galien* without any previous instruction in French? Certainly not. Munday could have combined his obligations as an apprentice with his attendance to French classes, because being over fifteen years he was considered an adult pupil and would attend his classes in after school hours; see M. St. Clare Byrne's introduction to Claudius Hollyband's *The French Littelton: The Edition of 1609* (Cambridge: Cambridge University Press, 1953), xvi, and Kathleen Lambley, *The Teaching and Cultivation of the French Language in England during Tudor and Stuart Times* (Manchester: Manchester University Press, 1920), 139. In his *Roman Life* Munday mentions that before traveling to the Continent he studied "the French tongue, to have some knowledge therein against I went over" (31.771–73), so it is not unlikely that he was already receiving French classes from Hollyband.

English prose. This probably explains why Munday decided to continue attending Hollyband's French classes, despite their high cost.[187]

In 1578 *Gerileon of England* (STC 17203) was published. It is the English translation of Étienne de Maisonneufve's *Gerileon d'Angleterre* (1572; FB 22671), which contains a revealing dedication in which the process of translation is described as follows:

> The Historie it self [i.e., *Gerileon*] beyng firste written in Frenche, was (in deede) for the greater parte thereof, after a kynde of sorte, translated by a certaine yonge man, more hardie and venturous in attempte, then luckie and Fortunate in atchieuaunce: whose good meaning, as it semeth to merite pardon, and perhappes some thankes: so vppon further scrutinie, examination, and conference of the copie with his Translation, it was easie to finde where he had tripped, and where (vnawares) he had vtterly loste his waie. Wherevpon I was driuen to sustaine a double labour: One in perfectyng his imperfections: The other in finishyng and supplying that parte of the Booke, where he had abruptly broken of, and absurdlie skipped ouer. (sig. *1r)

In this excerpt the publisher Miles Jennings adopts a patronizing attitude toward the young translator, although he prefers not to disclose this man's identity, probably to avoid exposing him to public ridicule and maybe ruin his career. There are sufficient indications that the unnamed *yonge man* could actually be Anthony Munday. The book was entered in the Stationers' Register to John Jugge on May 20, 1577 (Arber, 2:312), and was finally printed by John Kingston for Miles Jennings the following year.[188] Son of the respected printer Richard Jugge (d. 1588), John Jugge was admitted into the livery of the Stationers' Company in 1573/4, although he is credited with the publication of only one book, and that was in collaboration with John Allde, the printer to whom Munday was at the time apprenticed. It is not impossible that Allde, as he probably did with *Galien*, encouraged the eager but inexpert Munday to accept another translation assignment. Evidence that this connection is more than purely circumstantial comes from the edition of the second part of *Gerileon of England* (STC 17206), translated by Munday and published in 1592. It is significant that the dedicatory epistle of the second part, signed by a more acknowledged and experienced Munday, contains no explicit comment about the first part and his possible involvement in translating it. But, on the other hand, if Munday did translate the first part, it seems natural that he wanted to avoid seeing himself associated with it, owing to the scathing criticism the translation of the previous part received. Instead, the

---

[187] See Berec, *Claude de Sainliens*, 138–39.

[188] On Jugge, see Joyce Boro, "Jugge, Richard (*c.* 1514–1577)," in *ODNB*, 30:816. On Kingston, see Blayney, *Stationers' Company*, 2:773–75; and Duff, *Century of English Book Trade*, 86.

second part's dedicatory epistle reflects on two issues affecting the new translation's quality. As part of a conventional exercise in modesty, Munday first states that the translation is not perfect because, as he was producing it, he had to attend to other commitments: "it should haue been better, if more respite had been graunted me" (sig. A2v). The second half of the epistle praises the translation for its reliability, but it is awkward—and unusual—how Munday puts all the emphasis on guaranteeing the translation's textual integrity:

> Yet this dare I saye beside, that except it bee a word here and there by mee left out, or by the Printer mistaken, I am assured verie little lacketh, I am certaine not so much as a line of the Historie: for in verie trueth, I followed the French (welneere) word for word. (A2v)

If we compare the two epistles from the two editions of *Gerileon* it can be argued that Munday's epistle to the second part is implicitly written in dialectical opposition to Jennings's admonishments in the epistle to the first part. It is not that Munday is trying to rectify Jenning. Instead he accepts the latter's assertions and calls attention to his having learnt the lesson by avoiding repeating the same mistakes when translating the second part of *Gerileon*. Yet, the progression as a translator that Munday is making an effort to contrive would have been fully comprehensible only to a reduced circle of people who were aware of his participation in the previous translation published by Jennings.[189] To this small circle Munday gives an assurance that his new translation meets the standard, since this time much labor should not be required "in perfectyng his [i.e., Munday's] imperfections" and in "supplying that parte . . . where he had . . . absurdlie skipped ouer," as according to Jennings happened with the translation of the first part. The text of the epistle of 1592, therefore, can be read as a response to the first epistle of 1578, although it refrains from flaunting the superiority of the 1592 translation, as could be expected from a paratext aimed at increasing the book's commercial prospects. This apparent oversight would seem reasonable if Munday were actually responsible for translating the two parts. Consequently, we would do well to associate Munday with the translation of *Gerileon I*, even if he was not answerable for its final, published version.[190]

---

[189] As explained by Wilson, "Paratexts," 122, Munday's paratexts can "maintain a private and exclusive system of address for a small number of readers in Munday's circle."

[190] See Hayes, "Romances," 58. Hayes was unaware of the 1578 copy and dated *Gerileon I* to 1583 (75); cf. Ronald S. Crane, *The Vogue of Medieval Chivalric Romance During the English Renaissance* (Menasha, WI: George Banta, 1919), 39, 40. Turner Wright, "Young Mundy," 151, also admits that in the 1592 edition of *Gerileon II* "Mundy implied that he had been the novice in question" that is criticized in *Gerileon I*. Note that neither Hamilton nor Hill assign him any involvement in *Gerileon I*, nor does Celeste Turner in her monograph, 180.

In view of *Galien*'s linguistic shortcomings, stemming from both a poor understanding of the original and an unpractised writing style, and considering that Munday failed to overcome such deficiencies in *Gerileon I*, he must have decided to improve significantly his linguistic competence. While Hollyband's classes were certainly useful to practice his nascent translation skills and increase his knowledge of the source language, they cannot compare with the experience of living in France and becoming acquainted with everyday language. In fact, the option of spending a substantial amount of time on the Continent was the one preferred by the gentry and nobility for supplementing the education of their children, aware that knowledge of foreign languages, and of French in particular, could contribute to their social and professional advancement in England. As they completed their studies between the ages of sixteen and twenty, the young members of the landowning classes embarked on a continental tour to expand their cultural horizons and linguistic education. This antecedent of the eighteenth-century Grand Tour had an estimated cost of at least £80 that was well beyond the reach of middle-class youngsters, unless they were sponsored by a noble patron. As a result, the continental tour not only provided cultural benefits, but played an active role in consolidating class distinctions and privileges.[191]

In the fall of 1578, maybe even before turning 18, Munday decided to undertake a continental tour of sorts. His ultimate goal was to improve his linguistic competence, but it seems that he was also attracted by the aspirational desire of enjoying an experience generally identified with the upper class. When describing this adventure, Munday seems to replicate the leisurely attitude of his social betters, without hiding the real purpose for undertaking it: "I had enterprised this iourney *for my pleasure*, and in hope *to attaine to some knowledge in the French tung*" (*Mirrour*, 8.42–43; cf. *Roman Life*, 8.149–52; emphasis added). But, unlike his high-class counterparts, who undertook their continental journey with the necessary wherewithal, almost as a natural rite of passage, Munday found himself in a much more precarious financial situation. It was not the kind of experience that he was really entitled to, but was instead his own personal attempt to move up in the social ladder by imitating the path well-trodden by the rich. Moreover, Munday took no small risk in applying all his financial means to this end: "I committed the small wealth I had into my purse" (*Roman Life*, 5.87–89). A man with a pragmatic and utilitarian mind-set, he established a direct relation between his ability "to attaine some vnderstanding in the languages," and the end result that "in time to come: I might reap therby some commoditie" (*Mirrour* 7.13–15). In other words, Munday considered this expenditure as an investment whose returns would be made later in the future.

---

[191] For the ideas expressed in this paragraph I follow Lambley, *Teaching and Cultivation of French*, part II, chap. 7; for the estimated cost of this kind of continental tour, see 231–32.

The journey did not go as originally planned. After crossing the Channel and going ashore at Boulogne-sur-Mer, at some point "betvveen Bulloin [i.e., Boulogne] and Abeuile [i.e., Abbeville], my Companion [i.e., Thomas Nowell] and I [i.e., Munday] vvere stripped into our shirts by Soldiers" (*Mirrour*, 7.22–23). Given the circumstances, it would have seemed reasonable to abort their travel plans and return to England, a possibility Munday admits to have entertained: "I vvished myself at home again" (*Mirrour*, 7.28). Nevertheless, they decided to go ahead with their initial plan and rely on the assistance of the network of English Catholic exiles in Paris, who welcomed them with open arms in the belief that the newcomers were there to take up the Catholic cause.[192] Munday and Nowell had to feign a personal inclination toward Catholicism, and Munday justifies this deception on practical reasons and necessity, arguing that if he entered into a discussion with the English Catholics on matters of faith and religion, "it might turn to my farder harme. For there no freends I had to help me, no welth to maintaine me."[193] The same practical disposition led him to agree to the Catholics' entreaties and accept their generous invitation to travel to Rome and enter the English College there: "we thought if we could go to Rome and return safely again into England we should accomplish a great matter, the place being so far off."[194]

In Munday's view, posing as a Catholic offered him opportunities he could not pass up. In particular he was given the chance to travel through France and Italy until Rome at the expense of the Catholic community, thus completing a tour much grander than he could have initially imagined. That way Munday could really feel privileged in partaking of "the fansie that many yong Ientlemen of England haue to trauell abroad, and namely to lead a long lyfe in Italie," as the

---

[192] For the Paris networks of English exiles, see Katy Gibbons, *English Catholic Exiles in Late Sixteenth-Century Paris* (Woodbridge: Boydell & Brewer, 2011). As Adam H. Kitzes, "The Hazards of Professional Authorship: Polemic and Fiction in Anthony Munday's *English Roman Life*," *Renaissance Studies* 31 (2017): 441–61, comments, "had the open highway not rendered them so vulnerable, Munday would not have needed to turn to the community of English Catholic exiles to rescue him" (455).

[193] *Mirrour*, 8.44–45; cf. *Roman Life*, 8.165–69. In Edmund Campion's trial Munday repeats the same argument and explains that "in France and other places he [i.e., Munday] seemed to favour their religion [i.e., Catholicism]," William Cobbett, *Cobbett's Complete Collection of State Trials and Proceedings for High Treason and Misdemeanors*, ed. Thomas Bayly Howell (London: T. C. Hansard, 1809), 1:1069. Cf. Kitzes "Polemic in Munday's *Roman Life*," 455.

[194] *Roman Life*, 16.370–73; cf. 24.581–88. Munday must have felt privileged and, in fact, satisfied his desire of being seen as a gentleman when he passed himself off as "a gentleman's son" (*Roman Life*, 19.473) and presented himself in Rome under an assumed identity (cf. *Roman Life*, 24.577, 30.753–57). The Latin name he adopted there was Antonius Auleus; see Anthony Kenny, "Anthony Munday in Rome," *Recusant History* 6 (1962): 158–62.

humanist Roger Ascham (d. 1568) commented a few years earlier about the fashion of traveling there.[195] Yet, the journeys to Italy, unlike those to France, were viewed with suspicion, even in the case of youths like Munday, whose main purpose was their own cultural enrichment. Ascham advises against these journeys, "not bicause I do contemne, either the knowledge of strange and diuerse tonges, and namelie the Italian tonge" (*Scholemaster*, 223), but because of the danger of moral and confessional perversion that prolonged visits to Rome could entail.[196] Munday arrived in Rome on February 1, 1579, and remained there during four months, first as a guest and then as a student of the English College, founded in 1576 by students from the English College in Douay. Four months in Italy was a sufficiently long period of time for Ascham to have raised an eyebrow, and the same feeling was invoked at Edmund Campion's trial, began on 20 November 1581, when it was denounced, "that he [i.e., Munday] was an Atheist; for that beyond the seas he went on pilgrimage, and received the Sacrament, making himself a Catholic."[197] These remarks' intent was to question Munday's moral integrity and sow doubts about the validity of his court testimony. Munday knew that in a religiously polarized society, like Elizabethan England was, it was difficult to interpret accurately the position of some who, like him, appeared to be equally at ease with the two opposing religious identities, i.e., Catholic while on the Continent and Protestant back in England. In an attempt to dismiss the accusations of Catholicism leveled at him and quell people's misgivings about his continental journey, Munday opens his *English Roman Life* with a declaration of his true intentions in traveling to France and Italy: "desire to see strange countries, as also affection to learn the languages, had persuaded me to leave my native country, *and not any other intent or cause*" (5.84–87; my emphasis).

The controversy about Munday's equivocal *pilgrimage* has lasted to the present day, since some scholars continue to consider his explanations as a pretext meant to conceal his true intentions in traveling to the Continent. In such a time of religious conflict many Englishmen decided to go abroad to live with adherence to their Catholic faith or to pursue studies in Catholic institutions, colleges, and seminars that were proscribed in England. In this respect Celeste Turner contends that before his journey Munday was converted to Catholicism by John Allde, and "since his master and his publisher [i.e., Charlewood] worked for Catholic men, and his patron [i.e., Edward de Vere] was a crypto-Catholic,

---

[195] *Scholemaster*, 223. Note that *The Scholemaster* was first published posthumously in 1570.

[196] Cf. the following remark by Euphues: "I meane not to trauayle to *Sienna* to wooe Beautie . . . nor to sue to Uertue, least in *Italy* I be infected with vice" (Lyly, *England*, 62.16–21).

[197] *Cobbett's State Trials*, 1:1069.

there is now little doubt that he [i.e., Munday] went as a convert."[198] Beatrice Thompson has tried to further advance Turner's thesis and has stated, "it is really certain that he [i.e., Munday] went with the full concurrence of Allde, with the idea of making literary capital in the Protestant interest out of what he could see of English Catholic life on the continent," as if his primary purpose was to carry out fieldwork and use the information to obtain financial gains with his *English Roman Life*.[199] By contrast, Ayres challenges these views because, he argues, there is no supporting evidence to substantiate their claims. Ayres concludes, "There is no evidence that Munday was ever a Catholic and a good deal in *The English Roman Life* to suggest that he was not."[200]

Indeed, Munday left no explicit textual evidence of his supposed Catholic tendencies, whereas he had no qualms in parading his anti-Catholicism, best epitomized by his activities as pursuivant of recusants.[201] However, he easily integrated into and benefitted from the support networks offered by the community of English Catholic exiles, even if it was only for the purposes of traveling abroad and learning languages. Can we then rule out the possibility that Munday harbored Catholic ideas? Absolutely not. In order to receive such deferential treatment from the exiled English Catholics, for at least ten months Munday must have adopted practices and attitudes showing his affinity with them in political and religious matters. That is why scholars like Hamilton may be right when portraying Munday as a calculating man that, underneath the Protestant ideology adopted for his public persona, hid a pro-Catholic sentiment.

Should we, therefore, consider Munday as a man full of internal contradictions? Recently Katy Gibbons has argued that people might have been required to assume shifting religious identities, depending on the social environment or other circumstances. About the case of Munday in particular, Gibbons asserts,

---

[198] "Young Mundy," 155. See further in her *Mundy: An Elizabethan Man of Letters*, 10–23. More recently Hamilton has also argued that Munday was a Catholic convert. Previously Munday was also branded as a spy that "was sent abroad, at the age of twenty-five [sic], for the purpose of obtaining damaging testimony against the English seminaries on the continent," John Garrett Underhill, *Spanish Literature in the England of the Tudors* (New York: Columbia University Press, 1899), 294.

[199] "Anthony Munday's Journey to Rome, 1578–9," *Durham University Journal* 34 (1941): 4.

[200] *Roman Life*, xiv. The hypothesis that Munday held Catholic beliefs has been propounded by Hamilton in her monograph. While her book has raised the visibility of Munday and his contribution to the literary culture of early modern England, Hamilton's views on his supposed Catholic sentiments have been received with scepticism by the scholarly community; cf. Brian Lockey, *Early Modern Catholics, Royalists, and Cosmopolitans: English Transnationalism and the Christian Commonwealth* (Burlington, VT: Ashgate, 2015), 98–100.

[201] See John Dover Wilson, "Anthony Munday, Pamphleteer and Pursuivant," *Modern Language Review* 4 (1909): 484–90.

"This sort of shifting behaviour, moving between Protestantism in England and Catholicism in Catholic Europe, was clearly subversive of the clear denominational lines that clerical leaders on both sides sought to enforce."[202] Gibbons's suggestion of a multivalent religious identity seems particularly apposite when applied to Munday. Taking into account that when traveling to the Continent he was barely 18 and his own personal identity was probably not yet fully forged, it would be easier for Munday to assume a different version of himself among English Catholics.[203]

Later on, when he was back in England, Munday changed tack and perverted the virtues of his assumed ambivalence. An example of this duplicity is offered by the way he treated Ralph Marshall. The same year that Munday accepted Marshall's patronage for the publication of *Gerileon II*, he also informed on Marshall and was instrumental in his arrest on suspicion of Catholic sympathies.[204] This unsavory incident evinces Munday's lack of moral scruples, since he was giving priority to his personal advancement over his loyalty to friends and acquaintances. By betraying Marshall Munday was trying to keep in with officialdom and hopeful of reaping some future political reward. Notice, however, that he denounced Marshall only after obtaining the latter's patronage, a further indication of his calculating nature.

Regardless of the continental journey's influence on Munday's religious conscience, we need to focus on discerning this adventure's effects on his literary career. One direct consequence was his enhanced linguistic competence in both French and Italian. Before undertaking his trip, Munday was already familiar with French, but as soon as he returned to England he seized the first opportunity he had of showing his newly-acquired knowledge of Italian and closed the dedication to Edward de Vere of *Mirrour* with a few words in Italian.[205] In addi-

---

[202] Katy Gibbons, "'When he was in France he was a Papist and when he was in England ... he was a Protestant': Negotiating Religious Identities in the Later Sixteenth Century," in *Getting Along? Religious Identities and Confessional Relations in Early Modern England—Essays in Honour of Professor W. J. Sheils*, ed. Nadine Lewycky and Adam Morton (Burlington, VT: Ashgate, 2013), 177. Lockey, *Early Modern Catholics*, states, "I would suggest that Munday's confessional identity is ultimately impossible to define," (100).

[203] Note that both Turner and Thompson wrongly believed that Munday was 24 when he set off on his tour.

[204] See Hamilton, xxxi; and Byrne, "Books," 231. For the dedicatory epistle to Ralph and Frances Marshall of Carlton, Nottinghamshire, see Louise Wilson, "'I maruell who the diuell is his Printer': Fictions of Book Production in Anthony Munday's and Henry Chettle's Paratexts," in *The Book Trade in Early Modern England: Practices, Perceptions, Connections*, ed. by John Hinks and Victoria Gardner (London: The British Library, 2014), 12.

[205] See *Mirrour*, 10.95–97; cf. Turner, 26. Note that Edward de Vere himself had already traveled to Italy in 1575; see Nelson, 121–31.

Introduction 63

tion, Munday was actively engaged in the English College's academic life. We know that he was registered as an *humanista* or grammar-student,[206] and therefore he must have become familiar with, if not received some formal education in, rhetoric, thus helping him to develop a personal style and overcome the problems he encountered with his translation of *Galien*. One further consequence of Munday's tour was his access to the literary texts that were being consumed on the Continent, in particular the Iberian chivalric romances that were circulating in translation in France and Italy. During this journey, most probably while he resided in Rome, Munday must have come across the literary corpus of the Palmerin romances, including *Palmerin d'Oliva*. In 1580, a few months after coming back to England, Munday wrote the prose romance *Zelauto* and named a female character in it "Polinarda" after Palmerin d'Oliva's beloved. Not only did he borrow her name from one of the characters in the *Palmerin* cycle, but placed this character in narrative contexts that seem to echo *Palmerin d'Oliva* as I have argued elsewhere.[207] Furthermore, when he finished his translation of *Palmerin of England*, possibly in 1581, there are clear indications that he was fully acquainted with the entire narrative in *Palmerin d'Oliva*. Considering that he consulted an Italian version of *Palmerin d'Oliva* when preparing the English translation and taking into account that his time in Rome was relatively long, it seems probable that he initially read this romance in Italian and first came into contact with the corpus of Iberian romances while in Italy.

When he arrived back in England in the summer of 1579 Munday did not return to work as apprentice to his master John Allde,[208] but instead chose to

---

[206] Elsewhere he is also designated a *grammaticus*; for this kind of occurrences, see Kenny, "Munday in Rome," 158–59. See also Turner, 20–21.

[207] See Sánchez-Martí, "*Zelauto*'s Polinarda and the *Palmerin* Romances"; note, however, that it is not impossible that Munday was instead inspired by the Polinarda in *Palmerin of England*.

[208] Munday did not serve the required seven years of apprenticeship, and this failure to comply with his contract provoked the attacks of Thomas Alfield in his *A true report of the death & martyrdome of M. Campion* (1582; STC 4537), where Munday is described as follows:"munday, who first was a stage player (no doubt a calling of some creditt) after an aprentise which tyme he wel serued with deceauing of his master then wandring towardes Italy" (sig. D4v–E1r). In order to protect his good name Munday decided to refute Alfield's accusation by giving the personal testimony of his master John Allde. In Munday's *A breefe aunswer made vnto two seditious pamphlets* (1582; STC 18262), he provides the following refutation: "Then he [i.e., Alfield] beginneth to rip vp the course of my life, *Howe I was an Apprentise, and serued my tyme well with deceyuing my Maister*: I referre my selfe to the iudgement of all men, reading this which my Maister vnrequested, hath heere set downe on my behalfe. 'This is to let all men vnderstand, that *Anthony Munday*, for the tyme he was my Seruaunt, dyd his duetie in all respectes, as much as I could desire, without fraude, couin or deceyte: if otherwise I should report of him, I should but say vntrueth.' By me *Iohn Allde*" (sig. D3r–v). Munday finally received freedom

devote himself to literary pursuits and seek the sponsorship of another master, namely Edward de Vere, 17th Earl of Oxford.[209] In need of gaining some public recognition, his patron's favor, and much-needed earnings, Munday experimented with a literary formula based on the imitation of works and styles that achieved considerable success and attracted public attention.[210] In the months following his return to England, Munday composed and published *Mirrour*, a text dedicated to De Vere, written in the tradition of the *Mirror for Magistrates*, which had been well received with editions printed in 1559, 1563, 1571, 1574, 1575, and three separate editions in 1578.[211] Another example of Munday's strategy of copying other literary models is his publication of *Zelauto*. In view of the sensation caused by John Lyly with his *Euphues. The Anatomy of Wit* (1578), and its sequel *Euphues and his England* (1580), he published the romance *Zelauto* in

---

of the Drapers' Company by patrimony on 21 June 1585; see Hill, 29; and Percy D. Mundy, "Anthony Munday, Dramatist," *Notes and Queries* 219 (1914): 181.

[209] For his patronage, see Nelson, 236–39, 380–84. Hill considers that Munday "was probably attached to Oxford's household in some secretarial kind of role" (84); Turner, while contending that "the title 'servant' covered many domestic and secretarial offices" (28), thinks it possible that Munday was "the one man who, in 1581, acted with the Earl of Oxford's nine boy players at Bristol" (28). Later on, Turner refers again to the possibility that Munday acted "perhaps as leader of the boy company patronized by the Earl" (39). There are references to Munday as an extempore actor that, together with his subsequent relation with the theatre world, suggest that it is not unlikely that he worked in this capacity. See Nora Johnson, *The Actor as Playwright in Early Modern Drama* (Cambridge: Cambridge University Press, 2003), 97–98, and James P. Bednarz, *Shakespeare and the Poets' War* (New York: Columbia University Press, 2001), 93–94. By the 1590s Munday appeared on the payroll of playwrights that supplied Philip Henslowe with theatrical material, as recorded in his diary, *Henslowe's Diary*, ed. R. A. Foakes, 2nd ed. (Cambridge: Cambridge University Press, 2002).

[210] As explains Edwin Haviland Miller, *The Professional Writer in Elizabethan England: A Study of Nondramatic Literature* (Cambridge, MA: Harvard University Press, 1959), 209, "Authors needed money, and even the pittance received for a brief pamphlet relieved their distress." Although Miller describes Munday as a *hack* because of his need to earn a living with his writing (cf. *OED*, s.v. *hack*, n.³ 4), he wants to free this term from all its negative connotations, since "Among the hacks have appeared not only those disinterred from obscurity by literary historians but also writers of genius like Skelton, Holinshed, Dryden, Dr. Johnson, and Whitman" (206).

[211] See STC 1247–52, 1252.5, 3131, 13443–44. Heinrich (Munday, *Mirrour*, xiv), thinks it unlikely that Munday composed any part of this work during the time he spent on the Continent. Previously Munday wrote *The admirable deliverance of 266 Christians*, which exists only in an edition published in 1608 (STC 18258), and *The paine of pleasure* (STC 18277), which was printed in 1580 but composed before his journey. For further discussion, see Hamilton, 6–7.

1580, written in imitation of Lyly's works.[212] From the very title page of *Zelauto*, Munday proclaims that it is *"Giuen for a freendly entertainment to* Euphues, *at his late ariuall into England,"* (1). By establishing a direct connection with Lyly's most recent creation Munday was hopeful "that his work can ride on the fame of Lyly's Euphues volumes," as Mentz suggests.[213] Despite his efforts to find favor with Elizabethan audiences by channeling his creative energy into the imitation of successful models, Munday's strategy failed to produce the desired result, since neither *Mirrour* nor *Zelauto* were reprinted in his lifetime.

In a way, this apparent literary failure is a consequence of his personal circumstances: pressing pecuniary needs compelled Munday to become a prolific and versatile writer that assumed various authorial roles. Other than *Mirrour* and *Zelauto*, and apart from participating in controversies with the publication of brief polemical tracts and pamphlets, there was one other successful model left for Munday to try his hand at, namely the translation of chivalric romances. Although he had previous experience of translating chivalric texts, the encouragement to revisit the genre came from the commercial success of Margaret Tyler's *Mirrour of Princely Deedes and Knighthood*, published in 1578 and reprinted in 1580. It appears that the taste of English readers for chivalric romances of a medieval character was still alive and demanded to be satisfied with new materials, different from the romance texts printed since the beginning of the sixteenth century. After his time in Rome, Munday was perfectly placed to turn this literary fashion to his advantage, not only because his linguistic competence and translating skills had improved, but also because he had become familiar with the literary corpus of the Iberian chivalric romances.

It is quite likely that the idea of translating Iberian chivalric romances originated in Munday, who then proposed it to his printer John Charlewood. But after listening to Munday's suggestion, Charlewood seems to be the one who devised the publication strategy, completely stealing the initiative from Munday's hands. Such is the sequence of events that can be guessed from the clues that Munday leaves in his paratexts. At the end of his preface to *Zelauto*, besides announcing

---

[212] Between 1578 and 1580 five editions of *Euphues. The Anatomy of Wit* (STC 17051–54) were published, and three of *Euphues and his England* (STC 17068–70). Note that both *Euphues and his England* and *Zelauto* (STC 18283) were dedicated to the same patron. Yet, the involvement of a patron does not mean that an author had obtained a stable source of income, but instead had to worry about the commercial side of his profession, as Munday does in the preface to *Zelauto*; cf. Miller, *The Elizabethan Professional Writer*, 211–12. For biographical information on Lyly, see G. K. Hunter, "Lyly, John (1554–1606)," in *ODNB*, 34:867–72. Cf. Turner, 20.

[213] Steve Mentz, *Romance for Sale in Early Modern England: The Rise of Prose Fiction* (Burlington, VT: Ashgate, 2006), 38. See also Andy Kesson, *John Lyly and Early Modern Authorship* (Manchester: Manchester University Press, 2014), 85–86.

the forthcoming publication of *Palmerin of England*, Munday explains that he was constrained by Charlewood to publish *Zelauto*, despite its being incomplete:

> *The last part of this woorke remaineth vnfinished, the which for breuity of time, and speedines in the Imprinting: I was constrained to permit till more limitted leysure ... Not long it will be before the rest be finished and the renowned* Palmerin *of England with all speede shall be sent you* (6).

In other words, Charlewood was the one making publishing decisions. It is to be supposed that *Zelauto* did not get the reception Munday and Charlewood would have hoped to, since it was never reprinted and never completed, as promised in the aforementioned paratext.[214] Moreover, Charlewood was also responsible for the decision to start the publication in English of the *Palmerin* cycle not with its inaugural work, i.e., *Palmerin d'Oliva*, but with one of its sequels. Later on, Munday expressed repeatedly his dissatisfaction with the order chosen by Charlewood for the presentation of this literary corpus to English readers. In the address "To the courteous Reader" included at the end of *The Second Part of Palmerin of England* (1616) Munday wrote: *"the History of* Palmerin d'Oliue ... *should haue bin translated before this* [i.e., *Palmerin of England*], *or* Primaleon *of* Greece, *because they are the originall of all the other stories.*"[215] If the natural narrative order of the *Palmerin* romances was upset against Munday's criterion, such an alteration must be attributed to Charlewood. It was Charlewood who, in part, was taking financial risks with the publication of the *Palmerin* romances, and he was also responsible for adopting a strategy contrary to Munday's desire for offering the *Palmerin* cycle in its original narrative sequence. The fact that Munday's preferred option was overruled also suggests that Charlewood did not trust the former's commercial instincts.

While Munday's enthusiasm for the *Palmerin* cycle seems to go back to his time on the Continent and, therefore, emerged prior to and independently of Tyler's translation, the publication of the *Palmerin* romances was not unaffected by the commercial fortune of Tyler's *Mirror*. The publication of Tyler's *Mirror* deserves credit for making the commercial possibilities of the corpus of Iberian romances visible to the community of English printers. The printer Thomas East, who had been successful with Lyly's *Euphues*, once again hit the nail on the head with his edition of Tyler's romance translation.[216] And one more time Charlewood tried to replicate his competitor's positive result by printing a work of the

---

[214] By contrast, Turner, 34, states, "The thoroughness with which the first and only edition of *Zelauto* was thumbed out of existence augurs popularity."

[215] STC 19163; sig. Ff6ʳ. For other examples of this same complaint, see Sánchez-Martí, "*Zelauto*'s Polinarda," 79 and 82 notes 27–28.

[216] For more information on East, see Jeremy L. Smith, "East, Thomas (1540–1608)," in *ODNB*, 17:587–89.

same literary genre that he thought could be more appealing to English readers because of its eponymous hero's Englishness. After having agreed that Munday would prepare the translation of *Palmerin of England*, Charlewood obtained the publication licence on February 13, 1581. The entry in the records of the Stationers' Company contains useful information for a better understanding of the publication in England not only of *Palmerin of England* but of the entire corpus of Iberian chivalric romances:

> Lycenced vnto him [i.e., Charlewood] by master watkins [i.e., Richard Watkins] a booke intituled *the historie of PALMERIN of Englande*, vppon Condic[i]on that if there be anie thinge founde in The booke when it is extante worthie of Reprehension That then all the Bookes shalbe put to waste and Burnte (Arber, 2:388).

First, it becomes apparent that when the licence was issued the English version of the romance was not yet ready ("in The booke when it is extante"). In addition, the members of the Stationers' Company imposed an unusual moral restriction in order to guarantee that the published version was free from "anie thinge . . . worthie of Reprehension." Why should the forthcoming *Palmerin of England* be licensed subject to such a special condition? What sort of criteria would be used to establish the reprehensible nature of the book's content?

In her monograph Hamilton analyzes the events narrated in *Palmerin of England* from a historical perspective and argues that the text lends itself to a troubling interpretation, with a destabilizing political and religious discourse questioning of royal authority: "the first half of *Palmerin [of England]* includes fictional narratives about the harm that had come to England with the abandonment of an old religion and the harm that England's oppressive measures have brought to Ireland" (85). Hamilton's topical interpretation would suffice to consider *Palmerin of England* politically dangerous and thus make the book "worthie of Reprehension." Actually, since the earliest extant copy of *Palmerin of England* is of the 1596 edition, Hamilton contends that Charlewood probably decided to abort the romance's publication in view of its supposedly subversive plot. This way Charlewood would be complying with the condition imposed by the Stationers' Company and avoid their severe punishment, which could have serious financial consequences for his print-house. Hamilton's hypothesis is not without risks, although it is based on an apparently solid logic and a convincing analysis of the literary text in its historical context. All the pieces of the puzzle seem to fall nicely into place, but there is one piece of evidence that went unnoticed to Hamilton and would appear to disprove her theory, namely the reference to "'Palmeryng,' 2 parts" in a bookseller's catalogue of 1585. This reference would seem to indicate that Charlewood did use the licence obtained in 1581 and printed an edition of *Palmerin of England* in or before 1585.[217]

If, as it seems, such an edition was printed and commercialized in the first half of the 1580s, it follows that the serious doubts voiced by the Stationers must have been removed. In other words, the underlying political discourse was not considered potentially subversive, as Hamilton contends, nor was the romance judged "worthie of Reprehension." What could then be the source of the Stationers' reservations? Their dissuasive injunction probably derived from the suspicion with which the romance genre was viewed, an attitude originating in the late Middle Ages. In the sixteenth century the genre came under scurrilous attacks from the humanists, who criticized it for representing questionable moral values and religious beliefs, as Alex Davis has discussed.[218] The humanist scholars were concerned about the deleterious effect that chivalric literature, labeled as idle and vain, could have on the readers' moral standards, but their censure was aimed not only at readers and writers, but also at the community of printers and publishers. They demanded tighter controls in the licensing process, as does Ascham: "It is pitie, that those, which haue authoritie and charge, to allow and dissalow bookes to be printed [i.e., the Stationers' Company], be no more circumspect herein, than they are" (*Scholemaster*, 230). Even though Ascham here refers specifically to books "of late translated out of *Italian* into English, sold in euery shop in London, commended by honest titles the soner to corrupt honest maners" (*Scholemaster*, 229), next he associates this kind of texts with "bookes of Cheualrie" that bear testament to a time "whan Papistrie . . . couered and ouerflowed all England" (230). The influential cleric and scholar Edward Dering (d. 1576) expresses similar views in his *A Briefe and Necessary Instruction* (1572), where he complains that "there is so great licentiousnes of printyng bookes, as in deede it maketh vs all the worse."[219] After running through some of the medieval chivalric romances that were available in print — the likes of "*Beuis* of Hampton, *Guy* of Warwike, *Arthur* of the round table, *Huon* of Burdeaux, *Oliuer* of the Castle, the foure sonnes of *Amond* [*sic*], and a great many other of such childish follye"— Dering incisively concludes in a nutshell that this kind of books "Satan

---

[217] For the reference, see Henry R. Plomer, "Some Elizabethan Book Sales," *The Library*, 3rd ser., 7 (1916): 328; cf. Sánchez-Martí, "*Zelauto*'s Polinarda," 80–81, n. 15.

[218] Davis, *Chivalry and Romance in the English Renaissance* (Cambridge: D. S. Brewer, 2003), 7; see 1–19 for an overview of the reception and criticism of the genre in early modern England. For the late medieval period and early sixteenth century, see Jordi Sánchez-Martí, "Reading Romance in Late Medieval England: The Case of the Middle English *Ipomedon*," *Philological Quarterly* 83 (2004): 13–17; and Robert P. Adams, "Bold Bawdry and Open Manslaughter: The English New Humanist Attack on Medieval Romance," *Huntington Library Quarterly* 23 (1959): 33–48.

[219] STC 6679, sig. A2r. On Dering, see Patrick Collinson, "Edward, Dering (c. 1540–1576)," in *ODNB*, 15:872–74.

had made, Hell had printed, and were warranted vnto sale vnder the Popes priuiledge" (sig. A2v).

Ascham and Dering concur in associating chivalric literature with a culture and ideology dominated by what the former describes as "Papistrie," a historical period supposedly ended in England. Dering reviled Roman Catholic culture because "it maketh vs all the worse," and as a result all texts descending from a Catholic cultural background, including medieval romances, were viewed with suspicion and considered agents of moral corruption.[220] Chivalric romances were deprecated not simply because they could represent a period and principles contrary to the views and teachings of Protestant ideology. In addition, as Ascham asserts, these texts make ostentation of two narrative features considered aberrant by humanists: "the whole pleasure of which booke[s] standeth in two speciall poyntes, in open mans slaughter, and bold bawdrye" (*Scholemaster*, 231). In the opinion of Ascham and Dering this state of affairs was made possible by the inaction and passivity of those who regulated the book trade and negligently oversaw the publication of works. These scholars called for new moral restraints to be imposed on the publication of books originating in countries aligned with the Roman Catholic Church, as is the case of the Iberian romances, that way preventing the surreptitious re-emergence of papistry in England. Whether in response to this kind of demand or not, the truth is that in the final part of the 1570s stationers became more involved and started closely to supervise licensed texts.[221] It is precisely in this moment of increased control that the stationers enjoined Charlewood to avoid the presence —inadvertent or otherwise— of contents that may be morally detrimental in *Palmerin of England*.

Charlewood could not ignore the special condition that the Stationers' Company attached to the licence granted to print his first edition of an Iberian chivalric romance. Aware that failing to obey their stern injunction would carry serious consequences, Charlewood must have given Munday specific instructions to delete descriptions of and allusions to Catholic rituals and beliefs, and also to dignify the descriptions of warfare and romantic love. Munday acted accordingly and, as Hamilton explains, "certainly sanitized the original by eliminating a great deal of the Catholic religious material" (78). In Hamilton's view, however, Munday's "preservationist" treatment of his source did not obliterate the Catholic structure on which the entire narrative rests. Moreover, since Munday "bypassed the opportunity either to remake the works as Protestant ... or to disparage or revise the ideology of the Iberian works" (Hamilton, 78), Hamilton concludes that Munday contributed to increase the public visibility of the

---

[220] Hamilton remarks, "the sixteenth-century Iberian romances celebrated a world in which the unity of Christendom defined, coexisted with, and was identical to Catholicism" (77).

[221] See Phoebe Sheavyn, *The Literary Profession in the Elizabethan Age* (Manchester: Manchester University Press, 1909), 42–54.

Catholic ideology, thus making him suspect of Catholic loyalism in Hamilton's opinion. Her insistence on imputing Catholic sympathies to Munday is carried to extremes when she considers that failing to remould the romance and imbue it with Protestant values is a clear indication of Munday's Catholic sentiment. That is to say, in the absence of positive evidence demonstrating that Munday had altered his source in order to promote the Catholic cause, Hamilton puts forward the argument that Munday had a hidden agenda in favor of Catholicism because he failed to invest the text with a recognizably Protestant identity and instead simply deleted all Catholic references in his source. Nevertheless, Munday's contemporaries must have considered his treatment of the source text acceptable and free of anti-Protestant suspicion, since his translation of *Palmerin of England* was allowed to be printed in or before 1585 and remained in print in the following decades. Expecting that the officers of the Stationers' Company would go through his translation with a fine-tooth comb, Munday asks in the dedication for "a courteous moderation in iudgement, that his [i.e., Munday's] *labours be not hastily reproched, nor hatefully receiued*" (1609; STC 19162, sig. A4r). In sum, Charlewood recognized the gravity of the Stationers' warning, knew how to interpret their demands, and provided Munday with clear instructions on how to proceed with the translation. This course of action saved the English *Palmerin of England* from being consumed by the flames, oddly prefiguring the events in *Don Quixote*, where the same romance faces the same destiny but is also spared. Both in England in the 1580s and in Spain in 1605 *Palmerin of England* was granted a historical and a fictional pardon because in the two cases the text was not found "worthie of Reprehension."

Unlike his previous translations of chivalric texts, it seems that Munday managed to raise the quality of his work and satisfy the expectations for the publication of literary translations.[222] So confident did he become of his translating abilities that, in the second part of his *Palmerin of England*, Munday was already announcing the forthcoming publication of his translation of *Palmerin d'Oliva*.[223]

---

[222] Not everyone agrees with this statement. Robert Southey, who published a corrected edition of Munday's translation of *Palmerin of England*, was so displeased with the translation that he even suggested, "if he [i.e., Munday] had hanged himself before he translated Palmerin of England, he would have saved me a great deal of labour . . . for certain it is, that at least three-fourths of the book were translated by one who neither understood French, nor English, nor the story he was translating," *Palmerin of England*, by Francisco de Moraes (London: Longman, 1807), 1:xlii. Note that Southey considered that the translation is not attributable to Munday in its entirety.

[223] Although no copy of the first edition of *Palmerin of England* has been preserved, the address to the courteous readers in *Palmerin d'Oliva* provides sufficient evidence to believe that the announcement of the forthcoming publication must have been included in the *editio princeps* of *Palmerin of England*; see 103.2–4 below. The announcement of forthcoming editions was a marketing tool used to create expectation among readers and customers, and Munday resorted to it for his translations of the cycles of *Amadis* and

Since these two romances are rather voluminous, translating them kept Munday busy for quite some time. Considering that in the 1581 licence to print *Palmerin of England* the work was described as still not extant, and taking into account that Munday's output in 1583 was exiguous, it seems likely that he completed the translation in 1583 and had it printed the following year.[224]

After the translation of *Palmerin of England* and before *Palmerin d'Oliva* appeared in 1588 Munday was also responsible for a play titled *Fedele and Fortunio* (1585; STC 19447), a free translation and adaptation of Luigi Pasqualigo's *Il Fedele* (Venice, 1576). Prior to its publication *Fedele and Fortunio* was performed before Queen Elizabeth I, although we do not know precisely when. Although the exact date of composition of Munday's version is also unknown to us, there is scholarly agreement that it was produced sometime between 1579 and 1584, but I am inclined to believe that Munday finished his *Fedele* closer to 1584 than to 1579.[225] While in his critical edition of the play Richard Hosley admits that it is "not of great artistic merit" (9), he also highlights that it was well-known, though not always well-thought of. Someone who seems to have cast aspersions on Munday's *Fedele* was Thomas Nashe when, in the epistle to his *To the Gentlemen Students of Both Universities*, he refers to "a few of our triviall translators" who have decided "to intermeddle with Italian Translations: Wherein how poorely they haue plodded, (as those that are neither prouenzall men, nor are able to distinguish of Articles,)."[226] This final comment about the inadequate use of articles is probably intended directly for Munday, since he does not retain the masculine determinate article *il* that is used in the title of the original Italian.[227]

The next literary translation to occupy Munday's time was *Palmerin d'Oliva*, published early in 1588. The first edition is dedicated to his patron Edward de Vere, but this time Munday describes him as "*sometime my honorable Maister*" (102.7) while himself assumes the role of the earl's "*late seruaunt*" (102.19). Hill has suggested that Munday's relation to Oxford started in 1577 with his *Galien*

Palmerin; see Louise Wilson, "Serial Publication and Romance," in *The Elizabethan Top Ten: Defining Print Popularity in Early Modern England*, ed. Andy Kesson and Emma Smith (Burlington, VT: Ashgate, 2013), 213–21.

[224] For a chronological overview of Munday's literary output, see Hamilton, 199–206.

[225] For a discussion of the date of this play, see Richard Hosley, "The Date of *Fedele and Fortunio*," *Modern Language Review* 57 (1962): 385–86. See also *A Critical Edition of Anthony Munday's "Fedele and Fortunio,"* ed. Richard Hosley (New York: Garland, 1981), 30–32, 93–94. Cf. Mary Augusta Scott, *Elizabethan Translations from the Italian* (Boston: Houghton Mifflin, 1916), 201–2.

[226] *The Works of Thomas Nashe*, ed. Ronald B. McKerrow, repr. with corrections and supplementary notes ed. by F. P. Wilson (Oxford: Blackwell, 1966), 3:315–16.

[227] I owe this suggestion to T. W. Baldwin, *On the Literary Genetics of Shakspere's Plays, 1592–1594* (Urbana, IL: University of Illinois Press, 1959), 25–26. See also Hill, 73–74.

and stopped in the early 1580s, after Oxford himself fell out of favor temporarily as he admitted at the end of 1580 when "Throwing himself on his knees before the Queen he confessed to a pro-Catholic conspiracy over the past four years involving himself."[228] But Munday had already managed to replace the emoluments he could have obtained from his patron with the salary he received from another, more controversial occupation as "one of the Messengers of her Maiesties Chamber" (99.15–17). This information is provided on the title page of the 1588 edition of *Palmerin d'Oliva*, which in fact is the first time that Munday styled himself as such.[229] His employment as Messenger of Her Majesty's Chamber officially required Munday to carry the queen's correspondence throughout the kingdom, but in reality he assumed the role of informer and was involved in tracking down recusants, working under the supervision of the notorious Richard Topcliffe.[230] Munday worked in this capacity until 1595.

Munday must have been busy translating *Palmerin d'Oliva* between 1585 and 1587. When it was time to print it, Charlewood, with William Wright's consent, modified the publication strategy used for *Palmerin of England*. As someone who throughout his career had been reluctant to conform to the regulations of the trade, Charlewood decided to go ahead with the publication of this romance without applying for a licence.[231] He took this shortcut to save time and also to spare themselves the trouble of having to deal with the potential conditions and constraints imposed by the Stationers' Company, who by this time appear to have taken the moralists' admonitions about chivalric literature more seriously.[232] In addition, further to allay any initial misgivings about the nature of the

---

[228] Nelson, 249. See Hill, 84; in her opinion, Munday's "decision to cease dedicating to Oxford for some years seems entirely understandable" (85).

[229] Note, however, that in the records of the Treasurer of the Queen's Chamber there are payments to Munday, dated in 1586, for "riding ... to diverse partes of the Realme"; see Hamilton, xxi. Prior to this official position, Munday was described as "poet" in 1585 in the Drapers' Company Freedom List; see Munday, "Munday, Dramatist," 181.

[230] With his dedication in 1588 of his *A Banquet of Daintie Conceits* (STC 18260), Munday leaves testament of his friendly relationship with Topcliffe. See also Byrne, "Books," 231; Hill, 36–37. For more information about Topcliffe, the notorious torturer, see William Richardson, "Topcliffe, Richard (1531–1604)," in *ODNB*, 55:28–30. Note that a royal proclamation dated January 10, 1581, established a financial reward for those who collaborated and denounced Jesuits that were newly-arrived in England: "the said informer or utterer shall have her highness' reward for every such person by him or them disclosed and apprehended ... such sum of money as shall be an honorable due reward for so good service," in *Tudor Royal Proclamations*, ed. Paul L. Hughes and James F. Larkin, C.S.V. (New Haven, CT: Yale University Press, 1969), 2:484.

[231] For the turbulent circumstances that affected the Stationers' Company in the 1570s and 1580s, see Phillips, 123–29.

[232] For instance, while the licence for the publication of Tyler's *Mirrour* is granted unconditionally, when East applies for a licence to print the second part of this romance

text, Charlewood and Wright adopted a marketing policy already criticized by Ascham: they chose to camouflage the contents of the book by providing one of those "honest titles the soner to corrupt honest maners" (*Scholemaster*, 229; cf. 217). Thus, *Palmerin d'Oliva* went on sale with the subtitle, "The Mirrour of nobilitie, Mappe of honor, Anatomie of rare *fortunes*" (99.2–4). This subtitle diverts the attention away from the narrative ingredients usually associated with the genre, such as battles, tournaments, love affairs, and romantic encounters, precisely the features moralists abhorred. Instead they wanted to give greater prominence to the edifying value of the romance, implying that it could be a useful read, since it provides a model of noble and honorable conduct for its readers. On the same title page, besides, we also find out that the book's narrative was sanitized and all tasteless scenes reworked to guarantee its high moral standards ("*handled with modestie, to shun offence*," 99.10–11). Still, in order not to frighten away the traditional readers of chivalric literature or those interested precisely in the more lurid aspects of the genre, the title page promises that the story's entertainment value has been preserved ("*yet all delightfull, for recreation*," 99.11–12). That is to say, with this title page readers were promised the kind of profitable pleasure they had become accustomed to expect from literary texts in the Renaissance.[233]

Louise Wilson is doubtful about the real effect of the edifying promises that populate the paratexts of Munday's translations. She argues, "It is unlikely that any early modern reader would be unaware of the genre and subject matter of the text, given the popularity of the romances and the widespread familiarity of the titles, *Palmerin* and *Amadis*, as generic signifiers."[234] She makes this remark about the 1596 edition of *Palmerin of England II*, but I am convinced that we can be equally certain that common readers were sufficiently familiar with those works in 1588, when the Iberian romances no longer represented a novelty to English readers. With regard to the subtitle to *Palmerin d'Oliva*, Wilson considers it "a hyperbolic and not entirely serious claim to the value of reading

---

on August 24, 1582, new control measures are introduced, suggesting that the perception of this literary corpus changed:"Licenced to him vnder the handes of master Barker and master Coldocke *the seconde parte of the mirror of knighthoode* to be translated into Englishe and soe to be printed, condic[i]onally notwithstandinge that when the same is translated yt be brought to them to be pervsed, and yf any thinge be amisse therein to be amended" (Arber, 2:414).

[233] For this tradition, see Robert Matz, *Defending Literature in Early Modern England: Renaissance Literary Theory in Social Context* (Cambridge: Cambridge University Press, 2000); and Brian C. Lockey, *Law and Empire in English Renaissance Literature* (Cambridge: Cambridge University Press, 2006), 20–21.

[234] "Paratexts," 126.

the text."[235] She is right in signaling the discrepancy between the nature of the text and the way it is presented, between the actual product and the way it is packaged. But, isn't this kind of disparity still central to the practices of modern advertising? As consumers, we are bombarded with commercial messages that want to delude us into believing that the package is an accurate representation of the content, that buying a particular product will enhance our lives in unique ways. More specifically, in the case of literary products, nowadays publishers also deploy a similar commercial code, with blurbs that describe the content of books in hyperbolic terms. What is significant is not that sixteenth- and twenty-first-century publishers agree in resorting to hyperbolic language to promote their literary products, but the particular attributes they attach to those products. Here they differ, as differ the values and expectations of their respective target markets. The title page of *Palmerin d'Oliva* advertises the book as morally innocuous and profitable, that way hoping to overcome or assuage the critical discourse of moralists like Ascham and Dering.

At the same time, the title page is also promoting this romance as entertaining in order to attract as many potential customers as possible. Note, however, that in the address to the courteous readers preceding the text of 1588 Munday elaborates only on one half of the Horatian dictum *prodesse et delectare*, namely on the delight that can be derived from reading this particular book, "a freendly companion for the long euenings, and a fit recreation for other vacant times" (103.5–6). It may be that Munday had not yet come up with an effective argument to counter the humanist attacks on romance, or simply he felt it was unnecessary to reproduce his position there.[236] He offers this book for readers to fill their moments of idleness with an enjoyable and decorous (*fit*) activity, and reassures everyone that it contains "nothing [that] can be reprooued" (103.33), strongly echoing the "nothing worthie of Reprehension" that the Stationers demanded for the publication of *Palmerin of England* a few years before.

---

[235] "Writing Romance Readers in Early Modern Texts," *SPELL: Swiss Papers in English Language and Literature* 22 (2009): 120.

[236] See the arguments Munday presents in the 1596 edition of *Palmerin of England II* and the useful analysis by Wilson, "Paratexts," 126–27. It is not unlikely that the same paratext was used for the *editio princeps* of *Palmerin of England II*, in which case one could argue that Munday didn't want to rehearse the same views in his *Palmerin d'Oliva*. We can presume that Munday was possibly acquainted with Ascham's criticism against chivalric literature at least since 1580, when he published his *Zelauto* and "appears to have taken Ascham's attack on chivalric bawdry and manslaughter to heart," as suggests Metz, *Romance for Sale*, 37. The same sentiment toward chivalric literature was echoed by Thomas Underdowne in his translation of *An Aethiopian Historie*; cf. p. 15, n. 55 above. This work was also dedicated to Edward de Vere; note, however, that this condemnation of chivalric literature on the same grounds as Ascham was not included in the first edition of 1569 (STC 13041), but added in 1577, that is, after the publication of Ascham's *Scholemaster* in 1570.

But it seems that Munday was reluctant, or thought it unnecessary, at this point to beguile his readers into buying the book for its ostensible edifying value, when the promotional text on the title page already insists in this idea.

Instead, Munday presents one additional argument to call into question the hostile attitude against chivalric literature that dominated public discourse in Elizabethan England: "what hath past with so great applause in diuers languages, can hardly merite to be despised in England, being matter altogether of delight, and no way offensiue" (103.25–27). Munday disapproves of the prejudice against the corpus of Iberian romances voiced by the humanists and seemingly endorsed by the Stationers' Company, whereas this literary fashion had gained the favor of readers across continental Europe, as we saw above. His essential point is that English readers were not different from their European counterparts and should not be prevented from enjoying the same works in their own language. Obviously, Munday had a vested interest in advocating the distribution of the Iberian romances in England, since he could directly benefit and earn a steady income as a translator, as he eventually did. While he made no reference to his personal interest, Munday emphasized the benefits of making this internationally acclaimed corpus available to English readers. Furthermore, by challenging the humanists' viewpoint and encouraging the dissemination of these romances in English, printers, publishers, and booksellers could also reap the benefits of the new business opportunities that would arise, as they eventually did. In sum, no one could really benefit from censoring the Iberian romances, Munday says, while many could profit from publishing them.

In order to trigger this course of events, Munday wanted to enlist the collaboration of readers, or at least their acquiescence, so that they refrained from adversely affecting the forthcoming publication of his translation of another Iberian romance: "to feede you with varietie of delights, his History [i.e., *Palladine of England*] by Easter tearme next will be with ye: till when, vse such fauour to *Palmerin*, as Prince *Palladine* be not hindered" (postface of *Palmerin d'Oliva II*, 596.7–9). This explicit request for his readers to abstain from inveighing against the romance may seem conventional at first sight, but it is not. It is rather unusual that Munday demands "fauour to *Palmerin*," i.e., to the protagonist that metonymically stands for the whole work, not to his translation of the text, as translators more commonly did. It is also surprising that there was a time limit for this request, namely, "Easter tearme next," i.e., the 23rd of April, 1588, when *Palladine* was published. Considering that *Palmerin d'Oliva II* was published on March 9, 1588, Munday was asking his readers to suspend making any negative comments about the book for just a few weeks, so that the printing of *Palladine* would not be compromised.

Yet, the best service readers could do him, undoubtedly, was to buy a copy of the book. The commercial success of this literary product is the ultimate proof that it made financial sense to continue translating and printing this literary corpus. In order to make the edition of *Palmerin d'Oliva* more attractive to a wider base of potential customers, Munday explains in his address to the reader that measures had been taken so that purchasing a copy of this book could also benefit their *pursse*. He is referring to the division of the whole text in two parts, that way limiting the customers' initial expenditure, when they purchased the first part, and giving them the option of buying the second, if and when they chose to, all at no additional cost. This marketing decision, which seems trite and self-evident to us, may have been less familiar to Elizabethan book buyers, since Munday made efforts to explain its advantages to them. The fact that this decision was adopted and the way its rationale is verbalized provide us with two clues about the type of readership intended for this literary product. First, when Munday comments, "to glut men with delight, may make them surfeit" (103.8–9), we can surmise that the public being targeted was not necessarily used to reading long texts, but possibly more familiar with pamphlets and other kinds of short texts.[237] Second, that "they looue not to buie pleasure at vnreasonable price" (103.12–13), implies a kind of customer whose disposable income was limited and could not afford high-end products. This class of readers could be described as a popular audience that was being enticed to buy a superior product, which posed new financial and intellectual challenges. The efforts required to both purchase and appreciate this book also had their reward, since customers were promised a taste of upper-class literary entertainment: "if then the inferiour sorte mislike [this book], it is because they are not capable of so especiall deseruinges" (103.29–30). The paratext is an invitation to experience the literary tastes of a higher social class. The transactional process of buying this book, therefore, assumed the character of a social transaction, representing an opportunity for upward cultural mobility. In sum, *Palmerin d'Oliva* was marketed as an aspirational product that became accessible to a socially diverse type of readers at a relatively affordable price.

In the paratexts to *Palmerin d'Oliva*, Munday further offers a glimpse into the fragility of his situation. First, he still had no guarantee that his translations of Iberian romances would continue to appear in print: it was contingent on sales performance. Second, he expresses some authorial anxiety, some insecurity as a translator: his *Galien* and *Gerileon I* fiascos were still fresh in his memory. Munday probably did all he could to achieve the desired commercial success, but was still uncertain of his translation's quality. One thing he was certain of: if he failed to deliver a competent translation—i.e., one that captured the sense of the original and rendered it in readable English—his hopes of "reap[ing] some commoditie" from his knowledge of languages, as he planned to do when he traveled to the Continent, was doomed. These fears did not come true, but his feeling of

---

[237] See Miller, *The Professional Writer*, 209. A pamphlet "typically consisted of between one sheet and a maximum of twelve sheets, or between eight and ninety-six pages in quarto," according to Joad Raymond, *Pamphlets and Pamphleteering in Early Modern Britain* (Cambridge: Cambridge University Press, 2003), 5.

insecurity, his lack of self-confidence as a translator did not entirely disappear either. He needed reassurance that his translations were up to the standard, and this is precisely what his friend Henry Chettle did in a commendatory epistle to the 1596 edition of *Primaleon of Greece II* when stating, "*I haue not seen a Historie more delectablie continued, nor (to be plaine with ye) anie thing by your selfe more pleasingly translated. I would not be here taken (for commending this) to be a condemner of anie Worke by you before Englished.*"[238] The following section discusses the translation principles and practices that inform Munday's rendering of *Palmerin d'Oliva* into English.

Munday's translation of *Palmerin d'Oliva*

The paratexts accompanying Munday's *Palmerin d'Oliva* reveal little information about how he approached the process of translating this chivalric text into English. So unconcerned was Munday about describing this process that he even fails to mention the language in which this work was originally written, nor does he inform us about the language or languages from which he translated. All he says, in the dedication, is that the work had been "*worthely set downe in other languages*" (102.23–24), which he identifies on the title page as "Spanish, Italian and French" (99.13).[239] The explanatory notes to this edition make it apparent that Munday's translation is based primarily on the French version produced by Jean Maugin. Most personal names in the English version, however, reproduce the form they have in the Italian version made by Mambrino Roseo da Fabriano but not in the French translation as one would expect.[240] Thus, it seems likely that in the process of translating *Palmerin d'Oliva* from French Munday was at the same time consulting a copy of the Italian version. By contrast, while it is not unlikely that he obtained a copy of the Spanish original, all we can say is that Munday made no consistent use of it.

As regards the translation itself, the translator describes it to his patron Edward de Vere as "*my bad translation*" (102.23) and admits to his readers that in the book "nothing can be reprooued but my simple translation" (103.33–34). These are conventional remarks, part of the customary humility topos, but of little help to discover Munday's approach to translating and his attitude as a translator. In this sense he includes only one comment in *Palmerin d'Oliva* that

---

[238] STC 20366a, sig. A3r.

[239] Galigani interprets these words as an indication that "il nostro scrittore aveva a mano l'originale e le due versioni" (251), although he admits that we have no evidence that Munday did understand Spanish. By contrast, Margaret Tyler is straightforward about the original language of the *Mirror of Princely Deeds*: "The first tongue wherein it was penned was the Spanish" (49.8), from which she translated it directly into English.

[240] See "Index of Personal Names," 871–75; and Galigani, 252–54.

is revealing: "to translate, allowes little occasion of fine pen worke" (103.34–35). Munday complains that in fulfilling his task as translator he was constrained by the source text and abstained from imposing on it his own stylistic preferences. Since he assumes responsibility only for accurately transferring the original work into English, Munday wants us to believe that the merits—and demerits—of the English version, both in content and style, should be attributed to the author of the original work, not to the translator.

In a later paratext Munday made another traductological statement that, owing to its literary and chronological proximity to *Palmerin d'Oliva*'s genre and date of publication, can help us unravel his stance as a translator. It appeared in the address to the readers of Munday's *Palladine of England*, a chivalric romance of Castilian origin that he rendered into English using a French intermediary version made by Claude Colet.[241] On April 23, 1588, a little over a month since the publication of the second part of *Palmerin d'Oliva*, *Palladine of England* was published. Munday comments in its preface,

> If you happen to fynde any mislike in the translation, or that it is not so currant English as fyne eares hunt after: let this serue as a sufficient excuse for mee, that in translating, men are bound to their Writers words, and such as roue at random, may set downe what they please. (sig. *4r)

Munday takes up the same concern about the role of the translator and the value of translation, but develops his arguments further than he does in *Palmerin d'Oliva*. The underlying position remains the same and is now articulated in the form of a *captatio benevolentiae*. Munday presents himself merely as a translator in the etymological sense of the word, that is, as someone who simply transfers the original material into English, without any additional intervention. As such Munday informs his readers that there are two aspects he is not accountable for: first, if there is any narrative element in the translation that causes "any mislike" to the reader, and second, if the style of the translation is not considered to be "currant English." In other words, the former refers to the existence of narrative events that may be perceived as inadequate or offensive, whereas the latter alludes to the linguistic expression in the English version that may be considered inappropriate by Munday's readers.

This dichotomy between the narrative discourse's *content* and its *form* can be connected to classical rhetoric's tripartite division of the compositorial skills required of an author or orator, namely, *inventio, dispositio,* and *elocutio*. Cicero, whom Munday took as a model of eloquence, states, "Inventio est excogitatio rerum verarum aut veri similium quae causam probabilem reddant; dispositio est rerum inventarum in ordinem distributio; elocutio est idoneorum verborum

---

[241] See p. 16, n. 59 above.

ad inventionem accommodatio."[242] By leaving the *dispositio* out of his dichotomy Munday implies that the arrangement of the narrative matter in the English text was not a source of concern for him, since it is already determined by the author of the original text. But Roger Ascham, in his *Scholemaster*, can provide us with a slightly different interpretation. For assessing the eloquence of classical authors Ascham appears to depart from Cicero in the understanding of each rhetorical category, since for Ascham *inventio* refers to the "choice of honestie of matter," *dispositio* to the "framing of Phrases," and *elocutio* to the "proprietie of wordes" (*Scholemaster*, 287). From this point of view it is reasonable that the *framing of phrases* and *the proprietie of wordes* should be considered as categories that impinge on the *currency* of the written discourse and are subsumed within the larger concept of *form* or *expression*, as Munday seems to do.[243]

More significantly, Ascham's explanation of these rhetorical abilities also includes some assessment criteria that can help us further understand Munday's intentions as presented in the preface to *Palladine of England*. When evaluating the content or *inventio*, Ascham invites us to take into consideration the *honestie* displayed in the narrative events.[244] Thus, the *mislike* mentioned in Munday's preface probably corresponds to episodes of dubious morality that display social behavior that might be deemed inappropriate by his readers. The amorous encounters and desires described or mentioned in *Palmerin d'Oliva* certainly fall in this class of improper behavior that Munday anticipated could cause his readers dislike.

Concerning the choice of words or *elocutio*, Ascham pays attention to their *proprietie*.[245] When Munday apologizes because the English used in his translation may be perceived as insufficiently *currant* or less fashionable than expected

---

[242] *De Inventione*, I.vii: "Invention is the discovery of valid or seemingly valid arguments to render one's case plausible. Arrangement is the distribution of arguments thus discovered in the proper order. Expression is the fitting of the proper language to the invented matter," translated by H. M. Hubbell, The Loeb Classical Library (Cambridge, MA: Harvard University Press, 1949), 18–21. To this idea of *invention* Munday does allude in his translation when referring to the arguments Polinarda wants to advance in a letter to Palmerin: "before she would forget the *inuention* her spirite offered, shee presently wrote an answere" (475.38–39; my emphasis). Note also that the opening words in his *Mirror* are "*MARCVS, TVLLIVS, CICERO*, that flourishing floure of all Eloquence" (24.6).

[243] Conversely, Tyler has a tripartite model in mind when stating, "The invention, disposition, trimming, and what else in this story is wholly another man's, my part none therein but the translation, as it were" (*Mirror*, 49.31–33; cf. 50.62–63).

[244] Here I interpret *honestie* as "the quality of being seemly or appropriate; conformity to accepted or suitable standards of behaviour; decency, decorum; propriety" (q.v. *OED*, n. 2).

[245] Here I understand *proprietie* as "the quality of being proper or appropriate; fitness, fittingness, suitability; the proper use or sense of words" (q.v. *OED*, n. 2).

by "fyne eares," it is implied that his choice of words could be seen as *improper* in certain contexts.[246] By associating his potential readers with refined taste for linguistic expression or *fyne eares*, Munday is making an a priori estimation of his audience and positioning them as educated and probably well-to-do people. Of course, this is part of a marketing strategy designed to attract the interest of an aspirational reading class, who is supposed to expect a certain kind of sophisticated language. Munday imputes the alleged stylistic discrepancy between his readers' expectations and the translation's inelegance to the fact that he was bound to his "Writers words." This kind of approach to translation reveals the hierarchical submission of the translated text to the source text, a position the translator adopts even if it "desfigures the English, and makes it impossible for the translator to write elegantly."[247] In so doing, however, Munday can escape the blame for the translation's stylistic deficiencies and place it on the author of the source text. Had he not been bound to follow his source closely, Munday would have done like those "such as roue[248] at random, [that] may set downe what they please," as he contends. If in 1579 he admitted that his translation of *Galien of France* was jeopardized by his inadequate *inventio* for not being sufficiently *ripe* (see p. 54 above), in 1588, after nearly a decade in the business of writing, he certainly matured and became a more confident translator. What's more, as a result of his considerable experience of translation, his traductological insight also evolved. He became aware that the expertise of a translator does not depend on his capacity for *inventio*, the sole responsibility of the author, but on his linguistic competence, both in the target and in the source language.

No theory of translation was available in Elizabethan England that could help translators better understand their function and articulate a personal

---

[246] I am inclined to interpret *currant* as "in vogue," although it would predate in five years its first known occurrence according to the *OED* (s.v. *current*, adj. 7); an alternative interpretation is "in general use, prevalent" (adj. 6). Note that Aristotle argues that from a rhetorical point of view language "will be appropriate . . . if it corresponds to its subject," *Rhetoric*, III.7, in *The Complete Works of Aristotle: The Revised Oxford Translation*, ed. Jonathan Barnes (Princeton: Princeton University Press, 1995), 2245 (1408^{a}10–11). Cicero also develops this correspondence when he establishes, "sunt genera dicendi: subtile in probando, modicum in delectando, vehemens in flectendo," *De Oratore*, xxi.69: "these are the kinds of styles: the plain style is for proof, the middle style for pleasure, the vigorous style for persuasion," adapted from H. B. Hubbell's translation for The Loeb Classical Library (Cambridge, MA: Harvard University Press, 1962), 356–57. Finally, Ascham comments on the correspondence between form and content and advises the use of a style "proper and fitte for euerie matter" (283).

[247] Massimiliano Morini, *Tudor Translation in Theory and Practice* (Burlington, VT: Ashgate, 2006), 52. That is, even if he would have liked to, Munday's number one priority was allegedly to render his source text accurately, not to impress his readers, or in Lyly's words, "your eares which I seeke to delight" (*England*, 2:154.18–19).

[248] I.e., "to utter at random"; *OED*, s.v. *rove*, v.^{2} 3b.

Introduction

translation policy.[249] Therefore, Munday developed his own theoretical approach not from reading any treatise, but from his translation experience and personal reflections on this activity. The empirical character of Munday's translation policy probably explains its lack of terminological precision, even though he received rhetorical instruction during his time in Rome that must have helped him distinguish the various activities involved in the process of translating. In sum, in the preliminaries to his romance translations published in 1588, Munday fashions himself as a responsible and serious translator, whose task is to reproduce the narrative content of his original without judging its moral appropriateness while respecting its sintactic arrangement and lexical preferences.

The translators' explicit statements about their modus operandi, however, must be taken with a pinch of salt, since "Tudor translators continued to claim faithfulness to their originals . . . even when they cut and add at their pleasure."[250] It is convenient, therefore, to examine Munday's translation practice in *Palmerin d'Oliva* to determine whether it agrees with his stated policy or not. To do so I will compare Munday's translation with his original and determine to which extent he follows or departs from it. In this examination I consider the three main rhetorical categories used in written composition—i.e., *inventio, dispositio,* and *elocutio*—according to Ascham's interpretation. Since the explanatory notes offer ample commentary of the translation, the discussion that follows is not meant to be comprehensive but simply illustrative of Munday's modus operandi as a translator, and of his concerns, preferences, and idiosincracies.

With regard to the publication of *Palmerin of England*, I mentioned previously how the Stationers' Company imposed specific requirements on the narrative content of this romance to the effect that it should be free of episodes "worthie of Reprehension" (see p. 67). According to this stipulation, all erotic scenes, religious references, and descriptions of warfare should be treated with utmost care. In a sense, the original had to be filtered and purified to guarantee that the text contained "honestie of matter," in Ascham's words. Not only are love relationships a central ingredient of romance as a genre, but they are intricately interwoven with the development of their narrative plot. In the case of *Palmerin d'Oliva* the problem of sanitizing the amorous dimension typical of the genre is compounded by the French translator, who has put special emphasis on enhancing the erotic scenes to portray "les amours à la moderne," as Maugin declares in the preface to his translation.

---

[249] Morini, *Tudor Translation*, 17–24. The only exception was Laurence Humphrey's *Interpretatio linguarum seu de ratione conuertendi & explicandi autores sacros quam prophanos* (Basel: Hieronymus Froben and Nikolaus Episcopius, 1559); however, it was written in Latin and published in Basel and doesn't seem to have had any significant influence in England. See Gabriela Schmidt, "Introduction," in *Elizabethan Translation and Literary Culture*, ed. Gabriela Schmidt (Berlin: De Gruyter, 2013), 1–3.

[250] Morini, *Tudor Translation*, 4–5.

One source of concern for Munday is the expression of female desire, which he finds in the opening chapters of the romance. In the absence of Florendos, Griana's lover, she wonders, "quand le pourray-je voir & baiser à mon aise?,"[251] a question that is replaced in the English version by, "Howe might I . . . ease this waightie oppression?" (121.18–19). While the French text conveys Griana's wish to be physically reunited with Florendos as a way to show him her love, the English translation expresses an altogether more vague feeling of suffering and anguish. The tangible acts of *seeing* and *kissing* of the French are turned into an intangible, abstract, almost unreal, allusion to *oppression* in the English. Griana's unladylike conduct in the French version is justified, and could be excused, since Love has gained control of her heart and as a result she is unable to exercise self-restraint and behave decorously. In contrast, Munday does not even allow Griana to succumb to Love's seductions, but instead states, "euery worde [from Cardina about her meeting with Florendos] tooke hold on the gentle hart of the Princesse" (121.14–15). What takes hold of Griana's heart is not here identified with all-powerful Love, but simply with words, whose import, however consequential it may be, does not prevent her from acting with decency and decorum. In the English version Griana has not lost control of the situation and can rein in her emotions, because she was "lothe to receiue shame in her loue, hauing caryed her selfe with such honour all her life" (121.17–18). In this context it was advisable that a woman should keep her inner feelings secret, particularly if they could compromise her good reputation: "what she desired inwardlie, shee shaddowed with modestie" (121.16–17). It is significant that here Munday is not translating his French source, but instead imposing on his text an ideological position about the way women of repute should comport themselves: when they feel an overwhelming desire that can cast doubt on their honor, rather than succumbing to it, virtuous women must repress those feelings or, at least, conceal them, never reveal them as Griana does in the French text.

Munday's intervention shows how he got involved personally with the moral value of the English text. It even offers a glimpse of some authorial awareness, since Munday was compelled to compose or *invent* a part of the text in order for it to reflect a more acceptable moral point of view. The narrative consequences of this type of intervention are relatively small, since Munday could, with minor changes, delete or alter actions that were deemed worthy of reprehension. In the same chapter, however, Munday faced the challenge of describing the clandestine conception of the romance's eponymous hero, Palmerin d'Oliva. Maugin has resource to the siege metaphor and equates the lady's virginity with a fortress, but despite Griana's strong resistance, her lover and husband "Florendos (à la quatriesme charge) prit entiere possession de la place tant assaillie."[252] Munday did

---

[251] Sig. B6v: "when will I be able to see and kiss him at my ease?"
[252] Sig. B7r: "Florendos (at the fourth charge) took full possession of the besieged place."

not consider the metaphorical language sufficiently modest and chose instead to write the passage anew using figurative language that was less suggestive and more ambiguous, thus obscuring the real intent of the events being narrated: "faire *Cynthia* amiablie fauouring this delicate encounter, added such courage to the minde of this louelie Champion: as breaking his Launce in the face of *Venus*, hee [i.e., Florendos] bequeathed the successe of his deuoire to the gracious aspect of that Planet" (122.34–37). Munday still uses a martial metaphor and refers to Florendos as "this louelie Champion," who with the consent and encouragement of Cynthia (i.e., the Moon) intends to break a lance or fight to win a victory understood to be of a sensual kind ("in the face of *Venus*"). In this lofty style the sexual union between Florendos and Griana becomes a mere "delicate encounter," whereas the erotic connotations of the French text are suppressed. Moreover, while Maugin describes how the stiff resistance put up by Griana was overcome at Florendos's fourth assault, Munday does not reveal the ultimate outcome of Florendos's efforts, since the result is subordinate to the aspect or position of Venus relative to the earth—where the action takes place—and to the Moon, who has facilitated the sequence of events.

Munday wanted to avoid controversy, but could not simply erase this episode without the romance's storyline being affected. Unable to suppress this scene, he replaced it with an elusive and ambiguous description, whose right interpretation demands the full engagement of his readers. Those who had the necessary interpretative competence and were willing to read between the lines could just guess that some titillating matter was being touched on, although it lacked the erotic tension built by Maugin as part of his project of modernizing the Castilian original. The English translation, therefore, departs from the French version, not in the events narrated (i.e., the *inventio*), but in the form of narrating them (i.e., the expression or *elocutio*). Unlike Maugin, the English translator preferred to discuss sexual subjects using a dispassionate, elevated style. If in the preface Munday contends that "to translate, allowes little occasion of fine pen worke," Florendos's encounter with Griana offers a clear example of how Munday felt compelled to modify his source text. Still, he did not miss the opportunity to display his capacity for "fine pen worke" and composed an original passage using recherché expressions and allusions that, in his view, were the marks of an accomplished and seasoned author.

Intended to veil the French version's erotic nature, this type of rewriting is laborious, since it requires the composition of a new, parallel text that preserves the narrative coherence of the romance. Since this translation strategy was time consuming, Munday soon abandoned it and chose instead to censor this kind of awkward scenes. When Palmerin and Polinarda have their first intimate contact, they make their marriage vows in private and consummate their union straightaway. At this point Munday informs his readers of how he intends to deal with this delicate topic:

> Where is the wit so daintie, the tongue so florishing, or the penne so dilligent, as can conceiue, report or set down in perfect coullers, the ioyes of these louers? You faire Lordinges, and you likewise sweete Ladies, that long haue trauailed in amorous affections, and in the ende receiued the rewarde of your passions, by your owne conceites can imagine the content of these twaine (250.21–25).

In Munday's view, to describe the details of this amorous encounter "in perfect coullers"—using the appropriate rhetorical figures—seems challenging and arduous, since it requires the perfect combination of *wit, tongue* and *pen*. He then adds one further consideration: since his readers, both male and female, can be assumed to have experience "in amorous affections" and know the minutiae of a sexual relationship, it is unnecessary that he should waste his time and effort trying to describe it. So, instead, he invites his readers, "by your owne conceites . . . imagine the content [i.e., pleasure] of these twaine." If in the sexual union of Florendos and Griana Munday's translation demanded the interpretative engagement of his readers, now he appeals to their personal experience and imagination so that they can supply the erotic information that is purposely left out. In this different strategy Munday refrains from translating, adapting or rewriting the scene of his French source.

The dominant morality in Elizabethan England, in a way, dictated Munday's treatment of sexual descriptions. But there are other issues that also seem to make him uneasy from a moral perspective. When Florendos and Griana begin their sexual relationship, they are already married by virtue of the mutual agreement they express *de verba praesenti*. These are the "irreuocable vowes" (122.17) made by a kneeling Florendos as he asks Griana's hand in marriage, who replies, "I am well contented to accept you" (122.28). Though common and legally binding, these unions were frowned upon, as is implied by Ascham: "as now, not onelie yong ientlemen, but euen verie girles dare without all feare, though not without open shame, where they list, and how they list, marie them selues in spite of father, mother, God, good order, and all" (*Scholemaster*, 204). Munday cannot delete this information, because it could alter the narrative coherence of the romance. Instead, he avoids calling unnecessary attention to the couple's being married, hoping that it may go unnoticed. Thus, when a few lines after having consummated their marriage Griana addresses Florendos in the French version as "mon mary," my husband, the English translation reads "my Lord" (123.5). While the form of address in the French text is unambiguous, Munday chooses a more equivocal term that further conceals the true nature of the relationship between the two characters. Notwithstanding his initial reticence, Munday seems to have become somewhat more tolerant of this kind of unions. Later on, when Palmerin also marries Polinarda in a "mariage commencé par paroles de present" (sig. K1r), Polinarda is more explicit than Griana in "accepting you [i.e., Palmerin] onely for my Lorde and *Husbande*" (250.19–20; my emphasis).

Munday is determined to eradicate any sexual innuendo or hint and, rather than rephrasing the original passages, sometimes he prefers an easier method and simply makes small changes to the source text. Before being intimate with Florendos for the first time, Griana commends herself to her servant's sister, hoping that she will be able to assist her "mieux qu'autre que je cognoisse, & par son moyen pourrez satisfaire au meilleur Cheualier de la terre" (sig. B6v). It is implied that the kind of advise her servant's sister can provide refers to sexual matters and its ultimate goal will be *satisfaire* Florendos when they are together. Munday's translation is faithful to his original, except for the problematic verb *satisfaire*: "my Sister can better aduise then I, or any that I know, by her meanes may you *speake* with your Knight, the brauest Gentleman in the world" (121.22–24). Any trace of a sexual connotation is deleted and as a result the passage loses narrative force.

Munday's treatment of erotic episodes and remarks is best exemplified by the way he alters Laurana's words. In the French we find her promising, "je ferai tout ce qu'il [i.e., Palmerin] voudra" (D6v; *I will do everything Palmerin wishes*), a promise that Munday rephrases as, "I will doo for his [i.e., Palmerin's] welfare what I may with modestie" (161.35–36). Therefore, any action or thought that contravenes Munday's idea of decorum and propriety is, at best sanitized, if not deleted. In Ascham's words, we could argue that Munday follows his sense of *modestie* to remove all the expressions of *bold bawdrye* from the English translation.

In addition to matters of love, the plot of chivalric romances is also driven by the description of military action, another source of concern to Ascham. He dubbed this narrative ingredient as *open manslaughter*, which could be defined as the slaughter of human beings, particularly in battles, performed without concealment, for all to be seen.[253] Munday seems to agree with Ascham's views, since in his translation he summarizes, condenses or deletes episodes containing martial descriptions.[254] For instance, in the first part of the romance, when Polinarda's father, the Holy Roman Emperor, summons a tournament, the translation simply includes the following comment: "a breefe report wherof may very wel serue, in that you can imagine there wanted no braue chiualrie" (197.21–22). Once again Munday invites his readers to use their imagination and fill the gap he has chosen not to translate but simply summarize. This strategy is similar to the one he deploys in the case of erotic descriptions, the only difference being that now his choice does not respond to a social taboo, and thus the readers are not denied the highlights of this episode. The same happens when the work deals with warfare, whose treatment is best exemplified by the translation

---

[253] For this definition, see *OED*, s.v. *manslaughter* n. 2b, and *open* adj. 25a.

[254] He shows the same attitude in his translation of *Palmendos*, as suggests Leticia Álvarez-Recio, "Spanish Chivalric Romances in English Translation: Anthony Munday's *Palmendos* (1589)," *Cahiers Élisabéthains* 91.1 (2016): 5–20.

of chapter 111 of the French version. Instead of closely following his source as Munday announces in the prefatory section, he makes the following summary of almost the entire chapter in his source: "The next day the king *Tyreno* assaulted the Cittie, who was slaine in the battaile by *Palmerin*, so afterward was *Maulerino* crowned king of *Nabor*, and all the Countrey enioyed their former quiet" (513.11–14).

This tendency to condense descriptions of warfare gets reinforced toward the end of the book, as Munday was moved doubtless by the desire of completing the translation of this sizeable work. But there was probably one other reason that prompted Munday to pay little attention to military matters. In chapter II.xlviii, as he is translating the description of how Palmerin jousts against Tomano, Drumino, and their knights, Munday makes a revealing remark: "But not to hold you with tedious discourse considering which way the victorie is intended, the two Princes and all their knights were manfullye foyled by *Palmerin*" (519.31–33). While this abridgement originates in Maugin, Munday interpolates the adjective *tedious* to characterize the events being condensed. His choice of adjective contrasts with the views expressed by Maugin, who thinks those events offer occasion that "je m'amuse icy" (Aa3r; *I busy/amuse myself*). Munday finds nothing amusing in this kind of episodes, which follow a predictable and repetitive pattern and have little or no narrative value. One can understand that translating them can be a tedious activity.

One other characteristic of Munday's treatment of military passages is that he forbears from translating the physical consequences that chivalric violence has on human beings, whereas Maugin gives a graphic account of them. When Palmerin fights against a knight that tries to steal the glass with the healing water from Urbanillo, Palmerin's dwarfish servant, we read how the enemy knight "fel from his Horse deade to the ground" (154.14), while the French version contains a more explicit description: Palmerin "luy passa la lance a trauers du corps" (sig. D3v; *pushed the lance through his body*). Similarly, when Palmerin fights against the giant Darmaco and his wife, he had to kill her and "sende her packing after her Husbande" (172.31–32), but in the French text we get a vivid account of the means Palmerin uses to kill her: he "luy mist l'espée au ventre" (E3r: *he plunged the sword into her belly*). One could argue that Munday does not want Palmerin to have the reputation of a violent and merciless hero, though it seems more likely that Munday feels uncomfortable with graphic violence, regardless of the agent or context. In another combat, Palmerin unhorses Count Passaco, who then "was troden to death with the trampling of the Horses" (159.24–25). Yet, Munday leaves out the more gruesome aspects of Count Passaco's death, "sur lequel tant de cheuaux passerent qu'il luy creuerent le cueur au ventre" (D6r; *so many horses trampled on him that they destroyed the heart in his body*). I mention above how Ascham criticized chivalric romance for relating numerous battles that caused heavy casualties and, moreover, for doing so *openly*, full of grisly detail, as if reveling in the destructive power of men-at-arms. In a sense, Munday seems to share Ascham's view and avoids narrating *openly* the frightful effects of using violence, thus departing from Maugin, who by contrast takes more pleasure in vividly describing violent acts.

Whether Munday was directly influenced by Ascham or not, the fact that they shared the same sentiment suggests that the explicit descriptions found in the French version would have been disliked by some of the romance's English readership. Munday had no choice but accept the presence of military action in his text, but he was certainly not partial to chivalric ethics, aesthetics, and ideology. When the French source contains carefully phrased armorial descriptions, Munday does not take the trouble to reproduce heraldic style, not even the meaning of those descriptions. For instance, "portant de sinople à nombre infiny de besans d'argent" (L4r; *wearing vert with an infinite number of silver bezants*), is rendered as "so rich in Armes" (272.43); "sable escartelé d'argent" (L4r; *sable quarterly argent*) as "so adorned with white Roses" (273.22). Munday did not concern himself with the linguistic technicalities pertaining to defensive tactics either, and instead of translating the specific terminology, he preferred to use the following clause: "and such defences as are requisit in warlike occasions" (396.12). It is not unlikely that these two sets of lexical items, dealing with heraldic and military language, posed a challenge to the translator, because of the difficulty both in understanding the original and in finding the exact equivalent in the target language. Additionally, Munday took no interest in translating the different parts of a knight's armor: the French text enumerates all the integral parts of Palmerin's suit of armor as he takes them off (sig. M7v), whereas the English version just states that he "put of hys owne Armour" (298.5–6). All this evidence indicates that Munday was not favorably disposed to chivalry, although it may simply be that he thought either that this information was inconsequential to the main story line, or that his audience would be unappreciative.

The third ingredient in the translation that Munday treated with scrupulous care were religious references. As mentioned above, both Ascham and Dering associated chivalric literature with a Catholic ideology, whose manifestation was being persecuted in Elizabethan England. In such a context of religious conflict and bearing in mind the Stationers' injunction on the publication of *Palmerin of England*, Munday was well aware that his romance translations would be seen with some suspicion, since the corpus of Iberian romances originated from a Catholic country and reached him by means of intermediate versions produced in Catholic countries too. It is natural, therefore, that Munday should be cautious and erased any possible reference and external expression that could be associated with Catholicism. Making the sign of the cross is a common gesture in Catholic societies to commend oneself to God before facing danger, and consequently in the French version Palmerin "fit le signe de la croix" (D2v; *made the sign of the cross*) before fighting the Serpent of the Mountain Artifaeria. Instead of transcribing the gesture, Munday gives us its intended meaning divested of any confessional attribute: "commending himselfe to God" (151.30–31). Another type of conduct suppressed in the translation because of its Catholic connotations is hearing Mass. In 1581, when the threat of the Jesuit invasion was all too real, the English parliament passed an act explicitly forbidding attending Mass: "that every person which shall willingly hear mass shall forfeit the sum of one hundred marks and suffer imprisonment for a year."[255] The characters in the romance are therefore not portrayed acting illegally. For instance, when Polinarda's father invites Palmerin to join him to "ouir messe en la grande Eglise" (F1v; *to hear Mass in the cathedral*), the translation just mentions that her father "sent to desire his [i.e., Palmerin's] companie to the Chappell" (187.7), leaving out the liturgical component. When the romance's plot takes the protagonists to England, the translation becomes more scrupulous, and even more so when the queen of England's religious behavior is referred to. In the French text the queen of England "alloit ordinairement ouyr Messe, & faire son voyage à vne petite chapelle de nostre Dame" (K6r; *attended Mass regularly in a small chapel of the Virgin Mary*), a passage that is rendered in the English version only as, the Queen "dailie went to a Chappell" (259.22–23). Not only is the practice of hearing Mass censored, but also the fact that the chapel is dedicated to the Virgin Mary, a figure that aroused strong antagonism during the English reformation.[256]

To do justice to this romance, we need to remember that when it was composed in 1511 all these references would have been unobjectionable in England, and when the French translation was published in 1546 the same references would not have been so controversial. But the socio-political context changed significantly in the 1580s, when Munday prepared his edition of *Palmerin d'Oliva* and England became a religiously intolerant society that saw the repression of Christian denominations different from official Protestantism.

Still, the great caution Munday exercised with the Christian dimension of the romance disappears in the second part, when the action moves to the eastern Mediterranean.[257] An example illustrating how Munday uses his source freely can be found when Palmerin feels deep inside that his greatest desire or ambition is "the ruine and generall destruction of these Heathen hounds, sworne enemies to Christ and his Seruants" (390.14–15), although his source simply refers to "ces canailles enemys de nostre foy" (R3r; *this rabble, enemies of our faith*). With the amplification of his source Munday spells out its implications, so that his English audience could identify the true enemy of Christianity. By highlighting Palmerin's antagonism to the Muslim infidel, Munday also lays bare how the dissent

---

[255] J. R Tanner, *Tudor Constitutional Documents, A.D. 1485–1603* (Cambridge: Cambridge University Press, 1922), 153.

[256] See Gary Waller, *The Virgin Mary in Late Medieval and Early Modern English Literature and Popular Culture* (Cambridge: Cambridge University Press, 2011).

[257] A discussion of Munday's treatment of the characters's presence in the Near East can be found in Alejandra Ortiz-Salamovich, "Anthony Munday's *Palmerin d'Oliva*: Representing Sexual Threat in the Near East," *Sederi* 26 (2016): 67–84.

among Christians of different denominations—i.e., Christ's "Seruants"—was undermining Christianity and making it more vulnerable to the Muslim threat. This belief is reminiscent of the spirit of the Crusades that mobilized the European *bellatores* and would appear to position Palmerin as a crusading knight, a soldier of God, that dedicated himself to defend the Christian faith. In order to dispel the notion that Palmerin endorses a dubious form of Pan-Christianity, Munday prefers instead to present Palmerin as an ideal knight devoted entirely to honor the code of chivalry. In the French version Palmerin is at one point trying to convince Olorico of his words' veracity by invoking what is most sacred to him, "par le haut Dieu viuant" (R4v; *by the high living God*), whereas in the English text Palmerin uses another form of appeal, "by the honour of my Knighthoode" (394.30). Although it may be that Munday wants to avoid swearing a sacred oath, since it was increasingly perceived that these were of little effect,[258] the truth is that the change identifies Palmerin as a knight whose main priority was to fulfill his chivalric obligations. But later on Olorico also swears "par tous noz Dieux" (sig. S4v; *by all our Gods*), and Munday replaces it by "on my Knighthood" (414.32). Despite their conflicting religious beliefs, both Palmerin and Olorico agree in their commitment to chivalry and its values, and thus they can share a common role in life while respecting their religious differences.

Munday intervenes on the religious manifestations of his romance with the ultimate goal of producing a version that is inoffensive. Hamilton has concluded that "Munday's romances helped create a public sphere in which the Catholic perspective remained a competing voice and offered a counter-narrative that represented the larger Catholic world as advantageous to England's safety and identity" (79). The evidence offered by Munday's treatment of religion in his translation of *Palmerin d'Oliva* contradicts Hamilton's view. I see no sign of a Catholic agenda in his translation. In fact, as I have shown, he suppresses any religious practice that could have a Catholic signification. His prime concern was not to promote a "Catholic perspective," as Hamilton contends, but something more practical: to escape censure for his work and not compromise his literary career. In this strategy he avoids being specific about the Christian denomination of the characters in his text, but instead places the emphasis on the common enemy to Christianity. This religious stance would have been acceptable to all his readers regardless of their religious persuassion. By attenuating religious tension, Munday can reaffirm the knights' commitment to chivalry, something that one can assume readers of romances appreciated. In sum, the translator's attitude to religion, sex, and warfare is consistent and aims in these three areas to make the translation as innocuous as possible by guaranteeing the *invetio*'s "honestie of matter" that Ascham advocated.

---

[258] See Melissa Mohr, *Holy Sh*t: A Brief History of Swearing* (Oxford: Oxford University Press, 2013), 142.

The other aspect I want to discuss is the abovementioned *currency* of the language used in the translation. When Munday feels insecure about how "currant" his English may be, he is verbalizing a concern for presenting the contents of the book according to the style and taste that were fashionable and expected by its intended audience. When in 1588 Munday composed the paratext that contains this reflection there seemed to be general agreement about who was the writer of greatest stylistic and narrative talent. The person to receive such recognition would be John Lyly, whom the contemporary critic William Webbe (d. 1591) praised in 1586 for having cultivated the English language with a supreme command of rhetoric, thus demostrating not only his own ability but also the huge potential of English, which would have deteriorated inevitably without Lyly's efforts:

> the great good grace and sweete vayne, which Eloquence hath attained in our speech, because it hat had the helpe of such rare and singuler wits . . . Among whom I thinke there is none that will gainsay, but Master *Iohn Lilly* hath deserued most high commendations, as he which hath stept one steppe further therein then any either before or since he first began the wyttie discourse of his *Euphues*. Whose workes, surely in respect of his singuler eloquence and braue composition of apt words and sentences, let the learned examine and make tryall thereof thorough all the parte of Rethoricke, in fitte phrases, in pithy sentences, in gallant tropes, in flowing speeche, in plaine sence.[259]

It could be argued that Webbe is stating only a personal, subjective opinion, but it is an informed one that is corroborated by other, more objective, supporting evidence. First, the spectacular success achieved by the publication of the adventures of Euphues from the very beginning. Lyly's *Euphues: The Anatomy of Wit* (1578) and *Euphues and His England* (1580) continued to be reprinted in the following years up until the publication of *Palmerin d'Oliva*: 1584 (STC 17072.5), 1585 (STC 17056), 1586 (STC 17073), 1587 (STC 17057), and even in 1588 (STC 17074). In view of the unprecedented public response to Lyly's prose narratives, other writers together with their printers wanted to imitate Lyly's successful formula. This influence on contemporary literary culture provides us with a second kind of objective evidence to substantiate the claim that Lyly's style was seen as exemplary. The desire to copy or be associated with Lyly's mode of writing or simply with his attitude and way of presenting himself to the readers shaped the production of prose fiction during the 1580s and 1590s.[260] It seems

---

[259] William Webbe, *A Discourse of English Poetry (1586)*, ed. by Sonia Hernández-Santano, Modern Humanities Research Association Critical Texts 47 (London: MHRA, 2016), 95–96.

[260] See Katharine Wilson, "'Turne Your Library to a Wardrope': John Lyly and Euphuism," in *The Oxford Handbook of English Prose, 1500–1640*, ed. Andrew Hadfield

Introduction 91

safe, therefore, to consider John Lyly's style as the standard that was recognized as tasteful, accomplished, and appreciated by the *fyne eares* of other writers, critics, and readers.

Not only can we sense that Lyly's style was considered a model, but more significantly Munday was of the same opinion too. He was quick to notice the merit and novelty of Lyly's *Euphues* and as quick to find himself associated with it, since in 1580 he published *Zelauto*, "the first non-Lylyan text to present itself as a *Euphues* book," as Kesson points out.[261] Munday's preference for Lylyan style did not wane after the publication of his *Zelauto*, but continued influencing him, as can be seen in his presentation of *Palmerin d'Oliva*. Lyly is the first writer that used the term *anatomy* in a literary sense,[262] and it is indicative of an imitative intention that Munday used the same word in the subtitle of *Palmerin d'Oliva*: "Anatomie of rare fortunes." Moreover, if Lyly was original also in presenting a single story organized around the biography of a central hero,[263] the wording Munday chose for the title of his translation aims to create the same effect: it centers all the attention on the protagonist, as if the romance contained a narrative unified by the hero's biography. Munday's construction of the romance's title, by selecting the word *anatomie* and unifying the narrative around the eponymous hero, provides sufficient evidence to suggest that he was tapping features that were unique to Lyly, thus marketing his translation in a way that could replicate the commercial success of the latter's publications.

From all the evidence presented above it seems to me not unlikely that with the phrase "currant English" Munday implicitly referred to Lylyan style, the so-called *euphuism*, which other contemporary authors of prose fiction strived to imitate as well. Moreover, when Munday comments that his translation's style may not be "so currant English as fyne eares hunt after," he seems to have found inspiration in Lyly and even echoes the latter's choice of words in the epistle dedicatory to his *Euphues: The Anatomy of Wit*: "It is a world to see how English men desire to heare finer speach then the language will allow" (1:181.16–18). Both Munday and Lyly agree that English readers were eager to savor *fyne speach*. Lyly is concerned that the readers' wish may be unreasonable and even counter-productive, since it could exceed the capacities of the English language and, hence, result in frustration. But Munday is worried not about failing to satisfy his readers' over-high expectations, but instead about attaining the stylistic standards that could be reasonably expected from a prose romance. In case he did not attain

---

(Oxford: Oxford University Press, 2013), 184–86; and Kesson, *Lyly and Early Modern Authorship*, 85–96.

[261] *Lyly and Early Modern Authorship*, 85. See also Alejandra Andrea Ortiz Salamovich, "Translation Practice in Early Modern Europe: Spanish Chivalric Romance in England," PhD diss. (University of Leeds, 2014), 126.

[262] See Kesson, *Lyly and Early Modern Authorship*, 34.

[263] See Kesson, *Lyly and Early Modern Authorship*, 48, 61–62.

the style readers *desire* and *hunt after*, Munday has a justification: as a translator he was bound by his source text and had little opportunity for exhibiting his own *fine pen worke*.

A place where Munday could show off his stylistic competence was the paratexts, which he composed especially for the publication of the English translation of Iberian romances. The English *Palmerin d'Oliva* opens with a dedication to Edward de Vere that starts by talking about two apparently historical figures from antiquity, namely, Mucronius and his master Hagarbus. There would be nothing unusual about them, were it not for the fact that both Mucronius and Hagarbus are invented characters. Precisely, the use of invented historical figures is one of the ornamental devices characteristic of euphuism.[264] Moreover, in order to explain the relevance of the opening example, Munday uses an antithesis, the rhetorical figure most typical of euphuistic style too: "*Though this example (my good Lord) be vnfit for me, in what respect, beseemes me not to speake: Yet that excellent opinion of the* Spartanes, *I count it religion for me to immitate*" (102.13–15).[265] Although translating does not allow for giving visibility to the translator's stylistic skills, when Munday finds a way to display them, he wastes no time in showing his potential for fine pen work, which bears the mark of euphuism, his ideal of "currant English" with which his patron was well acquainted.

The use of euphuistic features is not limited to the the paratexts, but emerges in the translation itself. It is particularly significant when a stylistic characteristic is not borrowed from Maugin and when it is part of an amplification, since in both cases the choice is attributable to Munday. Some of these features include the following: word repetition ("sweet *death*, too long desired *death*," 343.13), simple alliteration ("*ma*kes way to *ma*nifold *mi*sfortunes," 321.35–36; "O *wo*nderfull *wo*rkeman of the *wh*ole *wo*rlde," 346.19–20), transverse or alternate alliteration ("*h*ad not *h*ope to see thee *l*eng*t*hened my *l*ang*u*ishing daies, thou hadst found my *b*odie *b*reathlesse," 487.6–7), and parison or parallel structure ("affection ballanced with desert, or loue measured by vertue as it is by opinion," 116.22–23; "that mine eies ouer-watched with tedious expectation, and my hart neere tyred with bootlesse wishings," 327.27–28; "the extremitie of his passions tooke away the libertie of his speeche," 116.27–28).

Euphuism is also characterized by the use of ornamental features, "those means of ornament and illustration which occupy a midway position between the matter and the manner of thought,"[266] and affect not only the verbal expression of the text but also its narrative dimension. These features include the introduc-

---

[264] See R. Warwick Bond, ed., *The Complete Works of John Lyly* (Oxford: Clarendon Press,1902; repr. 1973), 1:130. See note to the epistle, p. 599, n. 4.

[265] See Bond, *Lyly*, 1:120–22. Another example of antithesis can be found in the address to the readers: "in expecting thanks for my paynes, I should remaine condemned by generall misliking" (103.9–10).

[266] Bond, *Lyly*, 1:130.

tion of historical and mythological allusions, knowledge from natural history and other sources, and proverbs. As I mentioned above when discussing the French translation, Maugin modified the Castilian original by introducing frequent classical allusions of a literary, historical, and mythological nature that provided an analogical explanation for the narrative events in the romance. For instance, when Palmerin's foster family are making preparations to travel to Constantinople, Maugin establishes a parallel relation with the journey to Troy of Paris Alexander's foster parents: "as sometime did the foster Father of *Paris Alexander*, his Wife, and their Daughter *Pegasis*, when they brought the Cradle and acoustrements of the infant royall" (467.8–10). Note that the reference to "Cradle and acoustrements" is introduced by Maugin to make the correspondence between the classical episode and the romance exact.[267] Since his source text was already provided with the desired classical flavor, Munday was not compelled to find relevant parallels to complement his translation. In fact, I doubt that he, without having attended grammar school and with the time constraints of his profession, could have made such an intelligent use of the classical knowledge as Maugin did.

Yet, occasionally Munday also wanted to leave his personal imprint and decided to modify a reference he found in the French version. Toward the end of the first part, after finding out that Agriola has eloped, her mother wails more than "Hecuba, ayant veu sacrifier sa fille Polixene sur le tombeau d'Achilles" (O3v; *Hecuba, after having seen her daughter Polyxena being sacrificed on Achilles' tomb*). The comparison of the Queen's response changes in the English translation, where we read how she fell "into such pittiful acclamations, far surpassing those of *Maguelona*, when she lost her freend *Peter of Prouince* in the wood" (324.12–14). This apposite literary allusion indicates that Munday was not merely closely following his source, but wanted to engage creatively with it, choosing in this case to underscore the emotional force of the narrative with a reference that was popular and more familiar to his readers than the classical one added by Maugin.

The second kind of ornamental elements of euphuistic style is "the introduction of recondite knowledge of all kinds, e.g., of medicine . . ., of magic . . . and above all the famous *similes from natural history*."[268] Once again, Munday depended on his source text for this sort of knowledge, and reproduces a description of the princess Zephira's medical condition she contracts when a worm comes into her nostrils, "So the venome and poysone of this little worme, engendred a putrifaction and other like worms, which gaue a smell so filthy and lothsome, as hardly could any abide to stand by her" (499.21–24). The English translation also demonstrates familiarity with magical practices such as ornitho-

---

[267] See my "Notes to the Text" for a discussion of classical references in *Palmerin d'Oliva*, the majority of them added by Maugin.
[268] Bond, *Lyly*, 1:131.

mancy (530.12–22) and necromancy, with a long list of names connected to thaumaturgy, including Zabulus, Orpheus, Hermes, Zoroaster, Circe, Medea, Petrus Alphonsus, Roger Bacon, and Apollonius of Tyana (587.8–11). As to the knowledge of natural history, we are told of the treacherous nature of leopards (355.25–30) and the physical aspect of the fire salamander (358.29–30). This kind of knowledge is also used to make similes: when the text describes Tarisius's blind hatred, it is compared to "the matter prouoking a fierie Meteore" (234.28–29). Most of the references to natural history derive from the French text, although sometimes Munday interpolates a simile of his choice: Palmerin confesses how beneficial to him is her beloved Polinarda, "whose verie rememberaunce gaue him lyfe, as the ayre dooth the *Camelion*" (285.10–11).

One further ingredient associated with euphuistic narrative is "the perpetual introduction of proverbs and pithy sayings."[269] The presence of proverbs in *Palmerin d'Oliva* is not as pervasive as in Lyly's prose, although they appear frequently. In spite of proverbs being culturally-bound expressions that are hard to translate, Munday retains most of those he finds in the French version, especially if there is not a great lexical distance from the French wording to the English form of the proverb. Munday has no difficulty in rendering how Gramiell's brothers "firent de necessité vertu" (R7v) as "they were constrained to make a vertue of necessitie" (401.8–9); when Munday's translation states, "to see presuming mindes payde with selfe same coyne" (225.27–28), we are reading the equivalent of the French "sont payez souuentesfois de tel salaire comme a esté le Duc" (H5v), or Munday's "to performe the debt we all owe to nature" (552.35) is his translation of "faire payer vne dette que nous deuons à nature" (Dd1v). Occasionally Munday also adds proverbs that are not inspired by his source. For instance, aware that he has censored the amorous encounter between Lewes and the Duchess of Burgundy, Munday uses the expression "by the halfe the whole may be discerned" (214.23) to excite the imagination of his readers and invite them to fill in the missing description. Additionally, Munday also demonstrates a liking for proverbial language. When translating the clause "que grand personnage ne peut donner que grandes choses" (O8v), which is not a proverb, Munday wants to infuse it with proverbial value and translates it as "*That great persons giue great presents*" (341.41–342.1), an expression that stands out by the use of alternate alliteration and typographical contrast.

The ornamental features in Munday's *Palmerin d'Oliva* are mostly attributable to Maugin, who imposed them on the Spanish original. This erudite elaboration matches perfectly with the narrative contents of the romance and could hardly have been prepared by someone without a formal education.[270] That these

---

[269] Bond, *Lyly*, 1:134.

[270] Peter Mack, *Elizabethan Rhetoric: Theory and Practice* (Cambridge: Cambridge University Press, 2002), chap. 5, has argued that grammar school education provided useful materials and techniques for the authors of romances. Munday did not receive formal

characteristics were already part of his source should not detract from Munday's euphuistic aspirations. Helen Moore contends that Munday's prose from the 1580s, including his romance translations, offers ample evidence of his sympathy with euphuism.[271] The following example also illustrates Munday's interest, at least in the opening sections of the translation, in adopting a euphuistic style using amplification, alliteration, and antithesis:

> Heereupon it chaunced, that *Tarisius*, Sonne to the King of *Hungaria* (who had beene brought vp in company with the yonge Prince *Caniano*) fell into such amorous conceite of the yong Princesse, as hee deuoted him selfe onelie to her seruice, beeing vnable to conceale the obiect of his affections, but that time made her acquainted with the cause of his alteration. Manie meanes he founde to entise her good opinion towards him, but she carrying a religious zeale to loue in some other climate, made no reckoning of his importunate and dilligent seruice, which drewe a Hell of tormentinge thoughts vppon *Tarisius*, seeing his sute and seruice so deeplie despised. (104.34–105.1)

> Qui fut cause que Tarisius neueu du Roy de Hongrie (nourri auec le jeune Prince Caniam) en deuint amoureux, de sorte qu'il delibera la seruir si qu'elle cognostroit euidemment l'affection qu'il luy portoit. Sa deliberation fut executée à son pouuoir, mais elle n'en faisoit cas, dont il enduroit vn merueillex tourment: toutesfois desirant paruenir à son intention (B1r).

We saw at the beginning of this section how Munday presents himself in the paratexts as a slavish translator whose stylistic, rhetoric, and narrative potential is subordinate to his faithfulness to the source text. Nevertheless, it has become apparent how this traductological stance misrepresents Munday's translation practice. Such discrepancy between translation theory and practice is not unusual in sixteenth-century England and has been explained "as a lingering of medieval qualities in a new context where the penetration of novel, humanistic ideas on language and literature, of a modern philological approach to texts, begins to be felt, but not quite strongly enough to stamp out old habits."[272] In voicing his commitment to fidelity, Munday adheres to the prevailing literary discourse, an unproblematic and safe choice for him, since it is sanctioned by convention and fits with his readers' expectations. Had Munday been a more confident writer,

---

education in a school, but got some kind of introduction to rhetoric from his tutor Hollyband and when he briefly attended the English College in Rome. Proof of his familiarity and interest in rhetoric is the following sentence, interpolated by Munday, that we hear from the mouth of the villain Domarto: "This needelesse exordium haue I made to so foule an occasion, albeit truth needes no coullers or eloquent figures" (176.3–4).

[271] See Moore, "Ancient and Modern Romance," in *OHLTE*, 340, and the example she gives from *Palmerin of England*.

[272] Morini, *Tudor Translation*, 4.

he could have qualified his theoretical position by taking his cue from Maugin, who is honest with his readers about his treatment of the Spanish original: "Et à fin (seigneurs) que soyez avertiz de ma maniere d'escrire, je n'ay prins de l'original que la matiere principale."[273] Maugin has no qualms in letting them know that his engagement with his source has been one of creative appropriation, in which he has freely modified the content and expression of the Spanish text without deviating from the main story line. With this approach Maugin contrives to imbue the French translation with its own identity, more ennobled and modern, less rustic and medieval. As Bettoni argues, "Maugin traduce sempre e comunque inventando all'interno dell'universo fantastico del romanzo" (191–92); the result is "solo in apparenza trasportato dalla Spagna, ed in realtà prodotto in Francia" (Bettoni, 185). The French *Palmerin d'Olive* is a text of greater stylistic elegance, endowed with a *nouvelle eloquence*,[274] more readable and accessible to present-day readers.

What prevented Munday from being equally honest? Considering that the paratext was written after completing the translation, was he fully conscious of lying to his readers? Certainly Munday did not transform his source text as considerably as Maugin did, but he failed to forewarn his readers about his amplifications, interpolations, deletions, summarizations, and other kinds of intervention on his French source. This discrepancy between theory and practice in the case of Munday reveals a desire to be perceived as a member of the literary profession that knows and adheres to the same codes. But it also reveals a degree of authorial anxiety, since he dared not question the established norm and follow Maugin's example. Munday probably lacked the authorial confidence to distance himself from his peers, and maybe he was also anxious about an unpredictable book market that required him to minimize risk for his *Palmerin d'Oliva*, which was only the second of his translations of Iberian romances to be published. There is yet one further issue we need to take into account. We know the Iberian romances circulated in England in French among members of the nobility before they became available in English translation. Now that the common readers were given the privilege of accessing the same works, it seems natural that they would prefer to buy the book if they were promised that it was a faithful rendering of the original.

To conclude, Munday used a French intermediary translation to make the Spanish *Palmerín de Olivia* accessible to a new English audience. Even though he treated his source with some liberty, his personal situation and the market conditions compelled him to conceal this fact. Still, he deserves credit for his conscientious interventions, modification, and adaptation of the source text,

---

[273] Weinberg, *Critical Prefaces*, 134: "To the end (gentlemen) that you may be informed of my way of writing, I have taken from the original only the main matter."

[274] For the use of this concept in relation to Maugin's translation of *Palmerin*, see Taylor, *Rewriting Arthurian Romance*, 188, 192.

without which not only would have the publication of the book been hindered, but it might not have been well received by English customers and readers. The distance that exists between the medieval *Palmerín de Olivia* of 1511 and its early modern instatiation of 1588 is the result of the alterations made by Munday on a French version that is only committed to preseving the "matiere principale" of the original Spanish. But it also gives us a glimpse of how stories that traveled in time and space had to be adapted to meet the expectations of their new readers, in a different context and culture. Munday was an interpreter of the French version but also of English society, and he must have struck the right note because the romance remained in print for another fifty years.

Palmerin D'Oliua.

The Mirrour of nobili-
tie, Mappe of honor, Anatomie of rare
fortunes,[1] *Heroycall president of Loue:*
Wonder for Chiualrie, and most accomplished
Knight in all perfections.
(∴

Presenting to noble mindes, theyr Courtlie desires, to Gentles,
theyr choise expectations, and to the inferiour sorte, howe to imi-
tate theyr vertues: handled with modestie, to shun
offence, yet all delightfull, for re-
creation.[2]

Written in the Spanish, Italian and French,
and from them turned into English
by *A. M.* one of the Messengers of her Maiesties
Chamber.[3]

Patere aut abstine.[4]

At London,
Printed by I. Charlewoode, for Willi-
am Wright, and are to bee solde at his Shoppe, adioyning to S. Mildreds Church in the Poul-
trie, the middle Shoppe
in the rowe.[5]
1588.

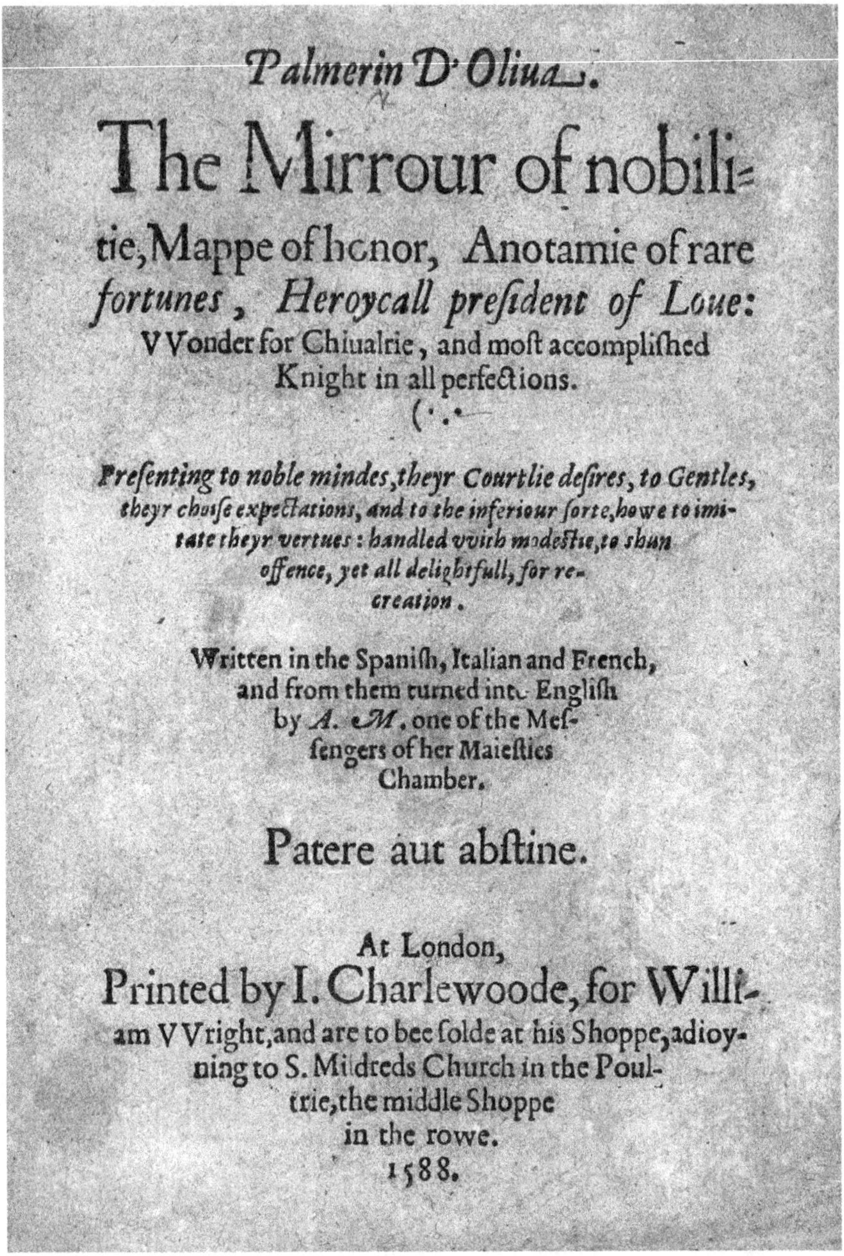

Palmerin D'Oliua.

The Mirrour of nobili=
tie, Mappe of honor, Anotamie of rare
fortunes, Heroycall president of Loue:
VVonder for Chiualrie, and most accomplished
Knight in all perfections.

*Presenting to noble mindes, theyr Courtlie desires, to Gentles,
theyr choise expectations, and to the inferiour sorte, howe to imitate theyr vertues: handled vvith modestie, to shun
offence, yet all delightfull, for recreation.*

Written in the Spanish, Italian and French,
and from them turned into English
by *A. M.*, one of the Messengers of her Maiesties
Chamber.

Patere aut abstine.

At London,
Printed by I. Charlewoode, for Willi-
am VVright, and are to bee solde at his Shoppe, adioyning to S. Mildreds Church in the Poul-
trie, the middle Shoppe
in the rowe.
1588.

Figure 2: Title Page of First Edition, Part 1, 1588. © The British Library, C.56.d.6.

Palmerin d'Oliva: Part I

Figure 3: Coat of Arms: Edward de Vere, 17th earl of Oxford.[1] *Palmerin d'Oliva* (London, 1588), sig.*2r. © The British Library, C.56.d.6.

To the right noble, learned, and worthie minded Lord, Edward de Vere,[1] *Earle of* Oxenford, Viscount Bulbeck,[2] Lord Sanford, and of Badelsmere,[3] *and Lord high Chamberlaine of England*: A. M. wisheth continuall happines in this life, and in the world to come.

Among the Spartanes *right noble Lord, and sometime my honorable Maister, nothing was accounted more odious, then the forgetfulnes of the seruaunt towardes his Maister: which made* Mucronius, *who had beene seruaunt to* Hagarbus *a poore Artezan, and for his vertues afterward called to the office of a* Senatour, *in all assemblies to reuerence his poore Maister, so that he would often say:* It was honour to *Mucronius, that he had beene seruaunt to Hagarbus.*[4]

Though this example (my good Lord) be vnfit for me, in what respect, beseemes me not to speake: Yet that excellent opinion of the Spartanes, *I count it religion for me to immitate. For if this vice*[5] *was so despised among such famous persons, what reproch wold it be to so poore an abiect as my selfe, beeing once so happy as to serue a Maister so noble:*[6] *to forget his precious vertues, which makes him generally belooued, but cheefely mine owne dutie, which nothing but death can discharge. In remembraunce therfore of my officious zeale, I present your Honour the willing endeuours of your late seruaunt: howe simple soeuer they be, right perfect shall you make them by your fauourable acceptaunce, this being added, that were I equall in ability with the best, all should be offered to my noble Maister.*

If Palmerin *hath sustained any wrong by my bad translation, being so worthely set downe in other languages: Your Honour hauing such speciall knowledge in them,*[7] *I hope will let slip any fault escaped, in respect I haue doone my good will, the largest talent I haue to bestowe.*

And seeing the time affoordes me such oportunitie, that with ending this first parte, the olde yeere is expired: I present it my noble Lord as your seruauntes New yeeres gift,[8] *and therewithall deliuer my most affectionate dutie, euermore ready at your Honours commaundement.*

Needelesse were it, by tediousnes to growe troublesome, when a woord suffiseth to so sound iudgement: I submit my selfe and my Booke to your gracious conceit, and the second part, now on the presse, and well neere finished I will shortly present my worthie Patrone.[9]

In meane while, I wish your Honor so many New yeers of happines, as may stand with the heauenly appointment, and my modestie to desire.

Sometime your Honours seruant,
yet continuing in all humble duty.
Anthonie Monday.

To the courteous Readers.

When I finished my seconde parte of *Palmerin* of *England*, I promised this worke of *Palmerin D'Oliua*, because it depended so especially on the other:[1] to discharge that debt, for promise is no lesse accounted, with the new yeere I send him abroad, a freendly companion for the long euenings, and a fit recreation for other vacant times.

But because some (perhaps) will make exceptions against me, that being but one Booke in other languages, I now deuide it twaine:[2] my aunswer is, that to glut men with delight, may make them surfeit, and so in expecting thanks for my paynes, I should remaine condemned by generall misliking. Beside, a Booke growing too bigge in quantitie, is profitable neither to the minde nor the pursse: for that men are now so wise, and the world so hard, as they looue not to buie pleasure at vnreasonable price. And yet the first parte will entice them to haue the second, when (it may bee alleaged) the cost is as great, as though it had come altogether: yet I am of the minde, that a man grutcheth not so much at a little mony, payd at seuerall times, as he doth at once, for this aduauntage he hath, in meane time he may imploy halfe his mony on more needful occasions, and raise some benefit toward buying the second parte. Againe, the other part will be new at the comming forth, where now it wold be stale: for such are affections now a daies, that a booke a sennight olde, is scant worth the reading.[3] Thus no iniurie is offered by deuiding my Booke, but profitte both to you and me: yours I haue rehearsed, and mine is, that a little pause dooth well in so long a labour, beside, this aduauntage would I take, that if my first parte deserued no liking, you should neuer be offended by me with the second.

Yet heerein I am encouraged, that what hath past with so great applause in diuers languages, can hardly merite to be despised in England, being matter altogether of delight, and no way offensiue: for noble and Gentle mindes, are farre from iniuring the Historie, that hath so highly pleased Emperours, Kinges and mightie potentates, if then the inferiour sorte mislike, it is because they are not capable of so especiall deseruinges.[4]

And yet *I* am perswaded, that both one and other will freendly entertaine *Palmerin D'Oliua*, because his History is so plentifully stored with choyse conceit, varietie of matter and exquisit conueyaunce: as nothing can be reprooued but my simple translation, yet that I hope will be pardoned too, in that to translate, allowes little occasion of fine pen worke.[5]

The second parte goes forward on the Printers presse, and I hope shalbe with you sooner then you expect: In the meane while let this haue fauourable acceptaunce, and that wilbe a spurre to hasten the other.

Yours to his vttermost.
A. Munday.

☙ The first parte of the auncient
and honorable Historie, of the valiant
Prince *Palmerin D'Oliua*, Emperor of *Constantinople*,
Sonne to the King *Florendos* of *Macedon*, and the
fayre *Griana*,[1] Daughter to *Remicius*, Emperour of
Constantinople: a History full of singuler and
Courtlie recreation etc.
(∴)

Chapter I.[1]
Of the secrete loue which the Prince Tarisius bare to the yong Princesse Griana: and the arriuall of the Prince Florendos at Constantinople.

The auncient Histories, of the famous Emperours of *Constantinople* doo record, that the eight Emperor[2] succeeding *Constantine*, the founder of that auncient and famous Cittie,[3] was named *Remicius*, who gouerned so iustlie, and with such exceeding honour: as not onelie his Subiectes intirelie looued him, but of the kingdoms about him he was so feared and reuerenced, that his Empire increased more large then in the time of his Predecessors. This *Remicius* was of such a princely and munificent minde, that no Knight whatsoeuer came into his Court, without verie honourable receite and bountifull rewardes: expressing the good nature of a vertuous Prince, whose deedes were helde of no small reckoning amongst his verie enemies. He maried with the King of *Hungarias* Daughter, a Princesse for witte and beautie, equall with any of her time, which caused her to be so especiallie loued of her Lord the Emperour, as hee altogeather gaue ouer the exercise of Armes:[4] notwithstanding, his Court did not diminishe one iote of the former glorie for good and hardie Knights, but dailie increased in such sort, as he tooke great delight to haue yong Princes, Knights and Gentlemen, nurtured and educated from their verie infancie in his Pallace, especiallie after the Empresse had brought him a Sonne, which was named *Caniano*, at whose birth was no little reioycing through the whole Empire. Within two yeeres after, she was likewise deliuered of a goodlie Daughter, named *Griana*,[5] who growing to fourteene yeeres of age, was of such rare beautie and singuler good grace, as those that behelde her, esteemed her for the chiefest peece of workmanshippe that euer nature framed.[6]

Heereupon it chaunced, that *Tarisius*, Sonne[7] to the King of *Hungaria* (who had beene brought vp in company with the yonge Prince *Caniano*) fell into such amorous conceite of the yong Princesse, as hee deuoted him selfe onelie to her seruice,[8] beeing vnable to conceale the obiect of his affections, but that time made her acquainted with the cause of his alteration. Manie meanes he founde to entise her good opinion towards him, but she carrying a religious[9] zeale to loue in some other climate, made no reckoning of his importunate and dilligent seruice, which drewe a Hell of tormentinge thoughts vppon *Tarisius*, seeing his sute and

Palmerin d'Oliva: Part I 105

seruice so deeplie despised. Neuerthelesse, (to compasse his intent) he desired his Cozin *Caniano*, to cause a Tryumphe bee published, whereunto all Knights might be summoned, as well straungers as others:[10] not doubting but hee should speede so well in deedes of Armes, as thereby hee might deserue the loue of the
5 faire *Griana*, and so afterwardes make meanes by the Empresse to demaunde her in mariage, all which hee concealed from his Cozin *Caniano*: who verie gladlie didde consent to what *Tarisius* had requested, watching oportunitie to finde the Emperour his Father at leysure, when he made his highnesse acquainted with the whole enterprise, of himselfe and his Cozin *Tarisius*, desiring him that all
10 Knights might haue warning for preparation, against a day the next Moneth[11] appointed for the purpose. The Emperour was verie well pleased with his Sonnes requeste, accounting himselfe highlie honoured by his demaunde: whereuppon he caused Heraulds of Armes presentlie to bee dispatched, to signifie his intended Tournament through al Countries farre and neere. In the meane while *Tarisius*
15 coulde not rest daie nor night, but still endeuoured to doo what he iudged might please the Princesse *Griana*, to whom as yet he had not vttered the effect of his longing desire, albeit, by exteriour actions he dailie made shewe sufficient of his tormenting passions. But it so fell out not long after, that one daie in her walking he had sorted her alone from al the other Ladies and Gentlewomen, in a
20 place commodious for a Louers discourses, where falling from one argument to another, the furie of his oppressions imboldened him so far, that at length he brake with her in manner folowing.

Madame, you are not ignoraunt of the honourable assembly, that is appointed at the feaste ensuing, when I hope to receiue the order of Knighthoode, and if it
25 shall like you to thinke so well of mee, as to graunt mee one request, easie enough for you to affoorde me, perswade your selfe that I shal imagine my fortune equall with the happiest Knights that euer liued, in that it may be the onelie meane, whereby I shall enioy the prize and honour of the Triumphe. *Griana* knowing assuredlie that *Tarisius* bare her great affection, as I haue before rehearsed,
30 returned him this aunswere. In sooth Cozin, it would please me meruailous well, to bee the meane of so good fortune as you promise your selfe. Neuerthelesse, I haue not learned so little modestie, as to grant anie thing, before I knowe what is desired. When *Tarisius* vnderstoode her modest excuse, he perswaded himself that he should nowe obtaine that of her, whereof vntill that instant he had
35 liued in despaire: whereuppon, the teares standing in his eyes, he began in this manner. I humblie beseech you good Madame, to take in worth what I am to acquaint you with, for when I determined to smoother my greefe in secrete, the extremitie of my affection grew to such a surplusage, as it brake the stringes of my thoughts almost vowed for euer silent, to reueale that to you which my selfe
40 dare but reuerentlie thinke, such is my feare to displease you: otherwise, I knowe no meane canne warrant me from suddaine and cruell death, so setled is the vnspotted loue[12] I bare you, which when I striue to ouercome, and my selfe also, the more I would decrease it, the more it augmenteth, and that so strongelie, as

while you are in presence, my spirite forsaketh euerie part of mee, to liue in you onelie. For which cause I haue determined (if you thinke it good) to request you of the Emperour your Father for my Wife, and if he regarde me with so much honour: the Realme of *Hungaria* may well challenge, and my selfe likewise, the highest roome in earthlie felicitie, hauing a Mistresse of such vnspeakable qualitie. In the meane time, if you please to bestowe on me anie Iewell or fauoure, commaunding mee to weare it as your Knight and Seruaunt: you shall wel perceiue how aduenturous loue will be in defence of my right, by the aduantage I shall recouer in the vertue of a gifte so acceptable.

Griana, who made but slender account of his passions, and beeing not well pleased that he held her with such vaine discourses: modestlie returned him this aunswere. If you had such regarde of me as I well deserue, you woulde not attempt me with speeches so vnfitting my hearing: for if your desire be such as you giue me to vnderstand, you ought to make it knowne to the Emperor or Empresse, who haue greater authoritie ouer me then I haue my selfe. Therfore I desire you hencefoorth not to aduenture the like on perill of your life, otherwise I shall let you knowe howe highlie you offend me: on which condition I am content for this time to pardon your want of discretion, in that I perceiue my selfe to be the onelie cause thereof, in graunting you time and leysure thus priuatlie to assaile me, for which ouersight I repent mee at the verie harte. With which wordes shee floong away and left him alone, declaring by her countenaunce to be offended with his request, in that shee desired rather to die then accept him for her Husband, or to allowe him the name of her freende. If then *Tarisius* was driuen into a quandarie, wee neede not meruaile: wherefore troubled as he was, and not caring greatlie whether hee went, he entred the Empresse Chamber, where shee and her Son *Caniano* stoode conferring togeather, without saluting the one or other, he satte downe in a Chaire, and gaue such bitter sighes, as the Empresse hearing, was somewhat mooued therewith, doubting he had either receiued some greate iniurie, or els coulde not prouide himselfe so sufficientlie as he would for the Triumphe, wherupon she left her Sonne, and calling *Tarisius* aside, thus began with him. Nephewe,[13] I see you verie melancholie, which makes me to iudge, that you want some needefull thing for the Tournament, which my Sonne hath caused to be published. With which words she beheld *Tarisius* more wishlie then she had doone before, and perceiued the teares to trickle down his cheekes, which made her more desirous to knowe the cause of his greefe, but his hart was so confounded and shut vppe in anguish, as hee could not speake one word to her. Neuerthelesse, the Empresse, who loued him as her owne Sonne, founde so manie meanes to perswade him, as in the ende he disclosed the loue he bare to *Griana*, and the aunswere likewise which shee made him: whereby I am assured (quoth he) that nothing but death can cease my torments. The Empresse (who of her selfe did manie times determine to make that marriage) perceiuing nowe howe fitlie the occasion offred it selfe, began to resolue on the consumation thereof: and to content her Nephewe, in excusing the Princesse *Griana*, spake as followeth. Doo you Nephewe mislike the aunswere of my Daughter? beleeue me therein she didde but her dutie: for she cannot dispose of her selfe beeing yong and vnder controule, but[14] the Emperour and I, whom you ought firste to make acquainted with your request.[15] But since I perceiue how you are affected, I promise you I will confer with my Lorde the Emperour, and hope to preuaile so well in the cause, as you shall speede of that you moste desire. As they continued these discourses, they were giuen to vnderstande by a Messenger, that the Prince *Florendos* the Kinges son of *Macedon*[16] was newlie arriued, with a braue companie of Knights. But his comming to the Emperour was not as his vassaile or Subiect, because the kingdome of *Macedon* was at that time no way beholding[17] to the Empire, but onelie to see the faire yong Princesse *Griana*, the renowne of whose beautie and vertues had so peirced his thoughtes, as before he sawe her, he loued and honoured her,[18] so that for this cause onlie he iournied to *Constantinople*, where he was verie honourablie entertained bothe of the Emperour and his Sonne *Caniano* as also of the Empresse and faire *Griana*, who oftentimes hearde him reckoned and esteemed amongst the most honourable and gracious Princes, that liued at that daie.

Chapter II.

Howe the Empresse conferred with the Emperour, as concerning the mariage of theyr Daughter Griana wyth Tarisius, Sonne to the King of Hungaria, whereof they both determined, and of that which happened in the meane time.

The Empresse was not forgetfull of her promise made to her Nephewe *Tarisius*, but endeuoured by all meanes possible to find the Emperour at such leysure, as she might impart the whole to him: and because shee had so hardilie taken the matter vppon her, shee would gladlie it should sorte to effecte, as commonlie Women are couetous of their owne desires,[1] therefore no meruaile if shee were earnest in following her intent. Soone after, walking alone with the Emperour, and smoothlie couering the baite she was desirous he shoulde swallowe, shee desired him to graunt her one request, whereof shee woulde not willinglie be denied. The Emperour neuer before hearing her so importunate, consented at the first to whatsoeuer she demaunded: nowe perswading her selfe sure to speede, thus shee beganne.

My Lord, hauing often considered with my selfe, that our Daughter *Griana* is of yeeres and discretion able for a Husband,[2] I am the more desirous to see her honourablie bestowed. And for that the yonge Prince *Tarisius* hath beene trained vp in your Court, and (which I little thought) some good will appeareth to be betweene them: I should thinke it not amisse to vnite them in mariage togeather, for hardlie shall we finde (in mine opinion) a Lord of greater blood and birth then he, beeing heire apparant to the Crowne and kingdome of *Hungaria*, besides they hauing beene so longe time conuersant togeather in their yonger yeeres, will entertaine a more speciall regard of loue betweene them, then can be in anie other that may mooue the question to her. Madame (aunswered the Emperour) she is your Childe, and I doo not thinke but you would her good: therefore I like the motion well, for that indeede I esteeme so well of *Tarisius*, as of mine owne Sonne, and since wee haue so happilie fallen into these discourses, we will foorthwith certifie the King his Father by our Ambassadours, that we may vnderstand his opinion heerein. The Empresse gratified her Lord with verie hartie thankes, beeing not a little glad she had so well preuailed, wherefore immediatlie shee aduertised *Tarisius*. But for *Griana*, her affection was els where, for she bare a certaine secrete good liking to *Florendos* so soone as shee behelde him, hearing so great reporte of his knightlie bountie and prowesse, so that beholding them togeather, and their eyes deliuering the good conceite of eache other: one might easilie iudge, that Loue hadde so mightilie maistered her thoughts, as (if he consented) she had sette downe her reste for her choise, and hee on the other side was drawne into the same compasse, notwithstanding eache of them (for the time) concealed, what they rather desired should be known betweene them. Yet this hidden fire stroue to gaine place of issue, for diuers times the Princesse *Griana* beeing amongst her Ladies, talking of such

Palmerin d'Oliva: Part I 109

Knights as woulde shewe themselues at the Tournament: the Prince *Florendos* was commonlie first spoken of, and so highlie would the Ladies commende him beyonde all the other,[3] as *Griana* coulde not refraine from changing coloure, so that the alteration she founde in her spirite might be euidentlie perceiued, howbeit none of the Ladies as then noted it, and thus shee continued till the feast of Saint *Maria d'Augusta*,[4] which was the daie appointed for the Tournament, on which daie the Emperour knighted his Sonne *Caniano*, and *Tarisius* Nephewe to the Empresse, in honour wherof, hee held a greater and more magnificent Courte,[5] then before time hee had doone, for he suffered the Ladies to accompanie the Knights at the Table, albeit they were not wont to doo so often at that time, yet full well it pleased the Prince *Florendos*, who satte opposite to the Princesse *Griana*, during which time of Dinner, though manie piercing lookes, and smothered sighes were sent from eache other, as messengers of their semblable opinions, yet cunninglie they shaddowed all from being discerned.[6] But after the Tables were withdrawne, and eache one preparing for the Tourney: *Florendos* so well behaued himselfe, as he founde the meanes to speake priuatlie with his newe Freende, and thus he beganne.

Madame, the Heauens haue not a little fauoured mee, in sorting vs so commodiouslie togeather, that I may shewe you before I enter the Lystes royall, the occasion why I left the Realme of *Macedon*, to visite my Lord the Emperor. I sweare to you vpon my knightlie faith, that your gracious selfe was the onelie cause of my iourney, and while I liue, I shall euermore aduenture my selfe, in ought that may stand with your fauour and liking: and the first argument of my happinesse I should account, if you would commaunde mee this daie to arme my selfe for your Knight: otherwise, I must be content to absent my selfe, beeing assured that without your regard, it is vnpossible for me to doo any thing that can returne me estimation or honour. And albeit I haue not as yet doone anie seruice to you, whereby I shoulde deserue to be so accepted: yet such is the hope I repose in your vertuous nature, as you will not refuse my honest request, beeing the first I euer desired of you, and not the last (I truste) shall doo you honour. Nowe (as you haue heard before) *Griana* earnestlie affected *Florendos*: neuerthelesse, as a modest and well aduised Princesse, doubting leaste hee faigned those speeches of course, dissembling her selfe to be somwhat displeased, returned this aunswere.

I did not thinke (my Lord *Florendos*) that you woulde so farre forget your selfe, to holde mee with speeches not beseeming the Daughter of so great an Emperour as I am: neuerthelesse, knowing you are a Stranger, and ignoraunt (it may be) of the modestie which shoulde defende Knights deuising with Ladies, I will not vse such rigour towards you as I ought, yet must I tell you that I finde my selfe offended.[7] You desire that as my Knight you may enter the Tourney: for that I graunt ye, to the ende I may perceiue the effect of the prowesse, which each one so much commendeth in you, the rest, it is my pleasure that you forbeare. Madame (quoth he) if I haue vsed anie such speeches as agree not with your patience: for Gods sake (in my excuse) accuse my small compasse of libertie, which remaineth onelie at your disposition. What (quoth she) thinke you that I wil loue anie but he that must and ought be my Husbande? Ah sweete Ladie (said *Florendos*) that is it I[8] so earnestlie desire, and thinke not that I sollicite you with anie other kind of loue, but onelie to make you the Mistresse of my self, and altogeather to dispose of me and mine: for proofe whereof, I will heereafter imploy my selfe in the Emperours seruice, in such sorte as (if you like it) I hope to purchase his consent. Truelie Sir (quoth she) that onelie appertaines to the Emperor and not to mee, to whom you are to make known what you intende: for hee hath authoritie to commaunde, and I am bounde by duetie to obey. At which wordes the Empresse called her awaie, when *Florendos* making her courteous reuerence, departed to his Chamber to arme him selfe, for manie Knights were entred the Lystes, and he in short space came thether for companie: where hee behaued himselfe with such valoure, as he not onelie got the honour of the first daie, but of the foure daies folowing while the Tourneie endured, and wonne the prize which *Caniano* had prepared for him that best deserued it, which made him bee greatlie esteemed of the Emperour, and of the whole Court in generall, especiallie of the faire *Griana*, whose harte by little and little Loue brought in subiection, to the no small content of *Florendos*, which doubtlesse had the Prince *Tarisius* behelde, I imagine hee woulde haue hardlie liked it. But nowe during the time of these great Feastes, and Triumphes, Fortune the sworne enemie to all quietnes, presented the Emperor with other occasions, to cut off these pastimes and courtlie deuises: for after many of the Knights assembled at his Courte, had taken leaue to returne into their Countries, *Gamezio* Sonne to the Soldane of *Babilon*, who was on the Seas with a mightie Armie, intending to conquer *Alexandria*, was by extreamitie of winde and weather, driuen into the straights before *Constantinople*. Which when the Pilots and Marriners perceiued, not one amongst them but greatlie reioyced at this good fortune, but cheefelie *Gamezio*, who perswaded himself that his Gods[9] had sent him thether, that the moste noble and florishing Cittie of the world might fall into his handes: whereupon the windes somewhat appeased, and the Seas calmed, he assembled the chiefe and principall Captaines of his Armie, and thus began.

    My good freendes, I beleeue assuredlie, that our great Gods would not suffer vs to arriue in *Alexandria*, because wee went against them of our owne Law and Religion, but rather it liked them better, that we should addresse our selues to this Countrie of Christians, either to ruinate it altogeather, or at least to bring it vnder our obeysance. Therefore I am determined for this time, to defer the reuenge of the iniurie, which the King *Calameno*[10] did to the Soldane, and as much as in me lyes imploy my forces in conquest of this Countrey: for which cause, I desire that each of you would particularlie encourage your people, assuring them (if wee can conquer this Cittie) the riches thereof will counteruaile their paine and trauaile. The Captaines failed not to accomplish their charge to the vttermost, summoning euerie one presentlie to Armes: so prouiding their Shippes, their Ensignes and all thinges els needefull for their defence, they hoysed their sailes, making towards the Shoare, where with such prouision as they had they tooke landing, making such a noyse with their Drummes, Trumpets, and Clamors, as was heard with no small feare in euerie part of the Cittie. Neuertheles, they were receiued with better resistance then they looked for, as following the discourse of the Historie, you shall at large vnderstand.

Chapter III.

Of the battayle fought before the Cittie of Constantinople, betweene the Emperours power, and the Armie of Gamezio.

Immediatlie was this huge Armie on the Sea, discouered by the Senternelles of the Cittie, whereupon the rumour arose so greate, as the people ranne on heapes to defende the Hauen, where the Moores thought to haue made their first entrie. In the meane while, *Caniano, Tarisius*, and the other principall Knights, with their men of Armes, put themselues in equipage, ordayning their Armie in such warlike maner, as nowe they marche forth of the Cittie, to succour those places where the Moores gaue most eager assault. The Prince *Florendos* beeing left behinde,[1] made no little haste to gather his companie, and as he galloped with them by the Emperours Pallace, hee espied the Princesse *Griana* standing at her Chamber windowe, casting manie a ruefull looke towardes the Gates of the Cittie, which so deepelie peirced the gentle Princes harte, as immediatlie hee saide within himselfe. By Heauen (sweete Ladie) either will I die this day, or remooue the greefe that seemeth so neere to touche you. And with this resolution he gaue the spurres to hys Horse, when it was not long before hee got among the thickest of the Moores, where he behelde the enemie so strong, and the Christians so weake, as the day was like to prooue dangerous and dismall. For the Prince *Gamezio*, was esteemed one of the best Knights through all *Asia*, and that daie hee behaued himselfe so roughlie amongst the Christians:[2] as sooth to say, they were enforced to retire towardes the Cittie. Which when the Emperour behelde, who remained with no great strength to defend the Cittie, he was not a little greeued to see his men turne their backs on their enemies, and disperse themselues in such fearefull and dysmaying sorte. But *Florendos*, and the Prince *Caniano* vsed such meanes, as they got them soone in aray againe, and returned on the enemie with a fresh and hardie charge. *Tarisius* shewed himselfe verie valiaunt and aduenturous, stryuing by all the meanes he could to equall the Prince *Florendos*, who that daie gaue testimonie of most rare exploits so these three noble Gentlemen past from rancke to ranck, sending all to the earth that durst withstande them. *Gamezio* seeing his menne so bloodilie slaughtered on euerie side,[3] meeting with *Tarisius* woulde take reuenge on him, deliuering him such a cruell stroke on the heade with his sword, as downe he fell to the grounde so astonished, as his enemie might euen then haue slaine him: and so hee had doone but for the Prince *Florendos*, who seeing the Moore auauncing himselfe on his Styrrops, to reach a full stroke at *Tarisius* on the ground, lifted him quite out of his saddle with his Launce, and bare him so rudelie therewith to the earth, as breaking his necke with the fal, he gaue vppe the ghost.[4] When the Moores behelde *Gamezio* their General slaine, and the Christians make such hauocke of them, theyr harts fayling them to make further resist, fled so fast as they could towards their Ships, when had not the night too soone preuented them, not one had escaped death or taken prysoner, notwithstanding, the greatest part were put

Palmerin d'Oliva: Part I   *113*

to the sworde, diuers making hast to get awaie by boates, were drowned in the Sea, and manie of account brought backe prisoners, thus with victorie returned the Emperours power to the Cittie. So manie of the Moores as escaped to theyr shyps, beeing not a little glad they were so farre from their enemies: sette sayle
5 and returned towardes the Soldane, to whom they declared the summe of theyr misfortune, as also the death of his Sonne *Gamezio*, which tidinges made him well nye mad with rage and anger. But beeing old and crazed with sicknesse, he could not goe in person to reuenge his death, which made him vowe and sweare, that so soone as his other Sonne came to yeeres to beare Armes, he wold sende
10 him with such a puissant strength, as easilie he should destroy the Emperour and his Countrie: in the meane time, he sent the raunsome to redeeme them that were taken prisoners, where we will leaue the Soldane, and returne to *Caniano* and the other Princes, who beeing nowe come againe to the Cittie, the Emperour hauing hearde the worthie seruice *Florendos* had doone that same day (and
15 how he had receiued some fewe daungerous woundes in the battaile) sent for him in all haste that might bee to his Pallace, because[5] his owne Chirurgions and Phisitions shoulde haue care of him. So was *Florendos* brought very honourablie to the Pallace, and conducted to a Chamber beseeming hys estate,[6] where the Empresse and *Griana* came presentlie to visite him: to whom the Prince *Caniano*
20 recounted, howe *Tarisius* had beene slaine by *Gamezio*, but that *Florendos* stepped betweene his death and him, but (quoth hee) the Moore excused *Tarisius*,[7] for in my presence he gaue his laste farewell to this world, so that nowe we may saie the victorie is ours, albeit before it hunge in hard suspence. While *Caniano* continued these and such like speeches, *Griana* cast manie a sweete looke on the Prince
25 *Florendos*, and hee aunswered his obiect with the selfe same messengers of hys hart: thus contented they their seuerall passions with such modest and vertuous regarde,[8] as none present could suspect their secrete meaning. The Empresse and her Daughter courteouslie taking their leaue, *Florendos* and his Chirurgions we leaue a while togeather, they to apply medicines to his woundes, and he the
30 remembraunce of his Mistresse to his hart.[9] On the morrowe the Emperour with his nobilitie rode foorth of the Cittie, to see the slaughtered bodies, among whom they founde *Gamezio*, who was easily known by the richnes of his Armour, which *Caniano* caused to bee taken from the deade bodie, and brought to *Florendos* as the deserte of his trauaile:[10] when the Emperour himselfe, (the more to honour
35 him) made present thereof to *Florendos* at his returne, with these speeches. My noble Cozin,[11] by your valour and Knightlie prowesse, haue I had the vpper hand of mine enemies, may I but liue to requite thy good desarts, I shall account my selfe happie and fortunate: notwithstanding, account of me as thy Kinsman and continual freende, and bee there ought in my power shall like thee to demaunde,
40 on the faith of a King I vowe to giue it thee.

   Florendos most humblie thanked the Emperor, as well for the great honour he did him, as also for his large and bountifull promise, wheron he builded so assuredlie, as he almost accounted faire *Griana* for his owne:[12] who with the

Empresse her Mother came dailie to visite him, by which meanes theyr mutuall loue encreased more and more, and *Florendos* recouered his health in the shorter time, when he solicited the Emperour with this sute following.

Chapter IV.

Howe Florendos intreated the Emperour, to giue him in mariage his Daughter Griana, and what answere the Emperour made him.

After that *Florendos* was throughlie healed of the woundes, which hee had receiued in fight against the Moores: finding the Emperour one daie at leysure, and alone in his Chamber, hee began to salute him as after followeth. My dread and soueraigne Lorde, so princely and gracious haue your fauours beene towards me, since first I entred your royall Courte, as the King my Father and I shall neuer aunswere such exceeding courtesie. And to the ende this kindnes may rather increase then any waie diminish, I beseeche your highnesse not to denie me one request, which among the infinite number of your princelie graces towardes me, I shall account it to exceede all other.[1] In breefe, it is the Princesse *Griana* your Daughter, whose loue and honourable fame, made me forsake the Realme of *Macedon*, onelie to desire her in marriage, if either anie desert in me, or your owne princelie good conceite, might repute me woorthie so high a fauour.[2] And for I woulde not your highnes should anie waie misconceiue of mee, as that the motion proceedeth from a youthfull and vnaduised heade, or that I haue enterprised it, without the good liking of the King my Father: I humblie desire your Maiestie to reste satisfied bothe in these and all other opinions, in that my Fathers consent, brought mee with no little speede hether, and the hope of yours during my aboade heere, hath taughte me to place my loue with discretion, and continue it wyth honourable vnspotted loyaltie. With this addition (vnder your highnesse correction) that were she mine as I am wholie hers: the faithfull seruice of a thankfull Sonne, shoulde aunswere the gentlenes of so good a Father, and the irreuocable vowes of holie loue, assure *Griana* of her *Florendos*. Right deerelie did the Emperour loue the Prince *Florendos*, as had he beene his owne Sonne *Caniano*, his knightlie valour and manifold other vertues iustlie inducing hym thereto: and gladlie he would haue consented to his request, if his promise made vnto *Tarisius* did not binde him to the contrarie, whereupon he returned him this aunswere. Beleeue me good Cozin, I am not a little agreeued that I cannot satisfie your gentle request, for that *Tarisius* Nephewe to the Empresse hath alreadie preuented mee: to him haue I past my promise for my Daughter, and dailie I expect the Ambassadours comming from *Hungaria* to finishe the mariage, so that I had rather loose the best of my Citties, then it should be said I falsified my worde.[3] Notwithstanding, of one thing I can assure you, that you are far higher in my grace and fauour then he: yet necessitie is without lawe,[4] and the regarde of mine honour must intreate you to hold me excused.

Greatlie abashed was the Prince *Florendos*, seeing in one instant that hope strooken dead, that had maintayned his life[5] since his comming to *Constantinople*: and so nypt in the heade was he with the Emperours answere, as hee stoode a good while in a studie not speaking a worde, at last he began thus. God forbidde that so great a Prince shoulde breake his promise by my occasion: neuerthelesse, my truth and loyaltie to your highnesse shall not any way diminishe, but I shall remaine the most forward in duetie, of any that owe seruice and alleageaunce to your Maiestie. Neyther will I (sayd the Emperour) imagine the worse of you, but loue you rather better then I did before. Then entered diuers Noble men and Gentlemen, which made them breake off from further speeches, and *Florendos* taking his leaue, went to his Chamber, so full of greefe and extreame heauines,[6] as easilie he could haue beene induced to commit some violence vpon himselfe: but casting himselfe vpon his bed,[7] he thus beganne to breath foorth the furie of his passions,[8] to ease the heauie burthen of his oppressed spirite.

    Vnhappy wretch that I am beyonde all other, what hope of life canst thou flatter thy self withal, seeing the meane that should maintaine the continuaunce thereof, forbiddes thee (fonde man) to hope any longer. What angry Planet gouerned thy natiuitie,[9] that he to whom thou gauest life, should this day be the cause to ende thine owne. Beleeue me *Tarisius*, had I made tryal of this inconuenience before, hardlie shoulde I haue put my personne in such daunger amongst the Moores, to sheelde thy life: but in defending the sworde out of thy throate, I haue deseruedlie thrust it in mine owne,[10] so that by lengthning thy daies, I haue expyred mine owne date, and that with a death so miserable and cruell, as no enemie whatsoeuer would wish to another. But were it not that my duetie to the good Emperour countermaundeth me, thou couldest not with such ease either outbraue me in my looue, or thus vsurpe the gracious fauoure of my Mistresse *Griana*, were affection ballanced with desert, or loue measured by vertue as it is by opinion. Notwithstanding, to die for her loue I shall account my selfe happie, in that she cannot but pittie my vnluckie death, and my spirite should passe with greater quiet to his ende, if she knewe with what content I take my destenie: but fayre *Griana*, would God I had either not seene thee at al, or Fortune had beene fauourable to me in choise. At which words the extremitie of his passions tooke away the libertie of his speeche,[11] so that he could not finish what hee woulde gladlie haue spoken, but falling from his bedde to the grounde in a swoune, amazed one of his Esquires that was in the nexte Chamber, who hearing the fall, ran in immediatlie, where seeing his Maister lying deade (in his iudgement) ran and called *Frenato*, who was Cozin to *Florendos*, and one that knewe most of his priuate affayres, notwithstanding, hee was ignorant in the cause of this accident, who taking him vppe in his armes, with colde water and vinagre caste in his face, at length he got life into him againe, when *Florendos* opening his eyes, and seeing his Cozin so busie about him, breathing foorth two or three bitter sighes, saide. My deere freende and Cozin, I beseeche you hinder not the ende and issue of my life, for beeing out of all hope to recouer my Ladie *Griana*, there is no meane left to maintaine my life. When *Frenato* heard these wordes, hee doubted that the Prince had receiued some contrarie aunswere from the Emperour, as concerning the marriage betweene him and his Daughter, for whose loue onelie hee left the kingdome of *Macedon*: wherfore, he perceiuing that she must bee the onelie meane to ease his torment, hee began thus roundlie to aunswere the Prince. And

Palmerin d'Oliva: Part I

what of this? must you therefore dispaire? Alas (said *Florendos,*) what would yee haue me doo? the Emperour hath long since past his promise for her to *Tarisius*, as his highnes assured me by his own wordes. Verie well Sir (answered *Frenato*) but doo you know if she haue giuen her consent? I promise you I am perswaded that she loues him not, but that her fauourable regarde is much more towardes you then him: and for you saye so much, to morrow will I sounde the bottome of this matter, so that (if I can) I will frustrate the Emperours intent towardes *Tarisius*. Doo you in the meane time but learne to dissemble your greefe, and shewe not your selfe *mal content*[12] for anie thing that hath beene saide: but bee of good cheere, and referre your fortune in this case to the successe of myne endeuours. These and such like perswasions *Frenato* vsed to the Prince, whom he thus left in his Chamber, and returned to the Pallace as was his manner. All this while the Emperour bethought himselfe, on the speeches that had passed betweene him and *Florendos*, which made him the night following, to discourse theron with the Empresse, perswading her, that hee coulde more willinglie accept of hym for his Sonne then *Tarisius*. But she who highlie fauoured her Nephewe, reprooued his opinion with manie answers, so that by importunate intreaties, teares, and other subtill fetches, which Women are wont to vse to accomplish theyr desires, she so farre disswaded the Emperour, as hee promised her againe not to giue her to anie other, then to him to whom he first past his worde. Of which wordes the Empresse was not a little glad,[13] and therefore all that night shee deuised, by what meanes she might from that time forward so much as in her laie, hinder *Florendos* from speaking to her Daughter: whereupon, she dailie kept the Chamber of presence, and helde a more strickt looke on *Griana* then before shee had doone, which greatlie increased the passions of *Florendos*, and brought him into so weake estate, as the learned Phisitions coulde not deliuer the cause of his sicknes, to the no small greefe of the Emperour, but especiallie of *Caniano*, yet for all this woulde not the Empresse at anie time visite him, because shee woulde hinder the occasion of her Daughters seeing him, remembring what speeches had past betweene him and the Emperour. And albeit *Griana* made no outward shewe thereof, yet in her harte shee was greatlie displeased at her Mothers dealings,[14] so that one day when her Brother *Caniano* came to see her, to recount vnto her in what extreamitie he had left his freendlie companion, and what greefe it would be to him if he died, as he greatlie doubted: What my Lord (quoth she) it is not so I hope? Yes certainlie (quoth he) and I feare he will very hardlie escape this day. At which wordes the water stoode in her eyes, yet so well as she coulde shee dissembled her passions: neuerthelesse, she could not holde it in, but said. I meruayle much that the Empresse my Mother makes so slender account of him, as since his sicknes shee woulde not vouchsafe once to visite him: I feare she hath forgotten what good hee did for vs, that day when he valiantly slew the Turke *Gamezio*. Beleeue me (my good Lord and Brother) I am hartilie sorrie for his sicknes, for if he die (as heauen forbidde quoth shee secretlie)[15] the Emperour my Father shall loose more then hee thinketh on, the great seruice hee hath doone for him already, may giue instaunce of my words,[16] and more he beeing the Sonne of so great a Prince as he is. By this time had such extreame greefe ouerburdened her hart, as she was constrained (feigning to goe to the Empresse Chamber) to leaue her Brother, that she might alone by her selfe bemoane her freends hard fortune.[17]

Chapter v.

Howe Griana sent a Ring to the Prince Florendos by Cardina her Mayde, desiring him (as he loued her) to comfort himselfe, and of the aunswere he sent her.

So soone as *Griana* hadde left her Brother, she went into her chamber, where more and more shee lamented for the sicknes of *Florendos*, and with her teares[1] shee coupled these discourses. May it be that anie liuing creature, can deserue so greeuous punishment as I doo, that endanger the life of the woorthiest Knight in the worlde? Vnhappy that I am,[2] that loue, yea the loue he beares to mee, should bring so braue a Gentleman to so hard an exigent:[3] but if he die, such iust vengeaunce will I take vpon my selfe, as I wyl not remaine one howre aliue after him, and let our ghostes seeke their owne quiet in death, that Fortune would not affoorde vs in life.[4] Yet will I thus farre first aduenture, and that before any sleepe enter these eies of mine, try if it consist in my power to ease his extreamitie, that buyes my loue at too deere a price.[5] And in this anguish of minde she called one of her Damoselles, the Daughter of her Nurse named *Cardina*,[6] whom aboue the rest she trusted most, and to her she began in manner following. *Cardina*, thou knowest the loue I alwaies bare thy Mother, and for her sake howe well I haue thought of thee, I haue knowne thee long time a true and faithfull Seruaunt: but nowe *Cardina* is a time beyonde all other, to make tryall of thy truth, and to witnesse thy loyaltie to me, onelie as thou art sure, so to bee secrete, and so secrete as I must put my life and honour into thy secrecie.[7] *Cardina*, who was wise, and of good gouernement, hearing *Griana* vse such earnest speeches: imagined that she would commit no common matter to her trust with such coniuration, whereuppon she modestlie returned thys aunswere. Madame, rather had I be torne peecemeale in sunder, then anie thing you commaunde for secrete, shoulde by me be reuealed without your licence: and so assure your selfe, that while I liue, you shall finde mee as faithfull in deede, as I promise in worde.[8] I neuer hitherto (quoth the Princesse) had other opinion of thee, listen nowe therefore what I shall commaunde thee. I haue vnderstoode for certaine *Cardina*, that the greeuous sicknes of the Prince *Florendos*, is caused by verie earnest loue which hee beares to me,[9] and for I account it great pittie to loose so good a Knight, doo so much as take the paines to goe to him from me: and saie I desire him to bee of good cheere, and if there bee any thing in my power may doo him good, I will gladlie accomplish it, as she that loues him as her own selfe, and to assure him thereof, saie I sende him this Ring, which I wyll him to keepe as a pledge of my loue. Madame (answered *Cardina*) Fortune[10] speede me so well, as my paines may giue ease to both your passions: and might my sentence like you Madame, I knowe no Knight so worthy your loue as *Florendos*. Goe then (sayd *Griana*) and returne againe so soone as thou canst. So went *Cardina* straite to the lodging of the Prince *Florendos*, at the entraunce whereof, shee met the Prince *Caniano* so heauie and pensiue as might be, because he perceiued his

Freend to consume awaie euerie day more and more. But *Cardina*, who had well learned her lesson, stept aside, and would not be seene of *Caniano*: who beeing gone, shee went vp to the Chamber, where when shee was readie to enter, she hearde the Prince complaine in this sort. Ah poore wretch, must thou needes die without anie hope of remedie?[11] And as he would haue proceeded on, *Cardina* stepped to him, and after she had saluted him, said to him secretelie, that the Princesse *Griana* had sent her to him, to vnderstand of his health, and beleeue me good Prince (quoth she) I neuer sawe Ladie so sorrowfull for your sicknes, as she is. She commendeth her selfe to your honour most hartilie, and hath sent you this Ring, as an earnest of the looue she beares you, desiring you to bee of good cheere and comfort your selfe, because she desires to see you, to confer with you of matters that concerne you bothe neerelie. These wordes so rauished the spirit of *Florendos*, as a good while he doubted, whether he dreamed, or that hee might giue credite to what he hearde: for albeit he knewe the messenger so well as anie in the Courte, yet coulde he not perswade himselfe that hee was so fortunate. At length (betweene hope and dispayre) he tooke the Ring, which he entertained with manie deuoute kysses, and embracing *Cardina* so well as hee coulde, thus answered. Alas my sweete freende, may it bee possible that my Ladie hath such regard of him, who neuer was able to doo her anie seruice? Doubt not thereof my Lorde (aunswered *Cardina*) and if you will declare your loue answerable to hers in vertue, you must giue testimonie thereof by comforting your person, that she may see you so soone as may be. Ah fayre Virgin (quoth he) let my whole life be imployed, in what shall like her diuine nature to commaunde me: and I assure you, that these tydings hath breathed such newe life into my verie soule, as alreadie I finde my selfe wonderfullie chaunged, yea, and that in such sorte, as before three daies bee past, I shall attende her gracious will with seruiceable dilligence. In the meane while, I shal desire you faire Freend, to let my soueraigne Mistresse vnderstand, that I kisse her highnesse hande[12] in humble duetie, and had ere this giuen farewell to this life, hadde not her sweete regard called me againe from death. Thus parted *Cardina* from the Prince, taking her way speedily towards *Griana*, who longed not a little to heare from *Florendos*, whom she had made Lord of her gentle affections.[13]

Palmerin d'Oliva: Part I   *121*

Chapter vi.
Howe Cardina recited to the Princesse Griana, what speeches had past betweene her and Florendos, and of the counsell shee gaue her Mistresse, to conferre with him in the Garden so soone as he was recouered.

5   *Cardina* thus dispatched from *Florendos*, made no little haste towardes the Princesse, who remained all this while silent in her Chamber, and no sooner perceiued she *Cardina* to enter, but she demaunded if *Florendos* receiued her token[1] in good part or no. Beleeue me Madame (answered *Cardina*) I thinke you neuer did anie thing in all your life, whereby you coulde obtaine more honour and applause,[2] then by that you vouchsafed to doo at this instant, for in my iudgment you haue performed a miracle, in giuing him life that was in the very iawes of death. Then from point to point shee recounted the talke passed betweene them, first howe she founde him in the midst of his regrets, and lastlie what message hee had sent by her. Thus while *Cardina* continued her discourse, euery worde tooke hold on the gentle hart of the Princesse,[3] and wounded her with such pittifull regarde of the Prince his torments:[4] as what she desired inwardlie, shee shaddowed with modestie, as lothe to receiue shame in her loue, hauing caryed her selfe with such honour all her life,[5] quoth shee to *Cardina*. Howe might I (good Seruaunt) ease this waightie oppression?[6] Verie well (said *Cardina*) when Fortune alloweth opportunitie. But thou knowest (quoth *Griana*) a Princesse as I am, to be seene secrete with so braue a Gallant,[7] dooth greatlie hazard my life and honour. As for that Madame, (saide *Cardina*) my Sister can better aduise you then I, or any that I know, by her meanes may you speake with your Knight,[8] the brauest Gentleman in the world, and one whom I knowe is so farre deuoted yours, as hee will rather loose his life, then impeache your honour anie waie: and otherwise then in loyaltie to make you his Ladie and wyfe, I am well assured he loueth not, which loue (Madame) you may well entertaine.[9] Returne then *Cardina* (quoth the Princesse) to my Lorde *Florendos*, and assure him that so soone as he is recouered, I wyll come and speake with him, in such place where we may well aduenture: and desire hym as he loueth me, that it may bee with all conuenient speede. *Cardina* without anie further delay, went with this message to the Prince *Florendos*: who hartened himselfe so well vpon these speeches, as within six dayes he found himselfe thorowlie amended, whereof the Emperour and *Caniano* hys Sonne, was not a little glad: but *Tarisius* was scant well pleased thereat, for he had conceiued a secrete iealousie, because he was so earnest in affection towards *Griana*, who by her Mayd *Cardina* had warned *Florendos*, that the night following he should come into the Garden, whereinto her Chamber had a secrete entraunce,[10] and there woulde he and she conferre of their loue, without suspicion of any. *Florendos* seeing these affayres sort to so good ende, purposed what euer happened, not to fayle the time and place: which made him thinke this day a yeere in length, so long hee looked and desired for the night. But nowe the wished howre is come, when *Florendos* with his Cozin *Frenato*

(who was priuie to the Princes secrete loue) departed from their lodginges, and comming to the Garden, they sawe the wall was verie high and harde to climbe, notwithstanding, greater thinges are possible to Louers, cheefely when a cause of such waight is in hand, so that in short time *Florendos* had gotte the top of the Wall, and afterward went to the place where *Griana* stayed his comming, who had no bodie with her but *Lerina*, Sister to *Cardina*, to whom likewise she thorowly bewrayed her secrets. He hauing espied them, came and fell on his knee before the Princesse, but she tooke him vppe in her armes, embracing him so sweetlie: as *Lerina* withdrew her selfe amongst the Trees, not with anie intent or feare to displease them, but with a certaine kinde of greefe which ouercame her, that shee wanted a Freende to participate with her in loue, as her Mistresse hadde, before whom *Florendos* beeing on his knee, sayd. Madame, by vertue of your commaundement I am thus bolde to enter your presence, yeelding my whole abilitie to you,[11] as to the diuine Goddesse that hath sheelded me from death, which grace seeing your princelie nature hath affoorded me, my life for euer heereafter remaines at your soueraigne pleasure: the vnfeigned promise whereof, I binde to you by irreuocable vowes, but especiallie by my faith, the onelie ornament of a true Knight, that I desire no longer to breathe this ayre, then to honour your name with my continual seruice, for life without your grace and fauour, is more yrkesome to me then a thousande deathes.[12] But by your fauour my Lorde (answered *Griana*) howe or from whence hath this hote loue[13] sprunge, let mee knowe I desire you? Madame (quoth he) as I haue heretofore, so at this time I assure you, that in my natiue Countrie of *Macedon*, I hearde the renowne of your excelling beauty, at which verie instant I dedicated my selfe onelie yours:[14] and euer since continuing in this religious seruice,[15] I haue so confidentlie set downe my rest, in gracious regard of your sweete selfe, as beeing yours in seruice, I liue, if otherwise, I die. In sooth (said the Princesse) I see then you haue giuen your selfe wholie mine, and so I am well contented to accept you. Then Madame (quoth he) to seale the assuraunce of this diuine fauour you haue doone me, let mee intreate to kisse those sweete lippes,[16] that deliuered the sentence I haue long looked for. Which to grant, though (for modesties sake) at first she seemed daintie, yet at length looue had so supprized her, as he needed not striue when no resistaunce was offered. Thus with teares and solemne kysses, they breathed into eache others soule, the mute arguments of their loue, and faire *Cynthia* amiablie fauouring this delicate encounter, added such courage to the minde of this louelie Champion: as breaking his Launce in the face of *Venus*, hee bequeathed the successe of his deuoire to the gracious aspect of that Planet.[17] And among a number of soft and sweete loue speeches, he discoursed to her his talke with the Emperour her Father, howe he had requested her in marriage, and howe he excused his consent by the promise he had made before to *Tarisius*, through the dailie and earnest perswasions of the Empresse. Notwithstanding (quoth he) in respect you haue not consented thereto, I hope they shall finde themselues farre beyonde their reckoning. Nowe for the Princesse, she neuer knewe that *Tarisius* had

Palmerin d'Oliva: Part I   123

laboured to haue her to hys Wife, because she made so light account of him, as she wold rather die then consent thereto, whereuppon shee returned *Florendos* this aunswere. The Emperour my Father hath reason to thinke hardlie of my Mother, and great discredite will it be to her,[18] to procure my mariage against my
5 wil, for neuer shall I consent thereto: and therefore my Lord[19] I desire your aduise, how I may preuent this ensuing daunger. Madame (answered *Florendos*) my deuise is layd already, so please you to accept thereof: I will conuey you hence secretlie, and before the Emperour or any one know of it, into my Countrey of *Macedon*, where I and mine shall entertaine you with great and reuerend honour,
10 and you shall be our gracious Lady and Princesse. Beleeue me (sayd she) it is doubtfull in such a iourney what daungers may happen, notwithstanding, hauing vowed my selfe onlie yours:[20] be it to the lyking or dislyking of my Father and Mother, I had rather breake through the straights of a greater hazarde, then be forced to marrie him, whome while I liue I can not like, therefore doo you expecte
15 the aduauntage of the time, and I will aduenture with you whether you please. Madame (answered *Florendos*) continue you this resolution, and referre the rest to my charge, which you shall see effected ere three daies be past: in the meane while I entend to take my leaue of the Emperour your Father, with this excuse,[21] that the King my Father commaundeth my returne home, for which cause I will
20 sende my traine before, reseruing onelie but tenne of my best Knights to accompany me. For that (quoth *Griana*) doo what you thinke best, and without anie further expecting me in this place, certifie me how things happen by your Cozin *Frenato*, or my Maide *Cardina*. But nowe you see the daie beginnes to breake, wherfore let me desire you to depart, that no scandall or suspition arise of our
25 meeting. *Florendos* kissing the Princesse hand, (though longer hee woulde haue stayde) humbly tooke hys leaue,[22] and by the helpe of *Lerina*, hee got ouer the Wall againe, where *Frenato* stayed his comming, to whom when he was entred his lodging, hee imparted the appointment betweene him and the Princesse, desiring him to discharge his trayne, except ten of his best approoued Knights,
30 to help him if any hinderance preuented his intent: as for the rest, they should be going on before, and stay his comming at an appointed place, three daies iourney from *Constantinople*. In the morning he awaited the Emperours comming abroad, to whom he said, that he had receiued Letters from the King his Father, with expresse commaundement to make speedy returne home: therefore my good
35 Lord (sayd hee) I desire to depart with your fauourable lyking, and in respect I may not contrary where I am bounde to obey, I intend to morrow to set forward on my iourney, assuring your highnesse, that in what place I shall chaunce to come, I am yours in loyall and faithfull seruice. My good Cozin (aunswered the Emperour) I giue you thankes with all my hart, for the honour you haue doone
40 me with your gentle presence: and if you haue occasion to vse mee in ought, you shall perceiue howe highlie I loue and esteeme of you. My Lord (said *Florendos*) I desire to deserue the great kindnes I haue found alreadie: so taking his leaue, the Emperour embraced him, and as he issued forth of the Chamber, he met the

Prince *Caniano*, of whom he tooke his leaue likewise, who desired him to staie three or foure daies longer.[23] In which time there came to the Courte certaine Ambassadours, which the Kinge of *Hungaria* had sent to the Emperour, to conclude the mariage betweene his Sonne *Tarisius* and the Princesse *Griana*, the Duke of *Gramay* beeing cheefe in this Embassade, who was accompanied with manie Knightes and Gentlemen of name and account, to whom the Empresse gaue verie gracious welcome, in that shee had priuatlie procured this their comming. As these Ambassadours entred the great Chamber, *Caniano* and *Tarisius* who accompanied them, perceiued *Griana* to withdrawe her selfe aside very sad and mellanchollie: whereupon *Caniano* came vnto her (greatlie abashed at her angry countenaunce) and thus hee began. Fayre Sister, at this time when you ought to shewe the moste cheerefull countenaunce, you are more sadde then of long time I haue seene you: me thinkes[24] you haue good occasion to be merrie, seeing the Emperour my Father hath prouided you so braue a Husbande, as is my Cozin the Prince *Tarisius*, who I am sure loues you as his owne life. Ah brother (quoth she) I knowe not what should mooue him so to doo, seeing I neuer thought so well of him: and more gladlie could I entertaine mine owne death, then bee constrained to loue where I cannot.[25] These words did *Tarisius* easily vnderstand, notwithstanding he made shewe as though he did not: but going to the Empresse he desired her to stay there with the Emperour, seeing the Ambassadours were come from the King his Father,[26] that what was begun as concerning him and *Griana*, might nowe be finished according to her[27] promise. Vppon this occasion, the Empresse called *Griana* aside, and with smoothe and sweete speeches began to breake with her, howe for her good shee had induced the Emperour, to giue her in marriage to her Cozin *Tarisius*, and what honourable aduantage she shoulde receiue thereby: wherefore faire Daughter (saide she) resolue your selfe with childlike[28] obedience, to thinke well of that your Parents haue determined. All these perswasions coulde not drawe one pleasing word from the Princesse, but shee excused her selfe still, by the desire shee had to remaine as shee was,[29] and rather then to marrie shee would take a religious life vpon her: with which words she brake into such teares as the Empresse was constrained to leaue her alone, not doubting to finde her the next time in better tune. *Griana* then considering with her selfe, how she shoulde be enforced at length to yeelde, whether she woulde or no, if *Florendos* did not the sooner accomplish his enterprise: called *Cardina* vnto her, and sent her with this charge to *Florendos*, that that present night he shoulde not fayle to meete her in the Garden, where she wold be readie to depart with him,[30] otherwise he should neuer gaine the like opportunitie, with which message *Cardina* departed.

Chapter VII.
How Florendos came that night to the Garden, to conclude what he and Griana had intended, and what happened to them.

Florendos vnderstanding the will of his Mistresse, with great dilligence laboured to execute what they had intended, and taking his leaue at the Courte, feigned he woulde returne no more, but take his waie straight towards *Macedon.*[1] *Tarisius,* whose iealousie increased euerie daie more and more, sette priuie spies to watch euerie night, who went in and out at the Princesse Chamber, and albeit of long time his labors were frustrate, yet at length he and his spies perceiued, how he whome hee most enuied, mounted the Garden Wall where the Princesse lay: for *Florendos* hauing left his companie without the Cittie, accompanied with *Frenato,* and both of them well armed, he priuilie returned againe to the Pallace, thinking about midnight to carrie her away, for whose loue hee had thrust himselfe into this daungerous hazarde. Thus hauing left their Horses without the Cittie with their Pages, and being come to the Garden Wall, *Frenato* helping the Prince to get vppe, *Tarisius* and his men, who vnhappilie lay there in ambush, ran violentlie vpon him, crying all aloude, kyll, kill these villaines that woulde dishonour the Emperours Pallace. At which wordes, *Florendos* and *Frenato* seeing themselues discouered, presentlie drewe their swordes, and beganne to laie about them verie valiantlie, *Florendos* giuing *Tarisius* so cruell a stroake on the heade, that hee fell downe to the ground as he had beene dead, and two or three of his companie with him: which when the rest behelde, they gotte ouer the Wall, and running with great clamour into the Cittie, cryed, helpe helpe *Tarisius,* whom *Florendos* (seeking to rob the Emperours Pallace) hath cruelly murdered. This noyse was heard by *Griana, Lerina,* and *Cardina,* who were in the Garden staying for *Florendos,* which did so amaze the hardiest of the three, as they knewe not what countenance to sette on the matter: especiallie *Griana,* whom this feare had strooken into a deade traunce, but *Lerina* and her Sister taking her vp in their armes, conueyed her into her Chamber, and soone after into her bed, when recouering her selfe, in extreame weeping thus spake. Alas miserable wretch that I am, dooth Fortune employ al meanes she can for my destruction? well, let her doo the vttermoste spight shee can, for I am well assured before it be long, that death shall tryumphe aboue all her discourtesies. *Cardina* seeing her so weepe and wring her handes, and as it were readie to fall into despayre, began to perswade her in thys sorte. Madame, it is no time nowe to vse these extremeties, for Gods sake learne to couer your passions: to the ende the Emperour may not detect vs, beeing assured that as yet we were not perceiued, and if you can but content your selfe, all this tumult will soone be ouercome. I pray thee (quoth *Griana*) leaue me alone, and goe see (if thou canst) what is become of *Florendos,* that I may know whether hee be taken or slaine. So went *Cardina,* and standing among others, as one that knewe nothing, behelde all. During this hote tumult, *Frenato* seeing trouble encreasing more and more, followed the matter with such dilligence, as he got *Florendos* forth of the throng, and the darknesse of the night was such, as they easily compassed to get out of the Cittie, where their Pages stayed with their Horses, wheron they mounted and set on away. But the Prince *Florendos* would manie times haue returned backe againe, so lothe was hee to leaue her whom he loued so deerely, for being out of all hope to see her againe, he esteemed his life of no value or account. In which impatience, he rent his comelie locks of haire, and haled his flesh with great violence, whereuppon *Frenato* thus spake to him. Why howe nowe my Lorde? wyll you in seeking honour wound your selfe with shame, or in arguing your loue to your Ladie, endaunger her life?[2] desire you to loose your selfe, and her also for euer? Beleeue me Cozin, this verie hardlie beseemes you, that the subtill dealing of a cowardlie Knight, should make you thus to forget your self.[3] No no good Cozin, it is now no time to declare these shewes: let vs therefore make speede to our companie, and if you thinke good, we will sende one secretlie backe to the Cittie, to vnderstand the ende of this troublesome broyle, and wee in the meane time may set forward towards *Macedon*. Ah sweete Cozin (quoth *Florendos*) you speake as the man that cannot comprehende my torments, thinke you it is possible for me to liue, leauing that rare creature in such perrill, for whose loue a Hell of greefes hath martired my soule?[4] By my knightlie faith I sweare, that death is a thousand times more welcome to me, then to be maistered by this one conceit, that I shold liue an hower out of her gracious seruice. Well well Sir (sayd *Frenato*) what you may not doo now, referre till better conuenience, and let vs set on before the daie light descry vs: otherwise, in seeking to defende *Griana*, your selfe shalbe witnes[5] of her reproche and condemnation. *Florendos* perceiuing his Cozin did aduise him for the best, was well contented to be ruled by him, so giuing the spurres to their Horses, stayed not till they ouertooke the rest of their companie: when he dispatched an Esquire presentlie backe to the Cittie, commaunding him straightly to direct soone to the King his Fathers Court, the successe of euerie thing that happened in his absence.

But now to returne where before we left, *Cardina* had not long staide in this hurlie burley, but shee perceiued the Emperour was rysen, who in all hast caused his Guarde to arme themselues to helpe *Tarisius*: for by this time hadde the two Knights which escaped, aduertised in the Courte, that they tooke *Florendos* as he was climbing the Garden wall, to goe to dishonour the Princesse *Griana*. At which report the Emperour was so mooued, as he went in greate furie to his Daughters Chamber, whom he founde in her bed, more likelie to die then liue: but necessitie (whereof manie doo often make a vertue)[6] made her couer her weakenes with a faire shewe of courage, so that when she see him enter, shee wrapped her selfe in her night Mantle, and came before him, to whom hee beganne in this furious manner. Thou leude Gyrle, darest thou conceiue the thought to doo mee this dishonour? by my Crowne for this thy presumption, I shall make thee such an example to all other, as thy heade from thy shoulders will scant quite thy fault.[7] *Griana* hearing him speake so roughlie, answered him againe thus mildlie.

My Lord and Father, I beseeche you to pardon me, you accuse me, and I know
not whereof: if I haue doone euil, it is in you to chastise me as you shal please, and
if I be innocent, vouchsafe good Father not to condemne mee. Ah varlet[8] (quoth
hee) this excuse shall little profite thee. So taking her verie rudelie, he locked
her in a strong Tower,[9] whereof he carried the Keye himselfe: then went he to
Tarisius his lodging to see how he did, for it was told him that he was in daunger
of his life, where he found the Empresse heauilie weeping, but he caused her to
goe to her Chamber, and commaunded his Chirurgions to looke dilligentlie to
his Nephewe, and not to spare any cost to purchase his health. Nowe because
they which searched for *Florendos*, could not finde him, the bruite and rumor
was qualified, and the Emperour went againe to his Chamber till the morning, when the Empresse hearing that her daughter was in prison, tooke it verie
heauilie, and kneeling before the Emperour, desired him that she might fetch her
foorth: but he was so angrie, as her wordes coulde doo nothing with him, yet he
graunted that shee shoulde goe see her, and tooke her the Key, when she entering the Tower, founde her sitting on the ground so blubred with teares, as was
lamentable to beholde, but when she behelde her Mother, she arose, and dooing
her reuerence, coulde not speake her teares so ouercame her.[10] The Empresse that
loued her deerelie, seeing her in this greeuous estate, had much a doo to dissemble what she thought, how beit, after a fewe light wordes passed betweene
them, she said. I am sorie daughter that you haue so lightlie throwne your affection vpon a Straunger, and that you forget your duetie, in following your Fathers
counsell and mine, who well knewe the loue *Tarisius* beares you, and no otherwise Daughter, then to take you to his wife. But you (carried awaie with that
loosenes, which ill agrees with your credite and calling) haue rather thought best,
to grant *Florendos* enterance by your Garden, at such a suspected howre, as while
you liue, your honour will be hardlie thought on: for two of *Tarisius* his Knights,
who thought to take the Traytour, are slaine, and my Nephew himselfe daungerouslie escaped. *Griana* hearing him called Traitour whom shee so highlie looued,
and that shee herselfe was accused, by that which ought to excuse her, answered.
Madame, and my gracious Mother, as yet I am ignoraunt of the cause, that hath
mooued the Emperour in such choller against me, and be it for this you speake
of, in soothe I am offered verie great iniurie, for I knowe not whether *Florendos*
or anie other haue entred my Garden, well I am assured hee came not where I
was. These are straunge newes to me Madame, I wold rather haue thought him
on his waie towards *Macedon*, in respect of the solemne leaue he tooke in the
Courte. For my part, I would that the Traytour which was the cause hereof, had
long since beene buried in the bottome of the Sea, then he should so abuse the
honor of *Florendos*, with a matter of such villanie, wherein I cannot iudge him
faultie: but were it he Madame, I am at a point, let him die the death, as he hath
well deserued, for my duetie to you my Parents hath taught me better nurture,
and loue canne be no priuiledge to me to offende.[11] Then good Mother, twit not
mee with impeache of honour in so innocent a cause, for defence whereof, were

the death present before mine eyes, I haue sorrowed as much as I would, and am more readie to embrace it then liue in suspecte, so shall my Father and you bee eased of prouiding me a Husband. As for the prison wherein I am, I will not denie his fauoure when it shall please him to deliuer me: but I coulde take it farre more contentedlie, to spende the remainder of my following daies thus solitarie, then to liue abroad misdeemed on by anie. Faire Daughter (said the Empresse) doo not discomfort your selfe in this sort, the Emperour had some reason (in regarde of the loue he beares you, and the outragious tumult which happened) to doo as he hath doone: but I hope in the end all will sort to the best, and that you your selfe shall remaine contented. Manie other speeches passed betweene them, till at length the Empresse left her and departed, for she thought long till she was with the Emperour, to let him know the talke betweene her and *Griana*: which shee didde without omitting anie thing, notwithstanding hee was more seuere to his Daughter euerie daie after. Then sent hee for the Ambassadours, and thus he began with them. My Lordes, at this time I am aduised, that you shall returne to your King my Brother, for in respect of the accidents which you haue seene to happen: I will craue pardon for this tyme, referring matters ouer till some other time, when thinges shall fall in better disposition. The Ambassadours vnderstanding the Emperours pleasure, the next daie tooke their leaue towarde the King their Maister, to whom they declared the whole in generall: whereat hee conceiued such dyspleasure, as he presentlie sent for his Sonne *Tarisius*, who had not as yet recouered his health. But he was so enamored on the yong Princesse, as he would not obey his Fathers commaund, but so soone as he was indifferentlie amended, he intreated the Emperour to pardon his Daughter, accusing his owne men, who vndiscreetlie had raised this false rumour of her and *Florendos*. By this meanes, the Empresse and her Ladies obtained libertie dailie[12] to accompanie *Griana*: but all the night time he caused her to bee locked vp as closelie as before, committing her to the charge of an aged Gentlewoman named *Tolomestra*, whom hee commaunded on paine of death, not to bee a minute of an houre forth of her companie.

Chapter VIII.
Howe Florendos arriuing on the frontiers of Macedon, made manie sorrowfull complaints, for not bringing Griana away, according to his enterprise.

No sooner had *Florendos* and *Frenato* ouertane their companie, but they rid on in such hast (fearing to be followed) as at length they got the Frontiers of *Macedon*. And because *Florendos* imagined himselfe without life, not hearing anie tydinges from his Mistresse *Griana*, he concluded to rest at the first Towne he came too, there to expect the returne of the Esquire he sent to *Constantinople*: who returned towards his Maister sooner then he looked for, by reason of the little aboad he made in the Emperours Court, for he staied not when he hearde that *Griana* was imprisoned, and that *Tarisius* was not slaine as his Maister was perswaded. These newes did wonderfullie afflict the Prince, as well for the harde vsage of his sweete Freende, as that he had fayled in killing him, by whose death he well hoped to recouer his losse: all the whole daie would he receiue no sustenance, but locked himselfe close in his Chamber, and tombled on his bedde as a man halfe desperate. But *Frenato* who would not be long absent from him, fearing least his furie woulde cause him worke some violence on himselfe, made such meanes that hee got into the Chamber, at what time the Prince was thus lamenting. Alas sweete Madame, was I borne in such an vnhappie houre, that without desert you must indure imprisonment for me? What satisfaction maie your *Florendos* liue to make, in requitall of this iniurie? When didde you euer merit to be so hardlie intreated for him? Beleeue me, coulde you bee discharged so soone as I coulde wyshe it, bolts, locks nor walles coulde holde you a thought whyle,[2] yet wyshing is no action,[3] euerie thing is contrarie to me, al helpes refuse me, and death likewise denies me: but by my sworde (and therewith he started vp) in spight of whatsoeuer I will deliuer you. *Frenato* seeing him rise in such a furie, came and tooke him by the arme, demaunding what he would haue. Death (quoth he) if I could, for it greeues mee to liue anie longer. You speake verie wiselie (quoth hee in mockage) is all this for the imprisonment of *Griana*? is it not better she should be there, then in the custodie of *Tarisius*? her captiuitie you know cannot long endure, but were she married she could neuer be recouered. Therefore let good hope perswade you, and now send an other Messenger with speede to *Constantinople*,[4] to know what accidents haue happened since, and to practise the meane to speake with *Cardina*, who will certifie you from *Griana*, what is or may be doone in these affayres. This counsell liked well *Florendos*, whereupon he presentlie dispatched a Gentleman of trust, who with all dilligence did execute the commaund of his Maister, for in good time he arriued at *Constantinople*, when *Griana* had libertie to speake with her Gentlewomen:[5] which when he hearde, he was not a little glad, whereupon he searched earnestlie till he hadde founde *Cardina*, to whom he deliuered his Maisters minde, as also in what sad and heauie plight he left him, desiring her with all speede to certifie the Princesse thereof, and what seruice she would commaunde him to his Maister. *Cardina* knowing how glad the Princesse would bee, to heare these tidings from *Florendos*, went to seeke her Sister *Lerina*, to whom she imparted what you haue heard, and she, well aduised of the time and place, discoursed the same to the Princesse, vnseene, and not suspected of old *Tolomestra*. How ioyfull she was of this message, I cannot vtter, nor you conceiue, but shee was resolued, neuer to haue any Husbande but *Florendos*, and therefore to comfort him, she deuised to write to him that he might hope as wel as she did: but wel she knewe not how to accomplish her intent, by reason shee wanted pen, inke and paper, and she was forbidden to haue anie. Notwithstanding, she so well perswaded her woman *Tolomestra*, as (feigning to wryte to the Emperour her Father) she recouered the meane to execute her desire. Then withdrawing her selfe apart, first she wrote a Letter to the Emperour, and afterwards one to *Florendos*, wherein she desired him not to be offended, albeit things fell out not to his lyking: for (with the fauour of Fortune) the end would be as pleasant to him, as the beginning had beene vnhappie to them bothe, withal, that as he desired to prolong her life, he shoulde doo nothing to the preiudice of his owne person.[6] These two Letters thus written and sealed, she called *Tolomestra*, and gaue her that she had written to the Emperor, desiring her to carrie it presentlie to his Maiestie, by whose departing, she had oportunitie to conferre with *Lerina*: in breefe she desired her to goe seeke the Esquire, that he might returne to his Maister with the Letter she sent him, which she did effectuallie, and the gentle Esquire made no little hast to his Maister. Who receiuing the Letter from hys Mistresse *Griana*, was not content alone to read it, but kist and rekist it a hundred times, saying. Ah sweete Letter, written with the hand of the only Princesse this day liuing: for her sake will I keepe thee, as the best token a true Knight can receiue from his Mistresse.[7]

Chapter IX.

Howe the Emperour promised Tarisius, that hee shoulde marrie Griana, whether she woulde or no: and howe she was deliuered of a fayre Sonne, without the knowledge of anie, but olde Tolomestra who had her in guarde.

When the Emperour had receiued the Letter, which *Tolomestra* presented him from his Daughter, albeit he found nothing therin might prouoke him to anger, sauing that she earnestlie desired him to pittie her estate, beeing innocent of anie thing was laide to her charge: yet he shewed him selfe more discontented then before, sending *Tolomestra* backe with this aunswere. Say to *Griana*, that seeing she was so aduenturous to incur my displeasure, shee shall well knowe that I will not spare to punish her offence: and let her assure her selfe, that I wyll neuer looke on her while I liue, if she match not with *Tarisius* to whom I haue giuen her. All this *Tolomestra* told to *Griana*, which rather then to obey, shee desired to die, wherefore when anie came to visite her,[1] she woulde shewe her selfe more pleasant in their companie then shee hadde doone, in respecte of vnexpected heauines that secretlye touched her, feeling herselfe so farre conceiued with Childe, as she knewe no meanes to saue it and her honour, if it should happen to be perceiued. One onelie helpe shee had in this extreamitie, that beeing so weake and sicklie, the Phisitions could not discerne her disease: but reputed her likely to die, which she with all her hart desired, yet doo what iniurie to her selfe she could, she had better health then she desired to haue. In the ende, feeling her selfe so grosse and vnweldie, she durst not leaue her bed, but kept it dailie, till her time drewe verie neere at hand, when the Emperour (by the earnest importunitie of the Empresse) happened to come and see her, bringing with him the Prince *Tarisius*: who beeing thus entred the Towre, they founde her in such greeuous and daungerous estate, as for all the anger the Emperour had against her, it mooued the teares to stande in his eyes, which he shaddowed so well as he coulde, framing his speeches to her in this sort.[2] Well Daughter, it likes you to contrarie me, in that which concernes your honour and profit, and without anie feare (as is thy duetie) thou hast boldlie refused the Husband which I haue appointed thee: but (by mine honour) I will cause thee know that thou hast displeased me, for wilt thou or not (before I leaue thee) I will giue thee to him whome I haue promised. Then taking her by the hande, and causing *Tarisius* to come neere, he saide. My Sonne, in regarde of my word, which I will keepe inuiolablie, I giue thee heere *Griana*, from henceforth account of her as thy Wife: and holde thee, heere is the Key of the Tower, keepe her in thine owne custodie, and heereafter thinke of her as thou findest occasion. Well sawe *Griana* that perforce she must obey her Fathers will: wherefore with great wisedome couering her secrete thoughts, with extreame teares deliuered this aunswere. Alas my good Lord and Father, I neuer thought that your highnesse would vse such crueltie towards me, as to enforce me take a Husband contrarie to my liking,[3] not (my good Lorde) but that *Tarisius* hath much better deserued: but that which toucheth me most in opinion is, that our neere alliaunce in kindred, is sufficient to continue the loue betweene the King his father and you, without anie such needelesse seeking of newe vniting. And moreouer good Father, his education in your Court with my Brother *Caniano* and me, since our verie yongest yeeres to this present, hath beene of such equall and familiar condition: as it seemes to mee impossible to reuerence him with that intire duetie, which women must and ought vse to their Husbands. Wherfore my good Lord and Father, I perswade my selfe (vnder your correction) that you should support me in this iust request: the rather in respect of my present estate, which may induce you somwhat to conceiue: that the obsequies of my buriall is more likelie to be solemnized, then those holie ceremonies that shoulde be vsed at my marriage. And with these words she powred foorth such aboundance of teares, as the Emperour knewe not what to answere: but ouercome with pittie withdrew himselfe, leauing *Tarisius* with her, who hoping to haue better words of her, said. Madame, I beseeche you not to offend your selfe, for anie thing the Emperour hath saide concerning me, for I wil not anie thing to your discontent, and rather would I suffer all my life, then cause the least doubt to encurre your dislike: hoping that in time to come you wyll take such pittie on mee, as beeing perswaded of the loue I beare you, and the reuerend desire I haue to doo you seruice you will graunt that with good will, which the Emperour striues to gaine perforce, assuring you that nothing can be more greeuous to mee, then the harde dealing which hetherto hath beene vsed towards you. And to the ende you may resolue your selfe of that I say, your Father hauing deliuered me the Keye of your prison, and the guarde of your personne, I here commit bothe to your gentle pleasure. So kissing the Keie, he laid it by her,[4] and without expecting anie aunswere, with great reuerence hee departed, leauing her with *Tolomestra*, so rapt into a slumber or traunce, as her Keeper would not for pittie trouble her.[5] The Princesse in this silent passion,[6] thought that shee sawe a fierce Lyon before her, with open throate readie to deuoure her, and neere at hand she espied an armed Knight, to whom shee laboured for her defence, crying, that for Gods sake he would sheeld her from the beast, but the Knight with stearne and angrie countenaunce thus answered. I wil not defend thee, but with my Sword will take thy life from thee. Thou hast so much offended the heauenlie powers in disobedience to thy Father, as I ought rather to deuide thy head from thy shoulders, then to hinder this beaste from deuouring thee. Thinkest thou to contrarie their diuine pleasures? Suffiseth not the fault thou hast committed with *Florendos*? content thee, and shroude thy shame, in regard of the fruite in thy wombe, whose woorthinesse thou shalt knowe more of heereafter. If thou dooest not, thou diest an euerlasting death, from which thou[7] canst haue no meane to defende thee. The Knight did so affright *Griana*, as she promised him to accomplish the Emperours commaundement without fayle: whereupon the Knight and the Lyon vanished awaie, leauing her (as she thought) by a fayre Fountaine, enuironed with Trees and diuersitie of flowers, the sweete sent wherof was so pleasaunt and odorifferous, as made the cheereful

bloode to reuiue againe in the Princesse, and with breathing foorth a vehement sigh,[8] she awaked, inuocating on the powers to pardon her transgressions, and promising to obey the wyll of her Father, albeit she could hardlie forget *Florendos* so soone.[9] Within two or three daies after, the Prince *Tarisius* came to visite her,
5 to whom she shewed better countenaunce then she had doone, and as they were deuising togeather in amorous talk, she said. Beleeue me Syr *Tarisius*, you haue vsed such honest and gentle courtesie towardes mee, as henceforth I giue my selfe wholie yours: therefore beeing sorrie for my long disobedience to my Parents and you, tryumphe nowe *Tarisius* in the honor of my loue.[10] If these wordes
10 pleased *Tarisius*, it is not to be doubted, for ioy whereof hee went presentlie to the Emperour, and made him acquainted with these happie tydinges: so that (to make short) after manie promises and solemne oathes to the Princesse, not onelie to accept her as his spouse and wife, but as his soueraigne Ladie and Mistresse, hee broughte her with him to the Emperour, who hearing the resolution of his
15 Daughter, embraced her, and tooke her into as good conceite as euer he did.

Notwithstanding, *Tolomestra* was commanded to attend on her still, wherefore *Griana* knowing her time to drawe neere, and hardlie could she conceale her fortune: after manie difficult doubts and feares debated in her thoughts, at last she imparted the whole to *Tolomestra*. The olde Gentlewoman after manie
20 motherlie rebukes, for the fault committed as the daunger imminent, thought better yet to couer this misaduenture, then to publish that which woulde displease manie, and profite none: so leauing to reprehende, when care and comfort was more required, at that instant the Princesse was deliuered of a goodlie man childe. Thus in the ninth Moneth, after the returne of *Florendos* towards
25 *Macedon*, on Mondaie at night about eight of the clocke,[11] the Princesse had her howre of deliueraunce: when *Tolomestra*[12] receiuing the Childe, sawe it so beautifull and wel fourmed, as it greeued her meruailouslie, to think what hard fortune it brought with the birth. For the honour of the Mother could not bee defended, but by the price of the infants life: wherefore hauing wrapped it in
30 swadling clothes which the Princesse had prepared of some valew, shee brought it to the sorrowfull Mother, saying. Trust mee Madame, it much displeaseth me that wee must thus loose this louelie childe, whom I could haue esteemed happy, and the Mother likewise, if it might liue without displeasure:[13] but he sweete babe must suffer the punishment for the offence, whereof he is not anie
35 way culpable. Alas (saide the Princesse) what shall we doo? would God it weare deade, or out of daunger: then taking it in her armes, and washing his face with flooddes of teares, after manie sweete kisses, thus said. Ah my little deintie, and must I needes leaue thee? must the safetie of thy life remaine in the mercie of a straunge Womanne, who not knowing thy Parents, may deale with thee discour-
40 teouslie? well, if thou die, thy Mother will not be long after thee. And as shee thus mourned ouer her infant, shee perceiued on his right cheeke a lyttle marke in likenesse of a Crosse:[14] which made her call her vision to remembraunce, and the words of the Knight, that promised good fortune to the Childe, which made

her conceiue a comfortable hope, whereupon, about his necke shee tyed a fayre Crucifixe of golde. Nowe was the night verie farre spent, and *Tolomestra* feared they shoulde be preuented, wherfore (quoth she) Madame it is time to determine of some thing, leaue muzing I pray you anie longer on the Childe, and let me goe carrie it to *Cardina* to be borne forth of the Court.[15] The weeping Mother seeing shee councelled for the best, for her last adiewe sealed manie sweete kisses on the face of the infant, and so in great greefe deliuered it to *Tolomestra*, who went and found *Cardina*, to whom she gaue it: and she without anie tariance mounted on Horsebacke, and not knowing what way shee tooke, rode on which way Fortune guided her. Verie doubtfull was she howe to be discharged of her carriage, for she feared to let any Woman in the neighbour Villages haue it, least so the Princesse might be discouered: for that it was commonlie blazed through the Empire, that the Princesse was imprisoned for the loue of *Florendos*. At length the daie began to appeare, when she perceiued herselfe on a high Mountaine, which was verie thicke sette with Palme and Oliue trees: then she alighted from her Horse, and made a little bed of sweete Hearbes, wherein she layd the Childe,[16] hoping some body would passe by that would take compassion on it. So committing the tender infant to the protection of the powers, she returned to the Cittie in very good time.

Chapter x.
Howe Gerrard passing where Cardina hadde left the Childe, heard it crye, and so brought it home with him to his wyfe to nourish it.

The Mountaine where *Cardina* had left the Princesse yong Son, was about a daies iourney from *Constantinople*, and was commonlie called the Mount of Oliues, where neere at hande dwelt a welthie Farmer, who hauing the occupation of the grounde, grew very rich by gathering the fruites of the Palme, Oliue, Date and other Trees, and like a good Husband he daily folowed his affayres, beeing named *Gerrard*. His Wyfe the same morning likewise was deliuered of a Male child, which being deade borne, caused this good man to walke foorth into his groundes in great heauines, for he had but one Daughter aged three yeeres, and his Sonne woulde haue beene a great comfort to him.[1] In these melancholique passions as he went neere the Tree, where *Cardina* had left the seelie infant, he heard it cry: whereat he greatlie meruailing, approched neerer, and sawe the sweete Babie pittifully mourning, wanting the nouriture that shoulde comfort it. Hee tooke it very tenderly in hys armes, and seeing it so sweete and louelie, was perswaded that God[2] had sent it him, in recompence of hys owne that was deade borne: and so ioyfullie went home with it to hys Wife, who was named *Marcella*, and to her he beginneth in this maner. Behold sweete Wife, in the place of your yong dead Sonne, God hath this day sent vs an other, which I haue brought you home. Then recounted he to her, howe he found it on the Mountaine vnder an Oliue Tree:[3] and therefore (quoth hee) I pray thee nourish it in stedde of thine owne, for a goodlier Childe did I neuer behold. The good woman tooke it, and vnwrapping the swadling clothes, sawe they were rich and of good valewe, but cheefelie the Crucifixe which hung about his neck: whereupon she iudged it of some noble house, and mooued with pitty, thus sayd. I beleeue sweete infant, that thy Mother is in no small greefe for the losse of thee, but seeing thy fortune hath brought thee to me, I wyll foster thee as thou wert mine owne Sonne. And from thence forward shee vsed it so louinglie, as euery one thought it to bee *Gerrards* owne Child: and bringing it to baptisme, because he found it so among the Palme trees,[4] hee caused the Childe to bee named *Palmerin*, who grewe on in yeeres, both in comelie feature and gentle behauiour. Not long after, *Marcella* brought her Husbande an other Sonne, whose name was *Colmelio*, and him did Palmerin loue as his own Brother and companion, as heereafter you shall more at large vnderstand: but heere I wyll craue leaue to pause for a whyle, and following the intent of this Historie, you shall vnderstand howe *Griana* gouerned herselfe, after she had escaped this hard aduenture.[5]

So soone as *Cardina* was returned to the Court, *Griana* sent for her, to knowe what shee had doone with the infant: to whom she discoursed in what sort she hadde left it, which greeued her as much as the weight of her offence.[6] Notwithstanding, considering howe happilie shee had escaped shame and disgrace, from thence forwarde shee dissembled her passions better, and shewed herselfe so well reclaimed, as the Empresse reioyced much thereat, hoping nowe to ende the matter for her Nephewe *Tarisius*: whereupon one day finding her Daughter alone, shee tooke occasion to conferre with her thus. Daughter, wil you now accomplish that, which your Father and I haue long beene importunate for, I pray you holde of no longer, least you driue him into anger againe, which can no way returne you benefite. When *Griana* heard her Mother speake so gentlie, and knowing well, that (whether she would or no) it muste sorte to that conclusion, she answered. Madame, you haue thought good (will I nill I') that I shoulde match with your Nephewe *Tarisius*, I must then by force doo that which wyllingly I cannot, nor while I liue shall I conceiue better opinion: yf then (Mother) hereafter our fortunes fall out so contrary, that any misaduenture happen by thys your wilfulnes, you neede not complaine but of your selfe, beeing the inuenter and procurer thereof.[8] All these speeches of *Griana* could not alter her opinion, but without regard of any danger, she went presently to the Emperour, desiring him (seeing *Griana* was recouered) to ende the marriage[9] betweene her Nephew and her: whereto he gaue such suddaine consent, as before a seauen night was finished, *Tarisius* and she were maried togeather, to her great greefe, as her countenaunce declared, for when euery one were at their feasting dauncing, and other delights, the woeful Princesse thought on the great iniurie she had doone to *Florendos*,[10] accounting herselfe the most vnhappy on the earth, and to herselfe thus sorrowed. Ah my deere freende, what wylt thou say when thou hearest these tydinges, that I am become so false and disloyall to thee? what excuse may pleade for me to thee? by good reason may I for euer bee excluded from theyr companie, who haue kept their fayth inuiolable to their freendes, and continue in profession of their vnchangable affections, for neuer did Woman commit such treason as this that I haue doone: and yet (my Lord) altogeather against my wil, as my wofull hart may giue euident witnesse, which shalbe thine while it remaines in thys miserable bodie, which *Tarisius* must nowe haue, though in iustice it be thine.[11] And in thys sort continued her dolorous complaints til night approched, when she must yeeld that honor to *Tarisius*, which with better wyll she could haue affoorded *Florendos*.

After the feastes and triumphes of the marriage were finished, *Griana* desirous to absent herselfe from her fathers Courte, because the remembraunce of *Florendos* passions was so greeuous to her: desired *Tarisius* to make short his staie, and set forward to *Hungaria*, whether the Emperour her Father caused her to be so honourablie conuaied, as beseemed the Daughter of so great a Prince.[12] But as shee was taking her leaue among the Ladies, the Empresse came to her sorrowfullie weeping, which when *Griana* beheld, shee said. Madame, I am abashed to see what heauines you shew for the departure of your Daughter, to whom you alone haue beene so cruell, as by your meanes shee is banished for euer from you and your Countrie: why lament you then? seeing it is your pleasure to make her vnfortunate while she liues? I hartelie desire the heauens to pardon you, and that the first newes heereafter you shall heare of me, maie be the true report of my death. This said, shee mounted on horsebacke, and without anie semblaunce of discontent took her leaue of her Father: so beeing honourablie accompanied, in short time she arriued in *Hungaria* with *Tarisius*, whose loue to her so vehementlie increased, as he reputed himselfe the most fortunate Prince in *Europe*, hauing gained the paragon among all Ladies.[13] Soone after the aged King died, by which meanes *Tarisius* came to the Crowne. *Griana* highlie esteeming such as shee brought with her from *Constantinople*, to witt, *Lerina* and *Cardina*, but especiallie *Tolomestra*, to whom she verie often imparted the whole secrets of her minde, leading so strickt and constant a life, as all the Court did wonder at her. But the remorse of conscience, which dailie touched her for the losse of her Sonne, caused her to spende day and night in deuout orisons, that the heauens would forget her hainous offence.

CHAPTER XI.
Howe Florendos vnderstoode by the Esquire hee sent to Constantinople, the marriage of Griana and Tarisius: whereat he conceiued such inward greefe, as hee would haue died with extreame sorrow.

A ll this while continued *Florendos* on the Frontiers betweene *Constantinople* and *Macedon*, til at length he hearde that *Griana* was released of her imprisonment, wherof he was so glad, as nowe he thought to deale more surelie then he did before: wheruppon he dispatched *Lyomenus* one of his Esquires towardes her, with a Letter of earnest and intire affection, wherein he desired to knowe, if he might compasse the meane to come and see her, and hee doubted not to bring her so secretlie on her iourneie, and with so good prouision, as before they should be againe discouered, they would be safelie arriued in *Macedon*. But this hope was soone frustrate, for *Lyomenus* beeing come to *Constantinople*, founde the marriage betweene *Tarisius* and *Griana* consumated: which he tooke so displeasantlie, as without giuing the Letter, or speaking to the Princesse, he returned hastilie againe to his Lorde and Maister. Who beeing aduertised of his comming, sent for him immediatlie vp into his Chamber, at whose entrance, the Prince discerned the newes by his countenance, wheruppon he demaunded if *Griana* were sicke, or howe shee fared? My Lord (quoth he) happie had she beene, if she had dyed tenne yeeres since: for I doubt (vnlesse you arme your self with wonderfull patience) that what is doone will highlie endaunger your person. Why (quoth *Florendos*) what is happened? Trust me my Lord (quoth he) the verie worst that can be for you, *Tarisius* hath espoused her, and (despight of her) the Emperour caused it to be doone. No sooner had *Lyomenus* spoken the word, but *Florendos* cast himselfe cruellie against the grounde, saying. O my God take pittie on my soule, for my bodie must needes suffer misfortune. At which wordes he fell in a swoune, when *Lyomenus* thinking him dead, ran hastilie and called *Frenato*: who knowing full well the cause of his passion, laboured by all meanes he might to perswade him, but notwithstanding all the intreaties he vsed, in foure and twentie houres hee coulde not get one word of him, whereuppon hee sent for an aunciant Hermit neere at hand, whom *Florendos* made verie much account of,[1] who beeing come, and applying diuers soueraigne Hearbes to his temples, whereof the olde Father knewe well the vertue, at length *Florendos* recouered his sences, and opening his eyes, beheld the olde Hermit, to whom with verie feeble voice he said. Ah good Father praie for me, for I feele mine ende nigh at hand. Not so my Sonne saide the Hermit, what? are you so vnprouided of diuine perswasion, as you will loose bothe bodie and soule for matter of so meane consequence? hast thou liued so long, and yet ignoraunt of the inconstancie of Women, which is no other then thou beholdest in *Griana*? Knowest thou not, that as the saile of the Shippe is subiecte to all windes,[2] so are their affections to continuall mutabilitie? and knowest thou not, that what they purpose to execute irreuocablie, in one moment they are suddainlie disswaded from? My Sonne,

beleeue my counsell, and with as much pleasure learne to forget this folly, as with
extreame paine thou diddest first imprint it in thy thoughts. Ah Father (quoth
Florendos) neuer seeke in this sort to perswade me, beeing assured if you knew
how things haue past, you wold not thus in tearmes disgrace my Ladie: for shee
is mine, and *Tarisius* hath no right to her, to whom the Emperour hath married
her perforce, els would she neuer haue broken her faith to me,[3] and while I liue
Father, none but she can bee called the Wyfe of *Florendos*, Sonne to the mighty
King of *Macedon*. The wise olde Father seeing him in choller, and beeing lothe
likewise to offende the Prince, would no longer crosse him in speeches, but fearing to mooue him too much, mildlie thus spake. May be (my Sonne) she hath
beene deere to you, and I would your consent in loue had aunswered your lyking:
but thus to dispaire, and endaunger your owne life, truste me it is not well doone,
therefore I desire you to perswade your selfe, and by your constancie condemne
her lightnes, taking patientlie what hath happened.[4] These and such like good
words vsed the old Hermit, but *Florendos* would take no sustenance, neither be
remooued from this opinion, for fiue daies while the old man staied with him:[5]
neither would he looke cheerefully as he was wont, but continued euermore sad
and melanchollique, nor could the King his Father cause him like of anie Wife,
but onely *Griana*, for whome continuallie he neuer left mourning.

Chapter XII.

How yong Palmerin sleeping, had a strange vision, which prouoked him to know whose Son he was, and of the talk which passed betweene him and Dyofena, the daughter of Gerrard.

Palmerin being now come to the age of fifteene yeeres, nourished in the Mountaine as the Childe of *Gerrard* his supposed Father, well beloued of him and *Marcella* his wife as their own Sonne: grewe in stature so tall, comelie and wel nurtured, as well might he be known of noble parentage. For albeit he companyed with *Gerrards* Children, who vsed him after their rusticall capacities: yet hee desired more to passe the Mountaines with his long Bowe, to chase the Beares and Bores thorowe thicke and thinne,[1] and to keepe Hawkes and dogges, rather then Sheepe and Cattell as the other Children did.[2] In these sports he had such wonderfull delight, as oftentimes he would come home verie late and sore wearied: but one time among the rest, he came home so ouerlaboured, as he was glad to laie him downe to rest, and he was no sooner fallen a sleepe, but he was solicited with a meruailous visyon, the effect whereof thus followeth. Hee thought (as hee was pursuing a goodlie Harte thorowe a Forrest) hee met with the fairest Ladie that euer eye behelde, who sat on the side of a goodlie Fountaine, and called him vnto her, saying. Be not abashed *Palmerin*, though I am come from the furthest parts to finde thee in this Countrey, for I am well assured, that ere many daies be past, thy bountie and prowesse shall make thee renowmed through the worlde, for one of the hardiest Knights that euer liued. Leaue therefore thys obscure and rusticall kinde of life, and henceforth lift thy mind to high occasions which are offered thee: and heereof beleeue me, as she that loueth thee as her owne life, beeing deuoted onelie thine at all times,[3] as nature may witnesse who hath marked me with thy like Charracter. Then shewing her arme, she saide. Beholde in this hande, and on this side of my hart, one like and selfe same marke, as thou broughtest on thy face from thy Mothers wombe. To which wordes *Palmerin* woulde haue aunswered, but the Ladie vanished awaie so suddainly, as he could not perceiue what was become of her. Whereuppon raising himselfe, and meruayling from whence this occasion should proceede, he admired the beautie of the Ladie he sawe in his sleepe, which was so liuelie in his remembrance, as he iudged her present before his eyes. But perswading himselfe that such apparitions happened by idle thoughts, or by some vapour of no effect:[4] made no account thereof, whereuppon, the next night following, the same Ladie that appeared to him in the Forrest, presented herselfe to him againe, holding in her hands a sumptuous Crowne of golde, and thus spake. See heere (my Lord) the honour which I holde, beeing giuen me onelie for the loue of you. In this sort continued this vision for foureteene or fifteene daies following, till at length the Ladie shewed herselfe verie angrie, saying. I am ashamed *Palmerin*, that you deferre so long to seeke me out, doo you thinke the promises I haue made you are friuolous? No, no, the time and trauaile thou takest (if thou giuest credite to my wordes) shall make thee knowe

Palmerin d'Oliva: Part I

that thou art the Son of a King, and not of the Countrey swayne that hath fostered thee. From henceforth therefore expect me no more in this Mountaine, but if my beautie haue found place in thy hart, seeke then to conquere me, that thou maist be the Lorde and possessour of mee.[5] Thus departed the Ladie, leauing a desire (more then accustomed[6]) in the hart of *Palmerin*, who till that time made little reckoning of so high matters, for the Pastorall life hee ledde with *Gerrard* and hys familie, seemed the most happiest[7] to him in all the worlde, not hauing seene any person of greater calling then he. But nowe newe affections so eleuated his minde, as he intended to goe seeke her, whom in sleepe he had beheld so often: For (quoth he) if she assure mee to discende of a royall linage, I may well presume she knowes me better then my Father *Gerrard*, els would she not so often induce me to folow my fortune, and the good that is prouided for me, well might I be accounted a foole, if I wold not aduenture on so especial an occasion, therfore happen what wil, I meane to search thorow the whole worlde till I haue founde her, and none but she shall euer be my Mistresse. But how can it be that I am discended from so high a place, seeing my Father is such a simple Countriman? Hath my Mother beene forgetfull of her reputation, that some Prince or great Lord hath so become my Father?[8] Well, I wyll knowe of her if I can before I depart, and if she will not tell mee, I will search for her that shall assure me. Thus was *Palmerin* confounded with remembraunce of his visions, as from that time he became maruailous pensiue and solitarie: then bethought he, howe he might knowe of his Mother *Marcella* the ende of his desire, wherof *Dyofena* (who loued him deerely) partlie aduertised him.

You haue heard heertofore, how when *Gerrard* founde *Palmerin* among the Oliue Trees, he had a daughter three yeeres olde, named *Dyofena*, indifferent fayre, who as shee increased in yeeres, became so amorous of her supposed brother, that hardly she could dissemble her affection: notwithstanding, shame and regard locked vppe her lippes, that she durst not speake what she gladlie would, but seeing *Palmerin* in like sadnes as she was, she immagined that one sicknes had strooken them both, wherfore casting manie doubts as she laie in her bed, in the same Chamber her Parents did, she heard them enter into this discourse. Haue you not seene *Palmerin* (quoth he) howe heauie and sadde hee hath beene a long time? Yea truelie haue I (quoth shee) it may bee that some haue tolde him hee is not your Sonne: so falling out of one matter into an other, *Dyofena* hearde them report the manner how they found him, which she desirous to let *Palmerin* vnderstande, arose earlie the next morning, and comming to *Palmerin*, thus conferred with him. Brother, if you knew so much as I doo, peraduenture you wold be not a little abashed. Why good Sister (quoth he) I pray you let me vnderstand the matter. In sooth (quoth shee) I euer thought till this time, that you had beene mine owne naturall Brother, but by chaunce hearing some talke betweene my Father and Mother this last night, I am no other then your freende, and shee that loues you dearelie:[9] which I haue euermore hetherto feared to let you knowe, doubting the nerenes of our consanguinitie, which I nowe perceiue cannot hinder our marriage, if you will request mee of my Father, who I am sure will not denie you. And so she rehearsed the manner of his finding, which so well lyked *Palmerin*, as he gaue the more credite to the visions he had seene, neuerthelesse, he thus dallied with *Dyofena*. It may bee Sister, you misunderstoode our Parents, my selfe will demaund the trueth of our Mother, if she assure me as you haue doone, then will I talke with them concerning our marriage. So shall you doo well (said *Dyofena*) to bee thorowlie assured, yet neede you not report mee to haue informed you, least thereby you bring mee into my Parents displeasure. *Palmerin* thus leauing *Dyofena*, chanced to find his Mother *Marcella* alone, to whom he said. Mother, I beseeche you graunt me one request that I shall demaunde of you. That will I my Sonne (quoth she) if it be in my power to doo. Understand then good Mother (quoth he) that I haue oftentimes dreamed how I am not your Son, so that I knowe not what to saie, vnlesse you please to assure mee better. When *Marcella* heard these wordes, she was strooken in a studie: but *Palmerin* was still so importunate, as at last she thus answered. In good faith (faire Freende) I neuer knew thine owne naturall Parents, yet haue I looued thee as if thou wert mine owne Sonne: and so what words *Dyofena* had before reported, *Marcella* confirmed, taking him with her into her Chamber, where she shewed him the costlie swadling clothes that he was founde in, and the Crucifixe likewise that hung about his necke,[10] which he intreated her to bestow on him, to the ende (quoth he) that for your sake I may keepe it while I liue. *Marcella* woulde not denie his request, but put it about his necke herselfe. From which time forwarde, *Palmerin* shewed himselfe of more cheerefull disposition, deuising how he might compasse the meane to goe seeke his fortune, wherto his sundry apparitions had so often incited him. And as none can shunne what is ordeined him by diuine prouidence, not manye daies after, as he was walking alone vppon the Mountain, he heard a voice cry verie pittifullie for helpe and succour: whereuppon *Palmerin* ranne that waie which hee hearde the voice, where hee behelde a Lyon greedilie deuouring a Horse,[11] and *Palmerin* hauing no weapon to defend himselfe withall but a staffe, verie hardilie sette vpon the beast, gyuing him such a stroake betweene the eyes,[12] as he fell down dead to the grounde, then comming to him hee hearde complaine, saide: I haue my Freende in some parte reuenged thy wrong. Alas Sir (quoth he) had you not beene, my life had perished, for as I trauailed on my iourney, this Lion furiouslie sette vpon me to deuoure mee: which the rest of my companie perceiuing, tooke themselues to flight, leauing mee as you founde mee. The best is (said *Palmerin*) that you haue escaped with life: and if you please to goe with mee not far hence, where I haue beene nourished, you shall haue the best entertainment that I can make you. My Freende (quoth the Straunger) you haue alreadie doone so much for me, as if you will goe with me into the Countrey where I dwell, I haue wherewithall to reward your trauaile richlie. Is it farre hence Sir, said *Palmerin*? In the Cittie of *Hermida* (quoth he) in the Realme of *Macedon* I dwel, from whence I parted a moneth since with my merchandise, which I haue left at *Constantinople*: from

Palmerin d'Oliva: Part I   *143*

whence returning homeward, this vnlooked for misfortune befell mee, which had made an ende of me without your assistance. As they were thus conferring togeather, one of the Strangers seruaunts came to looke him, and finding him so happilie escaped, was not a little ioyfull, reporting that he had left his companions not farre off. Returne then said his Maister, and wil them come to me to the next Village, where I meane to haue my wounds dressed,[13] which the seruaunt performed immediatlie, and all this while stoode *Palmerin* in debating with himselfe if he should thus leaue his Father *Gerrard* or not: at length (after manie opinions) fearing if hee returned home againe not to finde the like opportunitie, concluded to depart with the Stranger. So was hee sette on a verie good Palfray, and setting forwards to *Macedon*, that night they were entertained in a verie good lodging, where the stranger caused his woundes to be searched, reporting to euerie one, howe by the ayde of *Palmerin* his life was preserued, for which cause he accounted of him as of his owne Sonne. All this while *Gerrard* and his Wife little thought of this mishappe, but exspected *Palmerins* returne till darke night, and seeing he came not as he was wont: both he and his wife the next daie searched the Mountaines, but they could not finde him, which made *Gerrard* to question in himself, what euil he had offered him, that should make him thus depart. Nowe durst not his Wife *Marcella* tell him, the talke betweene her and *Palmerin*, but accompanied her Husband in sorrow for their losse: especially *Dyofena* and her Brother *Colmelio* were most sory, *Dyofena* for losse, as she thought, of her Husband, and *Colmelio* for the companie of his supposed Brother, whose absence went so neere his hart, as he intended neuer to giue ouer searche till he hadde founde him.

Chapter XIII.

How Palmerin went with this Merchant named Estebon to the Cittie of Hermida, who afterwarde gaue him Horse and Armour to be made Knight.

Estebon the Merchant thus conducting *Palmerin* on his way, at length arriued at the Cittie of *Hermida*, where he was louingly welcomed home by his Wife, both yong and beautifull as anye in that Countrey, to whom he reported his daungerous assault by the Lyon, and without *Palmerins* help he had beene deuoured: but (quoth hee) good fortune sent him at the verie instant that slewe him, for which I shal be beholding to him while I haue a day to liue, therefore good Wife entertaine him in the best sort you can deuise, for he hath well deserued it. This speeche had the Merchant with his fayre Wife, who embracing *Palmerin*, said: That nature had omitted nothing in her workmanship, making him so amiable and ful of hardines. *Palmerin* seeing himselfe so fauoured of so beautifull a woman, hauing before spent his time among Sheepheards, Swineheards and loutish Swaines of the Country, with modestie began to blushe, and was so well stored with ciuilitie to make her this answere. I desire Mistresse that my behauiour may bee such, as may continue my Maisters good liking and yours towards me. So from that time hee followed Merchandise, and profited so well in the course of traffique, as *Estebon* committed all his affaires to *Palmerins* trust: who rather gaue his mind to martiall exercises, and followed Knightlie dispositions so much, as verie nature declared the noblenes of his minde, for he delighted to mannage great Horses, to fight at al maner of weapons, to see daungerous Combats, to frequent the assemblye of Knights, to talke of Armes and honourable exployts, and in breefe, to exercise all the braueries of a noble Courtier.[1]

Whereat *Estebon* meruailed so much, as faling in talke with him, he said. Me thinkes it is strange *Palmerin*, that thou beeing the Sonne of a drudge, and nourished on the Mountaine of Oliues (as thy selfe hath often tolde me) disdaynest the life of a Merchant, frequenting the company of hardie Knights, as though thou shouldest take Launce and sheelde to enter the Combat. Sir (said *Palmerin*) I know not if my Father be such as I haue told you, but I wot wel my hart so serues me, as I can thinke of nothing but actions of honour and knighthoode. The Merchant was contented to heare *Palmerin* in these tearmes, because he perceiued that his Wife fauoured him greatlie, wherat he became a little iealous, and gladly would remooue the occasion, wherfore he said. Seeing it is so *Palmerin*, that thou hast no mind to follow my affaires, I am well contented thou shalt exercise chiualrie, beeing the thing thou naturallie affectest, and whereby thou mayst attaine to credite and account. For mine owne part, because I will not hinder so good forwardnesse, thou shalt haue of me money, Horse and Armour, that thou mayst goe to *Macedon* to the King, where if thou request it of the Prince *Florendos* his Sonne, he will not refuse to giue thee thy order. *Palmerin* returned him verie hartie thanks, and hauing prouided al things expedient for his iourney: tooke his leaue of the Marchant *Estebon* and his wyfe, hoping to speede well in his aduenturous enterprise.

Palmerin d'Oliva: Part I   *145*

Chapter xiv.
How Palmerin arriued at the Court of Macedon, hoping to receiue the order of knighthood at the hande of the Prince Florendos, Sonne to the aged King Primaleon, by the fauoure of the Ladie Arismena.

Such speede made *Palmerin* beeing departed from the Marchant, as on the fourth day following, riding by a Riuers side, he found a Dwarffe sitting heauilie weeping, of whom he demaunded the cause of his mourning. Alas Syr (saide the Dwarffe) as I was riding by the commaundement of my Maister, to a Lady whom he deerelie loueth, a Knight euen nowe tooke my Horse from me, and very villainously offered me outrage, which yet dooth not so much greeue mee, as (beeing thus on foote) I know not howe to get ouer this Riuer. Mount vp behinde me (said *Palmerin*) and at the first Towne wee come to, I will prouide thee of another Horse. Then mounted the Dwarffe vp behinde him, and hauing past the Riuer, desired to know of *Palmerin* whether he trauailed: for (quoth he) I neuer sawe man whom I had greater desire to serue, then you. Dwarffe (answered *Palmerin*) I nowe iourneie towarde the Court of *Macedon* to the King, where I hope to find the Prince *Florendos*, who is accounted one of the worthiest Knights in the world, and by his hande I desire to be knighted if I may. And after you haue receiued your order (said the Dwarffe) I hope you will not be so vnwise to hazard the aduenture, wherein so manie haue failed and lost their liues. What aduenture is that quoth *Palmerin*? To goe to the Mountaine *Artifaeria* (said the Dwarffe) in hope to kill the Serpent, which hath beene the death of so manie valiant Knights. And what occasion said *Palmerin*, mooued them to fight with the Serpent? That will I tell you, answered the Dwarffe. The King *Primaleon*, father to the Prince *Florendos* whom you seeke, three yeeres since fell into a verie strange disease, for which no remedie can yet be found,[1] notwithstanding the dilligent endeuours of the Queene, and Ladie *Arismena* her Daughter, one of the fairest and most vertuous Princesses that euer was hearde of: who seeing her Father in such daungerous estate, hath often assembled the best Phisitions in the whole worlde, who haue practised al possible means to recouer his health, yet hitherto all hath beene to no purpose. Whereupon she sent to an aunctient Knight, the most skilfullest in the arte of Nigromancie this daie liuing, who returned this answere: that he should neuer bee healed, except hee bee first washed with the water of a Fountaine, which standeth on the top of the Mountaine *Artifaeria*, whether fourtimes a yere resort three Sisters, Magitians of the Isle *Carderia*, to gather vertuous Hearbes which there they wash, and wherof they frame all their enchantments.[2] This place is so defended by the Monster wherof I tolde you, that no man as yet durst approche it. Which newes when the Princesse *Arismena* vnderstood, hoping by strength of men to recouer the water and vanquish the Beast, leauied a great number of Souldiours well appointed, who were no sooner entered the Mountaine, but the Serpent came furiouslie foorth of his Den, throwing fire and smoake out of his mouth,[3] and beating his winges togeather with such terror, as the very hardiest durst passe no further, but were all glad to take themselues to flight, yet coulde they not depart with such expedition, but the greater part of them paid their liues for their bolde attempt, the Mountaine was so stored with Lions, Beares, Wolues, Harts, Tygres, Ounces, and other wild rauenous Beastes that deuoured them. Nowe at length manie Knights haue tryed themselues in this aduenture, thinking by their Prowesse to performe more then the other: but all the worse, for not one of them returned backe againe aliue. And why goes not the Prince *Florendos* him selfe, said *Palmerin*, that is esteemed the most valiant Knight thorow all Greece? Alas Sir, said the Dwarffe, some other matter hath so drowned his minde in mellancholique, as he liues like one that dispiseth himselfe. While the Dwarffe continued his discourse, the desire of honour and renowne did so liuelie touche the spirit of *Palmerin*, as he said to him selfe. It may be that *Arismena* was the Lady, which in my sleeping thoughts visited mee so often,[4] if the Destinies haue vowed her mine, why should I feare the Serpent, or all the other Beastes wherewith this Dwarffe doth so terrifie me? Haue not I slaine a Lyon alreadie with a staffe?[5] Tush the more daunger is in the place, the more honor depends vpon the victory. If I leaue my life there, I am not the first, if I returne with conquest, I shall be beyonde anie yet in fortune: therefore fall out as it will, no perrill shall dismaie me from giuing the aduenture, whereupon he sayd to the Dwarffe. But tell me my Freende, hee that bringes the water from the Mountaine to the King, what aduauntage shall he deserue? My Lord, (quoth hee) it hath beene manie times published, that his rewarde shall be the best Cittie in all this Realme. See then Dwarffe said *Palmerin*, one man more will hazarde his life in this enterprise, albeit I should receiue but thanks for my trauaile, wylt thou goe with me? That will I (aunswered the Dwarffe) if you please, and neuer will I forsake you while breath is in my bodie. Thus set they on till they came to the great Cittie of *Macedon*, at what time *Florendos* was gone to the Temple in such heauines, as he seemed a man of another world, beeing accompanied with manie Knights, and his faire Sister the Ladie *Arismena*, to whom *Palmerin* boldlie addressed himselfe: and as though hee had beene a Courtier all his life time, with seemelie modestie he set his knee to the grounde before her, and thus began. Madame, I humbly beseeche you to vouchsafe mee one request, which well you may not denie me, in that I am a Straunger, as also in respect of the desire I haue to doo you seruice. And trust me Sir (quoth shee) you shall not bee refused, what is it you woulde haue me doo for you? That at your request (said *Palmerin*) the Prince *Florendos* your Brother, wyll giue me my Knighthoode. *Arismena* seeing *Palmerin* so amiable and well disposed of bodie,[6] meruailed of whence hee was, and said. In good sooth Sir, such matter nothing appertaineth vnto me, for (as I iudge) such a motion shoulde proceede from your selfe: yet taking him by the hande, shee presented him to her Brother, saying. I pray you my Lord graunt to this yonge Gentleman as yet not knighted, the thing he hath desired mee to demaunde. *Florendos* hauing not as yet behelde him, looked vppon him, when an exceeding passion, presenting the Princesse *Griana*

Palmerin d'Oliva: Part I   *147*

to his thoughts, suddainlie touched him,[7] and beeing rapt into more conceite of ioy then he had beene accustomed, demaunded of *Palmerin* if he would be made Knight. With right good wyl my Lorde quoth he, if it shall like you to doo me so much honor, for aboue all thinges els it is my onelie desire. My freende, said *Florendos*, it is necessarie I should first know, whether you be noble borne or no. My Lord, quoth *Palmerin*, as yet I neuer knewe my Father or Mother, nor any of my kindred: notwithstanding, mine owne hart makes mee iudge no lesse of my selfe, and more gladlie would I die, then doo anie thing that were not vertuous, and well woorthie the name of a Gentleman. And trust me, said *Florendos*, I am of the same opinion: this night therefore you must obserue the religious watch as is accustomed, and to morrowe will I giue you your order, and put the spurre on your heele my selfe.[8] *Palmerin* on his knee humblie kissed the Princes hand, and continuing in talke togeather, *Florendos* tooke a great delight in beholding him, so that hee demaunded his name and Countrey. My Lord, quoth he, they which found me amongst the Palme Trees, on the Mountaine of Oliues, not farre from *Constantinople*, haue giuen me the name of *Palmerin*.[9] By mine honour said *Florendos*, I ought wel to know the Cittie whereof you speake, as the place wherein my deerest affections tooke their first life, and not long since, are bequeathed to death, awaiting nowe but the howre to be discharged of the burden.[10]

Thus hauing in his companie his vnknowne Sonne, begotten by him on the Princesse *Griana*, knew little that his loue had sorted to such effect: neuerthelesse, nature prouoked him to like so well of *Palmerin*, as none in the Courte contented him more then he. And longer woulde they haue continued their talke, but that faire *Arismena* interrupted them, asking *Palmerin* if he woulde discharge her of the request he demaunded. That doo I Madame (quoth hee) and in requitall thereof, dedicate the whole circuit of my life to your gracious seruice: and to begin my deuoire on your behalfe, so soone as I haue receiued my Knighthoode, I wyll take my iourney towards the Serpent, in hope to bring the water that must recouer the King your Fathers health. Alas good Sir, said she, God forbidde that you should fall in such daunger by my meanes. I know well aunswered *Palmerin* that I can die but once, and if it be nowe, then am I dispatched, and if I escape, I shall doo that whereof many other haue failed, and this is my resolution faire Madame. Beleeue me, said *Florendos*, me thinkes you are as yet too yong, to finish an action wherein consists so great daunger, I praie you therfore referre it vnto such, as haue had more experience in Armes then as yet you haue. My Lorde, saide *Palmerin*, in other matters I shall obey when you command, but this I must desire you not to disswade me from. Well then, quoth *Florendos*, seeing you will needes haue it so, I am content, you shall in the meane while keepe mee companie: as for Sworde and Armour, trouble not your selfe to prouide anie, because my selfe will furnish you sufficientlie. Thus all daie *Florendos* accompanied *Palmerin*, demaunding of him what things he had seene in *Constantinople*, and falling from one discourse to another, he asked him what Esquire he had to attend on him. Then he shewed his Dwarffe called *Vrbanillo*, such a deformed

and euill fauoured felow, as euerie one that saw him laughed hartilie,[11] whereup‐
pon *Palmerin* said to *Florendos*. By my faith my Lorde, as vnseemelie as he is, I
thinke so well of him, as I should be displeased if he were anie waie iniuried.
Assure your selfe, said *Florendos*, that he will stand you in great stedde when you
haue no neede of him, and looke that you leaue nothing behind you, that you
neede to fight against the Serpent, and trust it in his discretion to bring after
you. When *Vrbanillo* perceiued euerie one iest so with him, he was halfe angrie,
and in some choller thus said to the Prince. I can no waie, my Lord, better my
shape or proportion, but if I liue, this little deformed bodie of mine shall giue
you to vnderstande, that I beare so good a minde, as where my Maister leaues his
life, I meane to finish mine, and though in meane while I can doo him no other
seruice, he shalbe assured of my trueth and loyaltie. Be not offended (Dwarffe
my good freende) saide *Florendos*, for I thinke well of thee and of thy behauiour:
And so because the Tables were couered for Supper, they brake of talke, *Palmerin*
preparing himself to his watchfull deuoire in the Chappell.

Chapter xv.

Howe Florendos gaue to Palmerin the Armour and Sword of Gamezio, whom hee slewe before Constantinople, and afterwarde Knighted him: and howe a Damosell came to the Court, who presented him with a Helmet and a rich Sheelde.

The time beeing come, that *Palmerin* should performe his deuoute watch in the Chappel, before hee receiued his Knighthoode, according to the aunctient custome: *Florendos* gaue commaundement that the Armour of *Gamezio* should bee brought him, which the Emperour had giuen him, after his conquest of the Soldan of *Babilons* army on the Sea, as you haue heard before,[1] and these he shewed to *Palmerin*, saying. My freend, this Armour sometimes belonged to the best Knight of his time,[2] whom (neuerthelesse) I conquered, beeing then more pleasant, ioyfull, and at better content, then I shalbe while I haue a daie to liue. And because I haue some speciall opinion of your prowesse, and that these ornaments of defence you will better imploy, then anie other on whom I shal bestowe them: I praie you henceforth to weare them for my sake. My Lorde, saide *Palmerin*, my desire is, that my seruice towardes your honour, maie be witnessed in my good imploying of this gentle gift. Then *Frenato* and diuers other Knights did helpe to arme him, and afterward accompanied him to the Chappell, where all that night hee spent in sollemne orisons, that God would endue him with strength to vanquish the Serpent, that so the King might againe receiue his health.

At the breake of daie, as *Florendos* went to the Chappell to giue him his order, there entred among them on the suddaine a comelie Damosell, bearing a Helmet and a Sheeld of Azier,[3] the goodliest and most beautifull that euer was seene, vpon the Sheelde beeing portraied a Ladies arme, hauing her hande fast closed togeather: the Damosell comming before the Prince *Florendos*, began thus. I pray you my Lord to pause a while, till I haue conferred a little with *Palmerin*. *Florendos* was greatlie amazed at this accident, in that he had neuer seene the Damosell before: notwithstanding he returned this answere. Faire Damosell and my Freende, good leaue haue you to saie what you please. Then comming to *Palmerin*, and falling on her knees before him, she saide. Sir *Palmerin*, a Knight that hath authoritie to commaund me, and whom as yet you doo not knowe, hath sent you by me this Helmet and Sheelde, wherein you shall find the verie secretes of your hart. And if you desire to know whence this honour proceedeth, it commeth from him who hath prooued the effect heereof, and that knowes more of your neerest affaires then you doo your selfe, albeit as yet he hath neuer seene you.[4] Damosell, saide *Palmerin*, where maie I finde the learned man that hath thus honored mee, whom I may remunerate with my cheefest endeuours heereafter? You cannot as yet know him, saide the Damosell. I praie you faire Virgin, quoth *Palmerin*, that you will aunswere on my behalfe, howe in anie place I shall come heereafter, I remaine readie to doo what likes him to commaunde me. It suffiseth (quoth she) looke that heereafter you remember your promise: then comming to the Prince *Florendos*, she said. My Lorde, the same Man from whom I haue saluted *Palmerin*, gaue me in charge to saie to you, that you should not feare or doubt to dubbe him Knight: but to perswade your selfe, that both by Father and Mother hee is so noble as he dooth well deserue it, and him heereafter you will loue beyond all other, for by him you shall enioy the thing you most esteeme and desire. Thus hauing no longer licence to staie with you, I humbly desire you to excuse my departure. Sweete Maide, saide *Florendos*, may your wordes sort to so good end, as you haue promised. So departed the Damosell, leauing *Palmerin* on his knee before the Prince, who taking the Sworde that sometimes belonged to *Gamezio*, Knighted him,[5] saying: And maist thou prooue as famous and fortunate, as my hope perswades mee thou wilt. Then was he honourablie conueyed to the Pallace, where the faire *Arismena* vnarmed him, and couered him with a rich Mantle of white Satten, imbroydered all ouer with sumptuous flowers of Gold: beside, no one in the troupe but highlie reuerenced him, for the woorthie report the Damosell made of him. And albeit the Princesse *Arismena* disswaded him so well as she could, that he should not endanger himselfe against the Serpent, because by him her Brother should ouercome his melancholly, and fearing his losse without hope of recouerie: yet needes would he be gone the same daie, but that her importunate intreatie perswaded him to staie eight daies longer. *Palmerin* beeing soone after alone by himselfe, he remembred the wordes of the Damosell, who promised him to finde the secrets of his hart in his Sheelde: whereupon he well aduised himselfe,[6] and sawe that the hand portraied in the Sheelde, had the same marke which the Ladie had, that appeared to him in his sleepe,[7] whereat not a little maruailing, he said within himselfe. It must needes be without all doubt, that he which sent mee this present, knoweth full wel the scope of my fortune, for I am well assured, that the Ladie which spake to mee in my sleepe, when I abode in the house of my Father *Gerrarde*, shewed me her hand, with the selfe same marke I see heere pictured: by which I may perswade my selfe, that she will not cease to follow and finde me out,[8] vntill such time as I maie speake with her. Whereuppon he founde himselfe so suddainlie inueigled with her loue, as he thus complained. Ah *Palmerin*, well maist thou see that long thou canst not resist this impression, but whence should this humour[9] proceede? To loue her thou neuer sawest, nor knowest where is her abiding? If it fall out that thou diest in thy pursuite, these passions shall so haue a finall ende, and I gaine the greatest felicitie that I can desire. By this time had he spent the eyght daies, which he promised *Arismena* for *Florendos* companie, when as well to begin the searche of her hee loued so well, as to ende the aduenture he intended of the Serpent: he prepared to depart, prouiding himselfe a great huge Mace of yron, which did him good seruice, as you shall reade heereafter.

Chapter XVI.

Howe Palmerin fought with the horrible Serpent on the Mountaine Artifaeria, and slewe him, bringing the glasse filled with the water of the Fountaine, whereby King Primaleon of Macedon recouered his health.

Eight daies had *Palmerin* stayed with *Florendos*, and in companye of the fayre Princesse *Arismena*, who fearing that hee woulde neuer returne from the Mountaine *Artifaeria*, was very pensiue and sad: and oftentimes she intreated him, not to hazard himselfe against those cruell, rauenous and supernaturall Monsters, but rather to witnesse his valour against Knights of account like himselfe, but all her speeches profited not, for he was resolute to depart. I shall yet desire you, sayde the Princesse, that for my sake you will take with you three Esquires which I will giue you, who may lend you succour if anie inconuenience should befall you. Then she called the Esquires, and presented them vnto him, with the glasse that he should bring the water in from the Fountaine, if Fortune stoode with him to finish the aduenture. *Palmerin* mounting on horsebacke, and *Florendos* accompanying him halfe a daies iourney on the way, left him on his iourney towardes the Mountaine *Artifaeria*, where he arriued on the last daie of *Aprill*.[1] Then he commanded the Esquires and his Dwarffe *Vrbanillo*, to expect his returne at the foote of the Mountain, for he would suffer none of them to goe vp with him: so ascended he the Hyll by a little trackt footepath, with hys yron Mace on his necke, and the Glasse for the water fastened at his gyrdle. Hauing thus trauailed vppe till about midday, he founde the passage so thicke set with Trees and brakes, as he was constrained to alight from his Horse, whom he vnbrideled and left there feeding: and much further had he not gone, but the night ouertooke him,[2] yet did the Moone shine bright and cleere, which made him still trauaile onwarde, till he beheld the Rocke where the water was, and the Serpents Den, who was come somewhat lower to recreate himselfe among the greene Hearbes,[3] where he hadde closelie couched himselfe. But when he heard *Palmerin* comming, he began to swell, and writhe his taile togeather verie strangely: all which could not dismay this aduenturous Knight, but commending himselfe to God,[4] sette downe his Glasse, and with his Mace marched stoutlie against his enemie, who said. Why *Palmerin*? didst thou so often request of *Florendos* and the Princesse his Sister, to try thy strength against thys deuill, and now thou art come in sight of hym wylt thou faint? Dooth it not beseeme thee better to die with honour, then to liue with shame? let the one encourage thee to follow thy enterprise, and the other kill thee when thou offerest to retire.[5] And with these wordes he aduaunced him to the Serpent, and the Serpent fiercelye began to assaile him, and with his taile had smote him down, but that hee nimblie preuented the stroke, deliuering the Serpent so sore a blowe on the head with his Mace, as made him reele and stagger, and cry so terribly, as the whole Mountaine resounded with a meruailous Eccho, and to reuenge himselfe, with his tallants he got hold on *Palmerins* Armour, which hee rent violentlie in two or three places, wounding his bodie verie daungerouslie. When *Palmerin* perceiued in what hard plight he was, he tooke hart a fresh, and watching his aduauntage, strooke the Serpent wyth his Mace so stronglie on the necke, as he fell to the grounde in a manner dead, and *Palmerin* plied him with so manie strokes one after another, as he left him not while any life was in him. After this happy victory, for which deuoutlie he praised God, binding vppe his woundes so well as he could,[6] with extreame wearines he laid him downe and slept, when he seemed to see the three Sisters whereof wee haue spoken before,[7] who were the Daughters to a Knight, Lord of the Isle *Carderia*, to whom none might be compared for knowledge in the Magicall sciences, and so well he had instructed his Daughters, as after his death, they alone excelled in this Arte, so that the men of that Countrey commonlie called them the Goddesses of destinie, because they coulde diuine before what should follow after. And if any one didde happen to iniurie them, they would reuenge themselues by their enchauntments, so that they were greatlie feared and helde in reuerence. They vsed diuers times this Mountaine *Artifaeria* as well to gather Hearbes for theyr necessarie vse, as also for the Water of the Fountayne, for the defence whereof they had there left this Serpent, who was in time growne so huge and monstrous, as he rather seemed a deuill then a natural Beast. Notwithstanding, howe hidious soeuer he was, *Palmerin* as you haue hearde ouercame and slewe him, finding the three Sisters in the manner as I haue tolde you: who were not greatlie discontented with him, but esteemed so well of him, as in his sleepe the eldest of them thus spake to him. Beleeue me *Palmerin*, thy beginning is so honourable, as great pittie it were to let thee die heere, cheefelie for the want that all *Greece* shal haue of thee in time to come, the whole Empire wherof is predestinated thine:[8] and therefore will I heale the woundes thou hast at this time receiued. I will then doo somewhat more for him, said the seconde Sister, I will enchaunt him so wel for his auaile, as heerafter no coniuration or witchcraft shall haue anie power to hurt him. Truelie said the third Sister, for my part, I will giue him such fortune, as the first time he shall see his Ladie *Polinarda*, (who so manie times saluted him in his Dreames)[9] shee shall looue him so intirelie: as no dolor or torment shall make her forget while shee liues, the happines shee shall receiue by his occasions. Then the eldest Sister tooke a Golden Cup, and filled it with the water of the Fountaine, and wringing the iuyce of certaine Hearbes into it, washed therewith *Palmerins* woundes, so that they were immediatlie healed.

Now felt he verie wel all they did, but his slumber tooke awaie the libertie of his speeche, vntill such time as they were departed, but first the eldest of them thus spake. Since this Knight hath had so good a beginning, and that his strength hath depriued our garde of our Fountaine, I praie you let vs suffer him to haue his Glasse full of our Water, that by his meanes the King of *Macedon* may be healed, which a number of other Knights haue failed of heeretofore. Wherto they all consented, and so it came to passe: then gathering their Hearbes as they were wont, and washing them, they tooke their waie to the Isle *Carderia*.

Chapter XVII.
Howe Palmerin discended from the Mountaine, wyth his Glasse full of the water of the enchaunted Fountaine, and how ioyfull Vrbanillo and the other Esquires were, seeing their Maister returne with so good fortune.

When these three Sisters were departed, *Palmerin* awaked and arose, not a little meruailing at that he had heard and seene: but most of al when he felt his woundes healed, and sawe his glasse ful of the water he came for, so rendering thankes to heauen for his good successe, hee went vp higher on the Mountain, thinking to see the Fountaine, but he could not,[1] wherfore without any longer staie he discended downe againe, thus saying to himself. How happie maie I count my selfe, to finde so good fortune in this desolate Mountaine? for now I know her name that is destenied to be mine, henceforth shal she not conceale her selfe from me, may I find the place where she abideth: and this I vowe by him that made mee, that I will not cease to seeke her through the world, til I heare some tidings of her: and were it not for the promise I haue made the Princesse *Arismena*, to bring her this water to recouer the King her Father, this daie woulde I begin my religious enterprise,[2] in hope (if the Ladies spake trueth that appeared to me in my sleepe) heereafter to be one of the happiest Knights in the world. So walked he on til he came where he left his horse, wheron hee mounted, and came to *Vrbanillo* and his other Esquires, who hauing heard the cry of the Serpent, when *Palmerin* gaue him his first stroke, perswaded themselues that their Maister was slaine: but when they saw him comming, *Vrbanillo* aboue all the rest was most ioyfull, and ran apace to meete him, desiring to know how he had sped. Verie wel I thank God, said *Palmerin*, who gaue me strength to kill the Monster, and to bring sufficient of the Water I hope, to winne the King *Primaleon* his health. Then haue I the thing I most desire, said *Vrbanillo*, albeit I greatlie feared that you had accompanied all the other Knights in death, that aduentured before you, and coulde not speede so well. So mounted they all on horsebacke, and made so good iourneies as they arriued at *Macedon*: whereof *Florendos* and faire *Arismena* were not a little ioyfull, especially when they were assured, that *Palmerin* had brought with him the Kings health, by meanes wherof it is not to be demanded,[3] if he were highlie honoured and receiued at the Court.

CHAPTER XVIII.
How foure Knights would haue taken the Glasse of fatall water from Vrbanillo, before Palmerin arriued at Macedon, and of the Combat betweene them.

You must heere vnderstande, that the same day, *Palmerin*, in companie of his Esquires, departed from the Mountaine, hee sent *Vrbanillo* the Dwarffe before towards *Macedon*, with the Glasse of water, when it so fortuned that foure Knights met with him, one of them saluting him in these hard tearmes. Deformed villaine, giue me that Glasse, or I shall take thy head from thy shoulders. *Palmerin*, who came not farre behind, seeing the Knights offer iniurie to his Dwarffe, gaue spurs to his Horse, and thus answered. Howe now Gentlemen? are you not ashamed in my presence to abuse my seruaunt? trust me I neither can nor wil so put it vp: and so couching his Launce, he encountred one of them so roughlie, as he fel from his Horse deade to the ground.[1] When the other three sawe their companion thus foyled, they altogeather set vpon *Palmerin*: but their fortune fel out so ill, as two of them were soone vanquished, and the third tooke himself to flight verie hardlie escaping. *Palmerin* made no account of folowing him, but leauing them rode on his way, his Dwarffe thus comming to him. Beleeue me my Lord (quoth he) hee is to be accounted ouer foolish hardie, that at the weapons point seekes to offende you: I dare boldlie affirme my wordes, by euidence of the fortune of these foure Knightes. In that, said *Palmerin*, thou maist be deceiued, but God is alwaies freende to iustice and equitie, and enemie to such as goe against them. But because you shall know the occasion why these foure Knights would haue taken the glasse from *Vrbanillo*, you must note that they were all Sonnes to a great Lorde of a Castell, which was a daies iourneie off the Mountaine *Artifaeria*, who hauing intelligence by Sheepeheards and other pesants, what good fortune had befallen *Palmerin*, to kill the Serpent, and bring away the fatall water, repined greatlie thereat: for the Lorde did highlie mallice the King of *Macedon*, because he had enforced him to surrender a Manour, which he against all right, held from one of his Sisters, and for this cause, knowing that by the vertue of that water the King shold recouer his health, hee sent his foure Sonnes to take it from *Palmerin*, whose successe in their attempt fell out as you haue heard. Now *Palmerin* by this time is come to *Macedon* to the King, whom with great reuerence he saluted on his knee: when the King embracing him so well as he could, saide. Trust me my good Freende, next God I must needes esteeme you dearest, for that as he by his Godhead hath made me breath this ayre, though weake and sicklie:[2] by diuine prouidence hee hath sent you to restore me my bodilie health, from hencefoorth therefore I shall intreate you to commaund mee and mine at your pleasure. My gratious Lorde, saide *Palmerin*, the heauens giue me successe to doo you seruice, for I knowe no Prince liuing this daie, for whom I would more gladly aduenture my life. I thank you good Sir, quoth the King, but the greefe I haue sustained for the sorrow of my Sonne

Florendos, brought me into such a long and lingering extreamitie,³ as well may I blesse the time, that by your good successe am so happilie deliuered: let me therefore entertaine you as my seconde Sonne, and perswade your selfe of such a Father, who wil loue you as if you were his owne naturall Childe, in that I and the greater part of my Kingdom shalbe at your disposition. Woorthy Sir, saide *Palmerin*, woorthilie might I be reputed amongst the worst in the world, refusing the honour you please to offer mee, especiallie in such an extraordinarie kinde of fauour: for the rest, (beeing thus accepted in your princely grace) I haue sufficient, beeing furnished with Horse and Armour to doo me seruice. With these wordes the King embraced him, and meere ioy caused the teares to trickle downe his cheekes: so that *Palmerin* staied longer with him then he made account to doo, till the Duke of *Durace* sent for him, as you shall reade in the discourse following.

Chapter xix.

How Duke Astor of Durace sent to the King of Macedon, desiring him to sende him the Knight, that had slaine the Serpent on the Mountain Artifaeria, to ayde him against the Countie Passaco of Mecaena, who laide straight siedge to one of his Citties.

So farre was spread the fame of this victory, which *Palmerin* had against the Serpent on the Mountaine *Artifaeria*, as at length the Duke *Astor* of *Durace*[1] hearde therof, against whom the Countie *Passaco* of *Mecaena*[2] waged battaile, and seeing himselfe vnable to resiste his enemie, minded to sende to the King of *Macedon*, requiring ayde of the Knight that slewe the Serpent at the enchaunted Fountaine: and heereuppon he dispatched one of his Gentlemen towards the King, who made good haste till he came thither, when dooing his reuerence, and deliuering his Letters of credite to the King, he saide. Dread Lorde, the Duke of *Durace* my Maister, most humbly salutes your Maiestie by me. The King hauing read the Letters, and noting the contents, bad the Messenger discharge the rest of his message. It is so Sir, said the Gentleman, that of long time my Lord and maister hath beene assaulted by the Countie *Passaco*, and in such cruell sorte hath warred on him, as he hath well neere destroyed his whole Countrie, for he hath taken the Cittie of *Mizzara*,[3] and againste all right dooth challenge it for his owne. After this, the Duke my Maister raysing his siedge to bid him battaile, Fortune hath beene so contrarie to my Lorde, as his noble Sonnes are slaine, and the greater part of his worthyest Gentlemen. Yet not contented with all this, the Countie pursues him stil to his very Cittie of *Durace*, which he hath begirt with siedge so stronglie, as hee is doubtfull of a further daunger. But within these eyght daies he vnderstood that your highnesse hath heere a Knight, that slewe the Serpent on the enchaunted Mountaine, in whose valour my Lorde reposeth such confidence, as woulde you graunt him licence to come thither, my Lorde will accompany him with so manie hardie men at Armes, as he doubts not to enforce the Countie to leaue his Country, and for that the matter requireth expedition, he desires your assistaunce with all possible speede. I am sorrie, quoth the King, that the Duke my Nephew is in such extremitie, and I promise you I did not thinke as yet to part with *Palmerin*: but seeing the necessitie is so vrgent, I will intreate him to goe with you, and so manie approued Knights with him, as the Countie shal perceiue, I am not well pleased with his hard dealing towardes my Nephew. Nowe was *Palmerin* present when the Gentleman deliuered his message, which pleased him not a little, because he would gladlie leaue the King to followe his fortune, and was thus held from his desire by importunate requestes: but seeing the King had graunted to sende him to the Duke, he fell on his knees, vsing these speeches. In respect my good Lord, that the Duke your Nephew hath vrgent occasion to imploy me, and in that his sute is onely for me, without any other of your people: I beseeche you suffer me to goe alone to him, for my hope is so good, in a cause of trueth and right, that wee shall bee sufficient there to ende the controuersie. Not so my good freende *Palmerin*, said the King, you shall not hazarde your selfe alone, but take such companie as I shall sende with you. My Lord, quoth *Palmerin*, he demaundes me without any other companye, and therefore let mee perswade you to satisfie his request: so turning to the Gentleman, he bid him prepare to set forward, for he was readie. Worthie Sir, answered the Messenger, with what expedition you please, for neuer was Knight expected with more earnest longing for, then you are. This suddaine resolution of *Palmerin* displeased *Florendos*: wherefore taking him aside, he said. I see then my deere Freende you will needes bee gone, albeit your companie hath giuen mee greater sollace and delight, then any thing els since I lost mine onelie content: yet is my regarde of your honor such, that I feare more to heare your misfortune, then I pittie the necessitie of my Cozin the Duke of *Durace*. Yet let me intreate you, that finishing your intent with fortunate successe, you make your present returne to the King my Father, whose loue, and whose liberalitye you neede not doubt of. My Lorde (quoth *Palmerin*) the King and you haue so highlie honoured mee, as wheresoeuer I shall come heereafter, I rest yours in my verye vttermost endeuours.

These wordes did *Ptolome* heare, the Sonne of *Frenato*, whom *Florendos* had kept since the time he was his Page, and was nowe olde enough to receiue Knighthoode: which made him desirous to purchase honour by some meanes, especiallie if the King woulde mooue *Palmerin* to take him with him, his request he perswaded himselfe would not bee denyed, whereupon, kneeling before the King, hee beganne thus. If it so please your highnes, that at your handes I might receiue my order of Knighthoode, before *Palmerin* departed from your Court: I am assured he would not disdaine me for his companion, especially if your Maiestie did mooue the question on my behalfe. Beleeue mee, quoth the King, so good a motion shall not be hindered by me, and therefore to morrow will I giue you your order, and such Armor as shall well beseeme a Knight, prepare you in meane time to performe your watch. Highly contented was *Ptolome* at these speeches, and gaue order for his prouision of needefull occasions, til euening came, when he entered the Chappell, where hee spent the night in deuout orisons, that heauen would so further the whole course of his time, as might stand with the aduauncement of iustice and his own honor. Earlie in the morning, the King accompanied with his Sonne *Florendos* and manie other Knights, entered the Chappel, where finding *Ptolome* on his knees, hee gaue him his knighthoode, wishing his fortune to prooue such, as might make him famous where euer he came: afterward he desired *Palmerin*, that this newe Knight might beare him companie in his trauailes, whereto *Palmerin* willingly consented, accepting so well of *Ptolomes* behauiour, as hee purposed thence forward not to forsake so good a companion. Then they both tooke their leaue of the King and *Florendos*, and departed with the Gentleman towardes the Duke of *Durace*, making such good expedition in their iourneye, as hauing crost the Seas with a prosperous winde, they landed in the Countrey of *Durace*. Nowe because the Cittie was besiedged on all sides, they were doubtfull howe to gette in vnseene of the enemie, which the Gentlemanne their guide performed so well: as by priuie signes made to the Sintinell, at length they got in without any danger. The Duke hearing tydings of their arriuall, left his Chamber and came to welcome *Palmerin*, whome hee entertained with great honour, spending the most part of the night in familiar conference with him, till hauing brought him to his Chamber, hee left them bothe to their good rest, till the next morning, when he came againe to visite them, thus saluting *Palmerin*.

Your arriuall, Sir Knight, dooth arme mee with such assured hope, as by the helpe I shall receiue at your hande, mine enemie (I trust) shal not outbraue me as he hath doone hitherto: and therfore you with your worthie companion, are bothe so welcome as you can desire. My Lorde, (quoth *Palmerin*) the King that sent me to you, hath bounde me to him by so manie courtesies, as for the loue of him and *Florendos* his Sonne, you may assure your selfe of my vttermost seruice, so long as I shall be able to holde my Sworde. The Duke returned his noble offer manie thankes, and walking into the Hall, the Duchesse there expected the comming of *Palmerin*, so after manie welcoms and courtlie embracings, the Tables beeing couered, they sat downe to Dinner: all which time, *Palmerins* eyes were fixed on the Duchesse Daughter, who was one of the fairest Vyrgins that euer he sawe, and so busied was his thoughts in beholding her, as hee gaue small regarde to the Dukes wordes, who reported what shamefull iniuries the Countie had offered him from time to time, and howe manie skirmishes had passed betweene them since the beginning of the wars. Thus spent they the Dinner time, till the Tables beeing withdrawne, and the Duchesse with her Daughter gone into their Chamber, the Duke questioned with *Palmerin* as concerning *Ptolome*, who was verie neere allied to the Duke: and so with discoursing of nouels of *Macedon*, as also the doubtfull affaires of the warres, they passed the whole daie till night came, when *Palmerin* and *Ptolome* departing to their Chamber, *Palmerin* coulde take no rest, the beautie of the Duchesse Daughter so troubled hys thoughts, which made him desirous to knowe her name: if this were shee the three Sisters spake of on the Mountain, and was beside promised him in his sleeping visions.[4] *Palmerin* was not alone thus passionate, but on the other side the yong Ladie became as amorous of him: but Fortune wold not permitte their loue, as you shall heare more heereafter. The Countie hauing al this while maintained very straight siedge, intending now to loose or gaine al, gaue fierce assault vppon the Cittie: first calling all the cheefest Lordes and Captaines of his Armie, moouing them with earnest and Souldiour like perswasions, to foresee all aduauntages, and to encounter their enemies with magnanimious and resolute courage. When he had thus imboldened his menne to the fight, with sound of Drummes, Trompets and Clarions they bad the Cittie battaile: then might you beholde howe they besturred themselues with Fagots to fill the Ditches and Trenches, set scaling Ladders to the walles, howe the one side assaulted and the other defended, that manie loste their liues or departed maimed, such hauocke did *Palmerin* and *Ptolome* with the Dukes power, make on their enemies, notwithstanding they were

Palmerin d'Oliva: Part I

in number farre beyonde them, and meruailous well prouided of all necessaries. But then *Palmerin* remembred a suddaine pollicie to preuent a mischeefe, for as the enemie retired to prepare for the seconde assault, he called the most part of the best Knights that the Duke had, willing each one betake himself to his horse and follow him, leauing the rest well appointed for defence of the walles. The Counties power sounding the alarme, and comming roughlie againe vpon the Cittie: *Palmerin* with his company priuilie issued foorth at the Posterne gate on the backs of the enemies, and gaue such a braue onsette, as they were forced to forsake their scaling Ladders to resist this encounter. There were manie strokes deliuered on either side, the Countie and most part of his Knights beeing on horsebacke, which made them holde the longer play with *Palmerin* and his men: notwithstanding, the Countie seeing such a hardie attempt giuen on a suddaine, and doubting freshe supplie woulde come from the Cittie, with feare began to retire, and with one of his Bretheren laboured to resist this sharpe assault, but *Palmerin* and his companie gaue them small time to rest, laying on loade with meruailous fiercenes, whereat the Countie was so offended, as comming to *Palmerin*, he gaue him such a cruell stroke on the Helmet, as he fell therwith to the ground, yet did he quicklie recouer himselfe againe, and requited the Countie with so sound a salutation, as he made him tomble from his saddle headlong to the earth, at what time on the other side *Ptolome* had so canuazed the Counties Brother, as he sealed him a quittaunce with his sword for his life. Then began the Counties Souldiours to dispayre of their successe, and *Palmerin* with his traine to follow them so closelie, as they were glad to take themselues to flight, leauing theyr Maister ouerthrowne in the Armie, where hee was troden to death with the trampling of the Horses.[5] Thus did the victorie remaine to the Duke, his enemies scattering in flight gladde to saue their liues, whom *Palmerin* commanded to follow no further, least gathering themselues togeather againe, and espying aduauntage, they might so endanger them: for oftentimes the vanquished too narrowly pursued, recouer courage and daunte the pride of the conquerers. For this cause he returned with his men into the Citty, the Duke vnderstanding the foyle of his enemie, which made him with a great number of woorthy Cittizens to goe meet *Palmerin* and *Ptolome*, whome embracing hee thus entertained. Ah good Knights,[6] by you is my estate recouered, and the death of my Sonnes reuenged on the murderer, therefore dispose of me and myne as you shall thinke beste: to which words *Palmerin* thus answered. My Lord, let heauen haue the honour of our victory,[7] as for me, I haue doone, and will heereafter what I can, for the great kindnesse of the King of *Macedon* your Vncle, who hath honored mee in sending me to you, and other recompence I neuer did or will seeke. As they thus parled togeather, the Duke perceiued by the blood on *Palmerins* Armour, that he was wounded in manie places, wherefore (quoth he) I see you are sore wounded, let vs make haste to our Pallace, where a Ladye attending on the Duchesse and well seene in chirurgerie, shall giue attendaunce on you till you are recouered. So mounting on horsebacke, they rode to the Pallace, where

Palmerin was lodged. Beeing brought into his Chamber, the Duchesse and her Daughter holpe to vnarme him, when the Ladie dressed his wounds, perswading him there was no daunger in them to be feared. Thus each one departing, *Laurana* the Duchesse Daughter called *Vrbanillo* the Dwarffe, saying to him. My Freende, desire thy Mayster to make bolde of any thing he wants, and that for my sake he will dispayre of nothing. Madame, said the Dwarffe, you haue good reason to wish my Maister well, as well for the good assistaunce he gaue the Duke your Father, as also in respecte of his deserts, which are as honourable as any that euer came in this Court. These words *Palmerin* verie well hearde, hauing his eye continually on her: wherefore when shee and all the other were departed, hee called *Vrbanillo*, demaunding what talke he had with the Princesse, which he reported, and his answere also. Gramercies, said *Palmerin*, I pray thee find the meane to let her knowe that I am her Seruaunt and Knight, ready to accomplishe anie thing that she shal commaunde me. Referre this matter to me Sir, quoth the Dwarffe, I knowe what Saint must patronize these affaires, and what offering must bee layde on his Altar.

Chapter xx.

Howe Palmerin became highlie enamoured with the beautie of the Princesse Laurana, thinking her to bee the Lady that sollicited him in his visions.

Vrbanillo the Dwarffe, not forgetfull of his Maisters commandement, the next day when *Laurana* came with her Mother to visite *Palmerin*, shee tooke the Dwarffe aside, demaunding what reste his Maister tooke the night past. Madame (quoth he) indifferent, I thanke God and you, for in you two consists the disposition of my Maisters health. As howe quoth shee? Thus Madame, said *Vrbanillo*, the first day that he behelde you, hee gaue the whole possession of himselfe so firmely to you, as day and night he meditates on your diuine perfections,[1] doubting in requital of his seruice to my Lord your Father, and his Countrey, whose liues and yours he hath defended, him selfe shalbe repayed with suddaine and cruel death: for had he not come for your safetie, well had he escaped this daungerous extreamitie. Then seeing (fayre Madame) that his valour hath beene the meane of your deliueraunce, doo not so degenerate from gentle nature, as to kill him that gaue you life.[2] Why my Freend (quoth she) what wouldest thou haue me doo? To loue him, sweete Madame, quoth he, as hee doth you. Alas, sayd she, thou mayst assure thy selfe, that none can wysh thy Maister better then I doo, beeing my duetie and his desert:[3] with which wordes shee chaunged colour with such modest bashfulnes, as it might be perceiued shee could hardly master her affections. Which when the Dwarffe behelde, as one not to learne his lesson in this arte, perswaded himselfe by the very lookes of *Laurana*, that his Maysters loue would sort to happy ende, and thereupon he followed the matter thus. I thinke Madame, that you wysh my Maister as well as anie, but that is not enough, vnlesse your wysh agree wyth his in this poynt: that you graunt your selfe his onely Lady and Mistresse, as hee hath vowed himselfe your Knight and Seruant. If it may please you to wysh this good to my Maister, vouchsafe this fauour as a president of your lyking: that so soone as he shall finde himselfe better in health, you wyll but consent to speake with him alone, in some such conuenient and vnsuspected place, as hee may haue liberty to acquaint you with the secrets of his thoughts. Alas (quoth she) how should I so doo, without offering too much impeache to mine owne honour? Madame, saide the Dwarffe, the night giues fauour to loues sweete enterprises. By this time the Duchesse was ready to depart, which *Laurana* perceiuing, sayd to the Dwarffe. Assure thy Maister from me, that I am more his then myne owne, and I will doo for his welfare what I may with modestie.[4] By reason of their departure, the Dwarffe coulde not make her answere, but shaddowing the matter as hee had doone before, went about his Maisters busines, till hee came and found him alone, when he discoursed all that had past betweene the Princesse and him, which so well contented *Palmerin* as nothing coulde more: because he perswaded himselfe, as I haue saide alreadie, that this was shee which the three Sisters promised him, by whom he shoulde receiue the honour that destinie allowed him. For thys cause thence forwarde he was verie desirous to knowe her name, commaunding *Vrbanillo* very straightly to enquire it, which hee did, informing his maister that her name was *Laurana*: whereupon he well sawe that hee was deceiued, in that the Sisters had named his Mistresse *Polinarda*, and therefore he resolued to withdraw his affection, and to depart thence so soone as he should be able to beare Armor. But it may be easilie presumed, that when one hath so far ventured in loue, that he perceiues himself beloued, as the Dwarffe perswaded his Maister: hardly can hee giue ouer so faire a beginning:[5] yet heere it fell out contrary, as you shall well perceiue, that the ende was more suddaine then the beginning. *Palmerin* now knowing the Princesse name, began to vse other countenaunce to her then hee was accustomed, but shee good Lady (in his excuse) conceiued better opinion then she had cause: yet as it euermore falleth out in loue, that when Ladies see themselues but slenderly courted by their Freendes, they growe importunate in their amorous desires, so came it to passe with *Laurana*, who perceiuing herselfe not solicited by *Palmerin* as shee was wont, one night somewhat late shee called the Dwarffe, and thus began. Howe comes it to passe (my good Freend) that thy Maister is not of so pleasaunt disposition, as heeretofore he hath beene? it may be thou hast not let him vnderstand my last salutation, or els feare with-holdes him from following his determination: I pray thee doo the message of my earnest good will to him, and tell him that I long to impart our affections togeather, to the ful resolution of our desired thoughts, which I haue found the way vnsuspected to accomplish, so please him to come to my Chamber to morrow at night, where I shall not faile to expect his presence.[6] When the Dwarffe heard *Laurana* vse these words, thinking his Maister was still in his former cogitations, thus aunswered. Trust me fayre Madame, within these fewe dayes my Maister is become so mellanchollie, as I haue manie times feared his death, and I am sure hee hath no other cause to torment him so, but onely the fury of the extreame loue he beares you: yet seeing you haue promised him such gracious fauour, let me alone to change this vnpleasaunt humour. Fayle not then quoth shee, to let him know my minde. I goe presently, said the Dwarffe, to acquaint him with these long desired tydings. So taking his leaue, he went to his Maisters Chamber, whom he founde fast a sleepe, when not daring to awake him, let stay hys message till the next morning, and so laide him downe to rest: at what time sleepe had thorowly possessed him, he began to cry and complaine so loude, as his Maister hearing him arose, and demaunded of him the cause of his lament. Alas my Lorde (quoth he) neuer in all my life was I so affrighted, me thought that one of the fayrest Ladies that euer eye lookt on, helde a naked sworde against my throate, saying. Vile and villainous creature as thou art, darest thou presume so much to offende me, as to make thy Lorde and Maister amorous of Lady *Laurana*, and to forsake me? iustly doost thou deserue to dye on this weapon for thy paillardise: and if heereafter thou carry any message to preiudice my right, assure thy selfe that I wil chastise thee in such sort, as all deformed villaines shal receiue example by thee. I tell thee Traytour, *Palmerin* his fortunes climbes higher then the name of

Laurana, and where he is more looued for the royaltie of his linage, then for his base and Pastoral education. With which wordes shee gaue me such a stroke on the heade with her sworde, as I (fearefull of my life) cryed so loude as you say you hearde me. This motion made *Palmerin* easily perceiue, that *Polinarda* had made thys threatning to the Dwarffe for *Laurana*:[7] which concealing to himselfe, he said in laughter. I think thou diddest forget to drinke when thou cammest to bed, and so thy hart beeing drie conceiued this fonde vision: I praie thee sleepe, and trouble me no more with such idle passions. The Dwarffe betooke him to rest, but *Palmerins* thoughts all night were hammering on this Dreame, so that he resolued to departe thence the next morning, and seeke els where his aduentures, seeing hee was admonished by so manie aduertisements. So at the daie rysing he called the Dwarffe, and commaunded him to prepare his Armour, for hee intended to take his leaue of the Duke. *Ptolome* hearing this, and hauing noted beside all that the Dwarffe tolde his Maister in the night. Dissembling the matter, as was his manner, he came and bad *Palmerin* good morrowe, who aunswered *Ptolome* in this manner. My deere Freend, I haue concealed none of mine affaires from thee, since the time we receiued our knighthoode, and parted togeather from the Courte of *Macedon*: nowe therefore shall I impart to thee what I haue determined.

   It is so, that vrgent occasions constraines me presently to leaue this Countreie, and henceforth to frame my course which way Fortune will direct me, by which occasion I see we must be enforced to leaue each other: notwithstanding, let me intreate that our absence may no way impayre our freendshippe, not doubting but in good time we shall meete togeather againe. In meane space, if you see the King or Prince *Florendos*, forgette not the humble duety of theyr vowed Seruaunt I beseeche yee, who dedicates his life and honour in all attempts to their gracious fauours. By God, said *Ptolome*, let who will doo the message for me, for neither death nor daunger shall seperate me from you: but I wil beare you companie while life and soule hold together. If you be so resolute, said *Palmerin*, shame were it for mee so to refuse you. Set forward then when you please (quoth *Ptolome*) for we neither must nor will depart, thats flat. So beeing bothe armed they came to the Duke, who meruailed much to see them so prepared, and therefore demaunded whether they went. My good Lord, answered *Palmerin*, in that your Countrey is nowe quieted, wee must intreate you for our departure, because waightie affaires in other places doo so commaunde vs. How happens it fayre Freendes, saide the Duke, that you will so soone leaue mee? My Lorde (quoth *Palmerin*) wee are so enforced, and therfore we humblie intreate you, not to be offended. If your affaires bee such, saide the Duke, lothe am I to hinder you, commaunde of me and mine what you please, for all remaineth at your disposition. Most humble thanks did *Palmerin* and *Ptolome* returne the Duke, and ere they went to horsebacke, they came to take their leaue of the Duchesse and *Laurana*, who was well nie deade, seeing her hope deceiued, for she expected the night comming, when shee and *Palmerin* should conferre togeather of their loue:[8] but seeing him now departing, she was out of all hope to see him againe, the extreame greefe whereof so ouercame her, as giuing a greate shrike shee fell in a swoune. The Ladies and Gentlewomen in great amazement came about her, ignoraunt of her euill but onelie *Palmerin* and his Dwarffe, which hee likewise woulde not reueale to anie, for the reason you hearde discoursed before: and rather would she entertaine her own death, then make knowne a secrete of such importaunce: wherefore hauing somewhat recouered herselfe, and not able to conceale her anguish, with an extreame sigh she thus breathed foorth her sorrow.[9] Ah *Palmerin*, easilie hast thou kindled the fire, which with great shame thou leauest consuming vnquenched. Who would haue thought such treason coulde harbour, where faire conditions and honourable valour shined so brightlie? Well may I condemne al men of disloyaltie, seeing thou hast failed resembling so excellent. Beleeue me Knight, thou hast doone mee great wrong, and thy selfe much more, for which where euer thou commest, be thou named the most vngrateful Knight that euer drew Sworde, seeking her death so cruelly, who loues thee deerer then her owne life. These complaints made the sorrowful *Laurana* before the Duchesse, not sparing to discharge the whole burthen of her oppressed hart, her Mother not daring to gainesay her, but expected when she shoulde depart this life: wherefore perswading her from dispaire, shee sweetelie promised to worke so with *Palmerin*, as he should staie and enioy her to his wife. But all was in vaine, for he mounted on horsebacke, and accompanied with *Ptolome* and *Vrbanillo*, left the Cittie of *Durace*, no one knowing which way they were ridden: *Palmerin* conuerted into such heauines, as nothing coulde torment him more, so earnest was his desire to see her, whome fate and Fortune had appointed for him.

Chapter XXI.

Howe Palmerin and Ptolome met with a Damosell, who made great mone for a Casket which two Knights had forcibly taken from her, and what happened to them.

Beeing thus departed from *Durace*, these Knights rode along, thinking in what heauines they had left the Dukes Daughter: when *Palmerin* accusing himself as guiltie of this mischaunce, within himselfe thus sadlie discoursed. Vnhappy man, that euer thou cammest into this Country, where thou hast left so harde an opinion of thy selfe, as while thou liuest thou shalt be the worse esteemed: and well worthie, for iustlie maist thou be accused of disloyaltie, in making meanes to obtaine the loue of the faire Princesse *Laurana*, and hauing conquered wher thou desiredst, to make so light account of her as thou haste doone. Had death preuented thee before, shee had beene satisfied, thine honour defended, and thy vnknowne *Polinarda* no way iniuried: which speeches made the teares to trickle down his cheekes, when *Ptolome* looking aside espyed him, and gessing the cause of his sadnes, said. Verily I neuer thought to see such womannishe behauiour in you, nor that any greefe or misfortune should haue teares so soone at commaundement. Howe will you heereafter withstande so manie casualties, hard aduentures, and daungerous stratagems, with manie and sundrie narrowe brunts that you must passe thorow, when I see you vnable to ouercome your own selfe: beeing supprized by her teares, to whome you haue doone honour to affoorde a good countenaunce? If you had receiued of her the sweetes of loue, reason might then plead in your excuse: but hauing no way misprised her honour, or offered offence to modest chastitie, what iniurie may shee saie that you haue doone her? Forget I praie you these vnseemelie fashions, hardly agreeing with a Knight of such report as you are, let vs finde some thing els to talke on, and tell me which way you intende to iourney. By my life, (quoth *Palmerin*) I knowe not: but let vs take which way Fortune shall please to conduct vs. I thinke it best then, sayde *Ptolome*, that we shape our course towarde *Rome*, where we shall finde people of all Nations, by whome we maie be instructed as concerning aduentures, worthy our trauaile, and guyding to honour. On then cheerelie, quoth *Palmerin*, and so they trauailed eight daies togeather, not meeting with any aduenture worthy to be spoken off: till at length they met a Damosell heauily mourning, who saide. Alas, what will shee saie whose trust was onelie in mee, hauing lost the thing wherein consisted her hope, to recouer the highest of her noble desires? *Palmerin* hearing these wordes, and mooued with compassion, rode to her, and demaunded the cause of her mourning. Sir Knight (quoth she) I was sent by a Ladye with a Caskette, wherein was one of the best Swordes in the whole worlde, which is so enchaunted, as none can drawe it out of the skabbard, but hee that is esteemed the worthiest Knight liuing:[1] but before any be admitted to make proffe of this aduenture, hee must graunt a request that I am to aske him. With this Sword haue I trauailed many strange Countries, as *Fraunce*, *Italie*, *Sclauonye*[2] and diuers other, where many haue tryed, but no one yet could finish the aduenture: whereuppon I was thys daie trauailing towarde the Emperours Courte of *Greece*, and heereby I met with two Knights, who hauing hearde the cause of my long trauaile, made proofe of their fortune one after another, and bothe failed, whereat they were so offended, as they tooke the Casket from me perforce, and are gone therewith I knowe not whither, which dooth so greeue me, in respect of her losse towards whom I am beholden, as death woulde be more welcome to mee then life. Faire Virgin, saide *Palmerin*, doo not discomfort your selfe, but shewe mee which way they rode that dealt with you so discourteouslie. Gentle Knight (quoth shee) if your hap be to restore my losse againe, you doo the most gracious acte, that euer Knight did for a distressed Damosell. These Traytors to honour (whereof the one is in Crimson Armour, bearing in his Sheelde three Lyons heades) tooke this waie by the woode, and as yet I am sure they canne not be farre hence. Then *Palmerin* clasped his Helmet, and taking his Sword and Launce, desired *Ptolome* to garde the Damosell and follow him, galloping that way which she had shewed him: and by the time he had rid two miles,[3] he espied them he looked for, talking with an other Knight they had mette, and they three togeather were assaying to open the Casket, to whom *Palmerin* cryed. Trecherous villaines, that can not meete with Ladies on the waie, but must offer them iniurie, deliuer the Casket, or yee die. One of the three turned presently, and seeing him that thus threatned them to be alone, not moouing a iote began to laughe, and scornefullie returned this aunswere. Softlie, softlie good Sir, God pardon their soules whome you kill so easilie: but for all hys words, *Palmerin* ran against them, and they at him, so that he receiued a small wounde on his shoulder, in recompence whereof, he gaue one of them a pasport into another world, and laid so lustilie on the seconde, as he set him quicklie beside his saddle. When the third sawe his companions at so harde a reckoning, he said to himselfe. By my faith he spake not vnaduisedlie, that said: *A safe escape is better then a bad tarrying.* And allowing this sentence for currant in his owne opinion, gaue the spurs to his Horse, making hast away with the Casket so fast as hee coulde: but *Palmerin* beeing somewhat better mounted, got such aduauntage of this runaway, as with his sword he parted his right arme from his bodie, whereuppon he fell to the grounde and the Casket with him. Then *Palmerin* alighted and tooke it vp, and leauing the Knight there, returned which way he came, when opening the Casket, he tooke great pleasure in beholding the Sworde, which was meruailous costlie: yet would he not prooue to drawe it foorth, because he knewe not her pleasure to whom it appertained. At length he espied *Ptolome* comming, who came apace (if neede had beene) to assist him: but when he knewe how he had ouercome the Knights, and recouered the thing was so desired, no man coulde bee better contented, especially the Damosell, who leaping from her Palfray, came and kissed *Palmerins* feete, saying. And may all happines repay this gentle deede, faire Knight, for but by you, my death had beene best welcome to me. Damosell (quoth hee) see heere the Casket according as I founde it, I know not whither they that

Palmerin d'Oliva: Part I   *167*

tooke it from you haue abused it or no. No, no, saide shee, they could no way wrong it, the Sword beeing heere that belongs to the best Knight. I praie you (quoth *Ptolome*) let mee make tryall of my strength, albeit I know my selfe no such man as you speake of: so taking the Casket, offered to begin, when the
5 Damosell desired him to forbeare, for (quoth shee) you must first graunt me one request. What ere it be, saide *Ptolome*, I graunt it: and so set all his might to his intent, but coulde not accomplish it, wherefore quoth he to the Damosel. Beleeue me Lady, he that wrought this enchauntment, dyd more by his arte, then I can by my cunning, and in my opinion you may trauaile long enough, before you finde
10 him that shall quit your expectation. The more wil be my trouble quoth the Damosell, beeing tyed by necessitye to such a Knights fortune. When *Palmerin* sawe that his companion had failed, he doubted whether he should take it in hand or no: yet seeing hee coulde speede no worse then other had doone, he said to the Damosell, will you any thing with me before I aduenture my selfe, for my
15 Freende shall not bee *mal content* for a fellowe. Gentle Knight, quoth she, I wyll nothing, but that you make me the like promise your freend did. Of that doubt you not saide *Palmerin*: so laying hande valiantlie on the Sword, without any great labor he drew it foorth,[4] beeing the richest and goodliest Sworde that euer was seene. Ah good Knight, sayde the Damosell, happy bee the day of thy nati-
20 uitie, for thou hast deliuered me from incredible labour. The Sword is yours, but by your promise you stand bound to goe with me where I shall conduct you, to doo that shall please my Lady to commaund you. Leade the way Damosell quoth *Palmerin*, and be sure we wil not leaue thy company. So mounted the Damosell on her Palfray, and tooke the way towards *Rome*,[5] where she that deliuered her
25 the Casket remained in deuotion, and with such speede they dispatched their trauaile, as they arriued at the Gate of a strong Castell, where the Damosell alighted, desiring *Palmerin* and *Ptolome* to expect her returne awhile. The Gate being opened, she went straight to her Mistresse and her Sister, who beeing gladde of her comming, demaunded if she had found the man shee went to seeke.
30 Ladies (quoth she) I haue, and hither he is come with me, but this I dare assure you before hande, that a more goodlie and valiant Gentleman liues not this daie: for in my presence he vanquished three Knights, who perforce tooke the Casket from me, and for the Sworde, he drew it foorth so easilie, as it had beene that he weareth by his side. Goe, said the Lady and cause him come neere, and come
35 Sister let vs goe to the Gate to entertaine him. Then was the Draw bridge let downe, when *Palmerin* and *Ptolome* riding to the Gate, met there the Ladies, whom they saluted with great reuerence, and each Ladye leading a Knight in by the hande, conducted them to their Chambers to be vnarmed.

Chapter XXII.

How the Lady of the Castell declared to Palmerin, what mooued the Gyant Darmaco to take from her her Daughter and her goods, whereuppon Palmerin promised to enter Combat with the Gyant: as much for pittie, as to acquite his promise made to the Damosell, that brought the Casket, and the enchaunted Sword.

Our two Knightes beeing thus entered the Castell and vnarmed, the Lady brought each of them a rich Mantle of Crimson Damaske, imbroydered with Golde and pearle, to couer them, and so came with them into the Hall to meate, where wanted no choyse of dainty delicates: so after the Tables were withdrawne, and manye other speeches passed beteene them, the Ladie thus began to *Palmerin*.

Sir Knight, as nowe I am a poore and disinherited Gentlewoman, that sometime was Wife to one of the welthiest Knights in this Countrey, with whome I long time remained not hauing anie Childe, till at length it pleased God to sende me a Daughter, so faire a creature as euer nature framed, who at my Husbands death was left with me but fiue yeeres aged. My Lorde and Husbande learned in the arte Magicke, and for his skill renowmed in this Countrie, the daie before his death hee called mee to him, vsing these speeches. Deere Wife, let it suffise thee that I knowe what shall happen to thee after my death, and that one shal take perforce from thee, not onelie such goods as I leaue thee, but also thy faire Daughter, to helpe which extremity, I haue somewhat prouided for thee before my departure.

Thou shalt finde in my Cabinett a Sworde, which I my selfe haue enclosed in a Casket, and haue sette so manie inchaunted spels on that Sword,[1] as no man shal be able to drawe it out of the scabbard, vnlesse he be the best approued Knight in the worlde, and he it is that must giue thee succour, and helpe to recouer againe thy losse. Too true fel out my Husbands speeches, for soone after *Darmaco* the Gyant came hither, and as his custome was to abuse whome hee listed, so tooke he from me the best of my Castelles, and in despight of me tooke my Daughter from me, saying that he would giue her to one of his Sonnes in marriage, a villain far more vicious then the Father, and so deformed, as nature standes ashamed at her owne workmanship. Nowe in respect I would not consent to this vnseemely marriage, such goods as was left me, hee violentlie tooke from mee, thys Sworde onelie excepted which you haue worthilie conquered, and that had gone with him too, but that my Sister hid it verie secretlie. Now woorthie Knight, if euer pittie tooke place in thy gentle hart, reuenge me on the villaine, that hath thus robde me of my goods and my Daughter, whose youth (beeing as yet but tenne yeeres olde) is the cause that the Giant hath not consumated the marriage.[2] And if it shal like you to doo thus much for me, you shall not onelie fulfil your promise to the Damosell that brought you hither, but you shall doo a deede acceptable to God, profitable to me, comfortable to my poore Childe, and

honorable for euer vnto your owne selfe.³ Madame (aunswered *Palmerin*) it is no meruaile if *Darmaco* haue doone you this wrong, in that Giants doo take a habit in trecherous dealinges:⁴ wherefore did not my promise binde me to your Damosel, I would not passe so lightlie out of this Countrie, ere I compelled him some-
5 what to recompence this iniurie, and this shall I (God willing) doo to morrowe, so please you I may bee conducted to him. Ah gentle Knight, saide the Ladie, what I am not able, Heauen will no doubt repay thee: And because it was nowe somwhat late, after they had spent a little more time togeather in conference, these Ladies accompanied him and *Ptolome* into their Chamber, and taking their
10 leaue, committed the Knights to their good rest for that night, which they passed with quiet repose, and on the next morning after they were armed,⁵ they demaunded their guide of the Ladie, that shoulde direct them the way towardes the Giant. Then she called the Damosell that carried the Casket, and two Knights of her owne, whom shee commaunded to goe with *Palmerin*: so committing him
15 to God and good successe, they tooke their waie straight to the Castell of *Darmaco*, where they arriued in the euening, when they espyed a Squire on the walles, who was appointed there to keepe the watch, to whom *Palmerin* saide. My Freende, I praie thee if *Darmaco* bee within, cause him to come foorth, for I would speake with him. And what woulde you with him aunswered the Squire?
20 I woulde intreate him, sayde *Palmerin*, to vse himselfe more courteouslie then hee hath doone heeretofore, and that hee woulde doo right to a good Ladie whom he hath disinherited, namely to sende her her goods and her Daughter againe: and if my intreatie may not preuaile with him, bidde him if hee dare come to the Combatt, wherein I will make him confesse vnder my Sworde, that his actions
25 haue beene villainous, traiterous, and disloyall.⁶ In good sooth Sir, aunswered the Squire in derision, you may seeme to haue reason, and they that sent you likewise, but your iourney I feare me will not amount to so much: therefore if you will be ruled by me get you going, vnlesse you are willing to leaue your heade for a signe to our Gates.⁷ My heade, said *Palmerin*, my Sworde holdes too good an
30 edge, and mine arme too sound strength, to leaue a Iewell of such price so easilie: goe therefore wher I byd thee thou wert best, otherwise assure thy selfe if I vanquish thy Maister, that thou with the rest shalt surelie dye the death. Too soone, said the Squire, shall I doo your message, and if anie harme happen to you, saie my good Freende you were councelled before: but as for my Maister *Darmaco*, he
35 hath not beene within for this howre and more, yet is his Sonne *Mordano* heere, who can bid you welcome as well as his Father. So departed the Squire, and in shorte time *Mordano* the Gyants Sonne came vpon the walles, demaunding of *Palmerin* what he sought for? I tolde thy Squire, aunswered *Palmerin*: but tell me, art thou the Son of the Giant, that delightest in offering villainie to Ladies? and
40 howe then, said *Mordano*, what if I am? I pray thee, said *Palmerin*, bid thy Father that without any further quarrell he deliuer the Ladie that he detaines violentlie, otherwise I shall cause him to doo it whether hee will or no. I shall make thee aunswere said *Mordano*, if thou darest tarrie but till I arme my selfe: and so

presently departing, in short time he came foorth very well appointed, with a
meruailous strong Launce in his hand, and mounted on a verie lustie Courser, so
prauncing towards *Palmerin*, hee saide. Wretch, art thou come to seeke thine
owne death? I pittie thee: yet if thou wilt yeelde thy selfe to my mercie, I will
spare thy life, and suffer thee to waste thy time in one of the base Dungions in
this Castel. From lodging there, God sheelde me, quoth *Palmerin*, and beeing
mooued wyth these rough wordes of his enemie, he encountred *Mordano* with
such courage, as their Launces beeing broken, bothe of them were dismounted,
Palmerin not hurt, but *Mordano* was wounded on the right side, the trunchion of
Palmerins Launce beeing left in his bodie. Notwithstanding he recouered himselfe quicklie, and came furiouslie towardes *Palmerin*, and gaue him such a cruell
stroke on the head, as the bloode beganne to trickle downe his face: which when
he perceiued, and howe it stoode him in hande now to be venturous, he requited
Mordano with so sounde a greeting, as he parted one of his armes quite from his
bodie, and astonied him likewise that he fell to the ground, but recouering himselfe, he ran towardes the Castell and *Palmerin* after him.[8] The Seruaunts of the
Castell, seeing their Lordes Sonne in such danger, with Iauelinges and other
weapons[9] came against Palmerin, whom they had murdered, if *Ptolome* and the
two Knights that were sent with him, had not speedilie come from their close
ambush to defende him, and so manfullie did they behaue themselues, as they
droue them into the base Court, where *Mordano* fell deade at *Ptolomes* feete, who
deferring no time, presently with hys Sworde tooke his heade from his shoulders.
The seruants this seeing, dispersed themselues and ran into corners, so that
Palmerin and his companie had no bodie left to resist them, some lying there
wounded to the death, and other escaping foorth at a backe Gate, which they
made fast after them least they should be followed. When *Palmerin* sawe all
thinges fall out so effectually, hee called for the Damosell and the Knights that
came with him, who beeing not a little glad of this great good fortune, desired
first to seeke for *Esmerinda* their Ladies Daughter, for they were well assured
that she was in the Castell. Searche in euery place, quoth hee, and because the
night drewe on, the Gates were made fast, and there they determined to lodge for
that night. In meane while, the Damosell went about the Castell, and neere the
Giants Chamber she founde *Esmerinda*, who immediatlie knowing her, came
running and caught her louingly about the necke: for before, (not knowing that
her companie had conquered the Castell) she and three other Womenne that
kept her companie, were greatlie feared, but nowe the Damosell gaue her perfect
assuraunce, that all was doone for her deliuerie, and by the onelie Knight for
prowesse in the worlde,[10] whom her Ladie Mother had thus sent thither. As they
continued this talke, *Palmerin* came to them, before whom the yong Gentlewoman *Esmerinda* humbled herselfe on her knees: but he taking her vp, embraced
her with these speeches. Prettie soule, your Ladie mother hath great desire to see
you, will not you goe with vs to her? Sir Knight, quoth shee, I neuer in my life
desired any thing more, then to see my Mother: but I greatlie doubt that the false

Darmaco will meete vs by the way, for he went this morning to the funerall of one of his Sisters, and it will bee to morrowe before his returne, when if hee hap to meete vs, we are but deade. Let me deale for that good Ladie, saide *Palmerin*: I haue learned alreadie to kill the Sonne, I doubt not but this smal practise, wil make me doo as much to the Father. While *Palmerin* and *Ptolome* thus deuised with *Esmerinda*, the Damosell and *Vrbanillo* had prouided Supper, which beeing ended they went to rest, expecting the morning, when they prepared the Women to horsebacke, and hauing taken what them best liked out of the Castell, they sette fire on the rest, and so tooke their way towards the sorrowfull Widdowe: who expecting good tydings, continued in earnest and deuoute orisons,[11] that the good Knight might ouercome her blood-thirstie enemie, and returne with victory and her Daughter *Esmerinda*.

Chapter XXIII.
Howe Palmerin returning with his company to the Ladies Castell, happened to meete with the Giant Darmaco, who lost his life in Combat with Palmerin.

Thus rode *Palmerin* and his company verie ioyfull of their good fortune, especially *Esmerinda*, aboue all the reste: but this pleasant humour lasted not long, for shee had espied *Darmaco* comming foorth of a woode, hauing with him his wife and tenne well appointed Knights, whereat the yong Ladie was so affrighted, as she cryed out, saying: O God, now are we all cast away. At which words the other women began to discourage themselues, and seeing the Giant so neere, knewe not whether they were best to goe forward or backe againe: whereupon *Palmerin* saide to *Ptolome*. I praie thee good Freende, while I fight with *Darmaco*, doo you and these two Knights deale with the rest: in the meane while, I thinke it good that my Dwarffe *Vrbanillo*, conuay these Ladies into the thickest of the woode. He had no sooner thus said, but he behelde the Giant make apace towards them, who not thinking what had happened, yet seeing faire *Esmerinda* so deliuered: in wonderfull rage, not taking either Sworde or Sheelde with him, he praunced towardes *Palmerin*, who entertained him so soundly on the head with his Fauchion, as the Giant tombled foorth of his Saddle, hanging in hys styrrop by the left foote, and was no way able to recouer himselfe.

The Horse feeling his Maister from his backe, and his burthen to weighe ouer heauie on his side, the Giants foote likewise tickling him in the flancke, began to course about, and to beate his Maister with his feete euery way he could reach him, when *Palmerin* on the other side laid him on such strokes, as at length he sent his soule to the deuils, the patrons of his villainous life.[1] Now thought *Palmerin* he had no more to doo, but goe helpe his companions against the other Knights, wherein he was deceiued, for the Giantesse to reuenge her Husbands death, gaue so cruell a stroke at *Palmerin* with her Husbands Mace,[2] as had he not shrunk aside she had slaine him, and so continued more like a Lyon then a Woman, redoubling stroke after stroke: which forced *Palmerin* for safegarde of himselfe, seeing no meanes or perswasions could preuaile with her, to sende her packing after her Husbande.[3] *Ptolome* and his Knights had dealt so well with the rest, as on the comming of *Palmerin* they had dispatched them all, if fresh supply had not come to them, as you shall heare more anon.

The Lady of the Castel mother to *Esmerinda*, so soone as *Palmerin* departed thence towardes the Giant, sent to seeke a yong Gentleman named *Crispino*, to whom shee promised her Daughter in marriage, if so be she could recouer her againe out of the Giants power: who staying not long after this message, made hast to the Castell, the Ladie entertaining him in this manner. Not long since, my good Freende, there departed hence a Knight, who intendes to reuenge my wrongs on the Giant *Darmaco*, and because I knowe not to what ende this enterprise will sorte: I pray you Arme you, and take tenne of your hardiest men

Palmerin d'Oliva: Part I 173

with you, to helpe the good Knight if he should be distressed. *Crispino* soone consented to this motion, and in his way towards the Castell, it was his chaunce to meete with the Dwarffe and the Ladies that fledde into the woode. It is not to demaund how pleasing this sight was to him, beholding *Esmerinda* whom
5 he loued as himselfe: of whom he demaunded where their companie was, and shee reported in what state they left them at time of their flight. Whereupon he commaunded fiue of his men to guide the Ladies, to a Kinsmans house of his that was neere at hande, and hee with the rest of his traine galloped to the place, where *Palmerin*, *Ptolome*, and the Ladies two Knights encountered wyth
10 the fresh supplie that came to *Darmacos* men. Hee was no sooner arriued, but he behelde *Palmerin* and *Ptolome* wounded very sore, and one of the Ladies Knights slaine among the rest, which mooued him and his men to bestir themselues: so that (short tale to make)[4] the Giants men were all vanquished in the ende, and then *Crispino* declared to *Palmerin*, howe he had sent *Esmerinda* and the
15 Ladies to his Cozins house not farre of, whether if it pleased him to walke, he should receiue what courtesie could be performed on so suddaine warning, in respect of the happy fortune the whole Country shoulde finde by him, beeing thus deliuered of *Darmaco* and his Sonne, but aboue all, for the safetye of his best beloued *Esmerinda*. Thus rode they togeather with *Crispino*, whose Cozin
20 made them verie gracious welcome, reioycing greatlie at this happy victory, and afterward they set forwarde to the good Widdowe, *Crispino* by the way reporting to *Palmerin* his loue to *Esmerinda*, and howe her Mother had promised him her in marriage, desiring him to assist the matter that it might bee finished: which he promised to doo, and so at length they came to the Castell, where
25 when the Ladie sawe her Daughter, and hearde howe her cheefest enemies were slaine, it is hard to expresse her exceeding ioy, which her cheerefull countenance somewhat made manifest, welcomming *Palmerin* with these wordes. Ah gentle Knight, howe might I be able while I liue to recompence this inestimable fauour? the comfort of mine age, and my oppressed soule haue you brought me, may
30 neuer harmes befal so good a Knight. Ladie, quoth he, giue the prayse to God, as for me, iudge if I haue beene as good as my promise to your Damosell or no: and if there be anie thing els to doo, Lady I am readie now to performe it. You haue doone so much for me, saide she, as nothing remaineth more to be desired, vnlesse of your bountie you will cause me to receiue what the Giant tooke from
35 me by force: for seeing he is deade, they that with-helde it from me, will nowe willinglie restore it againe. That shal be likewise accomplished, quoth *Palmerin*: but because hee and *Ptolome* were sore wounded as you hearde, they staied to be cured, and sent *Crispino* with his Cozin and a good sufficient traine, to demaunde the Ladies Castell and her goods. They that helde it of the Giant, vnderstanding
40 his death, made present deliueraunce thereof, and committed themselues to the Ladies mercie: whether shee sent her Daughter, so soone as *Palmerin* and *Ptolome* were healed, to whom the Subiects vowed their faith and allegeaunce, and with great Triumphes honoured the mariage of *Crispino* and *Esmerinda*. On the

morrowe, as the Knights sat at meate, there entred the Hall a Squire, who said to *Palmerin*, that a Damosel staied without to speake with him. Let her come in, quoth he, and saie her pleasure. The Squire bringing her into the Hall, she fell on her knees before *Palmerin*, saying. Sir Knight, doo you not knowe mee? No in good sooth, aunswered *Palmerin*. Beleeue mee (quoth the Damosell) then hath my seruice beene euil imployed which sometime I did you, and whereof I am sure you haue heard good account. Then *Palmerin* knewe her (she bringing the Sheelde and the Helmet when *Florendos* knighted him)[5] whereuppon he rose from the Table, and embracing her, said. Faire Damosell and my freende, I pray you pardon me, for the length of time since I first saw you, did quite exempt you from my remembrance: pleaseth it you to commaunde me anie seruice? Sir Knight, said the Damosell, when I presented you the Helmet and Sheelde, wherwith you tooke your order of Knighthoode, you promised mee (if you remember) that you would vse it with right good will, in anie affaires the Knight had that sent it you, and when he should require such performaunce: nowe is the time to confirme your deede with your worde, for hee hath sent mee to you with humble intreatie, that without anie staie, you goe where I shall conduct you, otherwise you are the onelie cause of his death. God sheelde him from such misfortune said *Palmerin*, rather woulde I goe with you presently from the Table. So doo I pray you, (quoth she) for I haue hast. Then he called for his Armour, and the table withdrawne, he went into his Chamber to arme himselfe, and so dyd *Ptolome* also: returning, they tooke their leaue of the Ladies and mounted on horsebacke, the whole companie beeing so sorrie for their departure, as *Esmerinda* came to the Damosell, saying. I promise you Damosell, you haue doone vs wrong in mine opinion, to hinder vs of the presence of so good a Knight. Ladie, aunswered the Damosell, thinke you he was borne for you onelie? content your selfe with the good you haue receiued by him, and suffer such as haue need of his prowesse, to receiue his assistaunce as you haue doone. And good reason saide *Esmerinda*, if it be to so good an end, that no resistaunce bee offered when helpe is required. So departed the two Knights with the Damosell which waie she guided them, and verie desirous was *Palmerin* to bee with the Knight that sent to seeke him: because hee would gladlie know, of whence hee was that wyshed him so wel, as his message declared by the Damosell the same daie hee was Knighted.

Chapter XXIV.

Howe Palmerin and Ptolome arriued at the Courte of the King of Bohemia, where they entred Combat against the Countie of Ormeque and his two Cozins, who accused the Knight and his Son of treason, that sent to seeke Palmerin.

Manie miles had these Knightes ridde with the Damosell, when *Palmerin* at length desired her to tell him, what hee was that sent him the Helmet and the Sheeld: whereto she aunswered, that seeing he was so desirous to knowe, listen, quoth she, and I shall report the whole vnto you. The Knight we speake of, is discended of verie royall bloode, beeing Vncle to the King of *Bohemia* that raignes at this present, as also to the Empresse of *Allemaigne* the verie best seene in Nigromancie this daie liuing. This noble man is named Prince *Adrian*, who neuer liked to liue in the Court of the King his Brother, but contented with what patrimonie his Father left him, at length maried with a verie beautifull Ladie, of whom in time hee begat a Sonne named *Dyardo*, which Sonne his Brother the King of *Bohemia*, nourished vppe in his Court with his owne Sonne. So mutually in loue agreed these two yong Princes, as after the death of the aged King, the yong *Dyardo* should ioyntlie rule with his Cozin the King: who tooke to Wife the Daughter to the Duke of *Lorayne*, bringing her with him into this Countrey, in companie of her Sister, a Princesse so wise and vertuous as euer liued. It so came to passe, that *Dyardo* my Lords most noble Sonne, framing his thoughts to the inspirations of loue, affected so highlie the other Sister, as he determined neuer to haue anie other to his Wife, if he might compasse what he intended. For her good Ladie, he coulde not be deceiued in his amorous desires, he found her loue so equall with his, yet did they shaddow their affections so discreetlie, as none coulde perceiue them, but *Domarto* the traiterous Countie of *Ormeque*, one of the best Knights in all this Country, were he as familiar with vertue and honestie, as he is with mallice and disloyaltie. This Traytour enterprised to match with the Queenes Sister, beloued as you haue hearde by my Lordes worthy Sonne, and thereuppon after manie sollicitings, made knowne his intent vnto her, whereof she made so slender account, as shee forbad him any more to trouble her. *Domarto* seeing my Lorde *Dyardo* his onely hinderaunce in loue, intended a mallicious villainie: and on a suddaine accused the Prince, that he intended to poyson the King, so to obtaine the Crowne, as discended of a neerer consanguinitie.[1] And as it often falleth out in such cases, when one seekes to crosse an others fortune, there is no time slacked[2] in following such drifts: euen so this Traytor, finding the yonge King alone, began his matter in this coullorable sort. My gracious Lord, the faith and allegeaunce I owe to your highnesse, bindes me to make your princelie eares acquainted with such newes, as, God is my witnes, said the Traitour (lifting his eyes and hands to heauen) mine own death were more welcome to me, such is the loue I beare them whom it concernes, beeing al so neere allied to you in birth, as sorie I am they shoulde bee detected: but in your regarde my gracious Lorde, the action touching you in such sort as it dooth, let me die rather then spare any liuing creature, no not mine owne Sonne, had nature giuen mee anie. This needelesse exordium haue I made to so foule an occasion, albeit truth needes no coullers or eloquent figures and therefore in breefe my Lord, this is the summe.[3] I am crediblie enformed, that your highnesse Cozin the Prince *Dyardo*, and Madame *Cardonia* Sister to the Queene, haue laid the platforme to poyson your Maiestie, and this haue they attempted, by the procurement of olde *Adrian* your Vncle, who pretends that the Crowne of *Bohemia* is his. I knowe not whether it be for want of discretion or no: but howsoeuer it be my Lorde, you shoulde not leaue such a villainie vnpunished. The King began greatlie to meruaile at these newes, and knewe not well what to think: wherupon he aunswered the Countie, that he coulde not beleeue this accusation. But the Traytour set so smoothe a countenaunce on the matter, and did auerre it still with such stout protestations, as hee induced the King to beleeue him: so that a daie or two after, the King beeing walking in hys Garden, seeing *Dyardo* and *Cardonya* at the Queenes chamber windowe, secretlie conferring of their amorous affections, commaunded them bothe to be carried to prison. The Countie glad thereof, prouoked the King still with such anger against them, as immediatlie he woulde haue them bothe doone to death: but that the Queene and the Lordes of hys Counsel, founde meanes to quallifie his displeasure, declaring what discredite his highnes shold receiue, if he did not suffer them to be openlie conuicted of their offences. Al this while good Princes, were they ignoraunt of this detection, till at length the King discoursed the whole matter to them, and likewise who was their accuser: nor did the Countie faile to maintaine his wordes openlie, offering to make it good in fight, against any that durst say the contrary, and because he had two Cozins, hardie and valiant Knights, conspirators likewise in this faction, there could be none found that would enter the Combat against them. Which when the noble Prince *Adrian* vnderstoode, very greefe had well neere slaine him, in respect he had no Child but this *Dyardo*, as also for that hee was accused with that hee neuer thought. Heereupon he went presently to the King his Nephew, and preuailed so well with him, as he obtained the space of two Monethes, to bring with him one or two that might maintaine the innocencie of him, his Sonne *Dyardo*, and the Princesse *Cardonia*, against the Traytour *Domarto* and his Cozins. And this is the cause he sent mee to seeke you foorth, in hope that you are as much his Freende as hee is yours, which you may somewhat perceiue, by the freendlie presents he sent you by mee to *Macedon*. So helpe mee God, saide *Palmerin*, you haue reported a most strange dyscourse, and neuer did I think, that such treason could enter the thoughts of any Knight, or other inferior person. Al this is true, quoth the Damosell, and it is appointed that the Prince *Dyardo*, with his aged and crazed Father, shal defend their owne causes, without seeking helpe of anie other: but he neuer as yet receiued the order of Knighthoode, and therfore is constrained to desire your assistaunce. And that shall I doo with all my hart, saide *Palmerin*, would God we were there where he expecteth vs, for the desire I haue

Palmerin d'Oliva: Part I   *177*

to see him, as also to vnderstande what he knowes of my following fortunes. Those matters are hid from mee, quoth shee, yet this haue I hearde him say diuers times, being in talk of you, that he accounted you the most honorable Knight in the worlde: and that if he euer chaunced to see you, he wold aduise you
5 to goe to the Emperour of *Allemaignes* Courte, to be the knightly Seruaunt to the Princesse *Polinarda*. When *Palmerin* heard the name of *Polinarda*, he remembred that it was her name, whome hee had so manye times seene in his traunces, for which cause he asked of the Damosell, what the Lady was of whom shee spake? My Lord quoth she, *Polinarda* is Daughter to the Emperour, and Niece vnto my
10 Lorde Adrian, the most beautiful Princesse that euer eye behelde. By my faith, saide *Palmerin*, the more easily may I be induced to graunt her my seruice, and thether intend I to trauaile, when I haue finished your Lords busines. So rode they with much more haste then before, tyl at length they came to the Cittie of *Almedya*, where the King remained, and the Prince *Adrian* expecting *Palmerins*
15 comming, which when he hearde, hee came to meete him, eache embracing other with meruailous courtesie, and the good olde man with the teares in his eyes thus saide. Ah good Knight, what may counteruaile this your exceeding paines, to maintaine the right of my Sonne and mee, who are falselie accused of such villainous treason, as (on the perill of my soule) we neuer did imagine?
20 Thereof am I certainlie perswaded, aunswered *Palmerin*, and therfore am I come to enter the Combat with him, that dare affirme otherwise. Mine olde age, quoth *Adrian*, might excuse mee henceforth from bearing Armes, but beeing vnable to endure so vile a slaunder, so long as life and soule will holde togeather, shal I doo my deuoire: so please your companion to make the second, as olde as I
25 am I will be the thirde, for the trayterous Countie hath two of his Cozins that take part with him. And if my fortune so fall out as I die in this tryall, I shall receiue my lot very contentedlie, if mine eyes might first beholde mine iniurie reuenged. I pray you said *Palmerin*, goe presently to the King, to the ende that hys highnesse may graunt vs the fielde, for my Freende and I thinke not long till
30 we haue made your accuser knowe his trecherie. *Adrian* immediatly went to the King, and on his knees thus began. My Lorde, you knowe that the Countie of *Ormeque* hath accused mee, my Sonne *Dyardo*, and Madame *Cardonya*, of the cryme of *Lesae Maiestatis*,[4] and in that we all are innocent, I am readie to maintaine, that he hath falsely and malliciously belied vs, which I my selfe will appro-
35 oue vpon him, or two more with me, against him and his Cozins, if they dare enter the fielde with him in this quarrell, where we will either make known their villainie, or receiue the reward belongs to disloyall Traitors. As for the wrong which you (my Lord) haue doone me, beeing your Vncle, and my Sonne *Dyardo* your Cozin germaine: that I referre to God to recompence, and to the better
40 knowledge you shall receiue of mee heereafter, beeing nowe too olde to bee a Traytour, and my Sonne too louing to proue disloyall. The King was abashed to heare his Vncle speake so audaciously, doubting nowe whether he should giue credite to what had beene reported, especially against him, so neere his highnes

in bloode, who so liberally offered to enter the Combat: notwithstanding his white heade and aged body made him vnfit for such actions, wherefore hee thus aunswered. Good Vncle, impute not mee any thing faultie in your accusation, and that the proofe shall manifest that must be made. The Countie beeing present, was strooken in a quandarie at these wordes, and gladly he wold haue denied his former slaunder, but he could find no waie cleanlie to doo it: wherefore seeing of force he must needes enter the Combat, he boldly fell on his knees before the King with these wordes. My Lorde, what I haue saide is verie certaine, and most true it is, that by the counsell of Prince *Adrian* heere present, his Sonne practised with Lady *Cardonya*, to poison you, that he might be King: which to make good, there is my gadge, on the behalfe of my selfe and my Cozins. Thou lyest Traytor in thy throate,[5] said olde *Adrian*, I take thine offer: and as he woulde haue gone on with further speeches, *Palmerin* stept before the King, saying. Worthy Lorde, seeing the effect of the wordes must be put in execution, which haue beene heere spoken on bothe sides before your Maiestie: may it please you the Prince *Dyardo* and Lady *Cardonya* may be sent for, to take with vs their oathes as in such cases is required, and in meane time let each one goe put himselfe in equipage for the Combat. Good reason said the King, and presently hee commaunded the Princes to be brought, who beeing come, *Palmerin* demaunded where they were that tooke part with the Countie: whereupon he presented his Cozins, the one named *Edron*, proude and arrogant, and the other *Edward* of selfe same qualitie. These two tooke their oathes with the Countie, that the Princes accused, conspired the Kinges death, in such sort as hath beene before declared: and olde *Adrian*, *Dyardo*, and fayre *Cardonya* sware the contrary. But it is true, and I wil not denie it (said the Prince *Dyardo*) that I haue and doo loue Ladie *Cardonya*, as much or rather more then mine owne selfe, yet neuer did I cary any other intent, but to request her in holie wedlocke, so pleased the King and Queene to like so well thereof as we coulde. But that euer I intended treason or villainie, it is most false, and Countie thou liest in thy throate, and thy copartners that haue sworne with thee. It is sufficient, said *Palmerin*: but my Lord, quoth he to the King, if wee be conquerers, the accused shall bee deliuered, and the accusers hanged? What saie you Countie, quoth the King? Good reason Sir, the like doo we request if we be victors. Will you (saide *Palmerin*) that eache shall helpe his fellow as he findes it conuenient? What els? said the Countie, that is expedient. While this talke endured, *Edron* regarded so well *Palmerin*, that hee espied the Sworde which the Damosell carried in the Casket, and brought to that Courte as she did to others, which shewing the Countie, he saide out aloude. Where did the deuils finde this Knight to giue him this Sworde? Belike they gaue him strength to drawe it out, els he might haue failed as manie other did: the Damosell was vnwise to bestowe it in such bad sorte. At which wordes *Palmerin* beeing angry, returned *Edron* this rounde aunswere. I see (Knight) there is in thee more brauery and foolishe glorie then manlie action, thou blamest mee before thou knowest me, but ere you and I part, Ile[6] finde better reason to bestowe on you, and beate better gouernment into

your pate with this sword that likes you not.⁷ This caused euery one wishlie to beholde *Palmerin*, the King remembring that he had seene the Sworde, which none in his Court coulde deserue to conquere: whereuppon he esteemed so well of *Palmerin*, as he commaunded *Edron* to silence, and all to goe arme themselues,
5 because hee intended that day to see the Combat fought.⁸

Chapter xxv.
Howe Palmerin, Adrian and Ptolome entered the Combat, against the Countie of Ormeque and his Cozins, whom they honorably vanquished.

After the King had commaunded the Knights to goe arme themselues, he gaue charge to foure of his auncientest Knights to see the fielde prouided, and there to place the Iudges, according to the wonted custome in *Bohemia*: the Knights beeing careful of the Kinges commaunde, had soone prepared all things in readines, wherefore the King, his Lords, Ladies and Gentlewomen, went to see the issue of this valiant enterprise. Then was the Prince *Dyardo* and faire *Cardonya* brought into the fielde, before whom was made a very great fire, wherein they should be burned, if the Countie conquered. Soone after came the sixe Combatants, who entered at two places appointed one against the other, the Challengers beeing conducted by two of the Iudges to their place, and the Defendants by the other two where they were appointed: so the Iudges beeing placed, the Marshal summoned the fielde, and the Heraldes bid the Champions doo their deuoire.

Palmerin had good regard to *Edron*, whose words sticking on his stomacke, called now for reuenge, wherefore couching his Launce, he encountered him with such a full carrire, as his Launce passed through his bodie, and *Edron* tombled dead to the ground. In the meane while, the Countie and Prince *Adrian* had vnhorssed eache other, *Adrian* so sore wounded as he could hardlie helpe himselfe: as for *Ptolome* and *Edward*, they had astonied each other with falles from their Horsses, but they recouered themselues quicklie, and with sharpe strokes beganne to charge eache other valiantly. Greatlie ashamed was the Countie to bee vnhorssed, and therfore to recouer his honour, he came with great furie towards his enemie: which *Palmerin* perceiuing, stept betweene them, saying. To me Countie, to mee, who wil bid more for thy heade then anie in the field. With which wordes he reached him such a sure stroke on the head, as made the fire flie foorth of his eyes: notwithstanding, as a man of good courage, he stept aside, and thrusting his sword into *Palmerins* Horse throate, enforced him quickly to take him to his feete: but all the worse for him as it fell out afterwarde, for *Palmerin* hauing beaten him out of breath, he flong away his weapon, and caught him about the middle, where they tugged so long togeather, that *Palmerin* getting him downe, and his knees on his belly, with his sword soone tooke his heade from his shoulders. All this while *Ptolome* had good play with his enemie, and after manie daungerous woundes receiued on either side, at length hee had the better of the daie by killing his aduersarie.[1] Then he and *Palmerin* went to the Iudges, who giuing them sentence of honourable victory, they tooke of their Helmets, and came to see in what estate the Prince *Adrian* was. Euill enough (quoth he) my noble good Freends, but the lesse account doo I make of my life, in that mine eyes haue seene due vengeaunce on mine enemies. Then was he nobly borne forth of the fielde, the King commaunding to lodge him in his owne Pallace, and the Chirurgions searching his wounds, founde them

Palmerin d'Oliva: Part I   *181*

mortall, which newes did greeue the whole Court in generall: the good olde Prince yet beeing of some courage, was ioyfull to die in so good sorte, hauing defended his owne honour and his Sonnes, whome he sent for, and in the presence of all the standers by, said. My Son, seeing it hath pleased God thus to sende for me, good
5 reason is it that his will bee fulfilled, but ere I depart, this I commaunde thee, that (next God) thou truely serue and loue my Lorde the King, bearing towards him a hart so faithfull, as I haue doone to the hower of my death: and conceiue no offence at what hath passed against thee and me, hauing come to passe (as I iudge) more by euill counsel, then any setled perswasion against vs. For the rest, to thy vttermost,
10 remember the good thou hast this daie receiued by that noble Knight, who is called *Palmerin*: then calling *Palmerin* to him, hee saide. Sir *Palmerin*, death hath seized so surelie on me, as I cannot let you know a number of things that concerne you very neerelie, I counsell you therefore to trauaile to the Emperours Court of *Allemaigne*,[2] where you shal heare tidings of that you seeke so earnestlie: with which
15 wordes hee deliuered vppe his ghost. And because it seemeth good ere I passe any further, to let you knowe how the Prince *Adrian* came by the knowledge of *Palmerin*, thus it is. I haue heretofore reported, that he was a notable Cabalist or Magitian, by meanes whereof fewe secrets were concealed from him: so casting the Callender of most honourable byrthes,[3] he happened on *Palmerin*, and perceiuing the
20 high fortune he was borne to, cheefelie that he shoulde prooue a most noble Knight, and the greatest Lord in *Europe*, hee was desirous to contract a marriage betweene him and his Niece *Polinarda*, presenting her to him in his visions, as hath beene declared.[4] Hee thus deceasing, the King highly discontented at his Vncles harde fortune, caused him to be buried in most sumptuous maner, making him a Tombe
25 in forme of a Piramides, the most excellent and stately that euer was in *Bohemia*, and ouer against it, were hanged the bodies of the Countie and his two Cozins, for his Trophe. Thus euery thing quieted, and the funeralles of the Prince *Adrian* solemnized, *Palmerin* woulde presentlie depart towardes *Allemaigne*: but *Ptolomes* woundes were so daungerous, as he was constrained to staie longer then he
30 intended. In the meane space, the King did them all the honour could be deuised, in hope to stay them still in his Court, but it was impossible, for *Palmerin* told him, he must needes goe to the Emperour, about affaires of very great importaunce. I knowe your meaning well enough, saide the King, you intende to goe Combat with the enchaunted Knight: and in so dooing, you shall loose both your paines and
35 your life, as manie other haue doone before you. What enchaunted Knight is it saide *Palmerin*? on my faith my Lord, I neuer hearde anie one talke of him but you. Then will I tell yee, (quoth the King) since I haue begun the matter. Not long since in the Country of the Emperour mine Vncle, in the Cittie of *Ymanes*[5] dwelled a welthie Knight, who had a fayre Daughter, amorous of a Gentleman, and their loue
40 kept so secrete as none knew it but themselues. It so fell out, that her Father marryed her to another Gentleman in his house, but for any good acceptation, or cheerefull countenaunce of the Gentlewoman, the bridegrome could haue none, so highlie esteemed she her first loue: and continued in opinion towards him so firme,

as she graunted him enteraunce into her Chamber at an appointed time, where hee murdered her Husbande, and carryed the Lady with hym whether he pleased. The bruite heereof was so soone spred abroade, as the mother of the murdered Gentleman heard thereof, whereuppon she made her complaint to the Emperour, who immediatlie sent to summon the other before him: but they refusing to come, and hauing taken themselues to a very strong Castell, were in the ende so straightly besieged, as the Lady with her louer, at length were taken, and hauing confessed the trueth of their offence, sentence was giuen on them that they should be burned. The Father to this Knight offender so greeued heereat, as hee went to one of his Sisters, entending neuer to see the Emperour or his Court againe. His Sister seeing him in this extreamitie, (as no mallice or bad inuention is comparable to a Womans) deuised to enchaunt one of her Sonnes, a good and hardy Knight, in such sort as he shoulde neuer bee ouercome in fight, but with an enchauntment of greater force. Beside, shee gaue him a Bow, and a great companie of impoysoned arrowes, wherewith he should kill the Emperour and his Children, or anie other whome himselfe pleased: which hee had not failed to haue doone, but mine Vncle *Adrian* vnderstanding thereof, did take such regarde to the matter, as hee coulde not hurt them, but many of his people, so that the Country is wonderfully perplexed. For hee is mounted on a Horse enchaunted as himselfe is, the swiftest in pace that euer was seene, wherewith he flies into manie out places of the Empire, committing a thousand harmes and cannot be stayed, for whosoeuer comes to him armed, Knight or pesant, all dies the death, and none escapes him. And that which is worst of all, it is commonly reported, that if mine Vncle will not giue him his eldest Sonne *Trineus*, and faire *Polinarda* his Daughter, to doo with them what shall like his humour, hee will neuer departe the Countrey, til he haue thorowly ruinated it. By my Sworde (my Lorde) sayde *Palmerin*, in all my life I neuer heard so strange a tale, were I sure to die a thousande deathes, I will fight with this deuill, and deliuer the Countrey if my strength wyll compasse it. Alas my good Freende, sayde the King, it would much displease me, that you should hazard your selfe in such daunger, for where such deuillish enchauntments are, the strength of man (howe great soeuer it be) dooth not auayle: and therefore for my sake I pray you to forbeare. Let come what pleaseth God said *Palmerin*, for if I die nowe, I shall be excused for euer heereafter. Well sawe the King that he coulde not chaunge him, therefore he left off any further to intreate him: and too long he thought hee tarryed for *Ptolomes* health, so desirous was he to be with the Emperour, hoping that his Combat with the enchaunted Knight, would graunt him meanes to see and talke with fayre *Polinarda*. Wherefore, when his companion had gotten a little strength, they tooke theyr leaue of the King and the Ladies, cheefelie of the Prince *Dyardo* and fayre *Cardonya*: who after theyr departure had such successe in their loue, as with the Kinges consent the marriage was finished. Nowe are *Palmerin* and *Ptolome* on their way to *Gaunt*, where the Emperour made his continuall aboade: the enchaunted Knight so persecuting him, as he durst at no time come foorth of his Castell.

Chapter XXVI.

Howe Palmerin and Ptolome arriued at the Cittie of Gaunt, where the Emperour of Allemaigne kept his Courte, and of the Combat betweene Palmerin and the enchaunted Knight.

Good expedition made these Knights in their iourney, tyll at length they arriued at the Citty of *Gaunt*, where the Emperor of *Allemaigne* then soiourned, not knowing howe to depart thence, because the enchaunted Knight watched him at all howres: our Knightes beeing thus come thether, lodged in the house of a welthie Burgesse, where they were entertained in very honorable maner. They were no sooner dismounted from theyr Horsses, but the whole Cittie was on a suddaine vprore, and the people ranne on heapes from one place to another: which made him remember what the King of *Bohemia* had tolde him, and presently he imagined what after followed, for his Hoste in great feare came running to him, saying.

Alas Sir, we all are vndoone, the enchaunted Knight hath gotten the Gates of our Cittie, and in despight of the guarde he is entered: wonderfull is the harme that he will nowe doo, if the Prince *Trineus* and fayre *Polynarda* be not deliuered to him. God defende such harde fortune, saide *Palmerin*, rather will I fight with him, and if I die, I shall accompanie many other in vnfortunate successe. With these words hee tooke his Launce, and galloped that way where hee hearde the tumult, which was at the Emperours Castell, where the enchaunted Knight was shooting his arrowes at the windowes he espied open. Ioyfull was *Palmerin* to finde him in so fit a place, where his Lady *Polinarda* might giue judgment of his valour, which opinion did so renewe hys courage, as presently he marched towards his enemie, who held in his hande a *Persian* Bowe, with an arrow in it, readie to shoote, hauing a great sorte more at his backe in his Quiuer: he was of vnreasonable stature, yet with a countenaunce sterne and couragious, all which could not dismay *Palmerin*, but called to him in this maner. Proud Knight, that by the ayde of deuils and euill spirits hast committed monstrous cruelties: it is nowe time that hee whom thou seruest should haue his pray, which is thy soule into endlesse perdition.[1] And so without staying for any aunswer, hee ran valiantly against him: but the enchaunted Knight taking his aduauntage, shot an arrowe at him so violently, as it pierced through his Armour to the bare flesh. *Palmerin* hauing broken his Launce, with an yron Mace he had, he reached such a stroke to the Knight, as hee brake his Bowe in two peeces, and the blowe falling on the head of his Horse, made him therewithall fall deade to the grounde. The Knight hauing recouered himselfe, tooke a Mace that hung at his saddle Bowe, and came against *Palmerin*, who was nowe on foote likewise: so layd they on loade terribly with their Maces, that the Emperour and his Lordes and Ladies hearing the strokes, came to the windowes to see the Combat, little thinking that any one durst presume to meddle with his enemie, yet all this while the Knights neuer breathed, though theyr Sheeldes and Armour were very much mangled, and their bodies wounded in many places. And because *Palmerin* sawe the fight endure so long wyth the Mace, he threw it downe and tooke him to his Sword, wherewith he did so bumbaste him about the heade, as hee could scant tell where to strike againe: but the Knight on a suddaine lifting vp his Mace, gaue *Palmerin* such a stroke betweene the head and the shoulders, as made him reele to and fro amazedly, yet comming to himselfe, and seeing the Knight faint with his great expence of bloode, closed with him, and casting his legge behinde him, threw him to the grounde, when setting his foote on his brest to keepe him downe, with his sworde he parted hys head from his bodie.[2] What question were it, whether the Emperour reioysed hereat or no? who for his whole Empire wold not he were aliue againe, beeing so well deliuered from his onely enemy in the worlde, that coulde so molest him and his Countrey with such crueltie. And to say sooth, the enchaunted Knight was altogeather inuincible, nor could *Palmerin* haue thus preuailed against his wonderfull enchauntments, but that the three Magicall Sisters of the Mountaine *Artifaeria* highly fauoured him, as you hearde before what promises they made him.[3]

The Combat beeing thus ended, and the enchaunted Knight dead, the Emperour (giuing thanks to God for this victory) let open the Gates of the Castell, and came foorth himselfe to welcome *Palmerin*, who kneeling on his knee before the Emperour, thus spake. Mighty Prince, such renowne haue I hearde through the worlde, of your exceeding honour and bountie, as I haue trauailed many straunge Countries to come offer you my seruice, desiring your highnes, (if my sute may seeme reasonable) to accept me henceforth amongst your Knightly Seruaunts. Ah faire Knight, aunswered the Emperour, it is for me to know of you, how I may remunerate this vnspeakable courtesie, for but by you, mine enemie had triumphed in my spoyle: so much then is my selfe, my Children and Countrey bounde to you, as no satisfaction is sufficient to regratiate. So taking him by the hand, and perceiuing his body wounded in many places, he conducted him into one of the fayrest Chambers in hys Castell, where he was vnarmed, commaunding his Chirurgions to take dilligent care of him, because in truth they much doubted his life. Wherfore getting him into his bed, all needefull things for his health were applyed to him, and no cost was spared, to saue his life that preserued the whole Countrey.

Chapter XXVII.

Howe the Empresse came to visite Palmerin, who kept his Chamber, because he had receiued such daungerous woundes, in the Combat with the enchaunted Knight, and of the speech he had with the fayre Princesse Polinarda.

The Empresse with her fayre Daughter *Polinarda*, gladde of the death of the enchaunted Knight, came to *Palmerins* chamber to visite him, who hearing of their comming, cast a night Mantle about him which the Emperor had sent him, and came with greate reuerence to welcome them: so desirous was he to see her, for whom he had trauailed so manie strange Regions. In this place it is necessary that you remember, what gratious gifts the three fatall Sisters bestowed on him, in the Mountaine *Artifaeria*, one of them graunting him this speciall fauour, that he should be highlie esteemed of her to whom he was destenied, so soone as she behelde him,[1] which came to passe as heere shall be declared. *Palmerin* expecting the entrance of the Empresse and her Daughter in his Chamber, meeting them at the dore, falling on his knee, did with great humilitie kisse their handes: but the Empresse taking him vppe in her armes, saluted him with these speeches. Gentle Knight, right happy may we count our selues by your comming hether, the Realme beeing more desolate then it hath beene seene heeretofore, and not without cause, in respect of the great iniurie the Knight did vs, whom you haue slaine, he hauing sworne the death of my children that neuer offended him: but God bee thanked the lot hath fallen on himselfe, which he determined to inflict on other, for which great grace they stand so deepelie bound to you, as to their Father that first gaue them life, which by your prowesse you haue happilie preserued, this second gift beeing of no lesse account then the first, worthelie may you bee called their seconde Father. *Palmerin* giuing eare to the Empresse salutations, had his minde more busied in beholding *Polinarda*, whose daintie regarde so maistred his opinions, as heade, hart, thoughts and all were nowe sette to work: yet couertly he shaped this answere to the Empresse. Madame, what I haue doone for you and yours, is nothing in respecte of my great good will: for since the time I first had knowledge of my selfe, and before I receiued the order of knighthoode, vnderstanding of my Lord the Emperour, and what honourable entertainment was in his Court, I dedicated my seruice to him onelie, and for this cause Madame came I hither. But howe is it possible Sir, saide she, that you can content your selfe to be one of his Knights, your deserts being so great? Very well Madame, quoth he, and yours too, so please your highnes to affoorde me such fauour. With all my hart Sir, said she, shall I entertaine you towardes the Emperour, and on mine owne behalfe will prouide better for you then I will speake of: and did it like you, I woulde accept you for a Virgins Knight heere, and none other. Whereuppon shee called her Daughter *Polinarda*, saying. Faire Daughter, this Knight as yet hath little acquaintance in the Court, I praie you see his entertainment maie be good, because his desire is to make staie with vs, and for your owne part, looke that you intreate him well, with this request, that you accept him for your seruaunt, and he shall be your Knight. And are you bothe agreed Ladies, said *Palmerin?* Heauen forsake me if I refuse honour of so high account. And as they woulde haue proceeded on, the Emperor came in and brake off their talke, and comming to the Empresse, saide. Madame, I beseeche you haue good regarde to the health of this Knight, and let our Chirurgions not trifle the time with him, for I perswade my selfe, that the enchaunted Knight with his venomed arrowes,³ hath wounded him with great daunger inwardlie, and hath besides sore brused his bodie with the weight of his Mace. But *Palmerin* hauing *Polinarda* so neere him, neither minded his woundes or what the Emperour had spoken, his obiect more delighted, then his woundes greeued him, then the Emperour taking him by the hande, saide. I pray you my deere Freende to bee of good comfort, dispayre not for anie thing I beseeche you, and bee aduised by them that haue care of your health, for you shall want nothing if my Crowne will purchase it. So departed hee and the Empresse, with their Daughter *Polinarda*, whome loue had already so inueigled, that she (beeing yet but tender of yeeres)⁴ found her selfe so restrained of her libertie, as scant she knewe howe to dissemble this suddaine affection: and from that time forward she became so sadde and pensiue, as one of her Ladies, the most fauoured and familiar with her, named *Brionella*, Daughter of the Duke of *Saxon*, well perceiued it, yet durst shee not presume to demaunde, whence proceeded this strange alteration, but so circumspectly did she regarde the Princesse, as she well noted the grounde of her greefes. Whereuppon it happened, that one time amongst other, they two beeing alone togeather, *Brionella* iudging that her Ladie delighted to heare speeche of *Palmerin*, nowe to hitte the nayle on the heade, she thus began. What say you Madame, (by your fauour) of the newe come Knight? did you euer see a brauer and more accomplisht Gentleman? Vpon my faith Madame, in mine opinion, I thinke that nature hath wrought all her perfections in him, and fauoured him aboue all other Knights in manhoode and Chiualrie. Ah *Brionella*, aunswered the Princesse, thou art not alone of this opinion, for I euer thought as much though I kept it in silence: would God I had as great authoritie ouer him, as he alreadie hath gotten ouer me. Is the matter so with you, saide *Brionella*? it shoulde seeme you are in looue with him then. To tell thee the trueth *Brionella*, quoth shee, I am, and did I not doubt some other hath preuented mee, I would aduenture to make him mine. In good sooth Madam, said *Brionella*, you two beeing vnited togeather in one reciprocall league of loue, well might it bee reported the most honourable match, and of the two noblest yong Princes through the whole worlde: and seeing you haue made a choyse so worthie, dismay not good Madame, but proceede in your determination. Thus deuised the two Ladies togeather on *Palmerin*, who was no lesse in affliction for the looue of *Polinarda*, whom hee had searched with so great payne and trauaile, and had nowe founde with so high good fortune. If loue was so earnest with him before in his sleeping visions, hauing not seene her: much more vehement was the impression nowe, hauing her in presence.

Palmerin d'Oliva: Part I 187

Whereupon the day folowing, he called for his garments, and as he was making himselfe readie, the Emperour by one of his Gentlemen sent him the good morrow, desirous to vnderstande in what plight he felt himselfe. Good Sir, aunswered *Palmerin* to the Gentleman, I beseeche you doo my humble dutie to the Emperour for this great courtesie, and you may thus assure him, that (heauen be praised) I feele my selfe in so good estate as euer I did. Which the Emperour hearing was highlie contented, and sent to desire his companie to the Chappell,[5] where *Palmerin* (neuer before so throughlie touched with the forcible assaults of looue) glaunced so manie sweete lookes on the Princesse *Polinarda*, and breathed so many sighes, the secrete Ambassadours of his harte, as it was a heauen to him to be in these passions.[6] The Emperour and all the traine returned from the Chappell, they went to meate, and *Palmerin* beeing placed right against *Polinarda*, was in such fits as hee knewe not what countenaunce to vse: for his couller went and came in such manner, as the Princesse might easilie iudge the cause of his dolour, wherupon she presentlie presumed, that she had more interest in his thoughts then ere she looked for. The like opinion conceiued he of her, yet was no other testimony deliuered on either side, then sad countenances, the reuealers of a tormented spirite. Thus continued these two louers, till the Tables were withdrawne, and then the Lords and Ladies fel to dauncing, in which delight and diuers other, the whole day was spent, till the Empresse and her Ladies departing to their Chambers, the good night on all sides was reuerently giuen: when *Palmerin* went to his lodging in such an agonie, as more likelie to die then liue, hee threwe himselfe on his bedde, where hauing sighed and sorrowed long time greeuously, at length hee brake foorth into these tearmes. Ah *Palmerin*, vnhappy, wretched and moste miserable, nowe art thou entred into such a Laborinth, as impossible is it for thee to get out again with life, but what shoulde mooue thee to so high an enterprise, beeing no way able to equall her that is second to none? Alas, nowe doo I plainlie see the small credite is to bee reposed in Dreames, and that the visions I saw in my Father *Gerrards* house, on the Mountaine *Artifaeria* and els where, are friuolous illusions, and of no account: with them may I ioyne the promise made mee by olde *Adrian*, who boasted to knowe so much of my fortunes,[7] for looue is not of such power on my behalfe, that faire *Polinarda* either can or will make anie reckoning of me. Then *Palmerin* resolue thy selfe suddainlie to die, that this inuisible and consuming fire, which by little and little melts thee away, may bee extinguished, and thy selfe eased.[8] With these wordes he breathed foorth such an extreame sighe, as *Vrbanillo* the Dwarffe (being neere) hearde him, who doubting least any newe mischaunce had happened, by the priuie woundes the enchaunted Archer gaue him, made hast to know the cause of this euill. Ah *Vrbanillo*, quoth *Palmerin*, I finde my selfe farre worse then deade. What my Lorde, sayd the Dwarffe, now you ought to be of best disposition, will you deceiue vs with this alteration? The Emperour neuer gaue you bad countenaunce since your comming, whence then shoulde proceede thys straunge conceit? No no *Vrbanillo*, quoth hee, it is not the Emperor, but a

Lorde of greater power then his Maiestie. It is Looue my Lad, the strickt commaunder of the stoutest mindes, he hath conquered mee, and well I knowe I shall die, if thou doo not finde the meane to helpe mee. By my fayth my Lorde (quoth the Dwarffe) so please you to tell me howe and wherein I may helpe you, let me die a thousande deathes if I doo it not. Vnderstande then my good *Vrbanillo*, sayd *Palmerin*, that this strange alteration, proceedes from the diuine lookes of my peerelesse Mistresse *Polinarda*, whose fiery beames haue searched so narowly euery corner of my thoughts, as I must die because I loue too deerlie.[9] But couldest thou make knowne to her the least parte of my insupportable vexations, may bee shee woulde haue some pittifull remorse of my martirdome: for well may it be iudged, that a Lady accomplished with so many vertuous perfections, must needes bee stored with sweetnes, fauour and pittie. Not vnlike my good Lord, said *Vrbanillo*, but doo not you remember how I was punished, when in the like case I ventured to sollicite your looue to *Laurana*,[10] Daughter to the Duke of *Durace*? by my fayth my Lorde, I shall not forget it while I haue a day to liue, and am afrayde to fall againe into the like daunger. And this spake *Vrbanillo* with such a grace, as *Palmerin* coulde not but laugh, noting with what feare the deformed felow gaue it foorth,[11] whereupon he sayd. Thou needest not be dismaid, if she that smote thee in thy sleepe bee that *Polinarda*,[12] for whose loue I am thus tormented, and for whom I was borne, as many haue enformed me: I pray thee therefore speake to her, and dreade no coullers. It is good, saide *Vrbanillo*, that you woulde haue mee more hardie then you are your selfe: speake to her your selfe if you dare, for I dare not aduenture it for feare of my life. If thou doost it not (quoth *Palmerin*) assure thy selfe thou shalt neuer henceforth serue me. Nay then (quoth the Dwarffe) I will rather put my selfe in ieoperdy, to be better beaten then I was the last time before I will loose so good a Maister. I pray thee doo, sayde *Palmerin*, in respect thou seest the earnestnes of mine affections. Feare not (quoth the Dwarffe) albeit you were a great deale more fit to breake the matter then I: but I wil gadge my life to gaine you the Ladie,[13] and heereupon they rested till the next morning.

Chapter XXVIII.
Howe Polinarda desired Palmerin to giue her his Dwarffe, and of the speeche which she and Vrbanillo had afterward togeather.

Early the next morning *Palmerin* arose, and hauing walked abroad to contemplate his desires, returned into the Chamber of presence, where he founde *Trineus* the Emperors Sonne, conferring with the Ladies: at which very instant the Dwarff entred, whose badde shaped body and face, made them all fall a laughing,[1] so that *Trineus* came to his Sister *Polinarda*, saying. Sister, did you euer beholde a more proper Page to attende on Ladies, then this gaunt Squire that serues my Lorde *Palmerin*? In good sooth Brother, quoth she, hee is farre vnlike his noble maister, yet wold I like well enough if he were mine. I beseech you Sir *Palmerin*, said *Trineus*, bestowe your Seruaunt on my Sister *Polinarda*. Madame, quoth *Palmerin*, were he better, hee is yours and his Maister likewise, then called hee *Vrbanillo*, who kneeling to vnderstand his Maisters pleasure, hee saide: *Vrbanillo*, I haue giuen you to my Ladie *Polinarda* as her man, will you not serue her honourablie and truelie aboue all other? Yea my Lorde, quoth he, next after you, but you will I not leaue while I liue, although you woulde disdaine my seruice. Good reason hast thou, said the Princesse, and wel am I pleased it shold be so: yet during the time of his stay heere, you shall forsake him and abide with mee. For that Madame, quoth the Dwarffe, I am well contented. Then looke you faile not, said the Princesse, henceforth to giue your attendaunce. These speeches were thus vsed as it were for pastime, that shee might thereby deceiue the iudgments of other: but her whole intent was, to know of *Vrbanillo*, if his Maister were affected to any other Ladie, by whose meanes her loue might be frustrate. For as you haue heard a little before, that loue had brought her vnder such obeysaunce, as did not the regarde of honour with-holde her, her selfe would first breake the Ise of her vexations, rather then staie too long and not be solicited. Many other deuises had the Ladies with *Vrbanillo*, who knewe so well howe to behaue himself, as from thence forward he grew so familiar amongst them: as he woulde enter their Chambers when himselfe pleased, vnder couller of attendaunce on the Princesse *Polinarda*, from time to time to mooue his Maisters messages. But at length she preuented him in this sort, for beeing alone at a windowe in the presence Chamber, shee called the Dwarffe, and making her entraunce by other occasions, she asked him whose Sonne *Palmerin* was. God knowes Madame, quoth hee, for I doo not, nor himselfe neither: but of this I can assure you, that neuer was Knightlie Chiualrie better imployed by any then by him, for since the time of my knowledge, he hath doone such noble acts, as it is not remembred that euer Knight in this age did the like. And then from point to point he discoursed, all that *Palmerin* had doone since he came to him: and can you thinke then Madame, (quoth the Dwarffe) that he is not discended of noble linage? Trust me Ladie, I haue my self heard by manie learned Magitians and other, that their diuinations were no lesse then I saie. When *Polinarda* heard the

Dwarffe thus speake on his Maisters behalfe, if before his loue had kindled her liking, no meruaile if hart and spirite were nowe enflamed: so that nowe she could no longer conceale what she had hetherto couered, and therefore sayde to the Dwarffe. I beseech thee *Vrbanillo*, by the faith and duetie thou bearest to thy Maister, tel me one thing that I desire to knowe of him, which shall bee nothing but to his honour and aduantage. You haue so coniured mee, faire Madame, quoth the Dwarffe, as death shall not make me hide what you please to command, if it lye in me to resolue you. Knowe then *Vrbanillo*, said the Princesse, that I looue thy Maister as well as my Brother *Trineus*, and am desirous to knowe of thee, what Ladie it is hee esteemes aboue all other, because when I knowe her, I may loue her the better for his sake: withall, that I may commend the Ladies happines, whose fortune is to be loued of so braue a Gallant. Well perceiued the Dwarffe, that now or neuer was the time to bestirre himselfe, according to the promise he made his Maister: wherefore hee aunswered the Princesse in this manner. Beleeue me Madame, were it to anie other, I would not reueale such secrets of my Lorde as you desire to knowe: but to you that are my Lady and Mistresse, I am content to bewraie the whole. Suffiseth then Madame, that he loueth in such sorte, as if the heauens sende him not remedie the sooner, vnpossible is it that his life should long endure: for I see him so far beside himselfe, and tormented with so manie passions, as euerie howre his death is expected. What will ye Ladie that I say? hee complaines, hee sighes, and daie by daie is in such dispaire for his Ladies loue: as happie might I haue accounted him, had he neuer seene her, or that his daies were as short as he desires. If then *Polinarda* were in doubt (not iudging herselfe to bee shee) it may easilie bee imagined, and presently was shee brought into such perplexitie, as the vermillion couller in her cheekes began to change, such suddaine feares possessed her, and so manie sundry opinions thwarted her conceite, as faine she woulde haue spoken, but coulde not of long time, wherby the Dwarffe discerned the cause of her alteration, yet he dissembled what he sawe, and thus continued on his discourse. Nowe considering (faire Madame) the high deserts of my Lorde, may she be esteemed happy (as you saie) that shall cause the losse of the best Knight liuing this day? Ah Mistresse, if he die (as God forbid) farwell the flower of all noblenes, and the most assured Freende to distressed Ladies. Wherefore I beseeche you pardon mee, if I shall name her vnto you, and let mee intreate you to deale with her so farre, that the courtesie wherein she is indebted to so good a Knight as my Master is, may be shewed effectually, as that she would loue and fauour him, as he dooth and hath verie well deserued. Trust me *Vrbanillo*, aunswered the Princesse, when I knowe the Ladie, I will, and beside, if she doo not regarde his passions as she ought, I wil intreate her at my request to be more pittifull. These wordes procured a suddaine iealouzie in her, that shee shoulde promise to another what she desired her selfe: yet earnest to bee resolued, she vowed to fulfill her promise, and therefore desired him to tell her name. So you will giue mee your worde Madame, quoth the Dwarffe, not to take in ill parte what I shall saie, I will satisfie your request presently. Beleeue me, saide the Princesse, I will not, rather perswade thy selfe, that heerein thou doost me great pleasure. Ah fayre Princesse, quoth the Dwarff, it is for you and no other that my Lord is thus tormented, it is for you that hee liues and dies a hundred times a daie: sweete Ladie haue pittie on him, and seeke not the losse of so good a Knight, who looues you deerer then his owne life. At which aunswere shee was supprized with incredible pleasure, yet feigning the contrarie, she saide: Is it I? and howe long I praie you? By my faith Madame, quoth he, that can I not well tell yee, but I haue hearde him say of long time, more then foure yeeres before he was Knighted, hee vowed himselfe yours: since which time, all his honourable actions hath hee onely dedicated to your praise. So that to finde you, hee left the King of *Macedon*, and his Sonne *Florendos*, of whom he was esteemed as no man the like, yet that honour hee forsooke to doo you seruice: and for your loue he yeelded himselfe as vassaile to the Emperour your Father, and gaue himselfe your Knight if you deigne to accept him. When *Polynarda* had well hearde the Dwarffe, (albeit her harte floted in ioyes) yet could she so well commaunde her thoughts, as shee seemed to make smal account of his words: notwithstanding, she returned him this aunsweere. I promised thee *Vrbanillo*, not to conceiue ill of ought thou shouldest tell me, nor doo I: yet wold I haue thee to regard my calling, beeing daughter to so great a Prince as is the Emperour. But if it bee so, that *Palmerin* thy Lorde beares me such speciall affection, I must let him knowe by thee, that it would haue beene farre more seemelie, himselfe to haue told me, then to make thee Ambassadour in such secrete affaires: neuerthelesse, I mislike not his honourable loue and good will, whereof I shall thinke better, when I knowe the effecte is conformable to thy protestations.[2] Madame (quoth the Dwarffe) so you would please to vouchsafe him time and place, hee will acquaint you with strange matter concerning bothe your destinies: which courtesie can no waie impeache your honour.[3] Why tell him, saide the Princesse, he shall haue mee dailie heere in the Chamber of presence, where he may saie his pleasure with safetie: in meane space, I accept him as my Knight, charging him, that he doo not depart the Court without my licence, if hee desire to doo mee pleasure. The Dwarffe well pleased with so good an aunswere, on hys knee kissing the Princesse hande, tooke leaue of her to returne towardes *Palmerin*: who meeting him by the waie, in place conuenient, saide. Howe nowe *Vrbanillo*? what newes hast thou brought me? life or death? So good newes Maister, aunswered the Dwarffe, as you haue good occasion to repute your selfe, the moste fortunate Knight that euer bare Armes. Then *Palmerin* embracing him, saide. Ah tell me what they are, hast thou spoken with diuine *Polinarda*? takes shee anie pittie on my consuming cares? That dooth she my Lorde, quoth the Dwarffe, and commandes you by me, (if you be so vowed hers as I haue perswaded) that hence foorth you depart not the Emperours Courte without her leaue. Then recited he the whole talke betweene them, and lastlie the pleasure she conceiued in so good tydings, so that she accepted him onelie for her Knight. While the Dwarffe continued this discourse, *Palmerin* was rauished with such inwarde ioy, as with a great sigh, he said. Oh heauens, how doo you fauour me? nowe see I well, that my seuerall apparitions on the Mounts of Oliues and *Artifaeria*, are predestinations ordeyned to mee by your gracious prescience:[4] I beseeche you therefore humblie, that what you haue promised, may soone come to effect, for the regarde of incomparable *Polinarda*. Then demaunded hee, by what meanes he might attaine to speake with the Princesse? She sayth, quoth he, that you shall dailie haue her in the presence, or in the Empresse Chamber, and there may you safely impart your whole minde vnto her. But I haue other newes to tel yee, for I vnderstand certainlie, that the Emperour intendes a matter greatlie for your aduauntage: he minds to morrow to visite one of his Castelles neere at hande, and there to passe the time in honour of the Ladies, will haue a Tourney. There (better then any where els) may you and *Polinarda* conferre togeather: therfore courage your selfe, and goe keepe companie with my Lorde the Emperour, it may bee himselfe will acquaint you with this enterprise. Now credite me *Vrbanillo*, saide *Palmerin*, thou hast doone so much for mee, as I shall neuer recompence thee while I liue: but I pray thee tell mee, did shee not at the first take my message strangelie? That did she (quoth the Dwarffe) when I perswaded her that you loued a Lady in such sorte, as hardlie coulde you liue without her fauourable regarde: then she thinking it was some other and not herselfe, changed couller meruailous passionatlie, but let it suffise you, that she is as deepe in loue as you are or can be. So went *Palmerin* to the Emperour, who calling him to him, saide. My noble Freende, I shal make knowne to you, what hath beene concluded in your absence, the Ladies of our Courte haue beene so long lockt in, for feare of the enchaunted Knight whom you haue slaine, as they haue desired to prograce[5] a little: for which cause, and to pleasure them, I am thus determined. Two leagues hence haue I a goodly Castell, enuironed with woods and pleasant Meddowes, there may wee hunte the wilde Harte and Bore with other pastimes: but nowe haue I caused Scaffolds and other prouision[6] to be made there for a Tourney, and fortie Knightes will I appoint in this action, tenne against tenne, and the first conquerers shall keepe the fielde against tenne other, that shall reuenge the tenne vanquished, so hauing all iousted, they shall fight at Barriers with rebated swordes, and the brauest Champion shall haue a rich Iewell, which the Empresse hath prouided for the purpose. Nowe woulde I haue you one of the ten challengers, and my Nephew *Ganareno* on the Defendants side, for him doo I esteeme one of the best Knights in my Courte: will you not doo thus much at my request? God forbid, saide *Palmerin*, that I shoulde refuse any thing you please to commaunde. These newes were immediatly published through the Courte, which made euery Knight speedilie to prepare himselfe, in hope to be of the number of the fortie, that should performe the Tourney: and thus they priuilie imparted to their Ladies, howe they would breake both Sword and Launce for their loue. Among whom *Ptolome* was not the last, for he so affected the yong Princesse *Brionella*, as he had made her sole Mistresse of his hart, yet coulde he not find the meanes to acquaint her therewith: but the next day, as shee rode among the

Palmerin d'Oliva: Part I 193

Ladies, they had good leysure to conferre togeather, and before they arriued at the Castell, they discouered thorowlie to eache other their affections, promising mutuallie such a iust consent in loue, as the one should bragge of the others happines. While they continued their amorous discourses, *Palmerin*, who had newlie
5 presented himselfe to *Polinarda*, was greatly discontented, because so soone as he came to her, the Empresse called her, and left not talking with her till they alighted from horsebacke: notwithstanding before night, he gayned recompence for that disaduantage, for after Supper, the Emperor and the Ladies went a walking by a goodlie Riuers side, there to disporte themselues in the coole of the
10 euening. Nowe was it the merrie Maie moneth, when the fieldes were richlie decked with Natures Tapistrie, and *Cupid* gaue oportunitie to hys Subiects, to contemplate theyr sweete and affable desires,[7] and well came it to passe for *Palmerin*, while *Trineus* and *Ptolome* were conuersing with the Empresse: that he taking his Mistresse by the arme, walked with her amongst the faire flowers, and
15 seeing the time and place serue him so well, trembling (as supprised with a vehement passion) thus began. Madame, your gracious nature will not count it strange, but rather take it in good part, that I a Knight errant, and as yet vnknowne among courtlie assemblies, should presume to make known a secrete to you, which my selfe dare not imagine without reuerence, and death can cause
20 me declare to none: nor may I proceede without some assurance of my vncertaine hope, by her diuine pittie that giues me life. And although the wordes of my Dwarffe haue acquainted me with your princely fauour, sufficient to expel all feare and suspition of reproofe: yet such is the height wher to I aspire, as the greatest Monarche in the worlde canne scantly deserue, then well may I esteeme
25 my selfe vnworthie.[8] But doubting whether your speeches were such, or that my Dwarffe (as such as he often may doo) hath reported more then he had in charge: I am desirous, (trusting on your benignitie and speciall fauour aboue all other) to vnderstande, if your pleasure bee so highlye to honour mee, as henceforth to accept me for your Knight and Seruaunt. And if such vndeserued grace[9] may fall
30 to my lot: I shall not onely acknowledge, that Fortune hath directed my course to the onely place of honour, but shall haue good occasion beside to make knowne by my knighthoode, that I am the fauoured of the most faire Princesse. Heerein good Madame, you shall not dissent from reason, if I hauing lost my libertie by beeing onelie yours, want the modestie that shoulde sheelde me in your high
35 regarde: therefore may you sweete Ladie in mine excuse, accuse loue and your celestial beauty, bothe stronger to commande then I to gainesay. My Dwarff hath let you knowe (as he tolde me) part of the paine I endure for your sake, which you cannot but thinke well off, in that my destenie so commaunded mee, long time before I sawe or knewe you, not alone in visions, but by manifest sollicitings, so
40 that in search of you, I haue suffered such trauaile, as maruaile it is that nature coulde make me able to sustaine. Notwithstanding, I account all right happily bestowed, if I may gaine fauour in your gracious eyes, without which it is vnpossible for me to liue: for there is no part possessing life or spirite in mee, that is not

vowed to your onelie seruice. These words were dipt in teares, and deliuered with manie a bitter sigh,[10] which mooued *Polinarda* to such compassion, as taking him by the right hand, she began to playe with his fingers, her trembling testifying her secrete afflictions: and breaking off *Palmerins* discourse, as he thought to haue continued longer, thus aunswered. Syr Knight, it seemes by your countenaunce that you dispayre of something, or els haue more fortitude then I can conceiue. Esteeme you mee of so simple iudgment, that knowing your valour and knightly perfections, I shoulde not account my selfe happy to haue so braue a Champion? Let it suffise you, that what *Vrbanillo* tolde you, is true, and in regarde of the paine you suffer for my loue, and fancying mee so firmelie as you doo: beleeue mee good Knight, you feele no greefe, but it is as familiar with me, so that what thought you haue of mee, the like haue I of you, as time and the vnspotted[11] loue I beare you shall witnesse, in meane time promise me not to depart my Fathers Court without my consent. And because I see the Ladies approching, refer we the rest till some other time, when wee shall haue more leysure to conferre togeather: and tell mee nowe if you bee determined to ioust to morrowe? That will I Madame, quoth hee, if it please you to commaunde me. In sooth saide she, I will not hinder ye, because I knowe the honor of the Tourney will be yours: for my sake therefore shall you were this Bracelet, as a signe of my fauour and pledge of my loue. So taking off her Bracelet, shee gaue it to *Palmerin*, who receiued it with no little content: and so concluding their talke, because manie Knights and Ladies came about them, they walked where the Emperor and the Empresse were, deuising with *Ptolome* and *Trineus*. Nowe because darke night drew on, and the euening dewe was dangerous,[12] they returned to the Castell, entending the next day after dinner to begin the Tournament.

Chapter XXIX.
Howe Palmerin gained the honour of the Tourney, and of that which happened afterward.

After the order of the Tourney was sette downe by the Emperour, as you haue heard, *Palmerin* did but expecte the howre to goe to it, not doubting to performe such chiualrie, that his Ladies fauour shoulde be woorthilie honoured: wherefore hauing prepared all his necessaries readye, immediatly after Dinner, accompanied with nine other Knights brauely Armed, whereof *Ptolome* was one, hee entered the Lysts royall. And espying his Mistresse *Polinarda* in the windowe[1] with the Empresse, after he had doone her humble reuerence, hee began to mannage his Horse with such braue carrires, as euerie one delighted to beholde him: but speciallie the Princesse, whose harte loue had thorowlye conquered, so that she gloried to be beloued of a Knight so worthy and commendable, as that her eye was neuer from the obiect of her sweete desires. And marking his Sheelde, she behelde in a Sable fielde, a Siluer hand fast closed,[2] the import whereof caused her to meruaile, in respecte what had passed betweene them before, and gladly would she haue knowne the meaning, but the place would affoorde no such conuenience: wherefore perswading herselfe for the time, shee was content in seeing her Bracelet, which her Knight wore vppon his right arme. And after manie courses and loftie poynts,[3] doone by *Palmerin* and other Knights before their Ladies, among whom *Ptolome* shewed so correspondent, as the presence of his Ladie *Brionella* highlie prouoked him. Then entered the Prince *Ganareno*, Nephewe to the Emperor, a Knight of no small reckoning amongst the *Allemaignes*, and with him nine other in most sumptuous Armour, and their braueries likewise ended to their Ladies[4] (yet nothing comparable to *Palmerin* and his companions) they went to their Tent, and while the Trompets and Clarions summoned the fielde, euery Knight prepared himselfe in readines. *Palmerin*, not so much to winne common applause, as her loue that had the soueraigne power ouer him, seeing *Ganareno* ordering himselfe to run first, tooke a strong Launce, and encountred him with such puissaunce, as Horse and man were bothe ouerthrowne, and very sore brused: notwithstanding, hee was soone recouered by his companions, and in a Chayre carried forth of the fielde. One of his Knights would needes reuenge his misfortune, and was himselfe in like sort serued: in breefe, the other eight had all one payment, not one of them beeing able to mooue *Palmerin* from his saddle. *Palmerin* ioyfull of his good successe, was departing away with his companie, when one of them thus spake vnto him. Sir *Palmerin*, you haue saued our labour, and got the honour that we desired. The time will come, (quoth *Palmerin*) when you may doo as much for me: but for this time (if you please) you may excuse me. All that were present, as well Lordes as Ladies, meruailed at the valoure of *Palmerin*: and among the rest the Emperour, who said aloud, that he neuer knewe a more valiant Gentleman. *Polinarda* beeing so neere as she heard her Fathers words, and had herselfe behelde his high good fortune, was suddainly sollicited with such affectionate pleasure, as forgetting herselfe and where she was, she thus spake to *Brionella* indifferent loude. What say you faire Freende? dooth not *Palmerin* worthily deserue to be loued? By my faith Madame, aunswered she, I neuer sawe Knight giue such rough encounters with the Launce, as he did to *Ganareno* and the rest of his companions. *Polinarda* wold haue proceeded further, but there entered tenne other Knights, the formost beeing *Ptolome*, not content (as it seemed) that hee ranne not at the first, and then entered tenne Knights more, of whome the formost was *Cormedes* an *Allemaigne* Knight. They raunging themselues in order, *Ptolome* and *Cormedes* brauelie encountred, but neither were vnhorssed: which greeued *Ptolome* to doo no better in presence of his Ladie, wherefore taking another Launce, at the seconde course *Cormedes* was cast quite out of his saddle, and three more of his fellowes after him for companie. Which when the Duke of *Lorraynes* Brother perceiued, a Knight well accounted of in that Countrey, desirous to recouer the honour his foregoers hadde lost, thus spake to *Ptolome*. It seemes that these *Grecian* Knights, are come to rob vs of the honor that is ours by inheritaunce, in vnhappie howre were the *Allemaignes* borne if they so suffer it: and so coutching his Launce, met *Ptolome* with so full a carrire, as loosing saddle and stirrops he fell to the ground, and foure more of his Knights after him had like entertainment, but a hardye Knight of the Emperours named *Menadus*, met the Dukes Brother so rudelie, as downe hee fell to the grounde with his saddle betweene his legs. Thus were manie braue encounters with the Launce to vanquish one another, and all for the loue of their Ladies, who delighted to see theyr Knights so brauelie behaue themselues. The Ioust finished, eache one allighted, and with their blunt Swordes fell to the Barriers, and so cruelly they laid on each other, as they wold not suffer one another to take breath: especially *Ptolome*, who buckled with the Duke of *Lorraynes* Brother, to winne the honor he lost in the Iousting. And now a fresh entered noble *Palmerin*, who as the onelie man to whome Loue and Fortune were fauourable, raunged among the thickest, and with his Sworde made way among them valiantlie: at length he came to the Duke of *Lorraynes* Brother, and so canuazed him about the pate with his blunt Fauchion, as he fell to the ground greatlie astonied, charging him to speake no more in disgrace of *Grecian* Knights. All the sport ended, the Knights withdrew themselues into their Chambers to be vnarmed, and eache Knight wrapping himselfe in his Mantle, *Palmerin* was in his Ladies liuery, for she had sent him a verie rich one, and so comming into the Chamber of presence, the Emperour welcommed him in this manner. Beleeue me my Lorde, I account the Prince happie that hath you for his Freende. As I am,[5] my gracious soueraigne, answered *Palmerin*, I am your humble and obedient Seruaunt during life, ready to accomplish what shall please you to commaunde me. The Emperour highly thanked him, and presently came the Empresse, one of her Ladies bringing with her a riche Cloke, all couered with pearles and stones of great valew, which she presented to *Palmerin*, as the prize and honour he had wunne in the Tourney, and saide to *Polinarda*. Faire Daughter, I am sure you will bestowe some gift on Sir *Palmerin*, in that he hath so worthilie deserued. These wordes raysed a sweete blushing in the Princesse countenaunce, not a little reioysing that he whom shee loued, had carryed awaie the prize from all the other Knights: so with a prettie modest smile, she tooke a chayne of Gold from about her neck, saying. See heere Sir *Palmerin* what I giue yee, this gift is to tye and chaine you in such sort, as you may neuer depart from the Emperours seruice. *Palmerin* with exceeding contentment receiued the Chaine, and on his knee humbly thanked the Empresse and the Princesse, to whom hee spake as followeth. Madame, I am well contented to abide in such a pryson, and neuer will I desire any other libertie, but still will bee his vassaile that hath power to commaunde mee.[6] This aunswere pleased the Emperour exceedinglie, in that he desired to haue *Palmerin* still abide in his Court. Wherfore he said to *Polinarda*, you haue doone well Daughter thus to binde *Palmerin*, for nowe he can not escape awaie when he list. So the Tables beeing couered, the Emperour and all the Knights of the Tourney satte downe to meate, where much talke was spent as concerning the successe on al sides, but *Palmerin* and *Polinarda* had enough to doo to view eache other, their eyes dooing their office, and carrying betweene them the message of their passions, yet so discreetlie shaddowed as none could perceiue them.[7] Supper ended, the Knights and Ladies went to dauncing, and afterwarde to their Chambers, because the Emperour had commaunded the next daie an other Tournament: a breefe report wherof may very wel serue,[8] in that you can imagine there wanted no braue chiualrie. What *Palmerin* did that daie, it were in vaine to tell, because the former daie makes knowne his woorthines, and *Ptolome* behaued himselfe in so good sort, that *Brionella* was as proude of him as the Princesse of her Knight, and therfore presented him with a very rich Diamond, as a token of his desert and her loue. Thus while the Ioustes endured, the Duke of *Lorrayne* had great familiaritie with *Palmerin*, because he had deliuered his Sister *Cardonya*, from the false treason of the County of *Ormeque*.[9] All pastimes thus finished, the Emperour returned to *Gaunt*, where *Palmerin* intreated his Mistresse to appoint him time and place, where they might more priuatlie discourse on their loue, the which she promised, and awaited oportunity.

Chapter xxx.
Howe Polinarda disclosed her secrets to Brionella, and of the talke she had with Palmerin.

Polinarda not forgetting the promise she made her Freend, to meete him in some place where they might argue on theyr loue, determined to discouer her affections to *Brionella*, the beloued of *Ptolome*: well perceiuing, that without her helpe, she could not attaine the end of her desires, wherefore without any longer stay, shee thus began with her. My chosen Freende, I would make known one thing vnto thee, which death can compell me discouer to no other, wherefore thou must haue care to keepe secret my speeches, in respect of my calling, not doubting but in time to recompence any paine thou takest for me. Fayre Princesse, said *Brionella*, in that you doo me such honor, as to impart your thoughts to me, rather will I die then fayle one iote of your commaundement, and therefore assure your selfe, that what you declare shall neuer be discouered. Then *Polinarda* reuealed to her the loue she bare *Palmerin*, what passions did torment her, and in what extreamitie her desires had driuen her: and therefore sweete Freende (quoth she with a deepe sigh) find thou the meane that I may priuatlie talke with him. *Brionella* admiring the earnest loue of the Princesse, knewe not readilie what to aunswere, but seeing that by these meanes she might more easily conferre with *Ptolome*, whom shee likewise intirelie loued, thus spake. It is no wonder Madame, you beeing so incomparable, as I knowe no Prince liuing of whom you are not woorthie, if you haue resolued your loue on noble *Palmerin*, in that there is no Knight in the worlde better deserues you, his rare chiualrie beeing such, as it cannot otherwise bee, but that he is discended of royall linage, beeing accomplished with so many speciall perfections. Therefore Madam, so like you, I haue deuised well for your purpose, as thus. You knowe my Chamber window standes so commodious, as you may with safetie confer with him at pleasure, which you may let him vnderstande by his Dwarffe, and appoint him time as you shall thinke conuenient. This counsel did not a little content the Princesse, because she longed to chatte with her louer, and therefore concluded at his departure to appoint *Palmerin* his time. Nowe was the Chamber of *Brionella* ioyning to the Cittie wall, and had a goodly prospect into the fieldes, and *Palmerins* lodging was neere vnto it, facing the wall as the other did: so that one might easilie passe betweene the lodgings, nothing beeing betwixt them but a little Garden, brauelie decked with flowres, and goodlie fruite Trees. The time appointed, *Polinarda* called the Dwarffe to her, saying. *Vrbanillo*, thou shalt goe to thy Maister from me, and after thou hast saluted hym with my manifolde well wishinges, wil him this night to come secretlie to Lady *Brionellas* Chamber, where at the windowe we may safelie talke togeather: and bid him not misdoubt my Lady *Brionella*, for I haue made her acquainted with all my secrets. And because thy selfe maist conduct him to the place, come, and I will presently shewe it thee. So went the Dwarffe with *Polinarda* to *Brionellas* chamber, where hauing seene the windowe, and gladde to carrie such tydings to his Maister, beeing well assured howe they woulde content him: he departed, and tarried not long on his message, because *Palmerin* thought each howre a yeere to heare from his Mistresse, wherefore hee beholding the Dwarffe comming, tooke him in his armes, and demaunded what newes he had brought him? The Dwarffe with a cheerefull countenaunce thus aunswered. My Lord, Fortune speede you as luckilie, as the newes that I bring you doo well deserue. By this beginning, *Palmerin* perceiued that he brought such tydings as he long looked for, which was, howe he might speake with the Princesse: wherfore embracing him againe, he commaunded him to make report of that his sweete Mistresse had giuen him charge. Then the Dwarffe deliuered, howe the Princesse had great desire to see him, and where shee did intende to speake with him. Which when *Palmerin* heard, filled with vnspeakable ioyes, he recorded the words to himselfe with many itterations, and the more often he spake the words, the more his delights increased. But tell me, (quoth he to the Dwarffe) didst thou marke the place well, where I must talke with my Goddesse?[1] Thereof doubt you not my Lorde, sayde the Dwarffe, for I shall not faile to bring you surely thither, if it be your pleasure I shall goe with you, because the Princesse her selfe, in company of Lady *Brionella* shewed it me. How am I beholding to her, said *Palmerin*, for this high fauour, which els were my death if I had beene denyed? Vppon this he called *Ptolome*, to whom he imparted euery circumstaunce, which *Ptolome* reputed for his great auaile: thys offering the meane for him to visite *Brionella*, and therfore they concluded to goe togeather the night ensuing, to the place appointed for this louing encounter. The howre of rest beeing come, and euery one in theyr Chambers as best beseemed, *Palmerin*, *Ptolome* and the Dwarffe remayned togeather, and seeing the time readie to countenaunce theyr enterprise, tooke eache of them a rich Mantle, and wyth theyr Swordes vnder their armes, went out at a windowe vppon the walles: and albeit the passage was somewhat daungerous, yet loue had so encouraged them, as without regarde of daunger or fortune, they came to the windowe which the Dwarffe shewed them, not seene by any. *Polinarda* who was most attentiue, hearing the trampling of theyr feete, sayde to *Brionella*. Is not this *Palmerin*? So opening the Casements, they sawe *Palmerin* and *Ptolome* attending like dilligent Seruants. If then bothe parties were pleased it is not to be doubted, nothing in the worlde more contenting them then the sight of each other. And truelye *Palmerin* and the Princesse had great reason, for beside that their fatall destenies did so prouoke them, theyr equal natures were so commendable and correspondent, as though they had neuer seene, yet were they borne to loue togeather. Now was *Polinarda* very brauely accoustred in a gorgious night Mantle,[2] and such soft white silkes, as she shewed more bright then the morning Starre, her firie pointed lookes so wounding *Palmerin*, as rapt vppe as it were into a second heauen, he remayned silent a long time, not able to speake a worde.[3] The Princesse was likewise in the selfe same conceit, and so ouercome with regarde of her Paramour, as she continued mute, and was loth to giue the onsette. *Palmerin* ashamed to accompany his Ladie with such silence, beganne thus mildlie to courte his Mistresse. I did neuer thinke, faire Madame, that Fortune woulde honour mee with such extraordinarie fauour, directing my course to your noble Fathers Courte, to bee thus entertayned into your gracious seruice, hauing no deserts in mee to induce you to your choyse: but it may be in respect of some good report by such, to whom I account my selfe highlie beholding, hauing thus founde the place where I was preordained to loue, my Starre hath appointed it,[4] and withall, to make me the happiest man liuing. And it may be Madame, that such as enuie not my happines, haue acquainted you with some of my exterior actions, which God (not I) hath brought to passe: but they ignoraunt of the intire and feruent loue I beare you, coulde make no iust report therof to you, beeing a secret so speciall, and not to be comprehended, beside, the depth and wonderfull nature thereof not to bee measured, therefore to be buried in your heauenly opinion,[5] which howe ample so euer you please to graunt me, the more am I bounde both in duetie and affection, which in despight of enuie and his confederates, shall remaine immooueable, and pleade the continuall loyaltie of your Knight and Seruaunt. And if I shoulde reporte howe manie times your diuine personne hath beene presented mee in sleepe, I shoulde therewithall discourse infinite passions, which I endured seeing my selfe frustrate of that I nowe beholde. How many Countries and Citties? what perrils and daungers haue I past to finde you, prouoked on still with neuer chaunging loue? If this then were sufficient to make me run through a worlde of daungers, I leaue it to your iudgment (sweete Madame) what it may doo nowe, seeing with myne eyes what I dreamed on before, and may with safetie saie, incomparable beautie. Heerehence proceedeth, that my extreame affections haue ouercome all other parts in me, not able to imagine howe manie reuerende opinions I vse of you: which must intreate you on my behalfe, that your accustomed clemencie will pardon my preiudicate conceite, because beeing not mine owne but yours onelie, I may easilie offende. These speeches moistened with the teares of his eies and luke-warme blood of his hart,[6] deliuered manifest euidence how truelie he loued the Princesse, who bearing him companie in all arguments of loue, thus answered. I doubt not Sir *Palmerin*, but the looue you beare mee is exceeding great, noting your earnest affections, and the great trauaile you haue sustained in search of me, and no other certaintie doo I request to be perswaded by, beeing as vehement in affection towards you, as you are to me, for proofe whereof, this attempt maie suffise, that against my duetie I should be seene thus secretlie, in a place so suspicious, and time so vnnecessarie. But if I haue offended heerein, accuse those seemelie perfections which I haue regarded in you, and the confidence I repose in your good conceit, coupled with the honourable estimation that is generallie reputed in your vertues. Pardon me (sweete Ladie) saide *Palmerin*, if by my longing desire to speake with you, I haue in anye thing displeased, for earnest good will to doo you seruice, constrained me to be thus importunate. The matter is far from anie desert of offence, quoth the Princesse, for hither are you come by my commaundement, to

Palmerin d'Oliva: Part I 201

the ende that wee might see one another, and talke of such thinges as neerest concerne vs: and therefore resolue your selfe good Knight, that I esteeme you aboue all other, and promise you by the faith of a Princesse and loyall Freende, to die rather then anie other shall be Lorde of me. Which verie words, so rauished his sences, as verie hardlie he could sustaine himself: whereuppon *Polinarda* put her hande out at the windowe, which he in often kissing well marking, behelde the Character thereon as you haue hearde before.[7] Ah Madame, quoth hee, this is the token that makes me the happiest man liuing. As howe I pray you? saide she, what know you heereof? Then *Palmerin* discoursed all his dreames and visions, and breefely ranne thorow repetition of his whole life, how the wise *Adrian* had sent him the Sheelde of Sable, wherin was figured a hand fast closed togeather, signifying the same hand I holde at this present, because this hath the same marke the other had in figure. In trueth said the Princesse, I was desirous to know the meaning of that Sheeld, wherin I sawe a Siluer hand closed, which you bare the first day of the Tournament, beeing nowe not a little glad that you haue so satisfied me. Afterwarde *Palmerin* made knowne to her, the marke himselfe had on his face, which agreed with hers in perfect likelihoode.[8] O God (quoth she) happie be the time of this meeting, blame me not my Lorde to bee thus supprised with your loue, seeing our fatall destenies haue so appointed: this will cause mee to liue in more hope of good successe, then before I did, and that our amitie will sorte to such ende, as our two harts shall bee combined in one, yet let mee see I beseeche you the marke on your face, howe neere it resembles this on my hand. She fetching a Taper which burned in the Chamber, lifted vp his comelie locks of hayre, and sawe them bothe shaped in one forme, wherefore suddainly setting awaie the light, shee embraced *Palmerins* heade in her armes, and sealed many sweete kisses on his amiable Charracter. The like louing salutation[9] passed betweene *Ptolome* and *Brionella*, at another Casement of the Windowe, with sollemne vowes and protestations neuer to faile in their loue, and this to be the place for conuersing on their desires, till Fortune affoorded them better opportunitie: and longer would they haue there continued, but that the Dwarffe came to his Maister in this manner. My Lorde, I thinke you can neuer finde time to make an ende, will you haue the day light preuent yee, and so discredite you all?[10] in sooth it is time you were in your Chamber. *Palmerin* who was lothe to depart from the pleasure of his thoughts, made small account of the dwarffes words and continued on in amorous deuises: but the Princesse a litle more fearefull then he, seeing the Dwarffe said true, and lothe to be seene suspitiously, said. My Lord, it is time to breake off, but I pray you faile not of your promise, let vs visite one another now you knowe the way and place. So *Palmerin* and *Ptolome* tooke leaue of their Ladies, and passed to their Chambers without suspition: the successe of their loue you shall vnderstande heereafter, as time and place shall fitte for the purpose: but nowe to satisfie you with choyse of delights, wee will returne a while to another discourse.[11]

Chapter XXXI.
Howe the King of Fraunce kept a royall and magnificent Courte, and howe his Sonne Lewes became enamored of the Duchesse of Burgundie.

During the time that the Emperour of *Allemaigne* liued in this happines, accompanied (as you haue hearde) with manie hardie Knightes: there raigned in *Fraunce* a mightie Prince named *Agariell*, valiant, wise and vertuous, hauing three Sonnes, whereof the second was the hardiest Knight at Armes, being named *Lewes*. This King *Agariell*, the more to honour hys Knights and noble Gentlemen abyding in his Realme, determined to keepe open Court for all commers, as none of his predecessors euer did the like before him: and therefore sent abroade his Heraldes, Gentlemen of his escuyrie and others, to summon his Lords and Barrons of *Fraunce*, that on a day appointed they would all meete at the Court. And because none shoulde be ignoraunt what hee intended, he requested that all Gentlemen professing Armes, at the feaste of Easter following, shoulde repaire to *Parris*, beeing the heade and cheefest Cittie of his Realme. The Queene likewise aduertised al Ladies and Gentlewomen, at whose commaunde euery one obeyed, so that in fewe dayes the Courte was furnished with Lordes and Ladies: nothing nowe intended but delights and courtlie pastimes, which made the Duke of *Burgundie* likewise repaire thither. Now was the Duke aged, a man of good prouidence, and a tryed Knight, hauing matched in marriage with the King of *Denmarks* Sister, a yong beautiful Ladie, and of vertuous education: the Duke hoping to haue issue by her, because by his first Wife he could not haue any. The King aduertised of the Dukes comming, commaunded his Son *Lewes* with an honourable traine to goe entertayne him, which he did, so that many solemne reuerences passed betweene the Duke and him, as also to the Duchesse, whom as he welcomed with manie salutations, so did he earnestlie contemplate her excellent beautie, reputing her fairer then the fayrest, and on a suddaine became amorous of her, such a violent breach made loue into his hart at the very first sight of her. In this great and vnlooked for vexation, hee conducted her to the lodging was prepared for the Duke, dissembling so well as hee coulde his newe desire: but so vehement was his oppression, as without returning againe to the King, he went to his Chamber. Prince *Lewes* beeing thus alone by himselfe, Loue not a little tryumphing of his new pray, tormented his thoughts with so manie conceits, as all the night he spent in sighes and dolorous laments, his mind stil trauailing by what meanes he might compasse his intent. Sometimes he thought it vnpossible in respecte of the Duke, then againe as easie because of his age, a contrarie too yrksome in his eyes for the sweete florishing youth of the Duchesse: all which imaginations wrought so diuersly in him, as his spirite forsaking counsell and reason, made him breake foorth into these exclaimes. Ah heauens, haue you fourmed beautie with such excellencie, as to cause me endure a torment more then mortall? Ah mine eyes, too lauishe were you in beholding her, who cannot chuse but vtterly disdaine thee, thou hast no acquaintaunce with

Palmerin d'Oliva: Part I 203

her, and therefore let thy death chastise thy boldnes. Yet mayst thou bee deceiued in thine opinion foolish man, perhappes in offering her thy seruice she may accept it, for the Duke is old, and likelie to die, howe happy were it for thee to be his executor for his Ladie? Dispayre not then man, for things thought impossible are easiest oftentimes in performance. In these and such like tearmes hee spent the night, and seeing the fayre morning salute him at his Chamber windowe, he arose, intending that day to bewray his passions to the Duchesse, and knowing that the Duke would goe visite the Queene, accompanied with many Knights he came to bid him good-morrow, which the Duke taking very kindly, requited him with many thankes, ignoraunt that for the faire Wyfe, he was so courteous to the olde Husband. The Duke hauing taken his way to the Queene, *Lewes* kept company wyth the Duchesse very mannerlie, wayting oportunitie to dyscouer his affections, and reuiewing[1] her beautie so perfecte and rare, not able longer to hold, beganne thus. It is maruaile Madam, if fayre beautie should be so bitter, as a man cannot surfette but hee must needes die. The Duchesse not knowing of whom the Prince spake, nor as yet regarding that he was in loue, aunswered. In sooth my Lord, the Ladie hath small reason, that shee shoulde vse you so hardlie, yf you meane it by your selfe. In breefe Madame, quoth hee, it is you haue wounded me, and none but you can ease my afflictions: if then (sweete Lady) you retaine such pittie, as all your other excellencies shewe you to haue, you wyll not disdaine to giue me remedie, which if you doo, for euer I remaine your Knight and loyall Freende. And in mine opinion Madame, you can not well refuse me, seeing Fortune hath beene such an enemie to you in marriage, the Duke beeing olde and full of mellanchollie, you yong, tender and daintie as may be, hee more meete to keepe companye wyth *Atropos* the mortall Goddesse,[2] then liue with a Saint of so rare perfections.[3] But had my luck beene such, before you were espoused to haue knowne you, I woulde with valoure haue hindered your briding so, or Fortune should haue foullie denied me: for such is my religion in looue, as better death then discontent,[4] and had I beene Lord of *Europe*, you had beene Ladie. Notwithstanding Madame, so like it you, I may be your Freende and knightly seruaunt: for Loue wants no wyles to compasse desire, and my sute is modest if you count it not vnseemely. The Duchesse, whom sweete loue could easilie entice to folly, hardly might resist a present conquest: wherefore chaunging countenaunce, and not daring to reueale what she gladly would, sayd. Trust mee my Lorde, your speeches are not comely, to violate chaste wedlocke is so monstrous, as you can haue no priuiledge to aske, nor I to graunt, and therefore content ye. This aunswere, albeit it was sharpe, and scant pleasing to the Prince, yet loue so perswaded him, that the Duchesse had another meaning then she bewrayed: for noting her countenaunce so full of change, he gessed that some sparks had fallen among her affections, wherefore he began againe. I beseeche you Madame accuse Loue, if I haue spoken to your dislyking, yet hope I to see the time, when I shall make knowne howe great my affection is to doo you seruice: and continuing this talke he brought her to the Queenes lodging, Loue following them bothe so narrowlie at the heeles, as the Duchesse was no lesse affectionate then *Lewes* was passionate. Which when he got some light of, in hope to purchase his desire, he sollicited her in more secrete manner then hee was wont, so that being one day in place where they might familiarlie talke: *Lewes* perseuering in his enterprise, declared what torments he suffered for her loue, whereuppon the Duchesse, not onely by the Princes reasons which were perswasiue, but as well to mittigate her owne oppressions, thus aunswered. Great is the force of your perswasions my Lord, but greater is that of looue, which hath made me yours: so that what you request, I cannot denie, and though it stand not with mine honour, yet such is my fortune. Let me intreate you therefore to conceale this loue so discreetlie, as none may knowe of it, especially my Lord the Duke, and expect the day that shall yeelde you content and make mee happy. This aunswere so highly pleased the Prince, as neuer man thought himselfe in greater felicitie, and rendering her manifold thankes, sayd. I sweare to you Madame, by the diuine force of loue that gouerns vs bothe, to bee for euer your Knight, and neuer shall any other desire abide in me, then you shall like and well allowe of, for otherwise I were not worthy this speciall fauour. The Duchesse thanking him, departed, and thenceforth so secretly shaddowed their loue, as none suspected that the Prince loued the Duchesse.

Chapter XXXII.
Of the enterprise of Lewes the Prince of Fraunce, for the loue of the Duchesse of Burgundie.

Long continued the King of *Fraunce* this state in all magnificence, there meeting many noble personages, as well Straungers as of the Realme, that it was meruailous to behold, as also the Ladies and Damosels that accompanyed the Queene: who on a day in the presence Chamber among many Knights, conferred of the bountie and prowesse of the florishing braue yong Courtiers, among whom the Prince *Lewes* making one, eache one spake in behalfe of his Ladies beautie, yet concealing their names to themselues, till better occasions might cause them deseruedly to be known. Al this talke the Prince well marking, who for the Duchesse loue was depriued of libertie, threw many sweete glaunces at the Mistresse of his affections, perswading himselfe, that nature neuer made a more perfect creature, and not able to make her like againe, burst her molde, whereupon hee said. Lordes and Ladies, who with such aduauntage haue chatted on beautie, vnderstand that such as you haue yet spoken of, or seuerally in your owne thoughts shall thinke vppon: may not be equall with one that I knowe, euen she that is Ladie and commaunder of my hart, whose beautie is so far beyond all other, as bright *Cynthia* from the goodliest star in the firmament.[1] And because that none shal imagine, how (being carried awaie with priuate opinion) I vse these speeches, I will make good my words by deedes of Armes, against anie Knight whatsoeuer that dare saie the contrarie. Nowe in regard that none shall pleade ignoraunce, I will aduertise all Knights, howe the first daie of Maie next ensuing, and seauen daies more immediatlie following, I will be in open fielde in my Tent, where I will erecte a statelie monument,[2] on the toppe whereof shall bee her figure whose Knight I am, and there will I defende it in this honorable quarrell, against such Knights as will Combat for the beautie of their Ladies, I affirming mine to excell all other in perfections. This condition must be obserued by such as enter the fielde, that they bring the Ladies figure with them whom they honor most: and if Fortune frowne on them in such sort as they be vanquished, they shall there leaue their Ladies Image, to be placed vnder my Mistresse as her subiect. Nowe if my vnhappy Starres so crosse me, as I loose the credite I would bee lothe, the conquerer shall enter in my Tent, and in my Ladies place shall his Mistresse bee mounted, if he meane to maintaine her with such conditions as I doo mine. And hee that last shall accomplishe these eyght daies, shall beare away the honour with the portraitures of the Ladies, which by him or anie other all the saide time haue beene gained. And this libertie shall be granted, that he which receiues the foyle with the Launce, shall Combat with the Sworde (if he please) before he yeelde. Nowe, that this mine enterprise may be openlie knowne, and put in execution as the vertue requireth: I will sende Horsemen through all the prouinces of Christendome, that all Knights willing thus to aduenture, shall be heere receiued.[3] His speeches ended, the Gentlemen present could not maruaile sufficiently, at this great and high enterprise of the Prince *Lewes*, and the daunger whereinto he thrust himselfe, yet not knowing who was the Ladie he woulde thus aduenture for: but she beeing present, perceiued that the Prince in honour of her loue, tooke in hande this perillous hazarde, wherein she conceiued such secrete content, as the passions of loue hauing penetrated her hart, made her feare his misfortune, which she would not for her life. In this assemblie was present the Duke of *Sauoye*, a yong Prince, braue, hardie and couragious as might be, and esteeming so well of himselfe, as he thought no Knight in the world coulde vanquish him, who to aunswere the Prince *Lewes*, arose and thus spake. My Lorde, I would not willingly haue entered the Combat against you, but that I heard you so farre outreache your selfe, as shee whose beautie you maintaine, is more perfecte then all other Ladies: but shee that is the commaunder of my hart, is such a braue accomplished Ladie, as (in trueth) her beautie may not be matched through the whole worlde. And to affirme what I saie, I sweare by the order of my knighthoode, that the morrowe after you haue finished your eight daies enterprise, I will enter the same fielde, and auerre against all Knights, that the Goddesse to whom I am dedicated, excelles all other Ladies in her heauenly gifts: and he that dare maintaine the contrarie, vnder my Sworde I will make him confesse it. All such therefore as will make proofe of their valour, shall find me there in my Tent at my appointed day, and nine daies after to sustaine the same quarrell in plaine Combat, either at the Launce, the Mace, the Sworde, on horsebacke or on foote, at his choise. And though I vanquish one Knight, it shall not be lawfull for me to rest a minute space, but presentlie take him in hande that shall followe:[4] and bee it my fortune to be foyled by him, he shall keepe the fielde in manner as you my Lord deuised. And to the ende all may be the better executed, pleaseth you that in such places where your intelligencers shall come, my enterprise may likewise bee declared, in respect I hope to behaue my selfe so well, as my Ladie will make speciall account of me. The Lady for whom the Duke of *Sauoye* thus attempted, was Daughter to the King, and Sister to *Lewes* named *Lucemania*, whom he loued intirelie, and aboue all thinges desired in marriage: which to compasse, and to honour his Ladie, he thus offered the Combat against all Knights. These Princes, intending to goe thorow with their intent, concluded betweene them, that the Duke of *Sauoye* shoulde break it to the King, to gaine his good-will: whereuppon the Duke departing towards the Queenes Chamber to finde the King, espyed him at very good leysure walking in his Garden, to whome hee went in all haste, and on his knee thus began. So please it your highnes to graunt me one boone, I shall be bounde to continue the loue I haue borne your Maiestie, which is to prolong my life in your seruice, as the most forwarde Knight in your royall Court. The King who had long time fauoured the Duke, taking him by the hande, thus aunswered. Demaunde my good Cozin what you please, and it shall bee graunted. Then the Duke deliberatelie discoursed, what the Prince *Lewes* and he had intended for the loue of theyr Ladies: wherwith the King scant content, and meruailing at this hastie enterprise, said.

Palmerin d'Oliva: Part I

Why Cozin? do you imagine your selues able to maintaine so hard a taske, in resistance of so manie hardie Knights, wherewith the worlde is now plentifullie stored? Beleeue me, in manie Countries are Ladies of greater beautie (I doubt) then is at this time in our Realme of *Fraunce*. I promise you, I hardly like what
5 my Sonne and you attempt, but seeing my worde is paste, you shall not nowe be hindered: doo therefore what your selues thinke expedient, with this consideration alwaies, that the ending of matters is greater then the beginning.[5] The Duke humbly thanking the King, aunswered. Wee doubt not my Lorde, but by the holpe of God and fauour of our Ladies, to ende our affaires with fortunate
10 successe, but if nowe we should giue ouer, and not goe forward with our promise, we might woorthily be reprooued of shame and cowardise, the most villainous reproches that can be to any noble hart. The King perceiuing the earnest affection of these two yong Princes, and that to denie their request would be more hurtfull then to graunt: commaunded him againe to proceede with their intent,
15 with such suretie against all strange Knights, as what losse or victory happened to them, they must be content with all that fell out. The Duke not a little ioyfull, kissing his highnes hande departed, and immediatly acquainted Prince *Lewes* therewith: but nowe the Queene vnderstanding her Sonnes enterprise, sent for him, and with sad countenance thus spake. I would (my Son) that the intent of
20 you and the Duke of *Sauoye*, were eyther awhile deferred, or vtterly forgotten, because I greatlie doubt, that the ende will bring a further consequence then you expect. For thinke you, that by all your forces and Chiualries, the beautie of your Ladies shalbe any iote increased? no beleeue me: but if they loue you as loyall Freendes ought to doo, as greatlie wil they dislike your enterprise, as feare the
25 daunger whereinto you may fall, a matter causing other desire then you thinke on, and more offensiue (perhaps) to them, then anie honor you may winne can please them.[6] *Lewes*, who by no meanes would be disswaded from his conceit, aunswered. Good Mother, if for no other feare, this matter shal not be reuoked, in regard of the shame, and neuer dying dishonor I shall gaine thereby, which
30 makes mee desire a thousande deathes, rather then not to bee so good as my worde: therefore perswade your selfe good Mother, that albeit her beautie for whom I enter the Combat, cannot bee more perfect hereby, in that it is without imperfection, yet such is my resolution in a matter so certaine, as her sweete lookes shall deliuer me strength enough to ende my taske, without dreade of any
35 inconuenience that may happen. The Duchesse (enflamed with loue) hearing these wordes on her behalfe, must needes speake, and thus began. I knowe not (my Lorde) who is the Ladie you loue, nor what are her vertues, but heereof I can assure you, that she is highlie beholding to you, and (except great reason to the contrarie) ought to loue you, considering what perill you thruste your selfe into
40 for her beautie. Madame (quoth the Prince) the trauaile I shall take, and the bad fortunes may befall mee, are little and of no account in respect of her gracious deserts, therefore for her honour, I will beare my inwarde paines with secrete content, and attempt these outwarde actions with the greatest courage I can

possible, desiring no other recompence then her fauourable conceit, whereof once assured, nothing can seeme difficult to me, no, were it to dye in her diuine seruice. And as he would haue continued longer, the King (not yet thorowlie content with his promise past to the Duke of *Sauoye*)[7] entered the Chamber, by whose countenaunce, *Lewes* wel knewe he was *mal content* wyth him, wherefore falling on his knee, hee saide. My Lorde, no one is ignoraunt, how all my welfare and reputation consisteth onelie in your Maiestie, as a Prince and Father, the most vertuous that I know, which great good in some part to recompence, I haue enterprised a matter vnwoorthie of dislike, so please your highnes (of your accustomed bountie) to excuse and accept it in good part, in respect that such as are borne to the highest places of dignitie, ought to bee more prompt and readie to all magnanimious actions, then theyr inferiors, cheefelie in prowesse, chiualry, and deedes of estimation. What brought such renowne to *Horatius, Mutius Scaevola, Marcus Curtius, Manlius Torquatus*, and a number more of *Romaine* Knights, if not the couragious folowing of occasions offered? What made for euer immortall the fame of *Marius* the *Romaine* Cittizen, *Hanniball* the *Carthaginian*, and *Agesilaus* the *Greeke*,[8] if not the vndaunted valour of their minds, deliuered in their deedes of kinglie consequence?[9] Assuredly I beleeue, that their Fathers, Vncles, and aunctent progenitours, neuer made them noble or ought renowmed: what then? onely vertue, the very formatrix of all nobilitie. For this cause my good Lorde and Father, hauing now oportunitie, as my Cozin the Duke of *Sauoye* hath informed you, may it please your grace to permit my endeuours with fauour, to the ende I may deliuer perfect testimonie, that I no whit degenerate from your heroycall and kingly vertues. The King somewhat moderating his former opinion, answered. Trust me Sonne, full well you know howe to disguise and couer your follye wyth vertues coullers, God sende it to fall out so well: arise, and be it as your Cozin and you haue requested. See in meane time that you prouide all needfull occasions, that when the daie comes nothing bee wanting. *Lewes* humbly thanking his Father, arose, euery one present not a little reioycing, because they feared all woulde be squandered. Then began the Lordes and Ladies to conferre togeather, and the Duchesse departing to her lodging, beeing manned by the Prince, did not (as I thinke) repent herselfe of her loue,[10] as a number of you (martching vnder the same Ensigne) wold doo the like in such a case. In fine, the Duchesse fearefull of the thwarts of Fortune, that she would work her disgrace by some bad coniectures or wounding reports, said. I know well (my Lorde) the good will you beare me, without anie further shewes or confirmations by actions so daungerous, which I had rather die then beholde, and therefore whatsoeuer you shall performe, will condemne mee as vnwoorthy of so good deserts: in this respect you shall therfore graunt me one thing, which is, that aboue all you haue care of your selfe, els will perpetuall discontent cut short my date, beeing bereaued of the honour of my greene desires.[11] Nowe Madame (quoth the Prince) may I boast of my fortune, not doubting to follow the deuise of a Ladie so vertuous, for your sweete wordes prolong my life, els ere this had death robd you of your Knight. The Duchesse heereto with an amiable smile, aunswered. I muste not loose you yet good Prince, for may I lengthen your life, it shall bee for euer. Many sollemne thankes the Prince returned, and by this time had brought her to her Chamber, wher hauing *baise la main*,[12] departed.

Chapter XXXIII.
Howe the Prince Lewes and the Duke of Sauoye, sent theyr Heraldes and Horsemen into all parts, to make knowne to all Knights their enterprises, and the conditions of theyr Combats.

The Prince *Lewes* ioyfull of the King his Fathers consent, but of the gracious aunswere of the Duchesse most of all, dispatched immediatlie his Heraldes into all the prouinces of *Europe*, who executed their charge with such dilligence, as there was no Court of Emperour, King or Prince, but they declared the enterprise of these two yong Princes. So that one of the Princes Heraldes, accompanied with the King of Armes[1] belonging to the Duke of *Sauoye*, came to the Emperors Court of *Allemaigne*, which then was furnished with a great number of Lordes and Knights, beeing there to sollemnize the day of hys byrth, but especially *Palmerin* aboue all the rest, tryumphing in the loue of his Mistresse *Polinarda*. The Heralds beeing entred the great Hall, founde the Emperour sitting in his chayre of estate, with many Princes, Barons and noble personages about him: who graunting them libertie of speeche, the Heralde of *Fraunce* began first in this manner. Illustrious and most redoubted Emperour, the cause why we thus presume before your Maiestie, is by the commaundement of the vertuous yong Prince *Lewes*, Son to our dreade Lorde *Agariel* King of *Fraunce*, as also of the Duke of *Sauoye* his Cozin, so good a Knight as may well commaunde: what our message is, so please your highnesse to call all your Knights in presence, because it cheefelie concerneth them, we with duetie will deliuer it. The Emperour presentlie called for all Knights and Gentlemen of his Courte, who desirous of the newes, were not long in comming, before whom he saide. Dreade Lord, the Prince *Lewes* of *Fraunce* my Maister, commends him to your Maiestie with this Letter, may it please your grace commande it to be read, and you shall soone see the effect of our Embassade. The Emperour caused his Secretarie to reade it openlie, and because it contained what you haue heard alreadie, it shall be needelesse to wast longer time in talke thereof: but the Letter beeing read, the Heralde thus proceeded. The Prince my Maister (woorthie Emperour) giues the Knights of your Court (as els where) to vnderstande, that he intendes to prooue by deedes of Armes, howe no Ladie in the worlde is comparable in beautie to the Lady he loues, which he will bee readie to maintaine in Combat the first of Maie next, and seauen daies following, in his Tent before the Gates of *Parris*, there will he verifie it against all commers that dare auerre the contrarie. Afterwarde he rehearsed all the conditions to bee obserued in this Combat, and the King of Armes to the Duke of *Sauoie*, made known his Maisters challenge likewise as you haue hearde. The Emperour meruailing at this message, said. Without doubt the Ladies had neede to be faire, and my Cozins your Maisters valiant and hardie, els it is doubtful howe such an enterprise will fall out, for the affections of persons are diuers, and theyr fortunes daungerous, neuerthelesse I desire the issue may sort to their honor. These Lordes and Knights haue hearde your message, and I iudge some of them will prouide to be there, because they prize the beautie of theyr Ladies at as high a rate, as your Masters doo esteeme their faire Freendes: yet let them doo what they thinke most expedient, because they are olde enough to make you answer. As for me, you may salute (on my behalfe) the King my Brother, and my Cozins, to whom I sende thanks with all my hart, that they thus acquainted me with their honourable endeuours. All this while the Knights conferred together, with diuers iudgments of these pretended Combats: some were either fearefull or too forwarde, others well aduised and prouoked with discreete courage. Among whome repute we noble *Palmerin*, all pensiue, his eyes fixed on the grounde, and not a worde,[2] hauing in his spirite discoursed, howe bitter the diuorce would be of the eye from his sweete obiect: in the ende concluded the Combat,[3] perswading him selfe, not in Christendome, nor in the other three habitable parts of the earth,[4] eyther Empresse, Queene or Ladie was more accomplished with perfections, then his gracious Mistresse *Polinarda*. And in respect of this Embassage, it seemed to him vituperous, and a dishonour not sufferable if he should not iustifie the trueth and haue so good occasion: wheruppon he desired a thousande deathes, rather then he would defer so braue a voyage, and so on his knee before the Emperour thus began. Gracious Lorde and my woorthy Patrone, I intende (with your good lyking and leaue) to depart with all speede possible, to the Ioustes and Combats of *Fraunce* and *Sauoye*: let it not therefore displease (for the honour of Chiualrie) that I leaue your Courte a while, but maie commit my selfe to this iourney with your fauourable opinion. The Emperour verie lothe to let *Palmerin* goe, aunswered. In sooth *Palmerin*, I greatly doubted (so soone as I heard these newes from *Fraunce*) that it would not passe without your presence, which displeaseth mee, not so much for their follie as your absence, which is and wilbe to mee greater greefe then you iudge: but let mee intreate that thy returne may be speedie, and stay no longer then thou hast good occasion.[5] I would gladlie knowe, would you graunt it me, what Ladie she is for whom you thus aduenture, you neede not *Palmerin* hide it from mee. My Lord (quoth he) the Dame for whome I enter the Combat, is such, as none may or ought compare with, so singuler, rare, and (aboue all) vertuous, and neuer would I think my selfe worthy to beare Armes, if feare of danger, misfortune, or death it selfe, should haue power to pluck me from my duetie. As for my staie, the Ioustes ended, within one Moneth or sooner, will I returne to your Maiestie: and let mee intreate you not to feare anie thing in my iourney, because I goe for your honour, and my sword shal ring on the stoutest Creast, the euer continuing honours of the Emperour of *Allemaigne*.[6] The Emperor vnwilling to forgoe him, and loth to hinder knightlie chiualrie, said. Without question *Palmerin*, the Ladie is indebted to you, and you declare vnspeakable loue, that for her beautie you deliuer your selfe to so great hazard: but as for your intent to my honor, I rather delight to haue it by your presence, then thirste after such applause with your absence.[7] But seeing you will needes to *Fraunce*,[8] happie fortune goe with you, and make you victorious in all your attempts: which I doubt not, but by your valour and vertues of your Mistresse, the *French* wil not braue so much on the seauenteene of Maie,⁹ as perhaps they wil on the first. Prouided, that before you depart, you demaund and haue all thinges for your iourneie, as well for such as goe in your companie, as for your owne necessarie prouision: and some wil I appoint to trauaile with you, that may preuent anie trecherous inconuenience. *Palmerin* not refusing thys bountifull offer, with great obeisaunce thanked the Emperour, and taking his leaue for that night, returned to his Chamber, determining to depart with expedition, because the daie of the Ioustes were at hande.¹⁰ Nowe was *Trineus* the Emperours Sonne a yong Prince, and had not yet receiued his order of knighthoode, hee hearing of *Palmerins* departure, was meruailous desirous to beare him company: whereuppon he kneeled before his Father, intreating him not to denie him one request. Demaunde what thou wilt my Sonne (quoth he) I graunt it thee. Then I beseech you good Father, saide he, to suffer mee see *Fraunce* with noble *Palmerin*, that I may bee acquainted with the courtesie and ciuilitie of that nation, not doubting but soone to deserue my knighthoode. And yet if before I receiue my order, I see these high and woorthie deedes of Armes, happilie they may entice me to follow their vertues: beside, if nowe I loose so good an occasion offered, I knowe not when I shal compasse the like commoditie, therefore (good Father) let me not be denied. The Emperor offended for his rashe promise to his Sonne, laboured to change his minde, but all woulde not serue, for the Prince promised to goe so couertlie, as none should knowe him. Wherefore he called *Palmerin*, who as yet was not departed the Hall,¹¹ saying. I see Sir *Palmerin*, you shall not goe alone in your voyage, for my Sonne *Trineus* desires to be your companion: for which cause I commit him to you, and desire you to conceiue so well of him, as at your returne we maie be all merrie togeather. Which *Palmerin* promised, whereuppon the Emperour called for the Maister of his Horse,¹² commanding him that all things might bee in readines against their departure: all which was doone with such dilligence, as the thirde daie following all thinges prepared, they tooke their leaue of the Emperour and the Ladies, who at their departure shedde manie teares (a common matter with them) wishing the victorie and honor to *Palmerin*. Thus with *Trineus* and twentie other Knights, a great number of Squires and seruants in good equipage, they iournied towards *Parris*, without anie hinderaunce by the waie, or matter of memorie.¹³

Nowe before we passe anie further, you shall vnderstand, that after the Heraldes of the Prince of *Fraunce* and Duke of *Sauoie* were departed, and that *Palmerin* had obtained leaue of the Emperor: the Princesse *Polinarda* aduertised heereof, was greatlie displeased with this suddaine departure, wherfore calling *Vrbanillo* the Dwarffe to her, she saide. *Vrbanillo*, thou must goe to thy Maister, and will him this night to meete me at our appointed place, that I maie confer with him of a secrete neerelie concerning mee. Which when *Palmerin* hearde, the earth beeing couered with her blacke Mantle, and euerie one in their dead sleepe, he called *Ptolome* and *Vrbanillo*, who were well acquainted with this loue walke,

and beeing there in presence of their Ladies, the Princesse with a great sigh thus began. Alas my Lord, what mind is this in you, thus to voyage towardes *Fraunce*, and leaue mee alone sad and sollitarie? Alas, not content to hazard so long a iourney, but a daungerous Combat beside for my beautie, which is of so slender
5 estimation, as may not parragon with the Ladies of *Fraunce*, beeing peereles[14] (as I haue hearde) among those of highest perfection. Ah my Lorde, more comfort and content is it to me to haue your companie, then to be crowned Queene of anie Realme conquered by your vertue and prowesse. Therefore (sweete Freende) I intreate you with all my hart, and by the vnfained loue you beare me, to leaue
10 such dangerous enterprises, where death is commonlie more frequent then life. These wordes came with such amiable coniurations from the Princesse, as *Palmerin* (though loth to be disswaded) answered. Let me preuaile with you so farre good Madame, as not to mislike my enterprise for your gracious loue, for the honour you haue doone me, in making mee your Knight, I prize at no lesse
15 valew then my deerest blood, and shoulde I be helde from these *French* exploits, vnwoorthy were I to bee your Seruaunt: in that (as you knowe) no Knight but caries the honour of his Ladie in such account, as he preferres that before his owne life. If then Madame in religion of this office,[15] I absent my selfe for a while, I shal accomplish nothing but my duetie, wherto your selfe bound me, and
20 I hope to execute with such successe, as you shall beare the prize for beautie, not onelie from the Ladies of *Fraunce* and *Allemaigne*, but from all Christendome, yea, the whole worlde may I liue to trauaile it. Doo not then (sweete Mistresse) mislike, if I absent my selfe for a cause so reasonable, and continue me still in your fauourable conceit, as he that was borne to doo you seruice. And albeit I
25 can not depart without exceeding greefe and anguish, yet perswaded of your rare arguments, I arme my selfe with patience and yeelde to reason, beeing present with you alwaies, in that I carrie your diuine Image in my soule, and leaue hart, life and all with you till I come. These wordes were sealed with manie deuoute kisses, and *Ptolome*, had like paine in perswading *Brionella*, yet this contented
30 them in the ende, that the honor of their trauaile was the renowne of their beautie, and so with forced content they louinglie departed.[16] The next morning the Princesse sent *Palmerin* an arming coate of greene Veluet, imbroidered all ouer with great Orientall Pearles, and verie thicke besett with Starres of Golde, and in the midst of each Starre a costlie Emeralde: and hee had caused her picture
35 to bee most curiously drawne in Golde, her face and hands formed wonderfull neere the life, and all her lineaments verie singulerlie fashioned, and this portrait caused he to bee sette in a fayre Litter couered with Crimson veluet, which hee had prouided onelie for the purpose, and so set forward.

CHAPTER XXXIV.
How the Prince Lewes came to see the Duchesse of Burgundie, and what happened.

So soone as the Heraldes and Horsemen of *Lewes* of *Fraunce* and the Duke of *Sauoie*, had dispatched their charge, their Lordes gaue order to prepare al things in readines so soone as might bee: but yet the Princes affection to the Duchesse so tormented him, as he dailie compassed new meanes to conferre with her, that shee might knowe the passions hee endured for her sake. At length it came to passe, that the King, the Duke of *Burgundie*, and diuers other Princes rode foorth on pleasure togeather, and returned not againe for two daies space, which made him thus begin with the Duchesse. I neede not tell you Madame, for you knowe it well enough, howe continuallie I languish in remedilesse afflictions, till nowe this opportunitie puts me in some hope of comfort, that you performing a sollemne promise, will deliuer me out of this extremitie. Wherefore faire Mistresse, since time and occasion hath pointed it, and Fortune (by nature froward and inconstant) fauours it, let mee intreate you to take the benefit of bothe, least heereafter we compasse not the like againe. My Lorde (quoth the Duchesse) you must thinke I am more yours then mine owne, and make that reckoning of you, as no Ladie can the like: howe is it possible then for mee (louing as I doo) to flie from that which loue commaunds me to fulfill? Let it suffise you then, that the regarde of mine honour defended, I am readie to doo ought may agree with your liking. What happened afterwarde, I leaue to your oppinions, but by the halfe the whole may be discerned,[1] notwithstanding, vertuous Ladies haue power to resist such motions, though time, occasion, and such amorous sollicitings did offer it them: but such may be accounted more diuine then humaine, and to them may worthilie be erected a Trophe, in disgrace of the temptresse *Venus*. But this little discourse, not much dissenting from the matter, is written in reproche of such yong daintie wantons, that attende on their ouer fonde and vnchast desires: and may likewise be a warning to vndiscreet olde men, that they choose theyr Pantofle fit for their foote.[2]

But nowe is come the first of Maie, the daie to beginne the enterprises of the Princes of *Fraunce* and *Sauoie*: *Lewes* to entertaine the Duchesse loue begun with such aduauntage, had greater desire nowe to execute his intent then before. Wherefore this daie was his Tent erected at the Citty Gates, beeing beautifull and verie sumptuous, and at the enteraunce thereof was placed a goodlie monument of black Marble, curiouslie sette foorth with collombes of white Marble, verie thicke imbossed with golde and pearle.[3] At the side of his pauillion, was placed another monument of greene Iasper, adorned with manie Bases, Pillers and antique imagerie of Golde,[4] whereon he intended the strange Knights that came should place the figures of their Ladies. On the other side was a seemelie place appointed for the Iudges of the fielde, who were the Dukes of *Orleaunce* and *Burgundie*, Princes greatlie esteemed for their nobilitie, and in theyr time had beene hardie and aduenturous Knights. Manie other Tents and Pauillions were that daie there set vppe, as well for strange Knights that came, as Noble men and Gentlemen of the Realme. And nowe[5] comes the Prince brauelie mounted to the fielde, accompanied with manie yong Princes, Knights and Gentlemen, the Heralds and Kings of Armes ryding before, the Drummes, Phifes, Trompets and Clarions sounding so gallantlie, as made the ayre deliuer a most sweete Eccho. Before him in a verye sumptuous Coche, was carried the curious counterfeite of the Duchesse, so superficiallie sette foorth with such perfection of arte, as though it had beene the liuely Duchesse herselfe. After followed Prince *Lewes* in gorgious gilt Armour, all ouergrauen with most artificiall flowers,[6] and mounted on a Courser of *Spaine*, esteemed one of the best runners in *Europe*, which made waie with braue and loftie voltages, as did not a little delight the beholders: one of the cheefe Princes of the Court bearing his Helmet, and another hys Launce. What neede I make further reporte of the Princes tryumphe, he comming to the fielde in such equipage, as well beseemed the house from whence he discended, and as beseemed a louelie Knight in presence of his Ladie: who as her fauour had sent him that morning, a costlie Girdle garnished with Rubies, Diamondes, great Emeraldes and other vnualuable stones, with a Sworde so good as euer Knight wore, and therewith rode he gyrded to the Fielde. Before he went, the King his Father thus spake to him. My Son, this daie and all the other following, Fortune speede thee so well, as thou maist winne the honour my hart doth wysh thee. My Lorde, aunswered the Prince, I hope before the sennight be finished, to accomplish your desire effectuallie, so fauour me she that may commaunde me. So leauing the King he came to the place appointed for the Combatte, the Iudges placing themselues where they shoulde, and the Prince himselfe in his Tent, where hauing his Mistresse picture set on the appointed place, he commaunded the Trompets to sound, and a Heralde to proclaime: that no Knight bearing Armes shoulde bee so hardie as to enter hys Tent, except he first grauntedhis Ladie to bee the fayrest creature in the worlde, and if any were so stubborne not to confesse it, by knightly prowesse he would force him doo it. The Heralde hauing doone his charge, and the Iudges caused the conditions to bee openlie reade, the people deuided themselues in conuenient places, and the Lords, Ladies and Gentlewomen betooke them to their Tents and Scaffoldes. The first that entered the field against the Prince, was the Countie *Durcell* of *Arragon*,[7] his foure Squires conducting before him in a great gorgious Litter, the stature of his Mistresse, Daughter to the King of *Arragon*, the fairest Ladie in all *Spayne*, and for whose beautie hee tooke in hande this quarrell. After him came foure other Squires, the formost leading his Courser, the seconde bearing his Helmette, the thirde his Sheeld, and the fourth his Gauntlets and Launce: and comming to the monument appointed for strange Ladies, caused the portrait of his Ladie to bee placed thereon, then comming to the Princes Tent, said. I know not Lord *Lewes*, if ouercome with glorie, presumption of your strength, or ouerweening your selfe, you haue made this large enterprise, to Combat with the best approoued Knightes in the whole worlde, in iudging no fairer Ladie to be this daie liuing then your owne: for mine own part, I am not so troubled in conceit as you are, to quarrell for such a fabulous matter, yet dare I tell yee, that my Ladie is much more beautifull then yours, which if you will denie, I am readie by the strength of mine arme to make you confesse it. *Lewes* feeling himselfe greeued with these iniurious speeches of the Countie, answered. Proude Knight, I am ashamed to heare thy iudgment so simple, as to thinke I am come hether for a matter of so light moment, as though I would not iustifie against thee and all other what I haue promised: but let that passe, before we part, I will cause thee know thy folly, by that time thy pate and thy bodie is[8] thorowly bumbasted, looke to thy selfe, for I intende to doo it. So mounting on horseback, and prepared as it had beene to a warre mortal, encountred eache other with such furie, as their Launces flying in shiuers vppe in the ayre, they met together so terriblie with their bodies, their Sheeldes, their Horsses and their heads, as they were bothe dismounted to the grounde. But earnest desire to vanquish, they beeing beside, stronge and well disposed Knights, made them quicklie beginne the second assault with their Swords, which was so dangerous, and handled with such dexteritie, as it was harde to iudge who should haue the honour of the Combat. But *Lewes* beholding the representation of his Ladie, and considering her so excellent and fauourable to him, tooke hart a fresh, and (as it were inspired with newe vigor) so laide on the Countie *Durcell*, as in short time he brought him vnder the mercie of his Sworde, when holding it against his throate, he said. Peremptorie Knight, if nowe thou confesse not my Lady to excell thine in beautie, thy vndiscreete heade shall raunsome thy follie. The Countie (for all this) woulde not aunswere one worde, by reason of the debilitie he felt himselfe in, hauing lost so much of his blood, as for the greefe hee conceiued to be thus vanquished: whereat Prince *Lewes* not content, would haue taken his heade from his shoulders, but the Iudges of the fielde came to him, saying. My Lorde, you ought to forbeare, hauing brought your enemie beyonde his owne defence, your victory beeing sufficient to content you, forbids his death. The Prince perswaded, entred his Pauillion, and ioyfull of his conquest, commaunded two Gardants of the field, to take the figure of the Princesse of *Arragon*, and place it at the feete of the Duchesse counterfeit, which was doone immediatlie, and the Countie *Durcell* brought into his owne Tent, where his Chirurgions tooke dilligent care for the curing of his woundes. Soone after came a Knight of *Myllaine*,[9] who giuing such defiances as the other dyd, was in the ende constrained with great shame, to confesse vnder the conquering Sworde of *Lewes*, the imperfections of his Ladie, and her stature placed by the Princesse of *Arragon*. The same daie were fiue great Lords of *Italie* brought in like subiection, and so the tryumphe ended till the next daie, when the first that came into the fielde was a braue Gallant of *Spayne*, a Knight of good estimation, and specially reputed, who after a vain-glorious Oration made (as the nature of the people[10] is that way affected) put hys fortune to the triall of his Launce, where hee sped so ill, as he was vnhorssed, and in the following Combat

likewise receiued the foile. After him seauen other Knights of *Castile* prooued as vnfortunate, their Ladies pictures all reuerencing the Duchesse, who beeing not a little proude of her Knight, and the memorable renowne he witnessed of her beautie: I leaue to your considerations, both of her conceite that waie, as also in
loue towards the Prince, who seeing no more readie to enter the quarrell, returned thence to the Pallace, to conferre with his sweete Mistresse of his high good fortunes.[11]

Chapter XXXV.

Of the Combat betweene Prince Lewes of Fraunce, and Crenus the Duke of Gaule.[1]

Great pleasure did the King conceiue, and all the nobilitie of the Court, at the gotten victories of Prince *Lewes*, against so manie woorthie Knights, so that they altogeather accounted him most fortunate. And nowe[2] the thirde daie when hee was entred his Tent, an English Knight (no lesse braue in termes then the former) defied the Prince, and betweene them began a dangerous conflict, in the midst whereof, the King with manie Princes, Barons and Lordes, as also the Queene and the Duchesse of *Burgundie*, came to their standing, and happily behelde the foyle of the English Knight, the Duchesse hearing him confesse her beautie, and behelde his Ladyes portrait placed vnder hers. But now the couragious Duke of *Gaule* named *Crenus*, came brauelie mounted into the fielde, dooing his duetie to the King, Queene and Ladies, who not knowing him, by his Armour iudged him some great Lorde, in that no Knight before caused so good opinion generallie, nor came with brauer countenaunce into the field: he beeing indeede a Prince of wonderfull possessions, and a Knight at Armes woorthilie approoued. The Duke (as all the other had doone) caused his Ladies counterfeite to bee placed where it ought by his Squires, to the no little admiration of all the beholders, noting what rare and excellent beautie it was adorned withall, the workman hauing performed such exquisite perfections, as it had beene the Ladie herselfe naturallie liuing: while the Squires were thus placing it on the monument, the Duke aduaunced himselfe to *Lewes* in this manner. The ouermuch selfe conceite (Lorde *Lewes*) of mindes but easily acquainted with matters of difficultie, hath often beene, and yet is the cause, to plucke great personages more lowe then they expecte: so that men haue seene them deceiued of their intents, and rewarded with ridiculous shame and confusion. This speake I to you, hauing heere begun a busines, the ende whereof will bee more harde to you, then as yet the beginning hath been: for *Europe* is sufficientlie stored with hardy Knights to asswage your presumptuous opinion, and Ladies much more faire and excellent, then she whom you contende for. And this (by the fauour of Fortune, gracious regarde of my Ladie and Mistresse, and helpe of my good Sworde) will I enforce you to confesse: that incomparable *Agriola*, daughter to the King of *England*, for vertue, for beautie and all diuine perfections, exceedeth yours whatsoeuer she be. Before such a leasing (quoth the Prince) shall passe the lippes of a Sonne of *Fraunce*, rather will I consent to bee peecemeale torne in sunder: and before fayre *Phoebus*[3] haue paced one howres iourney, I doubt not to make thee repent thy pride and arrogancie. By the soule of King *Arthur*,[4] said the Duke, looke thou garde thy selfe well, for I haue with my courtelax, abated the pride of a brauer man then thy selfe, and ere we two part, I meane to trie if I can doo it againe, therefore resolue thy selfe to thy best defence, for (by my life) I will not fauour thee. Without any further speeches they encountred with such violence togeather,

Palmerin d'Oliva: Part I 219

as Prince *Lewes* was throwne betweene his horsses feete, and he for *England* lost
his stirrops, but recouered himselfe well enough by the mayne of his Horse: then
he seeing his enemie not vppe againe, cast himselfe out of his saddle to haue
taken his aduauntage, but *Lewes* preuented him, and came marching against the
5 Duke with his Sworde drawne, who staied him thus. Me thinks Prince of
Fraunce, before any worse befall thee, thou wert best to yeelde thy selfe, and
remember that our Combatte beginnes for the excellencie of beautie. By God
man of *England*, aunswered *Lewes*, thou canst not perswade me to a thing so
farre from my thought, therfore goe too, and he that hath the fairest Freende,
10 shall soone be knowne. In this great choller, he reached the Duke such a stroke
on the head, as made him sette one knee to the ground, but recouering himselfe
quicklie, and both thorowly angry, they laid on eache other so cruellie, as the
very hardiest of the beholders feared the successe. Thus fought they for matter of
speciall value, the defence of theyr owne reputations, and honor of their Ladies,
15 whose loue was more precious in their harts then their owne liues. So long these
eager charges continued on bothe sides, as Prince *Lewes* hauing receiued more
then twentie woundes on his bodie, feeling himselfe fainte, fell downe before his
enemie, saying. O noble hart of *Fraunce*, the true succeeder of thy famous predecessours. The victorious *Englishman* setting his foote vpon him, saide. Lorde
20 *Lewes*, if now thou declarest not my Lady to excel thine in beautie, it costs thee
thy life, a matter nothing pleasing to me, in respect of the chiualry, and singuler
prowesse I haue founde in thee, as also this magnanimious enterprise of thine,
which in despight of thy foyle, and death it self, shall make thee liue for euer. But
Lewes made no aunswere, eyther for his weakenes, or sorowful conceite of his
25 misfortune, wherefore the Iudges came, who granting the Duke victorie, desired
him to proceede no further, which he honourably graunting, was as ioyfull of the
conquest, as the Duchesse sad and pensiue, thinking Prince *Lewes* had beene
slaine outright, wherfore she floong away to her lodging, not tarrying for the
King or any of the Ladies, who likewise departed the fielde in maruailous sorow,
30 seeing theyr Sonne so pittifully wounded: but aboue al, the Duchesse made more
lamentation, then shee woulde haue doone for the death of her Husbande, yet
fearing what shee thought secretly, shoulde by her greefe bee openly suspected,
comforted herselfe so well as she coulde: and beeing by herselfe, with one of her
trusty Gentlewomen, shee thus breathed foorth her mones. Ah trecherous For-
35 tune, enemye to all actions of regarde, why hast thou suffered the man thou most
fauoured, thus to be vanquished? and (which is most to be pittied) without hope
of life? Ah deceitfull tromperesse, seeing thou hast offered him so much wrong,
doo mee the fauour to beare him company in death, that liued and died so honourably for my loue. Ah death, let it suffise thee that Loue hath wounded him,
40 and make not thou experience of thyne ineuitable stroke, vnlesse thou wilt doo
as much for mee. Ah false and flattering Sonne of *Venus*,[6] is this the guerdon
thou rewardest them withall, that serue thee faithfully? So ceasing her complaint
awhile, in great impatience she thus began againe. Alas, neyther the one or other

are cause heerof, but my most vnhappy selfe, when (prouoked by my beautye) he tooke in hand this enterprise: but if it bee so (deere Freende) that enuious fate deale so harde with thee, soone mayst thou be reuenged on her that caused it. And wyth these wordes she fell betweene the armes of one of her Ladyes present, whom she specially trusted, who thus spake to her. Why howe nowe Madame? Wil you perswade your selfe no otherwise? beleeue me there is no remedy but you must change this conceite. What wyll you forgette your selfe? it is no time if you remember your selfe well, for if he whom you loue and endure these paynes for, shoulde vnderstande heereof: in stedde of seeking his health, you wyll shorten hys dayes, if (as you say) hee liue not without your welfare. More requisite is it, that you goe comfort him wyth your cheereful presence, then thus to bee the argument of bothe your deathes. Beside Madame, if my Lord suruiue, as no doubt he shall: what may he presume? trust me, matter sufficient (if you gouerne not your selfe better) that you seeke to discouer,[7] what most of all beseemes you to conceale. Alas (my Freende) aunswered the Duchesse, I knowe you speake the trueth: but howe is it possible for me to content my selfe, seeing what estate he is in onely for my loue? But if he dye, small reckoning will I make of my life: for let my honour bee blamed or otherwyse, let all aduersities and misfortunes goe togeather. Yet will I somewhat bee aduised by thee, and I wyll goe see if my presence wyl any thing comfort him. To breake off this talke came an Esquire from the Queene, to intreate her come to her Maiestie, which she did, and went with the Queene to the Princes lodging, who beholding the Duchesse so pale and full of greefe, with this conceit his woundes opened and bledde afresh: for which cause his Chirurgions, who imagined the occasion to proceede, by shame the Prince conceiued, that any one should see what woundes he tooke by the Duke of *Gaule*, wherfore they forbad any to enter his Chamber, vntill the peril of death was better passed ouer, which was within short time, when the Duchesse by her often visiting him, conuerted his sorowes into many ioyful conceits. But because our History appertaines not onely to hys deedes, or the loue of the Duchesse, we will returne to the Duke of *Gaule*, who after he had thus conquered Prince *Lewes*, followed the conditions of the fielde, taking the portraite of his Ladye *Agriola*, and placed it where the Duchesse picture stoode, setting it among the other conquered Ladyes. That day dyuers other Knights came on behalfe of their Ladies, whom the valiant Englishman entertained with such valour, as all his paines tourned to the honour of his Mistresse *Agriola*, who nowe was seated as paragon of the fielde.[8]

Chapter XXXVI.
Of the Combatte betweene Palmerin, and the Duke of Gaule, with the successe thereof.

On the same daie that the Prince of *Fraunce* was vanquished by the Duke of *Gaule*, arriued at *Paris*, *Palmerin*, *Trineus*, and theyr trayne, but the Combat was first ended, wherefore they commaunded their Squyres to prepare theyr Tent. *Palmerin* vnderstanding that the Duke was conquerer, greeued not a little, in that he came no sooner to winne the honour of the Prince: yet knowing if nowe he coulde conquer the Duke, more glory shoulde arise to him then by the Prince *Lewes*, he contented himselfe, passing that night in his Tent with the Prince *Trineus*, in diuers arguments of the Combat between *Lewes* of *Fraunce* and the Duke, yet was *Lewes* highly commended to *Palmerin* though he were ouercome, because hee had so brauely doone the two former daies against al the Knights that came. All this night could not *Palmerin* sleepe, thinking on the day ensuing, but rising earlie in the morning, and commending himselfe to God in his prayers, hee put on the Coate of Armes his Ladye *Polinarda* gaue him before hys departure, and tooke the counterfeite of his Lady in hys armes, not thinking any of hys Knights or Squyres woorthie to beare it, and thus accompanied with *Trineus* and other *Allemaigne* Lordes, entred the Lystes with so braue a gesture and countenaunce, as euery one commended him for a good Knight. And hauing placed the picture on the accustomed monument, as it had beene to the liuely creature herselfe, he thus began. Ah perfect mirrour of all beautie, vertue and excellencie, resolue thy selfe this daie to beare the palme of honour from all Ladies in the worlde, in that your Knight craues a thousand deathes, before he giue consent to the contrarie: and perswades himselfe so assured of your present fauour, as he durst venture on a whole Army, to keepe his religion in your diuine seruice.[1] These wordes were spoken so loude, as the Duke of *Gaule* hearde him, wherwith not contented, he aunswered. What now Knight? demaundest thou courage of a Ladie to defend her beautie, ill canst thou performe what thou speakest, if thou bee no better prouided. For all that Sir, saide *Palmerin*, I hope to make you graunt what I saie, and that there is not a fayrer Ladie liuing, then shee whose figure thou heere beholdest, otherwise I shall constraine thee whether thou wylt or no. That shall we see, quoth the Duke, so departing into their Tents to be armed, and readie to Ioust, they met so valiantlie togeather, as they broke their Launces brauelie without moouing eache other, and taking newe staues encountred againe, when the Duke was vnhorssed, and *Palmerin* verie sore wounded: so betaking them to their swords, continued a daungerous and doubtfull Combat, till in the ende *Palmerin* ouercame the Duke, and holding his sworde readie to cut off his heade, said. Knight thou art dead, if thou graunt not my Ladie to excell thine in beautie. Ah sir, saide the Duke, vnhappy be the howre that you tooke in hande this voyage, to depriue me of that which made mee the moste happie Knight of the worlde, with what countenance may I present my selfe before her, seeing Fortune hath beene so aduerse to me? thus filling the ayre with his regrets, the Iudges came, desiring *Palmerin* to saue his life, whereto he consented, which words were more bitter to the Duke then death, who in these complaints was leade into his Tent by his Squires. *Palmerin* not forgetting the honour due to his Ladie, tooke downe the Image of *Agriola*, and set his Ladies in the roome,² saying. Nowe are you in the place Madame, which is your owne by right. This victory was not a little pleasaunt to the *Frenchmen*, but especially to Prince *Lewes* when he hearde thereof, who the better to make his ioye knowne to *Palmerin*, sent him two of the best Horsses in his stable, as glad of the reuenge on the Duke, as that *Palmerin* remained conquerour. *Palmerin* sent hartie thankes to the Prince, as well for his present as his good-will, and continued in his deuoire to his Ladies beautie, as that daie hee honoured her with the conquest of foure *French* Knights, and the submission of their Ladies portraitures: yet aboue all, *Palmerin* commended to *Trineus* the valour of the *Englishman*, confirming the Duke for a chosen Knight at Armes,³ and neither *Frenchman*, *Italian*, *Spanyard*, *Englishman*, *Romaine*, or *Greeke*, that attempted against *Palmerin* in the following daies, but still he bare awaie the victory, and *Polinardas* picture their Ladies obeysaunce. The last of the eyght daies came into the fielde the Lord of *Albret*,⁴ greatlie esteemed for prowesse and chiualrie, and hee woulde defend the beautie of his *French* Ladie: but *Palmerin* after a long and tedious fight, brought him and his Mistresse among the vanquished, and so concluded the *French* Princes enterprise to his own immortal honor. Afterward came the King *Agariell*, with the Princes and Lords of his Court to *Palmerins* Tent, making him the greatest entertainment could be deuised, whereof *Trineus* and the other *Allemaigne* Lordes were highlie contented, and after his wounds were healed, caused him and his companie to be lodged in his own Pallace, where the Queene and her Ladies would often visite him, and the Prince *Lewes* likewise, who by many intreaties with *Trineus*, vnderstoode her name for whom *Palmerin* thus aduentured. But when the King vnderstoode, that *Trineus* was the Emperour of *Allemaignes* Sonne, and all this honourable companie came from his Fathers Court, their welcome cannot be sufficiently sette downe, nor *Palmerins* praises effectuallie rehearsed, whome the Prince *Lewes* thus entertained. In sooth Sir *Palmerin*, the Prince may imagine himselfe happie, that is honoured with your knightlie seruice, but aboue all, the noble Emperour of *Allemaigne*. My Lorde, quoth *Palmerin*, it likes you to speake your pleasure of me, yet did I neuer knowe Knightes more worthy in fight then your Countrimen, among whom your deserts may not escape vnreported, no more then the deeds of *Scipio* can among the *Romaines*.⁵ Manie other honourable and familiare speeches passed betweene the Prince and *Palmerin*, about the Ladies figures that were brought to the Ioustes: *Polinarda* onely tryumphing beyonde all the rest, hauing no seconde but faire *Agriola* of *England*, the Goddesse and Mistresse to the Duke of *Gaule*.

CHAPTER XXXVII.
Of the Combat which the Dukes of Sauoye and Lorrayne had togeather, for the beauty of their Ladies, and what was the issue thereof.

You haue heere before heard, the enterprise of the Duke of *Sauoy* for the beautie of his Ladie, and howe after Prince *Lewes* hys daies of Combat were finished, he shoulde maintaine nine other in the like quarrell:[1] wherefore the day after *Palmerins* victory, hee put himselfe in order as the time required, and hauing in the field erected two Pillers of Porphire, displacing them that belonged to the Prince *Lewes*, his Tent was there set vp all of Crimson veluet, verye curiouslye imbroydered with Golde and pearle, and rounde about within were manie braue sentences of loue, drawne from Historiographers and Poets, as well Greeke as Latin, in prayse of the Mistresse of his deuoted affections. In the morning hee went to gyue the good morrowe to the Princesse *Lucemania* Daughter to the King of *Fraunce*, whom he had chosen for his spouse and Wife. After many solemne courtesies passed between them, fearing the Queene shoulde finde them togeather, hee tooke his leaue of her, she giuing him from her arme a sumptuous Bracelet,[2] garnished with sixe great Diamondes, and sixe fayre Rubies, which gift encouraged him to follow his enterprise. Beeing come into the Field, the Iudges appointed, were the eldest Sonne of *Fraunce*,[3] and the Countie of *Armignac*, wise Princes and valiant Knights, and standing in the Gate of his Tent vnarmed, because he sawe none readie to offer him battell: the Duke of *Lorrayne* at length entred the Fielde, attended on by a braue company of Knights and Squires, who brought the portrait of his Ladie, beeing a figure of rare beautie, and hauing a Crowne on her heade, where ouer was written in great Letters of Golde, *Thys is Polinarda, exceedyng in beauty al Ladyes in the world*, which was read by manie, who coulde not satisfie their eyes in beholding so braue a spectacle, and being sette on the Pillar appointed, he came to the Duke of *Sauoye*, saying. Blasphemous Knight, detractour of the beautie of Ladies, heere may thine owne eyes witnes how thou hast belyed beautie, in presuming to thinke any more fayre then this incomparable creature, to whome thy Ladye may not worthilie be handmaide. And if thou will not presently confesse what I commaunde thee, sheelde thy head from my weapon, which I meane to knocke well for thy great vndiscretion. The Duke of *Sauoy* enraged with these words, armed himselfe presently without any aunswere, and mounting on horsebacke with a strong Launce in his hande, encountred his enemie so couragiouslye, as breaking their staues brauely in shyuers to their verye Gauntlets, passed on without any further harme. The Duke of *Sauoy* angrie that he had not dismounted his enemie, with hys Sworde drawne returned furiously vpon him, and laide on such strokes as the fire flew foorth of his Helmet: yet the Duke of *Lorrayne* like a good and hardie Knight, defended himselfe valiantly, and reached the Duke of *Sauoy* many shrewd woundes, so that bothe of them throughlie netled, rent eache others Armour in such sort with their swords, and mangled theyr flesh so vnmercifully, as the Iudges coulde not imagine who had the better vauntage. The Duke of *Sauoye* wondering to see the Duke of *Lorraine* holde out so long, began to storme more like a Fiend then a manne, rayling on Fortune, that (in respect of his Ladies beautie) shee asisted him no better, and beeing at the very point of dispaire, tooke hart a fresh, and redoubling his strokes vpon his aduersarie, at length slewe his horse vnder him, who falling downe, and his Maister vnder him, by reason he was so sore wearyed, and beside, had broken his thigh in the fall, coulde not recouer himself, before the Duke of *Sauoie* (being alighted) sette foote vpon him, and in furye woulde haue parted hys heade from his shoulders, but that the Iudges ran quicklie and stayed him. Then was the Duke of *Lorraine* halfe deade carried into his Tent, and the Duke of *Sauoie* caused *Polinardas* picture to be set at *Lucemanias* feete, a thing verye strange in respect of their great difference.[4] Afterwarde hee was vnarmed to haue his woundes bounde vp, which were so dangerous, as gladlie he would haue beene excused from the Combat with any other Knight for that day, didde not shame, and the Lawe hee made himselfe prouoke him to the contrary. But within an howre after,[5] he was defied by a Knight of *Scicilie*, who woulde Combat on foote with the battel Axe, in which conflicte the Duke was verye neere ouercome, he had lost so much bloode before: but in breefe,[6] the *Scicilian* Knight lost the daie, hys Ladyes picture was yeelded conquered, and the Duke of *Sauoie* went to rest him in his Tent.

Chapter XXXVIII.
Howe the Duke of Sauoye entered the Combatte against Ptolome, and howe he sped.

Palmerin not as yet in perfecte health,[1] was aduertised, how the Duke of *Sauoie* hadde conquered the Duke of *Lorraine*, fighting for the beautie of the Princesse *Polinarda*, the conceit whereof so greeued him as nothing coulde more, to see her honour so badlie defended, whom aboue all other he esteemed deerest, which made him in great choller say before the Prince *Trineus*. By God (my Lorde) Looue made a slender choyse of the Duke of *Lorraine* for his vassayle, and Madame *Polinarda* scant wise to chuse him for her Champion, in respect of the excellent beautie Nature hath bestowed on her. And yet it could not be imagined, howe the Duke of *Lorraine* shoulde gayne the victory without shame, in seeking honor beyonde his desert, because he is vnwoorthy such extraordinary fauoure: which makes me repute it rather of a faynt hart, then anie want of a iust quarrell. *Trineus* hearing *Palmerin* so affectionate in his speeches, in a merry laughter, sayd. In good sooth Sir *Palmerin*, the Duke of *Lorraine* was but ill councelled, to enter the Combat for my Sisters beautie without her licence, in that he once learned, howe you coulde defend it much better then hee. *Palmerin* fearing hee had spoken more then he ought, because he discoursed his loue too openly, excused the matter thus. If it were not (my Lorde) that I doubt to offer wrong to a Lady, on whome dependeth my lyfe, and whom I loue more deere then my selfe: I woulde cause the *Frenchman* well to vnderstand, how Madame *Polinarda* your Sister, surpasseth in all perfections eyther of grace or beauty, all the Ladies of this Country, yea, I dare say of the whole world, therefore one may easily coniecture, that the Duke of *Lorraine* during the Combat, had his mind fixed on baser occasions. Then *Trineus* smyling to see *Palmerin* so dilligent to shadowe his loue, sayd. It is no strange matter Freende *Palmerin*, to see presuming mindes payde with selfe same coyne,[2] as the Duke is: and yet I can not meruaile enough, that my Sister *Polinarda* wold not commit this matter to your charge, she hauing had so good knowledge of your valour and prowesse. These speeches pleased not *Palmerin* a little, and did in such sort encourage him, as for the iniury doone his Ladie by the Duke of *Sauoye*, in setting her figure at the feete of *Lucemania*, as had not *Trineus* perswaded him wyth fayre speeches, all sicke and sore as he was, he would haue gone to reuenge this dishonor. Notwithstanding, hee called *Ptolome* secretly, saying. Thou knowest (my deere Freende) what shame is offered her, to whom I was destenied before my byrth, by the presumption of an ouerbolde Knight, and what greefe it is to mee, that I cannot at this present reuenge this wrong my selfe, I pray thee therefore supply my insufficiencie, and enter the Combat with that vaine-glorious Duke, of whom thou maist gaine honor and yeelde me content, in giuing ease to my afflictions, which els are insupportable. I promise you my Lorde, aunswered *Ptolome*, before you made the motion I intended it, and I will accomplish it with such good will, as I doubt not to ouercome the Duke of *Sauoy*. And for my Mistresse *Brionella*, will I enter the fielde, whose beautie is sufficient to enriche me with the victory, for in my conceit, shee farre passeth *Lucemania*. Therefore my Lorde let me request one courtesie, which I am lothe you should denie me: that if you shall be able to morrow, but to accompanie me with your presence in the fielde. If the ayre will suffer me, quoth *Palmerin*, I will, in meane while I will pray, that thy fortune may fall out to my harts desire. Thus *Trineus, Palmerin* and *Ptolome*, were passing the time, conferring with other noble men, of the valoure of the Duke of *Sauoy* against all strange Knights, and how he had not foyled the Duke of *Lorraine*, had not his Horse fallen on him and maimed him, otherwise hee brought the Combatte to so good a iudgment, as he had wunne the honour of the fielde. Wherat *Palmerin* was more offended then before, because himselfe was not able to reuenge this misfortune, heerewithall he conceiued a kind of iealousie of the Duke of *Lorraine*, because hee hadde chosen his Ladie *Polinarda* for his Mistresse, and on her behalfe had entred the Combatte, and howe he durst place her picture on the Piller wyth her name, without he had receiued some commandement from her, which conceit so greeued him, as his woundes began to be as daungerous as at the first, continually labouring in his thoughts, nowe with the lightnes, then againe with the constancie of Women,[3] neuerthelesse, he could not iudge (affecting earnestly the vertues of his Lady) that she would be of such a double lyking, and in this doubtful estate, sayd. Ah God, I see that Women winne lightly, and loose againe more easilie. Then repenting his words, followes on thus. O heauens, and what shall I say? it is impossible that shee (meaning *Polinarda*) should be so forgetfull, and neuer will I beleeue, that a Princesse so wise and vertuous, wold reward me with such treason, which may not, nay I dare sweare cannot, once enter her thoughts. Yet would not all opinions serue to allay thys newe iealousie, but still it had power to confounde reason, and al the night continued he in this variable conceit, till the next morning, when *Ptolome* (so soone as the Sunne arose) accompanyed with *Trineus*, went to his Tent, where beeing armed, all sauing his Helmet, hauing his Launce and Sheelde, he came to the Duke, saying. Thou knowest Knight the cause of my comming, stand vpon thy guarde, for I fight for beautie. The Duke suddainly at these words mounted on horsebacke, and ranne against his enemie with such strength, as *Ptolome* cast the Duke forth of his saddle, and suddainly alighted wyth hys Sworde drawne: but the Duke recouering himselfe, entertained him in sharper sort then he expected. Nowe beganne betweene them a cruell and pittious Combat, as their Armour, sheeldes and swords, flewe about in peeces, and the blood trickling downe their bodies in manie places, so that it was generally reputed, how the fight could not end without the losse of both their liues. Yet in the ende, the Duke beeing of stronger constitution then *Ptolome*, and greedy of victory ouer his enemie, ranne so violentlie vpon him as hee got him on the grounde, and he beeing vppermost, offered to take the aduauntage of his life: but the Iudges forbidding it, caused *Ptolome* to be carried into his Tent, where the Prince *Trineus* staied not a little sorry for this great misfortune. The Duke likewise sore wounded was carried into his Pauillion, but first hee sawe the portrait of *Brionella* sette in the ranke of the conquered. The same daie dyd the Duke fight with a Knight of *Scotland* at the Mace, who not nimble enough in vsing that weapon, in the end had the foyle, and three other Knights afterwarde at seuerall weapons, so that it was admirable to beholde the exploits of Armes the Duke did,[4] in that no Knight as yet medled with him, but departed with shame, and their Ladies pictures placed as vanquished. And nowe was *Palmerins* Combatte against the Duke of *Gaule* not talked on, for the Duke of *Sauoy* was accounted the onely Knight in the world, to the no small ioy of the Princesse *Lucemania*, who perswaded herselfe now, that her beautie was most excellent. But she was not so pleasant as *Palmerin* was pensiue, and enraged out of measure, notwithstanding his weakenes, and the often intreaties of *Trineus*, he would needes to the fielde, saying. Good my Lord perswade me not, for I reckon not my life, so I may take vengeaunce of the dishonour doone to my Ladie your Sister: the manifolde courtesies of the Emperour your Father, haue so bounde me to her and you, as exceede my life farre, and therfore I beseech you not to hinder me. *Trineus* yet ouercame him by perswasions, assuring him to haue time sufficient for his reuenge, whereat greatlie displeased, he feigned himselfe to be whole sooner then he was indeede,[5] for the great desire hee had to deale with the Duke. And Prince *Lewes* angrie, to see the Duke hold the fielde longer then hee did, not able to bee ouercome by anye Knight, came to *Palmerin* saying. I knowe not my Lorde, whether you vnderstand the Duke of *Sauoyes* victories against so manie hardie Knights, but belike his strength is much better then mine was, or Fortune allowes him more fauour then she did to me. In my conceit if you enter not the Combat, you doo me wrong and your selfe too, and if hee depart hence with victory, then shall I haue cause to complaine of you: in that his successe hath made him so braue and presumptuous, as though no Knight is able to answere him in the field, let me intreate you Sir *Palmerin* to abate his pride, and (as well hee deserues) make him knowe his folly. *Palmerin* hauing greater desire to execute this matter, then thus to be intreated, returned the Prince this answere. My Lorde, God giues honour and victory to whom he pleaseth, without either regarde of the cause or the persons. If according to bountie or nobilitie of minde he distributed such gifts, then had you beene among the better sorte, as furnished sufficientlie with valour and magnanimitie: yet if your enterprise haue not sorted to your desire, account this for certaine that it is for your good, and for other reasons then are to you known, for such matters are his secrets, and he dooth ballance them by his diuine wisedome. Notwithstanding, as well to satisfie your request, as ease mine owne minde, to morrowe morning will I enter my Tent, albeit my present estate would haue me stay awhile,[6] there will I Combat with the Duke, not certaine how Fortune meanes to deale with me. But happen what shall, I goe with a minde to conquere, and doubt not but the issue wyll be such, as shall yeelde you content, and me the victory, so shall your sadnes and mine be conuerted into pleasure. With this aunswere the Prince satisfied, departed, yet was hee ignoraunt of *Palmerins* intent, which was farre otherwise then he imagined: but pleased as he was he went into the presence Chamber, where manie Knights were conferring of deedes of Armes past, to whom hee opened the fantasie of *Palmerin*, which caused a generall doubting of the Duke, setting him downe for vanquished, except *Palmerins* weaknes were his greater Freende.

Chapter XXXIX.
Of the perillous Combat between Palmerin and the Duke of Sauoye, and the issue thereof.

Sixe daies togeather had the Duke of *Sauoye* maintained this quarrell, for the beautie of his Ladie *Lucemania*, and no Knight as yet could get anie aduauntage of him, vntil the seauenth daie, when *Palmerin* prepared himselfe to the fielde, and entred his Tent, accompanied with Prince *Lewes* of *Fraunce*, *Trineus* and many other Princes. The King with all his trayne taking theyr standing to behold the Combat, *Palmerin* came armed foorth of his Tent, sauing his Helmet, which was carryed before him by two Squires with his Sheeld and Mace, and next to them came two Princes, who bare the portraiture of his Ladie *Polinarda*, which beeing sette on the Piller, hee clasped on his Helmet, and taking his Mace in his hande, martched to the Dukes Tent, and thus summoned him. Knight, thou hast long enough defended the field, and to my great greefe that it hath beene so long, my turne is nowe come, and it is good reason I shoulde keepe it the rest of the time: for the Ladie whom I loue, is not onely much more beautifull then thine, but beside, excelleth all other whatsoeuer, and if thou wilt not confesse the same, I wil not leaue thee with this Mace till I haue forced thee to doo it. I know not saide the Duke, what thou canst doo, but I am of the minde, that I shall soone quallifie thy ouer bolde brauing. At these words the Duke taking his Mace, deliuered *Palmerin* so sounde a stroke on the heade, as made him to stagger, but *Palmerin* requited him well againe for it, and long had they fought togeather, and brused eache other very pittifully, till at length *Palmerin* gaue the Duke such a cruell stroke betweene the heade and the shoulders, as he fell to the grounde cleane bereft of sence: when *Palmerin* taking off his Helmet, would not offer him any further violence, but setting his sworde against his brest, said. Now am I sufficiently reuenged on him, that so ill intreated the figure of the most fayrest among Ladies. The Iudges of the fielde, thinking *Palmerin* would haue slaine the Duke, came running to him with these words. Content you Sir, he is vanquished, and hath no power to defende himselfe. Whereuppon *Palmerin* put vppe his Sword againe, and leauing the Duke, went presently to the Piller where his Ladies portrait stoode, which embracing in his armes, he placed highest, and *Lucemania* at her feete, saying. I beseeche you Madame to pardon your Knight, in that he did no sooner repell the famous iniurie offered you, and impute it not to feare, or want of courage, but debility of bodie, which once a little recouered, I came to maintaine your honor, and heere confirme you for the most beautifull Ladie liuing.[1] While *Palmerin* thus contemplated his Mistresse figure, the Iudges commaunded the Duke to be carried into his Pauillion, where with soueraigne drinks[2] life was got into him again, but when he knewe himselfe to be vanquished, and that in one howre hee lost the greatest honour of all his life time, very[3] conceit of greefe had well neere slaine him. No lesse was the sorrowe of Madame *Lucemania*, but she and her Knight were not so much discontented, as

Palmerin, Trineus, and *Ptolome* were ioyfull, but aboue all other Prince *Lewes* of *Fraunce,* more pleasant then if himselfe had tryumphed in victory, thinking he could not sufficiently extoll the renowne of *Palmerin,* calling him the onely puller downe of the proude. That day did *Palmerin* encounter with seauen other Knights, and in his conquests shewed himselfe not onely magnanimious, but mercifull, sauing their liues, and honoring his Mistresse with the humilitie of theirs.[4] The next day likewise after many braue exployts, beeing readie to leaue the fielde because none came to resist him, on a suddain there entred a Knight in blacke Armour, stripte all ouer with Golde, and bearing in hys sheelde of Azur the Golden Sunne, whose braue order of entraunce declared him to be a hardie Knight at Armes, who aduauncing him selfe to *Palmerin,* said. My intent of comming hether (Sir Knight) is to let thee vnderstand, that I am the Seruaunt and beloued of a Ladie, who may not bee equalled with any other, and because I am enformed, that thou maintainest thy Freend, to excell all Ladies whatsoeuer, I offer to prooue the contrary, and will make thee confesse it. I neuer spake wordes more true, aunswered *Palmerin,* and heere abide to iustifie them: but this place is ordeyned to no other ende, then to make thee and thy like know, what vnaduised enterprises you take in hande. And one thing is required of thee, that before thou begin the Combat, thou sette vppon thys Pyller the counterfeite of her, whom thou perswadest thy selfe to excell my Lady in beautie, according to the conditions of this field published through all *Europe.* That cannot I doo, answered the Knight of the *Sunne,* for I haue no other picture of her then is imprinted in my hart, where loue hath so liuely figured her person, as she is daily presented to mee by her incomparable beautie, which cannot be taken from me but onely by death. And if loue follow the soule, (as diuers holde opinion) whole worldes cannot seperate mee from her. And therefore are all men vnworthy to receiue fruition (by their regard) of a thing so precious, which makes me imagine, none but my selfe woorthy to looke on her diuine figure. Prepare thee therefore to thy Horse, and defende thy selfe. *Palmerin* desirous to know the name of this fayre Ladie, sayd. I see Sir Knight, that thou art meruailous proude and surlie, which make mee desire rather to Combat wyth thee then any other, to abate this hote humour:[5] albeit this is contrarie to his conditions, who was the principall Author of this enterprise, which is, that thou shouldest set on this Piller her portrait whom thou so esteemest, yet thys exception shall be graunted thee, for the desire I haue to knowe what thou canst doo, as also her name, if thou darest reueale it. To tell thee her name (aunswered the Knight of the *Sunne*) I will not sticke with thee, and because in concealing it, I shall offer her wrong, nature hauing in her set downe the onely worke of beautie: know therfore that her name is *Polinarda,* Daughter to the mighty Emperor of *Allemaigne.* These wordes were so yrkesome to *Palmerin,* and troubled his thoughts in such sort, that hee knewe not readily what to aunswere: notwithstanding in midst of his choller, thus spake. By God Knight thou hast made a good choyse, for against her beautie will not I contende, hauing it in greater estimation and reuerence then thou canst haue: but I am

ready to prooue, that thou deseruest not to be named her Knight, no[6] not so much as her meanest Seruaunt. That shall we try, said the Knight of the *Sunne*, before we part: and albeit her excellencie deserue farre greater seruice then mine: yet so it is, that for the looue I beare her, and the affection I haue to obey her by some
5 agreeable seruice, I may by good reason name my selfe hers. At these speeches *Palmerin* conceiued such iealousie, as without attending any further matter, mounted in great anger on horsebacke, and met the Knight of the *Sunne* so forcibly, as bothe of them were sent to the ground: whereuppon they drewe their Swordes, and charged eache other with such furie, as their Armour and Sheeldes
10 were hacked in peeces, and the ground coullered with their expence of blood. No permission of breathing was suffered betweene them, but blood and death earnestly desired on either part, so that the King, the Lordes and the Iudges, reputed this for the strangest Combat that euer they sawe, nor could they say who was likest to winne the fielde, but if the one died, the other could not escape, so that
15 the King mooued with compassion, caused them to be seuered, and commaunded them to enter theyr Tents. Which motion liked well the Knight of the *Sun*, for long he perswaded himselfe he could not hold out, wherfore he mounted on horsebacke so well as he coulde, and withdrewe himselfe, *Palmerin* beeing wonderfully displeased, that he could not obtayne the victory of thys Knight. Soone
20 after, the King and the Prince *Lewes* came into his Tent, and seeing him very sore wounded, woulde not let him staye there, but sayd. Beleeue me (Sir *Palmerin*) you haue great neede of rest, and your wounds I see are very dangerous, you shall therefore be conueyed to my Pallace, where all helps that may be deuised shall be giuen, assuring you, that greater honour could neuer Knight purchase, then you
25 haue doone. And though this last Combat were not ended, you neede not be displeased, the issue thereof importing the death of the one or the other, and perhaps of both, which I would not haue seene for two of the best prouinces in my Realme. And me thinks you should content your selfe, hauing receiued before, such honour ouer so many Lords and Knights of name, come you therfor with
30 me, and Lord *Trineus* beare vs company. Great thanks receiued the King of them for this honourable courtesie, and *Palmerin* went with him to the Pallace, where the Kinges Chirurgions tooke care of his woundes, he beeing lodged in the most stately Chamber in the Courte. Nowe the Prince *Lewes* beganne to loue *Palmerin* so deerely, as he coulde not be an howre foorth of his companie, desiring his
35 health as his owne welfare: wherfore all thinges that he imagined *Palmerin* tooke pleasure in, would he performe with his vttermost endeuours, and would suffer none to hold him talk, but only of matter that might yeeld pleasure and delight. Notwithstanding, diuers Knights conferring with him that euening, as concerning the Knight of the *Sunne*: *Palmerin* aunswered them, that his mind should
40 neuer be thorowly quieted, vntil such time as he fought with him againe. The Prince, who still endeuoured to keepe him from sadnes, saide. I beleeue (my Lord) that he will not easilie be induced to deale with you again, for you brought him into such estate, as hee will keepe himselfe heereafter out of your handes:

and well I am assured, that had you continued but a little longer, the victorye had beene yours, for the Knight was so weakened, that he did nothing but defend your blowes. It pleaseth you (my Lord) to say so quoth *Palmerin*, but had he felt such valour in me, or such courage as beseemes a vertuous Combatant, hardlie coulde he escape as he hath doone: neuerthelesse, I hope (with the fauour of Fortune) to meete him once more, and then we will trie who is the strongest. Much other talke they had, but *Palmerin* intreated the Prince, that all the portraits of the conquered Ladies might bee brought him, which were aboue an hundred, of diuers beauties and most strange fashions, and among them all could be founde none seconde to *Polinarda*, but (as we haue said already) that of *Agriola* the Princesse of *England*: who (by the report of a Gentleman present that had seene her) was much more beautifull then her figure presented. Such speeches they continued so long of the *English* Virgin, as *Trineus* (albeit he neuer sawe her) became amorous of her,[7] and at that instant he so solemnly vowed himselfe hers, as thence forwarde he swore neuer to loue any but her, so that for her sake he thrust himselfe into manie perrillous fortunes, as in the folowing discourse of the History you shall reade more at large. From whom let vs returne to the Prince *Lewes*, who seeing so many portraitures of Princesses and Ladies, would dailie congratulate *Palmerins* good fortune, and embracing him, said. So helpe me God, my noble companion, I woulde neuer desire greater riches in the world, then to resemble you, especially in chiualry, which in you is so surpassing al other, as you haue ended to your honor, what a number haue fayled in. Oh howe happy may the Ladie account herselfe, that hath such a Knight? and were not the condition too cruell towards my selfe, I could wish I were a Woman in her place, to haue so high rule and commaunde ouer you. At which words all present began to smile, yet shewing good countenaunce to *Palmerin*, for the affection they sawe the Prince beare him, which is yet to this day a common vsage and practise among Courtiers: but *Palmerin* somewhat ashamed of such superstitious prayses, aunswered. Trust me my Lorde, I account my happines the greater, that I haue doone seruice to so high a personage and so good a Knight as you are, desiring to meete you in such place heerafter, where you may perceiue the good wil I beare you, not only for this high entertainement, which is more then I can deserue, as for the pleasure I haue to honour so good a Prince, which if the occasion happen, you shall perceiue the experience. I haue spoken nothing (quoth the Prince) but what is more acquainted to others then my selfe, and if I would conceale them, then will they be most openly knowne, because vertue doth so apparantlie shine in them.[8] Manie other speeches passed betweene them, and longer had continued, but that manie Lords which came to see the Ioustes, were now vpon departing, and therefore woulde take their leaue of the King, whereuppon they were constrained to breake off, the Prince going to the Chamber of presence, where hee gaue thanks to a number that honoured the Courte with theyr presence: and so one after another all departed, the Duke of *Sauoye* beeing one of the first, ashamed (God knowes) to be so conquered by *Palmerin*, and not bidding his

Lady *Lucemania* farewell. But *Lewes* did not serue the Duchesse so, for her loue continued as resolute as before, and shee loued him as wel conquered, as had he beene the conquerour, whereof she assured him by many amorous meetinges, by which meanes the Prince stayed the Duke at the Courte, longer then himselfe would haue doone. *Lewes* thus louing *Palmerin* as you haue hearde, intreated the Duchesse to come and visite him, which she accomplished the day folowing, when *Palmerin* spent manie discourses with her, rather of loue then entring into religion, for he perceiued by her countenaunce, that she had no will to become a Nunne:[9] where we will leaue them togeather, to tell you who the Knight of the *Sunne* was, that fought the last Combat with *Palmerin*.

Chapter XL.
Who the Knight of the Sunne was, and of his strange aduentures.

The King of *Hungaria*, Father to the Prince *Tarisius*,[1] that maried the faire *Griana*, Mother to *Palmerin*, had in his latter yeeres a Sonne named *Netrides*, and after he had long lyued in rest and prosperitie, hee dyed, leauing the yong Prince *Netrides* fifteene yeere olde, and in the custodie of his elder brother *Tarisius*. This *Netrides* growing in good constitution of bodie and behauiour, beeing well beloued generally, so gracious, gentle and well gouerned he was: as the Lords, Knights, Gentlemen and the people of *Hungaria*, esteemed him more then their King *Tarisius*, who beeing crowned after his fathers decease, loued *Netrides* as brotherhoode required, till Fortune (enuious of this concorde) not willing that the vertues of this yong Prince should be there extinguished: changed his affection into exceeding hatred, by an occasion heereafter following. One daie the King *Tarisius* walking in his Garden to take the ayre, left his Brother *Netrides* in his Chamber accompanied with the Queene, who without imagination of any harme, nor that his fatall stars woulde sort him anie misfortune, satte downe in the Kings chayre as he talked with the Queene, and continued there so long, till *Tarisius* came vp and founde him there sitting, which he tooke in such ill part, as in a great rage he thus beganne. Who made thee so audacious and presumptuous to sitte in my seate, against thy duety and my liking? By mine honor thou hast doone more then thou weenest, and if I see the like againe, or I may but heare thereof, thy heade shall pay the price of thy folly.[2] *Netrides*, who of his owne nature was humble and gentle, fell downe on his knee, intreating the King his Brother to pardon him, for what hee had doone, was not with any intent to displease his Maiestie, but an ouersight, and that so he would permit it to passe. The King made him no aunswere, because hee tooke *Netrides* reasons for no payment, but conceiued a secret hatred in his minde, by this occasion of so slender moment, which increased thence forward, as the matter prouoking a fierie Meteore:[3] so that he did repine at his Brother so much, as he wold not speak to him, nor affoorde him a good countenaunce. Then called he to remembraunce the loue of his people towardes hys Brother, and if this hatred should come to their knowledge for so small a cause, he imagined they woulde displace him, and make *Netrides* King. For which cause hee intended to haue him slaine, and the execution hereof hee committed to one of his Archers, but God (who is euermore the preseruer of the innocent) would not suffer such a damned deede of paracide to take effect.[4] Which *Tarisius* perceiuing, and finding one day his Brother alone, enflamed with this dyscontented humour, sayd. *Netrides*, thou hast offended mee more then I will now stand to argue on, I therefore banish thee my Court and Kingdome, and looke that within three daies thou get thee hence, and on thy life not to discouer it to any man, or take any one with thee to beare thee company. The yong Prince obedient to his Brother, made answere, that he wold accomplish his charge, and so withdrew himselfe into his Chamber, not declaring to any one

Palmerin d'Oliva: Part I 235

hys cause of heauines. Then willing one of his Squires to saddle hys Horse, departed so closely as he coulde, forbidding anie of his Seruaunts to follow him, and such expedition he made, as not resting but one night in any lodging, he left his brothers kingdome, wandering without anie care of himselfe, or which way
5 he tooke, but went heere and there, as fortune pleased to guide him. Hauing long time trauailed in *Allemaigne*, his money fayled him, in that at his departure hee was but badlie prouided: yet could not his princelie minde abase it selfe to begge, so that beeing without meate or drink, or anie place to rest himselfe in, ashamed of himselfe, hee sought to shroude him where none might discrye him, and so
10 entring a great Forrest, very thicke set with Trees, shrubs, and bushes, hee esteemed this a conuenient place to rest in, wherefore alighting from his Horse, and turning him to feede, layd himselfe downe at the roote of a Tree, and thus began to breathe foorth his complaints. Ah inconstant Fortune, and to me most of all inconstant,⁵ didst thou erecte me so high, and reiect mee nowe thus lowe?
15 well then may I saie, that more wrong thou doost a man in one houre, then right all his life time: for if heeretofore thou diddest lende me pleasure and delight, thou nowe makest me pay for it, (and that with vsury too rigorous) not leauing anie hope to comfort mee. Ah tirranous King, cruell and vnmanlike Brother, thou hast with shame banished me, and brought me into this poore estate,
20 wherein I must die? Oh happy if I might, rather then to liue in the vile estate of beggery. So saying, he layde him downe among the Hearbes, and was supprised with such extreame feeblenes, as he fell into his lamentations againe, thus. Ah my Lord and Father, too soone diddest thou leaue me, woulde God I then had borne thee company, or that at this instant I could come to thee. Ah men of *Hun-*
25 *garia*, I am well assured (knowing the loue you euer bare me) that you will pittie when you heare my afflictions and calamities: alas, I neuer deserued this vnhappy ende. And beeing vnable to continue longer speeche, he there determined to finish his life. But better fortune befell him then he expected, by the meanes of an auncient Knight named *Lombardo*, who beeing neere, hearde all his dolorous
30 complaints. This Knight beeing rich and of noble blood, had neere that Forrest a strong, delightfull and sumptuous Castell, and delighted to walke among the woods for his recreation, as good hap it was for *Netrides* that he walked this euening. He hearing these sad and sorrowfull regrets, pittie so touched his hart, as the teares bedewed hys cheekes: yet would he not trouble him while he continued his
35 mones, but afterward came and tooke him by the hand saying. Arise my Freende and take courage, for you are in the place, where you shall finde more good to benefit you, then harme to offende you, therefore cherrish your spirites, and forget this heauines, which may endaunger you beyond recouerie. *Netrides* seeing this honourable Gentlemanne, with his bearde so white as snowe, hearing his
40 courteous offer, and for him nowe so necessary: with ioy, feare and bashfulnes all coupled togeather, accepted it, and humbly thanked him, albeit (quoth he) a contented death is better to me, then a miserable and dispised life. The Knyght comforting him aunswered, that it was not in his power to chuse lyfe or death, but the

founder of the heauens reserued that authoritie in his owne handes. With these wordes hee tooke him by the hand, and conducted him to his Castell, where he was worthilie entertained by the Knight himselfe, his Ladie and her Daughter, one of the fairest Virgins in all that Country. *Lombardo* hauing heard all his misfortunes and hard aduentures, in the night discoursed the whole to hys Ladie, wherefore (good Wife) quoth he, entertaine him so well as may be, for I assure you he is discended of high degree, and if his manners and vertues bee correspondent to his byrth, wee will giue him our Daughter in mariage, if so himselfe accept our offer. The good Ladie misliked not her Husbands opinion, wherefore the next morning shee went to entertaine her guest, saying. My Lorde, your comming hither hath well contented my Lorde and Husbande, and so please it you to staie heere, he wil bee glad and fayne of your companie: which gentle offer *Netrides* accepted, thanking God and the Ladie for his good fortune. Thus remained he with this auncient Knight *Lombardo*, who afterwarde neuer remembred him of his miseries in the Forrest, but intreated him so well as though hee had beene his owne Sonne. *Netrides* seeing the Knights Daughter so faire and well conditioned, and she regarding not onely the vertues of his minde, but also his comely and well featured bodie, they began amorously to affect eache other secretlie, but loue inuented the meane to reueale it openlie: for *Lombardo* well noting the great discretion of this yong Gentleman, and knowing him to bee discended of bloode royall, resolued to cause him marry his Daughter, demaunding the question of *Netrides* among other speeches, if so he liked to marry his Daughter? My Lorde, quoth he, it is the sum of my desire, and greater honor cannot you bestowe on me, so please her to conceiue the same opinion I doo.[6] The marriage was sollemnized with all expedition, with the presence of manie Gentles, neighbours thereabout, who meruailed the Knight bestowed his Daughter so, in that they esteemed *Netrydes* but a poore Knight errant. It fortuned afterward that the auncient Knight and his Ladie deceased, leauing theyr Daughter great with childe, to the no little content of *Netrydes*, that after all his sorrowe he shoulde become a Father. Three daies before this Ladie fell in trauaile, shee dreamed that she was shut vppe in a very dark Chamber, whereout she coulde by no meanes get, and therfore called for helpe to one of her Gentlewomen. Then was she aduised to take her childe in her armes, and to staye there still, whereuppon she behelde her infant, and sawe that his face resembled the beames of the Sunne, the brightnes whereof chased away the darknes, so that shee might beholde the place as cleere as any other, saying. My Lord, forgette thys heauines, and you shall reioyce by this infant, for this is he shall reestablish you in the place you haue lost, and shall seate you in that Chayre with honour, for which you were exiled thence, giuing you his crowne, that traiterously chased you from his kingdome. He, comforted with these words, tooke the childe in his armes, and sayd. Little soule, I pray God thy mother speake trueth, and that thou maist be able to execute it. So saying, hee espyed a furious man who snatched the infant foorth of his armes, and notwithstanding all his intreaties and supplications, caryed it

away with him. This sorrowe for *Netrydes* made her giue a loude shryke, when he calling his Wife, demaunded the cause of her suddaine affright, whereupon she rehearsed to him the whole manner of her Dreame, and reioysing thereat, said. I hope my Lord that it will so happen to you as I haue dreamed, and therefore
5 comfort your selfe without feare of misfortune: notwithstanding, he remained in many doubtfull opinions, till they vnderstoode by effects the certaintye of this dreame.[7] Nowe was come the time of the Ladies deliueraunce, which was a goodly man Childe, so fayre and well fauoured as one should lightly beholde, beeing named *Frysol*, and shee woulde suffer none to nursse it but her owne selfe,
10 for the certaine hope shee reposed in him. The Chylde growing in time to such comely stature, as eache one tooke great pleasure to beholde him, whereof the Mother was so gladde, that albeit she had afterward two other Sonnes, yet shewed she no such speciall loue towards them as vnto *Frysol*, which procured some hatred betweene his brethren and him. This yong Lord growing to four-
15 teene yeeres of age, was in stature verie tall, delighting himselfe in ryding great Horsses, shooting in the long Bowe, casting the Barre,[8] and diuers other Gentle-manlike exercises, as also to chase in the Forrest, where olde *Lombardo* mette with his Father.[9] So that one daie after long and wearie chasing of the Hart, hauing sweated very sore, and meruailous drye for want of drinke, finding a little
20 spring by the foote of a Tree, he laie downe and dranke, but afterwarde he became so yll and sicklie, as hee trembled verie sore, so that one of hys Squires could hardlie leade him againe to the Castell. *Netrides* seeing him so exceeding ill, was meruailous sorrie, commaunding his Phisition to seeke some present helpe for him, who plied him with such wholsome potions, as his feuer left him, but his
25 face and all his bodie was so painted, as he had beene a Leaper: which made him bee mocked of his other Brethren, and scorned of all the Seruaunts, except his Father and Mother, which was such greefe to him, as he would haue died with fretting at them, but his Father rebuked them, and comforted him in this manner. I did hope my Sonne by thy meanes, to be restored againe to the Realme of
30 my deceased Father: but nowe, howe long it will be before, God knowes, if this strange malladie of thine be neuer holpen. *Frysol* amazed at his Fathers wordes, desired him earnestly to report the whole circumstance, which *Netrides* at length did, rehearsing how he was Brother to the King of *Hungaria*, the hard intreataunce he vsed towardes him, and lastlie hee tolde him the Dreame of his Mother.
35 *Frisol* studying a long space on his fathers words, at length aunswered. My Lord, you are not ignorant of the soueraigne power of the highest, who by his diuine iudgement hath sent mee this disease that thus torments mee: euen so when pleaseth him he will take it from me againe, and giue me health and strength much more then euer I had, with meanes sufficient to giue you ayde and suc-
40 coure, according to the matter whereon you haue diuined. And albeit I feele so extreame anguish, as death may not be likened to it, yet doth thys hope comfort mee in such sorte, that me thinkes already I am become more healthfull: therfore my Lord dismay of nothing, but perswade your selfe there is comfort behind.

These words were so pleasing to *Netrides*, as meere ioy caused the teares to trickle downe his cheekes, meruailing at the wonderfull courage of his Son, enduring such terrible paines as he did: wherfore what hee thought, he could not reueale, but withdrewe himselfe into his Chamber.

Chapter XLI.
Howe Frisol persecuted with his disease, and the mockery of his Bretheren, determined to goe seeke strange aduentures.

Frisol hauing heard the originall of his birthe, as also the vision that appeared to his Mother, was thence forwarde more pensiue then he had beene before, and perceiuing his Brethren continued their bad disposition, and day by day mocked him more and more: he determined to forsake his fathers house, to seeke aduentures,[1] and remedie for his sicknes, if any were to be found. And being one daie in the Forrest, more mellanchollie then accustomed, hee espied a Knight vexed with Leprosie come by the high waie, mounted on a poore Palfray, to whome he said. My Freend, I am infected with the same disease thou art, wherefore wilt thou suffer me to beare thee companie, and I will be readie to doo what thou shalt commaund me. The Knight perceiuing hee might gaine some benefite by *Frisol*, was well contented, and so bad him mount vppe behinde him. So was he glad to doo what was contrarie to his nature, and in this life continued two yeeres, trauailing many Countries, bearing continually the wallet, and what profit came he deliuered his Maister, reseruing nothing for himselfe but what he gaue him, and bearing a minde so noble and vertuous, as he desired rather death, then to enrich himselfe by anie villainous or dishonest act. So many Countries and prouinces had they trauailed, as at last they came into the Realme of *Hungaria*, when *Frisol* remembred that he was in his Vncles Land, who ledde a life so base and ignominious: hee was ouercome with exceeding heauines, which ill agreed with his daungerous disease, so that his companion desired to know the cause of his sadnes, but *Frysol* prayed him to content himselfe, saying that death was more agreeable to him, then a life so dolorous and miserable. At which words the Knight growing in choller, thruste him beside the Horse, and rode away leauing poore *Frysol* there, hauing no other comfort then to fill the ayre with his teares and complaints, till at length he receiued succour by a yong Maide named *Leonarda*, the Daughter of a riche Countriman that dwelt on a Mountaine neere at hande. This Maiden leading her Fathers Beastes and Cattell to pasture, tooke great delight in gathering hearbes and roots, wherewith to make oyntments for all woundes and diseases: and this daie (by the diuine permission) shee chaunced that way where she hearde the mornefull lamentations of *Frysol*, whom when she behelde, ouercome with pittie and compassion, said.[2] Alas my Freend, howe came you into this desert and comfortlesse place, beeing oppressed with such a bad and daungerous sicknesse? In good sooth Mistresse, (quoth hee) by no other meanes then the misfortune and displeasure of my life: Oh howe happy were my death at thys instant, then to liue any longer in this monstrous languishing. Freend, aunswered the Mayden, you ought not thus to dyspayre in sicknes, but consider, that the Lord and gouernour of the heauens and earth, dooth by these meanes trye and prooue his people, whom if he perceiue thankfull and patient in their afflictions: of reprobate enemies, he makes them his Freends and Children, onely by the raunsome that his beloued Sonne paide.[3] If then you will put your whole confidence in him, I am perswaded you shall soone finde remedie. So causing him to arise, shee conducted him to her Fathers house, where for certaine daies, she bathed him wyth wholesome Hearbes,[4] and annoynted him with such precious oyntments, as in short time his disease forsooke him, and he was as cleane as at the time hee dranke the water,[5] for which he humblie thanking the Maiden, said. God make me able (faire Vyrgin) to requite this wonderfull kindnes receiued at your handes, accounting my selfe more indebted to you, then to my parents that gaue me first life, and this perswade your selfe, that wheresoeuer my body bee seperated from this place, my hart shall remaine readie to doo you any seruice.[6] That is my will and intent, quoth *Leonarda*, but thanke him cheefelie that made me able to helpe you, and in so dooing shall I account my labour well bestowed. *Frysol* for this vnexpected good fortune, was thence forward verie dutifull and louing towardes *Leonardas* Father and her Brethren, as the readiest Seruant he had in his house: but the good man esteemed so well of him, as by no meanes hee wold suffer him to be so painfull, but with such fare as God sent him, entertained and welcommed him, not suffering him to departe thence in the space of a yeere and more. *Frysol* often accompanying *Leonarda* to the fielde, shee seeing him so faire and comelie a personage, began secretlie to affect him, yet would she not acquaint him therewith, fearing more to offend then to be refused. So soone as *Frysol* had thus recouered his strength, he determined to stay no longer there, wherefore finding *Leonarda* at leysure conuenient, he said. I know very well (fayre Mayden) how much I am beholding to you, for the speciall grace and good I haue receiued by you, which induceth mee to make you this promise, that you shall not commaunde any thing, but I wyll gladly accomplish it. And because I am desirous to trauaile after strange aduentures, I would request that it might be with your willing consent, promising you to stay no longer hence then the tearme of three yeeres, in which time I will not fayle to visite you againe: and if my fortune so fall out, as I am perswaded, I doubt not to recompence what you did for me. That which I alway feared (Sir *Frysol*) quoth she, is nowe come to passe, notwithstanding, seeing it is conuenient I should loue honour, more then mine own pleasure, I am content that you shall goe seeke your aduauncement so well begunne: but I pray you not to cast your promise in obliuion. I will not to the death (quoth he) doo anie thing to dislike you, or against your wil, and since you haue so freelie graunted me libertie, perswade your selfe my word shall be my deede.[7] So taking his leaue of her Father and Brethren, he trauayled towards *Allemaigne*, where hee hearde that chiualrie was more maintained then in anie other place, and so rode hee foure daies togeather without anie aduenture: till passing through a Forrest, he hearde a great noyse of people fighting, wherefore making hast that way, hee espyed an aunceint Knight, assaulted by sixe villaines that sought to murder him, whom he resisted so well as he could, albeit he had nothing but his sworde to defende him. The Knight espying *Frysol*, called to him for helpe, when he (suddainly finding a strong yong Tree

pluckt vppe by the roote) came therewith to the villaines, saying. Why traiterous varlets, who prouoked you to offer such shame to a Knight? with which hee tooke one of them so soundlye on the pate with his Tree, as he neuer rose to tell who hurt him. The Knight and he togeather so behaued themselues, as three of the
5 villaines were layd dead before them, which the other three perceiuing, tooke themselues to flight: wherupon the old Knight seeing himselfe so well deliuered, came and embraced *Frysol* with these wordes. Nowe may I say my good Freend, that my life had perished without your assistaunce, bethinke your selfe therfore howe I may gratefy this gentlenes: in meane time, I haue a house not farre hence,
10 let me intreate you to lodge with me this night, and I will make you the best entertainment the Country wyll affoorde. Whereto *Frysol* agreed, promising to leaue him in safety before he departed, for which the olde Knight thanked him, and as they went he discoursed to him, howe these villaines assailed him, because he had enforced them to surrender certaine heritages, which vniustly they
15 detained from poore Orphanes, and for that cause set spyes to watch him, that they might set vppon him and kill him, which surelie they had doone (quoth he) without your succour. In the continuaunce of these speeches, they arriued at his Castell where many of his Squires meruailed to see him so sore wounded, but especially his Lady and his two Sonnes, to whome hee rehearsed the summe of
20 his aduenture, and the great fauour and helpe he founde by *Frysol*, for which cause they entertained him with exceeding honour. And so long aboade *Frysol* there with the Knight, till beeing desirous to receiue the order of knighthoode, hee came to the Knight in this manner. May it please you Sir to bestow on me Horse and Armour, I wyll goe to the Emperors Court of *Allemaigne*, he beeing
25 the most renowned Prince in the world. The good Knight seeing him so forward to chiualry, gaue him Horse, Armour and money for his iourney, wherupon he sette forwarde, and the third daie after hee arriued at the Emperors Court, from whence (a little before) *Trineus* and *Palmerin* were departed towards *Fraunce*: which newes made *Frisol* earnestly desire his knighthood, because he intended
30 with all speede to trauaile thither likewise, in respect of the honour was there to be wunne. *Frysol* vnderstanding the Emperour was in the Chappell hearing diuine seruice, went thither, where beholding the Princesse *Polinarda*, he reputed her the onely fayre Lady of the world, thinking hee could neuer glut his eyes with regarding her,[8] whereupon, seruice beeing ended, he fell on his knee before the
35 Emperour in this manner. Because I knowe (inuincible Lorde) that you are renowned beyonde all other potentates whatsoeuer, and that you make no small accounte of Knights aduenturous: I desire that by your hande I may be numbred among them. The Emperour seeing him so yong and yet valiantly giuen, aunswered. I would be lothe my Freende to deny a request so reasonable, but I wil
40 first knowe if you be Gentle borne or no. My Lorde, quoth he, I sweare by the fayth I owe to God and your Maiestie, that I am noble borne, and of the bloode royall by my Fathers side. God forbid then (sayd the Emperour) but you shoulde be Knight, and Fortune sheelde you so well in chiualry, as she hath indued you

with comely shape and beautie. Then was the Spurre put vpon hys right heele, and the Emperour bad him ryse a Knight, commaunding his Daughter *Polinarda* to gyrde hys Sworde to him, which she did, saying. Worthily and with happines (Sir Knight) may you imploy the order you haue receiued. Madame (quoth *Frysol*) if heereafter any vertue or valoure abyde in me, it shal be imployed onely for you, hauing thus honoured mee with my Sword, wherewith I hope to accomplish such deeds of Armes, as shall renowne her name that gaue me my weapon: but *Polinarda* made him no aunswere, because *Palmerin* was the onely Image of her thoughts. After *Frysol* was thus Knighted, taking his leaue of the Emperour and his Daughter, he departed, making no small hast till he arriued at the Ioustes at *Parris*, where he determined for his first deed of chiualry, to enter the Combat for the beauty of *Polinarda*. But he could not get thither so soone as hee intended, for hee was hindered by the way with an vnexpected aduenture, which was in a fayre Forrest, where hee behelde foure Knights carry away a Ladie perforce, who seeing him, cryed. Ah good Knight, for Gods sake succour mee: whereuppon *Frysol* coutching his Launce, sent one of the Knights headlong to the grounde, and in short time wounded another in such sort, as nowe hee had but two left to resist him, on whom *Frysol* made tryall, howe well he coulde imploy the gift of *Polinarda*. The Knights seeing the hard fortune of their two other fellowes, the one hauing broken his necke in the fall, and the other wounded past hope of recouerie: tooke the wisest way for themselues, posting thence so fast as they coulde ride, but *Frysol* would not folow, least they had some other companie in ambush that might haue intrapped him, wherefore he conducted the Ladie to her Mothers Castell, where hee remained that night, and the next daie set forwarde to *Parris*, where hee arriued at the time he fought with *Palmerin*, according as hath beene before rehearsed.[9]

After the Knight of the *Sunne* (who hencefoorth shall passe by the name of *Frysol*) had left *Palmerin*, and was departed the fielde, the night was so obscure as hee knewe not which waie he rode, so that the moysture of the euening dewe did great harme to his woundes, as if God had not armed him with the better strength, he was in daunger not to escape with life. The verie same daie was the Duke of *Gaule* departed from *Parris*, to goe ayde the King of *England* against the Kings of *Scots* and *Norway*, who were Nephewes to the Emperour of *Allemaigne*, for that they molested him with troublesome warres: and the Duke beeing benighted, was glad to pitch his Tents in a faire fielde, through which it fortuned *Frysol* to passe, complayning of the daunger he felt himselfe in. The Duke of *Gaule* beeing abroade foorth of hys Tent to recreate himselfe, hearde this sorrowfull noyse, which made him send his men to see who it was, and to bring him with them to the Tent, whither when they had brought him, the Duke pitting his estate, demaunded whence he came, and who had wounded him in that sort. Then discoursed he the whole matter, how hee had fought with the Knight that ouercame the Duke of *Sauoye*, and so long their fight endured, that the darke night and the King caused them to be parted, neyther of them as yet conquered,

and because he woulde not returne into the Cittie, sought some Village where he might conuenientlie lodge. The Duke of *Gaule* hearing the wordes of *Frysol*, esteemed him for a hardy and valiant Knight, hauing so long endured against *Palmerin* vnuanquished, wherefore he saide. Sir Knight, you are very welcome
5 to mee, all the ayde and succour I can giue you, you shall bee sure to finde with hartie good will: assuring you, that there is no Knight liuing to whom I wysh more euill, then him whom you haue this daie fought withall. So causing him to bee vnarmed, willed him to rest himselfe vpon his owne bedde, and made his woundes be dressed, abyding there eyght dayes for the health of *Frysol*. In which
10 time, the Duke had imparted to him the warres of the King of *England*, which made him make more hast to be gone, or els he would haue kept him company longer. My Lord, quoth *Frysol*, so please you to accept my companie, I hope to behaue my selfe so well, as you shall not be discontented with me. The Duke thanked him, and reioyced that by his meanes so good a Knight was preserued,
15 and did him all the honour hee could deuise, taking him with him into *England*, where he founde the Countrey very much desolated with warres, to his no little greefe: but leaue we them, and returne to *Palmerin*.

Chapter XLII.

Of the great courtesie the King of Fraunce vsed to Trineus and Palmerin: and of their returne into Allemaigne.

So dilligently were *Palmerins* woundes attended, which he had receiued by the hand of *Frysol*, as not long after hee recouered his health, whereof the King and Prince *Lewes* were highly glad, and much more *Trineus*, to whome the King desired to giue his Daughter *Lucemania* in marriage, which to compasse, hee intended a sumptuous banquet, whereto hee woulde inuite these twaine, yet first he would acquaint the Queene therewith, and therefore began the matter with her thus. I see Madame, that our Daughter *Lucemania* is of yeeres sufficient for a Husband, and because I euermore desired her highest preferment, and that I would know if the Prince *Trineus* to whom I could wish she were espoused, were anie thing in loue that waie affected, for hardlie in my iudgment shall we finde a greater Lord, beeing heyre to the famous Emperour of *Allemaigne*: for this intent (I say) will I ordaine a banquet, whereto hee and noble *Palmerin* shall bee inuited, and our Daughter to beare them company in the best sorte you can deuise. The Queene, who more desired this marriage then the King her Husbande, aunswered. You doubt not (my Lord) that I request her cheefest aduantage, wherefore let it be as you haue determined, and shee shall be present as you haue appointed. This matter thus proceeding, two daies after were *Trineus* and *Palmerin* called to this banquet, and to honour them the more, the King caused his Sonne *Lewes*, with a braue companie of Knightes and Gentlemen, to conduct them into the Pallace, where they were royallie receiued by the King and Queene, and so led vppe into the Chamber appointed for their banquet. After they had washed, the King caused *Trineus* to sitte by him, and *Palmerin* against him, aboue whom sat faire *Lucemania* his Daughter, beeing placed iust opposite to the Prince *Trineus*, the Queene to furnish the Table, satte downe by the King. And albeit nature had bestowed on the Princesse most exquisite beautie, yet her sumptuous accoustrements made her appeare most amiable: but all coulde not mooue the hart of *Trineus*, to forget her to whose shrine hee was dedicated. The banquet ended, and the Tables withdrawne, *Trineus* daunced with the fayre yong Princesse, courting her with manie honest and decent speeches, which made *Lucemania* suppose he loued her, but the Prince noted it well enough, albeit his affections were bound to *English Agriola*. In this time the other Ladies were conferring of *Palmerins* knightlie valour, when the Countie of *Armignac* his Sonne, intreating the Duke of *Orleaunce* Daughter to daunce, was thus staied by her speeches to the other Ladies. You see faire Ladies (quoth shee) that *Palmerin* hath misprized our beauties, to reuenge our iniurie, let vs all fall vppon him, and shut him in some place where hee may neuer come foorth, for if he escape vs, the *Allemaigne* Ladies shall beare the honor from the *French*, which will bee to vs perpetuall discredite. These wordes she spake with such a pleasant countenaunce, as mooued all the other Ladies to smile, whereupon the Duchesse of *Burgundie*

Palmerin d'Oliva: Part I 245

answered. In sooth it is necessarie we should doo so, and let vs not suffer him to gette out of our handes so easilie, as he did from the Knights that came to the Combat. All the companie lyked this motion well, but the King said. Ladies, I will not consent that *Palmerin* shall haue anie wronge, because I haue taken him
5 into my guarde. And who shall make recompence (quoth another Ladie) for the wrong hee hath doone vs? You ought to suffer for satisfaction, saide the King, and bee glad that you had the meane to see the best Knight in the world, for mine owne part I promise you, I rest so contented. *Palmerin* hearing the King so commende him, bashfullie thus aunswered. Alas my Lorde, there is no such matter
10 in me as pleaseth your Maiesty to report, but what my abilitie is, it remaines to doo you seruice: accounting my selfe more then happy by comming to your Courte, to haue knowledge of a Prince so noble and vertuous, and no man liuing (next my Lord the Emperour) that maie commaunde me more then your highnes. Among other speeches, the King broke the matter of his Daughters marriage to
15 *Palmerin*, desiring him to labour in the cause to *Trineus*, which hee promised: but al in vain, for after they had taken their leaue to returne towards *Allemaigne*, though *Palmerin* was earnest in the matter, in respecte of the beautie and nobilitie of the Princesse, as for the support he might haue by matching with the Daughter of *Fraunce*, yet *Trineus* thus answered. I thanke you my Lord for the
20 good you wish mee, as also the honour the King affoordes mee: but another beyond her (whose renowne hath conquered me) is Lady and Mistresse of my affections. And because you are hee from whom I will not hide my most secrete thoughts, know that it is *Agriola*, Daughter to the King of *England*, to whom though my Father be an enemie, yet by your aide and mine owne good endeu-
25 ours, I doo not doubt to compasse my loue. You knowe my Lord (quoth *Palmerin*) that I wish as wel to you as mine owne hart, and when occasion serues, tryall shall make manifest. And seeing you haue fixed your loue on faire *Agriola* of *England*, imparting likewise the same so confidently to me: I am perswaded you coulde neuer make a better choise, therefore let nothing chaunge your opinion.
30 Thus rode they on with manie sundrie speeches, not a little gladde they were returning to the Emperour, but *Palmerin* much more then was *Trineus*, for the desire hee had to see his Ladie *Polinarda*: wherefore with the consent of the Prince, he sent a Squire before to aduertise the Emperour of their comming, before whom he had no sooner doone reuerence, but he was presentlie knowne,
35 and demaunded in what estate his Son *Trineus* and *Palmerin* were, where he had left them, and what accidents had happened in *Fraunce*? Then the Squire rehearsed the Combats and victories of his Maister against the Princes of *Fraunce* and the Dukes of *Gaule* and *Sauoye*, with their royall entertainment by the King and his Sonne, howe manie portraits of Ladies *Palmerin* had conquered, with the
40 whole discourse of euerie action. Whereof the Emperour, the Empresse, and all the Lords and Ladies were maruailous glad, yet was not theyr ioy comparable to the Princesse *Polinardas*, hearing the Squire reueale the honourable deedes of her loue, so that her conceit might be discerned by her countenance, and needes she

must thus demaunde of the Squire. I praie thee tell me my Freende, howe fares my Lord and Brother, with his noble companion Sir *Palmerin*? The Squire wel aduised, because he knewe the loue betweene her and his Maister, sette his knee to the grounde againe with this aunswere. I left the Prince your Brother, accompanied with my Lord *Palmerin*, well and in good health: but cheefely my Lorde, who since you sawe him, hath wunne the greatest honour that euer Knight did. Afterward he reported the manner of the Combats to her, and what greefe his Maister sustained in his sicknes, when he coulde not be reuenged on the Knight that lost her counterfeit, which the Duke of *Sauoye* placed at the feete of *Lucemania*, and last of all, the perillous Combat betweene his Maister and the Knight of the *Sun*. Which she tooke such delight to heare, as she made him repeate one thing manie times, and could not satisfie herselfe sufficientlie with these worthy reports. Which the Squire perceiuing, delighted as much to itterate euerie thing, and said. Beleeue me Madame, the loue my Maister beares to her, for whose beautie he entered the Combat, in my opinion is incredible, for he is much more hers then his owne, and I haue seene him in such sort thinking on her, as one coulde hardlie iudge him aliue or deade, fearing least anie other shold rob him of his loue, such is the iealousie of his vnspotted affection, albeit my Maister reputes his Ladie immouable.[1] *Polinarda* changing countenance oftentimes at the Squires wordes, aunswered. The Ladie shoulde be very ill councelled, beeing honoured with the looue of so good a Knight as *Palmerin*, to make refusall of his worthie seruice: and I promise thee, by the faith of a Princesse, that if I knew her, for the vnwillingnes I haue to heare him complaine, I wold endeuour to cause her like none but him, and therein to thinke herselfe the most happie among Ladies.[2] Wherfore (if thou maist bee so bolde) tell thy Maister at his returne, that I will be a meane to aide him towards her he loues: and therewithall present him my fauourable salutations, in that I euermore desired the fortunate ende of his enterprise, not so much for the lyking of his Ladie, beeing beloued of the best, as for the renowned chiualrie that harbours in his hart. These speeches ended, the Squire returned to meet the Prince *Trineus* and his Maister, to whom he reported his talke with *Polynarda*: which *Palmerin* reioycing at, let fall all iealousie, esteeming her nowe the truest Lady liuing. The men of *Gaunt* for ioy of his returne, that so worthilie deliuered them from the oppressions of the enchaunted Knight, went foorth in seuerall companies, according as honor, yeeres and office directed them, to meete him,[3] and so conueied him with signes of ioy to the Pallace, where the Emperour so much abased himselfe, as he came downe into the open Court to entertaine him, and glad likewise to see the safe returne of his Sonne *Tryneus*, saying. My Sonne, right happie is thy returne, and you Sir *Palmerin*, perswade your selfe so welcome as hart can deuise, assuring you, that your successe hath not a little pleased me. And needes must I account the Ladie especially bounden to you, for whose loue you haue past so manie dangerous Combats, good reason hath she to loue you, in respect of your trauailes for her, renowning her so much by your knightlie chiualrie, so that if she recompence you

not according to your merits, woorthilie may she be condemned of ingratitude. Alas my Lorde (quoth he) her beautie commaundeth higher matters then all my labours. *Polynarda* beeing in presence, remembred well her Fathers words, and therfore she intended to shun that condemnation, saying to herselfe. He that
5 deserues honour ought to were it, and he that commaundes the soule, may easilie ouer-rule the passions of the minde: let my Knight then be rewarded as he hath rightly deserued.[4] All this while, the eyes of these two louers so well discharged their office, as *Palmerin* wished that *Iuno* had graunted him so much, as she did somtime to *Argus* her sheepehearde,[5] that he might haue more ease in his afflic-
10 tion: for he thought it not enough, onelie to behold the beautie of so rare and excellent perfection. Againe, he was not a little tormented, because *Polynarda* (to couer what she woulde gladlie none should discerne) cast her lookes on the ground, which sometimes shee likewise compelled him to doo: but her presence whom he esteemed aboue all other things, would not allow him that consider-
15 ation. The Emperour at length commanded, that all the figures of the Ladies which he had wunne in Combat, should be brought before him: but when hee sawe so manie, and of so contrarie qualitie, hee coulde not but commende Sir *Palmerins* victorie. Then were diuers iudgments giuen of the beauty of the por- traits, eache one of the beholders after their seuerall opinions. *Ptolome* made
20 description of whom they were, and who did enter Combatte on their behalfe, omitting at no time the honour of *Palmerin*: whereat they all admired, some commending their complexions, others their sweete yong yeeres, and altogeather the prowesse of him that brought the conquest with him, whereupon the Emper- our said. In good faith Sir *Palmerin*, I blesse the time that Fortune sent me so
25 good a Knight, and thinke not to carrie awaie all the glory of your victorie your selfe, for I meane to haue part because you gaue your selfe mine. And woulde the Ladie you loue were in thys Courte or in my Realme, to the ende I might so assist you in your sute, as you might both be mine. My Lord (quoth *Palmerin*) the vic- torie is wholie yours, beeing gotten by your Knight, and if the Ladie I loue were
30 not vnder your regiment, then shoulde I complaine of a greater matter[6] then abyding with you, beeing obedient to your highnes as your humble subiect and Seruaunt. With which aunswere the Emperour was highlie contented, and *Tryneus* comming to his Sister *Polynarda*, saide. Trust mee faire Sister, you are more indebted to *Palmerin*, then to anie other Knight in the worlde beside, and
35 rather accept of him then of the Duke of *Lorrayne*, who maintaining your beau- tie, was ouercome by the Duke of *Sauoy*, and your picture placed at the feete of *Lucemania*, where yet it had remained, but that *Palmerin* conquering the Duke, remooued the figure of the *French* Princesse in obeysaunce to you.[7] *Polynarda* not content with the vndiscreete enterprise of the Duke of *Lorrayne*, aunswered. In
40 sooth good Brother, the Duke of *Lorrayne* is none of my Knight, and I repute *Palmerin* to haue more bountie and valour, then the Duke can haue of wit or courage, therefore great meruaile that hee was not slaine. The Emperour seeing *Polynarda* was offended with the Duke of *Lorrayne*, aunswered. You cannot

(Daughter) forbid men to execute their owne pleasure, and if the Duke liked to enter the Combat for your beautie, it was for the honourable good will he bare you, and albeit hee could not reache his desire, yet haue you no cause to thinke the worsse of him. *Polynarda* beeing a Princesse of rare wit and iudgment, as anie of her time, would multiply no more words, but continued silent: neuerthelesse, *Palmerin* remembring her aunswere to *Tryneus*, intreated her to keepe all the portraits of the Ladies, determining to sende them to whom they belonged, according to their degrees in birth and honor. Which she thankfully accepted, and spending this whole daie in diuers delights, *Palmerin* beeing in the euening in his Chamber accompanied with *Ptolome*, sent his Dwarffe to the Princesse to appoint the time of their meeting: and she seeing the Dwarffe, caught him about the necke, demaunding of him what newes hee brought. None but good Madame, answered the Dwarffe, my Maister hath sent you the *Bon soir*, and therewith his humble duetie to your highnes, for, being your Knight, and liuing onelie to doo you seruice: he hath good hope that your vertuous nature wyll not forget, howe many daungers he hath past for your sake, and nowe dooth loue appeale for his desired reward. Therefore good Madame, as you are hartfast,[8] vnite your selues handfast, giue my Maister life, your selfe comfort, and make me happy by carrying of this message: for I vowe by the reuerend faith I beare you bothe, that I will not depart without some gracious aunswere. *Polynarda* smyling to heare *Vrbanillo* speake so earnestlie, sayd. The assuraunce thou giuest me of the trustie affection thy Maister beares me, dooth not a little content mee, and pitty it were so good a Knight shoulde labour all this while in vaine: therefore perswade thy Maister, that to morrow at night I will meete him where we were wont, and there will I resolue him to his owne content.

Chapter XLIII.

How Palmerin went in the night to the appointed place, to conferre with his Lady Polinarda, and the amorous communication they had togeather.

<small>5</small> *Vrbanillo* with cheerefull countenaunce returned to his Master, declaring to him his talke wyth *Polynarda*, her sweete lookes, her gracious aunsweres, how choiselie she loued him, and lastlie her promise to meete him in the accustomed place: yet is not this all, for before you depart with her, shee hath assured mee to resolue you to your owne content. And that is it I want (quoth he) for might I once receiue my content, then shoulde I thinke my trauailes rewarded.
<small>10</small> And doubt you not thereof saide the Dwarffe, if she be a woman of her worde. Then *Ptolome* beeing present, asked the Dwarffe if he saw *Bryonella*. No in sooth (quoth he) she was not in the Princesse Chamber, nor (to my knowledge) was she acquainted with my comming, yet dare I thinke she will be there with my Lady. The time beeing come, the Ladies were at the place with deuotion answerable to
<small>15</small> those silent howres,[1] and theyr Knights not fayling their appointment, what pleasure on eache side was conceiued, is not to be enquired, for all wyshings are nothing in respect of their contentments. *Polynarda* hauing her freendly Knight before her, so sweete a blush ecclipsed her countenaunce, as woulde driue nature into a studie to frame the like, and thus she began. Alas my sweete Freende, in what
<small>20</small> paine, anguish and heauines of hart, hath your absence brought me? what teares haue fallen from mine eyes, and drops of blood from my hart, by renting sighes and ceaselesse acclamations, remembring our pleasures past, our present comfort, and the hope of better hap to come? What dolorous conceits hath often wounded me, thinking on so many hazards and perrils as might hinder me from
<small>25</small> seeing you againe? and not without cause, beleeue me, for had you miscaried, neuer Ladie sustained such a losse, in respect of your Knightlie valour, and the vnfeigned loue I beare you, whereof (before I depart) I meane assuredlie to resolue you, in requitall of your honourable trauailes for maintenaunce of my beautie. And heereof perswade your selfe good Knight, that to haue you, I refuse all
<small>30</small> other good fortunes whatsoeuer: and therefore I care not though it were openlie knowne, how especiallie I prize, desire, loue and esteeme you. *Palmerin* confounded with this long expected comfort, and not able to endure with silence, interrupted her in this manner. By the faith of your sworne Seruaunt, sweete Madame, the perrils, mishaps, and dangers I haue past since my departure, neuer
<small>35</small> deserued the verie least of your complaints, nor could my endeuours prooue such, as your incomparable perfections merited, the onelie remembraunce whereof was sufficient to make me inuincible: wherefore faire Mistresse, if I haue wunne anie honor, your fauour was the meane, and your beautie gaue mee the vertue, streaming so plentifullie from your chaste eies,[2] as the water from the Fountaine.
<small>40</small> To little purpose were it nowe to rehearse, the strange assaults, massacring thoughts, and violent flames, wherein I haue burned and continuallie beene crucified, since the howre it pleased you to let mee see *Fraunce*: vndoubtedly, the

verie meanest of my sufferings was able to destroie me, without the resolute
assuraunce of your diuine fauour, which triumphing ouer death, shall make me
liue continuallie. So that the desire to let you knowe how assuredlie I am yours,
and the continuall wyshing to see you againe, gaue mee victorie ouer your enemies, and brought me safe thorow all extreamities, to honour you, as I doo at this
present. It nowe remaines Madame, that you regarde the trueth of my loue, the
permanence thereof, and the instant passions worsse then death to mee, yet with
this prouiso, that I presume not of anie action meritorious,[3] but your grace, which
is able to strengthen me in greatest debilitie. And no where know I to seeke for
pittie and support of my cares, if not onelie by her, who hath the soueraigne
power to chase hence, the cruell and euer threatning menaces of death. Forbeare
good my Lorde, quoth she, thus to talke of death, considering I cannot liue one
howre without you, nor holde I any comfort of my life, but onelie in loouing you,
to enioy you: so that what you endure, I suffer, and no passion torments you, but
I haue a share therein, so deuoutlie is my spirit consorted with yours. And therefore thinke not your oppressions greater then mine, for if you doo, it proceedeth
by want of experience of feminine passions, the extreamitie whereof farre surmounteth your sexe. For which cause, to giue some rest to our long and ouertrauailed desires, I giue you heere my hand, and therewithall a chast hart, accepting
you onely for my Lorde and Husbande, and to my promise call Heauen and
Earth to witnes. Where is the wit so daintie, the tongue so florishing, or the
penne so dilligent, as can conceiue, report or set down in perfect coullers, the
ioyes of these louers? You faire Lordinges, and you likewise sweete Ladies, that
long haue trauailed in amorous affections, and in the ende receiued the rewarde
of your passions, by your owne conceites can imagine the content of these twaine:[4]
for *Palmerin* was of this opinion, that *Iupiter* had not the like pleasure with faire
Alcmena, for whom hee caused one night to endure the space of three daies,[5] as
hee hadde with his gracious Mistresse *Polinarda*. For nowe the manifolde strokes
he gaue for beautie, were heere remembred, his daungerous trauailes in all places,
recounted, his absence, with kinde gratulations welcommed, his teares, sighes,
complaints and feares, resolued, and lastlie, his long, vnchangeable and most
faithfull loue, freendlie rewarded. Let vs not heere forget, that *Ptolome* and *Brionella* were in the same predicament, for he knowing her to be of the noble and
auncient ligne, beside, sole heyre to the house of *Saxon*, might count himselfe
highly honored with such a Wife: and therefore the like coniunction was made
betweene them, so that nowe these Knights and Ladies were espoused before
God, there wanted nothing but the ceremonie of the Church to confirme it.[6] But
nowe comes *Vrbanillo*, and hee breakes of this pleasure, because the time was so
farre spent, as they must needs depart: which with much a doo they did, leauing
their Ladies examining theyr content, the Princesse soone after thus conferring
with *Brionella*. Alas faire Freende, it is doubtfull what danger maie arise, because
you haue contracted your selfe to *Ptolome* without the Emperors consent: howe
will you answer when you are charged with the fault? *Brionella*, who now feared

nothing but the preuenting of her loue, aunswered. In sooth Madame, you speake with great reason, you nowe giue counsell when the deede is doone, and cannot bee reuoked till it be dispatched: woulde you haue all the good fortune your selfe, and suffer your Freende to enioy no part with you? trust mee that is vnconscio-
5 nable dealing, for he that made you to loue, framed me of the selfe same mettall.[7] But I see you make the occasion to me, to learne howe to aunswere your owne deede: let vs referre all to him Madame, that appointed your choise by destinie, and mine by mine owne lyking. Manie other pleasaunt speeches passed betweene them, and diuers times their Knights came to visite them, till Fortune who will
10 neuer suffer thinges long in one estate,[8] sent an occasion to hinder this delight of theyr loue: for there was a Messenger come to the Courte from the King of *Norway*, Nephew to the Emperour, who beeing admitted audience, thus deliuered his message. Woorthie Lord, the King of *Norway* my Maister, requires your assistaunce in his great distresse, against the King of *England*, who with a mightie
15 and puissaunt Armie is entered his dominions, where he hath made great wast and slaughter of his people, in diuers skirmishes and conflicts passed betweene them, so that he neuer had like neede as at this instant. Trust me (quoth the Emperour) I will assiste him with right good will, and his misfortune dooth not a little greeue me, but I will take order for it immediatlie, and my power shall be
20 with him so soone as possiblie maie be, with which aunswere the Messenger departed. Nowe as concerning the cause of these warres, betweene the Kings of *Norway* and *England*, it was procured by displeasure of succor, that the King of *Norway* gaue to the King of *Scots* his Brother,[9] who helde warre with *England* about the taking of certaine Shippes: the Emperour likewise his heauie enemie,
25 and for that cause he promised helpe so soone to the King his Nephew. Which when *Trineus* vnderstoode, that his Father declared himselfe displeased with the Father of his beloued *Agriola*, (whose loue no occasion coulde alter) hee was greatlie discontented: yet dissembling his conceit, determined rather to aide the King of *Englande*, then his Cozin, and therefore intreated *Palmerin* to accompa-
30 nie him to his Chamber, where hee woulde acquaint him with some part of the sorrow he conceiued, by the succour his Father would sende to the King of *Norway*, against her Father whose Seruant he had vowed himselfe, and therfore (quoth he) let me desire you to conceale[10] a request I shall make to you. You knowe my Lorde, said *Palmerin*, that I will no lesse obey you then the Emperour
35 your Father, commaund therefore what you please, and be it in my power, it shal be executed. So it is, quoth *Trineus*, that I woulde haue you not accompanie the power my Father sendes by Sea, but doo so much for me, that you, *Ptolome*, and my selfe (vnknown to anie) may assist the King of *England* in his warres, by which meanes I doubt not to compasse the thing I most of all desire. And this I
40 dare tell you, that my life is only dedicated to her seruice, and so well doo I hope to imploye my paines, that she shall haue cause to loue me, and regard the paine I suffer for her sake: and but I gaine the fortune to purchase my loue, right soone and suddaine shall you heare of my death. You that haue felt the like torments

can censure of mine, which I dare not impart to the Emperor my Father, because
of the hatred hee beares the King of *England*, aduise mee therefore good Freende
what I shall doo. These speeches were nothing pleasing to *Palmerin*, seeing he
must nowe againe depart from his Ladie: but because he earnestly affected *Trineus*, and knew how wel he might helpe him in his loue, answered. Assure your
selfe my Lord, that I will labour dilligentlie for your good, and shall assist you to
my vttermost, in that you beare such loue to the Princesse. And I am of the opinion, that hauing receiued the order of knighthood, which the Emperour your
Father wyll not denie, it woulde auaile you much, to tell your Father howe you
desire (vnknowne) to aide the King of *Norway*. For my part, if he demaunde my
aduise, I will like it so well, as because the Armie cannot bee readie so soone,
your honor, *Ptolome* and my selfe will ryde before towards the King, and so may
we accomplish what you so earnestlie desire. This counsell pleased so well *Trineus*, as he intended on the morrow to request his order of the Emperor: as also
how gladlie he wold assist the King of *Norway*, and howe necessary it was for him
to goe before the Armie, as *Palmerin* and he had deuised togeather.

Chapter XLIV.
Howe Trineus was knighted, and what happened to him afterward.

On the morrow, this yong Prince seeing that to accomplishe his intent, it was necessarie hee shoulde be knighted, he gaue attendaunce to finde the Emperour at leysure, when he might sollicite his highnesse with his sute: and vnderstanding that hee was walking in his Gallerie, hee went to him, and on his knee thus began. Dreade Lord and Father, so pleased your Maiestie, it is nowe time I shoulde receiue my order of Knighthoode, and more necessary now then at any other time, in respecte of my earnest desire to aide the King of *Norway* my Cozin in his warres. The Emperour meruailing whence this humour shoulde proceede, answered. Why *Trineus*, doo you thinke your selfe able to take so waightie a charge in hande? truely such honor is soone receiued, but to maintaine it as it ought to be, and preuent the dangers incident therto, is more hard then you weene, and maketh proofe of the most couragious stomacke, in that neither paine, feare or danger must hinder, what a matter of so great consequence dooth command. And perswade your selfe, that such as councelled you thereto, knowe scant themselues their duetie in those affayres, wherefore for a time haue patience, and referre it tell better abilitie: for I wil send good store of other Knights in this expedition, who shall well excuse you to the King my Nephew. *Trineus* not contented with this answere, replyed. In truth my Lord, if I were not desirous to fulfill what is required in chiualrie, I wold not so boldly haue made this demaund, therefore for such exceptions as you admitted, let mee not I beseeche you be denied at this time: and let this induce you, that such as are borne to gouerne Kingdoms, if they giue themselues onelie to pleasure, without passing through the pykes of some dangerous hazarde, they are not woorthie to be lifted to such honor. The Emperor hearing the braue minde of his Sonne, and that his wordes sauoured of courage, conceiuing well thereof, answered. Since your desire is so earnest to be made Knight, I am well contented, but I wold haue it doone honorablie, and before a greater assemblie then now is in our Court. Alas my Lord, said *Trineus*, there is no neede of tryumphe before victorie:[1] let such pomp remaine I pray you,[2] til I haue wunne honor and accounte by my deedes. The Emperor ioyfull of the Princes good opinion, perswaded himselfe he wold prooue fortunate, wherfore he graunted his request, so that *Palmerin* might accompanie him in his voyage. Of which condition *Trineus* was not sorie, because in him consisted all his hope of successe: so his Father commaunded him to prepare himselfe for hys order, whereupon *Trineus* made himselfe a costlie Armor, and another for *Palmerin*, the deuises beeing changed, because they intended to passe vnknowne.[3] Nowe had the Emperor leuied an Armie of tenne thousande good Souldiers, the conduct wherof was appointed to the Countie *Tolano*, a Knight valiant and hardie, hauing had like charge in sundrie occasions of war: therefore so soone as all things were in readines, they were embarqued, and sayled with such benefite of winde and weather, as soone after they tooke landing in *England*. Where a while we will leaue, returning to *Polynarda*, greatlie discontent with her Brothers departure, because of *Palmerin*, and *Brionella* no lesse troubled for her freend *Ptolome*: but the Princesse feeling newe afflictions for the absence of her loue, came to her Brother, saying. I knowe not (Brother) who hath aduised you to venture so dangerously, our Cozin hauing assistance sufficient without hazarding your personne, let mee then intreate you (good Brother) to affect occasions that promise better securitie. Better occasions Sister? quoth hee, it is impossible, if it be a thing allowable and vertuous to succour a stranger, howe much more then is it to our Kinsman, especially such a one as is our Cozin of *Norway*? therefore I pray you be of good comfort till my returne. And if it so happen, that my Father in my absence intend your marriage, looke that you consent not til I come home againe, for my not being heere will serue you for a sufficient excuse. Which *Polinarda* promised, and her word so past, stoode her in no small sted afterward, as you shall finde in the discourse following. So soone as *Trineus* was prouided of all thinges for his knighthoode, he came to the Emperour in this maner. I desire you my Lord to accomplish your promise, hauing doone my duetie as you commaunded me. With right good will my Sonne, saide the Emperor, goe Arme your selfe. Then went hee, *Palmerin* and *Ptolome* armed to the Chappell, *Trineus* beeing in Greene Armour, figured all ouer with harts of Golde,[4] and in his Sheelde was portraied a Knight vnarmed, holding in his hand a Bowe bent, with an arrow readie to shoote against a greene Tree, whereon hunge a scrole, which had written in it in Letters of Gold this mot: *Madame, quand mourray-ie?*[5] Whereby he meant, that the loue which made him enterprise this voyage, should beare him companie till death. *Palmerins* Armor was all blacke, declaring his mourning for his absence from his Lady, and in his Sheelde for his deuise was figured, a goodlie Eagle, shrouding a little Birde vnder his winges, declaring therby the fauour he had receiued of his Mistresse. Soone after came the Emperor into the Chappell, where hee Knighted his Sonne, put his Spur on his heele, and girded his sworde about him:[6] afterward they went to dinner, and spent the whole daie in manie pleasures, for ioy of the newe Knight. *Palmerin* and *Ptolome* to comfort their Ladies[7] before theyr departure according as they were wont, when the Princesse *Polinarda* thus began. Alas my Lorde, what greefe wyll your departure be to me? with what patience doo you think I am able to endure it? perswade your selfe, the very conceit of your absence will be my death, or at least a cause of such danger as I shall neuer recouer. Bee well aduised therefore how you deale with me, for the intent of my Brother maie be broken if you would labour in it: but if it may not be, then saue my life by your speedie returne. These words were deliuered with such teares and reking sighes, as *Palmerin* might well perceiue the vehemence of her greefes, and answering her heauines with as earnest oppression, said. Sweete Ladie bee perswaded, and temper your sorrow with patience, considering the vnion of our spirites makes a simpathie of afflictions, if then for my sake you will not pacifie your selfe, yet to sheeld your owne perril let me intreate you to be resolued, in that my returne shall bee with such

Palmerin d'Oliva: Part I   255

expedition as you will commaunde. But if you continue thus melanchollie, you will bewray what as yet shoulde bee concealed, and so may great harme ensue to vs both. Wherfore I desire you to moderate your impatience, and thinke well of my departure, which is cheefelie to seeke out a Knight, against whome I fought
5 in *Fraunce* for your beautie, as for anie other matter you may beleeue me.

   Whereuppon he reported his Combat with the Knight of the *Sunne*, which made the Princesse (as well for *Palmerins* promise, as the account he made of *Frysol*) somewhat better quieted, to answere. If it be so my Lord, that your returne will bee with such speede, I shall enforce my selfe to beare the burthen
10 of my cares with as much patience as I can, and see you faile not your appointed time: but tell mee I praie you, what Armes beares the Knight of the *Sunne* you spake off? which *Palmerin* discribing, *Polinarda* remembred him, saying. My Lorde, I know nowe very well what he is, for eight daies after your departure towardes *Fraunce*, the Emperour my Father knighted him, commanding mee
15 to gird him with his Sworde, which I coulde not but obey: wherein the Knight glorying, sollicited me with affections not liking me,[a] which I pray you reuenge, beeing the man whom the matter neerest concerneth. After manie other amiable conferences, the Knights humbly tooke their leaue of their Ladies, and in the morning betimes, the Mariners called on *Trineus* and his companie to hast
20 aboorde, because the winde serued well for *England*, which they performed with all speede, hauing first taken their farwell of the Emperour and the Court. So hoysing sayle, they sette on to Sea, and in good time came within the kenning of *England*: where we will forsake them awhile, and returne to the Emperors Armie, which he sent to the King of *Norway* his Nephewe.

Chapter XLV.

Howe the Armie of the Emperour of Allemaigne arriued in England, vnder the conducte of the Countie Tolano: and howe they were discomfited.

Rehearsed it hath beene alreadie, how the Emperor of *Allemaigne* promised the Messenger of *Norwaye*, to sende his Maister the ayde of tenne thousand men at Armes, of whome the Countie *Tolano* was made General, and they arriued in *England* without any resistance. The Countie vnderstanding by his auaunt courers, the order of the Enemies Armie, and where the King of *Norway* was encamped, raunged his men in good order, and marched toward their Forte, which the King had made in the Duchie of *Gaule*, and which he had destroyed during the time the Duke was in *Fraunce*, hauing there fortifyed the strongest Cittie, and the Hauen that stood best for their commoditie. *Crenus* at his returne with *Frisol*, as you haue hearde,[1] vnderstanding the spoile of his Countrie, assembled his people togeather, and with the ayde of the King of *England*, came within a dayes iourney of his enemies. The Countie *Tolano* hearing thereof, appointed his men in seuerall companies, and the next daie gaue such sharpe skirmishes to the *Gaulles*, as they were constrained to keepe within their defences. Heereuppon the Duke determined to bid them battaile, and to helpe him in his attempt, hee caused an ambush of a thousand light Horsemen, to place themselues in a Forrest neere adioyning, of which companie *Frisol* was the leader, and to prouoke the *Norwayes* to the field, he sent out certaine men at Armes well prouided, who scouted heere and there, to the ende the *Allemaignes*, who had beene so hote the daie before, should be compassed with the secrete ambush, which fel out according to *Crenus* his expectation. For so soone as the *Allemaignes* saw the *Englishmen* so scattered, they dislodged themselues and followed them, with the whole Armie of the King of *Norway*, because they were perswaded that they tooke themselues to flight: but the *Gaulles* not dismayed with their comming, beeing but foure thousande Horse, and tenne thousand footemen, came valiantlie against the *Allemaigne* Ensignes, and then began a verie fierce encounter, but the *Englishmen* wise and pollitique, fearing misfortune, came on with their reregard towards the Forrest where the ambush lay, when the King of *Norway* ignoraunt of their intent, suddainlie made after them with the greatest part of his power, but they had a worsse welcome then they expected, for the *Englishmen* aduertised what they should doo, gathered vppon the Forrest side, charging their enemies with such a sharpe assault, as in lesse space then an howre, two thousand of them were slaine. *Frysol* perceiuing the time was come to show himselfe, calling his squadron togeather, cryed. Vpon them valiantly my freends, the spoyle is ours. So entred they pel mel among the *Allemaignes*, making such slaughter of them as was wonderful to behold, for albeit they thought not of this deceit, they were so ouerwearied with dalliance, as when they cam to the exploit they could doo nothing, but were slaine downe right, such valour shewed *Frysol* and his fresh supplie, forcing them to flight, and they following them, beeing glad to take the

Palmerin d'Oliva: Part I 257

Cittie of *Tomar* which was stronglie fortefied. Which when the King of *Norway* perceiued, he staied not long after them, because he sawe it was not best for him, and therefore fled after them for companie at the hard heeles, and got the Cittie in good time, els had they all perrished. Thus remained *Crenus* Maister of
5 the fielde, and following his successe, the next daie begirt the Cittie of *Tomar* with siedge, swearing neuer to depart thence, till hee sawe the Cittizens eyther through the Gates or the walles. Yet had this courage of his beene soone cooled, if *Frysol* like a good Captaine had not cherished vp his men, when *Crenus* at one saillie of the enemie lost two thousand men, and therefore saide. Why howe
10 nowe my louing Freendes and companions? wil you flye or faint at the hower of good fortune? desire you not to purchase the vertue so highlie esteemed? know you not that you deale with people halfe conquered, and altogeather dyscouraged? courage then my Brethren, courage, and let vs not exchange our reputation with their feare and faynting: you giue mee double strength good Freendes, if
15 but wyth good countenaunce, you will make them know, what cowardlie crauens they are. Follow me braue *Englishmen*, and this very daie will we giue them punishment, as their treason and rebellion hath well deserued. These words renewed eache ones courage meruailously, so that the Duke with a fresh supply beganne againe thus to animate them.[2] You knowe my good Freends, that although we
20 are but a handful in respect of them, what successe we haue alreadie had in our encounters, so that with greater ease may wee nowe conquere, weakening them so mightily as wee haue doone: let vs not dismay then, but witnes that the worst manne amongst vs, is more valiant and hardie in Armes, then the greatest Lord that is in their companie, eache man therefore cherrish his hope, and bearde
25 our enemies to the very teeth. The daie following, the enemie came foorth at a posterne Gate, and held the Dukes power very good playe, and the *Norwayes* very well appoynted with Bowes and arrowes, gauled the Horsse so cruelly, as they were glad to take their Campe, wherupon the Countie *Tolano* in hope of the daie, followed vpon them with his *Allemaigne* courtlaces, which *Frysol* perceiu-
30 ing, mette him in the face with his *English* squadron,[3] and giuing the spurres to his Horse, ran with his Launce quite thorow his bodie: whereat the *Allemaignes* much amazed, when they saw their Generall fall dead from his Horse, determined valiantly to reuenge his death, but *Frysol* and his men dealt with them so roundlie, as the stoutest was glad and faine to make them waie. Yet had they
35 hemde in *Frysol* with such a troupe, as if the Duke had not speedilie come with reskewe, they had taken him, and then began the sharpest bickering, for the Duke of *Gaule* and *Frysol* with their men so bestirred them, as the *Allemaignes* cleane discouraged, beganne to disorder themselues, and with the *Norwayes* fled to the Cittie so fast as they coulde, where *Frysol* and his men had entered, but
40 that the King of *Norway* not daring to come into the fielde, was there with men sufficient to resist his entrie. Thus remained the victory to the Duke of *Gaule*, by the braue pollicies of *Frysol* and his men, he beeing generally commended of the Armie: and thus retired the *Allemaignes* and *Norwayes* to their shame and

dishonor. After the retrait sounded by the King of *Norway*, hee sent to the Duke to demaunde truce for foure and twentie howres, that they might burye the dead, among whom was the Countie *Tolano*: which beeing graunted him, he caused the Counties bodie to bee embalmed, who by the counsell of his Lordes and Captaines, was sent home into his Country. The King and his company secretlie in the night embarqued themselues, to ioyne with the King of *Scots*, who expected his comming, and then did the Cittizens sende word to the Duke, that by the breake of daie they would yeelde the keyes of their Gates to him: whereuppon *Frysol* was Lieuetenant generall for the Duke of *Gaule*, and entred honorably the Cittie of *Tomar*, where the *Englishmen* rested themselues for two or three dayes, to recompence their paynes with profit and pleasure. The enemie was no sooner departed vnder sayle, but there arose such a terrible tempest, as the most part of their vessels perished in the Sea, and the other were so scattered, as they had lost the sight of one another: yet was some small number remayning with the King, as well of *Allemaignes* as his own Countreimen, so getting safe to shore in his kingdom, he determined a reuenge for his great ouerthrowe, but hee could not compasse his intent, as you shall reade heereafter.

Chapter XLVI.

Howe after the Prince Trineus, Palmerin and Ptolome, were arriued in England, they went to the Court, and what torments the Prince endured for his looue to the fayre Lady Agriola.

Trineus, *Palmerin* and *Ptolome*, beeing landed within foure dayes iourney of the Kinges Campe, which was prouided against the King of *Scots*, were aduertised, that the King stayed but the comming of the Duke of *Tintriel*, and then he meant to bid his enemie battaile, that had so boldlie presumed vpon part of his Realme. The garders of the porte where they landed, seeing they were strangers, woulde suffer them passe no further, till they knewe their names, whether they went, and what they came for. *Palmerin* answering on the behalfe of them all, said. Good freendes, we are *Grecian* Knightes, and trauaile strange Countries to seeke aduentures, and because we heard that your King menaceth warre, against his auncient and maleuolent enemie the King of *Scots*, wee come to offer our selues and our seruice to him, so please his Maiestie to accept it. This aunswere so well contented the Officers, as by their meanes they were conducted to the Court, where they were honorably entertained, and two daies togeather were there feasted with the King, in which time *Trineus* vnderstood, that the Queene and her Daughter, were aboue twentie miles[1] thence, whereupon the next morning they tooke their iourney thither, and by dinner time came where the Queene laie. But it fell out so happilie for *Trineus*, as before they came to the place where the Court aboade, they mette the Queene and her traine, who dailie went to a Chappell,[2] not a quarter of a mile from the Cittie, to heare diuine seruice, as she kept it for a continuall exercise, and with her was faire *Agriola* her Daughter. The Queene and all her Ladies alighted from their Palfrayes, they entred the Chappell, the Prince well regarding the Goddesse of his hart, who belike making her prayers more breefe then her Mother, came foorth with her wayting Ladies, to walke vnder a companie of greene Trees[3] neere adioyning. *Trineus* seeing her a creature so rare and excellent, made doubt in a matter of assuraunce, least he should bee surprised as *Acteon* was, when he found *Diana* bathing among her Nimphes.[4] He being thus caried away with meruailous conceit of her beautie, saluted not the Princesse as shee passed before him, nor heard *Palmerin* who reprooued him for omitting his courtesie: but wading further and further into this amorous furie,[5] spake so loude as he was easilie hearde, in this manner. O heauens, will you suffer the perfections of a Ladie so diuinelie accomplished, to be the cause of my vndeserued death? when may the time come for me, to let her vnderstand my desire to doo her seruice? or howe might she know the loyal affection I beare her? One of the Ladies of honor attending on the Princesse, reputing his wordes vnwise and ouer-bolde, answered. Why Sir Knight, where learned you so little courtship, as when the fairest in the Westerne world[6] passeth before you, you make no gentle gesture or salutation? I doubt that what is counted honestie and vertue among men of quallitie, with you is esteemed harsh and vnciuill, which makes me repute you more meete for the Kitchen, then to beare the honorable office and rich Armes of a Knight, as you doo. *Trineus* as it were awaked out of a traunce, saide. Ah sweete Ladie pardon me, for by my faith I can neither tell what you said, nor well where I am my selfe: for euen as you ended, I felt such a passion strike me to the very hart, as death will soone arrest me without remedie. The Ladie, who knewe not his meaning, checked him againe, thus. Were it not better then for you to be in the field, then heere in this foolish and vndiscreete pensiuenes? It is true Lady, (quoth the Prince) that at this time I haue shewed my selfe vnmannerlie, and a slender Courtier, yet is not the blame altogeather to be throwne on me, ignoraunt who the Lady was which you speake of: for wee are strange Knightes, and are come farre from this Countrey, with intent to aide and succour the King in his warres with our vttermost endeuours. Notwithstanding, because we haue with no more regard doone our duetie to your Mistresse, may it please you to entreate her on our behalfe, to pardon this offence: for satisfaction wherof, we wil goe serue the King her father in battell, where we doubt not so wel to behaue our selues, as shall deserue our pardon, if so be she will not at this instant so fauour vs. And I gladlie woulde, faire Ladie, that such seruice shoulde bee doone by her commaundement, for our strength and vertue by her perfections augmented, will attribute the honor to her that so graciously assisted vs, wherfore, so please you to make known our good intent towards her, we shall for such kindnes remain indebted to you. The Ladie tooke pleasure in hearing *Trineus*, especially perceiuing the zeale of him and his companions, to imploy theyr valour on the Kings behalfe, which caused her immediatlie doo this message to the Princesse, who at that instant (as a thing fatall to her) was wounded with loue: whereuppon she sent them answere by her Gouernesse, that shee entertained them as her Knights, and as her Seruants desired them to goe aide the King her Father, yet woulde shee not consent to pardon them, till the renowne of their exploites might shewe them to deserue it. *Trineus* tooke this answer for better aduantage then the Princesse thought on, accounting himselfe happy by such a good beginning, and therefore saide to the Ladie. I think my selfe (faire Ladie) one of the most fauoured by Fortune, hauing the meane to obey your Mistresse in her commaund, and hope to execute her charge in such sort, as I shall deserue the grace she dooth nowe denie me, yet with all humilitie on our behalfe, I intreate you to yeelde thankes for her princelie kindnes. The Ladie returning to *Agriola*, accomplished what *Trineus* desired her, wherupon she turned herselfe, and gaue them a countenaunce of fauour, which was answered by *Trineus*, *Palmerin* and *Ptolome*, with great reuerence, and the Princesse, (shewing herselfe not too statelie towardes the Knights) with her hand and gesture gaue a signe of her content, which was not a little welcome to *Trineus*. Then the Queene comming foorth of the Chappell, with *Agriola* and her traine mounted on horsebacke, taking their waie to the Courte againe: but when *Trineus* had lost the sight of them, wonderfull vexations began to assaile him, so that hee saide to *Palmerin*. Ah my good Freende, howe happie may that man account himselfe, whose

fortune honors him with the beauty of *Agriola*? Ah Sir *Palmerin*, I feele my self so exceedinglie tormented, as I doubt my death will be ineuitable. But tell me the trueth and dissemble not, how thinke you of my Mistresse? is shee not a Ladie more then diuine? In good faith my Lord, said *Palmerin*, what the Knight in
5 *Fraunce* told vs,[7] was but fables, in that she exceedeth report beyond all opinion: notwithstanding, it is necessary for you to nourish your hope, hauing thus spoken to her, and bewrayed your afflictions, not doubting but this good beginning of your enterprise, will cause the ende fal out to your content.[8] So rode on these three Knights, pleasing their humors with their seuerall iudgments of their
10 Ladies, yet *Palmerin* had seene such matter in *English Agriola*, as, but his plighted promise to *Polynarda*, was of force sufficient to change hys fancie. The next daie they arriued at the King of *Englands* Campe, where because they would not be known, they pitched their Tents behinde all the other: and soone after came the Duke of *Tintriel*, bringing with him a number of hardie men at Armes, so that
15 in short time the Kinges strength was such, as they exceeded their enemies in number. Heereupon the King assembled his counsell, and concluded, that the next daie they woulde goe seeke out the King of *Scots*, who in two encounters had the vpper hande, which made him so peremptorie, as he perswaded himselfe vtterly to confound the King of *England*: who raysing his power, followed so dil-
20 ligentlie, as the third daie after, he encamped within halfe a mile of his enemie, that had besieged the Towne of *Corfania*, and had brought it readie to yeeld, but that the King preuented it by the strength he brought.

Chapter XLVII.
Of the cruell battayle, betweene the King of Englande and the King of Scots.

When the King of *Scots* vnderstoode the comming of the King of *England*, and that in all hast he would bid him battaile, he wold no longer busie himselfe in besiedging *Corfania*, but retired a litle for his better aduantage, conferring with his Capitaines about their present affaires, concluding to offer the ennemie no skirmishes, because thereby they would know their intent: notwithstanding he gaue order to prepare for battaile, because he knewe the King of *England* came for no other purpose. The *Englishmen* not suffering the *Scots* to haue anie leysure to fortefie themselues, were by the King the next morning commaunded in array, and all winges and squadrons appointed, the Duke of *Tintriel* was made leader of the auauntgarde, wherein likewise were *Trineus*, *Palmerin* and *Ptolome*, and to the Dukes Brother was committed the charge of the arrieregarde, and beeing all ready to martch on, the King himselfe beganne this Oration. I thinke my Freendes that no one of you, but sufficientlie is acquainted in what respect we continue this warre, namelie, to defend the honor and reputation of our Realme, and to saue the liues of you, your wiues and children, and your goods, which the enemie wold violently spoile and take from you, intending to throwe perpetuall bondage and slauerye on your necks. Will you not then defende your liberties? will you not maintaine your aunciente renowne, which is, to bee Lords and commaunders of the *Scots*? assure your selues, that howe strong soeuer our enemie be, I hope with the aide of God, your vndaunted courages, and the right of our cause, to make a noble and victorious conquest. For I knowe, that our enemie hath not one man in his Armie, endued with such an intire hart and magnanimious courage, as you are, nor that valueth his title of honor with his life, as you doo: and therefore if we martch on valiantlie, continuing resolute and confident togeather, euery man laboring for his Prince, Countrey, freende and fellow, and God for vs all, your forwardnes will make them fearefull, and your verie countenances enough to conquere.[1] Euery manne then bee cheerefull, with a desire to vanquish, and heere I vowe to you on the worde of a King, that if Fortune stande so well with vs, as to winne the daie, neuer shall the *Scots* heereafter dare to lift vp themselues against vs. Thus did the King of *England* animate his men, and so martched on in good araie to the sight of their enemies, who by this time hadde ranged themselues for battaile, their auauntgarde conducted by the Marques of *Monthel*, the King of *Scots* himselfe in the maine battaile, and the arrieregarde led by the King of the Isle *Magdalen*: and as the King of *England* had encouraged his Souldiers, so began the King of *Scots* to harten his men in this manner. The time is nowe come (loyal Subiects and deere Freendes) that the pride of the *English* must bee abated by the vertue and valoure of the *Scots*, so that if you set before your eyes the occasion calling vs to the fielde, there is no one of you but will blame his predecessor, for staying so long time to recouer, what by true patrimonie belonged to them, and by the Kings of *Englande*,

(tirannous vsurpers) againste all right violentlye taken from our Auncestors. Will you not then recouer your losse, and reenter on those possessions, from which your Fathers (against all reason) were expulsed? Duetie doth chalenge it at your handes, beeing the good not onely for your selues, but for your children and suc-
5 cessors. Would you then loose so good oportunitie, to reestablish things so lost? Are your harts more timorous then your enemies? are your mindes made of worse mettall then theirs? No no, wel am I assured that the least among you, is of higher vertue and account then the best in their companie. If it hath beene their custome, (as they themselues vaunt) to tryumphe ouer vs, let vs learne them to
10 confesse with patience, that they haue no such right or custome to vanquish,[2] as in three skirmishes alreadie we haue sufficiently made knowne, with what fortune and vnconquerable spirits you entertained your enemies. Dismay no more nowe (my good Freendes) then you haue doone, let eache mans sworde make his entraunce amidst his foes, and fauour one anothers life, so shall sweete successe
15 returne you with victory.[3] The King hauing ended, they discerned the *English* power eager to encounter, and so the Armies meeting, began a dreadfull and dangerous battaile. There might you heare the Drummes thunder, the Trompets sounde, the Clarions ring, the Phifes warble, Launces shyuered, Knights dismounted, Footmen scattered, heads defended, armes and bodies wounded, some
20 crying, other dying, a matter more then lamentable to beholde, and so long continued this cruell and bloodie conflict, as the most part of the auauntgarde[4] were slaine, sore wounded, or taken prisoners. Which when the King of *Scots* perceiued, beeing a Prince so hardie and valiant as might bee, commaunded the maine battaile to giue the charge, in middest whereof he was in person: wheruppon, the
25 fight beganne again much more fierce then before, so that you might haue heard the Horsses storme, the Armour clatter, and on euery side behelde good and venturous Knights giue vppe their liues. At this furious onset, *Palmerin* seeing the *Scots* to retire for aduantage, cryed to the King of *England*. Why how now my Lord? doo you forget your selfe? why doo you not folow on with your maine bat-
30 tell, seeing the enemie playes vpon aduantage? cheerefully let vs vpon them for the daie will be ours. The King seeing that *Palmerins* counsel was verie expedient, commaunded his men to martch on valiantlie, which they did with such courage, as not one of them but was thorowlie busied. *Palmerin* fearing least *Trineus* would be ouer venturous, because the yong Prince was meruailous for-
35 ward, desired him not to runne so farre into danger, but keepe by him, to the ende the one might succour the other, if necessitie required. With these words he ranne vpon the *Scots* like an angry Lyon,[5] and no man durst withstand him, they sawe him make such slaughter: the King of *England* following him at an inche, deliuering true testimonie of his inuincible hart. On the other side, *Trineus* met
40 with the Kinges Brother of the Isle *Magdalen*, piercing his Launce quite through his bodie, so that he fel deade among his owne Souldiers: and *Ptolome* all this whyle was not idle, but where ere he came, he laid his enemie at his feete, so that the *Scots* wondered at the behauiour of these three Knights. When the King of

the Isle *Magdalen* vnderstood the death of his Brother, incensed with vnquenchable anger, ran fiercelie among the *English*, till hee came where *Trineus, Palmerin* and *Ptolome* were, one of his Knights shewing the King the man that slew his Brother, whereupon he making towards *Trineus*, lifted vppe hys Sword, and thought to haue slaine him: but *Palmerin* stepping beetweene them, said. To me Captaine, to me, and so the King and he encountered togeather so terribly, as *Palmerin* was wounded in two or three places, for which hee made such recompence to the King, as fastening his Sword on his Helmet, cleft his head in twayne, that doone he fell deade to the grounde. The sight heereof enflamed the *Scots* with such rage, as like mad men they ranne cutting and killing among the *English*, as wel to reuenge the King of the Isle *Magdalens* death, as to defend their own King whose danger they feared. In this hote skirmish the Kings of *England* and *Scots* met togeather, who charged each other with such forcible strokes, as the King of *England* was vnhorssed and sore wounded: but *Trineus* beeing at hand, seeing his deere freendes Father in such perrill, buckled with the King of *Scots* so valiantlie, as he gaue him many a cruell wounde, and had not his men made hast to conuay him through the throng, he had beene slaine by *Trineus*, so was the King of *England* mounted againe, and reuenged hys foyle on his enemie with meruailous valour. There tryumphed the three *Grecian* Knights with inexplicable honor, the *Englishmen* making such hauocke among the *Scots*, as vtterly dispayring, they fled, one part to a Forrest neere at hande, and the other towardes the Sea to their Shyps, the King getting into one of them to saue his life, by the meanes of one of his Knights, that lent him a good Iennet of *Spayne* to escape away withall. And so sayled thence the King with greater shame, then did the Emperor *Antonius* from *Octauius Caesar*,[6] leauing his men fiercely pursued by the *English*, who terrefied them in such sort, as many of the poore *Scots* chose rather to run into the Sea and drowne themselues, then to fall into the handes[7] of their conquering enemies.

Chapter XLVIII.
Of the retrait of the King of Englands Armie, and the honor he did to the three strange Knights.

After the King of *Englande* was maister of the field, he caused the retrait to be sounded, and hys men called togeather, commaunding likewise that search shoulde bee made through the fielde, to succour such as were sore wounded, and to burie the deade, least the ayre should be infected: wherupon the *Englishmen* tooke the spoile of their enemies, cheefely their bag and bagage which they had left behind them. In meane while the King withdrew himself into his Tent, where remembring the great seruice of the three strange Knights, hee commaunded his Nephewe *Cerides* to seeke them immediatlie, who founde them in a *Scottish* Tent binding vppe their woundes, and beeing not a little glad of his good fortune, hee came to *Palmerin*, saying. Gentlemen, the King my Vncle earnestlie desireth you to come to him, because hee will neither enter the Towne, nor vnarme himselfe, til he heare some tidings of you. Seeing it pleaseth him, said *Palmerin*, to commaund, we humblie obey, wherefore we pray you Sir to returne his Maiestie our dutifull thanks, and dilligent attendance. After *Cerides* was departed, they resolued among themselues (at the earnest request of *Trineus*) that *Palmerin* shoulde bee the cheefest among them, and him they woulde honor as their Lorde, because the Prince feared to be known if such account shoulde bee made of him: so went they presentlie to the Kings Tent, where they were no sooner entered, but the King (albeit he was sore wounded) arose from his Chaire, and embraced them louingly one after another, not suffering them to kneele before him, but honorably thus spake to them. Woorthie Gentlemen, howe welcome you are I cannot expresse, for I account my selfe so highlie beholding to you, as the Realme of *England* had sustained this daie great foyle, but by your fortunate valour: think then woorthie Lords, wherein *England* may recompence you, and on my worde it shall not be denied, in meane while I praie you let me haue your companie, because I will see your hurts carefully attended. The Knights with great reuerence accepted the Kings noble offer, and were conducted into a faire Tent next the Kinges, where the Chirurgions with great dilligence dressed their wounds, and afterward they came and supped with the King.[1] And because the King intended on the morrow to goe refresh himselfe at the Towne of *Corfania*, which before had beene cruellie besiedged by the *Scots*, to giue God thanks for his happie victorie, a famous Sermon was made before him by the Archbishop of *Canterburie*:[2] to whom likewise he gaue order for enterring such as had beene slaine of account, and in that place for memorie of his good fortune, hee caused a goodlie Monasterie to be builded, and dispatched a Poste presently to aduertise the Queene of his good successe. Now was his Maiestie verie desirous to know the three strange Knights, that had so valiantlie assisted him, especiallie the man that saued his life: whereupon the next morning he went to see them, demaunding howe they fared, for (quoth he) we will nowe set forwarde to *Corfania*, where wee will make you better entertainement then we can heere in the field. Then mounted they all on horsebacke, and rode to *Corfania*, where the King remained till he and his Knights were better recouered, and where the King made the Duke of *Tintriel* high Marshall of *England*, committing to his charge sixe thousand men, commaunding him to chase all the *Scots* foorth of his Kingdome, wheresoeuer he could find them, and to seaze to his highnes vse the Townes and Castelles, which they before had in vse: which the Duke executed with such expedition, as hee left not a *Scot* in anie Village or Hamlett, placing faithfull Officers for the King in euerie iurisdiction. During these labours of the Duke, the King euery daie visited these three Knights, and finding *Palmerin* at a time conuenient, he requested to knowe of whence hee was, and the names of his companions. Let me intreate you (quoth hee) not to hide your selues from me, because I shall not be in quiet till I know, that I may remunerate your deserts according to your persons. *Palmerin*, who feared to bee discouered, coulde not readilie deuise what aunswere to make, yet at length in great humilitie, thus said. We would desire your Maiestie, that it might stande with your good liking, at this time to excuse the knowledge of our present affaires, as also what wee are: yet thus farre will I resolue your highnes, that we are all Gentlemen of *Greece*, nourished in the Court of the King of *Macedon*, who in seeking strange aduentures, haue trauailed manie prouinces, and nowe at length came into your Kingdome, wel stored at this time with Knights errant, and gouerned (as wee well perceiue) by a King so gracious, as to such persons alloweth honor and good affection, as no King where we yet haue come, doth the like. For this cause my Lord, as also vnderstanding that the King of *Scots* menaced warre against you, came we into your Countrey, to serue you in all obeysaunce, as the verie simplest among your Souldiers. Trust me (said the King) I haue wel noted your seruice, and a man might bee deceiued in expecting better assistaunce, for which I rest yours in ought I may while I liue: but if you would name your selues, then should I knowe to whom I were indebted, as also that my Subiects might honor you accordinglie.[3] That (quoth *Palmerin*) will neither profit or preiudice your Maiestie,[4] let suffise then I beseeche you, the vnfeigned good will and seruice we owe to your highnes. The King seeing hee coulde not gette what he would, changed his talke, saying. Was it you Sir, that on the daie of battell was armed all in blacke? Yea my Lord, said *Palmerin*, and this Knight (pointing to *Trineus*) is my Brother, who sheelded you from daunger against the King of *Scots*. Ah deere Freends, quoth the King, this made me so importunate, and may it like you to stay in my Courte, I will regard you according to your especiall deseruings, as the onelie Knights of the worlde in my fauour, yeelding thankes to heauen, for the good I haue receiued by your meanes. Humblie did the three Knights regratiate the King, promising for a while to soiourne with him.

Chapter xlix.

How the Queene of England was aduertised of the victorie against the King of Scots, and the ouerthrowe of his whole Armie.

After the King of *Englande* had sent tidinges to the Queene of his good fortune, and the honour he intended to the three Knights of *Greece*: the Messenger was so speedie, as the seconde daie following, he arriued at the Cittie wher the Queene kept her Court, and presented her the Letters from the King her Husbande, reciting the whole manner of the battell, with the rare exployts of the three *Grecian* Knights, and how one of them preserued the Kings life: omitting nothing that was needfull to be reported, as how the King intended to come with the three Knights in great royaltie to *London*, and therfore she should prouide equall entertainment. The Queene highlie contented with these newes, demanded of the Messenger, if hee knewe the three Knightes that gaue such assistance to the King. No indeede Madame, answered the Messenger, neither did I see them, but at the time I was dispatched with my message. *Agriola*, finding in herselfe the puissaunce of the little God that made looue,[1] suddainlie suspected, that these Knights were they which shee sawe at the Chappell, and therefore saide. I pray thee tell mee my Freend, what Armes beare the Knights? One of them Madame (quoth he) the verie best Knight in the worlde, is in Greene Armour, and that is he that saued the King your fathers life, when the King of *Scots* had neere slaine him, but he remounted my Lord,[2] giuing his enemy such a dangerous wound with his Launce, as it was greatlie doubted he had kild him, he lost so much blood, and this was one of the principall occasions of our victorie. This Knights companion in Blacke Armour, behaued himselfe with wonderfull chiualrie, for as a Lion makes hauock in a heard of Cattell, so did he cut, slashe and mangle the *Scots*, as the very hardiest durst not abide before him. The third is in Black Armor, sparckled all ouer with white Roses, a Knight of no lesse courage then his companions, and one that fought for *England* with incredible prowesse. Let me die, said *Agriola* to the Queene, if these be not the Knightes that past by this Cittie, when we went to the Chappell to performe our exercise: and therwithall she rehearsed what speech her Gouernesse had with them, and what she commaunded them.[3] In sooth Daughter, quoth the Queene, your Gouernesse and you may well bee blamed, for the slender account you made of them: I praye you therefore when they returne, let your former faulte be sufficientlie recompenced. That shall I not fayle to doo, said *Agriola*. So the Queene honorablie rewarded the Messenger, sending him backe with answer, that the Kings charge should be effectuallie executed. The King aduertised of the Queenes replie, set forwarde with the Knightes of *Greece* and his traine to the Courte, and by the way, remembring the power sent by the Emperour of *Allemaigne* to the King of *Norway*, he said to *Palmerin*. I cannot sufficientlie maruaile gentle Knight, why the Emperor should declare himselfe mine enemie, and giue assistance to the King of *Norway* against mee, considering I neuer did any thing might deserue his displeasure: but I sweare by the faith of a king, that I will reuenge my wrong, and let him assure himselfe, that while I haue one foote of ground, or a dozen of my Soldiers to helpe me, I will neuer haue peace with him: to mollest me so within mine owne dominions, by God, my Freends, I cannot forget it. These words greatlie displeased *Trineus*, but especiallie *Palmerin*, who aunswered. In my opinion my Lord, the Emperor did but reason, and as duetie bounde him, in respect he could not honestly refuse to ayde the King of *Norway* his Cozin, and heereof I can assure you, in that I haue sometime beene in his Court, that he is one of the wysest and best gouerned Princes that euer I hearde of. Wherefore, bee it spoken vnder correction, your Maiestie should forget this light offence, and consider if the like had beene towards you, you woulde haue doone no lesse. When the King hearde him so support the Emperors cause, he presently iudged him to be of his Courte, and therefore said. Are you he Sir, that wunne such honor and renowne in *Fraunce*, at the Combat maintained by the Prince *Lewes* for the loue of his Ladie?[4] If you be so, I pray you doo not denie it, for I shall henceforth thinke my Court most happy, to harbour the most excellent among all Knights: and I promise you I am so iealous of mine owne conceite, as you can hardly perswade me otherwise, such experience haue I made of your bounty and vertue. *Palmerin* blushinge at these wordes, and doubting he should nowe be certainlie knowne, answered. Wee humblie intreated your Maiestie heeretofore, and so we doo nowe againe, that you would not enquire whence we are: suffiseth your highnes, that wee are his humble Seruants, in any thing that shall like him to commaunde vs. The King this hearing, repented hymselfe that he had beene so importunate, for hee feared leaste his speeches would make them forsake his company, wherfore by this time beeing come neere his Pallace, hee sayde. What I haue said Gentlemen, I hope shall not offend you,[5] in my excuse admit my earnest desire to know you. By and by ouertooke them the Duke of *Tintriel*, who went to restore to the Crowne (as you haue hearde) what the *Scots* vsurped, and he aduertised the King, that the Queene and her Ladies were rydden to a Castell foure myles[6] from *London*, to sollace themselues, whereupon the King resolued to ryde thither: whereof the Prince *Trineus* was not sorrie, such was his desire to see his faire Freende, whose loue still crossed him with so manie passions, as hee seemed a man of another worlde,[7] and did not his woundes serue somewhat to couer his disease, hardlie could he haue founde anie shyft to conceale it so closelie, wherefore hee began with *Palmerin*, thus. You knowe my chosen Freende, that the hope of my loue made me leaue my Fathers Court, and to preuent my meaning consists onelie in you, nowe in respect of my forcible captiuity, beeing vnprouided of strength, sence, or anie meane, to discouer my greefe to her who only can help mee: I intreate you by the inuiolable league of our amitie, that when you chaunce to speake with the Goddesse of my lyfe,[8] my paynes and anguishes may serue for my salutations, and imparting to her the extreamitie of my sorrowes, shee may perceiue in what estate I am, and what neede I haue of her gracious pittie. These wordes were deliuered wyth such sighes and teares, as *Palmerin* was amazed therat, albeit he knewe howe heauie the burthen was, and howe it exceeded patience in suffering, comparing his absence from his Mistresse *Polynarda* to be as insupportable, as the presence of *Agriola* (not daring to speake to her) was to *Trineus*, whereupon he answered. My Lord, repose your truste in this matter on mee, which I doubt not to handle in such sorte, as you shall haue no cause to bee *mal content*, or the Princesse any reason to be ingratefull. But what thinke you if my Dwarffe did carrie this message? in my opinion (through the whole world) you could not finde a more fitte fellow, such is his subtiltie and present inuention, as hee wyll prooue the onely string to your bowe.[9] Alas said the Prince, I care not who were imployed heerein, so I were sure of comfort. Then was the Dwarffe called, to whom *Palmerin* in this sort began. It is well knowne to thee *Vrbanillo*, with what good will I would doo any seruice I could to my Lord *Trineus*, as well for the incomparable kindnes I haue receiued of my Ladie hys Sister, as for the affinitie I hope shall one daie be betweene vs, by his meanes. So often haue I made experience of thy loyall seruice and fidelitie, in my cheefest and very neerest affayres, as well may I impart to thee the secrets of my noble companion, perswading my selfe of thy suretie and secrecie. It now remaines that thou pleasure the Prince *Trineus*, in breaking his loue to the Princesse *Agriola*, as thou diddest for me to my Mistresse *Polynarda*:[10] but aboue all thinges haue regard, that thou bewray not of whence or what we are,[11] yet maist thou assure her, that the Prince is one of the greatest Lords in *Europe*. My Lord, quoth the Dwarffe, I neuer was yet disobedient to you in all my time, and verie lothe were I nowe to begin: but because I am such a little writhen fellowe, you make me your Broker in these perillous loue matters. Notwithstanding, I will doo it though I died for it, esteeming my life well bestowed to pleasure such Princes. There can no inconuenience arise heereby to thee, quoth *Palmerin*, but profit euerie waie: be not enemie then to thine owne good. That will I neuer saide the Dwarffe, and well might the Ladie be iudged vnprouided of reason, and verie farre from vnderstanding, if she make refusall of the Princes honorable offer, the King himselfe if he knewe it woulde imagine his daies blessed, the issue then of this enterprise can not but sort to good. The Dwarffes words pleased so well *Trineus*, as he tooke him in his armes, saying. I commende my selfe and my happines to thee. Let me alone, quoth *Vrbanillo*, if I bring you not hearbes that shall coole this hote feuer, then let mee neuer be counted for a tall man: so went he about it, as you shall vnderstand heereafter.

Chapter L.
Howe the King of Englande went to the Castell to the Queene and her Ladies, and of the honourable entertainment made to the three strange Knights.

Newes beeing brought to the Queene, that the King was not far off, shee sent a verye honourable traine to meete him, and with them his Son the yong Prince *Frederick*, tenne yeeres olde, but beautifull and of such perfection, as promised great hope in time to come. Hee hauing made reuerence to his Father and the other Princes, demaunded for the strange Knights, and saluting them with such kindnes as was rare in a Childe, hee rode between *Trineus* and *Palmerin*, giuing them harty thanks for their freendlie succour to his Father, without which, said he, as the Queene my Mother tolde me, hee had dyed, and we all beene distressed. By this time they were come to the Castell, all the waie so thicke pestred with people, as there was no roome to stirre among them, euery one crying. Happie be the Knights that foyled our enemies. So entring the Castell, in the vttermost Courte they mett the Queene and her Ladies, among whom faire *Agriola* shyned, as beautifull *Venus* among the other starres,[1] wherewith the Prince of *Allemaigne* was so nipt in the head, as an offendour with his guilt before a Iudge,[2] so that not regarding what yong *Frederick*, or the other Lordes courteouslie said to him, he was readie to fall beside his horse with ouermuch gazing, but *Palmerin* suddainlie twitching him softlie, said. Fie my Lorde, what meane you to forget your selfe thus? see you not her that is ordeined yours, and wyll you not tryumphe in your happie sight, but sitte as one vtterlie discouraged?[3] For shame let passe this pusillanimitie, and with cheereful countenaunce goe giue her the good morow. The Prince did so, but with such timerous conceits, as hauing saluted the Mother, hee durst not speake to the Daughter: who imagining the best, and that bashfull reuerence did so with-holde him, she came to him in this manner. Are not you Sir the Knight in the Greene Armor, that not long since promised one of my Ladies to ayde my Father in his warres? I am faire Princesse, quoth hee, and what I haue doone, was at your commaundement, the vertue whereof gaue me such strength, as some of the *Scots* haue felt to their cost: but had I gone vnprouided of such fauor,[4] I am perswaded I could neuer haue returned aliue. It now remaines, sweete Lady, that according to the request I then made by your Ladie, it woulde please you to remitt his offence, who deserued the sharpest punishment can bee deuised, for not honoring that Princesse, which carries the Palme from all Ladies liuing.[5] In trueth my Lorde, sayde the Princesse, not onelie is your fault to bee forgiuen, if it could be named a fault, but also ought I to recompence you to my vttermost power, seeing by your meanes my father in safetie, and the Realme of *England* deliuered from the tirannous seruitude of the *Scots*: wherefore you may assure your selfe, that if I can stande you in anie stedde towards the King my Father, you shall commaunde mee to my vttermost. The Prince returned her a thousand thankes, and saide.

Beleeue me Madame, the very least title of your good will, is recompence to me more then sufficient, and would prouoke such affection in me towards your seruice, as you coulde not commaunde the thing, but I shoulde with duetifull willingnes performe it, as I doubt not but better occasions shall make manifest vnto you. Then entred they the great Hall, where such a sumptuous banquet was prouided, as will aske more time to report then leysure wil admit.⁶ Likewise heere to set downe the wonderfull passions of the amorous Prince *Trineus*, in regarde of a Ladie so exceeding in perfections, surpasseth my capacitie: but he that is seated opposite to so faire a creature, and loues so earnestlie as *Trineus*, yet dare not speake least he should be spyed, maie iudge of that which I cannot vtter. But seeing the libertie of speeche was denied, the speedie eye posted between them with sweete conueyances,⁷ and still must shee countenaunce the stranger Knightes, till fearing to be taken tardie, she closelie conferred with the Princesse *Eufemia*, daughter to the Duke of *Norgalles*, saying. What thinke you Cozin of these strangers? are they not the seemeliest personages that euer you sawe, both in fauour, countenaunce, good grace and hardines? I am of the opinion, that although they report themselues but as simple Knights errant, they be doubtlesse great Lordes, discended of noble and princelie parentage: as one may easilie gather by their ciuill and vertuous behauiour, which is euermore the witnes of true nobilitie. These words caused *Eufemia* to marke wel *Trineus* as her Cozin *Agriola* did, which hee perceiuing, and iudging that they talked of him, his alterations were so sensible as they might be easilie discerned: for the more they eied him, the greater was his torment, till the Table beeing wythdrawne, he had some ease in opening his mind to *Palmerin*, whose comfortable wordes were as good to him as restoratiues. *Agriola* on the otherside escaped not free, for her ease was no greater when she arose, then when she satte down, and that must be little, hauing so daintie a dish before her to fill her stomacke.⁸

The next morning, the King and the Ladies mounted on horsebacke, setting towards *London*, and God knowes the Prince was not farre behinde them, liuing onelie by the regard of her, with whose rare beautie hee coulde neuer satisfie his eyes.⁹ And as they rode thorowe a Forrest, the King seeing the Trees so greene and delightful, and because the heate of the daie hindered their trauaile, hee caused his Pauillions and Tents to bee there presentlie pitched, and intended to dine there vnder the coole Trees. Dinner beeing ended, he would needes goe course the Hare, wasting the afternoone in that pastime, and on the next daie, rode to chase a Hart which was taken in the toyles, and therwithall a huge wilde Bore, the mightiest that euer was seene, hauing wounded him in so manie places, as the Dogs and Bloodhoundes might easilie tracke him. Afterwarde they roused a fallowe Deere, when the Huntsmen made the woods ring so brauelie with winding their Hornes, and the Greyhoundes pursued the course so speedilie: as *Palamedes* chase was not comparable to this, till in the ende the Deere was fallen.¹⁰ These pleasures finished, the King with his companie returned to his Tents, shewing to the Queene and her Ladies the fruites of their pastime, saying. I promise you Madame, I thinke these *Grecian* Knightes excell in euery thing, for as in chiualrie, so this daie haue they shewed themselues excellent woodmen, as none in our trayne may compare with them. By this time the Tables were couered for Supper, all which time was spent in discoursing of their sports: till the good night giuen on al sides, the three Knights withdrewe themselues into their Tent. All these pleasures made not *Vrbanillo* forgetfull of his Maisters charge, wherefore practising howe to accomplish it effectuallie, he founde meanes to come acquainted with the Ladies attending on the Princesse, and in respect he attended on the Knights of *Greece*, he was licensed the oftener in to theyr companie. The next morning the King and the Knights walking into the woods, the Dwarffe watching time to deliuer his message, made so manie walkes and returnes before the Princesse Pauillion, as at last she espyed him, and calling him to her, said. I pray thee my Freend, by the faith thou bearest thy Maister, tell mee the trueth of a matter I shall aske thee. Madame, quoth the Dwarffe vpon his knee, commaund what you please, for there is nothing (my Maisters preiudice excepted) but I will truelie tell you. Which of the three, said the Princesse, is thy Maister? My Maister (quoth the Dwarffe) hath not his second in al perfections, he it is that was in the blacke Armour, who in the battaile for your Father did so manie wonderfull exploits, as farre exceedeth the fabulous reports of Sir *Gawen*, or *Launcelot du Lake*.[11] In sooth, quoth she, so haue I hearde, and beside thy duetie reserued to thy Maister, I see thou canst sette him foorth for a most hardie Knight: but tell mee of whence he is? what are his companions? and why do they make it so daintie to be knowne? Heerein Madame, saide he, I cannot with my duetie answere you, for I am restrayned by a former promise, not to reueale the least matter that may be hurtfull to them. Neuerthelesse, in regard of the reuerent good will they beare you, and that I would not haue you offended with such an abiect creature as I am, I would gladlie tell you some thing to your content, so you will promise me on your princelie worde, that what I reueale shall neuer be discouered by you. Perswade thy selfe thereof, said the Princesse, and looke what thou saist, by mine honor, shal neuer turne to thy after harme. Then know faire Madam, (quoth he) that the Greene Knight is of the most noble and illustrious house in *Europe*, loouing a Ladie as his proper life, for whom he hath left his Country, Parents and freends, to come and doo her seruice. The blacke Knight, as I haue alreadie tolde you, is my Maister, and further then this I may not tell you. What am I the neerer my desire, quoth shee, by this aunswere? either thou shouldest haue said nothing, or els thorowlie satisfied mee, for nowe I cannot be quieted, tell[12] thou tell me what Ladie it is, that the greene Knight loues so deerelie: let me not make so many intreaties, for I promise to thee againe, by the faith of a Princesse, that neuer shall anie creature know it by my meanes. You vrge me so farre, quoth the Dwarffe, and haue made mee such great promises, as I am constrayned (beyonde the charge giuen by my Maister) to acquaint you with the trueth, in respect, the fault wil be greater in you to make refusal, then in yeelding. Resolue your selfe therefore good Madame, that the braue greene Knight, so rich in Armes, but

Palmerin d'Oliva: Part I

more in minde, is the Prince *Trineus*, Sonne to the Emperour of *Allemaigne*, so passionate in loue, and so depriued of liberty, by deuoute seruice to your excellent bountie: as against both duetie and nature, he hath deceiued his Father, feigning to come ayde his Kinsman the King of *Norway*, where contrariwise, he hath shewed himselfe his mortall enemie. And to no other ende hath he thus offended both Father and Cozin, then to make known his long and labourous desires, to make you Lady and Mistresse of him and his: and such is his feare to be refused, as he endures more torments, then the martired body of poore *Prometheus*.[13] Bee not then the cause sweet Ladie, that a Prince so famous, and a Knight so gentle, shall buy his great good seruice to your Father and Countrey, yea the most loyal loue he beares to you, with vntimelie, vnfortunate, and cruell death. Thinke wyth your selfe, is it not the highest among all honours, to be Wife to such a Lord, and Empresse (in time) of renowned *Allemaigne*? Is it not perpetuall report, to be Lady and commaundresse of the principall parte of *Europe*? Let not him beare recorde that a bodie so adorned, and countenaunce so milde and gracious, can entertaine tirannie or crueltie: yea Madam such crueltie, as if you receiue him not into your fauourable conceit, you shall procure the death of the truest Knight in loue, that euer liued. The blacke Knight is the renowned *Palmerin d'Oliua*, the wonder of the world for valour, conquering in *Fraunce* the Duke of *Sauoy*, in maintenaunce of hys Ladies beautie, fayre without compare: conforming hys Sheelde and Armour equall to his mourning thoughts, for his absence from her that tryumphes in his loue. The third Knight, so adorned with white Roses,[14] is called *Ptolome*, looued by a Ladie well woorthy of him. It now remaineth fayre Princesse, that you make the Prince *Trineus* equall with them in felicitie, for you haue the maydenhead of hys loue, which with honor you may entertaine in your chaste thoughtes.[15] Thus haue I acquainted you with such a secrete, as no creature but your selfe coulde haue got of mee, and the danger to fall into your misconceit, hath made mee such a blab: leauing al you haue heard to your gracious construction. *Agriola*, meetlie farre enough in loue before, but now vtterly denyed of longer libertie, hearing the wordes of *Vrbanillo*, was surprised with such a strange alteration, as a long time she was driuen to silence, not able to vtter the secrete conceits of her minde, yet at length (to shadowe her suddaine change from the Dwarffe) shee sayde. Ah my Freende, thou acquaintest me with matter altogeather incredible, is it possible that *Trineus* Sonne to the Emperor of *Allemaigne*, would venture into this Court, considering the mortall enmitie betweene our Fathers? Trust me my Freende I cannot credite thee. I renounce mine own soule said the Dwarffe, if it be not as I haue told you, then iudge Madame what acceptaunce shoulde be made of his seruice, when loue to you exceedeth nature: may it not bee termed loue surpassing all other, either registred in antiquities, or present memorie? If it shoulde be, quoth she, as thou sayest, it is beyonde my power to returne condigne recompence, yet (in respect of thy secrecie) I dare assure thee, mine own opinion of him hath so ouer-maistred me, as in honorable modestie he may commaund, and I am not so ill nurtured to disagree. But if eyther by my words thou hast gathered, or by any chaunge of countenaunce perceiued, the suddaine yeelding of a flexible nature: interprete it in this good sort, that Princes afflictions make eache other melt, as framed of one mettall, which I charge thee conceale from him, as thou regardest my word and hys safetie.[16] Pardon me Madame, quoth the Dwarffe, it standeth not with my allegeaunce to obey you heerein, what a villaine might I bee accounted, and vnwoorthy the name of a faithfull seruaunt if I shoulde hyde these happy tydings from him, to ease those torments that euery howre threaten his death? Yea Madame, did my Maister but think I would so abuse him, well deserued I to be torne in peeces. Well quoth shee, if thou findest time conuenient, tel him, but no other I charge thee on thy life: and withall certifie him, that I woulde not for my Fathers crowne he should be knowne. Feare you not good Madame, said the Dwarffe, they are alreadie so well aduised, as none but your selfe can anie waie endaunger them. It suffiseth that the Prince vnderstande your pleasure, which I will impart to him when the King is returned: so kissing her hande hee departed, leauing her so highlie contented, in assuraunce of the loyall loue of *Trineus*, as she neuer determined anie other Husband, yet would she not disclose her mind, no not[17] to *Eufemia* her secrete companion, thinking herselfe too much bewrayed, because the Dwarffe knewe it. Soone after the Queene sent for her, to walke in the coole shaddowe of the Trees, where not long they staied before the King returned, who reported what pastime they had all that morning. The Knightes hauing saluted the Queene and her Ladies, *Trineus* saluting the Princesse *Agriola*, was so transported as hee scant knewe where he was, the Princesse likewise fixed such a stedfast eye on him, as wounded both him and her selfe togeather, her complexion so aptlie deciphering her sicknesse, as the Prince perceiuing it, said to himselfe. Ah looue, hast thou wrought so happilie for mee, as my Ladie knowes my secrete afflictions? shall I be so fortunate, as she wil take remorse on my passions? sweete hope perswades mee so, for the often change of her diuine countenance, telles me there is some mercie in working. The King and Queene departing into their Pauillion, *Trineus* and *Palmerin* did the like into theirs, the Prince taking *Vrbanillo* aside, demaunded if he had anie good newes for him. If you will graunt mee one thing, said the Dwarffe, I will tell you such tydings as cannot but content you. Demaunde what thou wilt, quoth *Trineus*, and by the faith of a Prince, thou shalt not bee denied. Then beganne he the whole discourse he had with the Princesse, and what deuotion shee had for the recouery of his health. Iudge you in what rare humour the Prince nowe felt himselfe, without question he imagined himselfe in a more beautiful paradise, then euer was inuented by *Epicurus* himselfe,[18] and embracing the Dwarffe he saide. Ah my good freend, what wilt thou that I giue thee? tel mee what thou demaundest? thou hast my whole life so much at thy commaund as thou maist liberally share out thine owne recompence, but seeing the beginning is so good, no doubt much better remaineth behind.[19] Why my Lord, quoth the Dwarffe, you know I was borne to doo you seruice, commaund what you please and I will accomplish it. Then shalt thou,

Palmerin d'Oliva: Part I

said the Prince, returne to my Mistresse againe, and kissing her hande, present her from me this Emerald, desiring her to weare it for my sake: with remembrance to pitty his painful miseries, whose life and death is onlie in her hand. *Vrbanillo* taking the Ring, *Trineus* and *Palmerin* went to passe the time with the King, and the Princesse at their entrance regarding *Trineus*, perceiued by his countenaunce that he vnderstood her message, for his blood was now risen cheerely in his face, which before was sunck downe with too much languishing, so that she imagined herselfe more happie, in beeing so beloued, then to loue, and knew not well howe to dissemble her ioy. Ah poore *Trineus*, the paine thou endurest, attending the wished howre to speake with her, far surmounteth the torments of *Leander*, awayting when *Phoebus* woulde goe bathe himself with *Thetis* and the Marine Goddesses, that he might afterwarde swim to his affianced *Heroe*: and had not shee giuen thee a better signe by her eye to aduenture, I would haue reckoned thee more infortunate, then the betrothed spouse to the prisoner of *Abydos*.[20] Nowe had *Trineus* bashfullie taken the Princesse by the hand,[21] when vnhappilie one came to aduertise the King, that the Hart he had chased the day before, was now againe gotten within the toyles, that if it pleased him to hunt in the morning, hee should no doubt kill him with little labor. These newes were so welcome to the King, that because he would the next morning more earelie goe to his pastime, hee withdrewe himselfe for that night, the Queene and *Agriola* likewise departing to their Pauillion: so that *Trineus* encounter was thus preuented, and he with *Palmerin* returned to their Tent, trusting still on the Dwarffes dilligence, that he should perfect all things to his harts desire,[22] and to perswade him the more, *Palmerin* thus began. I haue this hope my Lord, seeing alreadie so manie good signes, that you cannot anie waie be deceiued in your loue, and this I wold aduise you, Fortune beeing so fauourable, and assisting you to her very vttermost: you shoulde not henceforth shew your selfe so feminine, but in hardie maner, reueale to the Princesse, when you shall find her at conuenient leysure, both howe you loue her, and what fauourable grace you expect at her hands. I must confesse, that Letters and messages are able to doo much: but the person being present, and knowing how to request, and how to be answered, is more auailable a thousande times, and in breefe, no Messenger can be like himselfe. I speake not this, as though my Dwarffe were not faithfull, but to this end, that she shoulde receiue no occasion of displeasure. In how manie dangers haue Gentlemen beene, only by the bad construction of their seruants message? the readiest wit that is cannot number them: therfore if you find oportunitie, attend no other suter but your selfe. This councell well liked the Prince *Trineus*, wherfore he determined to speak to her himselfe, so soone as time and leisure woulde permitt him, and in this resolution they went to take their rest: but the remembrance of *Polinarda*, would not suffer *Palmerin* to sleepe, comparing his ioy in her presence, with his tormenting passions nowe in her absence breathed foorth manie sighes, and shed manie teares, til at length hee began to slumber, wherin he thought he discerned this sight. Beeing in companie with the King, he sawe come foorth of a darke caue a dreadful Lyon, who with open throat set vpon him, and assailed him in such maner, as with his nailes and teeth he rent his Armor, and put him in verie great daunger of his life, so that he stroue in such sort in his sleepe, as *Trineus* beeing in bed with him, awaked him, demaunding why he strugled so earnestlie. *Palmerin* thus awaked desired God to withstand all his euils, and afterward recounted to *Trineus* the whole effect of his dreame,[23] and said. It will not be amisse my Lord that to morrow we ride armed in the Kings companie, for such illusions, albeit they commonly fall out vntrue, yet can presage no good to followe. I like your counsel well, answered *Trineus*, and that *Ptolome* goe armed as well as we. In the morning they arose and armed themselues, all saue their Helmets and Launces, which theyr Squires caried, and in this sort came to bid the King good morrow, who meruailed much to see them so prepared, and doubting they had receiued some occasion of offence, demaunded what mooued them so to be armed. You know my Lord quoth *Palmerin*, that a Knight ought euermore to be ready for all aduentures, and not knowing what inconuenience or danger may happen, before such time we shall returne againe, we haue armed our selues to preuent the worst. The King not discontented with this answer mounted on horsebacke, and comming to the chase, had excellent game at Deere, Hart, Bore and wilde Buffell, wherein hee tooke such exceeding pleasure, as he determined to staie there fiue or sixe daies longer. But in the place where he supposed himselfe safe, and free from all hazard, suddainlie hee was sollicited with the chaunges of fortune, for the Queene and her Daughter *Agriola* were in meruailous danger, as you shall reade in the discourse following.

Palmerin d'Oliva: Part I 277

CHAPTER LI.
How the Queene of England and Agriola her daughter, were in danger to be rauished by the Giant Franarco, and of the succour they had by Trineus, Palmerin and Ptolome.

The King returning from the chase with his companie, little minding any infortunate euent, and conferring with *Palmerin* till they drewe neere vnto their Tents: at length they hearde a great tumult, and beheld a Squire making towards them so fast as his Horsse could gallop. *Palmerin* doubting some vnhappye chaunce, and remembring his Dreame, saide to the King. Neuer credite me my Lorde, if this Squire come not to you about some speciall affayres, as well may bee gathered by his speedie pace. At these wordes the Gentleman came to the King, reporting howe the Gyant *Franarco*, Lorde of the Castel of *Garbones*, since his departure came to his Tents, and from thence had violently taken the Queene and her Daughter *Agriola*, notwithstanding the resistaunce of manie Knights, who striuing to defend her, lost their liues. The King with these words strooken in wonderfull greefe, said. Ah Gentlemen, this villainous Traytor hath notoriously wronged vs. Howe is it possible to recouer them again before they be dishonoured?[1] *Trineus* and *Palmerin* mooued at these newes, asked the Squire, which way he went with the Queene and her Daughter? In trueth my Lord quoth he, I cannot tell ye which way he tooke, we all were so troubled and misused by his traine: except they went along the Forrest, and so are gone to the next village. Then *Palmerin* clasping on his Helmet, and snatching his Launce from his Dwarffe, galloped amaine after the Gyant, not speaking a word to *Trineus*, who accompanied with *Ptolome*, rode apace after him, and as they passed by the Queenes Tent, they sawe the Ladies and Gentlewomen heauily lamenting, especially *Eufemia*, the cheefe companion to the Princesse *Agriola*. Diuers Knights beside armed themselues to pursue the Giant, but *Trineus* not a little enraged, followed the track of the horse, demaunding of al he met, if they saw the villaine that had stollen away the Ladies. As concerning this Giant *Franarco*, you must note that he was the cruellest tyrant and most notable fellon in all the Realme, hauing a dayes iourney from the Forrest where the King hunted, a Castell so well fortefied, and furnished with munition and all things necessary, as in all *England* was not the like, which was left to him by the death of his Father, who forciblie tooke it from a Lorde his neighbour, and diuers other places, especially the Isle *Magdalen*. There succeeded he the royall dignitie, after the death of the elder Brother, who (as you haue hearde) was slaine in the battell by *Palmerin*,[2] and hee vnderstanding the death of the King of the Isle *Magdalen*, was so highlie displeased, that although hee had alwaies before borne allegeaunce to the King, hee nowe solemnlie swore to reuenge his Brothers death, being so feared of the whole Countrey, as none durst enterprise to deale wyth him. So to reuenge the slaughter of his eldest Brother, with diuers of his kindred and Freendes likewise slayne in the battaile, he strengthened himselfe with thirtie hardie Knightes, intending to displease the King so much as hee coulde. And hearing that he was comming to *London*, to feast the Knights that were the cause of his victory, but cheefelie him that slew his brother, came with his company this way, in hope to finde them all vnprouided. And comming that morning the King was gone on hunting, he found not those hee desired to meete withall, for the hatred he bare them, thinking himselfe sufficiently reuenged, if hee coulde carry away with him the Queene and her Daughter: which he accomplished to his owne desire, causing them mount vp behinde two of his Knights. The Gentlemen that were left to keepe the Queene company, offended to see such villainy offered theyr Ladie and Mistresse, defended her so well as they coulde, but all auayled not against the Giant and hys power, because they were armed, and they with the Queene were vnprouided, so that a number of them were slaine and sore wounded, and more had beene, but that he feared the return of the King, which made him in hast ride thence wyth hys spoyle, sending them[3] somwhat before, and loytering behind himselfe, to fight with any that shold come to reskew them. *Trineus* hauing gotten the sight of them, came posting to the Gyant, saying. Stay trayterous theefe, for thou maist not so carry her away that is worthy the greatest Lord in the world. With these words they ran fiercely together, *Trineus* gyuing the Giant a sore wound on the shoulder, but the Prince receiued such a mightie stroke from the Giant, as he fel from his Horse with his heeles vpward. *Palmerin* beeing not far of, and doubting least the Prince had beene slaine, came in a great rage to *Franarco*, saying. Monstrous enemy to manhoode, who made thee so saucie, to lay violent hands on Ladies of such account, by my Swordе villaine, I shall make thee deerely to pay for thy folly. So coutching theyr Launces they met together, the Gyant fayling, but *Palmerin* gaue him a shrewd wound on his body, and their horsses roughlie shouldring one another, as their Masters were both thrown to the ground. *Franarco* (beeing heauie and vnweldie) had such a fall, as easilie he could not recouer himselfe. *Palmerin* nimbly getting vp againe, gaue the Giant such a wound on his right legge, as the flesh hung downe pittifully to beholde. The Giant beeing not able to stande any longer on that leg, set his knee to the ground, beeing glad to defend the strokes of *Palmerin*, who reached him such a sound blowe on the foreheade with the hilts of his sworde, as the Giant fell along on his backe, when *Palmerin* soone setting his foote on his breast, with his sworde deuided his heade from his shoulders. During this fight, *Trineus* and *Ptolome*, made after the Queene and her Daughter, whom the Giants Knights droue cruelly before them. Nowe was it a matter well worthy memory, to see the braue behauiour of these two Knights, but cheefely of *Trineus* before his sweet Mistresse, whose presence endued him with such exceeding courage, as hee thought himselfe able to conquer the whole world, and therefore sufficient for all them, were they as many more in number. But strength dooth not alwayes equall courage, and louers thinke more then they are able to doo, as to *Trineus* perrill it had now fallen out, but that a company of the Kings Knights arriued, whereupon began a hote encounter betweene them, and *Trineus* comming to the Knight that

Palmerin d'Oliva: Part I

had *Agriola* behinde him, set him soone beside his horse, with his neck broken in his fall, so that the Princesse getting forth of the throng, and seeing her beloued so valiant in prowesse, betweene ioy and greefe, she said. Ah happy Knight, the mirror of all such as follow armes, I desire thy fortune may prooue such, as thou and thy company may haue victory ouer these traytors. Now may I bee well assured of the loue thou bearest me, for which, (if we may escape thys harde brunt) perswade thy selfe not to passe vnrecompenced. *Trineus* hearing the words of *Agriola*,[4] was enflamed with such a spyrite of conquering desire, as breaking in among the thickest, hys strokes gaue witnes he fought for a wife.[5] But the Giants Knights were men of such proofe, as the fresh supply that came were all well neere slaine, and doubtlesse the rest had borne them company, but that the King and *Palmerin*, with fifty Knights more, came to assist them: for *Palmerin* hauing slayne the Giant, mounted on his horse, because it was one of the goodliest that euer he saw, and espying the King comming with his traine, set on with him, and found *Trineus* in great danger, because so many of his side were slaine, but this fresh assistance brought by the King, was the meane that all the Giants Knightes were slaughtered, and they kneeled down thanking God for their victorie.[6] The King alighting, came and embraced the Queen saying. How happy may we thinke our selues Madam, hauing so well preuented this trecherous villanie? for neuer did I think to see you againe, but that God and these Knights so highlie befreended vs. The Queene and her Daughter were as yet so dismayed, in remembraunce of theyr former daunger, as beholding so manie lye slaine before them, and ioyful beside beeing so fortunatelie deliuered, as betweene these extreames they knew not what to say, but desired speedilie to set forward thence, which they presentlie did, the King commaunding his Nephew *Cerides*, to see *Franarco* and his men burned to ashes, and honorable Sepulture to be prouided for the other.[7] When the Queene hearde that *Franarco* was dead. Tell me my Lord (quoth she) who hath doone such a gracious acte to kill that monstrous villaine? Euen he Madame, said the King, that was cause of my victorie in battell, the Knight heere in blacke Armor, to whome I am so far indebted, as I cannot imagine anie recompence sufficient for him: and this can I not speak without great maruaile, seeing so rare valour performed with so little danger on his behalfe. Long may the good Knight liue saide the Queene that hath so defended vs, and may they all three prosper in their affaires, for their knightly seruice to the Realme of *England*.[8] While these speeches endured, *Trineus* beeing sore wounded, was brought between two Squires and set vpon his horse, but the King, the Queene, and cheefly fayre *Agriola* was glad, when she heard there was no such danger but he might well escape it. Wherfore mounting al on horsebacke, they rode to see the Giants bodie, which made *Agriola* repute *Palmerin* for no lesse then his Dwarffe commended him. Then the King commaunded to vnarme the bodie, and one of his Knights shoulde bring away his Helmet and Sheelde which would be tokens sufficient for him to recouer the Castell of *Garbones*, which he seazed on, and all other things belonging to the Giant, he sent the County of *Bonneroy* with fiue hundred men to confiscate and return to his Maiesties vse. The Countie well knowing such matters would not be easilie accomplished, if they in the Castel should make resistance, therefore pollitiquelie hee sent the Giants Targe and Helmet before, as sent from *Franarco*, who was with the King, and they should open the Gate because they were comming thither, for witnes whereof they shewed the Giants signet of Armes. The guard too credulous and thinking it vnpossible for anie man to conquer the Giant, opened the Gates, wherupon the Countie presentlie entred with his power, putting al to the sword, not sparing any, not so much as the Giants yonger Brother, who escaping aliue from the battaile, was the cause why *Franarco* dealt thus villainously. Thus did the Countie yeelde the Castell into the Kings obeysaunce, remaining Captaine thereof vnder the Kings authoritie, the like he did in manie other places, where the people aduertised of the Giants rebellion, and that the Castell of *Garbones* was taken: there was none would resist the Kings commaundement, whereof the Countie was not a little glad, returning so soone as he could with the glad tydings of his successe, to the Court, certefying the King how all things happened.

Chapter LII.
Of the conference Palmerin had with the Princesse Agriola after he had slaine the Giant Franarco.

By this time the King was come to his Pauillion, where hee caused his Chirur gions dilligentlie to attend on the three Knightes,[1] for the curing of their woundes, who founde that the Prince of *Allemaigne* was worst of al hurt, yet the King vnderstanding he was in no danger of life, was the better pacified, because he loued him deerelie, and intended to honor him so much as laye in hys power, promising not to depart thence till he recouered hys health, and because he would preuent the like mischaunces, he caused dilligent watch to be made euerie night, as though he had lien in field encamped with the enemie. During the Princes sicknes, he was oftentimes visited by the Queene and fayre *Agriola*, not vnthankfull for the courtesie receiued by him and his companions, and for which they requited him with manifold thanks. *Trineus* esteeming himselfe worthilie recompenced, seeing that heauenlie spectacle,[2] whose presence healed a greater wound then any hee had receiued in fight, desiring the continuance of the outwarde hurts, for comforting of his inward oppressions. And while the Queene thus conferred with *Trineus, Palmerin* came to the Princesse *Agriola*, seeing the time so lawful and commodious, that he might thorowlie acquaint her with matter long enough before premeditated, but because she was desirous to talke with him, she first began in manner following. I know not Sir Knight, how the King my Father will satisfie the great seruice you haue doone him, in so manie hazardes to his Realme and himselfe: but for mine owne part, I think my selfe so bounden, that after life, which hee gaue me by generation, my deuoted soule shall remaine to honor you.[3] And if these occasions passed, doo giue me iust cause to thinke my selfe happie, what lesse account may I make of that vertuous Prince *Trineus* your companion, who came into thys Countrey onely for my loue as I am perswaded, yet doubtfull to be lightlie carried awaie with report, I shold accept it for more sound assurance, so pleased you to speake the truth heerein. Madame (quoth *Palmerin*) if I haue doone any seruice to the King or you, it is rewarded with much more then sufficient, seeing it pleaseth you to make such account thereof, and I promise you, you haue two Knights wholy at commaund for the loue of the third: who is so confidently vowed your Freend and seruant, as no man in the worlde can bee more, and this is he that lieth wounded in his bed, the princelie Son and heire to the Emperor of *Allemaigne*, in which report my Dwarffe hath not deceiued you. And giue my word thys credite (Madame) that since the time he first hearde of your excellent beautie, beeing then in *Fraunce*, he neuer had other determination, but to spend his life in your gracious seruice: and making refusall of manie faire Ladies, especially of *Lucemania*, daughter to the most christian king of *Fraunce*,[4] set down this princelie and commendable resolution, neuer to espouse anie other but you, so it may stande with your liking to accept him for your husband, think then aduisedlie sweet Madam, of the incomparable happines ordeyned for you, and stand not in your owne light to loose so good fortune. In trueth my Lord, quoth the Princesse, I were well worthy to be reputed, among the number of most hard harted and ingratefull Ladies, if I should not loue the Prince *Trineus*, were it but for the danger he remaines in for me, and the vnfeigned loue which you say he beares mee. And thus farre I presume my Lorde on your credite, that if it were otherwise, you would not disguise the matter to me in this maner, much lesse deceiue such a Lady as I am, which (notwithstanding) would be to you but a slender conquest. Therfore you may assure him on my behalfe, that the loue I beare him is more then he thinks, and very far exceedeth his iudgement, as the proofe thereof (in time) shall deliuer true testimonie. Madame, quoth *Palmerin*, his onelie desire in this world you haue faithfully vnderstood, in you then it consisteth to preuent the contrarie, by mercifull regarde of his afflictions, and your presence will appease the anger of the Emperour his Father, in that so nobly he would enterprise (though against his will) to ayde the King your Father, onelie for your loue. And this will be the meane, that the conceiued displeasure of the Fathers, shall conclude in the happie coniunction of their Children. My Lorde, quoth the Princesse, I wil doo what shal please my Father and Mother to commaund me and no otherwise, considering the danger I may fall into, by yeelding my honor to any preiudiciall occasion. *Palmerin* who had no other feare but to bee knowne what himselfe was, thus answered. I am perswaded Madame, that your iudgment is so perfect, that to attaine a place of such dignitie, and a Husband so royal as the Prince *Trineus*: you wil not stand on friuolous Tearmes, nor be caried awaie with anie light or feminine feares, seeing that (setting apart these doubts) you shall worthely accomplish the thing that shall make you the most renowned Lady vnder the Occident. I pray you Sir *Palmerin*, quoth she, referre this talke till some other time, for the answere of such a high and weightie matter, deserueth to be excogitated with leysure, for oftentimes wee see, that such actions suddainly and slightly performed, causeth more repentance afterward then is expected. Yet thus farre I venture, and so faithfully perswade him, that he is the onelie Prince in the world I would accept for my Husband, if they were so agreed to whom God, nature and duetie hath bounde mee: and to let him vnderstand my willing desire towards him, I will speake to him my selfe, so soone as the Queene is departed. Not long after, the Queene returned to the King, leauing her Daughter with two of her Ladies to comfort the Prince, whereupon *Palmerin* taking her by the hande, brought her to the bedde side where *Trineus* lay, to whom she made very courteous reuerence, and trembling with modest bashfulnes, said. How fare ye gentle Knight? trust me your hard fortune dooth greatlie displease me, and if I could beare part therein, beleeue me I gladly woulde endure the paine: for it is good reason, that the causer of the harme, should haue a portion of the torment, gratifying you with a Maydens thanks, for your good assistaunce without any desert. *Trineus* was so rauished with her presence, and hearing her speake so freendlie, in whom consisted the safetie of his life, as he coulde not vtter the ioy hee

Palmerin d'Oliva: Part I 283

conceiued: which the Princesse well noted, and *Palmerin* likewise, who aunswered her in this manner. It cannot bee Madame but my Lord *Trineus* will soone amend, hauing the soueraigne medicine so neere him, that is onely able to helpe him: and with these wordes hee left them togeather, to acquaint each other with their secrete afflictions, when the Prince, giuing a greeuous sighe, sayd. Fayre Madam, to accomplish what you commaunded the first daie I sawe you, I did my deuoire to execute the effect of my charge, albeit not so sufficientlie as I could wish: yet since that time I neuer enioyed one minute of rest, till this instant, when mine eyes delighted with your sweete presence, gaue hope to my hart of further comfort. For this onely cause (fayre Mistresse) haue I forsaken my Parents and Countrey, regarding nothing more then this present happines, whereby my woundes are cured, my spirite contented, and my hart from all dangers sufficientlie recouered, so that no greefe canne now molest me, when your gracious fauour thorowlie confoundeth all. And nowe might I imagine my fortune beyonde all other, were not this fearefull doubt left to crosse it, that scanning disdaine should be hid in such rare perfections, as oftentimes it commeth so to passe: therefore I beseeche you Madame, may it so stand with your liking to resolue all doubts by your direct opinion, and heerein shall I account my selfe more honoured, then were I Monarche of the whole worlde. Loue hauing then so wounded the Princesse, as for a while she was driuen to silence, at length withdrew the passion, and caused her returne this answere. Alas my Lorde, I was (ere this) so certaine of your affection towards me, in respect of the daungerous trauailes endured for my sake, as you neede not seeke any other prooues, then what mine owne hart was fully resolued on: and so I continue still, expecting the day to make vs bothe fortunate, which I wolde haue you as yet dissemble, least crooked mishap any way preuent vs. As she was proceeding in her dyscourse, the Queene entred the Tent againe, by which occasion *Trineus* could not say what he intended, wherefore taking her secretlie by the hand, wrung her fingers with such a trembling passion, as all the night following he lay meditating on his Goddesse *Agriola*, and the comfortable aunswere she gaue him.[5] If the yong Prince were in such torments, his Lady bare him companie, thinking on the speeches past betweene her and *Palmerin*, and this euening the Dwarffe (not compassing before to speake with *Agriola*) presented her with the Emeralde from the Prince, which she kindly receiuing, in recompence therof sent him a fayre Diamond, rewarding the Dwarffe liberally for his paynes, who among the rest of his talke, highly commended the vertues of the Prince, which increased her looue so confidentlie, as he assured him of the Princesse loue, that death could not chaunge her setled affection. *Tryneus* fullie resoluing heereon, gaue such cheerefull phisicke to his hart, and the Chirurgions such dilligence to his wounds, as within seauen or eyght dayes hee was able to beare Armour:[6] whereuppon the King departed thence towardes *London*, where the strange Knights were entertained with meruailous honor, the Lords, Knights, Burgesses, Officers and other Cittizens, welcomming them with great pompe and royaltie, saying. Welcome are the Knightes that deliuered the Queene and her Daughter, from the cruell Gyant *Franarco*, with diuers other salutations, whereat *Palmerin* and his Freendes were greatlie abashed. Passing on to the Pallace, all the way they were still presented with rare shewes and deuises, and the Knightes Lodgings were appointed in very statelie Chambers in the Court, causing open Court to be kept for eyght dayes space, for the honour of these Knights, and entertainement of all freendlie commers, in all which time there wanted no sports and delights, as such times and occasions doo necessarilie require. Nowe came all the Princes, Lordes, and renowned Knightes in *England* to the Courte, except the Duke of *Gaule*, who excused himselfe by the warre in his owne prouince, which yet was not the cheefest cause of his absence: but the shame hee reputed to himselfe for his foyle in *Fraunce*, when he entred the Combatte for the beautie of the fayre Princesse *Agriola*.[7] These Knights thus worthilie intreated, they were at no time denyed entraunce into the King and Queenes Chambers, by which meane *Tryneus* myght when himselfe pleased conferre with the Princesse, till this instant among all other, the Prince thus began to his Ladie and Mistresse. You may easily presume sweet Madam, what secrete Combattes I continually endure for your loue, and no helpe is expected but the onely hope of your fauour, which as you haue promised to my speciall Freend Sir *Palmerin*: I doubt not but you wyll perseuere in that gracious opinion, and what promise hee hath made of my seruice to you, thinke not but I obserue with religious care and deuotion, though not sufficient to equal your deserts, yet because ingratitude shall not insult against mee. So manie thankes (quoth the Princesse) I returne you my Lord, as good opinions can bee imagined betweene vs bothe, and accounting you for my Freende, which is a higher degree, I heere discharge you of my seruice, and (myne honor guarded from blame) I shall iudge my selfe happy to yeelde you any content, which I will fulfil, notwithstanding any daunger towardes mee. But I praie you tell me my Lord, what is the intent of your looue in this action. Madame, (quoth the Prince) Sir *Palmerin*, who is nowe come to beare vs companie, shall crediblie enforme you, so please you to rest contented therewith. *Palmerin* thus entred, imagined theyr talke was not about affaires of Merchandise,[8] wherefore hee saide to the Princesse. God speede you Madame,[9] pardon me, I shoulde call you Ladie, and Wife to the Prince of *Allemaigne*, for I doubt not but you haue chosen him your Husbande in hart.[10] *Agriola* blushinge and smyling heereat, made no aunswere: wherefore *Palmerin* went forwarde in this manner. In faith Madame if you haue not doone so, I would counsell you to accomplish it presentlie, and prouide to goe with vs to *Allemaigne*, where the Emperour will entertaine you with such gracious fauour, as you will not loose if you beare the minde of a Princesse, beside, you shall be the meane of euerlasting peace between the King your Father and his Maiestie. To which words, *Agriola* thus discreetlie answered.

    I promise you my Lord, there is no Prince thys daie liuing, whom I would more gladlie accept for my Husbande, then the Prince *Trineus*: notwithstanding, for mee to departe without the knowledge of the King or Queene my Parents,

Palmerin d'Oliva: Part I 285

is an acte (in mine opinion) farre dissenting from duetie and honest report. Therefore my Lord, louing mine honour as you saie you doo, I praie you let our behauiour be with better wisedom, least we both fal into dangers not recouerable. *Palmerin* perceiuing *Agriola* contrarie to the most necessarie occasion, vsed
5 such arguments, and played so well the Oratour, that the poore Princesse had no power to resist: considering the greate loue she bare the Prince *Trineus*, which made her yeelde more easilie to his perswasions, so that she agreed to accomplish their determination, and depart with them towards the Realme of *Allemaigne*. *Trineus* ioyes nowe exceeded measure, and *Palmerin* (for his sake) was no lesse
10 contented, in respecte hee shoulde the sooner see his Mistresse *Polynarda*, whose verie rememberaunce gaue him lyfe, as the ayre dooth the *Camelion*.[11] But Fortune beholding eache thing prosper as liked their fancies, woulde nowe needes beginne to plaie her Pageant, crossing them with the vnhappiest stratageme, that euer coulde happen to so noble Princes, as in the sequel shall be largelie dis-
15 coursed.[12] They little expecting such a chaunce, are earnestlie folowing their serious enterprise, which was secretlie to carrie *Agriola* with them into *Allemaigne*, for which purpose they prouided Shippes and skilfull Pilots to conduct them, conueying all their necessaries aboorde, at what time this aduenture folowing happened in the Court of *England*.

Chapter LIII.

Howe in the time of this pleasant and great assembly, there came a Damosell to London, who desired the King to doo her iustice, against a Knight of his owne Court.

During the time that this royall companie continued at London, minding nothing but pleasures, pastimes, and courtly recreations, there came a Damosell, so faire as might bee, accompanied with two auncient Knights, and a lustie Champion brauelie armed, with six Squires attending on him. The Damosell entring the Pallace, came before the King, and on her knee beganne in this manner. Dreade Lorde, hauing long time hearde your good iustice towardes your Subiects, without anie fauour or exception of persons: I am the more bolde, (albeit hee that hath iniuried mee, is reputed for a Man of good quallity, and holdeth place of authoritie in your Court) humblie to craue of your highnesse one request, against the most false and disloyal Knight that euer was: whom when I but remember, more weightie and greeuous oppressions fall vppon my soule, then this wretched bodie of mine is able to endure.

Damosell saide the King, I shall right gladlie releeue your heauines, if it lie in my power to doo it: therefore tel mee the cause of your offence: and what hee is that hath so wronged you. Knowe my good Lorde (quoth shee) that I looued a Knight so deerelie, as contrarie to the lyking of my Parents and Freendes, and too much forgetfull of mine owne selfe, I tooke him to my Husbande, thinking he looued mee so faithfullie, as his shewes and behauiour gaue demonstration. But the Traytour had no other meaning, then to beguile and falselie deceiue mee, for after I had made him Lorde of mee and mine, and brought him to a Castell of mine, so strong and faire as anie in your highnesse dominions: the Traytour expulsed mee thence violentlie, pretending that wee were so neere allyed, as hee might no longer account mee for his Wife.[1] Since which time, notwithstanding all the humble intreaties I haue made: hee will neither restore mee my goods and possessions againe, nor yet accepte mee as his espoused Wife. Therfore I beseeche you my Lord, as becomes a good and vertuous Prince, for the honour of nobilitie and regarde of womanhoode, you will take pittie on a poore distressed Ladie, and that in such a rightfull demaunde, you woulde doo mee iustice, which I had sooner demaunded, but coulde not by the occasions of your troublesome warres.

Ladie, saide the King, as yet you haue not named the man that hath offered you this surpassing iniurie. My Lord (quoth shee) this is the man in your presence, named *Miseres*, a vile Traytour, and publique adulterer. And if he dare affirme that I haue spoken vntrueth, I haue heere brought a Knight with me, who by Combatte shall make him confesse his falshood and treason, so please your Maiestie to fauour my request. *Miseres*, (quoth the King) howe aunswere you this accusation and offence, wherewith this Lady chargeth you? *Miseres* beeing suddainlie driuen into his dumps, knewe not well what to saie: yet at length[2]

Palmerin d'Oliva: Part I

(with humble reuerence) hee thus beganne. My soueraigne Lorde, if credite may be giuen to the first countenaunce of accusations, without hearing howe the partie accused can iustifie himselfe, I doubt not but your Maiestie will presentlie condemne me: but when the matter is well debated and discided, they which seemed at first vnreproouable, are founde malicious and slaunderous persons, and the accused, innocent and free from blame, as heere your highnesse shall most plainelie beholde. The matter whereof this Ladie detecteth mee, is forged, and most villainouslie inuented: for to mee belonged the Castell shee quarrelles for, discended from my Predecessours, to whome I am the true, lawfull, and legitimate inheritour. True it is that this dissembling Womanne, by sweete speeches, feminine guiles, and secrete deceits, oftentimes practised to winne mee for her Husbande: but knowing her behauiour such as beseemed not a Woman of modestie and vertue, I would not heere her, much lesse consent to match with her. And this is the cause of her complaint, in hope that you, (beeing aboue all other Princes most benigne and honourable) will constraine mee to wedde her, in respecte of your absolute authoritie, as the duetifull obedience wherein I am bounde. When the Knight which came with the Ladie, heard *Myseres* blame her in this sorte, hee stepped before the King with these words.

    It is great follie (my Lord) in *Miseres*, to deny a matter so apparantlie knowne, although, if it were put to the iudgment of honeste personnes, his common good reporte might cause him bee beleeued: but the poore Ladye desires that her right may bee cleered by Combatte, wherein let him confounde her if he can, or els receiue rewarde for his notorious offence. On her behalfe therefore my Lorde, I saie and will maintaine, that *Myseres* is a most disloyall Traytour, and his mouth shall confesse it, or this day will I take his heade from his bodie. *Myseres* feeling himselfe somewhat touched, grewe into great anger, and albeit the shame he did the Ladie deliuered him culpable, and made him doubt the issue of the Combatte: yet in meruailous choller hee aunswered the Knight, that hee falselye belyed him, and was readie to make proofe thereof in Combatte, if it pleased the King so to appoint it. And I doubt not (quoth hee) to make thee paie for thy rashnes, and force thee confesse thy lacke of dyscretion, in gyuing credite to the trothlesse complaints of this deceitfull Woman. Then was it ordeined, that this difference shoulde bee tryed by Armes:[3] wherupon the Ladies Knight thus spake to the King. Seeing it hath pleased your Maiestie, to graunt the Fielde to *Miseres* and me, may it plese you (as is the custome) to commaunde, that hee deliuer hostages: to the ende, if hee be vanquished, the Castell may bee deliuered into your handes, to deliuer it in iustice where it appertaines. Good reason, saide the King, and therefore *Miseres*, you must before you enter the Fielde, accomplishe what the Knight in equitie hath demaunded.

    Then *Miseres* called one of his Bretheren, whom he required to stande as his hostage: and doubt not before the Sunne be sette, but I will discharge my selfe and my pledge, with which wordes hee departed the Hall to arme himselfe: but because the daie was too farre spent, the matter was deferred till the next morning. The King and his Lords, seeing the Ladies Knight in such resolute assuraunce, merueiled of whence and what he was, for none there knewe him but *Palmerin*, who neither coulde gesse assuredly what hee was, but by the golden Sunne in his Azure Sheelde: which made him remember that at the Ioustes in *Fraunce* the perillous Combatte without victorye on eyther side, was fought betweene him and this Knight.[4] *Palmerin* beeing gladde to see the man he long looked for, and purposing nowe to be fully reuenged on him, secretly went foorth of the Hall, commaunding one of his Squires, to conueye hys Horse and Armour the next morning out of the Cittie, because if hee vanquished *Miseres*, at his returne he intended to fight with him, or if *Miseres* had the better, yet hee shoulde not depart thence againe with life.

Nowe you must vnderstande, that this Knight which came with the Ladie, was the Knight of the *Sunne*, named *Frysol*, who euer since the Combatte betweene *Palmerin* and him, remayned with the Duke of *Gaule*, and was of him highlie honoured for his woorthy chiualrie. Of whome when this distressed Ladie hearde, she made her complaint to him of the wrong *Myseres* had doone her, and *Frysol* pittying her case, promised to ayde her in recouerie of her ryght: and so came with her to the King of *Englands* Courte, to the great greefe of the Duke of *Gaule*, who made *Frysol* promise him to returne againe after the Combatte: but *Frysol* was more desirous thereof then the Duke, in respecte of his fayre Sister, because hee was especiallie beloued of her. Thus *Palmerin* following his enterprise, feared to bee preuented, because the Fielde was appointed by the King, in the same place where hee intended to meete with *Frysol*, and beside, *Palmerin* and the Duke of *Norgalles* were ordayned Iudges of the Fielde, which he would not willinglie haue taken vppon him, doubting by that meane to bee hindered of his other determination. The time beeing come that the Knights shoulde to the Combatte, the King and the Ladies came to their Scaffoldes, and the two Iudges were placed in their Tent, accompanied with many Princes and honourable persons.

After that the Heraldes had commaunded the Champions to doo their deuoyre, then they clasped theyr Helmets and fetching their carrire, mette with such puissaunce as *Miseres* brake his Launce on *Frysols* Sheelde, not moouing him in his Saddle: but *Frisol* driuing his Launce through *Myseres* bodie, caused the Traytour to fall deade to the earth. Then he allighting, and opening *Miseres* Helmette, sawe no life in him, came to the Iudges, saying. You may nowe perceiue my Lordes, whether hee that offered this Ladie such villainy, hath receiued his due deserte, or no, if there yet remaine any thing els to doo for recouering of her right, I am heere readie to maintaine her cause. *Palmerin*, who was not verie well pleased with this victorie, answered. Knight you haue doone enough at this tyme, pray that other affayres may prooue as prosperous to you heereafter, and so in anger went foorth of the fielde, commaunding the bodie of *Miseres* to be brought thence, which was afterward interred with great honour.

Frisol hauing thus vanquished *Myseres*, the Ladie for whom he entred the Combatte, fell on her knees before the King, desiring him to surrender the Castell which *Myseres* vniustlie detained from her. In sooth Ladie, quoth the King, it is reason you should haue iustice, and your owne deliuered you, but knowe you
5 his name that defended your quarrell? My Lorde, (quoth shee) in concealing his name, I shoulde offer him great wrong, considering the bounty and prowesse of the man, which hath not beene sparingly shewed heeretofore, in presence of the Duke of *Gaule* against the King of *Norway*, whose Armie was discomfited by the worthie valour and policie of this Knight, who calleth himselfe by the name of
10 *Frysol*, the Duke of *Gaule* bringing hym foorth of *Fraunce* at his last voyage, and euer since hath so deerelie loued him, as hee were his owne naturall Brother.[5] I promise you Ladie, sayde the King, you made no ill choyse of your Knight, for I haue heeretofore hearde of hys actions, and am not a little glad that I know him, wyshing he were of my Courte, because a King accompanied with such per-
15 sonnes, must needes imagine his Countrey happie. And in respecte he is so braue a Champion, it is impossible but hee shoulde bee a wyse and vertuous Knight, wherefore I praye you cause him come to mee: which shee presentlie dyd, and hauing saluted his Maiestie with honourable reuerence, the King embraced him with these wordes. Woorthy Sir, you are most hartilie welcome, I could wysh you
20 were one of my Knightes, in respecte that my Court shoulde bee the more honoured, and I might requite your paynes better then I can on a suddaine.

Mightie Prince, (quoth *Frysol*) in assisting this distressed Ladie, I haue doone but my duetie: but if I coulde anie way doo your highnesse seruice, I knowe no Prince liuing, for whome I woulde more gladlie employ my selfe. And
25 at this time vrgent affayres excuse mee from staying heere anie longer: neuerthelesse, I intreate you my good Lorde, (if it may stande with your fauourable lyking) to repute mee among the number of your Souldiours and Seruaunts. If it must needes be so, sayde the King, you shal doo what please you, yet will I reckon you among those to whome I owe continual loue and affection. And
30 although the death of *Myseres* dooth somewhat greeue me, because I made some estimation of him: yet for your sake shall I deliuer the Ladie her Castell, which you haue conquered with so Knightlie chiualrie. *Frysol* humblie thanked hys Maiestie, and departed with the Ladie, which way they came: but *Palmerin* very much offended at hys departure, and earnestlie desiring to bee reuenged on him,
35 commaunded his Dwarffe to mark wel which way they went. The Dwarffe dilligentlye fulfilling his Maisters charge, returned and tolde him which way they tooke, whereuppon hee[6] being desirous to followe, without giuing any knowledge thereof to his companions, left *Trineus* to confer with his fayre Mistresse *Agriola*. And departed the Court so secretlie, as neither the Prince or *Ptolome*
40 suspected any thing, and so accompanied with his Dwarffe *Vrbanillo*, hee came to the place where his Squire stayed with his Armour, where when hee was armed, hee mounted on horsebacke thus speaking to his men. Returne you to the Cittie, and there expecte my comming, as for thee *Vrbanillo*, thou shalt saie

to *Tryneus*, that hee must pardon mee, though I did not acquaint him with the cause of my departure, which I was more enforced to doo then he thinkes on: neuerthelesse, praie him take no paine to enquire after mee, because I doubt not to returne very shortlie, although not so soone as hee woulde, yet praie him to vse so little speeche thereof as may bee. The like maist thou saie to *Ptolome*, and to them bothe commende mee most hartilie: with this charge to you bothe, that vppon paine of your liues neither of you doo followe mee, nor cause anie other to seeke after mee.

So taking his Launce, hee galloped that way which his Dwarffe shewed him they were gone, and hee wyth the Squire returned to the Cittie, making verie sorrowful lamentation because they thought their Maister woulde returne no more, in that hee woulde not bee knowne whether hee went, yet woulde they bewraie nothing their Maister had forbidde them. *Trineus* and *Ptolome* were meruailous sorrowfull, especially the Prince, who without the Dwarffs assuraunce of his Maisters short returne, had followed to seeke him: yet not thorowlie contented with *Vrbanillos* perswasions, the King came to comfort him, saying. You must thinke good Sir, that your noble Freend is gone about some strange aduenture, for you knowe he neuer enterprised anie thing, but it returned him honour. If heeretofore for the loue of his Ladie, hee shewed himselfe without his Peere in chiualrie, thinke you hee will not regarde his reputation, and premeditate his actions before hee runne too farre in daunger? Content your selfe I praie you, for if his returne bee not the sooner, I will cause such prouision to be made, as he shal be founde againe. The Princesse *Agriola* likewise intreated him not to bee displeased at the absence of *Palmerin*, for with the helpe of God and his Freendes, quoth shee, his returne will cause as much ioy, as his departure dooth greefe. All this coulde hardlie content *Trineus*, for hee dreamed in his sleepe,[7] that the Knight which slewe *Myseres*, was hee against whom *Palmerin* entred the Combat in *Fraunce*, at what time they coulde not ouercome each other. And remembring what ill will *Palmerin* bare him, vehementlie suspected that for this cause hee followed him, which imagination somewhat comforted him, and he reputed the Knight vnwise if hee medled anie more with *Palmerin*.

Chapter LIV.
Howe after the death of Myseres, Palmerin followed Frysol, whome hee had slayne, but that a Damosell intreated his life.

All that day *Palmerin* trauailed, and most parte of the next, yet coulde he heare no tidings of the Ladie and *Frisol*, which made him ride in greate mellancholly, till at length meeting with a Damosell, mounted on a goodlie Palfray verie richlie harnessed, of whom he demanded, if she met not a Knight armed, who bare in a Sheelde of Azur a Golden Sunne, and with him a Ladie attended on by manie Squires. Truelie Sir, quoth the Damosell, if you will graunt me two requests that I shall demaunde, I will bring you to him you seeke for, before to morrowe the thirde howre of the daie.[1] *Palmerin* who was wonderfull desirous to finde his enemie, graunted to anie thing shee woulde desire: on condition (quoth he) that you shewe mee the Knight.[2] Followe mee then sayde the Damosell, for I will accomplishe what I haue promised. So rode they togeather, and among other speeches, *Palmerin* asked her if shee knewe the Knight, and what hys name was? The Damosell aunswered, that shee knewe not the Knight, but shee was verie well acquainted with the Ladie in his companie, and this night (quoth shee) they mind to lodge at a Castell of mine Auntes. In the euening they arriued within sight of the Castell, where they allighted from their Horsses, and entred a little thicket, for feare of beeing seene, and the Damosell hauing a flagon of Wine, and a pastie of redde Deere in a maunde at her saddle bow. *Palmerin* and shee refreshed themselues therewithall: but all that night coulde not *Palmerin* settle himselfe to sleepe, watching the Castell Gate, least in the time of his sleeping hys enemie shoulde escape him. The next morning, so soone as the breake of daie appeared, *Frisol* came foorth of the Castell with his companie, whereof *Palmerin* not a little gladde, saide to the Damosell. Nowe (Ladie) is your promise perfourmed, for this is the Knight I seeke: if therefore you will anie thing with mee, I must intreat you to followe mee, for I woulde be verie lothe that he shoulde escape me.

With which wordes hee mounted on horsebake, galloping after *Frisol* so fast as the Horse coulde awaie, and ouertaking him, saide. Staie a while Sir Knight, thinke you to passe awaie in such sorte? haue you forgot your wordes at *Parris*, to the Knight that guarded the Duke of *Sauoyes* Tent?[3] nowe is the time I hope to correcte your presumption, when thou shalt well perceiue, that thou neyther deseruest to bee Seruaunt to the Princesse *Polinarda*, nor art woorthie to talke of her honourable name. *Frisol* thus staying, knewe by *Palmerins* wordes, that it was he against whome he fought the Combatte in *Fraunce*, wheruppon he answered. Truelie Sir Knight, I haue not as yet forgotten what I then sayde, nor is the beautie of *Polynarda*, or my looue to her so little, that my desire to doo her seruice should not bee nowe remembered, nor will I forbeare to confesse it still, for feare of thee or anie other whatsoeuer. And if thou hast sought me foorth in this quarrell, thou hast found mee so readie to defende it: as I will more willingly choose to die, then denie anie parte of my duetie to that gracious Princesse. *Palmerin* beeing so angrie, as he would multiply no more wordes, encountered his enemie so valiantlie, as they brake their Launces, and yet coulde not vnhorsse each other, then drawing their Swordes, they laide so cruellie vppon their bodies, as theyr Sheeldes beeing broken, theyr Helmets battered, their Armour defaced, and their fleshe so greeuouslie mangled, as neither of them both could iudge who was likest to winne the victorie.[4] Tyll at length *Frisols* Horsse fayling vnder him, fell to the grounde, and hee so weakened with his great losse of bloode, as hee coulde not recouer himselfe, before *Palmerin* came to him, thinking to haue parted his heade from his shoulders with his Sword, which when the Ladie sawe, for whome *Frisol* had slayne *Myseres*, she fell into most pittifull acclamations, not sparing her loouely tresses of hayre, but with great impatience renting them violentlie, made the ayre to eccho her lamentable complaints. Which the Damosell seeing that guyded *Palmerin*, and mooued with compassion of her exceeding greefes: fell on her knees before *Palmerin*, intreating him to giue ouer the fight. But he, feigning that hee hearde her not, because *Frisol* with rough strugling had got on foote againe: charged him with such violente strokes, as *Frisol* (beeing of inuincible courage) requited him wyth as woorthye chiualrie.[5]

Againe the Damosell came on her knees to him, intreating him to giue ouer the fight, saying. You know my Lord, that before you came hither, you promised me two requests, and this I make one of them, that you continue no longer Combatte against this Knight, and in so dooing I shall acquite you of part of the promise which you made mee. *Palmerin* chasing like a furious Lyon, aunswered. I pray you Damosell aske some other thing, for in this matter, of force you must pardon mee. In sooth saide the Damosell, if you denie mee my demaunde, I will complaine at the King of *Englands* Courte, and there will I declare you periured, for ill it beseemes such a Knight as you are, to make promise to a Ladie and not obserue it. By God Ladie, saide *Palmerin*, you doo mee greate wronge, in withholding mee from reuenge on him, whom aboue all menne in the worlde, I hate moste deadlie, vnhappie was the howre wherein I mette you: and so mounting vppe on horsebacke, he galloped awaie in verie great anger. When the other sorrowfull Ladie sawe, that *Palmerin* was gone, and had left her Knight, with great ioye shee embraced the Damosell that had procured it, thanking her for sheelding the life of a most noble Knight, for which courtesie shee remained bounde to her during life.

What I haue doone, (quoth the Damosell) is for the loue of you and this Knight, swearing to you by the fayth of a Gentlewomanne, that I haue another thing to aske of the Knight which is gone, that concerneth mee very neerelie. Notwithstanding, your teares mooued mee with such compassion, that I stande in daunger to loose what I shall neuer recouer, yet in respecte the cause was so honest and vertuous, I doo not repent what I haue doone: but because he remaineth indebted to mee for an other request, I must needes leaue you and followe him, so mounting vppon her Palfraye, shee rode after *Palmerin* with all the

haste shee possiblie coulde make. And in her iourney wee wyll leaue her, returning to *Frisol*, whose woundes beeing verye dangerous, the Ladie bounde them vppe so well as she coulde, tyll they came at theyr next Lodging, where by good fortune was a Ladie so well seene in Chirurgerie, as in shorte time she cured his
5 woundes whole and sounde. *Frisol* not well recouered, departed thence with the Ladie, because the thirde daie following they shoulde bee at the Castell, whither alreadie was come *Hermes*, one of the King of *Englands* Knights, beeing sent by his Lord the King to deliuer the Ladie her right: which *Hermes* did according to his charge, entertayned the Ladie honourablie, deliuered her the Keyes of the
10 Castell, and commaunded all the Subiects to reuerence the Ladie, which they refused not to doo, but were gladde of her comming. For ioy heerof, were very sollemne feastes prepared, and the Ladie recounted to *Hermes*, Commissioner for the King, howe *Frisol* fought the Combatte by the waie, against the Knight in the black Armour: whereby *Hermes* presentlie knewe, that it was the strange
15 Knight, who had left the Courte, vnknowne to his companions or anie of his Freendes, whereof hee was not a little glad, because hee iudged that these newes woulde bee welcome to the King. Wherefore so soone as he had accomplished his charge, and seated the Ladie quietlie in her Castell, hee departed, intending to follow *Palmerin* till he founde him, trauayling the way was assigned him by
20 the Ladie.

Frisol stayed there with the Ladie till he had perfectlie recouered his health, and then without any other recompence for his paynes, but onelie a Horsse, because his owne was slaine, and a newe Armour, his owne beeing spoyled, he returned to the Duke of *Gaule*, who reioyced greatlie to haue his companie. But
25 when the Duke vnderstood howe discourteously he had beene vsed by the blacke Knight, who was so highly fauoured in the *English* Courte, hee deuised by all the meanes possible to bee reuenged on him: so that beeing in a Castell on the Frontiers of his Duchie, yet within the King of *Englands* dominion, hee vnderstoode the blacke Knight should passe that way, because he coulde not els returne to the
30 Court. Nowe perswading himselfe for resolute vengeaunce, hee pitched his Tents in a fayre Meddowe neere a Bridge, and there placed twelue Knights, the most hardie and valiant men in all his Dukedom, who shoulde maintaine this order: that no Knight shoulde passe ouer the Bridge, vnlesse hee entred Combat with those twelue Knights one after another, and such as were vanquished, shoulde
35 submitte themselues to the Dukes mercy, eyther for their deliueraunce, or to remaine his prysoners, and the Horsse of the partie foyled, should belong to the conquerer, but if they were dismounted, the passenger shoulde goe on his iourneie, and take their Horsses with him.[6] Thys aduenture thus established, many good Knights were ouercome, because it was a very harde matter to vanquishe
40 twelue Knights, and yet escape: but the Duke tooke no little pleasure heerein, who detained *Frisol* more by constraint then otherwyse, for his anger so vehementlie encreased agaynst *Palmerin*, as no delight or pleasure coulde expiate his reuenging desires.

Chapter LV.

Howe Palmerin went with the Damosell to accomplishe the promise he made her, and what befell him.

Palmerin (as you haue hearde) departed from the Damosell in a great rage, because he coulde not execute what hee intended, wherefore hee deuised to deale some other waie, and to single foorth *Frisol* in such conuenient place,[1] as one of them shoulde die before they departed. And as hee was imagining some other way to ouertake *Frisol*, the Damosell had nowe againe recouered his companie, saying. I pray you Sir Knight, conceiue no il opinion of me, for hindering you from killing your enemie, whom you haue left in verye great ieopardie,[2] considering what bountie and courage is in him, and which your selfe perhaps wil be sorrie for. Wherefore I pray you forget this displeasure, and determine to fulfill what you haue promised, which if you will doo, you must goe with me. Beleeue me Damosell, saide *Palmerin*, you shewed but little courtesie, so often hindering me from the thing, which aboue all other in this worlde most tormenteth mee. What vnhappie bodie are you? but more vnhappie the howre I mette with you? but seeing it is reason I should keepe my promise, leade the waie, and I will not faile to follow you. So rode they on, and for foure daies space hee woulde not speake one word to her, and faine hee woulde haue left her companie, but that hee could not with honour forsake her. The next daie, as they rode by a Riuers side, *Palmerin* espyed a Knight standing with a Bowe and arrow in his hande, which he let flye at his Horsse and killed him.[3] *Palmerin* impacient by remembraunce of *Frysol*, and angrye that the Knight had thus killed his Horsse, made towardes him so fast as hee coulde, but the Knight was suddainlie gotte on the further side of the Lake, and *Palmerin* vppe to the middle in Water before hee was ware of it, and nowe he coulde neyther see the Knight that slewe his Horsse, nor the Damosell that came in his companie. *Palmerin* beeing in great perplexity, when he sawe nothing but water rounde about him, and feeling he was vppon a Bridge, behelde a meruailous deepe streame running vnder it, and at the ende thereof a goodlie Castell. Walking along the Bridge toward the Castell, amazed at this contrarie aduenture, hee espied a Knight on the battlements of the Castell, who saide. Staie a while Sir Knight, one shall come presentlie and open the Gate. *Palmerin* knewe not what to saie, but determined to defende himselfe if anie came to assault him, so the Castell Gate beeing opened, hee entred with his sword drawn, yet was there no man that displeased him, but euery one made him humble reuerence, with verie good wordes and gentle countenaunce, declaring by their behauiour, that hee was more then welcome thither. Thus walking on to the inner Courte,[4] there came towardes him a Ladie, accompanied with manie Damosels and Knights, all shewing cheerefull gestures, and the Ladie taking *Palmerin* by the hande, saide.

Ah gentle Knight, right welcome are you to this place, and Heauen be praysed for the good it dooth mee, to see you heare, that is able to accomplishe the thing, which no other as yet coulde bee able to finish: enter hardilie in good assuraunce, for to you will wee make all the honour we are able. *Palmerin* beleeuing the Ladie, was brought into a meruailous goodlie Chamber, where certaine Squires holpe to vnarme him, bringing him a gorgious Mantle to wrape about him. This doone, he was conducted into a large Hall, where the Table was couered, the Ladie entertaining him so noblie, as in the King of *Englands* Courte hee coulde not be better. The feaste ended, and the Tables withdrawne, the Ladie beganne to deuise with *Palmerin*, saying. Long time (my Lorde) haue we desired your comming, as the man in whome our onelie helpe consisteth: for by your valour wee are perswaded to be deliuered from the miserie, wherein I and mine haue too long time beene detained. I beseeche you Madame, quoth *Palmerin*, to tell mee your affayres, as also what the Knight meant to kill my Horsse, and why you entertaine mee with so great kindnes. If you will promise mee, saide the Ladie, to accomplish a needfull occasion, and which I thinke is destenied to you: I will resolue you, otherwise, I shall but loose my labour. If it be a matter resonable, (quoth *Palmerin*) and that a Knight may compasse, spare not to tell mee, for I will doo my endeuour therein. Gramercies gentle Knight saide the Ladie, the circumstance of the occasion followeth in this sort.[5] This Castel (my Lord) sometime belonged to my noble Father, a Knight so hardie and valiant as anie in these parts, in whose yonger yeeres loue so ouer-ruled him as he affected a Ladie, of no lesse qualitie and condition then himselfe,[6] by whom he had a daughter, at whose byrth his Ladie and Wife deceassed. My Father beeing yet in the flower of his youth, matched the seconde time with a Ladie of verie honourable and auncient discent, by whom he had mee the first Childe. My Sister come to fourteene yeeres of age, my Father oftentimes would haue richlie maryed her, whereto she beeing vnwylling, by my Fathers consent, shee remayned with her Mothers Sister, whose skill was verie great in all sciences, by whose counsel my Sister caused a goodly Pallace to be edified, and a strong Towre in an Isle on the otherside of thys Castell, where afterwarde they made their continuall abyding. During this time, my Father loouing me deerelie, matched me with a welthie and noble Knight, excelling in all perfections, but cheefelie in chiualrie, by whom I had a Daughter a yeere after our espousall: but the more my greefe, my Husbande and Father bothe dyed, within little space after my Childes birth. My Daughter beeing come to the yeeres of mariage, her beautie made her desired of manie noble Lordes: but because I still reputed her too yong, I denied all her suters, which afterward turned mee to verie great detriment. For my Sisters Aunt had a Son, the most mishaped, deformed and worst conditioned Knight, as all the Countrey could not shewe such another, yet became hee so amorous of my Daughter, as hee requested his Mother to demaunde her of me for his wife: but when I heard thereof, you may well perswade your selfe, that neuer woman dislyked anie thing more, and yet to this time doo as much as I then did, so that I made her aunswere, howe I woulde rather desire my Daughters death, then so to dishonour her, because he was altogeather vnwoorthy such speciall fortune.

Notwithstanding this sharpe repulse, he continued his amorous desires to my Daughter, so that hee earnestly perswaded his mother, to permitte him to take her from me perforce: to which sute the vndiscreete Mother consented, eyther mooued with pittie, or ouercome by the importunate sollicitings of her, so that one daie (vnder couller of a freendlie meeting to be merrie) he robbed me of my Daughter. This wicked Traytor, had long before that time intended this trecherie, compacting the mater secretlie with villaines and theeues, by whose assistance he caried away my Daughter, shutting her vppe in the strong Tower whereof I tolde you. And because he feared I wold gather some strength to reskewe her, considering how well I was beloued of my neighboures, hee preuented mee by a strange enchauntment, enuironing the Castell and the Tower with such a meruailous Water, as no Knight shoulde enter vppon them without theyr consent. Now that themselues might come foorth and returne againe at their pleasure, they deuised a little Boate, which is guarded by two fierce Lyons, and a puissaunt Knight that hath charge of them, so that none comes to them but whome they lyst. Since thys vnhappie time did I neuer see my Daughter, whome this damnable villaine (which most of all greeues mee) immediatly violated and rauished at his pleasure, swearing nowe neuer to take her as his Wife, but to vse her as his Concubine: and beside all this, the Traytour in despight of mee, and to reuenge the wordes I gaue him, dooth monstrouslie abuse her, and (vnmanlie) whippeth her dailie with Roddes, which my Sister hath often intreated to be spared, but he by no meanes wil be perswaded.[7] Thus seeing my selfe out of all hope to recouer her againe, haue euer since continued in earnest inuocations to Heauen, that some notable vengeaunce might punish this villainie: and such fauour haue I founde in my deuoute imprecations, as firste his Mother was chastised, with a disease called Saint *Anthonyes* fire in one of her legges,[8] which so greeuouslie torments her, as no remedie canne bee founde to asswage the vexation. Her Sonne vnderstanding heereof, woulde haue slayne my Sister, accusing her to procure his Mothers infirmitie, by her learned knowledge: whereuppon my Syster fearing her life, and watching time conuenient for her purpose, escaped from the villaine hither to mee, beeing sorrie that her Aunt shoulde thus iniuriouslye deale with mee, and promised to worke the meane that I should recouer my Daughter. These wordes not a little pleasing me, I woulde needes knowe howe I shoulde come by my Daughter againe, whose misfortune had beene so yrksome to me, whereto she thus answered.

It is so good Sister, that I cannot nowe reuersse the enchauntments I haue alreadie made for your daughter, though gladlie I woulde if it laye in my power,[9] wherefore you must attende the comming of a Knight, who exceedeth all other in vertue and prowesse: for he shall passe the water, kill the Knight, enter the Tower, and deliuer my Niece your Daughter againe into your custodie. As concerning this Knight, good Sister, that shall so hardly passe the water without feare, and fully accomplish my former enchauntment: for him will I leaue with you a Sworde, a verye sumptuous Armour, and diuers other gyfts to bestowe

Palmerin d'Oliva: Part I 297

on him, because my selfe shall not liue to see him, which came so to passe, for very shortlie after, my Sister died. Nowe knowe you Syr Knight, what matter is preordayned for you, therefore take pittie on mee a poore desolate Mother, and aduenture your selfe in this cause of honour, as bounde thereto by vertue and needefull occasion.

Beleeue mee Madame, sayde *Palmerin*, your dyscourse hath beene strange, and good reason mooues you to request vengeaunce, because your wrong is the greatest that euer I hearde of: which may somewhat perswade you, that the offender cannot long escape, without shame aunswerable to hys villainie, for Heauen wyll not suffer it, by assistance whereof, I hope to reuenge your Daughters rape. And trust me Ladie, I am sorrie I came not in your Systers life time, because she coulde haue resolued mee in a doubtfull matter: neuerthelesse I will doo so much for you as if she were liuing. But I meruaile what is become of the Knight that slewe my Horsse, and the Damosell that conducted me hither. As for the Damosell, (quoth the Ladie) she shall come anone to attend vpon you: but the Knight was onely a matter of enchauntment, deuised by my Sister to discouer the man that should ende this aduenture. And the Damosell whereof you speake, hath brought hither many Knights to the Lake, but when theyr Horsses were slayne, none of them durst bee so hardie as to enter the water, but onely you, beeing predestinated for this aduenture. In this and other such like talke, they spent the day tyll Supper time, and afterwarde was *Palmerin* conducted to his Chamber, and beeing in bedde hee coulde take no rest, first for greefe that hee had not slayne *Frysol*, then againe by the strange tale the Ladie tolde him: wherefore rysing the sooner in the morning, he went with the Ladie to seruice in her Chappell, where hee desired of God that he might preuaile against these coniurations, and vanquish the Knight that had so much abused his order. Returning from the Chappell, the Ladie among other talke, thus sayde. I see Sir Knight that your Armour is broken and much defaced, that one may iudge you haue not kept it idle in your Armorie, wherfore I think you met not with your freend, when you were enforced to so dangerous tryall: but as I vnderstande by the Damosell that was your guide hither, you returned him good payment for his paynes. To supplie your want, I wil bestow an Armour on you, which my Sister long since prouided for you, and with careful regard kept close in her Chest: therfore let me intreate you not to refuse it, in respect it was not prouided but for special purpose, beeing needfull for the present occasion you must now enterprise. *Palmerin* would not refuse her offer, wherefore opening the Cheste, there lay the Armour couered with white Taffata, whereon was wrought in Letters of Gold this inscription: *These Armes were made for the good Knight Palmerin d'Oliua, Sonne to the most royall King that this daye liueth in all Greece.* That woorthy present greatlie delighted *Palmerin*, because heerin his desire was somewhat satisfied, which was to knowe the estate of his Father: wherefore in midst of this pleasing humour hee saide to the Ladie. I perceiue fayre Madam, that your Sister knewe more of my destenie then anie other, for seeing she coulde so truelie describe my name, I neede make no great doubt of her further iudgment. So taking away the Silke, behelde there a more sumptuous Armour, then that which halting *Vulcan* made for noble *Achilles*, at the earnest intreatie of beautifull *Thetis*,[10] beeing curiouslie chased ouer with flowres of Gold, and the Sheelde of Steele, engrauen with rare deuises, as wel might beseeme the greatest Prince in the worlde. *Palmerin* presently put of hys owne Armour,[11] and inuested himselfe with the Ladies gift, which so well agreed with him in euerie point, as the like coulde hardlie be framed for his bodie.

When he was thus armed, he desired the Ladie to shew him the waie, that might conduct him to the place where he should discharge his promise, for he would delaie no further time in a matter of such weight. The Ladie commaunded three of her Squires to conduct him, who leade him along a narrowe pathe waie, which brought him to the enchaunted water so deepe and daungerous, and there they shewed him the boate to passe ouer in, which was fastened with a great Chayne to a Tree, whereupon *Palmerin* sought the meanes to vntie it: but so soone as hee laide hand on the Chayne to plucke it towardes him, there rushed presentlie foorth of the enchaunted Water, two mightie Lyons, who assaulted *Palmerin* in such forcible manner, as they got him down on the ground vnder them, yet he recouered himselfe quicklie, and valiantlie encountered these hidious monsters, who had such a deuillish charme on them, as no Sworde coulde anie waie hurt or wounde them. *Palmerin* perceiuing that all his labour was in vaine, called to Heauen for helpe in this necessitie, and commending his abilitie to the highest protection, and his hart to the gracious regard of his Mystresse: hee gaue one of the Lyons such a cruell stroke betweene the eyes, as he tombled headlong into the Water, and was afterwarde seene no more, and soone after he sent the other after for companie,[12] but had not his Armour beene of meruailous vertue, doubtlesse this shoulde haue beene his last aduenture.

Not a little ioyfull of this happy victorie, he entred the Boate, and with one of the Oares beganne to rowe, but nowe was hee surprised with a wonderfull daunger, for the Water arose in huge byllowes, beating and tossing the Boate so fearefullie, as he had much a doo to keepe the bottome from turning vpwarde. In this perplexitie, which hee coulde not deuise howe to mittigate, a matter of greater mischaunce yet befel him, for a meruailous great and ouglie Monster suddainlie started out of the Water, which laboured by all meanes possible to ouerturne the Boate. Nowe was hee constrayned to forgoe his Oare, and drawe his weapon to resist this Monster, which terrefied him so cruellie on the one side, and the rough Waters so daungerouslie on the other, as hee was not in the like hazarde, when hee fought with the Serpent on the Mountaine *Artifaeria*.[13]

To comfort him in this contagious extreamitie, hee implored his diuine assistaunce, whose onelie prouidence must nowe defende him, els had the raging and distempered Water, or the rauenous Monster that gaped for hys life, deuoured him. But he that in greatest perrilles, was euer of vndaunted spirite, made such harde shyfte to rowe with his Sworde, as in despight of the Monster, and the hurling waues of the Water, hee landed on the otherside: when immediatlie all the coniuration ceassed, so that neyther Water, Monster, Boate or any thing els might then bee discerned. I leaue you to imagine, whether *Palmerin* were gladde or no, that he had so happilie escaped this danger: for ioye wherof hee fell vpon his knees, and with heaued handes and eyes to Heauen, gaue thankes vnto God for his deliueraunce. His prayer beeing ended, hee went to the Castell, where hee hearde a most greeuous and dolefull complaint of a Ladie, saying.

Vnhappie bee the howre of my natiuitie, alas, is it possible that in all the whole worlde, anie Ladie may compare with my miseries? *Palmerin* attentiuelie marking these speeches, knewe well it was the imprisoned Ladie, wherefore mooued with compassion, hee called aloude for one to open the Gate, and so long hee called, that the Knight heard him, who looking foorth at a Windowe of the Fortresse, saide. In an euill howre (Knight) cammest thou hyther, and I meruaile what foolishe presumption guyded thee to this place, seeing thou canst no waie escape my handes, but in my courtesie it remaynes, eyther to spare thee, or put thee to a moste cruell death, although my enchauntment haue suffered thy passage. Thou art maruailous hardye, quoth *Palmerin*, there at thy Windowe, but if thy courage bee such, as to deale with mee hande to hande: I shall let thee vnderstande, that thy great wordes cannot sheelde thee from my Sworde, for I will pull downe that proude stomacke, and rewarde thy inexorable tirranie, to that good Ladie I hearde complaine, whom villainously thou tookest from her Mother. Come downe I pray thee if thou bee not afraide, and thou shalt see what entertainment I giue to such as thou art.

Are you Sir (quoth the Knight) such a corrector and reformer of vices? Darest thou but tarrie tell I come downe I shall teache thee the way to be better aduised. So arming himselfe presentlie, he mounted on horsebacke, and came foorth of the Castell: whereuppon *Palmerin* thus spake to him. There is ouer great ods Sir Knight, you to bee on horsebacke, and I on foote, you shall shewe small manhood in offering me such wrong: I pray thee (of courtesie) allight, otherwise I shall bestowe such a currying on your Palfray, as your Seruaunt afterwarde shall take but small paynes with him. The Knight of the Castell made as though hee hearde him not, and ran fiercelie with his Launce against *Palmerin*, who escaping his enemie, with his Sworde gaue the Horsse such a stroke on the leg, as he past by him, that the boane beeing cut in twain, he fel to the ground, hauing one of the Knights legges so fast vnder him, as hee was not able to recouer himselfe. *Palmerin* willing to help him vppe againe, gaue him halfe a dozen such raps aboute the pate, as hee laye quiet enough without any moouing: whereupon he vnclasped his Helmet, when the Knight hauing some ayre, beganne to striue with him, and drawing his pocket Dagger, gaue *Palmerin* a sore wounde therewith in the thigh, in recompence whereof, at one stroke hee tooke his heade from his shoulders. The Squires and Seruaunts of the Castell, who came foorth to see the issue of the fight, ranne apace to the Castell againe, to shutte the Gate for their owne safetie: but *Palmerin* (albeit hee was hurte) preuented them, laying about him so rowghlie on euerie side, as he sware if they woulde not bring him to the imprisoned Ladie, they shoulde all presentlie die the death. Manie of them with feare tombled headlong into the Ditch, other on their knees asked for mercy, promising to doo what euer he commaunded them, whereupon he saide to him that had the Keyes. Arise quicklie villaine, and conduct mee to the prison, or I shall paie thee for thy lazines. The poore fellowe almost frighted out of his witte, brought him to the Towre where the Ladie was, whome they founde naked from the middle vpwarde,[14] and so greeuouslie beaten, as all her bodie was gore bloode, which the Knight had doone that morning, for a Dreame he had the night before, howe her Mother woulde sende a Knight, that should take her thence perforce, and murder him,[15] in which opinion hee came to the Ladie, saying. I perceiue that thy Mother and Freendes labour to get thee from mee, and practise my destruction by all the meanes they maie: but for their sakes thou shalt deerlie abye their dealing. And with these words, the villaine so cruellie whipped her, as shee was readie to giue vp the ghoste, and so left her in hope she would haue dyed. *Palmerin* finding the Ladie in this lamentable plight, saide. Arise good Ladie and leaue your sorrowful acclamations, for the villaine that thus misused you, hath had such absolution for his deserts, as he hath left his heade in signe of his penaunce:[16] and if you wil depart with me towards your Mother, I will shewe you the Traytour where he lies nowe quiet enough. Ah my Lorde, (quoth the Ladie) is the trecherous *Scloto* deade, that so monstrouslie wronged me? Hee is Ladie, saide *Palmerin*, you neede feare him no more. Then Heauen be praysed (quoth she) for this happie daie, and among all Knights bee you the most renowned for euer, with which wordes shee arose, and wrapping a furred Mantle about her, without anie other garments on her bodie, shee went with *Palmerin*, and passing by the place where *Scloto* lay slaine, lifting her eyes and hands to Heauen, she saide. O my God, how is thy name to be praysed, so iustlie punishing the trecherie and disloyaltie of this villaine: Ah Traytor, howe worthilie hast thou receiued this death, which is not so rigorous, as thy mercilesse tyrranie hath been to me.

Heere you must note, that so soone as the Knight was deade, all the enchauntments about the Castel were presentlie finished, the great Lake beeing consumed after *Palmerins* passage, so that the Ladies Mother aduertised therof, came to meet *Palmerin*, embracing her daughter with such exceeding ioy, as they coulde not speake to eache other theyr teares so hindered them,[17] at length the Mother kneeled before *Palmerin* with these wordes. Ah woorthie Knight, howe happie haue you this daie made me? all my former greefes (by your meanes) beeing now conuerted into singuler contentation. As she would haue proceeded in her gratulations, she perceiued the bloode to trickle downe *Palmerins* Armour, which she sorrowing to beholde, saide. Me thinkes Sir Knight you are very sore wounded, I beseech you graunt me so much honor, as to repose your selfe a while within my Castell, where I doubt not to vse such dilligent care, as you shall be whole and sound in very short time. *Palmerin* not minding to refuse her offer, returned with the Lady, and beeing vnarmed, was brought to his Chamber, where the Lady dressed his woundes, and hee was so well entertained as hart coulde deuise.[18] Then went the Ladies squires and seruants to *Sclotos* Castel, from whence bringing al things that were of anie value, they burned the Traytors body, and putting his head on the point of a Launce, they placed it on the top of the Towre for a perpetuall memory.[19] The next daie came people from all parts of the Island, to see the Knight that ended the enchauntments, and among other, the Damosell that conducted him thither was one, who on her knee thus spake to him. Nowe am I satisfied Sir Knight, and you discharged of the promise you made mee, which was onely for the deliueraunce of this Ladie, whom you haue valiantlie conquered from the tyrant that tormented her. I beseech him, who euermore hath regard of the poore afflicted, that his pleasure may be to send you the like, or a better aduenture, whereby you may accomplish all your hautie enterprises. So wyll he I doubt not, said *Palmerin*, and that was one from which you disswaded me: but I shall neuer be merry till I finde him againe, though then at your entreatie hee escaped my hands so well. And Fortune speede the matter so happilie, quoth the Damosell, as peace and freendshyp may be vnited betweene you: for if eyther of you miscarrie, it were great pittie, considering the woorthy valoure wherwith you are both noblie furnished. Let come what will, said *Palmerin*, neuer shall other agreement be betweene vs. With these wordes the Damosell helde her peace, for she perceiued by his answers, that hee was not halfe pleased with the other Knight.[20]

Chapter LVI.

Howe Palmerin trauayling through a great Forrest, espyed a Dwarffe enter into a Caue, whom he folowed, and founde there a Knight, with whom he had much conference.

So long continued *Palmerin* in the Castell with the Lady, till his wounds beeing healed, and he able to beare Armour, hee saide to the Ladie. Madame, by the helpe of God and your dilligent endeuour, I finde my selfe in good constitution of body, wherfore with your fauourable licence, I meane to morrowe to depart hence, because occasions of great importaunce so commaundeth me:[1] yet this assuraunce will I leaue with you, that in anie place where I shall come heereafter, your wonderfull courtesie hath gained such power ouer mee, as at all times I remaine to doo you anie pleasure. The Ladie right gladde of *Palmerins* noble offer, and her Daughter thankfull for her benefit receiued,[2] returned him manie thankfull gratulations: but seeing they could no longer detaine him, for his speeches were such as hee woulde needes be gone, she sayd. Gentle Knight, seeing it likes you no longer to soiourne heere, but that you thinke it expedient to departe, I woulde gladlie present you with a simple gift, not as recompence of your painefull trauailes, but onely that heereafter you might remember from whence it came. Then tooke shee out of a Coffer two riche and precious Ringes, and presenting him one of them, she saide. You shall gyue this Ring to her whome aboue all other you moste esteeme, the Ring contayning this special vertue, that the longer she weares it, the more shee shall looue you, and daielie shall her looue so vehementlie encrease, as all aduersities and troubles shee shall beare with patience that by meanes of your loue may anie way endaunger her.[3]

This other Ring is of a contrarie vertue, which you must giue to the Ladie your deere Freende beloueth, and to him may you safelie saie, that anie occasion whatsoeuer, canne not plucke it from his Ladies finger: for this is the nature thereof, that the Ladie which weares it, shall not be disparaged, and neither intreaties, gyfts, or whatsoeuer beside, cannot compell her, to doo any thing contrarie to her lyking. If it came so to passe that shee were belooued by anie other, then him shee nowe affecteth, shee shall be able by vertue of this Ring, to quench all such libidinous desire in her sollicitour, and cause him neuer afterwarde to mooue her with anie dishonest request. As for these stones of so rare and excellent quallitie, you must note that they were preciselie chosen for you by my Sister, and placed as you see them, by her superficiall knowledge in the Magicall sciences, that in time to come they shall doo such seruice, as no Iewels (of what value so euer they were) might bee able to doo the like.

Beside these, shee gaue him diuers other Iewells to carrie to his Ladie, for which he humbly thanked her, and taking his leaue of her and her Daughter, who shed manie teares for his departure, hee mounted on horsebacke, and trauailing thorowe a great Forrest, hee espyed a Dwarffe, whom hee iudging to bee his Seruaunt *Vrbanillo*, because hee was of his stature, and very much resembled

him, he called aloude. Hearest thou tall fellow,[4] howe camest thou in this place, so vnfrequented and inhabited? The Dwarffe beeing in a great feare, ranne so fast as hee coulde into a great Caue betweene two Bushes, which made *Palmerin* allight and followe him, and verie farre went he into the Caue not seeing anie
5 bodie, till at length he came into a little roome, as it had beene cut out of a quarrie, which had light into it by a lyttle chincke cutte through the Rocke: and there he founde a yong Knight layde vppon a bedde, at whose feete lay the Dwarffe, quaking and trembling with his late feare, whome *Palmerin* nowe sawe that hee was not *Vrbanillo*, wherefore he saluted the Knight, saying. I must intreate you
10 Sir Knight to pardon mee, because I entred so boldlie, neyther knocking first, or calling for any of your Seruaunts: albeit I desired to speake with thys little man, but nothing coulde induce him to tarrie my comming, for hee fledde from mee as I had beene a deuill. Whereuppon perswading my selfe, to finde some other bodie heere more courteous, I followed him at the harde heeles, with no other
15 intent, but onelie to knowe howe I might possible gette foorth of this desolate Forrest, wherein by misaduenture I haue lost my waie, for I woulde not willinglie stray too farre, least I shoulde be forced to remaine heere as an holie Hermit, considering my profession is cleane contrarie.[5] To preuent such chaunce, I thinke it was Gods will I shoulde followe your Seruaunt, let mee therefore intreate you,
20 to know what you are, and wherefore you liue heere so solitarie, shunning as it seemes the companie of menne: protesting to you, that if I may in ought assist you, whereby to drawe you from this obscure life, I will with all my hart accomplishe it, though it were matter that shoulde concerne my life.

The Knight raysing vppe himselfe, and sighing so bytterly as life and soule
25 woulde haue parted in sunder, aunswered. Alas noble Knight, seeke not to vnderstande the depth of my sorrowe, in respect the remedie is altogether impossible: yet in that your demaund proceedeth from such a gentle spirite, as pittieth the miseries of despysed creatures,[6] I will acquaint you with some parte of mine estate.
30 Know then gentle Knight, that I am the most forlorne *Varnan*, whose vnfortunate life exceedeth all mens whatsoeuer, for this worlde affoordeth me nothing but mishappe, disgrace, contempt, and al tormenting greefes, as for delight and pleasure, they are lothsome to mee, my monethes, weekes, dayes, howres and minutes, beeing continually accompanied with all extreame passions. My great-
35 est ease consisteth in dolorous lamentations, remembraunce of passed infortunes, sad regrets, and insupportable mellanchollie. In breefe, I am onely hee, whose companions are, a trauailed spirite, thoughts confounded with frustrate hope, hauing vtterlie loste the light of those gladsome Sunnes, whereof the one shyned in my face, the other in my hart, so that nowe nothing is left for me but a life
40 despysed, yet welcome to me that am so disdained.

These wordes were vttered with so manie sighes, such floods of teares, and haling his flesh with such impatience,[7] as would haue relented a hart of Adamant, which mooued *Palmerin* by gentle perswasions, to request of him the cause of his disquiet, and so long he continued his importunate intreaties, that the Knight at length thus answered. Gentle Sir, so well contenteth me the sorrowes which I suffer, that in hope of any remedie, I woulde not bewray them: but seeing Fortune hath thus conducted you hither, in respecte of your gracious and affable nature, as also that you shall not repute me vndiscreete and misgouerned, I will satisfie you in the cause of my sadnes.

True it is Sir Knight, that I haue hetherto, and euer shall, loue a Ladie, Daughter to a Knight my neighbour, shee beeing (in my iudgment) one of the fayrest Ladies in the whole worlde. And perceiuing by her behauiour that she loued me as well, or rather more, which indeede shee did not: for her I accomplished all thinges that a Knight coulde for his Ladie, aduenturing mine honour and my life in all daungers for her sake, yea, nothing might bee refused for the diuine Mistresse of my thoughts. Perceiuing my selfe to bee so equally looued, and my passions to growe beyonde my abilitie, finding occasion to acquaint her with the secrets of my harte, I desired her to pitty my oppressions, which if she refused to do, she should loose her louer, and his life withall. For I was so sollemnly vowed to her seruice, as she could not commaund any thing so hard or daungerous, but by her fauourable regarde would bee most easie to mee. These words could draw no pittie from her, but displeased and in great anger she answered. That I might not bee reckoned among those Knights, who deserued the loue of a Ladie of her calling,[8] and thenceforth I should not bee so hardie, as to speake to her, or come in her presence. Goe quoth she, and followe her loue that gaue thee thy Faulcon, wherein thou takest such pleasure, and neuer mayst thou turne againe to me.

With these wordes shee floong from me to a Windowe, where I was wont always to stande and talke with her, beguiling the time in no lesse contentation, then those happy soules in the *Elysian* Fieldes,[9] such was the rare beautie, good grace, and singuler courtesie of my (sometime) beloued Ladie *Valerica*. I cannot denie, but that a Ladie bestowed the Falcon on me, but in any such respect as my Ladie imagined, God knowes is most vntrue,[10] nor could death compell mee so much to abuse my chosen Mistresse.

Seeing my Ladie then so rigorous, and her answere so seuere, yet assured of mine owne innocencie and loyaltie: I was supprised with such surpassing heauines, as euery howre I expected when my feeble spirite, woulde forsake his long despysed habitation. My Ladie beeing thus resolute in her owne opinion, and disdayning all meanes I shewed to perswade her, despayring likewise of anie after hope: I determined with my selfe, to abandon all companie, as vnwoorthie of theyr societie, and then betooke my selfe to this brutishe kinde of life,[11] where I might without anie impeache, breathe foorth my continuall complaints.

In this resolution I came to this place, without the knowledge of my Ladie or anie other, this Dwarffe onelie excepted, who euermore hath beene my most trustie Seruaunt, and fetcheth my necessaries at a village neere adioyning, and by his honest perswasions, hath manie times with-helde me from committing violence on my selfe. Thus haue you hearde in breefe the cause of my sorrowe, the depth whereof cannot bee considered or valued, but by such as haue in like manner tryed and suffered, the dysdaine and ingratitude of vnconstant Ladyes. *Palmerin* hauing hearde the fortunes of the Knight, repeated to him the graces and fauours of his Ladie *Polynarda*, what honor shee did him in her Fathers Courte, and howe he was in daunger to receiue the like reward, as the Knight did of his *Valerica*:[12] and fearing indeede that his mishappe woulde sorte to that issue, he fel down at the feete of this poore refused Loouer. The Knight perceiuing, that the repetition of his misfortune was cause of this alteration, breathing foorth a vehement sighe, he sayde.

Alas wretched Caytife that I am, hath my destinie made mee so vnhappie, that enduring an extreamitie worse then death, I cannot dye, and yet he that did but heare my miserie hath lost his life? I will not liue anie longer to preiudice anie other man,[13] but will nowe make waie to the ende of myne owne troubles. So drewe hee foorth *Palmerins* Sworde, and offered to thrust it into his bodie: but *Palmerin* reuiued to his former estate, started suddainlie vppe, and catching him in his armes, saide.

Howe nowe my Freende? will you be so inconsiderate, that for a little temporall paine which your bodie endureth, to condemne your soule to euerlasting perdition?[14] And though your passions touch you so seuerelie, as you will affoorde no pittie to your selfe: yet let mee intreate you to forbeare this humour.[15] For not without reason haue I sustayned this suddaine motion, remembring the vnspeakable comfort I receiued by one, who by false suggestions, or slaunderous reports (which woundeth more deepe then the fatall weapon) may in like sort be chaunged into such conceit, as her iudgment may exceede a hell of torments.[16] Yet canne I not denie (your Ladie hauing with such shame refused you) but you haue great occasion to greeue thereat, yet not to stretch the extreamitie so farre as to dispayre, or worke iniurie to your selfe, calling to memorie howe light the opinion of a Woman is, how suddaine she will alter, and howe prompt shee is to iealousie, especiallie where shee loueth effectuallie. And if heeretofore shee loued you so feruentlie, it is impossible but shee should feele some part of your anguish, and more violentlie (I thinke) then your selfe can. Trust then in him that hath all harts at commaunde, repose your selfe constantlie on his prouidence,[17] for hee will not leaue you frustrate of your honourable intent, standing with iustice and perfect integritie.

As *Palmerin* continued these comfortable perswasions, the Dwarffe couered the Table, and sette before them such a small pittaunce, as he had prouided, and when they had refreshed themselues: *Palmerin* tooke hys leaue of the Knight, promising him (if hee could by anie meanes) to giue some ease to his oppressions. *Varnan* returned him manie thankes, commaunding his Dwarff to conduct him to the high waie, beeing not a little sorrowfull to leaue his companie, who had so well aduised and comforted him. *Palmerin* beeing come into his readie waie, sent backe the Dwarffe, and rode on till hee was gotte out of the Forrest, intending to find out the Castell where *Valerica* remained, because he woulde somewhat sollicite the cause of sollitarie *Varnan*. Ryding along in this determination, hee espyed a Knight and two Squires before him, the Knight thus speaking to one of his Squires. I know not whether it bee time as yet to enter the Garden, or if Madame *Valerica* bee as yet come thether. Goe see if shee bee there, and returne quicklie to mee againe. *Palmerin* hearing the name of *Valerica*, knewe well it was shee, for whome the solitarie Knight liued in such pensiuenes: wherefore mooued with pittie of his miseries, hee sayde to himselfe. See heere the trecherie of a trothlesse Woman, so vnhonourablie to forsake the man that loues her so deerelie, and preferre the villainie of this intercepting Traytour: but I shall teache him ere I goe, what a penaltie belonges to the preuenting of a loyall Knight, and so comming to the Knight hee sayde. Art thou the man villaine, that wouldest forestall the loue of the best Knight in *England*? By my Sword, thou shalt deerelie pay for thy disloyaltie. With these wordes he gaue him such a stroke on the head, as he cleft it therwith to the verie teeth.

The Squires seeing their Maister slaine, began to haste awaie: but *Palmerin* caught him that was sent to the Garden, to whom he saide. Come on Sirra,[18] if thou louest thy life, bring mee to the Ladie, if thou doost not, thou shalt neuer followe thy trade anie longer. The Squire durst doo no otherwise, so hee brought him to the little Gate, where *Valerica* was wont to receiue in her louer, and knocking with his finger as his Maister was accustomed, *Valerica* opened the doore, and thinking it was her Freende, cast her armes about *Palmerins* necke, who brought her in his armes forth of the Garden, commanding the Squire presentlie to followe him. *Valerica* abashed heereat sayde. Howe nowe sweete Freend? whether will you carrie me? Knowe you not if my Father hearde heereof, that neither of vs durst approche before him? Tush Madame, sayde *Palmerin*, these are but wordes, there is no remedie but you must goe with me. So neither with teares nor requests would he bee intreated, but mounting on horsebacke, caused the Squire to helpe the Ladie vppe before him, because he would be sure shee should not escape from him, and ryding on towardes the Forrest, because the night drew on, he left the rode waie, seeking some place where they might conueniently repose themselues for that night. At length hee founde out a little thicket, where they allighted, and he turning hys Horsse to pasture, tooke off his Helmet and came to the Ladie, desiring her to bee content with such harde lodging for that night: but when she behelde that it was not her Freende, wringing her handes shee thus exclaymed. Alas vnhappie wretch that I am, how trecherouslie am I deceiued? what mishap may bee comparable to mine, hauing lost my Freende, and abyding at his pleasure that hath cruelly murdered him? Ah Fortune why art thou so inconstant,[19] to chaunge my former pleasures into this greeuous stratageme?

Palmerin hearing her so impacient, saide.[20] You must thinke Ladie, that what hath happened, is by diuine permission, who hath thus appointed to punish your loosenes, and your exceeding disloyaltie towardes him, who loues you deerer then his owne soule, and for your looue leades a most austere life, in the very desolate and vncomfortable place of the worlde. If hee haue thus long endured such hardnes for your sake, it is good reason that you should participate a little with his miserie. Feare not therefore, for I speake nothing of him but what I haue seene, and by great chaunce, haue I thus brought you from your Fathers house: meaning by Gods grace (this humour forgotten) to cause you match with him, whose true loue aboue all other hath deserued you.[21] Ah miserie incomparable, saide the Ladie, I see nowe it is in vaine to shunne what the destenies haue appointed, howe falles my fortune from ill to worsse? Must I nowe goe to that cowarde *Varnan*, whom hetherto I haue continuallie despised? let mee rather die a most shamefull death.

I know not Ladie what you thinke, said *Palmerin*, but in my opinion, *Varnan* is much better then you esteeme him, and a better Knight then he, that coulde defende his pate with no wiser pollicie: worthilie may you call him coward, and loue the other that liues to doo you seruice. So long they stood on these tearmes, vntill a Knight passed by them, to whome *Valerica* cryed. Helpe gentle Knight, for Gods sake pittie me, and deliuer me from thys Traytour, who falselie hath beguiled me, and violentlie brought me hether against my will. What art thou sayd the Knight, that thus dishonorest this Ladie? I shall teache thee better knowledge of thine order before wee part. *Palmerin* quicklie bridling his Horsse, and clasping on his Helmet, sayd to the Knight. What art thou that wouldest take her from me, whom I conquered euen nowe by my Sworde? follow thy way, or I shall shewe thee what discipline I vse to fooles, that will meddle with matters aboue their capacitie.[22] Doost thou so obstinatlie stand in thy trecherie? sayde the Knight: Marke what will be the ende of thy presumption.[23]

Chapter LVII.

Howe Palmerin hauing thus brought away Valerica, conducted her to the Caue to her beloued Varnan, and there confirmed the agreement of theyr loue.

Before we passe any further, you shall vnderstand that the Knight thus contending with *Palmerin*, was *Hermes*, whom the King sent after the Ladie with *Frysol*, to make deliueraunce of the Castell, as you haue hearde before:[1] he beeing *Palmerins* Freende, yet neither knowing the other. For *Hermes* tooke such regard of the Ladies complaint, as he marked not *Palmerin* before he put on his Helmet. *Palmerin* seeing that *Hermes* would needes try his fortune, encountred him with such a rough stroke, as downe hee fell to the grounde, *Hermes* thinking his head was shyuered in a hundred peeces: so *Palmerin* called *Hermes* Squire, commaunding him to helpe vp the Ladie, or els he woulde sende him after his Maister.[2] The Squire alighted and holpe vppe the Ladie, rewarding her with an infinite number of cursses, because his Maister hadde sped so ill by her meanes.

Trust me Ladie, quoth *Palmerin*, though you think my labour but ill bestowed, yet such is my regarde of the solitarie *Varnan*, as ending the Hel of torments he suffers, I must needes hold better opinion of my paines. With these and such like speeches he beguiled the time, till they came neere to *Varnans* Caue, who to take the ayre, was there walking vnder the Trees: but when he sawe *Palmerin* returned, and a Ladie with him, yea, perceiuing well that it was *Valerica*, they were no sooner allighted but he caught her in his armes, saying. Is it possible sweete Fortune, that after so long mishap, and when all hope was vtterly gone, thou canst affoorde me this gracious fauour? Ah happy eies that haue powred forth such showres of teares, what felicity may compare with yours, contemplating nowe the rare beauty of your Mistresse? May it be, that after so many insupportable torments, the meane therof shold return such pleasure, comfort and sollace? Depart then teares, pack hence lamentations, greefe, torments and al mellancholly conceits, get you els where, and in the most barbarous Countries of the world make your abiding, for she commaundes you hence, in whom consists my special contentment. O fortunate Knight, how may I recompence this inexplicable kindnes, surmounting all other that euer was heard of, impossible is it for me to requite this fauour, though al my possessions, life, body and spirit were bound to your seruice. But heauen will supply my want, and continue you in as great happines, as your noble bounty hath brought me comfort. Forbeare these speeches said *Palmerin*, albeit I had doone a thousande times as much, yet shold I but accomplish what one Christian owes to another. I pray you therfore let vs goe into your Caue least we be espied, and so preuented, beside, I am so ouer-watched, as I cannot stand on my feete through want of sleep. *Valerica* seeing herselfe in such an vncouth place, and in his custody she most detested, her angry stomack wold not suffer her speak one word, but when she had a whyle rested herselfe, on a seate of hearbs and flowres which *Varnan* dilligently prepared, *Palmerin* said. Behold Madam *Valerica*, see in what place, in what solitary, austere and sharp kind of life, your *Varnan* liues by your commandement, now seeing time and fortune is so fauourable, let not your rigor and disdaine exceede their mutability. Consider a little, what greefes he hath endured in this comfortlesse place, which verily haue been so great, as al the pleasures in the world, can not recompence the very least of them. I beseech you then, if heertofore you haue borne him hard liking, let it now be forgotten, and if vnaduisedly he hath any way offended you, let his long torments and surpassing loialty serue now for satisfaction, and take him to your husband, as the most perfect and faithful louer in *England*. You likewise sir *Varnan*, without remembraunce of your passed miseries, or her too rigorous refusals heeretofore, take her as your Lady and wife, and in al honor vnite your selfe to her by present speeches,[3] for seeing I haue brought her hether, it wil remain a continual reproche to mee, if you shold not accept her as your spouse and wife. Ah my Lord quoth *Varnan*, with right good will shall I accomplishe your command, so it may stand with my Ladies liking, for heerin is comprised the whole sum of my desires. Ah miserable beyond al other, said *Valerica* to *Palmerin*, must I by a varlet be subiected to so vile an extreamity, and constrained to take him for my husband whom I cannot affect? he beeing the most false and cowardly Knight that euer I knew? must I against my fathers wil, and by a Traytors procurement that hath so abused me, as no vertuous Knight woulde so haue wronged a Lady, be compelled to my mariage? heauen cannot like heereof, and rather wil I die, then doo the thing shal return me such reproch. Then shriked she so pittifully as though shee had beene quite distraught of her sences, which *Varnan* beholding, beganne thus to complaine. Ah gentle Knight, what greefe is it to heare her in these torments, whom I loue much better then mine own life? and for whom I rather desire to die, then not to enioy her with her owne liking. I cannot liue seeing her in these afflictions, and therefore conuay her again to her fathers house, and no sooner shal she be departed hence, but life wyl forsake this forlorne carkasse, then shal my death assure her how faithfully I loued. *Palmerin* seeing the obstinacie of *Valerica*, said. By God Lady, I think in all the world, is not a more cruell and disloyall woman then you are, perswade your selfe, that if I take the paine to carie you againe to your fathers Castell, I shall doo your errande there in such sorte, as all your life time repentance will hardly excuse you. And to speake the truth, *Varnan* dooth much more then you deserue, if you well remember your selfe, and for you are so stubborne,[4] I shall giue you the desart (offering to drawe his sword) that such ingratefull and trecherous women worthily merit. *Valerica* afrayde when she saw him in such choller, and doubting he would discouer her incontinent loue past, threwe herselfe at hys feete, desiring him to appease his anger, and she would obey what ere he commaunded. For (quoth she) seeing my fortune hath brought me into his companie, who for his vnfeigned loue to me, hath so long suffered wonderfull calamities: wel might I be esteemed of brutish nature, if I dyd not acknowledge it, therefor I will be his wife, and gyue him my faith heere in your presence. *Palmerin* wel pleased with this aunswer, tooke her vp by the hand, and taking *Varnan* by the other, espoused them there together by sollemne promises, and afterward laid him downe to rest himselfe awhile. Then *Varnan* taking *Valerica* in his armes, with sweet kisses and amorous speeches, expelled all former heauines, esteeming himselfe the happiest Knight in the whole world, hauing now at length obtained the fauour of his Mistresse, giuing her to vnderstand, howe acceptable the gift of pittie was, comming from so rare a creature to her languishing beloued. *Palmerin* seeing them so wel agreed, would nowe depart and leaue them to their fortune: but by earnest importunitie of these louers, he staied there longer then he intended. Nowe was the loue between these twaine, far greater then theyr hatred had beene, so that after they had staied three or foure dayes[5] in the Caue, with such entertainment as the Dwarffe could make them, they departed to one of *Varnans* Castels, and there obtained peace with the sad Parents of *Valerica*, continuing long time togeather in comfort of their loue, and ending their liues in loyalty thereof.

Chapter LVIII.

How Palmerin, after he departed from Varnan and Valerica, met with two Ladies in chase, one of them giuing him a Faulcon. And what happened to him against the Duke of Gaule his twelue Knights, out of whose handes he deliuered Hermes.

When *Palmerin* saw *Varnan* and *Valerica* so well contented, after many offers of theyr seruice, and kinde adiewes deliuered on all sides, hee left them in their Vault, and set forwarde on hys iourney, lodging that night in an auncient Knights Castle, where he vnderstoode, how the brethren of the slaine Knight,[1] besieged *Valericas* father in his Castell: Wherefore he turned an other course, and leauing the broad way that guided to *London*, he met two Ladyes accompanied with three Squires, who had cast off a Faulcon and a Martin[2] to flie, the sight wherof so highly contented him, as hee would needes tarrie to see the ende thereof, which made one of the Ladies thus speake to him. I see Sir Knight you haue no hast on your iourney, because you staie to behold our pastime, therfore if you will goe with vs to a water heereby, you shall there see a braue flight indeede, such woorthie game is there so plentifull, and my Faulcon so good as she will neuer faile. *Palmerin* who aboue all pastimes looued Hauking,[3] rode with the Ladies to the Marshes by their Castell, where they had such excellent sporte at Heron, Duck and Mallard: as the day beguiling them, *Palmerin* was forced to stay with them that night. When they were come to the Castell *Palmerin* manned the Ladies Faulcon so well, as though all his life time he had beene a Faulconer. The Lady seeing him so braue a Gentleman, so courteous, affable and comelie in behauiour, and that he tendered her Hauke so gently: was immediately supprized with his loue, so that she desired to knowe of whence he was, whom she could so gladlie affoord to chuse for her belooued, and hauing long earnestly behelde him, she sayd. Sir Knight, that I may entertaine you as your estate beseemeth, I pray you tell me your name, and whether you trauaile. Lady (quoth *Palmerin*) I am a stranger, who by fortune on the Sea was brought to this countrey, and because the king had warre against the Emperour of *Allemaigne*, I remained a while here as a Souldiour, attending a prosperous winde, to conuay me home againe into my natiue Countrie. The Lady hearing this, and iudging him one of the famous Knights that came to the Courte: looued him more earnestlie then she did before, prouiding such surpassing delightes for him, as shee wished that night had beene a yeere in length. The Tables withdrawen, and many pleasaunt speeches past betweene *Palmerin* and the Ladies daughter, she conducted him to his Chamber, wishing if her honour might so auouche it, that *Palmerin* neuer might haue any other bedfellow. But leauing him to his good rest, she departed to her Chamber, where little sleepe suffised her that night. In the morning, *Palmerin* called for his Horsse to be gon, the Lady verie sorowfull to forgoe his company: but seeing she had no meane to holde him, she sayd. Seeing your departure Sir, may not be denied, I would present you with the Faulcon, which yesterday did so specially content you, which if you please to accept for my sake: I shall not forget the honour you haue doon me, cheefely that you vouchsafed to stay heere this night beeing as welcome hether as the King him selfe. Seeing it is your pleasure Madame, sayd *Palmerin*, to bestowe your Faulcon on mee, I accept it as the onely thinge you could giue me, and by the faith of a Knight I promise you, that I will keepe it for your sake, and neuer part therewith, if by force or villainie it be not taken from me. The Lady so ioyfull heereof as might be deuised, caused the Faulcon to be brought to him. Heere must you note, that this is the selfe same Lady, which sent the Faulcon to *Varnan*,⁴ and looued him so deerely as after she vnderstood he had forsooke the Countrie, she gaue her selfe altogeather to this recreation. Her Father perceiuing how she was affected, suffered her to take her pleasure, sending her euermore the best Haukes that could be gotten. But it came so to passe, that two Faulcons so freendly giuen, and in the lyke sorte taken, prooued very vnfortunate to both the Knightes, causing them to cursse the hower, that euer they accepted the Ladies liberalitie, came neere her Castell, or sawe her Haukes, as you haue already heard by solitary *Varnan*, and hereafter shall perceiue in *Palmerins* fortune. He beeing departed from the Lady, rode two daies togeather without any aduenture, till at length he came to the Tents, where the Duke of *Gaules* Knights guarded the passage,⁵ whych scant pleased *Palmerin*, because he imagined if hee fought with them, he should be deceiued in his intent, and not see *Trineus* so soone as he would, whom he left at the Court expecting his comming, wherefore he would haue turned another way, but one of the Knights called to him. Returne coward returne, thou shalt not escape without tryall of thy manhood, for we must make proofe if there bee any in thee. *Palmerin* not knowing where to set his Hauke, and verie loth to loose it, was not desirous to Ioust: but seeinge that with honour he could not refuse it, answered. It is small courtesie Sir Knight, to challeng the man that hath no will to your sporte: but if there be no remedie, your will be fulfilled, albeit I hope you will first repent it. I see thou canst prate well, quoth the Knight, and beleeue mee thou wert wise if thou couldest so escape: but seeing thou art so long before thou art ready,⁶ Ile bring thee to such a place where Haukes shall not hinder thee, and in one yeere thou shalt spare the wearing of Bootes and spurres in such a comfortable place, as the Sunne nor day light shall offend thine eyes. I hope I haue learned, sayd *Palmerin*, to keepe my selfe from such places: but I would faine knowe the gentle Chamber Page, that is so skilfull in waiting with his Pantofles, as he can teach Knights errant how to were them. The Knight being angry, called forth the rest of his companions, among whom he espied *Hermes* prisoner, his Helmet lying by him, and his armes pinniond: therefore to reuenge his wronge, he called his Squire, saying. I pray thee my freend looke to my Hauke a while, for I am come to defende thy Maisters honour: and calling to the Dukes Knight, sayd. Come Sir, let vs dispatch quickly, for I haue earnest busines in an other place: the Knight laughing at him, answered. Why how now Captaine? thinke you to passe hence so easilye? Heere are sufficient to stay your hasty iourney, eleuen more must talke with you, the wurst of them able to abate your pride, for your horsse lackes a stable, and we will prouide him one. So coutching their Launces, they mette together with such force, as the Dukes Knight was throwen from his Horsse, his shoulder beeing broken with the weight of his fall, *Palmerin* arresting the Knightes horsse for hys owne, gaue him to *Hermes* squire in keeping, saying. Because the Knight is not willing to get on horsse-backe againe, holde this for me, and he may lie at ease to see the fortune of hys fellowes. Then came another Knight from the tent, whom *Palmerin* welcommed in so freendly manner, as he lay not able to stirre hand or foote: with this one Launce he vnhorssed foure more, and brake it so valiantly on the seuenth[7] Knight, as while he liued he meant to Ioust no more. With a fresh Launce he dismounted all the rest, none of them beeing willing to deale with him any further, wherefore *Palmerin* came to *Hermes*, saying. What doo you sir Knight? Why take you not the best horsse amonge all the dozen? That shall I Sir, seing you commaund me, albeit not long since you serue me as these Knights are: yet God be thanked that by your meanes I am deliuered from imprisonment, wherein these Knights intended to keepe me, because I vnhorssed foure of them, and at the fift encounter my horsse was kild, which was the cause of my foyle and taking. The Knights (quoth *Palmerin*) haue now leisure to rest them, for they were troubled before with watchinge for passengers: I doubt not now, but we may quietly passe the bridge for I see none of them offer to hinder vs. *Hermes* mounting on horsse-backe, commaunded his squire to take a fresh one for him likewise, and so they rode on together reioysing at this good fortune. They had not ridden the space of a myle, but *Hermes* demaunded *Palmerins* name, which when he knew in great reioysing he sayd: Ah woorthy Knight, now is my trauaile ended in search of you, trust me, I would refuse the best Cittie in *England*, in respect of the great freendship I haue found at your handes, as also for the comfort your presence will bring to our dread Lord and your noble companions, who long time haue expected your desired returne. As they rode on in these speeches, they came to a faire fountaine, where *Palmerin* would alight to refreshe hymselfe, and to binde vp such small woundes, as he had taken in Iousting against the Knightes of *Gaule*.

Chapter lix.
Howe Frisol was deliuered out of Palmerins handes, by the meanes of Colmelio his Squire.

The same day that *Palmerin* iousted with the Knights of *Gaule*, the Duke himselfe was gon on hunting, by meanes wherof he lost the sight of the pastime, which afterward he repented, because hee had with him the most parte of his Knights, so that no one was left in his Castell but *Frisol*, that might bee counted of any value: who beholding so many Knights foyled by one, meruailed not a lyttle what he might be, and after long consideration of his haughtie exploits, he said to himselfe. I cannot thinke this Knight to bee the man, against whome sometime I combated in *Fraunce*,[1] yet knowe I no man liuing but he, that could perfourme so rare chiualrie. Now, because *Palmerin* had changed his Armour, verely imagined that it was not hee, yet was he desirous to knowe, but doubtfull to followe him by reason of his former experience: againe, if he should suffer him to passe without some trial, he iudged it would returne to his great dishonour, wherefore he resolued to aduenture his fortune. And in this determination hee came to the Dukes sister, who looued him intirely, as you heard before[2] she beginning with him in this manner. I cannot sufficiently meruaile Sir *Frisol*, how you haue suffered in your owne viewe, my brothers Knights to be so shamefully confounded by one passenger: I desire you sweet freend, if euer you brake Launce for a Ladies looue, that for my sake you will deale with that proud Knight, and make him knowe that you can abate his courage, were his head framed of the hardest hammered brasse.[3] If you fulfil my request, you shal doo an acceptable deede to my brother, and to me such seruice, as I shall hereafter requite to your own content. Madame, quoth *Frisol*, I did intend to fight with him, but seeing it pleaseth you so graciously to commaund me, no daunger can withholde me, because the world shall witnesse, what great auaile so honorable a Ladies fauour is, to the Knight that liues to renown her name. So departing from his Lady, he presently armed him selfe, and mounted on a lustie Courser, followed the way that *Palmerin* was gon, the twelue Knights not a little glad therof, well hoping that he would reuenge their dishonour. *Frisol* continued his trauaile so long, till at length he came to the Fountaine where *Palmerin* refreshed himselfe, who had no sooner espyed him, but supprized with great ioy, sayd to *Hermes*. I am sure thys Knight comes hether to seeke me, wherfore I intreate you, by the reuerend looue you beare to your best belooued, not any way to hinder the fight betweene vs, till the ende deliuer victory to one side or other: for he thinking to reueng the reproch of his fellowes, hath followed me to perfourme what they were not able. Then *Palmerin* suddenly clasping on his Helmet, mounted on Horssebacke, and taking aduauntage of the playne feelde, because it was most conuenient for the combate, which *Frisol* perceiuing, scornefully sayd. I think Sir Knight, you are some kinde of Prophet, because you deuine so well the cause of my comming: vnhappy was it for you, to preuaile in such sorte against the Duke

Palmerin d'Oliva: Part I 315

of *Gaules* Knights, which you must now pay for with too late repentaunce. If I dyd them any harme, sayd *Palmerin*, it was theyr owne seeking, and by your arrogant speeches it may be presumed, you are one of the same company: but the loue of the Dukes Sister, cannot sheelde you from your deserued recompence. At these
5 wordes *Frisol* well perceiued, that this was the Knight he so much doubted: Neuerthelesse his courage was so good, as remembring the promise he made to his Lady, gaue spurres to his horsse, and they encountred with such braue chiualry, as the shiuers of their Launces flewe vp into the ayre, and then they assaulted eche other so roughly with theyr Swordes, as well they might bee esteemed right
10 valiant Champions. No mercie was intended on either side, for *Frisol* was determined to die or conquere, and *Palmerin* held the same resolution, so that the ground was coullered with their blood, theyr Armour and Sheeldes battered in peeces, and no hope left on either side of life. But as alwaies some mischaunce or other followes a noble minde, so fel it out with *Frisol*, for in their close buckling
15 together, *Palmerin* had got sure holde on hys sheeld, which *Frisol* striuing forciblie to recouer, the buckles brake in sunder, and with the sudden breach thereof he fell downe backward, when *Palmerin* leaping from his horsse, sayd. And let me neuer hereafter be called *Palmerin*, if now I doo not reuenge my selfe sufficiently. Which wordes when *Frisols* squire heard, he came hastily and fell at hys feete,
20 saying. Noble Knight, I beseech you for the honor you beare to Armes, to pause awhile, and tell me if you be *Palmerin d'Oliua*, for if you be, I am your brother, who haue suffered great paine and trauaile to finde you out. *Palmerin* presently knew *Colmelio*, the sonne of *Gerrard* his foster father, whose sight was so ioyfull to him, as casting away his sword, he ran and embraced him about the necke,
25 saying. My deere freend *Colmelio*, the most welcome man in the world to me. Howe happy may I account my selfe, quoth *Colmelio*, to finde you when all hope was past? hauing trauailed so many countries, and all in vaine: if then you looue me as you make protestation, let me intreate one fauour at your hand, that you forget your anger towardes my maister *Frisol*, and giue ouer your fight, for long
30 time haue I serued him as my Lord, and well hath he deserued much better seruice then mine. *Colmelio*, saide *Palmerin*, the thing thou demaundest is meruailous great, neuerthelesse, such is my comfort hauing met with thee, as I graunt thy request, and happily hath he now escaped with life, considering what occasions haue past vs heretofore. So taking *Colmelio* by the hand, he said to *Frisol*. Sir
35 Knight, at your squires intreatie, I suffer you quietly to departe, and meete with me againe at any time you thinke good: but you shall goe looke an other squire, for *Colmelio* at this time goes with me. *Frisol*, who was wounded in many places, and very faint with losse of his blood, might easily be induced to this agreement of peace: but comming to *Colmelio*, he sayd. Wilt thou forsake thy master, and
40 goe with his enemie? Trust me sir, quoth *Colmelio*, you must needs pardon me, if in this matter I chaunce to offend you, for to seeke him I forsooke my fathers house, and haue continued a very laboursome search.[4] If thou wilt needes goe, said *Frisol*, and that my intreaties may not disswade thee, I wyll pray for the

successe of thy desires, and thy aduauncement to honour, and while I liue will I
account of thee as my freend and brother. So returning as he came, he began in
this manner to exclaime against Fortune. Ah cruel and inconstant Ladie, suffised thee not to dishonour mee before mine enemie, but thou must rob me of my
squire I looued so deerely? but so hast thou dealt with them of highest calling, for
infinite Kings and Potentates hast thou deceiued, and (before their very cheefest
enemies) dishonoured: suche hath beene thy trecherie to me at this instant, that
I may iustly complaine of thee while I liue. As he continued these complaintes,
he met diuers armed Knightes that came to assist him, and the Duke himselfe in
company among them who demaunded of *Frisol*, whether his enemie were slaine
or sent away vanquished. Vanquished? sayd *Frysol*, thinke you so good a Knight
may be so easilie vanquished? Then he discoursed his whole successe, which the
Duke hearing, exclaimed on his hunting, that he was not present when *Palmerin*
passed: wherefore he would needes followe him, but that *Frisol* intreated him to
the contrary, because the night approched so neere, as it was impossible for him
to ouertake *Palmerin*. The Duke in a meruailous rage, for that his enterprise fell
out no better, returned with *Frisol*, and an hower within night they came to his
Castell, where hee called for his Chirurgions, charging them to giue dilligent
attendaunce on *Frisol*. When the Dukes sister hearde the misfortune of her
freend, she came hastily to him in his chamber, and after many sweete kisses,
sayd. I beseeche you my Lord forget my folly, for I was the cause of your mischance. Madame, sayd *Frisol*, where no offence is committed, what needes any
remission? If my fortune haue beene ill, it is not for me to complaine of you, for
your request tended to mine owne honour: but I must be content with my happe,
though it hath sorted to so bad effect, and this doth yet comfort mee, that I receiued my foile by the onelie Knight in the worlde. And if the heauens please to
lengthen my dayes, I shall be desirous to doo him seruice, for there is no man
liuing to whom I could better affoord it. Nowe neede I not mislike (hauing tryed
him so often) if he be woorthie the looue of diuine *Polinarda*, for he (beyond all
other) dooth best deserue it. Why how now? quoth the Lady, are you so vnwise,
to honour him so much, that hath so iniured you? and, which is most childish, to
desire his seruice? Goe then, and seeke him whom thou so loouest, for by mine
honour, I more despise thee now then any man in the world, thou making such
reputation of him, whome thou oughtest to persue with mortall hatred. *Frisol*,
smiling hereat, sayde. Madame, I must needes say so, seeing no ill wordes can
amend my mischaunce: so without any aunswer, she floong foorth of the Chamber. The next day the Duke called all his Knights, commaunding them to
restraine the passage no longer at the bridge,⁵ intending to goe to the Courte, so
soone as *Frisol* had recouered his health.

Chapter lx.

Howe Palmerin, Hermes and Colmelio returned to London, and the good entertainement the King of England made them.

After that *Frisol* was returned from the Combate, *Palmerin* after many embracings of *Colmelio*, went with him to the Fountaine where he left *Hermes*, all three together making no lyttle ioy: *Colmelio* for his happy finding of *Palmerin*, and he for the loue of his supposed brother, and *Hermes* for the comfort he shold bring the King his Maister, being able now to acquaint his highnesse with *Palmerins* name, which he was loath any in the *English* Courte should knowe, wherefore he sayd. Now can you not my Lord hereafter hide your name, though you haue beene daintie of it all this while. It is true Syr, quoth *Palmerin*, albeit I little thought to bee discouered so soone: but seeing it is so come to passe, my hope is in the highest, who will defend me in all mine attemptes: nowe tell me *Colmelio*, what newes in *Greece*? Truely my Lord, quoth he, the discourse wilbe long and tedious: therefore if you please to mount on horssebacke, it wil serue wel to shorten the thought of our iourney.[1] So as they rode towards *London*, *Colmelio* began to discourse, in how many places he had sought him in *Greece*, and how at length he heard of him at *Macedon*, by reporte of his conquest of the Serpent at the mountaine *Artifaeria*, which was the meane that brought the King of *Macedon* to his former health.[2] Afterward, how he left *Greece*, trauailing into *Allemaigne*, and from thence into *England*, at what time the Emperours power was discomfited: and hearing great fame of *Frisol* his late Maister, he spent some time in his seruice, not doubting but by his meanes to finde the man he looked for. *Palmerin* was somewhat mooued, hearing *Colmelio* so commende *Frisol*, wherefore he demaunded of him, if hee knewe any thing of that Knights linage. No my Lord, quoth he, but I can assure ye, that he is one of the most gentle Knights in the world, and he concealeth his parentage very secretly, which makes me iudge he is discended of royall birth. After *Colmelio* had ended his discourse, he repeated to him some parte of his fortunes, in the end perswading him, that he would remunerate his paines in seeking him, and in tyme manifest the looue he bare him. By this time they were come to the Cittie of *London*, *Hermes* riding before to the Pallace, where he aduertised the King, how *Palmerin* was returned to the Cittie, which newes so highly contented the King, as often times he imbraced *Hermes*, for bringing the man he long desired to see: but *Trineus* and *Ptolome* exceeded him in ioy, and mounted presently on horssebacke to goe meete theyr freend, when so many embracinges, courtesies and kinde gratulations had passed betweene them, as is vsuall at the meeting of long absent loouers:[3] Ah my Lord and freend, quoth *Trineus*, howe long hath Fortune kept you from me? and why did you depart not vouchsafing a farewell?[4] What earnest occasion might cause such an vnkinde departure? trust me, I perswaded my selfe in respect of the long continuaunce of our amitie, that death coulde not procure such a seuere enterprise. My Lord, quoth *Palmerin*, it seemeth you haue some cause to complaine of mee: but when you vnderstand how matters haue happened, you will not condemne me altogether. For at the time of my departure, I thought verely to returne the next day following: but such importunate affayres continually fell out, as I could not returne till this very instant. *Ptolome* sayd as much as *Trineus* did, notwithstanding, this fortunate meeting forbad al further accusations, and they became as good freendes as euer they were. So rode they to the Pallace, where the King attending theyr comming, perceiued at length they were entred the Hall, when *Palmerin* falling on his knee, kissed hys highnes hand,[5] who very honourably embracing him, sayd. Where hath my noble freend beene so long? What crooked fortune hath caused your so long absence? you departed from vs in blacke Armour, I praie you tell vs, where dyd you conquere these sumptuous Armes? by the looue you beare to Chiualrie, and to me, satisfie me in my demaund. *Palmerin* seeing the King coniured him so straightly, reported the trueth of all his aduentures, how he had that Armour of the Lady whose daughter he deliuered, and left his owne there broken in peeces.[6] The King embracing him againe, sayd. I cannot be perswaded, but all especiall aduentures, high good fortunes, and cheefest honors in the world, are only reserued for you, and among all the rest, most meruaylous is this of the Castell in the enchaunted Lake, which many Knights hath heretofore attempted, but returned with the losse of theyr horsses, Armour, and with great dishonour. Thrise welcome are you for these happy tidinges, as also for your gentle courtesie to *Frisol*, who is a Knight of most honourable reputation. But in regard of your wearisome trauailes, it is verie requisite that you now goe rest your selfe, therefore let some body helpe to disarme you, and betake your selfe (on Gods name) to your Chamber. *Palmerin* reputed the Kings councell most expedient, and therefore dyd as hee commaunded him, so hauing reposed himselfe a while, hee came to see howe the Queene and her daughter fared, who would not suffer him to depart, before he had likewyse acquainted her with all his Fortunes, especially the whole circumstaunce of his trauaile at the Castell of the Lake. But night being come, and euery one betaking themselues to rest: *Palmerin* demaunded of the Prince, how he followed his desires, and what hee had concluded as concerning hys looue? Ah deere freend, sayd *Trineus*, why aske you mee that question? doo you not thinke that hauing so lost you, I likewise was disappointed of any meane to helpe mee? Know then, that at this instant I am in the middest of all my misfortunes, for so badly hath it happened, that I am now further from *Agriola* then euer I was, and I shall tel you how. Not many dayes since, as I was familiarely deuising with my Lady, the Duke of *Gaules* daughter chaunced to heare, such amorous speeches as passed betweene the Princesse and me, wherby she gathered, that *Agriola* made some estimation of me: whereupon she laboured, to cause my Mistresse in shorte time mislike, what I had so long trauayled to perswade her with, as thus. That it ill beseemed a Princesse of her account, of so gracious discent, and daughter to such a mightie King, to conferre with straungers,[7] or vouchsafe a listening to any thing they sayd: for they were none such as she reputed them, but after they had brought a Ladyes honour in daunger, they then were not satisfied, as they vsed it for a custome to vaunt themselues among theyr companions. And so well could she feede the Princesse humour, with these suborning⁸ and spightfull detractions, which seemed to her as sweete and freendly perswasions: that in steede of the little looue I lately conquered, I finde nothing but frownes and disdaine, that she wil scant affoord me a looke. Which discourtesie hath well neere driuen me to despayre, in regard of her slender opinion of me, as being so hindered only through your absence. Often I determined with *Ptolome*, to leaue the Courte and followe you in trauaile: but the King by no meanes woulde permit me, sending many of his owne Knights, because I should not goe: yet was I resolued, that had you not come, no displeasure whatsoeuer should haue helde me heere, but to finde you I intended, or loose my life. This falles out very hard, quoth *Palmerin*, for by these meanes we shall stay heere God knowes how long, beside, *Hermes* knowes my name, which makes me doubt least we shalbe reuealed, the Emperour likewise may be offended at our long tariance. In regard of all this, good Prince, I thinke it best, that we send your squire and *Vrbanillo* my Dwarffe, to aduertise hys Maiestie of our affaires, and how by reason of the tempest, we were cast quite out of course so farre, as we cold not by any meanes assist his Armie, not doubting but to see hys highnes in very shorte time. In the meane while, we may practise meanes to win the Princesse fauour againe, and so in good time depart hence, with the honorable prize that we came for. *Trineus* was newly reuiued with these speeches, wherefore he desired, that betimes in the morning hee would dispatche theyr seruauntes towardes *Allemaigne*. Which *Palmerin* fayled not to doo, in respect of a dreame he had the night before, for he imagined that he sawe his Ladie *Polinarda* in meruaylous heauines, and that she sayd to him. Alas my Lord, what shall become of me? for I am narrowly sought to be seperated from you. This feareful vision so discouraged him, as he sent thence his Dwarffe, to shewe her what trouble he had with his dreame,⁹ and how constant he remained in his looue to her.

CHAPTER LXI.
How Palmerin promised the Princesse Agriola, to conuaie her out of England, with his freend, which he perfourmed, to the speciall content of the Prince Trineus.

Earlye on the next morning *Palmerin* arose, and wrote a letter to his Lady *Polinarda*, wherein he secretly put the Ring, which the Lady of the Castell in the Lake gaue him when he departed from her, straightly commaunding *Vrbanillo*, that hee should dilligently attend on the Princesse till he came, which should be with all the speede hee could possible. *Ptolome* likewise wrote to his Lady *Brionella*, and these letters dispatched, the messengers immediatelie set forward on theyr iourney. From this time *Colmelio* was *Palmerins* Squier, which pleased him very well, because hee nowe knew that *Palmerin* was noble borne, so that by his meanes in time hee should rise to preferment. This day the King would ride abroad a Hauking, which gaue *Palmerin* occasion to see his Faulcon flye, beeing reputed by the King and al his traine, to be the best that euer flew. In this time of recreation, *Hermes* reported to the King, that the Knight so long absent was named *Palmerin*, and the same Knight that wunne so much honour in *Fraunce*, which so well contented the King, as he more and more desired his company: summoning all his Barons and Lordes to his Courte, where he made such feastes, triumphes and other sportes, for the honour of the noble *Palmerin* and his companions, as the lyke had not beene of long tyme before. At night, when the Maskers, Momeries and Moriscoes[1] were in presence, that *Palmerin* espyed conuenient time to talke with the Princesse, hee tooke her aside to a windowe, and thus began. Madam, before I begin what I haue to acquaint you with al, I must giue you this ring, as I was commaunded by the Lady of the Castell in the Lake: the singuler vertues thereof are such, as I intreate you to keepe it continually on your finger.[2] Which *Agriola* receiuing, with a courteous reuerence, faithfully promised to accomplishe his request: then *Palmerin*, with earnest affection on hys freendes behalfe, thus continued his discourse. I cannot but meruayle fayre Princesse, you beeing a Lady of so speciall qualitie, renowmed among the most vertuous creatures in the world, for your rare integrity and profound iudgement, that you will be gouerned by the vnaduised perswasions of other: which I would not beleeue, had not the Prince *Trineus* certainly assured me, how since my departure, in steed of fauorable countenance, and the intreataunce beseeming so great a Lord, he can haue nothing but frownes, disdaine and coy regard, which is as easie for him to endure, as a thousand deathes one after another. Assure your selfe so farre beguiled, as your councellers disswade you from your cheefest good, desirous to withholde you from the height of honour, whereof you cannot fayle, beeing matched in mariage with the most vertuous Prince *Trineus*. Make you so small account, that hee beeing one of the most noble states on the earth, hath left his parentes, his freends and countrey, hath past so many strang and vncouth regions, hath aduentured the iniurie of the Seas, beaten

Palmerin d'Oliva: Part I 321

with so many bitter blasts and raging billowes, euery minute in daunger of Shipwracke, and al for your looue? Thinke you that he beeing Son to the Emperour of *Allemaigne*, attending euery day the rule of the Empire: that hee came hether to you in hope of your riche dowrie? No trust me Madame, and I thinke your owne conscience dooth so resolue you, that neerer home he could haue found other, endued with larger possessions then this Realme affordes you. But hearing the fame of your manifolde vertues, rare life, choyse beautie, and all other good gifts: he was willing, without regard of his own estate, to thrust him selfe in daunger, yea, to forget him selfe for your looue, which hetherto he hath with religious seruice intreated, and except you entertaine him with more gracious fauour, he is in daunger of life. Which if it should happen by your occasion, for euer you shall be noted of monstrous ingratitude, and Christendome should sustaine a losse vnrecouerable, how farre such a thought ought to be from you, I leaue to your own construction.[3] If hitherto you haue knowen me, a Knight readie to support the causes of Ladyes farre beneath your height, thinke you I haue not greater reason to honour you? yea, not to mooue you with any request, but what may euery way aduaunce your credite. And though my Lord *Trineus* were not of the blood imperiall, yet might his gentle hart, vnfeigned looue, and surpassing humanitie, cause you to make choyse of him, aboue all other whatsoeuer they be. But seeing it so falles out, that you will not regarde good councell, following rather the perswasion of meane capacities, whose iudgements may not reache to so high occasions: continue in your obstinacie, and marke the ende of such indiscreet censures. I see that our company is irksome to you, therefore (sooner then you imagine) we will remooue that occasion. I knowe well enough, that you intend to match with the Duke of *Gaule*, who is but your fathers subiect: so refusing the degree of an Empresse, you shall tarrie in *England* and be a Duchesse. Thinke you, that if my Lord matched not with you, the greatest Princesse in *Europe* would not triumphe in his looue? Yes certainly Madame, when you may at leasure sit down and recount your losse, which you sustained by flatterers and Parasites. Thinke what will be the daunger after our departure, the Emperour his Father, not minding to pocket the losse of his late Armie, will send such a puissante strength into *England*: as the King your father, nor the Duke your husband that must be, will scant excuse the whole ruine of this countrie. The meane to preuent this mishap, and assure your continuall tranquilitie, is in entertayning the councell I haue giuen you: where otherwise, your selfe conceit, makes way to manifold misfortunes and dangers.[4] Thus concluding his speeches, in great heauines he turned from her, whereat the Princesse inwardly greeued, for the Ring which he had giuen her was of such vertue, that after she had put it on her finger, she was wunderfully affected toward *Trineus*, as she could not thinke on any other: wherfore in this sudden chaunge, and trembling with the doubtfull conceit of her owne spirit, she called *Palmerin* to her, thus aunswering. Alas my Lord, and only comfort, in these heavy passions, what feare hath these harde and rigorous speeches brought me into? It is very true, that following the councell of young Ladies like my selfe, I haue beene perswaded to cast off the Princes looue, accounting him but as a simple Knight errant: but now being assured of his nobility, loyalty, and great gentlenes, and that he would not request (as I hope) any thing contrary to vertue and honour, I beleeue what you haue sayd, and submit my selfe to your discretion, as willing to obey any thinge you shall commaund me. Yet this I must request, that aboue all things mine honour may be defended, for rather would I suffer mine owne losse for euer, then this famous Realme of my father should be any way endangered. Beleeue me Lady, quoth *Palmerin*, if thus you continue, you may well venture to gaine this generall benefit, for hencefoorth there will none be so hardy, as to molest your father with warre, hauing matched his daughter with the great Emperours sonne of *Allemaigne*. To confirme this promise, you shall giue me this sweete hand which I kisse, as the hand of the soueraigne Lady and Empresse of high *Allemaigne*, that you will not shrinke hereafter from this honorable determination: but for your owne regard, you must conceale this contract from your most trustie freendes, and dispose in such sorte of your selfe, for I hope to compasse the meane and opportunitie, that you shall leaue *England*, and goe to the noble regions of your worthie Lord and husband. What I haue promised, sayd *Agriola*, I will perfourme, and with what speede you shall thinke conuenient: albeit I repose such trust in you, that hauing beene so fortunate hitherto in your enterprises, you will be carefull in accomplishing these daungerous intentions. Thus before they departed, the mariage of *Trineus* and *Agriola* was concluded, and because they would not as then bee suspected, they stept into the daunce next the young Prince, shewing very amiable and pleasant gestures: which *Trineus* (in his often turning) dilligently noted, imagining that *Palmerin* had not so long conferred with his Lady, but some assured resolution was determined, yet hee dissembled his inward ioyes so cunningly as he could. Eche eye was fixed on these two braue Knights, the Ladies and Gentlewomen perswading themselues, that they neuer beheld more noble personages, deseruing like estimation for theyr speciall chiualrie, as also for their bountye and Courtly ciuilitie. Thus passed the feast in all kinde of pleasures, and these two Knights with-drawing them selues into theyr chamber, *Palmerin* discoursed to *Trineus* his talke with *Agriola*, and how he had with such cunning pursued the matter, that in the ende he obtayned what he demaunded, reporting the gentle conclusion hee made with the Princesse. These ioyfull newes droue the Prince into such a quandarie, as he cold not expresse his secret content, wherfore *Palmerin* awaking him out of hys musing, sayd. As I am true Knight, I neuer thought that a man of your estate coulde be of so slender courage. What countenaunce would you vse in a matter of sorrowe, when such dainty tidings make you so effeminate? Be of good cheere man, *Agriola* is your owne, and none but *Trineus* must be her Lord and husband.[5] I must confesse my Lord, sayd *Trineus*, that my behauiour but little beseemes my calling: but the cause therof is, that I know no desert in my selfe that may be esteemed worthy the least fauour of my Lady. Beside, these newes brought me such special

Palmerin d'Oliva: Part I

contentment, as I am no longer mine own, but in her only I liue, and she holdes the ballaunce of my daunger or felicitie, in that I was borne to be her seruaunt. But now I desire you my Lord, seeing the occasion offereth it selfe, we hinder it not by any negligence: for if now we loose the fauour of the time, we neuer (I feare) shall recouer the lyke, therfore let vs so soone as we can prouide all thinges ready for our departure. Referre that to me, quoth *Palmerin*, be you as ready as I shall make prouision. The next day he went to the Maister of a Ship to knowe when tyme would serue for theyr secret departure, who answered hym, that the tyme was then very conuenient, the winde seruing prosperously, and the Sea calme and nauigable, and hee would furnishe hym with all necessaries for hys passage. Quoth *Palmerin*, see that your men and all things be in readynes, that we may launch away vpon halfe an howers warning. So departed the Maister about hys busines, and *Palmerin* to the Prince *Trineus*, whom he infourmed with these glad tidinges, now nothing remaining but to know the Princesse pleasure, she beeing lykewise as ready to depart as the most forward. But (quoth *Palmerin*) how shall we safely get you foorth of the Courte? I will, sayd the Princesse, this night feygne my selfe sicke, and for my greater quiet, cause my Ladyes to absent my Chamber, and so secretly wyll I escape disguised to the back gate of the Pallace, whych is not far from your lodging, wherto I may passe vnseene of any, and from thence goe wyth you safely to the Hauen. This practise was faythfully concluded betweene them, and *Agriola* withdrewe her selfe closely to her Chamber, where at nyght she began her counterfeit sicknes, commaunding her Ladyes to leaue her alone, because she would see if she could sleepe a little. Her Ladyes lyttle thinking of her secret deceit, went to theyr owne lodgings very pensiue and sorrowfull, which *Agriola* perceiuing, couered her selfe with her night mantle, and came to the place where the Knights stayed her comming. *Palmerin* taking her vnder his arme, conuaied her in that manner to the Princes chamber, where they altogether laid down the order for theyr embarquing, *Trineus* extolling his happy fortune, seeing his Lady so ready to accomplishe his desire. They arming themselues, and taking with them the Princesse costly iewelles, whereof she had plentifully stored her selfe, they came to the Hauen, where they found the Ship and Mariners ready, and getting all aboord, the wind seruing for theyr auaile, they set sayle, and before day they got farre enough from *London*.

Chapter LXII.

Howe the King of England and the Queene were aduertysed, how their daughter Agriola was conuayed away, and of their sorrowe for her departure.

The Duke of *Gaules* daughter, who continually was bedfellow to the Princesse, absented her selfe very long from bed, fearing to disquiet her Lady, beeing sicke as she supposed: but comming at length to see howe she fared, finding the bed emptie and *Agriola* gon: she presently made a great out-cry, wherat the other Ladies came, and altogether amazed at this sudden aduenture, went to the Queenes Chamber, where they reported, how the Princesse was gon, but how or when, they knewe not. The Queene at these tidings suddenly arose, and comming to her daughters chamber found it too true, which made her fal into such pittiful acclamations, far surpassing those of *Maguelona*, when she lost her freend *Peter of Prouince* in the wood.[1] In these lamentings she returned to the King, whose heauines exceeded iudgement, for the losse of his daughter, and then came diuers Lordes and Gentlemen, who declared that the straunge Knights were likewise departed. Which raysed such a rumour through all the Cittie, that they had stolen away the Princesse. The King vnderstanding the generall sorrow for his daughters absence, sayd. In sooth my freendes, if these Knights haue doone such seruice for mee, they haue sufficiently recompenced themselues, in dooing me the greatest dishonour they could deuise: yet will I not condemne them so much as my daughter, for that I am perswaded shee procured this mischaunce. But nowe I wel perceiue, what credit a man may repose in his enemie: for *Palmerin* euermore serued the Emperour of *Allemaigne*, then hardly could he be true to mee. Yet is it in vaine for me to blame him or his companions, if they tooke the aduauntage of their owne intents. But now there is no remedy, my daughter is in the company of most chosen Knightes: if she haue doone well or ill, hereafter her deserts wyll aunswer her misdemeanour. Thus the King would not suffer any pursute after them, though the Queene and her Ladies earnestly intreated him: he answering, that no such mone should be made, for a child so ingratefull and disobedient, but hauing committed an action so vile and enorme, she should no more account of her as her childe. And well may wee (quoth he) so refuse her, in that she would leaue her parentes and depart with straungers, happie might we haue accounted our selues, if we had lost her in her infancie. The Queene seeing her Lord so impatient, appeased his displeasure so well as shee could, because shee would not mooue him too much. Within fewe daies after, the Duke of *Gaule* arriued at the Courte, who most of all greeued at these vnhappy tidinges, wherefore hee perswaded the King, to proclaime open warre against the Emperour of *Allemaigne*, assuring him, that the Knight whych most commonly accompanyed *Palmerin*, was *Tryneus* the Emperours sonne. When the King heard the Dukes speeches, forgetting his anger, he reioyced, esteeming himselfe happy, and hys daughter wyse, in matching her selfe with such an husband: and if she had made her choyse among all the Princes of the world, she could not haue sorted out one comparable in honour. In breefe he aunswered the Duke, that for a daughter so lost, hee would not seeke the death of his loouers and subiects: but beeing one of Fortunes chaunges, he could not withstand it, and thus the King wisely and patiently endured his greefe.

Chapter LXIII.
Howe Vrbanillo and the Prince Trineus Esquier, arriued at the Emperours Court, and what great ioye their comming procured.

In this place our history taketh this occasion, howe the King of *Fraunce* daily expecting newes from *Palmerin*, as concerning hys intent of mariage, between his daughter and the Prince *Trineus*: but seeing he heard no tidinges at all, he determined to send hys Ambassadours to the Emperour, electing for cheefe in this embassade the Countie of *Armignac*, to whom he gaue ful power and authority, to conclude the mariage betweene *Trineus* and his daughter *Lucemania*, as also of the Princesse *Polinarda* with his son and heyre. The king dispatching all thinges for his Ambassage, sent many Barons and Knightes of name to accompany the Countie, to contenaunce the matter with more royalty and magnificence, and in this manner they came to *Gaunt*, where the Emperour being aduertised of theyr arriuall, made no great account thereof, such was his greefe for his sonnes absence and *Palmerins*, of whom he could not heare any tidings, as also for the foyle his Armie sustained in *England*. But whyle the messenger from the Ambassadours of *Fraunce* stayed with the Emperour, *Vrbanillo* and the Princes Squyer entred the hall, whose presence so highly contented the Emperour, as embracing them very louingly, he demaunded for *Palmerin* and his sonne *Trineus*, when they deliuering theyr letters, and the Emperour perswaded therby of theyr speedie returne, was greatly contented, saying to the Ambassadours messenger. My freend, seeing I haue heard such long looked for tidinges of my sonne, you may returne to the Countie your maister, desiring hym to come when hee thinkes conuenient, and he shal be hartely welcome to me: with this answer the messenger departed. Then the Emperour taking *Vrbanillo* by the hand, said. Tell me now I pray thee, how fares thy Maister? where is he? is my son with him? My gratious Lord, quoth the Dwarffe, where your noble sonne abideth, there is my maister, both of them in good disposition, and highly honored. And heereof I can assure your Maiestie, that you haue a sonne, who by good reason ought to bee numbred, among the best Knights liuing, for such honourable experience hath he made of his worthines, that perpetuall memorie, will record his deedes of chiualrie: what els remaineth you shall know at theyr comming, which will be so soone as they can possible. I euer perswaded my selfe, sayd the Emperour, that in the company of so good a Knight as *Palmerin*, my son could not but purchase credite and honour: therefore seeing they haue such prosperitie of health, I care the lesse for theyr stay, but welcome are they whensoeuer they come. By this time *Polinarda* heard of the Dwarffes arriuall, which greatly pleasing her she sayd to *Brionella*. I pray thee sweet freend, goe speedilie and seeke the Dwarffe, that we may knowe what is become of our Lordes, and my brother *Trineus*. *Brionella*, who longed to heare of her looue Sir *Ptolome*, whom well she knew to be one of the company, with all speede accomplished the Princesse commaundement, and found the ioyfull messenger with the Emperour, who tooke great delight in the

Palmerin d'Oliva: Part I 327

Dwarffes reportes: but his Maiestie perceiuing, with what cheerefull countenaunce she came, to bring *Vrbanillo* to her Lady the Princesse, bad him goe with her, hoping by his meanes his daughters extreame sadnes would be comforted. *Brionella* beeing foorth of the Emperours presence, embraced hym many times to
5 knowe hys tidinges, when the Dwarffe not ignoraunt of the Ladyes passions, deliuered *Ptolomes* letter to cheere her: but when the Princesse sawe *Vrbanillo* comming, with the teares in her eyes she ranne apace to meete him, and casting her armes about his necke, embraced hym very often, saying. Tell me *Vrbanillo*, tell me, how fares my brother and thy Mayster *Palmerin*? Madame, quoth the
10 Dwarffe, so well as your owne hart can wishe, and will ere long bee heere with you. Then deliuered he the letter from *Trineus*, which certefied her of hys shorte returne, and that he would bring with him the thing she most esteemed. But the wagge knowing she expected other matters, and that her brothers medicine was not sufficient for her cure, he gaue her his maisters letter, when she hastily brek-
15 ing open the seale, found the Ring which her loyall freend had sent her, and after she had welcomd it with many deuout kisses, she put it on her finger, with these wordes. I charge thee keepe this token safely, in witnesse of the Knightes gentlenesse that sent it, whome my hart hath made speciall choyse of abooue all other. Then reading the letter, and discreetly considering (not without great effuse of
20 teares) the sweet wordes, humble suplications, entire excuses and extreame passions, that her freend continually suffered for her looue, deliuering many bitter sighes, she sayd. Ah my true and loyall freend, I beleeue well, and take in good part your cause of absence, beeing assured, that if possible you could returne sooner, nothing should stay you from the place, where the only remedie of your
25 dolorous greefes abydeth. But seeing for my looue, you may not forsake my brother, I will pray for your continuall safetie, and speedy conduction to your longing desires, that mine eies ouer-watched with tedious expectation, and my hart neere tyred with bootlesse wishings, may by your presence be thorowly comforted.[1] Afterward, *Vrbanillo* breefely reported to her, the noble actions of his
30 Lord and Maister, the looue of *Trineus* to the Princesse *Agriola*, discribing her beautie and rare perfections, whereupon *Polinarda* thus answered. Beleeue mee *Vrbanillo*, if the Princesse be so fayre as thou saiest she is, her great vertues and firme loyaltie likewise comparable: enuie and false report shall not impeach her, to be reckoned among the most happy Ladies of the world, and her desires will
35 bee as honourably effected, as with vertuous thoughts she first began them. The like (I doubt not) will happen to thy maister, for fortune hath euermore so specially fauoured him, as now it were against reason shee should alter her countenaunce. So departed the Dwarffe from the Princesse, returning to the Emperour, who by no meanes could get any other tidinges of his son, then what you
40 haue heard, which made him doubt the Dwarffe iuggled with him. The next day, the Emperour sent his cheefest Lords and Barons, to conduct the *French* Ambassadors to the Courte, which was sumptuously hanged with Tapistrie, especially the great hall, which was adorned with costly cloth of golde, and rich purple, as

it had beene the Pallace of *Salomon*.[2] The Ambassadours entertained with meruaylous royaltie, and hauing deliuered the summe of their embassadge: the Emperour answered, that hee would conferre thereon with his Councel, in mean while they might returne to their lodgings. After they were departed the hall, the Emperour demaunded of the Princes Electours,[3] and the rest of his nobilitie, if these mariages of his sonne and Daughter, with the heire and Princesse of *Fraunce*, might not be graunted, as well for the vtillitie and honour of the Empire, as for the generall benefit of Christendome, commaunding them to speake theyr iudgementes without feare. The Lords altogether answered: that the motion was so good, and the aliaunce so honorable, as it was no way to be misliked. I will then (quoth he) talke with the Empresse, that she may vnderstand her daughters opinion, and then my Lords of *Fraunce* shalbe aunswered. So leauing them, he went to the Empresse Chamber, to whom he reported hys agreement with his Councell, which pleased her likewyse meruailous wel: but when she had a little considered on the matter, she aunswered, that but little could be sayd, before *Trineus* returned home againe. You reason well, quoth the Emperour, but in meane time I pray you, sound your daughters iudgment, that we may returne our Brother of *Fraunce* some certaine answer. Which she promised to doo, and so departing from her Lord, she went to her daughters Chamber, where hauing commaunded her Ladies aside, she thus began. Faire daughter, it is the Emperours pleasure and mine, that you marie with the eldest Sonne and heire of *Fraunce*, and your brother *Trineus* with his sister, for he is one of the most renowmed Kings of *Europe*, and his Sonne recounted among the best Knights of the world: for which good fortune you may thanke the heauens, that so great a Prince offers hys Sonne to be your husband. Aduise your selfe of your aunswer, for by your opinion must the Ambassadours be dispatched hence, who came to the Court for nothing els, but to conclude these honorable mariages. *Polinarda* hearing the words of her mother, was supprized with such sudden heauines, as she could not tell what to answer: but fearing the Empresse should perceiue, that her looue was already determined, with sad countenaunce thus replyed. Madame, you know what promise I made my brother, the day when he departed from the Courte, in the presence of you and all the nobilitie, that I would not mary before his returne:[4] and me thinkes I were greatly to bee blamed, and well woorthie greeuous reprehension, if I should so falsifie my woorde, which I can not doo without impeache of mine honour. And herein, shall I follow the laudable vertue of the Emperour my father, who euermore esteemed his promise aboue all earthly possessions. Beside, I can assure you that my brother will neuer marie with the Princesse *Lucemania*, for he looues one many degrees beyond her, and (may I speake it without offence) one of the most beautifull Ladyes that euer nature framed. Thus Madame, my Father and you haue excuses sufficient and auaileable, wherwith to aunswer the King of *Fraunce*. It may be, quoth the Empresse, that your brother loues els where: but I can tel ye, that neither he nor you shal doo any thing, contrary to the Emperours commaundement. *Polinarda* seing her mother persist in her opinion, bit in her sorowes with many secret sighes: yet knew she so well how to dissemble her passions, as the Empresse could not discerne her priuate meaning. So returned she to the Emperour, aduertising him of her daughters answere: whereat he was so offended, and in great anger hee came himselfe to his Daughter, saying. Why how nowe daughter? are you so bolde to disobey my commaundement? or dare you repugne against my wil? all is to no ende that you haue babled with your mother, for (will ye or no)⁵ it shall bee as I haue appointed. I knowe right well, dread Lord and Father, quoth she, that I ought no way to deny your pleasure, but rather will I die a thousand deathes, then consent to match with the Sonne of *Fraunce*, considering what promise I haue made my brother: and if I should so farre dishonour my selfe, as not to regard what I haue promised, I were not woorthie heereafter to be named your daughter. Thus stoode she resolute in her answer, and therewith shed such aboundaunce of teares: as the Emperour was constrayned to tell the Ambassadours, that the mariages could not be concluded til the returne of *Trineus*, notwithstanding, hee graunted all the other articles of theyr embassade. The Princesse quallifiing her greefes so well as she could, sent for the Dwarffe, and taking him by the hand, sayd. Alas my freende, I am now in the greatest perplexitie in the world, neuerthelesse, one thing comfortes me: that thou beholdest the true looue and loyaltie I beare thy maister, which neuer shalbe broken, what euer become of me. And would to God he were now heere: then would I speake it openly, without feare of any, that I am his, and hee mine. Madame, quoth the Dwarffe, if you continue faythful to my Maister, perswade your selfe of his assurance, for he building on your constancie, takes such continual pleasure in remembring you, that it is the only meane that preserues his lyfe: and you may be bolde to credite mee, that if your brothers looue did not with-holde him, he would haue bene heere long ere this, but he will come soone enough (I hope) to ende this doubt. As for me, I am of the opinion, that heauen will not suffer so good a Knight to dye, but first will permitte him to see hys Mistresse. Dye? quoth the Princesse, sooner let al the Knights in the world ende theyr dayes, and the eldest Sonne of *Fraunce* likewise, though he looue me to deerely, so might I be rid of these importunate Ambassadours. The Emperour seeing he could get no other answer of his daughter, concluded with the *French* Ambassadours, that so soone as his sonne was returned, hee should be aduertized, and so for that time they might departe: but the Empresse and he first bestowed on them many riche presentes, and so in short time they arriued againe in *Fraunce*, where great ioye was made in hope of these mariages, albeit they little thought, the Prince *Trineus* would tary so long. Aboue all other, the *French* Prince was most ioyfull, hearinge the Countie of *Armignac* reporte the wonderfull beautie of *Polinarda*: but she good Lady was of an other minde, for she had rather betake her selfe to a Cloister, then to breake her faith to *Palmerin*, whom she looued so constantly. Thus leaue we her conferring with *Vrbanillo*, returning to *Palmerin* and the Prince *Trineus*.

Chapter LXIV.

Howe Palmerin beeing thus on the Sea, caused Trineus there to marie the Princesse Agriola.

This noble company beeing thus on the Sea, hauing winde at will, sayled with such expedition, as in foure[1] dayes they had gotten farre enough from *England*: and the Prince seeing *Agriola* very pensiue and sad: comforting her with many sweete kisses, and taking her by the hand, thus spake. O soueraigne Creatour, how shall I render sufficient thankes and praise to thee, in graunting me the only thing that I desired? Ah sweete Madame, and my only Mistresse *Agriola*, howe much is your seruaunt indebted to you? hath any Knight more cause to honour and extoll his Lady, then I? Beleeue me fayre Princesse, such are the rare effectes of your gratious nature, and I so ioyfull of my happy fortune, as neither freende or father shall fetche you againe from mee. If my life might endure the length of tenne mens,[2] and euery day I should accomplish wunders in your seruice: yet could I not remunerate the least parte of your Princely deserts. But if your looue be such to me, as I am right well assured it is, let me intreat you forbeare this heauines, and banish from your thoughts these mellancholly humours: for seeing you so sad and pensiue, I suffer a torment wursse then death it selfe. For let me perceiue (how little soeuer it be) that my presence may be to your liking, and our present enterprise somewhat more pleasing: I flie to the heauens with conceit of happines, and value my fortune aboue the reach of humaine capacitie. In steede of teares, let vs vse quaint tearmes, and for these dumpes, pleasaunt imaginations. Perswade your selfe Madame, you are now in his custody, that honours you for your vertues, reuerenceth you for your diuine perfections, extolles you for incomparable merites, and liues for you with his very vttermost endeuors.[3] Thinke not though you haue left your parentes, the faulte is not pardonable, for the new aliaunce wherein you haue combined your selfe, shall one day glad you with such speciall content: that what you doo imagine now a daungerous offence, will be reputed an act of prouident and Princelie discretion. Then shall you finde true, what *Palmerin* hath spoken, and his promises of preferment and imperiall dignitie, shalbe both rightly and sufficiently perfourmed. Let these perswasions, if not my intreates, expell these passions, and procure better comfort. Madame, quoth *Palmerin*, though you haue left your country, consider the occasion, the looue of a mightie Prince, and the heauenly appointment, that your noble vertues should be coupled together, hath brought you from *England*, to sit on the imperiall seate in *Allemaigne*. How carefull we haue beene of your honour, your selfe can witnesse, no motion being offered to preiudice your liking. That you are contracted before the onlie immortall witnesse, you will not deny: therfore to preuent all ensuing daungers, the actuall ceremonie shalbe heere celebrated, and the royaltie thereof sollemnized when wee come into *Allemaigne*. So, if *Himen*[4] claime his due, you may graunt it without reproche, and *Iuno*[5] will as well smile at her sacred offering heere, as if it were in bower or hall. The credite of Princes are charie, and angrie parentes may hinder, what heauen dooth further: but the deede doone, it cannot be recalled, nor can you be diuorced but onely by death, and pittie were it, looue so well begun, but should continue, therefore (so please you) let it bee perfourmed. The Princes both agreed, they were ther maried, requiting theyr chast looue, with a simpathie of vertuous desires:⁶ but this time of delight and pleasure had small continuaunce, for Fortune enemie to prosperitie, accompanied with her eldest sonne Mischaunce, conuerted their ioies into sorrow, teares and paynes vnspeakeable, as you shal reade hereafter. These Loouers thus riding merily on the streame, suddenly the Sea began to swel, the winde chaunged roughly, the Skyes were troubled, and such a daungerous tempest beate vpon their Ship, as the Pilot, Maister, and Mariners knew not what to say, and fiue⁷ dayes together they were in this perplexitie,⁸ sometime forwarde, then againe backward, that no hope of lyfe was expected, but euery one prepared themselues for death, the implacable messenger of God, for they could discerne no other remedie.⁹ *Agriola* not accustomed to these daungers, was meruaylously discomforted: but *Tryneus* perswaded her with many examples, in that such stratagems were vsual on the Sea, albeit, she to ende the feare she sawe before her eyes, would oftentimes haue cast her selfe into the raging waters. At length the tempest ouer-passed, they discryed an Island, whereto with the helpe of theyr Oares they coasted, shrouding themselues vnder the sides of an highe mountaine: and although the place seemed casuall, yet there they determined to caste Anker, vntil the Seas were more calme and quiet. Beeing thus vnder the lee, and defended from the winde with the huge Rock, *Palmerin* came vp on the hatches, to see what iudgement he cold make of the Island, and so delectable the country seemed vnto him, as he was desirous to go on shore, taking his Faulcon on his fist that was giuen him in *England*,¹⁰ so with no other defence but his Sword, he went to viewe the soyle, not suffering any body to beare him company. *Trineus* and *Agriola* perswaded him to the contrary, but all would not serue: for the scituation of the Countrey pleased him so well, as he walked on in great contentation, not minding to returne againe to the Shippe, till toward the euening.

Chapter LXV.

How Trineus, Agriola, Ptolome and al their Mariners, were taken by the Turkes, after that Palmerin was gone to viewe the Island.

The History reporteth, that while *Palmerin* was thus absent, there arriued foure or fiue *Turkishe* Gallies, who likewise glad to shun the tempesteous weather, cast Anker neere to *Trineus* ship, and seeing no body on the deck of this straung vessell, because (fearing no harme) they were all at rest: they enuironed it about, and hauing boorded it, the Captaine of the *Turks* called to them, saying. What? are yee a sleepe within, that ye let vs boord yee without any resistaunce? by the reuerence of our Gods, we shall awake yee, but little to your ease. So came the Soldiours on boorde after theyr Captaine, who put the Pilote, the Maister, and many of the Mariners to the Swoord, sparing none but such as they pleased to ransome. Then searching the Cabins, they found *Trineus, Agriola* and *Ptolome*, whom they tooke prisoners, by reason they were vnarmed, as also somewhat sicklye after their roughe[1] passage. This rouing Captaine or Pirate, named *Olimael*, noting the singuler beautie of *Agriola*, commaunded her to be caryed on boord his Galley. When the Princesse sawe her selfe so hardly handeled, and that her Lord was prisoner with these villainous *Moores*, so that perforce they must abandon one another: she brake foorth into pittifull acclamations, and looking on her husband, thus spake. Ah my Lord, how hard and straung is this fortune? haue we escaped a tempest so dangerous, now to fall into this mercilesse extremitie? Oh that you and Sir *Ptolome* had beene Armed, that these *Moores* might haue bought our liues with the sword: but despightfull chaunce hath so thwarted vs, as no meane is left to preuent our perill. Ah *Palmerin*, how greeuous is thine absence, and how displeasaunt will our mishap be to thee? how much would thy valour now auaile vs, beeing vtterly destitute of any succour or refuge? I know our misse will so offend thee, as I feare thou wilt vse some outrage on thy selfe. With these woordes she fell downe among them in a dead traunce, the sight whereof so enraged *Trineus* and *Ptolome*, as snatching weapons out of the *Moores* handes, they layd about them so lustely, that in short time they had slaine halfe a score of them. But vnable were they to contend against so many, wherefore beeing taken againe, they were bound so cruelly with cordes and chaynes, as rente theyr tender and delicate flesh in many places: and being so conuayed into an other Galley, theyr squires likewise prysoners with them, the *Moores* tooke what they pleased out of the Ship, and when they had doone, set it on fire. Then presently they weyed Anker, and launching away, made hast, least any reskewe should followe them, so that quickly they lost the sight of the Island, and *Olimael* comming to se *Agriola*, assaied by many meanes to asswage her heauines, embracing her in his armes, and promising her great riches if she would be pacified. But all his speeches were in vaine, for she seeing the *Moore* imbrace her, with angry stomacke like a Lion enraged, caught him by the haire and the throat, saying. Thou villaine Dogge, thinkest thou I take any delight in thy company? How darest thou

Palmerin d'Oliva: Part I 333

traitourly theefe lay hand on me? And so roughly did shee struggle with *Olimael*, as if his men had not assisted hym, she had strangled him: Notwithstanding, he tooke all patiently, perswading him selfe, that by gentle speeches, smooth flatterings, and large promises, he should in time win her to his pleasure. So came he foorth of the Cabin, with his throat and face brauely painted with *Agriolas* nayles, washing away the blood, which made comely circles about his phisnomie: then called he the Captaines and cheefe of his companie, willing them to share the bootie among them, and hee would haue nothing but the Princesse for his parte, for hee was so inueigled with the beautie of his prisoner, as he had no delight but only in beholding her. In this manner then he bestowed his prisoners, *Trineus* he gaue to one of hys Cozins, and *Ptolome* to a Knight that serued the Soldane of *Babilon*, the Squires and the pelfe hee gaue among the common Soldiours. But when the Prince sawe he must needes leaue his Lady, and eche man would carie his prysoner whether him pleased: his greefe for his wife, and sorrowe for his freendes, I leaue to your iudgement, as not able to be expressed. Yet some hope of comforte he reposed in *Palmerin*, that by his meanes (beeing escaped theyr hands) he should get againe *Agriola*, else was there no way lefte to helpe him. *Ptolome* who deerely looued the Prince, before they parted, thus began. Why howe now my Lord? where is your wunted prudence and discretion? Where is that constant magnanimitie, which in so many fortunes heeretofore you vsed? what? is it lost, or haue you forgot it? What meane ye? will ye be subiect to passions, as a weake effeminate person? You that are sprung from the most ancient, noble and generous race of Christendome, esteemed for a most couragious and vertuous Knight: will you bee driuen into these sad and desolate opinions? What then would a *Turke, Moore* or barbarous *Mirmedon*[2] doo in lyke aflictions? when he that hath assurance of his God, and knows that all persecutions, fortunes and mishaps, are prooues of his fidelity, and the meanes to attaine eternal quiet: shews these vndutifull behauiors, as though he had lost all meanes of hope and comforte. If the body be afflicted, let the spirit be animated, and armed with patience, against all infirmities of the flesh. Leaue these soft countenances for women, and if you will not perswade your selfe, that these troubles happen for the encreasing of our ioy, it may be the meane that God will forsake vs. Then neither feare or dispayre I pray you, for he that suffered vs to fall into these *Moores* handes, both can and will deliuer vs againe. As for your Lady *Agriola*, doubt not of her vnconquerable loyalty, for she hath in her custody a iewel of such vertue, as no one can dishonour her against her owne lyking.[3] Comfort your selfe then in the power of the highest, and repose your selfe on the constancy of your Lady, with this certaine perswasion: that this crosse and aduersitie hath fallen vpon vs, for our greater good and aduauncement hereafter. Then came *Olimael* and interrupted their talke, commaunding nine or tenne of his people, to conuay *Trineus* into another Galley, and *Ptolome* into that where his Maister was, that so they might depart, to recouer the rest of theyr Gallyes, which were scattered from them by reason of the tempest. And so they departed one from an other, the

Galley wherein *Trineus* was descrying a goodly Ship of Christians, whereof they beeing glad, set sayle with the winde towardes the Christians, who roode away so fast as they could, and had escaped, but that they met full with certaine Pirattes of *Natolia*,[4] who ioyning with the Gallies, in the ende boorded her, and parted the spoyle among them: the winde suddenly began to chaunge, so that they were constrayned to flye for succour to an Island in the kingdome of *Persia*, which they reached in good tyme, glad to sheeld themselues from daunger: These Pirattes thus come to the Hauen, went all on shore to refresh themselues: but they had no sooner set foote on land, such enchauntments were there dispersed through the whole Isle, as they presently knewe not one another. But to acquaint you with the manner of these enchauntmentes, you must note, that the Isle where they landed was called *Malfada*, which name was giuen it by the Lady thereof, who was called likewise *Malfada*,[5] the most subtill Magitian of her tyme: so that wee may say of her, as the Poets feigned of the auncient *Circes*.[6] And albeit she was issued of Christian parentes, yet hauing such familiarity with the deuil and his maligne spirits, she would not accquaint her selfe with any goodnes towardes Christians, but daily practise theyr harme and destruction. And for this intent, she had of long time enchaunted this Island with such charmes, that what Ships ariu'de there, could neuer depart thence againe, much lesse such as entred within the Isle. They beeing thus stayed, *Malfada* would come her selfe, and chuse such as she lyked, the rest she transformed into Hartes, Wolues, Dogges, Bores, and all manner of beastes. Such likewise as she tooke with her into her Fortresse, when she had abused them to content her owne pleasure:[7] she would cast them foorth, transforming them as shee dyd the other: in breefe, she was wursse then a Deuill, and the whole Isle a very disguised hell. This wicked woman knowing, that more vnfortunate people were landed at the Hauen, called her seruauntes, and came to see them: but she made no great account of them, wherefore she commaunded her seruauntes to take all the riches foorth of the Ship, conuerting it by her enchauntment, that it seemed lyke sunk in a bottomlesse gulfe. Afterward at her pleasure, she transformed them that came in it, amonge whome *Trineus* was chaunged into the shape of a very fayre Dogge, not that hee was so, for that is a thing against nature, and which God no way will permit, that man shal take any brutish shape, or a brute beast any humaine forme. For the Magicall dispositions thus holde theyr Arte, that the enchaunted esteeme themselues beastes, and of that sorte was this disfigured Mastiue: notwithstanding, these distressed captiues had naturall reason and humaine power, but the benefitte of speech was taken from them. And thus was *Trineus* transformed, which he seemed not to mislike, for not remembring him selfe, he forgot all his heauie passions, marueiling only at his sudden mutation.[8] And heere will we leaue him in hys strange deformitie, to report what befell to the Princesse *Agriola*, after that dolorous separation beetweene her Lord and her.

Thus Gentlemen haue we lefte the Prince *Trineus* transformed into the shape of a Dogge, in the Isle of *Malfada* by the Enchauntresse: the English Princesse *Agriola*, in the custody of the Turkish Pirate *Olimael*: *Ptolome* and *Colmelio* caried into *Aethiopia*, and *Palmerin* raunging in the Island with his Hauke for his delight. Right straunge will be the meeting of all these freendes againe, after the hazardes of many perillous fortunes. For *Agriola* thus seperated from the Prince her husband, is maryed to the great Emperour of *Turkie*: how wunderfully the ring which *Palmerin* gaue her, preserues her chastitie, will be worth the hearing. How *Palmerin* counterfeiting him selfe dumbe, dooth many rare exploites in the Isle of *Calpha*, wil be as acceptable. How *Palmerin* gaines his *Polinarda*, *Trineus* his chast wife *Agriola*, *Ptolome* his *Brionella*, and al honors meeting together in the Emperours Court of *Allemaigne*, will be so straung as the like was neuer heard: and all this perfourmes the second parte, which shall be published so soone as it can be printed.

FINIS.

A. Munday,
Honos alit Artes.[1]

THE
Second Part of the
honourable Historie,
of *Palmerin d'Oliua:*

Continuing his rare fortunes, Knightly deeds
*of Chiualrie, happie successe in loue: and how
he was Crowned Emperour of*
Constantinople.

Herein is likewise concluded the variable troubles of the
Prince TRINEVS, and faire AGRIOLA, the
Kings daughter of ENGLAND: with
their fortunate Marriage.

Translated by A. M. *one of the Messengers of*
her Maiesties Chamber.

Patere aut abstine.

LONDON
Printed by Thomas Creede.[1]
1597.

THE
Second Part of the
honourable Historie,
of Palmerin d'Oliua:

Continuing his rare fortunes, Knightly deeds
*of Chiualrie, happie successe in loue: and how
he was Crowned Emperour of*
Constantinople.

Herein is likewise concluded the variable troubles of the
Prince TRINEVS, and faire AGRIOLA, the
Kings daughter of ENGLAND: with
their fortunate Marriage.

Translated by A. M. *one of the Messengers of*
her Maiesties Chamber.

Patere aut abstine.

LONDON
Printed by Thomas Creede.
1597.

Figure 4: Title Page of Second Edition, Part 2, 1597. © The British Library, C.56.d.7.

TO THE RIGHT HONOVRABLE AND HIS VERY GOOD LORD *EDWARD DE VERE, EARLE OXEN-ford,* Viscount Bulbecke, Lord Sanford of Badelesmere, and Lord high Chamberlaine of England.

A. M. wisheth the full issue of his noble desires

Promise is debt, my good Lord, as the Prouerb auoucheth,[1] and debt must needes bee paide, as reason requireth: the one not arguing so much liberalitie in speech, as the other doth vertue in accomplishing. When I presented your honour the first part of this Historie, I promised to hasten the other to the selfe same Patrone:[2] whereto I haue bene vehemently induced, by the gracious and affable receite of the former, and therefore (kissing your hand) I offer the conclusion of worthy *Palmerin*. Nor hath it beene so tedious and troublesome to mee in the translation, as I hope you will conceiue delight thereby in the reading: howsoeuer it prooue, I neede not despaire, hauing a Iudge so honourable, who measureth good will farre beyond abilitie.

Your Honours in all humilitie. A. M.

᛫ To the Freendlie
READERS.

Though long, yet at length Palmerin *is finished, and hauing endured so manie bitter brunts in search of aduentures: after all, nowe remaineth either to bee commended or condemned by your censure. Condemne him you cannot with reason, considering all his actions haue beene so honourable: as too malicious were the man would deale so hardly with him that hath giuen no occasion of offence. Commend him then you must, in respect of his manifold vertues, thrust altogither in the face of Fortune, onelie for your delight and recreation.*

As concerning his Sonnes, Palmendos *and* Primaleon, *the one is kept vnder his mothers wing, the Queen of* Tharsus, *and the other sporting in the Court at* Constantinople: *not daring to sette foote in the stirroppe after Knightly exercises, til they heare how their Father speedes. If he haue that fauour his deedes deserued, then on goes their Armor, and in the cheefest places of Christendome wil they shewe themselues, with repetition to the world of wonderfull aduentures.*

But while they expect good newes or bad, Paladine *sonne to the king* Mylanor *of* England, *is posting to you: what he and the noble Prince* Manteleo *of* Millaine *doe, in knightly affaires of most noble Chiualrie, the Historie shall deliuer: which is already on the presse in good forwardnesse.*[1] *From my house at Cripple-gate this ninth of March.* 1588.

Yours to his vttermost,
Anthony Monday.

ꙮ The second part of
the aunciernt and honou-
rable Historie of Palmerin
D'Oliua.
*Continuing his rare fortunes, Knightly deedes of Chiual-
rie, happie successe in loue, and how he was crowned Emperour of Constantinople. Herein is likewise concluded the variable troubles of Trineus, and faire
Agriola of England, with their fortunate mariage, etc.*

CHAPTER I.

*How Olimael presented the Princesse Agriola to the great Turke, who
immediately became amorous of her: and what rewardes and preferment the
Pyrate receiued, for his gift.*

As yet I am sure you remember in the first part, how the Pyrate *Olimael* diuided his prisoners reseruing for himselfe none but the King of *Englandes* daughter,[1] hoping in time to purchase her lyking.[2] And beeing alone with her in the fayrest Cabin in the Gallie, hee deuised all meanes hee could to comfort her: but all his labours were bestowed in vaine, for shee woulde receyue no kinde of sustenaunce, desyring euerie houre to die, hauing so lost her Lord *Trineus*. He seeing that fayre speeches, offers, gifts, and other inticements proper to perswasion, could not compasse the thing he desired, he grewe into choler, intending to gaine his pleasure perforce, so that after manie threatnings, with rough violence hee woulde needes rauish her. *Agriola* seeing that her feeble strength coulde not long withstand the Turke, albeit she stroue and resisted so well as shee coulde: therefore with deuout prayer shee called on God, desiring him to take pittie on her, and not to suffer that villainous Ruffian to dishonour her. Her prayer beeing ended, *Olimael* beganne in such sort to tremble, as hee staggered backewarde foure or fiue times, and so exceedingly was hee surprised with feare, as hee was constrayned to leaue her, and withdraw himselfe into another place. The Princesse, though shee were amazed at this suddaine chaunge, noting with what terrour the Captaine departed, yet was she greatly comforted by her deliuerance, imputing the whole worke thereof to the Almightie prouidence, and the vertue of the Ring that *Palmerin* gaue her:[3] wherefore with thankfull heart, and eleuated eyes to heauen,[4] shee sayd, O celestiall Father, howe great and infinite is thy goodnesse? howe happie is the creature, whom thou regardest with the eye of pittie? assuredly I nowe perceyue, that such as in extremitie haue recourse to thee, shall no waie perish. Then taking the vertuous Ring, and kissing it many times, sayd:

Vnualuable Iewell, giuen me by the best Knight in the worlde, howe carefully will I keepe thee? howe true is that saying: *That great persons giue great presents.*[5] Hencefoorth shalt thou bee kept (for the loue of him that gaue thee, and for thy singular vertue) in the place where I vsually store things of greatest price. So taking a little Chayne of Golde,[6] which serued her as a Bracelet, shee fastened this worthie Iewell thereto, and put it about her necke, so that the sumptuous Stone laye glistering betweene her milke white breasts,[7] a prospect so rare and delicate, and of no lesse power to drawe the beholders eyes, then the Adamant, the Amber, or the Ieate, can by their vertue: beside, so woonderfully repleat with sweete regard, as I dare affirme that the most cruell Tyrant in *Turkie*, would stand amazed at those two daintie Mountainets, more mortifyed and humbled then the aged Hermits of *Thebaida*.[8] *Olimael* yet quaking at his suddaine alteration, durst presume no more to offer her villaynie, but by rich gifts and presents sought to perswade her: all which auailed not, for as hee got but little profit by his violence, so wonne he much lesse by his trecherous offerings. So sayled they eight dayes togither, *Olimael* not able to compasse *Agriolas* loue, nor hearing anie tydings of the vessels that were lost, neyther of his Cozin who had *Trineus* captiue, which grieued him as nothing could do more, in that he was so vnprouided, as well he could not present himselfe before his Lord, to whom hee had promised to bring store of Christian prisoners, and now hee had in his bootelesse loue so lost his time, as either the tempest or shipwracke, had spoyled him of his owne companie.[9] In this doubtfull opinion, he debated with himselfe, that the great Turke did earnestly affect fayre Ladyes,[10] so by the meane of his beautifull prisoner, he imagined to bee entertained with good countenaunce, and his losse woulde be past ouer with forgetfulnesse: wherefore hee commaunded the Pilot to make toward the port of *Ottobant* where as then the great Emperour of *Turkie* soiourned, and thither they came in short time after. Notwithstanding, as a Seruant well instructed, not daring to abuse the familiaritie of his Lorde, hee sent one of his Knights to excuse his cause, and to report, that by casuall mischaunce he had lost his men and Gallies:[11] but if his Maiestie pleased to forget his misfortune, and receyue him into his accustomed fauour, he would bring him one of the fayrest Ladies in Christendome, and discended of most royall parentage. The Emperour beeing lasciuious, and more addicted to vnchaste desires[12] then any in his Realme, hearing this message, was so supprised with the onely report of her beautie, as immediately he became passionate for her loue: sending the Pyrate worde that hee could not bring a more desired present, and therfore remitted all his offences, promising him greater fauour then euer he had. And because no contrarie occasion may hinder his comming, quoth the Emperour, thou shalt carrie him this Letter, sealed with mine owne signet, that hee may no way doubt of his assurance. The Knight taking the Letter, and kissing the Emperours feete, according to the custome, returned to his Maister, deliuering him the aunswere hee had receiued. *Olimael* ioyfull thereof, caused *Agriola* to cloath her selfe in her most sumptuous garments, and so with all his men set forwarde towarde the Court. Nowe although the Princesse was all blubbered with teares, and halfe deade to see her selfe in the power of these Straungers, professed

Palmerin d'Oliva: Part II   *343*

and sworne enemies to her faith and religion: yet could not the rare perfections of her beautie be shadowed, but the glimse thereof set euery eye to wonder.[13] And as she looked about her, to see if any of her companie were landed with her, she espied *Ptolome*, whom they minded secretly to conuey from her, but shee beholding him so sad and sorrowfull, stept towards him,[14] saying. Ah, my deere freend *Ptolome*, what wreakfull chaunce hath Fortune throwne vppon vs: but well may I content my selfe, for this is a iust scourge for mine offence, and vndutifull obedience[15] to the King my father. Ah my Lord and loyall husband *Trineus*, neuer shall I see thee againe, for God dooth know[16] whither these villaines hath sent thee. Ah noble *Palmerin*, who was woont heeretofore to comfort me, too much hast thou failed vs, all thy former promises are nowe altered: for in steede of imperiall soueraigntie, pleasure and honor I am requited with pouertie, greefe, shame and mockerie. Ah death, sweet death, too long desired death:[17] why commest thou not to end all these miseries? But God will not permit thee, because by my torments and afflictions, I may feele the weightie burthen of my offences, and large bountie of his mercies.

    Ptolome seeing her in this mournfull vexation, sayde. It is no time nowe (Madame) thus to offende your selfe, but rather (as wise and well gouerned) to beare these aduersities, euen with as great content as your former prosperities, taking in good part whatsoeuer shall happen: for I am in good hope, and my minde perswades me, that wee shall be deliuered by noble *Palmerin*,[18] who I am sure endureth greater greefe in his libertie, hauing lost vs, then wee can doo in our imprisonment. *Olimael* exceeding angry to see *Agriola* weepe, violently puld *Ptolome* from her, charging his men, not to suffer him once to come in her sight, which he suffered patiently, because he saw it was in vaine to kicke against the pricke.[19] When they were come to the Pallace, and admitted to the Emperours presence, *Olimael* kneeling downe and kissing his foote, presented *Agriola* to his maiestie: who seeing her of such rare and wonderfull beautie, said to *Olimael*. This present (my Freende) is of such surpassing value, as thou couldest neuer honour me with the like:[20] good reason is it therefore, that a gift so precious should be rewarded with like recompence, and so perswade thy selfe I will, and thou shalt say the Emperour is bountifull.[21] As for the Ladie thou hast giuen me, I perceiue her so faire and gracious, as I intend neuer to haue any other wife: and that I may espouse her with the greater magnificence, I will stay till the hallowed day of my coronation, when all my Princes, Barons, and Knights, wil be heere assembled, and then in their presence shal our nuptialles be solemnized.[22] Nowe had the Emperour a Woman captiue, named *Hippolita*, who was a Marchants Daughter of *Scicilie*, and better skilled in all languages then anie Ladie in the Court, for which he made speciall account of her, reposing great confidence in her, and acquainting her with his cheefest secrets, wherefore hee sent for her before *Agriola*, and sayd. *Hippolita*, I giue you this Ladie in keeping, commanding you to intreat her as our owne person, and that all meanes may be practised,[23] to cause her forsake this sad mellancholy. In conference, you may shewe her what honour and happinesse she shall receiue by falling into our handes, and what incomparable fortune it is to her, whom we shall please to accept for our Wife. All which *Hippolita* (with great humilitie) promised to accomplish, and so conducted her into a maruailous princely Chamber, the floore couered all ouer with cloth of Tissue, and hung about with such sumptuous Tapistrie and cloth of Gold, as hardly might the richnesse thereof be valued. There *Hippolita* caused the Princesse to sitte downe in a Chayre of state, which was purposely prouided for her,[24] demaunding her name, and of what countrey shee was. The Princesse answered, that shee was of *England*, but further of her state shee would not bewray. *Hippolita* speaking perfectly the *English* tongue, tooke great delight daily to commune with her, and because *Agriola* should the better like of her conuersation, she tolde her that she was likewise a Christian: but by constraint she followed the Law of *Mahomet*, and his *Alchoran*.[25] In further speeches shee acquainted her with the estate of the *Sultanes*, in the Court of the great Emperour of *Asia*: which communication serued well to weare away the time, albeit the Princesse tooke small pleasure therein. *Olimael* in consideration of his noble present, was created high Admirall of the *Mediterranean* sea, and furnished with greater store of Foystes and Gallies then had before.

Chapter ii.
How the great Turke summoned all the Kings and Princes his Subiects, because hee minded to hold open Court: and howe he married with the Princesse Agriola his prisoner.

Hippolita daily conuersing with *Agriola*, because shee had so good knowledge in her language, at length the Emperor came to her chamber, and because he might the better behold the princesse, hee sate downe in a Chaire opposite to her, and there he sate a long time, not able to content his eyes with looking on her: for, speake to her he could not because shee vnderstood not the *Turkish* language.[1] Wherefore he commanded *Hippolita* to request her name, and what her Parents were, which to satisfie his maiestie, shee did, *Agriola* thus answering her. In vaine Lady seeke you to know of me the thing which death cannot force mee bewray: let this suffice you, that I am a poore Gentlewoman, the most infortunate that euer liued, with which words shee wept very greeuously. The Emperour moued with pittie, departed to his Chamber so surprised and enflamed with her loue, as hee could take no rest one minute of the night, considering with himself, that seeing she esteemed so little of the riches she sawe in his Pallace, and refused the offers made her by *Hippolita*, that doubtlesse shee was extract of some noble linage.

The next morning he called his foure Secretaries, commaunding them to write to all the Princes of his Empire, that they should not fayle to honour the day of his coronation with their presence, and to bring with them theyr Queenes and Daughters, and this they should do on paine of displeasure: all which was performed with present expedition. In the meane time, hee caused sundrie sumptuous ornaments to bee prepared, with all manner of precious Iewels could be deuised, and these he daily sent to *Agriola*, but all these presents, promises, and munificent entertainment, could no way mooue her, not so much as to grant him a gracious countenance. He likewise sent for the brauest Ladies in his Court, that they should keepe the Princesse companie: but she would be conuersant with none but *Hippolita*, of whom she had so prettily learned the *Arabian* tongue, as many times she could indifferently answere the Emperour. But when he beheld her continually so pensiue, and that by no meanes shee would bee comforted, hee doubted least his presence did offende her, and therefore hee forbare so often to visit her. For so deerely he loued her, as for the halfe of his Empire hee would giue her no occasion of discontent, hoping in time (which is the Lorde and conquerour of all things[2]) to alter that humour, and purchase her loue, which he desired with earnest affection. But now at this day, where may we find a Lady so vertuous and wel gouerned, being captiue as *Agriola* was, that could not be woon by such a mightie Emperor, considering her youth and beautie, and the wonderfull riches incessantly offered her. Yet the highest Lord so protected her, that the more liberall the *Turke* was in honors and perswasions, the more loyall continued her loue to *Trineus*, whose perfect image was engrauen in her heart.[3] And not fearing torments or death, she boldly answered the Emperor that he trauailed in vain, for she might not loue him, in that she was married to an husband, more noble euery way then he, and none but him shee would loue while she liued[4]: yet made he no great account of her words, considering what frailtie commonly is in women.[5] The day being come of this great preparation, and al the Princes present to vnderstand their soueraignes will: he beeing placed in his imperiall seate, said. That hee intended to take to wife, one of the most beautifull Ladyes in the world, and for that cause he sent for them, to vnderstand howe they liked thereof. Their aunswere was, that they liked well thereof, and would gladly honour her as wel beseemed them. Then sent he for *Agriola*, and before them all, saide vnto her: that it was his pleasure to accept her for his wife, and therefore shee should prepare her selfe on the morrow to be married. The Princesse abashed at these speeches, fell downe before him in a dead traunce, where vpon, by the Queenes and Ladies present, shee was conuayed into her Chamber, where beeing againe reuiued, she began most pitifull and dolorous lamentations: so when all the companie had left her, that shee was alone with *Hippolita*, falling downe on her knees at her beds feete, she thus began.

O my God and benigne Father, pittie thy poore distressed creature, and forget the offences I haue heretofore committed: for what is a sinner, vnlesse thou in mercie suffer her to come before thee? Wilt thou then vouchsafe (O wonderfull workeman of the whole worlde)[6] one eye of pittie vpon thy humble forsaken seruant? and suffer her not to fall into subiection, to the vowed enemie of thy holy worde, arming me so strongly in this temptation, that I no way iniurie my Lord and husbande *Trineus*, but rather graunt this desolate spirit, may leaue this bodie and the worlde togither. Ah my honourable Lord *Trineus*, where art thou nowe? that thou art not heere to defende the shame and wrong this Tyrant offers thee? what? art thou dead? or hast thou forgotten me? No, no, so well am I assured of thy fidelitie, as no torment can diuert thee from mee. Yet if I knewe directly that thou art not liuing, the lesse woulde bee my feare to follow thee: for then the greatest pleasure this Pagan could doe mee,[7] were to make mee happie onely by death. But for the matter is vncertaine, and that I liue in hope once more to see thee: I will patiently endure all afflictions whatsoeuer, for so sweete a reward as is thy loue.[8] These sorrowes of the Princesse so greeued *Hippolita*, as one coulde hardly iudge who was most passionate, yet at length shee thus spake to *Agriola*. I beseech you good Lady to leaue these greeuous lamentations, and regarde the high estate, honour and dignitie, that you shall haue in marrying with my Lord. Neuer perswade me (quoth the Princesse) to manifest disloyaltie:[9] for such preferments, if they bee not gotten iustly and by vertue, they ought not to bee coueted, but to be shunned as diuelish Serpents. Thus spent they the whole night, and in the morning came the Queenes and Ladies newlie come to the Court, to bid the sorrowfull Bride good morrow in her Chamber, attyring her in wonderfull gorgious vestures, after their Country maner, farre beyonde the royaltie of *Helena*, after her arriuall at *Troy*.[10] Betweene foure Kings shee was brought into the greate Hall, and from thence conducted to the Temple,[11] where they were

Palmerin d'Oliva: Part II 347

espoused by the *Mofti*. To recount here the royall solemnitie in the temple, the Maiestie and vnspeackable dignitie at the pallace, the excellent Comedies, rare triumphs, Maskes, Momeries, Moriscoes, and such like courtly pleasures, would bee a matter too prolixious: for they are not to our purpose. Let it then suf-
5 fice yee, that after they were magnificently entreated at Dinner and Supper, the daucing began, and God knowes how the *Turks, Moores, Arabes,* and *Medes*,[12] set foorth themselues in their deuises, and sports before their Ladies, much lyke the Satyres and horned Faunes, giuing new inuasions on the Nimphes of *Diana*.[13] But all these maruayles, ioyes and follies, coulde not chaunge the Princesse counte-
10 naunce, for shee continuing in her pensiuenesse, these sports were worsse to her then the torments of death: aboue all, fearing the losse of her chastitie, which was a Iewell neuer to be recouered.[14] The Pastimes ended by the Queenes and Ladies, shee was conducted to the nuptiall bedde, so braue and stately as the Prince *Aeneas*, when he came to Queene *Dido* of *Carthage*,[15] and there was the vnfortu-
15 nate Bride committed to her rest. Soone after came the hastie Bridegroome, calling for Torches that hee might beholde the Goddesse hee honoured, and as hee was preparing himselfe to bed,[16] he was troubled with such feares, passions, and apoplexie, as nowe he seemed more lyke a ghost then a man. Perforce hee was constrained to forsake the Chamber, when the extremitie of the fit somewhat
20 asswaging, and his former loue passions freshly assayling him, comming to the Princesse againe, heauily hee thus spake.

Ah, *Agriola*, Ladie and sole Mistresse of my heart, I thinke thou art some Goddesse, or (at least) exceeding all humanitie: so strange is this aduenture, as neuer any man (I thinke) heard of the like. Alas, cannot thy anger be appeased?
25 nor thou induced to loue him, who for thy sake endures most horrible torments? I pray thee bee not the cause of my death: or if thou needes wilt, suffer mee first to enioy the fruites of my desires. Know, my Lord, answered *Agriola*, that with my will you neuer shall enioy it, and if perforce you seeke to dishonour me, assure your selfe, I am resolued rather to suffer endlesse miseries, then to violate my
30 faith to my loyall Husbande: for such is my trust in God, that hee will not forget such as call on him. But in respect thou hast not beene cruell to mee, nor hast exercised mee with any tyrannie, I shall suffer thee to lye vpon the bed by mee, as my Brother might doo, and sometime (though it be more then modestie) embrace thee in mine armes:[17] but if farther thou presumest, thou mayst not bee permit-
35 ted, but shalt loose that fauour, thy selfe, and mee togither. Madame, quoth hee, in graunting mee that courtesie, you saue my life, for I haue many Concubines to qualifie those passions, and neuer will I attempt your dishonour while I liue: if I but offer the motion, refuse mee foreuer. I shall therefore account of you as my Sister, and death shall not make me doo contrarie to your appoyntment. The
40 yong Princesse glad of this solemne promise, gaue him a kisse or twaine, and suffered him to embrace her:[18] but other kindnesse could he neuer obtaine, contenting himselfe with this, because hee loued her so specially. At fifteene dayes end, the feastes beeing ended, the Princes tooke their leaue of the great *Sultane*, who

with many rich presents sent them home into their Countryes. Thus remained *Agriola* with the great *Turke*, and the Knight to whom *Olimael* had giuen *Ptolome* and *Colmelio*, sailed with his prisoners into *Aethiopia:*[19] and thenceforward vsed them not as slaues, but as Gentlemen of good qualitie, especially *Ptolome*, whom hee reputed a hardie Knight, and a man borne to great enterprises.

Chapter III.

How Palmerin after his recreation, returned to the sea side, and seeing the Ship and his companie gone, made great lamentation, and what after followed.

Before in this Historie you haue heard,[1] how *Palmerin* walking on shore with his Faulcon on his fist, desired to see the pleasantnesse of the Isle, and finding so manie delights to with-holde him, returned not towarde the Ship till it was neere night: but when hee came thither againe, and could not see the Shippe, nor anie one to question withall, he was greatly amazed, running heere and there, yet all to no purpose. Sometime hee imagined that *Trineus* had betrayed him, because he had acquainted him with his loue toward his Sister: and then againe resolued himselfe on the contrarie. All about hee looked for his companions, not knowing what to think: whether, they were carried away by Pirats, or taken prisoners by the Inhabitants of the Island. In the end, hauing compassed in his minde all imaginations hee could, and seeing that by his regard of pleasure he had lost his Friendes, hee entred into many sorrowfull lamentations, farre exceeding *Cadmus* when hee lost his Souldiers by the horrible Serpent, cursing and exclaiming on himselfe,[2] as he had beene guiltie of the death of his father. Alas (quoth hee) why did I not remember these wretched misfortunes by poore *Varnan*? whose sorrowes was likewise procured by a Hawke: in haplesse houre was this wicked Byrde giuen me.[3] Ah trecherous and deceiuing strumpet, I thinke thou art some incorporate Fiende sent from Hell, to iniurie the most constant Louers: and therefore gentle Owle, or rather enchanted Diuell, thou shalt neuer hereafter displease any other, so taking her by the necke, hee pulled her in peeces, and said:

Ah sweete Lady *Polynarda*, how contrarie is Fortune? and howe vnhappily our desires preuented? well am I assured, if *Trineus* come to the Court without me, it will endanger your life, and the onely thing that sheeldes mee from death, is comfortable hope to see you once again. Therfore diuine mistresse, I call for your succour, that by your gracious assistance, I may endure these vehement occasions. Ah gentle Princesse *Agriola*, howe haue I deceiued you? but in requitall of your wrong, no rest nor ease shall possesse my soule, till I haue brought *Trineus* and you to as great ioy, as by my meanes you haue receiued discomfort. In these complaints hee laide him downe vnder a tree, and so wasted the time till morning came, when seeing no creatures to speake withall, nor any meane for him to passe the Sea, hee determined to passe through the Island till hee might meete some body to conferre with. Thus hauing no defence but his sword vnder his arme, hee walked along, and at length he met a Moore with foure Spanielles, and a Marlin on his fist: whome hee humbly saluting, demaunded the name of the Countrey, and if there were any shipping neere for his passage. The Moore perceiuing by his language that he was a Christian, in great anger answered. Art thou come so farre to seeke thine owne misfortune? by Mahomet

I shall welcome thee hither with a vengeance. So laying hande on his Semitary, *Palmerin* perceiuing by his gesture (though hee vnderstood not his talk) that he wished him no good, wherefore drawing his sword, hee gaue the Moore such a stroke on the head, as he cleaued it to his very teeth, and sayd. By God villaine, thou shalt not take me prisoner, or send me into the sea to seeke my raunsome, and so may all discourteous varlets be serued, as resemble thee in conditions. Thus leauing the Moore dead, hee tooke another way, least if he should bee followed, hee might fall into danger: but seeing hee was vnarmed, and could not speake the *Arabian* tongue, hee imagined that at length he must needes be taken. Hereupon he returned backe to the Moore, and taking his garments, left his own there, and thence forward determined to counterfeit himselfe dumbe:[4] by which subtiltie he thought to escape vnknowne, and preuent his imprisonment, till hee founde meanes to returne towards *Allemaigne* againe. The day stealing on apace, and darke night approching, he came to a fayre Fountaine, of the cleerest water (in his opinion) that euer hee sawe, where laying him downe to rest, consumed the night as quietly as he could. On the morrow he began to remember his miseries, his dangers past, and such as were imminent, the conceit whereof made him very melancholy: so after hee hadde eaten a little bread which hee found in the Moores budget, according to the maner of *Diogenes*,[5] he layd him downe againe and slept.

Chapter IV.

How Palmerin counterfeiting himselfe dumbe in the Isle of Calpha, was found by certaine Turkes, as he lay a sleepe by the Fountaine: and howe hee was receiued into the seruice of Alchidiana, Daughter to the Soldane of Babilon.

Now that you may the more easily vnderstand in that which followeth, the full intent of our discourse, you must call to memorie how *Gamezio*, who was slaine before *Constantinople* by the Prince *Florendos*, as you haue heard in the first parte of this Historie:[1] was Sonne to the Soldane of *Babilon* named *Mysos*, and brother to *Maulicus*, who at his death was a verie yong prince. *Mysos* vnderstanding by his Subiects, that *Gamezio* the hope of his declining age, was gone by the summons of *Atropos*[2] to the habitation of the Gods, could not afterward enioy the health of body, or quiet in minde: and therefore ere a yeere was fully expired, hee went to seeke his sonne among his equalles in the fieldes of *Elysium*.[3] Before hee tooke his iourney wherein no creature returneth againe,[4] hee charged his succeeding Sonne *Maulicus*, to reuenge his brothers death, beeing perswaded that himselfe should not be discharged of his infortunate remembrance in the other world, if hee failed to accomplish his latest commaundement. *Maulicus*, not to hinder his departure, promised he would, yet could hee not fulfill it, beeing troubled in his own Kingdoms more then 20 yeeres after. But after he had reduced the rebellious Prouinces into obedience, he married with the King of *Armeniaes* Daughter, by whom he had the Princesse *Alchidiana*, one of the most beautifull and gracious Ladies of her time: who beeing come to age of experience, was so loued of her father, as he would neuer suffer her out of his sight, so that he made deniall to all such as requested her in marriage. *Alchidiana*, when shee vnderstood her owne singularitie, desired the companie of the most beautifull Ladies in *Asia*, because she held this opinion, that when the fayrest were present, beautie would then bee most splendant. For this cause shee sent to Prince *Guilharan*, Sonne to *Polidia* her mothers sister, that he should bring his Sister *Ardemia* to the Court, who was counted the Paragon through all the Monarchie of *Babilon*.

She being come to the Citie of *Calpha*, from whence the name of the Island was deriued,[5] hir Couzin *Alchidiana* deuised all the meanes she could to entertaine her withall, and among other courtly recreations, they daily vsed hawking and hunting.[6] It so came to passe, that these princesses and Gallants of the Soldans Court, now ryding to theyr pleasure, the knights delighting the Ladyes in beholding the braue voltages of their horses, and their swiftnes in course like the wings of *Pegasus*:[7] after the choyse of many places for game they came by the Fountaine where *Palmerin* lay a sleepe so soundly, as he neither heard theyr hornes nor hallowing.[8] Which when one of the Moores perceiued, intending to make all the other laugh, he alighted from his horse, and comming to him that meant no bodie harme, said. By *Iupiter* this sleepy fellow is drunke, but I will awake him, that hee may iudge the prize of our course: with which words he gaue *Palmerin* such a blow on the eare, as made him turne his head on the other side. *Palmerin* sodainely starting vp, and seeing him stande scorning that thus had strooken him, hee drewe his sword, and therewith sealed the Moore a quittance for his life, whereat the other abashed, came to reuenge their companions death: but *Palmerin* casting his Mantle about his arme, layde about him so lustily, as hee sent six more after their fellow, and any one that came neere him he layde at his foote, either maimed or slaine outright. *Alchidiana* maruayling at this stratageme, as also to heare the outragious noyse of the Moores, came riding towards them, demaunding what hee was that made such hauocke in her presence. The Knights gaue place to the Princesse, so that shee came verie neere to *Palmerin*, who enraged like a sauage Bore in the Wood, made a bloudie massacre among the Moores, and when shee behelde his braue featured bodie, and hardie courage, shee perswaded hirselfe that he was descended of high birth, and if she sought not means to cease this turmoyle, it would proceede to a greater daunger: therefore (mooued with pittie) shee commaunded her people on paine of theyr lyues, to holde themselues quiet while shee demaunded the cause of this tumult.

Palmerin wel pleased that the Princesse so succored him, imagined by her exceeding beautie, and sumptuous ornaments, that shee was their Soueraigne, wherfore casting himselfe at her feete, offered her his Sworde, which courtesie not a little contenting her, sayd: I knowe not my friend whether thou be Knight or Squire, but whatsoeuer thou art, seeing (of thine owne good will) thou hast thus yeelded to me, I will defend thee against all other. Therefore tell me what he was, that agaynst my will did first assaile thee. *Palmerin* with reuerent obeysaunce, made signes of his thankfulnesse, and with such good countenance dissembled to be dumbe, as one would haue iudged hee had neuer spoken. This poore man, quoth *Alchidiana*, the Gods offered great wrong in depriuing him of speech, for this I will say, (hadst thou vtterance) thou wert one of the brauest accomplished men of this world, both in sweete complexion, courtesie and hardinesse. Notwithstanding, thou must needes bee high in their grace, beeing able to encounter with so many, and defende thy selfe so woorthily as thou hast done. Then was shee certifyed by an auncient Knight, that one of the squyres of her Chamber smote him as he lay a sleepe, which he reuenged in such sort as she had seene. Trust me (quoth she) the dumbe man did as well beseemed him, wherefore, in respect of his ciuilitie, and that he can so well correct the ouerboldnesse of fooles: I will intertaine him as one of our Court, forbidding any to wrong him, as they tender my fauour, and their owne liues. So commaunding buriall for the dead, and prouision for the wounded, shee went to her Pauilion, which was not farre off, willing *Palmerin* (by signes) to go with her, deliuering him his sword again, and saying he should be her seruant. Humble graces did *Palmerin* requite her withall, and in signe of his obeysance offred to kisse her feete, but she would not permit him, and taking him vp by the hand, sayd: Looke that hereafter thou go not from me, whereto by signes he consented, knowing that by her meanes he should be safely protected.

Palmerin d'Oliva: Part II   353

    While these courtesies on eyther side endured, the Princesse *Ardemia* and the other Ladies entered the Pauillion: but *Palmerin* earnestly beholding *Ardemia*, was amazed at her woonderfull beautie, imagining that shee much resembled his Ladie *Polynarda*, so that breathing foorth a vehement sigh, he could hardly with-holde
5 himselfe from speaking. The Tables being couered for their hunting banquet, very choyce delicates were serued in on great plates of Golde, garnished with verie precious and costlie stones, which caused *Palmerin* to maruell not a litle, whom the Princesse seeing so sad, sayde. Howe now my Freend? doost thou not thinke thy selfe safe in my presence? Beleeue me on my worde, if any one displease thee, he
10 shall presently die the death. So causing him to sit by her at the Table, intreated him so well, as he had beene one of the cheefest Barons in her Fathers court. The Tables withdrawne, the Hunters had started a Hare, which was so narrowly pursued by the Houndes, as to saue her life, she ranne into the Princesse Pauillion, but the Greyhounde was so speedie of pace, as he caught her in the presence of *Alchidi-*
15 *ana*, who with her owne handes tooke her from the Dogge, and gaue her in keeping to one of her Pages. By this tyme it drewe towards night, wherfore each one mounting on their Palfrayes, set forwarde to the Cittie: the two Princesses hauing no other talke all the way, but of the singuler behauiour of the dumbe Knight. They riding faire and easily, because *Palmerin* trauayled by them on foote, *Ardemia*
20 beholding his goodly Sworde, demaunded of him if hee were a Knight, which he by signes made knowne vnto her, wherof *Alchidiana* verie ioyfull, sayde, that shee woulde present him to the Soldane her Father, and for this cause, the more she beheld him, the greater pleasure shee conceyued in him. Beeing nowe come to the Gates of *Calpha*, there stood manie Knights readie with lighted Torches, to con-
25 duct the Ladies and their traine to the Pallace, which was so rare and sumptuously edifyed, as *Palmerin* was amazed to see such royaltie.

    All the way *Alchidiana* had the dumbe knight by her side, giuing him her hand to alight from her Palfray, which hee did with exceeding reuerence, and nothing discontented with his office:[10] but manie Kings and Princes there pres-
30 ent, murmured thereat, thinking him not worthie to come so neere her, nor might he so be suffered, but that the Princesse somewhat enamoured of him, would suffer none to contrarie her pleasure: and leaned on his arme al the while shee went vppe the stayres of the Pallace, to giue the good euen to the Soldane, who stayed his Daughters returne in the great hall. Still leaned shee on *Palmerin*,
35 till she came to her Father, who satte in a magnificent Chaire of estate, hauing the resemblaunce of the firmament ouer his heade, (after the Turkish maner) so garnished with Rubies and Dyamonds, which with the lights of the Torches shined most gloriously: whereat *Palmerin* wondered, conducting the Princesse with so braue gesture, as many reputed him some noble person, and other (enui-
40 ously) thought the woorst of him.

    The Soldane, who loued his Daughter, as you haue heard before, arose from his Chayre to welcome her home, demaunding what sport shee had on hunting, and if shee had brought any venison home with her? Certes my Lord, quoth she, we haue had better fortune then you thinke on: but before I declare the manner thereof to you, will it please you to giue mee what I haue found this day? The Soldane, not able to denie his Daughter any thing, liberally graunted her request. A thousande thankes good Father, quoth shee: this dumbe Knight hath your Maiestie giuen me,[11] who (in his owne defence) hath this day slaine certaine of your Knights, and hereof you may assure your selfe, that hee is one of the most hardy Gentlemen that euer came into these partes. Seeing it is your request Daughter, quoth hee, I coulde bee well contented to graunt it, but how shall I aunswere the Freendes of the murthered, to whom I haue alreadie promised, that for his offence he shall be deliuered to the Lions? So, which of these graunts ought best to bee kept: yours beeing my Daughter, wherein nature ruleth, or theirs beeing my Subiects, which the Lawe commaundeth? I may not bee iudge herein, sayde the Princesse, notwithstanding, me thinkes (vnder your highnesse correction) that you haue been but hardly counsailed, to giue a sentence so cruell, hauing not heard or seene the partie.[12] And albeit hee were guiltie of blame, as hee is not, yet before his condemnation, hee ought to bee heard howe hee could cleere himselfe: but if hee must die, I hauing assured him life, and taken him into my defence: the disgrace is so great to mee, as mine honour must remaine for euer condemned. And you my Lord and Father, whose authoritie may discharge me of this reproch, if you refuse now to assist me, the greefe hereof will bee my death. These words she spake with such affection, and so heauily weeping, as woulde haue mooued a stony heart to pittie her: wherefore *Maulicus* touched with naturall remorse, sayd: You shall perceyue Daughter what I haue deuised, to the ende my worde may not bee impeached. He shall be put into the Lyons Denne, and suddenly taken out againe, by this meane I shall keepe my promise to his accusers, and satisfie your earnest desire. And the better to content you herein, his enemies shall bee perswaded that he escaped the Lions with life, and then will I giue him safetie thorow all my dominions. The Princesse fearing the bloodthirstie desire of the Lions, coulde not so content her selfe, which *Palmerin* perceyuing, that the Father and daughter thus contended for him, fel downe on his knee before the Soldane, making signes that hee should accomplish his promise, for hee feared not the daunger of his life. *Maulicus* maruailing hereat, perswaded his daughter that being so hardie, hee might escape: therefore to content her selfe, for things should bee handled in such sort, as the Knight should no way be endangered. These words somewhat contented the Princesse, causing *Palmerin* to be conducted to his chamber, charging him that was appoynted to attend on him, to see that he were very honourably vsed, and in the morning to bring him againe before her father. The Soldane and his Knights spent all that euening in diuerse iudgements on the dumbe Knight, each one being glad of the Soldanes sentence: but *Alchidiana* was so pensiue (considering the dangerous hazard he should passe), as she floong to her Chamber, refusing all sustenaunce, and spending the time in dolorous complaints, desiring rather her own death, then the dumbe knight should be any way harmed.

Chapter V.

How Palmerin was put into the Denne among the Lions and Leopards, and hauing killed three of them, escaped valiantly.

Palmerin beeing brought to his Chamber, which was one of the most sumptuous in all the Pallace, according as the Princesse had appoynted, he made signe to the Gentleman that attended on him, to withdrawe himselfe, for he was accustomed to bee alone in his chamber, which he immediatly did, being loath to offend him. *Palmerin* beeing alone by himselfe, gaue thanks to the God of heauen, who in midst of his misfortunes, caused such a gracious Ladie to fauour him so kindly, as defended his life when hee was in daunger, and by whose means hee conceyued good hope to escape his enemies hands, and to returne safely toward *Allemaigne*. His meditations ended, he betooke himselfe to rest, and in the morning *Linus* the Gentleman that had him in charge, came and presented him before the Soldane, who commaunded him to bee carryed presently to the Lions. *Alchidiana* vnderstanding that the dumbe Knight was with her Father, sent him a rich Mantle of scarlet, desiring him to weare it for her sake: which hee putting about him, went frankely with his Keeper to the Lions Denne, where the doore beeing opened, hee boldly entered, desiring God to assist him in this perill. *Palmerin* being in the Denne, because none of the Lions should get forth to hurt any other, howe euer God disposed of him, made fast the doore after him, and with his sworde drawne, and his Mantle wrapped about his arme, went to see how the beasts would deale with him. The Lions comming about him, smelling on his cloathes woulde not touch him: but (as it were knowing the bloud royall) lay downe at his feete and licked him, and afterward went to their places againe. But there were among them three Leopards, that furiouslie came and assayled him,[13] the formost whereof hee paunched with his Sworde, that hee was able to doo no more harme. The other two, although they had torne his Mantle, and put him in verie great daunger, as they that looked in at the windowes and crennels perceyued, yet to their no little admiration, in the end hee slue them both, and so went forth of the Denne againe, to whom *Linus* came, and louingly taking him by the hand, brought him to the Soldane, to whom hee discoursed his fight with the Leopardes, and howe gentle the Lions had beene to him.

The Soldane greatly astonished hereat, made more estimation of him then hee did before, and because the Lions refused to touch him, reputed him of royall parentage. Whereupon he sent for his Daughter, praying her to intreate him not as a Knight, but as a noble and vertuous Prince, considering his behauiour so well deserued. The Princesse entertayned him very graciously, and hearing the successe of his happy fortune, spake thus in the hearing of them all. Because euery one shall know, Sir knight, how much I honour your good gifts, I will cause my Father so well to loue you, as hee shall repent himselfe a thousande tymes of the daunger hee put you to: and so verie louingly embracing him, desired pardon on her own behalfe, because she suffered him to be thrust to the Lions. *Palmerin* in signe of attonement, and that hee was nothing displeased, kissed her hand, and sitting downe in a Chaire by her, behelde *Ardemia*, who resembled his Mistresse so equall in beautie, and could not holde his eye from her, so that hee conceiued such pleasure in his regard, as he iudged it sustenance enough to maintaine life. But she that was ignorant of the cause, presumed that he loued her, wherfore thenceforward, she began so amorously to affect him, as shee enioyed no rest but in his presence. Thus were these two Ladies *Alchidiana* and *Ardemia* touched with one disease, and that so sharpely to the quicke, that the least torment they endured (seeing hee could neither speake nor vnderstand their language) was woorse to them then death. And so it fell out, that each of them thinking her selfe best beloued: concealed her thoughts from the other, and would in no case be reputed amorous, least so her desires should be discouered. *Alchidiana* for arguments of her loue, gaue him horses, esquires, seruants, and pages, so that the greatest Prince in the Court was no better equipped then he: and in this fortune such was his mind, that for all the honor and fauour the Soldane and his daughter bare him, he did not outreach himselfe in behauiour, but was benigne and full of courtesie, that each one loued and desired to be familiar with him. And if any enterprise of Ioustes or Tourneyes were in hand, *Palmerin* was the formost in the field, and carried the prize away from all whatsoeuer, which incited *Maulicus* to loue him in such sort, that he entertained him into such speciall credite, as he would neuer resolue on any matter of importance, without his shew of good liking. And albeit the Princes of the Court shewed him good countenance, yet Enuy (that neuer can rest in ambitious hearts) caused them in the ende to raise slaunder against him: which *Palmerin* perceiued, but being vnable to remedie, awaited conuenient time for his departure, notwithstanding the earnest affection *Alchidiana* bare him. He knew likewise so well to disguise his matters, that so often as the Princesse would hold him in talke, he still feigned not to vnderstand her: which made her iealous towards *Ardemia* her Cozin, who by *Alchidianaes* iniuries and *Palmerins* refusall of her loue, lost her life, as you shall read in the chapters folowing.[14]

Chapter VI.

How the Prince Maurice sent his Ambassadors to the Soldane, to desire safe conduct for his comming to the Court: to trie if he could find any Knight there, able to deliuer him of an extreame trouble that hee dured by enchauntment.

During the time that *Palmerin* was thus esteemed and beloued in the Court of the great Monarch of *Assiria*, vpon a Sunday after dinner, as the Soldane was in the great Hall conferring with his Daughter, and many other great Princes and Lordes present: there entred a Moore Knight armed, except his Helmet and Gauntlets, which were carried after him by two Squires, and making his solemne reuerence, humbled himselfe at *Maulicus* feete, saying. Most high and redoubted Monarch, my soueraigne Lord *Maurice*, sworne Prince of whole *Pasmeria*,[1] kisseth your highnesse hand, sending to require your gracious safe conduct, that himselfe may come to your Court, to trie among all your knights, if there bee any one so loyal and valiant, as can deliuer him from a torment he endures, the most cruell and straunge that euer was heard of, and happened to him in this sort.

The King of *Pasmeria*, great gouernour of the Moores, and father to my Lord, beeing vnable (through extreme age) to weilde the gouernment of his Realme, gaue the administration thereof, and made his Lieutenant generall, my Lord *Maurice*, a Knight so hardy and puissant as any of his time, and so renowned for his bountie, sagacitie, and braue lineaments of body, as there is none of the Kings of *Iudea*, *Egypt*, *Ethiopia*, and neighbour Countreyes round about, but gladly desire his aliaunce and friendshippe. So that many haue sent their Ambassadours to him, presenting their Daughters and Kingdomes to him, the greater part whereof he hath hitherto refused, excusing himselfe by his fathers age and his owne youth. But as often times it happeneth, Fortune enemie to all good endeuours, not suffering him to remaine in quiet, permitted that the queene of *Tharsus*,[2] the fayrest of the Orientall parts, a young Widdow and rich, as is very well knowne, after shee had sent him many presents of incomparable value, intreated him to come and see her, shaddowing in this message, the great desire shee had to match with him. The Prince being benigne and courteous, would not denie her, but in short time after iourneyed to her. The Queene entertaining him with great royaltie, and seeing in him farre more gracious and beautifull gifts then before she heard reported: was so surprised with loue, as in steede of looking to be wooed, her selfe was constrained to demaund, knowing so well to declare her desirous and affectionate passions, as the Prince mooued with amorous pittie, granted what she requested, without any further condition or promise, presuming on himselfe, in respect of her great and fauourable entertainment, that hee would not leaue her for any other. But herein was she deceiued, for the yong Prince hauing staied with her tenne or twelue dayes, desired leaue to departe, saying that hee had receiued Letters from his Father, which commaunded his speedy returne home againe, promising her, (if so his father consented) to take her in marriage, and that with such expedition as might bee. The Queene somewhat contented with this answere, thinking hee would performe what hee promised, let him depart. He being come home into his owne Countrey, forgot his loue to his newe Freend, and by his Fathers commaundement, marryed with a yong Princesse, Daughter to the King *Lycomedes*. The Queene hearing these newes, was almost dead with conceit of greefe, and conceiued such hatred against my Lord *Maurice*, as she determined to be reuenged on him, whatsoeuer came after. And the better to compasse her intent, shee sent to search out one of her knights, a learned Magitian, promising him, if he would help her to be reuenged on him that so deceiued her, shee would make him one of the cheefest in her Realme. The Magitian, who euermore was desirous to please her, promised her to worke such a deuise, that *Maurice* should endure such cruel torments, as her selfe should be constrayned to pittie him. And to accomplish this practise, hee onely desired the King her Fathers Crowne, which was one of the richest in the whole world: which Crowne he coniured in such sort, as the diuell himself could not imagine the like, and comming therwith to the Queen, said.

Madame, you must sende this Crowne to the Prince of *Pasmeria*, desiring him for your sake hee will weare it on his head, in the cheefest affayres of his estate, which hee immediatly will accomplish: but this I dare assure you, that hereby hee shall suffer so many vexations, as hee would endure a thousand deaths if hee could possible, to be deliuered from this torment, which he neuer shall be till the most loyall louer in the world take it from his head. The Queene so ioyfull hereof as could be, sent the Crowne to the prince, who receiued it thankfully, and beholding it so sumptuous, sodainely put it on his head: but presently flew out of his head such a flame of fire, as it had beene the blaze that commeth from a discharged Cannon.[3] Then called hee for ayde and succour, making the greatest lamentations that euer were heard, but all was to no ende, for no Knight or Lady there could do him any good, and so all the whole day hee remained in this cruell martirdome, burning aliue, yet not perishing, resembling the *Salamander* in the extreame fire.[4] When his people saw that they could procure him no ease, they sent two of the greatest Lords of the Realme to the Queene, who humbly intreated her to pittie the Prince, and to recompence the fault he had committed, hee should take her to his Wife, and endow her with those honourable possessions belonging to him. The Queene entertained them very nobly, and after she had vnderstood their message, answered.

My Lords, the marriage betweene your maister and me, is intollerable, and no way can hee nowe contract himselfe againe, for I remembring his disloyaltie, and hee the torments hee suffers by my meanes, it were impossible that wee should louingly liue togither, therefore in this matter you shall excuse me. And let him know, that seeing hee was so presumptuous contrarie to his faith and promise, to refuse me for his Wife, I now so much disdain and contemne him, as my heart by no meanes can be induced to loue him. And no other remedie is there for his torments, but that hee seeke through *Asia, Europe*, and *Affrica*, a

Palmerin d'Oliva: Part II

louer so perfect, who by his loyaltie may cease the paines he suffers for his trecherie and treason. With this short answere depart my Countrey, for your Maister is so vnworthie of fauour, as for his sake I hate his people.

    The Ambassadours maruailing at this fatall destenie, returned to their Lord, to whom they reported the Queenes answere, and what remained to ease his affliction, which more and more encreased his greefe: wherfore seeing what he was enioyned to doo, the next day hee left the Court, entending not to stay a day in any place, till he should finde a Knight so vertuous and loyall. Thus hath he trauailed *Ethiopia, India, Tartaria*,[5] and the greater part of your realmes, but as yet hee hath founde none to remedie his misfortune: but if any other disloyall Knight in triall touch the crowne, his vexations are far more greater then before. For this cause most mighty Lord, hauing heard the great fame of valiant knights in your Court, especially of a stranger Knight being dumbe, who came hither but of very late time: he desires your maiestie, his assurance graunted, to suffer him trie his fortune heere, if in your presence he may finde any helpe, or else to seeke further in other Princes Courts. These are the principall points of my charge, may it please your highnesse to consider of mine answere, how I shall returne and certifie my Maister, that you may likewise see an aduenture maruailous.

Chapter VII.

How the Prince Maurice came to the Court of the Soldane of Babilon, where he was deliuered of his burning Crowne that tormented him, by the loyaltie of Palmerin.

Maulicus wondering at this strange discourse, thus answered the Moore. You may (my friend) returne to your maister when you please, and say from vs, that hee shall be welcome to our court, with as safe assurance as our own person, as well for his valour and bountie, which I haue heard greatly esteemed, as for that wee are desirous to see so strange an aduenture ended in our presence. And wee cannot sufficiently maruaile, howe he could bee so forgetfull of himselfe, that after his faith so broken, hee could extinguish her remembrance that loued him so vnfeignedly: but heerein may wee beholde the soueraignitie of confident louers. Go then and certifie him of our pleasure, and that we pray our gods his comming may be in such an houre, as hee may depart hence to his owne content: yet am I greatly afraid, that he shall not finde any Knight in our Court, but hath eyther forfeited or failed towardes his Lady. The Moore kissing the Soldans hand, and humbly taking his leaue, returned to his Lord, leauing the Soldane and his Knights, admyring this rare accident, so that hee exhorted euery one to aduenture his fortune at this Crowne, to giue the greater assurance to their Ladies, of their loyall fidelitie: but many of them were herein deceiued, for in steede of prayse and glorie, they receiued shame and reproch, as you shall see heereafter.

The Prince aduertised of the Soldans aunswere, in hope of good successe sette forwarde on his iourney, and the next day following hee came to *Calpha*, where *Maulicus* caused him to be honourably lodged in the Cittie, because that day he would not come to the Pallace. On the morrow, after that *Lethea*, wife to the Soldane, her Daughter *Alchidiana*, the fayre *Ardemia*, with many other Ladies and Princes were come into the Hall, to see the tryall of this noueltie: Prince *Maurice* vnderstanding how the Soldane with all his courtly assistants, stayed his comming, went to the Pallace accompanied with a hundred Knights, all clad in mourning blacke, in signe of their continuall sorrow for their Princes misfortune. There he was very royally entertained, the Soldane causing him to sitte by him in a sumptuous Chayre of estate, of purpose prouided, and after many welcomes and kinde gratulations, the Soldane demaunded how hee felt himselfe, and whether hee sustayned any ease of his torment. Ah my Lord quoth the prince, I can not expresse to your maiestie the paine which I feele, being a thousand times worse to mee then death, and euerie hour enforcing mee to despayre, but I must endure it with what patience I can, till incomparable loyaltie discharge mee of this burthen.[1] With these words he lamented exceedingly, so that each one was mooued to pittie him, for such a burning flame continued in the Crowne,[2] and so furious heate proceeded from his mouth, as sette the Hall in maruailous hotnesse, yet consumed hee nothing at all, but in euery part was as

Palmerin d'Oliva: Part II 361

formall as any other man. Beloued Couzin, said the Soldane, for my selfe I will not enterprise to meddle with your Crowne, for I doo not imagine my selfe so fauoured of loue, as I can finish that wherein so many haue fayled, nor would I willingly seeke mine owne dishonour, being farre vnable to profit you: as for my
5 knights, let them make proofe of theyr loyalty and spare not, and see which of them can winne the honour of this aduenture.³ Hereupon *Guilharan*, brother to faire *Ardemia* first entred, and comming to the enchaunted Prince, sayd. Trust me my Lord, since I began my profession in loue, I neuer committed any preiudice to my Lady, therefore will I trie to end this enchauntment.

10 Then earnestly beholding *Alchidiana*, for whose loue onely hee came to Court, hee approched to the enchaunted Prince, and puld so hard as he could at the Crowne, but hee crying aloude, sayde. For Gods sake Sir knight striue no longer, for if by disloyaltie I could be cured, I see you are able to giue me remedie. Alas, in all my life I neuer felt like paine by any Knight that tried his
15 fortune, great neede haue you to doo seuere pennance, if you will bee fauoured by loue any more, towards whom you haue so haynously offended, for my infirmitie may not be holpen, but by loyaltie, firmnesse, faithfull persuit, constant perseuerance, and such other honoured vertues esteemed in loue, whereof you haue not the least particular. Thus retyred this newe louer, more ashamed then a
20 Virgin to bee seene lightly disposed,⁴ and so sate downe among the other knights, whose fortune prooued as effectuall as the first, to their owne disgrace, and great torment of the languishing Prince. The Kings and auncient Princes seeing the young Knights could doo no good, put themselues in deuoire, each one conceiuing so well of himselfe, as if theyr fortune serued to ende the aduenture, their
25 yeeres should carrie the honour, and they be renowned for euer by their Ladies:⁵ but their vaine conceit and desire to accomplish an impossibilitie, much abused them, so that they shamefully remained frustrate in their intents, and the paines of the enchaunted Prince greatly augmented, who thus spake to them. Truly my Lords, it is the custome of your auncient and audacious opinions, to extoll your
30 loues and valour: but for any thing I see, your olde yeeres haue much lesse merited amorous mercy, then the indiscreete and vnconstant dealing of these yong Princes. Then seeing that no other offered to prooue his vertue, deliuering many greeuous sighs, he sayde. Vnhappie wretch that I am, howe much more had it beene to my ease and benefit, if the Queene of *Tharsus* (whome I so heynously
35 offended) would haue contented her selfe in her reuenge, to cause mee be peecemeale torne in sunder, then thus haue deliuered me into this insupportable vexation, the ende whereof will neuer be accomplished, seeing that in this honourable Court of my Lord the Soldane, I find no one can giue me comfort.

Palmerin hearing the lamentation of this amorous martyre, fell into a pro-
40 found imagination, and after he had long regarded *Ardemia*, who so liuely resembled his Mistresse *Polynarda*, saide within himselfe. Ah sweet Madame and onely mistresse, vouchsafe at this instant to assist mee, for by your succour I shall nowe make proofe of my faithfull and inuiolable loyaltie, which neuer in ought

offended you, if not at *Durace* in affecting *Laurana*, whom I simplie thought to be the Lady, who was so often promised in my visions.⁶ But seeing my thoughts neuer sorted to effect, as also that I was deceiued in your name: that ought not be imputed to me for any trespasse,⁷ and therefore diuine Goddesse bee fauourable to me. Then surprised with sodaine ioy, hee beganne againe earnestly to beholde the Princesse *Ardemia*, who imagining her selfe onely beloued of him, cast foorth a bitter sigh, and turning to *Alchidiana*, saide. Ah Madame and my deere Couzin, what great fault hath this cruell Queene committed, appointing her Magique in such sorte, as loyall and faithfull Ladies maye not be suffered heerein, for deliueraunce of this yong and beautifull Prince: doubtlesse hee should sooner receiue helpe by them then by Knights, for much more loyally doo they loue, then men, and are in their affections firme and constant. *Alchidiana*, who felt her selfe touched with this intricate furie, whereof the faire *Ardemia* complained, suddainly coniectured, whereto her sighes and faultering speeches tended, which raysed priuate conceit, and such a vehement attaint of iealousie, as she would not aunswere any worde, but feigning to smell some discontented sauour, turned her face the contrary way. *Palmerin* looking round about him, and seeing no one would meddle with the aduenture, fell on his knee before the Soldane, crauing leaue by signes to trie his fortune, which he graunted, and in a laughter, saide. Goe thy wayes dumbe Knight, and in such an houre maist thou touch the crowne, that all the honor may fall to thy share. Then *Palmerin* hauing his eye fixed on her, who in beautie did paragon his onely Mistresse, exalting his minde with an intire sighe, secretly said.

Ah mirrour of excellencie, although my body bee farre distant from you, yet am I in spirit daye and night in your presence, beeing so confidently assured of your loue, that is no iote inferiour to mine, which verie thought makes me thinke you present before mee. Wherefore cheefe Mistresse and Gouernesse of my life,⁸ you shall nowe receiue the honor, that by the vertue of your faithfull Seruant you ought to haue: for I hold my selfe towards you, so innocent and pure, as needes must aunswerable successe repay so good deseruing.⁹ Then laid he hand on the burning Crowne, which hee tooke from his head so easily, as though no enchantment at all had helde it: and then ceased the vehement heate in *Maurice*, and from his mouth came so odifferous and sweet sauours, as euery one present delighted to feele them. The Prince so ioyfull as could bee for his deliueraunce, as may well be coniectured, prostrated himselfe at *Palmerins* feete, and with vnspeakable ioy thus said. Most noble and fortunate Knight, how much am I bound and indebted to thee? right happie was the howre of thy byrth, but much more happie my iourney to see thee: let my word suffise, I so far deliuer my selfe yours, as my selfe, my Subiects, my possessions, or whatsoeuer else is mine, I freely offer to your disposition. *Palmerin*, who euer bare the most noble minde of a Knight, was displeased that so great a Prince shoulde honour him with such reuerence, wherefore with great humilitie hee tooke him vppe in his armes, causing him to sit downe where before hee did: but the Soldane and all his Lords

greatly amazed, not so much at his courtesie, as his gratious fortune, did him all the honour could be deuised: but hee bashfull of this ouergreat kindnesse, kneeled down before *Maulicus*, shewing by signes[10] that himselfe was altogither vnwoorthie of such honor, but his Maiestie, to whome that rich Crowne woor-
thily appertayned, which he presenting the Soldane, kneeled downe to kisse his feete, but *Maulicus*, would not suffer him, and taking him vp by the hand, said. Sir knight, we heartily thanke you for the great pleasure you haue doone vs, promising you by the faith of a Prince, that this Crowne shalbe kept in our Treasurie, in witnesse that we had in our Court, the most loyall and honourable among all Knights. In recompence whereof, we giue you this Cittie, with all th'appurtenaunces thereto belonging, and to morrowe will wee put you in possession thereof. Oh that it pleased the immortall powers, and their great Prophet *Mahomet*, to deliuer you speech, whereof you are destitute: for I sweare by their high and immortall name, we would make you the greatest in all our kingdoms. *Palmerin* with humble gesture returned his thankfulnesse, signifying that he would haue neither Cities nor castles, but that it suffised him to be one of his knights: notwithstanding, the Prince by importunat meanes gaue him rich gifts, and for his sake staied there more then two monethes.

Chapter viii.

How the fayre Princesse Ardemia, enduring extreame passions and torments in loue, made offer of her affections to Palmerin, which he refused: wherewith the Princesse (through extreame conceit of greefe and despight) suddainly died.

Easilye may be coniectured, the great pleasure of the two Ladies, *Alchidiana* and *Ardemia*, beholding the man whome they loued as their liues, to haue the honour of the enchaunted crowne: for each of them seuerally perswaded her selfe, that he had thus aduentured in honor of her loue. And as they returned from the Hall to their chambers, *Alchidiana* came and tooke *Palmerin* by the hand, and walking on with him, thus spake. Ah gentle knight, how are you to bee regarded aboue all other? I knowe not why the Gods should depriue you of speeche: except that in all things, this onelie excepted, you should be perfectly resembled to them. Oh how happie is shee, that might aduenture to make you her Seruant, doubtlesse, if in her appeare so singuler perfections, as apparantly shew themselues in you: well might it be reputed a rare coniunction, when the celestiall dispositions gouerning their humaine affections, hath vnited you in so amiable alliaunce.

The Gentlemen that attended on the Princesse, greatlie murmured at this priuate familiaritie: but shee was so immoderate in her affections, as virginall modestie was now forgotten, and carelesse of regarde, openly shewed her desires. Thus were these two Ladies now, much more amorous of the dumbe Knight then before: so that they were not well, but eyther in his companye, or thinking on him. *Alchidiana* remaining iealous of her Cozin, seemed not to loue her as she was woont, but deuised all the meanes shee could, that she might be sent to her Fathers Court againe: yet she that little made account thereof, sought opportunitie to bewraye her loue to *Palmerin*, and by hap seeing *Alchidiana* in the Gallerie, conferring with two of her Ladies, shee entred alone into her Cozins Chamber, where sitting downe on the bedde, shee compassed many imaginations, howe she might discouer to the dumbe Knight, the secrete fire that was kindled in her brest.[1] So long shee staied there, till *Palmerin* came, because about that time hee was woont to visite the Princesse *Alchidiana*. *Ardemia* so glad heereof as could be possible, suddainlie started vppe, and saluting him with more then common reuerence, taking him by the hand, and causing him to sit downe by her vpon the bedde. Then enflamed with woonderfull passions, surpassing *Pasiphaes* desire to the brutish Bull, when shee mette him in the wood cow made by *Dedalus*,[2] shee beheld him with such a piercing countenaunce, as the least glimse whereof, was able to confounde the reason of the most constant person, as the aspect of the Sunne in the signe of *Leo*, dooth the eyes of the beholders,[3] and of force to warme the coldest complexion,[4] although it were an Eunuche himselfe in her presence.[5] Then deliuering three or foure bitter sighes, fetcht from the verye bottome of her heart, as cruell as the striuing pangs of death: she tooke a rich Diamond from her finger, and put it on *Palmerins*, with these words.

Oh sweete Freende, and onely comforte of my soule, let me intreate you to weare this as an argument of my loue, thereby to knowe, howe well you esteeme of mee, assuring you, that I am so deuoted yours, as if you vouchsafe to deigne me the fauour and honour, by iournying to the Court of my Father with mee, I neuer will haue any Husband but you, and there shall such account be made of you, as wel beseemes a Knight so noble and vertuous. Ah diuine defence of my life, and more woorthie to bee loued then Loue himselfe, misdeeme not of these speeches so aduenturouslye vttered, by a yong Ladie and vnmaried: for the loue I beare you is such, as I am constrained (forgetting the decent regard of a bashfull Virgin, who naturallie is shamefaste) to esteeme of you honestlye, and as is conuenable to mine estate. Then seeing the Gods, the place, the occasion, and the time, permits me to bewraye, that which I dare not otherwise manifest: haue then faire Knight some pittie on mee, and let mee enioy assuraunce of that grace, for which I liue in ceaselesse torments. With which wordes shee embraced him, and sealed so many sweete kisses on his hand, as apparantly deciphered her earnest affection.[6]

Palmerin amazed at this strange accident, because shee was a Pagan, and contrary to him in faith, that making no aunswere, but following the example of chaste *Ioseph*, who refused *Zephira*, Wife to *Putiphar*, great prouost to the King of *Aegipt*:[7] started from her suddainlie, and mooued with displeasure, departed the Chamber, thinking in himselfe, that such occasions more ouer-rule the hearts of men, then all other matters that might bee deuised, and onely the practises of hellish *Pluto*.[8] Then calling to his Ladie for assistaunce, said to himselfe. Ah sweete Mistresse, succour now your seruaunt, for I rather desire a thousand deathes, then to violate the chaste honor of my loue, or to giue that fauour to this Lady which is onelye yours. *Alchidiana*, by chance seeing *Palmerin* when he entred her Chamber, and perceyuing him now to depart againe: imagined presentlie the truth of the cause, wherefore entring the guarderobe which was adioyning to her Chamber, shee closely stood and hearde all that had passed, and at his comming foorth staied him in this maner.

Not without great cause (good Knight) didst thou take the fatall Crowne from the head of *Maurice*, for in thee is more firmnesse and continencie, then is in the disloyall *Ardemias* vnchaste desires and villainie: but in vnfitte time did shee rip open her vnmaidenlike affections, for I will publish her shame to euery one, and cause her to be lesse esteemed then a knowne offender.[9]

Palmerin fearing that in her choller she would doo no lesse then she said, fell on his knee before her, intreating her by signes to forbeare, otherwise it would be his death. She seeing him so faire and gracious, and thus to humble himselfe at her feete, quallified her displeasure, promising to keepe it in secret. So *Palmerin* withdrewe himselfe to his Chamber, leauing the two Ladies nowe togither: but *Ardemia* agreeued at the dumbe Knights refusall, woulde not reueale her wrong to *Alchidiana*, (who so soone as *Palmerin* was out of hearing) thus began. Why?

shamelesse *Ardemia*, thinkest thou thy beautie of such value, that the Knight, to whome my Father and I haue doone so great honours, would leaue vs, and depart with thee? trust mee thou art farre from thine account: for if thou vauntest to doo him such honor in thy Fathers Courte, as his nobilitie deserueth, it consisteth in my power to exalt him more in one howre, then thou canst doo in a thousand yeeres, mightest thou liue so long. I did neuer thinke that such audacious and incontinent tempting a man, could any way enter thy heart: but if such bee thy disposition, thou oughtest rather to abide in thy Fathers Courte, where thou maist haue leysure to followe thy base affection, with some of the varlets or youthes attending on thy Father, then to offer the motion heere in my Chamber. Hence, hence, foorth of my presence, for I will not keepe company with such an intemperate Woman. What regard hadst thou of thy great linage, or the place from whence thou art discended? Yea, what comfort will it be to me when I shall heare, that a Ladie, issued of the blood royall, should bee more shamelesse and impudent then a strumpet,[10] a villaine, or an high way begger? Many other such like hard speeches vsed *Alchidiana*, all which greeued her not so much, as to bee despised of him, whom she reputed as passionate for her loue, as shee was for his.

These high words of the Princesse, caused the Ladies attending on *Ardemia* to enter the Chamber, which made her then breake off, because she woulde not haue euerie one knowe the matter: and they seeing their Mistresse so sad and discomforted, brought her to her owne Chamber, where on her bedde shee sorrowed so impatiently, as each one feared she would iniurie her selfe, and faine shee woulde, but that their presence hindered her: therefore shee deferred it till better opportunitie. And because shee had spent the most part of her yonger yeeres, in reading the workes of Poets, as wel *Greekes* as *Arabians*, she remembred the mournfull Tragedie of *Biblis*,[11] which caused her to frame a Dittie, that shee had translated from the *Greeke* poesie of *Sapho*, into her vulgar speech:[12] and turning towardes her Ladies and Gentlewomen, she began in this maner.

The lamentable Dittie of
Ardemia, dying for loue.[13]

M*use not (fayre virgins) at* Ardemia,
    Although her end be hard and dolorous:
For death is pleasant as mine elders say,[14]
    To any Ladie sometime amorous.
For as the Swan in cold Meander[15] *glide,*
    By mournfull notes foretelles her speedy death:
So my complaint doth bid me to prouide,
    For sweetest loue makes hast to stop my breath.
The ill that endlesse and vncessantly
    Torments my heart, is fayre and choysest beautie:

And this vnhappie awkwarde desteny,
Falles to my lot through spotlesse loyaltie.
For fond conceit that ouer-rulde my wit,
More wretched then fayre Biblis *maketh me:*
5 *And he I loue more stony hard is knit,*
Then Caunus, *who could ken no courtesie.*

Yet Biblis *oftentimes could ease her heart,*
By sweete deuising with her louely freend:[16]
But he I honor, recks not of my smart,
10 *Nor will vouchsafe one gracious looke to lend.*

And as her sorrowes cheefely did arise,
Because the secrets of her loue were knowne:
So I reueald, each one will me despise,
Which death can stint ere it too farre be blowne.

15 *Vnhappie wretch, that could not this foresee,*
And be more chary of so choyse a thing:
But all too late I wish the remedie,
Therefore my folly doth due guerdon bring.

If loue that is esteemde a power diuine,
20 *Vnto his Seruaunts giue so sharpe reward:*
What merit may vile hatred then resigne,
Vnto his vassayles that his Lawes regard?

Oft haue I heard mine auncient elders say,
That such as loue not, are vnwoorthie life:
25 *Yet doth my loue imagine my decay,*
And throwes my hope into whole worlds of strife.

And yet the paynes I wish for my mischaunce,
May not be valued with my present woe:
For to compare them is meere dalliaunce,
30 *And neither sence or reason should I showe.*

Life is to me lothsome and burdenous,
All pleasure seemes to mee tormenting hell:
Ah poore refused, and abused thus,
Must thou needes die for louing all too well?

35 *O sacred* Venus, *patronesse of loue,*
In this distresse wilt thou not pittie me?
And thy fayre Sonne that thus his shaft did proue,
Will he forsake me in this ieopardie?

If you forsake me in this iust request,
40 *And will not fauour what you did procure:*

> *Giue leaue to him that bringeth all to rest,*
> *And he will ease the torments I endure.*
> *You fatall Sisters that haue spunne my thred,*[17]
> *And now thinke good it should be cut in twaine:*
> *Fulfill the taske as you are destenied,*
> *And let my heart abide no longer paine.*
> *Come sweetest death, expected too too long,*
> *Ende all the euils vnhappie loue begun:*
> *If thou delay, I challenge thee of wrong,*
> *Hast then good death, that loue and life were done.*

    Her complainte thus finished, shee commaunded her Ladies to depart the Chamber, and being alone by her selfe, shee againe began to consider, the rigorous refusall of *Palmerin*, the conceit whereof greeued her so extreamely, as also the reproachfull wordes of her Cozin: that making a conscience of her sorrowes, and raging with extreamitie of this despight, brake the vaines of her heart in sunder, and the artiries of her bodie, as the bloud issued foorth at many places aboundantly, and therewithall in short time she was strangled.

    The next morning, her cheefest Lady that attended on her, and loued her exceedingly, came to the bedde side to see how shee fared: but finding her dead, and so besmeared with her owne bloud, gaue such a loude shrieke, as *Alchidiana* and her Damoselles, affrighted at the noyse, ranne in all haste to the Chamber. The Princesse knowing the cause of this mischaunce, was maruellous sorrowfull, assuring her selfe, that the wordes shee spake in her anger, occasioned this bloudie stratageme. And the rumor of this mishap was so soone spread through the Palace, as all the Ladies, Damoselles, Knightes, Squires, and other, came to beholde the harde fortune of *Ardemia*. What lamentation was made on all sides, is not to be expressed: especially the Ladies attendant on *Ardemia*, and her Brother *Guilharan*, who brought her with him thither: but her Gouernesse, not able to endure the burthen of her heauinesse, without feare or dread of any, thus openly complained. Ah sweete Princesse *Ardemia*, the flowre of beautie, howe deare hast thou bought this precious gift? for I knowe assuredly, that for this cause onely thy death happened: vnhappie was the houre, when thou didst leaue thy Fathers Court, to accompanie the Princesse *Alchidiana*. After her mones and the funerall pompe accomplished, the Soldane erected for her a most beautifull Tombe, with a sumptuous Coronet on the toppe thereof, being vpheld by two inestimable Pillers of engrauen and guilded Alablaster,[18] the like whereof were neuer seene, since the first King of *Greece*. Yet was hee ignorant in the cause of her death, and *Palmerin*, not imagining whence this inconuenience did arise,[19] was so sorrowfull for the death of the Princesse, as day and night hee mourned for her, and at length remembring her wordes to him, and doubting his vnkindnesse to be the cause of her death,[20] sayd within himselfe:

Palmerin d'Oliva: Part II   *369*

    Alas faire Princesse, must I (at the first motion) driue thee to dispaire? had I dissembled a little, or temporized the matter, thou hadst not fallen into this extremitie, but my onely wilfull indiscretion, is cause of thy losse. O Female sexe, howe are you subiect to casuall passions? Yet neede I not wonder at this present mishappe, for from the beginning of the worlde, the Woman hath beene so suddein and voluntarie to the effect of her desires, were they good or euill, but especially in the action of loue: as neyther feare, honor, shame, torments, no nor death, could diuert her from her vndiscreete fantasies. Hereof beare record *Hypermnestra, Myrrha, Deianira, Scylla, Phedra, Thisbe, Oenone, Phyllis, Salmacis, Hero* and *Dydo*, whose deathes were procured onely by lauish loue.[21] O diuine wisedome, that hast suffered me to fall into this lucklesse accident, protect mee from any further disaduauntage: seeing thou hast taken her hence, who gaue some ease to mine affections, in that so liuely shee resembled my sweete Mistresse, whome I desire to serue with continuall loyaltie. I nowe perswade my selfe, that this loue was not accompanied with vertue, and that for my good it hath so chaunced: forgette mee not then, but so enable me, as in such badde occasions I swarue not from my duetie. And such is my confidence in thy promises, as no temptation shall preuaile against mee: but this captiuitie once discharged, I hope to direct my course pleasing in thy sight, and to performe such gracious seruice, as thy name shalbe exalted and glorified for euer. So long continued he in this silent contemplation, as *Alchidiana* perceiued him, which greatlie displeased her: but fearing any way to offende *Palmerin*, shee durst not saye what shee thought, liuing in hope, that her Cozin being dead, she should now compasse the effecte of her desires. *Ardemia* enterred in her honourable Tombe, *Guilharan* her Brother with his traine, and the Ladies that attended on his Sister, returned into *Armenia*, where great sorrowe was made for the death of the Princesse, and the renowne of her beautie, blazed the report of her death through euery region.

CHAPTER IX.

How Amarano of Nigrea, eldest son to the king of Phrygia, vnderstanding the death of the faire Princesse Ardemia, who was newly promised him in mariage: made many greeuous lamentations for her losse. And how Alchidiana discouered her amorous affections to Palmerin.

So farre was spread the reporte, of the strange death of the Princesse *Ardemia*, as at length it came to the hearing of *Amarano*, eldest sonne to the king of *Phrygie*,[1] the most valiant and redoubted knight of that country: as wel for his great prowesse and deedes of Armes, which he before that time accomplished in *Asia*, as for his affable nature, vertue and courtesie. This yong Prince being in the King his fathers Court, and hearing commended beyond al other Ladies of the East, the faire *Ardemia* Daughter to the King of *Armenia*, at the verye sounde of the Trompe of this blazing Goddesse,[2] and setting the newes downe for true, from her affecting speech, he became so amorous of her, as he had no content but in thinking on her. Heereupon, he sent his Ambassadours to her Father, to request her in mariage, wherto right willingly he condiscended, and nowe at the instant, when he intended to go visite her, newes came to the Court of her admirable death, which for a while was concealed from him, because each one doubted the conceit thereof would cause his death. For they knowing the loue he bare her to be so vehement, as hee vnderstanding her strange kinde of death, they thought it impossible, but it would arise to very scandalous inconuenience, yet in the ende he hearde thereof: but to sette downe heere the greefe, teares and complaints of this yong Prince, is more then I am able: let it therefore suffise you, that his sorrowes were such, as euery houre his death was likewise expected. It was likewise told him, howe through the enuie of *Alchidiana*, shee dyed, and that (for certaintie) shee was one of the cheefest causes thereof: which mooued him then into such an alteration, as hee swore by the great Prophet Mahomet, to reuenge her iniurie, so that the Soldane shoulde for euer remember the daunger in suffering so great a treason. In conclusion, hee intended to take with him, two hundred chosen Knights, all clad in mourning for the greefe of their Maister, and foure of his Brethren, Knights of great hardinesse and so well they iourneied, as they came within twentie miles of the Soldans Courte. But that wee may not too farre swarue from our intent, *Alchidiana*, ioyfull (as you haue hearde) for the departure of *Guilharan* and his companie,[3] from thenceforwarde sought all the meanes shee could, to conferre with *Palmerin* alone at her pleasure. And labouring thus in her tormenting passions, as it is common to all louers, such account she made of her beautie and riches, as she imagined that *Palmerin* would not disdaine her: but rather would repute himselfe happy, to haue that at his pleasure, whereof so many Kings and great Lordes had beene denyed. And in this opinion, the next time that *Palmerin* came to her Chamber, she beganne with him in this manner.[4]

Now Syr Knight, what thinke you of the death of *Ardemia*, who so falselye would haue seduced you to goe with her hence? did shee not commit great treason against mee if shee had preuailed? but right well is shee rewarded, and as I desired. Thinke then no more of her presumptuous follie, or the ridiculous conceit of her vaine loue, which shee made her pretence, to cause you forsake my Fathers Court: where you haue receiued so many speciall honours, cheefelie of his Daughter, who loues you deerelie, and intends to make you Lord ouer all her possessions.[5] Beleeue mee Sir Knight, if hitherto I deferred to acquaint you heerewith, it was in respect I doubted her: but now shee being gone, esteeme henceforth of me as your owne,[6] and to begin this alliaunce, I honour you with all that is mine, and my selfe to be disposed at your pleasure. For my heart which is onely subiect to you, applyes it selfe to your lyking, and can wish nothing but what you will commaund. How long haue I desired this happie day? howe often haue I contemned and despised my selfe, in not daring to breake the seale of my affections, which nowe I haue aduentured to your knowledge? As for that which now troubleth mee, is the want of your speech, which the Gods haue depriued you off, being enuious of your manifolde perfections. Alas my Lord, why did they not endue thee with that benifit, that in declaring my desires, thy answeres might returne reciprocall pleasure?

Some in their loue delight themselues, with embracing, kissing, and such ceremoniall behauiour: as for mee, amourous, priuate and familiar conference, I repute a cheefe content. Yet hath Loue one shaft in his Quiuer more pleasing then all these, beeing the onely argument of each others resolution: in respect whereof, I commit my honour into your protection, prizing, esteeming, and chusing you aboue all men in the world beside.[7] *Palmerin* exceedingly abashed at these vnseemelye speeches, knewe not what signes to make for his aunswere, and hauing recourse to his onely comforter, lifting his eyes to heauen, thus priuately inuocated. My God, deliuer me from this enemie, and suffer me not to fall in consent to this temptation, for I thinke her a Deuill incarnate, and sent to deceiue me. Impossible is it that a maiden, by nature modest and bashfull, would let slip such effronted wordes and audacious. The conceit heereof so vexed and offended him, as the Princesse feared he would haue dyed: not with conceit that like hap might come to *Alchidiana*, as did to *Ardemia*, but because he shuld so wickedly sin against his owne soule, and falsefie his loue to his sweetest Mistresse. Yet knowing that this sadnesse would not satisfie the Princesse, he feigned to swoune, his colour changing in such sort, as one would haue iudged him past recouerie.

Alchidiana was so greeued heereat, as she could not imagine what to saye: but seeing that *Palmerin* seemed nowe not to vnderstand her, and before had by signes still reuealed his meaning, saide. By our great God, it may well bee said, that this man is a huge lumpe of flesh, which the deuil hath enchaunted to torment me withall, or else some other shaddowe and resemblaunce: for hee refuseth what all men desire, yea, and often despayre, because they cannot attaine it. But fearing least her ende would imitate her Cozins, or that the dumbe Knight should die in her presence, shee durst presume no further: but threwe her selfe downe vppon a Pallet, not able to speake her stomacke was so enraged.[8] Which *Palmerin* perceiuing, arose out of his feigned traunce, and giuing a great sighe, departed the Chamber, and went to his owne. The Princesse seeing him gone, began to weepe and lament very greeuouslye, and in midst of her melancholy, fell into these speeches. You Gods, how can you suffer one so contrary to nature, as is this dumbe Knight, to liue among men? Can you behold that he whom I deliuered from death,[9] brought into the grace of my father, and to whom I haue doone more honour then had hee beene mine owne Brother, will not regarde me? but against all reason, disdaineth, refuseth, maketh no reckoning of my dolours, and setteth at nought my earnest intreaties? Ah vndiscreete and carelesse Girle, thy folly at this time too much ouerruled thee, that knowing thine owne estate and high linage, wouldest submit thy selfe to loue one vnknowne to thee, and of whom thou canst haue no answere, more then of a sencelesse stocke or stone. If I can now learne to hate thee, it will be some comfort to me: but the more he iniurieth mee, the more am I deuoted to his loue. Then againe she contraryed her selfe in this sort. Yet seeing it is so, ingratefull wretch that thou art, I will cause thee (ere it be long) to repent thy villainie. In this anger she continued all the day, not comming foorth of her Chamber, intending thenceforward vtterly to despise him: but the first time shee sawe him againe, shee reputed him so louely, faire and gracious, that (to dye) shee could not wish him any harme, but loued him much better then before. Yet to couer her owne inconstancie, shee sent him no more presents, nor did him such honor as she was accustomed, which *Palmerin* well perceiued: but hee could dissemble it in such sort, as the Princesse hardly might decipher him. For hee liued in hope of the Soldans promise which hee had made to his deceased Father,[10] to sende his Brethren to *Constantinople*, in whose company hee might trauaile thither, and so escape the Turks and Moorish Infidelles.

Chapter X.

How Amarano Prince of Nigrea, came to the Soldans court, to accuse Alchidiana, as causer of the death of the fayre Princesse Ardemia her Cozin.

During the time that the Princesse *Alchidiana* dissembled not to loue *Palmerin*, the Prince *Amarano* of *Nigrea*, came within a dayes iourney of the Isle of *Calpha*, where hee remayned to rest himselfe a little. In the meane time he sent an Ambassade to *Maulicus*, crauing assuraunce for his comming to his Court, to accuse one that was neare about him. The Ambassadours arriued, and their message vnderstoode, the Soldane aunswered, that hee shoulde haue what securitie he would demand: for to the Prince *Amarano* (quoth hee) nor the meanest of his people, shall anie thing bee misdone, nor to him or them that shall defende the cause of the accused. And greatlie amazed was the Soldane at these tydings, considering the distaunce betweene *Calpha* and *Phrygia*. Wherefore he supposed, that some bodie had iniuried the Prince since his arriuall. Notwithstanding (quoth he to the Ambassadours) that your Lorde may stand in no doubt of treason, you shall haue our louing letters to him: and let presently be proclaimed through the Citie, by sound of Trumpet, the safe conduct of the Prince and his traine. The Ambassadours returned with their Letters to the Prince, who ioyfull of these newes came to the Citie: but before hee would approach the Court, hee went to the Tombe of the Princesse *Ardemia*, and if hee made such lamentations, when hee but heard of her death, what iudgement may bee set downe of his mones, beeing nowe at the Sepulchre of his best beloued. Ah inconstant Fortune, quoth hee, why wouldest thou not permit mee to see her liuing? Ah *Ardemia*, accomplished with admirable beautie, great was her sinne, who enuying thy perfections, procured thy cruell death: yet this is my comfort, that I shall come in time inough to reuenge thy vndeserued mishap, and he that dare gaine-say mee, with her the authour of thy tragedie, shall receyue such condigne punishment, as shall remaine for euer in memorie.

These complaints deliuered with exceeding sorrowe, his Brethren perswaded him, that such behauiour beseemed not so great a Prince: therefore he should referre those offices to effeminate persons, who make a God of their silent passions, as for him, hee should thinke on nothing, but his mortall manner of reuenge. *Amarano* ashamed of his owne follie, mounted on Horsebacke, and came to the Pallace, where hee and his Brethren entred armed, and the Prince beeing a man of goodly personage, had so stearne and fierce a countenance, as hee was generally reputed a hardie Knight, and his Brethren verie little inferiour to him. He being come into the presence of *Maulicus*, saluted him with great reuerence, and not kissing his hande as others were accustomed, because hee was not his Subiect, neyther came for peace, but matter of fight and death: after long pause, in that the remembraunce of his greefe somewhat impeached him, he began to the Soldane in this maner.

Mightie Lord, and redoubted Monarch of *Asia*, beeing assured of the equall iustice, which you affoord to all persons without exception: I doubt not but you will punish the partie abyding in your Court, be his or her calling neuer so great, who by disloyall treason hath too much dishonoured mee. For which cause, reposing my hope in your noble vertue, I haue left my Countrey, and aduentured into your presence, to accuse your Daughter *Alchidiana*, whom (so please you) to call before this assemblie, I will charge, that she by false and spightfull hatred, as a most cruell and disloyall Ladie, trayterously murthered her Cozin the Princesse *Ardemia*. And because this villainie hath hitherto beene concealed verie secret, in respect it could not easily bee verified: I am heere readie to proue in open fielde, agaynst any of your Knights that dare maintaine her cause,[1] howe the treason before rehearsed, was committed by her: in reuenge whereof, she ought to bee rewarded with sharpe and shamefull death.

The Soldane maruayling at this accusation, said. By the reuerence of all our Gods, Prince *Amarano*, I cannot be perswaded, that it coulde at anie time enter my daughters thought, to perpetrate an offence so abhominable: but because reason commaundeth that I doo iustice, I will send for her, promising you, that if shee be found culpable in your accusation, shee shall haue such punishment, as your selfe shall rest contented therewith. Then he commaunded two Kings to goe fetch the Princesse, who beeing come, satte downe by her father, her accuser not deigning to salute her, or once to mooue from the place where he satte. This day had *Maulicus*, for the better defence of his person, caused fiue hundred armed Knights to attend on him, the greater part whereof (seeing the pride of the Prince of *Nigrea*) would furiously haue runne vpon him, saying, that hee should repent his follie: but the Soldane offended thereat, caused a Herauld presently to proclayme, that on paine of death, no one should harme or offende the Prince, nor anie in his companie, and whosoeuer did otherwise, shoulde presentlie die for breaking his commaundement: then framing his speeches to the Prince, sayde. *Amarano*, nowe maist thou behold my Daughter before thee: disburden the greefe of thy minde to her, and iustice shall bee doone thee to thine owne desire. Imagine, quoth the Prince, that such as knowe you Madame *Alchidiana*, will not a little maruaile, seeing you accomplished with such gracious beautie, that you should so farre forget your selfe, as to commit treason. But because a matter so vnlikely, demaundeth as hard a proofe, I will auerre with mine owne person in Combat, agaynst any one that dare support your quarell, that you are guiltie in the accusation alreadie alleaged, and principall cause of the death of the *Arminian* Princesse your Cozin. To reuenge such famous wrong, I haue forsaken my countrey, trauelling night and day, and haue presented my accusation before your Father, with this condition: that if your Knight shall bee vanquished, you are to bee punished as a cause of such weight requireth. If it be my fortune to bee foyled, and your Champion victor, I shall yeeld my selfe as conquered, and demaund no better recompence, for it can not greeue mee to remaine with her bodie, whose verie remembraunce keepeth me aliue: this said, he went and satte downe againe. The Soldane who was a man of great wisdome, and well considering the matter, seeing the accuser persist so confidently in his wordes, knew not what to aunswere. Yet as a vertuous Prince, he spake to his Daughter in this maner. *Alchidiana*, you haue heard the speeches of the Prince, aduise your selfe well of your answer: for which of you both shall be found attainted in the cryme, be it *Lese Maiestatis*, or other kinde of treason, shall be punished as the cause requireth.

Chapter XI.
Howe Palmerin seeing that none of the Soldans Knights would aduenture for Alchidiana against Amarano, enterprised himself her cause in combat. And how the Queene of Tharsus sent him a sumptuous helmet.

Alchidiana hauing heard the accusation of *Amarano*, and that he had spoken so slaunderously of her in the presence of the Soldane: incensed with maruailous anger and disdaine, returned him this aunswere. *Amarano* the most rash and vndiscrete Knight that euer I sawe, I wonder howe thy folly could make thee so audacious, to come and accuse me of treason (against all truth) before my Father and his Nobilitie. But thy speeches well noted and considered, shew nothing but carelesse youth, arrogancy, and too vainglorious conceit: chiefly in this, that thou armed *Cap a pe*, and accompanied with so many well appoynted Knights, commest in this sort to molest a poore maiden, who neuer to thee or thine committed any offence, but all seruiceable honour, especially to her, on whose behalfe thou offerest the combat. As for the valour thou reputest in thy selfe, that moitie which this slaunder doth encourage thee withall, colouring thy hardinesse and resolution of heart, thou oughtest rather oppose against a Knight able to aunswere thee, then a siely Virgin, who hath no weapon but her honour wherewith to defende her selfe.[1] I confesse I am a Ladie, but not traiterous or false, as thou auouchest, yet of so noble courage, as were I of thy sexe, thou neuer shouldest depart this Hall, before I had that conspyring head from thy shoulders, to witnesse thy falshoode and maleuolent spirit.[2] Notwithstanding, as I am, so please my Lorde and Father, with a Kitchin cudgell I shall let thee know, that thou dotest in thy speeches, and against thine owne conscience chargest me, with the murder of my Cozin. Examine thy thoughts, what likely reason might induce mee to such an offence? If shee was fayre, thanks to our Gods, mine owne talent is so good, as I neede not enuie her beautie. If shee made account of her rich dowrie, I beeing sole heyre to the Signories of the Soldane, might iudge my selfe farre beyond her, being desired in mariage by many Kings and Princes, whereof I am well assured shee neuer had the like. I knowe not then what cause should anie way induce me, to request her death. But what neede I make such protestations to thee? seeing that by some one of my Fathers Knights thy pride will bee abated, and I reuenged of the iniurie thou hast doone me. *Amarano* not aunswering her a worde, spake to the Soldane in this sort.

It is not decent my Lord, that a Prince or Knight of qualitie, should stay on the wordes of a Woman so little considerate, who more by anger then vertue, thinkes to reproue and annihilate a true accusation. Wherefore, according to the agreement before determined, cal for the knight that dare vndertake the quarrell of your daughter, to whom I will manifest in plaine Combat, that what I haue said, is trueth: and if hee bee vanquished, your Daughter *Alchidiana*, and he shall bee burned togither, as the greatnesse of the offence well deserueth: contrariwise, if Fortune denie mee successe, I will request no other iustice,

Palmerin d'Oliva: Part II 377

then what shall please you to appoynt for me. *Maulicus* seeing that well he could not denie the Prince, though to his greefe, pronounced the sentence, that his Daughter that day shoulde present a Knight, to sustaine her cause, according to his conditions alleaged. This hard prescription, made neuer a Knight willing
5 to aduenture the Combatte, so much they feared *Amarano*, for the great report they heard of his prowesse, but stoode all silent, as though themselues were condemned to death. *Alchidiana* seeing the courage fayle of so manie Knights, whom shee esteemed for men of great account, knewe not to whom shee should haue recourse: and therefore ouercome with exceeding sorrowe, but that her Ladies
10 assisted her, had twise or thrise swouned before her Father. *Palmerin* beholding her, and knowing that his refusall was greater cause of *Ardemiaes* death, then the iniurious wordes of *Alchidiana*, pityed her estate, and hauing before his eyes the loue she bare him, the great honours was done him for her sake, and the pusillanimitie of the Soldanes Knights, was so mooued, as forgetting all daunger,
15 and his dissembled dumbnesse, which hitherto hee had so cunningly obserued, as though he had beene borne in that Countrey, hee thus began in the *Arabian* tongue. Ah cowardly catiues, vnwoorthie henceforth the name of Knights, how can your hearts endure, that a proude and presumptuous Prince shall come into your presence, falselie to accuse your Ladie and Mistresse, and not one of you
20 daring to defende her right? By the celestiall powers, well may you bee accounted heartlesse men, and (in suffering this wrong) to be depriued of all noble titles, and to bee solde in the market as slaues and villaines. Thinke you the Prince *Amarano* is come hither for anie other intent, then to make tryall of his great hardinesse? Can you be destitute of reason, and so easily abused, as to thinke that
25 the Princesse *Alchidiana*, whom nature hath so worthily enriched with beautie, and with whom no other may make comparison, could be prouoked to murther *Ardemia*, for this onely occasion, because she was faire? And you Lord *Amarano*, for a matter so slender, haue you enterprised to blame a Ladie so vertuous, as is the Princesse *Alchidiana*? I accept the Combat on her behalfe, auouching, that
30 shamefully and without reason you haue accused her, behold me readie likewise to maintaine in open fielde, that falsely and maliciously thou lyest in thy throate:[3] in witnesse whereof, there is my gage, and I beseech your highnesse affoorde vs presently Iudges, that may discerne the issue of our Combat.[4] I take thy offer, quoth the Prince, and before the Sun set, will giue thee the payment that belongs
35 to such a frollicke companion.

Who can nowe imagine the ioy of *Maulicus* and his Daughter, seeing him whome they reputed dumbe by nature, thus to recouer his speech? assuredly they were all so amazed, that they thought Mahomet had come from the clowdes to performe this myracle. The Soldane thus surprised with vnspeakeable comfort,
40 forgetting the maiestie of his person, caught *Palmerin* in his armes, saying: Ah, good Knight, howe may this bee? dreame I? or dooth but my fancie delude me with your speech? O Mahomet, for euer bee thou praysed for this great grace. By the highest God, I am more ioyfull of this good fortune, then had I gained

the fayrest Island in the *Mediterranean* Sea. Nowe will I dismay no longer of my Daughters fortune, seeing that you take her quarrel in hand, and for her sake wil combat with *Amarano*: with all my heart I graunt you the Fielde, and thinke that my Daughter will not denie it. But tell mee, noble Freend, howe you haue so happily recouered your speech. *Palmerin* abashed that hee had so forgotten himselfe, knewe not what excuse to make, neuerthelesse, seeing nowe there was no remedie, and that the stone throwne could not bee recalled,[5] imagined some likely similitude of his suddaine speech, saying: I promise you, my Lord, that the certitude of your Daughters innocencie, and the great griefe I conceyued, seeing your Knightes so cowardly and faint in courage, mooued mee into such choller, as the Catarre, which of long time hath hindered my speech,[6] dissolued it selfe, and hath giuen my tongue libertie to reueale, what I was enforced to bewraye before by signes.[7] And this is not a thing altogether strange, for I haue heretofore read in Histories, that a Knight called *Aegle Samien*, dumbe from his byrth when one of his companions would vsurpe the honour of a victorie, which iustly appertained to him, was so enraged and incensed with displeasure, as that very passion, with the helpe of the Gods, restored his speech.[8] And thus hath it happened to mee, for which I honour theyr names with immortall thanks, not so much for my speaking, as that I may nowe declare my earnest affection to do you seruice, and fayre *Alchidiana* your Daughter, to whome I am so greatly indebted, for the manifolde honours shee hath doone mee without desert, as I shall neuer be able to recompence. Ah my noble friend quoth the Soldane, this liberall offer for the defence of my Daughters honour contents mee in such sort, as both shee and I remaine to requite your paines. *Amarano* amazed at the braue disposition of *Palmerin*, but specially at the great honour *Maulicus* did him, knew not well what to thinke: and did not the feare of reproch ouer-rule him, I thinke hee would haue deferred the Combat till another yeere. Notwithstanding, to couer his new opinion, he bethought him of a pretie subtiltie, and saide. I beseech your Maiestie to tell mee of whence this dumbe Knight is, to whome our Gods (by miracle) haue restored such brauing language. It is necessarie that I know what hee is, and whence he is discended, because the fight beeing enterprised for two such Princesses, as sometime was fayre *Ardemia* and your Daughter present: if hee be not the Sonne of a King, as I am, hee may not be permitted the Field with me. *Amarano*, answered the Soldane, I know not what hee is, for till this time hee hath continued dumbe in our Court: to him therefore you shall frame your demaund, for this opinion I holde of him, that hee will answere you nothing but truth. But if you go about so craftily to excuse your selfe, each one may iudge that in you which but ill beseemes the mind of a noble man, that is, to bee double in your speech. And (which is more) hee beeing a Knight as good as your selfe, you may not refuse him, because you demaunded the Combat against any Knight in my Court, and in your challenge made no exception. Perswade your selfe (quoth the Prince) that if hee be not the sonne of a King, hee shall not enter the Fielde against mee: therefore if hee bee none such, hee hath not to meddle with Armes

Palmerin d'Oliva: Part II 379

in this cause, and so the fight on his behalfe is finished. If thou make such doubt, said the Soldane, aske him the question thy selfe, I hope hee is able to resolue thee in these subtill cauils and sophisticall questions.

During this contention, there entred the Hall a fayre yong Damosell,[9] bearing betweene her handes a goodly Helmet, the richest and most beautifull that euer was seene, and falling on her knees before the Soldane, with such gracious salutations as stood with her dutie, shee demaunded which was *Amarano* of *Nigrea*, who had accused his Daughter, and which was likewise the dumbe knight, who enterprised her defence. *Maulicus* without any other inquisition, shewed them both to her, whereupon the Damosell arose, and comming to the Prince, thus began. *Amarano* of *Nigrea*, the Queene of *Tharsus* my Lady and mistresse beeing certaine that this day thou wouldest be in this place, sent mee hither to aduertise thee, that the dumbe knight is of higher linage then thou art, and such a one he is, as the greatest Lorde or Prince may not compare with him in bountie. And if thou wilt knowe the certaintie of his discent, more then any other as yet dooth: shee aduiseth thee (for thy profit) to desist from the Combat whereto thou hast challenged him, in defence of thy false accusation against *Alchidiana*. And further shee doth admonish thee, that if thou doost not as shee commandeth, the knight late dumbe, surpassing all other in knightly chiualrie, shall ouercome thee, and thou shalt not bee able to stande against him. Damosell, quoth the Prince, you may answere your mistresse, that ouerlate shee sent me her counsell, and I am not accustomed to giue credit to such sorcerers: besides, I will not loose mine honour at the simple wordes of a Woman I knowe not. And it doth not a little content mee, that this knight is such an one as hee should be, wherefore, being so sure of his bounty, I am the more desirous to Combatte with him, to make experience of his renowne: yet this I still maintaine, that what I haue spoken is true, and thereon wee will presently enter the Feeld, so please the Soldane to giue consent. *Maulicus* seeing the day was too farre spent, adiornde it till the day following, wherefore the Prince withdrew himselfe to his lodging, reposing great confidence in his owne strength, and after his departure, the Soldane taking *Palmerin* by the hand, sayde. I knowe not my Lorde how I may acknowledge the honour you do my Daughter, whom I esteeme as mine owne selfe: but if the Gods affoord me life, I will deuise some such recompence, as I hope shall returne your owne content. Then the Damosell sent from the Queene of *Tharsus*, approching to *Palmerin*, presented him the Helmet, saying. Noble and vertuous knight, the Queene saluteth you with this token of her good will, in remembraunce of your speciall loyaltie, whereby you deliuered the Prince *Maurice*,[10] for which she so much remaineth yours, as you shall command her any seruice hence forward, albeit she could haue wished him longer torment, that proued so vnfaithfull to her. She likewise desireth you to weare this Helmet in fight with *Amarano*, for it will greatly auayle you, and more then any other: for such is her hope, that after you know this present seruice, you will not deny her one request, which one day shee intendeth to craue of you. *Palmerin* taking the Helmet, answered.

Fayre Virgin, most humbly thanke the Queene on my behalfe, and tell her that wheresoeuer I am, she shall finde mee ready to fulfill any thing shee will commaunde. The Damosell departed, and made such speede, as in short time she came to the Queene, her Mistres, whom she acquainted with her whole message: whereof she was very ioyfull, especially of *Palmerins* great courtesie, whom she beganne to affect very greatly.

Chapter XII.
How Palmerin entred the Combat with the Prince Amarano of Nigrea, whom he slew, and the great honors the Soldane and his Daughter did him.

The Princesse *Alchidiana* hearing the words which the Queene of *Tharsus* damosell reported before the Soldane her Father, beeing likewise glad that *Palmerin* was of so noble parentage, and so renowned in the region farre thence distant, began to loue him more extreamely then euer she did before, and resolued with her selfe, that seeing for her sake hee vndertooke the Combate, hee bare her more secret affection then hee durst bewray, and in this opinion shee practised howe to conferre with him againe, which this day shee could not compasse, because hee was continually with the Souldane. But when *Palmerin* tooke his leaue for that night, the Princesse had a little leysure to thanke him for his honorable kindnes, and how glad she was that the Gods had restored his speech againe. Soone after she sent him a most sumptuous golden Armour, desiring him (for her sake) to weare it in the Combate: which *Palmerin* thankfully accepting, assured the messenger that hee would sufficiently reuenge his Ladies iniurie. In meane time, the Soldane commanded his Knight Marshall to see the field prepared in readinesse, and the Scaffolds for the Ladies prouided, and to haue two thousand Armed men in place, for defence of his owne person. All which the next morning was duely executed, the Soldane appointed two Kings, and *Amarano* his two brethren, Iudges of the field: who going to their tent, and all the nobilitie to their appointed places, expected nowe the issue of the fight. The Ladies came to their standing, among whom *Alchidiana* shewed like fayre *Vesper* among the other stars,[1] and soone after came the two Combattants, so brauely and richly appointed, as nothing wanted that could be imagined, especially *Palmerin*, before whom a King bare his Helmet, and the great Admiral of *Assiria* his Sword, and so brauely did hee mannage his Horse, with such sightly behauiour and gallant countenance, that each one iudged hee had learned his knowledge before he came thither into *Turkie*: and caused *Maulicus* to perswade himselfe, that the victorie was destenied to him. In the ende, that they might the sooner begin the Combat, the Iudges tooke their seates, commaunding silence through the field, which was pestered with wonderfull resort of people: and then the Heralds fulfilling their charge, gaue liberty to the Champions to doo their deuoire. *Palmerin* clasping his Helmet, gaue the Spurres to his Horse, and encountred *Amarano* with such furie, as they were both dismounted headlong to the grounde: but *Palmerin* ashamed to be so foyled before the Soldane, recouered himselfe quickly, and aduauncing his sheeld, gaue *Amarano* such a sound stroke on the head with his Sword, as made him stagger in great amazednes. Notwithstanding, his courage and agilitie was such, as well declared hee had followed those affaires, so that the fight was so fierce and cruell betweene them, as in many yeeres before the *Assirians* sawe not the like: for *Amarano* was the most hardie Knight in all those parts, yet *Palmerin* assaulted him with so many sharpe charges, as he made him forget his cunning points of defence, and with head and shoulders to awarde his strokes. Which when the Princes two Brethren behelde, they were maruailously abashed, for they imagined that through the East parts, no Knight might bee founde to equall him, wherefore one of them sayde. I thought my brother would haue dispatched this companion at the first encounter, but seeing he hath held out so long: no doubt hee is more expert in Armes, then wee at first made account of him.

The two Kings were somewhat mooued with these words, willing him to be silent, vntill such time as the end was determined. *Amarano* hearing what his brother had spoken, offended with himselfe because hee could not ouercome *Palmerin*, began to encourage himselfe, and albeit hee was sore wounded in many places on his body, yet he followed his intent so nobly, as taking his sword in both his handes, hee stroke *Palmerin* so violently on the Helmet, as made him set one of his knees to the ground to saue himselfe. But hee perceiuing that if he had many such blowes, it would returne his disaduantage, intended to play double or quitte,[2] and remembring the honour of his Mistresse *Polynarda*, he ranne with such valour on *Amarano*, as cleauing his Sheelde in two peeces, cut away a great parte of his arme. The Prince feeling himselfe so maimed, began to faint, hardly enduring to defende his enemies strokes, which *Palmerin* perceyued, and chased him about which way him listed, first heere, then there, where best the Prince had hope of safetie: but all these delayes little auayled him, for *Palmerin* left not till he got him downe, when *Amarano* thinking to helpe himselfe, drewe a little pocket Dagger, and therewith thurst *Palmerin* vnder the short ribbes, which wound so mooued him, as renting his Helmet from his head, immediatly smote it from his shoulders,[3] *Palmerin* beeing then so gladde and well disposed, as though hee had but newlie entred the fielde, tooke the heade of his enemie by the haire, and presented it to the Princesse *Alchidiana*, saying. Madame, I nowe thinke my selfe acquited of the promise, which I made to my gracious Lord your Father, for heere is that conspyring head that first accused you: bethinke your selfe therefore, if there be any thing else to bee doone for you, because I remaine heere readie to accomplish it.

The Princesse exceeding ioyfull for this worthie victory, aunswered. Truely my Lord, you haue doone so much for mee, that although my Father, my selfe, and all my friendes should bequeath our liues to your seruice, yet could wee not recompence the very least of your noble courtesies, cheefely this one, surpassing all the other, and beyonde our abilities to remunerate. Yet let me intreate you to carrie the Traytours head to the Iudges, that they may censure my innocencie in this slaunder, and whether the accuser hath not receiued condigne punishment. Which he did, and threw the head before the Princes brethren, whose greefe exceeded measure for their brothers ill fortune, and taking vppe the head with the body likewise, they caused it to bee sorrowfully conueied foorth of the fielde. Immediatly was *Palmerins* Horse brought him, whereon he mounted, and was conducted with great pompe by the two Kings that were the Iudges, and other mightie Princes, as well *Califfes, Agaz,* as *Taborlanes,*[4] to the gate of the

Pallace, where the Soldane (to doo him the greater honour) attended in person his comming, the like hee neuer did before to any king or Prince, how mightie soeuer hee was, and therefore his Subiects maruailed not a little hereat. *Palmerin* would haue done him reuerence on his knee, but he would not suffer him, for taking him in his armes, he thus sayd. For euer (gentle Knight) be the honour of thy victorie against our enemie, and the false accuser of our Daughter, for which I account my selfe so bound to thee, that all the dignities and riches I am able to giue thee, may not counteruaile thy vnspeakeable deserts: therefore I will remaine so much at thy disposition, as I and mine shall be at your command. So taking him by the hand, he conducted him to his Chamber, where himselfe holpe to vnarme him, commaunding his Chirurgions to be so carefull of him, as of his owne person. Thus leauing him to haue his wounds dressed, he returned to the great Hall, where hee found his nobility attending his comming, to whom he sayd. What think you my Lords of our state, if our Champion had beene foyled? I had beene the most forlorne and abiect Lorde in all *Assiria*,[5] to haue beene forced to do iustice on myne owne Daughter. But thanks to our Gods, hee deliuered mee from that daunger, therefore maruaile not, if (beyonde my custome) I welcommed him with reuerence and honour: for one that renowmeth himselfe by vertue and prowesse through the whole world, ought to bee so entertained, rather then such as liue in vayne pompe and glory, whispering deceitfull tales into Ladyes eares.[6] Neyther can you (in my iudgement) honour him sufficiently, because my Daughter and mee hee hath sheelded from death, expulsed our ignominious slaunder, and slaine our false accusing enemy, to make vs liue in perpetuall fame and memory. The most part of them well noting his words, and confounded with the remembrance of theyr shame, when they durst not enterprise the Combat for their Lady, knew not what to answere, but fearing to grow in further offence, sought how to change his minde to some other talke.

Alchidiana beeing all this while in her Chamber, prepared her selfe to goe visite *Palmerin*, not knowing how to shape her course, for fresh bewraying of her secret afflictions: for the Goddesse *Iuno*, when shee stoode before Syr *Paris* for sentence of her beautie, was not more sumptuously adorned then the Princesse.[7] Nowe beginnes shee to dispute in her thoughts, the honourable graces of *Palmerin*, his nobilitie so farre renowmed, his knightly prowesse and magnanimitie, whereof herselfe had so good experience, as shee resolued neuer to haue any other Husband. Then demaundes she of her Ladies, how she might recompence her Knight, if her head-tyre stoode orderly, if her locks of haire were tressed as they ought, and if her garments were braue enough. For conclusion, the louely Mayden knew not how to dispose of herselfe, to gaine his loue shee so earnestly longed for.

In this equipage she goes to see her Friend, and in his Chamber shee findes her Mother, who hindered her languishing Daughter, from discouering her sicknesse to him, that onely had the power to helpe her: wherefore liuing in hope of some better oportunitie, for this time she smothered her greefes so wel as she could, finding other talke with her Ladies, least her mother should suspect her.[8]

Chapter XIII.

How the brethren of Amarano, would haue buried his bodie in the Tombe with Ardemia, which Alchidiana would not suffer, but constrained them to carrie him home againe into his Countrey.

Amarano thus slaine, his Brethren (according to his charge thus giuen them, before hee entred the Combat) tooke his bodie, and with great mourning they brought it to the Princesse *Ardemiaes* Tombe, thinking to burie him there with her: but *Alchidiana* aduertised heereof came presently and intreated her Father, that hee woulde sende an Herauld to the Brethren of the vanquished Prince, to charge them not to leaue the bodie of *Amarano* in his Dominions,[1] for if they did, he would cause it to be burned as a Traytor deserued. Moreouer, that they themselues should depart within foure and twentie hours, and on paine of the daunger should ensue by their default. For good Father (quoth she) if you should permitte their boldnesse, it will be great blame and dishonour to you: in that it is commonly knowne, with what great pride and arrogancie he came to your Court, thinking to iniurie your good report, and eyther to shut mee from your presence for euer, or else with open scandale[2] to ende my life. The Soldane well regarding her wordes, willingly graunted her request, whereupon the Princes Brethren were certified of the Soldanes pleasure, by a Trumpet: whereat they maruailed not a little: but seeing they could no way remedie it, they said. Herauld, it is reason that your Lord should bee obeied within his owne territories, neuerthelesse you may say vnto him, that the crueltie he shewes to a dead bodie, is verie great, and against all equitie, which he heereafter happilie may repent. So opening the Tombe againe, they tooke foorth their Brothers bodie, and the Princesse *Ardemiaes* likewise, conuaying them into a Litter of Cipres,[3] to keepe them from corrupting, and thus returned with them to *Phrygia*, where the Princes death was greatly lamented, but cheefly by the aged King his Father, who seeing his Sonne dead before him, after many dolorous passions, thus complained. Ah Fortune, howe cruell doost thou shew thy selfe to the mightie, as well as the meanest? Ah my Sonne *Amarano*, too deere hast thou bought thy loue to *Ardemia*. Wretched and dispised olde man, howe vnfortunate art thou among all other? For when thou perswadest thy selfe to haue ioy and comfort by thy Sonnes, thou findest the cheefe cause of sorrowe and discontent. O death, thou sufferest me too importunate. Yet if the Soldane had graunted thee buriall, where thou diddest desire it before thy death, the lesse had beene my greefe. But soone shall I cause him repent his hard dealing, and reuenge thy death with sufficient requitall. The second brother to *Amarano*, named *Gramiel*, seeing his father in such extreame heauinesse, assayed by all meanes he coulde to comfort him: promising in the presence of all his Knights, with all possible speede to reuenge his Brothers death, and so did all the six Brethren solemnly vowe togither. Which speeches did somewhat comfort the aged King, who commaunded the bodies of the two louers to be taken from his presence, and for a perpetuall memorie of his Sonnes death, he caused a sumptuous monument to be made of marble and Porphire, whereon was grauen the cause of their vnhappie death. All this while, *Gramiell*, who vndertooke his Brothers reuenge, gaue charge to the people round about him, as also to the Kinges and Princes of *Suria*,[4] who were then enemies to the Soldane, to prepare themselues in readinesse, so that within a Moneths space, hee had assembled a power of fiftie thousand hardie Soldiers, himselfe beeing appointed leader and generall ouer them. In this sort they tooke themselues to the Feelde, hoping to ruinate the Soldanes Countrey with fire and sworde: but they were better entertained then they expected, as hereafter shall bee largely discoursed.

Chapter XIV.

Howe Alchidiana ouercome by vehemencie of her loue, offered her selfe to Palmerin as his wife, and of the aunswere he made her.

Remembring what hath past in the chapters before, we may not forget, how by the message of the Queene of *Tharsus* sent to the Soldanes Court: *Alchidiana* (who began as it were to despise *Palmerin*) was constrained to renue her loue:[1] thus conferring with her selfe, that if so great a person as the Queene of *Tharsus*, commended, esteemed and honoured him, hauing neuer seene him, the better meane had she, beeing dayly in his companie, to practise the furtheraunce of her earnest desires. Shee therefore continually awayted oportunitie, to discouer the fire newly raked from the embers, and which day and night consumed her with languishing:[2] but so well it came to passe, that not many dayes after the Combat with *Amarano*, hee came to visite her in her Chamber,[3] right ioyfull of the talke hee had with the Soldan, as concerning the prouision of his strength, to goe ruinate the Citie of *Constantinople*, which gaue him hope of his returne to *Allemaigne*. *Alchidiana*, hauing courteously saluted him, and shewing better countenaunce then before shee did, caused him to sit downe by her, and soone after began in this sort.

I desire you, Sir Knight, by the reuerence you beare our Gods, and the fayth you owe to her, for whose loue you tooke the enchaunted Crowne from the Prince *Maurice*:[4] to tell me your name, what your Parents be, and of whence you are. For I sweare to you by the honour of a Princesse, that the guerdon you shall receyue in so dooing, is my heart, hauing once conquered those desires that long haue tormented me: intending to make you Lorde of my selfe, and all the possessions of the Soldane my Father, without anie sinister meaning, you may beleeue mee. Consider therefore good Knight, that without feare or dissimulation, I haue tolde you what neerest concerneth mee, if then you desire not my present death, make aunswere as honourable dutie requireth, ballancing in your owne thoughts, howe vehemently the impressions of loue haue touched me: in respect that now I haue twise for your sake, exceeded the limits of mine owne regard, whom bashfulnesse should protect from such boldnes. And if patiently I endured your sharp repulse when last I bewrayed the state of my loue:[5] thinke it was caused through mine owne good conceit, that beeing denyed the libertie of speech, you did not perceyue the extremitie of my passions. But seeing our Gods haue beene so fauourable, as to restore the thing was earst taken from you, and likewise hath brought you into her companie, who loues you dearer then her owne life: shew not your selfe so hard of nature, to flie the howre that Loue and Fortune presents you withall. Therefore my onely beloued Lorde, in recompence of your sharpe Combat with proud *Amarano*, receyue me as your wife, whom you haue woorthily deserued.[6]

Palmerin seeing himselfe assayled by so faire an enemie, who coulde sooner bring in subiection an other *Hercules*, then euer did *Iole*, and as easily giue life to a statue of Marble, as *Venus* sometime did, at the request of *Pigmalion* the Caruer:[7]

was in maruellous affliction, hauing before him, on the one side, feare to offende God, on the other, the loyaltie he ought his Mistresse, and then the immediate death of *Alchidiana*, if he denied her. In the ende, remembring what the Soldan had spoken, concerning his voyage to *Constantinople*, hee deuised by this meane to make her such aunswere, as she should rest contented, and neither God nor his Mistresse be offended, he thus began. Vertuous and most excellent Princesse, thus I am assuredly perswaded, that there is not any Monarch or Prince so noble in all *Asia*, but might reckon himselfe among the happiest, in respect of your perfections and vnaluable riches, to espouse you as his wife. By farre greater reason, I that am poore, a Knight errant, vnknowne, and whose life you haue saued, may say, and name my selfe aboue all other in fortune. But knowing my selfe so simple, and of so slender deseruing towardes you, I esteeme it impossible for the Gods, and nature likewise, to lift mee to so wonderfull degree of happinesse. Wherefore, seeing the cause such, and greater then I can desire or imagine: likewise that it is conformable to your commaundement, doubtlesse I were vnwoorthie any fauour of Fortune, and to bee esteemed among the most vngratefull Knights in the worlde, if in anything I should disobey your pleasure. My reason is, that you (beeing reckoned as cheefe among the most perfect and accomplished Ladies) deigne so much to abase your selfe, as to make mee Lord of your loue, which hath beene desired by so many worthie personages.[8]

For these causes, most gracious Mistresse, I am bound to loue you aboue all other Ladies liuing, which henceforth I hope to doo, and loyally to serue you with my vttermost endeuours. And as I ought (sweete Madame) to loue none but you, so is my dutie to hold your regard in cheefest commendation: therefore will I with such secrecie, as so honourable a conquest will permit, conceale this extraordinarie grace. And had I not this morning made promise to your Father, to accompanie his power to *Constantinople*, there to reuenge the death of your deceassed vncle *Gamezio*, soone should our loue sort to wished effect, and I gather that sweet flower, which aboue all other would beautifie my Garland.[9] Notwithstanding, my hope is such, that in this voyage I shall do such seruice to the Soldane your Father, as at my returne hee will recompence mee to your content, and good lyking of his Princes and Subiects: which may no way nowe bee mooued, least his minde otherwayes busied, should conceyue displeasure against me, and so all our fortune for euer squandered.[10] In this respect (sweete Madame) if euer hereafter I shall doo you seruice, let me intreate you to patience till my returne, resoluing your selfe in the meane while, that I am more yours then mine owne, and dedicate my life to your gracious seruice.[11] As concerning the rest of your demaund, my name is *Palmerin d'Oliua*, and what my Parents are, the Queene of *Tharsus* within these three daies will tell me more, then hitherto I could vnderstand by any, when you shall vnderstand more of my estate and Country also: but so farre as I yet gather by mine owne knowledge, my discent is from *Persia*.[12]

This excuse hee made, because *Alchidiana* should not suspect him to bee a Christian: and with this aunswere shee was so ioyfull and contented, as nothing was able to inspyre more cheerefull life into her languishing soule, which *Palmerin* perceyuing, and the better to continue her in this opinion, verie often he kissed her hande in signe of his affectionate obeysaunce, and in this sort hee departed to his owne Chamber, leauing the Princesse triumphing of her conquest.[13]

He was no sooner come into his Chamber, but solicited with the remembraunce of his Ladie *Polinarda*, hee imagined how she blamed him with mournfull complaints for his late promises: which thought so diuersly afflicted him, as he spent all the rest of the day in teares, and as shee had beene present, humblie requesting her to pardon what had past him, in respect hee did it not willingly, nor gaue anie consent with his heart thereto, but dissembled the matter, least the Princes by his deniall shoulde fall into despayre: and rather then he would violate his solemne vow to his gracious Goddesse, hee woulde aduenture on infinite dangers. Yet did this feigned answere to *Alchidiana* greatlie auaile him, and caused him to bee more honoured then euen hee was before: as also to bee continually accompanied with her presence, whose onely delight was in dayly beholding him.

Chapter XV.

Howe the Soldane hauing determined to send his armie to Constantinople, would elect Palmerin his Lieutenant generall: which he refused, intreating him to giue the charge to the olde King of Balisarca.

Now was the Soldan continually mindfull of the promise hee made to his deceassed Father *Misos*, to reuenge the death of his Brother *Gamezio*:[1] wherefore seeing all his dominions in peace, and that hee had with him the valiaunt *Palmerin*, hee concluded to leuie a mightie Armie, to finish that which dutie daylie called for. And hauing prouided a huge number of Galions, Foysts, Gallyes and other vessels,[2] hee sent abroade to aduertise all the Kinges, Princes, Califfes, and Taborlanes his Subiects, of his will and pleasure: who likewise gathering their forces togither, were numbred to bee aboue an hundred and fiftie thousand fighting men. All this while the Soldane so fauoured *Palmerin*, as he had bestowed on him diuerse Dukedomes, which he made but slender account of, because hee continually expected time to see his *Polynarda*. *Alchidiana* likewise building on his passed promises, daylie presented him with many rich gifts, and practised all the deuises shee coulde to please his fancie: for so deuoutly did the Princesse loue him, as shee rather desired her owne death, then to giue him the least occasion of dislyking. And *Palmerin* by fayre and affecting speeches, perswaded such setled opinions in her, as shee helde his promises with greater pertinacie, then euer did any Logitian maintaine his *Aristotle*.[3] By this time were the men of Armes come from all places, wherefore the Soldane calling to *Palmerin*, beganne with him in this manner. Syr *Palmerin*, considering how much I am indebted to you, my affections are so resolutely perswaded, that I esteeme of you as you were my Sonne, and much more then I am able to vtter: not so much for seruices you haue done mee from time to time, as for the incomparable deedes of armes and chiualrie, which makes you honoured through the whole world. Hauing nowe determined to sende my forces to *Constantinople*, my onely hope I repose in you, and well it liketh mee that you beare the office of my Lieutenant Generall, and principall gouernour of the Kings and Princes in this expedition. Therefore my noble and approoued good Friend, vsing your wonted magnanimitie and discretion, my people shal think well of my appointment, referring the honor of their victorie, to the generall hauocke and confusion of their enemies.

Nowe I perceiue (my gracious Lord) answered *Palmerin*, that by your manifolde fauours and courtesies, you would depriue mee of acknowledging mine owne dutie: notwithstanding, in respect it is your pleasure, I would aduenture the vttermost of my life for you, which I cannot with greater honour loose, then in your noble seruice. Yet, may it be spoken within compasse of your highnesse controll, me thinks you should rather giue this charge to the King of *Balisarca*, a man wise, experienced, and farre more skilfull in Armes then I am. Beside, your people hauing a man of their owne nation for theyr head, will obey him more willingly, and serue with much more cheerefull courage, then vnder him whom they know not, but onely by your Princely and liberall bountie, which hath beene such, that from the meanest estate, where fortune helde mee as altogether despised, your Maiestie hath lifted mee to the highest earthly honour. Thus speake I, dread Lorde, as not gainsaying your commaundement, but for this consideration, that taking this honourable charge, the Souldiers may mutinie against me, and so your seruice be altogether disappointed.

 And thinke you (quoth the Soldane) that my people will be more obedient to the King of *Balisarca* then to you? Yea doubtlesse my Lord, saide *Palmerin*, that is my opinion. Know then, quoth the Soldane, that for this counsell you haue giuen mee, my loue is nothing diminished towardes you: for I see by this noble regarde, how deseruedly you gaine the fauours of Kings and great personages: it shall be therefore as you haue appointed. This counsell gaue *Palmerin*, not for any good he wished to *Maulicus*, or the King of *Balisarca*, but (desiring nothing more, then the ruine and generall destruction of these Heathen hounds, sworne enemies to Christ and his Seruants[4]) to ridde himselfe of that charge, which would bring him so great and shamefull report, to fight against his Lord and maker:[5] therefore premeditating on all these inconueniences, he but expected the meane to gette footing in Christendome againe. *Maulicus* thus contented with his aunswere, the King of *Balisarca* was appointed generall of his Armie, yet he gaue commandement that *Palmerin* should bee reuerenced among them, as the second person to himselfe, and on paine of death none to offende him.[6] As all this strength was readie to take shipping, newes came to the Court of *Gramiell* and his brethren, what slaughter and spoyle they made through all *Assiria*, whereat the Souldane beeing greatly offended, seeing his prouision against Christendome thus chaunged, came to *Palmerin*, and sayde. My Sonne, what thinke you of our enemies? What shall I doo to these followers of their Brother in pride? I pray you counsell mee in this necessitie. *Palmerin* perceiuing his desire preuented, was ouercome with maruailous passions: yet to hide his discontent from the Soldane, he thus answered. Seeing it hath so fallen out my Lord, that without any summons our enemies haue presumed vppon vs, I thinke it most expedient that your Armie prouided in so good readinesse, beginne first with these arrogant inuaders: for I doubt not, their attempt beeing so trecherous, and the courage of our men so resolute, but they shall deerely buy their presumptuous aduenture. A matter soone begunne, will bee as soone ended,[7] and our shipping readie, wee may afterwarde set forwarde to *Constantinople*, for this will bee a good whetting to our stomackes, to deale with our enemies of greater multitude.[8] This counsell was accepted, wherefore it was immediatly proclaimed through the field, that euery man should be readie to depart within three daies.

Chapter XVI.

How the Prince Olorico, sonne to the King of Arabia, came and offered his seruice to the Soldane, bringing with him fiue hundred armed Knights, and of his entertainment.

Somewhat before the Soldanes Armie was readie to depart, the Prince *Olorico*, eldest sonne to the King of *Arabia*, came to the Court, and with him fiue hundred Knights, so hardy, braue, and comely personages, as both for the Court and the war, better might not be imagined. This yong prince reputed among the most valiant of his time, hearing report of the rare beauty of *Alchidiana*, vnder colour of offring the Soldane his assistance, determined to behaue himselfe so brauely in his court, that by his liberalitie and honorable actions, he would obtaine the Princesse to his Wife, wherefore beeing come to the Court, and hauing doone his obeysance to the Soldane, hee began in this manner.

Right mightie Lorde of all *Assiria* and *Palestine*, hauing of long time heard your great forwardnesse to the encreasing of our faith, cheefely of the last honourable councell you held, to reuenge the death of your famous deceased Brother *Gamezio*, whom our Gods nowe entertaine at their celestiall banquets: I tooke my selfe to trauaile, with aduised resolution to doo you such seruice as might stande with my abilitie, and your pleasure to command. And for I now beholde, that my arriuall is in a time so fortunate, I celebrate theyr names with immortall thankes, assuring your Maiestie so farre to stretch my endeuours, as the sonne that is bounde by dutie to his Father. The Soldane who had heard great report of his bountie and valour, his Father likewise beeing one of his friendes and confederates: after he had made him very gracious welcome, thanked him for the succour he brought him, and henceforth he would not esteeme of him as a stranger, but as his Sonne and most especiall Friende. All this while *Palmerin* noted the behauior of the yong Prince, and iudging by his complection that hee was of better nature then the other *Assirians*, began to affect him, so that after the Soldane had giuen them all the good night, *Palmerin* accompanied the Prince to his Chamber, where they could deuise no other conference, but of this new and warlike enterprise, which made *Olorico* demaunde of *Palmerin*, if hee should go in those affaires. That will I verily (quoth he) if sicknesse or prison do not withhold mee. Let me intreate you then, sayde the Prince, to doo me so much honour, as to accept me for your companion. Whereto *Palmerin* right soone condiscended, and then began such a league of amity betweene them, that it endured to the death,[1] as you shall reade heereafter. But because it was nowe late, they tooke their leaue of each other till the next morning, when *Maulicus* would haue *Olorico* dine at his Table with *Palmerin*, where wanted no prouision that beseemed so great a person, beeing now set foorth in most rich and honourable pompe. The Tables being withdrawne, the Prince began the daunce, thinking to see faire *Alchidiana*: but hee was deceiued, for she kept her Chamber in her amorous opinions,[2] and would not be seene till the appointed day, when the Armie should make shewe in open field.

This day the Soldane went to order the battaile, and to appoint the wings and squadrons, which made *Alchidiana* likewise take delight to walke abroad with *Palmerin*, who was now in maruailous sumptuous Armour, bearing a sheeld of Sinople, with a barre of Gold figured therein, signifying his inward ioy, that in so short time he should get from these barbarous and vnchristian helhounds. Before them went two[3] yong Lords bareheaded, and behinde a great number of Ladies and Knights, so rich in apparrell as could be deuised. Beeing thus brought to their Palfrayes, *Palmerin* beganne to carrire and braue with his Horse before the Princesse, who tooke no little delight in her supposed louer, and riding along with him, fell into many discourses, nothing tending to Religion as I gesse, but such deuout seruice as loue teacheth his Schollers.[4] In the midst of their communication, came the Prince *Olorico*, so altred with his affection to the Princesse, that they which haue felt like assaults, might easily iudge the cause of his passions. Hauing made two or three humble reuerences to her, he offered to kisse her hand: which shee would not permit him, excusing the matter so modestly, and wishing his welfare as her owne, that he imagined himselfe greatly fauoured.

Palmerin regarding the afflictions[5] of this new come louer, and that hee might giue him the better meane, to deuise with her so priuatly as he desired, turned his Horse to the other side of the Princesse, thus speaking to her. What thinke you (Madame) of the gentle succour which my Lord *Olorico* hath brought your Father? beleeue mee, the courtesie is so surpassing great, as your selfe ought especially to thanke him, if it were but for his forwardnesse, in qualifying the haughtie courage of *Amaranos* brethren. Doubtlesse (quoth she) his companie is to be esteemed, and among tenne thousand Knights, hardly may bee founde so braue men as is in his troupe, in recompence whereof, I will not denie the Prince any thing, that hee with honour will request of me. *Olorico* perceiuing this sodaine inuention of *Palmerin*, returned him many thanks, and after the accustomed dissimulations vsed in such causes, albeit Loue had for a while depriued him of speech: earnestly beholding the rare beautie of the Princesse, he thus began. Madame, although I should doo to my Lord your Father all the seruices that a Knight is able to yeelde his gracious patrone, yet the very least of these fauours, which it hath pleased your excellencie to bestowe on mee, may bee reckoned for much more then deserued recompence. Wherefore beeing perswaded that my seruice is placed in your good conceit, I shall not henceforth feare to put my life in hazard, so much I desire to see these present promises accomplished: whereof you Sir *Palmerin*, beeing esteemed among the most famous persons liuing, shall beare mee witnesse, when time graunteth conuenient opportunitie. I haue promised nothing, sayde the Princesse, but what I will right gladly accomplish, requiring nothing but your good opinion, which so many choyse Ladies haue heretofore desired. And I demaund no better pay (quoth the Prince) then her gracious fauour whom I desire to please.[6] Thus beguiled they the time, till the Armie marched forward in array, which they faire and softly followed, till tenne Pages belonging to the Princesse, leading tenne goodly Coursers most richly caparassoned, came before them. Another Page brought a seemely Launce, the bandrole whereof was the Princesse colours, and a Golden Sheeld, wherein was portraied the head of *Amarano*, helde vppe by the haire by a Knights hands signifying the victory of *Palmerin* against him:[7] the Sheeld beeing bordered rounde about with Pearles, Rubyes, Emeraulds, Crisolites, and other precious stones of inestimable value, then beganne the Princesse thus to *Palmerin*.

My noble Friend, in this warre I desire you to bee my Knight, and for my sake to beare this Launce and Sheeld, that the proude Brethren may see the shame of *Amarano*. And such is my hope, that as you serued the eldest, so will you deale with the other, while one of them remains aliue.[8] These Horses likewise for the warre I bestow vppon you, they beeing accounted the very best in *Turkie*, and these will serue you well when you are in fielde: our Gods bearing mee witnesse (faire Friend) that did not my estate hinder me, and the regarde of mine honour withhold me, with right good will would I beare you companie, to see your noble and Knightly deedes of armes. And this I dare boldly say, that *Hipsicratea* neuer followed her Husband *Mithredates* with greater affection, were he on sea, or on lande, on Horsebacke, or on foote, then I could doo the noble *Palmerin d'Oliua*.[9] Notwithstanding, though my body may not be there, yet shall my spirit bee continually present, to comfort my languishing life, which will be but a shadow of death to me till your returne. But because I see many eies are fixed on vs, all the Kings likewise taking their leaue, of my father, I will leaue you to the protection of our Gods who send you happily and right soone againe. These words were coupled with such sighs and teares, as shee had fallen from her horse, but that one of her Ladies of honour stayed her.

Palmerin after hee had with great kindnesse thanked her, kissed her hande, saying. Perswade your selfe sweete Madame, your sheeld shall be shewne in such place, where his Brethren that detracted your honour, shall easily see it, though but little to theyr aduantage. Thus tooke they leaue of each other, and *Olorico* likewise bad the Princesse farewell: then doing their dutie to the Soldane, followed the armie, leauing him and *Alchidiana* sorrowfull for their departure.

Chapter XVII.

How the prince Olorico being with Palmerin in his Tent, demaunded of him if hee loued the princesse Alchidiana, and of the answere he made him.

These two young Princes *Palmerin* and *Olorico*, conferring still as they rode, with what greefe and sorrow *Alchidiana* parted from them, and falling from one imagination to another, they concluded to lodge together in one tent. And because *Palmerin* was the better and more richly prouided of all things necessarie for the field, *Olorico* was the more glad of his companie: so the day beeing spent, and the Tents pitched in a goodly plaine, *Palmerin* inuited the Prince of *Arabia* to suppe with him, for the Souldane had appointed him such honourable prouision, as better hee could not for his owne sonne. The Tables withdrawne, and spending the time a while at Chesse play, they went to bed,[1] where *Olorico* (not able to sleepe) beganne in this manner to his friendly companion.

Most fortunate *Palmerin*, howe much more could I wish to resemble you, then the greatest King or Lorde in the world, to be likewise beloued of her, who in beautie, good grace, and sweete speech, hath not her like. And because my good Friend and Brother, I haue noted the speciall loue of the Princesse *Alchidiana* towardes you, let me intreate you to tell me, who shee is you aboue all other loue, and intend to make your espoused Wife: vowing to you on the word of a Prince, whosoeuer it bee, to conceale it with secrecie, and to disswade my selfe from my loue newly begunne for your sake, albeit I died therefore. For your noble minde and braue gentilitie, hath gained such soueraigntie ouer me, as all other pleasures whatsoeuer I despise, onely to haue your companye and fauour. Thus quallifying the passions, which day and night doo secretly torment mee, I will sette downe such order, as my Father shall not neede to send his Ambassadours, nor imploy any of my Freendes to demaunde her for mee: albeit for this onelye cause, I left my Countrey in such sort as you haue seene. *Palmerin* hearing the wordes of the yoong Prince, and perceiuing him wounded with her loue, whom he desired to be furthest from, smyling said. My Lorde *Olorico*, I sweare to you by the honour of my Knighthoode,[2] I neuer thought of the loue which you demaunde, nor haue I any desire to followe that humour. But true it is, that I would doo so much for her, as a Knight may for his Ladie, for so shee well deserues, her fauour and gentle behauiour woorthye farre better abilitie: wherefore my deere Freende, if you will beleeue me, giue not ouer your intent, but practise to gaine her to your Wife: and I promise you that I will so mooue the matter to the Soldane and her, as happilie maye effect the end of your desires. Yet let me intreate you to continue so iust a Freende to her, as her high calling well deserueth: otherwise I had rather die the death, then once to speake a word on your behalfe. These newes so cheered the Prince, as embracing him manie times, and returning him manifold thanks, he said. Assuredlie my noble Freend, I am greatly beholding to my father, who gaue me my present being: but much more owe I to you, because my estate had now ended, but that your gracious speeches called me againe to life. My second selfe, hauing thus lost my libertie, I despaire of attaining what you haue promised, and endure a death more then mortall: but that you breath hope of successe into me, assuring mee of immediate felicitie and ioyfull dayes heereafter, which no father, but so good a freende was able to doo.³ After other such like speeches, the Prince slept, but *Palmerin* touched in another sort, was sollicited with the remembraunce of his lost freendes: and perceiuing his companion slept soundlie, he began thus to deliuer his sorrowes. Ah vnfortunate and wretched *Palmerin*, how can thy mind so long beare this yoke of seruitude, onely standing in feare of death? Hast thou so forgot those two perfect louers, *Trineus* and *Agriola*, with thy true freend *Ptolome* not knowing whether they bee aliue or deade? what? wilt thou not searche for them? The Emperour of *Allemaigne*, hath not hee good cause to complaine of thee, yea, and to blame thee, if his sonne be not returned? Darest thou present thy selfe before him? Ah touch of loyaltie,⁴ faire *Agriola*, how iustlye mayst thou call mee thine enemie, inuenter and first motion of thy misfortunes? O wretched and miserable that I am, for leauing thee so discourteouslye, I well deserue a million of torments, farre worse then those exercised by the cruell *Dyonise* on the *Scicilians*.⁵ Nor coulde they be sufficient to expiate my hainous guilt, in that forgetting thee fayre Princesse, I liue in daylie delights among these *Moores* and *Tartars*. But were I such as I ought to bee, mindfull of a fault so foullie committed, I shoulde not liue one houre in rest or quiet, till I had found my deerest Freendes againe.⁶ Ah disloyall Traytour, how canst thou thus waste thy time heere slothfullie,⁷ knowing the great and continuall trauails, thy Ladye and Mistresse endureth for thee? But I vowe to God, this warre finished, I will not abide in the Soldanes Courte tenne dayes, but intende to sette forwarde to see the Iewell of my welfare.⁸ And were it not to my perpetuall discredit, as also that I should be iudged a faynting coward, I would begin my iourney presently.

    Thus all the night continued *Palmerin* such like complaints, considering his Freendes misfortune and his owne, with such deepe impressions, as thence forward hee liued in meruailous melancholie, and would not delight himselfe, as before hee was accustomed.

Chapter XVIII.
Of the Combat betweene Palmerin, and two of Amaranoes Brethren, whom he valiantly ouercame, and killed.

Following the true discourse of our historie, the King of *Balisarca*, Lieuetenant generall of the whole Armie, caused the next morning to bee proclaimed by sound of Trompet, that euery man should attend on his Ensigne: and not go robbing and forraging the Villages, on paine of death to be inflicted on the offender. So marching on in good array, in short time after they encamped themselues before a citie, where the enemies kept themselues in garison: and planting themselues there for their aduantage, the next morning they determined to giue the assault. All the night they were ordering the maner of their batterie, the Pyoners making Trenches, and such defences as are requisit in warlike occasions.[1]

Euery thing in due and perfect order, at Sun rysing they beganne to assaile the Cittie rounde about: following their intent with such courage and alacritie, as with scaling Ladders and other Engines, in lesse then two howres they gotte vpon the walles, and (in despight of their enemies) entred the Cittie, murdering and expulsing the *Phrygians*, and sharing the spoyle among themselues. All other Cities, Townes and Villages, that were taken by the enemie, within six dayes after were recouered, they not daring to withstand the Soldans power. *Gramiell, Amaranoes* eldest Brother amazed heereat, hauing vndertaken to reuenge his Brothers death, with his Forces betooke himselfe to open Fielde, determining to giue the *Assirians*, battaile, and that way to make triall of their fortune, in which resolution they came within halfe a dayes iourney of theyr enemies.

The King of *Balisarca* aduertised heereof, dislodged immediatlie, taking aduauntage of a little Mountaine, which was in the open sight of the enemie. And *Palmerin* who desired nothing more then the fight, that hee might accomplish his promise to the Princesse *Alchidiana*,[2] when hee receiued of her his rich Sheelde and Launce: perswaded the Generall, that hee should the next morning summon the Brethren of *Amarano*, that within foure and twentie howres, they should depart the Soldanes confines, or else endure the daunger of the Sworde. The King of *Balisarca* aduising heereon in counsaile, founde it verie necessarie and expedient: wherefore calling his Sonne, Sir *Palmerin*, and the Prince *Olorico*, hee committed the charge thereof to theyr present dispatch. They beeing come to the Armie of *Gramiell*, were immediatly conducted to the Princes Tent, who was then deliberating with his Brethren, and other Captaines of the Armie. So soone as he vnderstoode the arriuall of these Ambassadours, he caused them to come before him, and their message beeing deliuered, the *Phrygian* Princes, who were of meruailous haughtie disposition, aunswered, that they would not obey any such commaundement. Moreouer, they intended to chase thence the Soldanes Lieuetenant, euen to the verie Gates of his owne Cittie: for that (contrarie to all equitie) hee withstoode the buriall of their Brothers bodie in his kingdome. *Gueresin*, Sonne to the King of *Balisarca*, could not suffer such iniurie to his

Palmerin d'Oliva: Part II

Lorde in his presence, wherefore he said: that the Soldane had doone them no wrong, but receiued their Brother and his traine with greater honour then they deserued, and that none of them should haue the like againe. So went hee foorth of the Pauillion, *Gramiell* and two of his Brethren following him, whereof the one had beene in *Asiria* with his Brother *Amarano*: who seeing *Palmerin*, that all this while kept himselfe without the Tent, and marking his Sheeld, where in mockage was painted his Brothers head: he knew him immediatlie, and in great rage pulling himselfe by the haire, said.

Villaine that I am, how can I suffer in my presence the Traytour that murdered my Brother? Bold and presumptuous catife, how durst thou aduenture before mee, thus to deride me with thy villainie? Trust me, saide *Palmerin*, I dare come before thee with better assuraunce of my selfe, then thy Brother had when he entred Combat with me. Wherefore, if thou be such a Gallant, as thou wouldest haue me iudge thee by these brauadoes, and likewise hast any stomacke to reuenge thy Brothers shame: Arme thy selfe, and an other of thy Brethren with thee, and come to me in place conuenient, where I my selfe will iustifie to you both, that *Amarano* was woorthilye slaine, and as such a false accusing Traytour well deserued. I desire nothing more, saide *Orinello*, for so was hee called that gaue these hotte speeches, but my Brother shall not deale with thee, till I haue tried my fortune alone: and if I faile of my purpose, then shall he afterwarde Combat with thee, this prouided, that thou assure mee from any in thy companie, but thine owne person. That will I vppon my Knighthoode, said *Palmerin*, thou perfourming as much on thy behalfe: yet I thinke before the sport be doone that thou wilt wish thy fellow with thee. Thus *Palmerin*, *Olorico*, and *Gueresin* withdrewe themselues, *Orinello* and his brother presently going to Arme them, and accompanied with manie Knights, came into the field, *Palmerin* likewise as readie as the formost, came in with a good traine of Souldiers hee had brought with him, least any treason shoulde bee wrought against him. *Olorico*, shewed himselfe greatly discontented, because hee might not accompanie his Freende in the Combat: but *Palmerin* perswaded him, that more needefull occasions were reserued for him, which should returne him greater honour, and whom he should court in better sort then euer he did, the Ladies of *Arabia*. *Gramiell* being verie richly armed, woulde needes come see his Brethrens Combat, which hee had good hope would sort to theyr honor: but *Palmerin* seeing *Orinello* readie to the carrire, encountred his enemie with such puissance, as his Launce passing through his body, caused him fall dead from his horse without moouing eyther hand or foote.

Hauing performed his course, hee returned to take his Launce out of his enemies body, striking him with the great Trunchion ende on the stomacke, to see if any life was left in him: but seeing his soule was departed to Lucifers Pallace,[3] hee coutched his stafe to receiue the other Brother, who met him with such strength, as he was well neere dismounted, yet in the ende hee was sent after his Brother, though manie hardie strokes first passed betweene them. Heereupon

was such a suddaine crie on all sides, some with ioy, and other with sorrowe, as
made the ayre resound theyr voices. And I thinke that the *Greekes* when they
receiued their libertie by *Quintus Flaminius*, made not the like clamour: when
(as *Valerius* rehearseth) the Byrds fell from the ayre with the furie of theyr cries.[4]
In the meane while, the King of *Balisarca*, hauing hearde heereof, came into the
Fielde, accompanied with manie Lords, and conducted *Palmerin* with great honour and tryumphe backe to his Tent: especiallie the Prince *Olorico*, who exceeding
ioyfull for the good fortune of his companion, embracing him, saide. Ah gentle
Palmerin, how brauelie haue you accomplished your promise to the Princesse? the
like successe heauen graunt you in labouring my cause. Beleeue me good Prince,
quoth *Palmerin*, so well will I imploye my selfe in that action, as I hope you shall
haue cause to thanke me. Now to returne to *Gramiell*, he caused his Brethrens
bodyes to be conuaied thence, and embalmed them in two Chests of leade, referring their Funerall till his returne: and with the teares in his eyes, he thus began
to encite his people. Not knowing howe (my louing Freendes and Countreymen)
to animate your mindes sufficiently, with remembraunce of the tirannie, exercised
by the Soldane on the bodye of my Brother and your Prince: vnhappie occasion
presents you with a fresh memory of reuenge, seeing these two yong Princes, the
beloued Sonnes of your King, so shamefullye slaine in your presence. For this
cause, deere Freendes, that each of you may take a newe couragious spirite, to
morrowe to encounter these effeminate *Assirians*: let vs all be resolute togither,
and cause them to vnderstand, that you, who haue lead your liues in the Deserts
of *Affrica*, much better know how to mannage Armes, then such loyterers in theyr
Mistresses Chambers, who can doo nothing but before theyr Ladies.[5]

 Heereupon two hundred Knightes aduaunsed themselues before him,
swearing and vndertaking, to bring *Palmerins* bodie to him the day following: and therefore all that night they prepared themselues, strengthening theyr
Sheeldes and Armour, and all other things necessarie for the fight, thinking the
next morning by Sunne rysing to bid them battaile, these knightes inuenting to
ambush themselues, as you shall heare. *Palmerin* beeing brought thus honorablye
to his Tent, called for the Chirurgions to visit his woundes, which they founde so
easie to bee cured, as they assured him of speedie recouerie.[6] Hee then summoning the whole Counsaile togither, aduised them, that in his opinion hee thought
it expedient, to dislodge that place about midnight with bag and baggadge, and
so to coast the Mountain, feigning a fearefull departure. For (quoth hee) the
enemie aduertised of our retyre, will imagine that we despayre of our successe,
by reason of the death of the two slaine Princes.[7]

 Thus our dissembled flight, will cause them disorderlie to pursue vs, which
we will suffer, till espying our aduantage: when returning valiantly vpon them,
I dare gadge my life we shall eyther kill them downe right before vs, or at least
driue them to a shamefull foyle. This deuise was generallie allowed for good,
and at the howre appointed was executed. By chaunce this morning *Gramiell*
came among his menne verie earlie, and vnderstanding the Soldans power was

Palmerin d'Oliva: Part II   *399*

departed with such silence: presentlye cryed alarme, charging all his men to followe them, for he doubted they woulde enter a Cittie neere at hande, which was so stronglye fortefied, as they should neuer entise them foorth to skirmish, therefore he desired to preuent them of that helpe.[8]

Heereupon the Horsemen galloped after them amaine, crying: vpon them (my Freendes) vpon them, the day is ours. *Palmerin*, the Prince *Olorico*, the King of *Balisarca*, *Gueresin* his Sonne, with a thousande men at Armes, seeing howe they were disordered: returned vppon them, and made such a slaughter among the *Phrygians*, as the Field was couered all ouer with their bodies. *Gramiell*, seeing, that of the first sallie not one came backe againe, sette forward with his battaile, wherein hee had a thousand Horsemen, and furiouslye running on the Soldans power: by misfortune hee mette with the Prince *Olorico*, to whome he gaue such a cruell stroke on the head, as had almost sette him beside his Saddle. *Olorico* greatly discontented heereat turned valiantlie towards his enemie, and betweene them continued a very daungerous fight: but in the ende, *Gramiells* Helmet beeing cutte from his heade, hee beganne to despayre, when *Olorico* following his intent, noblie at one blowe smote his heade from his shoulders. This mishap was seene by one of his yonger Brethren, who running fiercelie with his Launce against *Olorico*, was suddainlye preuented by *Palmerin*, in that hee stroke him beside his Horse, where hee was troden to death with the trampling of the Horsses.

Then came foorth the two hundred swoorne Knightes from their ambush, who had vndertaken *Palmerins* death, and him they hemde in so subtillie, as hee was brought into very great daunger. Which the Prince of *Arabia* beholding, made way through the thickest to assist his Freende, after whom followed *Gueresin* with an hundred Knights: without which supply, both *Palmerin* and *Olorico* had been slayne, for theyr Horsses were killed vnder them, and they enforced to fight on foote. But when they beheld this fortunate succour, theyr courage nobly increased, and then beganne the sharpest encounter, for the winges on eyther side approched, the Archers and Crossebowes likewise, sending their Arrowes as thicke as hayle among them, so that the battaile endured till darke night. Then the Brethren sounded the retraite, for which the King of *Balisarca* was not sorrie, hauing so ouertrauailed himselfe that day, as he could no longer sitte on Horsebacke: notwithstanding, before hee woulde enter his Tent, he sawe the Fielde assured, the watch placed, and all the Souldiours planted in good order.

Chapter XIX.

How the Brethren of Gramiell, with all their traine, tooke themselues to flight, and how Palmerin suddainly pursued them with his power, and tooke them prisoners.

Immediatlie after that these two *Phrigian* princes had thus sounded the retrait, and considered how they had lost fiue of theyr brethren, three in single fight with *Palmerin*, and the other in the battaile,[1] the greatest part of their power likewise almost vtterly dismaid: to know the certaintie of their strength, they commaunded a deuision to bee made of the whole and wounded, and seeing how small their number was, they concluded not to stay in any place, til they came to the Realme of *Pasmeria*, whereof *Maurice* was King, and their kinsman, from whom *Palmerin* tooke the enchaunted Crowne,[2] where they thought to supply their want, with men actiue and able to Armes.

The next day, the king of *Balisarca* raunged a thousand men in order, to giue a fresh assault on the enemie: but he was suddainlie aduertised by his espiall, how the *Phrygians* were fledde. He not a little glad of these newes, sent word to *Palmerin* thereof, who though he was sore wounded, Armed himselfe, commaunding his Captaines to prouide sixe thousand men presently, to goe see the certaintie of these tydings. With this strength he ioyned the Kings power, and so went to the enemies Campe, where they found no resistaunce, nor any but such as laye greeuouslye wounded, of whome hee enquired which way the cowards were fled: which the poore Souldiours reporting to him, hee vowed to followe till hee ouertooke them. The resolution agreede vpon, betweene the King of *Balisarca*, and him with tenne thousand light Horsemen hee determined to pursue them: and the King to staye there with the rest of the Armie, to recouer the Townes againe to the Soldane, which before had beene taken by the enemie, and to bee in readines with assistaunce, if he shoulde happen to stande in any neede.

While *Palmerin* made election of his company, a horseman was dispatched with these newes to the Soldane, how the enemies had beene foyled, and of their flight. The messenger beeing come before *Maulicus*, and the Letter opened and read, how valiantly *Palmerin* dealt with his enemies: before all his nobility, the Soldane sayde. By all the Oracles of *Delphos*,[3] I may well perswade my selfe, that whersoeuer *Palmerin* is for vs, wee are assured of the victorie. The Princesse hauing heard these newes, sent for the messenger, and after shee vnderstoode by him, howe *Palmerin* bare her Sheelde in the face of her enemies, and had slaine in Combat two of *Amaranos* Brethren: shee was meruailous ioyfull, and rewarded the Messenger so well for his paynes, as for euer hee might extoll the bountie of the Princesse.

The Messenger dispatched againe with the Soldans Letters, brought speedie aunswere to the King of *Balisarca* and *Palmerin*, of their packet: wherein the Soldane hartylie thanked them, desiring them to followe theyr fortune. *Palmerin* vnderstanding the will of the Soldane and *Alchidiana*, and howe they desired him

Palmerin d'Oliva: Part II

to pursue the Brethren of *Gramiell*: determined to set forwarde next morning, aduertising the Prince *Olorico* thereof, that hee might put himselfe in readines. But notwithstanding all theyr dilligence, their enemies gotte before them into *Pasmeria*, where they rested themselues, in hope to be assisted by their Cozin *Maurice*. And he was giuen to vnderstand, how the dumbe Knight named *Palmerin*, followed them: wherfore he commaunded them to depart his Realme, for hee would not ayde them against his deerest Freende.[4] This repulse droue them into great dispayre, yet seeing they coulde not helpe it, they were constrained to make a vertue of necessitie,[5] and so secretly as they coulde deuise, by little and little stole toward their owne Countrey. *Maurice* hearing how *Palmerin* was come into his Realme, rode three or foure daies iourney to meete him, and entertaining him with exceeding honor, offered himselfe, his people and substance to his seruice. *Palmerin* verie thankfull for the Princes kindnesse, woulde haue nothing but certaine Horsses of him, because diuers of his owne had miscaried. By this time were the Brethren entred the confines, which belonged to the Admirall of *Tharsus*, where they had doone verye much harme, by exactions and great misusing of the people. This Admirall was a verie gentle Knight, and named *Alfarano*, which seeing what iniurie they did him, and vnderstanding that they had beene conquered, and now fledde without anie place of assuraunce: leueyed an hoste of hardie Souldiours, wherewith he intended to keepe a straite, through which they must of necessitie passe, beeing so narrowe as they could passe but two togither: and no way else coulde they escape him, except they woulde climbe the tops of the Mountaines.

In this place lay the Admirall ambushed, with so manie men as he thought conuenient, and within three dayes after, *Palmerin* with his power came to assist them. The *Phrygians* hauing heard heereof, were greatlie amazed at this vnexpected aduenture, and had no other helpe but to climbe the Mountaine, where in holes and Caues they were glad to hide themselues: and there they continued fiue or sixe daies in safetie, albeit they were readie to die for want of sustenaunce. *Palmerin* foreseeing the incommoditie of the place, and that they could not escape him, nor needed hee anie further to followe them: caused the Mountaine to be enuironed on all sides, thinking the ende heereof woulde bee such, as indeede it afterward prooued to be. For these poore distressed menne, hauing neyther foode or other prouision, came foorth of their Caues, and assembled togither on the side of the Mountaine, where entering into conference of their estate, some gaue counsaile to goe fight it out, but other (better aduised) would not consent thereto, for better is it (quoth they) to yeelde our selues to the mercy of our enemies, then to aduenture our fortune where no hope of successe is to be expected.

Heereuppon they concluded, and the two Brethren of *Gramiell* were the first that vnarmed themselues, and comming in this manner to *Palmerins* Tent, thus they began. Noble Knight *Palmerin*, more fortunate then any man in the world, we, Brethren to the renowmed Prince *Amarano*, whom thou hast with thine owne hand slaine, and three other of our brethren likewise,[6] whereof the noble *Orinello* deserueth speeche, all sonnes to a King, and themselues heeretofore worthy accomplished Princes, though nowe foyled and consorted with the deade: we (noble Lord) more certaine of thy clemencie and courtesie, then any successiue ende of a battaile so vnreasonable and desperate, come to yeelde our bodies and goods to thy disposing, desiring thee to pittie our estate, and regarde the works of Fortune, to whom thou art Subiect as well as we. Beside, that the more shall greater persons bee praised for honorable fauour, then by vsing rigour and vnnaturall crueltie, which maketh them euery where hated and despised. When *Palmerin* sawe them so humble, considering his owne estate, and how time might frowne on him, returned them this aunswere. Now (my Lords) haue you doone wiselie, to laye by Armes, and submit your selues, for otherwise your destruction was at hande. Notwithstanding, in respect you haue thus yeelded your selues to me, I entertaine you into my safe defence, assuring you peace with the Soldane, so that you sweare your faithfull loue, and doo him homage. So gaue hee them in keeping to one of his Knights, whome hee especially trusted, and returning to *Alfarano*, in recompence of his wrongs and losse sustained by the *Phrygians*, gaue him all theyr spoyle, and the raunsome of all the Knightes taken prysoners. The Admirall all humblye kissing his hand, desired him to rest himselfe in one of his Citties, which was within fiue or sixe miles of the place: which gentle offer *Palmerin* would not refuse, because he was sore wearied with trauaile: wherefore by the Admiralles appointment, the Pallace was prouided for *Palmerin* and his Freende *Olorico*.

Chapter XX.

How the Queene of Tharsus came to see Palmerin, in the Citie belonging to Alfarano her Admiral, where by the meane of an enchaunted drinke, shee accomplished her pleasure with him.

Here our History willeth vs to remember, how in our former discourse was mentioned, that the Queene of *Tharsus* sent a rich Helmet to *Palmerin*,[1] and at the Damoselles returne, was acquainted with his singular composed feature, rare courtesie, and Knightly chiualrie: the reporte whereof, caused her amorously to affect him, and in such vehement maner, as she determined her own death, vnlesse she might enioy his louelie company.

Which the better to compasse, shee discouered her desires to a cunning Magitian, hee by whose meanes she sent the Helmet to *Palmerin*: who gaue her such an enchaunted powder, as *Palmerin* drinking it in wine or otherwise, should soone after become so forgetfull of himselfe, as the Queene might accomplish whatsoeuer shee desired. He likewise did reueale to her, the seuerall loues of *Palmerin* and *Olorico*, which tale made her more earnest in following her intent. And vnderstanding his arriuall in the Realme of *Pasmeria*, concluded in person to goe see him: furnishing her selfe with all things necessary, both rich Tapestry, and great store of Gold and Siluer plate, habillements, precious stones, rings and vnualuable Iewels. With these shee adorned her Knights, Ladies and Gentlewomen to the vttermost, and when she had finished her traine to her own liking, shee sette forward with such expedition, as within three dayes shee arriued at the Cittie where hee was, but first shee aduertised her Admirall of her comming, that hee shoulde imagine nothing by her suddaine presence. The Admirall so ioyfull heereof as could be deuised, in that by this meane hee shoulde the more honourably entertaine his guestes: acquainted *Palmerin* and the Prince *Olorico* therwith, who likewise were exceeding glad of the newes, especially *Palmerin*, desirous to know by her his ofspring.

Therefore in most magnificent order with theyr men at Armes, and the Admirall *Alfarano*, they rode to meete the Queene for her greater honour: who by the speciall intelligence was giuen her, knewe *Palmerin* among them all, in that hee marched formost with the Prince *Olorico* and the Admirall of *Tharsus*. Shee regarding in him farre more singularities, then sparing report had acquainted her with all: after that *Palmerin* had saluted her with very great reuerence, as he was not to learne courtlye courtesie, the Queene requited him with a sweete kisse, and thus began. Sir Knight, the fayrest beyond all other that euer I sawe, well woorthie are you to be esteemed among the most happie, beeing able to winne the loue of Ladies that neuer sawe you. Aduise your selfe well of this great fauour, and what a precious Iewell you receiue of them, in requitall of your seruice, or acceptaunce of any amorous contentment. Then wonder not, (Gentle Knight) if to see you I haue left my Country, for beside your great valour, bountie and loyaltie, which neuer can be sufficiently commended, your beautie, affabilitie and most rare perfections, deserue not onelye the loue of the greatest Ladye and Princesse, but their continuall seruice likewise, if they but consider theyr owne dueties. If then your vertues and gifts of nature are of such value and merit, what may shee imagine of her selfe, who is your onelie Ladie and Mistresse, and aboue all other is honored with your faithfull seruice, as well records the memorye of the burning Crowne?[2] *Palmerin* hearing himselfe so commended by such an excellent Queene, blushed with bashfulnesse, and humbly shaped this aunswere. Madame, so far vnable am I, to deserue the loue and good will you beare me, as neuer will Fortune fauour me sufficiently, to recompence the least part of this princelie kindnesse. Yet heereof (faire Queene) you may assure your selfe, that you haue a Knight so forward in your seruice, as nothing shall withholde him from executing your commaundement, though the penaltie of my life were ioyned thereon. Trust me (quoth the Queene) your behauiour promiseth no lesse then you speake off, and if I haue taken anie paine for you, I thinke my selfe now thorowlye satisfied: lette it suffise you then, that I account my fortune not the least, hauing gayned such place in your good opinion. These and such like speeches passed betweene them, till they came to *Alfaranos* Pallace, where they spent the rest of the daye in diuersitie of pleasures: the Queene intreating *Palmerin* and *Olorico* the next daye to dine with her in her lodging, where shee intended honorably to feast them. The next day at ten of the clocke, these two yong Princes came to see her, finding her in a goodlie Hall, which was richlie hanged with cloth of Golde, and therein stoode a Cupboorde, garnished with the most costly plate that euer was seene, for the basest peece was cleane gold, imbelished with precious stones, beside diuerse other inestimable strange Cups, and Glasses of *Agatha*. What their seruice at Dinner was, I leaue to the iudgement of Ladies desirous of fauour. Yet this I dare say, that the viands were so rare and exquisite, and abounding in such plentie, as though shee had them dayly at commaund. The Tables withdrawne, the Queene tooke each of the Princes by the hande, and sitting downe betweene them, with a sweete smiling countenance beganne thus.

 I pray you gentle Knights, to tell mee which of you is most affected to the seruice of Loue, and followes it with greatest endeuour: gladly would I be resolued by you, albeeit I know the certaintie as well as your selues. Madam (quoth *Palmerin*) if you haue such knowledge of our affections, well may our answere bee excused. Verie true, sayde the Queene, especially you, of whose loyaltie the Prince *Maurice* is so notable a witnesse. Notwithstanding which of you doth most mistrust the attainment of her grace, to whom he is most deuoted in loue, let him not giue ouer the pursuit of his desire: but rather let me intreate you to continue your loue with much more feruencie, as to those renowmed Ladies, who by their vertues and graces, doo woorthily challenge you from all other: for I dare assure you such a successiue end of your loue, as with especiall content you shall finish your affectionate desires.[3]

If they were ioyfull of this assurance, it is no question to be demaunded, chiefly *Olorico*, who till then dispaired: but now so happily resolued, gaue place to *Palmerin*, who was desirous to conferre more priuately with the Queene, therfore in the meane time he deuised with another Lady, and *Palmerin* seeing the occasion so fit, began his tale in this maner. I cannot forget, fair Queene, when you sent your Lady to me at the Soldans court, that after her message deliuered she saide to me, that you were acquainted with further secrets concerning my estate.[4] For this cause I intreate your highnesse, if you doo not imagine mee too importunate, that it might please you to acquaint mee with my Father and Mother, for that aboue all other things I most desire. The Queene amazed at this demaund, thus answered. Knowe (gentle Knight) that what the Ladie in this matter saide to you, as also what my selfe euen now promised you, commeth not from mee, for one of my Knights acquainted mee therewith, hee beeing the most skilfull in the Magical sciences that is in all *Turkie*. As now he is returned into his owne Countrey, and no other answere could I get of him: but that you are the Sonne of the most loyall redoubted and valiant Prince in the worlde, whom before you haue anie further knowledge of, you shall deliuer from death, and that very shortly.[5] Beside you loue a Ladie, who in all perfections of nature, fortune or spirit, hath not her equall.

In sooth (quoth *Palmerin*) I shall account my selfe right happie, to deliuer my Father from such daunger, and Heauen I beseech that it may so bee. On these tearmes came *Alfarano*, and the dauncing began, which constrained them to breake of talke, and step into the daunce, in which delight they spent the time till Supper was summoned, till which aduertisement, they were just like was *Ogyer* the *Dane* in *Faeria*.[6] For neuer was *Dido* such an affectionate auditrice of *Aeneas*, recounting the ruine of the *Troians*,[7] then was the Queene of *Tharsus* to *Palmerin*: towards whom her heart was so enthralled, and with secret fire so wasted and consumed, as dooth the Waxe before the fire. Being set at the Banquet, *Palmerin* and *Olorico* on the one side, and the Queene and *Alfarano* on the other, the Tasters attending on them were two Ladies, who had in charge to giue the one the sleeping and daungerous drinke, and to the other, the amorous and delicate, yet in effect to prouoke forgetfulnesse. So well did the Ladies discharge their office, and the Princes tooke this mixed drinke so substantially, as they coulde hardly forbeare sleeping at the Table: wherefore euery one arysing, the Queene gaue the good-night to *Alfarano*, who presently went to his lodging. Then were these two sleepie Princes conducted to their chamber, where beeing in bed, they slept soundly, and the Queene comming to them, accompanied with those trustie Ladies that wayted at Supper, tooke the Prince *Olorico*, conuaying him to another bed, for he was so charmed as hee coulde not awake.

Afterward the Ladies departed, and the Queene went to bedde to *Palmerin*,[8] whom she abused at her owne pleasure. A matter not to bee esteemed fabulous, in that other haue beene brought into the like case, as well may witnesse *Brangiena*, who endured these sweet skirmishes, because she should not manifest

the Historie of *Yseul* her Mistresse, and *Tristram*.⁹ The Queene hauing satisfied
her vnchast desire, caused *Olorico* to be brought into his place againe, and then
returned to her owne Chamber. But now this enchauntment loosing his operation, a fantasie appeared to *Palmerin*, resembling his Ladie *Polynarda*, who sayd:
Ah *Palmerin*, disloyall Traytour and adulterer, howe much are they deceyued,
that repute thee a loyall and faithfull Louer? Ah wretch vnworthie of so good a
name, hauing so iniuriouslie forgotten mee. Doost thou not consider thy great
offence, committed against the God of heauen: medling with a Woman more
brute then brutishnesse it selfe, and thy disloyall treason agaynst my selfe? Be
assured, that if thou presently forsake not her companie, I will neuer forget thy
fault, but chastise thee continually as a dissembling reprobate. So she departed,
Palmerin intreating her to pardon this iniurie, which she would not heare, but
floong away in great anger: and he awaking, brake foorth into these speeches.¹⁰

    Ah vnhappie wretch that I am, thus to loose the gracious fauour of my Mis-
tresse. These wordes awaked the Prince *Olorico*, who embracing him in his armes
demanded the cause of his sorrow: but *Palmerin* was so surprised with greefe, as
he would make no answere, but fell from the Bedde in a swoune. *Olorico* fearing he was dead, cried out for helpe, whereat the Queene arose, and casting her
night Mantle about her, came to know the occasion of this clamour: and finding
Palmerin breathlesse, shee called for so many present remedyes, as extinguished
the passionate fitte. *Palmerin* seeing the Queene so neere him, clothed himselfe
immediately, and departed the Chamber, commaunding all his people to prouide
themselues, for he would depart thence within an howres space. Neither could
the earnest intreaties of the Queene, nor courteous perswasions of *Alfarano*, cause
him to stay till Dinner time: but his carriage beeing sent before, and his men
attending him, hee came to take his leaue of the Queene, who verie sorrowfull
for this straunge accident, said to him at his departure. Noble *Palmerin*, my heart
attainted with such extreame greefe, as the sight of you doth somewhat remedie, expected further hope of ease by your presence: but seeing your departure
may not bee withstoode, I pray you vouchsafe to weare this Ring for my sake,
and keepe it safely, till my messenger bring you another like vnto it. Madame
(quoth *Palmerin*) beeing vnable to remunerate the great honours you haue done
me, I will not denie you so small a request, that I may the better fulfill the bond
of allegiaunce, wherin I stande bound to you while I liue. Go then in the safe
protection of the Gods, quoth shee, for thou hast left me such a recompence,
as all my life time will be ioyfull to mee. *Palmerin* not vnderstanding her darke
speeches, departed, putting the Ring on his finger, beeing the most rich and
curious peece of worke that euer was seene: for in it was a goodly great Rubie,
cutte in faces, so liuely as could be deuised, which shone so brightly, as in the
night time it sparckled great light. The Queene likewise, after shee had giuen
great riches to the Admirall, returned to her Countrey, leading thenceforwarde
a verie chaste and continent life, onely for his sake, by whom (in short time) shee
founde her selfe conceyued with Childe. And at the time appointed, by nature,

Palmerin d'Oliva: Part II   *407*

shee was deliuered of a goodlie Sonne, resembling his Father in braue constitution: whome the mother caused to bee named *Palmendos*, as well in memorie of his father *Palmerin*, as also of his Graundsire *Florendos*, from them deriuing his name,[11] as beeing the onlie flower of Chiualrie. And as *Palmerin* was vertuous, so did his Sonne follow him in all bountie, prudence, magnanimitie, loyalty, liberalitie, courtesie and humanitie: in briefe, he had all the noble vertues that a Child might receiue from his father, as you may at large perceyue in his Historie.[12] But because his deeds as yet serue not to our purpose, we will leaue him growing vnder his mothers charge, and returne to them whom lately we left.

Chapter XXI.

Howe Palmerin, to colour his intended and desirous voyage into Christendome, perswaded the Soldane to sende his Armie to Constantinople, and what followed thereon.

Greatlie desirous was *Palmerin* to returne towards the Soldane, and therefore would not make his way by *Pasmeria*, but iourneyed thitherwarde, where the King of *Balisarca* staied his comming, who came to meet him with all the Lordes and Captaines of his Armie. Thus hauing brought the Countrey in quiet obeysaunce of the Soldane, with theyr prisoners they returned towardes his Maiestie, sending worde before of their speedie comming. The Soldane was not a little ioyfull of these tydings, as also of the fortunate victorie against his enemies, wherefore he left the Cittie of *Calpha*, and determined to meete them at a Castell of pleasure,[1] which hee had lately edifyed, cheefely because hee would see the good order of his Armie, which was now conducted in better equipage, then before was woont to bee seene in *Assiria*. The King of *Balisarca* caused the captiues to be ledde before, who (by his commaundement) when they came in the Soldanes presence, threw their Armour to the ground, and three times fell on their knees kissing the ground,[2] prostrating themselues before him with great reuerence. All these ceremonies finished, *Palmerin*, the Prince *Olorico*, with the other Gouernours of the Feelde, came, and kissing his highnesse hande, hee intertained them verie graciously: and after he had embraced *Palmerin*, he woulde needes ryde betweene him and the King of *Balisarca*. In this order rode they on to the Pallace Gate, where his Ladie *Lethea* and *Alchidiana* her Daughter, trickt vp in vestures of surpassing value, attended their comming: and after the accustomed reuerences on all sides, entered the great Hall, where the Princesse taking *Palmerin* by the hande, before her Father and all his Barons, thus spake.

Sir *Palmerin*, so well is your prowesse and haughtie deedes of Armes knowne to euery one, as my prayse cannot extoll them to aduauntage: notwithstanding I dare say before my Father, and all his Lords heere present, that hee is so much indebted to you, as he can neuer returne sufficient recompence. These words vttered with such affection, were noted by euery one, especially the Prince *Olorico*, when *Palmerin* made this answere to the Princesse. Madame, heere may you behold the Prince of *Arabia*, one of the best Knights that euer I knewe, and who hath doone more seruice to your Father and you in this warre, then any other beside: for with his owne hande he slue *Gramiell*, who was chiefe leader of the *Phrygian* Armie. Beside, such and so many haue beene his rare exploytes, as no one that I knowe may be equalled with him. And all this hee admitteth to your fauour, wherein hee earnestly desireth to continue, so please you to accept him for your Knight: deliuering this assurance before hand, that heereafter hee will aduenture his life in your cause, whersoeuer it shal like you to commaund him. For this cause (Madame) you may not refuse him, being the man that among all the *Assirians*, dooth best deserue to be your seruaunt. *Alchidiana*, who well

Palmerin d'Oliva: Part II 409

vnderstoode to what ende his speeches tended, and the occasion why *Palmerin* thus spake, aduised her selfe well, and returned this answere.

So helpe me our Gods, I know well that the Prince *Olorico* is so puyssant and renowmed, as any man of whom I yet heard: notwithstanding, I hope the Soldane my Father will not be ingratefull in the knowledge thereof, and that sufficiently I dare awarrant yee. But I desire you faire sir, to tell me howe the Queene of *Tharsus* intreated you, and what is your opinion of her? In good faith, Madam, aunswered *Palmerin*, shee is one of the most honest and vertuous Ladies that euer I came in companie withall, and to whom I greatly desire to do any seruice. You haue good reason, quoth the Princesse, in that she came so farre to see you, and discouer her loue: which other coulde as well accomplish, as good, or rather in honor beyonde her, if they might hope of anie ease in their passionate desires. *Palmerin* feigning not to vnderstand her meaning, entred into other kinde of talke, vntill supper time, which finished, each one returned to their Chamber, when the Prince seeing himselfe alone with his Freend, thus sayd. Ah my deere Freende *Palmerin*, howe worthily may you be sayde to bee without compare, in all perfections that a Knight ought to haue, loue onely excepted? yet heerein (if I be not deceyued) you doe for mee agaynst all reason, for a thousand times are you more beloued, then your selfe can loue anie. Notwithstanding, for this default, if so it may bee named, and for the wordes this day vsed in my presence to *Alchidiana*, I remaine vowed to your seruice: for in trueth you know not the good you did me, supporting my imperfection of speech when I was before my Mistresse. Yet know I not whence such imbecilitie should proceede, if not by beeing rauished with regarde of her celestiall countenaunce, my ouer laboured spirite forsooke me, and beeing too much tormented in this languishing bodie, abandoned all the partes sensatiue,[3] placing it selfe onely in mine eyes, which neuer could imagine themselues satisfied, contemplating beautie of so rare and especiall estimation. And were it not that my hope onely consisteth in you, comparing my small desert, and the excellencie of my Ladie, long ere this had my soule forsooke her infortunate habitation, which so indiscreetlie fell into these oppressing passions. And this I earnestly intreate you to let her vnderstand: in that I feare least shee impute my happie alteration, to want of wisedome and ciuilitie. Trust me, quoth *Palmerin*, I promise you my vttermost abilitie, and so much will I do, as one Friend may for another, to discharge my selfe of the promise which heeretofore I made you.

And let me intreate you on mine owne behalfe, to remooue that opinion of speciall loue, which you report the Princesse beares me, beeing not such as you doe imagine: for (noble Prince, and my deare Freende) you neede not despayre of the benefit whereof I haue so solemnely assured you. After many other speeches, they slept till the next morning, when clothing themselues in their richest garments, they went and gaue the good morrow to the Soldane, who verie honourablie thanked them: and *Palmerin* espying conuenient occasion, thus began.

My Lord, you haue sufficient experience, that by the bountie and great fauour of the Gods, you haue obteyned victory against your enemies, to the no little content of your Subiects: all which beeing so happily finished, base were the thought, to feare the perfection of higher enterprises. Therefore my Lord, I thinke it expedient, so it may stand with your good liking, considering your prouision for the sea is in such readinesse, your people likewise acquainted with your intent, before we meddle with the Brethren of *Amarano*, came daily in troupes to offer their seruice: that now you send your Armie to *Constantinople*, for your answere once heard, right soone will we embarke our selues, and set forward on our voyage. For the rest, I pray you deliuer these prisoners to be vsed as your slaues: but as for the Princes, I thinke (hauing seene the fortune of theyr Brethren, and their owne badde successe in Armes) that they will serue you with continuall loyaltie.⁴ My Sonne, quoth the Soldane, let all bee doone as you haue appointed, for such is my confidence in you, that your intent cannot but sort to good ende: wherefore my Gallies and al things readie furnished, depart when you please, hauing first sent your Souldiers aboard.

The Prince *Olorico* beeing present, offered againe to go in this voyage, with like number of men, as he brought against the Brethren of *Amarano*: for which the Soldane greatly thanked him, promising him such satisfaction at his returne, as should agree with his owne content. *Alchidiana* taking in ill part the words of *Palmerin* on the Prince *Oloricos* behalfe, sent for him to come speake with her, which hee did, and finding her very sad and melancholy, hee demaunded if any one had doone her displeasure, and what the cause might bee of her pensiuenesse. Ah my deere friend, quoth shee, how can I but be agreeued, seeing no one Lady in the world, hath so many contrarie fortunes as my selfe? Alas, my heart hath chosen you for my onely Lorde and Friend, thinking to finde place woorthy my conceite, and that your loue would answere me with the like: but in ought I can perceiue, I am too much beguiled, for you, either as ingratefull or carelesse, vse affecting speeches to me, importing no other ende, but that in leauing you, I should take the Prince *Olorico* for my Husband. Do you imagine me so mutable and inconstant, that I will or can loue anie other but you? or that my affection intirely setled so high, can brooke such a downefall, as to like the man so much inferiour to you?⁵ And (which most of all offendeth me) not contented to mocke me, in disdaining my knowne loue, so discourteously would perswade me to choose another? Let all our Gods be iudge, if I haue not iust cause to complaine of you, albeit I haue greater cause to hate and despise my owne selfe: for in that I haue more then deserued your loue, yet (as too much vnwise) I cannot consider, that in the heart of an ingratefull person, loue hath no place of certaine abyding. But seeing our gods haue in such sort subiected mee, as (against my will) I am constrained to loue mine enemie: in vaine were it for me to resist against them, that they beholding the vnspotted loue of the one, may in the ende punish the ingratitude of the other. Thus thinking to continue longer speech, so many violent sighs intercepted her, as she was not able to proffer one word more, whereby

Palmerin enforced, thus answered. I beseech you Madame, crosse me not with these needelesse words, for although the Prince is so worthie to be loued, as any man that euer I saw: yet were I very much vnprouided of witte, and a meere stranger to good consideration, if I would refuse that speciall felicitie, then which I can desire no greater.

I knowe (sweete Lady) that you loue mee intirely, perswade your selfe then, that my loyaltie is no lesse, nor can death make mee gainesay the promises I haue made you: and were it not to the great disaduantage of mine honour, to leaue the honourable warre your Father hath intended, which might procure each one to misconceiue of mee, assure your selfe, that I would forsake dignities, Armes, and all, to do you the seruice you worthily deserue: all which at my returne, feare not, shal be effected. So well could *Palmerin* dissemble the matter, as the Princesse was somewhat better pacified, and taking his leaue of her, returned to the Soldane: before whome he caused to bee brought, the Princes and Lords that were prisoners, and at his request *Maulicus* gaue them libertie, with this charge notwithstanding, that they should serue him in this warre. Which that they might the better accomplish, he commanded them horse, armour, and all other things necessarie, making all possible speed could be deuised, that his armie might set forwards to sea.

Chapter XXII.
How Palmerin sailing with the Soldanes armie, was brought by tempest into the Sea of Allemaigne, where hee tooke landing with the prince Olorico.

Quickly *Palmerin* consented to embarke the Armie, desiring the Prince *Olorico* to accompanie him to the Hauen, to make choyse of the best vessel for themselues: and suruaying them all, they found a goodly Carricke, new and very well appointed, wherein many prisoners lay chained, which had beene taken by the Soldanes gallies, and other Rouers of the Moores, of whom *Palmerin* demaunded what people they were, they answered that they were christians, and had long time liued there in that thraldome.[1] *Palmerin* not a little glad of these newes, asked of what Countrey they were, whereupon one of them that could well speake the *Arabian* tongue, answered. Wee are all of *Allemaigne*, to whome Fortune hath exceeded in crueltie. These wordes were maruailous welcome to *Palmerin*, and for which inwardly he thanked his God: but the better to dissemble his ioy, he thus spake. This Countrey should seeme to be very farre from hence, because I neuer heard thereof before. So finding this vessell fitte for his purpose, hee appointed it for himselfe and the Prince *Olorico*, discharging all other that were therein, two Knights onely excepted, to whose charge hee committed the Christians: causing his Horses, Tents, and all other necessaries, to be carried aboard, as well the Prince *Oloricos* as his owne, accomplishing euerie thing in such order, as within three dayes after the Souldiers were readie to depart: and nowe the day is come to launch away, when the Soldane and other Taborlanes, accompanied the King of *Balisarca* to the Hauen. But the faire *Alchidiana* would not bee seene, by reason of her great greefe for her Friendes departure: for when shee came to take her leaue of *Palmerin* in his Chamber, shee fell (in a manner) dead at his feete, soone after shee deliuered these lamentable speeches.

This is no common farewell my beloued Lord, which you now take of me, but say it is my very last adiew: for my heart perswades mee that I shall neuer see you more, because the extremities of my sorrowes are such, as well I know I cannot long endure. Adiew then sweete Freende, who in steede of ioy and comfort, leauest me in despayre, which neuer can haue ende but by immediate death. Good Madame say not so, quoth *Palmerin*, for I hope right soone to see you againe. So leauing her, *Olorico* and he went towards the Hauen: the Prince beeing so passionate to leaue her sight, by whose sweete lookes his life was maintained: as had not his friendly companion comforted him, vnable was hee to departe the Pallace. But beeing nowe come to the Port, and seeing the winde and sea seruiceable, loth to trifle the time with any longer stay, they came to take their leaue of the Souldane, who tooke great care for theyr contentment, and many times embracing *Palmerin*, commending to him the disposition of all his affayres, sayd. My noble Sonne and friend, I vowe to you in presence of our Gods, that if you returne hither againe with victorie, with such honours I will endowe you, as shall be sufficient for the whole worlde to talke on. *Palmerin* humbly kissing

Palmerin d'Oliva: Part II   413

his hande, went aboord, the Marriners hoysing sayle, launched foorth into the Sea, with such a braue noyse of Drums, Trompets, Clarions, Cornets, Fifes, and other instruments, as though Heauen and earth would haue encountred together. *Palmerin* thus floting on the gouernment of *Neptune*,[2] imagined how with safety he might forsake his companie, wherefore he commanded to vnbinde all the Christians. For (quoth hee to *Olorico*) seeing they are Marriners, and well skilled in the art of Nauigation, they may stand vs in good steede, if time so require, or any sodaine tempest should assaile vs: but the better to beguile his owne people, he caused them to sweare their faithfull seruice to him.

    The night being come, and he seeing that euerie one slept soundly, called two of the Christians, and in the *Allemaigne* tongue thus beganne. My Friends, giue thanks to God for your fortune, in that you Christians haue founde one of your faith and religion, who hath good hope shortly to deliuer you from these heathen helhoundes: therefore set feare apart, and regarde well your Quadrant, if you can compasse any meane to get the coast of *Allemaigne*. The Christians more glad then can be expressed, answered, that they would accomplish his commandement, and therefore he should repose his trust in them. About midnight, as God would, beganne a great tempest and blustring of winde, so that in despight of the *Pylots* and Marriners, the Fleete was seuered in many parts: but the Christians perceiuing that this winde[3] serued well for their auaile, knew so well how to order their course, that in short time they got farre inough from their companie, and thus continued the winde for tenne or twelue dayes, for which *Palmerin* deuoutly thanked God.

    So happily strayed *Palmerin* with his *Allemaignes*, that one of them at length tolde him they were neere the straites of *Gibraltare*, for which *Palmerin* not a little ioyfull, said, that they might passe *Spaine* without any feare, and so the sooner reach *Allemaigne*. But when they began to coast the straight, the Turkish marriners were amazed, saying that the Christians knew not their course, beeing more then eight hundred leagues foorth of theyr compasse.

    Palmerin fearing to be discouered before hee came to his intent, aunswered in choler, that the Christians knewe their course much better then they did, and they to prate no more[4] on paine of their liues: which threatning presently droue them all to silence. Afterwarde they sayled with so good winde, as they tooke landing at a Port in *Allemaigne*, which at this day is called *Tolledo*,[5] when the Christians said to *Palmerin*, how that was the place where they were borne, where (if so he pleased) they desired their libertie. *Palmerin* assuring them of their request, answered that hee himselfe would land there, and therfore went first on shore, feigning to seeke fresh water, and all things accomplished to his owne desire, he caused his Horse to be brought forth, and *Oloricos* likewise, who was importunate to beare him companie. No sooner was *Palmerin* on shore, but he kneeled downe, giuing thanks to God for his safe deliuerance. The Marchants and Marrines of the Citie, seeing them whome they thought lost in the Sea more then tenne yeeres before, were greatly abashed, welcomming them home with exceeding ioy, but they answered, that they ought rather to thanke the Knight in greene Armour, for hee deliuered vs from the Moores and Infidels, without request of any ransome.

Olorico amazed at these signes of ioy, as also when hee sawe *Palmerin* pray, knew not well what to thinke, which *Palmerin* presently perceiuing, and to resolue him of all doubts whatsoeuer, sayd. No longer neede I now my good Lord and Friende, to hide the affaires and secrets of my heart from you, know therefore that I am a Christian, and a Gentleman of the Emperours Court of *Allemaigne*. But that which most of all greeueth me, is, that I am constrayned to forsake your companie, and returne againe to my Lorde, for too much should I offend my God, to go with you to the Soldanes seruice. Wherefore my louing friend, let me intreate you to holde me excused, swearing to you by the faith of a Knight, that whether else it shall like you to go, I will accomplish your minde in any thing. I intreate you likewise, to entertaine al my Squires and Gentlemen into your seruice, and among them to share all my treasure in the Shippe, because I will haue nothing with me but my Horse and armour. And notwithstanding all this, feare not to present your selfe before the Soldane and *Alchidiana*: for to them will I write such matter of you, as they shall accept you in my place, and with as great honour as euer they did mee. If heauen so fauour mee as I may come to the knowledge of my father, I will certifie you with the truth of all. As for my counterfeiting to be dumbe, was onely but to awaite opportunitie, when with safety I might escape thence.

If *Olorico* at the first was amazed, what may be iudged of him nowe? notwithstanding, hee loued *Palmerin* so perfectly, as hee returned him this answere. Although Syr *Palmerin*, wee are of contrary faith and opinion, yet hath your noblenesse and humanitie gained such priuiledge ouer me, that as you haue long time liued a Christian among the Turks, so for your sake will I liue a Turke among the Christians, dissembling in like sort as you did, and neuer shall any occasion force mee to forsake you, till you haue found your Father, and know if he be discended of the Soldanes bloud. No honour will it be for me nowe, to returne again to the *Assirian* Princes, and as for my people, I force not though they go backe againe with my treasure: for on my Knighthood,[6] I will bee no richer then you, nor will reserue any thing with mee, then what belongs to a Knight errant, which is Horse and Armour. For the rest, let Fortune do the worst she can, I hope for all this, one day to be King of *Arabia*. Then noble friend, be not offended, for I will beare you companie, if death or strong imprisonment doo not withhold mee. *Palmerin* embracing him, saide.

Ah worthie Prince, so noble is your minde, and repleate with fidelitie, as perswade your selfe to find me your loyall Brother, and fellow in Armes, neuer to forsake you while I can lift my Sword, so please you to abide with mee. So calling the cheefest of them in the ship, they sayde as much to them as you haue heard, commaunding them not to stir from *Arabia* before they heard some other tydings. As for their strange conceit at these newes, I bequeath to your iudgements,

Palmerin d'Oliva: Part II 415

yet durst they not gainsay their Maisters, but launching into the deepe, sayled backe again into their own Countrey.

    Palmerin and *Olorico* for this night lodged in the Cittie, to refresh themselues, and the next morning,[7] after they had taken leaue of the Merchants they deliuered, they set forward on their iourney. Continuing their trauaile three daies together, at length they mette a Knight, who seeing them armed after the Turkish manner, sayde. Gentlemen, God saue ye, if I should not seeme troublesome to you because I iudge you to be strangers, I would gladly knowe if you could tell me any tidings of two Knights, which long since left this Countrey. Howe were they named? (quoth *Palmerin*). Syr saide the Knight, one of them is *Trineus*, Sonne to our dread Lord the Emperour, and the other, the most valiant *Palmerin d'Oliua*. Two yeeres and more since they left the Court, without any newes what became of them, sauing that wee heard they were a while with the King of *England*, and thence they conuayed his Daughter, the Emperour continuing so sorrowfull for theyr losse, as euery houre his death is expected. May it be (quoth *Palmerin*) that all this while *Trineus* is not returned? What daunger will noble *Allemaigne* receiue, by loosing their young Prince? Ouercome with exceeding griefe and sorrow by report of these vnhappie tidings, to himselfe he beganne in this maner.

    What shall I doo? dare I be so presumptuous, as to present my selfe before my Mistresse? what sufficient excuse can I make for the losse of her brother? Doubtlesse, if it were such a hell to me, to finde the meane for my departure, from that long captiuitie in the Soldanes Court, much more will it be to me now in the search of the Prince, for without him I dare not approch the Emperours presence. While he thus secretly discoursed with himselfe, he became so exceeding passionate, as *Olorico* thought he had lost his sences: which was the cause, that without any further enquirie, the *Allemaigne* Knight departed from them: when *Olorico*, amazed at this suddain alteration, said. How now Sir *Palmerin*, what hath moued you to this heauinesse? I beseech you conceale not the cause from me: for if it be by any offence, that the Knight offered which spake to you, soone shall I deliuer him his penance. Therefore tell me I pray you, for vndoubtedly I will not suffer you to rest, vntill you haue acquainted me with the truth. *Palmerin* knowing how deerly the Prince loued him, and that for his sake he had left Country, parents and friends, reposing on his loyaltie, imparted his loue to him, as also the losse of *Trineus* and the Princesse *Agriola*. *Olorico* then laboured to perswade him, aduising him to compasse some secret speech with his Ladie, of whome hee might learne how to recouer her lost brother, and the faire *Agriola* of *England* againe. *Palmerin* following this counsell, pacified himselfe, and kept himselfe so closely as he could, from being knowne to any.

Chapter XXIII.
How Palmerin by the meanes of Vrbanillo his Dwarfe, spake with his Lady Polynarda, with whom he stayed fiue daies,¹ to recompence some part of his long absence, and to the great contentment of them both.

Such expedition in their iourney made these noble companions, that at length they arriued neere a castle, which was foure leagues from *Gaunt*, where the Emperour as then was, disposed to hunting for the delight of the Ladies: but cheefely to expell his owne melancholy, for the losse of his sonne, as also to recreate the Princesse *Polynarda*, who shadowing the cause by her Brothers absence, lamented continually for her noble Friend *Palmerin*, of whome shee could vnderstand no tydings, albeit she had trauailed her verie vttermost endeuours, which forced her to so manie extreame imaginations, as the very least was worse then death it selfe.

The Emperours trayne lodging each way about the Castle, hindered our two Knights from any good hostage, so that they were constrained to abide in a little simple house, where they demaunded of a Courtier that lay there, what time the Emperour would depart thence, who aunswered, that his highnesse was minded that day to returne to *Gaunt*, to conferre with the Princes electours of speciall affaires concerning the Empire. *Palmerin* ioyfull heereof, caused his Horse to bee brideled, and accompanied with *Olorico*, went and ambushed themselues in a little thicket, neere the high way where the Emperour must needes passe, to the ende he might beholde his Ladie *Polynarda*. *Palmerin* attending her comming who was the onely support of his life, his heart leapt with conceite of his ioy to come, yet trembled likewise because hee durst not present himselfe before the imperiall maiestie, without the noble *Trineus*.

Soone after, by the Guarde of Archers that came formost, hee well perceiued the Emperour was at hand, when remembring the honors and fauours he had receiued in his Court, the teares trickled downe his cheekes, cheefely for want of his highnesse sonne, who was so especially committed to his trust, then followed the Empresse, and with her the faire Princesse *Polynarda*, clothed all in black, witnessing by her outwarde habit, the secret sorrowes of her heart. Her thoughts still hammering on her priuat greefes, yet assailed with a sodaine motion, shee gaue such a sigh as *Palmerin* easily heard it, which troubled him in such sort, as without the assistaunce of *Olorico*, hee had fallen downe from his Horse. *Polynarda* beholding his sodaine alteration, without any regarde of her Mother, called *Vrbanillo* the Dwarfe to her, who since his comming from *England* neuer boudged from her, and to him she sayd. Hast thou heeretofore (*Vrbanillo*) seene these two Knights, which shaddow themselues in the wood side while wee passe by? No trust mee Madame (quoth the Dwarfe) I neuer sawe them to my remembrance. I pray thee, said she, ride to them so fast as thou canst, and demaunde of them from me, of whence they are, and if they can tell any tydings of thy maister, and my Brother *Trineus*. The Dwarfe, who was more then a Doctor in such affaires,

Palmerin d'Oliva: Part II   417

dissembling that his Horse would stale, suffered the traine to passe by, and then rode towards the knights, who were deuising on the Princesse beautie. *Palmerin* well knowing *Vrbanillo*, and seeing him come in such hast, was not a little glad, thinking now he should heare some newes of his Mistresse, wherefore he saide to *Olorico*. I pray you let vs goe meete this Horseman, for I thinke his returne is onely to vs. Nowe was the Dwarffe come to them, and hauing humbly saluted them, said. I beseech you faire Knights to tell me whether you belong to the Emperour, or are straungers, for the Ladie whome I serue, is verie desirous to knowe, and that for matters neerely concerning her, whereof if you can any way truely resolue her, your rewarde shall aunswere your owne contentment. What *Vrbanillo?* quoth *Palmerin*, lifting vp his Beuer, didst thou not knowe thy Maister? Oh Heauen, (quoth the Dwarffe), praised be thy maker for euer for this aduenture. And moued with extreame ioy, he fell at his Maisters feete, saying. Ah my Lord, what comfort will this be to the Princesse *Polynarda*, when shee shall vnderstande of your presence? and not without iuste cause: for by this meane is shee deliuered from the greatest torments in the worlde. And that nothing may want to furnish this long expected ioy, tell me if the Knight in your companie, be the Prince *Trineus* or no? It is not hee, quoth *Palmerin*, for it is more then a year since, that of him, and faire *English Agriola* (after that I vnfortunately lost them)[2] heard anie certaine report. For this cause *Vrbanillo*, it behooues thee to be faithfull and secrete, not discouering my beeing heere to any but my Ladie, of whome thou must learne, by what meanes I may best come to see her. The Dwarffe taking his leaue of his Maister, turned his Horse to be gone: but comming backe suddainlie againe, saide. Is this Sir *Ptolome* that is with you? Madame *Brionella* wil not be a litle glad to hear of him likewise. Nor is it he, (quoth *Palmerin*) I lost him in company with the rest. God will restore them one day againe, saide the Dwarffe, so giuing the spurres to his horse, he galloped till he came to the Princesse, who seeing him returned in such haste, knew not well what to think: yet fearing to be discouered by a knight that accompanied her, determined not to request his tidings, vntill shee came home into her Chamber. But neuer was poore Louer in greater agony, when she expected her friend in some priuat place, then was the faire Princesse at this present: wherefore, so soone as shee came to her Chamber, shee called for the Dwarffe, who being come, shee said, I pray thee *Vrbanillo*, by the reuerend dutie thou owest mee, whence are the two Knights, and what answere did they make thee? They are such sweet Madam, quoth the Dwarffe, as when all the men in the world could tell no tydings of, my selfe by happie fortune haue found: for by them I bring you the Key of Paradise, if your self wil but find the meane to enter. Tush, I pray thee quoth the Princesse, iest not with me in this sort, for now is no time of sport or meriment: tell mee who they are I desire thee? Know then fair Madam, quoth he, that one of them is my Maister *Palmerin*, who thus concealeth him, because he hath not brought the Prince your brother with him, and he (humbly kissing your hand) commends him to your gracious fauour, desiring you to send him answer, how he may secretly speak with you, because he wold not be knowne to the Emperor, or any other of the Court. How welcome these long expected newes were to the Princesse, I leaue to the opinion of long absent friends.[3] O heauens, quoth she, doth *Palmerin* liue, and is so near at hand? now hath my hart his only desired comfort: and such is my hope, that seeing he is come, my brother (by his meanes) shall not be long hence, to such good fortune are all his actions destenied. Presently she ran to tell *Brionella* these newes, who likewise was exceeding ioyfull, because she imagined *Palmerins* companion to be her *Ptolome*. Whereupon they concluded togither, that *Palmerin* should the night following come to the Gardein, where first his sweet Amours were sollicited,[4] and by a Ladder of Cords he should ascend their Chamber. This resolution set downe, the Dwarffe departed to execute his charge, when *Polinarda* thus began to *Brionella*. Ah my deare friend, how impossible is it for me to hide the ioy my heart conceiueth, that was so late in such surpassing heauinesse?

What will my Ladies now thinke, when they behold their Mistresse so pleasaunt? Let them speake what please them, (quoth *Brionella*) should you render them account of your behauiour? yet this I thinke, that your discretion is so good, when you haue seene the onelye comforte for your cares, that you can so wel dissemble your thoughts, as the most warie eye can hardly discerne you. Well haue you said, (quoth the Princesse) if loue could be gouerned by wisedome: but the pleasure which the wisest haue receyued by his rules, hath in the ende discouered their vanitie and folly. Such were the speeches betweene these two Ladies, attending the night in good deuotion, when each one thought to see her Lorde and best beloued, that their long sorrowes might somewhat be quallified.

The Dwarfe beeing gone on his message as you haue hearde, the Knights reposed themselues on the greene grasse till Sunne setting, that they might the more couertly enter the Cittie: and the time beeing come that they woulde sette forward, *Palmerin* said to *Olorico*. My Lorde, wee will take this by waye which leadeth to the Cittie, for I intende before I depart, to heare some newes from my Mistresse. Goe which way you please (quoth the Prince) yet must I needes meruaile at you, that you woulde bee so long absent from such an excellent Princesse: trust me, *Alchidiana* is fayre, yet may not shee be equalled with your Lady. The greefes I haue endured, said *Palmerin*, by my long absence, are not to be spoken off: yet could I no way compasse my returne sooner. By this time they were come to the Cittie, and to a lodging appointed them by *Vrbanillo*, who beeing now come to his Maister, deliuered the message hee was commaunded. *Palmerin* vnderstanding his Mistresse pleasure, presently vnarmed himselfe, and wrapped a scarlet Mantle about him, taking his trustie Sworde vnder his Arme: hee intreated *Olorico*, to staye there till hee returned, or heard further tydings from him, leauing *Vrbanillo* in his companie, with charge to vse him as his owne person. He beeing come to the walles of louelie Paradise, founde the Ladder readie prepared for him, whereby hee made a speedie passage: and finding *Brionella* there staying his comming, embracing her sweetly, saide. Trust me Ladie, the want of Sir *Ptolome* your Freende, dooth not a little greeue me: but by the grace of God, ere it be long I hope to bring him with me. Ah my Lord quoth she, right happie is your comming: for your presence hath beene heere most of all desired. But albeit shee sette a good countenaunce on this aunswere, yet were her secret sorrowes innumerable, beeing deceiued of the comfort shee expected.

Palmerin who thought hee stayed too long from his desire, woulde trifle no further time, but entred his Ladies Chamber: who angerly had throwne her selfe on a Pallet, because hee staied to speake with *Brionella*, then falling on his knee before her, hee offered to kisse her hande, which with dissembling disdaine she would not suffer him, saying. Truelie you shall receiue no fauour of mee, before I knowe certainlie who you are: for I stand in doubt to bee deceiued, and that you are some other then my *Palmerin*, seeing you haue been so long time from me, and (which is more) would neuer vouchsafe to send to me.

Then taking a light in her hand, and earnestly beholding him, hardlie coulde shee sette it from her againe: when welcomming him with an infinite number of sweete kisses, shee saide. Now knowe I well that this is my *Palmerin*: what Countrey might be so delectable, or fortune so contrarie, that could withholde you all this while from me? O that it might haue stoode with mine honor, for my selfe to seeke you foorth: with good will could I haue endured the trauaile, yea much more then you haue doone for mee. How often (considering the daungers of the Sea) hath very death surprised me? and into how manie sundrie opinions haue I fallen, sometime to disguise my selfe into a mans attire, to enter the estate of a Knight errant, and beginne a search which neuer shoulde bee ended, till I founde you? For this hath bene receiued as a generall rule, that by too long sufferance and expectation, one may endure a thousand deaths: and thinke not but the very least of my afflictions, haue bene of force to depriue my life. Consider that griefe, desire, remembrance, languor, sorrow, hope, suspition, teares, complaints, and other such like passions common in loue, continually beate vpon the heart with burning affection: and to such inconuenience their issue growes, as the vitall spirit is chased from the bodie. For Gods sake Madame, quoth *Palmerin*, leaue these wounding speeches, and suffer me to take a litle life, in beholding that which is no lesse diuine then humane, for my offence deserues not these accusations. Then discouered he all his fortunes passed, which droue the Princesse to no litle admiration, when she said.

Beleeue me my Lord, seeing that by your meanes my Brother *Trineus* is lost, for my loue, and to satisfie your promise to my Lord and Father, you must needes goe finde him againe. That shall I Madame, quoth *Palmerin*, but before I begin this iourney, let me intreate that fauourable regard: which is the comfort in loue, and vniteth life and soule togither, which heretofore you haue graunted, and I hope will not now deny me.[5] What may I iudge (quoth she) of your constancie since your absence? for not long since I was sollicited with a vision, which tolde me that you committed breach of loyaltie with a Queene, to my no litle griefe: although full often I reprooued you therefore, to cause you forsake that sinne, when me seemed the Queene thus answered. Be thou assured *Polynarda*, that although *Palmerin* esteeme thee aboue all other, yet shall he leaue some part of his loue with me. Hearing these words, I brake forth into tears, wherewith you seemed to be moued, and so forsaking her, followed me: and herewith I awaked, finding (indeed) my face besprent with teares, and my heart ouercome with insupportable griefe. *Palmerin* abashed hereat, remembred what entertainment the Queene of *Tharsus* made him at the Banquet, of her sundry delights and great fauours for his arriuall, her piercing, amorous, and alluring speeches, wherewith incessantly shee did sollicite him: and such was his conceit, as he verely perswaded himselfe, that by enchaunted practises she had abused him, wherupon he said. I sweare to you Madame, by the religious vowes of our loue, that neuer did I commit such wrong against you: if the Queene of *Tharsus* of whome you haue spoken, did not one night deceiue me by an enchaunted drinke, which vnwittingly I receiued as I sate at supper, causing me to loose both sence and vnderstanding: and so acquainted her with his dreame that night likewise.[6]

Doubtlesse my Lord, quoth she, considering the extremitie of her affection, she practised some meanes to compasse her desire: but seeing it fell out in that sort, and beleeuing you would not willingly offend me, I am contented to pardon that fault. In these and such like speeches, they spent that night, and foure more afterward,[7] all which time *Palmerin* was kept vnseene in her Chamber: till his departing time being come, when the Princesse attiring her selfe in her wonted mourning garments, and shaping her countenance to her former sorrow, shrowded her pleasures past, and thus we will leaue them, returning to our *Assirians* sayling on the Sea.

Chapter XXIV.

How after the tempest was past, the soldans Armie assembled togither, and came against Constantinople, where by the Emperours power they were discomfited: and the King of Balisarca, his sonne Gueresin, and diuers other great Lords of Turkie slaine.

The tempest which had thrown *Palmerin* on *Hercules* pillars,[1] after many long and contagious stormes, began now to cease, the Sea beeing faire and calme, and the windes very quiet, whereupon the king of *Balisarca* General of the Armie, in short time assembled togither the most part of his Fleete, and came vpon the Coast of *Natolia*,[2] where hee attended the rest of his Foystes and Galleyes. And hauing there stayed about fifteene dayes, among all the Shippes that came, hee could heare no tidings of *Palmerins* Carrick: the long stay wherof caused him to doubt, least he had vnhappily perished in the Sea, and ouercome with exceeding greefe, hee thus began.

Ah gentle *Palmerin*, the flower of all Chiualrie, in lucklesse howre didst thou betake thy selfe to the Sea: what answere shall I make the Soldane for the losse of thee, and the Prince *Olorico*, beeing so especially committed to my trust? Nowe cannot Fortune bee so fauourable to vs as she would: for by thy losse I vtterlye despayre of expected victorie. To cut off these bootelesse complaints, he was counselled by the Lords, Knights and auncient Captaines, to sette forward to *Constantinople*, to discharge themselues of their promise to the Soldane, least in returning without dealing with the enemie, they should be reputed for fearefull and faint-harted Cowards. Setting their sailes to the wind, at length they came to the *Bosphor*.[3] Now was the Emperour verie aged and sickly, hauing altogither committed the superintendaunce of the Empire, to his sonne *Caniano*, who had a son aged seauenteene yeeres, named *Cariteos*. And being aduertised of the comming of so manie *Assirians*, *Turkes*, and *Moores*, hee sent to all the Christian Princes for succour: the greater parte whereof, was there as nowe arriued, with resolute determination, to welcome these Infidels.

When the Emperours scoutes had espied the enemie to enter the straight, yong *Cariteos* beholding the Knightes on all sides, some on the walles, and other in the Fielde, came and kneeled before his Graundfather, earnestlye desiring him to graunt him his Knighthood. For my Lord, quoth he, a better time and occasion cannot be then nowe. The aged Emperour graunted his request, and with the teares in his eyes, said. In the name of God, my Sonne, maist thou receiue thy order, and to the glorious maintenaunce of the Christian faith: albeit thy youth forbids thee to venture so soone.[4]

Presentlye arose the yong Knight *Cariteos*, and clasping on his Helmet, was the first that went foorth of the Cittie, accompanied with tenne thousand Horsemen, and twentie thousand Footemen, to hinder the landing of the enemies: which a great while hee did with such valour, as the Hauen was chaunged with the bloud of the slaughtered. The King of *Balisarca* hearing thereof, commaunded his Archers to their taske, whose shafts flewe so thicke in such multitude, as it were the Hayle that falleth from the Cloudes: and on the other side hee gotte thirtie thousande men on land, who assayled the Christians so furiouslye, as yong *Cariteos* was slaine, and a great number of noble personages, which was the cause that the Christians retired to the verie Gates of the Citie. The Prince *Caniano* aduertised of his sonnes death, and the great daunger wherein the Armie was, issued foorth of the Cittie with eight thousande Horsmen, and foure thousand hardie Archers, who like hungry Tygers ranne vpon the Turkes, beating them to the earth in such heapes, as twelue thousand of them were slain at this encounter, and the rest repulsed backe to their ships, where many entred for sauegard of their liues, and a great number were miserably drowned in the Sea.

At this mishap the King of *Balisarca* was greatly enraged, who with his power presently went on shore: the fight enduring so cruell and bloudie three howres space, as neyther side could be reputed likeliest of victorie. In this encounter ended their liues, the King of *Balisarca*, his Sonne *Gueresin*, and a great number of Califfes and Taborlanes of *Turkie*: and of the Christians, the Prince *Caniano*, with diuers other great Princes and Lords, whose deathes are to this day lamented in *Greece*: yet were the Pagans and Christians so animated one against another, as darke night was the cause of their seperation. When the Emperour vnderstood the death of his Sonne and Nephew, hee was readie to die with conceit of griefe: but seeing the necessitie of the time required other matter, then sorrowing teares and vnprofitable lamentations, hee presently dispatched Postes and Messengers, to hasten the succour was comming from Christendome. In short time arriued a mightie Christian power, and despight of the Turkes entred the Cittie, when the Emperour presently sent tenne thousand into the Field, and prouided a signall for the other, to set fire among the Turkishe Fleete, at what time they receiued the signe from the Cittie. The Infidelles seeing the Christians to sallie abroad, left their Shippes and came to meete them: whereupon the Christians diuided themselues into squadrons, and running furiously on the *Moores, Arabes*, and *Assirians*, made such hauocke and slaughter of them, as happie was he coulde best defend himselfe. Then suddainly was the signall of fire made, on the highest steeple in *Constantinople*, to the Emperours power wafting on the Sea: which immediately launching among the Turkish Fleete, suncke the greater part of them, and burned the rest with their wilde fire. When the Turkes beheld this stratageme, and that they were now destitute of any helpe, they beganne to faint: so that at the comming of the Emperour, who came himself vpon them, with a fresh sallie of fiue thousand[5] men, they were all slaine, except a fewe that escaped into Galleyes, that brake from the rest vpon sight of the pollicie.[6] Great was the spoyle gotten by this conquest, which the Christians taking with them, entred *Constantinople*, where they gaue God thankes for their happie victorie.

But although the Emperour sawe his enemies vanquished, after the Princes were departed that came to his succour, right greeuous was the losse of his Sonnes to him: wherefore his Lordes aduised him, to send for his daughter the

Palmerin d'Oliva: Part II   *423*

Queene *Griana*, and King *Tarisius* her husband, and to commit the gouernment of the Empire to him. For the accomplishment of this generall determination, the Duke of *Pera*[7] was appointed Lord Ambassadour, being one of the most auncient Princes of *Greece*: who accompanied with many noble Gentlemen, made such expedition in his iourney, as hee arriued in *Hungaria*, before the King and his Queene *Griana*, whose sorrowes may not be expressed for the death of her brother. When they vnderstood the Emperours pleasure, they resolued on their obedience, which caused the King to sende for two of his Nephewes, who were sonnes to the Duchesse of *Ormeda* his sister, the one named *Promptaleon*, and the other *Oudin*, to be his Lieutenants in *Hungaria* during his absence. Vpon their presence, before the Ambassador of *Constantinople* the King *Tarisius* tooke their oathes, for their loyall and faithfull gouernment. But because we must now reuiue matter long expected, as concerning the noble Prince *Florendos* of *Macedon*,[8] I am loth to spende any further time in vaine, and will now report what happened at *Buda*, during the time of this determination.

Chapter xxv.

How the Prince Florendos of Macedon, accompanied with none but his Cozin Frenato, departed from his Countrey in a Pilgrims habit, iourneying in Hungaria, where he killed the King Tarisius: and how he and the Queene Griana were taken prisoners.

Lordings, let vs nowe remember how after that *Palmerin* was departed from *Macedon*, hauing recouered the health of the olde king *Primaleon*,[1] Father to the noble Prince *Florendos*, who during the time of *Palmerins* presence, was somewhat more pleasant then of long time he had beene, appeasing his complaints for the Princesse *Griana*, by the happie tidings of the ancient knight, that sent the sheeld to *Palmerin* at his knighting.[2] But now *Florendos* hearing no newes of him, returned to his former heauines, and languished much more then euer he did: so that when the *Macedonian* Princes and Lords pressed him with continuall request of marriage, that hee might haue issue to succeede in the Kingdome, hee was constrained by their importunitie, to make them promise of their request, crauing a yeeres respite before, in which time he intended to make a deuout voyage, whereto they consented in respect of his promise. Nowe did he not demaunde this time of his Subiects, for any desire he had to bee a Pilgrim, or any superstitious zeale to the Spanishe Leather Cape, Shooes, Frocke,[3] and such like: but for he longed to see his sweete mistresse *Griana*, whom he serued in heart with such loyall affection, as till death he would not marrie without her consent and licence.[4]

The day being come that he would depart, he tooke his leaue of all the Princes, Lords and Gentlemen, and accompanied with *Frenato* Father to *Ptolome*, both caped after the manner of Pilgrimes: mounted on two Palfrayes of small value, and without anie weapons, except each of them a little short Dagger, departed the Cittie, making such haste in their iourney, as they arriued at *Buda*, where as then the King kept his Court,[5] prouiding to set forwarde to *Constantinople*. There were they lodged in one of the best Osteries in the Cittie, and the next morning went to the great Church, where the Queene was euer woont to heare diuine seruice: and so well it fortuned, that at the time these two Pilgrims entred the Church, the Queene her selfe was in the Chappel. *Florendos* who was maruailously disguised, stoode not in doubt to bee knowne: but seeing the Chaplaine had begunne seruice, hypocritically he approched to the Aultar with holie deuotion, to the ende hee might the better beholde the Queene. Regarding her sweete countenaunce, he remembred the courtesies he sometime receyued of her, and what exceeding affection as then shee bare him: but now being in the custodie of another, and he out of hope to haue any more gracious pittie, his spirits were so wonderfully troubled, and so manie passionate sighes hee breathed from his heart, as he fell downe in a swoune, that euerie one reputed him for dead. The Queene, who manie times had noted his pittious lookes, commaunded *Tolomestra* one of her Ladies, shee that had the charge of her in the Tower of

Palmerin d'Oliva: Part II 425

    Constantinople, that shee should go vnderstand the Pilgrims disease, and do the best to recouer him againe, which *Frenato* had done before she came.
    Tolomestra demanded of *Frenato*, the cause of his sicknesse, who answered. Madame, we are newly come from the holy voyage of *Ierusalem*,[6] and hee (who was wont to endure many vehement alterations, which the contrary ayres by the waye doo breede) feelyng the freshe coolenesse of this Church, hath therewith beene ouercome as it should appeare.
    My friendes, quoth *Tolomestra*, withdrawe your selues to the Court, and enquire for the Gallery, in which place the Queene dooth daily giue her almes: there shall be prouided some remedie for you, and I will giue you certaine precious Drugges, which shall heereafter comfort you, when any such humour offendeth you. A thousand thankes (good Ladie) sayd *Frenato*, we will doo as you haue commaunded vs. Seruice beeing ended, they went to the Gallery, whither soone after came the Queene, and opening the Casement of her Window as shee was wont, stood to behold the Almes giuen to the poore Pilgrims. *Frenato* and his companion had gotten so neare the Windowe, that the Queene might easily heare any thing they sayd. After most humble reuerence made, *Florendos* thus beganne. Most excellent Queene, renowmed beyond all other Ladies, among so many of your daily charities, may it please you to pittie the most poore and miserable Knight in the world? The Queene at these wordes knewe him, and was in such feare least the King should know of his being there, as shee could hardly sustaine her selfe, but satte downe on a Pallet by *Tolomestra*, who seeing her suddaine alteration, sayd. What ayle you Madame, that your colour changeth in such sort?
    Ah my trustie friende (quoth the Queene) the Pylgrime that swouned in the Church, is the Prince *Florendos* of *Macedon*. I pray thee goe to him, and intreate him presently to depart hence: for if the King come to the knowledge of him, all the worlde cannot sheelde him from death. For the rest, will[7] him follow no further, what he lost by his owne default: and that the fauour heeretofore graunted, my duetie and honour now forbiddeth mee. *Tolomestra* entring the Gallerie, saide the message to the Prince *Florendos*, who vnderstanding this sharpe answere, shed manie teares with greefe, saying. Ah my deere Freend *Tolomestra*, desire my gracious mystresse *Griana*, that in requitall of so manie tormenting passions, which nowe twentie yeeres I haue patiently endured, shee will affoord me once to speake with her, and kisse her hand before I depart. *Tolomestra* brought this answere to the Queene, perswading her to heare him speake, which shee might do with safetie, vnder colour of requesting to know the maruailes of *Palestine*, with the precious and worthie monuments of the holie Citie.[8]
    I am content to graunt so much (quoth the Queene) but I greatly feare the issue of his speeches, go then and cause him secretly to enter. Ah gentle habit, where-under many doe often beginne their delight, which in the ende proues woorsse then Tragicall. The two Pilgrims beeing entred, *Florendos* fell on his knee before his Ladie, and kissing her hand, sayd.

O my God, thy name be praysed through all worldes, permitting mee to kisse these handes so long time desired. See heere sweete Mistresse your *Florendos*, that with such loyaltie hath loued you, and hitherto hath kept the fayth, which hee vowed to you at *Constantinople* in your fathers Pallace,[9] and which no death can make me falsifie or change, vnlesse you please to suffer me take another wife, wherein I shall satisfie the importunate requests, which daylie the Lords of *Macedon* make to me for marriage, that I might leaue them an heyre of my linage. Which is a matter so greeuous to me, in that I failed of you to whom I first gaue my fayth, as I resolued neuer to take any other, which I knowe not how I shall performe without losse of my life. As he thought to haue proceeded further in speeches, and the Queene hauing not answered one worde, vnhappily the King entred, which the Queene beholding, swouned with feare. But she was immediately recouered by her Ladyes. When the King seeing her in such estate, and in what secrecie the two Pilgrims talked with her, hee gathered some suspition, and ouercome likewise with the force of iealousie, saide.

Madame, what make you here at this time? and in so slender companie of Ladies, how dare you stande talking with these Straungers? I woulde gladly know the matter, and what hath made them so bold to enter your Chamber? *Florendos* seeing his affaires to growe from badde to woorsse, and that his Ladie was so threatned, entring into choler, he drew his Dagger from vnder his Frocke, and taking the King by the bosome, said: *Tarisius*, I will not hyde from thee who I am: it is more then twentie yeeres since I promised thy death,[10] and nowe I am come in person to performe it. With these wordes he stabde the Dagger to his heart, and downe fell *Tarisius* dead at his feete: which when the Queene saw, she on the other side fell in a swoune again. *Frenato* greatly amazed hereat, sayde to *Florendos*. For Gods sake my Lord let vs shift for our selues, before this misfortune bee blazed abroade. Content thy selfe, sayd *Florendos*, neuer shall it bee reported that I left my Ladie to suffer for mine offence: or that for the feare of death, which is the ende of all mishaps, I will endure such intollerable anguishes and torments.

Now by ill fortune one of the Pages of honour attended on the King, and hauing seene this homicide, hastilie ranne downe the stayres, crying aloude. Arme ye Knights, arme ye, and reuenge the Kings death, who by a trayterous Pilgrime is slaine in the Queenes Chamber. *Cardino* one of the Queenes Squires, her brother that caried yong *Palmerin* to the mountaine,[11] had no leysure to take anie other armes then a Sword and Sheelde, wherefore he was the first that came to the Queenes Chamber, where hee found *Florendos* guarding the entraunce, who presentlie knew him, saying. Depart my good Friend *Cardyno*, vnlesse for the Queenes loue I shal take thy life from thee. And what art thou (sayde *Cardyno*) that knowest mee so well? I am thy Freend (quoth the Prince) the most vnfortunate *Florendos*.

Straunge it is my Lord, quoth *Cardyno*, that you durst venture into this Court: but take heere my Swoorde and Sheelde, and defend your selfe, for I

Palmerin d'Oliva: Part II 427

thinke you will stande in great neede thereof. In the meane while, I wil go aduertise the Duke of *Pera* of this mishap, he is your good freend, and by his meanes you may haue some succour: for oftentimes haue I heard him say at *Constantinople*, that he wished you as well as my Lord the Emperour. Dispatch then said
5 *Florendos*, that thou be not found heere with me, assuring thee, if I may escape this daunger, I will acknowledge this seruice to thine owne content. *Florendos* armed himselfe with the Sword and Sheeld, whereof hee was so glad, as if hee had beene backed with manie trustie freends: vowing before he died, to make such a spoyle among his enemies, as should remaine for an after memorie. *Car-*
10 *dyno* went with all diligence to the Duke, and secretly acquainted him with all this misfortune: whereat the Duke greatly amazed, answered. I will do my vttermost for his safetie, because full well he hath deserued it. And so accompanied with many *Grecian* Knights, he went to the Queenes Chamber: and thrusting through the throng in despight of them that guarded the stayres, hee got to the
15 Chamber. At the entrance whereof he found *Florendos* defending himselfe with such manly courage, as nine or ten lay slaine at his feete.

The Duke and his men caused the *Hungarians* to withdraw themselues, saying: that himselfe would not suffer the matter so to escape, for the offence ought to bee punished by iustice, after the truth were knowne and thorowlie vnder-
20 stoode. Hereupon the kings two Nephewes came in great rage, saying to the Duke of *Pera*, that the Queene and the Pilgrime ought presently to die.[12] What? quoth the Duke, depart you likewise, your willes shall not heere stande for Lawe, nor is the Queene to bee intreated with such rigour.

So drawing his swoorde, and his Knights likewise, resisted the *Hungarians*,
25 so that manie of them were slaine, vntill certaine Gentlemen came, who louing and esteeming the Queene, appeased this tumult. Then was it agreed vpon, that the Duke should take him into his charge, who had murthered the King, on whom such punishment should bee inflicted as the cause required: and heereupon the Duke tooke his oath before all the companie. In this sort the Kinges
30 Nephewes were quieted, who presentlie departed the Chamber, causing the dead and wounded to bee conuayed thence, that the people might receiue no further occasion of offence, and the Duke comming to the Prince *Florendos*, said.

Yeeld your selfe to me my Lord, and I promise you on the faith of a Prince, that I will maintaine both your right and the Queenes, whatsoeuer daunger I haz-
35 ard therby. If you will not, assure your selfe, that your bodies cannot suffice the villainous furie of these people, for they haue confidently sworne your deathes. I know my Lord, (quoth *Florendos*) that you speake the trueth, and I repose my trust on your nobilitie, which is such, as you will not suffer anie iniury to the man beeing in your guarde: I yeelde my selfe to you, and earnestly intreate you not to
40 imprison the Queene, for (on mine honour) she is guiltlesse. And if any offence hath beene committed, it was by me: yet not without iust cause, and in defence of mine own life. My comming hither was, because I am newly returned from *Ierusalem*, and remembring the manifold honours, which sometime I receyued of

my Ladie in the Emperour her Fathers Court: in my passing by, I was desirous to do my dutie to her. At the instant time I was saluting her, the King came into the Chamber, who moued with an aunceint hatred, which you verie well know, would haue slaine me, but I preuenting his intent with the ayde of my weapon, bestowed that on him which he wished to mee. I beleeue well what you haue sayd, quoth the Duke, yet must you needes abide triall in this case.

Frenato perceyuing his Cozin in such daunger, sought about the Chamber for some weapon to defende him: and finding the Kings Sworde by the Queenes bed side, shewed it to the Duke, that he might giue the better credite to the Princes wordes. Yet notwithstanding all their excuses, these two Pilgrims were taken into sure custodie, and shut vp both togither in a strong Towre, which was verie long before they could accomplish, because in leading them thither, many sought meanes to kill them, and they had done it, but that the Duke verie strongly defended them.

Chapter XXVI.

The sorowfull complaints made by the Queene Griana, seeing her Husband dead, and her friend taken. And howe the Duke of Pera conueyed her to Constantinople, causing Florendos and Frenato to be brought thither by fiue hundred armed Knights.

Verie sorrowfull was the Queene *Griana*, seeing so manie misfortunes succeede one another, as euerie houre her death was expected: and faine she woulde haue committed violence on her selfe, but that *Cardyno* with diuerse Knights attended on her, that none of the Kinges kindred shoulde offend her, while the Duke of *Pera* led *Florendos* and *Frenato* to the Tower. At whose return, as he thought to comfort her, shee fell on her knees before him saying: Ah noble Duke of *Pera*, if euer pittie had place within your heart, for Gods sake make an end of my vnfortunate life: and execute on me (without any fauour) the sharpest rigour of equall iustice, not suffering longer life to a woman so dispised and miserable.

O God, doost thou permit a happie life, to enioy so bad an end? Thou that onely knowest the inward secrets of the heart, seeing I stand suspected in this treason, let my speedie death deliuer mine innocencie. Ah inconstant Fortune, that in my yonger yeeres was so aduerse to mee, how might I credit thy continuall mallice but by this strange and vnexpected accident?[1] Ah gentle Prince *Florendos*, it was not for loue that thou camest to see mee, but for a secret hatred more then deadly, seeing that by thee (and that with great shame) I shall remaine for euer defamed. Where was that loyaltie, and the great feare to offend mee, which sometime thou seemedst to haue? Knowest thou not that in a royall and noble minde, one onely note of infamie is an extreame torment? Doubtlesse, if thou wouldest well consider the wrong thou hast done me, thou shalt finde it to exceede all other worldly iniuries. But I may perswade my selfe, that my destinie was such, for being long since by thee dishonoured, it must fall out for a finall conclusion, that by thee also I shall receiue death.

In this maner the Queene complained, with such effuse of teares and bitter sighes, as the Duke pitying her case, sayd. I beseech you Madame, to endure this mishap paciently, seeing now it cannot be recalled, and consider that these teares and lamentations can yeelde yee no amendes, but rather threaten daunger, and will in the ende not onely weaken your bodie, but hazard desperation. The King is dead, he must be buried: *Florendos* hath offended, hee shall be punished: your people are wounded, they must be cured. Offende not then your selfe with these bootlesse regreetes: but commaund that the proofe of your innocencie be followed. Hereupon the Duke caused preparation for the funerall pompe, and brought the king to the bed of honor, not without many teares and lamentations of his Subiects. When the obsequies were finished, *Promptaleon* and *Oudin* came and exclaimed on the Duke, because hee brought not the Queene and *Florendos* to open punishment. My friends, quoth the Duke, haue I not heretofore tolde you, that wee must not inconsiderately put such persons to death? let the Councell bee called togither, and as they determine I will proceede.

Then were all the Princes and Lordes assembled, among whome the Duke was intreated to speake his opinion, which hee did in this maner. I thinke it conuenient, vnder correction of you my noble Lords, that the Prince *Florendos*, and the Queene, ought to bee sent to my Lord the Emperour, and there to haue iustice extended on them, as well for the suretie of your owne persons, as for the conseruation of the Realme. For except iustlie and by probable causes you condemne the Prince *Florendos*, hardly may you perswade the *Macedonian* Princes: beside, the Lordes may say, that without hearing hee was cut off, and likewise by his open enemies. Againe thinke you that the Emperour will let passe in silence so great a wrong, to punish his Daughter, and not acquaint him with her offence? Considering this indifferently, you shall find your selues on eyther side endangered: your goods will be spoyled, your liues endamaged, for hardly can you resist agaynst such power. So well coulde the Duke sette foorth his discourse, with confirmation of Hystories both auncient and moderne, that in despight of the Kings Nephewes it was concluded, how the prisoners should be sent to *Constantinople*. If they were hereat offended, it is not to bee doubted, but hearing the Counsailes resolution, prepared themselues to goe to the Emperour, determining a sharpe and seuere accusation: trusting so much in their strength and prowesse, that if the Emperour (for proofe of the cause) shoulde committe it to the Combat,[2] they easily thought to compasse their intent. So were the two Pilgryms committed to the Dukes Nephew, with an hundred Knights of *Greece* for their guard, and foure hundred *Hungarians*, who would needes followe for the loue they bare the Queene: she beeing maruellouslie fauoured in her countrey, for her many vertues, and chiefly charitie.

The Queene her selfe, with the yong Princesse *Armida* her Daughter, and all her Ladyes and Gentlewomen, were committed to the Duke of *Pera* his charge, and the rest of the traine that came with him in the Ambassade. When the Queene vnderstoode shee should be caried to the Emperour, shee was further out of pacience then shee was before, rather desiring a thousand deaths, then to come with this reproach before her Father:[3] yet notwithstanding all her intreaties, shee was conueyed into a Litter, and not so much as a pinne left about her, for feare of inconuenience.

To comfort her, her Daughter *Armida* was placed in the Litter, without whose companie (such was her greefe to come before her Parents), shee was diuerse times in daunger of death by the way. But the yong Princesse beeing twelue or thirteene yeares of age, coulde so well comfort her sorrowfull mother, as her talke expelled many bitter imaginations. If the Queene was in heauinesse, wee must thinke *Florendos* griefes nothing inferiour, seeing his Ladie led in such sort, and accused of a crime wherein none but himselfe was culpable: yet made hee no account, beeing reuenged of his auncient enemie, so the Queene were deliuered, though himselfe endured the death. But nowe are they come to *Constantinople*, yet not so soone, but the Nephewes of the deceassed King were before them, where they had blazed a false and most shamefull reporte. And but for the aduise of certaine noble Princes, that fauoured *Florendos* and the Queene *Griana*, vpon the trothlesse speeches of these twaine: the Emperour had concluded to burne his Daughter and the Prince so soone as they came, such horrible slaunders had these traytours spread of them. Namely, that the King was murdered, finding *Griana* committing adulterie with *Florendos*. At which words the Emperour was so enraged, that like a man depriued of reason, he violently pulled himselfe by the beard, saying.

Ah wretched and infortunate olde man, haue the heauens suffered thee thus long life, that after the death of thy sonnes *Caniano* and yong *Cariteos*, thou must see thy daughter conuicted of treason, adulterie, and murder? If I haue had some comfort by my Sonnes, lying now in the Hearse of honour, for maintenance of the Christian faith: doubtlesse this iniurie is so great and enorme, as no ioy or comfort can now abide in mee. Ah my louely Daughter *Griana*, whom I had good hope would bee the onely support of mine age, and for that cause sent to haue thy companie: commest thou now with such shame and monstrous report? *Florendos*, if heeretofore against the *Turke Gamezio* thou didst me seruice,[4] with great wrong hast thou now reuenged thy selfe, taking from mee that good which thou canst neuer restore againe. But let it suffice, that knowing the truth of thy disordered dealing, such shall bee thy punishment, as shall remaine for perpetuall memorie. The Empresse likewise forsaking her Chamber, came and kneeled before the Emperour, desiring him to put *Florendos* to the first councell, and he to be dispatched with dilligence. At which words the choler of olde *Remicius* augmented, hee answering.

Madame, for Gods sake gette you gone, for you are the onely cause of my dishonour: and then you beganne it, when you would not suffer the Prince *Florendos* of *Macedon* to match with our daughter, but gaue her to your Nephew perforce, and contrarie to her owne liking.[5] The Princes seeing him so offended, intreated her to depart, perswading her that the accusers of *Griana* were her cheefest enemies, and that might easily be gathered by their proude and maleuolent detractions, which happily would proue false rather then truth. For if they might heerein speede of their purpose, and theyr accusation passe for currant, the princesse *Armida* should be disinherited, and themselues be the onely heyres of the Kingdome. This was their principall drift, not any deuotion to reuenge their Vncles death, as they in outward shew declared: and hereupon all opinions were set aside vntill the next day, when the prisoners arriued.

Chapter XXVII.

How Florendos and Griana were brought to Constantinople, and there were appointed by the Emperours Councell, to purge themselues of their accusation, by the combate of two knights, against their accusers Promptaleon and Oudin.

The Duke being arriued at *Constantinople*, immediately caused the Queene *Griana* and *Armida* her daughter, to be conducted to the Pallace, by manie noble Lords and Gentlemen. When *Griana* saw shee must needes go before her father, she began again her wonted pittifull complaints, notwithstanding shee was so comforted by the Lordes of *Greece*, by theyr solemne promise to defende her right, as shee encouraged her selfe, and comming before her Father, fell on her knees, and thus beganne. My gracious Lord and father, inconstant fortune euermore hath beene, and still will continue, a most cruell enemie of them of highest calling: and no further neede I seeke for proofe of my words, then the History of your last warres against the Turks, and the present slaunder of mine enemies against mee. I cannot likewise forget that twentie yeeres and more are nowe expired, since (to my great greefe) I was seperated from you: but with much more exceeding heauines am I now returned, if by my misaduenture you receiue any impeach, or I deserue to loose the name of your Daughter. Therefore my Lord, forgetting the name and office of a Father, let naturall regarde be exempted from you; and exercise on mee tyrannous torments, with the greatest rigour that may be deuised. Yet all too little in respect of my deserts, not for any offence in this matter, as God is my witnesse, but for the suspition of the common and vulgare people, more credulous of the faults of Princes and noble Ladies, then of their discreete and sober vertues. Neuerthelesse, receiuing death for a matter neuer committed, and with patience, despight of mine enemies, it will redound to my immortall honour.

Vpon these speeches, the Princesse *Armida* making great reuerence to the Emperor, and with the teares trickling downe her cheekes, saide. Dread Lord, my cheefest desires euermore haue beene to see your maiestie, but so it falleth out nowe, that in steede of ioy and pleasure, it is with greefe, teares, and tribulation. Yet gracious Lord, for the first request that euer I made to your highnesse, I beseech you to credit me, that my mother hath committed no treason, or any dishonour to the deceased King my Father, neither euer permitted any man entrance into her Chamber, but hee whom now the question concerneth,[1] and at that time, I with these other Ladies were present, and are credible witnesses of the whole action. Such efficacie wrought her words in the Emperours minde, as he beganne to defie the accusation, perswading himselfe that it was nothing but falshood: and louingly taking the yong Princesse vp by the hand, addressed his speeches in this manner to the Queene.

Well hast thou sayde, that Fortune hath beene too contrarie towards thee, for when my whole hope remained in thee, and that the Crowne of mine Empire

Palmerin d'Oliva: Part II   433

should haue beene placed on thy head, thou hast fallen into such wounding reproch, as both thou and I shall be for euer dishonoured. My Lorde, quoth *Griana*, vnder correction, and sauing the reuerence of your imperiall Maiestie, neuer imagine the case any thing to your defame: if you credite not mine enemies or common report, from whence is engendred all vntruth. This speake I not to excuse my death, which I know to be the refuge for the desolate, and ende of al afflictions, but to declare mine owne innocencie, and that mine honour shall at length be founde vnspotted. But now consider good Father, with what violence you enforced mee to match with the King *Tarisius*,[2] my heart being still against it, and the neerenesse of linage betweene vs forbidding it. Nor were you ignorant of my loue to the Prince *Florendos*, the most gentle Knight of *Greece*, and whose only trauaile hither was to make mee his Wife: all this will I not denie, nor can my heart permit to passe in silence. Notwithstanding, by your commaundement I was constrayned to forsake my best beloued, and take the man I was not borne to fancie. After I sawe it must needes be so, acknowledging him my Lord and Husband, and my selfe his Wife and Subiect, neither in word or deede, nor so much as very thought, did I dispose my selfe to any disobedience, but liued in most loyall and honourable dutie. Verie true it is, that he founde *Florendos* talking with mee, but I protest before Heauen, that it was with such chaste and modest regarde, as the Sister might conferre with her Brother. And so little time our talke endured, as I had not the meane to answere the Prince, for the King comming in, and prouoked with frenzie or wicked iealousie, woulde haue slaine him, whereby such fortune fell out, as the King receiued what he would haue giuen. Nor can *Florendos* bee worthily blamed for comming to see me, in respect of the long time since our last companie: beside, hauing not forsaken his Pylgrims weede, wherein hee trauailed to the holie Lande, he came to acquaint me with the maruailes in his iourney.

See heere in breefe the whole truth of this Historie, and if the Kings Nephewes auouch otherwise, I say (my Lord) they lie falsely. In this respect, as well to protect mine owne honour as the Princes, I humbly desire your Maiestie, that our innocencie may be discided by Combate: for such is my hope in a rightfull cause, as I shall find some Knight to fight for me. The Lords of the Empire were altogether of the same opinion, and instantly desired the Emperour, to graunt his Daughter her lawfull request: whereto hee answered that he would take counsell thereon, and iustice should be doone her as it ought. Heereupon the Emperour went into his Chamber, and the Queene was brought to the Empresse her Mother, where the poore Lady was assaulted afresh, for shee was no sooner entred the Chamber, but her Mother thus beganne. I knowe not Daughter how badly thou hast beene counselled, that since the day of thine espousall to the Prince *Tarisius*, who loued thee so deerely, thou hast continued such hatred against him, that at length thou art become the onely cause of his death.

Madame, quoth the Queene, you speake your pleasure, but (in regarde of my reuerence to you) I aunswere, that I neuer thought it. Wherefore I intreate you to forbeare such speeches, and if you consider all things well, your selfe will be founde in greater fault then I. For contrarie to my solemne promise which I had made to the Prince of *Macedon*, you compelled mee to marrie with him: and if *Florendos* had the opportunitie, and in defence of his owne person hath slaine him, ought you then to impute the crime to me? With these words the Empresse held her peace, and sate conferring with the yong Princesse *Armida*: in meane while came the Duke of *Pera*, who had the Queene in charge, and conducted her to her Chamber, and afterward (by the Emperours commandement) he shut *Florendos* into a strong prison.

The next day, *Promptaleon* and *Oudin* came to the Pallace, where with great and audacious impudencie they came before the Emperour, saying. Why haue you not my Lord, prouided the fire to burne your Daughter, and her adulterer *Florendos*? Soft and fayre,[3] aunswered the good *Remicius*, bee not so hastie, I finde them not so faultie as your accusation deliuereth: for no other harme was committed then talking together, and because *Florendos* was disguised, is that a consequence my daughter must die? Nor will I encurre such infamous report, in putting such a Prince to death, without hearing how he can answere for himselfe:[4] you therefore my Lord of *Pera*, go fetch *Florendos*, that hee may answere to their propositions. The Duke obeyed his commandement, and brought the Prince so spent with extreame greefe, because hee had caused the Queene into such danger, as hardly he could sustaine himselfe, but after he had with great humilitie, prostrated himselfe before the Emperour, he began in this manner. Most mightie Lord and Emperour of *Greece*, maruaile not that with such heauinesse I come before your maiestie, when in steede of dooing you seruice according as my dutie commandeth me, I bring you cause of offence and displeasure. Neuerthelesse, I repose my self on your benignitie and princely iustice, wherein I must intreate you, to haue regard on the Queene your Daughters innocence, for the fault that is committed, if it deserue to be called a fault, was doone without the Queenes knowledge, or so much as a thought of the matter on her part, before it happened. Moreouer, there is none of so harsh iudgement or reason, but will consider what familiaritie and friendship, doth passe betweene Princes and Ladies in occasions of honour. Which may serue to answere the cause of my comming to see the Queen, being thereto bound by dutie and honest loue, wherewith in my yonger yeeres I faithfully serued her. And this I did without any iniurie to her honor, much lesse occasion of offence to the King, which hee would needes interprete in that sort, when with so good indiscretion hee came and assailed me.

These are fables, quoth *Promptaleon*, for the conspiracie and treason betweene thee and the Queene is so manifest, as euerie one knowes it. And if the Emperour doo not this day consumate your liues both together in one fire: he offereth the greatest iniustice that euer Prince did, and before the whole world wee will heereafter accuse him. Darest thou maintaine by Combate in fielde, saide *Florendos*, what thou with such brauerie affirmest in this Hall? that will I by mine

Palmerin d'Oliva: Part II 435

honour, quoth *Promptaleon*, and let the Knight come that dares aduenture, on this condition, that if I be the conquerour, the Queene and thou may bee burned as ye haue deserued, and the Princesse *Armida* declared not legitimate, and so disinherited of the Kingdome. Now hast thou reuealed thy villany, saide *Flo-*
5 *rendos*, and for the last condition doost thou follow the cause so earnestly, rather then by any matter of truth and equitie: but thou art deceiued in thine intent, and thy death (villaine) shall deliuer assurance of her succession. So please my Lord the Emperour of his grace, to prolong the day of Combate till I haue recouered some health: my selfe alone, against thee and thy Brother, will prooue ye false
10 Traytours, and that maliciously yee haue accused the Queene. The Emperour seeing the Prince so weake and sickly, and yet with so good courage willing to defence his Daughters wrong, resolued himselfe that shee was innocent. Remembring then his noble seruices in defence of his Empire, and howe iniuriously he denied him his Daughter: he was mooued in such sort as he could not refraine
15 from teares, thinking for vengeance of that offence, that heauen had iustly permitted the death of *Tarisius*, wherefore beholding *Florendos* with pittiful lookes, pronounced the sentence in this manner. You *Promptaleon* and *Oudin*, Nephewes to our deceased, deere, and beloued sonne, the King of *Hungaria*, shall mainteine your words in open Fielde, against two such Knights, as my Daughter and
20 the Prince *Florendos* can deliuer on their behalfe, and that within twelue dayes⸳ after this instant, one of which the Prince himselfe shall bee, if he be not furnished with another to his liking: alwayes prouided, that the vanquished shall be declared Traitors, and attainted of the crime of *Lese Maiestatis*, and so punished according to the exigence of the case. The two Brethren accepted these condi-
25 tions, beeing so farre ouercome with their owne pride, as they reputed themselues the most valiant Knights of the world. *Florendos* feeling himselfe so weake of body, would gladly haue demaunded a longer day, but the sentence being giuen, the Emperour likewise promising to appoint another knight in his steede, hee was contented, and committing all to the Emperors pleasure, was carried backe
30 againe to prison in such pensiuenesse, as he was iudged not able to liue til the combat day. The Queene likewise was kept in sure guarde, despayring howe she shoulde finde a Knight, that would aduenture on her behalfe in fight, because the strength and prowesse of the Challengers was so renowmed. Leauing thus these two louers in doubts and feares, let vs returne where we left before, to noble
35 *Palmerin*, that hee may bring them some better comfort.

CHAPTER XXVIII.

How Palmerin hauing staid with his Ladie fiue dayes, in so great pleasure as his heart could desire, fearing to be discouered to the Emperour, tooke his leaue of her, promising to begin the search of Trineus and Ptolome.

Polynarda hauing her Freend in her custodie, would not presume so farre vpon her selfe, or the faithfulnesse of her Ladies, as shee would suffer him to stay there in the day time: and doubting likewise least his comming in the night should be espyed, committed the whole matter in such trust to *Bryonella*, as they performed their ioyes without any impeachment. During these delights and amourous contentments, which these timorous Louers passed togither, the Princesse among other talke rehearsed to her Freend, how the King of *Fraunce* sent his Ambassadours to the Emperour, to treate on the marriage beweene her and his eldest Sonne, as also her Brother *Trineus* with his Daughter *Lucemania*. And howe importunate the Empresse had beene with her, discouering what honour and felicitie it should bee to her, to bee Queene of so great a Kingdome as *Fraunce* is. And trust mee my Lord, quoth shee, I know my Parents are so affected to this alliaunce, as if my Brother *Trineus* were come, I know no meane whereby to excuse my selfe. Alas Madame, quoth *Palmerin*, herein you may consider, if the Emperour by violent force constraine you heereto, what continuall greefe it will bee to your Seruaunt *Palmerin*? What torments? What tyrannous paines of strange conceit, may equall themselues with the verie least of my passions? nor can I any way bee able to endure them. The doubtfull feares of this misfortune strooke to his heart, with such an impression, as hee fell in a swoune betweene his Ladies armes, shee embracing him with such ardent affection, as the soule of the poore tormented Louer, feeling with what equall desire his Ladie requited him, receiued fresh strength into his languishing bodie, and beeing come to his former estate, the Princesse said. Alas my Lord, at the time I supposed to be in assuraunce with you, and to thinke on no imaginations, but new pleasures and delights, forgetting the regarde you haue long continued, in expectation of the wished fortunate houre, will yee bee nowe the cause of my death? Thinke you, that if loue bee so violent on your behalfe, it exceedeth not a thousand times more in mee? Beleeue me, you men make your vaunts of the great passions, feares and doubts you haue to offende your Ladyes, whom to serue loyally you haue especially chosen: but in no wise may these oppressions be compared to ours. Where is hee among ye, who hath experimented, howe great the paine of dishonor is, and can couer his extreame loue with dissimulation? What a death is it to constraine violence agaynst it selfe? to containe the piercing eye, and subdue an heart so affectionate, as bringeth death to the rest of the bodie: if shee shewe not some part of her desire, by lookes (the faithfull and secrete messengers)[1] to him she hath chosen, loueth, and wisheth? The torment of the will likewise, when one dare not come in presence, nor behold her fauoured, to languish, and yet may seeke no meane of helpe: all these insupportable miseries we poore Ladies must endure, beeing giuen by nature, or forced for a custome. Wherefore my Lorde, present not me with your passions, considering each thing as it ought, they may not be compared to the least of mine: for loue who hath ouermaistred me, reigneth with such resolute authoritie, as I must sooner die, then offer you anie wrong, seeing that as my Lord and Husband I haue elected you, and bestowed those fauours on you which are most desired, to wit, willing obedience, and that (then which) nothing is more precious.² Hauing then made you soueraigne of my selfe, the Prince of *Fraunce* cannot enioy an other mans right. And if my Father vsing his authoritie, shall enforce mee, although it be greeuous to mee, I will tell him what hath happened, and no menaces whatsoeuer shall alter mine opinion.

Palmerin seeing his Ladie so firme and loyall, was not a little ioyfull, thus answering. Doubtlesse my deare and most gracious Mistresse, hitherto I durst presume on my selfe, that by my manifolde loyall seruices, I shoulde one day deliuer recompence, for some part of the honours you haue done mee: but nowe I perceiue, that abounding in your graces, you depriue me of all meanes to acknowledge your bountie, which commonly men desire to shew by their obedience, nor shall I be able to deserue the inestimable value, contained in the simplest worde of your last most honorable promise.

Nowe the Princesse discerning by the Window, that *Aurora*, *Phoebus* his faire Porter,³ began to let foorth the morning light, and prouide way for his Maisters iourney, withdrew her selfe to her Chamber, and quicklie layde her downe by *Brionella*, who the better to hide her Ladies affayres, dissembled that she had a feuer *Quotidian*,⁴ by which meane shee compassed to keepe her Chamber, and entertained *Palmerin* as her selfe desired. All this while *Vrbanillo* brought newes from the Prince *Olorico*, who was so desirous to see the Princesse againe: as hee vowed not to depart the Cittie, before hee accomplished what hee intended. *Palmerin* who loued him as his Brother, was in great doubt howe hee shoulde safelye bring it to passe: till *Bryonella*, whose deuises were euer readyest, sayde. My Lord, the man beeing no way able to hurt you, of the lesse importance neede you make the matter: will yee see howe we will a little iuggle with the Emperour? Let it be sayd, that the Prince is Cozin to *Vrbanillo*, and the cause of his comming into this Countrey, was to seeke you: then because he vnderstandes how my Ladie loues the Dwarffe, his Maiestie (without anie doubt) will suffer the two Cozins to take their leaue of her: will not this deuise then shadow his seeing the Princesse? Without question, quoth *Palmerin*, I shoulde neuer haue inuented such a subtiltie, be it then as you haue determined, but with great policie, that the Emperour misdoubt nothing, for if he discouer vs, we are shamed for euer. Referre it to me, sayd *Brionella*, if I discribe not their kindred cunningly, neuer beleeue that a Woman can inuent a lie without studie.⁵ *Brionella* conferring with the Dwarffe, layde downe the platforme in such order, as the next day the Prince came before the Emperour: when *Vrbanillo* on his knee desired leaue, that hee might depart with his Cozin there present, to seeke his Maister, in whose search he woulde trauaile, till he heard certainly of his life or death.

Ah, *Vrbanillo*, quoth the Emperour, in such a luckie howre maist thou goe, as to finde both him and my Sonne *Trineus*, good leaue hast thou to goe when thou wilt. But when I beholde you both aduisedly, verie hardly doo you seeme to bee Cozins: for if there be anie alliaunce betweene you, it neuer came by the Fathers side:[6] and if it be by the Mother, the one was then married in *Barbarie*,[7] and the other in *Scotland*. Why my Lord (quoth the Dwarffe) rather had I die, then tell an vntruth before your highnesse: and with such protestations did the Dwarffe sooth his tale, as they of greatest doubt gaue credite to him. Hereupon the Emperour commaunded them to goe take their leaue of his Daughter, willing her to write to her Brother. Hauing obtained what they desired, they stayed not long in returning thankes: but went presently to the Princesse Chamber, where shee (aduertized of their comming) staid for them. Honourable salutations on each side deliuered, a Chayre was brought for the Prince, and he sitting downe by *Polynarda*, she thus began. Albeit my Lord I am verie loath to forgoe my Seruaunt: yet hauing found him so honest, and for the good will I wish to all his kindred, especially you, who haue enterprised to seeke his Maister and my Brother, I am the better contented to part with him.[8] If the Prince commended her beautie, when being ambushed[9] hee sawe her passe by:[10] what may wee imagine of his opinion nowe? For beholding her, the comfort of her long absent Freende, had called all her beauties togither, enriched with so many sweete and amiable graces, as hee coulde not repute her of humaine linage, but rather some Angell discended from heauen, to make the glorie of *Palmerin* more ample: whereupon, to deceiue the Ladies beeing present, hee returned this answere. Vndoubtedly Madame, if I and all mine had spent our soules in your seruice, we should holde our selues sufficiently recompenced, with the princely fauor you affoord our Cozin, which he is no way able to deserue. And perswade your selfe faire Princesse, that if he be your obedient Seruaunt, my selfe am no lesse, in all things that your excellencie shall please to commaunde mee: so that if there were not vrgent occasions to excuse my departure, it would be my onely content to remaine at your disposition. Yet such is my hope, that this greefe shall bee changed into ioy by a speedie returne, when wee shall bring the Prince *Trineus* and our noble Maister *Palmerin*. The sooner, the better welcome will they be, quoth the Princesse, for therin consisteth my cheefest comfort. And after many other speeches betweene them, she gaue him manie rich gifts, wherewith he helde himselfe so honoured, as if he had gained the Monarchie of *Asia*: so kissing her hande, the Prince with his newe Cozin, returned to his lodging. Now was it concluded betweene *Palmerin* and the Princesse, because the Empresse on the morrow would come to see her daughter, that he should depart the same way he came, wherefore the hower beeing come that hee shoulde passe the Wall, *Polinarda* thus spake. Nowe is the time (my Lorde) that you must leaue me, and I be forced to consent, because there is no remedie: but perswade your selfe, that with this parting begins my sorrowes. Yet if I knewe where you trauailed, my greefe woulde be the lesse, and my life prolonged with better hope: but beeing

vncertaine of your way, and knowing what misfortunes and daungerous perilles, may incounter you in vnknowne Countries, I knowe not howe I shall dissemble my torments.[11] Notwithstanding, sweete Freende, if your stay be long, send *Vrba-nillo* againe, to comfort poore *Bryonella*, and my selfe: for loosing the onely main-
5 tenaunce of our languishing liues, impossible is it but our spirits will soone forsake their miserable habitations. For Gods sake Madame quoth *Palmerin*, neuer talke of such a separation, for the remembraunce thereof, is death to me: and it so offendeth mee to see you in this perturbation, as I loose both courage and hope of well dooing. Continue then the humour you haue done since my comming,
10 that I beholding you pleasaunt, may be comforted thereby during the search of your Brother, which I hope will bee both short and sudden. Otherwise, before the earth bee readie for mee, I shall bee forced to take vp my endlesse Hostage.[12] So after many sweete kisses, and gracious courtesies passed betweene them, they tooke their leaue each of other, with such effusion of teares, as the verie inwarde
15 soule bemoned their departing. So with his Ladder of Cordes hee gotte ouer the wall againe, and came to the lodging where he left *Olorico*: then arming themselues, they rode away in great haste, because they feared to bee knowne by any.

Chapter XXIX.

Howe after Palmerin was departed from his Ladie, there appeared to him one of the Fayries of the Mountaine Artefaeria, who declared to him part of his fortunes following. And of a Combat which he and Olorico had against ten Knights.

Great haste in their iourney made these two knights, so that in short time they came into the Kingdome of *Hungaria*, where passing through a great forrest, they ascended a high Mountaine, at what time the ayre beeing calme and cleare, was suddainly obscured by manie darke Clowdes, and such outragious windes and rayne beganne, as they were glad to shrowde themselues vnder certaine Pine Trees neere at hande. Hauing there rested themselues a while, they behelde a verie thicke miste about a Fyrre Tree, and heard withall a verie terrible thunder: and the fogge somewhat clearing, they behelde a comely Ladie vnder the Tree, whereat they were strooke into no little admiration, yet *Palmerin* desirous to vnderstand the effect of this aduenture, made towards the Tree, when the Ladie began in this maner to him.

Palmerin d'Oliua, meruaile not at this accident, which hath happened onely for thy sake and profite. Heretofore I came to thee on another Mountaine, where I and my Sisters healed the woundes thou didst receiue by the Serpent.[1] At this time I am come to thee, to wish thee followe thy iourney begunne: assuring thee that they whom thou seekest, are yet liuing, and in the custodie of Turkes and Infidels: but before thou canst find them, thou shalt be deliuered from death by him thou hatest most. And after thou hast founde this fauour by him, hee shall ayde thee in restoring from prison and death, thy best and dearest Freendes:[2] and so I leaue thee to thy happie successe. Then suddainlie vanished the Woman away, and coulde not afterwarde bee seene againe, leauing *Palmerin* verie pensiue for what hee had heard, which he esteemed to bee true, because hitherto hee had found no lesse, all that the Sisters sayd to him on the Mountaine *Artifaeria*.

Returning to his companie, *Olorico* demaunded what Goddesse had talked with him, and what made him on a suddaine so cheerefull? Trust me my noble Freend, quoth he, the matter is such, as for all the Golde in the worlde, I would not but haue knowne, which *Vrbanillo* can better declare vnto you, then I am able: but because wee woulde meete no more strange aduentures in this Mountaine, let vs speedily set forwarde on our iourney. All that day they rode without any occasion to stay them, and the next day likewise till towarde the Euening, when they espyed tenne Knights comming before them, the formost of them leading a Ladie, who made verie greeuous and pitifull lamentations: whereupon *Palmerin* clasped his Helmette, desiring *Olorico* to do the like, because (quoth hee) for anie thing I see, we shall haue pastime with some daunger. The Prince did as his Freende requested him, and when the Ladie was come somewhat neerer them, shee framed her speeches to them in this maner. Gentle Knights, for Gods sake helpe me, for these Traitors haue forcibly brought me hither: and

Palmerin d'Oliva: Part II   *441*

to compasse their villainous intent, they haue murthered my Husband and two of my brethren. *Palmerin* without answering one word, approched to him that ledde her, and gaue him such a rap on the pate, with a Mace that hee carryed at his Saddle bowe, as with the stroke he fell dead to the earth, making him sure
5 not to escape, during the time that hee dealt with the other. *Olorico* had taken his carryre against another of them, whom he encountred so puissantly, as the Knight breaking his Launce, *Olorico* thrust his quite through his bodie, whereof *Palmerin* being glad, said.

To the rest noble Prince, for wee are sure two of them can doo vs no harme.
10 With such courage did these Gallants bestirre themselues, as in lesse space then halfe an howre, six more of them were slaine: for *Palmerin* neuer gaue stroke, but either he brake an arme, head, or necke. The two which were left, seeing the hard fortune of their fellowes, would bide no further daunger, but tooke themselues to flight with all the speede they could. When the Lady sawe her selfe
15 deliuered of her enemies, she came and humbled her selfe at *Palmerins* feete, earnestly desiring him not to leaue her, but that it would please him to conuay her to her Castle neere at hand: whereupon *Vrbanillo* alighting, holpe her to mount on one of the vanquished Knights Horses.

By the way shee rehearsed how hee that led her, had of long time loued her,
20 but because he was proude and of euill conditions, her Father could not like of the match, but gaue her to a yong Gentleman his neighbour, who was a verie vertuous and worthie minded Knight. This seemed displeasing to him that was refused, so that he brought nine of his kindred and Friendes with him, and hid themselues in ambush neere my fathers Castle, whereto I haue intreated you to
25 conduct me. They staying there thus vnknowne to any all the night, and the most parte of the day, till my husband, two of my brethren, and my selfe, tooke Horse, intending to go hunt at the Riuers side, they seeing vs far inough from any reskew, violently set on vs, killed my Husband and Brethren, and brought me away with them, the Traitour himselfe saying, that after hee had rauished
30 mee of mine honour, he would commit me to the like vsage by the Groomes of the Stable, who when they had satisfied their villainous willes, should put mee to cruell and shamefull death.

Beleeue me Madame, quoth Olorico, you are happily deliuered from such violence, and I thinke if all such like Ruffians were so serued as they are, Ladyes
35 might passe through the Countrey safely and without danger. By this time they were come to the Castle, where (because it was night) the Bridge was drawne, but when the guard heard that the Lady was come, it was presently let downe, and one of them ranne to the Ladies mother, who fearing shee had lost her Daughter, was now greatly comforted, especially when shee vnderstoode, that they which
40 had slaine her Sonnes, were likewise killed themselues: and certainely both the Mother and the Daugther reputed themselues so beholding to these Knights, as they knew not in what sort to entertaine them, whereby they might expresse their comfort.[3]

Beeing very honourably vsed by these Ladies, after supper they were conducted to their Chamber, where they reposed themselues that night, and the next morning came to take their leaue of the Ladies, to the no little greefe both of the one and the other. All this day they trauailed without any aduenture, till at length they came to a goodly fountaine, where they alighted to let their Horses pasture a while: and hauing refreshed themselues with certaine victualles that *Vrbanillo* had prouided for them, *Palmerin* laide him downe and slept, and *Vrbanillo* by him, finding themselues somewhat wearie with riding all the day. *Olorico* being a yong Prince, and desirous to see any strange occasion, walked about into diuers places, regarding heere and there the scituation of the Countrey, the Mountaines and goodly Castles builded vppon them. Hee was no sooner departed, but there arriued fiue armed Knights, two of them beeing they that escaped, when *Palmerin* so nobly deliuered the Ladie, they hauing that night past lodged at his Fathers house who ledde the Lady, and which *Palmerin* first killed with his Mace. And thinking nowe to reuenge themselues, had brought three of his Couzins in their company, and watched at the Ladies Castle the comming forth of the Princes, but their stomackes would not serue them to meddle with them there, wherefore they followed them all that day, till they behelde them seperated as you haue heard.

When they sawe that *Palmerin* slept, one of them (fearing least the noyse of the Horses should awake him) alighted, and drawing his Sword, came therewith to haue slaine him: but by good fortune there arriued a Knight, who had beene hunting there about all that day, and hee cried to him with his Sword drawne. Ah villaine, kill not the man that sleepes. The Traitour seeing this new come Knight so braue a person, beganne to be afraide, and therefore stept backe again a little, at what time *Palmerin*, by the knights crie, awaked, and seeing him so neere that thought to giue the mortall stroke, was greatly amazed, sodainely drawing his sword to defende himselfe, not hauing the leysure to put on his Helmet, by which occasion he receiued a small wound vpon his head. The Knight seeing the cowardly villainie of them that assailed *Palmerin* altogether, bestirred himselfe so worthily among them, as hee that gaue the wound died soone after vnder his sword. Whereupon the foure Knights diuided themselues, two against *Palmerin*, and two against him, who defended themselues so worthily, and had brought their enemies into such danger, as they two that before escaped, seeing to what danger the fight would tende, gaue the spurs to theyr Horses, and galloped away so fast as the horse could pace. By this time the prince *Olorico* heard the Dwarfes clamours, beeing greatly afraide of his maisters death, came running thither with all speede, when the Knight that had saued *Palmerins* life, sayde.

Noble Knight, well may you giue thanks to Heauen, in that your enemies, who thought to kill you sleeping, are foyled: for if God had not permitted my course this way, without all doubt you had lost your life. But since it hath beene my good happe to preuent your ominous fortune, I must aduise yee heereafter to beware of like hazard:[4] and may it please you to accompanie me to a Castle within two miles distance, your entertainment shall be good, and your wounds cured by a Ladie very expert in Chirurgerie. I accept your offer gentle Sir, quoth *Palmerin*, with right good will, as well to haue your friendly companie, as to sheelde you from any other such like villanies, who happily may seeke your harme for this noble fauour. So they rode on altogether, *Palmerin* remembring the wordes of the Fairie Ladie, and could not imagine who the knight should be that had so honourably preserued his life: this made him more to maruaile, that hee should be his enemie, whom (to his remembrance) hee had neuer seene in any place before.

To put him from these cogitations, *Olorico* ashamed of his absence in such a needfull time, came to *Palmerin* with these words.⁵ Certes my noble Friende, I am henceforth vnworthie to beare armes, seeing that in such daunger I left your companie: vnhappie that I am, might not former experience teach me what sodaine aduentures doo often happen to Knights errant? what punishment may be sufficient for my hainous offence? Leaue such speeches to Women, quoth *Palmerin*, for if we knewe before what would happen afterward, neuer should we fall into any inconueniences, but it is sufficient that we haue so well escaped, and let God haue the glorie for so happie deliuerance. By this time they were come to the Castle, and entring the base Court, the Seruants came to take their Horses to the stable: meane while the Knight himselfe went to aduertise the lady of the other knights arriual, saying. Faire *Leonarda*,⁶ I pray you vouchsafe the best honour and entertainment you can deuise, to two Gentlemen I haue heere brought with me, for I imagine by their rich armes and courtly behauiour, that either they are Princes, or discended of very honorable parentage. Trust me my Lord, quoth she, for your sake I will endeuor my selfe to welcome them as they ought.

And comming into the hall to salute them, after many courtesies deliuered on either side, the Lady seeing *Palmerins* armour besmeared with bloud, by reason of the wound he receiued on his head, saide. I feare my Lord you are very sore hurt, therefore the sooner it be seene to, the better ease you shall finde. Heereupon her selfe holpe to vnarme him, and afterward brought him into a goodly Chamber, where when shee had staunched his bleeding, and bound vp the wound, he was laide in a maruailous rich bedde prouided for him, she promising within ten dayes and lesse to restore him so well, as he would at pleasure trauaile without any danger.

For this kindnesse *Palmerin* returned her many thanks, and because hee might the better rest without disturbance, shee caused euerie one to depart the Chamber, her selfe likewise courteously bidding him good night. *Palmerin* beeing alone, looked rounde about the Chamber, to see if by any armes or deuise, hee might knowe the Knight that so happily deliuered him: at length, hard by his bed side he espied the Sheeld of *Frysol*, with the Sunne painted therein, which hee well remembred to be his deuise,⁷ whom for *Polynardaes* loue he hated, according as you haue heard in the former part of this Historie,⁸ which when he beheld, the teares trickling down his cheekes, he thus began to himself. I perceiue that the lady which saluted me on the mountaine is of excellent knowledge, for though the Knight bee my cheefest enemie, yet for the honorable kindnesse he hath this day shewed me, I wil forget all former iniuries, and loue him henceforth as hee were my brother, and what I could neuer compasse by rigour and force of Armes, I will nowe seeke to conquer by loue and courtesie. While he continued these priuat speeches, *Frysoll* opened the Chamber doore, and entred to bid Sir *Palmerin* good night, who not a little glad of his comming, said.

I pray you Sir knight, by the honourable loue you beare to Chiualrie, to tell me your name, and if heeretofore you were neuer in the Realme of *England*? My name, quoth the Knight, which hitherto I neuer hid from any man, is *Frysoll*, and two yeeres I remained in the Realme you speake of, with the Duke of *Gaule* in his Court. You remember then a Knight, saide *Palmerin*, with whom in lesse space then twelue dayes together, you had two seuerall Combats? Very true, quoth *Frysoll*, and some good reason I haue to remember it, for the fight on my behalfe was so dangerous, as but by the fauour of a Lady and a Squire, I neuer had escaped with life.[9] Nowe hast thou in thy custodie, saide *Palmerin*, the man that did thee such wrong, no more an enemie, but for euer thy vowed, true, and trustie Friend: and by the order I haue receiued, there is no man this day liuing, that shall withdraw me from thy friendshippe, because thou better deseruest it then any Knight in the world.

And hath by my meanes, quoth *Frysoll*, the onely flower of Chiualrie beene deliuered from death, and the resolute hatred betweene vs, vnited nowe with loue more then brotherlike? in happie howre went I on hunting this day, and fortune could neuer honour mee with more desired successe. For confirmation of this new alliance, hee ranne and called *Leonarda*, *Olorico*, and the rest, and before them all kissed *Palmerin* in the Bedde, to seale the perpetuall league of amitie betweene them.[10] Then was recounted their aduentures and hatred past, whereat euery one greatly maruailed, seeing this sodaine change to such surpassing loue.

Frysoll also rehearsed, how after the rape of *Agriola*,[11] the Duke *Crenus* his Lord, went to the Court, where hee aduised the King to pursue his Daughter, or to sende him in search of her, whereto he could not any way perswade the King. Moreouer, howe his Maiestie would haue kept him still in his seruice, whereto he might not graunt, for the promise he made the Ladie that came thither, whome after hee had brought to her Castle, hee trauailed by the Emperour of *Allemaignes* Court, where hee certainely vnderstood that *Trineus* and *Agriola* were not as yet there arriued, nor could any newes bee heard what became of them.

Yet during all these speeches, he concealed all his owne noble deeds of chiualrie in *England, Allemaigne*, and other places: so vertuous and debonaire was this gentle knight, coueting in nothing to extoll himselfe.[12] He forgot not likewise to report how that Lady cured him of a long and greeuous disease,[13] for which hee had so giuen himselfe to her seruice, as for euer he vowed himself her knight. *Palmerin* not a little contented with this discourse, said. I thinke the King of *England* would not sende his Shippes after his daughter, remembring her happinesse to come, beeing nowe the espoused wife to Lord *Trineus*, and the honour thereof had beene alreadie seene, but that the tempest of the Sea was too much their enemie. Then declared hee their troublesome time on the Sea, in what manner he lost them, and how he now trauailed to finde them againe. Since fortune hath so appointed (quoth *Frysoll*) that this loue and friendship should bee begunne betweene vs, to continue the same I will beare you companie, and will not forsake you till yee haue found them, may it like you to accept me for your companion.

If it like mee? quoth *Palmerin*, you neede not doubt thereof, and rather you then any man that I knowe, for which noble kindnesse I thinke my selfe most fortunate. In this manner beganne the concorde betweene *Palmerin* and *Frysoll*, which continued with vertuous and perfect constancie, as in the Chapters following you shal perceiue. Thus soiourned these Knights, there louingly togither,[14] till *Palmerin* being recouered and able to beare armes, they departed thence, leauing the poore Lady *Leonarda* in great heauinesse, because her friend *Frysol* left her so soone.

Chapter xxx.

How Palmerin, the prince Olorico, and Frysoll, went to Buda, thinking to finde the Court there, where beeing arriued, they heard newes howe the prince Florendos was taken, whom they went to succour with all diligence at Constantinople.

Frysol, because he would not haue his Ladie *Leonarda* too much discontented, made promise of speedie returne to her: which words somewhat pleasing her, he departed with his two friendes, and such quicke hast they made in theyr iourney, as within six daies after they arriued at *Buda*. There were they aduertised of the Kings death, whereof the Prince of *Macedon* was accused, and the Queene likewise: for which cause they were as prisoners conuaied to the Cittie of *Constantinople*.

At these tydings *Palmerin* was very displeasant, wherefore he sayde to his companions. Beleeue mee good Friends, my heart will neuer be in quiet, till I haue beene before the Emperour, who ought to bee an indifferent Iudge to *Florendos*, and hee is the onely man of the world, to whome most gladly I would do any seruice: therefore let vs make hast to *Constantinople*, to the end we may succour him, if he stand in any neede of our ayde. I am ready, quoth *Frysoll*, and let vs sette forwarde when you please. Heerewith hee remembred his father, to whom the Crowne by right appertayned, if *Tarisius* deceased without anie heire: whereto (by this meane) hee might attaine right soone. Perswading himselfe with assuraunce heereof, hee was now more earnest to be gone, and hastened his companions in such sort, as they came to *Constantinople*, two daies before the appointed time for the Combat. As they entred the Cittie, they met a Knight riding on hunting, whome after they had saluted, *Palmerin* questioned with all: if hee knew any thing of the Prince *Florendos* his misfortune, and what the Emperor intended to doo with him. Sir, quoth the knight, the Emperour hath resolutely set down, that the Prince and his daughter shall receiue their triall by Combate, against the two Nephewes to the deceased King: and furnished they must bee of their Champions, before the limitted time of ten dayes bee expired, and nothing else as yet is doone, to my knowledge. I thank you good Syr,[1] quoth *Palmerin*, it is happie the matter is no further forward. So leauing the knight, they praunced merrilie into the Cittie, and because it was too soone to take vp their lodging,[2] they rode to the Pallace, to knowe at full the certainetye of the matter: thus beeing all Armed, except their Helmets, which their Squires carried after them, they made a seemely shew as they rode, in that they were all three of one stature, and verye beautifull young Princes, they were especially noted, and followed by many Knights and Gentlemen, who imagined such persons went to the Pallace, for other matters then Courtlie dauncing.

These three companions beeing entred the great Hall, which was hanged rounde about with blacke veluet, in signe of mourning, they meruailed what might bee the occasion thereof: wherefore *Palmerin* falling on his knee before the

Palmerin d'Oliva: Part II   *447*

Emperour, and hauing humblye kissed his hande, thus spake. Most renowmed Monarch of the worlde, my Freendes heere and my selfe, within these fewe dayes, as we trauailed through the Realme of *Hungaria*, were aduertised that you keepe in pryson the Prince of *Macedon*, whom (so please your Maiestie to vouchsafe) I woulde gladlie see, in respect that hee is my Lord, as for the desire I haue to deale in the Combat appointed, if it like him to make choyse of me.

    The Emperour perceiuing *Palmerin* so faire, modest, and couragious, began with himselfe to conceiue well of him: and imagined that his Sonne *Caniano* was againe reuiued, so neere did he resemble him in countenaunce, stature, and all proportions of the bodie, wherefore hee returned him this answere. It shall not in ought displease mee, my Freende, to let you see him, to the ende you may conceiue no suspition of iniustice. So calling a Gentleman Vsher, commaunded him to conduct the Knight to the Towre where the Prince *Florendos* was: afterwarde enquiring of the Prince *Olorico* and *Frysoll*, what the Knight was that so hardily did enterprise the Combat. Dreade Lord, quoth *Frysoll*, he is called *Palmerin d'Oliua*, a Knight (in my iudgment) of the verie highest qualitie in the worlde. Then hee and the Prince *Olorico*, rehearsed the prowesse and deedes of Chiualrie by him accomplished, in *France, England, Allemaigne, Bohemia* and *Turkie*: which beeing heard by a *Bohemian* Knight then present, he came to *Frysoll*, saying.

    I pray you Sir, is this that *Palmerin* who kild the Serpent on the Mountaine *Artifaeria*, and brought the water from the Fountaine, which healed the good King *Prymaleon* Father to *Florendos*? It is he Sir quoth *Frysoll*, and no other. Then dare I say, gracious Lorde, quoth the Knight, that you haue seene the most valiant and vertuous Gentleman, that euer came in *Thrace*.[3] Heereuppon he discouered the noble victorie he obtained in *Bohemia*, against the two Gyants *Darmaco* and *Mordano*, whome hee slew before his woorthy Combat on the behalfe of *Dyardo*, Cozin germaine to the King and fayre *Cardonya*: against the Counte of *Ormeque* and his Cozins, in the Companie of Prince *Adrian*, and *Ptolome*.[4] Heereat were all the Princes and Knights present amazed, so that the Emperor himselfe saide.

    Well maye *Florendos* nowe aduenture the tryall of his cause, hauing the onelye Champion of the worlde on his side:[5] and in this manner they deuised of him, till his returne from the pryson againe. *Palmerin* entring the Towre, *Florendos* was astonied, because no person was wont to come see him: but chiefly when he sawe him on his knees to him, vsing these speeches. Alas my Lord *Florendos*, how greeuous to mee is your imprisonment? in vnhappie time did you knowe him, that hath caused you to bee so ill intreated. I pray you my Lord comfort your selfe and take courage, for heere may you beholde your Seruaunt *Palmerin*: who will be hewed in a thousand peeces, but hee will deliuer you from this miserie. *Florendos*, whose eyes and face were greatlie swolne with incessant weeping, onelye with the sorrow hee conceiued for his Ladie, knowing him to bee the same man indeede: was so exceeding ioyfull, as infinit embracings and kissings, woulde not serue to bewraye his comfort, for such gracious welcomes, reuerence and courtesie he vsed, as *Palmerin* (bashfull to bee vsed with such honour) said.

Vnseemelie is it my Lord, that you should thus much abase your selfe to mee: for (vnder correction) it ill agrees that the Maister should honour the Seruaunt. The poore Prince could not but still holde him in his armes, and with teares and meruailous affection, thus aunswered. Ah *Palmerin*, mine onelie hope and comfort in trouble, where hast thou beene? what fortune hath kept thee so long from mee? My deere Freende, howe manie yrkesome thoughts haue I endured, expecting thy comming? so that when I saw thou didst not returne, and I could no way heare what was become of thee: the verye conceite of thy absence had neere slaine me. Then carelesse what became of my selfe, being depriued of my loue and honour of my life,[6] I am fallen into these miseries farre exceeding death: which Fortune I see hath permitted, because I am perswaded that thou must deliuer me from all mishappes, and by thee shall I attaine my cheefest desires. Ah happie and fortunate hower, well worthie for euer to be celebrated with tryumphes, finding thee the onely cause of my good, whome long since I feared was consorted with the dead: but seeing thou art now so happilie come,[7] acquaint me with the fortunes that staied thee thus long, for very desirous am I to knowe them. *Palmerin* was so greeued to see him in such weake and sicklie estate, as hee could hardlie make any aunswere, yet striuing with himselfe, said.

My noble Lord, the time requireth now other occasions, heereafter shall I tell you the whole discourse. Graunt mee I beseeche you, without further intreating, that I may enter the Combat in your name, against one of those Traitours who haue accused you: for such is my hope in God, that I shall speede luckilie, and bring him to the end such a villaine deserues. With all my heart, quoth the Prince I am contented, assuring my successe so well in your vertues, as if fiue hundred of my Knights did enter the fielde for mee. And to the ende that without feare or doubt you maye take my cause in hand, I sweare to you by the liuing God, that since *Tarisius* espoused *Griana*, I neuer sawe her, till when the King came and found me with her: which was so short a time, as she had not the leysure to make mee any answer. True it is that I kild the King: but howe? I did it in respect hee was mine enemie, and abused my Lady and lawful wife. What though they were espoused togither? the mariage was not to be allowed, in that it was doone against her will: she beeing (as I haue said) my Wife, by solemne speeches before God married to me.[8] It suffiseth, said *Palmerin*, I haue enough. You shall likewise vnderstande my Lord, that I haue brought with me another Knight, who will gladlie aduenture the Combate on the Queenes behalfe, and such a one he is, as the other accuser will scant dare to stande against him: wherefore let mee intreate you to comfort your selfe, expecting our happy and fortunate successe.

Florendos falling on his knee,[9] gaue thanks to Heauen for this luckie euent, and hauing an indifferent while conferred togither: after *Palmerin* had aduertised *Frenato*, of his Sonne *Ptolomes* health, and that in short time hee had good hope to finde him, he returned to the Emperour, to whome making great reuerence, he saide. Now my gracious Lorde, I come to vnderstand your answer.[10] I pray you sir Knight quoth the Emperour, holde me excused, if I haue not welcomed you, as your nobilitie, bountie and highe Chiualrie deserueth: but after the Combat is ended, which for my part I graunt ye, what hath wanted now shall bee supplyed, so that your selfe shall rest contented. I thanke your Maiestie for this extraordinarie fauour, said *Palmerin*, and seeing the Prince hath committed his cause to my fortune, I beseech you send for the Kings Nephewes, that the appointed daye may not bee preuented by any further delayes. And if the Queene your Daughter be not prouided of a Champion, this Knight (poynting to *Frysoll*) my vowed Freende and companion, shall vndertake her cause, in that he came hither for no other businesse: and such good experience haue I made of his valour and hardinesse, as if by knightlie Chiualrie her right may be defended, assure your selfe my Lord, this is the man. I thinke, said the Emperor, she is not as yet determined of anie one, albeit full manie haue made offer of themselues: and for wee will expect no further, this Knight shall be preferred before all that come. I humbly thanke your Maiestie for this fauour, aunswered *Frysoll*: yet would I bee loth to presume too farre, before I vnderstand the Queenes pleasure. The Emperour caused him to be conducted to the Queenes Chamber, and his two companions with him, who desired to see the Ladies: where beeing entred, *Frysoll* humbly vpon his knee, began in this manner. Right noble and excellent Queene, so far through Christendome, is spread the report of your rare vertues and integritie of life, especially your innocencie in the crime wherewith you are accused: as from farre Countreyes I am come to be your Knight, if you will vouchsafe me such honour as to accept me. Assuring you, that vnder your commaundement, and in the companie of my noble Freend, who vndertakes the Combat for my Lord *Florendos*, right willing am I to aduenture life and credit. Alas Gentle Knight, quoth the Queene, this offer proceedeth from your courtesie and bountie, not by any vertue on my parte deseruing: for too contrarie hath Fortune euermore sette her selfe against me. But verie ingratefull might I bee accounted, and neuer be reckoned among Ladies of regard, if hauing taken such paines for me, I shoulde not accept you for my Knight, especiallie in so vrgent occasion. Therefore I entertaine you into this seruice, and I desire of God, that you may be as easilie deliuered from the charge you take in hand for me, as my conscience is cleere from the faulte wherwith I am accused.

I hope Madame quoth *Frysoll*, that my Lord your Father shall ere long perceiue, your loyall, perfect, and pure nobilite, which neuer can keepe companie with seruile and detestable treason. All this while *Palmerin* beholding the Queene, seeing her sweete face so stained and blubbered with teares: mooued with naturall remorse, was constrained to turne his head aside, to hide the teares that trickled down his cheekes.

The Queene likewise regarded him so earnestlye, as when she behelde him weepe, she imagined that one gaue a violent pull at her heart: which shee dissembled so well as she could, determining not to demand the cause thereof, vntill such time as the Combatte were finished. So taking their leaue of the Queene and the Princesse *Armida*, they returned to their lodging till the next morning, when the Emperour sending for them to the Pallace, where *Promptaleon* and *Oudin* staied their comming, the Emperour himselfe thus began. Now *Promptaleon*, heere maist thou behold two yong Knights, who speake the contrarie of that thou hast reported: wilt thou yet maintaine that my daughter hath committed treason, and hath beene disloyall to her Husband, thy deceased Vnckle? I will my Lorde, quoth he, and sweare by my Baptisme, for that cause she shal die the death: and if anie dare vndertake the contrarye, I am readie to prooue it by force of Armes. I thinke it conuenient, said *Palmerin*, my Good Lord, that no Combat should be graunted, without the presence of the accused. Immediatelie *Florendos* and *Griana* were sent for, and being come before the Emperour, *Palmerin* said to the Prince. How saye you, my Lorde, doo you permit in maintenance of your right, that I giue these false accusers such discipline, as their wicked and treacherous dealings deserue?[11] I doo, (quoth the Prince) and Heauen prosper thee in thine enterprise. What saye you Madame, quoth *Frysoll* to the Queene, doo you affoorde the like to me? Shee aunswered as *Florendos* before had doone, whereupon *Palmerin* thus spake to the accusers.

We two Knights will maintaine, that you both are Traitours, and that by couetous and greedie desire of rule, and to enioy the Kingdome, you woulde (against all right) disinherit the yong Princesse *Armida*: for which cause you haue shamefullie accused the Queene her Mother, to haue committed murder, and more then that, charge her with disloyall lubricitie. For if the Prince *Florendos* talked with her, when the King founde him in her Chamber: it was in no other sort then honor allowed, and according to the dutie of honest loue, wherein all Princes are bounde to their Ladies. Beside, if your King was slaine by the Prince, it was in defence of his owne life, and in repelling the iniurious speeches he gaue him: to approoue what I say, wee present our gadges to the Emperour, so please him to receiue them. The like did the two Brethren, desiring his highnesse to appoint the Combat presentlie, in the wide and necessarie place[12] before the Pallace. For (quoth they) wee will teache these vaine-glorious Strangers, the price of such iniurious speeches, spoken to those that know how to correct them.

I thinke (quoth *Palmerin*) thou shalt neede to teache thy selfe: but if thou hast learned anie newe dexteritie, practise it well thou art best,[13] for I can tell thee the time will require it. The good Emperour *Remicius* commaunded silence, and taking the gadges of these foure Knights, bad them goe arme themselues, saying hee woulde see the ende thereof before he tooke any sustenaunce.[14] The Duke of *Mensa*, and the Counte of *Redona*, auncient Princes of *Greece*, were appointed to bee Iudges of the Fielde: who commaunded two hundred knights to Arme themselues, for assurance of their owne persons.

Chapter XXXI.

Of the noble Combat in the Cittie of Constantinople, by Palmerin and Frysoll, against the two Nephewes of the deceased King of Hungaria, whome they vanquished, by which meane the Prince Florendos and Queene Griana were deliuered.

Promptaleon, and *Oudin* being departed the Hall, *Palmerin* and *Frisoll* taking their leaue of *Florendos* and the Queene, whom the Emperour caused to be shut vppe in their prisons againe: went to their lodgings to Arme themselues. The Duke of *Mecaena*, an honorable prince, discended of the most ancient race in al *Greece*, with many other great Lords went after them: and when they were Armed, the Duke would needes beare *Palmerins* Launce, and the graund Squire attending on the Emperor, caried *Frysols*. In this maner came they to the place appointed for the Combat, where the two Brethren were alreadie staying for them, the eldest thus beginning in mockage. Beleeue mee Knights, for men that shewed themselues so hardie in a Hall, mee thinks you haue beene very long Arming your selues. I thinke you came on your footcloth Mules to the Fields entraunce, for feare of falling to hurt your selues: but soone shall ye be taught better horsemanshippe I warrant ye. If there were in thee so much wisdome and exercise of Armes, aunswered *Frysoll*, as are high words and brauing behauiour, it would bee a little better discerned then it is: notwithstanding ere wee haue doone, I thinke they that came first into the Fielde will tarrie last heere, vnlesse some bodie for pittie carrie them out before.[1] Heerewith the Trompets sounded, and the Heraldes commaunded the Champions to doo their deuoire, which was the cause, that these hotte words were chaunged into deedes: and running fiercelie against eache other, they encountred with such puissaunce, as *Palmerin* cast *Oudin* foorth of his saddle, with a verie great wound on his left side, and *Promptaleon* was receiued by *Frysoll* so roughlie, as he fell backwarde on the crupper of his Horse, because hee was lothe his Brother should fall without companie.[2] The two Brethren, enraged to bee thus foyled at the first, came with their swords drawn to kill their aduersaries Horsses: so that they were constrained quicklie to alight, when they assayled each other with meruailous furie, for either side expected victorie, the one in hope of a kingdome, the other to saue their Freends liues.

Strange was it to beholde this violent fight,[3] yet the two Brethren seemed vnable long to holde out, for theyr Armor was so cut and mangled, and themselues so driuen foorth of breath, as hardly they coulde sustaine themselues: so that *Promptaleon* desired *Frysoll* to rest a while, who mooued with anger, thus aunswered. Nay Traytor, now shall I teach thee how to defende thy selfe, and not one minute will I graunt thee to trauerse with mee:[4] but will send thy soule to the Father of thy villainie,[5] vnlesse with speede thou denie thy slaunder. With these words he laid so many sounde strokes on him, as at length hee fell downe deade at his feete, which when *Oudin* perceiued: hee threwe his Sworde at *Palmerin*, and caught him fast about the middle, thinking that way to get him downe, but

Palmerin striking away his feet, caused him fal on his backe, and without attending for his reuolt, noblye stroke his head from his shoulders.

So comming to *Frysol*, he asked if he were wounded. No my Lord (quoth he) I thanke God, the greatest wound I haue cannot with-holde me to doo you further seruice, if so be you haue anie neede. Then putting vp their Swords, they demaunded of the Iudges, if any thing else remained to be doone, for deliueraunce of the prisoners. Nothing worthy Lords, answered the Iudges, and them will the Emperour nowe deliuer, with all possible speede. The good *Remicius* heartilie thanking God for this victorie, sente a Knight to the Champions, with request to come and lodge in his Pallace, as also that they should presently come speake with his Maiestie: yet could not the Messenger make such haste, but they were come foorth of the Fielde, the Duke of *Mecaena* and the Prince *Olorico* bearing them companie.

When the Knight had ouertaken them, hee saide. Returne woorthie Knightes to my Lord the Emperour, for hee would conferre with you, and haue your wounds attended by his owne Chirurgions. So turning again to the Pallace, they entred the Hall, where the Emperour meeting them, said. Right welcome are ye my noble Freendes, who haue so happilie defended my Daughters honor: for whose sake I shall make ye such recompence, as shalbe henceforth an encouragement to all Knights, to aduenture the Combat on the behalfe of anie distressed Ladye. Imediatlye in theyr presence, by sounde of Trompet hee caused to bee declared, that the Prince *Florendos* and the Queene *Griana*, were innocent of the trayterous accusation, and therefore in open Fielde bad they should bee deliuered: commaunding likewise his most expert Chirurgions to giue diligent attendaunce on the wounded Knights, causing them to be lodged in the most statelie Chambers of his Pallace. Afterwarde, hee suffered the bodies of the vanquished to bee buried, giuing expresse charge on paine of death, that none of the knights of *Hungaria* should depart from *Constantinople*, without his leaue: because hee woulde while they stayed there, prouide for the gouernment of the kingdom, as appertaining to his yong Daughter the Princesse *Armida*. The Empresse was so ioyfull for the deliueraunce of *Griana*, as shee had soone forgotte her Nephewes misfortune: the Queenes Ladies likewise were not a little glad, but aboue all, the yong Princesse *Armida*, her comfort could not be expressed, that her Mother was so graciouslie defended:[6] and now the Duke of *Pera*, who hadde the Prince *Florendos* in custodie, fetching him foorth of prison, said. My Lord thanke God and the Knights that fought the Combat for you: for by theyr meanes the Emperour declareth you absolued and set at libertie.

The Prince lifting his eyes to Heauen, thus began. Ah my God, how happie is the man that trusteth in thy mercie? doubtlesse, he that beleeueth in thy promises, shall neuer perish. Noble Duke, in all mine afflictions I haue euermore founde your speciall fauour: but if God prolong my life, I will not be vnmindfull of your gentlenesse.[7] In sooth my Lord, quoth the Duke, for so good a Prince, any honest minde would gladlie endeuour himselfe: and if I haue pleasured you

Palmerin d'Oliva: Part II 453

in anie thing, I did no more then my dutye, which christian amitie requireth of each other. So taking him by the hand, hee brought him before the Emperour, when falling on his knees, the Prince thus spake. If heeretofore dread Lord, both I and my people gaue our selues to trauaile, and aduentured desperate hazard in your defence: at this time I count my selfe sufficientlie recompenced, seeing your displeasure qualified, and the hard opinion you conceiued against me, chaunged into princely and honorable iustice.

Syr *Florendos*, aunswered the Emperour, when I remember the wrong you did my Daughter, leauing such a scandalous report of her, at the first time you came to this Cittie, I thinke you woorthie of the sharpest death. But placing mercie before rigorous iustice, I am desirous to let you knowe, that it liketh me better to be loued then feared: forgetting quite the offence against our person, the murder of our Sonne, without any regard to the murmur of the people, whose ignoraunce cannot consider of Princes mercie. Nor will I stayne mine aged yeeres with mine owne proper bloud, or the death of a Prince so noble, whereby I shoulde leaue to my following posteritie, as a Trophe of my life, an endlesse memorie of tirannous crueltie: but rather shall my cheefest aduersaries stop their mouthes,[8] with remembrance of my clemencie and princelie bountie, as your owne conscience shall well witnesse with me. You therefore my Lorde, the Duke of *Pera*, see that the Prince *Florendos* be lodged in the best place in our Cittie, and keepe him companie vntill his traine shall come from *Macedon*. With great humilitie the Prince kissed the Emperours hande, acknowledging his manifolde and princelie courtesies: desiring the Duke likewise before his departure, that hee might speake with the two Knightes, *Frysoll* and *Palmerin*.

Beeing brought to their Chambers, the embracings and gracious courtesies hee vsed to them, I am not able to vtter, and verie loth was hee to parte from them, but that hee woulde no way preiudise theyr health: wherefore giuing them the good night, he was conducted to his lodging, leauing *Palmerin* verie sadde and pensiue, remembring what the Queene of *Tharsus* had saide to him, howe hee should deliuer his Father from death, before he could know him, which was likewise confirmed by the apparition of the Ladie to him, vnder the name of his best and deerest of Freendes.[9]

O that the Heauens did so fauour me, quoth he, that I were the Sonne of the Prince *Florendos* and Queene *Griana*, then woulde I imagine my selfe the happiest man in the world. Yet can I not forget, that the Fayries tolde mee on the Mountaine *Artifaeria*, that one daie I shoulde bee Lord of all *Greece*:[10] but God is my witnesse, that I couet not such honor and preferment, were it not for the loue of my Ladie, to the ende her Father might not dislike of our contract. And hence will I not depart before I vnderstand the truth heereof, and to what ende this aduenture will happen. *Frysoll* on the other side, he deuised how to make himselfe knowne to the Emperour and Empresse: because he had good hope when himselfe might bee knowne, that his Father *Netrides* shoulde enioy the Kingdome of *Hungaria*. The Prince *Florendos* likewise coulde take no rest, for his great desire to recouer the Queene *Griana*. Such were the passions of these three Princes, eache one liuing in hope of good successe, which happens according to their expectations, as you shall reade heereafter.

Chapter XXXII.
How the Queene Griana with the yong Princesse Armida, went to visit Palmerin and Frysoll, and howe the Queene knew Palmerin to be her sonne, to the no litle ioy of the Emperour and the Prince Florendos.

Two daies after the deliueraunce of the Prince *Florendos*, the yong Princesse *Armida* deuising with the Queene her Mother, said. Me thinks gracious Madame, we are to be reprooued of ingratitude, in that we haue not as yet visited the poore wounded knights, considering how greatly we are beholding to them: I beseech you let vs this morning go see how they fare.

Alas Daughter, aunswered the Queene, hast thou the heart to bring me among such persons, when I am saide to bee the cause of thy fathers death? Then the Princesse breaking foorth in teares, replied. Beleeue me Madame, if you remember your selfe well, you are in as little faulte as I am, and so hath an honorable victorie declared:[1] but had you beene anye way culpable therein, yet nowe you ought to comfort your selfe, hauing had such a famous proofe of innocencie. In signe whereof, and to declare your thankfulnesse to those gentle Knights: it will bee counted a speciall point of courtesie, to visite them that ventured for you.[2] Go we then, said the Queene, seeing you thinke it so necessarie, and are so desirous. So accompanied with manie Ladies, clothed all in mourning blacke, they went first to *Frysoll*, greatlie thanking him for the paines hee had taken, putting his life in daunger, for the conseruation of their honors. Not to mee Ladie answered *Frysol*, ought you giue these thanks, but to him that onelye giueth strength to man: and if from my byrth I had continually trauailed in your seruice, yet your graces are such as I shoulde neuer deserue to bee reckoned among your meanest fauorites. The yong Princesse thinking her selfe greatlie bounde to him, woulde not giue him good morrowe with so little talke: but sitting downe on the bedde by him, taking him by the hand, began againe thus.

I knowe not Sir Knight, how the Queene my Mother will proceede in requitall of your noble seruice, for mine owne parte, not forgetting howe the Traytours threatned me,[3] whom (to their endlesse shame) you haue vanquished and slaine: I find my selfe so indebted to you, as it far exceedeth my power, to guerdon you with answerable recompence. *Frysol* perceiuing the yong princesse affection, whom Loue had caught somewhat within his reache, knewe immediatlie by her sober bashfull lookes, the cause why so manie sighes were coupled with her words, himselfe likewise suddainlie sicke of the same disease, returned this aunswere. Madame, if Fortune the Freend to your happinesse, would fauour mee so much, as the enterprise doone by your commanding, might sorte to an ende fitting my desire: I shoulde then accounte my selfe more then sufficientlie gratefied in this, that the act is agreeable to your liking, and the fauourable countenaunce of such a Ladie, is more then so meane a Knight as my selfe can merit.[4] Beside, from the daye that the high renowme of your prudence and gracious beautie, assured me of those exquisite gifts, wherewith nature hath plentifullie enriched you: I tooke such a religious vowe of bondage on mee,[5] as (considering your high calling, and my selfe so far inferiour) I shall neuer obtaine the fauour of libertie, if your benignitie, exceeding all things else, graunt me not that speciall grace. The Queene loth to trouble this forme of confession, withdrewe her selfe into *Palmerins* Chamber, where (as it fell out) shee founde no bodye but himselfe: by which occasion, remembring the loue she bare to *Florendos*, after shee had humblie saluted him, shee thus began.

Beleeue me gentle Sir, your knightlie Chiualrie hath shewed it selfe of such desert, as the Prince *Florendos*, for defence of whose honor, you haue not feared to aduenture your life, your daungerous woundes well witnessing the same, shall neuer deuise sufficient satisfaction. For in my iudgement it may well bee said, that goods, honor and life, hath beene restored him by your noble magnanimitie. Madam, quoth *Palmerin*, these wounds that for these two daies haue made me keepe my Chamber, thankes be to God are not so daungerous, as if occasion were offered, either for you or my Lord *Florendos*: but full well could I bee seene therein, to purchase entertainment into your gracious conceite. The Queene then sitting downe in a Chaire by him, and viewing him verie earnestly, his lockes of haire kept down by a gorgious wrought Cap, embroidered with Saphires and small Emeralds, shee behelde the mole on his face like a Crosse, which made her remember that her Son had the like, and in the selfe same place, when *Cardyna* tooke him from her and caried him to the Mountaine.[6] Heereupon she tooke greater occasion to regard his countenaunce, and imagining him verie much to resemble the Prince *Florendos*, immediatlie shee perswaded her selfe that hee was her Son. Which conceit mooued her to such alterations, as of long she continued silent, though *Palmerin* (in meane while) demaunded manie questions of her. These changes ouer-ruled by reason and discretion, shee commaunded her Ladies to depart the Chamber, and to goe accompanie the yong Princesse *Armida*: they beeing no sooner gone, but shee began in this maner.

Let me request Sir *Palmerin*, to know your Parents and the name of the Countrey where you were borne. *Palmerin* some what amazed at this demaund, was nowe in the midst of his onely desire, verilie perswading himselfe that the Queene was his mother,[7] wherefore he thus aunswered.

Madame, I sweare to you by my faith, that I knowe no Ladie this day liuing, to whom I woulde willinglie reueale more then to your selfe: but so contrarie was Fortune to mee in mine infancie, that as yet I could not get anie knowledge either of my Father or Mother, nor of the Countrey where I was borne. Yet thus I haue beene certified, that I was nourished on a Mountaine not farre from this Citie, which is called the Mount of Oliues, where (as I haue beene many times tolde) my Foster-father founde mee in rich swadling cloathes: and more then this, so please you to credite mee, cannot I bewray of whence or what I am.

O heauens (quoth the Queene) how greatly am I bound to prayse your infinite bountie and pittie, for so safe protecting mine infant, whom I forsooke so cruelly? Ah gentle Knight, see heere thy Mother, euen shee that commaunded

Palmerin d'Oliva: Part II 457

thou shouldest bee caried to the Mountaine: and the Prince *Florendos*, whom so lately thou diddest deliuer from death, hee (noble *Palmerin*) is thy Father. Notwithstanding my Sonne, I desire thee by the reuerent loue thou bearest mee, to conceale secretlie what I haue sayde, vntill I gaine the meane to dis-
5 couer my shame to the Emperour: yet such a shame, as neuer came greater good to thy Mother: nor can I nowe account the deede sinfull, in that my fortune hath brought mee such an honourable Sonne. So rauished with ioy was both the Mother and the Sonne, as neither coulde expresse their inward contentation, for such was their alteration as they reputed for an illusion or dreame, what was
10 most certaine indeed: such wonderfull comfort brought this vnexpected chaunce, wherewith the greatest indowments of honour or riches may not bee compared. Beeing in this extasie, the Mother for her Sonne, and the Sonne for his Mother: *Palmerin* hauing now againe recouered his forces, sayd.

My God I render thy name immortall thanks, in that I drewe my breath
15 from so noble and vertuous persons, as also for graunting mee knowledge of them in a time so fortunate: forbeare then (good Mother) to misdeeme of any thing, for I will discourse the matter in such sort to the Emperour, as forgetting all things past, hee shall receiue both the mother and sonne with greater ioy then you can imagine. But to the ende (Madame) you may be more certaine of your
20 sonne, see heere a Crucifixe of Golde, which was tied about my necke when I was founde, and hath of long time beene kept by the most perfect Lady in the world.[8] The Queene knowing it right well, after shee had kissed it manie times, answered. Assuredly my sonne, it is the verie same that my selfe tied about thy necke, when I was in the greatest greefe that euer distressed mother might bee: to
25 see her infant violentlie rapt from her, so soone as Nature had brought him into the world.[9] But if my mishap as then surpassed all other womens: yet now is it recompenced with such a fortunate houre, as no Ladie may compare her felicitie with mine. Ah, my sonne, by thee are my sorrowes chaunged into ioy, my dispaire into content, and from death it selfe am I brought againe to life: for if my
30 husbands hard hap made me despise life, now may you be assured how much I desire it.

Then declared shee, how to saue the Prince *Florendos* life, whose faithfull loue brought him to such extremitie by sicknesse, she aduentured her honor for his safetie, and entering the paradise of loue, bestowed that iewel on him, which
35 she most of all esteemed.[10] And so maist thou (quoth shee) report to the Emperour, yet in this manner, that not by carnall impudicitie I so consented: for God is my witnesse, that notwithstanding the perill wherein I sawe him, no perswasion could cause me yeeld him that especiall remedie, before he had first solemnly vowed marriage to mee,[11] which against all right was broken by the Emperours
40 commaundement.

Madame, quoth *Palmerin*, *Florendos* is of such valour, and his honorable actions so well receiued among men, that albeit he had made you no such promise, yet reason may excuse you in this matter. But if by promised faith, and to saue the life of so gentle a Knight (who happilie by your refusall might haue miscaried) you honoured the Temple of Loue with so sweete an offering:[12] among people of good minde, it ought rather to bee tearmed a vertue, then anie bad affection or vnlawfull lust. And therfore, Madame, comfort your selfe, for shortly I hope to assure your peace with the Emperour: and seeing I haue you for my mother, and the Prince *Florendos* for my Father, I feele my selfe free from any greefe or vexation, assuring you, that I will driue it to no further delay, but this morning will I confer with his Maiestie.

The Queene beeing fearefull, that her long stay should cause anie bad opinion, hauing kissed her sonne, gaue him the good morrowe, and so went to her Chamber, where shee found *Cardyna* her Gentle woman, to whom she shewed the Crucifixe her sonne had giuen her, saying. Tell me, I pray thee *Cardina*, doost thou remember that heeretofore thou hast seene this Crucifixe, and in what place? Beleeue me, Madame, quoth shee, I thinke I haue seene it before nowe, but in what place I am not certaine? Why? forgetfull creature, knowest thou not that this is the Crucifixe which was tied about my sonnes necke, when thy selfe did carrie him to the mountaine? In good faith, the Knight is hee, who fought the Combate for my Lorde *Florendos*. Nowe see the great mercie and bountie of our God, who preserued his life then, and from infinite daungers hath defended him hitherto. Notwithstanding, bee thou secret, and on perill of thy life reueale it to none, vntill the Emperour my Father be acquainted therewith. *Cardyna* was so ioyfull heereof, as shee must needes goe presently to see *Palmerin*, and finding the Chirurgions with him visiting his woundes, shee fetched a gorgious Mantle of purple Veluet broydered round about with Pearles, Diamonds and Rubies, as wel might beseeme the greatest Monarch to weare. As *Cardina* holpe him to put on this Mantle, she noted the marke on his face, which she remembred since the time of his birth: and in this maner goes *Palmerin* cheerefully to the Emperour, whom he founde conferring with his Lords and Barons, but his presence caused them breake off talke, imagining him the comeliest person that euer they sawe. The good olde Emperour *Remicius*, reioycing to see him in so good and able plight, demaunded of him howe he fared? Right well, quoth he, I thank God and your highnesse, readie to aduenture on any occasion shal like you to commaund me: and now am I come to aduertise your Maiestie of such matters as will not a little glad ye in the hearing, so please your grace to vouchsafe me priuate audience. Hereupon the Emperour commaunded euery one to depart the Hall, and they beeing nowe alone, *Palmerin* thus began. Dread Lord and mighty Emperour, till this time haue I frequented the Courts of manie Kings and Potentates, without desire of requesting anie thing, vntill this present: when faine would I request one boone of your Maiestie, the grant whereof shall returne you both profit and honor. My noble Freend *Palmerin*, aunswered the Emperour, what euer thou pleasest, demaund, and on my worde it shall bee graunted.

Palmerin with humble obeysaunce kissing the Emperours hand, sayd. In sooth, my Lorde, all that I haue to request, is onely to desire your highnesse, that

all offences committed by the Prince *Florendos*, and Madame *Griana* your Daughter, may not onely be forgotten, but also forgiuen. For thy sake *Palmerin*, quoth the Emperour, I forgiue all their offences whatsoeuer. May it then please your Maiestie, quoth he, to remember, howe when *Florendos* came to doo you seruice
5 during your warres agaynst *Gamezio*, because you denied to giue him your Daughter, hee was so sicke, as euerie howre his death was expected?[13] It then so fortuned my Lord, the Princesse your Daughter, acquainted with the cause of his sicknesse, to giue him some comfort, as also to defend so good a Prince from death: by gracious speeches shee gaue him some hope of loue, and such (for trueth) as before
10 they parted, a solemne promise of marriage was concluded betweene them. I know not the conditions of their agreements, but it seemed the Articles consisted on no difficult accorde, for each receyued of other the sweete desires of loue, in so much as that night was I begotten. And for a trueth, my Lord, I am the Sonne to the Prince *Florendos*, and Madame *Griana* your Daughter, who (as I vnderstand) by the
15 Empresse perswasion, against all right you compelled to marrie with the Prince *Tarisius*. *Florendos*, notwithstanding my Mothers wrong was verye great, hath continued so loyall, as hee would neuer accept anie other for his Wife, nor as yet will, but onely her. Nowe my Lord, that this matter may not seeme a fantasticall inuention, I can resolue you of the place of my byrth, which was in the Tower, where my
20 Mother remained prisoner by your commaundement, vnder the charge of a Ladie named *Tolomestra*: who to defende your daughters honor, caused me to be carried to a place not far hence, which is called the Mount of Oliues, from whence my surname is likewise deriued, and in that place was I found by a Countrey pesant vnder a Palme Tree, who in signe thereof named me *Palmerin d'Oliua*. My sorrowfull
25 Mother, hoping one day to see me againe, diligently noted diuerse markes I haue, and hung about my necke a golden Crucifixe, which this day I gaue her againe: and by this marke on my face like a Crosse, shee well remembers me to be her Sonne. In this respect my Lord, that your Daughters offence, was occasioned by true and faithfull loue, and hauing likewise promised to forgiue all causes of displeasure:
30 graunt my father nowe at length to enioy his lawfull Wife, that I beeing their Sonne, may not bee esteemed as illegitimate, the dooing whereof will renowme your name for euer, and loue tryed in so manie afflictions, shall be crowned with his long and desired reward.

The Emperour amazed at this strange discourse, could not imagine what
35 answer to make: wherefore hauing sitten a prettie while silent, lifting his eyes to heauen, hee thus began. O mightie King of Kings, onely good and full of mercie, I render thy name euerlasting thankes, for thy gracious regarde to the distressed Empire of *Greece*: for though in our last warres thou tookest away my Sonne *Caniano*,[14] thou hast at this instant sent me another, who well hath learned to
40 defend this state, from the proude inuading Gouernour of *Turkie*. Ah my Sonne *Palmerin*, right well doo I beleeue what thou hast said. And albeit thou hadst not shewen such probable arguments, yet doost thou so perfectlie resemble my Sonne *Caniano*, as easily may be coniectured whence thou art discended.[15] Whatsoeuer

thou demaundest my Sonne, is already graunted. And with these words the teares trickled downe his milke-white Bearde,[16] such was his inward earnest conceyt of ioy: and imbracing *Palmerin* in his armes, he called his Lords, who maruelled not a little at this euent, and thus spake the Emperour. See heere my Freendes your liege Lorde and Soueraigne, the Sonne of my Daughter *Griana*, and the Prince *Florendos*, how may you applaud the bountie of Heauen, prouiding for you such a noble Prince? The Lords all wondering at these speeches, came and entertained him with manie signes of honour: so that it is not registred in any auncient memorie, that euer King or prince had such suddaine and gracious welcome.

By this time these newes were spredde through the whole Pallace, and the Empresse hearing thereof, sent one of her Squires for *Palmerin*: when the Emperour taking him by the hand, brought him to her Chamber, saying. See heere Madame your Sonne, who by your meanes hath long time beene banished our Court: heereafter looke hee bee better vsed.

The Empresse surprised with incredible ioy, louingly embracing him, said. Welcome my Sonne, forget my heynous offence, when I would not suffer thy Mother to enioy the Prince *Florendos*,[17] which fault Heauen hath reuenged, with the death of my three Nephewes, whereof I nowe make no reckoning, seeing God hath sent vs such a gracious comfort. The Emperor on the other side welcommed the Queene his Daughter, which as yet hee had not doone since her comming from *Hungaria*. Lay by (quoth hee) fayre Daughter, these blacke garments, the witnes of your inward mourning, and decke your selfe presently in reioycing habits: for now before all my Lords of *Greece*, will I haue you espoused to the Prince *Florendos*. So departed the Emperour and the Princes, leauing the Queene with her Ladies, who disrobed her of her mourning garments: his Maiestie commaunding *Palmerin* to go seeke the Prince of *Macedon* his Father, accompanied with all the noble men of the Court.

In the meane while, he caused all the ornaments of black to bee taken downe, and the Pallace to bee hanged with sumptuous cloth of Golde: and gaue in charge to the Empresse, that the Queene, the Princesse *Armida*, and all the Ladies, should adorne themselues, as to receiue the verie greatest Prince in the worlde. Likewise he saide to all his Knights. Reioyce my good Freends with mee: for God tooke away my Children, and hath double restored them: for those that bee dead, hee hath raysed vs more. *Palmerin* hauing with him all the Emperours Knights, went to the lodging of the Prince *Florendos*, and by the way the Cittizens of *Constantinople*, Nobles, Marchants, and Artezans, welcommed him verie honourablie, making bonfires and Garlandes of tryumph, in euerie streete, crying. Welcome to this noble Cittie our newe Lord and Maister: and such cheerefull delights did they solemnize the time withall, as though it had beene the feast of Christmasse. *Palmerin* and his train being come to the Princes lodging, found two squires at the Gate, sent thither by the Emperour, the one holding a Horse verie richly caparassoned, and the other costly garments of cloath of

Palmerin d'Oliva: Part II   461

Golde, which he caused to be brought vp after him into the Chamber, where falling on his knee before the Prince, he said.

    Nowe come I my Lord to kisse your hande, not as I haue done heeretofore, but as becommeth a Sonne to his Father: for I am your Sonne, begotten on the Queene *Griana*, whom the Emperour will nowe bestow on you in marriage. *Florendos* was so rauished with these speeches, as hee was readie to swoune betweene *Palmerins* armes: but at length fetching a great sigh, saide. O celestiall Soueraigne, what am I, whom thou shouldest so respect, and lift to such surpassing happinesse? Ah poore *Florendos*, not long since the most wretched among men: what man may nowe compare with thy fortune, hauing such a knight to thy Son, and fayre Queene *Griana* to thy Wife? Go wee my sonne, quoth hee, embracing *Palmerin*, for it is no reason to stay, when such happie newes hath sent for vs. And credit mee, the verie first time I did behold thee, my heart was solicited with greater ioy then I am able nowe to expresse, which euer since made me coniecture, that there was more betweene vs then freendly alliaunce. Then was hee cloathed in the rich garments sent by the Emperour, and his Cozin *Frenato* in like maner: so comming on horsebacke, the Duke of *Pera* rode on his right hande, and his Sonne *Palmerin* on the left, with many Princes, Lords, Knights, and Gentlemen, ryding both before and behind them. In this manner came they to the Pallace, where the Emperour himselfe staied their comming at the Gate: and after they were alighted, the Prince making humble reuerence to his Maiestie, thus spake. Mightie and redoubted Lord, I knowe not how to render sufficient thanks, in that your highnes is pleased to honor me with your daughter, which is the thing I alwaies desired. Notwithstanding, I hope to shew such deserts heereafter, as neither shee shall be miscontented, nor your maiestie repent your gentle gift. Noble Lord, quoth the Emperour, well haue you deserued her, and mine Empire with her, in respect of your worthy sonne *Palmerin*, whome all *Europe, Asia,* and *Affrica* honours. Wherefore in the presence of all my Lords I will giue her to you, deferring the day of solemnitie, vntill the states of *Macedon* come, therefore Sonne *Palmerin* go for your Mother.

    Presently hee departed, the Dukes of *Pera* and *Mecaena* with him, and soone they returned, bringing with them the Empresse, the Queene, and his Sister the yong Princesse *Armida*, whom hee had schooled with such gracious speeches, as she had nowe forgotten her displeasure towardes the Prince *Florendos*, for the death of the King her Father. There openly in the Hall, by the Archbishop of *Constantinople*,[18] the Prince *Florendos* and *Griana* were affianced together,[19] to their no little contentment, as also to the good lyking of all the Princes and Lords of *Greece*, who spent the rest of the day in ioyfull disports and tryumphs.

CHAPTER XXXIII.
How Frysoll declared to the Empresse, that he was sonne to her Nephew Netrides.

All this pleasure of the Princes and lords of *Greece*, for so many ioyfull and vnexpected accidents, might not be compared with the pleasures of the Prince *Olorico* and *Frysoll*, who would nowe no longer keep his bed, in respect of his ioy for the good fortune of his friend, wherfore putting on his garments, and accompanied with *Olorico*, he came downe into the great Hall, as the Prince of *Macedon* was betrothed to his Ladie, when *Palmerin* stepping from al the rest, welcommed them with very gracious courtesie. After they had beene generally saluted, *Frysoll* came before the Empresse, and on his knee began in this manner.

Most excellent and gracious Madame, may it please you pardon mine offence in shedding the bloud of your kinsman. Notwithstanding, as the Law of iudgement and reason[1] exhorteth me, of two euilles I choose to take the least:[2] so did I rather thinke it good to bathe my handes in the bloud of mine owne Couzin, then permit him (by the Prince *Florendos* offence) to suffer open violence.[3] This speake I Madame, as being the Sonne to your Nephew *Netrides*, whom long since his eldest Brother disinherited, and banished him his Countrey to a little Castle,[4] where at this time he remaineth in good disposition. Now iudge which of these euents is most admirable, that of your noble sonne *Palmerin*, or this which I haue now rehearsed. But may it be (quoth the Empresse) that my Nephew *Netrides* is yet liuing? and can it be possible that thou art his Sonne? Trust me Madame, saide *Frysoll*, I haue tolde you truth, and by Gods leaue you shall haue more ample proofe therof within these few dayes.

Heereuppon the Emperour, the Empresse, *Florendos*, and *Palmerin*, with inexplicable reioycing, embraced *Frysoll*, not a little extolling theyr fortune, that such hardie knights were discended of their linage. Then *Frisol* rehearsed before them all, the three Combats hee had with *Palmerin*, and what great honour he woonne at the Tourney in *France*,[5] which report greatly contented the Prince *Florendos*, hearing the honourable Chiualrie of his sonne, nor would hee forget to ioyne therewith, his conquest on the Mountaine *Artifaeria*, with his Combats both in *Bohemia* and *Durace*.[6]

At these reports the Emperour somewhat amazed, saide before all his Lords. I beleeue my Friendes, that the maruailous and rare fortunes of these two Cozins *Palmerin* and *Frysoll*, with the strange aduentures they haue finished in their youth, promise greater matters in their following yeeres. Then an auncient Knight of *Hungaria*, who was named *Apolonio*, said to the Emperour, how in time past hee had beene Page to the Father of *Tarisius*, by which meane hee knew *Netrides* right well if hee might see him. And if he be yet liuing, quoth hee, in regard of his manifolde princely vertues, the Realme of *Hungaria* neede no better Gouernour, nor will the people themselues mislike of so good a change. Wherefore, may it so stande with your highnesse pleasure, to grant mee companie beseeming the cause: I wil do my dutie in the search of him, and bring him hither with mee to the Court. Willingly the Emperor consented thereto, and like order tooke the Prince *Florendos*, that *Cardyna* with her Brother and other Gentlemen, should go to the Mountaine of Oliues, and enquire for *Gerrard Palmerins* foster-father, *Marcella* his Wife, and *Dyofena* their Daughter. *Palmerin* seeing all things sort to so good ende, falling on his knee before the Emperour and his Father, saide. Seeing it hath pleased God to make me knowne for your Sonne, I will not conceale a matter from you, which concerneth mee very neerely, and although it be of great importaunce, yet will I not further proceede without your aduise. So discoursed he all his seuerall apparitions, while he continued with his supposed Father, whereby he was prouoked to go seeke the lady, who by fatall destenie was promised him: nor did he hide his troubles in her search, but therewith bewrayed that her name was *Polynarda*, daughter to the Emperour of *Allemaigne*, and his Wife by solemne vowes passed betweene them.[7] He declared moreouer, how he trauailed to find the Prince *Trineus*, whom hee lost on the Sea with the Princesse of *England*, and them hee would recouer againe, in respect of his faithfull promise to his Ladie. Notwithstanding, quoth he, if you thinke it conuenient, I would gladly sende to aduertise the Emperour and my Lady his Daughter of my present good fortune, that his Maiestie may confirme our priuate agreement, because I doubt the Prince of *Fraunce*, whose Ambassadours haue beene there to conferre on the matter, may otherwise preuent me of mine onely choyse. In like manner, if *Netrides* shall be founde to bee made King of *Hungaria*, and the Princesse *Armida* to be bestowed in marriage on Syr *Frysoll*, who is such a Knight in my iudgement, as well deserues one of the cheefest Ladies in the world.

So God helpe me my Sonne, quoth the Emperour, no reason were it to disappoint what thou hast so well contriued: for seeing things haue beene forepointed by fortune, meere folly it is for men to contrarie them. And because I haue heeretofore heard, that the Emperours Daughter is the flower and choyse Ladie among all other, whose vertues challenge the man beyonde compare in Chiualrie: I will sende mine Ambassadours to the Emperour, as well for the perfection of the marriage, as to comfort her in her despayres, with certaine assurance of our health and welfare, and so shall your intended trauaile not bee hindered. Notwithstanding, before you begin your iourney, you shall receiue the homage of all the Princes and Lords of *Greece*, as their liege Lord and supreme Gouernour, which beeing doone, I will likewise take order for my Nephew *Frysoll*, so soone as his Father shall come to the Court. Then calling for the Maister of his Horse, commaundement was giuen for speedie dispatch of messengers to all parts. So leauing the Emperour busied in these affayres, *Florendos* and *Palmerin* went to the Queene, who causing them to sitte downe by her, after shee had very graciously welcommed them, sayde.

I pray you tell me, which of vs three is most beholding to Fortune, the Father, the Mother, or the Sonne? Doubtlesse, who so considereth the condition of our aduenture, will finde it such, as seldome hath the like beene seene heeretofore.

And in sooth my Lorde *Florendos*, the greeuous torments I haue endured since the losse of my Sonne, and my great disloyaltie towards you by breach of my promise, I iudge may bee equalled with the burthen of mine offence. Neuerthelesse, if you esteeme not your selfe satisfied, let your noble regarde excuse what nature hath perfected, which is, to endure much more then as yet wee haue done. Madame, answered *Florendos*, in time of ioy remember not our passed misfortunes, but thinke what now is doone, our happy starres haue graciously furthered and limitted to this end, that my loyaltie, with the bountie and prowesse of our sonne, should be laid open to euerie iudgement. Heere had the Prince occasion to rehearse his afflictions in loue, endured twentie yeeres space and more for her sake, which *Palmerin* hearing, either fearing to offend them, or induced by modest bashfulnes, he went to his Sister the Princesse *Armida*, whose thoughts hee sounded by such subtilties and dissimulations, as he found the effect of her desires, which was to enioy Sir *Frysoll* to her Husband. He not a little contented heerewith, confirmed her choyse to be commendable, sealing the assurance thereof with an honourable report of his knightly deedes of Armes. Then the Emperour called for the Duke of *Mecaena* and the Counte of *Reifort*, as also his principall Secretarie, whom hee commaunded to write to the Emperour of *Allemaigne*, touching the marriage of the Princesse *Polinarda* and his sonne *Palmerin*, shadowing the secret agreement betweene themselues, and committed the rest to the discretion of the Ambassadours.

The Letters sealed with his great Signet, was deliuered to them that had the charge of this message, who could not so speedily departe from *Constantinople*, because the winde and weather was not nauigable.[8] Now had *Palmerin* promised *Frysoll* that he would speake to the Princesse his sister, and solemnely resolue vpon their marriage: wherefore (meeting with this earnest Louer) hee thus laboured to please him.[9] Trust me Cozin, I haue so surely imprinted your especiall generositie in my Sisters minde, as the carracters can neuer be defaced, but remaine more perfect by your speedie marriage. *Frysoll* reuiued with these newes, as all pretenders of loue may well imagine, offered to kisse his hande, which *Palmerin* would not suffer, whereupon hee thus proceeded. Ah my Lorde, howe am I more and more indebted to you? right wise was hee which saide, that affabilitie and liberalitie are continuall companions with noblenesse and magnanimitie. And though by al my seruices I cannot deserue the honour you do mee in accepting me for your Brother, yet am I so faithfully vowed yours, as the honours of my Father, nor loue of the Princesse your Sister, can seperate mee from your companie, vntill you haue founde your long desired Friende *Trineus*. And for this cause my Lord, I earnestly intreate you to hasten *Apolonio* towards my Father, for I will sende him to the place, where he shall be assured to finde him. *Palmerin* accorded thereto immediatly, and so labored with the Emperour, that the Letters were deliuered, and the oathes taken of all the *Hungarians*, they were sent home into theyr Countrey, with a Lieutenant appointed to gouerne them vntill the comming of *Netrides*, to whom *Frysoll* wrote the truth of all his fortunes, with earnest request of his speedie presence.

And to enduce him to the greater haste, hee feigned that many Princes laboured for the Crowne of *Hungaria*, and were in likelihood to obtaine it: all which was but to enioy the faire princesse *Armida*. The same day *Florendos* sent to the King his Father at *Macedon*, that hee should send the cheefest states of his Realme, against the day that *Palmerin* should be sworne the Prince of *Greece*.

Chapter XXXIV.

How Cardyna the Gentlewoman attending on the Queene, accompanied with her Brother and diuers other Squires, brought Gerrard, his wife and daughter to the Court, and what entertainment Palmerin made them.

Cardyna, with those that were commanded to keepe her company, in short time came to *Gerrards* house, whom shee found sitting at dinner with his familie. The good man was at first amazed, seeing such courtly personages enter his house, a matter esteemed rare among the persons dwelling on the mountaine: but seeing they came in decent and modest sort, not proffering any discourtesie, he entertained them very friendly, when *Cardyna* taking him by the hande, said. Good Father, are you the man that is called *Gerrard*? I am the same quoth he, gentle mistresse. You are then the man, aunswered *Cardyna*, that I seeke, and therefore I pray thee tell me what thou didst with a Childe, that twentie yeeres and more since, thou foundest in swadling clothes vnder a Palm Tree on this Mountaine: for certaine I am that thou didst take him home with thee to thy house? Ah mistresse, quoth the good old man, you haue killed my heart in remembring me of him, whom I loued deerer then any of mine owne. The infant of whom you speake, I founde not farre hence vnder a Palme Tree, for which cause at his Baptisme I named him *Palmerin*. From that time forwarde, I nourished him as hee had beene mine owne Sonne, till hee came to tall stature, and as he grew in yeeres, so did hee in vertuous and noble qualities, which made him not a little beloued in these parts, for when hee attended my Cattell, he tooke pleasure to course the Wolfe, Hart, Beare, Bore, and Lion, and oftentimes would kill them when him listed, which none of mine owne Children durst at any time aduenture.[1]

Ah sweete Mistresse, when I remember his many seruices, the dutifull reuerence and loue hee bare mee, I am readie to die with conceite of greefe, that it was my ill hap so soone to loose him. Yet came not this misfortune alone, for mine eldest Sonne, who loued him as he had beene his owne Brother, immediately went after him, and yet could I neuer heare any tidings of them. Notwithstanding Mistresse, if you know of whence hee was, I can shewe you all the clothes wherein I founde him. I shall be contented to see them, quoth *Cardyna*, but what will ye giue the partie that can tell ye where he is? *Gerrard* at these wordes fell on his knee before her, and with the teares trickling downe his graie beard,[2] saide. By my troth mistresse, if it shall like you to doo me so great pleasure, of all my substance I will giue yee the one halfe: or all my heard of Beastes, which ye saw feeding on the Mountain as ye came, beside my continuall seruice while I liue. Gramercies Father, sayd *Cardyna*, but call for your Wife and Daughter, and then shall I tell ye newes that will content you. As for him, whose friendly Parentes you were so long time, hee is nowe at *Constantinople*, and is the Sonne of Madam *Griana*, daughter to the Emperour: who commaundeth you three to come to the Court, that she may content ye for nourishing so well the noble young Prince. The olde man exceeding ioyfull, without ordering his affaires, or appointing his Seruaunts their course of labour, saide to his Wife and *Dyofena* his Daughter.

Make ye readie presently in your best garments, and let vs goe see that noble Gentleman: for all the Golde in the world cannot make me staie, nowe I haue heard so happie tidings. The good woman and her daughter, trickt vp themselues in their countrey fines,[3] and taking the rich swadling clothes, sette forward to *Constantinople* so merely, as sometime did the foster Father of *Paris Alexander*, his Wife, and their Daughter *Pegasis*, when they brought the Cradle and acoustrements of the infant royall, to the Cittie of *Troy*, after he was knowne by his Father King *Priam*, and Queene *Hecuba* his Mother.[4]

Palmerin being aduertised by one of the Ladies of Honour attending on the Empresse, that *Cardyna* had brought *Gerrard*, to prouoke greater contentation, he would needes goe meete him, and so went downe into the Court, accompanied with many yoong knights lately come to the Emperours seruice. *Gerrard* seeing this goodly troupe, among them all knewe *Palmerin* perfectly, wherefore alighting from his Horsse, and without giuing him in charge to any Page or Lackie, ran and fel downe at his feete, but *Palmerin* staying him in his armes, said. Father *Gerrard* and my deare friende, the God of Heauen bee euermore praysed, in that by bringing me to the knowledge of my Parentes, I haue the meane to satisfie your paine and trauaile for me, sauing my life in my yongest yeares, and nourishing me to the state of discretion.[5]

Ah my Lord, quoth *Gerrard*, I thinke in all the world is no man so happie as my selfe, hauing defended from perill so noble a person, therefore needelesse is it to make offer of money for your nurriture: in that I prize your golde and siluer lesse then drosse, such is my content to see you so well. *Palmerin* likewise, whose match might not be founde in courtesie and nobilitie of heart, louingly welcommed *Marcella*, and her daughter *Dyofena*, walking along with them vp into the Pallace, where in this sort hee presented them to the Emperour. See heere my good Lord, they that from mine infancie, with exceeding kindnesse and loue nourished mee: let mee therefore intreate your Maiestie so to conceiue of them, as their paines and charges may be sufficiently requited. The Emperour taking great pleasure to beholde them, saide they should continue in the Court with him, commaunding them to bee brought to his daughters Chamber, who entertained them verie graciously: but when they came to vnfold *Palmerins* little pack of cloathes, hardly can you imagine the inwarde ioyes of the Mother. For *Tolomestra* well knew the Scarlet mantle, which her selfe had all embroydered with curious knots of Gold, and all the other prettie trinkets, saying. Doubtlesse Madame, it cannot bee but that *Palmerin* is your Sonne: for well I knowe hee was wrapped in these cloathes, when *Cardyna* carried him hence to the Mountaine.[6] Then did *Gerrard* discourse before all the Ladies, in what manner hee founde yong *Palmerin* among the Trees: not forgetting to report euery thing, from that day till his departure without his knowledge.

Many sweete smiles did the Queene intermedle with her forced teares, hearing the sundrie daungers her Sonne had endured: and for the great loue shee bare to *Marcella*, she made her one of the Ladies of her Chamber, and gaue *Dyofena* a worthie dowrie to her marriage. As for *Gerrard* himselfe, the Emperor made him one of his cheefest Barons, and dubbed his Sonnes Knights, who proued afterward of hardie courage, as heereafter in the Historie you may perceiue. This done, the Emperour brought *Florendos* and *Palmerin* into his Treasurie, saying. My friendes, take, beare away, all is yours, dispose thereof as you please: furnish your selues with all needefull thinges, against the day of my Daughters marriage. Giue bountifully to the poore Knights, that they may likewise prepare themselues in readinesse, all which will redound to your perpetuall honour.

In sooth my Lord, answered *Florendos*, it is against all equitie and reason, that during your life I should presume so farre: well worthie were I of the sharpest reprehension, to vsurpe that, which by right appertaines to him who gaue me life and honour. When the Emperour sawe hee coulde not perswade them, hee sent a sumpter Horsse loaden with Golde, to the Prince *Olorico* and *Frysoll*: beside diuers other Iewels of inestimable value, that they might the better furnish their estate, against the solemnitie of the *Macedonian* Prince. On which day, these two Knights determined a Tryumphe at Armes, for the loue of their friende and companion *Palmerin*: who the same day should bee sworne Prince, and sole heire to the Empire. Vpon this occasion, and by his highnesse commaundement, the Heraldes were sent abroad to publish the Tourney, which should endure tenne dayes togither: with the excellencie of the prize to them, that should beare the honour of the Ioust each day. These disports so prouoked the Lords of *Greece*, as neither King, Duke, Countie, Barron, or Knight, that was able to mannage Horsse and Armes, but repaired to *Constantinople*, in such troupes, as though a new world had bene to be conquered.[7]

Chapter xxxv.

Howe the Knight that Florendos sent to Macedon, rehearsed to the King Primaleon the effect of his charge: and how Palmerin entertained his fathers Princes and Knights.

Florendos hauing sent one of his knights to *Macedon*, in verie short time the Messenger arriued at a Castle of pleasure, where as then the King remayned for his delight, with the Princesse *Arismena* his Daughter, to expell such contagious thoughts as daily troubled them, for the absence of the Prince, of whome they coulde vnderstande no tydings. The knight beeing come into the Kinges Chamber, where his Maiestie satte deuising with his Daughter: and setting his knee to the grounde, in this maner beganne his message. Right high and mightie King, I bring you the very straungest tidings, yet replete with ioy and speciall comfort, whereof your Maiestie neuer heard the like. My Lorde the Prince *Florendos* your Sonne, with humble dutie saluteth your excellencie, and the faire Princesse *Arismena* his Sister, certefying you, that the aduenturous knight Sir *Palmerin*, euen hee by whose meanes your health was recouered,[1] is his owne Sonne, begotten on the princesse *Griana*, Daughter to my Lord the Emperour, to whom hee is nowe betrothed, by the consent of all the Princes of the Empire, and Sir *Palmerin* your Sonne[2] shall be Emperour, after the decease of his noble Grandfather. The good king *Primaleon* olde and decrepite, was so surprised with these newes, as he imagined he heard some fantastical illuding voice, rather then matter of trueth and certaintie: with which inwarde oppressing conceite, his weake estate not able to support it selfe, beeing ouercome with ioy, doubt and suspition, as hardly could *Arismena* his Daughter keepe life in him, so often hee swouned with hearing this reporte, yet at length taking the Knight by the hande, he sayde.[3] My good Freend, God I trust will blesse thee with honour and prosperitie, for bringing mee the tidings I haue long desired. Nowe may I well say, that neuer anie Princes age was more beautified with happinesse, then mine is, hauing my Sonne allyed in such an house, and another Sonne excelling all the Knights in the worlde. But if the Heauens vouchsafe me so much grace and fauour, that I may once see him before I ende this life, it will be such sufficient content to mee, as then I force not though I liue no longer. Then calling for one of his Secretaries, to reade the Letters his sonne had sent him, and hauing heard the contents thereof, commaunded present dispatch of Messengers, to aduertise the Lords and nobilitie of his Realme, who likewise were so gladde of these newes, as each one prepared himselfe agaynst the day appoynted. The King hauing written Letters to his Sonne, as also to *Palmerin*, whom hee entreated to come and see him, gaue them to the Messenger, and withall such an honourable gift for his paynes, as well might content a greater personage.[4] He returning to *Constantinople*, effectually discharged his aunswere: and *Palmerin* reading his Grandfathers Letters, vowed to fulfill his request, and afterward to follow the search of *Tryneus*.

Now the day beeing come, when the Lords of *Macedon* shoulde set forwarde to *Constantinople*, they came to take theyr leaue of the King, who began to them in this manner. Ah, my good Freends, God is my witnesse, with what good will I would beare you companie, if my aged yeeres did not forbid me: neuerthelesse, let mee desire yee to behaue your selues in such sort, as if I were in person with ye, and honour Prince *Palmerin* no lesse then my selfe. So creating the Duke of *Pontus*⁵ his Lieutenant in this Ambassade, because hee was a braue and comely yong Prince: bequeathed them to happie Fortune in their iourney, commaunding a Knight to poste before them, that *Palmerin* might be first aduertised of their comming. On the same day as they should arriue at the Cittie, *Palmerin* accompanied with the yong King of *Sparta*, the most subtill and ingenious Prince of his time, (as well instructed in the manners and conditions of the auncient Kings his predecessours, especially imitating cautelous *Vlisses*)⁶ and diuerse other yong Princes and Knights, rode to meete the Lords of *Macedon*, at the Gates of the Citie. There alighted all the Lords to kisse his hand, which hee woulde not permit them to doo: but casting himselfe likewise from his Horse, embraced them all one after another. And mounting on horsebacke againe, entered the Cittie, which was so plentifullie stored with Knights and gentlemen against the tryumph: as the Prince *Olorico* and *Frysoll* were appoynted by the Emperour, to see the Lords lodged according to their estate, and to erect Tents and Pauillions without the Cittie, where the rest of their traine might be decently entertained.⁷

This choyse made the Emperour of these twaine in this matter, because in all his Court were not two more courteous Princes: beside, they were the onely men in the worlde, for affable and gracious entertaining straungers. All this businesse ended, and *Palmerin* deuising with the Queene his Mother, *Frysoll* beeing in his companie, sawe her enter the Chamber, to whom he had vowed his seruiceable deuotions: wherfore feigning some occasion at the windowe where the Princesse stood, he went and stood by her a prettie while, and at length entred into these speeches. Madame, as yet in all my life I neuer requested any thing of a Ladie, and now would I gladly moue one sute to you, (as to her that is the onely Mistresse of my heart) if I should not seeme ouer-bold in this petition: assuring you, that hauing obtained this fauour of you, you shall not commaunde anie thing, how difficult so euer it bee, but I will gladlie enterprise it for your sake. Beleeue me, Sir *Frysoll*, aunswered the Princesse, you speake but reason, demaunde then what you please, and you shall obtaine it: because I holde this opinion of you, that you will not request any thing, that shall in ought be preiudiciall to mine honour. A thousand thanks good Madame, said *Frysoll*, this houre I hope hath boaded mee good fortune, and this is my request, that you would so much honor me, as to permit me enter the Tourney vnder the name of your Knight, because I would enterprise nothing but by your commaundement. And this (in my iudgement) is such an especiall fauour, as I durst not presume to solicite you withall, without the graunt my Lorde your Brother *Palmerin* made mee: with this addition, that according to my deserts in the Tourney (if you can so fancie) to accept me as your

Lord and husband. With these wordes the Princesse was touched to the quicke, in that her desires were that way addicted: and her colour chaunging with her priuate conceyte, shee shadowed so artificially as shee could, and with wordes fearefull and trembling, thus aunswered.

In sooth my Lord, neuer was I mooued with any such sute heeretofore: but my Brother may so farre commaund mee, as what liketh him I would be loth to gain-say. As for your demaund, to enter the field vnder the name of my Knight, with right good will I graunt it: assuring you thereof with this Iewell, which henceforth so please you to weare, shall remaine as a token of my loue to you. So taking a goodly Emeralde from her finger, kissing it, with great courtesie gaue it him. Nowe am I sure Madame, quoth *Frysoll*, to haue part of the prize, seeing I shall aduenture in your seruice: nor is this ring of so little value, but when in the Combat I shall behold it, my forces will be redoubled, and newe life enter my fainting spirit. Moreouer I dare say, that neuer did the Ring of *Giges* bring him more honour, then this will to mee: for this could not profite or aduantage him, but onely by beeing inuisible.[8] On the contrary, I haue no pleasure but in your presence, nor shall I thinke my selfe at better ease, then when among Launces and Swordes I may labour for your loue. Then entred the Empresse, with other Ladies newlie come to the Court to see the Iousts: which brake of their talke, wherefore taking leaue of each other, they departed the Chamber.

Chapter XXXVI.
Howe the Duke of Mecaena, and the Counte of Reifort, arriued at Allemaigne, at the Emperours Court, and after theyr Ambassage dispatched, the Emperour sent backe with them to Constantinople, the Duke of Lorraine, and the Marquesse of Licena, as his Ambassadours.

Nowe is the day come, when the Fleete appoynted for the Ambassade to *Allemaigne*, should depart, wherefore beeing furnished with all things necessarie for their voyage, the winde and Sea likewise verie seruiceable: came to aduertise *Palmerin* thereof, to knowe if he would commaund them any further seruice.

Palmerin walked with them to the Hauen, and by the way gaue a Letter to the Duke of *Mecaena*, saying. Worthy Duke, present my humble dutie to my Lady *Polynarda*, and giue her this Letter, whereof I pray you bring mee an answere. And pleased God that I might go with you, neuer could any voyage better please me: therefore lette me intreate you returne so soone as possible may be. The Duke promised to accomplish his desire, and taking leaue of each other, they went aboord, where hoysing theyr sayles, with a merrie wind away they went, and arriued in *Allemaigne* sooner then expected. When they were come on shore, they sent a Knight before to the Emperour, that hee might bee acquainted with their comming, yet could not his Maiestie but maruaile at this Ambassage, because in all his time he neuer had the like,[1] and therefore thought this strange occasion would sort to as strange an ende. At length, to doo them the greater honour, he sent all his Knights and Gentlemen to receiue them, who conducted the Duke of *Mecaena* and the Counte of *Reifort* to the Pallace, and afterwarde to the presence of the Emperour. When the Duke entred the Chamber, hee saluted his Maiestie with great reuerence, yet not kissing his hande, because he came from as great a state as hee was: afterward he beganne in this manner.

Mightie and redoubted Monarch of *Allemaigne*, the most high and excellent Emperour of *Constantinople* my Maister, vnderstanding the losse of your Sonne *Trineus*, greeteth you with health and continuall happinesse. Giuing you to vnderstande, that within these fewe daies such good fortune hath befallen him, as in all his life time hee neuer had the like. And albeit in his last warre with the Turkes and Moores, he lost both Sonnes, Nephewes, and many great Lords of his kindred, and since that time hath beene troubled with the hard hap of his daughter *Griana*, Queene of *Hungaria*, and the sodaine death of her Husband the King: yet hath his Maiestie changed all these greefes into ioy, by knowledge of the good Knight Sir *Palmerin*, whose renowne liues as wel in Heathenesse as in Christendome, beeing now found Sonne to my Lord the Emperour, and therefore created sole heyre to the Empire. And the noble Prince *Palmerin* on his behalfe, humbly saluteth your imperiall maiestie, beeing the Lord to whom he is most affected in seruice, so that to finde out your Sonne *Trineus* and the faire *Agriola* Daughter to the King of *England*, whom two yeeres since and more hee lost in the East Seas:[2] he abandoneth all honorable preferments, vntill his

Palmerin d'Oliva: Part II 473

trauaile shall be finished: and he hath brought him hither before your highnesse. And hauing alreadie searched in many Kingdomes, at length hee vnderstood that they were liuing and in health, also that himselfe should in the ende recouer them,[3] hee thought it necessarie to acquaint you herewith, because he doubted of your extreame sorrow and heauinesse.[4] The Emperor astonied to heare the good fortune of *Palmerin*, as also the losse of his Sonne *Trineus*, could not subdue his passions, which mooued the teares to trickle downe his cheekes, with conceit of ioy and greefe together: yet shadowing his alteration so well as he could, thus replyed. In truth my Lorde Ambassadour, I alwaies imagined by *Palmerins* woorthie actions, that he was discended of noble or royall linage, and greatly it contenteth me, that he so happily hath founde the house of his discent, expelling altogether (considering his promise and prowesse) what hath beene long imprinted in my heart, concerning the losse of my Sonne *Trineus*. For so fauourable are the heauens to *Palmerin*, in all his enterprises and admirable aduentures, as one may imagine, that deeds of honor and account are reserued onely for him, cheefely the recouerie of my Sonne, which I hope hee will effectually bring to passe. And trust me, not without great and sufficient reason, doth the Emperour your Maister repute himselfe happie: this onely good fortune beeing of force enough to discharge his mind of all sorrowes and cares, that former occasions mooued him with all. Nor know I howe to recompence his princely kindnesse, honoring me with so good and happy tidings, but that it may please him to accept of mee heereafter, as his louing Brother and faithfull Friend. No other thing my Lord (quoth the Duke) dooth his Maiestie desire, and to beginne this amitie and alliance betweene you, hee requesteth that if his Sonne *Palmerin* hath heeretofore founde such fauour in your eyes, you would now confirme it, by giuing him to wife the Princesse *Polynarda* your Daughter, whom he will not marrie vntill he haue brought home your Sonne *Trineus*. As for the other conuentions of the marriage, these Letters shall certifie you: so kissing them, hee deliuered them with very great reuerence.[5]

And her shall he haue with right good will, sayde the Emperour, for a fitter husband can shee not haue: I thinke likewise her selfe will consent thereto, for the good opinion she had of him while he remained in our Court. But because I will not displease the King of *Fraunce*, who in like manner requesteth her for his Sonne and heyre, I will conferre with the estates of the Empire, and then deliuer you certaine answere. So the Ambassadours withdrew themselues to their lodgings, and the Emperor caused the Letters to bee read before all his Princes and Lordes, who could no way mislike of this marriage, and therefore great ioy was made through the Empire, in hope the Prince *Trineus* should soone be recouered. These ioyfull newes soone spreading through the Court, at length were brought to the Princesse *Polinarda* in her Chamber, who not able to conceale her sodaine ioy, ranne to *Bryonella*, saying. Sweete friende, nowe maist thou reioyce with me, in that our loues are nowe assured vs, whereof before wee vtterly despayred. Ah my *Brionella*, Heauen hath now confirmed our fortunate successe, in that my *Palmerin* is founde to bee the Emperours Sonne of *Constantinople*, whereof he hath certified my Lord and Father by his Embassage, and howe *Palmerin* hath heard tydings of my Brother *Trineus*, whom shortly he will bring home againe, yet not without thy *Ptolome* I hope. Therefore (my onely copartner in loue and feare) let vs abandon all greefe and sorrow, which greatly may preiudice our health and welfare: and nowe dispose our selues to a contented resolution of life, attending our long desired fortune. God graunt it may be so, quoth *Bryonella*, yet my minde perswades mee that wee shall not see them so soone as you weene. The Emperour hauing conferred with the Lordes of *Allemaigne*, who very well allowed the marriage of his daughter with *Palmerin*: determined to send to the Emperor of *Constantinople* ambassadours, for perfect confirmation of the marriage. And by generall consent, the Duke of *Lorrayne* and the Marquesse of *Licena*, were chosen for this present Embassage. Which being doone, the Emperour went to the Empresse Chamber, and sent for his Daughter *Polynarda*, who was so ioyfull of these happie newes, as she could scant imagine how to dissemble her content, when shee should come in her Fathers presence, yet shadowing it from any open suspect, after shee had saluted her Father with great reuerence, the Emperour, thus spake.

Daughter, you haue hitherto refused so many noble offers, as hardly can I permitte to mooue you with any other: yet once more will I trie you againe, in hope you will stand vpon no more refusals, but ioyne with me in opinion, as beyonde all other best beseemes you. The man of whom I speake, is noble *Palmerin*, of whose honourable behauiour you haue some knowledge, and for no other cause hath the Emperour sent his Ambassadours, aduise your selfe then what you answere, for all our nobilitie allow the match, and thereto haue generally subscribed their consent. The Princesse couering her inwarde ioy with modest bashfulnesse, thus answered.

If heeretofore my good Lorde, I excused my obeysance to your commandement, especially for taking a husband, it was onely for the promise I made to my Brother *Trineus*:[6] but nowe seeing it is your pleasure, and the good lyking of al the estates, as also that the marriage shall not be solemnized till my Brothers presence: I will not disobey your commaund, assuring your Maiestie, that more content am I to match with him, then any other you named heretofore. And this one speciall cause, that he laboureth to bring home my noble Brother, which Heauen graunt hee may: otherwise can I not marry, without verie great impeach to mine honour.

The Emperour well perceiued by the grace of her answere, and her countenance nowe nothing sadde or melancholie, that shee was nothing offended with this motion, wherfore he said. Happie may I count my selfe faire daughter, that among all the Christian Princes you haue chosen such a Husband: therefore apparrell your selfe to morrow in the best sort you may, for then shall my Lordes the Ambassadours see you. So departed the Princesse to her Chamber, and no more speeches were vsed till the next day, when the Emperour sent for the Ambassadours of *Constantinople*, and in the presence of the principall estate of the Empire, ratefied the mariage between *Palmerin* and his daughter. And for further confirmation thereof, promised to send his owne Ambassadours with them, to satisfie (on his behalfe) the Emperour, *Florendos* and *Palmerin*. For which exceeding gentlenesse, the Duke of *Mecaena* (in the Emperours name) thanked his Maiestie, earnestly entreating him to dispatch them thence so soone as might bee, because their charge was to returne with all possible speede. This resolution absolutely sette downe, the Emperour (for the greater honour) caused them to dine with him at his owne Table, and grace being said by the Lord Almoner,[7] the Duke of *Mecaena* desired his Maiestie, that hee might see the Princesse *Polynarda*: whereof hee made promise so soone as Dinner was done, when taking the Duke of *Mecaena* by the one hande, and the Countie of *Reifort* by the other, brought them to the Empresse Chamber, where they founde the Princesse in such sumptuous ornaments, and accompanied with such rare grace and exquisite beautie, as they iudged her rather an Angell then anie earthly creature.[8] And greatly was the Duke abashed at such a singular spectacle, not knowing how to frame his opinions: but hauing humbly saluted the Empresse, came to the Princesse, and on his knee reuerently kissed her hand, with these speeches. Let it not displease ye faire Madame, that I vse this honourable dutie to you: for I doo it in this respect, as to the gracious Ladie and Empresse (heereafter) of *Constantinople*.

By this meane hee secretly conueyed *Palmerins* Letter into her hande, for which the Princesse gaue him many deuout thankes, which were coupled with such magesticall gestures, as neither to *Nero* or *Galba* were done the like, no not by *Constantine* himself to the Pope.[9] And though the Dukes words had raised a sweete blush in her cheekes, yet could she with such choyse answeres excuse the same, as gaue greater countenaunce to all her behauiour. Then turned the Duke to the Emperour, and smiling, saide. Trust me my Lord, nowe doo I verely beleeue what hath heretofore bene told me of the Prince *Palmerin*, that hee is an especiall Iudge of the beautie of Ladies, for in mine opinion, hee hath chosen one without a second: and of her may truly be affirmed, what the Poets described of *Helena*, tearming her the Goddesse of beautie. With this rare Princesse to be matched an Husband so famous, well may be saide, the couple to be without compare: for the faire formed *Paris* may not be equalled with *Palmerin*.[10] So the Ambassadours departing, the Princesse withdrewe her selfe to her Chamber, where reading her friends Letter, her ioyes and pleasures redoubled, because shee might now boldly credite her fortune.

And before she would forget the inuention her spirite offered, shee presently wrote an answere: earnestly entreating him to hasten his returne, to abreuiate her languishing desires, which nowe made her life but a shadow of death. Hauing close sealed her Letter, shee sent it to the Duke by one of her most trustie Ladies, with diuers other rich gifts and presentes. The Duke of *Lorraine* and his companie readie, departed thence with the Ambassadours, and winde and weather seruing so well, they arriued at *Constantinople* the day before *Florendos* his nuptialls. Newes being brought heereof to the Courte, *Palmerin* accompanied with many Princes and Knightes, went to the Hauen, and at the landing of the Ambassadours, *Palmerin* embraced the Duke of *Lorraine*, and the Marquesse of *Licena*: and so ryding to the Pallace, beguiled the time with diuers discourses, where among, the Duke of *Lorraine* thus spake. Syr *Palmerin*, I alwayes did imagine, that those straunge aduentures atchiued by you, during the obscuritie of your yonger yeares, would in the end reueale your honourable parentage, and make your name for euer immortall: and were the Prince *Tryneus* with you nowe, for the verie best condition in the world would I not leaue your companie. Gentle Duke, answered *Palmerin*, if I did not perswade my selfe, how greatly I should comfort your minde, by recouering your Prince *Tryneus*: I should account my life so vnhappie, as presently I would desire my death. God graunt quoth the Duke, that you may finde him againe, for that will bee the greatest good that euer came to our Empire: considering the vertues, magnanimitie and speciall chiualrie, which is as currant in our yong Prince as in any other. And thus they spent the time till they came to the Pallace, where the Duke of *Lorraine* after hee had saluted the Emperour and the Princes, deliuered the message committed to his charge. Wherewith *Palmerin* was not a little pleased, considering what he had read in his Ladies Letter, which discouered the sorrowes shee endured for his absence: but being assured of her firme loyaltie, as also that shee was now promised him in marriage, his cares were the lesse, commaunding the Duke to be lodged neare his owne Chamber, that he might the better conferre with him of his Mistresse, whom he loued as deare as his owne life.

Chapter XXXVII.

Howe after the Prince Florendos and Queene Griana, were espoused togither, Palmerin was sworne Prince and heire of Greece and Macedon, by the consent of the Lords of the Empire and the Realme.

The Ambassadours of *Allemaigne* being now come, the Emperour was aduertised thereof, and considering that the Princes of *Thrace* and *Macedon*, had expected their presence for the space of sixe dayes, it was appointed, that on the morrow the Prince *Florendos* and *Griana* should be married. And the day being come of this long desired wedding, shee was cloathed in such rich and costly garments, as though she had bene still a virgine. But heere to set downe the sumptuous vestures of her, her husband, the Emperour, the Empresse, with diuers other Lords, Ladies and Gentlewomen, also the solemnitie and ceremonies, both at the Church and at the Pallace, would waste a great deale of time in vaine, and without any pleasure or profit to the Readers, and therefore I will let it passe vnder your conceit, and speake of such things as are most needfull.[1]

After that the Prince *Florendos* and *Griana* were espoused by the Patriarche of *Constantinople*,[2] the whole traine returned to the Pallace, where before the Gate was erected a goodly Theater, hanged rounde about with cloth of Golde, and therein were set manie Chaires and Canapies of estate. There was the Prince *Palmerin* placed in the cheefest seate, the Emperour and *Florendos* on the one side, and the Empresse and *Griana* on the other: then was *Palmerin* sworne Prince of *Greece*, with all the obseruations in such causes accustomed, by all the Lords of the Empire, from the Emperor himselfe to the verie meanest Gentleman. In like sorts did the states of *Macedon*, his Father *Florendos* first beginning, the Duke of *Pontus* next, and in the selfe same order as the Imperialistes had doone. This doone, the Tables were couered, and all the Princes placed according to their dignities: the Emperour and Empresse at the cheefest, the newe married couple at the second, and the Prince *Palmerin* at the third: so consequently the Kings, Princes, Dukes, Marquesses, Counties, and all the rest in order. As for the magnificence of the seruice, the royal order obserued, the Tryumphes, Momeries, Masques, and dauncing: would but fill paper with needlesse reports, in that your iudgements can conceiue thereof sufficientlie. But the Tabels beeing withdrawne, the noble Gallants went and Armed themselues, and entred the field which was appointed without the Cittie, and furnished with Scaffoldes and standings for the Lords and Ladies, where the afternoone was spent brauelie at Tylt and Tourney, with daintie chiualrie performed by *Frysoll*, *Olorico*, the King of *Sparta*, the duke of *Pontus* and many other knights. When night was come, and Supper ended, the Bride and Bridegroome were honorablye brought to their Chamber, and *Florendos* beeing alone with his Ladie, thus beganne. Ah sweete Madame, how manie sorrowes haue I endured, in expectation of this long desired houre? but hauing at length compassed my wish, I holde my selfe sufficientlie satisfied: giuing credite to the auncient prouerbe, *That true loue neuer wanteth his reward*,³ and that which I thought woulde haue beene my death, hath now returned me greatest honor and profit. In sooth my Lord, answered the Queene, I was euermore perswaded of your loyaltie: but where necessitie ruleth, reason hath no place.⁴ And if by the exteriour action I haue beene disloyall to you: yet my heart, which first of all I gaue to you, neuer diminished in will to loue you firmelie. For which *Tarisius* verie often reprooued me, notwithstanding in the ende, and by the sufferaunce of God I think, he receiued the rewarde, that the vsurper of another mans right deserueth. But why should we (my Lorde) call now to memorie things past, or remember matters which breed nothing but heauinesse? it is for you to excuse mee, and for my selfe to loue and honor you. All the points of theyr former diuorce debated betweene them, to such effecte theyr pleasures sorted in the end, as that night shee conceiued with a Daugther, which prooued to bee beyond all other in beautie. On the morrow the Prince *Palmerin* entred the Lists royall, because this daye he desired to Ioust: before him went the cheefest Princes of *Greece* on foote, and sixe Trompets to make him waye: he managing his Horse with such loftie voltages, as euerie one delighted to behold him. After he had doone his reuerence to the Emperour, hee gaue the spurres to his horse to encounter *Frysoll*: but when they came to meete, *Frysoll* threwe by his Launce and would not touch him. The like did the Prince *Olorico* and diuers other Knights, whereat *Palmerin* somewhat angry, strooke his Launce into the ground and brake it: and causing himselfe to be vnarmed, went vp to the Emperour in his standing, to see the pastime of the other Knights, and hee was no sooner come, but the Emperour thus spake to him. Bee not offended my Sonne, because you haue vnarmed your selfe without tryall of the Ioust: for the Knightes haue doone as best beseemed them, not to aduenture on their Lord and Maister. But if you would so faine haue some sporte with them, you must heereafter disguise your selfe from beeing knowne: otherwise I see you shall but loose your labor. When *Palmerin* heard these words, to the ende hee might somewhat delight the Emperour and the Ladies, especiallie such as neuer sawe his behauiour in chiualrie: hee was determined the last day of the Tryumphe to come suddainlie among them, and Armed in such sorte as none shoulde knowe him.⁵ In breefe,⁶ now is the last daye come, and the Emperour vnderstanding that *Palmerin* woulde enter the Listes disguised, went to his standing, and *Palmerin* secretlie entring his Chamber, found there a white Armour, such as the yong Knights was accustomed to weare, which his Dwarfe had there prouided for him: Armed himselfe presentlie therewith, and mounted on a Horse of the same colour, entred the Fielde on the assailants side, because he had heard, that this daie the King of *Sparta* would encounter the Duke of *Pontus*, *Frysoll*, *Olorico*, and other of the most gentle Knightes in the companie. The Emperour knewe *Palmerin*, among all the rest, and said to *Florendos*: what thinke you (Sonne) of the white Knight? Doo you know him? No my Lorde, quoth the Prince, I know not what hee is but me thought hee entred with a iollie countenaunce, it now remaines to see what hee can doo. At the encounter, *Palmerin* vnhorssed the Prince *Olorico*, afterward the Duke of *Pontus*, and fiue other Knights in his companie: then hauing broken his Launce, the Emperor sent him another by a Squire, willing him (for his sake) to imploy it as he had doone the other, but hee would make no answer because he feared to be knowne. Now was *Frysoll* much offended at the Prince *Oloricos* misfortune, wherefore hee would reuenge his Freendes cause: but the king of *Sparta*, esteemed a hardie and approoued knight, stept betweene them, and being cast from his horse, was so hurt with the fall, as he was caried foorth of the Field to his Chamber. Then *Frysoll* gaue spurres to his Horse, and encountred *Palmerin* with such puissaunce, as hee made him loose his styrrops, and had hee not caught holde about his horse necke, hee had fallen to the ground: but *Frysoll*, his fortune was so bad, as his Horse stumbling fel down, and his Maister vnder him, whereupon the Emperour said to *Florendos*, that the Knight in white Armour was his sonne *Palmerin*. In sooth my Lord, quoth the Prince, his fortune is good if it be hee, and well may he be esteemed the worthiest in the companie. The duke of *Lorrayne* hearing their talke, said.

Meruaile not my Lorde that Prince *Palmerin* hath so good successe, for in *Allemaigne* haue I seene him doo much more then this, and so much, as my Lorde the Emperour hath beene constrained to commaund them giue ouer. *Palmerin* seeing himselfe Maister of the Fielde, departed as secretlie as hee came thither, and so did the Emperour, *Florendos*, *Griana*, and all the other Ladies, among whome the yong Princesse *Armida* was most pensiue for her Freendes misfortune, so that by her countenaunce her inwarde affections might easilie be discerned. But on the morrowe, when *Palmerin* sent for all the Knights of name with whome he had Iousted, and euerie one knewe that hee woonne the prize of the last daies Tryumphe: the sorrowe of the Princesse *Armida* was conuerted into pleasure, reputing it an honor to her Knight to bee vnhorssed by her Brother.[7]

When the Emperour vnderstoode that *Palmerin* was iesting with the Knights, hee came into the Hall, and taking him by the hande, merrilie saide. See heere my Freendes the white Knight, whome you all were so desirous to knowe, but if you finde your selues agreeued with him, you must laye the blame on mee: for I was the onely cause of this enterprise, to the ende that hauing made open proofe of himselfe, you all might witnesse his valour and bountie, who after my decease must be your Lord and Gouernour.

Nowe were all the Knightes well contented againe, especially the Prince *Olorico* and *Frysol*: who though hee was somewhat brused with his Horse falling on him, came and embraced *Palmerin*, saying. In sooth my Lorde, the strength of your arme and Launce yesterdaye, hath giuen vs good experience of your vertue: yet our desire to reuenge our companions foyle was such, as had you beene our Father we shoulde not haue knowne yee. It may bee (said *Palmerin*) that yee made no reckoning of the Knight, who handled ye in this rough manner: or that you thought him not woorthie to beare a Launce, because you refused to Ioust with him the other daye. A kinde floute (quoth *Frysoll*, perceiuing how *Palmerin* iested) and queintlie deliuered, is this your recompence to the Knights that Freendly spared you? If I had knowne so much before, I should haue cryed quittance with you before wee parted. These words *Frisoll* spake in such sorte, as *Palmerin* imagined he was in choller: wherefore he thus answered. Good brother I pray you excuse mee, if in dooing my deuoire I haue offended yee: when you please I will doo penaunce for it, if it be but to please her, who cannot hide her good will towardes you.

    Heereuppon all the three Freendes embraced togither, taking leaue of each other till the next morning, when a newe Tourney was begunne againe, and continued for fiue daies togither: the honour whereof (to make shorte) happened to *Frysoll*, vntill the last daye, when a strange Knight came into the Fielde, and brought one with him resembling a Giant in stature, who with a Turkish Bowe and enuenomed arrowes, slewe and wounded verye many. So that *Palmerin* seeing the spoyle of his Freendes, was constrained to go Arme himselfe, and defying the Giant, ouercame both him and the Knight that brought him.

    Some haue reported this Giant to be a Monster, in forme of the *Centaures* that encountred *Hercules* at the nuptials of *Hippodamia*: but such rediculous follies are not heer to be inserted, and though the *Spaniard* in his Historie affirme it, yet carries it no likelihoode, wherefore leauing such impertinent discourses, let vs proceede as occasion doth lead vs.[8]

Chapter XXXVIII.
How the aged Knight Apolonio, found Netrydes, father to Frysol, and brought him to Constantinople, where hee was made Gouernour generall of Hungaria: and how Frysol espoused the Princesse Armida.

Apolonio hauing receiued *Frysols* Letters, and a briefe direction for his iourney, to the place where he should finde his father *Netrydes*: followed his intent with such diligence, as he came to the Castle where hee remained, and founde him sitting at the Gate, being newly returned from hunting in the Forrest. No sooner had *Apolonio* beheld him, but he presently knew him not, wherefore feigning that he and his company were Knights errant, saluted him, and demaunded if he woulde giue them entertainment for that night, because they knew no place of lodging neare at hand. *Netrydes*, who was euer of a most noble minde, welcommed them verie courteously, commaunding their Horsses to the stable, and themselues to be honourably feasted at Supper. All supper time, *Netrydes* verie earnestly eyed *Apolonio*, perswading himselfe that hee had seene him before: and *Apolonio* likewise well regarded *Netrydes*, neither daring to question with other for feare of misconceit.

In the end, *Apolonio* thorowly resolued that this was the man hee sought, and seeing two yong Gentlemen sitting at the Table by him, hee thus beganne. I pray you Sir tell me, are these two Gentlemen your Sons? They are Sir, answered *Netrydes*. Haue you not one more (quoth *Apolonio*) elder then these? Then *Netrydes* remembred his sonne *Frysol*, whom he iudged to be dead because of his long absence: wherefore breathing foorth a verie great sighe, saide. In trueth sir, I knowe not whether I haue or no, for it is long since I lost mine eldest Sonne by great misfortune, and hetherto hearde no tydings of him, nor know I whether hee is liuing or dead. By what mishappe I pray you Sir, quoth *Apolonio*, did you loose him? Whereupon *Netrydes* discoursed the whole circumstaunce, in selfe same manner as *Frysol* had reported: whereby he was now assured that *Frysol* was his sonne, and so without dissembling any longer, said. I can resolue ye my Lord, that hee is yet liuing, and in very good disposition. O my God (answered *Netrydes*) if these newes may be true, then am I the most happie Knight in the world. And so are you, said *Apolonio*, for hee is liuing, recouered of the disease hee had when hee departed from you,[1] and is nowe one of the most esteemed Knights in all *Greece*: so that hauing deliuered the Queene *Griana* from prison, which victorie hee obtained in the company of noble *Palmerin*, against the two Nephewes of King *Tarisius*,[2] hee is found to be neare kinsman to the Empresse. For which cause he hath sent, and I am expreslie hither come, to bring you with me to *Constantinople*, to the ende you may receiue your owne by right, I meane the principall regiment in the Realme of *Hungaria*. Ah Heauens, answered *Netrydes*, for euer be your prayses, in reuealing the wrong my Brother did, when causelesse he banished me my natiue Countrey: but that I may bee resolued in one doubt, I praye ye tell me, were ye not sometime of my Brothers Court? Yes truelie answered *Apolonic*, and to your Father I serued as a Page in his Chamber,³ nowe in respect of the manifolde courtesies I receiued at your hands, for euer I vowed my selfe to doo you anie seruice, desiring you with all possible speede to hasten your departure: for I greatlie doubt wee shall not else finde your Sonne at the Courte, because hee determineth to iourney with *Palmerin*, in the search of *Trineus* the Emperours Sonne of *Allemaigne*.

Heereupon *Netrides* leauing the charge of his house to one of his Cozins, departed with his Wife and his two Sonnes: making such speedie dispatch in their iourney, as not manie daies after the Tryumph, they arriued at *Constantinople*. Which when *Frysoll* vnderstood, hee went to meete them: beeing accompanied (for the greater honour to his Parents) with *Palmerin*, the King of *Sparta*, and manie other yong Princes. There were manie salutations and welcomes, giuen with great ioy by the Sonne to his Father, Mother, and Brethren, and by the Parents likewise to their Sonne, with such exceeding signes of loue, as you can better conceiue, then I expresse. After all these courteous greetings, they went to the Court, where began a fresh occasion of ioy, betweene the Empresse and her Nephewe *Netrydes*: shee then embracing him in her Armes, thus spake.

Ah my noble Nephew, how haue the Heauens blessed me with speciall fauour, in suffering me before my death to see my cheefest Freendes,⁴ whom I was out of all hope to behold againe: especiallie you, whose long absence from your Countrey, hath rather deliuered imagination of your death then life. Neuerthelesse, it is the prouidence of the highest, that after all the troubles you suffered in your youth, you might receiue the recompence in your age, by the knightlie honour and bountie of your linage. In sooth Madame sayd *Netrydes*, not so pleasant to mee is high preferment, as that I liue to see my sonne againe, for hauing contented my selfe in my little Castle, with a life free from offence and sollitarie, I did account it to exceede all other: but nowe seeing in my declining yeeres, the God of Heauen hath thought good that I might profit his people, the thought were base and abiect in me to make refusall.⁵ So long were they deuising on these and other matters, as the good night beeing giuen on all sides, the Emperour caused these newe come Freendes to bee conducted to theyr lodgings.

But on the morrowe when *Palmerin* came to bid the Emperour good morrow, he thus began. You knowe my Lord, that a Common wealth without a heade and Gouernour, (as for example) is the Realme of *Hungaria*, cannot long endure without sedicious tumults or rebellion: wherefore, vnder your Maiesties reuerende regarde, I thinke it expedient that my Sister *Armida* shoulde bee giuen in mariage to Sir *Frysoll*, because in nobilitie of minde and perfection of iudgement, hardly may so good a Knight be found, nor shee enioy a fitter Husbande, and so may the Realme lineallie discende, from *Netrides* nowe aged, to his noble sonne.⁶

The Emperour liked well of this aduise, wherefore the same day were *Frysoll* and the Princesse *Armida* espoused togither: to the good lyking of all, but especially of the louers themselues, whose secrete desires were now effectuallie requited.[7] After the feast was ended, *Netrides* instituted Gouernour of *Hungaria*, departed with his wife and Sons to his Kingdome: where hee was receiued very honorablie by his subiects, who had not forgot their former loue to him: and the vnnatural dealing of their king his deceased brother.[8]

Chapter XXXIX.
How Palmerin tooke his leaue of the Emperor, his father and mother, to follow the search of the Prince Trineus.

Certaine daies after the solemnitie of this honorable mariage was ended, betweene *Frysoll* and the yong Princesse of *Hungaria*, *Netrides* likewise gone to his seate of gouernment: all the Lordes and Princes of the Empire, except such as continuallie aboad in the Emperors Court, returned to their own homes, the like did al the strange knights that came to the tryumphs, except the king of *Sparta* and the Lords of *Macedon*. Wherefore *Palmerin* nowe remembring his promise to his Ladie, and how long he had stayed slothfull at *Constantinople*, determined to departe, and vnderstanding that his Father was with the Emperor, came to them with these speeches.

My gracious Lords, it is now three monethes and more, that I haue remained heere by your commaundement, contrarie to the promise that I made my Ladie: wherfore (by your leaue) I am nowe determined to departe hence, before the Duke of *Lorrayne* returne backe againe, that hee may assure my Lord the Emperour that I am gone to seeke my Freendes. My Sonne quoth the Emperour, vnwilling am I thou shouldest leaue vs so soone, but if the matter may not be contraryed, in respect you are bounde to her by faithfull promise, who aboue all other deserueth loyall seruice: I neither maye or will gaine-saye you, but intreate your returne so soone as may be. You shall therefore take with you a good companie of Knightes, who may preuent anie sinister occasions, which your trauaile in strange Countreyes happilie may offer: that my hart enioying life by your presence, may once more see you before my date bee expired.

I beseech you my Lord aunswered *Palmerin*, greeue not your selfe by my absence which shall not be long I hope, neither will the multitude of Knights auaile in my enterprise, for more by fortune then by force of Armes must the aduenture bee finished. Doo then as you thinke good aunswered the Emperour, in meane time I will cause prouision for your traine. *Palmerin* hauing now licence to depart, perswaded *Frysoll* so earnestlie as hee coulde, to abide at *Constantinople*, as well for the loue he bare his Sister *Armida*, as because he was loth to depart the new maried couple:[1] but all the circumstances he could vse, might not perswade him, for his religious vowe to his Freend, exceeded his affection to the Princesse: so that for a flat resolution, he aunswered, that nothing but death shoulde seperat their companie. *Palmerin* seeing *Frysoll* continue in his former amitie, and that the desire which conquers all men,[2] coulde not preuaile in his noble minde: reioysed greatlye thereat, determining to recompence his princelie kindnesse, if Fortune did not contrarie him in this enterprised iourney.[3] And fearing least anie newe occasion should arise to delaye this intent, dispatched presently his Letters to the Emperor of *Allemaigne* and his Ladie *Polynarda*, honoring his highnesse Ambassadours with manie sumptuous gifts. Hauing nowe ordered all his affayres, and euerie one beeing ready to mount on horsebacke, hee came to bid the Queene his Mother farewell, for well he knewe, that if shee could any waie hinder his departure, his iourney should be soone preuented.[4] The Queene with motherlie loue embracing her Sonne, saide. Ah my Sonne, hast thou beene so short a time with me, and wilt thou now leaue mee? trust me it is a point of great vngentlenesse, to deale so hardly with thy mother: but seeing the Emperour and my Lorde haue giuen their consent, my gain-saye will bee to little purpose. And nothing would it auaile mee to sette before thine eyes, the inconstancie of Fortune, her sleights and trecherie, commonly against great persons: when they are in the waye to prosperitie, honor and renowme. Therefore my sonne, I committe thee to the protection of Heauen, desiring thee to regard mine honor, which by thee ought to be defended, and now may runne in daunger of common reproche, in that the vulgar sort iudge after their owne humours, not according to the quallitie and estimation of vertue.[5] For this cause let thine returne be the sooner, as thou tenderest my life and thine owne good.[6]

All which *Palmerin* promised to doo, and so comming downe into the Court, founde there the Emperour and his Father mounted on horsebacke, who bare him companie two miles from the Cittie: where after many courtesies betweene them, the Emperour and *Florendos* returned to the Courte againe, where the Duke of *Lorrayne* stayed their comming, when taking his leaue likewise, went aboorde, and sayled with so good a winde, as in short time he arriued in *Allemaigne*, where hee was graciously welcommed by the Emperour, and especially by the Princesse his Daughter, to whome he reported the honorable behauiour of *Palmerin*, and howe he was sworne Prince of *Greece* and *Macedon*. Heereof was she so ioyfull, as neuer coulde shee be satisfied, with the discourse, making many demaunds to the Duke, as well of the Tryumphes, Tourney and disports, as also of the marriage celebrated at *Constantinople*: whereto the Duke returned such fitte aunswers, as nothing wanted to extoll her Freendes honor, yet without anye occasion of iealouzie to the Princesse,[7] wherto amorous Ladies are commonlie subiect.

But nowe returning where wee left before, you must note, that *Palmerin* beeing departed the confines of the Empire, entred his Fathers Realme, where in euery Cittie he was entertained with great tryumphing: especiallye in the Cittie of *Hermida*, where the Merchaunt dwelt that was *Palmerins* Maister,[8] for whom he sent, but hee was aduertised by his Wife, that her Husband was gone to the Sea, and his two Sonnes with him, wherefore he gaue her manie rich gifts, and Letters for his Maisters free enfranchise and libertie. At his departure from thence, he came to the place where *Vrbanillo* his Dwarfe was borne, whose father was there liuing a poore auncient Knight, and his Sister of as tall stature as *Vrbanillo*, whom *Palmerin* (at her Brothers request) sent to *Constantinople* to his Mother. And for the honor of the order his Dwarfes Father had receiued, hee gaue him the Village wherein he dwelt, and in the presence of the *Macedonians* put him in possession thereof, who not a little commended the discreete and liberal mind of the Prince.

From thence he iourneyed to the cheefe Cittie of *Macedon*, where remained the aged King his Grandfather: but how the Cittizens entertained him, and what honorable Tryumphes were made at the Court, I list not heere sette downe, because it would be more tedious then benificiall. As for his Aunt the Princesse *Arismena*, shee at his comming mette him in the base Court with all her Ladies: and as *Palmerin* fell on his knee before her to kisse her hande, she stayed him in her armes, saying. God forbid Sir *Palmerin*, that the Knight of the greatest fame in the world, should reuerence so simple a Damosell as my selfe: but rather am I bound by duetie to honor you, as the man by whose especiall vertues, our linage is this daie crowned with perpetuall memorie.

Fayre aunt, answered *Palmerin*, if before I knewe you to be my Fathers Sister, I deuoted my selfe to your seruice, with much more affection shall I desire to followe it nowe: wherefore suffer me (sweete Madame) to kisse your hand, as being the Ladie to whome I rest continually bounden. I beseech you my Lord, quoth the Princesse, to pardon me, for neuer shall a *Macedonian* Maiden be so reproued, but that she well knowes her dutie to her betters. At these speeches came the King of *Sparta*, the Dukes of *Pontus* and *Mecaena*, and the Prince *Eustace*, whom the Princesse welcommed with exceeding honor. After all courtesies ended, *Palmerin* said.

I vnderstand Madame, that the king your Father is crazed and sicklie: if it be so I am verie sorrie, I praye you therefore let vs goe see howe his Maiestie fareth. When you please my Lord, quoth the Princesse, for I thinke if heeretofore hee receiued health by you, Fortune may at this time affoord the like: and yet (as I haue read) there is no remedie for troublesome age, but onelie death it selfe,[9] which is the Gate to immortalitie, and endeth all diseases whatsoeuer. So entred they the Kings Chamber, and the Princesse going to the bed side to her Father, saide. My Lorde, see heere the good Knight *Palmerin* your Nephew, may it please you to speake to him, and bid him welcome? Well know I that he is right welcome to your Maiestie, were there no other cause then the happye recouerie of your former health, which his aduenturous trauaile heeretofore brought ye.

The good olde King, whome the palsie caused to shake and tremble: raysed himselfe vppe a little, and beholding *Palmerin*, with weake and feeble voice, thus spake. Come neere my noble Sonne, that these armes halfe deade may embrace thee, and my lips now drie and withered, may once kisse thee before I die. So holding him betweene his armes, and lifting his eyes to Heauen, said. O my God, for euer be thy name honored and praysed, in vouchsafing me to see my Sonne before my death. Ah sweete death, the ende of all miseries, and beginning of felicitie, now art thou welcome, forbeare not thy stroke, in that I haue now seene the honorable defence of my Subiects heereafter, yea such a worthie Freende for them, as neuer had they the like. Ah my Son, howe deerelie ought I to loue thee? how gracious hath thy remembraunce beene of mee? yet feele I my selfe so weake and feeble, as nature cannot prolong my life three daies. Alas, I knowe not which of vs twaine hath greatest cause to reioyce: eyther the Father seeing his Sonne, euen when he is readie to leaue him, or the Sonne finding his Father attending his comming before he giue vp the ghost. I hope my good Lord, said *Palmerin*, that you shall not leaue vs so soone, therefore take a good heart, and that no doubt will prolong your life. Alas my Sonne, quoth the King, vnweldie age hath so weakened my body, and euen dried vp my vitall blood,[10] as longer I may not liue: and had not hope to see thee lengthened my languishing daies, thou hadst found my bodie breathlesse, which yet sustaineth feeble life, onely by thy presence.

Now that I may leaue this worlde with content, and trauaile with better quiet to mine ende: tell mee (good Sonne) the whole matter concerning thy Father *Florendos*, with the perfect discourse of thine owne fortunes.[11] Then *Palmerin* rehearsed euery circumstaunce, both of his Fathers deliuerie, howe hee had maried the Queene *Griana*, and in what estate he left them both at his departure.

Chapter XL.

How the aged King Primaleon of Macedon, graundfather to Palmerin, dyed, and how the King of Sparta espoused the faire Princesse Arismena, Sister to the prince Florendos.

Not two dayes had *Palmerin* stayed in the Court of his Graundfather, but the aged king resigned his life to the celestiall powers: for which cause all the triumphes ceased, and generall sorrow entertained for the losse of their good king. *Arismena* who so reuerently loued her father, as in his life time she would not match in mariage with any one, because it was his will it should be so:[1] neuer shewed her selfe discontented therewith, but her Father beeing now dead, shee committed the whole affayres of the Realme to the Counte *Roldin*,[2] one appointed for that office by generall good liking.[3] With such honorable pompe was the funerall obsequies executed, and the Princesse gracious behauiour therein so especially commended: as the young King of *Sparta* became amorous of her, and discouered his mind to *Palmerin*, intreating him so to fauour the cause, as he might make *Arismena* his Queene.

Palmerin verie ioyfull of the Kings motion, in that he was one of the cheefest estates of *Greece*, acquainted his Aunt with the Kings request, and what an honor it was to her to be so matched. Nor was the Princesse heart so colde by her Fathers death, but seeing the yong beautifull King loued her so well, it began to warme againe: so that considering her owne estate, beeing nowe in yeares past foure and twentie, shee made some excuses by her Fathers late decease, but *Palmerin* perceiued by her modest yeelding lookes, that the heart consented, although the mouth was loath to vtter it. Wherefore the next day they were espoused togither, by which meane the King was more affected to follow *Palmerin*, as he determined before hee came from *Constantinople*, as well for the great kindnesse he found in him, as for his fauour in furthering him with the ende of his desires.

Now was the King more importunate on *Palmerin*, to accept him for his companion in his trauaile, who at length condiscended, although he imagined that his Aunte had rather haue her newe Husbande tarrie with her. The day beeing appoynted for their departure, *Palmerin* concluded with the King of *Sparta*, that hee should sende *Arismena* to *Constantinople*, there to stay his returne with her Brother *Florendos*. For her safe conduct thither, all the cheefest Knights that came thence with him were chosen, except the Prince *Eustace* Son to the duke of *Mecaena*. And *Palmerin* fearing his voyage woulde be longer then hee expected, commaunded *Vrbanillo* his Dwarffe to returne to the Queene *Arismena*: and if I stay (quoth hee) longer then a yeare from *Constantinople*, go then to *Allemaigne* with this Letter to comfort my Ladie, and take with thee thy Sister, whom I sent to the Queene my Mother.[4]

The Dwarffe (although he had rather haue gone with his Maister, then attend on Ladies) not daring to gain-say him, returned with *Arismena*, who in short time after arriued at *Constantinople*, where the Prince *Florendos* very

Palmerin d'Oliva: Part II 489

ioyfully receiued her, beeing not a little contented that shee was ioyned in marriage with the King of *Sparta*, yet his Fathers death hee tooke verie heauily. How welcome she was to the Emperour, the Empresse, and Queene *Griana*, I doubt not but you can sufficiently imagine, who continuallie comforted her till her
5 Husbands returne. Before *Palmerin* departed from *Macedon*, he established all things in due and decent order, creating the Counte *Roldin* Lieutenaunt generall for the Realme, commaunding as dutifull obeysaunce to him, as to their souereigne Lord the King his Father. Afterward hee tooke order that his shipping might be ready, because he would delay no longer the search of *Trineus*.

Chapter XLI.

Howe Palmerin and his companions sayling on the Mediterranean Sea, were taken by Olimaell, Admirall to the great Turke: and of their fortunes in Greece, where Palmerin saued Laurana the princesse of Durace.

Roldin established in the gouernment of *Macedon*, and the Ship readie which *Palmerin* had appoynted, hee went aboord with his vowed Freendes that would not leaue him, vz. *Frysoll*, the Prince *Olorico*, the Duke of *Pontus*, the King of *Sparta*, and *Eustace* sonne to the Duke of *Mecaena*. These sixe hauing sworne the search of *Trineus*, committed themselues to the mercy of the winds and Seas, not knowing where they should first take landing. Hauing thus sayled sixe or seuen dayes[1] togither, and the Seas nothing rough or tempestious: they went vp on the decke to see if they coulde descry any shore. And as they were deuising merily togither, they suddainlie espyed a great Fleete of Ships, which with wind at will made apace towards them: but because you shall vnderstand of whence and what they were, attend the sequell and you shall be resolued. The Moore *Olimaell*, as ye haue read in the former part of this Historie, after he had giuen the Princesse *Agriola* to the great Turke, entred into so great credit,[2] as in recompence of his gift, hee was made high Admirall of *Turkie*,[3] so that beeing renowmed for a Knight of Peerelesse desert, the Turke gaue him the charge of his great Armie, wherewith he shoulde continually disturbe the Christians. This *Olimaell* was Generall of this huge Fleete descried by *Palmerin*, wherat somewhat amazed, he called one of the Pilots, demaunding if hee knew the ensigne of whence they were. The Pilot had no sooner behelde them, but hee presently saide they were Turkes, and no way there was for themselues to escape, because he saw sixe light Gallies were made out to hem them in, and the rest came mainly vpon them. But *Palmerin* as a Prince experimented in daungers, thus spake to his companions.

Noble Freendes, where Knightlie force or bountie cannot auaile, it were meere follie to vse it, we are but sixe and all in one vessell, and farre wee cannot flie before we shall bee taken: I thinke it best therefore that wee vse sound dissimulation, and so expect when Fortune will better teach vs the way to recouer our losse, and reuenge vs on our enemies to their confusion. Withdraw your selues, and leaue me alone to talke with them, because I can well speake the *Arabian* language.[4] Yet thinke not that cowardise or feare of death makes mee vse these speeches: for in an action inuincible, hardinesse and knightly prowesse will bee esteemed as follie and indiscretion. Haue then patience my good Freendes, I hope that all shall turne to our good. No sooner had he ended his speeches, but hee heard the Captaine commaund them to yeeld, or else they should die. Die? quoth *Palmerin*, that goes verie hard: assure vs our liues and we yeeld, otherwise not. I promise thee, said the Captaine, neither thou nor thy companie shall haue any harme. So seazing vpon the ship, they brought it to the Admirall *Olimaell*,

Palmerin d'Oliva: Part II

presenting to him all the Knights they tooke therin: for which he hartily thanked them, saying.

Tell me Gentlemen and dissemble not, are ye Turks, or Christians? Sir, quoth *Palmerin*, seeing Fortune hath beene so contrarie to vs, you shall vnderstand truly what we are. We are Christians and poore Knights, searching aduentures to gaine honour and profit, in some Princes seruice be he Heathen or Christian. And because we can not now shew you what we are able to doo, so please you to suffer vs enioy our libertie, and graunt vs the benefite of our Armour, we will promise you loyall and faythfull seruice. *Olimaell*, who was by nature sterne and austere, seeing these sixe Knights so yong and braue accomplished persons, imagined theyr assistaunce woulde greatlie auaile him: wherefore he thus answered. Gentlemen, if you wil sweare to me by your fayth, that you will not depart from me without my licence, but will loyally imploy your selues in what I shall commaund, you shall haue your Armour againe, and I will not vse you as my slaues and prisoners, but as my honest companions and Friends. Which oath they all tooke to him, wherefore they were immediately armed againe, and remained in the Galley with *Olimaell*, who seeing their armour so rich and costly, esteemed them to bee of noble blood, and therefore caused them to be verie honourablie intreated.

So sayling on, at length they came neare the great Cittie of *Albania*, when *Olimaell* commaunded two or three Foystes, to goe vnderstand in what estate the Citie was, who were aduertised by certaine Fischermen, that the people were vnprouided of anie fortifications, so that winning the Port, the whole Cittie might easily bee conquered. These tydings caused them forciblie to enter the Hauen, where setting all the Shippes on fire, they went on shore, and murthering the Warders of the Gates, tooke the Cittie at the first assault, when *Palmerin* and his noble Freends (to their great sorrow) declared howe well they could skill of such affayres.[5] The Citie was ouercome, and the chiefest Citizens therein taken prisoners, the Turkes following their fortune, marched further, and came to the Cittie of *Durace*, where the faire Princesse *Laurana* abode, of whom *Palmerin* sometime was amorous: when he imagined by her excellent beautie, that it was shee who so often solicited him in his dreames.[6] *Palmerin* beeing there come on land, presently knewe the Countrey, wherefore hee sayd to his companions.

I nowe perceiue deere Freends, that fortune forceth vs from ill to worse, this speake I in respect of this Cittie, agaynst which wee must be compelled to fight: and not manie yeeres since, with the price of my blood I laboured to defende it.[7] But because the Dukes Daughter is so good a Ladie, as in my heart I reuerence and honor, I beseech you euery one imploy your selfe, to preserue her and her Ladies, and demaund them of the Admirall for our part of the spoyle.

While *Palmerin* thus conferred with his Freendes, *Olimaell* vnderstoode by certaine prisoners, that the Cittie was verie slenderly defended, and therefore no great maistrie to winne it quickly.[8] Yet at their first assault they were so valiantlie repulsed, as *Olimaell* and his men began to despaire of victorie: wherefore hee made open proclamation, that hee who first could enter the Cittie, should haue anie boone of him hee woulde request. *Palmerin* ioyfull of this promise, caused sixe scaling Ladders to be sette agaynst the wall, whereon hee and his Freends ascended, and on the wall cryed, the Citie is ours: wherewith the people within were so dismaied, hauing endured a long and furious skirmish,' as they all fledde out at the further Gate. The Turkes then burned the Gates on the Sea side, and entering the Citie, put olde and yong to the Swoord. But *Palmerin* and his companions feigning to pursue them that fled, ranne strait to the Pallace, at the entraunce whereof they found many Moores, who had taken the Duke, wherefore they went to finde the Princesse *Laurana*, who sate in her Chamber, well neere deade for greefe, because shee heard that her Father was slaine. Her hee committed to the custodie of the King of *Sparta, Frysoll, Olorico,* and *Eustace,* desiring them to comfort the Princesse, in that neither shee or her Ladies should fall into the Tyrants power, and so comming to *Olimaell,* on his knee he began in this manner. You knowe my Lord the promise you made to day, by vertue whereof because I first got ouer the wall into the Cittie, for my share I request the Dukes Daughter, and for my Freendes that followed mee, her Ladyes and Gentlewomen: for other spoyle of the riches and treasure we desire not.

Olimaell graunted his demaunde, charging his people on paine of their liues, not any way to offende the Ladies. In this manner was the Princesse saued, whereupon the Duke of *Pontus* presently went to her, and taking her by the hand, acquainted her with this ioyfull newes, whereto shee thus replied. Can it bee possible that *Palmerin*, who heeretofore ventured his life in my fathers defence, against the Count *Passaco* of *Mecaena*, should now become so familiar among Turkes and Moores? Hath hee so forgot his honour to God, that himselfe is not onely a vassaile to the enemies of his faith, but dooth likewise seeke their destruction that serue Christ Iesus? Be silent good Madame, aunswered the Duke, for if his name be knowne, we all perish: what hath beene doone, is for the safetie of your life, and our owne likewise, which hee hath obtained of the Generall of the Armie.

With these words she was somewhat pacified, and the old cinders of loue, which nowe began to spreade abroade, caused her to returne this answere. In sooth, my Lord, seeing I am become *Palmerins* prisoner, I thinke my honour in better assuraunce, and my Fathers death is the lesse greeuous to mee, in that this matter may sort to better effecte then I can conceiue. By this time was *Palmerin* come to her, who intreated her to keepe all things secretly, for hee woulde endure a thousand deathes, before shee should be any way dishonoured. In time (quoth he) wee may be deliuered from these Hell-houndes: as for you and your Ladyes, the Admirall hath openly commaunded, that you be reuerently vsed.

A thousand thanks my Lord, quoth the Princesse, and seeing matters are so come to passe, yet do I reioyce that I fell into your power. The Citie of *Durace* left in the same state as *Albania* was, the Turkes went all aboorde, taking no prisoners thence, but *Laurana* and her Ladies, whome *Olimaell* intended to giue

Palmerin d'Oliva: Part II   493

to the great Turke. So passing along the Coast of *Thessalie*,[10] they spoyled many Citties on the Sea side, tooke the King and many noble men: so that nowe they were stored with a number of Christian prisoners. Now *Olimaell* feared, that the Christian Princes hearing what spoyle he made in their Dominions, woulde rayse a mightie power agaynst him, wherefore hee gaue charge to his Pilots, to order their course towards the Cittie of *Tubant*, where as then the great Turke kept his Court.

    The King of *Thessalie*, three dayes before his taking, sent his Queene (who was great with Childe) to one of his Castels, a good dayes iourney from the Sea: but when shee heard her Husbandes misfortune, the greefe shee conceyued caused her presently to fall in trauell, when shee was deliuered of a goodly Daughter, named *Francelina*. At this time the three Magical Sisters, who appeared to *Palmerin* on the Mountaine *Artifaeria*, and one of them afterwarde in his going to *Buda*,[11] made theyr aboode in an Isle thereby named *Carderia*. When they (by their hidden Philosophie) heard how the King was taken, and should be kept in perpetuall prison, without the helpe of his Daughter which was newly borne: they concluded to frame such an enchauntment, as mauger the Turke and his power, as hee that would not deigne to kisse his shooe, should be deliuered from imprisonment. Heereupon the yongest of these three Sisters, went to the Castell where the wofull Queene remained,[12] where shee was verie honourablie entertained, because the Queene desired to know, if the King her Husband was dead or aliue, and if any hope might be expected of his deliuerance.

    The Damosell Enchauntresse aduertised the Queene, that in departing with her Daughter *Francelina*, the King her Husband should enioy his libertie, and in time to come, she should be maried to one of the best Knights of the world.[13] Wee neede not doubt that the Queene was heereat amazed, yet the loue of the Mother to her infant, cannot conquer the loue of the Wife to her Husbande, which among all loues is the most honest and loyall: so that in hope to free him againe, on whom depended her wealth and welfare,[14] shee gaue her Childe to the Damosell, intreating that shee might be vsed as beseemed the Daughter of a King, and as the sweete beautie of the infant deserued. Shee returning to *Carderia* with the Childe, made her Sisters verie ioyful by her comming, who there nourished the infant till shee was three yeeres olde, when the beautie of the yong Princesse beganne to shewe it selfe, as fayre *Cynthia* dooth among the Starres.

    Nowe did the Sisters inclose her in a strong Tower, made of purpose for young *Francelina*, wherein was the most goodly Garden in the worlde, there was shee attended by her Nursses, and sixe waiting Gentlewomen: and such enchauntments were imposed on the Tower, as no man should euer see her, vnlesse he were the best Knight of his time. The entraunce into the Tower was verie strayte and narrowe, barred vppe with a great Gate of yron, and guarded with two furious Lyons. Ouer the gate stoode a huge Image of Copper, holding a mightie Mace of Steele, wrought by such cunning, as if anie Knight but he that was destenied to end the aduenture, should assay to enter, hardly might he escape to returne againe.[15] Moreouer, the conquerour should not denie the first demaund of the princesse, which was the deliuerance of her Father, and for this cause the Sisters enchaunted the faire *Francelina*, whose Historie wee must yet forbeare, proceeding where wee left before.

Olimaell beeing thus on the Sea, laden with Christian spoyles and prisoners, at length entred the port of the great Cittie of *Tubant*, where hee made such a cheerefull noyse of Droms, Trumpets, Clarions, and Cornets, as though the greatest Monarch in the worlde had come to take landing.[16] The great Turke maruailing at this sodaine melodie, sent one of his Knights to vnderstand the cause, who beeing certified by *Olimaell*, what great victories hee had obtained against the Christians, and the number of prysoners he brought with him, returned to the Pallace, where he told his Lord that the Admirall *Olimaell* was come, and had brought with him great spoyles from the Christians: where among (quoth hee) is a Christian King in person, many worthy Knights and Gentlemen, and a young Princesse of incomparable beautie. Not a little ioyfull was the Turke at these newes, wherefore comming into his great Hall, where the imperiall seates of maiestie were erected, himselfe sate downe in the one, and faire *Agriola* of *England* in the other, expecting the comming of *Olimaell*, who in tryumphant manner set forward with his prize, brauely mounted on a lustie Courser sumptuously caparasoned, and aduauncing his sword drawne in signe of victorie. Beeing come to the Pallace, *Olimaell* saluted his Lorde with great reuerence, standing by him to make report of his conquest, and make present of his prisoners after their estate and calling.

First he caused all the riches to be brought, and all the meanest captiues one after another to kisse the great Turks foote, then commaunding them to be carried thence, he began in this manner. It is not to be doubted, most high and mightie Monarch, that this victorie gotten on the Christians, enemies to our Gods, hath beene obtained onely by your fauour, therefore it is good reason, that to the principall head of this enterprise, the great and cheefest honour should be doone. The witnesse heereof are the treasures present, and these prisoners abyding your mercie, who from the very meanest to the highest, shall humble themselues at your maiesties foote.[17] When very many had doone theyr reuerence, and the King of *Thessaly* shoulde next follow, who though his handes were pinniond behinde him, yet had a Crowne of Gold on his head to shewe what hee was: although he sawe himselfe in the Tyrants power, and *Olimaell* had commaunded him to kisse his Maisters foote, boldly made this answere. Nor will I so much displease my God, vncircumcized Tirant as thou art,[18] in such sort to abase my self, being a king, and administratour of iustice to faithfull Christians, to kisse the foote of the most nastie and vncleane creature in the world, profaning the worship which I onely owe to my maker. It is in thy power to take my life from mee, but not to constraine me do the thing wherein consists my damnation, and a thousand deathes I will endure, before I yeelde so much as in thought to thee.[19] Villaine (quoth the Admirall) darest thou speake so vnreuerently in the presence

Palmerin d'Oliva: Part II   495

of my Lorde? did not my regarde of him withholde mee, soone should I seperate thy cursed head from thy shoulders. With these words he gaue the King such a blow on the face, as made him fall on his knees to the ground.

    Ah Traytour, quoth the King, well hast thou shewen the nature of a villaine, that without commaunde strykest a King captiue, and vnprouided of Armes: but might it so please thy Lorde, in open Fielde will I prooue thee a disloyall and vnchristened Curre, that thus abusest the bloud royall. The great Turke seeing the King so moued and angrie, the bloud likewise trickling from his nose and mouth: commaunded him to be carried thence, to one of the strongest Castles in *Natolia*,[20] where he should be enclosed without any companie, that his captiuitie might be the more greeuous to him.

    When the King of *Thessaly* was departed, *Palmerin* approched, leading the Princesse *Laurana* by the hande, hee and his fiue companions beeing Armed, except theyr Helmets, Gantlets, and swords, whereat the great Turke maruailing, demaunded of *Olimaell* why hee suffered them to be armed? My Lord, quoth hee, these sixe Knights were the first prize I tooke, who (after they had giuen me theyr oathes) haue done such seruice to your Maiestie, especially this, poynting to *Palmerin*, one of the best knights that euer I saw: as full well do they deserue libertie, which in recompence of aduenturing their liues in your seruice, vnder your highnesse correction, I promised them. By Mahomet, answered the great Turk, for thy sake I likewise confirme it, and if heereafter they will abide with mee, I will make them greater then euer they were. While the Turke was making these promises, *Agriola* hauing well noted *Palmerin*, knew him, and with the sodaine conceit thereof was readie to swoune: but staying her selfe on her Chayre, said. O sole bountie, who is this? are not mine eyes deluded and my thoughts beguiled? At these wordes *Palmerin* knewe her, which before hee did not, by reason of her strange disguysed apparrell: yet thought hee best to conceale his inward ioy, least crooked fortune should now againe preuent him.[21]

    The great Turke seeing *Agriola* looke so pale and wan, started from his Chayre, and taking her in his Armes, said. Alas Madame, hath any sodaine ill befallen yee? hath any one in this companie offended yee? By our Gods, if I knew him, presently shoulde he die the death. The Princesse trembling with feare, seeing *Hippolyta* was not present,[22] spake thus in English. What will my Lorde and Husband *Trineus* say, if hee be in this companie, seeing I haue so disloyally forsaken him, and thus (though God knowes perforce) in steed of him, haue taken the enemie to him and our faith? Yet one comfort haue I, that this Infidell hath not carnally knowne me, for which perfection I thanke the heauenly maiestie. At these speeches *Palmerin* was so glad, as the feare of death could not withholde him, but in the same language he thus answered.

    Feare not good Madame, *Trineus* is not in our companie, but so please you to say I am your Brother, you may happily saue my life and practise your deliuerance. The Turke misdoubting by *Palmerins* perswading, that hee had caused this sodaine alteration, imagining him to be her husband of whom he had heard her talke so often, in a great rage said: Knight, how durst thou presume my Ladies presence, knowing the sight of thee would any way displease her? By the Prophet Mahomet thou shalt immediately die, that all such audacious villaines may take an example by thee.

Agriola knowing the Turks censures were very peremptorie,[23] and commonly no sooner saide then executed, embracing him, thus replied. Ah my Lorde, do not the thing in haste, for which afterwarde you will be sorrie,[24] for I assure you on my honor, the Knight that spake to mee is my Brother, and hath left his Countrey onely to finde me, and him I do loue so effectually, as if you put him to death, impossible is it for me to liue afterward. When the Turke heard her speake with such affection, qualifying his anger, saide. I promise ye Madame, for your sake hee shall haue no harme, but bee entertained with loue and honour, conditionally that you forgette this melancholy, and henceforth shewe your selfe more pleasant: for in seeing you sad, I am more greeued, then if I had lost the moitie of dominions. In sooth my Lorde, answered *Agriola*, now shall I be merrie, seeing you intende to loue my Brother, for greater good cannot happen to me then this gentle entertainment, and henceforth shall I tread vnder foote, the sad remembraunce of my Countrey and Parents, hauing him with me, by whom I hope to gaine my greatest comfort. So the Turke arising from his Chayre, caused *Palmerin* and *Laurana* to accompanie *Agriola*, and the other fiue Knights hauing kissed his hande, hee went to his Chamber, commaunding *Olimaell* (for his greater honor) to vsher *Agriola*, who as she went, thus spake.

Beleeue me Admirall, if I was offended when thou broughtest me prisoner hither, thou hast now made mee sufficient amendes, in that by thee I enioy my Brother, whom I was out of all hope to see againe. Alas Madame, quoth he, little did I thinke him to be such a one, for had I: his vsage should haue beene much better, which fault I hope heereafter to recompence. I commend him to thy courtesie, sayde *Agriola*, let him and his friendes haue all things they want, according as my Lorde hath appointed. So taking her leaue of them, she entred her chamber, where she and *Hyppolita* conferred with *Laurana*, of all her fortunes passed, and the aduentures of her Brother. Nowe was *Palmerin* and his companions by the Turks commaundement, lodged neere the Pallace, and to each of them he sent a goodly Horse with costly furniture, thinking by these meanes to conquere *Agriola*, and purchase that of her which he long had desired, and talking with *Palmerin*, sayde. Right well may you be Brother to my Lady *Agriola*, in that your beautie and complexion deliuers great likelihood, seeing then our Gods haue permitted that for her comfort you shoulde be brought hither, perswade her I pray yee, that she be no longer repugnant to my will, for could I haue a Child by her, I would thinke my selfe the happiest Lord on the earth. Beside, I would haue you forsake the follie of your Christianitie, and yeeld your selfe to our Law,[25] which is much better then yours, and you shall see how our Gods will fauour you, likewise what great good you shall receiue therby. My Lord, quoth *Palmerin*, I will labour with my Sister so much as lies in me to doo, as for your Law, as yet I

Palmerin d'Oliva: Part II   497

am vnacquainted therwith, but when I shall find it to be such as you assure mee, easily may I bee drawen thereto, and to serue you with such loyaltie, as so great an estate doth worthily deserue. I confesse my selfe likewise greatly bounden to your maiestie, in that you haue accepted my Sister as your Wife, and to mee a poore slaue giuen life and libertie, which I beseech you also graunt to the Marriners, in whose Vessell it was my chaunce to bee taken, in so dooing she may be greatly mooued by your magnificent liberalitie and mercie.

    The great Turke presently gaue his consent, causing their safe conduct to bee openly proclaimed, so *Palmerin* and his Friendes humbly departing to their lodging, the Turke went to *Agriolaes* Chamber, where sitting downe by her, he thus began. Now shall I perceiue Madame, how much your Brother may preuaile with you: for hee hath promised me so to order the matter, as you shall graunt my long desired sute. My Lord, quoth shee, my Brother shall command me nothing, but I will doo it with all my heart: as for your request, it is not in my power, but in the hande of God, who defendeth me as best him pleaseth. Nor can I change the opinion I haue held so long, though by hauing my Brother with me, I enioy farre greater content then I did before.

    It sufficeth me, saide the Turke, to see you so well pleased, and as for your Brother, that you may perceiue howe well I loue him, before one moneth be expired, I will make him the cheefest Lord in my Court, next mine owne person: so kissing the Princesse, he departed to his Chamber. The day following *Palmerin* saide to his companions. You see my friendes, how friendly Fortune smileth on vs, but least shee change, as euermore she is wont, wee must practise some meanes to escape from these Turkish infidels. Beside, seeing wee haue founde the Princesse *Agriola*, I hope *Trineus* is not so secretly hidden, but we shall heare some tydings of him. Of her will I therefore enquire, if she know what became of him and *Ptolome* when I left them: in meane while you may closely conclude with our Marriners, that they be euer readie at an howres warning, for I hope we shall set hence before eight dayes be past. *Palmerin* went to *Agriolaes* Chamber, and there by good hap hee found her alone, whome after he had humbly saluted, the Princesse thus spake to him. My noble friende, you must be carefull howe you speake to me, especially before the aged Lady you sawe heere yesterday, for shee vnderstandeth all languages, and if we be discouered, there is no way but death, therefore when you see her with me, conferre rather with *Laurana*, and say to her what you would haue mee know, because shee is a Lady both vertuous and faithfull. No lesse (Madame) haue I alwaies found her, quoth *Palmerin*: therefore I beseech you make account of her, and acquaint her with your greatest affaires, for shee is daughter to one of the most gentle Princes in the world. But Madame, I would gladly know what became of *Trineus*, after that so vnhappily I departed from you.[26] The Admirall *Olimaell*, quoth shee, came with his Gallies so soone as you were departed, who tooke vs, and then seperated vs in sunder, scant permitting me to speake to him or *Ptolome*, nor knowe I what is become of them. It sufficeth then Madame aunswered *Palmerin*, that I haue founde you, for on you dependeth the life of *Trineus*, who shall not long (I hope) bee concealed from vs, therefore aduise your selfe on the day when you will departe, for I haue a shippe readie to carrie you from this seruitude. Thanks be to heauen quoth she, for so good fortune, I will be so readie as you shall not stay for me. Now entred *Hippolyta*, who brake off, theyr talke to other occasions, where we will leaue, and returne to the Prince *Trineus*.

Chapter XLII.
How Trineus beeing enchaunted into the shape of a Dogge in the Isle of Malfada, there came a Princesse of the Moores, who requested him of the aged Enchauntresse, to whom he was giuen, and what happened to him afterward.

I thinke as yet you remember, without repetition of the former discourse, in what manner the Knight, Cozin to the Admirall *Olimaell*, to whome the Prince *Trineus* was giuen, arriued by tempest in the Isle of *Malfada*, and how he with his people were transformed into diuers shapes of Beasts, among whom *Trineus* bare the likenesse of a goodly Dogge.[1] Beeing thus disguised, a yong Princesse named *Zephira*, Daughter to the King of the same Countrey, came to demaund counsell of the aged Enchauntresse *Malfada*, for the cure of a certain disease, which by strange aduenture happened to her in this manner.

This yong Princesse one day beeing pleasant in her Fathers Court, among many of her waiting Ladyes, entred a goodly Garden, which abounded with great diuersitie of sweet flowers, and after shee had walked a prettie while in an Arbour of Muske-roses, shee espied a Gille-flower, which seemed so faire and beautifull in her eye, as shee was prouoked to goe crop it from the stalke. Hauing this dellicate flower in her hand, wherein (by misfortune) a venemous worme was crept, she tooke such delight in smelling it: as her breath drewe vp the worme into one of her nose-thrilles, not beeing able to get it out againe. So the venome and poysone of this little worme, engendred a putrifaction and other like worms, which gaue a smell so filthy and lothsome, as hardly could any abide to stand by her.[2] Her Father not a little agreeued at this mischaunce, sent for the most skilfull Phisitions, to see what remedie might be deuised: but all their paine and trauaile was in vaine, for the disease continued still without any amendment. In the end, the King fearing it would change to a Canker incurable, and hauing heard what straunge actions the Enchauntresse *Malfada* performed, sent the Princesse *Zephira* to her, where shee beeing arriued without anie daunger, because she would not hurt anie inhabiting in the Isle, declared to the Sorceresse the whole manner of her misfortune.

The Enchauntresse answered, that shee could giue her no remedie, and hardly should she finde any at all: except it were by an ancient Knight, who remained in the Court of the King of *Romata* and *Grisca*, Realmes subiect to the Soldane of *Persia*, and the knight was named *Muzabelino*. The Princesse was so displeased at this answere, seeing her intent frustrated, as shee would receyue no sustenaunce: wherefore walking in the Feeldes to represse her anger, and so to the Sea-side, where the Ships lay confused, shee behelde the Dogge which was the Prince *Trineus*, and so farre in liking was shee with him, as she desired the Enchauntresse to giue him her, and hauing obtained her request,[3] returned to her Father, who lay sicke in one of his Citties called *Nabor*, whereof the whole Realme bare the name.

When the King saw his Daughter returned without cure, his Melancholie conceit so strooke to his heart, as with in three daies after he died. Hauing made his Testament before his deceasse, hee gaue his Daughter as her portion a Citie called *Elain*,⁴ one of the greatest and surest strengths in the Realme, with all the signories belonging thereto. To *Maulerino* his yongest Sonne, he gaue an other like portion, which was a dayes iourney distaunt from *Elain*. After the Kings funerall rytes were solemnized, the Princesse with her brother *Maulerinc*, went to their owne possessions, doubting the furie of the Prince *Tyreno*, their eldest Brother, who alwayes had showen himselfe proude and contentious.

Shee beeing thus in quiet by her selfe, tooke no other pleasure then in playing with her Dog, because hee seemed verie subtile and politique: so that shee prepared a Couch for him at her beds feete. *Tyreno* beeing crowned King after his Fathers deceasse, began greatly to despise that his Sister should enioy the fayrest Cittie in the Realme: for which cause hee practised all the meanes he coulde to put her to death. And that he might the better compasse his purpose, hee secretly sent a Messenger to the maister of the Princesse horses, that if hee woulde kill or poyson his Brother and Sister, hee would giue him fiftie thousande Seraphes, and make him gouernour of *Elain*. The wicked noble man, greedie and couetous, seeing the large promise of the Tyrant, consented thereto: so that one night the Princesse beeing asleepe, he entred her Chamber with his Sword drawne, there to haue murthered her, and afterward the Prince her Brother. *Trineus*, who had lost nothing belonging to a man but bodily shape and voyce, seeing the Traytour enter his Ladies Chamber with his weapon drawne, started vp presently, and setting his two forefeete on the villaines breast, bit him so cruelly by the face and throate, as he being vnable to helpe himselfe, was constrained to crie out aloude. With this noyse the Princesse awaked, and her Brother likewise, who lay in the next Chamber, comming in haste to see the cause of this outcrie, and knowing the Traytour, beate him so sore with the Pommell of his Sword about the stomacke, as in the end enforced him to confesse his treason. Whereat *Maulerino* not a little maruailing, and wrathfull at his villainous intent, smote his heade from his shoulders. In the morning he appoynted such guarde in the Cittie, as no straunger might enter without great examination. The Princesse knowing howe her Dog had saued her life, loued him afterwarde so tenderly, as shee would feede him at her owne Table, and none but her selfe might giue him anie foode. Heere will we likewise pause a while, and declare the deliuerance of the Princesse *Agriola*.

CHAPTER XLIII.
Howe the great Turke became enamoured with the Princesse Laurana, by means wherof he was slaine, and Agriola deliuered.

Palmerin being vpon a day in his Chamber with his Companions, practising some meane for the deliuerance of *Agriola*: the Princesse *Laurana* of *Durace*, came to them, framing her speeches in this maner. Gentlemen if any of you be desirous to deliuer vs from this cruell enemie, who holdes vs in this thrall and bondage, I haue deuised the best meanes that may be, and thus it is. The Turke the most luxurious and vnchast man in the worlde, not contented with infinite number of Concubines,[1] hath many times made loue to me,[2] so that to compasse mine intent, I haue made him promise within three dayes to graunt his request. In this time I haue intreated the Princesse *Agriola* to shewe him the most disdainefull countenaunce that may bee, which shee hath faythfully promised, and for this cause hath sent mee to you, to conuay hence all the riches he hath giuen yee, and which shee her selfe will likewise sende ye: so that when the houre is come for me to fulfill his pleasure, one of you beeing priuilie armed, shall in my place murther him, in reuenge of the ill Christendome hath sustained, by the last vnhappie voyage of *Olimaell*, who determineth verie shortly, as I vnderstand, to goe spoyle to Isle of *Rhodes*.[3] *Palmerin* very glad of the Princesse notable inuention, thus answered. Because (Madame) I lately promised the Turke, not to depart his Court, but to keepe him companie, when he denied his Admirall, that I and my companions shoulde go with him to the *Rhodes*: I cannot be the man to ende this woorthie reuenge, therefore one of you (my Freendes) must resolue to performe it. In meane while, you Madame *Laurana* may returne to the Turke, pleasing him with faire and freendly speeches: for if neuer so little suspition bee gathered, not one of vs can escape with life. Feare not, sayde the Princesse, I will vse the matter so carefully as you can desire, right well knowe I howe to enflame his heart with queint lookes, coy disdaines, faint yeeldings, and other such like ceremonies vsed in loue, as feare not you to prosecute the stratageme, in that a beginning so good, must needes sort to a successiue ende.[4] The yong Duke of *Pontus*, who began to growe affectionate towards the Princesse *Laurana*, sayd.

In sooth my Lord, so please you to commit the charge heereof to me: so well hope I to execute the same, for her sake that did so woorthily inuent it, as I dare warrant to deserue no reproch thereby. For my first earnest to gentle Loue, shall be so gracious, as in qualifying the vnlawfull heate of our enemie, I will binde my selfe neuer to loue anie other: and her faith receyued, if I bring not his head to Madame *Laurana*, let mee bee accounted as one of the most slothfull Knights that euer bare Armes. Aduertise mee therefore of the place and houre, and doubt not of my faithfull performance. At this pleasant answer they all beganne to smile, whereupon *Palmerin* thus spake. Beleeue mee noble Duke, considering your youth and braue disposition, I knowe no one in this companie more meete for the Princesse *Laurana*, then you are: but I thinke when the appoynted houre shall come, you will bee a little more angrie with the Turke then her, if she haue you in that subiection as it seemes she hath. Yet let vs not nowe trifle the time in vaine, when such waightie occasions commaundeth our diligence.[5]

So returned *Laurana* to the Princesse *Agriola*, acquainting her with the Knights determination, when not long after, the great Turke entred the Chamber, accompanied with *Palmerin* and the King of *Sparta*, and that he might the better speake to her hee so earnestly desired, hee caused *Palmerin* to sit betweene him and *Agriola*, then turning to *Laurana*, he began to deuise familiarlie with her. Which when *Palmerin* and *Agriola* perceiued, the better to beguile him, hee made a signe to the King of *Sparta*, that hee should enter into some talke of hunting: wherat the Turke presently arose, and taking *Laurana* by the hand, led her to the window, with these speeches. Mistresse of my heart, and the very fairest creature that euer mine eyes behelde, will ye graunt the request I made to you yesterday? See you not what great honour I haue done to Madame *Agriola*? Notwithstanding, if you will loue me, I will make you my Wife,[6] that I may haue issue by you to succeede in my kingdome, and your honours shall be nothing inferiour to hers. And though she still denie me the fauour, which with long and continuall pursuite I haue desired: yet doe you consider my greefe, and if in short time you vouchsafe me no pittie, the extreame afflictions I endure for your loue, are rated at the price of my life. God forbid, quoth *Laurana*, that so great a losse shoulde come to the Orientall Empyre by me, rather will I forget the accustomed regard of mine honour, to bee accepted in your grace and fauour. And the cause that made me deferre so long from this answere, was the feare I haue of Madame *Agriola*, and her Brother, to whome I was giuen by your Admirall after my Fathers decease.

But to the ende, my Lorde, that none of them may suspect our loue, I thinke it conuenient that *Hyppolita*, who alway lyeth in your Chamber, remoue her selfe to the Ladies attending on *Agriola*, and her shall you commaunde to giue me the Key of my Ladies Chamber, which hitherto shee hath vsed to carrie. By this meane may I the more safely, and without suspition of any one, come in the night to fulfill your desire. The Turke imagining he had gayned the Princesse loue indeede, was not a little ioyfull, wherefore he said.

Sweete Ladie, you shall haue the Key as you request, nor shall she longer lodge in my Chamber, whom you feare so much. Moreouer, this night will I perswade *Agriola*, that I feele my selfe not halfe currant:[7] and therefore to keepe her selfe in her owne Chamber, and so may you come boldlie to me this night. If any one chaunce to meete yee, say that I sent for you: and if they dare bee so bolde as to hinder your comming, in the morning shall my Ianizaries[8] put them to death, whatsoeuer they be. So taking a Ring from his finger, wherein was a stone of inestimable value, hee gaue it to the Princesse, saying. Holde Madame, take this as a pledge of my promise: for which *Laurana* humblie thanking him, thus replied. My Lord, I see *Agriola*, hath foure or fiue times earnestlie noted you, I thinke it good therefore that we breake off talke, assuring you, that I will not

Palmerin d'Oliva: Part II

faile at midnight, when euerie one is fast a sleepe, to keepe my worde, and in the Mantle which you sent mee yesterday, I will couertly enter your Chamber, conditionallie that you keepe your promise to mee afterwarde. Doubt not thereof, said the Turke, and so taking his leaue of her, went presently to his Chamber, where finding *Hyppolita*, he commaunded her to take thence her bed, and carrie it to the Ladies Chamber, likewise taking the Key from her, hee sent it by one of his Pages to *Laurana*, who hauing it in her hand, came laughing therewith to *Palmerin*, saying.

Howe say you my Lord, haue I not handled the matter as it should be? the Turke mooued with pittie of our straite imprisonment, hath giuen me the charge of Madame *Agriola*: for by his Page hath he sent me the Key of her Chamber, and *Hyppolita* shall lodge nowe among other Ladies. And because this night the action must bee fulfilled, doo you aduertise the Duke of *Pontus*, that at midnight he faile not to come, to vse drunken *Holofernes* as hee hath deserued.' *Palmerin* and the King of *Sparta*, praysing God, that their affaires went forwarde so luckily, returned to their lodging, intreating *Agriola* to be ready at the houre, that their intent might not be hindered by her. Afterwarde they rehearsed to their companions, what was concluded by the Princesse *Laurana*: wherefore, quoth hee to the Duke, prepare to bring your Armour secretlye to *Agriolaes* Chamber, where you shall finde the King of *Sparta*, and my selfe. Meane while, *Frysoll, Olorico,* and *Eustace,* see that all our baggage be conueyed into our shippe, which may safely be done without suspect, considering what great multitude of Souldiours are embarquing, and therefore prouide all things readie agaynst our comming. The houre being at hand, *Palmerin,* the King of *Sparta,* and the Duke of *Pontus,* went to the Princesse Chamber, where the Duke was immediately Armed, except his Helmet, which he left on the Table, couered with the Mantle whereof *Laurana* spake, putting on the attyre the Princes wore vppon her heade, and so finely was he disguised in those habits, as in the dark he might be reputed rather a woman then a man, and beeing readie to depart about the practise, he saide to *Palmerin*.

I thinke it best my Lord, that you and the King of *Sparta*, conduct the Ladyes before to the Porte: for if in mine attempt I should happen to faile, yet should you loose but the worst in your companie. So importunate was hee with them to follow his aduise, as he caused them to depart presently to the Hauen, where they were ioyfully welcommed by *Frysoll*, and the rest, without meeting anie by the way to hinder them. When the Duke saw himselfe left alone, and now he was to dispose himselfe to his intent, falling on his knee, he thus spake.

O my God, that suffered the mightie *Holofernes* to bee beheaded by thy Seruaunt *Iudith*: affoorde me at this time the like grace, and giue mee strength to worke his death, who is the greatest liuing enemy to Christians. This said, hee went to the Turks Chamber, where he found the doore readie open, and approching the bed, the Turke (who verilie thought it was *Laurana*) raysed vp himselfe, and taking him by the arme, said. Welcome, sweete Ladie, for verie long haue I expected thy comming. Ah Traitour, quoth the Duke, I am not she thou lookest for, regarde of honour will not suffer her to sinne in such sort. With which wordes hee stabbed him to the heart, and smiting off his head, wrapped it in the Mantle that *Laurana* gaue him: so going to *Agriolaes* Chamber, and clasping on his Helmet, went presentlie to his Freendes, whom hee founde in prayer for his good successe, and throwing the head into *Lauranaes* lappe, said.

Madame, hee that was so importunate for your dishonour, as a witnesse of his loue to you, hath sent you his head here by me: wherwith I present you so deuoutlie, as henceforth I dedicate my life and seruice to your disposing. A thousand thanks my Lorde, quoth the Princesse, this vertuous act hath made mee so constantlie to bee yours: as in anie thing that toucheth not the impeach of mine honour, I remaine with my vttermost endeuours to pleasure you. As the Duke woulde haue replied, the other Knights came to looke on the head, which when they had cast into the Sea, they presently hoysed saile, and before day had gotten farre enough from thence.

In the morning, as the marriners came from theyr Gallies towardes the Cittie, they espied the head floting on the water, and taking it vp, shewed it to their companions, to know if they could tell whose it was. When they behelde it so dreadfull, the mustachoes[10] strouting out like stiffe bristles, and the locks of hayre hang shagging downe, they knew not what to thinke, and one of them hauing well marked it, said.

By all our Gods, if I be not deceiued, this is the head of my Lord the great Turke, at which words all the other began to scorne and mocke. *Hyppolita* seeing faire *Phoebus*[11] let foorth the morning light, came to the Princesse *Agriolaes* chamber, where not finding her nor *Laurana*, the chamber likewise dispoyled of many things, she doubted immediatly that they were fled, whereof to be resolued, she went to the great Turks Chamber, and seeing the Pages standing at the doore, saide. Why enter ye not? the howre is past, and my Lorde is not yet risen. Lady, quoth they, as yet hee hath not called vs, and you knowe as yesternight he forbad our entrance till we were called: it may bee hee slept but badly this night, and therefore now is contented to take his rest. I feare, quoth she, some other matter then sleepe dooth hinder his calling you, so thrusting open the doore, and entring the Chamber, sawe the bloud dispersed on the ground, and the headlesse truncke hanging beside the bed, with which sight they made a verie pittifull outcrie, whereat many noble men and Gentlemen came, who likewise beholding what had happened, ioyned with them in sorrowfull complaints. Soone was the report of this murder blazed through the Cittie, so that *Olimaell* hearing thereof, ranne thither with all haste, where he was no sooner present, but *Hyppolita* thus began. Ah *Olimaell* thou broughtest the Traytours hither that haue slaine my Lorde, and by thy meanes hath this treason beene committed. By all our Gods, sayde one of the Turks Nephewes present, it is true, but because thou hast suffered *Agriola*, her Brother, and the other Knights to escape, thou villaine shalt abie it deerely. So drawing foorth his Semitarie, killed *Olimaell* therewith, saying. Such be their reward that trayterously betray theyr Soueraigne: mine Vnckle of a poore Ianizarie made thee his cheefe Admirall,[12] and thou for his kindnesse hast requited him with death, but now thy villainy is worthily recompenced.

Olimaell thus slaine, his men ranne furiously on the Turks Nephew, and slew him, with fiftie Knights beside that defended his quarrell, and had it not beene for an auncient Basso,[13] who with an hundred Souldiours came to part them, they were in danger of a greater sedition, because they sawe none pursue *Palmerin* and his companions.

The Basso that had thus pacified this tumult, by promises perswaded the Ianizaries, and preuailed so well with them, as the same day he proclaimed a yonger Brother to the Soldane deceased, great Emperour of Turkie. Many iniuries did he to Christendome afterwarde, in reuenge of his Brothers death, which yet we will forbeare, to rehearse what happened to *Palmerin* and his companions being on the sea.

Chapter XLIV.

How Palmerin and his companions mette two Turkish Ships, from whom they deliuered Estebon the Merchant and his Sonnes: and came to the Isle of Malfada, where Palmerin lost them all, and of the sorrow hee made for his mishap.

Laurana was so ioyfull, that shee had so fortunately escaped the Turks hands, and beside was so reuenged of hir cheefest enemie, as nothing could yeeld her greater contentation: but howe much more would shee haue reioyced, if shee had known the slaughter at the Pallace? As she sat discoursing heereon with *Palmerin* and the Duke of *Pontus, Frysoll* beeing aloft on the decke, espied foure ships comming towards them with full saile, whereupon hee called to his companions, that they shoulde presently arme themselues. For (quoth he) I see two Rouing Shippes, and they haue taken two other, or els my iudgement fayleth: let vs therefore labour to withstand them, least we sustaine a further danger.

No sooner had he spoken these words, but they all put themselues in readinesse, so that when the enemie closed with them, and many entred the shippe, thinking it was yeelded, they had a sharper entertainment then they expected, for not one escaped aliue that came aboord, but either were slaine or thrown into the Sea. In breefe,[1] they ouercame both the Pirates, and left not one aliue to carrie tydings hereof into *Turkie*. Afterward, as *Palmerin* searched the Cabins, to see what prisoners the Moores had taken: he espied his maister *Estebon* the Merchant of *Hermida*, and his two sonnes by him, with two other Merchants, chained by the handes and necke, in like sort as the poore slaues are in the Gallies, whereupon he saide. Trust mee Maister, hee that put this coller about your necke, was little acquainted with your honest humanitie. So looking vp and downe for the Keyes that opened the locks of the chaines, hee espied a Turkish marriner, who fearefull of his life had hid himselfe, to whom he said. By God villaine, if thou shewest me not quickly where the Keyes are, I wil sende thy soule after thy fellowes.[2] Spare my life most noble Knight, cryed the Turke, and I will giue ye not onely the Keyes, but also shew you such secrets heere within, as no other now but my selfe can shew ye, wherein is infinite wealth and riches.

Dispatch then, sayde *Palmerin*. The Moore fetching the Keyes, opened the locks, tooke off their chaines, and brake the manacles bounde about their handes, when *Palmerin* lifting vp his eyes to Heauen, saide. Thanks to my God, that so happily sent mee to succour *Estebon*, by whose meanes I came to the knowledge of my Friendes and Parents, and who first gaue me horse and armour for knightly seruice.[3] *Estebon* hearing *Palmerins* words, maruailing not a little, fell on his knee, saying. I beseech you my Lorde to tell me your name, to the ende I may be thankfull to him, by whom I haue escaped the cruell Infidels, and receiued such an vnspeakeable benefit. Why maister, quoth *Palmerin*, know ye not me? I am your seruant *Palmerin*, who you first prouoked to follow armes by your liberalitie, and euer since haue I followed that profession, and nowe haue requited

Palmerin d'Oliva: Part II

some parte of your kindnesse. Ah my noble Friende *Palmerin*, said old *Estebon*, suffer me to kisse thy hande, for if heeretofore thou didst deliuer me from the Lions throat:[4] what may I say of the daunger from which I am nowe defended? In happie houre was that knightly furniture giuen, and with successefull fortune haue you imployed them, but may it please ye to goe with mee, I will prouide you of all things necessarie, and giue you my Sonnes heere to be your Seruants.

The King of *Sparta* seeing *Estebon* vse such zealous speeches, saide to him. Father, you are very much deceiued, imagine you the sonne to the Emperour of *Constantinople*, a simple Souldier? your age (Father) makes you forgette your selfe. At these words the good olde man somewhat astonied, excused himselfe to the King, and turning to *Palmerin*, saide. Alas my Lord, in not knowing you otherwise then one of my seruants, I haue offered your excellencie very great wrong, and great hath beene my desert of punishment, vsing the great Lorde of *Greece* so vnreuerently. But pardon my boldnesse, noble Lorde, and let mine ignoraunce excuse the offence committed: for vnwittingly did I fall into this error. Content thy selfe good maister, quoth *Palmerin*, in nothing hast thou offended mee, but if thou wilt returne to thy Countrey, these vesselles belonging to the Moores, and all the treasure in them, will I frankely bestow on thee. Ah my Lorde, answered *Estebon*, since Fortune hath so happily brought me into your companie, so please you to licence me, loth am I to departe from you, for such store of Theeues and Robbers are on the Seas, as hardly can I escape their handes aliue. And sorrie would I be, saide *Palmerin*, that you or these merchaunts should any way miscarrie, though perhaps your Wiues would gladly haue ye at home: but this I must tell ye, that I cannot returne to *Constantinople*. I shall be contented, saide *Estebon*, to stay your good leysure, for a poore life is better to mee in this companie, then welthie possessions among mine enemies.[5]

Heereuppon, *Palmerin* commaunding all the riches in the Moores Shippes to bee conuayed into the other, sette fire on the vessels, and hoising sayle, rode on merrily. Within three daies after arose a mightie winde at Northeast,[6] which carried them with such violence, as the Pilots told *Palmerin* they were nowe come on the borders of *Persia*, and very neere the Isle of *Malfada*, where they arriued before the Sunne setting. They seeing the Countrey so faire and delectable, would needes goe on shore to refresh themselues, for the Ladies were so distempered with the rough storme, as they were very desirous to recreate themselues a little.

Palmerin not able to shun this fatall chaunce, went on shore with his friendes and the two Princesses, all the other likewise speedily followed them, where they had not long stayde, but they were all diuersly enchaunted. The two Ladyes were transformed into the shape of Hindes, the other to Dogges, Wolues, and Leopards, all of them running with such swiftnesse, as though the furies had stood to chase them:[7] but *Palmerin* could not be enchaunted, by reason of the gift hee receiued of the three wise Sisters on the Mountaine *Artifaeria*,[8] whereat hee greatly greeued, for such was his impatience thus to loose his friendes, as hee entred into these lamentations.

    Ah peruerse and vnconstant fortune, how diuers and daungerous are thy trecheries? Ah stepmother too cruell,[9] why dost thou not exercise thy rage on simple and forsaken soules, but on such as exceede in honour and vertue? Doubtlesse my sinne hath caused this mishap, when I perswaded my Friendes to goe against their Christian Brethren,[10] onely by feare of my wretched life. As he stoode thus complayning, hee behelde the Ladie of the Isle with her Seruants, comming to take the spoyle of their bootie, whereof beeing ioyfull, and thinking by her meanes to finde some succour, he ranne apace towards her, and falling on his knee, thus spake. Alas noble Ladie, if euer pittie had power to mooue ye, instruct me howe to recouer my companions, and two woorthie Ladies transformed into brute Beastes. *Malfada* swelling with anger, to see that he was not likewise enchaunted, aunswered. Wretched Knight, accursed bee their power that defended thee from my incantations, liue not thou in hope to finde any remedie heere: for these enchauntments are of such strength, as they may not be vndone, but by the most skilfull magitian in the world, which thou art not I am well assured, and therefore dost thou but loose thy labour. But because by mine art I cannot be reuenged on thee, some other meanes will I seeke for thy destruction. You therefore my Seruants, lay handes on him, and carrie him to the darkest of my prysons, that his following dayes may be spent in greater miserie. Vncourteous and despightfull, quoth *Palmerin*, are these speeches, especially comming from one that vaunteth of her knowledge, nor can they bee measured by loue or charitie, and therefore shall I chastise such bad creatures, as refuse a matter no way hurtfull to themselues, but wherein theyr owne honour might be discerned. With which words hee smote her head from her shoulders, and valiantly buckling with the other, in the ende left not one to carrie reporte of this massacre:[11] afterwarde hee fell into his lamentations againe in this manner.

    Infortunate *Palmerin*, seest thou not how mishap will neuer leaue thee? for where thou thoughtest with comfort to finde thy Brother *Tryneus*, nowe hath Fortune ouerwhelmed thee with a whole world of mischaunces. Ah noble *Agriola* and gentle *Laurana*, two of the most modest Princesses that euer the earth bare, howe may you iustly blame me? bringing you from where you liued in honour, in this accursed place to bee transformed to brute Beastes. Neuer did *Circes* deale so cruelly with *Grillus*, and other Souldiers to the wise *Vlysses*,[12] as this villainous olde hag hath doone with me. Had you yet beene altered to Lyons and Tygers, you might haue defended your selues from the crueltie of other Beasts: but this damned Sorceresse hath transformed you, to the most fearefull and timerous among all other creatures, and therefore subiect to euerie inconuenience.[13]

    Ah loyall companions, who loued me deerer then your Father or Brother: from the Turks which cherished you with such kindnes and loue, haue I brought you to the cruell and mercilesse *Malfada*.[14] My noble Friende and Brother *Frysoll*, what now will auaile thy haughty Chiualrie? And gentle Prince *Olorico*, who for my sake forsooke countrey, Parents, Friendes and all: how maist thou iustly condemne me of infamous reproach? What answere shall I make to mine Aunt *Arismena*, for her noble husbande the King of *Sparta*? And vertuous Duke of *Pontus*, a Knight of high and especiall qualitie: greatly maist thou blame thy fortune to bee acquainted with mee. Not forgetting the magnanimious Prince *Eustace*, how can I excuse thy hard hap, to the good olde Duke of *Mecaena* thy Father? Had it pleased the soueraigne Creator of all things, that among you my selfe had taken the strange shape, my quiet would haue beene the better, to accompanie you with mishappe, as I haue doone in good fortune. Ah sweete Sister *Armyda*, little thinkest thou what offence thy Brother *Palmerin* hath committed: and gracious Mistresse *Polynarda*, what torment will this bee to your heauenly thoughts, when you shall vnderstand the summe of my ill successe? Wandering along in these mones, he came to the Enchauntresse Castle, where at the gate he sawe two Damoselles,[15] who humbly saluting him, saide. Welcome Sir Knight, heere may you repose your selfe if you please. Alas Ladies, quoth he, it is nowe no time for me to rest, because the Ladie of this place I thinke, beeing the most ingrate and despightfull woman that euer I sawe, hath depriued mee of all my ioye and comfort: but I hope I haue so well paide her for her paines, as heereafter shee shall do no further harme. Yet if any of you haue beene so well instructed by her, as to finish the deuellish coniurations, and will accomplish it, or tell me, if by force they may bee reduced to their former shapes, who remaine enchaunted heere in this Islande, for euer will I bee her Knight, and will preferre her in honour beyond all other of her race. The Damosels (who thought their Ladies cunning had brought him thither, that shee might abuse him,[16] and afterwarde transforme him as was her custome) beeing amazed at this aunswere, thus spake. Accursed villaine, of an euill death maist thou die, whom our Mistresse by her knowledge cannot transforme, now knowe we that thou hast murdered her: but assure thy selfe to finde vs thy two most mortall enemies, and though we can change thy Freendes to their former shapes, yet in despight of thy villainie, wee will not, nor shalt thou knowe how it may be doone.

Awaie strumpets, quoth hee, get yee going, or I will sende your soules after your Mistresse:[17] and were it not a disgrace to mine honor, to defile my hands with the bloode of such wicked creatures, by heauen I would cutte yee as small as flesh to the pot. Then came a knight foorth of the Castell, who embracing *Palmerin*, said. My Lord *Palmerin*, what fortune hath brought you into this accursed Iland? *Palmerin* seeing such strange euents succeede one an other, knewe not what to imagine: but at length returned this answer. You must hold me excused Sir, for in truth I knowe ye not. Why my Lorde, quoth the knight, haue you forgotten *Dyardo*, whose life you defended in the king of *Bohemiaes* Court?[18] By heauen, said *Palmerin*, I could not call you to remembraunce, but tell mee good Knight, what aduenture brought you hither? for my chaunce hath beene so vnfortunate, as the rehearsall woulde bee most dolorous. Then *Dyardo* declared, howe the King had sent him with some small assistaunce, to pursue fiue Foystes of

Moorish Pirats, who had doone manie iniuries to his subiects. And, quoth hee, after I had long time chased them, fiue other Galleyes came, and ioyning with them, tooke mee, and slue all my men.

    At length, by tempesteous wether we were cast on this Isle, where we landing to seeke fresh water, all the Moores were changed into Harts, Dogs and Bores: but the Ladie sparing me in regard of amorous desire, hath kept mee in this Castle a yeere and more, abusing mee at her owne pleasure, and neuer could I compasse any meane to escape hence againe, for if I had but made offer neere the Gate, by forcible strokes haue I beene beaten backe, yet not able to discerne who smote me.

    Your hap, quoth *Palmerin*, hath beene verie harde, but her cursed head lying on the shore side, perswades me heereafter she shall doo no more harme. But tell me good *Dyardo*, is there no one within so skilfull in her Science, as wee may winne to doo vs some good? Not one, aunswered *Dyardo*, therefore am I lothe you shoulde staie long heere, in doubt of further daunger. I will then, saide *Palmerin*, goe seeke such a one as shall ende these enchauntments: and because you shall not be iniuried by anie in the Castle, wee will make them fast in prisons till my returne. After they had so doone, they went to the stable, where *Dyardo* gaue *Palmerin* a lustie Courser, and taking leaue of him, set forward on his iourney.[19]

Chapter XLV.
How Palmerin departing from the Isle of Malfada, came to the Court of the Princesse Zephira, shee that kept Tryneus transformed: where he was entertained, to ayde her against her eldest brother, who vexed her with dayly troubles.

So soone as *Palmerin* had thus left the Isle of *Malfada*, and had that day likewise passed a very dangerous riuer, at night he came to a little village, where taking vp his lodging, he fell in talke with his host in the *Arabian* tong, if he knewe any one that was expert in Nigromancie. I knowe none, quoth the Hoste, but an olde Ladie in an Islande harde by, to whome our Princesse not long since went, for remedie of a strange disease wherewith she is tormented. Where abideth your Princesse? saide *Palmerin*. Not past thirtie miles hence, (quoth the Hoste) in a Cittie called *Elain*. Perhappes, quoth *Palmerin*, by her I may be better resolued. So bidding his Hoste good night, withdrewe himselfe into his Chamber, where many imaginations passed him concerning the Princesse *Zephira*.[1]

It may bee, (quoth hee within himselfe) that the Enchauntresse vnable to helpe her, hath yet assigned her to some man more expert in that diuellish Science: who compassing her health, happily may giue mee some counsell to amende my misfortune. In this opinion the next morning he rode to the Cittie of *Elain*, heauie and sadde, yet in hope of comfort: and as hee came neare the Cittie, hee was enclosed with two or three hundreth light Horsse men, whome the Prince *Maulerino* Brother to *Zephira* had there ambushed, to take all auaunt-currers and Knights passing by them. Yet obserued they these conditions, that who so would take the Princes paie, and sweare faithfull seruice, shoulde sustaine no harme: but such as refused so to doo, were carried into the Cittie, their Horsse and Armour taken from them, and they enclosed in strong prison. These Moores were amazed to see *Palmerin* so richly armed, and much more beholding him so brauely mounted, wherfore they said to him.

Yeeld your selfe Sir knight, and sweare to maintaine our Princesse quarrel: or else be assured thy death is present. The condition is very harde, said *Palmerin*, but for I haue heard the wrong offered by the king to your Princesse, I will sustaine her cause, not as a prisoner enforced heereto, but of mine owne good will, as all knights errant are bound by dutie, to defende the iust quarrell of distressed Ladies.[2] Presently was *Palmerin* brought to the Princesse and her Brother, who were conferring togither about these earnest affaires: when the Knight that conducted *Palmerin*, stept to the Prince *Maulerino*, and thus spake. See heere my Lord, a Knight latelie taken, whome for that wee haue found honest and courteous, we haue suffered him to remain Armed, and commit him to your opinion. While the knight continued these speeches, transformed *Trineus*, who laye at the Princesse foote, seeing *Palmerin* with his beuer open, ran and leaped on him, whining and fawning on him so louingly, as euery one greatlie meruailed thereat. In breefe, they might discerne by his cries, colling about his legs, and pittifull mourning, that faine he would haue spoken, and shewed his loyall Freende his inward complainings. The Princesse meruailing at this strange occasion, said. I thinke (Sir Knight) my dog knowes you, for since *Malfada* gaue him me, I neuer could see him so faune on anie body. In sooth Madame, answered *Palmerin*, to my remembraunce, I neuer sawe your dog before this present. Heereupon shee called him to her, and made many meanes that hee shoulde come to her, yet would he not leaue *Palmerin*, but shaking his head, still whined to his Freende, as crauing aide and succour at his hand, wherewith the Princesse mooued, thus spake.

I praye thee Knight conceale not any thing from mee, for I perswade my selfe, that thou hast beene heeretofore some Freende to the Enchauntresse *Malfada*, seeing my dogge is so loth to come from thee. Let mee vnderstand the truth I praye thee, and if thou likewise wilt assist mee against my cruell Brother, thou shalt be honourablie vsed, and thy ordinarie paye redoubled. Madame, answered *Palmerin*, heere may you beholde the most distressed Knight liuing, and a Christian, whose harde fortune hath beene such, as arriuing in the Enchauntresse Isle whereof you spake, I haue lost fiue Freends, my true and honourable companions, and with them two Ladies, who in all vertues may not be equalled. Yet haue I reuenged their losse on the olde hagge and her seruaunts, whose breathlesse bodies remaine for foode to the foules of the ayre. And because I hearde (fayre Princesse) your selfe was not long since with her, for councell in some vnhappie fortune befallen you, faine woulde I knowe, maye it please you to graunt mee so much fauour, if shee assigned you to anie other more skilfull then her selfe, by whom you not alone shall finde remedie, but my tormenting greefes maye likewise bee comforted. Good Knight, aunswered the Princesse, the Gods themselues will trauaile to helpe thee, and it may be I haue learned of her, by whose death thou hast reuenged the wrong of manie noble persons: some hope of further good, to ease those passions which thy speeches bewray. True it is, that I stayed with *Malfada* the space of eight daies, yet not learning any thing of her woorthie the rehearsall, this onelie excepted: she tolde me that in the kings Court of *Grisca* and *Romata*, remained an auncient Knight named *Muzabelino*, by whome (if my maladie were curable) I should finde helpe, and by no other man whatsoeuer, so did she extoll him beyond all other. And had not the king my Father died soone after my returne, and my iniurious brother euer since molested mee, long ere this had I gone to that skilfull man, whome I meane to finde, so soone as I can bring my troubles to anie good ende.[3] By all our Gods, quoth the Prince *Maulerino*, seeing *Malfada* is deade, *Muzabelino* maye finish all the enchauntments: but during her life, neither he nor all the Magitians in the world were able to compasse it.

As for the kingdome of *Romata*, it is very farre from this Countrey, the greater will your paine and daunger be in trauailing thither. Right pleasant will the paine bee to me, said *Palmerin*, so may I recouer my deerest Freends againe: and for you sweete Madame will I aduenture my life, eyther to winne you peace

Palmerin d'Oliva: Part II 513

with your Brother, or a happie victorie by his death, that wee maye the sooner sette forward to *Romata*.

    A thousand thankes good Knight, quoth the Princesse, and this day shall we knowe what our Brother intendeth: if peace, it is welcome, if warre, we must defend our selues so well as we may. Still did the dogge cling about *Palmerins* feete, so that hee demaunded of the Princesse, if shee brought him from the Isle of *Malfada*, for doubtlesse, quoth he, I thinke it is some Knight transformed by that cruell woman, who heeretofore belike hath knowne me. At which words the dog howled exceedingly, when *Palmerin* tooke an oath that hee would searche all the worlde ouer, to finde some meane to bring him to his former shape, that hee might know from whence this loue proceeded. The next day the king *Tyreno* assaulted the Cittie, who was slaine in the battaile by *Palmerin*, so afterward was *Maulerino* crowned king of *Nabor*, and all the Countrey enioyed their former quiet: whereupon the Princesse *Zephira* gaue *Palmerin* her dogge, who requited her with many gracious thanks, because he greatlie suspected, that it was his freend *Trineus* transformed into that shape: but now let vs returne to the soldane of *Babilon*, vnderstanding how his Armie was discomfited at *Constantinople*.[4]

CHAPTER XLVI.
Howe one of the Nephewes to the King of Balisarca, brought newes to the Soldane of his vncles death, the foyle of his Armie, the losse of Palmerin and Olorico. And how the Princesse Alchidiana bought Ptolome, whom she greatly honored for Palmerins sake.

The King of *Balisarca*, (as you haue heard before) being slaine, his Armie discomfited and al his Galleys burnt before *Constantinople*,[1] one of his Nephewes that kept the straight of the *Bosphor*, with two foysts, least any succour should come that way to the Christians, by one Galley[2] that escaped, hearde all this misfortune: wherefore making haste backe againe fearing to be taken, at length arriued in the Soldans Kingdome, where not staying long, hee posted to the Courte, and to the Soldane reuealed all that had happened. When the Soldane heard how his Armie was thus ouerthrowne, *Palmerin* whom he loued so well, and the Prince *Olorico* lost in the storme on the sea: vexed with greefe and rage, hee called his Lorde Ambassadour *Maucetto* to him, saying.[3]

Haste thee good *Maucetto* to my Brother the Soldane of *Persia*, and desire him to leuey me a strong Armie against the Moneth of March next ensuing, to encounter with the Emperour of *Greece*: promising him the spoyle whatsoeuer it bee, reseruing for my selfe nothing but the fame of reuenge.

Maucetto departed presentlie on his iourney, and by the way mette sixe Moores, leading two Christians to the Soldans Court to sell, which were *Ptolome* and *Colmelio*, of whome hee demaunded why they were so bounde in chaines?

My Lord, quoth one of the Moores, they be Christian slaues, who not long since were taken at the Sea by *Olimaell* Admirall to the great Turke. And how came you by them? said *Maucetto*. The Admirall, quoth the Moore, gaue them to one of his Cozins, who now is deade, and his wife beeing loth to keepe them anie longer, sendes them to the Court to be solde for money. *Maucetto* bought *Colmelio* of them, refusing *Ptolome* because he was somewhat sicklie, and so passed on his Embassade. The Moores comming to the Court with poore *Ptolome*, and placing him among other slaues that stoode to bee solde, there came a deformed Moore, farre worsse mishapen then was *Thersites* the *Greek*,[4] and he would needes buy *Ptolome* of the Merchaunt: but *Ptolome* disdaining to be subiect to so vile a creature, gaue him such a stroke on the stomacke with his fiste, as made him tumble ouer backward, saying. Thou monstrous Villaine, let me rather die, then come into thy subiection. At this instant passed by the Princesse *Alchidiana*, smiling to see the Moore lie along: but when shee behelde the good personage of *Ptolome*, shee remembred her louer *Palmerin*, and was therewith mooued thus to speake. Howe durst thou take such hardinesse vpon thee, beeing a bondslaue and a captiue, thus to strike a Moore, free of this Countrey? *Ptolome* perceiuing by the Ladies attending on her, that shee was the Soldanes Daughter, falling on his knee, thus aunswered.

Assuredlie Madame, rather desire I death, then to liue at such an ill fauoured villaines controll, my selfe beeing a Knight at Armes. Are you then a knight? said the Princesse. I am good Madame, quoth he, although my seruitude hath very much altered mee. *Alchidiana* without any further questions, deliuered the Merchant two hundred Seraphes, and by two of her Squires caused him to bee conducted to her Chamber, where he was presentlie disroabed of his vnseemelie garments, and cloathed in such as well became a knight to weare: afterwarde, she commaunded her attendants to depart the chamber, and comming to *Ptolome*, she thus began.

Nowe Syr Knight, I intreate you by the holy faith you owe to your best beloued, that you will truelie tell mee, by what misfortune you happened first into thraldome. Madame, quoth he, seeing of your owne grace and bountie, you haue deliuered mee from these villaines that made sale of my life, I will not fable with you in any one point, but tell you a Historie repleat with wonderfull sorrowe. Hauing reuealed the manner of his taking, and all the mishaps hee endured euer since, the teares trickling downe his cheekes, he said. And yet sweete Ladie, all these passed miseries, and still abiding your slaue, greeues me not so much, as the losse of my deerest Freende, the best knight in the worlde, who went to see his Falcon flie, when the Pirates came and vnhappilie tooke vs.[5] Tell me good freende, quoth the Princesse, what may the knight bee called, of whom you make such estimation? Quoth *Ptolome*, he nameth himselfe *Palmerin d'Oliua*.

O soueraigne Gods, said *Alchidiana*, haue you beene companion to the noble *Palmerin*? That haue I in truth Madame, quoth he, and knowe more of his affayres then anie other man doth. Vnhappie that I am, said the Princesse, nowe see I well that I am deceiued in all my hope. Saye good knight, naie more, I coniure thee by thy faith to the soueraigne Creator of all things, to tell mee, if he bee of our Lawe, and hath beene dumbe of long,[6] or no? By God Madame, answered *Ptolome*, your adiuration is such, as rather will I make a sacrifice of my selfe, then bee found vntrue to you in any thing. Hee is a Christian, borne in *Greece*, and neuer had defect in his speech: if discreet consideration of following euents, eyther to escape captiuitie or death, did not inforce him to feigne such a deceite, for hee is most expert among all other, in dissembling anye matter may turne him aduauntage. Then such hath beene my fortune, quoth *Alchidiana*, as his vertue, bountie and wise foresight, vsed for the space of a yeere and more in my Fathers Court, made me so religiously vowed to him in loue, as neuer intend I to make other choise: and I sweare by all our Gods, that if I heare not the better tydings of him by thee, my spirit will forsake this wretched bodye, and expect better fortune among the soules in *Elisium*. Ah imperious loue, how wonderfull is thy strooke? My freende is contrarie to me in lawe and profession,[7] a Knight errant, vnknowne, absent from mee, and loues me not: for these occasions, were I the onelie Daughter to the great Emperor of *Turkie*, I neither can or will change my former opinion.

Happe then what shall, and let my Father make an oblation of my blood to his secret Idoll, I will not desist from louing him. And thou my Freend (quoth she to *Ptolome*), because thou hast not hid the truth from mee, bee thou at this instant free, and vse thy libertie as thou pleasest: for rather let me abide the death, then the companion to my noble Lorde suffer shame by mee. *Ptolome* falling on his knee, humblie kissed her hande, and began to reueale the knightly chiualrie, that *Palmerin* and *Tryneus* sometime did in *England*: likewise howe they brought the Kings Daughter from thence, who remained captiue among the Turks, and her Husband giuen as slaue to the Admiralles Cozin. It is enough said the Princesse, talke to me no more heereof, for by the great God, the verie remembraunce of him is greater greefe to me, then the mercilesse seruitude a poore slaue endureth. The loue he bare to you, to the other knight, and the yong *English* Princesse, whose misfortune I cannot sufficiently bewayle: calleth mee hence to trauaile in search of him, and may I find him with them, right gladsome will the iourney bee to mee, because hee is the onelie darling and fauorite of Fortune. And now shall I tell you howe I meane to couller mine intent. My Father not knowing your captiuitie, to him shall I saye how you are the onelie companion to *Palmerin*, and hither are you come to seeke him, as hauing hearde before that hee remained in your seruice: of this I dare assure you, his Maiestie so deerelie loueth *Palmerin*, that hee will deliuer you all things necessarie for his search, be it by land or sea. And if your God shall fauour you so much, as in your trauaile you happen to finde him, or else to send mee certaine tidings of him, you shall doo me the greatest honor, that euer Knight did to distressed Ladie. So forwarde was the Princesse in her amorous desire, and loth to waste time with tedious delaye: as that daie shee acquainted her Father therewith, and so cunningly shee plaid the Oratrix, as the soldane gaue *Ptolome* Armour, Horsses, Seruants, and fortie Knights to attend on him. Beside, he furnished him with two great Ships, that he might enquire at all the Ports on the Sea for *Palmerin*.

The daye beeing come of his departure, hee tooke his leaue of the Soldane, the Princesse *Alchidiana* accompanying him to the Porte, where for her adieu shee gaue him a sweet kisse, saying. Sir Knight, if your fortune bee such as to bring mee the man, who onelie hath power to mittigate my torments: beside the continuall fauours of a Princesse,[8] I will make you one of the greatest Lordes in the Orient. Madame (quoth hee) I will doo my diligence, and till I returne let good hope perswade yee.[9] So hoysing saile they set to Sea, where we will leaue him till hee meete with *Palmerin*.

Chapter XLVII.

How Palmerin and the princesse Zephira, departed from Elain towards Romata, to seeke Muzabelino, and what happened by the way in their iourney.

After that *Maulerino* was crowned king of *Nabor*, the rebellious Subiects brought to obedience, and the bodie of the slaine king *Tireno* enterred, the yong Princesse *Zephira* and *Palmerin* thought long to set forwarde on their iourney, wherefore the king allowing them a very honourable trayne, bequeathed them to their desired fortune. Hauing passed many regions, and sundrie dangers incident in trauaile, chiefely of a Basilisque, whome *Palmerin* with the helpe of the dog *Tryneus* valiantly ouercame,[1] at length they entred the realme of *Romata*, where by commandement of the king *Abimar*, their entertainment was according to their estates, the occasion thereof being thus. This king *Abimar* holding the greatest possessions in that region, would neuer yeeld himself as subiect to the signorie of *Persia*: wherat the soldan now growing offended, sent an Ambassadour to commaund him, presently to determine on his obedience, or else he would ouer-run his Countrey with a mighty Armie, and put both olde and yong to the Sworde. *Abimar* abashed at this threatning Embassade, demaunded counsell of the wise *Muzabelino*, what answer hee should make the Ambassadour, whereto the Magitian thus aunswered. Feare not my Lord the threatning menaces of the Soldane, for in that you haue two noble Sonnes, to witte the Princes *Tomano* and *Drumino*, knights of high and speciall account: yet come there two others, (one whereof maye not be knowne) with the Princesse *Zephira*, Daughter to the King of *Nabor*, who shall deliuer you from his tirannie, and make him your Freende, therefore dismaie not to sende him a hardie answer, as well beseemeth a Prince free, and not to be commaunded. And though one of the knights that commeth with the Princesse shall a while bee vnknowne to you, by the bountie of his companion, with whom no other may well compare: yet ere long you shall knowe him, to your no little ioye and contentation. *Abimar* giuing credit to *Muzabelinos* speeches, gaue charge in all the Citties where through the Princesse should passe, that shee shoulde be entertained with honorable tryumphes, as if himselfe had beene in companie. And though the Prince *Tomano* greeued heereat, who loued the yongest Daughter to the Soldane of *Persia*, yet the King answered the Ambassador, that hee woulde maintaine his right by the Sworde, and if the Soldane came to assayle him, he would defend his Countrey so well as he could.

The Ambassadour dispatched with this answer, *Tomano* came to *Muzabelino*, saying. Ah my deere Freende *Muzabelino*, what wrong haue you doone mee, in perswading my Father to holde warre with the Soldane? whose Daughter you know I loue in such sort, as if I obtaine her not in mariage, hardly can my life long endure. Content your selfe my Lord, answered *Muzabelino*: for if the two knights that come, bring fortune for your father, you must expect the like for your selfe. But, said the Prince, maye I not knowe their names? Let it suffise (quoth *Muzabelino*) what I haue saide, yet heereof I dare assure you, that they are Christians, and extract of the greatest linage on the earth, in bountie and valour incomparable:[2] whereof if you list to make experience, and thereby to credit what I haue said beside, I shall shewe you a meane auaylable for the purpose. You shall cause two Tents to be erected by the Cedar Fountaine, which is halfe a mile distant from this Cittie, in the one of them let be your Brother *Druminc*, and your selfe, with tenne of the best Knightes in your Fathers Court, and in the other let be your Sister: accompanied with tenne of her cheefest Ladies, and about a bowe shot from thence towards the high way side, you shall sette vp a Marble Pillar, whereupon let these lines be engrauen.

> Sir Knight, in these pauillions doth remaine,
>   A Lady fayre, kept by a Princes sonne:
> Foyle him by Ioust, and winne her hence againe,
>   Thou maist not passe before the deede be doone.[3]

If it happen that they passe by and see not the Pillar, send one of the Ladies to them, to let them vnderstande that they may not passe, before one of them haue Iousted with the Prince and his Knights. If they be vnhorssed by him, the Ladie must be deliuered to him: yet with this condition, that he refuse not to graunt her one demaunde. By Mahomet, sayd *Drumino* husband to the Lady, I will not meddle in this matter, he may be such a one, as if he hap to winne my Wife, he will be loth to restore her backe againe. Feare not that (quoth the Magitian) hee is so courteous, and hath so faire a Freend himselfe, as he neyther may or will with-holde her. By heauen said *Tomano*, I will cope with him, and to morrowe let the Piller and Pauillions bee erected, there will I with my companions stay his comming. See heere the cause why the King *Abimar*, commaunded the Princesse *Zephira* and her Knights to be so honourablie entertained. By this time is the Princesse come within a daies iourney of *Romata* and *Tomano* with his Brother, Sister, Ladies and knightes, betake themselues to the pauillions, hearing that *Zephira* was come so neere: and being themselues Armed, their sister decked likewise in most sumptuous ornaments, they vowed to breake many launces for her sake.

Chapter XLVIII.
How Palmerin Iousted against Tomano, Drumino and their knights, whome he all dismounted, and what entertainment the king Abimar, and the wise Nigromancer Muzabelino made them.

By this time is the princesse with *Palmerin*, and her companie, come to the place where the pauillions were erected, and not seeing the Piller,[1] they passed on: wherefore *Tomano* sent a Damosell to declare the conditions of the passage. *Palmerin* feigning himselfe somewhat wearie, made this answer. Damosell, you may saye to the Prince and his knights, that the Princesse *Zephira* is not in our guarde, as the Lady he fights for abideth with him. Nor comes she hither to be fought for, rather doth she intreat him to spare vs the Ioust, in that it will be small honor to him to conquer knights ouerlaboured in trauaile, and whose horses are not able for that exercise.

The Damosell certifying the Prince of this aunswer, he grew into anger, swearing they should not passe before they tryed their fortune: wherefore hee sent the Damosell againe, who thus spake to *Palmerin*. Sir knight, your excuses may not serue you, you must eyther Ioust or leaue the Princesse behind you. Trust me Damosell, answered *Palmerin*, sorrie woulde I be to accompanie her so far, and leaue her in the custody of one I know not, did your Prince shewe more courtesie, it woulde agree much better with his order: but because he shall not think, that we refuse the Iouste through feare or cowardise, say hee shall haue his desire, both he and all his shall try their fortune ere wee passe further.

This answer returned to the Prince, *Drumino* first shewed himselfe in the Fielde, and by importunate intreatie, certaine of the Princesses Knights would first try their valour: but such was their ill fortune, as *Drumino* vnhorsed them one after another. *Zephira* somewhat offended heereat, intreated *Palmerin* eyther to win them passage, or else with his successe[2] she was content to staye Prisoner. I goe Madame (quoth *Palmerin*) and Fortune speede mee, as I regard the safetie of your honor. *Muzabelino*, hauing acquainted the King with this pastime, they came in habits disguised to beholde it, at what time the Prince *Drumino* encountred *Palmerin*. But not to hold you with tedious discourse considering which way the victorie is intended,[3] the two Princes and all their knights were manfullye foyled by *Palmerin*.

The Ioust beeing ended, and the king returned again to the Cittie, *Muzabelino* came to *Palmerin*, and hauing saluted him with great reuerence, thus spake. Woorthie Lord, who onelie deseruest the name of chiualrie, let mee intreate you to excuse the kings Son, who to make proofe of your valour, by my meanes attempted this noble aduenture, from which you haue escaped with great honour, and to their shame that made the challenge. What are you Syr, said *Palmerin*, that know me so well, and the cause why I came into this Countrey? Your Freend *Muzabelino* (quoth he) whome you haue taken such paines to finde, and who knowing you to be a Christian, will keepe you from all dangers among these Mahumetistes. *Palmerin* suddainlie allighting from his Horsse, came and embraced him, saying. Noble Freend, suffer mee to kisse your hand, as a witnesse of my reuerence to your honourable age. Not so my Lord, answered *Muzabelino*, rather suffer me to doo my dutie, to that incomparable person, by whose meanes ere sixe Monethes be past, the greatest nobilitie in the world shall receyue incredible honour.[4]

While these courteous ceremonies endured, the conquered Princesse with her Ladies came from the Pauillion, and saluting *Palmerin* with great courtesie, sayde. See heere, Sir Knight, the Lady, who trusting in your honourable benignitie, commeth to submit her selfe at your disposition, beeing woonne with more choyse chiualrie, then euer any other Ladie was. Notwithstanding, I hope that you will not refuse to graunt me one demaund, according to the conditions agreed in the Ioust. *Palmerin* seeing her so discreet and modest, so sumptuous in apparell, and accompanied with so manie Ladies, iudged that she was the Kings Daughter, and Wife to the Prince *Drumino*, wherefore entertaining her verie graciously, hee thus replyed. Vnfitting it is, faire Ladie, that a Princesse of so high and speciall qualitie, shoulde bee subiect to a poore and vnknowne Knight: and though the agreement of the Ioust bee such, yet do I humblie thanke you for this honour, bequeathing you to your former libertie, and restoring you to him that hath best right to you.

A thousand thankes worthie Lorde, said the Princesse, now I see the words of *Muzabelino* to my father are true, that the Knight who conducted Madame *Zephira*, as in chiualrie hee surpasseth all other: so in franke minde and liberalitie, hee hath not his seconde, which was the cheefest cause why I aduentured my selfe in this hazarde of Fortune. Madame, quoth *Palmerin*, if the wise *Muzabelino* hath vsed any speach of mee in mine absence, and to my honor, it proceeded not by my vertue, but his good will in so dooing, which if I liue, I will one day acknowledge. Right welcome are you, saide the Princesse, and faire *Zephira*, the rather for your sake: and such be the houre of your arriuall heere, as you may obtaine the ende of your desires. *Zephira* humblie thanked the Princesse, *Tomano, Drumino*, and all the rest embracing *Palmerin*, thinking it no dishonour to be conquered by him: they mounted all on horsebacke, and comming to the Cittie, founde the King there, readie with an honorable traine to receiue them, who saluting the princesse *Zephira*, verie kindly, said. No maruell Madame, if you durst vndertake so long a iourney, hauing the only knight of Fortune in your companie, as my Sonnes haue good occasion to witnesse: and shee that commits her selfe to his charge, may bee well assured of speciall defence. *Zephira* with humble thanks requiting the King, *Palmerin* and all the rest graciously welcommed, they rode all to the Pallace, where being intertained in choysest sort, *Muzabelino* still accompanied *Palmerin*, who forgot not his woonted kindnes to his louing Dogge.

Chapter XLIX.

The talke that the princesse Zephira and Palmerin had with the wise Muzabelino: and how Palmerin departed from Romata to the Castell of the ten Rocks.

The Princesse *Zephira*, who had not yet talked with *Muzabelino*, in the morning sent for him and *Palmerin*, shee causing them to sit downe by her, began in this manner. My Lord, if your great iudgement haue acquainted you with the cause of my comming, and that you will doe anie thing for the loue of Sir *Palmerin*, let pittie perswade you, for in you onely consisteth my remedie. Madame, quoth *Muzabelino*, vse not such speaches, for what my studie and practise hath taught me, you must make no account of, but referre your selfe to the supreame Creator, who by the meanes of noble *Palmerin*, will restore your health, and him will I acquaint with the manner how it must be compassed.[1]

Your disease happened by smelling to a flower,[2] and by the smell of another it must be recouered. The flower appoynted to giue you health, groweth in an Arbour in the Castell of the tenne Rocks, and kept by the enchauntment of a Ladie, more skilfull in all artes, then euer was the skilfull *Medea*.[3] This Ladie deceassing an hundred yeares since, and more. Shee seeing before her death the vertue of this flower, and of a Bird which is kept there by the selfe same meanes, hauing inchaunted them in a Garden, the most sumptuous in the world, raysed ten Rocks of Marble without the Castell, each one ascending higher then an other, and by these Rocks was the Castle named.[4] Such enchauntment did the Ladie exorcise on them, as when anie one thinketh to passe them, presently starteth out of each Rocke an armed Knight, who returneth the aduenturer so forciblie, as to this day they haue not beene passed by any. Couragious therefore must he be that passeth these Rocks, which if *Palmerin* by his bountie and prowesse doo not accomplish, no man liuing can ende the aduenture: for by force, not cunning must the enchauntment be ended. When the Princesse heard, that by the daungerous trauaile of noble *Palmerin* her health must be restored, she thus sorrowfully complained.

Ah Gods, suffiseth it not that heeretofore this good Knight aduentured his life, in the daungerous battell when my Brother was slaine:[5] but nowe he must abide the diuellish coniurations, where death is dayly and hourelie expected? shall I consent to offer him such wrong, and bee guiltie of his blood, who surpasseth all other in chiualrie? rather let my death be a warrant for his safetie, then noble *Palmerin* shoulde endure such perrill for me. Lament not Madame, quoth *Muzabelino*, before you haue cause, hee that slewe *Malfada*, and her Seruaunts,[6] is so specially fauoured of the heauenlie powers, as no enchauntment whatsoeuer hath power to hurt him. Why Madame, said *Palmerin*, thinke you my good will is lesse to doo you seruice, then when I was first brought to your Court? Forbeare these teares, I pray you, and offend not your selfe: for such is my hope in God, that what is done by man, shall bee destroyed by man: besides, it will bee great reproach to mee, if comming into straunge Countries to seeke aduentures, I shall depart without triall of my fortune. *Muzabelino* hearing him speake so couragiouslie, tooke him aside, saying. Noble and hardie Knight, whom feare of death cannot dismay, happie shall I account my selfe to doo thee anie seruice.

And to the ende thou mayst with better affection followe this enterprise, assure thy selfe to passe the Rockes, and enter the Castell with happie victorie, where ending all the aduentures therein contained, thou shalt finde a part of remedie for recouering thy companions, but not all, for the rest is in the Tower of *Malfada*, where as yet thou canst not enter, but at thy returne shalt easily open, and in the ende ioyfully finde all thy Companions and Freendes. For the rest, feare not my discouerie of thy secrete loue and parentage, which is the most noble in all Christendome, for rather will I bee torne in a thousand peeces, then so good a Knight shall bee iniuried by mee. Seeing you know so much quoth *Palmerin*, I commit all to God and you, let me therefore right soone craue leaue of the King for my departure, because I long that the Princesse were eased. Right sorie was the King to part with him so soone, yet the hope of his short returne somewhat pacified him. And when the newes were spreade abroad that *Palmerin* should trauaile to the Castell of the tenne Rockes: *Tomano, Drumino*, and the Princesse *Zephira* woulde needes beare him companie, which hee being not able to gainesay, because they were importunate on him, gaue his consent. So departing from *Romata*, they made such haste in their iourney, as within fewe dayes after they arriued at the Castell: and comming to the first Rocke, they behelde a goodly Sworde, enclosed therein vp to the crosse. The two yong Princes maruailing thereat, allighted from their Horsses, and assailed by strength to pull it out. Which they were not able to doe: wherefore *Tomano* entreated *Palmerin* to trie his fortune, who after many courteous refusals offered to pull it foorth, but a fearefull flame of fire suddenly issued foorth of the Rocke, which compelled them to retyre back, wherfore *Palmerin* said to the Princes: This Sword I see must be none of ours, therefore it is in vaine to striue any further.[7]

Chapter L.

Howe Palmerin passed the tenne Rockes, vanquished the tenne enchaunted Knightes, and entered the Castell, where hee finished all the enchauntments: Trineus returning to his former shape, and what happened to them afterward.

Palmerin when hee had failed in drawing the Sworde out of the Rocke, hee prepared himselfe to the Combat with the enchaunted Knights, whome as yet hee coulde not anie way discerne: but first he began his orisons in this manner. O soueraigne Creator, who euermore hath succoured me in all my aduersities and fortunes, this day giue mee strength to confound these diuelries and enchauntments, and let thy name haue the honour of a glorious victorie.

Then giuing his horse the spurres, gallopped onward, saying. Sweete Mistresse *Polynarda*, if euer your remembraunce gaue mee ayde and fauour, now let your diuine regard comfort your seruaunt. Beeing then betweene the two foremost Rocks, a mightie Knight mounted on a lustie Courser, with a huge Launce in his hande, called to him, saying.

Turne Sir Knight, you may passe no further, then furiouslie encountering one another, they met so roughlie togither with their bodyes, as they were both cast foorth of their saddles. The Dog that still followed *Palmerin*, seeing his Freends horse offered to stray, caught the bridle by the raignes with his teeth, and would not let him passe anie further. In the meane while, *Palmerin* hauing fought with the Knight, and after a long and cruell combat, smote his head from his shoulders. In breefe,[1] he was so fauoured of Fortune, as hauing vanquished all the tenne Knights, he passed the tenne Rocks: and no sooner was he mounted on the foremost, but a darke Clowde compassed him about, so that the two Princes, *Zephira* and their Knights, to theyr great amazement lost the sight of him, yet his former victorie, exempted all feare from them of bad successe.[2] There stayed they *Palmerins* returne till Sunne setting, when the two Princes demaunded of *Zephira*, if shee woulde depart thence, or stay there all night? Depart? quoth shee, no by my life, heere will I abide the good knights returne from the Castell: wherupon her seruants hauing erected theyr pauillions, they there tooke vp their lodging for that night. By this time *Palmerin* was come to the Castell Gate, where looking on his Armour which was hacked in peeces, his flesh cut and mangled in manie places, breathing foorth a bitter sigh, sayd. If yet this trauaile may auaile the Princesse, and my noble companions that are enchaunted, let happe to mee what please the Heauens, for theyr libertie is more deere to mee then life. Then looking on his Dog, who all this while held the Horses bridle in his mouth, hee remembred, that he had not demaunded of *Muzabelino* anie thing concerning him, wherefore he said. Ah gentle dog, yet no Dog (I thinke) but rather some Knight thus transformed, howe forgetfull haue I beene of thy seruice in my necessitie? why did I not demaund the trueth of *Muzabelino*, what thou art? But mayst thou prooue to be my good Freend *Trineus*, when all the enchauntments of this Castell shall bee ended, thy former shape (I hope) shall bee restored.

So striking at the Castell Gate, to see if anie way hee could get it open, at length hee looked vppe to the battlements, and beheld an auncient Knight, with a long beard so white as snowe, who furiously thus spake to him. Proude Knight, who made thee so bolde thus to beate on the Gate? enter, vnto thy further ill I hope: with these wordes the Gates opened of themselues, when presently *Palmerin* with his Dog entred, and the olde man, who seemed ouer-spent with yeeres and weaknesse, meeting him in the Gate, taking him by the arme, threw him violently agaynst the ground, saying. Thou that hast ouercome the ten Knights, yong and armed, what canst thou doo to an olde man without defence? Wretched villaine, aunswered *Palmerin*, wherefore hast thou strooken me? by the liuing God, did not thine age excuse thee, soone should I lay the breathlesse at my foote.

Soft and faire, said the olde man, thou shalt haue work enough to defend thy selfe. So catching *Palmerin* about the middle, he wroong him so cruelly, as one might heare his bones cracke. O my God cried *Palmerin*, defend me against this cursed diuell. At length hee forced the olde man to let goe his holde: when began such a furious fight betweene them, as neuer was *Palmerin* in such daunger, in that euerie blowe was giuen him, hee thought did breake all his bones in peeces. The dog seeing his Maister in such extremitie, caught the olde man by the throate, and neuer left tugging till he got him downe, when suddenly he vanished away, and was no more seene afterward.[3] For this victorie *Palmerin* thanked God, and hauing cherished his Dog, entred further into the Castell. Where he behelde most stately Galleries, erected on great colombes of Porpherie and Alabaster, as neuer did hee beholde a more sumptuous spectacle.

In the middest of the Court was a goodly Tombe, enclosed with barres of beaten Golde, and ouer it stoode a goodly Table of Christal, vphelde by foure Satyrs of Agatha: and on the Table was pictured the personage of a Ladie, drawne by such curious arte and woorkmanship, as hardly could it bee equalled through the world. *Palmerin* approched to behold the counterfeit, which helde in the one hande a Booke fast shutte, and in the other a Key of Golde, poynting with the Key towarde the Gate of the Pallace: whereupon he imagined, that this was the Tombe of the Ladie Enchauntresse, whereof *Muzabelino* had told him before, and putting his hand betweene the golden Barres, the Image presently offered him the Key. Heereat beeing somewhat abashed, he iudged that this happened not without great cause, wherefore taking the Key, hee went and opened the Pallace Gate, and entering the great Hall, hee founde it so richlie paued, and garnished rounde about with such costly Tapistrie, as the greatest Monarch in the world had not the like.

Looking behinde him for his Dog, he beheld him suddainlie chaunged to his former shape, and running to embrace *Palmerin*, said. Happie be the houre of thy comming deere Freend, to whom I remaine for euer bounde, in acknowledging the speciall graces and fauours receiued. But *Palmerin* deceiued with so manie illusions before, woulde hardlie giue credite to what he now behelde, reputing him rather some hellish furie so disguised, onely to entrap him with further danger, which *Trineus* perceiuing, spake againe. Ah my noble Friend *Palmerin*, for Gods sake doubt no more, I am thy Brother *Tryneus*, who since thy comming from *Elain*, followed thee in the enchaunted forme of a Dogge: reioyce then with me, for since thy long desired hope hath now so good an ende, doubt not but the residue of thine affaires will prooue as fortunate. *Palmerin* beeing nowe thorowly resolued, I leaue to your iudgements the kinde gratulations betweene them, who well can conceiue the wonderfull ioy of long absent Friendes, especially of such as liue and die for each other. Ah my Lord quoth *Palmerin*, why did I not sooner acknowledge thee? the great succour thou gauest me by the way, might well haue perswaded me, yet though I still imagined thee my friend transformed, hardly could I resolue thereon till further experience.

Ah fortune, if heeretofore thou hast beene enuious towardes mee, yet now hast thou recompenced me in such sort, as now I haue no cause to exclaime on thee. So sitting downe together, *Trineus* reuealed the manner of his taking, and all that befell him till his transformation. Which *Palmerin* to requite, discoursed the knowledge of his Parents, how he was betrothed to his Lady *Polynarda*, and howe he recouered the Princesse *Agriola*, who afterwarde was likewise enchaunted in the Isle of *Malfada*.[4] *Tryneus* at these newes, was readie to die with greefe, but *Palmerin* perswaded him of the wise *Muzabelinos* promise, that shortly hee should returne againe to the Isle, and there finish all the enchauntments whatsoeuer. While they thus conferred together, they sawe sodainely sette before them a Table furnished with all kinde of meates, and a hand holding two great Golden Candlestickes, wherein burned two faire waxe Tapers, beside, they heard a trampling of their feete that brought the meate to the Table, but they could not discerne any liuing creature. Trust mee, quoth *Palmerin*, I thinke some bodie knowes I haue an hungrie appetite, sitte downe with me good friend, for these two moneths[5] had I not a better stomacke. After they had well refreshed themselues, the table was presently taken away againe, and they entring a goodly wardrobe, where vnder a Canapie of cloth of Golde, they founde two maruailous costly greene Armours, so beset with faire Emeraldes and great Oriental Pearles, as neuer proude Pagan wore the like in heathenesse. By them stood two goodly Sheeldes of proofe, in the one beeing figured the Armes of *Constantinople*, and in the other the Creast of *Allemaigne*, whereat *Palmerin* not a little maruailing, saide to *Trineus*. I think my Lord, that these Armours were prouided for vs, let vs trie if they bee fitte for our bodies, so helping to arme each other, they founde them so fitte as they had beene purposely made for them. There founde they likewise a Siluer Casket, wherein were two sumptuous Kingly Crownes of Golde, and betweene them stood a rich Golden Cup, hauing in it a Ring, with the most beautifull stone in it that euer was seene.

Wondering at these euents, and doubtfull to take thence those rare presents, immediately a Damosell came before them, and humbly on her knees thus spake. Most mightie and magnanimious Princes, the Iewels you haue founde in the Casket are yours, and them must you carrie to the Ladies of your affections, because they were purposely made for them, as these worthie Armours were for you. As for her that deuised them, in this shee accounteth her selfe right happie, that this day they are fallen into your power, and by you shall all the aduentures heere be finished.

You my Lord, quoth shee to *Trineus*, must take the Ring that is in the Cup, and leaue it not wheresoeuer you come, least you be changed into the shape of a dogge againe. And you my Lord *Palmerin* must take the Cup, to put the flowers therein, which you must beare to the Princesse *Zephira*, assuring you that no one must drinke therein, but she to whom you must carrie it. Faire Damosell, saide *Palmerin*, tell me howe I shall finde the Garden, where those flowers grow of such soueraigne vertue, and howe I may come to the Arbour where the strange Birde remaineth pearched: likewise if any other then your selfe is in this Castle?

My Lord, quoth shee, the Ladie of this Castle at her decease, left all the persons in this Castle a sleepe by enchauntment, except my selfe that am her Neece, and such coniurations hath she charmed them withall, as they shall not stirre till you haue taken the Birde you aske for: at whose fearefull crie they shall all awake,[6] in all this long time no whit consumed. And heere haue I euer since remained forepointed by her to doo you seruice, in shewing you the manner howe to gather the flowers, and to take the fatall Birde pearched in the Arbour, whether I will bring you at an appointed houre. In meane while rest your selues on this rich bedde, which hath beene prepared onely for you, and here repose your selues till my returne. By my sword Damosell, quoth *Palmerin*, you tell vs matters full of wonder, notwithstanding, seeing we finde some parte of them true, we giue credit to the rest. So bidding her good night, there slept they till the next morning, when the Damosell came to call them, conducting them into the Garden, the most braue and stately that euer they behelde, and after she had shewed them the Arbour, departed. *Palmerin* looking round about him, maruailed at the ingenious foundation of the Castle, the surpassing faire Galleries, and the beautifull Fountaines in the Garden, where hee heard an exceeding pleasant harmonie of Birds. Then calling *Tryneus* to him, entred the Arbour, where taking the fatall Birde by the wings, shee gaue three great cryes so loude and fearefull, as made both the Princes greatly amazed.

At this instant were all the enchauntments there ended, and the Seruants restored to their former libertie, when *Palmerin* hauing tied the Bird to his fist with a threed the damosell gaue him, and filling his Cup with the soueraigne flowers, they came foorth of the Garden, and in the great Hall mette them the Lord and Ladie of the Castle, so olde, withered, and decrepite, as it seemed hardly they could sustaine themselues, casting themselues at *Palmerins* feete, they saide.

Ah noble Prince, flower of all chiualrie, the highest God hath blessed thee from thy Cradle, and in the end shall make thee the happiest in the worlde, for the especiall good thou hast this day doone, restoring all them to life that here slumbred, except the aged Ladie my Wiues Sister, who for these hundred yeeres past hath slept in her Tombe. After many courteous speeches passed betweene them, *Palmerin* and *Trineus* departed the Castle, and as they went downe the Rocks, *Tomano* and the Princesse *Zephira* came to meete them, she courteously embracing him, saide. How fares my noble Lord? greatly did I despaire of your health, for this morning I heard such a fearefull crie from the Castle, as wee were out of all hope to see you againe. By the ayd of God, Madame, answered *Palmerin*, and this Knight my deere Friende, whom in the shape of a Dogge you brought from *Malfada*, I finde my selfe in perfect content, and heere haue I brought you the soueraigne remedie for your so long and vnfortunate disease. But may it bee, quoth the Princesse, that so faire a knight shoulde bee so transformed? No lesse do I reioyce for his good fortune then mine owne. So entred they the Princesse pauillion, discoursing all the maruailes they had seene.

Chapter LI.

How the Princesse Zephira was cured of her disease, and Trineus ended the aduenture of the enchaunted sword in the Rocke.

After that the Princesse *Zephira* had felt the sweete odours of the flowers *Palmerin* brought her, the enuenomed wormes which so long time had tormented her, fell from her head dead to the ground, and the lothsome smell of her Canker beganne to cease. Yet all the scars on her face were not throughly healed: but the sodaine ease that she found by the flowers, gaue hir hope that in time they would weare away. Meane while the two Princes of *Romata*, conferred with *Palmerin* about the strange Birde, and also of the costly Armours they brought with them from the Castle, which beeing past ouer with no little admiration, they remembred the Sword enchaunted in the Rocke, whereuppon the Prince *Tomano* entreated *Trineus*, to trie if that aduenture were reserued for him.

Nay quoth *Trineus*, if you haue alreadie failed, hardly may I hope of better fortune, yet can I but loose my labour as you haue doone, and shame were it for me to passe hence without triall. So taking the Sword by the handle, with very great ease he puld it out of the Rocke, being the goodliest Sword in workmanshippe that euer was deuised. Trust me, quoth *Trineus*, he that made this weapon doubtlesse hath tride the vertue thereof. That may bee, answered *Palmerin*, but had hee likewise knowne the valour of the Knight, who nowe is worthily become maister thereof, of greater count would he haue esteemed his labour, and to thy perpetuall honour deere friende maist thou imploy it. But now woorthy Lords? seeing the Princesse *Zephira* hath found so good ease, and my louing Brother *Trineus* hath wonne this Sword, I thinke it best that wee set forwards to *Romata*, which (after they had seene the sumptuous buildings in the Castle, the rich Tombe, the beautifull Garden, and all other monuments worthie view) they did.

Beeing come to *Romata*, and there receiued with speciall signes of honor, the wise *Muzabelino* caused the fatall Bird to feede of the flowers, which *Palmerin* hadde brought from the Castle of the tenne Rocks. No sooner had the Bird tasted the flowers, but presently shee deliuered such melodious notes, as sweeter harmonie was neuer heard before, and during the time of her singing, fell so many droppes of precious water from her beake, as before Dinner time the Cuppe was well neere filled. Which when the wise Nigromancer perceiued, hee brought a verie faire Lute to *Palmerin*, saying. I beseech you my Lorde play some exquisite peece of Musique, that the Bird listening to your melodie, may cease her owne recordes, els shal we loose the soueraigne vertue contained in the Water. *Palmerin* taking the Lute, plaide thereon so artificially, that the Princesse of *Romata* whom he woonne in the Ioust,[1] was enforced to vse these speeches. How can wee sufficiently maruaile at the perfections of *Palmerin*? for if in prowesse he surpasse *Hercules* of *Libia*, who ouercame Tyrants and Monsters at his pleasure:[2] well may wee name him another *Amphion* or *Orpheus* of *Thrace*, who with theyr melodie tamed the Fishes, Beasts, and Birds.[3] *Trineus* taking the Cup, brought it

Palmerin d'Oliva: Part II 529

to the Princesse *Zephira*, who dipping her handkercher therein, bathed her face therewith: the precious vertue whereof was such, as all the enuenomed scarres the wormes had made, were presently washed away, and her face so delicate as euer it was before: whereupon the Princesse falling at *Palmerins* feete, ioyfully
thus spake. Doubtlesse my Lord, I am greatly beholding to the Prince *Trineus*, who saued my life when the Traytour would haue slaine mee in my bedde:[4] but I must confesse my selfe much more indebted to your worthinesse, by whose paines the venomous putrefaction is extinguished, whereby I endured torments farre exceeding death.
    Madame, answered *Palmerin*, your happie recouerie must not be imputed to me, but to the soueraigne Lorde that so prouided for you, and seeing your health is so worthily restored, I thinke best that wee sette forward to morrow on our iourney, that we may finish the Magicall coniurations of *Malfada*, as wee haue alreadie doone those at the tenne Rocks. The Princesse of *Romata* hearing these words, preuented the answere of *Zephira*, and comming to *Palmerin*, said. I beseech you Sir Knight, in honour of that God which you reuerence, that you will not refuse me one demaund, according to your promise made me, when you ouercame my Brother and his Knights in the Ioust. Aske Lady (saide *Palmerin*) what you will, and you shall not bee denied, so that the matter consist in my power to performe. Well may you performe it (quoth she) and to your endlesse honour I hope. The summe of my request is, that you wil not forsake the King my Father, till his warre against the Soldane of *Persia* be finished. And that you would entreate your Friende to accompanie you therein. Denie mee not good Sir, for no greater shame is to a Knight then breach of promise: nor will I stirre from your foote, vntill you haue graunted what I request. In sooth Madame, answered *Palmerin*, although my Friend and I haue great affaires in our Countrey, yet (in respect of my promise) we will assist your Father, let vs in meane while intreate you, to pardon our returne with the Princesse *Zephira*, who thinks the time long before shee come to *Nabor*. Doubtlesse my Lorde, quoth *Zephira*, rather then you and my Lorde *Trineus* shall breake your promise to the Princesse, in giuing succour to the King *Abimar* her Father: I can content my selfe to stay heere more willingly then to returne to the King my Brother. Madame, saide *Muzabelino*, assure your selfe that *Palmerin* is the onely meane whereby you haue attained your present felicitie, and by him shall you with honour see your Countrey againe. In sooth my Lord, saide the Princesse, full well I know his owne gracious nature induced him, first to aduenture his life for the safetie of my Countrey: then to passe strange Countreyes with daunger, onely to finde you, and lastly his rare fortune at the Castle of the tenne Rocks, from whence hee brought those precious flowers, and the fatall Byrd, wherby my long infirmitie hath beene cured. To offer him fauour or all my possessions in way of recompence of so great paines, they are not comparable: for though I made him Lorde of my selfe, and all those territories my father left me, yet doth my conscience tell mee they are too base. In breefe, I know his deserts so exceeding my

reach, as well may I sitte downe to imagine, but neuer bee able to contriue a sufficient rewarde. Beleeue me Madame, aunswered *Muzabelino*, you haue spoken truth, and his noble magnanimitie must onely helpe my Lorde, and this I assure you, that were it not the daunger of his kingly honour, and hazard of the whole Monarchie of *Asia*, hardly might the knight be stayed heere, of such waight and importance are his other affaires. Then calling *Palmerin* to him, whose inward thoughts were busied with the remembrance of his Lady, he said.

Let not your stay heere my Lorde offende you, though well I knowe the waight of your greefe, for that God who hath called you to this present estate, hath forepoynted things that you cannot shunne, in recompence whereof, before your departure from this countrey, great and victorious honours are appoynted you. Beside, for a perfect resolution in your further doubts, take you no care for nourishing your Birde: for when your Musique made her cease singing, at that instant I threw such a charme on her, as henceforth shee shall liue without taking any foode. And when you returne to your Citie of *Constantinople*, let her bee pearched in some conuenient place, in the great hall of your Pallace, and there shall she remaine as a certaine Oracle vntill the day of your death, to deliuer tydings of good or bad. If anie Knight or Ladie shall enter your Court, either with intent of treason, or bringing ill newes, the Birde shall giue such fearefull shrikes, as she did at the time when you tooke her in the Arbour: but if the newes be of ioy, and for your good, then shall she sing more sweetly, then when the souereigne water fell from her beake, wherewih the Princesse *Zephira* was cured.[5]

In breefe my Lorde, at the time when you must leaue this life, for the glorious habitation among the blessed, shee shall foretel such strange occasions, as shall dismay the most resolute courage. By this meane shall you be guarded from all inconueniences, and your good fortune continued in such sort, as you shall bee the most peaceable Emperour that euer liued in *Greece*. Certes my Lord, answered *Palmerin*, not by any desert in me, am I thus honoured with so high a present, which I will keepe so charie as mine owne person: but that the name of *Muzabelino* may for euer be imprinted in my heart, giue mee some one of your name or kindred, who euermore may bee neerest to my person. My Lord quoth *Muzabelino*, to you will I giue one of my Sonnes, begotten by me on a Christian Ladie, agreeing with you in faith, and opinion: whereof I am not sorie, yet feare I that the King should knowe so much, least his religion might cause his death.

Deere freend, said *Palmerin*, for Gods sake giue him me presently, and him will I loue as hee were my brother. Your request (quoth he) can I not yet satisfie, till wee goe to my Castle where he is kept, which because I will no longer deferre, to morrow will I perswade the King to iourney to his great Cittie of *Grisca*, there to take view of his Armie, when I shal compasse the meane to giue him you. Vpon this conclusion they departed to their chambers.

Chapter LII.
How Muzabelino gaue Palmerin his Sonne Bellechino, entertaining the King and all his companie royally at his Castle, and how the two Armies of the King Abimar and the Soldane of Persia encountred, with the successe therof.

Muzabelino perceiuing by his art, that the Soldane of *Persia* with his power was neere at hand, thinking to ruinate the great Cittie of *Grisca*, aduertised the King thereof, willing him with all speede to muster his Armie, and preuent the soldanes determination. The King not misliking his aduise, set forward presently to *Grisca*, and by the way, at the earnest intreatie of *Muzabelino*, the King with all his courtly companie, lay at his Castle, where many rare deuises were shown them by enchauntment, which I passe ouer as matter altogether impertinent.[1] There did the Magitian giue *Palmerin* his Sonne *Bellechino*, one of his Daughters likewise to the Queene, and another to the Princesse *Zephira*.

Afterward they iourneyed to the Cittie of *Grisca*, where all his armie was ranged in readines, beeing numbred an hundred thousand fighting men: the auantguarde he committed to the two Princes, *Palmerin* and *Trineus*, consisting of twentie thousand horsemen, his two battailes of 10000 Archers on horsebacke, the two Princes *Tomano* and *Drumino* had in charge, and the rereward was gouerned by the two Kinges of *Sauata* and *Garara*. The Soldanes power beeing ordained in battaile wise, within few dayes after the fight beganne, which continued with such danger on either side, as the victorie hung very long in suspence. In the ende, after a mightie massacre made of the *Persians*, among whom was *Donadel* Prince of *Siconia* slaine, with many other great Califes and Lords, the Soldane himselfe was taken prisoner by *Palmerin*, and sent bound with fetters of Gold to the Princesse *Zephira*. The Messenger comming to the Princesse Chamber, declared how *Palmerin* had sent her that prisoner, to entreate him as her selfe liked best. In sooth my Lord quoth the Princesse to the Soldane, you are right welcome for his sake that sent you: heere shall your entertainement be as fittes your calling, and mislike not your mishap, in that the knight who sent you, is wont to conquere where himselfe pleaseth. The Soldane angrie at his hard fortune, yet seeing hee was prisoner to a Lady so beautifull, was immediately so surprised with loue,[2] as hee was not able to answere the Princesse one word. But she perceiuing he was very sore wounded, caused him to bee conducted to a goodly Chamber, commaunding her Chirurgions to attend him dilligently.

On the morrow shee came to see how hee fared, when Loue ouermastering all his senses, made him forgette his hatred to the King *Abimar*, resoluing to become his friend by marriage of the Princesse, and vnable longer to suppresse his waighting passions, which more troubled him then his dangerous wounds, hee thus beganne. Fairest among the daughters of men, tell me I desire you, if you bee the Childe of the King *Abimar*, or els of whence you are, to the ende I may one day acknowledge this fauour, which your milde nature affoordes your prisoner. Heereunto the Princesse answered, howe shee was Daughter to the King *Onodius* of *Nabor,* coupling therewith all her passed fortunes: concluding in the ende, that in all actions agreeing with honour, shee remained his humble Seruant. Fortune, quoth he, neuer constant but in vnconstancie, once yesterday was I the greatest Prince in the worlde, and now none in my Kingdome so miserable as my selfe, beeing brought in subiection to my inferiour, and snared in loue with my vassailes Daughter. Wisely sayd the Poet, *That badlie doo loue and Maiestie agree togither:*[3] for though the height of mine estate forbids my desire, yet loue and mine owne lyking are two such seuere enemies, as I must not nowe stand to dispute the cause. Happie is the Knight in whose power remaines a Ladie so excellent: but much more happie is the Ladie that can commaunde so great a person, by whom such honours are this day affoorded you fayre Princesse, as wel may you vaunt to bee the greatest in *Persia.*

If by a Knight surpassing in prowesse I was conquered in battaile, by one in beautie and curtesie incomparable am I againe ouermaistred: so that I am enforced to present you my heart, and all the signories I possesse, to vse at your pleasure, vowing (for your sake) perpetuall peace with *Abimar* mine enemie. The Princesse abashed at this vnexpected offer, a sweete blush coloured her daintie cheekes, and fearing to be imputed too indiscreete, shaped her answere to the last poynt of the Soldanes speeches, as thus. In sooth my Lord, well could I like, that peace were concluded betweene the King and you, though not by any meane in mee, but by the omnipotent power of the Goddes: who letting you know the weaknesse of your owne strength, would not haue any warre betweene you and the King *Abimar.* And if it like you so much to abase your selfe, as to like the simple Daughter of a King, who while hee liued, was your highnesse Subiect: well may I with modestie giue consent: for if my Father all his life time obeyed you as his Lorde, vnseemely were disobedience in his Daughter. By the holie Alcaron of Mahomet, aunswered the Soldane, your benigne humilitie hath more conquered me, then the proudest enemie in the worlde coulde doo: doo you therefore appoynt the Articles of our peace, and I as vnpartiall will agree thereto.

Thus began the peace and the promise of mariage betweene the Soldane and the Princes *Zephira,* which beeing thorowlie agreed vppon, the King *Abimar, Palmerin, Tryneus,* and all the states subscribing thereto, the Camps on either side were discharged, and the Soldane with his great Seneshall openly in the Citie of *Grisca,* protested peace in this manner. That the Soldane shoulde espouse *Zephira,* and *Tomano* the Princesse *Belsina* the Soldanes Daughter. Beside, hee renounced all pretended rights to the Realmes of *Grisca* and *Romata,* nor would he demaund anie tribute of them afterward, or enter his confines with anie violence, but assist the King continually against all his enemies.

Moreouer, within two Moneths, hee would deliuer tenne thousand talents of Golde, and two millions of Seraphes, in recompence of his wrong doone to the King *Abimar.* All this my Lord, quoth the Soldane, will I faythfullie performe, and all the Kinges my Subiects shall subscribe thereto: on this condition, that you accompanie the Princesse to the Cittie of *Harano*, there to honor with your presence our espousall, where your sonne *Tomano* shall likewise match with our Daughter. To this the King willingly consented, whereupon the Soldane sent his Seneshall, to cause his Armie march homewardes into *Persia*, except sixe thousand men at Armes, to guard the Soldanes person: then openly in the field was the peace proclaimed, and the Captaines on either side freendly embracing each other. Afterward the soldane comming to the king *Abimar* and in the presence of *Palmerin* and *Trineus*, thus spake. Needlesse were it now (my Lord) to remember our passed displeasures, but generally to conferre of loue and peace: yet hereof I can assure you, that the Princesse *Zephira*, and these two strange Knights, preuailed more agaynst me then all the rest of your Armie. But least your people should thinke, that our concluded peace is not thorowlie grounded, to morrowe will I bee openlie affianced to the Princesse *Zephira*, and afterward set forward to *Harano*, that my Sisters may bee present at our nuptials, in the meane while, our Seneshall and sixe other noble Lordes, shall remaine with you as our hostages. These determinations fulfilled, the Soldane posted to *Harano*, where hee heard of the death of the Prince *Donadel*, and the Kinges sonne of *Rosillia*, with diuerse other Princes of his kindred slaine in the battell: but the heate of his newe loue caused him to make small account therof, preparing all things readie for the solemnitie of his marriage.

Chapter LIII.

The conference that the Soldane of Persia had with his Sisters, thinking by theyr meanes to stay Palmerin, and Tryneus in his Court, and the honourable entertainement hee made them at the arriuall of the Princesse Zephira. And how by good fortune Palmerin recouered his Squire Colmelio, from the Ambassadour Maucetto.

No sooner was the soldane come to *Harano*, but hee presently dispatched Messengers to his sisters, that they might bee present at his honourable marriage: and calling for his Daughter the yong Princesse *Belsina*, he thus began. Faire Daughter, I thinke you are not ignorant, for report flieth quicklie far,[1] that I haue promised you in mariage to the Prince *Tomano*: therefore I account it verie requisite, that your solemnitie bee done on the same day, when I shall espouse the Princesse *Zephira*.

My gracious Lorde and Father, quoth shee, I remaine altogither at your highnesse direction: and if for conclusion of peace you match with so faire a Princesse as is *Zephira*, it were agaynst reason I should refuse the worthie Prince *Tomano* of *Romata*. When hee perceyued the readie good-will of his Daughter, and his two sisters by this time were come to the Court. After hee had welcommed them in most gracious manner, hee entred into these speeches. I thought it verie expedient (fayre sisters) since you vnderstand the peace concluded betweene the King of *Grisca* and my selfe, to acquaint you with other matters greatly concerning you.

There commeth hither in the companie of the Princesse *Zephira*, two strange knights of very rare perfections, to whom I would willingly haue you vse such especiall behauiour, as wee might purchase the meanes to enioy them continually in our Court, for no other intent I promise you, but onely that they may match with you in marriage. You sister *Lyzanda*, (quoth hee to the eldest) I commit to the cheefest Knight, the verie same man that most valiantlie tooke mee prisoner in the battaile: and you *Aurecinda*, (for so was the yongest named) I bequeath to the other, who is one of the goodliest personages that euer Nature framed.

Heereunto they were right soone entreated, especiallie *Aurecinda*, who though her elder sister were graue and well aduised, yet was shee pleasant, quaint and so subtile, as easily could shee practise the meane to deceiue the wisest man, whereof shee made some experience, as you shal hereafter perceiue in the Chapters following. The Soldane hauing sent for all the Kings, Princes and Lordes his subiects, to bee present on the day of this great solemnitie: the Prince *Tomano*, earnestlie desiring to see his best beloued, desired *Palmerin*, *Trineus*, and the Princesse *Zephira*, that they might set forwardes to *Harano*. But *Muzabelino*, who knew what troubles would succeede the marriage, aduised the King *Abimar* not to goe, and counsailed the two Princes, *Trineus* and *Palmerin*, to keepe themselues continuallie Armed, because the Soldane was a man continually subiect to incertaine chaunces. So giuing to each of them a Cote of Armes of Crimson Veluet,

Palmerin d'Oliva: Part II 535

most curiouslie embroidered with Pearles, hee departed from them, returning backe againe to the Citie of *Grisca*. Nowe ride these Princes ioyfully to *Harano*, where they were receiued by the soldane with wonderfull pompe and honor, each one admiring the rare beautie of the Princesse *Zephira*, who was conducted with
5 such a royall traine, as neuer was the like seene before in *Harano*. At the Cittie Gate the Soldane mette them, and in a sumptuous Coche accompanied them to the Pallace, where after many solemne curtesies on each side deliuered, and such magnifical royaltie beseeming the time and place, the Soldane came to his Sisters, who had not yet talked with the two strange Knights, and thus spake.
10   Sisters, to the ende that heereafter you shall not be beguiled, the Knights that accompanie my Ladie the Princesse, and whome I haue so much commended to you, are Christians, notwithstanding they bee such, as they twaine deserue greater honor then I am any way able to expresse. As for their comely stature, after that your eye hath conferred with your heart, I referre my opinion to your
15 iudgement, regarde then that they bee loued and esteemed as their perfections doo worthily deserue. *Aurecinda* the yongest and most voluntarie Sister, hauing her eye continually fixed on the Prince *Trineus*, thus conferred with herselfe.
    My Brother verie lightly commaundeth vs to loue these strange Knights, I knowe not what my Sisters opinion is, as for mine owne, the beginning alreadie
20 of my loue is such, that if I do not quickly obtaine my desire, I feare that my affection is rated at the price of my life. The time is passed ouer with many delights, and daily pastimes after the *Persian* manner, but all this while *Lizanda* and *Aurecinda* are tormented with loue, so that all patience was vtterly denied them, yet bearing this waightie burden so well as they coulde, at length the
25 two Sisters came to the Princesse *Zephiraes* Chamber, where they founde *Palmerin* and *Trineus* conferring together, feigning the cause of their comming to bid the Princesse good morrow. *Palmerin* perceiuing that *Lizanda* sodainely chaunged her colour, imagined the cause of her secret disease, and beeing loth to bee tempted with anie such occasion, dissembling that he sawe her not, tooke
30 *Zephira* by the hande, and leading her to the window, founde some cause of conference, which *Lizanda* perceiuing, in anger shee flong forth of the Chamber, yet *Aurecinda* would not follow her, for she being thorowly conquered with loue, neither regarding feare, shame, or other such like behauiour seemely in Maidens, tooke *Trineus* by the hand, and causing him to sitte downe by her, thus beganne.
35 I doo not a little maruaile Syr knight, that when Ladies come to see you, their entertainment is no better. It is not the manner of Gentlemen to be so sollitarie, without hauing some friend or beloued, which you shall soone finde in this Court, of higher calling then you imagine, if Ladies may discerne some signe of your fauourable liking. In good faith Madame, answered *Trineus*, if to you and
40 your sister I haue not done such duety as beseemed me, it proceeded by forgetfulnesse, or my minde carried away with other occasions, for nature made me obedient to Ladies. If these words Sir knight (quoth she) proceede from your heart, I can assure you to be loued of such a one, who is not vnworthie the like good will,

and of such account is shee with the Soldane, as he shall create you one of the greatest Lords in *Persia*, so please you to stay in his highnesse Court. That may not be (quoth *Trineus*) for so soone as the Soldane and the prince *Tomano* shall be espoused, I must needs depart with my companion, about affaires of very great importance. *Palmerin* who with one eare listened to the Princesse *Zephira*, and with the other to the words of *Aurecinda*, after she was departed to her Chamber, thus spake to *Trineus*.

Good Friende, beware of this Ladie, that shee cause you not to offende God, and violate the loyaltie you owe to Madame *Agriola*. Such experience haue I had in these actions, as when Ladies haue enterprised theyr amorous furies, if they cannot compasse it by the meanes of men, they will aduenture it with hellish familiars, that can deceiue the very wisest, especially in this wicked Countrey, where is no knowledge of God or his Lawes. Beside you know, that such impudent loue cannot bee carried about without such apt messengers, and from whence proceedeth manie inconueniences. Brother, aunswered *Trineus*, feare not my constancie, for my Ladyes loue hath taken such sure foundation, as death cannot make me false to her, yet prooued his words contrarie in the end, and for which hee repented afterwarde.

While these delights continued, *Maucetto* Ambassadour to the soldane of *Babilon*, arriued at the Courte, where the Monarch of *Persia* receiued him verie honourably, willing him to conceale the newes till the marriages were past, which on the morrow was performed with maruailous royaltie. As the Princes and Lordes accompanied the soldane to the Temple, it happened that *Aurecinda* was conducted by the Prince *Trineus*, whereof she beeing not a little glad, by the way entred into these speeches. Ah my true Friend and Lord *Trineus*, when will the day come that I may be thus led, to espouse the man whom I loue more deere then my life? Madame, quoth *Trineus*, I cannot maruaile sufficiently to see you thus changed, considering the greatest Lord in the Orient may be thought too simple for such a Wife: yet did you choose one that perhaps would not espouse you, my Lorde the soldane beeing your Brother, may constraine him thereto. Heere-hence (quoth shee) proceedeth my sorrow, for hee whome I loue is not the soldanes subiect, nor dooth agree with mee in faith and opinion, he will giue no eare to mine intreaties, much lesse to such a one, as can make him one of the greatest Lords in *Persia*.

But thinke you my Lorde that I can conceale what you may plainely discerne in mine eyes? You are the onely man my heart hath chosen, and whome the soldane loueth more then his Brother. Alas Madame, quoth the Prince, vnfitting is it that a Knight errant, shoulde espouse the Sisters of so great a Lord as is the Soldane of *Persia*. And would his Maiestie so much honour me, yet the contrarietie of our faith is such an impeach, as flatly it may not be, for rather will I be torne in peeces then match with a Pagan, or renounce my faith for her loue. No, no, my Lord, saide the Princesse, I will renounce mine for your loue, and worship Iesus Christ the sonne of the blessed Virgin. Well worthie then were I of

Palmerin d'Oliva: Part II 537

reproch, quoth *Trineus*, if I should not requite you with loue againe, considering what you aduenture for my sake.

As they would haue proceeded further in talke, *Colmelio, Palmerins* Squire whome *Maucetto* hadde bought,[2] standing to see the traine of *Persian* Lords and
5 Ladies passe by, espied his maister and the Prince *Trineus*, wherefore preasing through the guarde of Archers, hee came to the Prince, and taking him by the Mantle, saide. Most happie be this houre my noble Lorde, to finde you and my Maister *Palmerin*. What fortune hath brought thee hither *Colmelio*, saide *Trineus*, hast thou yet spoken to thy Maister? No my Lord, aunswered *Colmelio*, he
10 conducteth the Princesse with the Calife of *Siconia*, wherefore I durst not presume to trouble him.

Beleeue mee, saide the Prince, but thou shalt speake with him, and while the Arch-Flamin[3] was performing the ceremonies in the Temple, *Trineus* presented him to his Maister *Palmerin*, who was thereof so ioyfull, as if he had gotten the
15 best Cittie in *Persia*. Hee demaunded by what meanes hee escaped the Pirates handes, the true discourse whereof *Colmelio* rehearsed, and howe *Maucetto* the Ambassadour bought him, as *Ptolome* and he were brought to the Soldane of *Babilon* his Court to be sold, and there doth *Ptolome* finde great fauour as I haue heard, of the fayre Princesse *Alchidiana* the Soldanes Daughter, onely for your
20 sake.[4] Thou tellest me wonders, said *Palmerin*, depart not from me till after Dinner, when I will goe to thy Maister *Maucetto* to demaunde thee, which I hope hee will not denie, because when I was Knight to *Alchidiana*, hee was one of my most specially good Friendes. After the solemnitie of the marriage was ended, and Dinner ended at the Pallace for preparation of pastime: *Palmerin* calling *Colme-*
25 *lio*, went with him to the Ambassadour *Maucetto*, who not a little abashed to see him, that was generally reputed dead in the soldanes Court, came and embraced him with these speeches. My Lorde *Palmerin*, what great God hath raysed you againe? The soldane was crediblie enformed, that you and *Olorico* were drowned in the sea:[5] for which both hee and Madame *Alchidiana* more lamented, then for
30 the losse of his whole Armie before the Cittie of *Constantinople*.

Palmerin dissembling as though he knew not thereof, seemed to maruaile thereat very much, and the better to shaddow his conceit, saide, that after the tempest was ceased, which cast him verie farre from the Soldanes Armie, thinking to returne to *Constantinople*, hee was by violent windes brought to the Isle of *Malfada*,
35 where the Prince *Olorico*, quoth hee, and all the rest of my companions remaine enchaunted, whom I hope to recouer againe after I can get hence. Little thought I my Lord, aunswered *Maucetto*, to finde you in this Countrey, but did Madame *Alchidiana* know so much, her sorrow would soone be conuerted into ioy.

But what newes with you my Lord? said *Palmerin*. What may bee the
40 cause of your Ambassage? I will not conceale the truth thereof from you, quoth *Maucetto*, I come to demaund ayde of the Soldane of *Persia*, for a fresh inuasion against *Constantinople*. I maruaile quoth *Palmerin*, that he will enterprise the voyage againe, which hath cost him so much, and returned so little profit: rather

would I counsaile him to forbeare, and so will I write to his maiestie before your
departure, as also to Madame *Alchidiana* his Daughter. But I would request one
curtesie of you Sir *Maucetto*, that you woulde giue mee your slaue *Colmelio*, who
in time past hath beene my Squire. Him shall you haue with all my heart, quoth
Maucetto, and not onely him but whatsoeuer els is mine beside, so please you to
accept thereof.

    I thanke you good Sir, aunswered *Palmerin*, and I doubt not in time to
requite your gentlenesse. While they thus talked together, the Soldane came to
Palmerin, saying. Will not you make one my Lord in this daunce? the Ladies say
they cannot haue your companie. In sooth my gracious Lorde, answered *Palmerin*, little doo I delight in any such exercises,[6] very earnest affaires haue I with
the Ambassadour *Maucetto*, which craue suddaine and speedie dispatch. Beside,
faine would I know some tydings of him from my Ladie *Alchidiana*, from whose
seruice I haue now discontinued a yeere and more. The Soldane abashed at these
wordes, saide. I pray you tell mee the truth, are not you hee that slewe the Prince
Amarano of *Nigrea* in Combat, and afterwarde two other of his Brethren, of
which exploits remaine such fame through all *Turkie*?[7] In sooth my Lord aunswered *Palmerin*, beeing vowed to my Ladies seruice, I neuer could suffer her
honour to be any way distained, and in that dutie I will continue, for the manifolde curtesies I haue receiued by her. By the liuing God, sayd the Soldane, now
think I my selfe the happiest prince in the world, hauing the man in my Court,
whose verie name maketh the stoutest to tremble. But seeing wee are thus farre
entred, tell mee, is the Princesse *Alchidiana* so beautifull as Fame reports her?
That is she my Lord, quoth hee, and much more then fame is able to vtter,
beside, shee is one of the most gracious and affable Princesses that euer I beheld
in any Kings Court.

    Nowe is night come, and after the Courtly pastimes were ended, the Bride-
groome went to receiue the honur of his Bride, commaunding *Palmerin* to bee
intreated as his owne person, which not a little contented the Princesse *Lyzanda*,
thinking heereby (alas too lauishly) to obtaine him for her husband, but heerein
she was deceiued, so that her rash loue procured her miserable death. *Aurecinda*
likewise continually courted *Trineus*, as though shee had alwaies beene trained
vp in his company, wherefore one day, after hee had beene warned foure or fiue
times by *Palmerin*, he thus spake to her. Madame, if your honesty and vertue
hath imprinted in noble mindes, an especiall conceite of your continencie and
chastity, I maruaile nowe what many will thinke, in that you should not shewe
any such signes of loue to me, for it seemes yee yeelde the Cittie before any
assault be giuen. Al these speeches could not qualifie her humour, for loue had
so emboldened her with such vnshamefastnesse, as shee made no conscience of
following the cause, giuing credit to one of her Ladies perswasions, that by good
pursuit all things enioy a happy ende.

Chapter LIV.
How Maucetto the Ambassadour to the Monarch Misos of Babylon, declared his message before the Soldane and all the princes of Persia. And of the Combate betweene Trineus, and the King Orzodine of Galappa.

After the mariage feast was fully ended, the Soldane sent for the Ambassadour *Maucetto*, who in the presence of al the *Persian* Lordes, thus began to deliuer his message. Mighty and illustrious Monarch of *Persia* the soldane of *Babilon* my lord and maister, hauing euermore continued in faithfull alliance to your maiestie, lets you knowe by mee his great and domageable losse, which he sustained before the Citie of *Constantinople*. For recouerie whereof, hee humbly intreateth your highnesse most fauourable assistaunce, which well you cannot denie him, in respect of the great sway you hold in *Turkie*, as also for the establishment of our faith and generall destruction of the *Grecian* Empire. Ambassador, quoth the Soldane, I will better consider heereon, and aunswere you accordingly. So calling all the Princes presently to counsell, diuers confused iudgements were amongst them: whereupon hee sent for *Palmerin*, and before them all demaunded his opinion, whereto hee shaped this aunswere. Might it stand with your highnesse liking, and the good conceit of all these noble Princes, gladly would I bee excused in this matter, wherein I may not speake without suspition, because the entent is against mine owne natiue countrey, and those whome I agree withall in fayth and opinion.

But seeing your Maiestie will needes know my iudgement, pardon in speaking boldly what I would be loth to dissemble. I thinke no one of you my gracious Lords, but well remembers the late warres against the King of *Grisca*, since which time the souldiers are hardly recouered, and extreamitie were it to endanger the liues of wounded men. Moreouer, the Soldane of *Babilon* who nowe demaundeth succour, sending his Armie into *Greece*, where raignes a Prince so mightie and puissant, as well coulde repulse them with shamefull confusion. Perswade your selues as yet there is no other, but he that tryumpht in conquest before, I feare can do the like againe, and thus my Lords is mine opinion.

Well haue you answered, quoth the Soldane, and this peaceable conclusion liketh me best, so arysing from counsell, they went into the great Hall, where before theyr comming, as the Princesse *Zephira* was deuising with many Lords and Ladies, entred an armed knight, accompanied with sixe other in Armour, and twelue Squires, who seeing the Soldane not in his chayre of estate, demaunded of the Queene where he was. Knight, quoth she, he is in counsell with the Princes and Lordes of his Realme, and long it will not be before he come: in meane while you may passe the time in conference with the Ladies. By God, said *Trineus* to the Queene, I thinke he scant knoweth howe to conferre with Ladies, for his indiscreete behauiour shewes him to be the woorst nurtured Knight that euer I sawe: saw you not (quoth hee to the Princesse *Zephira*) how vnmannerly hee sat downe without vsing any reuerence to your Maiestie?

The Knight sitting strouting in a Chayre, and hauing vnclasped his Helmet, said to the Queene. I pray you tell me Madame, are those two strange Knights in this Court, that were against your Husbande in the battaile and tooke him? They be Sir Knight, quoth she, well and in good disposition thanks to the soueraigne Creator. I aske not of their health, quoth he, how are they called? The one said the Queene, is named *Palmerin*, the other *Trineus*. And I quoth he, am *Orzodine* King of *Galappa*,[1] to whome fortune hath beene more fauourable in loue, then in riches: making me Freende to the faire *Oronia*, Daughter to the Calife of *Siconia*, and Sister to the Prince *Donadell*, who was slaine in the battaile against the King *Abimar*:[2] shee in my iudgement, not hauing her second in beautie, at whose request I haue trauailed the greatest part of *Asia*, to spread her name and honorable reputation, which I haue doone to her perpetuall fame: and returning to her when my labours were finished, in sted of ioy and pleasure, I found her sad and pensiue for the death of her Brother. These newes were worse to me then death, and to comfort her, I promised to reuenge her Brothers misfortune: and this is the onelie cause of my comming, for hauing Combatted with him that slew the Prince, her loue to mee will be the greater, and mine honour shall be spread with more aduantage. I beleeue well, quoth the Queene, if you escape with life from the Combat: but tell me Sir Knight, why beare you such ill will to him that slew the Prince? considering that it was doon in plaine battaile, and he his enemie who would haue doone as much to him if he could. Not for this cause alone will I enter the Combat, said *Orzodine*, but for I am desirous to let him knowe that I am more fauoured in loue then hee: and as I am one of the most happie Louers, so am I the best Knight in the world, which I will maintaine against anie that dare gain-say it. Happy louer, *Dieu Vous gard*,[3] said *Trineus*. If the Poets had hetherto spared the discription of *Cupid*, Sonne to the Goddesse of loue, now might they iustly haue sette him downe for blind: yet is hee worthie to be condemned, that hee would vouchsafe anye fauour to the most foolish among men, hee hauing dedicated me to the seruice of a Ladie, to whom your gentle *Ironia*, *Oronia*, I should saye, dooth not deserue the name of her seruant.[4]

For the rest, where you vaunt your selfe to bee the best Knight in the world, your follie is too apparaunt, for there are manie Knightes errant in the worlde, who can giue you a braue canuazado at the Launce: and after they haue foyled you in the Ioust, bestowe a little paines to take your greene head from your grosse shoulders. My selfe that slew the Brother to your Goddesse of beautie,[5] will doo you so much pleasure, as to heale the incurable disease wherewith you are day and night tormented. O diuine spirites cryed the Pagan, fauour me so much, that this Knight may but dare to enter the Fielde with mee. Yes I dare, sayde *Tryneus*, and before we part, I doubt not but to make thee quiet enough.

Orzodine presentlie threwe his Gauntlet as his gage, and *Tryneus* a Golden bracelet, which *Aurecinda* had giuen him, entreating *Zephira* to keepe them, which she refused to doo, fearing the daunger of the Prince *Tryneus*. Heereupon the Soldane entred the Hall, leading *Palmerin* by the hand, but when they sawe

Palmerin d'Oliva: Part II 541

the Armed Knight thus contend with *Trineus*, they meruailed greatly what might be the occasion thereof. When *Orzadine* sawe the Soldane was sette, he entred into these speeches. Soldane, I am hither come to accuse thee, of a villainous act which thou hast committed, harbouring in thy Court, the man that slewe
5 the valiant *Donadell*: whose murther thou canst not so cunningly couer, but thy treacherie shall be openly discouered.

What art thou, said the Soldane, that darest speake thus presumptuously in our presence? *Orzodine* King of *Galappa*, quoth he, of whom thou hast heard heretofore, and now haue I presented my gage against this Knight, which I will
10 maintaine in despight of the proudest. The Soldane abashed at this euent, sought to disswade them from the Combatte, because hee had heard great speeches of the Kings prowesse, but all was in vaine, for *Orzodine* was so obstinate, and *Tryneus* so earnest to reuenge the Turks proud blasphemie against his Ladie, as they would not be pacified till the Fielde was graunted them. Let vs haue Iudges
15 presently, quoth *Orzodine*, and the Fielde assured for our Combat, that I may discipline this glorious straunger.

Make not such haste, sayd *Tryneus*, for I feare thou wilt thinke thy comming too soone. Immediately were the two Combattants Armed, the Iudges placed in their Tent, when the Soldane and *Palmerin* with manie Princes, went
20 to beholde this exployt. But such a mightie man was the King of *Galappa*, as *Palmerin* feared his freends successe. The Trompets sounding, the Knights brake their Launces brauelie, and mette togither so furiouslye with their bodies, as they were both throwne out of their Saddles: but they quickly recouering themselues, drewe theyr swordes, and marched against eache other with lyke courage, as did
25 *Achilles* against noble *Hector*.[6] Long continued the fight with danger on either side, but the king of *Galappa* strooke such pessant strokes, beeing a man of equall stature with a Giant, as hee wounded *Trineus* in manie places: and such was his ill fortune, after long trauersing about, hee sette his foote vnwarilye on the Trunchion of a Launce, whereby he fell downe backward to the ground. *Orzodine* tak-
30 ing aduauntage of this fall, sette his foote on the Princes breast, striuing to pull his Helmet from his head: but God knowes in what agonie *Palmerin* was nowe, when he breathed foorth these speeches to himselfe. Ah Heauens quoth he, haue I taken such paine and trauaile to finde my Freend, and must he now die among his enemies, *Aurecinda* likewise readie to yeeld vp her ghost with greefe, seeing
35 *Palmerin* readie to swoune as he stood. Alas, quoth she, is it not enough that my Freend must die, but his noble companion will beare him companie? While this doubtfull feare was among the Courtiers, *Tryneus* had so well scufled with *Orzodine*, as he laye along by him likewise, when drawing a pocket dagger, he stabbed it through his Helmet, into one of his eyes, so that he nailed his head to
40 the ground. *Orzodine* feeling himselfe wounded to the death, gaue a very loude cry: when *Tryneus* hauing gotten his Helmet off, presentlie smote his heade from his shoulders. If the Knights of *Galappa* were now dismaide, and the soldane, *Palmerin*, *Zephira*, *Tomano*, and all the rest ioyfull, I leaue to your iudgements:

especially *Palmerin*, who reioycing that *Trineus* had thus conquered his enemie, entred the Lystes and embraced him, and bringing him foorth of the Fielde, he was welcommed to the Pallace with wonderfull honor.

 The bodie of the dead King was giuen to them that came with him, with meruailous reprehension of theyr Maisters audacious challenge, and so with great heauinesse they returned home againe.[7] Nor would the Soldane longer stay in his Court the *Assirian* Ambassadour. But excused himselfe to the *Babylonian Mysos*, that he could not giue him anie assistaunce, couering this aunswer vnder his vnfortunate battaile against the King *Abimar*. *Maucetto* seeing that to staye longer would not auaile him, tooke his leaue of the Soldane, saying. Albeit my Lorde, you cannot giue my Maister anie assistance, yet let *Palmerin* returne to him at his departure from your Court. What I can doo heerein, aunswered the Soldane, your Lord shall be assured to finde, although I thinke his minde bee otherwise adicted: but you were best to knowe his minde your selfe, because I heard him saye he would write to Madame *Alchidiana*.

 Maucetto departing to *Palmerins* lodging, the Soldane went to see his Sisters, of whome hee demaunded, if they had as yet practised anie thing with the Knights. My Lord, aunswered *Aurecinda*, who in all things was more prompt then her eldest Sister, I haue fixed my loue on the knight *Trineus*, with full resolution neuer to loue anie other: yet dooth not he intend to staye heere in your Courte, much lesse (I feare) to make me his wife. As for my Sister, shee cannot compasse the meane, howe to impart her loue to Sir *Palmerin*. Right strange is it, quoth the Soldane, that the promises you haue made them, and so apparant signes of ardent affection, cannot disswade them to make choyse of you: Doubtlesse they bee some great Princes, who to see the fashions of the worlde haue thus disguised themselues. Continue your loue as you haue begunne, and if by other meanes you cannot stay them, aduenture your honors as a meane to entrappe them. And now dooth occasion well serue you Sister *Aurecinda*, for by courteous intreating *Tryneus* now he is wounded, you maye more profit in one houre, then you haue doone during this tedious pursuit.

 Needlesse was it for the Soldane thus to perswade her, in that she laboured for no other matter, keeping *Trineus* companie both day and night: but *Palmerin* offended thereat, secretlye thus rebuked the Prince. What meane you my Lord? If you mend not this order I must be angry with you. You see this Princesse exceedes in her desire, and you giue her occasion to continue it: I know not what will happen heereon, but my mind perswades mee that you will hardlie depart hence with honour. Be aduised I desire you and take this of me: that if the wisest man will lende his eares to loose persons, and followe theyr affections: hee shall become more vnreasonable then a bruite Beaste, regarding nothing but what is obiect[8] to his eyes, and what the flesh, (the onelie mortall enemie to the spirit) shall soonest perswade him.

Chapter LV.

How Aurecinda Sister to the Soldane of Persia, pursued the Prince Tryneus so neere, as in the end, she had her desire, and what followed thereon.

Palmerin hauing thus schooled the prince *Trineus*, that he should giue no eare to the enticements of *Aurecinda*: *Lyzanda* came to his chamber, and feigning vrgent businesse with him, tooke him aside, deliuering her affections in this maner. Right happie wold I think my selfe Sir *Palmerin*, so you would deigne to continue in the Soldans Court, who doubtlesse would aduance you to the highest step of honor, and giue me to you in mariage that am his Sister, and a Lady worthie some reckoning.

Palmerin offred to depart the Chamber, but *Lyzanda* stayed him, proceeding thus. Alas my Lord will you neuer vouchsafe to speake to mee? nowe see I well that you are the most disloyall Knight in the worlde. Madame aunswered *Palmerin*, rather will I die then one iote of disloyaltie shall be found in me: nor can I graunt your importunate requests, without committing notorious treason to my Ladie, and offending my God, whom foolish loue shall neuer make me to displease. So without any further speeches he went to the Prince *Tomano*, leauing the poore Ladie well-neere dead with this vnkinde refusall, who going to her owne cabbanet, thus began to breath foorth her sorrowes.

Ah Loue, the most cruell passion that euer entred the hart of anie Ladie, how great and meruailous is thy power? Some thou enforcest to desire and intreat, without being heard or regarded: others thou causest to be happily fauoured, esteemed of their Freends, Seruaunts and louers. Vnhappie that I am, but much more vnhappie Brother, accursed be the houre when thou diddest commaund mee, to loue the most cruell and vnkinde among men. Can there be anie Ladie in the worlde more disgraced then I am? had I not reuealed my loue to him, some comfort I might thereby enioy among my sorrowes: but the frozen minde knowing my loue, dooth holde mee in the greater contempt. My Sister tolde me, that by too long concealement of loue, many haue lost them they most esteemed: but I (alas) doo finde it cleane contrary. Now was *Aurecinda* (by chaunce) in the Chamber next her Sisters Cabinette, and hearing her thus sorrowfully complaine, shee came to her, and thus spake.

Good Sister discomfort not your selfe by your friendes refusall: I would not thinke my selfe woorthie the name of a woman, if I could not winne you the man that thus torments you. As for me, I haue founde the meane to compasse mine owne desire. Yet could not all these speeches appease her, wherfore shee left her, and vnderstanding by one of her Ladies, that *Tryneus* should this night suppe in the Soldans Chamber, whereupon shee went to the Ladies hote house, and there prepared his bed, and such sweete delicate bathes, as might mooue the spirits of a verie staied Gentleman.[1] This doone, she came to one of the Pages of honor, Brother to the Ladie whome shee most of all trusted, saying.

I praye thee good Page, goe to the Prince *Trineus* his Chamber, and there attende till he come foorth: then feigning that some one hath doone thee iniurie, thou shalt intreat him to helpe thee against him that abused thee. If hee condiscende, as doubtlesse he will, bring him to the bathe, where I will stay his comming with thy Sister, and so soone as he is entred, make fast the doore on him, and gette thee gone, but in anie case be secret heerein, and I will recompence thee to thine owne content. The wagge was so well instructed in his arte, as he failed not in any one point of his charge. But as the Prince *Tryneus* came alone from his Chamber, he fell on his knees before him saying. My Lord, if euer you pittie a Gentleman abused, let mee intreate you to reuenge my cause, on a villaine that hath too much wronged me.

Tryneus, who had often seene the Page in his Chamber with *Aurecinda*, answered. Beleeue me Page, it were pittie to denie thy request, considering thou doost demaunde it so courteously: shall I neede to bee better prouided then I am? No my Lord, quoth he, your sword is sufficient. So was he conducted by the Page along the Gallery, and beeing come to the appointed place, he opened the doore, thus speaking to the Prince. My Lord, the partie you must deale withall is in this Chamber, accompanied but with one Ladie, wherefore you may enter secure from daunger. Hee was no sooner in, but the Page clapt to the doore and departed. Now was *Tryneus* not a little amazed, when he saw no bodie but the Princesse with her Ladie, shee being come thither to bathe her selfe, and layd in her bed: but in such surpassing brauerye, as *Iupiter* with his lightning, *Neptune* with his three forked Mace, and *Pluto* with his *Cerberus*,[2] would stand and wonder thereat. So finelie had she tressed the golden wyres of her hayre, and her heade attyre embellished with such goodlie Orientall Pearles, as made her seeme a beautifull Angell, beeing couered with a gorgious Canapie, resembling the Sunne vnder a faire cloud. Betweene her daintie Breastes hung a precious Carbunckle which supplied the office of *Venus* her firebrand:[3] when she sawe *Tryneus* stand so agast, she said. Why? my Lord, are you more afraide of a naked Ladie, then of the most puissaunt Knight in *Persia*, armed *cap a pe*? I can iudge no lesse, seeing you dare approch no neerer. In sooth my Lord, quoth the Pages Sister, you may thinke your selfe happy to be desired of such a ladie, whome mightie kings and princes haue earnestly sought, and woulde gladly haue had the least fauour shee bestowes on you. So taking him by the hand, shee caused him to sit down in a Chayre by the beds side, and giuing her Mistresse her Harpe, she departed, leauing them together. Ah page, quoth *Trineus*, howe hast thou deceiued mee? What? saide the princesse, you forgette where you are, you must at this time somewhat pittie my sorrowes, and heare a dittie which I haue made for your sake. Then taking her Harpe, shee thus beganne to sing as followeth.

The Dittie sung by Au-
recinda to the Prince Trineus.[4]

Palmerin d'Oliva: Part II 545

 T*he God of warre, fierce, stearne, and rigorous,*
  when he beheld faire Venus heauenly beautie:
 Made small account of her disloyalty,
 But suddainlie became full amorous.[5]
5 *Beautie had then her power vigorous,*
  Chaunging rough lookes to sweetest secrecie.
 But he I loue, incenst with crueltie,
  Doth not regard my torments langourous.
 Why should I then pursue that stubborne minde,
10   *That with excuses kils my hope out-right?*
 Yet if he helpe not, death must me acquite
 Ah mightie loue in nature most vnkinde
   Thou doost constraine me to affect the man:
   That neither fauour, loue nor kindnes can.
15 *What haue I sayd? the Knight of my desire,*
  Is meere diuine, and furthest from compare:
 Whose Eagles eyes can well discerne my care,
  And with sweete pitties droppes alay this fire.
 The little God hath made him gracious,
20   *His Mother, mild, to rue the Ladies smart:*
 That shrines his liuely Image in her hart,
  Then to despaire beseemes no vertuous.
 Regard sweet freend the passions of thy Freend,
  Whom God and nature hath appointed thine:
25   *Giue loue his due, and then thou must be mine,*
  So shall long sorrow haue a happie ende.
   The Persian mayd, say boldly thou hast wonne:
   That Monarches, Kings and Princes neere could donne.

  With excellent cunning did shee handle her instrument, but with farre better
30 grace and affection deliuered her dittie, gracing it with such sadde countenaunce, mournfull lookes, and renting sighes, as forced the Prince *Tryneus* to become exceeding amorous. And burning in this newe fierie impression, beheld the singuler beautie of *Aurecinda*, which rauished his sences in such sort, as (trembling like the Aspen leafe) hee satte downe by her on the beddes side. The Princesse
35 laying her Harpe from her, embraced him very louinglie with these speeches. Alas my Lord, will you still continue in this rigour and cruell inhumanitie? your heart is more harde then Adamant, that will not bee mollified with so manie intreaties: I sweare to you by the Sunne that lightneth the worlde, vnlesse you graunt me one request, before your face will I presentlye sleye my selfe.[6] Full well
40 doo I perceiue, quoth *Tryneus*, that hardlie can I escape misfortune: the Seruaunt hath deceiued mee, and now the Mistresse seekes my death. Ah Madam, quoth

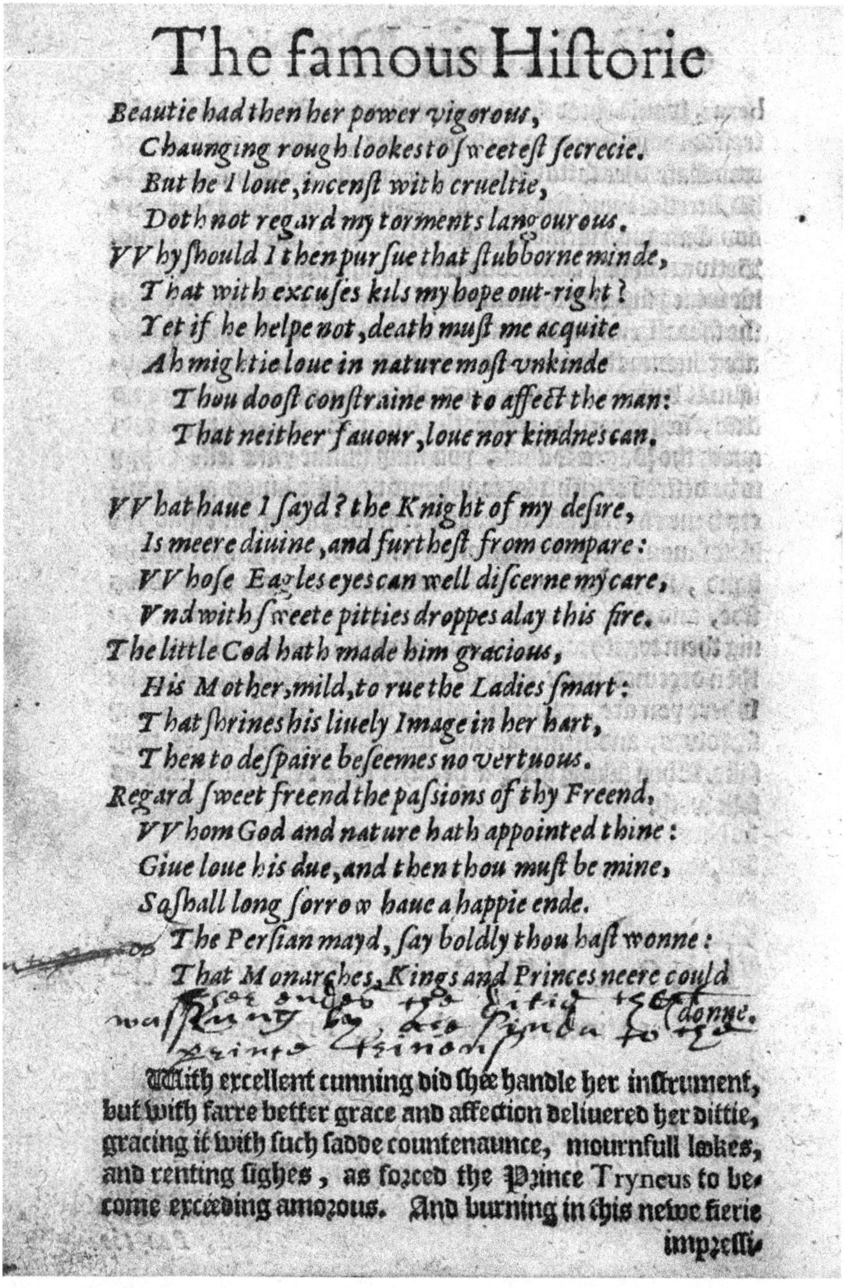

The famous Historie

Beautie had then her power vigorous,
  Chaunging rough lookes to sweetest secrecie.
  But he I loue, incenst with crueltie,
  Doth not regard my torments langourous.
VVhy should I then pursue that stubborne minde,
  That with excuses kils my hope out-right?
  Yet if he helpe not, death must me acquite
  Ah mightie loue in nature most vnkinde
    Thou doost constraine me to affect the man:
    That neither fauour, loue nor kindnes can.

VVhat haue I sayd? the Knight of my desire,
  Is meere diuine, and furthest from compare:
    VVhose Eagles eyes can well discerne my care,
    Vnd with sweete pitties droppes alay this fire.
The little Cod hath made him gracious,
  His Mother, mild, to rue the Ladies smart:
  That shrines his liuely Image in her hart,
  Then to despaire beseemes no vertuous.
Regard sweet freend the passions of thy Freend,
  VVhom God and nature hath appointed thine:
  Giue loue his due, and then thou must be mine,
  So shall long sorrow haue a happie ende.
    The Persian mayd, say boldly thou hast wonne:
    That Monarches, Kings and Princes neere could donne.

With excellent cunning did shee handle her instrument, but with farre better grace and affection deliuered her dittie, gracing it with such sadde countenaunce, mournfull lookes, and renting sighes, as forced the Prince Tryneus to become exceeding amorous. And burning in this newe fierie impressi-

Figure 5: Annotation in contemporary hand. *Palmerin d'Oliva* (London: Thomas Creede, 1597), Part 2, sig. V5^v. The Huntington Library, San Marino, California (RB 330331).

he, how can I graunt your request, considering mine offence to God, and she that loueth me loyallie? Eyther bee as good as thy worde, quoth she, else stand to the danger that may befall thee.

Why? Syr Knight, is my beautie of so slender account, as I am not woorthie to bee helde betweene thine armes?[7] wilt thou suffer me to consume in this violent flame, which thou maist with such ease and honor extinguish? hadst thou rather see a Ladie split her heart before thee, then thou wilt vouchsafe to preserue her life? Come, come sweet Freende, see how Loue and his Mother hath made waye for thee, refuse not opportunitie so fauourablie offered. What blemish is on this bodie, that shoulde deserue disdaine? If the King of Gods would thinke himselfe honored with this conquest: much more estimation shouldest thou make heereof. In breefe, she was so perfect in her subtiltie, and knewe so well how to inueigle the Prince with queint speeches and sweete embracings: that she made him forget God, his Ladie, loyaltie, and himselfe, so that of a Maiden, he made her the fayrest woman in *Persia*.[8] When the time came that hee should depart, the Princesse saide to him. Yet haue I a further request, my Lord, you must promise to meete mee in this place at times conuenient, and endeuour with your companion that he may likewise loue my Sister. *Trineus* made promise hee would, but rather hee desired to stab himselfe with his weapon: then that *Palmerin* shoulde knowe this great abuse, so heinous did his offence seeme to himselfe.

Aurecinda perswaded her Sister, still to pursue *Palmerin* with her loue, and what had passed betweene her and the Prince *Trineus*, she declared: whereupon her desire grewe the greater, yet all was in vaine, for *Palmerin* would giue no eare to her complaints, which was the cause of this mishap following. *Lyzanda* aduertised by her Sister, that *Tryneus* still thus vsed her companie in the Bath: enuious of her Sisters benefit, and despightfull at *Palmerins* obstinate refusall, she went to the Soldane, and with manie teares thus deliuered her greefe. Ah my Lorde, how much better had it beene, that wee had neuer knowne these cruell Christian Knightes? whose ingratitude will bee the cause of my death: for the yonger of them is meruailouslie beloued of my Sister, who forgetting her faith, honor, and her obedience to your Maiestie, hath dishonored both her selfe and you, onelie to make proofe of the other knights Crueltie to me. The Soldane admiring his Sisters report, answered.

I did not will my Sister to abuse her selfe, without promise of marriage: but seeing it hath so fallen out, by my Fathers soule they shall both repent it. Durst the Traytour abuse me so much in mine owne Courte? Why? my Lord, quoth *Lyzanda*, you are the onelie cause thereof, and therefore you must bee angrie with no bodie but your selfe. Let me not liue an houre sayde the Soldane, if I be not sufficiently reuenged on him: Sister, be you but secrete, and referre the rest to my direction. Then calling for the Captaine of his Guard, willing him to take fiftie Knights, and when his Maiestie was at Supper, they shoulde goe take his Sister and the Knight with her in the Bathe, and afterwarde carrie them to strong pryson. But see it doone secretlye, quoth he, for if his companion know thereof, it may arise to further incouenience. And because *Palmerin* should not misdoubt this treason, all Supper-time the Soldane held him in familiar talke: he hoping by this fetch, to staie them still in his Courte, but it fell out afterward to bee the cause, that manie of his best and cheefest Knightes were slaine.

Not long had the ambushed Knightes waited where they were appointed, but the Princesse *Aurecinda* opened the doore, and came foorth with her Freendes as she was accustomed: where they were suddainlie taken, *Tryneus* not hauing the leysure to drawe his sworde, so was hee caried prisoner to one of the strongest Towers in the Pallace, and *Aurecinda* at the same time to another. *Tryneus* seeing himselfe thus betraide, fell into these lamentable discourses. Vnfortunate wretch that I am, haue I so lately escaped by my freende, the cruell enchauntments of the hellish *Malfada*,[9] wherein I endured so manie paines and torments, and am now come to the place where they shall be redoubled?

Ah *Palmerin* my good Brother and companion, what wilt thou say when thou hearest of my taking, but most of all when thou vnderstandest the cause thereof? Miserable wretch, how often did my Freend warne mee of this inconuenience, yet had not I the grace to credite his Counsaile: doubtlesse, my very conceit of shame, when thou shalt bee acquainted with my foule offence, will bee more greeuous to me then death. What dishonour, paine, torment and punishment, shall bee sufficient for my misdeede? Forlorne and despised Catife, could not the feare of God, which hath hitherto so graciously protected thee, nor the loyaltie of *Agriola*, who forsooke Parents, Freendes, and all for thee,[10] haue kept thee from this monstruous acte? O eternall God, the man that forsaketh thee is vile and abhominable. When I had thy feare before mine eyes, I was at rest and quiet in conscience, esteemed and beloued of all men: but when thou gauest mee raynes of libertie, I became dissolute and forgetfull of thee, as also of them that honoured me so much. Ah miserable occasion, and those deceits, entisements, and subtill perswasions, howe mightie are they in operation? neither men nor diuels could bring mee into such daunger, as you haue plunged mee in vp to the eares. Ah villainous Page that first brought mee thither, and thou the falsest Ladie in the world art cause of my euill. Nor are they to be accused but my wretched selfe, who seeking mine owne hurt, found it, and hauing found it, continued in it. Thus sorrowfully wayled *Tryneus*, where on the contrarie side *Aurecinda* reioyced: for when shee considered the estate of her Freende, shee perswaded her selfe by this meane, that the Soldane her Brother woulde enforce him to marrie her, which hope made her as ioyfull, as *Tryneus* was sadde and pensiue.

When the Captaine had imprisoned *Tryneus* and *Aurecinda*, he came to the Soldan sitting at the Table, saying. Will your Maiestie commaund me any further seruice? I haue enclosed the knight *Tryneus* in one Tower, and your sister *Aurecinda* in another. Why? quoth the Soldane, did you find them togither? I did my Lord, quoth the Captaine, your sister leading him by the hande out of the Ladies hote-house. By Mahomet, quoth the Soldane, but that you speake it, hardly coulde I beleeue it, what shamefull villainie is this committed in our

Pallace? by the greatest God, the facte shall be so worthily punished, as it shall remaine for a perpetuall memorie. At these speeches *Palmerin* was not a little amazed, and dissembling his anger so well as he could, said to the Soldane. I cannot be perswaded my Lord, that *Tryneus* would commit so vile an acte, without entisement thereto by your sisters treason: shee beeing (vnder your Maiesties correction) the most shamelesse Girle that euer I sawe, for twentie and twentie times haue I seene her followe him, with gestures farre vnfitting one of her calling. Then starting from the Table, quoth he. Consider what hee is, and what thou intendest against him, for neuer was imprisonment so dearely bought as this will be, and before thou puttest him to death, it shall cost mee my life, and the liues of an hundreth thousand Knightes beside, in reuenge of his wrong.[11] Beeing thus enflamed with ire, hee could not so giue ouer, but thus beganne againe. By God Soldane, thy treason is so manifest as thou canst not hide it, full well doo I vnderstand thy flatteries, whereby thou hopest to keepe vs in thy seruice, but farre art thou from thy reckoning, for rather will I be torne in a thousande peeces, then endure the reproach of such a mans seruice, who vnder colour of friendship imprisoneth his Knightes, and afterward threatneth them with death. *Tomano, Drumino, Corax,* and many other knights belonging to the King *Abimar,* seeing *Palmerin* in such a rage, as it seemed the fire did sparkle from his eyes, endeuoured to perswade him, and *Tomano* thus spake to the Soldane. My Lorde, vnder my safe conduct and your faith promised, are these two Knights come with vs to your Court, and you haue now imprisoned one of them, aduise your selfe of speedie iustice: for this shame doone him is against all right, and for euer shall you be noted with breache of faith: beside, I repute his iniurie as done to my selfe. The Soldane seeing the Princes thus mooued, although himselfe procured those fiftie Armed knights to take *Tryneus*, yet with smooth countenance hee thus answered. Content your selues my friends, *Tryneus* in right shall be defended: and if I finde my Sister culpable, shee shall be punished as she were a straunger. More I demaund not, said *Palmerin*, for I am assured that by her flatteries *Tryneus* hath bene seduced. So departing to his Chamber, he met his two Squires, *Bellechino*, and *Colmelio*, of whom he demaunded, if they at any time perceiued the loue betweene *Tryneus* and the Princesse *Aurecinda*.

They answered that they did perceiue it, and diuers nightes they sawe him goe to the Princesse Chamber. And why did you not reueale it to me? quoth he, worthily haue you deserued death, in concealing the shame of your Maisters Freende, wherein my selfe cannot escape vntouched. Heereupon he Armed himselfe, and sending for the Prince *Tomano*, said to him.

I thinke it best my Lord, that you keepe your ordinarie guarde about your person, till we knowe how the soldane will deale with *Trineus*. As for my selfe, I intende (if your Brother *Drumino* and the Prince *Corax* will ioyne with mee) to keepe the Fielde with the thousand Knightes that came hither with vs, that none may enter into the Cittie without our licence. In meane while, you may sende a Courrier to the King your Father, that he presentlye sende vs what helpe he may. Sir *Palmerin*, answered *Tomano*, not onelie my Knightes shall enter the Fielde for you, but my selfe likewise, so please you to commaund mee, and what you thinke best for the deliueraunce of your Freende *Tryneus*, I will bee willing to accomplishe to my vttermost. Presentlye will I send a Horseman to *Grisca*, and conferre with my Brother *Drumino*, that his Knights and Gentlemen may be Armed that came from *Sauata*, as also they that came with my Nephewe *Corax* from *Garara*, which will be in number a thousand more: your selfe in meane time may get foorth your necessaries.

Who then had seene the Knights Arming, the horses prouiding, the bag and baggage carrying, would haue said that *Palmerin* was as much feared and beloued in a strange Countrey, as in his owne. Such was the dilligence of the Nobles and Souldiours of *Grisca, Sauata* and *Garara*, as they were right soone before the Pallace attending for *Palmerin*: who commaunded *Tryneus* his Horse and rich Armour shoulde be brought foorth by his Squires, leauing in his Chamber all the riches and treasure, that the soldane and the Princesse *Zephira* had giuen him: and mounting on his owne Courser, he came and embraced the prince *Corax*, saying. Let vs depart (my Lord) from these ingratefull people, that neuer knew how to entertaine straungers: well may the soldane thanke the Princesse *Zephira* his wife, else I had smitten his head from his shoulders. Then were the Ensignes displaid, the Drummes and Trumpets sounding cheerefully, as the noise was heard through all the Cittie.

And in this manner went *Palmerin* to the field, which raised such a tumult among the people, and such sedition among the Nobles of *Persia*, as they boldly told the soldane, that vnaduisedly he had imprisoned the straunge Knight, and the Princesse his sister, and faith ought euermore bee defence for a stranger. The soldane perceiued his follie well enough, but as a man delighting in his euill, without altering his humour, regarded not their speeches: commanding that they should all arme themselues, and charging each one expressely not to speake to *Trineus* without leaue. Why? quoth he, the foole that is gone, too much abused me in my Pallace: by my Crowne, I will punish both his pride and his companions, mauger all them that dare say the contrarie. And so he floong from them into his Chamber.

Chapter LVI.

Howe the Soldan seeing hee coulde not perswade Trineus to marrie his sister, condemned him to death, and what followed afterward.

Tomano, who by the aduise of *Palmerin* remained in the Cittie, with two hundred Knights for defence of his person, sought all the meanes he coulde for the deliueraunce of the Prince *Trineus*, and comming to the Queene *Zephira*, thus spake. Madame, seeing men can no way perswade the Soldane, trie what the pleasing speeches of Ladyes will doo: who (in my iudgement) cannot come from him without obtaining their request.

The Soldane hauing forgotten the especiall fauour, which heeretofore hee receyued by Sir *Palmerin*, for whose safetie he gaue both faith and promise, at the simple report of Madame *Lyzanda*, hath this night past committed Sir *Trineus* prisoner in the strongest Tower, saying hee was founde in the Bath with *Aurecinda*. And so earnestlie dooth hee prosecute the matter, as notwithstanding the intreatie of all the Princes and my selfe, he will not discharge him, but hath sworne that in despight of vs all, hee shall bee punished. What? quoth the Queene, dooth my Lorde so forget himselfe, that he will seeke his harme who hath done him such honour? Beleeue mee Madame, answered the Prince, I haue tolde ye the truth, therefore when you shall walke to his Chamber, which is the place where all demaundes are graunted to Ladies, you may put him in remembrance of the Prince, and giue some good wordes for him, that so willingly aduentured his life for you. Ah my Lord, sayd *Zephira*, I feare the Soldane will hardly heare mee: for when such mightie persons are in anger, little account make they of loue or vertue, yet will I willingly doo what lies in me.

So bidding the Prince good night, shee went weeping to the Soldanes Chamber: which his Maiestie perceiuing, came and embraced her, demaunding who had anie way offended her. Euen you my Lorde, quoth shee, and in such sort, as if presently you doo not helpe it, I doubt the danger will be verie great. I vnderstand you haue sent *Trineus* to prison, and withall haue sworne that hee shall die: if you suffer such an infamous deede, thinke not but my life will speedilie follow him. Madame, aunswered the Soldane, what I haue done is to no other ende, but to stay him, and his companion in my Court, because their renowne is so famous in *Turkie*. With this excuse hee so qualified the Queene, that shee durst not moue anie further questions. The next day hee sent for the Prince *Tomano*, and with manie other great Lordes went to see his sister *Aurecinda*, framing his speeches to her in this manner. Sister, you haue showne your selfe of good gouernement, and great estimation made you of honour and vertue, in daring to think so foule a thought as you haue committed in act. Didst thou not consider thy place of honour in my Court? what shame hast thou doone to the house of *Persia*, which hitherto neuer sustained blemish, and now is foyled by thy immodest dealing with a straunger? So much dooth thy heynous fault offende mee, that if hee make thee not his Wife, thou shalt die the death as the Lawe hath ordained. Soldane,

answered the Princesse fiercely, in vaine seekest thou to recall the act committed. Doost thou thinke my fault so offensiue, which first was perpetrated by thy
perswasion? To loue a Gentleman, faire, well spoken, comly, sweet, gracious and
benigne, and who is of highest desert among all other: is it a matter deseruing
death? Cheefelie to a Princesse, whose youth may well excuse her trespasse? If
it be worthie the name of a sinne, it is more to thee then me: for thou didst first
intreate, perswade and commaunde mee to loue him, yea thou didst inuent the
meane how to winne him.

By thy deuise did I first make offer of that, which is the onelie sweete solace
in loue.[1] If thou therefore wilt put me to death, my care is the lesse, seeing that
with the most perfect among men I haue obtained my desires. And for the fault
shall not be laid on the best knight in the world, my selfe induced him thereto, I
called him, I deceiued him: and in breefe, more by force then loue I constrained
him to yeelde, to ease those passions that hourely tormented mee. When the Soldane behelde the impudencie of his Sister, he thus replied. Verily true it is, that
I commaunded thee to loue him, but not in this sort, whereof I can request no
better proofe then thine owne shamelesse speeches, which I will seuerely correct
before it bee night. So departing from her, he went to *Trineus* with these words.
Sir knight, I did neuer thinke that a man wise and valiant, as thou hast beene
esteemed, hauing seene and frequented manie Princes Courts, could imagine
an act so foule and detestable, in his Pallace that hath so highly honoured thee.
It behooueth thee therefore to take thy choyse of two things, either to amende
thy fault by espousing my sister, whom I frankelie giue thee, and therewithall to
renounce thy Baptisme, or suffer cruell death in rewarde of thine offence. Soldane, answered *Trineus*, thou abusest thy selfe in thinking to beguile mee.

My God, first arme mee with patience to the death, rather then for riches
and honours momentarie, I shoulde forsake my faith to my Sauiour, by whom
I hope to enioy euerlasting happinesse. As for the fact thou twittest me withall, well may it be excused, for I haue neither rauished or violated, but by force
of loue erred, with her that threatened her owne death before my face, except I
consented to her desire: yet in respect of mine honour, much better had it beene
to haue suffered her die: but to shunne the reproch of too seuere and inhumane
nature, I yeelded to her amourous petitions. Notwithstanding, if thou therefore
wilt put mee to death, thou canst not doo mee so much shame as thou imaginest,
but shalt cause me to performe the debt we all owe to nature,[2] and for which we
enioy our byrth in this worlde.

To conclude, thy flatteries and menaces cannot make me thine, much lesse
hers that hath so falsely deceiued mee. By the Starres,[3] quoth the Soldane, the
audacious behauiour of these Knights makes mee woonder: the one hath villainouslie iniuried mee in the presence of my Barons, and the other (for nothing
I can say) will not exchaunge his opinion, which hee shall soone and deerelie
repent. So causing the Tower to be fast locked, he went to the great Hall, and
there before all his Knights, said. You haue heard my Lordes, the confession of

Palmerin d'Oliva: Part II 553

them both, and withall haue seene their great obstinacie: therefore by sentence irreuocable I condemne them to death, and this day shall they be burned in the place accustomed, none of you all mooue me to the contrarie, for I will not be otherwise perswaded. By heauen, saide the Prince *Tomano*, vnhappie should I be to stay with you any longer, wherfore at this instant I forsake your alliaunce, and henceforth will shew my selfe your mortall enemie. Alas my Lord, quoth the yong Princesse *Belsina*, will ye so soone abandon my companie? Follow me then answered *Tomano*, where I go, for no more will I be seene in this tyrannous Court, where nothing but dishonour and crueltie is vsed.

Presently the Princesse and hee mounted on Horsebacke, and with their traine came to *Palmerins* Campe: who hauing heard the Soldanes sentence, was readie to haue slaine himselfe, but that hee hoped to saue the life of *Trineus* at the fatall houre. Alas my Freendes, quoth hee, to his companie, this day must you assist mee, to deliuer the most gentle Knight that euer bare Armes. Set forwarde couragiouslie agaynst the Tyrant, whom with the ayde of my God, wee shall easily vanquish. *Zephira* hearing that *Tomano* and *Belsina* were gone, and how the Soldane had iudged *Tryneus* and *Aurecinda* to death, entred into maruailous regrets and acclamations, whereat the Soldane was so enraged, as hee commaunded that *Tryneus* and his Sister, shoulde presently bee led to the place of execution, and vnder the charge of fiue thousand soldiours, they were brought on horsebacke foorth of the Cittie: but when *Aurecinda* sawe herselfe so hardly vsed, wringing her hands, and renting her comely locks of haire, shee brake forth into these pittifull speeches.[4]

Alas Gentlemen, why are you the instruments to execute a Tyrants will? what recompence can you expect at his handes, that for greedie desire of my patrimonie, sendeth mee to death? So piercing were these wordes in the eares of the Souldiours, as they verie much lamented her case: but *Tryneus* neuer chaunged colour, ryding on with resolute constancie, not once listning to the mones of the Princesse.

When they were come within sight of *Palmerins* power, they raunged themselues in battell array, committing *Tryneus* and *Aurecinda* to fiftie Knights, who should conuey them to the Furnace where their death was appoynted, which was a good quarter of a league from the Cittie. *Trineus* nowe seeing death before his eyes, and no succour neere to reskewe him, prepared himselfe to the latest extremitie, and with many sorrowfull farewels to *Agriola* and *Palmerin*,[5] was fully perswaded to endure the torment. *Palmerin* knowing which way his Freend should be led to death, with a sufficient traine lay secretlie ambushed, and espying oportunitie, gaue summons to his men, whereupon they all issued foorth verie couragiouslie. But as they rushed out from their secrete ambushment, the ayre was suddenly obscured, and such thunder, haile and raine fell, as neuer was the lyke heard or seene before, the Soldanes squadron seemed to bee all in a flaming fire. The poore *Persians* thinking the end of the world was come vppon them, fledde towards the Cittie: but notwithstanding all theyr haste, the greatest part of them remained dead in the field. If the natural fire (prepared for *Tryneus*) made him fearful, doubtlesse this fire raysed by coniuration made him much more afrighted, but suddainly came to him an Armed Knight with his Sworde drawne, and mounted on a horse of mightie bignesse, who tooke the Horse of *Tryneus* by the brydle, saying.

Come Sir *Tryneus*, in despight of the Tyrant thou shalt not die. At these wordes arriued *Palmerin*, who embracing *Tryneus*, said. Ah my deere Freend and Brother, what villanous minds beare they that would doo you this outrage? alight and put on your Armour which my Squire hath brought hither, that wee may with honour reuenge this shame. As they thought to goe set on the enemie, the Armed Knight, who was *Muzabelino*, thus spake. My Lorde, let vs not tarrie tryfling time heere, but summon your people togither, and sette forwarde to *Grisca*, where you shall finde better succour then in this place. The disolate *Tryneus*, what with his former feare, and present ioy to beholde his Freende, was not able to speake one worde, but *Palmerin* hauing well noted the Armed Knight, at length knewe him to bee *Muzabelino*, wherfore embracing him, sayd.

Ah my Lorde, for euer be the King of Kings praysed, in graunting me to haue knowledge of you, let me be worthilie condemned of ingratitude, if I doo not acknowledge this great fauour to my Freend, which I account as deere as doone to my selfe. After many courteous salutations passed on all sides, they set forwarde to *Grisca* with theyr men and prouision: where wee will leaue them, to shewe what afterward befell to the Soldane and his people. After a long and verie dangerous tempest, with whirle-windes, lightnings, and straunge apparitions, to the great discomfort of all the *Persians*: one of the Princes, came to the Soldane, saying.

My Lord, the lightning hath fallen so terriblie in the Court, as all the Ladies of honour are slaine therewith. An other brought newes, that three partes of the soldiours, which conducted *Tryneus* and *Aurecinda* foorth of the Cittie, lay all slaine in the rough tempest. While these strange mishappes were discoursing,[6] *Aurecinda* entred the Chamber, saying. Now soldane maist thou behold thy sinne. Seest thou not that the celestiall spirits, haue reuenged our wrong with the death of thy people? and for my escape I render thanks to the highest, not to thee that gaue my life to the fire, yet much better would my death haue contented mee, then to liue without him whose absence is my torment: and did not the hope of his life giue mee some comfort, thou shouldest perceiue how little I esteeme of my life. Then entred the Queene *Zephira*, and she falling at the Soldanes feete, thus began. Ah my Lord, the dishonour you haue this day done mee is vnspeakeable. Haue my deserts beene so simple in your eyes, that I might not intreate the libertie of one Knight, who this day (I feare) hath perished by your ingratitude? Neuer shall I see those noble Knights againe, whose liues haue beene endaungered for my welfare. Ah my Lorde, if you looke into the weight of your offence, you shall perceyue my teares are not shedde without great reason.

Madame, quoth the Soldane, and you faire Sister, at this time excuse my fault committed, and patientlie beare what hath happened: for I vowe to you by the fayth of a Prince, that I will make sufficient amendes for my trespasse. When hee now thought to bee no further troubled, his Sister *Lyzanda* entred mad and raging, and snatching his Fauchion from his side, said. See villaine, see what happeneth by thy commaundement, one of thy Sisters is for euer defamed, and the other will presently end her life before thee. Heerewith shee stabd the weapon to her heart, and fell downe dead at the Soldans feete, to the no little sorrow of his Maiestie, and all that were present: but *Zephira*, causing the bodie to bee taken away, the Soldane commanded she should be honourablie buried, and erecting a goodlie Tombe of Marble ouer her graue, caused the maner of her death to be thereon described. Afterward, by the counsell of the Lords of *Persia*, hee sent the Prince *Tomano*, and the straunge Knights, all the riches and treasure they had left behinde them: the Princesse *Aurecinda* remaining in continuall heauinesse, and within short time shee felt her selfe to be conceiued with Childe. Heerein shee somewhat comforted her selfe, though Fortune would not suffer her to enioy the companie of her Freend, yet one day shee hoped to see his liuely image: which at the time appoynted by Nature shee did, beeing deliuered of the goodlyest male Childe that euer was seene in *Persia*, naming him *Ryfarano*, who carried the beautifull complexion of his Mother, as hee did the hardinesse and magnanimitie of his Father.

Chapter LVII.

Howe Palmerin and Trineus hauing soiourned a while at Grisca with the king Abimar, departed to the Isle of Malfada, where by the meanes of Dulacco and Palmerin, all the enchauntments were finished.

By the way as the Princes rode towards *Grisca*, *Palmerin* vsed these speeches to *Trineus*. Howe happie is the Prince that giues credit to good counsell, and will not be led by flatteries, or subiect himselfe to his own passions? and how vnfortunate are they that fall into the contrarie? Can ye haue a better example heereof then the trayterous Soldane? who first (causelesse) disquieted the good King *Abimar*, and afterwarde at his sisters motion, imprisoned his Friend: for your good successe heerein my Lord, you must thanke *Muzabelino*, and the Prince *Tomano*, whose power was so readie to defende you. *Tryneus* remembring his follies past, was still so ashamed thereof, as hee could make no aunswere, wherefore *Palmerin* thus spake againe.

Why? my Lorde, hath the imprisonment for fayre *Aurecinda* strooke you dumbe? leaue this bashfulnesse to Women, and remember your former courage. Stoute *Hercules*, whose honors are yet so rife in memorie, did not hee for the loue of *Iole*, weare feminine garments, and spin among women? Did not *Achilles* the like, when hee was with his faire friend in the Courte of King *Lycomedes*, *Marke Anthonie* the *Romaine* Emperor, did not he follow *Cleopatra* before *Octauius*, although his armie on the Sea was twofolde the number of his enemies?[1] And you, for a little familiar loue to a yong Princesse, who conquered you onely by importunate sute, remaine thus confounded. Doo you imagine your selfe to excell in strength, prowesse, and knowledge, *Hercules, Achilles,* and the Emperour *Anthonie*?

Alas deere Brother, aunswered *Tryneus*, well may you boast of your especiall graces, beeing able to tryumph ouer concupiscence, but so yrkesome is my offence in mine owne conceit, as I thinke my selfe vnworthie to be seene among men of vertue. What shall I say to my *Agriola*, when she shall vnderstand my hainous offence? howe shall I dare to present my selfe before her? For that, saide *Palmerin*, we shall doo well enough, but I would it were so wel come to passe, that we were with her to abide her censure. Continuing these speeches, they arriued at *Grisca*, where the king beeing aduertised of their comming, came to meete them, vsing these words at their gracious entertainment. Right welcome are ye my noble Friendes, no maruaile though the Soldane sought to wrong you, remembring howe for my sake you vsed him in the battaile. In sooth my Lord, aunswered *Palmerin*, well doth your nobilitie deserue our seruice, and his iniurious dealing sharpe reuenge, which happily heereafter hee may feele to his cost, vsing strangers so vnhonorably: but heere we present your Daughter *Belsina* to your Maiestie, after whose marriage al these troubles began.

Welcome faire Daughter, saide the King, much better then my sonne hath beene to your Fathers Court. When my Father, quoth the Princesse, hath

Palmerin d'Oliva: Part II 557

considered his furie, doubtlesse he will be heartly sorrie therefore, and make satisfaction for any thing misdoone, till then I beseech your highnesse to conceiue the best. And according as the Princesse had spoken it came to passe, for within three dayes after, the Soldane sent Ambassadours to the King *Abimar*, to excuse the imprisonment of *Trineus*, and the sentence of death hee gaue against him, sending to him and *Palmerin* all their treasure and sumptuous presents, in signe of satisfaction, and to his Daughter *Belsina* and the Prince *Tomano*, he sent sixe Camelles laden with gold, as the dowry of their marriage.

Nowe are *Palmerin* and *Trineus* wearie of theyr so long stay from their friendes, wherefore they desired leaue of the king to depart, who seeing hee coulde not well intreate their longer aboade, right thankfully yeelded to their request, giuing them all things needefull for theyr iourney, as Horses, Armour, men, money, and diuers other gifts of inestimable value. For which kindnesse they humbly thanked his maiestie, refusing to trouble themselues with such riches in their trauaile, nor would they take that the Soldane sent them, or what they brought from the ten Rocks, except the Birde and the two Crownes, giuing all the rest to *Muzabelino*, desiring him to continue them in remembrance.[2] My Lordes, quoth he, no seruice can bee lost that is doone to such liberall Princes, as nowe you giue mee good occasion to confesse, and though both I and mine should spend all our following daies in your seruice, yet can wee not recompence the verie least of your courtesies, recommending my sonne *Bellechino* once more to you my Lorde, in hope he will prooue a loyall and faithfull Seruant, otherwise I could part his head from his shoulders in your presence.

And because the way you brought Madame *Zephira*,[3] is verie long, troublesome, and dangerous: I haue prepared a Shippe for you, which without any perrill shall speedily carrie you to *Malfada*, and a yong Knight my brother[4] haue I appointed Pilot therein, who shall direct you howe to finish all the enchauntments in the Isle, and afterwarde I desire you to order the matter with the King *Maulerino*, that my Brother may haue the gouernment thereof after your departure. Beleeue me noble Friende, aunswered *Palmerin*, your Sonne will I intreate as well beseemes him, and your Brother shall not onely haue the charge of the Isle, which I will freely giue him, but I will so worke with the Brother to *Zephira*,[5] that he shall endow him with greater possessions. So taking theyr leaue of all the Courtiers, *Muzabelino* brought him to the Shippe, wherein they were no sooner entred, but it presently cut through the waters with such violence, as they were verie quickly come to *Malfada*. They going on shore, *Dulacco* Brother to *Muzabelino*, demaunded of the Prince *Trineus*, if he had the Ring he founde in the Cuppe at the Castle of the tenne Rocks.[6] I haue it on my finger sir,[7] aunswered *Tryneus*. Let vs three then enter the Isle, saide *Dulacco*, as for you *Bellechino* and *Colmelio*, stay you in the shippe till you heare the sounde of a Cornet, and then may you safely venture on the land.

Dyardo standing in one of the Turrets in the Castle, sawe when the shippe came and cast Anker, wherefore hee expected if any durst come foorth thereof on the shore, and so amazed hee was that the three knights were not transformed, as till *Palmerin* spake to him, hee knewe not what to imagine, but afterward he made hast downe, and letting downe the Bridge, came and embraced him, saying. Welcome is my noble Lorde to *Malfada*, haue you learned or brought any remedy with you, whereby to recouer your Friendes heere enchaunted? in happie houre did you bestow your labour, if so it came to passe, but what may these two knights bee that come in your companie? The one is the Prince *Trineus*, quoth *Palmerin*, whom I so long time sought for, and the other is the man that must giue vs assistance.

After many friendly embracings, *Palmerin* demaunded what was become of the two Damoselles he left there. My Lord saide *Dyardo*, they remaine prisoners to doo pennaunce for the hard speeches they gaue you.[8] So went they all to the prison, where *Palmerin* demanded which of them had the Key of the enchaunted Tower: but they continuing in their former obstinacie and mallice, would not aunswere one word. False harlots, quoth *Palmerin*, why speake ye not? if you giue me not the Key quickly, all your sorcerie shall not saue your liues. Then beeing fearefull of death, presently fell on their knees,[9] and one of them taking the Key foorth of her pocket, opened the doore of the Tower, saying.

Enter Knight, I hope thou wilt repent thy hastinesse. *Palmerin* and his three companions went in, where they behelde a huge Idoll of Copper, holding a Bowe with an arrow readie drawn to shoote: by him hung a goodly Cornet of Iuorie, and on the other side a faire Booke. My Lord, said *Dulacco*, we must haue both the Cornet and the booke: and if you faile in getting them, no one aliue can ende the enchauntments. My God will strengthen me, sayd *Palmerin*, so drawing his Sword, and couering himselfe with his Sheeld, he boldly stept to the Image. And in despight of the deuils that fiercely strooke at him, hee puld the Bowe violently from him, when sodainely such a fearefull crie was heard through the Castle, as made them all to shake and tremble. The booke and Cornet he easily reached, and giuing them to *Dulacco*, willed him to finish the rest. That will I, quoth he, but you must be readie to assist me: let vs nowe go foorth and you shall see maruailes: when I am reading the first leafe of the Booke, doo you sounde the Cornet so loud as you can possible. *Palmerin* did as he was commaunded, and by the reading of *Dulacco*, and the sounde of the Cornet, all that were enchaunted in the Islande came running thither,[10] being so many, as *Palmerin* was amazed thereat.

Dulacco, hauing ended his Lecture, they all returned to their former shapes, the first were the couragious *Frysoll*, the King of *Sparta*, the Duke of *Pontus*, the Prince of *Mecaena*, the Prince *Olorico*, *Laurana*, and *Agriola*, whome *Trineus* ranne and embraced, seeing her so perfect in beautie as euer she was.

Now the remembrance of his offence with *Aurecinda*, stopped the passage of his speech, and her fauours shewne to the great Turke made her likewise ashamed, yet kisses and embracings with teares and sighs, deliuered theyr inward ioy for this happie meeting. Heere must we imagine the comfort of the other fiue

Palmerin d'Oliva: Part II   559

    Princes and *Laurana*, then which doubtlesse could be no greater, seeing theyr noble Friend that had deliuered them, and beholding each other in good disposition. Now are all those which were enchaunted, brought to their former shape, as well Turks as Christians, and theyr shippes by *Dulacco* restored them againe:
5 cheefely they that belonged to the Merchaunt *Estebon* and his sonnes, to whome *Palmerin* gaue such aboundance of treasure, as afterward they had no cause of want, discharging each one to their owne countrey, who departed thence to their no little contentation. *Agriola, Laurana*, and the other Princes, beeing altogether conferring of their good fortune, *Palmerin* commeth cheerefully among them,
10 and discoursed what had happened since the seperation, wherein hee reuealed all that you haue heard alreadie, which to repeate againe would bee but troublesome: it sufficeth you to conceiue, that all the friendes beeing met together, are so well acquainted with each others mishappe, as nowe they ioyntly reioyce in this happie successe.[11] The next morning, *Palmerin* called *Bellechino* his Squire,
15 saying to him.

    Thou must presently poste to *Elayne* to the King *Maulerino*, and hauing saluted him on my behalfe, deliuer him these Letters, wherein his maiestie shall bee acquainted with all that hath happened, but make all possible speede thou canst, because at thy returne wee wil sette to Sea presently. The Squire bee-
20 ing gone, *Palmerin* gaue in charge to *Dulacco*, to see his Shippes victualed and prouided, and that withall which *Muzabelino* had giuen him.

    Afterward hee went to bid *Agriola* and *Laurana* good morrow, and then comming to *Frysoll*, the king of *Sparta*, and *Olorico*, who were all pleasantly discoursing together in their Chamber, hee saide to them. Assuredly my good
25 friendes, if fortune had beene so aduerse to me, that I could not haue found *Tryneus*, or the meane to deliuer you from the enchauntment, I had giuen my farewell to Armes, riches, and honor, and would haue haunted those paths where neuer man trode. For with what face could I approch the presence of my sister and Aunt, hauing lost them whome they liue onely to loue. And you noble Prince
30 *Olorico*, haue iust occasion to complaine on me, that haue caused you to endure such paine and trauaile: but in recompence of this ouer great wrong, I will cause you to enioy her whom you haue so long faithfully loued, and so soone as I am arriued at *Constantinople*, I will send Ambassadours to my Lord the Soldane, that he may accept you as his sonne in my steede.

35   My Lorde, aunswered *Olorico*, the honour you haue doone me in accepting my companie, I account to exceede al other curtesies, and though for a time I haue beene vnfortunate, I take it patiently, assuring you by the word of a Prince, that I imagine the man not woorthie to taste the sweete, that cannot abide to feele the sower.[12] By this time are *Palmerins* Letters come to the King *Maulerino*,
40 who hauing vnderstood their contents, ioyfull of *Palmerins* returne, and of his good fortune in finishing the enchauntments, hee came presently with his traine to *Malfada*, where to discourse the pleasure on each side conceiued, the honourable and gracious curtesies bestowed, with all the especiall fauours beseeming

a king and so woorthie personages, is farre beyonde my capacitie, and therefore I referre it to your gentle consideration.[13] But at *Palmerins* intreatie, *Dulacco* was made Lorde and cheefe Gouernour of *Malfada*, and diuers other territories neere adioyning, which mooued *Palmerin* thus to thanke the King. Seeing your maiestie for my sake, hath bestowed this Islande on my woorthie good friende, to the ende that the name of the wicked *Malfada* may be vtterly raced forth, let me intreate that it may henceforth be called the Isle of the two Louers, because therein was enchaunted two, the most loyall Seruants that euer Loue had,[14] hauing endured wonderfull and variable fortunes, and yet heere met in the ende to their no little comfort.

Let it be, quoth the King, as you haue appointed, and whosoeuer henceforth calleth it otherwise, shall be held among vs as an open blasphemer. Afterwarde the King accompanied *Palmerin* and his friendes to their Shippes, and there committed them to their prosperous voyage: so *Palmerin*, his seauen companions, the two Princesses, with his Squires *Bellechino* and *Colmelio*, entred the shippe that *Muzabelino* gaue him, and an hundred knights which the King *Maulerino* had giuen him, were embarqued in an other shippe well appointed, so hoysing saile, with a merrie gale of winde they launced into the sea, and the King with his traine returned to his Court, leauing *Dulacco* quietly possessed of the Isle of the two Louers.

Chapter LVIII.

How Palmerin and his companions sayling on the Sea, met with Ptolome: and of the honourable entertainment the Emperour Florendos, and the Ladies made them, when they arriued at Constantinople.

Three dayes sayled our Knights without anie aduenture, and on the fourth, as *Phoebus* gan enter his Chariot, to display his golden beames on his Vncle *Neptunes* regions,[1] *Palmerin* standing aloft on the decke, espied a great Carricke, which with full saile made haste towards them, and by the Banners he discerned that it was of *Turkie*, wherefore he cried to his companions to arme themselues. Suddenly were they all come aloft on the Deck armed, and the hundred knights in the other ship were likewise in readinesse, when the Carricke being come neere them, they might behold the Turks strongly prouided, and *Ptolome* their Captaine brauely encouraging them. At length they buckeled togither, and a daungerous fight began betweene them, so that seuen of the King *Maulerinos* Knights were slaine, the King of *Sparta* sore wounded by *Ptolome*, and *Dyardo* in great perill of his life.[2] When *Palmerin* saw the King of *Sparta* fall, and that the Moores had daungerouslie hurt diuerse of his Freends, fearing the King was slaine, hee came to *Ptolome*, and after manie sharpe strokes on either side, at last got him downe, when pulling his Helmet furiouslie from him, thinking to haue smitten off his head, *Ptolome* cried: Kill me not sir Knight, for I yeelde my selfe to thee. *Palmerin* knowing his freend, sayd to his companions and the rest. Giue ouer my freends and fight no longer, for false fortune hath too much deluded vs.

Ah, worthie *Ptolome*, why haue I dealt so hardly with thee? is it possible that any man may bee likened to mee in mishap? no sooner am I out of one, but presently I fall into another: by heauen (deere Freende) if I had slaine thee, right soone woulde I haue beene reuenged on my selfe. See then, sweet *Ptolome*, how *Palmerin* greeues for his offence, more then if he had lost the best limme on his bodie.[3] When *Ptolome* behelde his Friend *Palmerin*, and by him the noble Prince *Tryneus*, embracing them, he said. O Sauiour of the world, howe highly hast thou this day fauoured mee, permitting mee to finde my deerest Freendes: then they brought him to the Princesse *Agriola*, in her Cabin, who was not a little glad to beholde the man, that endured with her some part of miserie, and *Colmelio* was ioyfull to behold Sir *Ptolome*, in that their hap was to bee parted when they were ledde to be solde as slaues:[4] but *Agriola* woulde needes heare all his fortunes, since the first time of their separation, which hee and *Colmelio* trulie recounted. Beleeue me *Ptolome*, said *Palmerin*, I see wee all haue had our shares in aduersitie, and hardlie can we iudge whose wrong hath beene greatest: but howe came you thus to bee Captaine among the Turks? My Lord, quoth he, the Princesse *Alchidiana* bought me, and charged mee to seeke you, both by Sea and Lande: and for my defence gaue mee fortie Knights, of whom there nowe remaines but ten[5] aliue. That Ladie am I highlie beholding to, sayde *Palmerin*, and for the wrong I haue done her by the death of her Knights, I will excuse my selfe by an honourable Ambassade, when I shall send the Prince *Olorico* to her againe. And that thou *Ptolome* maist knowe some of my good happe, vnderstande that I haue founde my Father and Mother, who are *Florendos*, the King of *Macedon*, and *Griana* the Daughter and heyre to the Emperour of *Greece*. I did euer perswade my selfe, quoth *Ptolome*, that your discent was of royall linage: but I intreate you for my sake, that these Knights which your men haue taken, may be gentlie vsed, and enioy their libertie. *Palmerin* calling them to him, said. For *Ptolome* his sake that was your Captaine, and her loue that commaunded you to trauaile with him, I wish to you as to my selfe: yet shall you all go with mee to *Constantinople*, that you may helpe to conduct the Prince *Olorico* backe againe, whom I meane to send with you to your Mistresse.

We abide my Lord (quoth they) at your direction, and willingly obey your will, in that wee haue knowne howe deerelie the Soldane loued you, and better fortune coulde not befall vs, then so luckilie to meete with you, and the Prince *Olorico*: as for our Companions that are slaine, there is no remedie, for such mishaps are common where Fortune frowneth. So sailed they on freendlie togither, and on the Sea we will leaue them, to tell you of the return of the Ambassadour *Maucetto* to the Soldane of *Babylon*, who hearing that the *Persian* had refused to assist him, was somewhat offended thereat, but when he saw what *Palmerin* had written, he pacified himselfe, saying. Ah gentle *Palmerin*, hadst thou beene in the battell at *Constantinople*, I had not needed to demaunde helpe of him whom I iudged my Freend: but seeing Fortune hath showne her selfe so contrarie, I will not attempt anie thing from which thou disswadest me.

Maucetto declared, that *Palmerin* had likewise sent a Letter to the Princesse *Alchidiana*, which hee commaunded him presentlie to carrie her: no sooner had she read the Letter, and thereby vnderstoode his knightly deedes of Chiualrie, but embracing the Ambassadour, thus spake. *Maucetto*, neuer couldest thou haue brought mee better newes, then of the man whose name flourisheth in all places. Ah sweete Letter, written by the hand of the most perfect Knight liuing, full charie and choisly will I keepe thee. Ah *Ptolome*, whom my noble Freend loues so deerely, thee haue I sent in daungerous hazarde of thy life: but may I once see thee againe, thou shalt perceiue my loue for *Palmerins* sake.

Happie art thou Princesse *Zephira*, hauing with thee the myrror of mankinde. My Lord, quoth shee, (as though *Palmerin* had beene present) wilt thou wrong thy selfe so much as to tarrie with her? Dare the Soldans Sisters vaunt that they loue thee? They be faire, as I vnderstand, but not so faire that thou shouldest refuse me for them. What haue I said? doubtlesse matter to mine owne reproach, for if thou wouldest, the kingly offers of my Father, and my importunate intreaties could no way mooue thee: hardlie may the *Persians* preuaile with thee, especiallie in such a weightie cause as loue is. *Maucetto*, what sayest thou? is Lord *Palmerin* like to stay long in *Persia* with the Soldans Sisters? No Madame, quoth he, I heard him say verie often that he woulde depart thence before a Moneth was expired.

Palmerin d'Oliva: Part II 563

In these and such like speeches they continued, wherin wee purpose to leaue them, for by this time is *Palmerin* and his Freendes arriued in the Hauen of *Constantinople*, and *Colmelio* is sent before to the Pallace, to aduertise the Emperour of these ioyfull tydings. As *Colmelio* entered the great Hall, the first man he mette was his Father *Gerrard*, who was newly made Lord Chamberlaine to the King *Florendos*: wherefore falling on his knee before him, he said. Father, little did I thinke to finde you exalted to such honour, happie was the day when you founde Prince *Palmerin*, and much more happinesse is this day, in that I bring the most ioyfull newes that euer man did to this Court. Olde *Gerrard* exceeding glad to beholde his sonne, catching him in his armes, said. Welcome *Colmelio*, to thy aged Father, hast thou heard any tydings of thy Lord and Maister? Go with mee Father, aunswered *Colmelio*, and you shall heare matter of maruaile. At that instant came the Emperour with the King *Florendos* into the Hall, and all the Ladies going to heare diuine seruice, wherefore *Gerrard* thus spake to his highnesse. My Lord, see heere my Sonne *Colmelio*, who long time hath trauailed in search of Prince *Palmerin*, hee hath some message of importaunce to deliuer to your Maiestie. Right welcome is hee, quoth the Emperour, say what thou wilt, my freend, thou hast free libertie.

Mightie Emperour, sayd *Colmelio*, your Son Prince *Palmerin* is arriued in the Hauen, and with him the yong Prince *Tryneus*, Sonne to the Emperour of *Allemaigne*, the good Knight Sir *Ptolome*, the fiue Princes which went with him from *Macedon*, the two Princesses of *England* and *Durace*, with diuerse other vnknowne to me: and saluting your Maiestie with his humble dutie, intreateth that Horses may be sent for them and the Ladies, that hee and they may come to kisse your highnesse hande. The Emperour, *Florendos* and the Ladies, were readie to swoune with ioy at these tydings, and hauing embraced the Messenger, commaunded a royall traine to goe meete his Son, and goodly Palfraies to bring them to the Pallace. Some ranne on foote to the Port, other on Horsebacke, so that before the Emperours traine came, such store of Gentlemen and Marchants were there to receiue them, as hardly they could stand one by another. After they were all mounted on horsebacke, with great ioy and triumph they rode towards the Pallace, where *Tryneus* falling on his knee before the Emperour, sayd.

Long liue your Maiestie in health and happinesse, here may you beholde the man, for whom my Lorde *Palmerin* your Sonne, hath endured such paine and trauaile. The Emperour perceiuing by his speeches that hee was *Trineus* the Prince of *Allemaigne*, thus aunswered. I hope my Lorde, that you will beare with mine age and weakenesse, which hinders me from entertaining you as fain I would, but I beseech you to aryse, for it ill beseemes so great a Prince, to humble himselfe in such sort. *Florendos* and *Griana* (in this time) welcommed their Sonne, *Arismena* the King of *Sparta*, *Armida* her *Frysoll*, and the olde Emperour and Empresse graciously entertained *Agriola* and *Laurana*, each absent Freend so embraced and welcommed, as all the day was spent onelie in those ceremonies. The next morning *Palmerin* dispatched his Dwarffe *Vrbanillo* to the Emperour of

Allemaigne, that he and *Polynarda* might vnderstand these long expected newes: and afterward comming to Sir *Frysoll*, he sayd to him. Brother, our Mother⁶ hath enriched vs with a Sister since our departure, and my Sister *Armida* me with two Nephewes, I pray you let vs go see them.

    Heereupon the Nurses brought the yong Princes, the eldest of them being named *Dytrius*, and the yongest *Belcar*, the yong Princesse, Daughter to *Florendos* and *Griana*, was called *Denisa*, so faire and comely were the infants, as if Nature had studied to make them most exquisite. Beleeue me Sir *Frysoll*, quoth *Palmerin*, if my sister continue as she begins, the Realme of *Hungaria* shall hardly want heires: what? two at a blow, bir Ladie⁷ it is a signe of good fertillitie. And when you are entred the estate of wedlocke, answered *Frysoll*, if your linage increase according to the greatnesse of desire, Madam *Polynarda* shall be as well sped as her neighbors. Thus iested the Princes togither, attending newes of the courrier, that went with *Vrbanillo* to the Emperor of *Allemaigne*, who at that time was at *Vienna*.

Chapter LIX.

How the Duke of Mensa, and the Countie of Redona, conducted the prince Olorico into Assiria, where hee was espoused to the princesse Alchidiana.

For the space of a Moneth and more, *Palmerin*, *Trineus* and *Agriola*, soiourned at *Constantinople*, till all things were prepared for them to trauaile towardes *Allemaigne*: during which time, *Palmerin* shewed such signes of loue to the Prince *Olorico* as he wold seldome be forth of his companie. And seeing that more and more his amourous passions encreased, hee sayde. Deere Freend *Olorico*, although I am no way able to recompence your long continued kindnesse, or remunerate the paine and trauaile you haue suffered in my companie, yet haue I determined (so you like thereof) to sende you to *Assyria*, and with you the Duke of *Mensa*, and the Counte of *Redona*, as Ambassadours to my Lord the Soldane, with such an honourable traine beside, as *Mysos* shall haue no occasion to complaine.

Nor doo I this (sweete Prince) as enuious of your companie, or that I stand in feare of the Soldane, but onelie to keepe my promise, which was, that I would ayde you to my vttermost, to accomplish the marriage betweene you and Madame *Alchidiana*,[1] for whom I see your minde is incessantly troubled. My Lorde, aunswered *Olorico*, if euer perfect loue might be discerned in a Princes heart, doubtlesse it is most amplie deciphered in yours. Where you can finde in anie Historie, semblable affecttion? or that a Christian would so fauour his enemie, that is contrarie to him in law and profession? Rare is the humanitie, that so great a Prince would so much abase himselfe, to accept as his companion in Armes, the poore Sonne of the King of *Arabia*, practising for his good, not the suretie alone of the Christians, but the alliance of the greatest Lord in *Asia*. Wherefore my noble Lorde, since of your accustomed good nature you haue made me this offer, of simple iudgement should I shewe my selfe to refuse it. I accept your gracious kindnesse, and assure your selfe of his readie seruice, whom your precious vertues hath so bound to you, as for euer I will name my selfe the seruaunt to the Prince of *Greece*. Heereupon *Palmerin* wrote to the Soldane of *Babylon* in forme as followeth.

The Letter of Prince Palmerin, to the
great Soldane of Babylon.

Right puissant Lord of *Assyria*, if the obedience we owe to Parents and Countrey, are causes sufficient to call home a Knight errant, with refusall of all straunge freendships and alliaunces, I hope your Maiestie will not mislike of my returne from *Persia* to *Constantinople*. And because I was there aduertised by your highnesse Ambassadour *Maucettc*, howe you haue resolued to vexe vs with open hostilitie, I will nowe reueale vnto you, that by the grace and fauour of the highest God, since my departure from your Court, I haue obtained knowledge of my Parents, who are such, as if you seeke the wracke of *Constantinople*, you goe about to destroy that *Palmerin*, whome heeretofore you haue so deerelie loued, and is nowe become the onelie heyre to that Empyre. Wherefore my Lord, if for my sake you will graunt so much, as to forget reuenge for your deceassed brother *Gamezio*:[2] both we and all ours shall continually name our selues, your Friendes and assistaunts against all your enemies. Contrariwise, if you will follow your former opinion, wee must defende our selues so well as we may. And for I can no more (with credit) forsake my Countrey, Parents and friendes, to returne againe to your seruice: I sende you the Prince *Olorico*, a Knight both valiant and hardie as anie in all *Turkie*, without exception of your Court, the great Turks, or the Soldane of *Persia*, and he to serue you in my steede. Desiring your highnes by that affection which you did beare me when the Prince *Amarano* was slaine in your presence,[3] that you accept him as your Sonne, and giue him in marriage your Daughter *Alchidiana*, as the man that hath best deserued her, if euer Prince might merit a Ladies loue by bountie and choyse chiualrie. So shall you performe an action of mickle honour, and binde me continually to acknowledge this kindnesse.

Your Palmerin d'Oliua.

Another Letter he wrote to the Princesse *Alchidiana*, the tenure whereof was thus.

The Letter of Prince Palmerin,
to the Princesse of Assiria.

To you Madam *Alchidiana*, daughter to the great Soldane of *Babilon*, *Palmerin d'Oliua* your knight, sendeth health condigne to your magnificence. Madame, sending to your Father the Duke of *Mensa*, and the Count of *Redona* our Ambassadours, to intreate of perpetual peace and alliance betweene his Maiestie and vs, whereto may it please you to giue fauourable assistance: I thought good by them likewise to write to your excellencie, with earnest intreatie to receiue as yours, the Prince *Olorico*, heire to the Crowne of *Arabia*. You know faire Madame, that neuer had he come to your Fathers Court, had not the perillous battaile against the proude Brethren of *Amarano* prouoked him, nor would he haue aduentured the dangers of the Sea, but in hope (at length) to purchase your gracious loue. For these considerations, good Madame, entertaine him into your sober thoughts, who hath no more feared to spend his bloud for your sake, and thrust his life into infinite dangers, then I haue doone to sette my hande and penne to this paper. I know that your grace, beautie, and great dowrie, commandeth the cheefest Prince on the earth for your Husband, and (to sheelde my selfe from blame) I know that I promised you my seruice, when I should returne from *Constantinople*:[4] but how hath it fallen out? your *Palmerin* is knowne by them that haue like authoritie ouer him, as your loue hath on the Prince *Olorico*. I am a Christian, a stranger, Sonne to the simple king of *Macedon*, and the Daughter to the Emperour of *Greece*, beside, of verie little or no desert at all. Hee is of your

Palmerin d'Oliva: Part II 567

Lawe, your Neighbour, sonne to the rich king of *Arabia*, and a Prince of as high vertue as euer was in my companie: witnesse whereof he made on the *Phrigians*, and in an hundred places since in my presence. Wherefore Madame, if noblenesse of hart, and loyall loue deserue so great an alliance, I know no Prince this day liuing more worthie then he. Assuring you withall, that more gladly would I die the death, then sollicite the cause of him, whome I would but imagine vnworthie your person.

Your Knight, Palmerin d'Oliua.

When he had sealed these Letters, hee gaue them to the Ambassadours, who accompanied with fiftie *Grecian* Knights,⁵ went to the Hauen where their shippes was prepared, after them followed the King *Maulerinos* hundred Knights, the number being supplied with other, in stead of them that were slaine,⁶ and after them went the Knights that came with *Ptolome*, then came the Prince *Olorico* and *Palmerin*, deuising by the way on manie matters.

My Lord, quoth *Palmerin*, I imagine you nowe remember our taking by the Admirall *Olimaell*,⁷ and feare that the like mishappe may againe befall you: I therfore (as your guarde) giue you the hundred Knights I had of the King *Maulerino*, and fiftie Knights naturally borne in *Greece*, as able in Armes as any other whatsoeuer, intreating you to holde me excused, if I giue you not such estate as beseemes your nobilitie. Woorthie *Palmerin*, answered the Prince, the greatest Lord that is, might well content himselfe with the honourable companie you haue giuen mee. And did not extreame passions ouer-rule me, and call mee hence to her seruice whom I haue onely chosen, I woulde renounce *Arabia* and the Lawe of Mahomet, onely to liue in your companie. But in what place my fortune guides me heereafter, neither Parents or Friendes shall hinder mee to saie that I am your vowed and affectionate seruaunt. The like doo you conceiue of me, sayde *Palmerin*. So with teares they left each other, *Olorico* and all his companie beeing aboord, such fauourable winde and weather they had, as without any danger they safely arriued where the Soldane lay: and first the tenne knights went on shore, they that were left of the companie which the Princesse *Alchidiana* gaue to *Ptolome*,⁸ and comming before the Princesse, saide.

Madame, your Knight sir *Ptolome* humbly saluteth you by vs, sending your excellencie this Letter. Beside, there is nowe arriued at the porte, the Prince *Olorico*, and certaine Ambassadours from the valiant *Palmerin*, Prince of *Greece* and *Macedon*, who come on his behalfe to kisse your hand. The Princesse hauing heard these newes, and read the Letter which *Ptolome* sent, containing the great good fortunes of *Palmerin*, was inwardly so rauished with delight, as a long space she remained silent, but at length brake foorth into these speeches. Ah Fortune, how well thou knowest to change matters which way thou pleasest, not according to the wil and desire of passionate minds, but on the behalfe of the highest in perfections. Ah *Palmerin*, the man whom my heart shall euer loue, howe may faire *Polinarda* iustly tearme her selfe happie, hauing thee for her Lord and loue, considering that the beautie and graces of so manie Ladies conquered with thy deserts, nor the sumptuous riches continually offered thee, could once diuert thee from thy first affection. Ah *Alchidiana*, that which hath made so many Ladyes and knights fortunate, in compassing the onely issue of their desires, dooth now remaine for thy torment alone, making thee the most vnhappie creature vnder the Sunne. *Agriola*, *Griana*, *Arismena*, *Armida*, and *Zephira*, are they (sweete Knight) by thy meanes in assuraunce of theyr loues? *Trineus*, *Frysoll*, the King of *Sparta*, *Maulerino*, *Abimar*, *Tomano*, and diuers other, are their Realmes quieted, and their Ladyes triumphing in their ioyes, onely by the price of thy bloud and daunger of thy life? And must I alone remaine disgraced, for euer confounded, hauing lost the knight I loued as my soule? While the princesse continued these complaints, the prince *Olorico* and the Ambassadours were come before the soldane, and being entertained by him with verie gracious countenance, they presented the Letters from *Palmerin*, which beeing read in presence of all his Lords, the Soldane thus answered.

My Friends, I will impart these newes to my Counsell and my Daughter, and afterwarde make you answere' as I may. Heereuppon the Duke of *Mensa*, the Counte of *Redona*, and the Prince *Olorico* withdrew themselues, and soone after the Soldane sent for his daughter, thus speaking to her. Daughter, our Princes thinke good, and haue counselled mee to make peace with *Palmerin*, who at this present is heyre of *Greece*, and requireth in witnesse of our truce, that I should giue you in marriage to the renowned Prince *Olorico*. Aduise your selfe hereon, for *Palmerin* hath earnestly intreated it by writing, and heere I haue a letter for you, I think to the same effect. The Princesse hauing read the Letter, returned this answere. It is verie true my Lord, his request to mee is for the selfe same cause: seeing therefore it liketh you, and the Princes of our Realme think it conuenient, in respect of the common profit and good may ensue thereby, it is not for me to make deniall.

Right glad was the Soldane of this aunswere, wherefore he saide, go then faire Daughter and decke your selfe accordingly, for after Dinner in the presence of the Ambassadours, you shall be affiaunced to the Prince. *Olorico* since his arriuall had talked but little with his Ladie, wherefore hee nowe determined to go see her, and meeting her as she returned from the Soldane, he saluted her with great reuerence, but the Princesse feigning that she knew nothing yet of their marriage, thus spake to him. I vnderstand my Lorde, that your companion *Palmerin* hath altogether forsaken vs. Madame, quoth the Prince, if hee haue abandoned your companie, it is onely by the fauour of Fortune, who hath beene a greater Friend to him then any man beside: yet cannot the great honours and possessions he now enioyeth, make him forgette you, in that at my departure he said, for euer he would liue and die your knight. God keepe him, said the Princesse, where euer he is, for still is my heart vowed to his remembrance, and gladly can I doo as much for him as for my Brother, though his present aduauncement hinder him from my seruice. Such is his trust Madame, quoth hee, in your fauour, that you will not refuse any honest

Palmerin d'Oliva: Part II   569

request he makes to your excellencie, in which respect hee hath sent mee to intreate you, that you will be assistant to the peace hee desireth with your father, and that you would vouchsafe me so much honour, as in his steede to entertaine me into your seruice: which to begin, I present you my heart, that neuer since the day of our departure from *Constantinople*, hath enioyed any rest, beeing absent from the onely meane of my comfort. If then I haue liued all this while in some hope, by remembraunce of your exceeding graces and courtesies, beyonde all other should I account my selfe in happinesse, if now at length you receiue me as your Seruant. I receiue you, saide the Princesse, for *Palmerins* sake, and for your owne deserts which haue beene so worthie, requiting you with equall affection, so that you denie mee not one request. Nothing shall you bee denied (sweete Princesse) quoth hee, if by my life it may be compassed.

    Nor will I demaunde any thing of so great value, said she, this is the fauour you shall graunt me, heereafter when time shal serue, that you wil conduct me to *Constantinople*, there to behold the faire princesse *Polynarda*, and the magnificent Court of noble *Palmerin*, in recompence whereof, I giue my selfe to be your wife, and accept you as my Lord and Husband. If *Olorico* was now well pleased, I referre to your iudgements, wherefore confirming their promises, by kisses and embracings, with solemne protestations and irreuocable vowes,[10] they departed thence to their Chambers.

    After Dinner, the Princesse attired in most sumptuous garments, came into the Hall with her waiting Ladies, when the Soldane sent for the Ambassadours, and thus spake to them. My Friendes, I now perceiue the man to bee ouer foolish that trusteth in himselfe, I thought by my power to destroy *Greece*, where on the contrarie my people are destroyed. I thought to continue vnquenchable hatred toward your Maister, and now I am constrained to graunt him peace, yet not constrained, but by the worke of the greatest God I am mooued so to doo, which in the presence of all my Lordes I protest, and with as good will as hee dooth demaunde it. See then the power of that Maiestie, which can subdue and conquere where he list, and I sweare to you by my Crowne, that the good fortune of *Palmerin* contenteth me as well, as if he were mine owne sonne. Mightie Soldane, answered the Duke of *Mensa*, if you resolue to loue the worthie Prince *Palmerin*, both hee and his will performe the like to you, and on his behalfe we promise faithfully, that against all your enemies (Christendome excepted) you shall be assured of his succour and assistance.[11]

    I request no better assurance, quoth the Soldane, then this that he hath sent, and that you may witnesse I am his faithfull Friend: at this instant shall the peace be ratified by all the Lordes and Princes here present, and to seale the same, as he requested, I giue my daughter to the Prince *Olorico*. Great ioy was generally made for this good agreement, and the two louers were espoused together within few dayes after: and the time being come for the Ambassadours returne to *Constantinople*, *Alchidiana* sent diuers rich gifts to *Palmerin* and *Polinarda*, the like did the Soldane and the Prince *Olorico*.

CHAPTER LX.

How Palmerin, Trineus, and Agriola, accompanied with many great Lords and princes, went to the Emperor of Allemaigne at Vienna, where great triumphs were made at the celebrating of the marriage between Trineus and the princesse Agriola.

Soone after the Prince *Olorico*, and the Ambassadours of *Greece* were gone towardes *Assiria*, *Palmerin* (although the aged Emperour very much disswaded him) made prouision for his speedy voyage to *Allemaigne*, and hauing conducted the King of *Sparta* and his Aunt *Arismena* some parte of their way homeward, at his returne to the Cittie of *Constantinople*, came to the Duke of *Pontus*, saying. I remember the time when you did cutte off the great Turks head,[1] an acte deseruing good and especiall recompence, and that you thereby deliuered vs, and performed it at the motion of the Princesse *Laurana*, her haue you loued euer since both on lande and Sea, and her Countrey is not farre hence: will ye now make her your Ladie and Wife? I promise ye my assistance so farre as I can.

My Lord, aunswered the Duke, fearing to offend you, I still deferred to mooue you in this cause, but seeing wee are nowe so happily fallen into these tearmes, I will not conceale the truth from you. In sooth my Lorde, when first I sawe her, I loued her, and haue euer since continued in this hope, that time at length would fauour my intent. It sufficeth, saide *Palmerin*, and presently hee acquainted the Emperour therewith, who thinking the match very meete and conuenient, they were the next day married by the Archbishop of *Constantinople*, and in short time after went to take possession of their Duchie of *Durace*, where they were receiued very honourably, and the whole state yeelded vp into the Dukes hande.

When *Palmerin* sawe that the most parte of his companions were departed, at the earnest intreataunce of the Prince *Trineus* and *Agriola*, he set forward to *Allemaigne*, accompanied with *Frysoll* and *Armida*, whome hee conducted into the Realme of *Hungaria*, where *Frysoll* was crowned King by reason of his Fathers decease: there went with him like wise *Diardo* of *Bohemia*, the Prince *Eustace*, *Ptolome*, and other Lords of great account. Such good speed they made in theyr iourney, as in short time they arriued at *Vienna*, where the Emperour beeing aduertised of their comming by the Dwarfe, came with his courtly trayne to meete them, and taking his Sonne *Tryneus* in his armes, said. I see it is the will of God my Sonne, that heereafter I shall haue as great ioy by thee, as in thy long absence I haue had greefe and sorrow, all which I patiently put vp, for the loue of thy brother, the noble Prince *Palmerin*, and faire *Agriola* of *England*, that well deserues it. But in good sooth my Children, had you not come in so happie time, I should haue bene driuen to meruailous feare. For the King of *Fraunce* perceiuing, that I would not giue my daughter in marriage to his eldest sonne, demaunded the King *Recinde* of *Spaine* his daughter, who graunted his request: so that they twaine, with the aide of the King of *England*, haue leueyed such an Armie on the

Palmerin d'Oliva: Part II   571

Sea, as neuer was the like seene to passe the *Rheine*.[2] But seeing you returned in good disposition, the lesse account I make of their angrie menaces: yet are they the three principall Kings of Christendome.

   My Lord answered *Palmerin*, be not you dismaide at their enterprise, for
5 ere manie dayes bee expired, I hope to see all matters quietly pacified, and that without anie effusion of blood. The lesse is my doubt, quoth the Emperour, in that with such good fortune you haue finished your intentions, for nothing you begin but comes to luckie ende. Witnesse heereof appeareth in the search of my Sonne *Tryneus*, whom the best Knights in Christendome haue laboured to
10 finde: but all their trauaile I see hath beene spent in vaine. By this time they were come to the Pallace, where they were graciously receiued by the Ladies. Alas my Freendes, said the Empresse, which of you shall I first embrace? Ah my Sonne *Tryneus*, howe sorrowfull hast thou made mee since thy departure from *England*? iust cause hast thou to thanke the Heauens, who protected thee still in so manie
15 daungers, and forget not thy Brother *Palmerin*, who hath endured such trouble for thy sake. Faire Daughter, quoth she to the Princesse *Agriola*, welcome are you indeed. God send you better fortune heereafter, then you haue had alreadie, which yet hath bene a Touch-stone of your loyaltie. But while these speeches continued, howe the other two Louers with piercing regard beheld eache other,
20 and how many gracious signes passed as secrete Ambassadours betweene them. *Polynarda* was clad in such costly accoustrements, for the pleasure she conceiued since the Dwarffes arriuall at the Court, as shee seemed another *Iuno*, when shee stood to abide the arbitrement of *Paris*, or like *Voluptas* following her Mother *Venus*.[3]
25   But fearing least this amiable encounter, should decipher some part of her former courtesies to her friend,[4] which as yet was vnknowne to any but *Bryonella*, she locked vp all secrets with so sweet a kisse, as would haue contented the rudest of the Gods, had it bene *Vulcan* or *Neptune* themselues.[5] And comming to salute the Princesse *Agriola*, sayd. No meruaile (faire sister) if your loue wrought won-
30 ders in my brothers minde, for vnfainedly I speake it, your exquisite graces deserue the greatest seruice in the world. Alas Madame, aunswered *Agriola*, if nature, or they that had the charge of me in my youth, could haue painted me with such beautie as I see in you, or enriched me with wisedome, able to deuise with my Lord when he came to see mee: then could I haue said somewhat of the paines he
35 hath taken for mee, but I know my selfe so full of imperfections, as the loue hee beares me proceedeth of his owne good nature, not by any merit he can behold in me. Then *Palmerin* kneeling before the Emperour, said. I beseech you my Lord graunt me one request, which shall be no way preiudiciall to your Maiestie. Arise sir *Palmerin*, quoth the Emperour, aske what thou wilt, and thou shalt haue it.
40   My Lord *Tryneus*, and the Princesse *Agriola*, saide *Palmerin*, are religiously married betweene themselues, let me intreate your highnesse to confirme it with open solemnization,[6] before the Duke of *Mecaena* heere present: whom I meane to send into *England*, that he may resolue the King howe himselfe was an eye

witnesse of their marriage. The Emperour liked so well of *Palmerins* motion, as soone after the wedding was solemnized, and he comming to *Bryonella*, courteously taking her by the hand, said. My good friend *Brionella*, I am now to be discharged of the promise I made at my last being here: in witnesse whereof, I haue brought your knight sir *Ptolome*, and him I commend to your further fauour. So highly am I beholding vnto you my Lord, quoth shee, as neuer shall I bee able to returne sufficient recompence: but were we equall in ioy with the Prince *Tryneus* and faire *Agriola*, then would I think no storme could wrong vs.[7]

   Palmerin at these words presently left her, and perswaded the Emperour so well, as *Ptolome* and *Brionella* were likewise espoused togither, when *Palmerin* conferring with the Princesse *Agriola*, thus spake to her. Now may you iudge Madame whether I deceiued ye or no, and if the estate of my Lord *Tryneus* be any lesse then I told ye. Had I not giuen faithfull credit to your speeches, answered *Agriola*, I would not haue forsaken my Parents and friendes so rashly: but I hope they will pardon me, in that I haue done nothing but to their honour. On the morrow, with exceeding ioy and rare tryumphs, were *Palmerin* and *Polinarda* married togither, and thus was long and faithfull loue worthily requited.[8] *Ptolome* was now created Duke of *Saxon*, and *Dyardo* tooke his leaue to goe see his wife *Cardonya*, whom he had not heard of since the time he was taken by the Pirates.

Chapter LXI.

Howe Palmerin sent Ptolome Duke of Saxon (as his Ambassador) to the King of France, and the Duke Eustace of Mecaena, to the King of England, to treate of the peace betweene them.

Certaine dayes before the departure of *Dyardo* toward *Bohemia*, *Palmerin* in the presence of the Emperour and all the Princes, gaue the charge of his Embassade to the Duke *Ptolome*: which he should deliuer not onely to the most Christian King of *France* himself, but also to his yongest sonne, who now had espoused the Duchesse of *Burgundie*. So departed *Ptolome* from *Vienna*, accompanied with many Lordes and knights, and at length arriued at *Digeon*,[1] where the Prince *Lewes* being acquainted with the cause of his comming, thus answered the Ambassadour.

My Lorde, sometime I had acquaintance in *Fraunce*, with the most renowned *Palmerin*, and because hee is the onely man of the worlde, to whom I owe all friendly affection, I will perswade my Father to ioyne in peace with him. Nowe was *Ptolome* in good hope that his trauaile woulde sorte to successiue ende: wherefore they presently iourneyed to the King, who as then was with his estates at *Paris*, and hauing hearde *Palmerins* request, who nowe was wedded to the Princesse *Polynarda*,[2] and therefore his intended warre with the Emperour, would extende to the hurt of the man he loued, thus answered. Duke of *Saxon*, I am sufficiently acquainted with the bountie of thy Maister, and verie well I doo remember, that at his beeing in *Fraunce* he combatted for his Ladie *Polinarda*:[3] yet was I ignoraunt till nowe of that[4] hath happened. But leaste hee should conceiue, that I seeke to make a commotion in Christendome, let him enioy his Ladie and Wife in peace, although shee was sometime promised to mine eldest Sonne,[5] reseruing the conditions of our amitie, that our first Nephewes and Neeces may match togither in marriage, therby to continue the honour of their predecessours. As for the Kings of *Spaine* and *England*, who moued me to giue them assistaunce, on their behalfe I can make you no certaine answere, vntill my Messengers be returned home againe. Gracious Lord, quoth *Ptolome*, I dare assure you in the name of my Maister, that hee hath euermore esteemed your fauour among the best Christian Princes, and will not refuse the marriage betweene your Children heereafter. And this coniunction of your amitie, will cause that neither the Kings of *Spaine* or *England* will seeke to molest him: but with your highnesse ioyne in loue and friendship. With this answer *Ptolome* returned to *Vienna*, where the Emperour and *Palmerin* welcommed him with exceeding honour: and by this time had the Duke *Eustace* taken landing in *England*, where deliuering the summe of his charge to the King, his highnesse returned him this answere. Although my Lord Ambassadour, both your Maister and the Prince *Tryneus* did me manifest dishonor,[6] yet not to withstand peace, which still ought to bee preferred before warre, I graunt his request, and will presently call home my Garrisons, shaking hands with him in honourable concord. As for the wrong doone to my Daughter, I am content to excuse it, beleeuing that shee was not conueyed hence but with her will: thanking the Prince for the honour he hath done her, seeing she would leaue her Parents and friendes so lightly. I thinke my gracious Lord, answered the Duke, that when you consider what your Daughter hath done, you will not touch her with want of witte or iudgement: for in respect of the long enmitie betweene the Emperour and you, shee desired that her marriage might sort to this happie ende. Nor would she haue departed hence with the Prince *Tryneus*, without a faithfull and resolued promise of marriage: which is performed, with as great honour as euer was done to the daughter of a King. Thinke you, quoth the King, that had not the great friendship of *Tryneus*, (when against his Fathers will, he came with *Palmerin* to assist me)[7] qualified the weight of mine anger against him, but I woulde haue pursued the iniurie he did to me? yet did I referre his seruice, to the iudgements of my Lords of *England*, who perswaded me to reuenge, which you well perceiue as yet I haue not done.

Prince *Palmerin*, quoth the Duke, is so vertuous, as rather woulde hee haue runne on a thousande deathes, then your daughters honour shoulde anie way haue beene impeached: but beeing assured of this fortunate issue, both hee and *Tryneus* aduentured as they did. And sorrie am not I, said the King, that all things are come so well to passe, but seeing we are entred thus farre in speeche, tell mee (I pray you) how *Palmerin* came to the knowledge of his Parents, and howe hee finished the aduentures at the Castle of the tenne Rockes, and the daungerous Isle of *Malfada*, which neuer any Knight could compasse before? Then the Duke rehearsed euerie accident, how amourous the great Turke was on the Princesse *Agriola*,[8] and each seuerall occasion as they fell out: at which report, the Queene with her Ladies were present, who hearing the discourse of so straunge and variable fortunes, said.

I thought my Daughter had learned more modestie, then leauing her Fathers Court, to followe a Knight vnknowne to her in straunge Countries: but seeing the ende hath fallen out so well, henceefoorth I shall remaine in better contentment, seeing a Prince of so great renowne hath now espoused her.

While this conference endured, the Duke earnestly beheld the Princesse *Sabinda*, Daughter to the Prince of *Sansuega*, and Neece to the Queene: and of such excellent grace and beautie he esteemed her, as forgetting the death of his Father, who deceased since his departure from *Allemaigne*, hee became so amourous of her, that he demaunded of the Queene if shee were her Daughter. Shee is not my Daughter, quoth the Queene, but the Daughter of my Brother, the Prince of *Sansuega*.

Right glad was the Duke thereof, and resolued to request her of the King in marriage, who knowing the honourable place he held among the Princes of *Greece*, and what account *Palmerin* made of him, consented thereto, so that within fewe dayes after they were espoused togither. Hereupon, to accompany the Princesse, and to confirm the peace, the King sent the Duke of *Gaule*, and another great Lorde with them into *Allemaigne*, the Queen likewise sent twelue English Ladies to attend on her Daughter.

 Thus returned the Duke of *Mecaena* to *Vienna*, where he was worthily welcommed by the Emperour, *Palmerin* and *Tryneus*, especially the yong Duchesse, and the Ambassadours of *England*, by whom the peace was faithfully ratified and confirmed.

CHAPTER LXII.
How Palmerin and Polinarda, departed from Vienna toward Constantinople, where after the decease of the aged Emperour Remicius, Palmerin was crowned Emperour of Greece, and what ioy was made at the byrth of Polinarda her first sonne.

After the Ambassadours of *England* were returned home, *Palmerin* perceiuing the Empire of *Allemaigne* was in quiet, tooke his leaue of the Emperor, minding to conduct his *Polinarda* to *Constantinople*, not without manie sorrowfull lamentations, of the mother to forgo her daughter, and faire *Agriola* her new acquainted sister, yet the Emperour pacified them well inough, by shewing what benefit this contract would be to Christendome, and so proceeded to his daughter in this maner.

Thou goest *Polinarda* to the seate of a great Empire, but more pleaseth mee the peerelesse name of *Palmerin d'Oliua* thy husbande, then the regiment of such a mightie Monarche. Farewell faire Daughter, continue in faithfull loue and obedience, remembring the reuerende honour a Wife oweth to her Husband. *Polinarda* hearing with what earnest affection her Father spake, was so ouercome with modest duetie of a Childe to her Father, as shee was not able to aunswere one word: which *Palmerin* beholding, kissed the Emperours hande, embraced *Tryneus*, and tooke a courteous farewell of all the Ladies, commaunding the Pages presently to bring away the Princesse Litter, saying to her. Madame, the longer you staie heere, the greater will be your conceit of sorrow, by absence the griefe will be forgotten: let vs then merely iourney to the Cittie of *Constantinople*, where they that neuer sawe you wil reioyce more at your comming, then all the *Allemaignes* can sorrow for your departure. With like comfortable speeches *Palmerin* frequented his Ladie by the way, till at length they entred the Realme of *Hungaria*, where *Frysoll* with his cheefest Lords attended their comming, to whom *Palmerin* in iesting, said.

Brother, I haue aduentured to bring your Sister *Polinarda* into your Kingdome, take heede if you laie claime to her now as sometime yee did, for I am readie to defende her against whosoeuer dare. I perceiue my Lorde, (quoth *Frysoll*) that you will haue my follie generally knowne, I pray you let no such youthfull pranckes be nowe remembred:[1] for as you are the cheefest in chiualrie, so haue the destenies giuen you a Ladie, whome no one in the whole world may paragon. Well may it be said, that God and Nature fore-pointed this match: nothing inferiour to louelie *Paris* and faire *Helena*, or puissaunt *Hector* and wise *Andromacha*.[2]

Frysoll accompanied them so farre as *Alba*,[3] where courteously parting from each other, *Frysoll* returned to his Kingdome, and *Palmerin* soone after came to *Constantinople*, where no litle ioy was made for his safe arriual, especially for the Princesse *Polinarda*, who was a right welcome Ladie into *Greece*,[4] the olde Emperour prouiding such deuises and tryumphes, as the Chronicles to this daye

Palmerin d'Oliva: Part II 577

recorde the memorie thereof. About tenne or twelue Monethes after, *Polynarda* was deliuered of a goodly Sonne, who was named *Primaleon*, whereat the good olde Emperour so inwardly reioyced, as his spirit onely comforted in the good fortune of his Sonnes, and fearing afterwarde to see anie sinister chaunce fall to them, departed this fraile and transitorie life, whose death was signified three dayes before, by the enchaunted Bird.⁵ His Funerall was performed as beseemed so great an estate, and faine woulde *Palmerin* haue had his Father the King *Florendos* crowned Emperour, earnestly labouring the Princes in the cause. But he desiring them to holde him excused, returned them this answere.

Great offence were it to God my Friendes, that the honour due to him, who gaue me libertie, defended my renowne, and saued my life, shoulde bee taken from him and giuen mee: for if vertue, authoritie, and good fortune, are the properties whereby to make choyse of an Emperour, *Palmerin* is verie many degrees before me. As for his generositie, it is so well knowne to you, that it were but lost labour to make report thereof. For his authoritie, the barbarous nations among whome hee hath liued and conqueringly controlled, deliuer sufficient testimonie. And for his high good fortune in all his enterprises, where is the man that may bee equalled with him? or what hath hee at anie time attempted, but he hath finished the same with wonderfull honour? I could name Kings and Princes that raign onely by his meanes. To speake of the victories he hath obtained, either in battell or single Combate, your eyes haue beheld, and the whole worlde apparantly witnesseth. This dare I boldly say, and some of you doo know it better then I, that his onely name will be more feared in *Greece*, then all your fore-passed Emperours haue bene by their greatest puissance.

So well did the people like what the King *Florendos* had sayd, as immediately was the Prince *Palmerin* proclaimed Emperour of *Constantinople*, and the same day he was crowned according to the accustomed rites and ceremonies. Not long afterward did the King *Florendos* stay with his Sonne, but returned with his Queene to *Macedon*, where hee gouerned in loue and iustice among his Subiects: daily sending Messengers to *Constantinople*, as well to vnderstand the health of the Emperour and Empresse,⁶ as also of yong *Prymaleon*, who daily increased in strength and beautie.

Chapter LXIII.

How the Prince Olorico and Alchidiana, thinking to trauaile to Constantinople to see the Emperour Palmerin and the Empresse Polinarda, strayed on the Sea. And what sorrowful mone she made, and how she was found by Palmerin.

In one of the Chapters before you haue heard, how *Olorico* promised the Princesse *Alchidiana*, that he would bring her to the Emperor *Palmerins* Court, which she imprinted so deepe in her fancie, as but for the common malladie incident to yong Ladies, which is to become great soone after they are espoused, she would haue betaken her selfe to trauaile, within three Monethes after her mariage. Notwithstanding, within short time after that trouble was past, she came to begge a boone of the Soldane, which he would not denie her, thinking shee would demaund no matter of weight. Father, (quoth shee) you must needs giue leaue to the Prince *Olorico*, that hee may accompanie me to *Constantinople*, for I desire to see the Emperour *Palmerin*.

Daughter, saide the Soldane, the trauaile on the Sea is verie perillous, and oftentimes great estates perish by shipwracke: but seeing you are so desirous, and I vnaduisedly haue past my promise, you shall not in ought be hindered by mee. Heereuppon was presently prepared tenne Shippes and Galleyes, the greater part whereof was laden with Horses, riche Tapistry, and other things of great value, which should be giuen to *Palmerin* and his *Polinarda*. In the rest were embarqued chosen Knightes for her defence, with Ladies and Gentlewomen to attende on her, and all needefull necessaries: thinking to shewe her sumptuous magnificence in the Emperours Courte, which in conclusion fell out otherwise. For Fortune who is euer variable and neuer permanent, at the instant when *Olorico* and *Alchidiana* builded most on her fauour, and were come within tenne dayes sayling of *Constantinople*: she altered their opinions in most doubtfull manner, as they expected nothing but the ende of their liues. The winde now ariseth contrary to them, a suddaine and terrible tempest ouertaketh them, and with such rough billowes their Shippes were beaten, as in their sight sixe of their Galleyes were drowned, the residue were verie farre scattered from them, and the great Carricke wherein themselues were, against a Rocke was split in the middest. Nowe are they left to the mercie of the waters, and *Alchidiana* wafting on a plancke for safegarde of her life: and had not one of the Pylots by swimming recouered a little Squiffe, wherewith he presently made to her and got her in, otherwise there had the Princesse vnhappily perished. This Pylot was so expert and cunning, as cutting through the vnmercifull waues, hee gained landing at a Porte distant from *Constantinople* about thirtie miles. The Inhabitants where they came on shoare, wondred to see her so gorgiously attired, and had not the Pylot friendly perswaded them, that shee was a Princesse trauailing to the Emperours Court, and by mishap had lost all her companie on the Sea, they would haue dealt with her verie hardly. But when they vnderstoode the cause of

Palmerin d'Oliva: Part II 579

her comming, they entertained her with fauour and ciuilitie, causing her to be lodged at a very welthy Merchaunts house, where she wanted nothing shee could desire. *Alchidiana* seeing that shee had escaped the daunger of the Sea, and was nowe in better assuraunce then before, comforted her selfe with this good fortune: but when shee remembred her losse, into what want and pouertie shee was now brought,⁴ and that through her foolish desire, her Husband was drowned, (as shee thought) shee was so ouercome with griefe, that neither her owne noble minde, nor the daily presence of the *Greekes* that came to see her, could disswade her from ceaselesse lamentations.

Ah wretch that I am, quoth she, how well haue I deserued this wreakefull aduenture? Ah ill aduised *Alchidiana*, what moued thee to crosse the Seas? if not an inordinate desire to see him, of whome thou maist expect no remedie for thy sorrow: or else to see her that is Mistresse of his heart, and so make thine owne conceites more languishing? My Lord and Husband *Olorico*, I am the vnhappie cause of thy death, thy loue hath euer beene to mee sounde and perfect: why could it not then make thee forgette the man, who always disdained my passions, and neuer loued mee but with dissimulation? If thou escape death as I haue done, iust cause hast thou to hate mee continually. Coulde not I remember, howe thy people spent their blood for me, onely to witnesse thy neuer daunted affection? and I haue requited thy loue with monstrous ingratitude. Why then did not our Gods make me alone to suffer the desert of my folly, but take reuenge on them that neuer offended? Ah noble Ladies, howe hard is your recompence in my seruice, that your tender and delicate bodies should be foode for the Fishes? And you worthie Knights and Gentlemen, in steed of purchasing honour and renowne with your Maister, you are lost for euer, to my no little greefe and vexation. The Merchaunt in whose house shee was lodged, hearing her heauie and lamentable complaintes, thus comforted her. Be of good cheare Madame, your Husband (by the grace of God) will well enough escape this daunger. As for your treasure, it is a matter soone gotten and soone lost: and to mourne for your Ladies and Gentlemen, it is to no purpose, because it can no way benefit them. When wee poore men loose our goods, wiues and Children, wee must with patience please our selues: you then hauing knowledge of vertue, and that we are all subiect to the transitorie chaunges of the worlde, to despaire is farre vnseemelye your estate.

My Lord the Emperour is bountifull and liberall, and the most vertuous Prince that euer raigned in *Greece*: hee will so well recompence your losse, as you shall not complaine of your comming. With these perswasions shee was somewhat pacified, and hauing stayed there nine or tenne daies to see if anie other of the Galleyes would arriue there, seeing none came, shee sold diuers of her precious Iewells that was about her, for halfe the value they were worthe, and prouided her selfe of sixe Horses, for her selfe, her Hostesse and her two Daughters, the Pilot that had saued her from drowning, and one of the Merchants Seruants, with which companie shee rode toward *Constantinople*, hauing chaunged her rich attire into mourning weedes. As they were in a great

Forrest sixe miles from the Cittie, the Princesse calling to remembraunce, howe poore and simple she should come before the Emperour, hauing beene one of the welthiest Ladies in the world: was so ouercome with this conceite, as hardly could her hostesse keepe her from swouning, wherefore seeing they were neere a goodlie Fountaine, there they alighted to rest her a little. And after shee hadde walked in the coole shaddowe of the Trees,[5] shee founde her selfe in better disposition, preparing to mount on horsebacke againe: but it came so to passe, that the Emperour *Palmerin* hauing beene hunting in that Forrest, and by earnest pursuit of the game lost all his companie, so that at length he came to the Fountaine where *Alchidiana* walked.[6] His arriuall greatly amazed the women, and before hee would demaund what they were, hee alighted and dranke of the Fountaine water. *Alchidiana* earnestly beholding him, and feeling inwardlie a strange alteration, presentlye swouned againe in her Hostesse Armes. Alas, said the Emperour, haue I so offended the Ladie, that the sight of mee should endaunger her life? tell me my Freende quoth hee to the Pilot, doost thou know of whence she is? No my Lord, aunswered the Pilot, but I vnderstand she is a noble Princesse, who comming to see the Emperour, hath lost her people and goods in the Sea. Me thinks I haue seene her heertofore, saide *Palmerin*, but I cannot remember the place where. Then beholding her more aduisedly, he said. Is not this the Princesse *Alchidiana*? that cannot bee: my Ambassadours tolde me that shee was married to the Prince *Olorico*.

    By this time was she a litle recouered, and seeing how he helde her in his armes, thus spake. Ah Syr *Palmerin*, why doo you hinder the departure[7] of miserable *Alchidiana*? thinke you shee can ende her life in better time and place, then in this Countrey, and betweene his armes whome she loued as her life, yet neuer receiued courtesie by him till this instant. Ah my Lorde, heere maist thou behold the foolish and indiscreete *Alchidiana*, who for thee hath lost her Husband *Olorico* that loued her deerelye: Knightes, Ladies and inestimable treasure hath shee likewise lost, all which she maketh no account off, but of her beloued whom she shall neuer recouer. But may it be Madame quoth the Emperour, that you are indeed the Princesse *Alchidiana*, Daughter to the Soldane of *Babilon*, the flower of all the Ladies in *Turkie*? The same am I, saide shee, who loued thee so vnmeasurably, as the loyaltie of mariage, feare of daungers of the Sea, nor thy too rigorous refusall, both in my presence and by thy Messengers, coulde not diswade me from this shame, onelie to see thy Court and the beautie of *Polynarda*. And that at length I might purchase my desire, I brought my Husbande with mee, who I feare the cruell waters haue swalowed, and as braue Ladies as euer were seene, with riches that well might decorate an Empire. By Heauen, Madame quoth *Palmerin*, if the Prince haue lost his life in this aduenture, neuer will my heart be merrie againe. Nowe see I the vnspeakable loue you beare me, which I haue in some part requited toward your *Olorico*: yet dismay not (sweete Ladie) nor feare his death before further tryall, for by mine honour I sweare, no sooner shall I come to *Constantinople*, but I will cause his search presently to be followed, not doubting but hee may be found againe.

And nowe faire Princesse, tell what vertue or desert you sawe in mee, that might value the least paine you haue endured? committing your gracious personne to so manie doubtfull hazards, of feares, affrightes, perturbations, heate and colde, which your choyse nature could hardly brooke in trauell: vnworthie were I the name of a man, if nowe I shoulde not pittie you. And I sweare to you by the liuing God, that if your mishap sort to an euill ende, neuer will I weare my Diademe longer. Alas Madame, if heeretofore I haue deluded you, consider it was a Louers deceit: that had bequeathed his heart to such a Ladie, as loues you as if you were her Sister. But haue you, quoth shee, among your amorous delights, acquainted her with my vnseemely boldnesse? what may she then conceiue of me, but as of a Girle giuen to loose and lauish appetite? The loue of wedlocke faire Princesse, said *Palmerin*, cannot make me disclose her preiudice that honoured me so much:[8] let it suffise you, that for the fauour I obtained when you found me in lyke place,[9] she remaineth to recompence you with all possible kindnesse. Let vs then depart hence toward *Constantinople*, that you may be vsed as beseemeth your high calling. Poore of spirit that I am, quoth the Princesse, had I entred into conceit of your former illusions, neuer had I fallen into so great daunger: but as for matters past, either of your rygour or disdaine, your present affabilitie compelles mee to forget, set on then when you please, and I wil beare ye companie.

The Pilot, the Marchants Wife and her Daughters, on their knees, desired the Emperour to excuse them, in that they had not reuerenced his Maiestie as they ought. Worldly honour I expect not, sayde the Emperour, come with mee, that I may recompence your paines taken for this worthie Princesse. So rode they on, and as they issued forth of the Forrest, there staied the Knights and Hunters, attending the Emperours comming, they all maruailing at the great courtesie hee vsed to the Ladie: then his Maiestie calling the Duke *Eustace* to him, sayd. Thou must presently with thy Companions goe Arme ye, and trauaile to finde the Prince *Olorico*, whom the tempestuous seas hath separated from his Ladie. Who brought these heauie tydings to your highnesse, sayd the Duke. This Ladie who is his Wife, quoth hee, hauing myraculouslie escaped shipwracke by the meanes of this Mariner. When they were come to the Pallace, the Duke of *Saxon* came to holde the Emperours Horse while he alighted. *Ptolome*, sayde *Palmerin*, know you no better your Mistresse *Alchidiana*? you must now remember her passed fauours, when shee redeemed you from base seruitude.[10] And that shall not I forget my Lorde, quoth the Duke, while I haue a day to liue: but I cannot thinke that this Ladie is shee. It is euen shee without further question, sayd the Emperour, doo you and the Duke of *Mecaena* helpe her from her Horse, and conduct her vp into the Pallace, while I in meane time goe to aduertise the Empresse.

Madame, quoth *Ptolome*, yet can I not be thorowlie resolued. In sooth *Ptolome*, said shee, I am *Alchidiana*, who to accomplish what thou and thy companions coulde not, am come hither in this pouertie: discouering my want of knowledge by an vnrecouerable losse, except you my Lords take the greater pittie on me. Thinke you Madame, quoth *Ptolome*, that my Lord *Olorico* is lost? neuer feare it I beseech ye, but thinke you shall finde as great fauour in this Court, as if you were with the Soldane your Father.

Palmerin comming to the Empresse, said. Madame, as I was hunting this day, I found in our Forrest the Princesse *Alchidiana*, of whom I haue so often tolde yee, shee beeing wife to the Prince *Olorico*, that named himselfe my Dwarffes Brother when I was with you last at *Gaunt*,[11] I desire ye to intreate her as her calling deserueth, because I am not a little beholding to her. So taking her by the hand, they came and met the Princesse, and *Palmerin* taking her courteouslie in his armes,[12] deliuered her to the Empresse, saying.

Faire Princesse, you shall remaine with my Ladie, till our knights haue found your Lord and Husband. God will requite your kindnesse to a distressed Ladie, said *Alchidiana*, although I feare for my offences his fortune will be much the woorse. Madame, quoth the Empresse, so noble and debonaire is your Lord and Husband, as no danger can any way preiudice his life, but thinke him as safe as if he were heere present with you, which doubtlesse will be right soone, and in good time: therefore let mee intreate you to bee of good cheere, as if you were now in *Assyria*. And although we cannot compare with the Court of *Babylon*, yet heere shall you be vsed as beseemes so great a Princesse.

I doubt not thereof good Madame, said *Alchidiana*, the more am I indebted to the Emperour and you: yet can I not forget the absence of my Lord, beeing separated from him in a place so vncouth. He that is the defender of the iust, quoth the Empresse, will send ye to meete againe in place more comfortable, and in that hope I pray ye to perswade your selfe, laying aside these mourning garments, the very sight therof cannot but offend yee. These gracious speeches somewhat contented her, and expelled all priuate conceit of sorrow: yet would she not chaunge her habite, till she heard either good or bad newes of the Prince *Olorico*.[13]

Chapter LXIV.

Howe the Prince Olorico was reskewed from the Moores, by the yong Knights that the Emperour Palmerin sent in his search: and what ioy was made at Constantinople at his arriuall.

Vpon the Emperours resolution for the search of *Olorico*, the Dukes of *Mecaena* and *Saxon*, with each of them fiftie Knights, were prepared to sea with two Gallies: and *Colmelio, Bellechino, Sergillo* Sonne to *Cardino*, and the Marchant *Estebons* two Sonnes, whom the Emperor had newly knighted, with thirtie hardie Souldiours departed in an other. Eight other vessels were sent on the Coast of *Propontida*,[1] and the *Bosphor*, to seeke the Prince.

It so came to passe, that the same day *Alchidiana* was preserued from drowning, *Alibarbanco*, a Pirat, was sayling towardes *Natolia*, and passed verie neere where the Princes Carricke was split, and him did hee espie floting on a Chest, which was filled within with Martin skinnes, being then with pittie mooued to behold him in such daunger, hee caused his men to take him into the Shippe, who readie to yeelde vp his ghost hee was so benummed with colde. When *Alibarbanco* sawe him so richly apparelled, and the Chest stuffed with things of such value, hee imagined him presently to bee some great Lorde, for whom he shoulde haue some large raunsome, wherefore he vsed him verie courteouslie. *Olorico* seeing he was so happily escaped, lifting his eyes to Heauen, sayd. Great is thy mercie O God, that hast so fauourablie vouchsafed to regard thy poore creature, nor were losse woorthie reckoning, so my Ladie *Alchidiana* were safe in *Assyria*. What angrie planet raigned when we betooke our selues to Sea? what answere shall I make to the Soldane your Father, that gaue me such charge of your person at my departure? hardly may I dare to come before him any more.

Alibarbanco hearing these complaints, reioiced thereat. By Mahomet, quoth hee to himselfe, nor shalt thou see him anie more if I can hinder it, for I will present thee to the great Turke his mortall enemie, and for thy raunsome I shall receiue a bountifull recompence. So thinking to strike toward *Natolia*, he happened among the Emperours yong Knights ere hee was aware: wherefore hee thought to take their ships likewise, yet therein hee found him selfe greatly deceyued. For *Bellechino* knowing them to bee Turkes by their Banners, said to his companions. We are now I feare in the daunger of Turkish Pirats, let vs therfore with courage winne our deliueraunce. Heereuppon they fiercely assayled *Alibarbanco*, and buckled so closelie that in the ende they boorded him, making such a slaughter among his men, and throwing him likewise slaine into the Sea, as none were left to resist their further entraunce, where they found the Prince *Olorico*, and beeing not a little glad of their good successe, they each one embraced him with gracious courtesie. Alas my Freends, quoth the Prince, how knew you my beeing heere? who gaue you in charge to seeke me forth? who hath beene the Messenger of my misfortune? My Lord the Emperour *Palmerin*, aunswered

Colmelio, vnderstoode thereof by your Ladie *Alchidiana*, whom hee founde by good happe as hee rode on hunting.

But may I giue credite to your woordes? said the Prince, is my Ladie with his Maiestie at the Court? Shee is in trueth my Lorde, sayde *Bellechino*, and the Mariner likewise that saued her life, whome the Emperour hath highlie recompenced for his faithfull seruice. I beseech you quoth *Olorico*, let vs hoise saile presentlie towarde *Constantinople*, for my heart cannot bee perswaded till I haue seene her, so great is my doubt, considering our vnfortunate separation.

Neuer may I beare Armes in Knight-hoode, said *Bellechino*, or lift my Sworde in honourable Chiualrie, if *Alchidiana* be not at *Constantinople*, where I both sawe her, and spake to her, before our departure. So taking the vessell that belonged to the Pirate *Alibarbanco* with them, in short time after they arryued at *Constantinople*, where their cheerefull sounding of Drums, Trumpets, and Clarions at their landing, deliuered testimonie of their good successe. If the Emperour was glad for the recouerie of his Freend, the Princesse *Alchidiana* of her Husband, and euerie one generallie for the man lost by such mishappe, I leaue to your iudgements, that can censure the rare ioyes of loue and freendship. What Triumphes, Tournamentes, Bonfires, Maskes, Momeries, and other delightfull exercises were performed, for ioy of the Prince *Oloricos* safetie, whome the Emperour made account of, as you haue heard before, it would demaunde a larger volume to set downe: you must therefore heere imagine, that you behold his Maiestie highly contented, *Alchidiana* thorowlie satisfied, and the whole Court well pleased by this happie euent, giuing themselues to expresse the same in open and manifest signes, beseeming so great estates to prosecute, and therefore of as great honour as may be deuised.[2]

The yong Knights are especially welcommed for their woorthie seruice, the Dukes of *Saxon* and *Mecaena* likewise, though they failed of bringing the Prince, yet they brought two Foystes belonging to the Pirate *Alibarbanco*, richlie laden with manie wealthie spoyles, which were giuen among the yong Knights, in recompence of their paines. During the time of these surpassing pleasures and delights, there entred the hauen of *Constantinople* three shippes, laden with maruailous sumptuous gifts and presents, from the Queene *Zephira*, and her Brother the King *Maulerino*, beeing sent to the Emperour *Palmerin*, and his Empresse *Polynarda*, by two great Lords Ambassadours from *Persia*, to request familiar loue and alliaunce with the Emperour, the Soldane confessing his iniurie to *Trineus*, while he was in his Court.[3] When the *Persians* came before the Emperour, who was honourably accompanied with Kings, Dukes, Princes, Counties, and many braue Ladies, they were greatly abashed, yet thinking on the argument of their Ambassade, one of them began in this manner.

It is no maruell (redoubted Emperour and Monarch of *Greece*) if thy subiects both loue thee, and visite thee, when thy behauiour hath conquered the mindes of forraine Potentates, who to enter amitie and peace with thee, some haue left their Countreys to sende their Ambassadours hither, other dare not stirre, or assemble their men in warlike manner, so is the name of *Palmerin* feared thorowe all *Asia*. Hereof beare witnesse the great Turke, the Califfe of *Siconia*, and the heyres to the Prince *Amarano* of *Nigrea*: not much inferiour in this condition, is the Soldane of *Babylon*, whose daughter with her Husband I heere beholde. The victorious *Abimar*, King of *Romata* and *Grisca*, the worthie *Maulerino*, and the puissaunt Soldane of *Persia* my Maister, Husbande to the vertuous Queene *Zephira*, who with their Brother haue sent your highnesse three Shippes, laden with the most wealthie riches their Countreyes can yeeld. My Lord and they humbly kisse your Maiesties hande, desiring you to forget his discourtesie to the gentle Knight *Tryneus*, when hee became enamoured on the Princesse *Aurecinda*.[4] But if their loue then sorted to a philosophicall trope or figure,[5] it hath sithence prooued effectuall in procreation, to the no little ioy of my Lorde and Maister.

The Princesse was deliuered of a goodly Son, growing in such exquisite forme and feature, as it is expected hee will one day resemble his Father in chiualrie, as he dooth alreadie his Mother in amiable perfection.

Ambassadour, quoth the Emperour, for the great vertue and nobilitie I haue founde, as well in the Princesse *Zephira*, as also her noble Brother, I graunt the freendly alliance thou demaundest. Yet heereof am I sorie, that the Son to the Prince *Tryneus*,[6] should be nourished and spend his youth among Mahumetists, without knowledge of his God and Redeemer: for in such sort should hee be instructed, after he is come to the yeeres of vnderstanding, that all the Alchoran is tales and fables, and doubtlesse God will so deale with him in time, as hee shall imitate the steppes of his noble Father. As for the presents sent vs by the King *Maulerino*, the Soldane, and his Queen *Zephira*, we accept them as from our Freends, and will returne them some remembraunce of our thankfulnesse. His Maiestie commaunded the *Persians* to bee lodged in his Pallace, and continued still their former ioyes and tryumphs: but to alter those Courtly pastimes and delights, this misfortune happened which heereafter followeth.

CHAPTER LXV.
Howe the great Turke refused to assist Lycado, Nephewe to the Admiral Olimaell, against the Emperor Palmerin: and what trouble happened to Constantinople by the Traitor Nardides, Nephew to the King Tarisius, Lycado, Menadeno, and their father.

Such was the humanitie and pittie of *Palmerin*, when hee finished the enchantments at the Isle of *Malfada*, as he gaue libertie to all the Turks and Christians, which were before transformed, as you haue heard:[1] among whom was *Lycado*, Nephew to the Admirall *Olimaell*, hee that at the taking of *Agriola*, had the Prince *Tryneus* for his prisoner.[2] This *Lycado*, seeing himselfe in his owne Countrey, and out of daunger, where he heard howe the great Turke was slaine, and his Vncle likewise, hee came before the Sultane that then raigned, saying. Worthy lord, as men are naturallie inclined to bemone their losses, so are Subiects bound to aduertise their Soueraignes, of any shame or iniurie done to their Maiesties. This speake I my Lord, because you haue not as yet reuenged the death of your deceassed Brother, now sleeping in the Armes of Mahomet, albeeit trayterouslie slaine by *Palmerin* and his Companions: at which time my noble Vncle was likewise murthered, with many Knights of cheefe and especiall account.[3] And least you should be ignoraunt in the truth of the deede, and who also carryed hence the Princesse *Agriola*, I haue credibly vnderstood, that *Palmerin* is Nephew to the Emperour of *Greece*, one of his companions is the Emperours Sonne of *Allemaigne*, and all the rest were Princes and Lords of *Greece*, onely sent as spyes into *Turkie*. Wherefore, seeing you now holde the state in such peace and quietnes, it were necessarie you should leauie a mightie Armie: and please you to commit the charge thereof to mee, I will loose my life, or make an absolute destruction of all *Greece*. I remember, said the great Turke, that your Vnckle made like entraunce into my deceased Brothers Courte, as you by your speeches now labour to doo, but I will so warilie looke to such intrusions, as no Traytors shall rest heere if I can hinder them. Your Vnckle vexed the Christians, what followed thereon? the death of his maister, and a daungerous confusion. By you likewise may ensue as bad fortune, departe you therefore from our Court, and but that we are loth to bee noted with tyrannie, thou shouldest presently be drawne in peeces with Horses. False Traytour, thou that commest to counsaile vs in a matter wherein we cannot meddle but with great dishonour, it behooues thee first to regard the end of thy intent, and what he is that gouerns in *Greece*. Go villaine go, and on perill of thy life neuer presume before our presence againe.

Lycado was greatly astonied at this sharpe answere, and seeing he could haue no better successe, hee went to his Father the Brother to *Olimaell*, beeing one of the cheefest Magitians in all *Turkie*, to him he made his complaints, saying, he would die in that resolution, but he would cause the Turke to knowe that hee was no Traytour, and this (quoth he) shall be the meane whereby I will compasse it. I meane to disguise my selfe, and trauaille to the Cittie of *Constantinople*, where priuily I wil murder the Emperor *Palmerin*, so shall my Lorde the great Turke touch mee with no further suspition, but will reward me with greater benefits then euer my Vnckle had. My Sonne, answered his Father, thinkest thou that thy deuise will sort to effect? thy Brother *Menadeno* would helpe thee heerein, but hee is too yong: yet when time serueth for thy departure, I will not onely tell thee, but conduct thee my selfe. I beseech you good father, saide *Lycado*, further me in what you may, for neuer will my hart be at rest, till I haue paid *Palmerin* with the selfe same coyne the great Turke was. In meane while do you studie, and search all your Bookes of Astrologie, Diuination, Magique, and Nigromancie, as *Zabulus, Orpheus, Hermes, Zoroastres, Circes, Medea, Alphonsus, Bacon, Apolonius*, and all the rest that write of the blacke speculatiue:[4] reade them againe and againe, deuise such spelles, exorcismes, and coniurations, as the very spirits may speake of the feast I will make at the Cittie of *Constantinople*.

Heereupon the olde man made his Sonne *Menadeno* Knight, and with *Lycado* betooke themselues to Sea, saying. My Sonnes I will bring ye to *Constantinople*, where (by vertue of mine arte) we will arriue before three dayes be expired: remember your vnckles death, and behaue your selues in such sort, as you may be Registred for euer.[5] The time doth nowe fauour you with sufficient reuenge, and therein shall you be assisted by a Christian Knight, whome we shall finde readie landed there for the same cause.[6]

Their Ankers being weyed, they launch into the deepe, and cut through the waues with such violence, as if the deuill himselfe were in their sailes, so that they tooke landing at the selfe same houre as *Nardides* arriued at *Constantinople*. As concerning what this *Nardides* was, you remember the two Traytors *Promptaleon* and *Oudin*, Nephewes to the King *Tarisius* of *Hungaria*, whome *Palmerin* and *Frysoll* slew at *Constantinople*,[7] hee was their Brother, and Sonne to the Duchesse of *Ormeda*. Shee vnderstanding the death of her two Sonnes, could not conceale it from the Duke her Husband, who presently died with very conceit of greefe: whereuppon, shee to reuenge this mishappe caused by her report, as also the death of her two Sonnes, made promise to *Nardides*, (then beeing eighteene yeeres olde) that so soone as hee was knighted, hee should go to *Constantinople*, and there (if it were possible) to murder the Emperour and *Frysoll*. All this he vowed to performe, and two or three yeeres after, hauing married the Kings Daughter of *Polonia*, hee embarqued himselfe with forty Knights, determining by a Combat or treason, to compasse his intent.

These wreakfull aymers at reuenge, landed all in one instant at *Constantinople*, when the old Magitian calling to *Nardydes*, sayde hee would gladly speake with him in secret, as concerning matters greatly for his auaile. Hereupon they went all closely together into one of the Cabins, and the olde man entred into these speeches. Sir *Nardides*, needelesse is it for you to hide your affaires from mee, for I knowe that you departed from *Polonia* with fortie Knights disguised like Merchants, onely with this determination, to destroy the Emperour, in reuenge of certaine iniuryes done to your Brethren. But if you will giue credit to mee, and go to worke in such sort as I shall aduise yee, yee shall happily obtayne the end of your desire. By God, sayd *Nardides*, you tell mee wonders, there is not one in the shippe that knowes mine intent, yet you haue sayde the truth, whereat I cannot maruaile sufficiently. Seeing then you know so much, it were but follie to dissemble, say then your minde and I will heare yee. This night, sayd the old man, the Emperour wil suppe in the great Hall with the Prince *Olorico*, and the Princesse *Alchidiana*, the King of *Sparta* and his Queene, with many other great Princes and Lordes, so that such store of people are in the Pallace, as little regarde will bee had of strangers or housholde seruants.

You then with my Sonne *Menadeno*, beeing Armed, as beseemes a cause so weightie, shall sodainely enter and kill the Emperour: my Sonne *Lycado* and I will stay your returne heere, and I that can commaunde the winde and weather,[8] will carrie ye hence without danger of following. And true it is, that there is a Bird pearched in the Hall, which the wise *Muzabelino* hath so enchaunted, as neither good or ill tydings can come to the Emperour, but she bewrayes the same by her song or fearefull crie:[9] yet doubt not you thereof, strike boldly, there will be none Armed, so shal you departe againe at your owne pleasure. My Friend, said *Nardides*, happie be the houre I mette with thee, assure thy selfe, that if I can kill the Emperour, and thou afterwarde deliuer me safely, such recompence will I bestow on thee, as both thou and thine shall for euer remember me.

Other recompence I demaund not, sayde the olde man, then the death of the Emperour, prepare thy selfe therefore to follow thine intent. The night beeing come, these Traytors Armed themselues, and casting their mantles about them, entred the Pallace, were among the Pages and seruants, without suspition they came into the Hall: leauing *Lycado* and his Father at the Port,[10] where hee threwe abroade such enchauntments, that all such as came foorth of their houses, presently fell downe a sleepe in the streetes. No sooner were the Traytours entred the Hall, but the Bird gaue a horrible and fearefull crie, beating her beake against her breast with such furie, as though shee would haue rent foorth her heart. My God, sayd the Emperour, in mercie behold mee, for the cry of this Birde dooth foretell great misfortune. Looke about my friendes, quoth he to his Guard, and see if any Stranger or vnknowne body is entred our presence. *Nardides* by these speeches knew hee was the Emperour, wherefore drawing his Sword, hee thought to haue cleaued his head, yet hee fayled of his intent, for the Emperour seeing the blow comming, with a great Golden Cuppe awarded it[11] indifferently, notwithstanding, the Sword in slipping from the Cuppe, gaue him a sore wound vpon the head. *Olorico* sitting on the other side of the Table, ranne at the Traitour, but the Emperour had receiued two strokes more ere he could come at him, so that his maiestie fell from his Chaire as he had beene dead.

As the Prince *Olorico* held the Traytor *Nardides* by the armes, *Menadeno* strooke at him so rigorously, as if *Ptolome* had not borne off the blowes with a great siluer plate,[12] *Olorico* there had lost his life. Duke *Eustace* seeing this shamefull outrage, wrong the Sword out of *Nardides* hande, and gaue him such a sounde

stroke therewith on the head, as made him tomble his heeles vpwarde, and by the helpe of *Bellechino*, who founde the meanes to gette off his Helmet, hee smote his head from his shoulders. *Bellechino* who had beene newly baptised, loued the Emperour as hee had beene his Father, and comming to *Menadeno*, whome Duke
5 *Ptolome* strongly helde in his armes, gaue him so many stabs on his throate, that he likewise fell downe at his feete. The Empresse seeing her Lord so wounded, rent her garments, tore her comely locks of hayre, and smote her faire face with maruailous violence. Ah my Lord, quoth shee, thou art not wounded alone, for if thou die, as God forbid, right soone will my ghost follow thee. Cease Madam
10 your complaints, saide the Emperour, and comfort your selfe so wel as you may, for this is the houre wherin I must leaue you: I haue lost such aboundance of my bloud, as longer may I not liue with you: O my God forgiue my sins, and receiue my soule. In vttering these words he swouned againe, and the Empresse with him for companie, to the no little amazement of all the Lords and Ladies,
15 who were well neere at their wits ende to beholde this vnexpected alteration. *Alchidiana* like wise was in wonderfull perplexitie, fearing also that her Lord was wounded to the death, but to comfort this sorrowfull and desolate Court, good fortune sent this helpe ensuing.

Chapter LXVI.

How the wise Muzabelino knowing by his arte, the cruell treason doone to the Emperour, came to succour him, and of that which followed.

Muzabelino the Nigramancer, of whom we haue alreadie spoken, by chaunce this day was turning ouer his Books, and found the dangerous stratageme deuised by these Traitours, and calling his familiars together,[1] demaunded the danger that would ensue by this treason: whereto one of them replied, that if hee went not speedily to *Constantinople*, the Emperour, the Prince *Olorico*, and their Ladies, would hardly escape that day with life. Then armed he himselfe, in the selfe same maner as he was when he succoured the Prince *Tryneus*,[2] and calling two spirits of the ayre resembling Giants, their faces so vglie and fearefull, as no humane creature durst beholde them: them hee commanded to carrie him to *Constantinople*, and with a great flaming fire-brand in his hand, he cut through the ayre with such horrible thunder, as each one thought the world had beene ended.[3] When he beheld the olde man that defended the Port, hee sayd to him. False and disloyall Traitour, darest thou meddle with the man whome thou knowest to bee in my guarde?[4] take him to yee, (quoth hee to his two spirits) and conuay him to your Courte, and there keepe him aliue for mee, for I will giue him a paine a thousande times worse then death: you know how to vse my gentle guest, let him be dealt withall as his behauiour hath deserued. The miserable olde man astonied heereat, and thinking to helpe himselfe by his Magique, was presently transformed into a Serpent. Now thou shalt perceiue, saide *Muzabelino*, that I am greater in power then thou art. So taking two great Golden Chaines, he tied the Serpent about the neck therewith, and his Sonne together, setting such a coniuration on them, as he should neuer be chaunged to his former shape.

Then came hee to the Pallace, where taking off his Helmet, hee entred the Hall, saying to the Knights. Ah my deere friendes, the Traytour that thus hath molested you, is taken, reioyce therefore, and be of good cheere, your Lord is not dead, he liueth, he must liue, and in despight of enuie shal florish more then euer he did. The princes and knights hearing him speake so friendly, and yet knew not what hee was, notwithstanding his promises they were greatly amazed, but when they sawe *Bellechino* and *Colmelio* so reuerently embrace him, they began to conceiue better opinion of him. Alas my Lord and Father, said *Bellechino*, in a happie houre came you hether, and your presence puts vs out of al further feare, vouchsafe to succour the Empresse *Polynarda*, for pittie it is to see her thus chaunged. Heereupon *Muzabelino* embraced the Empresse, whose face was colde, pale, and wan. Why Madame? quoth he, where is your former wisedome and discretion? leaue these desolate countenances to common people, your Lorde is in no danger, but within three dayes hee shall be well againe. Conuey her hence, saide he to the Ladies, I am ashamed to see your follie, suffering her to lye in this sort and no one helpe her. Then was shee conducted to her Chamber, and *Muzabelino* with the ayde of his Sonne and Duke *Eustace*, carried the Emperour to his bed,

Palmerin d'Oliva: Part II 591

where staunching his woundes with a precious Oyntment, *Muzabelino* gaue him some of the water to drink, which before had healed the Princesse *Zephira*,[5] and which hee had brought with him in a little viall of Christall, when the Emperor beeing somewhat better recouered, lifting his eies to Heauen, said. How great
5 art thou in mercy my soueraign Redeemer, sending *Muzabelino* from the furthest regions, to helpe me in so great necessitie? Ah my noble friende, what haue I doone at any time for thee, that might induce thee to fauour me so much? My Lord, answered *Muzabelino*, so precious are your deserts in mine eies, as I can do no lesse, except I should be accounted the most ingratefull among men. So bath-
10 ing his woundes with the iuyce of certaine vertuous hearbs, he willed al that were present to depart the Chamber, and on the morrow they should see their Lord in better estate. So left they the Emperor to his rest, and al the princes, Knights, and Ladies, came to welcome *Muzabelino*, who comforted the Princesse *Alchidiana*, assuring her that the Prince *Olorico* should do wel enough, for he had like-
15 wise bathed his woundes, and left him in his chamber quietly sleeping. On the morrow hee commaunded the bodies of *Nardides* and *Menadeno* to be burned,[6] afterwarde he loosed *Lycado* from his father, causing him to be put in prison till the Emperour were amended, and taking the Serpent by the chaine, he brought him by the helpe of his two spirits into the great court, where by his cunning he
20 erected a goodly Marble piller, and on the top thereof a strong Cage of yron, saying to the olde man transformed. Accursed creature, to the ende thy paine may bee the greater during the Emperors life, thou shalt remain in this monstrous shape, and die thou shalt not, till the God of heauen call him hence whose death thou diddest contriue. Incontinent the spirits thrust the Serpent into the Cage,
25 and afterward vanished away, leauing the monster casting fearefull flames of fire out at his mouth, and howling with strange and pittifull cries. Then went *Muzabelino* to the Empresse, who still remained sad and pensiue, and bringing her to the Emperour, said. See Madame, am I not so good as my word, your Lord is well and perfectly recouered, be you then pleasant and mourne no longer. Not a
30 little ioyfull was she at this sight, embracing his highnesse with such affection, as though she had been absent from him a long time: but when the Emperor saw her face so martered with lamenting, and her sweete countenance so much altred, Alas Madam, quoth he, why doo you offend that seate of heauenly beautie, which God ordeined to excell all Ladies liuing? albeit I had dyed, yet should
35 not you haue vsed such tirannie on your selfe. If such a wreakfull chaunce had happened, answered the Empresse, soone had my ghost followed my Lord. For my heart hath no comfort but onelie in you, and that once lost, farewell life and all. Then must you both, said *Muzabelino*, consider the mightie worke of God, especially you my Lord, who as you are loued of manie, so are you hated likewise
40 of a number: you must therefore heereafter stand vpon your guard, hauing before your eyes, that the more renowne encreaseth, the more doth spightfull enuie seeke to deface it. *Alexander* the great, and *Iulius Caesar*, are examples thereof.[7] You Madame must wash your face with the water in this viall, which will restore

your former beautie, as sometime it did to the Princesse *Zephira*.[8] Within fewe daies after, the Emperour shewed himselfe to his subiects, who were meruailous ioyfull to see him so well recouered, the Prince *Olorico* likewise was perfectlie cured, and all things so well as if this had not happened. Then was *Lycado* deliuered to the people, who in recompence of his treason, haled him into the Market place, and there binding him in an yron chayne, made a small fire vnder him, and so by little and little broiled him to death.

Chapter LXVII.

How the Soldane of Babylon sent for the Prince Olorico, and his Daughter Alchidiana, and of the sorrow the Emperour and Empresse made for their departure.

The report of this mishap at *Constantinople* was so spread abroad, as the king *Florendos* of *Macedon*, and the Queene *Griana* hearing thereof, presently poasted to *Constantinople*, where by the good means of *Muzabelino*, they found their Sonne in verie sounde estate of health, for which they highly thanked the wise Magitian, giuing him many rich and honourable rewards. And *Muzabelino* seeing all matters quietted, that the *Persian* Ambassadours were likewise readie to returne to the Soldan, not a little contented with the league of peace, hee tooke his leaue of the Emperour, and sailed home with them to the king *Abimar* of *Grisca*, whom he certified of all things that happened, and how fortunately the daunger was preuented. *Frysoll* the king of *Hungaria*, came with his Queene *Armida* to *Constantinople*, a Messenger likewise came from the Emperour of *Allemaigne* and *Tryneus*, to vnderstand the health of the Emperour, such was the brute of this suddaine mischance. While all these Princes remained there at the Court, the Princesse *Alchidiana* was deliuered of a faire Daughter, who at the Emperor *Palmerins* request was baptized, and named *Philocrista*,[1] and not many dayes after the Empresse had a Daughter likewise, named *Belliza*, and the Queene of *Hungaria* had another, called *Melicia*: no little ioy beeing made at the byrth of these children.[2] But now the Soldane of *Babylon* seeing his sonne and daughter returned not all this while, sent the young King of *Balisarca* to enquire of them, and no sooner was he entred the Hauen of *Constantinople*, but newes of his arriuall was brought to *Alchidiana* and *Olorico*, who to honour the King, went and met him at the Porte. The King being landed, seeing himselfe vnarmed, and remembring the death of his Father before that Citie,[3] with the teares in his eies, said: Wretched that I am, must I venture thus nakedly on the shore, where my father, brother, and deerest friends were slaine? Ah *Constantinople*, the enemy to our Law and Religion, doost thou flourish by the blood of the greatest Lords in *Turkie*? a day will come to abate thy pride and insolency.[4] I hope King of *Balisarca*, said *Oloricc*, if thy father and brother were slaine, it was like worthie Princes in their Masters seruice, whose death if thou remember, and (withall) the valour of them that slew them: thou must think how Fortune fauours the *Grecian* successors in the Empire. Beside, thou commest now in peace, but ill beseemes it thee then to remember passed troubles: say thy message to the Emperor that thou commest for, and think not on such friuolous matters. By this time they were come into his Maiesties presence, when the King began in this maner. Mighty and renowned Emperor, the Soldan of *Babilon* my Master, perceiuing that age hasteneth on his death, sendeth to intreat your highnes, that his son and daughter may returne home to him, that while he liues he may inuest them in the Kingdome, to behold some part of their worthy gouernment. I think their absence, said the Emperor, is as irksome to him, as it is pleasing and contented to me, nor wil I with-hold them contrary to his liking: desiring you good Princes to hold me excused, if I haue not vsed you as your vertues worthily merit. *Alchidiana* hauing heard her fathers request, brake foorth into teares, and though nature made her desire to see the place of her birth, and to behold her parents and kindred: yet piercing affection which conquereth all things, drew backe her mind in such sort, as shee could more willingly haue staied in the Emperors Court. But beholding the mutuall loue betweene *Palmerin* and *Polynarda*, she resolued to vse the like to her Husband, and forget the folly that too much conquered her appetite.[5] When the day was come of their departure, maruellous was the sorrow at this friendly parting: yet seeing there was no remedie, she kissed her daughter *Philocrista*, and courteously bidding the Emperor and Empresse farewell, with her Lord *Olorico*, who was as loth to leaue his noble friend, went aboord, and hoising saile attained safe arriuall at the Soldanes Court. Great ioy was made for their returne, the Pilot that saued the Princesse life,[6] the Soldane made chiefe Captaine of his Guard: and he dying, *Olorico* was created Soldane, whereof soone after he aduertised the Emperor, sending to him and the Empresse many precious iewels, not forgetting somwhat to his daugther *Philocrista*. When *Olorico* and *Alchidiana* sailed from *Constantinople*, the King of *Sparta* and his Queene *Arismena*, the Duke *Eustace* and the Duchesse *Sabinda*, with diuers other Princes returned to their countries. The like would the King *Florendos, Griana, Ptolome* and *Bryonella* haue done: but that the Emperour intreated their longer stay. *Griana* gaue her Dwarfe *Amenada* sister to *Vrbanillo*, to the young Princesse *Belliza*, and the Emperor gaue his Dwarfe such welthy possessions, as he maried with a rich Gentlewoman of the city, by whom he had a sonne of the stature of the *Pygmees*, named *Risdeno*, who afterward was giuen to wait on the yong Prince *Primaleon*. Now the Emperor calling to mind, his former paine and trauell in search of aduentures, so loued and honored Knights errant: as from each place in the world they came to his Court, as wel to behold his magnificence, as the three yong Princesses, *Philocrista, Beliza,* and *Melicia* whose beauties were renowned farre and neere. Great Iousts and Triumphes were daily made in honor of them, wherein *Belcar*, sonne to King *Frysoll*, and *Tirendos* son to Duke *Eustace* of *Mecena*, hauing receiued the order of Knighthood, shewed themselues both forward and valiant. Dailie came such store of Knights to *Constantinople* from *Allemaine, Italie, France* and *Spaine*, as they exceeded the number of them in King *Arthurs* time, when he made the great Tourney before the Castell of Ladies.[7] And one euening as the Emperour was deuising with the Princes, to censure of them that had best deserued: suddainly entred the Hall a Lady richly attired, who without saluting or speaking a word to any body, a good while stood viewing the Emperor and his Knights. At length, making as though she would returne againe, she thus spake. Noble Emperor *Palmerin*, I haue more delighted to behold thy Chiualrie, then any of the Princes on the earth: but a time shal come, that the renowne of them and thee, shall be vtterly abolished by Strangers, chiefly by one, whose vertue and bountie shall be such, as thy selfe shalt account him the best that euer bare Armes.[8] So departing, she mounted on her Palfray, and rode away in exceeding great haste. The Emperour maruelling at these words, said. Ill aduised was I, in not demanding of the Lady the Knights name, which shal surpasse all other in prowesse, gladly would I know his name, of whom she made such a glorious report. These speeches so enflamed the minds of the Knights present, as many of them secretly Armed themselues, and rode after the Lady, among whom was *Cardyno* and *Colmelio*, whom we will leaue in their iourney till they find her: and heere conclude our History, til time bring on the following booke of *Primaleon* and *Palmendos*,[9] desiring your fauourable acceptations for these two parts, the better affection I shal haue to proceede in the other.

FINIS.

M y promise performed,[1] and *Palmerins* famous Historie finished: for my long labour, Gentlemen, I request but your friendly speeches, an easie matter to be giuen by you, yet nothing can bee more welcome to me. If I may speed in so small a request, *Palmendos* will leaue his Mother the Queen of *Tharsus*, and *Primaleon* hasten his order of Knight-hood, that you may bee acquainted with their rare aduentures.[2] In meane while, the famous *Palladine* of *England* is arriued, and to feede you with varietie of delights, his History by Easter tearme next will be with ye:[3] till when, vse such fauour to *Palmerin*, as Prince *Palladine* be not hindered.

Antonie Monday.

Honos alit Artes.

FINIS.

Notes to the Text
Part I

Title Page

1 **The Mirrour of nobilitie, Mappe of honor, Anatomie of rare** *fortunes* This subtitle departs significantly from the ones in the Spanish, French, and Italian versions, which refer primarily to Palmerin's lineage, praising him for his valor and nobility. In contrast, Munday chooses to eulogize the protagonist's moral virtues and, by extension, highlight the edifying value of the romance, a choice that may have been motivated by the humanist attacks against the genre; see "Introduction," 67–69. By failing to mention the chivalric nature of the work and the love episodes it contains, Munday is actually misrepresenting the contents of the book. To do so Munday piles up the terms "mirrour," "mapppe," and "anatomie," whose semantic difference is not apparent and can in fact work as synonyms. Richard Sugg, "The Anatomical Web: Literary Dissection from Castiglione to Cromwell," in *Rhetoric and Medicine in Early Modern Europe*, ed. Stephen Pender and Nancy S. Struever (Burlington, VT: Ahsgate, 2012), 83–109, discusses the subtle differences implicit in these terms and describes Munday's lexical choice for the subtitle as opportunistic, combining "more traditional catchwords and the highly modish 'anatomy'" (92–93). Indeed, "'Anatomies' were something of a vogue in the latter part of the sixteenth century. The name implied an attempt to get to the bottom of things and reveal everything fully and methodically," as J. B. Bamborough remarks in the introduction to The Clarendon Edition of Robert Burton's *The Anatomy of Melancholy* (Oxford: Clarendon Press, 1989–2000), 1:xxv. Note that Munday used the word *mirror* previously in the title of his *Mirrour of Mutabilitie* (1579). For the fashion of including the word *mirror* in titles, see Herbert Graves, *The Mutable Glass: Mirror-imagery in Titles and Texts of the Middle Ages and English Renaissance* (Cambridge: Cambridge University Press, 1982), esp. 4–5. The subtitle, therefore, is best understood as a pose or as part of a commercial strategy, even though it conceals the contents, style, and nature of the book. The departure between the title and the contents of the book seems to have been a practice adopted at the time to attract the interest of potential customers, as Robert Burton criticizes in his *Anatomy of Melancholy*: there is "a kinde of pollicie in these daies, to prefix a phantasticall Title to a Booke which is to

bee sold," ed. Thomas C. Faulkner, Nicolas K. Kiessling, and Rhonda L. Blair (Oxford: Clarendon Press, 1989), 1:6.15–16.

2 *Presenting to noble mindes, theyr Courtlie desires . . . yet all delightfull, for recreation* Munday paints a picture of his reading public that comprises all social classes, from the nobility to the laboring classes, and suggests that all of them can benefit from the book according to their social status. In the case of the nobles and gentles Munday simply states that in the book they will find "*theyr Courtlie desires . . .* [and] *choise expectations.*" The work, however, seems to be more advantageous for "*the inferiour sorte,*" since "the text assures its readers that it will put the laboring classes . . . to work imitating virtues" (Phillips, 141). In addition, Munday reassures his readers that the book contains moral values presented in a "*delightfull*" mode "*for recreation,*" thus agreeing with the Horatian dictum, to instruct and delight. While this Horatian doctrine was a commonplace among Renaissance poets, it was less frequently found with other genres; see Nicholas Cronk, "Aristotle, Horace, and Longinus: The Conception of Reader Response," in *The Cambridge History of Literary Criticism, vol. 3: The Renaissance*, ed. Glyn P. Norton (Cambridge: Cambridge University Press, 1999), 200. Cf. Louise Wilson, "Writing Romance Readers in Early Modern Paratexts," *SPELL: Swiss Papers in English Language and Literature* 22 (2009): 115.

3 **one of the Messengers of her Maiesties Chamber.** This is the first time Munday styles himself as such. As Messenger of Her Majesty's Chamber Munday was officially responsible for distributing some of the Queen's correspondence around the country, although it seems he got involved in the persecution of recusants. For more information, see "Introduction," 72; James P. Bednarz, "'Histriomastix' and the Origin of the Poets' War," *Huntington Library Quarterly* 54 (1991): 13; Byrne, "Books," 231; Hamilton, 62–65; Hayes, "Romances," 62.

4 **Patere aut abstine** I.e., suffer or desist. One of the two mottoes adopted by Munday in his works. This motto was used by the French printer Denis Janot, although it is likely that Munday took it from Janot's successor, Etienne Groulleau, as suggested by Louise Wilson, "The Publication of Iberian Romance in Early Modern Europe," in *Translation and the Book Trade in Early Modern Europe*, ed. José María Pérez Fernández and Edward Wilson-Lee (Cambridge: Cambridge University Press, 2014), 211. See also Hill, 49.

5 **I. Charlewoode . . . the rowe** For information on the printer and the location of Wright's shop, see "Introduction," 44–45.

Coat of Arms

1 **Vero nihil verius** I.e., nothing is truer than truth. This is the motto of Edward de Vere's family. It is constructed with the form of the family's name, Vere, and may be related to Martial, epigram VIII.76, line 7: "vero verius ergo quid

sit audi" (*Hear, then what is truer than truth*), *Epigrams*, ed. with an English translation by Walter C. A. Ker (Cambridge, MA: Harvard University Press, 1961), 60–61. In his *Adagiorum* Erasmus discusses the adage "Vero verius" (*truer than truth*); see *Adages: IV iii 1 to V ii 51*, trans. by John N. Grant and Betty I. Knott, Collected Works of Erasmus 36 (Toronto: University of Toronto Press, 2006), 420, no. IV.ix.2. This wood-block coat of arms began being used in 1586 with the publication of Angel Day's *English Secretarie* (STC 6401), and differs from the one used up until that moment, visible for instance in Munday's *Mirrour* and *Zelauto*. For facsimile reproductions of the earlier and later wood-blocks of de Vere's coat of arms, see Nelson, figs 12 and 13, and discussion on 238 and 381.

The Epistle Dedicatorie

1 **Edward de Vere**, seventeenth earl of Oxford (1550–1604); for a biographical account, see Nelson.

2 **Viscount Bulbeck** The title Bulbeck is derived from Isabel de Bolebec, wife of the 3rd Earl of Oxford; see Nelson, 20.

3 **Badelsmere** This family title comes from an estate in Kent; see Nelson, 446 n. 5.

4 *Among the* **Spartanes** . . . **seruaunt to** *Hagarbus* I have been unable to locate this reference to the Spartans Hagarbus and Mucronius, here presented as an analogy of the high regard Anthony Munday had for his former master Edward de Vere. It seems quite likely that this is an apocryphal story invented by Munday. Note how the names *Hagarbus* and *Mucronius* seem Latin rather than Greek. There is nothing unusual in making up this kind of opening anecdote; e.g., Lyly also opens the epistle dedicatory of his *Euphues: The Anatomy of Wyt* with the invented story of Paratius (Lyly, *Euphues*, 1:179.7–9).

5 *this vice* I.e., forgetfulness of the servant toward his master.

6 *beeing once so happy as to serue a Maister so noble* Munday's relationship with Edward de Vere as his servant started in 1577 and finished in the early 1580s. For more information, see "Introduction," 71–72. Even though he was no longer Oxford's servant, Munday insists on this connection: first, he calls him "*sometime my honorable Maister*" (102.7), then "*your late seruaunt*" (102.19), and finally "*Sometime your Honours seruant*" (102.36).

7 *Your Honour hauing such speciall knowledge in them* Edward de Vere is believed to have been taught Latin during his time in Cambridge, and must have attained a working knowledge of French and Latin as he traveled on the continent; see Nelson, 23–25, 121–37.

8 *as your seruauntes New yeeres gift* It was not uncommon in the sixteenth century that books were offered as gifts to patrons at New Year's time. For a tentative

list of books, both printed and in manuscript, presented as New Year's gifts, see Edwin Haviland Miller, "New Year's Day Gift Books in the Sixteenth Century," *SB* 15 (1962): 233–41.

9 *the second part, now on the presse, and well neere finished I will shortly present my worthie Patrone* The second part was printed on March 9, 1588, according to the preface to the readers included in the third edition of 1616 of the second part of *Palmerin d'Oliva*, believed to reproduce the text of the now lost *editio princeps* of the second part; see 340.19–20. For more information, see "Introduction," 50.

To the Courteous Readers

1 **When I finished my seconde parte of *Palmerin* of *England*, I promised this worke of *Palmerin D'Oliua*, because it depended so especially on the other** The first edition of *Palmerin of England* has not been preserved but was probably completed in 1583; see "Introduction," 71. Considering Munday's tendency to announce the forthcoming publication of translations, it seems likely that he referred to his *Palmerin d'Oliva* in the postface to the second part of *Palmerin of England*. Although the latter was printed first, Munday was well aware of the *Palmerin* romances' natural order and favored that their appearance in England should have started with *Palmerin d'Oliva*, instead of *Palmerin of England*. The alteration of this order is therefore attributable to the printer John Charlewood. See further in Jordi Sánchez-Martí, "*Zelauto*'s Polinarda and the *Palmerin* Romances," *Cahiers Élisabéthains* 89 (2016): 78–79.

2 **But because some (perhaps) will make exceptions against me, that being but one Booke in other languages, I now deuide it twaine** When editions of *Palmerin d'Oliva* were printed in other European countries, they tended to be printed in one volume. See "Introduction," 42. See also Wilson, "Publication of Iberian Romance," 214.

3 **for such are affections now a daies, that a booke a sennight olde, is scant worth the reading** A similar complaint was voiced by Lyly in the address "To the Gentlemen Readers" of his *Euphues*: "It is not straunge when as the greatest wonder lasteth but nyne days: That a newe worke should not endure but three monethes. Gentlemen vse bookes, as gentlewomen handle theyr flowres" (1:182.9–12).

4 **what hath past with so great applause ... not capable of so especiall deseruinges.** For the European publication of this romance, see "Introduction," 27–41. See Wilson, "Publication of Iberian Romance," 211–12.

5 **to translate, allowes little occasion of fine pen worke** This is the only traductological statement Munday makes in *Palmerin d'Oliva*, although it is not a faithful description of his translation policy. See "Introduction," 78.

Head-title

1 **The first parte ... the fayre *Griana*** The head-title used in the edition of Munday's translation reveals Palmerin's progenitors from start, thus departing from both the Sp. and Fr. versions. While the Fr. makes no allusion to Palmerin's parents, the Sp. states that Palmerin conducted himself "sin saber cúyo hijo fuesse" (7; *without knowing whose son he was*).

Chapter 1

1 Munday follows the chapter division of the Fr. The contents of chapter 1 correspond to the prefatory material in the Sp. text.

2 **the eight Emperor** The use of cardinal for ordinal numbers was common in Middle English, but gradually disappeared in early Modern English; see Mustanoja, 306.

3 **the founder of that aunciert and famous Cittie** This phrase has no parallel in the Fr. text, but expands the Sp. "que la edificó" (7; *who built it*). Although the reference to Remicius is the only one with an air of historical authenticity, there was no emperour of Byzantium named Remicius; cf. Patchell, 26 n. 3, 82.

4 **gaue ouer the exercise of Armes** The Sp. describes Remicius's previous main military endeavor as follows: "la guerra qu'él de contino hazía a los moros, enemigos de nuestra fe" (7; *the war that he continually fought against the Moors, enemies of our faith*). This information is omitted by Maugin, and therefore not included by Munday.

5 ***Griana*** This is a portmanteau name, a combination of *Grima*, the heroine of *El Cavallero Cifar*, and *Oriana*, heroine of *Amadis de Gaule*; see Thomas, 89 n. 1.

6 **the chiefest ... framed** This phrase amplifies the Fr. "vn chef d'œuure de Nature" (B1r; *a masterpiece of nature*); see Galigani, 274. Romance heroines are traditionally presented as the most beautiful women, but rarely do we find a physical description of them, as in the case of Griana; see Patchell, 53–54.

7 **Sonne** Fr. "neueu" (B1r; *nephew*), Sp. "fijo" (7; *son*).

8 **fell into ... seruice** An amplification of the Fr. "en deuint amoureux" (B1r; *fell in love*); Munday writes this amplification "con gusto tipicamente barocco" (Galigani, 274).

9 **religious** This adjective is added by Munday to suggest both the uprightness and devotion of her love; cf. Galigani, 274.

10 **a Tryumphe ... as others** Tournaments are a typical feature of chivalric romances. In their literary presentation tournaments are declared for a number of reasons, including as a test of valor (motif H1561.1; see Bordman, 50, and

Bueno Serrano, "Índice," 764). In the Elizabethan period tournaments became an anachronistic manifestation of medieval chivalric values and were appreciated for their social and also symbolic force. There is no denying the fact that real life imitated fiction, in particular the romance tradition. For an account of the tournament tradition in Renaissance England, see Alan Young, *Tudor and Jacobean Tournaments* (London: George Philip, 1987); for the literary connections of chivalric practices after the Middle Ages, see Alex Davis, *Chivalry and Romance in the English Renaissance* (Cambridge: D. S. Brewer, 2003).

11 **a day the next Moneth** Munday omits the date of the tournament, given in the Sp. as "el día de Santa María de Agosto" (8; *the day of St. Mary of August*), i.e., the 15th of August, the feast of the Assumption of Mary rendered in French as "le jour de la Myaoust" (B1r; *the day of mid-August*).

12 **vnspotted loue** This is Munday's rendering of the Fr. "tant est grande l'amytié" (B1v; *so great is the affection*); Galigani suggests that Munday is trying to "transformare questi lubrici amori in qualcosa di più puro" (284); cf. n. 9 above.

13 **Nephewe** The designation of Tarisius as the empress's nephew corresponds to the Sp. "Sobrino" (9) and the Fr. "neueu" (B2r). Note, however, that the empress is described as "the King of *Hungarias* Daughter" (104.21) and Tarisius as "*Sonne to the King of Hungaria*" (108.3). We must understand that these are two successive kings.

14 **but** I.e., without. The form *but* here is in fact a preposition meaning "without, apart from" (see *OED*, s.v. *but*, prep. 2).

15 **the Emperour... your request** Freedom of choice was rarely exercised among the aristocracy in Tudor England. Thus, it seems natural for the contemporary readers of the text that Griana's mother takes control over her daughter's marriage prospects. For a short overview of marriage in Tudor England, see Jeremy Boulton, "Marriage and Marriage Law," in *Tudor England: An Encyclopedia*, ed. Arthur F. Kinney and David W. Swain (New York: Garland, 2001), 467–68. Note that the Fr. reads "jeune & sote" (B2r; *young and foolish*), which Munday renders as "yong and vnder controule" (107.3).

16 **the Kinges son of** *Macedon* In this noun phrase the head *son* splits the prepositional phrase *the King of Macedon*. This construction, known as split genitive, was common throughout the Middle English period but was gradually abandoned in the sixteenth century. See Mustanoja, 78–79; and Matti Rissanen, "Syntax," in *CHEL*, 202–3.

17 **beholding** a common mistake for *beholden*; cf. Lyly, *Euphues*, 1:187.6. Further occurrences of this mistake are not indicated in the notes.

18 **the renowne ... honoured her** Prince Florendos falls in love with Griana based only on her reputation as beautiful and virtuous, an instance of the medieval topos of *amor de lonh* or love on hearsay, in which the mere description of the desired one excites passion (motif T11.1; see Bordman, 88, and Bueno Serrano, "Índice," 898). For a discussion of the medieval origin of the topos, see Irénée Cluzel, "Jaufré Rudel et L'Amor de Lonh," *Romania* 78 (1957): 86–97.

Chapter 2

1 **as commonlie ... desires** Munday makes explicit the term *maladie* in the vaguer Fr. "ainsi que telle maladie est commune aux femmes" (B2r; *since such a disease is common among women*).

2 *Griana* **is ... Husband** The age of marriage in medieval canon law, which in England survived the Reformation, was twelve for women and fourteen for men. In chapter 1 Griana is said to be fourteen years old. See Martin Ingram, *Church Courts, Sex and Marriage in England, 1570–1640* (1987; repr., Cambridge: Cambridge University Press, 2003), 128.

3 **the other** I.e., all the remaining ones. For the use of the form *other* with the value of a plural, see *OED*, s.v. *other*, pron. 4a.

4 **the feast of Saint** *Maria d'Augusta* Here is the first reference in the English text to the date of the tournament. Note that at this point no mention of the date is made by Maugin, whereas the Sp. reads, "el día de Santa María de Agosto" (10; *the day of St. Mary of August*).

5 **the Emperour ... magnificent Courte** It was common in the late Middle Ages to dub knights when the emperor held a solemn court, as happens in the text. See Keen, 79.

6 **though manie ... discerned** Here Munday amplifies the Fr. "l'vn & l'autre eurent assez affaire à dissimuler leurs affections" (B2v; *the two of them had difficulty in dissembling their affections*), thus revealing his interest in elaborating the finer points of the secret love relationship between Griana and Florendos. Here they are shown communicating their love using *verba visibilia* or non-verbal signs, namely, sighs and looks. That way, not only do they hide their feelings from other people, but express their affection more comfortably than using verbal communication; e.g., their first verbal exchange misrepresents their actual feelings. For a discussion of the literary use of non-verbal communication, see J. A. Burrow, *Gestures and Looks in Medieval Narrative* (Cambridge: Cambridge University Press, 2002), esp. chap. 3. As Burrow remarks, "most often for fear of discovery by others ... lovers resort to looks" (95). Cf. the Sp. "Florendos ... nunca quitó los ojos de Griana ... ; e ansimismo ella lo mirava a él e conosció, según él tan afincadamente ponía los ojos en ella, que por amor suyo havía venido a aquella tierra" (10; *Florendos kept his eyes fixed on Griana; she also stared back at*

him and realized, as he was looking intently at her, that he had come to that land for the love of her).

7 **I did not thinke ... offended** Despite her sincere love for Florendos, Griana decides to observe the moral exigencies imposed by her society so that their genuine love can be also perceived as virtuous; cf. Patchell, 66.

8 **that is it I** I.e., that is the thing which I. As Mustanoja (205) points out, the non-expression of the relative pronoun becomes more common in literary prose at the end of the sixteenth century.

9 **Gods** In contrast to the Fr. ("Dieu," B3r; *God*) and the Sp. ("Dios," 11; *God*), Munday prefers to use the plural to refer to the Muslim divinity, as was conventional in English medieval romances. Below (110.32) Munday also decides to omit the qualifier *almighty* when alluding to Gamezio's God, whereas the Fr. reads "Dieu tout puissant" (B3r; *God Almighty*) and the Sp. "Dios Todopoderoso" (11; *God Almighty*).

10 **King *Calameno*** We learn in the Sp. that Calameno is the king of Alexandria, against whom Gamezio and his men initially intended to fight. The relevant passage did not get translated into Fr. and therefore is not included in Munday's translation.

Chapter 3

1 **The Prince ... left behinde** Munday reproduces the error in the Fr. text that states that Florendos "estoit demouré derriere" (B3v; *had remained behind*), while the Sp. reads, "Florendos no fue de los postreros mas antes salió con todos sus cavalleros el primero" (12; *Florendos was not among the last ones but rather he sallied forth the first with all his knights*).

2 **For the Prince ... Christians** Munday condenses the description of the battle but leaves out details that would have contributed to a better understanding of the events, as for instance mentioning that Gamezio goes ashore: "il print terre" (B3v; *he went ashore*).

3 **seeing ... euerie side** This phrase amplifies the sense of the Fr. "les auisant" (B3v; *seeing them*); cf. Galigani, 278.

4 **lifted him quite ... ghost** Munday departs from Maugin in the description of Gamezio's death at the hands of Florendos: "luy mit l'espée dedans le fondement jusques à la croysée, & tomba mort" (B3v; *he put his sword into his bowls as far as the crotch and Gamezio fell dead*).

5 **because** I.e., in order that, q.v. *OED*, conj. 2.

6 **and conducted ... estate** Munday's interpolation.

7 **the Moore excused** *Tarisius* The English text departs from the Fr. "le Payen y est demouré pour gage" (B4r: *the Pagan is dead*); see Huguet, s.v. *gage*: "*demeurer pour gage, pour les gages*. Subir un dommage, être pris, maltraité, tué, mourir." Here *excuse* means "to save from punishment or harm, esp. by suffering (in a person's stead)" (*OED*, s.v. *excuse*, v. 4). Galigani considers it a case of "cambiamento intenzionale" (263). The Sp. here reads, "Florendos . . . mató aquel cavallero moro" (13; *Florendos killed that Moorish knight*). Note that Munday chooses systematically to render the Fr. *payen* as *Moore* in order to highlight the religious, but also racial, antagonism between Christians and Muslims.

8 **such modest and vertuous regarde** Munday reassures us that the love relationship between Griana and Florendos remains pure and is, so far, limited to the exchange of looks (cf. note 6 in chap. 2), whilst Maugin states that such exchanges occurred "in moderation" ("si modestement," B4r; see Huguet, s.v. *modestement*: "modérément, avec modération"). This understated encounter between the two lovers substitutes for a brief but unnatural dialogue in the Sp.

9 The English text omits a passage from the Fr. where the sentries inform Caniano of the flight of the enemy ships.

10 **his Armour . . . as the deserte of his trauaile** In Munday's translation Florendos receives Gamezio's armor as a reward for his exertions, whereas in Maugin's version it is offered to Florendos in recognition of his being the "cause de si belle deffaicte" (B4r; *cause of such a beautiful defeat*).

11 **Cozin** Remicius addresses Florendos as his cousin, not because they are related but "as a term of intimacy, friendship or familiarity" (*OED*, s.v. *cousin* n. 5).

12 **bee there ought . . . his owne** Remicius makes a rash promise that raises Florendos's hopes of obtaining Griana's hand. Unfortunately we know that the emperor has already pledged his word otherwise and therefore cannot honor his promise to Florendos. The emperor's impetuosity contrasts with Griana's caution when she tells Tarisius, "I haue not learned so little modestie, as to grant anie thing, before I knowe what is desired" (105.31–33).

Chapter 4

1 **My dread . . . all other** As Galigani (274) suggests, Munday elaborates on this scene by adding epithets such as "dread and soueraigne," while the Fr. simply reads "Monsieur" (B4v). Besides Munday adds the following phrases not present in the Fr.: "then any waie diminish" (115.10), "your highnesse" (115.10), and "among the infinite number of your princelie graces towardes me" (115.11–12).

2 **if either . . . fauour** This clause is the result of Munday's direct intervention, since the Fr. succinctly states, "s'il vous plaist me faire tant d'honneur & de grace"

(B4v; *if it pleases you to do me so much honor and grace*). Munday infuses the remainder of Florendos's talk with the same elaborate and verbose style, which emphasizes the latter's good manners and obliging attitude toward his beloved's father.

3 **it should be said I falsified my worde** Of course, Remicius has fallen in a contradiction, since he previously, in a rash promise, made it possible for Florendos to legitimately hope to obtain Griana's hand (113.35–40). Remicius gives precedence to Tarisius over Florendos, when both could have been treated as equally rightful suitors.

4 **necessitie is without lawe** Proverbial; cf. Tilley, N 76.

5 **that had maintayned his life** This clause is a mistranslation of the Fr. "qu'il auoit taschée à viuifier" (B4v; *which he had aimed to invigorate*); see Galigani, 260.

6 **so full . . . heauines** This phrase amplifies the Fr. "si triste" (B4v; *so sad*) because Munday "sente che il semplice epiteto francese non basta in questo caso" (Galigani, 274).

7 **casting himselfe vpon his bed** This phrase represents a specification of the Fr. "il fut entré en sa chambre" (B4v; *he went into his chamber*) and is closer to the Italian "postosi ne'l letto," (*lay down on the bed*; *Historia del valorosissimo cavalliere Palmerin d'Oliva* [Venice, 1544], 11r), whether by imitation or coincidence we do not know; cf. Galigani, 278.

8 **he thus . . . of his passions** This clause shows the rhetorical elaboration of the more direct Fr. "commança a se plaindre" (B4v; *he started to moan*), Munday thus heightening the pathos of the situation; cf. Galigani, 275.

9 **Vnhappy wretch . . . natiuitie** Munday interpolates the opening of this paragraph, since the Fr. reads only "Helas pouure malheureux que je suis!" (B4v; *Alas, poor wretch that I am*).

10 **I haue . . . owne** This clause is added by Munday in order to emphasize Florendos's perception of injustice in a more effective way than the Fr. "vous me rauissez, pour recompense, tout mon bien & mon seul reconfort!" (B4v; *in recompense you take away from me all I have and my only comfort*).

11 **At which . . . speeche** This clause makes apparent Munday's liking for the baroque and euphuistic. By contrast, its Fr. counterpart succinctly reads, "Et lors la parole luy faillit" (B5r; *and then he was at a loss for words*); cf. Galigani, 276.

12 *mal content* Fr. "mal contant" (B5r; *discontented, dissatisfied*). Note that the word *malcontent* is attested in English for the first time in 1586 (see *OED*, s.v. *malcontent*, adj.) and it would therefore be perceived as a neologism, hence the choice of italics.

13 **Of which ... glad** Munday's text departs from his source in order to highlight the empress's success, achieved by means of wiles, when the Fr. simply illustrates the empress's courtly manners: "Dequoy elle le remercia tres humblement" (B5r; *for which she humbly thanked him*).

14 **shee was ... dealings** Munday makes explicit the Fr. "si en portoit elle vn merueilleux desplaisir en son cueur" (B5v; *because of that, deep down she was greatly displeased*), thus locating the source of Griana's displeasure unequivocally in the actions of the empress.

15 **as heauen ... shee secretlie** These words are interpolated by Munday.

16 **may giue ... words** This phrase is Munday's interpolation.

17 **that she ... hard fortune** This clause makes explicit the Fr. "pour mieux l'amollir de pleurs" (B5v; *in order to better soften him up more with tears*).

Chapter 5

1 **her teares** Munday introduces this phrase to enhance the sentimental force of the situation.

2 **Vnhappy that I am** This clause is added by Munday. Note that these added words are uttered not by Florendos, as Galigani states (273), but instead by Griana.

3 **that loue ... exigent** Munday follows his euphuistic taste in adopting the repetition of words (*loue*) and parallel constructions (*so braue ... so hard*); see Galigani, 276.

4 **and let ... in life** Griana's remarks are Munday's interpolation, which departs from the Fr.: "Ne vaut il donques mieux que luy & moy viuions contans?" (B5v; *is it not preferable that he and me live happily?*).

5 **that buyes ... price** This clause is interpolated by Munday.

6 **the Daughter ... named *Cardina*** Munday turns the male servant *Cardin* of the Fr. and Sp. into a female one, probably thinking that a confidante is better suited to serve Griana. Note, however, that Munday's decision of changing the gender of this character was used by early critics to discredit both his translation and him as a translator, as the following quotation suggests: "honest Anthony [Munday] little regarded the language, actions, or even sexes of his original.... The Cardin here spoken of, Munday without the least scruple, has emasculated into Cardina" (*British Bibliographer*, 138). The change in gender of this character requires that Munday makes minor adjustments to the text, which he does consistently throughout the translation. In chap. II.xxv, however, the adjustment consists in inventing a brother to Cardina; see 426.34–35.

7 **and so . . . secrecie** This clause is interpolated by Munday, who wants to emphasize the secretiveness of Griana's intentions, first, by repeating the word *secrete*, and later by using the word *secrecie*. Similarly Cardina next describes her lady's request as **commaunde for secrete** (119.26–27), while the Fr. uses the verb "commander" alone (B5v; *to command*).

8 **while I . . . worde** In his translation Munday finds ways of elaborating on and improving the expression of his original, in this case by imposing a parallel structure to the more basic Fr.: "je viuray loyal & obeïssant Seruiteur" (B5v; *I will live a loyal and obedient servant*).

9 **the greeuous sicknes . . . beares to me** Lovesickness was a common motif in medieval literature (motif T24.1; see Bordman, 88, and Bueno Serrano, "Índice," 899), but it also had great currency in the literature of the early modern period; see Lesel Dawson, *Lovesickness and Gender in Early Modern English Literature* (Oxford: Oxford Uniuersity Press, 2008).

10 **Fortune** Munday generally tries to avoid using the word *God* (Fr. "Dieu," B6r) and prefers to translate all references to divinity evasively, as in this case. For a similar practice elsewhere, see Munday, *Amadis*, xxiv.

11 **must thou . . . of remedie?** In the Fr. the question is asked in the first person and addressed to "Dieu" (B6r).

12 **her highnesse hande** In early Modern English the possessive case with singular nouns ending in sibilants was marked by position; see Görlach, 81.

13 **whom she . . . affections** There is no Fr. equivalent for this relative clause.

Chapter 6

1 **token** This word replaces the phrase "ce qu'elle luy auoit mandé" (B6r; *that which I had sent him*), a case of concentration and explicitation that shows how Munday was actively engaged with the narrative, instead of mechanically translating it.

2 **whereby you . . . applause** This clause is Munday's interpolation.

3 **euery worde . . . Princesse** In the Fr. what takes hold of Griana's heart are not Cardina's words but "Amour"; Galigani considers the addition of the adjective "gentle" as another example of *amplificatio* (273).

4 **the Prince his torments** This type of construction, known as the possessive dative, combines a noun with a possessive pronoun *his* instead of the genitive case of the noun. The possessive dative already existed in Old English, was common in Middle English, and frequent in early Modern English. See Mustanoja, 159–62; and Charles Barber, *Early Modern English* (London: A. Deutsch, 1976), 200–1.

5 **what she desired . . . all her life** Munday changes the sense of the Fr. with the purpose of dispelling any suspicion of impious thoughts in Griana. The Fr. suggests that, once Love has got control of her heart, Griana fails to act with her characteristic self-possession and abandons her previous code of conduct based on "son honneur & la crainte de receuoir honte" (B6v; *her honor and the fear of receiving shame*); by contrast, Munday insists that she is still capable of controlling her desires for fear "to receiue shame."

6 **Howe might . . . oppression?** Munday decides to censor Griana's passionate impulses by substituting this question for the more explicit Fr., "Helas, mon amy, quand le pourray-je voir & baiser à mon aise?" (B6v; *Alas, my friend, when will I be able to see and kiss him at my ease?*); as Galigani states, "Mundy [*sic*] ricorre alla sostituzione della frase incriminata con una più innocua" (283).

7 **to be . . . a Gallant** This phrase is interpolated by Munday in order to make explicit the implicatures of the Fr.

8 **may you . . . Knight** Munday substitutes the neutral verb "speake" for the Fr. "satisfaire," which could invite morally awkward interpretations in this context: "pourrez satisfaire au meilleur Cheualier de la terre" (B6v; *you will be able to satisfy the best knight on earth*).

9 **and otherwise . . . entertaine** This sentence departs from the Fr. and its sole purpose is to guarantee the morality of Florendos's feelings toward Griana.

10 **the Garden . . . secrete entraunce** In the Fr. there is no access from the garden into Griana's chamber, but instead her chamber overlooked the garden: "sur lequel [i.e., the garden] sa chambre auoit regard" (B6v; *her chamber overlooked the garden*). The garden represents a *locus amoenus* traditionally chosen by lovers for their trysts; cf. Patchell, 64.

11 **I am thus bolde . . . abilitie to you** This clause amplifies the Fr. "je suis venu vers vous, prest à vous obeïr" (B6v; *I have come to you ready to obey you*).

12 **as to the diuine Goddesse . . . thousande deathes** This passage preserves the sense of the Fr. but departs from it at the level of expression. Munday intervenes most notably to infuse the couple's loves with a quasi-religious ethos that presents Griana as a "diuine Goddesse," whom Florendos joins by meanes of "irreuocable vowes" and with his "faith." Munday is using a language typical of courtly love.

13 **hote loue** Munday's interpolation of the adjective "hote" ("hauing or showing intensity of feeling; fervent, ardent, passionate"; *OED*, s.v. *hot* 6a) contrasts with his efforts to sanitize the love relationship between Florendos ang Griana.

14 **in my natiue Countrie of** *Macedon* **. . . I dedicated my selfe onelie yours** Cf. 107.9–13.

15 **this religious seruice** Munday confers a religious dimension to the Fr. "seruitude" (B7r; *service*), but he is referring to the religion of love; cf. n. 12 above. See Galigani, 284. As Helen Hackett argues in *Women and Romance Fiction in the English Renaissance* (Cambridge: Cambridge University Press, 2000), 73, in the Iberian chivalric romances "love is elevated to the level of a religion of which suffering heroines are the saints and martyrs."

16 **to seale ... lippes** As Galigani states, "qualche volta la richiesta di un bacio dà luogo ad abbellimenti ed infiorettamenti di stile" whose purpose is the "nobilitazione delle passioni amorose" (285). Note the interpolation of the adjective *diuine*.

17 **But by your fauour ... of that Planet** Munday censors and changes this scene. Firstly, Florendos appears as the initiator of this sexual encounter ("you [i.e., Florendos] haue giuen your selfe"), while Griana is left in a passive stance limited to accepting his desires. Conversely, in Maugin's version Griana is the one who asserts her desires and invites Florendos's advances: "je [i.e., Griana] veux que soyez mien, & pour tel je vous retiens" (B7r; *I want you to be mine, and for that reason I detain you*). Munday also tries to suppress or minimize any possible erotic suggestion by describing the encounter between Florendos and Griana as *delicate* and their kisses as *solemne*; likewise he refers to Griana as *Cynthia*, alluding to the Moon. The Fr., however, implies a fully-fledged sexual encounter: "Florendos faisant petit à petit ses aproches se trouua en telz termes, qu'il eut d'elle ce que plus il eust peu souhaiter" (ibid.; *Florendos making his approaches little by little found himself on such terms with her that he had from her the most he could have desired*) and "Florendos (à la quatriesme charge) prit entiere possession de la place tant assaillie" (ibid.; *Florendos, at the fourth charge, gained full possession of the assailed fortress*). As Galigani remarks, Munday's text seems "quasi preludere alla poesia amorosa dei metafisici" (287–88) by obliquely alluding to the sexual encounter of Florendos "breaking his Launce in the face of Venus," the goddess of love. The same scene in the original Sp. shows how Florendos forces himself on Griana much to her discontent: "E como se sentaron y él la vido tan fermosa, no se le acordó de usar con ella de cortesía mas tomóla en los braços sin nada le dezir e fizo tanto que la tornó dueña" (*Palmerín de Olivia*, 18; *And as they sat and he saw her so beautiful it didn't occur to him to treat her with courtesy but instead he took her in his arms and so much did he do to her that he made her a woman*).

18 **and great discredite will it be to her** The Fr. says nothing about the Emperor thinking harshly of Griana's mother, but states instead, "Monsieur a eu raison de complaire à ma Dame" (B7r; *my father has reason to please my mother*). This clause is added by Munday to increase the negativity associated with the Empress.

19 **my Lord** Fr. "mon mary" (B7r; *my husband*). Munday avoids explicitly acknowledging Griana's relationship with Florendos as a marriage, whereas Maugin has no qualms about doing so. Note, however, that the wording of the

Notes to the Text: Part I   611

English text implicitly invites the understanding that Griana and Florendos are united in matrimony. First, Florendos declares to Griana, "I binde to you by irreuocable vowes" (122.17), a proposal that Griana accepts willingly: "I see then you haue giuen your selfe wholie mine, and so I am well contented to accept you" (122.27–28). As stated by Diana O'Hara, *Courtship and Constraint: Rethinking the Making of Marriage in Tudor England* (Manchester: Manchester University Press, 2000), 10, "By the law of marriage, the mutual consent of a couple, as expressed by words of contract spoken in the present tense (*per verba de praesenti*), constituted an indissoluble marriage bond." These conditions (i.e., mutual consent and present tense) apply in the case of Griana and Florendos, who therefore are legally married. A direct consequence thereof is that the sexual act they engage in results in the legitimate conception of a child, in this case the eponymous hero of the romance. For the theme of marriage in the Iberian romances of chivalry, see Michael Harney, *Kinship and Marriage in Medieval Hispanic Chivalric Romance* (Turnhout: Brepols, 2001), esp. 105–227.

20 **hauing vowed my selfe onlie yours** Cf. the Fr. "je me suis faicte vostre" (B7r; *I have become yours*), which suggests that their union has been sealed by their sexual encounter.

21 **with this excuse** This phrase is added by Munday for a better understanding of the text.

22 *Florendos* **kissing . . . leaue** This passage is interpolated by Munday; hence, the restrained hand-kiss should come as no surprise. This scene actually replaces a passage in the Fr. of no narrative consequence. Note also that Munday endows his translation with greater referential precision, most notably in the case of the characters' names: for instance, the next occurrence of "*Lerina*" in the English text (123.26) corresponds to the Fr. "la Damoiselle sœur de Cardin" (B7r; *the damsel sister to Cardin*); above, it reads "your Cozin *Frenato*" (123.22–23) for the Fr. "vostre cousin" (B7r; *your cousin*). The result is a text that lends itself to less confusion.

23 **three or foure daies longer** Fr. "encores pour quatre ou cinq jours" (B7v; *for still four or five days*). Munday pays little attention to numerals and tends to alter his source when they carry no narrative implication.

24 **me thinkes** This verbal form, meaning *it seems to me*, is an impersonal construction, itself a vestige of the Middle English period, that survived throughout the Early Modern period; see Barber, *Early Modern English*, 285–86; Görlach, 106; and Rissanen, "Syntax," in *CHEL*, 249–52.

25 **then bee . . . cannot** There is an impediment to Griana's marriage to Tarisius; it is tacitly implied that she is already married. This clause makes explicit the more ambiguous sense of the Fr. "qu'il me soit de sa vie plus qu'il est" (B7v; *that he mean more to me than he does*).

26 **the King his Father** Munday corrects an incongruity in the Fr., which states that the diplomatic mission is dispatched by Tarisius's grandfather ("ayeul," B7v), when it was his father.

27 **her** It refers not to Griana (she never promises Tarisius to marry him), but to her mother the Empress, who did promise to Tarisius her daughter's hand (106.31–107.6); cf. Fr. "ce qu'elle luy promist" (B7v; *that which she promised him*).

28 **childlike** Munday introduces this adjective.

29 **by the desire . . . as shee was** This clause departs from the Fr. "l'ennuy qu'elle auroit de s'eslongner d'elle & de l'Empereur" (B7v; *the sadness she will have for moving away from her and the Emperor*).

30 **to depart with him** This clause makes explicit the Fr. "pour paracheuer ce qu'il sçauoit" (B8r; *to bring to an end that which he knew*).

Chapter 7

1 *Macedon* Fr. "Grece" (B8r; *Greece*). Munday's translation is not inaccurate but shows consistency in associating Florendos with Macedon, although it is true that the region of Macedonia encompassed the northern part of Greece. Cf. Odile Sassi and Mathilde Aycard, *Atlas historique de la Méditerranée* (Beyrouth: Presses de l'Université Saint-Joseph, 2009), 125.

2 **wyll you in seeking . . . endaunger her life?** Munday presents a free translation of two questions from the Fr. containing two idioms: "voulez-vous rompre l'Anguille au genou, & jecter le manche apres la congnée?" (B8v); see Huguet, s.v. *anguille*: *"rompre l'anguille au genouil*. User de violence mal à propos, employer de mauvais moyens." The expression *jeter le manche après la cognée* still means "to throw in the towel"; see *The Oxford-Hachette French Dictionary*, 4th ed. (Oxford: Oxford University Press, 2007), s.v. *cognée*.

3 **this verie hardlie . . . forget your self** Munday introduces these words in order to avoid reproducing the more compromising Fr.: "vous auez tort de faire maintenant cest office, & de mener l'estat d'vne femme publique" (B8v; *you are wrong to do this service now and lead the life of a prostitute*).

4 **leauing that rare creature . . . martired my soule?** In the Fr., Florendos takes pity on Griana, "qui pour l'amour de moy receura desormais tribulations innumerables" (B8v; *who for the love of me will now receive innumerable tribulations*); the appellation of Griana as "rare creature" is Munday's.

5 **witnes** Fr. "cause" (B8v; *cause*). Munday prefers to place Florendos in a passive position.

6 **necessitie (whereof manie doo often make a vertue)** Proverbial; see Tilley, V 73. Cf. 401.9.

7 I shall make thee ... quite thy fault The Fr. establishes a direct relation between the two clauses: in order that other young women may be discouraged by this exemplary punishment, "je [i.e., Remicius] ne t'aualle la teste de dessus les espaules" (B8v; *I do not cut off the head from your shoulders*). Munday obscures the causal connection by subtly altering the sense of the second clause and highlighting the gravity of Griana's offense.

8 varlet In the Fr., "malheureuse" (C1r; *dishonest*).

9 he locked her in a strong Tower There is a long literary tradition for the motif of a father locking his daughter in a tower (cf. motif P234.3, *daughter imprisoned*; Bordman, 74, and Bueno Serrano, "Índice," 838). In classical mythology Acrisius locks her daughter Danae to prevent her from bringing into the world a child who would kill him as an oracle predicted. Ovid refers to this myth in his *Amores* when stating, "the doors were bronze, the tower / Iron, the father hard, the daughter prim" (III.viii.31–32; trans. A. D. Melville, *The Love Poems* [Oxford: Oxford University Press, 1990], 70; cf. II.xix.27–28). In Marie de France's *Yonec* (lines 25–72) an old man out of jealousy decides to keep her beautiful and young wife locked in a tower with the company of an old woman; in *Aucassin et Nicolette* (4.20–22) Aucassin's father has Nicolette locked away in a tower in order to upset his son's love for her; ed. F. W. Bourdillon (Manchester: Manchester University Press, 1970), 5. While Remicius does not act as a cruel father, his decisions become increasingly arbitrary. He decides to lock Griana in a tower to protect her from the advances of Florendos. Cf. Guillaume de Lorris's section of the *Roman de la Rose* (lines 3911–36), in which Jealousy puts Fair Welcoming in prison in a tower to deter Love, and also to punish her for betraying the principle of filial obedience; cf. also how in *Paris and Vienne* Vienne's father decides that she "shold be enclosed in a chambre" (42.31–32) as a punishment for having tried to elope with Paris.

10 coulde not speake her teares so ouercame her This clause alters the sense of the Fr., "se mist à gemir & souspirer mieux que deuant" (C1r; *she began to moan and sigh more than before*).

11 for my duetie to you ... to me to offende This passage is Munday's interpolation.

12 dailie This word must be understood as "occurring during the daytime," as opposed to "the night time"; cf. Fr. "sur jour" (C1v; *during the daytime*).

Chapter 8

1 in requitall of This is the first occurrence of this phrase in the *OED* (q.v. *requital* n., phrase b).

2 a thought whyle I.e., a very little amount of time; see *OED*, s.v. *thought* n. 6.

3 **coulde you bee discharged ... wyshing is no action** This passage is Munday's interpolation.

4 *Constantinople* The 1572 edition of Maugin's translation mistakenly reads "Thrace" (C2r; *Thrace*). By contrast, the English reading is correct either because Munday correctly decided to amend the Fr. or because he used a different edition of the Fr. text, since the 1546 edition reads "Constantinople" (B6r).

5 *Griana* **had libertie to speake with her Gentlewomen** The English text is not equivalent to the Fr., "Griana auoit deliberé de parler de jour à ses femmes" (C2r; *Griana had decided to speak by day to her women*); it is instead closer in sense to the Sp.: "con Griana podían hablar sus donzellas" (23; *Griana's maids could talk with her*), as decided by the Emperor.

6 **he shoulde doo nothing to the preiudice of his owne person** Munday reverses the suicidal disposition of the two lovers and attributes it to Florendos, instead of Griana as happens in the Fr.: "si elle auoit retardé sa mort, n'estoit que pour luy conseruer sa vie" (C2r; *if she had delayed her death it was but to preserve his life*).

7 **as the best token a true Knight can receiue from his Mistresse** This clause is interpolated by Munday, who wants to highlight the knightly dimension of a purely sentimental epistolar exchange; cf. the Fr., "comme ce dequoy j'ay receu plus de resiouïssance, que de chose qui m'auint onques" (C2r; *as that from which I have obtained more rejoicing than from anything that ever happened to me*).

Chapter 9

1 **anie came to visite her** The Fr. suggests that her only visitors are "ses ennuyz" (C2v; *her afflictions*).

2 **framing his speeches to her in this sort** Amplification of the Fr. "luy disant" (C2v; *telling her*).

3 **for wilt thou or not ... a Husband contrarie to my liking** This is a textbook example of a forced marriage, and as such the union of Griana and Tarisius would have been perceived as legally fragile by the contemporary readers of this book. This argument is later put forward by Florendos himself when saying that Griana's marriage with Tarisius "was not to be allowed, in that it was doone against her will" (448.31). Cf. as Vienne explains Paris, "I haue not consented to ony maryage / And ye knowe wel that maryage is nothyng worth / wythout the consentyng of bothe partyes" (*Paris and Vienne*, 30.34–36). See also B. J. Sokol and Mary Sokol, *Shakespeare, Law, and Marriage* (Cambridge: Cambridge University Press, 2003), 31. Since a forced marriage was legally reversible, the interpretation offered by Petruccelli seems not applicable at least to the English version: "Al casarse con Tarisio [Griana] es desleal a Florendos (. . .), al que sin embargo no deja de amar y, de esta manera, también traiciona a su marido"

(307). The theme of forced marriage is familiar from the Middle English verse romances and occurs in other Iberian chivalric romances too (motif T108.1; see Bordman, 92, and Bueno Serrano, "Índice," 911).

4 **So kissing the Keie, he laid it by her** This sentence is probably the result of a translation problem. The Fr. reads, "Ce disant luy bailla la clef de la tour" (C3r; *thus speaking he gave her the key to the tower*), but Munday probably read *baisa* (kissed) instead of *bailla* (gave), as suggested by Galigani, 262–63.

5 **so rapt into a slumber . . . for pittie trouble her** The clause represents a baroque amplification of the more straightforward Fr.: Griana was "si faschée qu'elle s'endormit" (C3r; *so tired that she fell asleep*); cf. Galigani, 275.

6 **in this silent passion** Munday here puts a rhetorical spin on the Fr. "en songeant" (C3r; *dreaming*); see Galigani, 275.

7 **thou** This pronoun refers to Griana, whereas the Fr. source gives "ton paillard" (C3r; *your lover*), alluding to Florendos.

8 **as made the cheerefull bloode . . . breathing foorth a vehement sigh** Munday's taste for ornate style is again visible in this passage, wich corresponds to the Fr. "elle n'eut soufert mal ou desplaisir: & sur ce poinct s'esueilla" (C3r; *she had suffered no harm or displeasure: and at this point woke up*).

9 **The Princesse in this silent passion . . . hardlie forget** *Florendos* **so soone** As González comments apropos Griana's dream in the Sp., it is "Griana misma quien se reprende y acusa a través de la voz del caballero" ("Sueños," 215, n. 15). González further proposes a tripartite division of the dream: the first part consists of a negative allegorical image (the lion attacking Griana), the second part of the knight's exchange with and censure of Griana, and the third part of a positive allegorical image (the fountain surrounded by flowers). González argues that the vision of the lion represents the "euerlasting death" awaiting Griana if she insists on disobeying her father, whereas the positive image represents her salvation if she changes her mind. Note, however, that the English version departs from the Sp. (and the Fr.) in a significant detail: while in the Sp. "la voz del caballero reprende y acusa a la princesa no tanto por sus aventuras con Florendos . . ., sino por su desobediencia al padre, por resistirse al matrimonio con Tarisio" (González, "Sueños," 215–16), in the English version Griana is reprimanded on account of "the fault thou hast committed with *Florendos*." In other words, Munday considers Griana's sexual encounter with Florendos a more serious transgression than her filial disobedience. Griana's dream is also discussed in Julián Acebrón Ruiz, "La aventura nocturna. Claves del sueño en la literatura castellana medieval y del siglo xvi." PhD diss., Universitat de Lleida, 2001, 307–9. The interpretation of dreams was a contentious issue in Renaissance England, that saw the publication of Thomas Hill's *The moste pleasaunte Arte of the Interpretation of Dreames . . .*, where he made available to his contemporaries a summary

of dream theories. Hill's work was printed three times in the decades preceding the publication *Palmerin d'Oliva*: 1567, 1571, 1576 (STC 13498.5, 13497.5, 13498); see Peter Holland, "'The Interpretation of Dreams' in the Renaissance," in *Reading Dreams: The Interpretation of Dreams from Chaucer to Shakespeare*, ed. Peter Brown (Oxford: Oxford University Press, 1999), 125–46. Munday omits a religious remark present in the Fr., "faisant le signe de la croix" (C3r; *making the sign of the cross*).

10 **tryumphe nowe *Tarisius* in the honor of my loue** This clause is Munday's interpolation.

11 **at night about eight of the clocke** Fr. "dix heures de soir" (C3v; *ten hours in the evening*).

12 ***Tolomestra*** The English text omits information in the Fr. about Tolomestra's sleeping in a different room than Griana. This omission was most probably caused by eyeskip, since Munday took as point of resumption the second occurrence in the same paragraph of *Tolomestre*: "Or auoit Tolomestre si bien ... elle fit vn beau filz, que Tolomestre reçeut" (C3v). Alternatively, the eyeskip may be attributable to the compositor of the English version when using Munday's manuscript as copy-text.

13 **if it might liue without displeasure** This clause alters the sense of the Fr., "si nostre Seigneur n'eust point esté offensé lors qu'il fut engendré" (C3v; *if our Lord had not been offended when he was begotten*).

14 **in likenesse of a Crosse** This phrase departs from the Fr. "en forme de croissant" (C3v; *crescent-shaped*). In like manner, Maugin changed the Sp., "una señal negra a manera de lunar e era redonda" (26; *a black mark in the manner of a mole that was round*). As Galigani (263–64) explains, Maugin interprets the Sp. "lunar" (*mole*) as "luna" (*moon*), but presents it as a crescent rather than full moon. Munday's departure from the Fr. is intentional and seems logical in the context of the narrative, since he substitutes the Christian cross for the Crescent, symbol of Islam and of Ottoman power. The presence of a birthmark indicative of the hero's nobility forms part of the romance tradition, and occurs both in the English metrical romances (as in the case of *Emaré*, lines 503–4, and *Havelok*, lines 1251–63; see Patchell, 27–28) and in the Hispanic chivalric romance; e.g., Esplandián, son to Amadís and Oriana, is born with this mark: "seaven Caracters under either little teate, some as red as blood, and the other as white as snow," Munday, *Amadis*, III.iii.552 (cf. Bueno Serrano, "Índice," 448–50).

15 **to be borne forth of the Court** This phrase makes the Fr. specific: "ainsy que nous auons auisé" (C3v; *as we have instructed*).

16 **her howre of deliueraunce ... wherein she layd the Childe** The circumstances surrounding the birth of Palmerin parallel those of Amadis de Gaule's: both

the two childbirths are kept secret; in both cases the aide of the hero's mother (Darioletta in *Amadis*) is entrusted the baby for mislaying and exposing it. While Palmerin is abandoned on a mountain, Amadis is placed in a "Cofer into the Sea" (Munday, *Amadis*, I.ii.19). Note, additionally, that the two babies receive recognition tokens placed around their neck, Palmerin a golden crucifix and Amadis a letter "with a little golden Chaine, fastened about the Childes necke" (ibid.). For the use of these same motifs with other Amadisian heroes, see John J. O'Connor, *"Amadis de Gaule" and Its Influence on Elizabethan Literature* (New Brunswick, NJ: Rutgers University Press, 1970), 118–9. For a discussion of Amadis's birth, see Juan Bautista Avalle-Arce, "El nacimiento de Amadís," in *Essays on Narrative Fiction in the Iberian Peninsula in Honor of Frank Pierce*, ed. R. B. Tate (Oxford: Dolphin, 1982), 15–25.

Chapter 10

1 **and his Sonne woulde haue beene a great comfort to him** This clause is interpolated by Munday.

2 **God** Note that Munday raises no objection to using the word *God*, since in this context it highlights God's power for benevolence.

3 **vnder an Oliue Tree** Fr. "sous vn Palmier" (C4r; *underneath a palm tree*); Sp. "encima de una oliva" (27; *on top of an olive tree*).

4 **he found it so among the Palme trees** There is no contradiction in having found him "vnder an Oliue Tree" and now saying it was found "among the Palme trees," since at the end of chap. I.ix Cardina leaves the newborn "on a high Mountaine, which was verie thicke sette with Palme and Oliue trees" (134.14–15). The hero's name serves as reminder of his place of birth (or rather discovery in this case); cf. Patchell, 79. The hero's name "es el clásico sintagma que caracteriza a los caballeros por su procedencia," as states Mª Carmen Marín Pina, *Páginas de sueños: Estudios sobre los libros de caballerías castellanos* (Saragossa: Institución Fernando el Católico, 2011), 226.

5 **after she had escaped this hard aduenture** Fr. "depuis qu'elle fut releuée" (C4r; *after she was recovered*).

6 **which greeued her as much as the weight of her offence** Munday emphasizes Griana's sense of guilt, thus differing from the Fr., "eut tel ennuy, que peu s'en falut qu'elle n'en trespassast" (C4r; *was so angry that she nearly died*).

7 **will I nill I** whether I like it or not; see *OED*, s.v. *will* v.1 50b.

8 **beeing the inuenter and procurer thereof** Munday expands the Fr., "qui en estes le motif" (C4v; *you who are the cause thereof*).

9 **to ende the marriage** Note that the verb *to ende* in this context means "to carry through to the end; to finish, complete" (see *OED*, s.v. *end* v.1 1a).

10 **on the great iniurie she had doone to *Florendos*** Munday departs from the Fr. "au mariage d'elle & de Florendos" (C4v; *on her marriage with Florendos*) and avoids making explicit reference to the marriage privately entered into and consummated by Griana and Florendos; cf. n. 19 to chap. I.vi.

11 **though in iustice it be thine** This clause is added by Munday, who chooses to suppress how Tarisius has tried to access her "corps" (C4v; *body*). In addition, Munday censors the sexual act on the wedding night, alluded to only implicitly: **she must yeeld that honor . . . she could haue affoorded *Florendos*** (136.30–31); cf. the passage omitted from the Fr. "Mais si tout le jour elle . . . la laissa en son lict triste & faschée" (C4v).

12 **as beseemed the Daughter of so great a Prince** This clause has no Fr. equivalent, but instead seems to summarize the import of the Sp. "El Emperador la embió muy acompañada de cavalleros e de donzellas" (28; *the Emperor sent her well accompanied by knights and damsels*).

13 **hauing gained the paragon among all Ladies** In the Fr. Tarisius considers himself fortunate for a different reason: because "tant luy sçauoit bien complaire la Princesse en tout ce qu'il prenoit plaisir" (C5r; *so well did the Princess know how to satisfy him in everything that gave him pleasure*). Munday offers a more conventional motivation and censors the Fr., thus avoiding its erotic overtones.

Chapter 11

1 **whom *Florendos* made verie much account of** This clause substitutes for a compromising appositional phrase in the Fr.: "confesseur de Florendos" (C5r; *confessor to Florendos*), since it could be connected with Catholic sacramental confession. Next Munday also omits the hermit's prayers to God: "supplia deuotement nostre Seigneur qu'il eust pitié de luy" (ibid.; *he devoutedly begged our Lord that he took pity on him*).

2 **the saile of the Shippe is subiecte to all windes** Proverbial; cf. Tilley, S 25.

3 **els would she neuer haue broken her faith to me** This clause is added by Munday.

4 **and by your constancie . . . what hath happened** This clause underscoring Griana's fault has no equivalent in the Fr. text.

5 **but *Florendos* . . . neither be remooued from this opinion, for fiue daies while the old man staied with him** Cf. the Fr. "si luy fit il changer d'opinion durant quinze jours qu'il sejourna auec luy" (C5v; *the Hermit did manage to change Florendos's opinion during the fifteen days the Hermit stayed with him*).

Chapter 12

1 **thorowe thicke and thinne** Note the alliteration of this expression (cf Galigani, 277; see *OED* s.v. *thick and thin*, n. 1), contributed by Munday and not warranted by the Fr. text (sig. C6r).

2 **hee desired more to passe the Mountaines ... as the other Children did** Chivalric literature in general has taken special interest in exploring the concept of nobility, not so much as an accepted form of social privilege but instead as a genuinely intrinsic quality. In the case of Palmerin, who is brought up unaware of his noble descent, there are indications that set him apart from his rustic social context and identify him with recognizable noble practices, such as his inclination for hunting, one of the preferred pastimes among noblemen throughout the Middle Ages and the Renaissance.

3 **beeing deuoted onelie thine at all times** Munday omits an idea that the Lady of the Fountain tells Palmerin in the Fr., "estant des deuant ma conception dediée à estre vostre" (C6r; *being devoted to being yours even before I was conceived*). This idea would contribute to better understand why in the dream's logic Palmerin's birthmark also appears on the lady's hand and at the side of her heart, since this is a clear indication that the two of them were destined to love each other.

4 **by some vapour of no effect** Munday omits other details in the Fr.: "du cerueau agité des fumees, de la digestion de l'estomac" (C6r; *of the brain agitated by the fumes from the digestion of the stomach*); cf. Galiani, 278. Contemporary dream theory considered these fumes as the main source of powerful dreams; see Holland, "Interpretation of Dreams in the Renaissance," 127.

5 **he was solicited with a meruailous visyon ... Lorde and possessour of mee** Palmerin's prophetic dreams, which haunt him for approximately a fortnight, determine to some extent the narrative development of the romance, thus suggesting that the Spanish author had planned the story's plot from the start. The main consequence of the hero's dreams is his infatuation for the lady, whose identity has yet to be revealed (see González, "Sueños," 221). About experiencing love in dreams, Andreas Capellanus states the following in his thirteenth-century treatise *De amore*: "si coamantem somnium repraesentet amanti, oritur inde amor et ortus sumit augmenta" (II.ii.3: "love grows and experiences increase if a dream depicts a lover to his partner"; ed. and trans. P. G. Walsh, *Andreas Capellanus On Love* [London: Duckworth, 1982], 228–29). Moreover, the unnamed lady makes two revelations with narrative implications. Palmerin learns, firstly, that a glorious future awaits him, ending with his coronation; and secondly, that he is the son, not of Gerrard and Marcella as he thought, but of a king. Finally, the lady incites him to abandon his current life in search of her (motif H1381.3.1.2.2: *search for lady seen in dreams*, Bordman, 49; Bueno Serrano, "Índice," 760) and of his own identity. For an insightful discussion of this dream, see González, ibid.,

219–27; further analysis can be found in Acebrón Ruiz, "*E como le vino el sueño soñava* . . . : Experiencia onírica y aventura en *Palmerín de Olivia*," *Scriptura* 5 (1989): 7–16, and in his "La aventura nocturna," 315–21.

6 more then accustomed Cf. Fr. "inacoustumée" (C6r; *unaccustomed*).

7 the most happiest Multiple comparison, combining the use of *most* with the inflectional superlative, became common in the fourteenth century and continued to be so in the fifteenth and sixteenth centuries; see Mustanoja, 281.

8 how can it be that I am discended . . . great Lord hath so become my Father? These are not rhetorical questions, but instead represent legitimate doubts of the protagonist. In Malory's *Le Morte Darthur* we find a good case in point that perfectly illustrates Palmerin's misgivings about his personal situation. Aryes, a cowherd, asks King Arthur to dub his son Torre, who "wylle not laboure for me for onythyng that my wyf or I may doo, but alweyes he wille be shotynge or castynge dartes, and glad for to see batailles and to behold knyghtes" (Malory, III. iii.82). Merlin, however, reveals that Torre, is not actually Aryes's son, but Pellinore's, as Aryes's wife confirms: "she told the kynge and Merlyn that whan she was a maide and went to mylke kyen ther met with her a sterne knyght, and half by force he had my maidenhede, and at that tyme he bigat my sone Tor" (Malory, loc. cit.). Palmerin shares with Torre a disinclination for menial work and a penchant for activities related with the nobility; Palmerin, first, shows interest in hunting and, in the next chapter, in knightly action. See note 1 in chap. I.xiii.

9 your freende, and shee that loues you dearelie In translating the Fr. "vraye amye" (C6v; *true friend and lover*), Munday chooses to expose the actual implications of his source's wording.

10 the costlie swadling clothes that he was founde in . . . that hung about his necke See 133.29–31.

11 a Lyon greedilie deuouring a Horse Munday leaves out crude detail from the Fr.: "durement naüré en la cuisse" (C6v; the man was *badly wounded in the thigh*); cf. Galigani, 279. Note that, instead of a *lion*, the Fr. ("vne Lyonne"; C6v) and Sp. ("una leona," 32) give a *lioness*.

12 betweene the eyes Fr. "entre les deux oreilles" (C7r; *between the two ears*).

13 to haue my wounds dressed Above Munday omits that the merchant is wounded by the lion; the Fr. reads, "ceste Lyonne . . . m'a abatu & faict vne grande playe en la cuisse" (C7r; *this lioness has attacked me and made me a great wound in the leg*).

Chapter 13

1 rather gaue his mind to martiall exercises . . . all the braueries of a noble Courtier Palmerin's natural preference for chivalric activities is a signal of his noble descent; see note 8 in chap. I.xii. Patchell argues, "his [i.e., Palmerin's] capacities and proclivities approached those of the ideal medieval knight" (29) and puts him on a level with Amadis de Gaule, Lancelot, and Tristram.

Chapter 14

1 a verie strange disease, for which no remedie can yet be found This strange disease remains unnamed in Fr.—and therefore in English—probably because Maugin failed to understand the meaning of the Sp. "gafo" (35; *leprous*), a word that is less recognizable than *leproso*; but when the Sp. uses the word *leproso* (101) to describe Frisol's illness, then Maugin has no qualms in translating it as *ladre* (I3r; *leper*), which then gets picked up by Munday (237.25). Leprosy was indeed an incurable disease, thus giving rise to a number of outlandish remedies adopted by physicians; see Luke Demaitre, *Leprosy in Premodern Medicine: A Malady of the Whole Body* (Baltimore, MD: Johns Hopkins University Press, 2007), 264–71. The whole episode as presented in the Sp. version is discussed by Bueno Serrano, "Las tres *fadas*," in the light of folkloric formulations.

2 he should neuer bee healed . . . and wherof they frame all their enchantments In the Fr. the three magicians wash themselves in the water of the fountain. Note that the tradition of the leprosy-healing bath can be traced back to the Bible (e.g., Lev. 14:7–8, 4 Kings 5:10), which influenced later medieval texts as suggested by Paul Remy, "La lèpre, thème littéraire au moyen âge: Commentaire d'un passage du roman provençal de Jaufré," *Le Moyen Age* 52 (1946): 195–242. In the Arthurian tradition the Spring of Healing "has the virtue that any man who drinks of it, however tired or badly wounded he is, will at once be recovered and whole" (cf. *Lancelot-Grail*, 9:348); cf. also the fountain mentioned in Lord Berners's translation of *Huon of Burdeux*, "the whiche founteyne as than was of such vertue that yf any sycke man dyd drynke therof, or wasshyd his handes & face, incontynent shulde be hole," 116.27–30, and see 804–5 for a discussion of the episode in *Huon of Burdeux*. Note also that in chivalric texts serpents can appear as guardians of valuable things; cf. motif N582, *serpent guards treasure* (Bordman, 68; N577 Bueno Serrano, "Índice," 822). The presence of the magical fountain on the mountain Artifaeria in the Sp. has been connected with the expedition by the Spanish explorer Juan Ponce de León to Florida in search of "a fountain of youth"; see Hugh Thomas, *Rivers of Gold: The Rise of the Spanish Empire from Columbus to Magellan* (New York: Random House, 2004), 283–84.

3 throwing fire and smoake out of his mouth Munday adds the special effects, since the Fr. simply reads, "le Serpent sortit de sa cauerne, siflant, grinsant les dens" (C8r; *the serpent came out of her cave hissing, grinding its teeth*). This adventure has clear resonances of Amadis's fight against the Endriagus, who also hides behind a rock and "all such as haue attempted his destruction, have fayled and finished their lives most cruelly" (*Amadis de Gaule*, III.x.632). For a discussion, see Patchell, 45, and Mónica Nasif, "Iniciación y heroicidad: Palmerín de Olivia y el mito del dragón," in *Nuevos estudios sobre literatura caballeresca*, ed. Lilia E. Ferrario de Orduna (Barcelona: Edition Reichenberger, 2006), 181–88. For other dragon encounters in the Spanish romances, see John K. Walsh, "The Chivalric Dragon: Hagiographic Parallels in Early Spanish Romances," *Bulletin of Hispanic Studies* 54 (1977): 198 n. 28.

4 **the Lady, which in my sleeping thoughts visited mee so often** See 140.15–141.4.

5 **Haue not I slaine a Lyon alreadie with a staffe?** See 142.29–32.

6 **well disposed of bodie** of a good physical constitution.

7 *Florendos* **hauing not as yet behelde him . . . suddainlie touched him** Unexpected meeting of father and son (motif N731; see Bordman, 68, and Bueno Serrano, "Índice," 823).

8 **this night therefore you must obserue the religious watch . . . and put the spurre on your heele my selfe** The night before his dubbing the would-be knight had to "spend the night waking in prayer and contemplation," as described in Keen, 10; the presentation of spurs is also part of the ritual (Keen, 7; cf. Cervantes, I.iii.60–61); "religious watch" translates the Fr. "la veille" (C8v; *vigil*).

9 **they which found me amongst the Palme Trees . . . the name of** *Palmerin* See 135.30–31.

10 **awaiting nowe but the howre to be discharged of the burden** This clause is a vague translation of the Fr. "de trop grand' regret je meurs en moy mesmes cent fois le jour" (C8v; *of great regret I die within myself one hundred times a day*).

11 **his Dwarffe called** *Vrbanillo* **. . . euerie one that saw him laughed hartilie** Dwarfs are familiar characters from medieval chivalric literature (motif F535; see Bordman, 38) and also populate the Iberian romances (motif F451 and ff.; see Bueno Serrano, "Índice," 707–9). In the case of Urbanillo, he is deformed and ugly, as well as loyal, resourceful, and exemplary. His very name presents Urbanillo as "the model of chivalric urbanity," as Daniels argues (29), although he becomes the laughing stock of the court. The following articles analyze the presence of dwarfs in Peninsular chivalric texts: Bueno Serrano, "Motivos literarios de la representación de la violencia en los libros de caballerías castellanos (1508–1514): Enanos, doncellas y dueñas anónimas," in *Actes del X Congrés Internacional de l'Associació Hispànica de Literatura Medieval*, ed. Rafael Alemany, Josep Lluís Martós, and Josep Miquel Manzanaro (Alicante: Institut Interuniversitari de Filologia Valenciana, 2005), 1:441–52; José Manuel Lucía Megías and Emilio

José Sales Dasí, "La otra realidad social en los libros de caballerías castellanos: 1. Los enanos," *Rivista di Filologia e Letterature Ispaniche* 5 (2002): 9–23; see also O'Connor, 59–71.

Chapter 15

1 **the Armour of *Gamezio* should bee brought . . . as you haue heard before** See 113.30–34. Note the use of the verb *to hear* (instead of *to read*), which suggests that an aural transmission of this text, or part thereof, was considered a likely possibility by the English translator. Malory's *Le Morte Darthur*, another romance text of comparable length, also anticipated an aural transmission as has argued Joyce Coleman, "Reading Malory in the Fifteenth Century: Aural Reception and Performance Dynamics," *Arthuriana* 13 (2003): 48–70.

2 **to the best Knight of his time** Fr. "au meilleur Cheualier de l'Orient" (D1v; *to the best knight of the Orient*).

3 **Azier** Fr. "acier" (D1v; *steel*).

4 **And if you desire to know whence . . . he hath neuer seene you** As Galigani (261–62) argues, this sentence misinterprets the Fr.: "& si vous mande, qu'il vous a en honneur & reputacion, comme celui duquel il a preueu l'excellence, sçachant plus de voz propres affaires que vous mémes, encores qu'il ne vous ait onques veu" (D1v; *and he sends it* [i.e., a shield], *he who holds you in honor and reputation, as one whose excellence he has foreseen, knowing more than yourself about your own affairs, even though he has never seen you*). The origin of the mistake lies in the mistranslation of the verb form *mande*, which Munday seems to read like a form of *to demand* and is rendered as *desire to know*. Because of this initial mistake, Munday invents the second part of the sentence to agree with his interpretation.

5 ***Palmerin* on his knee before the Prince, who taking the Sworde that sometimes belonged to *Gamezio*, Knighted him** As is the case with Amadis (Munday, *Amadis*, I.v.40) and Galahad (*Lancelot-Grail*, 6:2), Palmerin is knighted by his unknown father; cf. Patchell, 30.

6 **aduised himself** This verbal phrase mistranslates the Fr. "se mist à le contempler [i.e., the shield]" (D2r; *he observed it [i.e., the shield]*), since the reflexive form of the verb *to advise* means not "to look at," but "to bethink oneself; take thought, consider, reflect" (*OED* s.v. *advise*, v. 5), also another sense of the Fr. *contempler*, but not the one valid in this context.

7 **the same marke which the Ladie had, that appeared to him in his sleepe** See 140.26–28.

8 **she will not cease to follow and finde me out** In the Fr. it is Palmerin who promises to search for the Lady: "je fay vœu presentement ne cesser jamais d'aller & chercher, jusques à ce que je l'aye trouuée & parlé à elle" (D2r; *I vow at present*

never to stop searching for her until I find her and talk to her). Notwithstanding Munday's alteration of the Fr. at this point, in the English translation Palmerin is the one who goes in search of the Lady.

9 **humour** The concept of *humour* refers to an understanding of the functioning of the human body, both physiological and psychological, as based on four essential bodily fluids, namely blood (hot and moist), phlegm (cold and moist), yellow bile or choler (hot and dry), and black bile (cold and dry), that could determine and explain certain kinds of human afflictions and behavior.

Chapter 16

1 **on the last daie of** *Aprill* Fr. "le dernier jour d'Auril" (D2r; *the last day of April*). The date in the English and French departs from the ambiguous Sp. "dos días de passar el mes de abril" (42; *at two days of passing the month of April*), which could mean the 3rd or 29th of April, or the 3rd of May (cf. Bueno Serrano, "Las tres *fadas*," 143).

2 **the night ouertooke him** This is the night of April 30, so the encounter of Palmerin with the Serpent happens on May Day. Bueno Serrano ("Las tres *fadas*," 142–43) suggests that in the Celtic calendar May Day corresponds to Beltane, a festival with which it seems more natural to associate the three fairies; Bueno Serrano also argues that the mountain Artifaria could be understood as a passage to the Other World. Moreover, she adds, "Según las creencias populares, entre las virtudes del agua de mayo está curar las cicatrices de la cara y las enfermedades de la piel, como necesita Primaleón" ("Las tres *fadas*," 143).

3 **the greene Hearbes** Munday decides to leave out crude details, since in the Fr. the Serpent was not lying only on "greene Hearbes," but also on "ossemens, tant d'hommes que de bestes qu'il auoit deuorez" (D2v; *skeletons, both of men and of beasts he had devoured*); cf. Galigani, 278.

4 **commending himselfe to God** Once again Munday avoids referring to the sign of the cross, which has open Catholic connotations; cf. Fr., "fit le signe de la croix" (D2v; *made the sign of the cross*).

5 **let the one encourage thee . . . when thou offerest to retire** Munday rephrases the dilemma honor vs. shame by composing a parallel construction to emphasize the antithesis between these two social values; see Galigani, 276.

6 **binding vppe his woundes so well as he could** Munday leaves out lurid details about the serious wounds suffered by Palmerin, who "tomba de l'autre costé, sans espoir de plus longue vie" (D2v; *fell on the other side with no hope of living any longer*).

7 **he seemed to see the three Sisters whereof wee haue spoken before** See 145.35–36. Note, however, that Palmerin does not physically see the three Sis-

ters ("he *seemed* to see," my emphasis), but instead he has a vision of them in his dream; cf. motif D1731.2.1.: *Fairy seen in dream*. See Bueno Serrano, "Las tres fadas," 149–50.

8 **the whole Empire wherof is predestinated thine** In the series of prophetic dreams that Palmerin had (see chap. I.12), he learns that he is predestined to be crowned, although his kingdom is not mentioned. The three Sisters now complete the information. The three Sisters, or "Goddesses of destinie" are reminiscent of "las Parcas romanas, las Moiras griegas, las Nornas de la mitología germánico-escandinava como responsables del destino del hombre" (Bueno Serrano, "Las tres *fadas*," 145).

9 **his Ladie *Polinarda*, (who so manie times saluted him in his Dreames)** The third sister reveals the name of the Lady of the Fountain that Palmerin sees in his dreams, viz. Polinarda. The three gifts are an instance of motif F341.1. *Fairies give three gifts*, all of them of significant narrative import.

Chapter 17

1 **hee went vp higher on the Mountain, thinking to see the Fountaine, but he could not** It remains unexplained in Munday's version why Palmerin is unable to see the Fountain. But in the Fr. we learn at the end of the previous chapter that the three Sisters agree "que desormais elle soit inuisible à tous autres" (D3r; *that from then on the fountain will be invisible to all others*).

2 **my religious enterprise** Fr. "la queste que j'ay entreprise" (D3r; *the quest that I have embarked on*). Munday adds a supposed religious component to Palmerin's quest.

3 **it is not to be demanded** The verb *to demand* as used in this context was actually a common false friend; see *OED* s.v. *demand*, v. 3: "to ask for (a thing) peremptorily [. . .]. † But formerly often weakened into a simple equivalent of 'to ask' (*esp.* in transl. from French, etc.)."

Chapter 18

1 **he fel from his Horse deade to the ground** Munday omits gruesome details from the Fr.: "luy passa la lance au trauers du corps" (D3v; *he drove the lance through his body*).

2 **as he by his Godhead hath made me breath this ayre, though weake and sicklie** This clause departs significantly from its correspondent text in the Fr.: "ainsi qu'il voulut descendre du ciel en terre pour me donner la vie spirituelle" (D3v; *just as he wanted to descend from heaven to earth to give me spiritual life*).

3 **the greefe I haue sustained for . . . such a long and lingering extreamitie** Primaleon's illness is caused by "the sorrow of my Sonne *Florendos*" (154.42–155.1).

By contrast, in the context of the Sp. original, Bueno Serrano, "Las tres *fadas*," 138, suggests, "Primaleón ha enfermado por el dolor de conocer el adulterio de su hijo Florendos con Griana"; such motivation is not warranted by the English translation.

Chapter 19

1 *Durace* The city of Durazzo in modern Albania; cf. 492.41–42, where Durace appears associated with Albania.

2 *Mecaena* Fr. "Messine" (D4v; *Messina*); Messina, a city in the island of Sicily.

3 **the Cittie of** *Mizzara* Probably the city Mazzara del Vallo in the island of Sicily.

4 **if this were shee the three Sisters spake of . . . promised him in his sleeping visions** For the two episodes mentioned, see respectively 152.29–31 and 140.17–141.4.

5 **hee was troden to death with the trampling of the Horses** Munday omits gory details, as he does throughout the book: "il luy creuerent le cueur au ventre" (D6r; *they destroyed the heart in his body*).

6 **goe meet** *Palmerin* **and** *Ptolome*, **whome embracing hee thus entertained. Ah good Knights** A passage from the Fr. is missing, most likely due to a mechanical error of either Munday or the compositors, as a result of which the point of resumption is mistaken: after finishing translating or composing the English text corresponding to the Fr. "sortirent pour receuoir Palmerin" (D6r; *they came out to welcome Palmerin*), the English text then moves to the next occurrence of the word *Palmerin* some ten lines below ("disant à Palmerin: Ah bon Cheualier!"; D6r, *telling Palmerin: Ah, good knight*), thus omitting all intervening words.

7 **let heauen haue the honour of our victory** This clause is Munday's interpolation.

Chapter 20

1 **your diuine perfections** Munday adds the *diuine* dimension to Laurana; Fr. "vostre grande beauté" (D6v; *your great beauty*). Cf. Galigani, 275.

2 **doo not so degenerate from gentle nature, as to kill him that gaue you life** This clause includes a moral judgment ("degenerate from gentle nature") that is absent from the Fr.: "ne soyez cause d'vn tel malheur qui auiendroit, s'il perdoict ainsi la vie" (D6v; *don't be the cause of such misfortune, which would strike if he lost his life thus*).

3 **beeing my duetie and his desert** This phrase is Munday's interpolation.

4 **I will doo for his welfare what I may with modestie** In this clause Munday introduces changes that tone down the erotic implications of the Fr., "je ferai tout ce qu'il voudra" (D6v; *I'll do everything he wishes*).

5 **when one hath so far ventured in loue ... giue ouer so faire a beginning** Palmerin seems hesitant about turning his back on Laurana, in spite of being fully aware of her identity and thus of his likely disloyalty to Polinarda (cf. also the opening of chap. I.xxi). The Sp. version is more explicit in presenting Palmerin's attitude as unfaithful: "¿qué haré, que mucho me ha vencido la fermosura d'esta donzella?" (51; *what shall I do, now that the beauty of this damsel* [i.e., Laurana] *has overcome me?*). Palmerin's feelings are reproved by Polinarda in Urbanillo's dream, or rather, nightmare (see note 7 below).

6 **I long to impart our affections togeather ... I shall not faile to expect his presence** Munday tempers the explicitness of Laurana's invitation in the Fr.: "j'ay moyen à ceste heure de contenter ses affections en toutes les sortes qu'il sçauroit demander: & s'il luy plaist se trouuer demain à l'heure de minuict en ma chambre, je l'attendray seule" (D7r; *at this time I have the means of satisfying his desires in every way that he could ask: if he is willing to be in my bedroom tomorrow at midnight, I shall wait for him alone*).

7 **one of the fayrest Ladies that euer eye lookt on ... *Polinarda* had made thys threatning to the Dwarffe for *Laurana*** Once again Polinarda appears in a dream and vents all her anger not on Palmerin but instead on Urbanillo, whom she admonishes vehemently for his direct involvement in the sentimental dealings of his master with Laurana. González, when discussing Urbanillo's dream ("Sueños," 227–32), explains that Polinarda's maneuver is typical of a jealous courtly lover. In the dream she first threatens Urbanillo and then compares her social rank with that of Laurana by saying, "*Palmerin* his fortunes climbes higher then the name of *Laurana*" (162.43–163.1); in other words, Polinarda's and Palmerin's social standing (i.e., of royal descent) is superior to Laurana's (i.e., of ducal descent).

8 **when shee and *Palmerin* should conferre togeather of their loue** Munday substitutes an unobjectionable clause for a more suggestive line in the Fr.: "car elle s'atendoit tenir la nuit prochaine Palmerin entre ses braz" (D7v; *since she was hoping to have Palmerin in her arms the following day*); see Galigani, 283–84.

9 **rather would she entertaine her own death ... she thus breathed foorth her sorrow** Laurana falls in a contradiction, since she first makes known her intention to keep the secret of her love for Palmerin, but right away reveals it to her mother. Her threat of suicide is reminiscent of a similar incident involving Lancelot, in which case the damsel, Elaine of Ascolat, does die of unrequited love (cf. Malory, XVIII.xix.529–30).

Chapter 21

1 **a Caskette, wherein was one of the best Swordes ... the worthiest Knight liuing** This is an occurrence of the motif *recognition by unique ability to dislodge sword* (motif H31.1), famous from the Arthurian legend; cf. the episode as narrated by Malory, I.iii-vii.35–39); see Bordman, 46, and Bueno Serrano, "Índice," 734. For a debasement of this motif, see 522.22–29.

2 *Sclauonye* It refers to the territories of eastern Europe populated by the Slavs.

3 **two miles** Fr. "trois lieuës" (D8v; *three leagues*); Sp. "más de dos leguas" (54; *more than two leagues*).

4 **so laying hande valiantlie on the Sword, without any great labor he drew it foorth** Cf. how Arthur in Malory is said to have "pulled it out easily" (I.vi.38). This incident is one further indication that Palmerin is destined to become a great hero and ruler.

5 *Rome* Fr. "la Romanie" (E1r; *Romania*); Sp. "Romania" (55; *Romania*).

Chapter 22

1 **and haue sette so manie inchaunted spels on that Sword** This clause is Munday's interpolation.

2 **(beeing as yet but tenne yeeres olde) ... hath not consumated the marriage** Being only ten years old, she fails to comply with the minimun age of marriage for girls, which was established at twelve years in contemporary England. It is, however, surprising that the giant observes this one human law.

3 **and honorable for euer vnto your owne selfe** This phrase is Munday's addition.

4 **Giants doo take a habit in trecherous dealinges** Chivalric literature is populated by giants, who form an integral part of the adventures befalling romance heroes, and Palmerin seems to be familiar with their treacherous nature; see motif F531ff. (Bordman, 35–38 and Bueno Serrano, "Índice," 710–14). For a discussion of their role in English Renaissance romances, see O'Connor, 62–67.

5 **on the next morning after they were armed** Munday here leaves out that "les deux Cheualiers furent ouyr messe" (E1v; *the two knights went to hear Mass*), most probably because of the Catholic associations of such an action.

6 **villainous, traiterous, and disloyall** Munday amplifies the Fr. "desloyautez" (E1v; *disloyal acts*) by means of these three adjectives (see Galigani, 272–73); moreover, Munday interpolates the clause **I will make him confesse vnder my Sworde** (169.24), with no equivalent in Fr.

7 **vnlesse you are willing to leaue your heade for a signe to our Gates** Darmaco's squire addresses Palmerin with the haughtiness and disdain typical of giants; cf.

below how the narrator describes the speeches of the giant Mordano as **these rough wordes of his enemie** (170.7); see José Julio Martín Romero, "'¡O captivo cavallero!' Las palabras del gigante en los textos caballerescos," *Nueva Revista de Filología Hispánica* 54 (2006): 20–21.

8 **he encountred *Mordano* with such courage ... ran towardes the Castell and *Palmerin* after him** The description of this combat is notably reduced by Munday; cf. Fr. sig. E2r.

9 **and other weapons** Munday uses this unspecific term possibly because he is unsure about the translation of the Fr. "vouges" (E2r; *pikes*).

10 **the onelie Knight for prowesse in the worlde** I.e., the best knight in the world on account of his prowes*s*.

11 **continued in earnest and deuoute orisons** The prayers of Esmerinda's mother are more explicit in Fr.: "implorant l'ayde & secours de nostre Seigneur Iesus Christ" (E2v; *begging for the help and succor of our Lord Jesus Christ*).

Chapter 23

1 **The Horse feeling his Maister from his backe ... patrons of his villainous life** As O'Connor comments, "Darmaco dies ignominiously as he is dragged and kicked by his horse" (66). It was to be expected that giants should die a shameful death, due in part to "the widespread assumption that they are allied to devils [as happens in the case of Darmaco, the devils being "the patrons of his villainous life"], and that may explain in part why they are so often laughed at" (O'Connor, ibid.). Giants were treated comically already in medieval literature, for which see Jeffrey Jerome Cohen, *Of Giants: Sex, Monsters, and the Middle Ages* (Minneapolis, MN: University of Minnesota Press, 1999), 156–59.

2 **Mace** Fr. "lance" (E3r; *spear*).

3 **to sende her packing after her Husbande** Munday leaves out a gruesome piece of information: "luy mist l'espée au ventre" (E3r; *he plunged the sword into her belly*).

4 **short tale to make** Munday actually summarizes the action, not only in this instance but throughout the entire chapter.

5 **she bringing the Sheelde and the Helmet when *Florendos* knighted him** See 149.23–25.

Chapter 24

1 The opening of this chapter combines two popular motifs: K2221 *treacherous rival lover* (Dyardo and Domarto love the same woman), and K2100 *false accusation* (Domarto accuses Dyardo of planning to poison his cousin the king); see Bordman, 57–58, and Bueno Serrano, "Índice," 789–90, 792).

2 **slacked** I.e., "spent wastefully," as explains John Jowett in *Sir Thomas More*, 205 n. to line VII.14.

3 **This needelesse exordium haue I made . . . in breefe my Lord, this is the summe** This rhetorically elaborate sentence is Munday's interpolation.

4 *Lesae Maiestatis* Munday prefers the more archaic Latin to the contemporary Fr. "leze Majesté" (E5v).

5 **Thou lyest Traytor in thy throate** Fr. "Tu as menty" (E5v; *you have lied*); Munday expands the Fr. for alliterative effect; cf. Galigani, 277.

6 **Ile** This cliticisation of "I will" becomes widespread around 1600; see Roger Lass, "Phonology and Morphology," in *CHEL*, 179.

7 **and beate better gouernment into your pate with this sword that likes you not** This clause is interpolated by Munday.

8 **nor did the Countie faile to maintaine his wordes openlie, offering to make it good in fight . . . goe arme themselues, because hee intended that day to see the Combat fought** In view of the accusation of treason levelled at Dyardo and Cardonia by Domarto, a trial by combat is called for ("offering to make it [i.e., the accusation] good in fight," 176.24–25). These events correspond to a "judicial *iudicium dei*—a judicial process designed to obtain proof by a direct verdict of God," as defined by Robert Bartlett, *Trial by Fire and Water: The Medieval Judicial Ordeal* (Oxford: Clarendon Press, 1986), 115; and the combat is organized precisely to obtain such proof: "the proofe shall manifest that must be made" (178.4). Munday first leaves out a direct appeal to God ("receiue the reward belongs to disloyall Traitors," (177.37); Fr. "auec l'ayde de Dieu," E5v; *with God's help*), but next makes an explicit remark, "that I referre to God to recompence" (177.39), thus confirming divine intervention in this conflict's resolution (or "tryall," 177.26). A common practice in medieval Europe, trial by combat declined throughout the fifteenth century, although in the sixteenth "charges of treason were settled by trial by battle" (Bartlett, op. cit., 108) and aristocrats still settled their disputes by means of the duel of chivalry. Any of the litigants could offer a proxy under certain circumstances, including old age (the case of Prince Adrian, although he renounces such possibility), youth (the case of Dyardo, who has not "yet receiued the order of Knighthoode," 176.41), and womanhood (the case of Cardonya); consequently, they entreat Palmerin to be their champion. In the following chapter the trial proceeds in a ritualized manner and in likeness of a judicial court with judges.

Notwithstanding its historical demise, the judicial combat remained alive in literature, particularly in chivalric texts from all over Europe, as best exemplified by the story of Amicus et Amelius, available in different versions in many European languages. For the presence of this motif (no. H218) in other chivalric texts, see Bordman, 48, and Bueno Serrano, "Índice," 740; for the story of Amicus et Amelius, see the discussion in MacEdward Leach, ed., *Amis and Amiloun*, EETS os 203 (London: Oxford University Press, 1937), lxxix–lxxxiv.

Chapter 25

1 **All this while *Ptolome* had good play . . . by killing his aduersarie** Munday prunes the fight between Ptolome and Edward and prefers to center his attention on Palmerin's combat.

2 **the Emperours Court of *Allemaigne*** This reference loosely signals to the Holy Roman Emperor.

3 **Cabalist or Magitian . . . Callender of most honourable byrthes** This passage is introduced by Munday; in the Fr. Adrian is knowledgeable in "Geomence, Negromance, & telles sciences noires" (E7r; *geomancy, necromancy, and such dark sciences*).

4 **hee was desirous to contract a marriage . . . presenting her to him in his visions, as hath beene declared** See 140.15–141.4. Adrian's revelations have serious narrative implications, since they suggest that the love between Palmerin and Polinarda is not as pure as one might think. Rather than being destined to love each other, the two lovers are puppets in the hands of the magitian Adrian, who has manipulated Palmerin's feelings and prevented him from exploring his own affections, as in the case of Laurana.

5 ***Ymanes*** Possibly Mainz.

Chapter 26

1 **into endlesse perdition** This phrase is interpolated by Munday.

2 **with his sworde he parted hys head from his bodie** Patchell cites the end of the fight between the Enchanted Knight and Palmerin as an example of how the heroes in the Palmerin cycle of romances can be "merciless in dealing with him [i.e., an enemy], even to the point of brutality" (74). One should note, however, that Palmerin is not gratuitously inflicting violence on the Enchanted Knight, but rather trying to defeat this dangerous enemy who has received "the ayde of deuils and euill spirits" (183.29).

3 **the three Magicall Sisters . . . what promises they made him** Here the text refers to the promise made by the second Sister, who cast a spell protecting Palmerin against any evil enchantment. See 152.26–28

Chapter 27

1 **what gratious gifts the three fatall Sisters . . . her to whom he was destenied, so soone as she behelde him** This is the gift offered by the third sister; see 152.28–32

2 **are you bothe agreed Ladies, said *Palmerin*?** In the Fr. this question is posed by Polinarda's mother: "ne le voulez vous pas ainsi tous deux?" (F1r; *don't the two of you want it this way?*).

3 **his venomed arrowes** This phrase is not in the Fr.

4 **beeing yet but tender of yeeres** Fr. "aagée peut estre de quinze ans" (F1r: *perhaps fifteen years of age*).

5 **sent to desire his companie to the Chappell** Fr. "aller ouir messe en la grand Eglise" (F1v: *go to hear mass in the great Church*). This is a case of religious censorship; cf. Galigani, 281.

6 **and breathed so many sighes . . . heauen to him to be in these passions** This passage is added by Munday.

7 **the promise made mee by olde *Adrian*, who boasted to knowe so much of my fortunes** See 181.12–23.

8 ***Palmerin* resolue thy selfe suddainlie to die . . . and thy selfe eased** Palmerin's lovesickness manifests itself in violent emotional distress that puts him on the verge of committing suicide. As Patchell explains, Palmerin experiences a "conflict between hope and despair, between ecstatic love and insupportable grief" (57; see also 59, 62).

9 **proceedes from the diuine lookes . . . as I must die because I loue too deerlie** This passage is introduced by Munday. Note the adjective *diuine*, previously used for Griana and her love for Florendos; cf. 122.14 and 122.29.

10 **when in the like case I ventured to sollicite your looue to *Laurana*** See chap. I.xx.

11 **with what feare the deformed felow gaue it foorth** This phrase is introduced by Munday, who also adds the alliterative effect; see Galigani, 277.

12 **if she that smote thee in thy sleepe bee that *Polinarda*** See 163.2–5.

13 **I wil gadge my life to gaine you the Ladie** Munday introduces the alliterative effect; see Galigani, 277.

Chapter 28

1 **the Dwarff entred, whose badde shaped body and face, made them all fall a laughing** In the Peninsular romances dwarfs become the object of ridicule; see O'Connor, 60–62.

2 **I promised thee *Vrbanillo*, not to conceiue ill . . . the effecte is conformable to thy protestations** Polinarda shows great self-assurance in both her attitude (above we read, "could she so well commaunde her thoughts," 191.15–16) and her words. As argues Petruccelli, Polinarda "bajo su frágil apariencia, encubre decisión y fortaleza ante los titubeos de Palmerín" (310). This position of female power contrasts with the disempowerment Palmerin experiences as a result of his protracted lovesickness. For the male implications of lovesickness, see Dawson, *Lovesickness and Gender*, esp. 5–7.

3 **which courtesie can no waie impeache your honour** This clause is Munday's interpolation.

4 **my seuerall apparitions . . . are predestinations ordeyned to mee by your gracious prescience** Note that Palmerin is inattentive to Adrian's meddling with his infatuation for Polinarda, but instead favors the idea that himself and Polinarda are genuinely destined for each other.

5 **prograce** I.e., progress, "to travel ceremoniously, as a royal, noble, or official personage" (*OED*, s.v. *progress* v. 1). This unusual spelling is also found in the manuscript version of *Sir Thomas More*, XVII.128 (see the editor's note to this line on 326).

6 **Scaffolds and other prouision** Fr. "lices" (F4r: *lists*). Next, the preparations for the tournament are described, with the scaffolds for ladies and other onlookers. Tournaments are a recurrent event in the Spanish chivalric romances (see Patchell, 30–31). This tournament is presented as a form of public entertainment in which safety measures are adopted, including barriers and blunted swords; see Keen, 205.

7 **to contemplate theyr sweete and affable desires** This clause departs from the Fr. "pour faire les petis larrecins amoureux" (F4r; *to do amorous petty thefts*); Munday is toning down the possible erotic implications of the Fr.

8 **then well may I esteeme my selfe vnworthie** This clause is Munday's interpolation.

9 **vndeserued grace** This noun phrase is added by Munday.

10 **deliuered with manie a bitter sigh** Munday adds these words for dramatic effect.

11 **vnspotted** As happens in the case of Griana and Florendos (105.42), Munday chooses the same adjective to describe the love between Palmerin and Polinarda, thus dispelling any moral doubt about their relationship.

12 **and the euening dewe was dangerous** This clause is introduced by Munday. See how below we read, "euening dewe did great harme to his woundes" (242.29–30).

Chapter 29

1 **in the windowe** Fr. "dans l'eschafaut des Dames" (F5r; *on the Ladies' scaffold*).

2 **marking his Sheelde, she behelde in a Sable fielde, a Siluer hand fast closed** This is the shield Palmerin received on the occasion of his being knighted (149.25–27). Now we have more information: the background surface of the shield is black and the hand is made of silver.

3 **courses and loftie poynts** Fr. "courses & voltiges" (F5r; *races and acrobatics*).

4 **their braueries likewise ended to their Ladies** I.e., having ended the displays of courage meant for their ladies.

5 **As I am** I.e., I am likewise happy.

6 **she tooke a chayne of Gold ... hath power to commaunde mee** This exchange contains elements proper to the prisoner-of-love motif, although Polinarda purports to tie Palmerin to the service of her father the emperor; cf. Daniels, 7.

7 **their eyes dooing their office, and carrying betweene them the message of their passions, yet so discreetlie shaddowed as none could perceiue them** Here again we have the lovers resorting to communicating their feelings using *verba visibilia*; cf. n. 5 to chap. I.ii.

8 **a breefe report wherof may very wel serue** Munday indeed condenses the remainding days of the tournament, although the action is of little narrative relevance since Palmerin takes no part in it. One significant piece of information is missing in the translation, namely, that the Duke of Lorraine "desiroit grandement auoir pour femme Polinarde" (F6v; *greatly wished to have Polinarda as his wife*).

9 **the Duke of *Lorrayne* had great familiaritie ... the false treason of the County of *Ormeque*** See 180.9–34.

Chapter 30

1 **my Goddesse** Munday turns Polinarda into a goddess to the eyes of Palmerin; the notion of divinity attached to Polinarda is not so explicit in the Fr.

2 **night Mantle** Its meaning does not exactly correspond to the Fr. "couurechef" (F7v; "sorte de voile complétant la coiffure féminine," Huguet, s.v. *couvrechef*).

3 **he remayned silent a long time, not able to speake a worde** Fr. "demoura comme transy, sans qu'il eust sçeu dire vn seul mot" (F7v; *he remained as in a trance, without even saying a word*). Galigani thinks it possible "che il nostro traduttore [i.e., Munday] non afferrasse il significato della parola 'transi' e la sostituisse con la parola che sembrava ovvia" (259). Munday's command of French was certainly very high, hence it seems unlikely that he failed to grasp the meaning of *transi* ("Être transporté hors de soi," see Huguet, s.v. *transir*); instead Munday did not think it necessary to find a semantic equivalent.

4 **where I was preordained to loue, my Starre hath appointed it** This clause is Munday's interpolation.

5 **therefore to be buried in your heauenly opinion** This clause is not a direct translation of the corresponding passage in the Fr.: "qu'il [i.e., Palmerin's desire] pourroit meriter quelque priuauté de vous" (F7v; *that it might deserve some kindness from you*). Probably Munday is once again censoring Palmerin's advances because of the seeming sexual overtones, while highlighting the purity of the characters' relationship by using the adjective *heauenly*. This change, next, allows Munday to depart from the Fr. when reading that the more *priuauté* she offers him "plus grande seroit l'obligation, non l'affection" (ibid.; *the greater would be the duty, not the affection*); instead the subtle distinction of his source is subsumed by Munday into an all-encompassing statement: **the more am I bounde both in duetie and affection** (200.14–15).

6 **luke-warme blood of his hart** This noun phrase is interpolated by Munday.

7 **behelde the Character thereon as you haue hearde before** See 140.25–28.

8 **which agreed with hers in perfect likelihoode** The Fr. reads, "laquelle estoit couuerte de ses cheueux" (F8r; *which was covered by his locks*).

9 **kisses on his amiable Charracter. The like louing salutation** Here Munday censors a passage from the Fr. in which Polinarda offers to satisfy Palmerin's sexual desires, although he manages to resist the temptation: "Ce qu'elle pouuoit facilement faire . . . ce que Palmerin luy promist" (F8v).

10 **and longer would they haue there continued . . . the day light preuent yee, and so discredite you all?** The light of day marks the end of lovers' secret encounters, since they can no longer move unobserved. This particular topic becomes the focus of attention of the Old French lyric compositions know as *aubes*, in which the lovers "voice their emotions as the watchman blows upon his horn to announce the approach of day," Urban T. Holmes, Jr., *A History of Old French Literature from the Origins to 1300* (New York: Crofts, 1938), 197. Here Urbanillo performs the role of the watchman.

11 **the successe of their loue you shall vnderstande heereafter . . . wee will returne a while to another discourse** This entire passage is interpolated by Mun-

day in order to engage his audience's interest in the relationship of the romance's protagonist, despite having censored a significant part of it.

Chapter 31

1 **reuiewing** This is the first occurrence of the verb *review* according to the *OED* (sense 5a).

2 *Atropos* **the mortall Goddesse** In Greek mythology Atropos ("Inflexible") is one of the three Fates, in charge of the destiny of humans. In particular Atropos is the most terrible of the three, since she decides the moment of every individual's death; see Mark P. O. Morford, Robert J. Lenardon, and Michael Sham, *Classical Mythology* (Oxford: Oxford University Press, 2011), 130. Lewes is therefore suggesting that the old Duke of Burgundy should meet his death shortly, thus legitimizing his desires. The narrative tension is caused by the motif T121.2. *unequal marriage: old man and young girl* (cf. Bordman, 92, and Bueno Serrano, "Índice," 911) or, in other words, by ignoring the wisdom in contemporary proverbs, e.g., "like blood, like good, and like age make the happiest marriage" (Tilley, B465).

3 **then liue with a Saint of so rare perfections** This clause is introduced by Munday and substitutes for the Fr. "qu'obeir à Venus pour si grande beauté" (G1v; *than to obey Venus because of such great beauty* [i.e., that of the Duchess]). Munday suppresses how in the Fr. the contemplation of female beauty may arouse romantic passions (implied in the allusion to Venus, goddess of love in classical Rome). Instead he prefers to underscore the Duchess's supposed probity by describing her as a saint, although one would be hard-pressed to consider the Duchess a saint in view of her response to Lewes's proposal; cf. Patchell, 66–67.

4 **Fortune should haue foullie denied me: for such is my religion in looue, as better death then discontent** This passage is Munday's and departs from the Fr. The danger of adultery worries Munday, who in the rest of the chapter makes further changes to highlight the immorality of Lewes's proposition and to condemn it, as he does below when stating, **to violate chaste wedlocke is so monstrous** (203.35–36; it has no equivalent in the Fr.).

Chapter 32

1 **as bright** *Cynthia* **from the goodliest star in the firmament** This clause is Munday's interpolation. Cynthia, another name for Diana, is the goddess of the moon, thus explaining literally the quoted text; cf. 493.34. But Cynthia is also the goddess of chastity; see Morford et al., *Classical Mythology*, 216–17. To draw an analogy between Cynthia and the Duchess of Burgundy seems therefore questionable and is a clear indication that Lewes's judgment is blinded by love.

2 a statelie monument Fr. "perron" (G2v; Huguet, s.v. *perron* n., "Pierre où un chevalier écrivait un défi"). In 1606 Jean Nicot, in his *Thrésor de la langue francoyse, tant ancienne que moderne*, defined *perron* "comme vne base quarrée, esleuée sur terre de cinq ou six pieds de haut, ou plus (terme vsité és Romans anciens) où les Cheualiers errants pendoyent ou affichoyent leurs emprinses pour s'essayer aux estranges & faëes aduentures. Il estoit fait pour la plus part de marbre ou d'autre pierre, ou bien de fer ou d'autre metail . . . les cheualiers anciennement en vn festin royal ou court planiere, ou autre grande assemblé de haut court, vsoient de ceste assiete de perrons en vn pas de combat"; a facsimile edition of the 1621 edition is available from the Fondation Singer-Polignac (Paris: A. et J. Picard, 1960); for a discussion, see also Sydney Anglo, "L'arbre de chevalerie et le perron dans les tournois," in *Les fêtes de la Renaissance*, ed. Jean Jacquot and Elie Konigson (Paris: Centre nationale de la recherche scientifique, 1975), 283–98, esp. 296–98. Cf. Patchell, 31–32. For a discussion of the presence and uses of *perrons* in the Iberian romances of chivalry, see Stefano Neri, "Algunos apuntes sobre los 'padrones' en los libros de caballerías," in *Il mondo cavalleresco tra immagine e texto (Trento, Castello del Buon Consiglio, 20–22 novembre 2008)*, edited by Claudia Dematté (Trento: Università degli Studi di Trento, 2010), 115–33.

3 I will make good my words by deedes of Armes . . . all Knights willing thus to aduenture, shall be heere receiued The challenge Lewes proposes is actually a *pas d'armes* or passage of arms. A *pas d'armes* was sponsored by an individual knight, in this case Lewes, although the permission of the promoter's lord was required; the king of France, Lewes's father, grants such permission a posteriori: "you shall not nowe be hindered: doo therefore what your selues thinke expedient" (207.5–6). Participation in a *pas d'armes* was not restricted to guests, as was the case in a round table, but open to all knights ("against anie Knight whatsoeuer," 205.21–22), who engaged in one-to-one combats. In order to increase the prestige of the challenge, it had to be widely publicized ("in regard that none shall pleade ignoraunce, I will aduertise" 205.22–23; "through all the prouinces of Christendome," 205.40–41; cf. 211.12–13), specifying the place ("I will be in open fielde in my Tent," 205.24–25, before the gates of Paris), the date ("the first daie of Maie," 205.23), and the duration ("these eyght daies," 205.35), and making explicit reference to the particular rules of engagement or *chapitres d'armes*, in this case, the weapons used ("he which receiues the foyle with the Launce, shall Combat with the Sworde," 205.37–38) and the rules applying to the provision and placement of ladies' portraits. The defendant or *tenans* proclaimed the joust with the desire of protecting a possession against all comers or *venans*, in this case the property is the Duchess of Burgundy's beauty. Yet the ultimate goal of this conventionalized ritual was to achieve greater individual knightly honor. Next, the Duke of Savoy announces another similar *pas d'armes* but with different rules of engagement. The *pas d'armes* became a *topos* in chivalric literature available to English audiences; see Anthony W. Annunziata, "The *Pas d'Armes* &

its Occurrences in Malory," *Studies in Medieval Culture* 14 (1980): 39–48, 154–56, to which I am indebted for the information in this note. As Annunziata states (42), Malory's Arthuriad contains at least thirty jousts that match the characteristics of a *pas d'armes*. Additionally, it seems likely that the author of the Spanish original found inspiration in historical occurrences of this chivalric activity, about which s/he could have had direct or indirect knowledge of. Martín de Riquer, *Caballeros andantes españoles* (Madrid: Espasa-Calpe, 1967), has pointed out how "la novela caballeresca ... refleja una auténtica realidad social, sin desfigurarla ni exagerarla," and adds that "caballeros reales e históricos estaban, a su vez, intoxicados de literatura y actuaban de acuerdo con lo que habían leído en los libros de caballerías" (12). The best-known example of a historical passage of arms in the Iberian Peninsula is that of the knight Suero de Quiñones, which took place in 1434 near the Orbigo bridge. This passage, chronicled by Pe[d]ro Rodríguez de Lena and preserved in a number of sixteenth-century manuscripts, was certainly the one that became more widely known in contemporary Spain, and could have served as inspiration for the author of *Palmerín de Olivia*, as argued by Lilia E. F. de Orduna, "Realidad histórica y edición novelesca. En torno al *Passo Honroso* de Suero de Quiñones, a la literatura caballeresca y al *Quijote* de 1605," *Rivista di Filologia e Letteratura Ispaniche* 2 (1999): 47–65, esp. 52–55. Rodríguez de Lena's *El Passo Honroso de Suero de Quiñones* is edited by Amancio Labandeira Fernández (Madrid: Fundación Universitaria Española, 1977), with selected passages edited with facing English translation in Noel Fallows, *Jousting in Medieval and Renaissance Iberia* (Woodbridge: Boydell, 2010), 399–501. For historical information about the development of the *pas d'armes* in Europe, see Richard Barber, *The Knight and Chivalry*, rev. ed. (Woodbridge: Boydell, 1995), chap. 8.

4 **it shall not be lawfull for me to rest a minute space, but presentlie take him in hande that shall followe** Munday departs from the Fr., "il me sera loysible me refraischir vne heure, deuant qu'entrer au combat contre le suyuant" (G3r; *it will be permissible for me to repose for an hour before fighting against the next one*).

5 **the ending of matters is greater then the beginning** Cf. Tilley, B260.

6 **then anie honor you may winne can please them** This clause is interpolated by Munday.

7 **to the Duke of** *Sauoye* Note that Munday here emends the Fr., which erroneously reads, "le Duc de Loraine" (G3v; *the Duke of Lorraine*).

8 *Horatius ... Agesilaus* **the** *Greeke* Probably Horatius Cocles, legendary Roman hero (6th c. BC), who defended single-handedly the city of Rome against the Etruscans; cf. Valerius, III.ii.1. *Mutius Scaevola* Gaius Mucius Cordus Scaevola, legendary Roman hero, who tried to assassinate the Etruscan king Porsenna in the sixth century BC; Porsenna himself admired Scaevola for his courage; cf. Valerius, III.iii.1. *Marcus Curtius* Roman hero who is said to have sacrificed his

life by plunging himself into a chasm in the Roman Forum in order to save the Roman Republic; cf. Valerius, V.vi.2. *Manlius Torquatus* Probably Titus Manlius Torquatus (4th c. BC), consul and dictator whose military victories earned him legendary fame, with his fortitude and valor exalted in popular stories; he sacrificed his son to uphold military discipline; cf. Valerius, II.vii.6. *Marius* the *Romaine* Cittizen Gaius Marius (ca. 157–86 BC) set the foundations for the Roman professional army; cf. Valerius IX.vii mil. Rom. 1. *Hanniball* the *Carthaginian* Hannibal (247–ca. 182 BC) passed into history as the Carthaginian general who, leading a land expedition from New Carthage in Spain to Italy, defeated the Romans on several occasions but failed to conquer Rome; cf. Valerius, passim, and Munday, *Zelauto*, 48, 54, 139. *Agesilaus* the *Greeke* Agesilaus II (ca. 445–359 BC), king of Sparta that successfully headed an expedition into Asia Minor in 396 BC, supported pro-Spartan interventions that eventually enraged Thebes and Athens and led to his humiliating demise at Leuctra; cf. Valerius, VII.ii, *ext.* 15. Note that all these references to the ancient world were not included in the Sp. original, but instead were added by Maugin and translated by Munday.

9 **if not the vndaunted valour of their minds, deliuered in their deedes of kinglie consequence** In this clause Munday interferes with his source to change it subtly; cf. the Fr. "sinon la magnanimité de leurs cueurs, cogneuë par leurs belliqueux actes" (G3v; *if not the magnanimity of their hearts, known for their warlike acts*).

10 **the Duchesse . . ., beeing manned by the Prince, did not (as I thinke) repent herselfe of her loue** Munday places more responsibility for the adulterous relationship on the Duchess than the Fr., in which she at least attempts to change Lewes's mind: "la Duchesse . . . ne luy [i.e., Lewes] persuadoit . . . de se repentir" (G4r; *the Duchess did not convince Lewes to repent*).

11 **els will perpetuall discontent cut short my date, beeing bereaued of the honour of my greene desires** Munday changes the tenor of the Duchess's words, since the Fr. contains a proposal, —deemed to be indecent by Munday— guaranteeing Lewes that, even if he calls off the *pas d'armes*, she is willing to grant him "ce que plus me sçauriez & voudriez demander, qui est de bien peu de pris, au regard de vostre valeur" (G4r; *the most that you would be able and want most to ask, which is very little recompense compared with your valor*).

12 *baise la main* Fr. "baisé la main" (G4r; *kissed the hand*).

Chapter 33

1 **King of Armes** I.e., the king of heralds; cf. Bradford B. Broughton, *Dictionary of Medieval Knighthood and Chivalry: Concepts and Terms* (New York: Greenwood Press, 1986), 283.

2 **not a worde** Fr. "sans sonner mot" (G4v; *without uttering a word*). In present-day English it would appear necessary to add the word *uttering*, but "Elizabethan authors objected to scarcely any ellipsis, provided the deficiency could be easily supplied from the context"; Abbott, *Grammar*, 279.

3 **concluded the Combat** I.e., he decided to take part in the combat; see *OED*, s.v. *conclude*, v. 14.

4 **perswading him selfe, not in Christendome, nor in the other three habitable parts of the earth** Fr. "n'estimant en la Chrestienté, non pas en toutes les trois parties habitables de la terre" (G4v; *considering that neither in Christendom nor in all the three habitable parts of the earth*). Maugin makes a point of stating that Polinarda's beauty is without compare in the whole world, whereas the Sp. simply reads, "a la fermosura de Polinarda ninguna se podía ygualar" (87; *no one could match Polinarda in beauty*). In doing so, Maugin seems to convey the idea that the world is divided into three parts throughout which Christianity is unevenly distributed. After the discovery of America such world view became obsolete, as can be read in *The Decades of the Newe Worlde or West India* (London, 1555), Richard Eden's translation of Pietro Martire d'Anghiera's *De orbe novo decades*, Gonzalo Oviedo's *Natural hystoria de las Indias* and other works: "The hole globe or compase of the earth was dyuyded by the auncient wryters into three partes, as *Europa, Affrica*, and *Asia* . . . All the reste . . . is discouered of late tyme, as the Weste India cauled the newe worlde, bycause none of the owlde autoures had any knowledge or made any mention therof" (sig. HHh2r); I quote from the facsimile published in March of America Facsimile Series 4 (Ann Arbor: University Microfilms, 1966). In contrast, Munday's translation subtly brings this geographical information up to date by tacitly identifying Christendom with Europe and mentioning three other land masses where Christianity is not the predominant religion. For evidence that Munday's contemporaries believed the world was made up of four parts, see Thomas Blundeville in *M. Blundevile his Exercises, Containing Sixe Teatresis* (London, 1594): "moderne Geographers . . . doe deuide the whole earth but into foure partes, that is to say, *Europe, Afrique, Asia*, and *America*" (sig. Ii7v).

5 **and stay no longer then thou hast good occasion** This clause is Munday's interpolation.

6 **and my sword shal ring on the stoutest Creast, the euer continuing honours of the Emperour of *Allemaigne*** This clause is Munday's interpolation.

7 **but as for your intent to my honor . . . after such applause with your absence** This clause is Munday's addition.

8 **you will needes to *Fraunce*** Already in Middle English, it was a common linguistic feature to find a modal verb without a following infinitive in expressions of motion, as happens in this case. See Rissanen, "Syntax," in *CHEL*, 232–33.

9 **on the seauenteene of Maie** Fr. "le quinziesme jour de May" (G5r; *the fifteenth day of May*). Munday's departure is caused by his desire to agree with the statements made first by Lewes ("the first daie of Maie next ensuing, and seauen daies more immediatlie following," 205.23–24) and next by the Duke of Savoye ("the morrowe after you haue finished your eight daies enterprise . . . and nine daies after," 206.15–20). Note, however, that Munday's calculations are not quite exact, since the correct date would be the eighteenth day of May (Lewes's enterprise ends on the 8th of May; the following day, the 9th, plus nine, adds to the 18th).

10 **because the daie of the Ioustes were at hande** Lack of concord, e.g., the use of a plural verb (*were*) with a singular subject (*daie*) was tolerable in Munday's time. The confusion is caused by the proximity of the plural *Ioustes*. See Abbott, *Grammar*, 298, and Görlach, 121.

11 **who as yet was not departed the Hall** While in Middle English *have* was increasingly the preferred auxiliary for constructing the pluperfect tense, mutative instransitives continue to use *be* in late Middle English and early Modern English. See Mustanoja, 501; and Rissanen, "Syntax," in *CHEL*, 213–5.

12 **Maister of his Horse** "the officer who has the management of the horses belonging to a sovereign or other exalted personage; in England, the title of the third official of the royal household," *OED*, s.v. *master* n. 18c(a); cf. Fr. "Maistre d'hostel" (G5v; *master of the household*).

13 **matter of memorie** matter deserving to be recorded or chronicled; cf. Fr. "auanture digne de memoire" (G5v; *adventure worthy of being remembered*).

14 **peereles** Fr. "perles" (G5v; *pearls*). Munday's *peereles* can be construed as a heteronym equivalent to present day *pearl* (q.v. *OED* for the spelling variant used in our copy-text) and *peerless*.

15 **in religion of this office** I.e., in compliance with my duty as your knight.

16 **I carrie your diuine Image in my soule . . . and so with forced content they louinglie departed** In this passage Munday once again censors the Fr. (G6r), which describes Palmerin's amorous encounter with Polinarda that lasts until dawn, when they say their farewells.

Chapter 34

1 **What happened afterwarde, I leaue to your oppinions, but by the halfe the whole may be discerned** Munday leaves what might have happened between Lewes and the Duchess to the readers' imagination. But in so doing he is censoring a long explicit passage from the Fr. (G6v–G7r) that relates the sexual consummation of these two characters' adultery during two consecutive nights.

The clause **by the halfe the whole may be discerned** is proverbial; see Tilley, H44.

2 **a warning to vndiscreet olde men, that they choose theyr Pantofle fit for their foote** I.e., one should marry his or her equal, or as put in Chaucer's *Miller's Tale*, "man sholde wedde his simylitude" (I.3228), *The Riverside Chaucer*, ed. Larry D. Benson, 3rd ed. (Boston: Houghton Mifflin, 1987), 68. This is also a common motif, J445.2: *foolish marriage of old man and young girl*; T121.2: *unequal marriage: old man and young girl* (Bordman, 51, 92; Bueno Serrano, "Índice," 771, 911).

3 **a goodlie monument of black Marble ... imbossed with golde and pearle** This monument is actually a *perron* "sur lequel il fit assoir le pourtrait de la Duchesse" (G7v; *on which he had placed the portrait of the Duchess*). This information completes that presented in 205.21–42 relating to the challenge issued by Lewes.

4 **Pillers and antique imagerie of Golde** Fr. "chapiteaux antiques" (G7v; *ancient capitals*). It is possible that Munday was not familiar with the Fr. word, since the English cognate *chapitel* is not attested until 1682 (q.v. *OED*).

5 **And nowe** Munday chooses to omit the information provided in the Fr. relating to the Catholic practices of Lewes: "Le landemain le Prince fut ouyr la messe deuant le jour en l'Eglise nostre Dame" (G7v; *the following day the Prince went to hear mass in the Church of our Lady before daybreak*).

6 **ouergrauen with most artificiall flowers** Fr. "tout semé de fleches" (G7v; *all strewn with arrows*).

7 **the Countie *Durcell* of *Arragon*** The personal name *Durcell* in fact refers to a place name as mentioned in the Sp.: "Conde de Urxel" (89), i.e., *Count of Urgell*, a Catalan county on the southern Pyrenees belonging to the Crown of Aragon.

8 **thy pate and thy bodie is** It was possible in the sixteenth century to have a verb inflected for the singular with two singular subjects; cf. Görlach, 121.

9 *Myllaine* I.e., the Italian city of Milan.

10 **the people** It refers to "the *Spanish* people" (Fr. "tel peuple," G8v; *that people*).

11 Note that Munday produces a condensed version of the two first days of action in the context of the *pas d'armes*.

Chapter 35

1 *the Duke of Gaule* Fr. "Galles" (G8v; *Wales*), Sp. "Gález" (90; *Wales*). The choice of the form *Gaule* indicates that Munday is not merely translating from French into English, but also infusing his translation with the exoticism and mystery associated with chivalric romances. In doing so, however, Munday obscures the meaning of his text, since the English *Gaule* is easily identifiable with *Gaul* (or

Fr. *Gaule*) but not so with *Wales*; cf. the reference in Malory to "Kyng Bors of Gaule, that is Fraunce" (I.x.42). Helen Moore argues, "for Munday's audience at least, the 'de Gaule' tag indicated France, not Wales" (Munday, *Amadis*, 973 n. to 199). Therefore, readers might have found it confusing when the Duke of Gaule is later described as "man of England" (219.8). Note, in addition, that in the Sp. *Amadís de Gaula* the place name "*Gaula* is not Wales nor is it France proper: it is a little feudal realm located in Brittany," as argues Edwin B. Place, "*Amadis of Gaul, Wales,* or What?," *Hispanic Review* 23 (1955): 107. I am grateful to Joan Ignasi Soriano for calling this article to my attention.

2 **And nowe** Munday omits the Fr. "ayant ouy le seruice diuin" (H1r; *having heard the religious service*).

3 ***Phoebus*** Epithet meaning "bright" used for the Greek deity Apollo and also identified with the sun. It is added by Munday.

4 **King *Arthur*** The invocation of King Arthur, a legendary figure of literary fame in the Middle Ages and beyond, seems appropriate for a Duke of Wales because of King Arthur's Celtic background.

5 **he for *England*** This is the Duke of Gaule who is fighting *for Agriola of England*, and below is referred to as "man of *England*" (219.8).

6 **Sonne of *Venus*** I.e., Cupid, god of love.

7 **matter sufficient . . . that you seeke to discouer** I.e., sufficent evidence to know that you seek to reveal (what should be concealed). Munday slightly departs from the Fr.: "pour descouurir ce que desirez estre entierement celé" (H2r; *to discover what you wish to keep entirely secret*).

8 Munday omits the Duke of Gaule's martial set pieces; Fr. H2v.

Chapter 36

1 **to keepe his religion in your diuine seruice** Fr. "pour estre premier reçeu en ton seruice" (H3r; *to be admitted the first to your service*).

2 **roome** Fr. "perron"(H3v); Munday seems to have struggled to find an English equivalent to the Fr. *perron*; above he uses *monument*, but here he chooses *roome* meaning "a particular place or spot without reference to its area" (*OED*, s.v. *room* n. 1.6). See further in n. 2 to chap. I.xxxii.

3 ***Palmerin* commended to *Trineus* the valour of the *Englishman*, confirming the Duke for a chosen Knight at Armes** This clause is added by Munday with the purpose of praising his audience's fellow countryman.

4 **Lord of *Albret*** Fr. "le Seigneur d'Albret" (H3v); Sp. "el señor de Labrí" (92).

5 **the deeds of *Scipio* can among the *Romaines*** Scipio Africanus (236–ca. 184 BC), Roman general famous for having defeated Hannibal in Africa in 202 BC. Cf. Munday, *Zelauto*, 48, 165.

Chapter 37

1 **he shoulde maintaine nine other in the like quarrell** It reads above that the Duke of Savoye would maintain his challenge for a total of ten days: "at my appointed day, and nine daies after to sustaine the same quarrell" (206.20–21).

2 **she giuing him from her arme a sumptuous Bracelet** In the Fr. she also bestows on him "sa manchette" (H4v; *her oversleeve*), a typical present in chivalric texts (motif T59.2. *sleeve as love token*).

3 **the eldest Sonne of *Fraunce*** I.e., the heir apparent to the throne of France.

4 **caused *Polinardas* picture . . . a thing verye strange in respect of their great difference** The narrator takes sides with Polinarda by finding it very strange that her picture should "be set at *Lucemanias* feete," since there exists a great difference in both the two ladies' beauty. Thus, since it is obvious that Polinarda's beauty is superior, something must be amiss in this combat that has failed to uphold the truth. The cause of the problem is not in "anie want of a iust quarrell" (225.14), but that the Duke of Lorraine is not entitled to claim Polinarda as his lady, and is thus "seeking honor beyonde his desert" (225.12–13).

5 **within an howre after** The Fr. does establish the rule of one hour respite in between fights, but it is not included initially in Munday's translation; see n. 3 to chap. I.xxxii.

6 **in breefe** Munday does actually condense the action of the Fr.

Chapter 38

1 ***Palmerin* not as yet in perfecte health** Palmerin is still recovering from the wounds received in his combat against the Duke of Gaule.

2 **payde with selfe same coyne** Proverb; see Tilley, C507. Note that the occurrence here of this proverb antedates the earliest record in Tilley.

3 **the constancie of Women** Fr. "la fermeté qui peut estre aux femmes" (H6r; *the firmness one may find in women*). Although traditionally women have been associated with *inconstancy*, Munday is being faithful to his source. Hence, the English translation suggests that in his thoughts Palmerin is pondering on the presence of the quality *constancie* among women, of which there is a notable lack. The compositors of the third edition emend the text to read "inconstancie," which sounds more idiomatic, but misrepresents Munday's translation.

4 **the exploits of Armes the Duke did** Munday fails to mention the duration of the Duke's success: "ce jour, & six autres ensuyuans" (H6v; *that day and the six days following*). The Duke is expected to fight off challengers for nine or ten days (see n. 1 to chap. I.xxxvii) and at least seven have already gone by.

5 **he feigned himselfe to be whole sooner then he was indeede** The English text heightens Palmerin's mettle in showing him willing to take the Duke on while still recovering from his injuries, whereas in the Fr. he has made a full recovery: "le troisiesme jour apres fut assez fort pour porter armes" (H6v; *the third day afterward he was strong enough to bear arms*).

6 **my present estate would haue me stay awhile** Fr. "ne santant aucune indisposition qui m'empesche" (H6v; *not feeling any illness that hinders me*).

Chapter 39

1 **I came to maintaine your honor . . . the most beautifull Ladie liuing** This clause is Munday's addition.

2 **soueraigne drinks** Fr. "vinaigre, & eau de vie" (H7v; *vinegar and brandy*).

3 **very** "Used as an intensive . . . to emphasize the exceptional prominence of some ordinary thing or feature"; q.v. *OED*, adj. 8(c) for other examples without the article.

4 **and in his conquests shewed himselfe . . . with the humilitie of theirs** This clause is introduced by Munday, who takes the opportunity to summarize Palmerin's combats leading up to his fight against the Knight of the Sun.

5 **this hote humour** This term here describes a choleric individual; see n. 9 to chap. I.xv.

6 **no** I.e., nor; see *OED*, s.v. *no* conj.1

7 ***Trineus* (albeit he neuer sawe her) became amorous of her** This is a case of *love through sight of picture* (motif T11.2; cf. Bordman, 88, and Bueno Serrano, "Índice," 898); see Patchell, 56.

8 **and if I would conceale them . . . because vertue doth so apparantlie shine in them** This passage is Munday's interpolation.

9 **she had no will to become a Nunne** This remark is to be interpreted ironically; cf. the Fr. "qu'elle estoit ja Nonnain renduë" (I1v; *that she had been already ordained a nun*).

Chapter 40

1 **Father to the Prince** *Tarisius* Fr. "son Neueu, ou petit filz" (I1v; *his grandson*); Munday corrects the inaccuracy in the Fr. For the marriage of Tarisius and Griana, see 131.34–133.15. Chapters I.xl and I.xli represent a flashback or analepsis since the chronological sequence of events in the narrative is interrupted in order to flesh out the life story of the mysterious Knight of the Sun. See González, "Sueños," 233–34.

2 **thy heade shall pay the price of thy folly** This clause provides more detailed information than the vaguer Fr. equivalent, "je vous monstreray vostre folie" (I1v; *I will show you your folly*).

3 **as the matter prouoking a fierie Meteore** In this clause Munday draws a phenomenal comparison of opposite proportions to that used by Maugin: "comme le Poussin en la coque souz le ventre de la Poule" (I2r; *as the chick in the shell underneath the hen's body*). For this kind of comparison in Maugin's version, see Freer, 218.

4 **a damned deede of paracide to take effect** The story of Netrides has all the ingredients of folk tales, including the presence of the parricide motif (S22), for whose occurrence in romance texts, see Bordman, 86, and Bueno Serrano, "Índice," 891.

5 **inconstant** Fr. "contraire" (I2r). The word *inconstant* is repeated twice in the same sentence. Since the English text departs from its Fr. source, one could argue that *inconstant* is repeated as a result of a mechanical error caused by attraction to a word previously copied, in which case the text should be emended by substituting the word *contrarie*. Instead, I retain the original reading because the repetition is introduced for rhetorical purposes: fortune is inconstant, and to *me most of all* inconstant.

6 **so please her to conceiue the same opinion I doo** This clause is Munday's interpolation.

7 **Three daies before this Ladie fell in trauaile ... the certaintye of this dreame** In contrast with the Fr. and Sp. texts, in the English version the dreamer is not Netrydes but his pregnant wife. Munday makes changes to the wording of the dream in order to ensure its own consistency and adjustment to the narrative (cf. e.g., at the opening of the next chapter the English text reads, "the vision that appeared to his [i.e., Frysol's] Mother" (239.4–5), while its source states "les visions qui s'estoyent apparuës à son Pere," I3v; *the visions that had appeared to his father*). Munday departs from his source on purpose and probably attributes the dream to Netrydes's wife because of the prophetic significance associated with the dreams of pregnant women in contemporary England; see Patricia Crawford, "Women's Dreams in Early Modern England," in *Dreams and History: The*

Interpretation of Dreams from Ancient Greece to Modern Psychoanalysis, ed. Daniel Pick and Lyndal Roper (London: Brunner-Routledge, 2004), 97. For a brief discussion of this dream, see González, "Sueños," 236.

8 **casting the Barre** This is a trial of strength to find out who is capable of throwing the bar (i.e., a thick rod of iron or wood; see *OED*, s.v. *bar* n. 1.2) the farthest away.

9 **where olde *Lombardo* mette with his Father** This clause is Munday's interpolation, "his Father" referring to Netrydes, Frisol's father.

Chapter 41

1 **to seeke aduentures** Munday mistranslates the Fr. "pour aller chercher son auanture" (I3v; *to go seek his fortune*). In this context the noun *auanture* means "ce qui doit arriver" (see Huguet, s.v. *adventure*), whose English equivalent is *adventure*, n. 1: "that which comes to us, or happens without design; chance, hap, fortune, luck" (q.v. *OED*). Frysol decides to explore his fortune and see whether he can find a cure for his illness or not. But in his rendering Munday uses the word in the sense "any novel or unexpected event in which one shares; an exciting or remarkable incident befalling any one" (*OED*, n. 6).

2 A passage from the Fr. is omitted in the English probably as a result of mistaking the point of resumption possibly due to the similarity of the ending of the words "complaignant . . . jettant" (I4r).

3 **onely by the raunsome that his beloued Sonne paide** Munday avoids the more explicit reference to Jesus Christ in his source: "par le moyen du merite de la passion de nostre sauueur & redempteur Iesus Christ son filz" (I4r; *by means of the merit of the passion of our savior and redeemer Jesus Christ, his son*).

4 **she bathed him wyth wholesome Hearbes** This clause is inserted by Munday, who chooses to link Frysol's cure with another cleansing bath, as happened in the case of Primaleon (see 145.23–34).

5 **at the time hee dranke the water** See 237.18–21.

6 **that wheresoeuer my body . . . my hart shall remaine readie to doo you any seruice** Here Munday subtly alters the phrasing of the more overt declaration of love in the Fr.: "que quand mon corps se separera de vostre presence, mon cueur demourera à jamais vostre" (I4r; *that when my body departs from your presence, my heart will remain forever yours*).

7 **my word shall be my deede** Proverbial; cf. Tilley, W 820.

8 **thinking hee could neuer glut his eyes with regarding her** This clause is Munday's interpolation.

9 **according as hath beene before rehearsed** Here is the end of the analepsis; now the action resumes where we left it at the end of chap. I.xxxix; see 233.9–10.

Chapter 42

1 **such is the iealousie of his vnspotted affection, albeit my Maister reputes his Ladie immouable** This clause is Munday's interpolation.

2 **for the vnwillingnes I haue to heare him complaine . . . the most happie among Ladies** In this passage Munday changes the sense of the Fr.: "pour l'enuie que j'ay de lui complaire, je m'efforcerois du tout à luy obeïr comme à la plus heureuse des Dames" (I7r; *since I wish to satisfy him, I would try hard to obey him completely as I would obey the happiest of Ladies*).

3 **that so worthilie deliuered them from the oppressions of the enchaunted Knight, . . . to meete him** This passage is Munday's interpolation. For Palmerin's fight against the Enchanted Knight, see 183.15–184.9.

4 **He that deserues honour ought to were it, and he that commaundes the soule, may easilie ouer-rule the passions of the minde: let my Knight then be rewarded as he hath rightly deserued** This passage is inserted by Munday to substitute for the more suggestive Fr.: "je luy monstreray vne telle priuauté, qu'il ne se deüra plaindre de moy" (I7r; *I'll show him such kindness that he will have no complaint about me*). Munday's intervention is aimed at presenting arguments that justify Polinarda's sense of moral debt toward Palmerin and her decision to comply with his amorous desires shortly, thus anticipating their sexual encounter in the following chapter.

5 ***Palmerin* wished that *Iuno* had graunted him so much, as she did somtime to *Argus* her sheepehearde** The text refers to Argus, a monster of one hundred eyes always vigilant (only two of his eyes rest at a time) to whom Juno, suspicious of her husband Jove, entrusted the guard of Io, who was turned into a cow (hence his treatment as *sheepehearde*). For Ovid's account of the story, see *Met.*, I.567–746.

6 **shoulde I complaine of a greater matter** Fr. "je vous voudrois complaire en plus grande chose" (I7v; *I would like to satisfy you in a greater matter*). The cause of the departure in the English text may lie in the orthographical similarity of the Fr. *complaire* and the English *complaine*. As a result of this confusion Munday's version makes poor sense.

7 **the Duke of *Lorrayne*, who maintaining your beautie . . . remooued the figure of the *French* Princesse in obeysaunce to you** See 224.11–12 and 229.30–33.

8 **hartfast** A nonce word formed to make a pun with *handfast* in the following clause; *hartfast* suggests that Polinarda loves Palmerin in a firm, fixed and unshaken manner.

Chapter 43

1 with deuotion answerable to those silent howres The clause departs from the Fr. "auec vne deuocion toute autre qu'à dire leurs heures" (I8v; *with a devotion completely different from the one for saying their hours*). Munday avoids mentioning the canonical hours in the Fr., not so much because of ignorance as Galigani suggests (261), but in keeping with his cautious treatment of all Christian references throughout the text.

2 streaming so plentifullie from your chaste eies This clause is Munday's insertion. As already stated by Lyly, "Loue commeth in at the eye, not at the eare, by seeing Natures workes, not by hearing womens words" (*England*, 2:59.13–14).

3 It nowe remaines Madame, that you regarde . . . I presume not of anie action meritorious This passage notably amplifies the Fr. (sig. I8v).

4 I giue you heere my hand, and therewithall a chast hart . . . by your owne conceites can imagine the content of these twaine As in the case of Griana and Florendos (see 122.12–28), Palmerin and Polinarda are here united in matrimony. Munday omits some ideas in the Fr. (sig. K1r), most notably in relation to the sexual details of their wedding night. Instead Munday appeals to the readers' imagination and experience to fill in the details he leaves out.

5 *Iupiter* had not the like pleasure with faire *Alcmena*, for whom hee caused one night to endure the space of three daies The text refers to the mythological story in which Alcmena is visited by Jupiter in the shape of Amphitryon, Alcmena's husband, and lies with her for one night that he extends for the length of three days. This incident provided the plot for Plautus's comedy *Amphitruo*, where we read that when Jupiter is lying with Alcmena, "haec . . . nox est facta longior" (Prol., 113; *this night has been lengthened*); ed. W. M. Lindsay, *Comoediae* (Oxford: Clarendon Press, 1904), vol. 1. Munday also shows direct knowledge of Plautus in his *Zelauto*, 139.

6 nowe these Knights and Ladies were espoused before God, there wanted nothing but the ceremonie of the Church to confirme it These two couples of lovers have already freely consented to their marriage and have physically consummated it. While these two actions would in principle have a legally binding effect, there existed in Elizabethan England the social perception that ecclesiastical solemnization was desirable, particularly when members of the nobility were involved. See further in David Cressy, *Birth, Marriage, and Death: Ritual, Religion, and the Life-Cycle in Tudor and Stuart England* (Oxford: Oxford University Press, 1999), 317–18.

7 woulde you haue all the good fortune your selfe . . . framed me of the selfe same mettall In this passage Munday departs from the Fr. Next he summarizes the action as presented in his source text.

8 **Fortune who will neuer suffer thinges long in one estate** Fortune's variability was proverbial; Tilley, F 606.

9 **displeasure of succor, that the King of *Norway* gaue to the King of *Scots* his Brother** I.e., the offence caused by the support the King of Norway lent to his brother, the King of Scotland.

10 **conceale** Fr. "ne me vouloir escondire de la requeste que je vous veux faire" (K2r; *do not reject the request I want to make you*). In the Fr. Trineus demands Palmerin *not to refuse* his request, rather than *to conceal* it. Munday seems to mistranslate the Fr., but with little narrative consequences: while in the Fr. Trineus trusts Palmerin, in the English version he first wants to be reassured of his friend's discretion. In his response Palmerin, however, guarantees Trineus not his secrecy but his assistance.

Chapter 44

1 **there is no neede of tryumphe before victorie** Proverbial; see Tilley, V 50.

2 **let such pomp remaine I pray you** These words are Munday's addition.

3 **the deuises beeing changed, because they intended to passe vnknowne** The use of incognito is common in chivalric literature (cf. 478.26–27). For a discussion of this motif, see J. A. Burrow, "The Uses of Incognito: *Ipomadon A*," in *Readings in Medieval English Romance*, ed. Carol M. Meale (Cambridge: D. S. Brewer, 1994), 25–34. Cf. motif R222.1(G) *Knight jousts incognito* (Bordman, and Bueno Serrano, "Índice," 890).

4 **harts of Golde** Cf. Fr. "besans d'argent" (K3v; *silver bezants*); Sp. "sobreseñales blancas" (110; *white devices*).

5 *Madame, quand mourray-ie?* I.e., "My Lady, when shall I die?"

6 **came the Emperor into the Chappell . . . and girded his sworde about him** The knighting ritual is divested of all its religious connotations, except for the chapel, with no reference even to the mass in the morning after Trineus's night watch. Consequently the ceremonial as presented in the English text becomes a much more simplified matter than in the Fr.

7 *Palmerin* **and** *Ptolome* **to comfort their Ladies** I.e., they *went* to comfort their ladies. Here the preposition *to* "means motion, 'with a view to,' 'for an end'" (Abbot, *Grammar*, no. 186). Fr.: "Palmerin accompagné de Ptolome la [i.e., Polinarda] fut voir" (K3v; *Palmerin, accompanied by Ptolome, went to see Polinarda*).

8 **eight daies after your departure towardes** *Fraunce* **. . . sollicited me with affections not liking me** See 241.35–242.3.

Chapter 45

1 *Crenus* at his returne with *Frisol*, as you haue hearde See 243.12–15.

2 with a fresh supply beganne againe thus to animate them This clause is Munday's interpolation.

3 wherupon the Countie *Tolano* in hope of the daie ... mette him in the face with his *English* squadron This passage has no equivalent in Fr. or Sp.

Chapter 46

1 miles Fr. "lieuës" (K6r; *leagues*).

2 who dailie went to a Chappell Fr. "qui alloit ordinairement ouyr Messe, & faire son voyage à vne petite chapelle de nostre Dame" (K6r; *who usually went to hear Mass, and made her way to a small chapel of our Lady*). Munday leaves out a number of details and imposes censorship, which is, as Galigani argues, particularly severe in the case of the Virgin Mary, "la cui venerazione era ritenuta dagli anglicani atto di idolatria" (281).

3 a companie of greene Trees Fr. "saussaye" (K6r; *plantation of willows*). Munday failed to find a one-word equivalent in English, but his solution, though vague, shows that his goal was to follow his original as closely as possible.

4 surprised as *Acteon* was, when he found *Diana* bathing among her Nimphes Acteon, a zealous hunter, got lost in the forest and accidentally stumbled on a secluded grotto in which the goddess Diana, aided by her nymphs, was taking a bath stark naked. Upset by Acteon's intrusion, Diana turned him into a stag. This mythological story is related in Ovid, *Met.*, III.138–255.

5 for omitting his courtesie: but wading further and further into this amorous furie In this passage Munday elaborates on the more prosaic Fr. "son imprudence: ains se delectant en son profond penser" (K6r; *his imprudence: rather delighting in his deep thought*).

6 in the Westerne world Fr. "Isles Occidentales" (K6r; *western islands*). Munday's translation is more accurate than a literal rendering, since Agriola is considered to be the most beautiful not of Britain exclusively, but of western Europe in general. The phrase "west iles" was already used by the fourteenth-century author of *Sir Gawain and the Green Knight* (line 7) to mean "a general, though unparalleled, term for western lands"; ed. J. R. R. Tolkien and E. V. Gordon, 2nd ed., revised by Norman Davis (Oxford: Clarendon Press, 1967), 71.

7 what the Knight in *Fraunce* told vs See 232.10–12.

8 this good beginning of your enterprise, will cause the ende fal out to your content Proverbial; cf. Tilley B 262.

Chapter 47

1 **euery man laboring for his Prince ... and your verie countenances enough to conquere** This passage is absent from Fr.

2 **let vs learne them to confesse with patience, that they haue no such right or custome to vanquish** In this passage Munday subtly alters his source and fails to reproduce cogently the sense of the Fr. "nous leurs apprendrons à auoir la pacience de delaisser ce qui ne leur vient de droit, & accoustumer d'estre vaincuz" (K7v; *we will teach them to have the patience to abandon what doesn't come to them by right and we will teach them to become accustomed to being conquered*).

3 **so shall sweete successe returne you with victory** This clause is Munday's interpolation.

4 **the auauntgarde** Fr. "l'auangarde d'Escoçe" (K7v; *the Scottish vanguard*).

5 **like an angry Lyon** It was usual in medieval literature "to compare brave, fierce, angry knights to a lion," as states Ernst Brugger, "Yvain and His Lion," *MP* 38 (1941): 277. Thus Munday wanted to make the same comparison with the hero of his romance, even if he had to depart from his source, since the Fr. applies the simile "comme vn Lyon eschauffé" (K8r; *like an angry lion*) not to Palmerin but to the King of the Isle of Magdalen, later described by Munday as "incensed with vnquenchable anger" (264.1–2).

6 **sayled thence the King with greater shame, then did the Emperor *Antonius* from *Octauius Caesar*** The text here refers to the naval battle of Actium fought on September 2, 31 BC between Mark Antony and Octavian and decisively won by the latter with little opposition from the former. Antony managed only to sail away with Cleopatra, although that seems to have been his goal when their armies joined battle: "For when he [i.e., Antonius] saw *Cleopatraes* shippe under saile, he forgot, forsooke, and betrayed them that fought for him, and imbarked upon a galley with five bankes of owers," as we read in Plutarch (6:377–78). For a brief explanation of the battle, see Christopher Pelling, "The Triumviral Period," in *The Cambridge Ancient History*, 2nd ed., vol. 10: *The Augustan Empire, 43 BC—AD. 69*, ed. Alan K. Bowman et al. (Cambridge: Cambridge University Press, 1996), 54–59. Note that the Fr. reads only "Cesar" (not *Octavius* Caesar).

7 **the handes** Fr. "mains cruelles" (K8v; *cruel hands*). Munday avoids reproducing the adjective *cruel* to describe his fellow countrymen.

Chapter 48

1 **and afterward they came and supped with the King** This clause is Munday's interpolation.

Notes to the Text: Part I 653

2 the Archbishop of *Canterburie* The Spanish author was certainly unfamiliar with English geography and social organization, as all references to places and people in England are fantastic. The reference to the Archbishop of Canterbury was inserted by Maugin (K8v) and retained by Munday. It surprises, however, that Munday did not try to restyle the place names in his original so as to match actual English geography and thus endow his text with greater realism.

3 as also that my Subiects might honor you accordinglie This clause is Munday's interpolation.

4 That (quoth *Palmerin*) will neither profit or preiudice your Maiestie The correlative construction with *neither . . . or* was not unusual; see Barber, *Early Modern English*, 274.

Chapter 49

1 the little God that made looue I.e., Cupid.

2 he that saued the King your fathers life . . . but he remounted my Lord See 264.12–19.

3 if these be not the Knightes that past by this Cittie . . . and what she commaunded them See 259.22–260.41.

4 Are you he Sir . . . at the Combat maintained by the Prince *Lewes* for the loue of his Ladie? Cf. 230.4–8.

5 What I haue said Gentlemen, I hope shall not offend you Fr. "Ie vous jure par ma coronne, qu'on ne vous en parlera plus" (L2r; *I swear you by my crown that we won't talk to you about it anymore*).

6 myles Fr. "lieuës" (L2r; *leagues*).

7 as hee seemed a man of another worlde Fr. "qu'il sembloit plus mort que vif" (L2r; *that he seemed more dead than alive*).

8 the Goddesse of my lyfe Munday amplifies the Fr. "elle" (L2r; *she*).

9 hee wyll prooue the onely string to your bowe This proverbial clause (cf. Tilley, S 937) is Munday's interpolation; cf. the use of the same proverb in Lyly's *Euphues*: "my counsayle is that thou haue more strings to thy bow then one" (1:255.13–14).

10 as thou diddest for me to my Mistresse *Polynarda* See chap. I.xxviii.

11 thou bewray not of whence or what we are The same instructions gives Ipomadon to his men as part of his strategy to preserve his anonymity: "And also his men comaundyd he / They schuld tell no man of no degre / Off whens ne whatte they were" (lines 1745–47). *Ipomadon*, ed. Rhiannon Purdie, EETS os

316 (Oxford: Oxford University Press, 2001), 52. The couplet version, known as *The Lyfe of Ipomydon* or *Ipomydon B*, was printed by Wynkyn de Worde ca. 1522 (STC 5733) and ca. 1527 (STC 5732.5) and reads "Ne no man tell what I am, / Where I shall go ne whens I cam" (lines 233–34). *The Lyfe of Ipomydon*, ed. Tadahiro Ikegami (Tokyo: Seijo University, 1985), 2:6.

Chapter 50

1 faire *Agriola* shyned, as beautifull *Venus* among the other starres Venus is the brightest celestial body after the sun and the moon.

2 as an offendour with his guilt before a Iudge Fr. "que le larron surpris au meffait" (L3r; *as the thief caught in the act*). Here Munday draws on his own personal experience in trials, e.g., his testimony against Edmund Campion and other priests in November 1581, for which see Munday's *Discovery of Edmund Campion and his Confederates* (1582).

3 and wyll you not tryumphe in your happie sight, but sitte as one vtterlie discouraged? This passage is interpolated by Munday and substitutes for the Fr. "pour participer à l'auenir en ses biens faitz, & obtenir ce benefice vnique de jouïssance" (L3r; *in order to share in her good acts in the future and obtain that unique benefit of pleasure*).

4 vnprouided of such fauor This phrase is an explanatory amplification of the Fr. "autrement" (L3r; *otherwise*); Munday displays his concern for making the text less vague and more reader-friendly.

5 not honoring that Princesse, which carries the Palme from all Ladies liuing See 259.31–42.

6 as will aske more time to report then leysure wil admit This clause amplifies the Fr. "qu'impossible seroit de mieux" (L3r; *a better one would be impossible*).

7 the speedie eye posted between them with sweete conueyances Munday decides to censor a suggestive passage in the Fr. ("Et ainsi que son œil ... de couleur"; L3r) in which Trineus and Agriola exchange amorous looks. By using the clause seeing the libertie of speeche was denied (271.11), Munday is, however, giving an indirect clue at the ultimate reason for his pruning of the original Fr.

8 and that must be little, hauing so daintie a dish before her to fill her stomacke This clause is Munday's interpolation.

9 with whose rare beautie hee coulde neuer satisfie his eyes This clause is an amplification of the Fr. "qu'il ne pensoit jamais assez voir" (L3v; *of whom he never expected to see enough*).

10 *Palamedes* chase was not comparable to this, till in the ende the Deere was fallen In Malory's *Morte Darthur* Palamedes is described hunting the Questing

Beast of Arthurian romance: "the questynge beest, that hadde in shap a hede lyke a serpents hede, and a body lyke a lybard, buttocks lyke a lyon, and foted lyke an herte" (IX.xii.254–55). Palamedes's chase and the King of England's are comparable in that they eventually catch their quarry; the difference is in the type of quarry. Patchell inaccurately states, "An allusion in *Palmerin d'Oliva* to Palamedes' quest indicates that the Spanish author probably knew this creature [i.e., the Questing Beast]" (47). The Sp. original, however, includes no allusion to Palamedes and in fact the whole hunting scene is limited to a simple sentence: "huvieron tan buena dicha que tomaron muchas aves e caçaron a su voluntad" (121; *they had such good luck that they caught many birds and hunted at leasure*). The hunting scene as it is presented in Munday's translation was actually introduced by Maugin (Fr. sig. L3v), who must have become acquainted with Palamedes's quest through its presence in the the Post-Vulgate *Queste del Saint Graal*. For the passage describing how Palamedes kills the Questing Beast, see *Lancelot-Grail*, 9:352.

11 **Sir *Gawen*, or *Launcelot du Lake*** Fr. "Gauuain, & Lancelot" (L3v). The text refers to the literary narratives dealing with the adventures of Sir Gawain and Lancelot, the most famous knights in the Arthurian tradition. While there are a number of Middle English romances about Sir Gawain, the adventures of Lancelot, though not unknown in England, received less attention prior to the publication of Malory's *Morte Darthur*. For the Gawain romances, see *Sir Gawain: Eleven Romances and Tales*, ed. Thomas Hahn (Kalamazoo, MI: Medieval Institute Publications, 1995), and for Lancelot, see *Stanzaic Morte Arthur*, in *King Arthur's Death*, ed. Larry D. Benson, rev. Edward E. Foster (Kalamazoo, MI: Medieval Institute Publications, 1994), 9–128. No allusion to these knights appears in the Sp.

12 **tell** I.e., *till*.

13 **the martired body of poore *Prometheus*** Munday refers to the torture Zeus inflicted on Prometheus, whose liver was eaten every day by an eagle. This torment was meant to be eternal, since the liver eaten during the day grew back every night. The reference to this episode, told in Hesiod's *Theogony*, 507–616, is inserted by Munday; the Fr. simply states, "qu'vn pauure martir n'en pourroit souffrir d'auantage" (L4r; *that a poor martyr could not suffer more*); cf. Munday, *Amadis*, 995 n. to 750.

14 **so adorned with white Roses** Fr. "sable escartelé d'argent" (L4r; *sable quarterly argent*). Munday devotes little effort to translating heraldic descriptions. Above he also uses the phrase "so rich in Armes" (272.43) for the Fr. "portant de sinople à nombre infiny de besans d'argent" (L4r; *wearing vert with an infinite number of silver bezants*). The difficulty here is possibly caused by the heraldic term *sinople*, although Munday adopts this word in his translation of *Palmerin of England*, II.lxii (cf. *OED*, s.v. *sinople* n. 3a).

15 **for you haue the maydenhead of hys loue . . . entertaine in your chaste thoughtes** This passage is Munday's insertion.

16 **the suddaine yeelding of a flexible nature . . . as thou regardest my word and hys safetie** This passage is Munday's insertion.

17 **no not** Cumulative negation was accepted and served to emphasize the negative; see Barber, *Early Modern English*, 283, and *OED*, s.v. *no*, adv. 3.

18 **a more beautiful paradise, then euer was inuented by *Epicurus* himselfe** In this context the English word *paradise* is to be understood as "a garden, esp. an enclosed one" (q.v. *OED*, 3rd ed., n. 4a), since it is a translation of the Fr. "Paradis" (L4v) meaning "Parc, lieu planté d'arbres" (q.v. Huguet). The text ultimately refers to the Garden of Epicurus, the Greek philosopher (341–270 BC), who bought a house in Athens and used the house's garden for his philosophical teachings. The Epicurean school, also known as "The Garden," was denigrated for its hedonism. See David John Furley and D. Sedly, "Epicurus," in *The Oxford Classical Dictionary*, ed. Simon Hornblower, Antony Spawforth, and Esther Eidinow, 4th ed. (Oxford: Oxford University Press, 2012), 513–14.

19 **seeing the beginning is so good, no doubt much better remaineth behind** Cf. the proverb in Tilley, B 259.

20 **the torments of *Leander* . . . then the betrothed spouse to the prisoner of *Abydos*** Phoebus drives the sun chariot across the sky until the end of the day, when Thetys and other nymphs receive him in the sea (cf. Ovid, *Met.*, II.62–70). When the night falls Leander of Abydos swims across the Hellespont to meet with his beloved Hero, who lives in Sestos, enemy of Abydos. Leander does the same every night until on one such occasion the light that guides him is extinguished and Leander drowns. Then, Hero, his "betrothed spouse," decides to take her own life (cf. Virgil, *Georgics*, iii.258–63). The story of Leander and Hero underscores that Trineus of Allemaigne and Agriola of England similarly love each other in spite of the enmity between their respective countries.

21 **had *Trineus* bashfullie taken the Princesse by the hand** Munday censors the Fr., "Trineus auoit ja la main sur le dur tetin de la Princesse" (L5r; *Trineus had already put his hand on the Princess's hard breast*).

22 **the Hart he had chased the day before . . . that he should perfect all things to his harts desire** In order to assist the king in the hunting of the hart, the animal is kept "within the toyles" (275.17); this is a hunting practice in which a semicircular net is placed at the edge of the forest where the animal is driven by beaters for the benefit of those waiting with bows and arrows or crossbows; cf. Peter Edwards, "Hunting," in *Tudor England: An Encyclopedia*, ed. Arthur F. Kinney and David W. Swain (New York: Garland, 2001), 373. Similarly, Trineus trusts that Urbanillo's actions together with the ring should assist him in his

own metaphoric hunt, so that the lady is inclined to agree with "his *harts* desire" (my emphasis). This parallel of pursuit between the cynegetic activity and the love-hunt is not unusual in chivalric romances, as for instance in the case of *Sir Gawain and the Green Knight*; see Anne Rooney, "The Hunts in *Sir Gawain and the Green Knight*," in *A Companion to the "Gawain"-poet*, ed. Derek Brewer and Jonathan Gibson (Cambridge: D. S. Brewer, 1997), 157–63.

23 he thought he discerned this sight ... recounted to *Trineus* the whole effect of his dreame Palmerin has another prophetic dream, which he interprets not literally but in a more general way instead: "such illusions ... can presage no good to followe" (276.8–9). That is to say, the dream prompts Palmerin to ready himself to face any eventuality, not specifically a lion. The impending danger announced in the dream materializes in the following chapter in the form of the giant Franarco. For a similar reading of the dream in the Sp., see González, "Sueños," 238–39.

Chapter 51

1 before they be dishonoured This clause is Munday's interpolation, which suggests that he was knowledgeable of the tradition of identifying giants with lustful creatures; cf. Geoffrey of Monmouth's *Historia Regum Britanniae*, X.165, ed. Michael D. Reeve, trans. Neil Wright (Woodbridge: Boydell, 2007), 224–25, where the giant of Mont St. Michel abudcts Helena and, after killing her, rapes her nurse (cf. Bordman, 37, motif F531.5.7.0.4: *Giant ravishes women*). Franarco's behavior is beyond the boundaries of human morality, thus posing a real threat to human society ("enemy to manhoode," 278.22) that demands "a firm human response ... spurred by anxiety about both transgressive sexuality and the capacity for reproduction," as argues Dana Oswald, *Monsters, Gender, and Sexuality in Medieval English Literature* (Woodbridge: D. S. Brewer, 2010), 13. The action following is parodied by Francis Beaumont in his play *The Knight of the Burning Pestle* (1607, printed 1613), act 1, lines 214–30, ed. Michael Hattaway (London: Ernest Benn, 1969), 26. Note, however, that the stage directions of the play attribute the text to *Palmerin of England*. For a discussion of the discrepancies between the text in the play and its source, see Richard Proudfoot, "Francis Beaumont and the Hidden Princess," *The Library*, 6th ser., 4 (1982): 47–49.

2 There succeeded he the royall dignitie ... was slaine in the battell by *Palmerin* See 170.3–22.

3 them This personal pronoun refers to the Giant's men, according to the Fr.. The long sentence in which this personal pronoun appears imperfectly condenses a long passage in the Fr. ("de sorte qu'ilz en estendirent ... viendroient au secours des Dames"; L6r), from which relevant information, such as the arrival of Palmerin and Trineus, is omitted.

4 **Trineus hearing the words of Agriola** In the Fr. Trineus hears Agriola but fails to understand what she is saying: "ne sçachant, toutes-fois, qu'elle disoit" (L7r; *not knowing, however, what she was saying*).

5 **hys strokes gaue witnes he fought for a wife** Munday departs from the Fr.: "comme vn Trigre ayant perdu ses faons" (L7r; *like a tiger that has lost its cubs*).

6 **they kneeled down thanking God for their victorie** While the English text suggests that the King and his men thanked God, in the Fr. they are "la Royne auec sa fille Agriole" (L7r; *the queen with her daughter Agriola*).

7 **and honorable Sepulture to be prouided for the other** This clause is Munday's addition.

8 **and may they all three prosper ... for their knightly seruice to the Realme of England** This clause is Munday's addition.

Chapter 52

1 **the three Knightes** I.e., Palmerin, Ptolome, and Trineus.

2 **seeing that heauenlie spectacle** Fr. "voyant celle" (L7v; *seeing that one, i.e., Agriola*). As in the case of Griana and Polinarda, Munday elevates Agriola to a divine status.

3 **my deuoted soule shall remaine to honor you** This clause modifies the Fr. "je tiens & vous doy celle que j'ay maintenant" (L7v; *I have and give you the life I now have*).

4 **since the time he first hearde of your excellent beautie ... daughter to the most christian king of Fraunce** See 232.12–14 and 244.6–34.

5 **taking her secretlie by the hand ... and the comfortable aunswere she gaue him** Munday has removed from this scene how Trineus kisses Agriola's hand in the Fr., "sa main la baisa" L8v; *her hand he kissed*); for a comparison between the Fr. and the English version of this passage, see Galigani, 286.

6 **within seauen or eyght dayes hee was able to beare Armour** In the Fr., after a six-day long convalescence, Trineus was capable to "monter à cheual & cheminer" (L8v; *ride a horse and walk*).

7 **the shame hee reputed to himselfe ... for the beautie of the fayre Princesse Agriola** See 221.34–222.5.

8 **theyr talke was not about affaires of Merchandise** Fr. "ilz parloient d'autre chose, que d'enfiler Perles" (M1r; *they were talking about something other than stringing pearls*).

9 God speede you Madame Given Munday's efforts to erase systematically most references to God, notwithstanding the formulaic nature of this expression, it is worth mentioning that it has no parallel expression in the Fr.

10 I shoulde call you Ladie . . . but you haue chosen him your Husbande in hart Palmerin's words appear in English as a statement, while they correspond to two questions in the Fr.

11 as the ayre dooth the *Camelion* This clause is Munday's interpolation. In Munday's times chameleons were "supposed to live on air" (*OED*, s.v. *chameleon* n. 1). Cf. *Hamlet*, III.ii.94–95: "of the chameleon's dish, I eat the air."

12 as in the sequel shall be largelie discoursed The text anticipates the great misfortune awaiting Agriola, Trineus, and Palmerin. Note, however, that the word *sequel* refers not necessarily to the second part of the romance, but simply to the "the ensuing narrative, discourse" (*OED*, s.v. *sequel* n. 7).

Chapter 53

1 pretending that wee were so neere allyed, as hee might no longer account mee for his Wife In order to avoid incest due to their supposed close kinship ("neere allyed," 286.26), this knight decides to effectively dissolve their marriage.

2 beeing suddainlie driuen into his dumps, knewe not well what to saie: yet at length This passage is Munday's interpolation.

3 Then was it ordeined, that this difference shoulde bee tryed by Armes A judicial combat is appointed to settle the difference; for more information on judicial combats, see n. 8 in chap. I.xxiv above.

4 at the Ioustes in *Fraunce* **. . . was fought betweene him and this Knight** See 231.5–19.

5 in presence of the Duke of *Gaule* **against the King of** *Norway* **. . . as hee were his owne naturall Brother** See 243.2–15.

6 hee I.e., Palmerin.

7 hee dreamed in his sleepe Munday departs from the Fr. "qu'il luy souuint" (M3v; *it came to his memory*). Although this dream is unique to the English text, it leaves the narrative sequence of events unaltered, since it has no premonitory value.

Chapter 54

1 the thirde howre of the daie The opening section of chapter I.liv in the Fr. text (most of the text on the left column of sig. M4r) is omitted in Munday's version. The third hour of the canonical day ends at 9 a.m.; see *OED*, s.v. *tierce* n. 1.2a.

2 *Palmerin* **who was wonderfull desirous to finde his enemie... that you shewe mee the Knight** This is an example of motif M223, *Blind promise: Person grants wish before hearing it*, which is a favorite of chivalric texts; see Bueno Serrano, "Índice," 808–9.

3 **haue you forgot your wordes at *Parris*, to the Knight that guarded the Duke of *Sauoyes* Tent?** The text here refers to the challenging words he uttered before fighting against Palmerin at the tournament in Paris (see 230.11–15). Note, however, that nowhere is it mentioned that these words are addressed to "the Knight that guarded the Duke of *Sauoyes* Tent." The Sp. original contains the exact same reference, "no se vos acordará de las palabras locas que dexistes ante la cibdad de París al cavallero que guardava la tienda del Duque de Savoya" (132; *you will not remember the crazy words you said in the city of Paris to the knight who guarded the Duke of Savoy's tent*), which Maugin accurately translates (sig. M4r-v). But in the Sp., when the Knight of the Sun utters those words, we are told, "estando [Palmerín] a la puerta de la tienda" (96; *Palmerin being at the tent's entrance*), although it is not explicitly stated that this is the Duke's tent. This passage is not included in Maugin's translation (sig. H8r), and thus Munday is not directly responsible for the lack of consistency of his text. In sum, we need to understand that "the Knight that guarded the Duke of *Sauoyes* Tent" is Palmerin.

4 **they brake their Launces ... who was likest to winne the victorie** A full paragraph from the Fr. (M4v: "Mais Palmerin ... à moitié") is not included in Munday's translation.

5 **charged him with such violente strokes ... requited him wyth as woorthye chiualrie** This passage is Munday's interpolation.

6 **no Knight shoulde passe ouer the Bridge ... and take their Horsses with him** This incident clearly reproduces the rituals established for the *pas d'armes*. By taking place near a bridge, it replicates more overtly Suero de Quiñones's *passo honroso* at the bridge near Órbigo, for which see n. 3 to chap. I.xxxii; cf. Patchell, 32–33.

Chapter 55

1 **to single foorth *Frisol* in such conuenient place** This clause represents a playful departure from the Fr. "deuancer Frisol, pour le trouuer en quelque autre addresse" (M5v; *to overtake Frisol and find him on some other road*), since Munday applies hunting terminology to Palmerin's search for Frisol (the verb *single* means "To separate (one deer, etc.) from the herd; to pick out and chase separately," q.v. *OED*, v.1 2). Note, however, that Munday opens the following sentence by describing Palmerin's thoughts as *imagining* and properly translating the Fr. *deuancer* ("to ouertake").

2 **whom you haue left in verye great ieopardie** This clause differs from the Fr. "qui eust esté vn grand dommage" (M5v; *which would have been great pity*).

3 **Bowe and arrow in his hande, which he let flye at his Horsse and killed him** Munday avoids providing details about the horse's death; cf. Galigani, 279.

4 **the inner Courte** It refers to an "enclosed courtyard accessed through the gates," as John Jowett explains in *Sir Thomas More*, 294 n. to line XIII.125.

5 **So rode they on, and for foure daies space hee woulde not speake one word to her . . . the circumstance of the occasion followeth in this sort** This episode follows the pattern of the Arthurian adventure of the Sorrowful Castle, going back to Chrétien de Troyes's *Ywain*, lines 5107–5809. The motif (F771.4.8; see Bordman, 40) was not created by Chrétien, who most probably found it in his source; see *Ywain and Gawain*, 128–29, n. to lines 2931–3358. Apart from the Middle English translation of Chrétien's romance, this motif also occurs in Malory's *Morte Darthur*, VI.x.147–48. This episode as presented in Munday's version shares the following points with the other English texts: (1) the hero becomes involved in the adventure at the request of a damsel that shows him the path to the perilous castle; cf. *Ywain and Gawain*, 2931–33, and to a lesser degree Malory, 147.22; (2) the hero chances to meet a knight, the Knight with a Bow, who kills his horse; cf. the "foule chorle" that attacks Lancelot and kills his horse in Malory, 147.24–29; (3) the castle can be entered by crossing a bridge; cf. Lancelot "rode ouer a longe brydge" in Malory, 147.24; (4) access to the castle is granted by a guardian or porter; cf. *Ywain and Gawain*, 2953–56; (5) the hero is welcomed by a number of gentlewomen and knights, who both in *Ywain and Gawain* (3339–48) and in Malory (VI.xi.148.3–10) express their happiness only after the hero's victory; (6) the hero learns that other knights have failed before, as happens in *Ywain and Gawain*, 3064–66, and Malory (148.12–13: "for many fayre knyghtes haue assayed hit and here haue ended"; (7) the hero is first unarmed and next receives "a gorgious Mantle" (295.4), just like Ywain, who is both unarmed (3102) and then provided with "ful riche wedes to were" (3107); (8) next the hero, like Ywain (3111–13), is offered food; (9) as happens in *Ywain and Gawain* (3005–67), the hero is informed of the circumstances that led to the present sorrowful situation; (10) the hero goes to bed ("afterwarde was *Palmerin* conducted to his Chamber, and beeing in bedde hee coulde take no rest," 297.21–22), like Ywain (3114); (11) the hero goes to a chapel ("rysing the sooner in the morning, he went with the Ladie to seruice in her Chappell" 297.24–25), just as Ywain "Went ful sone til a chapele" (3120); (12) the hero comes across a woeful lady, comparable to the gentlewomen in *Ywain and Gawain*, 2966–76, and Malory, 148.5–7; (13) finally, the hero fights the oppressor, Scloto, who is described as "the most mishaped, deformed and worst conditioned Knight" (295.37), and thus comparable in his deformity to the two opponents in *Ywain and Gawain*, "Men sais þai er þe devil sons, / Geten of a woman with a ram"

(3018–19), and in Malory, VI.xi.147.38, "two grete gyaunts." Unlike the medieval English analogues, the castle in *Palmerin d'Oliva* is enchanted (motif D6.1., *enchanted sorrowful castle*; see Bordman, 24), but as soon as Palmerin kills Scloto, "all the enchauntments about the Castel were presentlie finished" (300.30–31). This last detail in Munday's narrative resembles one adventure of Lancelot in another sorrowful castle called the Dolorous Guard, which is also enchanted, although it is predicted that once Lancelot proves victorious "lors charroient tuit li anchentement del chastel dom il estoit toz plains," *Lancelot do Lac: The Non-Cyclic Old French Prose Romance*, ed. Elspeth Kennedy (Oxford: Clarendon Press, 1980), 1:183.36–37: *then all the enchantments of the castle, of which it was full, will disappear.*

6 **he affected a Ladie, of no lesse qualitie and condition then himselfe** Fr. "qu'il deuint amoureux d'vne Damoyselle de moindre qualité & condicion que luy" (M6r; *he fell in love with a Lady of less quality and condition than himself*).

7 **he continued his amorous desires to my Daughter . . . but he by no meanes wil be perswaded** This episode represents an unusual instance of rape, because it combines the two early modern senses of *rape*, namely, abduction and violation of a woman. Rape, as the clearest representation of a damsel in distress, forms a recurrent topic in chivalric narratives, including the English translations of the Iberian romances. For a useful discussion and interpretation of the role of rape in this literary corpus, see Jocelyn Catty, *Writing Rape, Writing Women in Early Modern England: Unbridled Speech* (New York: Palgrave, 2011), 25–42, and 9–24 for the ways in which the concept of rape was construed in contemporary England.

8 **a disease called Saint *Anthonyes* fire in one of her legges** St Anthony's fire describes "an intensely painful burning sensation in the limbs and extremities caused by a fungus . . . that can contaminate rye and wheat. The fungus produces alkaloid substances known as ergotamines, which . . . in excess . . . are highly toxic and cause symptoms such as hallucinations, severe gastrointestinal upset, and a type of dry gangrene. Chronic ergot poisoning (ergotism) was rife during the Middle Ages due to the consumption of contaminated rye," *Webster's New World Medical Dictionary*, ed. Mitzi Waltz (Foster City, CA: IDG Books Worldwide, 2000), s.v. "St. Anthony's fire." Here Munday is more specific than the Fr. "chancre, ou estiomene" (M6v; *cancer or gangrene*).

9 **I cannot nowe reuersse the enchauntments . . . though gladlie I woulde if it laye in my power** Expansion of Fr. "je ne puis maintenant deffaire l'enchantement que j'ay fait, dont il me desplaist" (M6v–M7r; *I cannot now undo the enchantment and that displeases me*).

10 **behelde there a more sumptuous Armour . . . at the earnest intreatie of beautifull *Thetis*** Thetis begged Vulcan (the lame Roman god equivalent to the Greek

Hephaestus), the metalworker, to forge arms for her son Achilles. The story is told by Homer in *The Iliad*, xviii.428 ff., and xix.12 ff.; cf. Ovid, *Met.*, xiii.288–95.

11 **Palmerin presently put of hys owne Armour** Munday avoids enumerating the various parts forming the armour as we read in the Fr. sig. M7v.

12 **two mightie Lyons, who assaulted *Palmerin* . . . and soone after he sent the other after for companie** The presence of a couple of lions to prevent the hero's advance is a common motif in chivalric literature (motif B847: *Lions placed in castle to prevent entrance*; Bueno Serrano, "Índice," 651); e.g., Malory describes how Lancelot "aryued afore a castel on the bak syde . . . . And there was a posterne opened . . . and was open withoute ony kepynge, sauf two lyons kept the entre" (XVII.xiv.495). For a list of romances, including the English translations of Iberian *libros de caballerías*, with the same motif, see Harold Golder, "Bunyan and Spenser," *PMLA* 45 (1930): 227 n. 35.

13 **when hee fought with the Serpent on the Mountaine *Artifaeria*** See 151.27–152.5.

14 **naked from the middle vpwarde** Munday specifies the comparatively vague Fr. "mal en ordre" (M8v; *in a bad way*).

15 **a Dreame he had the night before . . . take her thence perforce, and murder him** Of course, this prophetic dream comes true. For a brief commentary on Scloto's dream, see González, "Sueños," 240.

16 **hath had such absolution for his deserts, as he hath left his heade in signe of his penaunce** Palmerin refers to Catholic religious practices to explain jocularly the outcome of his fight against Scloto. Absolution and penance are two of the seven sacraments in the Catholic Church enabling people to obtain complete forgiveness for their sins when these are confessed to a priest and the assigned penance is done. In Palmerin's view there is no absolution for the treatment Scloto gives to the lady, and therefore the penance he deserves for those sins can be only death. Munday's translation follows the Fr. text closely.

17 **as they coulde not speake to eache other theyr teares so hindered them** This clause is Munday's interpolation.

18 **beeing vnarmed . . . and hee was so well entertained as hart coulde deuise** Munday omits the following information from the Fr.: "il fut desarmé & couché en vn riche lict, & la jeune Damoyselle en vn autre, qui auoit autant ou plus mestier d'estre traictée que Palmerin" (N1r; *Palmerin was unarmed and lying in a rich bed, and in another was the young damsel, who was in the same or greater need of treatment than Palmerin*).

19 **putting his head on the point of a Launce, they placed it on the top of the Towre for a perpetuall memory** Note that in the Dolorous Guard Lancelot also

finds "desus mains des creniax si avoit testes de chevaliers atoz les hiaumes, et androit chascun crenel a tombel ou il a letres qui dient: 'Ci gist cil, et veez la sa teste,'" *Lancelot do Lac*, 1:194.7–10 (*on many battlements there were the heads of knights equipped with helms, and in each battlement a tomb-stone with an inscription that reads: 'Here lies so-and-so, and there you can see his head'*).

20 the other Knight I.e., Frisol. In the Fr. the damsel decides to fall silent, "craignant par ses repliques l'ennuyer, ou fascher" (N1r; *fearing to annoy or bother him with her rejoinders*).

Chapter 56

1 occasions of great importaunce so commaundeth me It was possible to have a singular verb with a plural subject. For the use of *-th* for 3rd person plural, see Görlach, 88–89.

2 The Ladie right gladde of *Palmerins* **noble offer, and her Daughter thankfull for her benefit receiued** Cf. Fr. "la Dame fut grandement faschée, & encores plus la Damoyselle sa fille" (N1r; *the lady was greatly upset and even more so her daughter*).

3 Then tooke shee out of a Coffer two riche and precious Ringes ... by meanes of your loue may anie way endaunger her This incident combines two motifs: *ring as parting token* (H82.3.1; Bordman, 46, and Bueno Serrano, "Índice," 736) and *magic ring* (D1076; Bordman, 26, and Bueno Serrano, "Índice," 666).

4 tall fellow This phrase is Munday's free, jocular rendering of the Fr. "mon amy" (N1v; *my friend*).

5 considering my profession is cleane contrarie This clause is Munday's interpolation. Although the activities of knight and hermit are poles apart, the distance between these two occupations is smaller than Munday suggests. For instance, Guy of Warwick, with a distinguished career as a knight, retires to a hermitage before his death: "And an ermitage he [i.e., Guy] founde at last, / . . . / There thought he, for sooth to say, / To dwell unto his ending day" (lines 7396–7400), as can be read in the edition printed ca. 1565 by William Copland, here quoted from the text edited by Gustav Schleich, *Guy of Warwick nach Copland Druck*, Palaestra 139 (Leipzig: Mayer & Müller, 1923), 222. The same is true of the hermit in Ramon Llull's *The Book of the Ordre of Chyualry*, trans. William Caxton, ed. Alfred T. P. Byles, EETS os 168 (London: Oxford University Press, 1926), 3–4.

6 as pittieth the miseries of despysed creatures This clause is Munday's insertion.

7 and haling his flesh with such impatience This clause is Munday's interpolation.

8 That I might not bee reckoned ... deserued the loue of a Ladie of her calling Motif T91.6.4.4: *Heroine will not marry knight of low rank*; cf. Bordman, 91, and Bueno Serrano, "Índice," 908.

9 those happy soules in the *Elysian* Fieldes In Greek mythology the Elysium (or Elysian Fields) was the place where some chosen heroes, after their death, were brought by the gods. It is thus understood as a place of ideal happiness.

10 God knowes is most vntrue This clause is Munday's interpolation; the Fr. makes no allusion to divine powers.

11 I determined with my selfe ... to this brutishe kinde of life Varnan adopts the lifestyle of a wild man ("brutishe kinde of life") as a result of his rejection by his beloved Valerica. It is an instance of motif T.93.1: *Disappointed lover becomes wild man* (cf. Bordman, 91; not included in Bueno Serrano, since the Sp. contains no suggestion of Varnan's becoming an *homo sylvaticus*; see Sp., 140). Varnan's reaction is recognizable from other English chivalric texts. In *Ywain and Gawain* Ywain experiences the same feelings of rejection by his wife Alundyne, "An evyl toke him als he stode; / For wa he wex al wilde and wode. / Unto þe wod þe way he nome" (lines 1649–51; *As he stood he got an illness; because of woe he became all wild and mad and took his way to the wood*); cf. a similar episode involving Tristram and Isolde in Malory, IX.xvii–xxi.260–64.

12 howe he was in daunger to receiue the like reward, as the Knight did of his *Valerica* Palmerin has a premonition that he may be affected by a similar turn of events. See 311.42–312.9 where Palmerin, like Varnan, is presented with a hawk by the same lady.

13 I will not liue anie longer to preiudice anie other man This clause is Munday's interpolation.

14 So drewe hee foorth *Palmerins* Sworde ... to condemne your soule to euerlasting perdition? In desperation because of his sweetheart's rejection, Varnan is determined to commit suicide by stabbing himself with a sword. While being not an uncommon literary motif (motif F1041.21.6.6: *attempted suicide from grief*; Bordman, 44, and Bueno Serrano, "Índice," 729), this incident also had direct resonances for the book's contemporary readers, since there was a sense that suicide was becoming more common; see Michael MacDonald, "The Inner Side of Wisdom: Suicide in Early Modern England," *Psychological Medicine* 7 (1977): 565–82, here 566. Therefore, the events contained in the romance could be felt to be realistic, because the method of self-destruction was the third preferred in suicides (cf. MacDonald, ibid., 567) and his motive was one of the four most common in England (cf. MacDonald, ibid., 569). Palmerin mentions the severe consequences that such an act would have on Varnan's soul. Since self-destruction was considered to be anti-natural and against God's law, suicides were denied "funerals and burial in the churchyard, the rites which marked the transmigration of Christian souls into the afterlife and membership in the community of the dead" (MacDonald, ibid., 567). For more information about the changing attitudes toward suicide, see also Gary B. Ferngren, "The Ethics of Suicide in the Renaissance and Reformation," *Suicide and Euthanasia: Historical and Contemporary Themes*, ed. Baruch A. Brody (Dordrecht: Kluwer Academic, 1989), 155–81.

15 **yet let mee intreate you to forbeare this humour** This clause is an amplification of the Fr. "ayez la de moy" (N2v; *have it* [i.e., pity] *on me*). The word *humour* became fashionable at the end of the sixteenth century and Munday has no qualms in forcing it into his text; see David Bevington's introduction to his edition of Ben Jonson's *Every Man In His Humour*, in *The Cambridge Edition of the Works of Ben Jonson*, ed. David Bevington, Martin Butler, and Ian Donaldson (Cambridge: Cambridge University Press, 2012), 1:115.

16 **as her iudgment may exceede a hell of torments** This clause departs from the Fr. "vn mal excedant dix mile morts ensemble" (N2v; *an evil causing in excess of ten thousand deaths altogether*).

17 **him that hath all harts at commaunde, repose your selfe constantlie on his prouidence** This passage expands the Fr. "DIEV." (N2v; *God*).

18 **Sirra** Form of address used for social inferiors.

19 **Fortune why art thou so inconstant** Proverbial; Tilley, F 606.

20 **saide** Fr. "se prit à rire" (N3r; *started laughing*).

21 **whose true loue aboue all other hath deserued you** This clause is Munday's insertion.

22 **that will meddle with matters aboue their capacitie** This clause is an amplification of the Fr. "qui vous ressemblent" (N3v; *who resemble you*).

23 **Marke what will be the ende of thy presumption** This clause is an amplification of the Fr. "vous verrez qu'il en auiendra" (N3v; *you will see what will happen*).

Chapter 57

1 **as you haue hearde before** See 293.5–17.

2 **or els he woulde sende him after his Maister** This clause corresponds to the Fr. "qu'il luy appresteroit de la viande pour toute sa vie" (N4r; *that he would prepare meat/food for the rest of his life*).

3 **vnite your selfe to her by present speeches** Palmerin is encouraging Varnan to marry Valerica *per verba de praesenti*; see n. 19 to chap. I.vi.

4 **and for you are so stubborne** This clause is Munday's interpolation.

5 **dayes** Fr. "mois" (N5r; *months*).

Chapter 58

1 **the slaine Knight** See 306.2–15.

2 **Martin** Fr. "Esmerillon" (N5r; *merlin*); note that a merlin is a falcon-like bird, unlike a martin. Note that in 349.39 Munday translates this word accurately as "Marlin."

3 **my Faulcon so good as she will neuer faile.** *Palmerin* **who aboue all pastimes looued Hauking** In George Turbeville's *Booke of Faulconrie*, published in 1575, we read, "the female of all byrdes of praye and rauyne [including the female falcon] is euer more huge than the male, more ventrous, hardie, and watchfull" (quoted in Catherine Bates, *Masculinity and the Hunt: Wyatt to Spenser* [Oxford: Oxford University Press, 2013], 150), thus explaining why a female falcon is used. Hawking was a fauourite pastime of the nobility in the late Middle Ages and the Renaissance, although it went gradually out of fashion; see Richard Grassby, "The Decline of Falconry in Early Modern England," *Past and Present* 157 (1997): 37–62.

4 **the selfe same Lady, which sent the Faulcon to** *Varnan***.** See 304.22–31; Palmerin's premonitory feelings in 305.6–7 are here confirmed.

5 **the Tents, where the Duke of** *Gaules* **Knights guarded the passage** See 293.30–35.

6 **but seeing thou art so long before thou art ready** Fr. "il y a trop long temps qu'estes à cheual" (N5v; *it has been too long a time that you've been riding your horse*).

7 **seuenth** Fr. "cinquiesme" (N6r; *fifth*).

Chapter 59

1 **the man, against whome sometime I combated in** *Fraunce* See 231.5–19.

2 **hee came to the Dukes sister, who looued him intirely, as you heard before** It is not mentioned that the Duke of Gaule's sister loves Frisol.

3 **were his head framed of the hardest hammered brasse** This clause is Munday's interpolation.

4 **to seeke him I forsooke my fathers house, and haue continued a very laboursome search** See 143.22–24.

5 **commaunding them to restraine the passage no longer at the bridge** Note that Munday provides more specific information than the Fr., "fit abollir la mauuaise coustume, que jusques adonc il auoit tenue en son chasteau" (N8r; *he caused to be abolished the bad custom that until that time he had kept in his castle*). Maugin chooses not to disambiguate the original Sp., "de allí adelante mandó quitar la

costumbre del castillo" (149; *from then on he commanded to abolish that custom from the castle*).

Chapter 60

1 **to shorten the thought of our iourney** To make the journey seem shorter (by spending the time listening to the news from Greece).

2 **his conquest of the Serpent . . . that brought the King of** *Macedon* **to his former health** See 151.37–152.5 and 153.24–32.

3 **as is vsuall at the meeting of long absent loouers** This clause is Munday's free translation for "qu'ilz furent vn bien long temps sans pouuoir parler" (N8v; *that they were unable to speak for quite a long while*).

4 **why did you depart not vouchsafing a farewell?** See 289.37–40.

5 *Palmerin* **falling on his knee, kissed hys highnes hand** Cf. Fr. "s'approcha du Roy pour luy baiser les mains: que le Roy ne voulut souffrir" (N8v; *he came up to the King to kiss his hands, but the King did not permit it*).

6 **he had that Armour of the Lady . . . and left his owne there broken in peeces** See 294.27–39.

7 **to conferre with straungers** Munday subtly alters the Fr. "s'amuser auec les estrangers" (O1r; *to enjoy herself with foreigners*); cf. Galigani, 284.

8 **suborning** This is the first recorded occurrence of the word according to the *OED*.

9 **a dreame he had the night before . . . what trouble he had with his dreame** Once again Polinarda addresses Palmerin in his dreams (cf. 140.15–141.4, and 162.33–163.8). She expresses fear about her imminent separation from her beloved that the text confirms in 327.19–29. This dream has an immediate effect on the narrative action of the romance, since it prompts Palmerin to advance his return, "lo cual posibilita indirectamente la peripecia que sufre la nao que lleva de regreso al héroe," as suggests González, "Sueños," 241.

Chapter 61

1 **Maskers, Momeries and Moriscoes** *Maskers* refers to people taking part in a masque; *momeries* are dumbshows; the word *morisco* is used to describe a morris dance. Cf. Munday, *Amadis*, 999 n. to 894.

2 **I must giue you this ring . . . as I intreate you to keepe it continually on your finger** This magic ring induces to love and not only does it preclude the possibility that Agriola can love any other different from Trineus, but also protects her from the unwanted advances of other suitors, as explained in 302.25–33.

3 how farre such a thought ought to be from you, I leaue to your own construction This clause is Munday's interpolation.

4 The meane to preuent this mishap ... makes way to manifold misfortunes and dangers The English version represents an amplification of the Fr.: "Et de tout ce (si vouliez croyre mon auis) ne seroit rien: ains à vostre fantasie en voulez estre la premiere cause & l'effait" (O2r; *And this would be nothing, if you wish to believe my opinion; instead, according to your fantasy, you wish to be the first cause and effect*).

5 Be of good cheere man ... none but *Trineus* must be her Lord and husband This sentence is Munday's interpolation.

Chapter 62

1 which made her fal into such pittiful acclamations, far surpassing those of *Maguelona*, when she lost her freend *Peter of Prouince* in the wood Munday alludes to the romance *Peter of Provence and the fair Maguelone*, which tells the story of Peter, son to the count of Provence. Having heard about the extraordinary beauty of Maguelone, daughter to the King of Naples, Peter decides to travel to Naples and take part in the tournaments being held there. After winning the battle on the day of his arrival, Peter meets Maguelone at dinner and they both fall in love. Though the two of them agree on their love, she knows that her father will oppose her marriage with Peter, who then asks her to elope with him. They run away at night riding a horse during two days, until they stop to sleep on the second night. Peter wakes up and, following a bird that has taken Maguelone's rings, gets onto a fishing boat, but is taken prisoner by Moorish pirates. When Maguelone wakes up she is completely unaware of the whereabouts of Peter. It is at this moment when the "pittiful acclamations" alluded by Munday occur. This story was highly popular throughout Europe, with versions in more than twenty languages including English. For a complete bibliography of all existing versions, see François Roudaut, ed., *Pierre de Provence et la belle Maguelonne* (Paris: Classiques Garnier, 2009), 255–78. The English version survives only in two manuscript fragments, one fifteenth-century manuscript used by Frederick Furnivall for his edition titled *Peare of Provence and the Fair Maguelone*, in *Political, Religious and Love Poems* (London: Kegan Paul, Trench, Trübner, 1866; reprinted 1903), 293–300; and a sixteenth-century manuscript edited by Arne Zettersten, "Pierre of Provence and the Faire Maguelonne: A Prose Romance Edited from Bodleian MS. Lat. misc. b. 17 and Bibliothèque nationale ms. fr. 1501," *English Studies* 46 (1965): 187–201. Both these fragments contain no reference to Maguelone's moans, which are included in the French version: "Quant elle vist qu'elle ne le ouyoit en lieu a peu que elle ne saillist hors de son sens et commença fort à plourer et aller parmy le bois criant son amy Pierre tant fort qu'elle pouvoyt crier ... Et après ... commença à faire les plus piteux plains que jamais homme ouyt" (Roudaut, op. cit., 104: *When she realized that she couldn't find him she nearly went out of her senses and started crying loudly and walking within the wood shouting for her friend Peter as loudly as she could . . . And later she started making the most pitiful laments ever heard*). It is important to note that the allusion to Maguelone's wails is introduced by Munday (and was not part of the original Sp. as mistakenly noted by Patchell, 98), who substitutes this reference for the mythological one in the Fr.: "Hecuba, ayant veu sacrifier sa fille Polixene sur le tombeau d'Achilles" (O3v; *Hecuba, after having seen her daughter Polyxena being sacrificed on Achilles' tomb*); cf. Ovid, *Met.*, XIII.448 ff. Munday's intervention is significant. On the one hand, it establishes a parallel with the events in *Palmerin d'Oliva*, since both Maguelona and Agriola decide to elope, while both their lovers are taken captive by the Turks; note, however, that Patchell disapproves of Munday's intervention and considers that this "analogy is poorly drawn," 87–88. On the other hand, the fact that Munday refers matter-of-factly to this story suggests that he could expect it to be widely known, although the exiguous textual evidence might have led us to think otherwise.

Chapter 63

1 **and speedy conduction to your longing desires . . . be thorowly comforted** This passage is an amplification of the Fr. "& conduire ou vous aspirez le plus: & que bien tost ces yeux vous puissent voir, & ces bras embrasser à mon plaisir" (O4v; *and conduct you where you most desire; and that very soon these eyes may see you, and these arms embrace you at my pleasure*).

2 **the Pallace of *Salomon*** It refers to the temple built by King Solomon. The construction of this building is described in 1 Kings 5–8, where it reads, "And the whole house he ouerlaid with golde vntill he had finished all the house" (1 Kgs 6:22). Munday refers to Solomon's temple in his *Mirrour*: "he [i.e., Solomon] made all the ornaments of the Lords *Temple* of pure Golde" (98.29–30).

3 **the Princes Electours** refers to "the Princes of Germany formerly entitled to take part in the election of the Emperor" (*OED*, s.v. *elector* n. 3).

4 **you know what promise I made my brother . . . that I would not mary before his returne** See 254.10–14.

5 **will ye or no** whether you like it or not.

Chapter 64

1 **foure** Fr. "deux" (O6r; *two*).

2 **If my life might endure the length of tenne mens** A hyperbole of the Fr. "tous les jours de ma vie" (O6r; *all the days of my life*).

3 **In steede of teares, let vs vse quaint tearmes ... with his very vttermost endeuors** This passage is added by Munday.

4 *Himen* Greek god of marriage.

5 *Iuno* Roman goddess of marriage.

6 **Let these perswasions, if not my intreates ... requiting theyr chast looue, with a simpathie of vertuous desires** This passage describing the marriage of Trineus and Agriola is authored almost entirely by Munday; cf. the corresponding Fr. text (O6r: "Palmerin voyant liurer ... telles choses"). In contemporary England this form of verbal contract, performed by the mutual consent of the couple but without a public ceremony or the sanction of a cleric, was legally binding, even if the parents chose to oppose it, as Palmerin anticipates. Munday includes a reference to the impossibility of divorce, which actually was never permitted in Tudor England; for the discussion about legalizing divorce in contemporary England, see Lawrence Stone, *Road to Divorce: England, 1530–1987* (Oxford: Oxford University Press, 1990), 301–4.

7 **fiue** Fr. "vingt" (O6r; *twenty*).

8 **they were in this perplexitie** Maugin here refers to the winds "Mestral, Nordest, Bise, & de Transmontane" (O6rv; "*mistral, northeasterly wind, bise, and tramontana*"); these winds all come from the north and thus would expedite the crossing from London to an island near Anatolia; cf. Bettoni, 187–88. Munday omits this information.

9 **for they could discerne no other remedie** Cf. the Fr. "quand il luy plairoit la leur enuoyer" (O6v; *when it should please Him to send them their death*).

10 **his Faulcon ... that was giuen him in *England*** See 311.42–312.8.

Chapter 65

1 **roughe** This is the first occurrence of this word in this sense recorded in the *OED* (q.v. adj. 10c).

2 *Mirmedon* "A member of a gang or army adhering to a particular leader; a hired ruffian or mercenary" (*OED*, s.v. *myrmidon* n. 3a); this is the sense in the *OED* that most closely represents Munday's use of it, although it predates the earliest instance recorded in the dictionary in more than sixty years.

3 she hath in her custody a iewel of such vertue, as no one can dishonour her against her owne lyking I.e., her ring. See 320.25–28.

4 *Natolia* Most probably the Anatolian Peninsula; but see also n. 2 to chap. II.xxiv.

5 the Isle where they landed was called *Malfada*, which name was giuen it by the Lady thereof, who was called likewise *Malfada* The name of the enchantress, Malfada, means in Sp. "bad fairy" (Sp. *mal hada*; Corominas and Pascual [see below] mention how "en los Libros de Caballerías se aplicó *hada* a un ser femenino sobrenatural que intervenía de varias maneras en la vida de los hombres"); but when it is used for the island, the name describes an ill-fated land (Lat. *fatum* > med. Sp. *fado* > *hado*). For this etymology, see Joan Corominas and José A. Pascual, *Diccionario crítico etimológico castellano e hispánico* (Madrid: Gredos, 1980), s.v. *hado*, and Marín Pina, "Maga", 78; This fabulous place and the events that happen there gave inspiration to the Spanish chronicler Álvar Núñez Cabeza de Vaca (ca. 1495–ca. 1560) to designate as *Malhado* an island he chanced upon in his expedition to America (1527–1537): "A esta ysla pusimos por nombre ysla de Malhado," *Los naufragios*, ed. Enrique Pupo-Walker, Nueva Biblioteca de Erudición y Crítica 5 (Madrid: Castalia, 1992), 226. This place name enjoyed no real currency, although Cabeza de Vaca chose to apply it probably to Galveston island, on the coast of Texas; see Cleve Hallenbeck, *Álvar Núñez Cabeza de Vaca: The Journey and Route of the First European to Cross the Continent of North America, 1534–1536* (Port Washington, N.Y.: Kennikat Press, 1971), 119–27. For biographical information, see Carmen Borrego Pla, "Núñez Cabeza de Vaca, Álvar," *DBE*, 38:60–62. For the parallels between Cabeza de Vaca's account and the Sp. romance, see Javier Roberto González, "Mal Hado-Malfado. Reminiscencias del *Palmerín de Olivia* en los *Naufragios* de Álvar Núñez Cabeza de Vaca," *Kañina: Revista de Artes y Letras* 23 (1999): 55–66.

6 the most subtill Magitian of her tyme: so that wee may say of her, as the Poets feigned of the auncient *Circes* The myth of the enchantress Circe goes back to Homer's *Odyssey* (X.133–466), where she is seen entertaining Odysseus while she is capable of turning men into "swine or wolves or lions" (X.433), but it was retold later on by other ancient poets including Virgil (*Aeneid*, VII.10–24) and Ovid (*Met.* XIV.247–307). For the historical development of this myth from classical to modern times, see Judith Yarnall, *The Transformations of Circe: The History of an Enchantress* (Urbana, IL: University of Illinois Press, 1994); Yarnall reproduces on 103 a woodcut representation of Circe from Geffrey Whitney's *A Choice of Emblemes* (1586). For a discussion of the use of this myth in the Sp., see Marín Pina, "Maga", 78–82. Note that Aeaea, the name of Circe's island in the *Odyssey*, XII.4, is located somewhere in the region of the Levant, where the sun rises and where the action takes place; see further in Alfred Heubeck and Arie Hoekstra, *A Commentary on Homer's Odyssey* (Oxford: Clarendon Press, 1989),

2:52, n. to lines X.135–39. Cf. Munday, *Primaleon*, III.iv.17, where we read how the giant Gataru's brother is changed to a dog when "he was inchanted in the Isle of *Malfate*"; see Patchell, 40 n. 100.

7 **when she had abused them to content her owne pleasure** Malfada's main goal is to satisfy her sexual desires, with no respect for the Christian morality of her parents and completely governed by the devil; cf. José Manuel Lucía Megías and Emilio José Sales Dasí in "La otra realidad social en los libros de caballerías (II): Damas y doncellas lascivas," in *Actes del X Congrés Internacional de l'Associació Hispànica de Literatura Medieval*, ed. Rafael Alemany et al. (Alicante: University of Alicante Press, 2005), 2:1008–9.

8 *Trineus* **was chaunged into the shape of a very fayre Dogge . . . marueiling only at his sudden mutation** In spite of the human degradation entailed by being metamorphosed into animals, Trineus can consider himself fortunate, since his existence in the shape of a dog carries the advantage of being treated like a domestic animal; cf. Campos, 282–84.

Postscript

1 **Honos alit Artes** This is a literal quotation from Cicero's *Tusculan Disputations*, I.ii.4: "Public esteem is the nurse of the arts"; trans. I. E. King, The Loeb Classical Library (Cambridge, MA: Harvard University Press, 1950), 7. Munday had already used this motto on the title page of his earlier works, *The Mirrour of Mutabilitie* (1579; for a facsimile reproduction, see Munday, *Mirrour*, 1), *A View of Sundry Examples* (1580), *Zelauto* (1580), *A Courtly Controversie, Betweene Loove and Learning* (1581), *A Breefe Aunswer* (1582), and the *English Romaine Life* (1582; for a facsimile, see Ayres's edition, xxix). At the beginning of the first book of *The Mirrour of Mutabilitie*, Munday expresses his deep admiration for Cicero (see Munday, *Mirrour*, 24 n. to line 6). Cicero's dictum became proverbial in the Renaissacne; cf. Hans Walther, *Proverbia Sententiaeque Latinitatis Medii Ac Recentoris Aevi*, ed. Paul Gerhard Schmidt, vol. II/8 (Göttingen: Vandenhoeck & Ruprecht, 1983), 282. Erasmus himself comments on it in his *Adages*, I.viii.92, trans. R. A. B. Mynors, Collected Works of Erasmus 32 (Toronto: University of Toronto Press, 1989), 174; it was included in Richard Taverner, *Proverbes or Adagies, gathered out of the Chiliades of Erasmus* (1569), sig. C8v. The English version of this adage, i.e., "Honors nourish arts," became proverbial in Elizabethan England; cf. Tilley, H584. See also Munday, *Amadis*, 979 n. to 297; Munday, *Mirrour*, 4; Munday, *Zelauto*, 189; and Hill, 49.

Notes to the Text
Part II

Title-page

1 **Thomas Creede** For information, see "Introduction," 45–49.

The Epistle

1 **Promise is debt, my good Lord, as the Prouerb auoucheth** For this proverb, see Tillley, P603. Note that Munday previously used this proverb in his *Zelauto*, 20: "promise is due debt we say."

2 **When I presented your honour the first part of this Historie, I promised to hasten the other to the selfe same Patrone** Munday used the marketing strategy of announcing the forthcoming publication of his translations of romances. To see how he organized his literary "debts" and how he usually fulfilled his promises, see Gary Schmidgall, "*The Tempest* and *Primaleon*: A New Source," *Shakespeare Quarterly* 37 (1986): 431 nn. 7, 8.

To the Freendlie Readers

1 **Paladine** *sonne to the king* **Mylanor** *of* **England . . .** *which is already on the presse in good forwardnesse* The next Iberian romance translated by Munday was *Palladine of England*, published on April 23, 1588, just a little over a month after making this announcement.

Chapter 1

1 **As yet I am sure you remember in the first part . . . the King of** *Englandes* **daughter** See 332.10–33.

2 **hoping in time to purchase her lyking** Munday suppresses the sexual overtones of the Fr. "pensant bien en jouyr & faire à sa volunté" (O8r; *thinking to have joy of her and to do what he wanted*).

3 **the Ring that** *Palmerin* **gaue her** See 320.25–28.

4 **and eleuated eyes to heauen** This phrase substitutes for the Fr. "en rendit louanges" (O8v; *he praised God for it*).

5 *That great persons giue great presents* This saying is not recorded in Tilley; see "Introduction," 94.

6 **Golde** Fr. "esmail" (O8v: *enamel*).

7 **milke white breasts** Munday amplifies the Fr. "tetins" (O8v; *breasts*).

8 **more mortifyed and humbled then the aged Hermits of** *Thebaida* These are the first hermits in the history of the Christian Church, known for their longevity and for practising austerity, humility, and mortification. Paul of Thebes, also known as Paul the First Hermit, took refuge in the Theban desert as he fled from the Roman emperor Decius, and lived well over one hundred years (d. ca. 345). His disciple Antony of Egypt also died a centenarian (251–356). For more information, see David Farmer, *Oxford Dictionary of Saints*, 5th rev. ed. (Oxford: Oxford University Press, 2011), 23–24, 347. For a collection of relevant sources about and by these hermits, see Helen Waddell, *The Desert Fathers* (Ann Arbor, MI: University of Michigan Press, 1957).

9 **and now hee had in his booteless loue . . . had spoyled him of his owne companie** This clause departs from the Fr. "Et tant s'en faloit, qu'il auoit luy mesmes tout perdu, par la tempeste & naufrage" (O8v; *And so it fell that he had himself lost all due to the tempest and shipwreck*). Munday introduces Olimael's ill-advised love as one of the causes of his misfortune.

10 **the great Turke did earnestly affect fayre Ladyes** From the sixteenth century, the Ottoman dynasty's survival did not depend on political alliances or interdynastic marriages, as was the norm among western monarchies, but instead it "chose to reproduce itself by serial concubinage with slaves" (Mansel, 82). Beauty, and not birth, was essential for concubines selected to enter the imperial harem. Thus Olimael knows that the Sultan will be pleased to welcome fair Agriola to his harem. See further in Leslie P. Peirce, *The Imperial Harem: Women and Sovereignty in the Ottoman Empire* (New York: Oxford University Press, 1993), esp. 28–112.

11 **by casuall mischaunce he had lost his men and Gallies** Fr. "par orage & fortune il auoit perdu ses gens" (O8v; *due to a storm and fortune he had lost his men*).

12 **more addicted to vnchaste desires** On this occasion Munday prefers to avoid the concreteness of the Fr. "conuoiteux de belles filles" (O8v; *desirous of beautiful girls*); but cf. n. 10 above.

13 **the glimse thereof set every eye to wonder** This clause amplifies the Fr. "chacun s'en esmerueilloit" (P1r; *everyone marveled at her beauty*).

Notes to the Text: Part II

14 **whom they minded secretly to convey from her ... stept towards him** These two clauses are interpolated by Munday.

15 **vndutifull obedience** Munday rephrases the Fr. "grand deshonneur" (P1r; *great dishonour*) in order to temper Agriola's feelings of guilt and more precisely identify her breach of the expected filial obedience.

16 **for God dooth know** For the first time Munday introduces a reference to God with no equivalent in the Fr.

17 **sweet death, too long desired death** This phrase is Munday's addition.

18 **my minde perswades me, that wee shall be deliuered by noble *Palmerin*** Palmerin facilitates the freedom of Agriola in chap. II.xliii and of Ptolome in chap. II.lviii.

19 **to kicke against the pricke** Acts 9:5; see Tilley F 433.

20 **as thou couldest neuer honour me with the like** Fr. "que j'en doy oublier tout le passé, ores que m'auriez meffait" (P1r; *that I must forget all the past, now that you have done me harm*).

21 **and thou shalt say the Emperour is bountifull** Fr. "qu'à jamais vous deürez contenter de moy" (P1r; *for you ought to be satisfied with me forever*). Below we read that that the Emperor appoints Olimael High Admiral of the Mediterranean.

22 **then in their presence shal our nuptialles be solemnized** Munday alters the sense of the original Fr. "pour luy monstrer amplement nostre magnificence" (P1r; *in order to fully show them our magnificence*). Regardless of the fact that she is a Christian, the Sultan here expresses his desire to marry Agriola and to treat her with respect, not just like another concubine. In fact Agriola's destiny is not without a historical precedent, since the Sultan Suleyman the Magnificent (r. 1520–66), for love, married his slave Hurrem, born Alexandra Lisowska, the daughter of an Orthodox priest. Hurrem had Suleyman forswear his other sexual partners, so great was his love for her; see Mansel, 82–86. In the case of Agriola, she takes advantage of his infatuation for her and imposes the following rule: they can share the same bed, but have to abstain from having sexual relations, for which the Sultan is allowed to turn to his concubines; cf. 377.36–37.

23 **and that all meanes may be practised** This clause is Munday's interpolation.

24 **a Chayre of state, which was purposely prouided for her** Fr. "vne chaire couuerte de drap d'or frisé & s'estant vn peu reposée" (P1v; *an armchair covered of cloth shot through with gold and having rested a bit*).

25 **the Law of *Mahomet*, and his *Alchoran*** I.e., Islam and its sacred book the Koran.

Chapter 2

1 **the *Turkish* language** The language used in the Sultan's court is interchangeably called *Arabic* or *Turkish*, although they are unrelated; the former is a Semitic language, whereas the latter belongs to the Ural-Altaic family of languages.

2 **which is the Lorde and conquerour of all things** Munday departs from his source, "qui domte toutes choses & les rend à leur poinct" (P2r; *who tames all things and brings out the best in them*).

3 **whose perfect image was engrauen in her heart** This clause expands the Fr. "le voyant en son cueur" (P2r; *seeing him in her heart*).

4 **none but him shee would loue while she liued** Munday alters the sense of the Fr. "qu'elle aymoit plus que soymémes" (P2r; *whom she loved more than herself*).

5 **considering what frailtie commonly is in women** This may be a precedent for *Hamlet*, I.ii.146: "Frailty, thy name is woman." See Per Hannibal Hamlin, *The Bible in Shakespeare* (Oxford: Oxford University Press, 2013), 155–56.

6 **(O wonderfull workeman of the whole worlde)** This vocative remark is added by Munday; note the alliteration.

7 **this Pagan could doe mee** The translation provides a specific agent in contrast to the Fr. "qu'on me sçauroit faire" (P2r; *that one could do to me*).

8 **for so sweete a reward as is thy loue** Munday elaborates on the Fr. "pour l'amour de toy" (P2v; *for the love of you*).

9 **Neuer perswade me (quoth the Princesse) to manifest disloyaltie** Explicitation of the succint Fr. "Ne m'en parlez jamais" (P2v; *never talk to me about that*).

10 *Helena*, **after her arriuall at** *Troy* See n. 10 to chap. II.xxxvi.

11 **Temple** Fr. "Mesquite" (P2v; *mosque*).

12 *Turks, Moores, Arabes,* **and** *Medes* The text makes a point of noting the existence of four different ethnic groups: the Turks refers to those belonging to the Ottoman empire; the Moors are African Muslim tribes, including those that invaded the Iberian Peninsula in the eighth century; Arabs are the people that originated from the Arabian Peninsula; the Medes are an Iranian group that established an empire in Media in the seventh century BC. Note, however, that throughout the book these terms are not always applied with such semantic precision.

13 **much lyke the Satyres and horned Faunes, giuing new inuasions on the Nimphes of** *Diana* Satyrs are mythological creatures of the woods characterized by their debauchery, in particular their love of wine and lust for nymphs. Fauns are another class of woodland gods represented as a man with horns. Nymphs are

mythological maidens inhabiting natural locations, like woods and rivers or seas, that are commonly associated with other gods; in the case of Diana, the virgin goddess of the forest and *nympha nympharum*, they may be understood as her followers forming her entourage; Spenser also connects Diana's nymphs with satyrs and fauns: "With all her [i.e., Diana's] Nymphes enranged on a rowe, / With whom the woody Gods [i.e., both satyrs and fauns] did oft consort: / For, with the Nymphes, the Satyres loue to play and sport" (*FQ*, VII.vi.39.7–9).

14 **chastitie, which was a Iewell never to be recouered** Chastity, as the foremost female virtue in early modern England, was priceless from a moral point of view.

15 **so braue and stately as the Prince** *Aeneas*, **when he came to Queene** *Dido* **of** *Carthage* When Aeneas presents himself before Dido, Virgil explains in the *Aeneid*,: "restitit Aeneas claraque in luce refulsit / os umerosque deo similis" (I.588–89; *Aeneas stood forth, gleaming in the clear light, godlike in face and shoulders*), in *Eclogues. Georgics. Aeneid: Books 1–6*, ed. and trans. H. Rushton Fairclogh, revised G. P. Goold, The Loeb Classical Library (Cambridge, MA: Harvard University Press, 1999), 302–3. Note, further that, as Helen Moore states, "these lovers are conventionally evoked at moments of betrayal"; Munday, *Amadis*, 978 n. to 273.

16 **as hee was preparing himselfe to bed** Munday prefers to censor the description of the wedding night as described in the Fr.: "Estant nu auec elle, luy commença plusieurs propoz joyeux: mais quand ce vint qu'il la cuyda traiter amoureusement il fut si surpris de paour, douleur & apoplexie" (P2v; *Being naked with her, he began to make many joyous remarks to her: but when it reached the point that he thought he could treat her amorously, he was taken aback by fear, pain, and apoplexy*). Munday's intervention prevents English readers from establishing a cause and effect relationship between the Great Turk's maladies and his impure desires, as previously happens to Olimael when attempting to rape Agriola (341.26–30).

17 **to lye vpon the bed by mee, as my Brother might doo, and sometime (though it be more then modestie) embrace thee in mine armes** Munday amplifies the Fr. "te tenir entre mes braz, comme mon amy & frere" (P2v–P3r; *to hold you in my arms as a friend and brother*); in doing so, he maintains the internal coherence of his version, especially as refers to her giving him permission to share the same bed. Now Agriola, with the help of the magic ring, has full control of the relationship.

18 **gaue him a kisse or twaine, and suffered him to embrace her** Munday's Agriola seems more generous than her French counterpart, since of her own will she kisses the Sultan, apart from letting him embrace her; cf. Fr. "l'embraça par bonne amour" (P3r; *she embraced him out of good love*).

19 *Aethiopia* Fr. "Ethiopie" (P3r); not in Sp. Since classical times the term *Ethiopia* was used to designate the region south of Egypt. According to our text, it

was possible to sail to Ethiopia, perhaps by sailing up the Nile. Conversely, the term might be used more loosely to describe the north-eastern region of Africa, extending to Turkey.

Chapter 3

1 you haue heard Fr. "auez vous ja leu" (P3r; *you have already read*); see 331.23–27.

2 hee entred into many sorrowfull lamentations, farre exceeding *Cadmus* when hee lost his Souldiers by the horrible Serpent, cursing and exclaiming on himselfe Cadmus is the legendary founder of Thebes. As told by an oracle, Cadmus had to follow a heifer and build a city in the place where the animal lay down; see Ovid, *Met.* III.1–137. When the heifer did lie down, he decided to make a sacrifice to Jove, "And bad his servants goe and fetch him water of the spring" (Golding, III.32, 62). The problem is that by the spring dwelt a serpent that "deales his dreadfull dole / Among the Tirians [i.e., Cadmus' men]" (Golding, III.52–53, 62). When Cadmus realized his men were too long delayed, he went to seek them out, but what he found were their corpses. Then he started crying: "Well trustie friends (quoth he) / I eyther of your piteous deathes will streight revenger be, / Or else will die my selfe therefore" (Golding, III.69–71, 63). This mythological episode reflects some of the narrative circumstances in our romance and conveys more vividly the pathos of Palmerin's perplexity and sense of guilt.

3 these wretched misfortunes by poore *Varnan* . . . this wicked Byrde giuen me See 303.30–305.3 and 312.3–9.

4 thence forward determined to counterfeit himselfe dumbe Dumb servants were highly valued by Ottoman sultans, since they were unable to reveal secrets; see Mansel, 96. For a brief discussion of this episode in the Sp., see Carlos Rubio Pacho, "'Acordó de fazerse mudo e jamás fablar': Palmerín entre moros," in *Palmerín: 500 años*, 114–17. Feigning dumbness as a defensive strategy is not uncommon in chivalric literature; e.g., in Munday's *Palladine of England*, Lyboran "to preserue his life, counterfeited himselfe to be dum" (sig. O3r).

5 hee hadde eaten a little bread which hee found in the Moores budget, according to the maner of *Diogenes* Diogenes (ca. 400–325 BC) was a Greek philosopher who advocated the individual's self-sufficiency, even when it involved breaking social conventions, as in this case of Palmerin taking bread from the Moor.

Chapter 4

1 *Gamezio*, who was slaine . . . as you haue heard in the first parte of this Historie See 112.35–39. It seems safe to interpret this comment as an indication that Munday knew that the romance would be published in two volumes, even before he finished translating the text (but see n. 2 to chap. II.xli).

2 **the summons of** *Atropos* I.e., the time of death. More information provided in n. 2 to chap. I.xxxi.

3 **the fieldes of** *Elysium* The resting place of heroes in Greek mythology; cf. n. 9 to chap. I.lvi.

4 **Before hee tooke his iourney wherein no creature returneth againe** It has been argued that these words could have provided Shakespeare with inspiration for *Hamlet* (III.i.79–80): "The undiscover'd country, from whose bourn / No traveller returns." See *British Bibliographer*, 148.

5 **the Citie of** *Calpha*, **from whence the name of the Island was deriued** The name *Calpha* seems to have been introduced in the story by Maugin, since the place remains unnamed in the Sp. It seems likely that it could refer to the seaport of Caffa, present-day Feodosiya, in the southern coast of the Crimea. Even though it is not strictly speaking an island, limited geographical knowledge of distant regions can explain the mistake. It was administered by Genoa until 1475 when the Ottomans conquered it. For a description of this town and its people in the fifteenth century, see the account of the Sp. traveler Pero Tafur, *Andanças e viajes de un hidalgo español*, edited by Marcos Jiménez de la Espada (Madrid: Miraguano / Polifemo, 1995), 89–95.

6 **they daily vsed hawking and hunting** Munday amplifies the information in the Fr., "chasser" (P4r; *hunting*). Hawking and hunting were activities in which women took part both during the late medieval period and the Renaissance. See Richard Almond, *Daughters of Artemis: The Huntress in the Middle Ages and Renaissance* (Cambridge: D. S. Brewer, 2009).

7 **the wings of** *Pegasus* Pegasus is a winged horse from Greek mythology.

8 **he neither heard theyr hornes nor hallowing** Munday departs from his source: "le bruit des coureurs ne le peut esueiller" (P4r; *the noise of the hunters did not wake him up*).

9 **sealed the Moore a quittance for his life** I.e., discharged the Moor from his life. Cf. Fr. "luy en donna tel coup en la jointe de l'espaule, qu'il le fendit jusques à la ceinture" (P4r; *he gave him such a blow at the shoulder joint that he split him down to the waist*). Munday prefers to use figurative language to signify the death of Palmerin's adversary.

10 **nothing discontented with his office** Munday deletes the description of Palmerin's newly-acquired occupation in the Fr., "Laquais" (P5r; *lackey*). But it is precisely in his capacity as manservant that he is allowed "to come so neere her [i.e., Alchidiana]" (353.30), so much so that in the Fr. Palmerin "la prit souz les esselles" (P5r; *took her below the armpits*).

11 this dumbe Knight hath your Maiestie giuen me Alchidiana considers Palmerin as the prey captured in her hunt. Previously her hounds give chase to a hare (see 353.12–16), but Alchidiana prefers to hand it to one of her servants. She is actually more interested in the metaphorical love hunt; for the presence of this motif in western literature from antiquity, see Marcelle Thiébaux, *The Stag of Love: The Chase in Medieval Literature* (Ithaca, NY: Cornell University Press, 1974), 89–143; for a late medieval representation of a lady trapping her lover, see Almond, *Daughters of Artemis*, fig. 26.

12 Seeing it is your request Daughter, quoth hee, I coulde bee well contented to graunt it . . . to giue a sentence so cruell, hauing not heard or seene the partie Maulicus rejects her daughter's request to bring the death of his subjects to a trial and conduct the hearing examination of the defendant (cf. how the Duke of Pera handles a similar situation involving Florendos, see 429.30–430.22). Maulicus wants to quench his nobles' thirst for vengeance without leaving his daughter's desires unfulfilled. In order to strike a balance he devises a legal artifice and thus satisfies both parties. Palmerin, confident of his martial abilities, decides to accept the sultan's unjust verdict and thus to enhance his reputation in the court.

Chapter 5

1 The Lions comming about him . . . three Leopards that furiouslie came and assayled him This episode is a manifestation of the reverent lion topos where fierce lions act docilely in the presence of a charismatic character. As noble animals associated with royalty, these lions detect Palmerin's royal descent and, with their friendly disposition, confirm his innocence. This theme has biblical antecedents: when King Darius decides to cast Daniel into the den of lions, but he is unscathed because of his innocence (Daniel 6:16–23; cf. 1 Maccabees 2:60). The same topic has also figured in European literature from classical times and was available to Munday's contemporary audience, e.g., in the Middle English romance *Sir Bevis of Hampton*, lines 2387–94 (available in print in Munday's time); *FQ*, I.iii.5–7; Shakespeare himself mentions how "the lion will not touch the true prince" (*1 Henry IV* II.iv.267–68). For more information about the origin and circulation of this topos, see Miguel Garci-Gómez, "La tradición del león reverente: glosas para los episodios en *Mio Cid, Palmerín de Oliva, Don Quijote* y otros," *Kentucky Romance Quarterly* 19 (1972): 255–84, esp. 276–77, n. 25 for Munday's *Palmerin d'Oliva*. The Sp. version of this episode is discussed in Campos, 275–76; Francisco Layna Ranz , "Itinerario de un motivo quijotesco: El caballero ante el león," *Anales Cervantinos* 25/26 (1987/1988): 193–209, at 200; Edith Rogers, "Don Quijote and the Peaceable Lion," *Hispania* 68 (1985): 9–14. Note how leopards, lacking the nobility of lions, display their treacherous nature, as they were believed to be.

2 by *Alchidianaes* iniuries and *Palmerins* refusall of her loue, lost her life, as you shall read in the chapters folowing See 368.8–14.

Chapter 6

1 *Pasmeria* Possibly the ancient city of Palmyra, present-day Tadmur in Syria.

2 *Tharsus* Possibly Tarsus, near the south-eastern coast of Turkey.

3 **you must sende this Crowne to the Prince of** *Pasmeria* **... flew out of his head such a flame of fire, as it had beene the blaze that commeth from a discharged Cannon.** This episode, already present in the Sp. version, describes a method for executing traitors known in continental Europe and apparently also used in England, although historical evidence of the latter is scarce; see Brian Innes, *The History of Torture* (New York: St. Martin's Press, 1998), 58. It seems that Munday's translation of this episode captivated the imagination of other contemporary writers that, in turn, introduced references to it in their own creations. See the use of the burning crown in texts published after *Palmerin d'Oliva*: William Kempe, *Nine Daies Wonder* (1600): "Call vp thy olde Melpomene, whose straubery quill may write the bloody lines of the blew Lady, and the Prince of the burning crowne: a better subiect I can tell ye: than your Knight of the Red Crosse," ed. G. B. Harrison (London: The Bodley Head, 1923), 33; *A Pleasant Commodie Called Look About You* (1600): "Eare on thy head I clap a burning Crowne, / Of red hot Yron that shall seare thy braines," lines 2858–59, ed. Richard S. M. Hirsch (New York: Garland, 1980), 89; *The Tragedy of Tiberius* (1607): first, in the stage directions it reads, *"Enter Spurius with a burning Crowne"* (line 2785), and next *"He sets the burning Crowne vpon his head"* (line 2791), ed. W. W. Greg, Malone Society Reprints (London: Oxford University Press, 1914), sig. L3r-v. Christopher Marlowe, *Edward II* (c. 1592): "But if proud *Mortimer* do weare this crowne, / Heavens turne it to a blaze of quenchelesse fier" (sc. 18.43–44), ed. Richard Rowland, *The Complete Works of Christopher Marlowe* (Oxford: Clarendon Press, 1994), 3:68, although Rowland argues that here it is "an allusion to the crown which Medea gave to Creusa, the woman for whom Jason had deserted her" (119; cf. Euripides, *Medea*, 1186 ff.); while it might well be that Euripides's *Medea* is the ultimate source of this episode, it seems unlikely that the anonymous author of the Sp. version could be familiar with it, since classical references are conspicuous by their absence from the original Sp. There is one further allusion in Henry Chettle's *The Tragedy of Hoffman* (acted 1602, printed 1631) that may originate in a source other than, or in addition to, Munday's *Palmerin d'Oliva*: "Fix on thy master's head my burning crown" (I.i.195), "And wear his crown made flaming hot with fire.– / Bring forth the burning crown there" (V.ii.2352–53), ed. J. D. Jowett (Nottingham: Nottingham Drama Texts, 1983), 10, 73. Paul Browne, "A Source for the 'Burning Crown' in Henry Chettle's *The Tragedy of Hoffman*," *Notes & Queries*, n.s., 51 (2004): 297–99, argues that Chettle found inspiration in

the circumstances of the Hungarian peasant leader György Dózsa. According to E. Koeppel, "The Prince of the Burning Crown und Palmerin d'Oliua," *Archiv für das Studium der neueren Sprachen und Litteraturen* 100 (1898): 23–30, esp. 27–28, Munday deserves credit for introducing this theme in England, although Koeppel was unable to consult the English version and relied only on the Fr. one. For historical evidence of the use of a burning crown in executions, apart from Browne's article, see Harold Jenkins, *The Life and Work of Henry Chettle* (London: Sidgwick & Jackson, 1934), 86–87. In addition, we should not ignore that the Turks were also familiar with how the Rufai or Howling Dervishes used "metal instruments, with points in their bulbous ends . . . [that] were heated in a brazier, and held red-hot against the dervish's skin" (Mansel, 38). Finally, the instant combustion of the crown sent by the Queen of Tharsus also parallels the immediate death of the person who puts on the Poisoned Mantle Morgan sends to King Arthur (Malory, IV.xv-xvi.107).

4 **resembling the *Salamander* in the extreame fire** I.e., the fire salamander, which has black skin with yellow, orange, and red markings.

5 *Tartaria* A region in Central Asia extending eastward from the Caspian Sea.

Chapter 7

1 **but I must endure . . . till incomparable loyaltie discharge mee of this burthen** This clause is Munday's insertion.

2 **for such a burning flame continued in the Crowne** This clause is added by Munday.

3 **let them make proofe of theyr loyalty . . . winne the honour of this aduenture** Fr. "à fin d'eux esprouuer, & faire (s'il est possible) que vostre tourment cesse" (P7v; *in order to test them and, if possible, to make your torment cease*). Munday highlights the virtue and identity of the knight that helps Prince Maurice, instead of calling attention to the benefit for the latter.

4 **then a Virgin to bee seene lightly disposed** Fr. "qu'vne pucelle priée d'estre femme" (P8r; *than a virgin who has been begged to become a woman*).

5 **their yeeres should carrie the honour, and they be renowned for euer by their Ladies** Munday departs slightly from his source: "qu'ilz en seroyent à tousiours louez, & pourroient par ce moyen meriter la grace de quelque Princesse" (P8r; *that on account of it they would be praised for ever and could thus deserve the grace of any princess*).

6 **if not at *Durace* in affecting *Laurana* . . . who was so often promised in my visions** See 160.3–162.5.

7 that ought not be imputed to me for any trespasse Munday amplifies the Fr. "celà ne se doit imputer" (P8r; *that should not be imputed*).

8 cheefe Mistresse and Gouernesse of my life Munday departs from his source to exalt Polinarda; cf. Fr. "seule Dame de mon cueur" (P8v; *only lady of my heart*).

9 as needes must aunswerable successe repay so good deseruing Fr. "qu'il ne me sçauroit fuir" (P8v; *he wouldn't be able to flee from me*).

10 shewing by signes Fr. "monstrant par sa mode accoustumée" (P8v; *showing in his usual way*). With the explicitation of the reference in his source, Munday facilitates the reading of his own translation.

Chapter 8

1 the secrete fire that was kindled in her brest This clause is Munday's interpolation.

2 *Pasiphaes* desire to the brutish Bull, when shee mette him in the wood cow made by *Dedalus* In Greek mythology Pasiphaë is said to have married King Minos of Crete, but as a curse was made to fall desperately in love with a bull. In order for her to sate her lust, Pasiphaë asked her husband's servant Daedalus to build a wooden cow inside of which she could fit and from their union the Minotaur was begotten.

3 as the aspect of the Sunne in the signe of *Leo*, dooth the eyes of the beholders The zodiac sign of Leo governs between July 23 and August 22. Leo is "a hot, summery sign, ruled by the sun and fire," as states Mary Ellen Snodgrass, *Signs of the Zodiac: A Reference Guide to Historical, Mythological, and Cultural Associations* (Westport, CT: Greenwood Press, 1997), 132; during the period of the sign of Leo the sun is particularly bright and has a dazzling effect.

4 to warme the coldest complexion The concept of *complexion* refers to an innate and defining characteristic of an individual acquired at the moment of conception. The ideal kind of complexion was temperate, although there were other types of relevant factors. See further in Nancy G. Sirasi, *Medieval & Early Renaissance Medicine: An Introduction to Knowledge and Practice* (Chicago: University of Chicago Press, 1990), 101–4. Munday departs from his source: "eschauffé le plus froid homme du monde" (Q1r; *warmed the coldest man on earth*).

5 although it were an Eunuche himselfe in her presence Notice that eunuchs together with mutes had free access to the imperial harem; see Mansel, 96.

6 shee embraced him, and sealed so many sweete kisses on his hand, as apparantly deciphered her earnest affection Munday modifies this scene with the purpose of toning down the suggestiveness of the Fr., "l'embrassoit & baisoit de telle affection, comme si elle eust deu trepasser apres telle caresse" (Q1v; *she* *embraced and kissed him with as much affection as if she would have to die after such a caress).*

7 chaste *Ioseph*, who refused *Zephira*, Wife to *Putiphar*, great prouost to the King of *Aegipt* In the Bible, Joseph is a Hebrew patriarch who was sold to the Egyptian officer Potiphar. Zephira, Potiphar's wife, tried to seduce Joseph but was refused, and in revenge accused him of trying to rape her; see Gen. 39.

8 hellish *Pluto* In Greek mythology Pluto is the god of the underworld.

9 a knowne offender Munday chooses this euphemism to avoid the more explicit words of the Fr.: "vne paillarde, ou vne garce publique" (Q1v; *a harlot or prostitute*).

10 strumpet Fr. "mechanique" (Q1v; *menial worker*).

11 Tragedie of *Biblis* Byblis fell passionately in love with her brother Caunus, who repeatedly rebuffed her. As a result Byblis went mad and finally was turned into a fountain. See Ovid, *Met.*, IX.454–655. As Ovid explains, "Byblis ought / To bee a mirror unto Maydes in lawfull wyse to love" (Golding, IX.540–41, 237); cf. Lyly, *Euphues*, 1:231.21. By bringing up her example it is implied that there is something unlawful about Ardemia's love for Palmerin.

12 a Dittie, that shee had translated from the *Greeke* poesie of *Sapho*, into her vulgar speech This reference is introduced by Maugin, but it is inaccurate since the poem is not attributed to the Greek poet from Lesbos, Sappho, whose work became available in France in 1547, one year after the publication of Maugin's translation. The first text authored by Sappho was included in the Greek edition of Dionysius of Halicarnassus's *De compositione* published by Robert Estienne (Paris, 1547; FB 65407); see Joan DeJean, *Fictions of Sappho, 1546–1937* (Chicago: University of Chicago Press, 1989), 30, although DeJean gives 1546 as the year of publication. On the contrary, Ardemia's circumstances rather parallel those underlying Sappho's epistle to Phaon as presented by Ovid in his *Heroides*, XV: the handsome youth Phaon enjoys a passionate relationship with Sappho until he leaves her. Finding herself in a desperate situation, Sappho decides to end her days by leaping to her death into the sea from the White Rock at Leucas (cf. Strabo, *Geography*, X.ii.9; see further Gregory Nagy, "Phaethon, Sappho's Phaon, and the White Rock of Leukas," *Harvard Studies in Classical Philology* 77 [1973]: 137–77). Before committing suicide she writes the epistle, whose tenor is imitated in Ardemia's ditty. Munday's readers could have read Ovid's text either in the English translation by George Turberville, *The Heroycall Epistles of the Learned Poet Publius Ovidius Naso* (London, 1567; STC 18939.5; a modern edition was prepared by Frederick Boas [London: Cresset Press, 1928]) and, if they knew Latin, in the Latin edition published in London in 1583 (STC 18928). Moreover, the story of Sappho was popularized by John Lyly in his court play *Sapho and Phao* (London, 1584; STC 17086); for a facsimile edition, see *Sapho* *and Phao 1584*, ed. Leah Scragg, Malone Society Reprints 165 (Oxford: Oxford University Press, 2002). For the fortunes of Sappho in Renaissance England, see Harriette Andreadis, *Sappho in Early Modern England: Female Same-Sex Literary Erotics, 1550–1714* (Chicago: University of Chicago Press, 2001), esp. 28–35, for the Ovidian version.

13 **The lamentable Dittie of Ardemia, dying for loue** Like Munday's Fr. source, this poem (EV 14967) is made up of fifteen quatrains (abab) in iambic pentameters. Note that this lament is not in the Sp. original, but comes from Maugin's pen. The English poem, however, does not reproduce the literal sense of the Fr. one, but instead uses the latter as inspiration to compose a poem in English that can approximate the sense and intent of the Fr. text, of a classicizing tenor. Munday, therefore, modulates his translating strategy to produce a text that meets his audience's expectations for poetical compositions. Cf. Freer, who thinks that "i versi sono piuttosto mediocri" (209).

14 *Although her end be hard and dolorous: / For death is pleasant as mine elders say* As Plato explains in his *Timaeus*, death is a natural outcome for elderly people and "the soul is then released in a natural way, and finds it pleasant to take its flight" (81d). Ardemia's death, however, is not the end result of a natural process and, therefore, it is "*hard and dolorous*," since "all that is unnatural . . . is painful" (Plato, *Timaeus*, 81e); Plato, *Complete Works*, edited by John M. Cooper and D. S. Hutchinson (Indiana: Hackett Publishing, 1997), 1281. Munday's contemporary John Donne also elaborates on this topic in his famous sonnet *Death be not proud*, composed about 1609, particularly in the following lines: "From rest and sleepe, which but thy [i.e., death's] pictures be, / Much pleasure, then from thee much more must flowe" (lines 5–6), in *The Variorum Edition of the Poetry of John Donne, vol. 7, part 1*, gen. ed. Gary A. Stringer (Bloomington, IN: Indiana University Press, 2005), 10, with relevant commentary on 313.

15 *the Swan in cold* **Meander** Meander is the name of a river in Phrygia, in the southern part of Turkey (cf. *OED*, s.v. *meander*). In mythological stories swans make no noise until just before death.

16 **Yet Biblis** *oftentimes could ease her heart, / By sweete deuising with her louely freend* Indeed in her letter to Caunus Byblis admits, "I have libertie to talke with thee asyde" (Golding, IX.667, 241).

17 *You fatall Sisters that haue spunne my thred* I.e., the Fates of classical mythology; cf. n. 2 to chap. I.xxxi.

18 **two inestimable Pillers of engrauen and guilded Alablaster** Fr. "douze colonnes Doriques d'Albatre" (Q3r; *twelve Doric columns made of alabaster*); cf. Munday, *Amadis*, 991 n. to 745.

19 not imagining whence this inconuenience did arise Fr. "cognoissant plus que nul autre dont procedoit l'inconuenient" (Q3r; *knowing better than anyone else the cause of this inconvenience*). By means of Munday's alteration of his source, the English version plays down Palmerin's feeling of guilt and thus his responsibility for the death of Ardemia.

20 and at length remembring her wordes to him, and doubting his vnkindnesse to be the cause of her death Munday adds this passage in order not to dispel entirely the suspicion or the possibility that his rejection may have contributed to the tragic outcome.

21 *Hypermnestra, Myrrha, Deianira, Scylla, Phedra, Thisbe, Oenone, Phyllis, Salmacis, Hero* **and** *Dydo,* **whose deathes were procured onely by lauish loue** The female mythological characters included in this list are reminiscent of those included in Chaucer's *Legend of Good Women,* who "For to hyre love were they so trewe / That, rathere than they wolde take a newe, / They chose to be ded in sondry wyse" (G.288–90). Hypermnestra was commanded by her father Danaus to kill her husband Lynceus on pain of death, but she preferred to save him since "is it bet for me / For to be ded in wifly honeste / Than ben a traytour lyvynge in my shame" (Chaucer, *Legend of Good Women,* F.2700–2). Myrrha was in love with her father but felt guilty about it; she contemplated the possibility of committing suicide but in the end was changed into a myrrh tree. Deianira killed herself when she came to realize she had unintentionally killed her husband Hercules. Scylla betrayed her city to obtain the love of Misos, the leader of her city's enemies; Misos, however, rejected her and she was turned into a bird. Phaedra fell in love with Hippolytos, her husband's son by an Amazon, but he rejected her; she found the means to bring destruction on Hippolytos, but when her passion came to light Phaedra hanged herself. Thisbe's lover Pyramus, mistakenly thinking she had been devoured by a wild beast, killed himself; when she found his dead body, Thisbe also committed suicide. The nymph Oenone refused to cure her husband Paris after he desobeyed her and abducted Helen of Troy; when Paris died Oenone hanged herself. Phyllis opposed her husband's decision to visit his own country and, seeing that time passed without his returning, eventually she killed herself. Salmacis was a nymph that fused physically with the unresponsive Hermaphroditus. Dido killed herself after Aeneas's departure (cf. n. 15 to chap. II.ii). For Hero, see n. 20 to chap. I.l. A list including Myrrha, Biblis, and Phaedra is adduced by Lyly to illustrate how "nature can no way resist the fury of affection"(*Euphues,* 1:231.20–23).

Chapter 9

1 *Phrygie* Phrygia, ancient kingdom in Asia Minor. Note that in Sp. Amarán was "fijo del Rey de Tracia" (176; *son to the king of Thrace*).

2 at the verye sounde of the Trompe of this blazing Goddesse I.e., Fame.

Notes to the Text: Part II

3 **ioyfull (as you haue hearde) for the departure of *Guilharan* and his companie** Munday avoids reproducing a scathing remark in the Fr. about Alchidiana, who is said to be pleased "de la mort de sa cousine" (Q3v; *for the death of her cousin*), although later he has no qualms in retaining similar comments.

4 **the next time that *Palmerin* came ... she beganne with him in this manner** Munday censors the scene in Alchidiana's room: "elle le fit asseoir sur l'vn de ses genoux: & tenant de sa main l'vne de celles de Palmerin, & ayant l'autre bras sur son col, luy dist" (Q3v; *she had him sit on one of her knees and holding in her hand one of Palmerin's, and having her other arm around his neck, she told him*).

5 **intends to make you Lord ouer all her possessions** Munday slightly but significantly alters the sense of the Fr.: "entend en brief vous faire le plus grand de toutes ses Seigneuries" (Q3v: *shortly intends to make you the greatest of her possessions*).

6 **esteeme henceforth of me as your owne** Fr. "je veux d'oresenauant que vous & moy ne soit qu'vn" (Q3v; *I want that you and I become one henceforth*). While in the Fr. Alchidiana proposes to have a romantic relationship with Palmerin, in Munday she offers to become Palmerin's possession.

7 **Yet hath Loue one shaft in his Quiuer ... all men in the world beside** This passage substitutes for another in the Fr. that obliquely refers to sex ("Il est bien vray ... de ce monde," Q4r).

8 **not able to speake her stomacke was so enraged** Fr. "elle se fust voluntiers nazardée deux heures" (Q4r; *she would willingly have spoken with a nasal voice for two hours*); *nazarder* means "nasiller," i.e., to speak with a nasal voice (see Huguet, s.v. *nasarder*).

9 **he whom I deliuered from death** See 352.20–39.

10 **the Soldans promise which hee had made to his deceased Father** See 113.3–11. The promise is originally made by his father, but must have later been assumed by Maulicus himself.

Chapter 10

1 **I am heere readie to proue in open fielde, agaynst any of your Knights that dare maintaine her cause** A judicial combat is here proposed; see n. 8 to chap. I.xxiv.

Chapter 11

1 **a siely Virgin, who hath no weapon but her honour wherewith to defende her selfe** This noun phrase together with the relative clause is introduced by Munday.

2 **thy falshoode and maleuolent spirit** Munday amplifies the Fr. "tes soties" (Q5v; *your foolish behavior*).

3 **thou lyest in thy throate** Proverbial; cf. Tilley, T268.

4 **I accept the Combat on her behalfe . . . Iudges, that may discerne the issue of our Combat** González ("Sistema," 72 n. 17) does not know whether to consider Palmerin's challenge as a prophecy or not. It can be interpreted as a prophecy if his decision is based on positive knowledge of Alchidiana's innocence. If, on the contrary, he lacks that certainty, "se trata . . . de una simple conjetura, de una apuesta, de una corazonada, por más fuertes que éstas sean."

5 **the stone throwne could not bee recalled** Proverbial; cf. "a stone once cast, and a word once spoken, cannot be recall'd" (Tilley, W777).

6 **the Catarre, which of long time hath hindered my speech** Munday follows Maugin, who departs from the Sp. in identifying Palmerin's supposed illness: "mi lengua, que mucho avía que la tenía atada con un grande mal" (178; *since long time ago my tongue was tied because of a great disease*).

7 **to reueale, what I was enforced to bewraye before by signes** This clause is Munday's interpolation.

8 **a Knight called *Aegle Samien*, dumbe from his byrth . . . with the helpe of the Gods, restored his speech** The text refers to the following episode, described among his miracles by Valerius Maximus: "Echecles of Samos, an athlete, was dumb; but being robbed of the title and prize of a victory he had won, fired with indignation he found his voice" (I.viii *ext.* 4, 117).

9 **a fayre yong Damosell** Fr. "vn jeune Damoyseau" (Q6v; *a young squire*). Munday maintains the consistency of his change of this character's sex, even though the Fr. uses other male designations to refer to this character, e.g., "Escuyer" (*squire*) and "Gentilhomme" (*gentleman*).

10 **in remembraunce of your speciall loyaltie, whereby you deliuered the Prince Maurice** See 362.24–34.

Chapter 12

1 **fayre *Vesper* among the other stars** It refers to the planet Venus.

2 **double or quitte** An expression from gambling applied figuratively to describe "a bold or desperate attempt to extricate oneself from present evils at the risk of greatly increasing them" (*OED*, s.v. *double* adv. 4); cf. Munday, *Amadis*, 997 n. to 849.

3 *Palmerin* **clasping his Helmet, gaue the Spurres to his Horse . . . his head, immediatly smote it from his shoulders** Munday abridges the description of the combat in his source.

4 *Califfes, Agaz,* as *Taborlanes Caliph* is the title of a Muslim religious and civil ruler during the Ottoman empire; *aga* is a military official of the Ottoman empire; *Taborlanes* (Fr. "Taborlans," Q8v) refers to "a mighty Prince, or Potentate (perhaps from Tamberlain)," see Randle Cotgrave, *A French and English Dictionary* (London, 1673), q.v. *taborlan*; it corresponds to the entry in the *OED*,'*Tamer'lane / 'Tambur'laine*, n., "used allusively for a person like Timur, a conqueror, a scourge, a despot." Knowledge of the Mongol ruler Tamerlane was popularized by Christopher Marlowe's play *Tamburlaine the Great* (1590).

5 *Assiria* Munday departs from the Fr. "l'Asie" (Q8v; *Asia*).

6 **whispering deceitfull tales into Ladyes eares** Fr. "viuent oyseux entre les Dames" (Q8v; *they live idly among the Ladies*). Munday's translation describes one activity that may fall in the category of idleness mentioned in the Fr.

7 **the Goddesse *Iuno*, when shee stoode before Syr *Paris* . . . more sumptuously adorned then the Princesse** The text refers to the judgment of Paris, who had to decide who was the most beautiful of three goddessess, namely, Juno (equated with Hera by the Romans), Athena, and Aphrodite. According to Lucian, Juno offered Paris to make him "lord of all Asia," but nonetheless he chose Aphrodite because she promised that he would obtain Helen as his wife. Thus the reference prepares the reader for Palmerin's rejection of Alchidiana, as happened to Juno. For the satiric version of the judgment of Paris offered by Lucian, see his *Dialogues of the Gods*, XX, trans. Howard Williams (London: George Bell, 1900), 38–48, quoting from 45.

8 **wherefore liuing in hope of some better oportunitie . . . least her mother should suspect her** Munday departs from the Fr. "Et prenant vn doux congé luy laissa trois de ses Damoyselles pour ses gardes à fin qu'il fust gouuerné & pensé plus plaisamment" (R1r; *and taking sweet leave of him she left three of her maids to guard him in order that he were governed and taken care of more plesantly*).

Chapter 13

1 **not to leaue the bodie of *Amarano* in his Dominions** An example of the motif *burial denied* (M2.2; see Bordman, 62). This vengeful measure reveals Alchidiana's lack of moral sense and her father's distorted sense of justice.

2 **else with open scandale** This clause is Munday's insertion.

3 **Cipres** A coniferous tree native of the Middle East traditionally associated with mourning, hence an appropriate choice.

4 *Suria* I.e., Syria (Sp. "Siria," 183).

Chapter 14

1 **by the message of the Queene of *Tharsus* . . . was constrained to renue her loue** See 379.11–15.

2 **the fire newly raked from the embers, and which day and night consumed her with languishing** Munday amplifies his Fr. source: "ce nouueau feu, qui la consommoit sans cesse" (R1v; *this new fire that ceaselessly consumed her*).

3 **hee came to visite her in her Chamber** Fr. "elle le vint voir" (R1v; *she came to see him*). The situation is reversed in the English version. It seems that Munday disapproves that Alchidiana could take the initiative and visit Palmerin in his room, although she does take control of the stituation and starts by addressing him and setting the tenor of the encounter.

4 **the fayth you owe to her, for whose loue you tooke the enchaunted Crowne from the Prince *Maurice*** See 362.24–34.

5 **if patiently I endured your sharp repulse when last I bewrayed the state of my loue** See 371.4–23.

6 **whom you haue woorthily deserued** This clause is Munday's addition.

7 **so faire an enemie, who coulde sooner bring in subiection an other *Hercules*, then euer did *Iole*, and as easily giue life to a statue of Marble, as *Venus* sometime did, at the request of *Pigmalion* the Caruer** Probably an allusion to Ovid's version of the Greek myth in which Iole uses erotic wiles to overpower Hercules and enjoin him to adopt effeminate ways (Ovid, *Heroides*, IX.64–80; see further in n. 1 to chap. II.lvii). In view of Alchidiana's advances, Palmerin fears he might fall in a similar kind of trap and be in her "subiection." The story of the statue that is brought to life is also told by Ovid in his *Metamorphoses* (X.243–97). Pygmalion, weary of prostitutes, decides to live without a woman and instead fashions a statue of ivory. After some time Pygmalion falls in love with his statue and, on the feast day of Venus, he asks the goddess permission to marry the statue and Venus grants it. The text invites the reader to draw a comparison between Alchidiana's and Venus's power.

8 **which hath beene desired by so many worthie personages** This clause is Munday's insertion.

9 **and I gather that sweet flower, which aboue all other would beautifie my Garland** Munday composes this fragment to render his source in a more flourished way: "me faisant auoir l'entiere fruition de ce que je desire sur tout" (R2r; *making me attain full fruition of that which I most desire*).

10 **least his minde otherwayes busied, should conceyue displeasure against me, and so all our fortune for euer squandered** Munday amplifies the Fr., "ains le pourroys destourber de son intention" (R2r; *instead you could distract him from his intention*).

11 **and dedicate my life to your gracious seruice** This clause is Munday's interpolation.

12 **my discent is from** *Persia* Fr. "j'ay hanté le plus communément la Perse" (R2r; *most commonly I have dwelt in Persia*). In the English text Palmerin's lie is more obvious, since we know with certainty that he is of Greek origin.

13 **leauing the Princesse triumphing of her conquest** Fr. "Puis se retira l'Infante, craignant fascher ou ennuyer son nouuel alié" (R2r; *then the Princess withdrew fearing to annoy her new ally*). Munday introduces this sentence so that his text is consistent in making Palmerin pay Alchidiana a visit in her chamber; cf. n. 3 above.

Chapter 15

1 **his Brother** *Gamezio* Munday corrects the error in the Fr., "son Oncle Gamezio" (R2v; *his uncle Gamezio*); cf. n. 10 to chap. II.ix.

2 **other vessels** Fr. "hurques" (R2v; *hurque* or *hulcque* is "a large ship of burden or transport, often associated with the carrack," q.v. *OED, hulk* n.2 1). Munday decides not to translate this word, either because he did not know its meaning, or because he could not find an English equivalent.

3 **shee helde his promises with greater pertinacie, then euer did any Logitian maintaine his** *Aristotle* Aristotle was the founder of logic. By "his *Aristotle*" the text means the philosopher's works on logic, such as his *Prior Analytics* and *On Interpretation*. For the currency in the Renaissance of Aristotle's teachings on logic, see E. J. Ashworth, "Logic, Renaissance," in *Routledge Encyclopedia of Philosophy*, ed. Edward Craig (London: Routledge, 1998), 5:767–72.

4 **these Heathen hounds, sworne enemies to Christ and his Seruants** Munday amplifies the Fr., "ces canailles enemys de nostre foy" (R3r; *this rabble, enemies of our faith*).

5 **to fight against his Lord and maker** Fr. "pour puis apres laisser son maistre au besoin" (R3r; *in order to abandon his master in need afterwards*). Munday departs from his source in order to underscore the religious division between Palmerin and the sultan, whereas the Fr. focuses on their natural affinity; "son maistre" refers to the sultan, not to God.

6 **and on paine of death none to offende him** This clause is introduced by Munday.

7 A matter soone begunne, will bee as soone ended Proverb; not in Tilley; cf. "the sooner the better" (Tilley, S641) and "He that never begins shall never make and end" (Tilley, E123).

8 for this will bee a good whetting to our stomackes, to deale with our enemies of greater multitude This passage is Munday's interpolation.

Chapter 16

1 accept me for your companion. Whereto *Palmerin* right soone condiscended, and then began such a league of amity betweene them, that it endured to the death The kind of relationship established between Palmerin and Olorico seems to replicate the spirit of medieval *compagnonage*, which implied obligations such as advice, vengeance for the death of the other, permission from the companion to marry someone or to establish new friendship, assistance, faithfulness to death, etc; in chap. II.xxii Olorico rehearses the continuance of their friendship and Palmerin calls him "loyall Brother, and fellow in Armes" (414.39). The medieval institution of *compagnonage* disappeared in the twelfth century but was kept alive in literature. For a useful discussion of this institution and its literary presentation in medieval literature, see J. Flach, "Le compagnonnage dans les chansons de geste," *Études romanes dédiées à Gaston Paris* (Paris: Bouillon, 1891), 141–80.

2 for she kept her Chamber in her amorous opinions This clause is Munday's interpolation.

3 two Fr. "douze" (R3v; *twelve*).

4 but such deuout seruice as loue teacheth his Schollers This clause is added by Munday to expand and clarify the irony in the previous clause introduced by Maugin; cf. Freer, 230.

5 afflictions Fr. "affections" (R4r; *affections*).

6 then her gracious fauour whom I desire to please This clause is Munday's insertion.

7 a Golden Sheeld, wherein was portraied the head of *Amarano* . . . the victory of *Palmerin* against him See 381.34–382.29.

8 while one of them remains aliue This clause is Munday's insertion.

9 *Hipsicratea* neuer followed her Husband *Mithredates* with greater affection, were he on sea, or on lande, on Horsebacke, or on foote, then I could doo the noble *Palmerin d'Oliua* Alchidiana uses Hypsicratea, wife to Mithridates VI, king of Pontus (120–63 BC), as an example. As Valerius Maximus states, "she [i.e., Hypsicratea] cut her hair short and accustomed herself to a horse and weapons the more easily to partake of his toils and dangers. She even followed him [i.e., Mithridates] as he fled through savage nations" (IV.vi, *ext.* 2, 409).

Chapter 17

1 **they went to bed** Munday leaves out that they slept "en vn mesme lict" (R4v; *in the same bed*).

2 **by the honour of my Knighthoode** Munday favors Palmerin's chivalric devotion over his religious one in contrast to what happens in the Fr., "par le haut Dieu viuant" (R4v; *by the high living God*).

3 **which no father, but so good a freende was able to doo** This clause is Munday's interpolation.

4 **touch of loyaltie** I.e., stroke of loyalty.

5 **the cruell *Dyonise* on the *Scicilians*** Fr. "Tyrans Denis aux Siciliens" (R5r; *Denis the Tyrant to the Sicilians*). Most probably Dionysius I (ca. 432–367), although perhaps his son Dionysius II (ca. 397–343 BC), both of them tyrants of Syracuse. See Valerius, VI.ii, *ext.* 2, 27: "In Syracuse, where everybody was praying for the destruction of the tyrant Dionysius because of his excessive harshness and the intolerable burdens he imposed." This tyrant's cruelty became proverbial, to the extent that reference is made by Dante in his *Divine Comedy*: "Dïonisio fero / che fe' Cicilia aver dolorosi anni" (*Inferno*, XII.107–8; "cruel Dionysius who made Sicily have woeful years," trans. Charles S. Singleton (Princeton: Princeton University Press, 1970), 1:124–25 and 2:198 for Singleton's discussion of the passage.

6 **in rest or quiet, till I had found my deerest Freendes againe** Munday introduces these words.

7 **how canst thou thus waste thy time heere slothfullie** Amplification of the Fr. "comment peux-tu arrester icy" (R5r; *how can you remain here*).

8 **the Iewell of my welfare** I.e., Polinarda; cf. Fr. "vous" (R5r; *you*).

Chapter 18

1 **and such defences as are requisit in warlike occasions** With this clause Munday avoids translating the military terminology introduced by Maugin (R5v).

2 **that hee might accomplish his promise to the Princesse *Alchidiana*** The only promises Palmerin makes Alchidiana are part of the "feigned answer" (388.15) he gives in order to distract her momentarily from her marriage plans with him. This reference may therefore allude to the following part of the text: "if euer hereafter I shall doo you seruice, let me intreate you to patience till my returne" (387.35–36). In other words, the fight Palmerin now joins in, in favor of Alchidi-

ana's father, and ultimately Alchidiana herself, serves to gain time and thus postpone his return and reunion with her.

3 **Lucifers Pallace** I.e., hell; see Freer, 217. Cf. John Milton's reference to and description of "The palace of great Lucifer" (*Paradise Lost*, V.760), ed. Alastair Fowler, Longman Annotated English Poets, 2nd ed. (London: Longman, 1998), 331 note to lines 760–66.

4 **the *Greekes* when they receiued their libertie by *Quintus Flaminius* . . . when (as *Valerius* rehearseth) the Byrds fell from the ayre with the furie of theyr cries** This incident is told by Valerius Maximus as an example of liberality: "after the defeat of king Philip of Macedonia . . . T. Quinctius Flamininus ordered these words to be proclaimed: 'The senate and people of Rome and T. Quinctius Flamininus, commander-in-chief, order that all Grecian cities formerly under the dominion of king Philip, be free and exempt from tax.' Hearing these words, men were overcome with a mighty unlooked-for joy . . . Then, when the herald's pronouncement was repeated, they filled the heavens with so enthusiastic a shout that according to general and sure report birds flying overhead fell to the ground in stupefaction and fear" (IV.viii.5, 433–35). For a similar reference occurring in a passage of the Fr. untranslated by Munday, Maugin states how when Palmerin frees Malfada's prisoners, they shouted so loudly "qu'aucuns oyseaux qui vouloient alors par là, tomberent en la mer" (Dd5r; *that some birds that were then flying overhead fell on the sea*). Freer (219) considers this type of comment to be a typical case of exaggeration on the part of Maugin, when it seems more likely to be inspired by this passage from Valerius.

5 **who can doo nothing but before theyr Ladies** This clause is Munday's addition.

6 ***Palmerin* . . . called for the Chirurgions to visit his woundes . . . they assured him of speedie recouerie** Munday's translation does not convey the impression that Palmerin has received any wound in his fight against Amarano's brothers. The Fr. text does describe how Palmerin is wounded when fighting against Gramiell: "neantmoins en glissant il fut vn peu attaint au costé" (R6r; *nevertheless by slipping he was wounded a bit on the side*).

7 **by reason of the death of the two slaine Princes** This clause is inserted by Munday.

8 **they should never entise them foorth to skirmish, therefore he desired to prevent them of that helpe** Cf. Fr. "s'ilz y entroyent sans auoir escarmouche, qu'ilz en seroient blasmez à jamais" (R6v; *if they entered there without having a skirmish they would be blamed forever*).

Chapter 19

1 they had lost fiue of theyr brethren, three in single fight with *Palmerin*, and the other in the battaile Munday departs from the Fr.: "voyans auoir perdu quatre de leurs freres, tant en combat singulier de Palmerin, que le jour de la bataille" (R7r; *seeing that they had lost four of their brothers, both in single combat against Palmerin and the day of the battle*). Munday corrects his source and provides information to substantiate his account. Palmerin, in single combat, kills Amarano, Orinello, and an unnamed brother, while Gramiell and another unnamed brother (this one's death is caused by Palmerin) die in the battle. Taking into account that Amarano had "sixe Brethren" (384.40), only two of the siblings now remain alive.

2 Maurice ... from whom *Palmerin* tooke the enchaunted Crowne See 362.17–34.

3 all the Oracles of *Delphos* It refers to Apollo's oracle at Delphi, the most famous oracle since ancient times. This oracle was consulted particularly to foretell the outcome of wars, but it seems to the Sultan that when Palmerin is involved they are destined to win. The oddity is that this reference is put in the mouth of a Muslim.

4 he [i.e., Maurice] **commaunded them** [i.e., Gramiell's brothers] **to depart his Realme, for hee would not ayde them against his deerest Freende** [i.e., Palmerin].

5 make a vertue of necessitie Proverb; see Tilley, V73. Cf. 126.37.

6 the renowmed Prince *Amarano*, whom thou hast with thine owne hand slaine, and three other of our brethren likewise Palmerin has indeed caused the death of four out of the seven brothers, although in one case he simply "stroke him [i.e., an unnamed brother of Amarano's] beside his Horse, where hee was troden to death with the trampling of the Horsses" (399.19–21). See n. 1 above.

Chapter 20

1 the Queene of *Tharsus* sent a rich Helmet to *Palmerin* See 379.34–380.2.

2 as well records the memorye of the burning Crowne See 358.17–26.

3 Notwithstanding which of you doth most mistrust the attainment of her grace ... with especiall content you shall finish your affectionate desires The one who "doth most mistrust the attainment of her grace" refers to Olorico, who is now given reassurance that he will be successful and manage to obtain Alchidiana's love; see their marriage in 568.12–569.20. Giving away this information at this point, however, has no effect on the narrative development of the story, because what is important is not the knowledge of future narrative events but instead the description of how those events unfold; see González, "Sistema," 38–40, where he analyzes the prophecy in the context of the Sp. original, in which the same successful outcome is predicted for both Palmerin and Olorico.

4 **when you sent your Lady to me . . .you were acquainted with further secrets concerning my estate** See 379.13–20.

5 **you shall deliuer from death, and that very shortly** See 451.6–452.24.

6 *Ogyer* the *Dane* in *Faeria* Ogier the Dane is the eponymous hero of a thirteenth-century chanson de geste titled *La chevalerie d'Ogier de Danemarche*, ed. Mario Eusebi (Milan: Istituto Editoriale Cisalpino, 1963). Ogier enjoyed literary fame beyond the thirteenth century by means of adaptations and reworkings of the same story, for which see Emmanuelle Poulain-Gautret, *La tradition littéraire d'Ogier le Danois après le XIIIe siècle: Permanence et renouvellement du genre épique médiéval* (Paris: Champion, 2005). The reference to this literary character is introduced by Maugin, who certainly expected his readers to be familiar with it and thus able to interpret it. The episode of Ogier in fairyland is preserved in an unedited fourteenth-century romance (Paris, Bibliothèque Nationale, fr. MS 1583), which tells the story of how Ogier, while in Faeria, became "irrité de ne rien trouver à manger (effet comique que l'auteur ne se lasse pas de répéter)," as explains Knud Togeby, *Ogier le Danois dans les littératures européennes* (Copenhagen: Munksgaard, 1969), 141. In this context the allusion to Ogier invites us to assume that Palmerin and the Queen of Tharsus are dancing with empty stomachs. However, we cannot expect that Munday's readers could have made this interpretation, since the story of Ogier the Dane is not attested to have had circulation in England (no English translation exists, unlike other European vernaculars; see Togeby, ibid.). In fact Munday himself fails to interpret the reference in his source and mistranslates it (see Textual notes to 405.24). See also my note "Anthony Munday's *Palmerin d'Oliva* and 'Ogyer the Dane in Færia'," *Notes and Queries*, n.s., 61 (2014): 217–18.

7 **For neuer was *Dido* such an affectionate auditrice of *Aeneas*, recounting the ruine of the *Troians*** In Virgil's *Aenid* Dido asks Aeneas to tell her the events surrounding the fall of Troy and he complies with her request in Bk. 2. Maugin introduces this mythological reference with the purpose of connecting the author of the Castilian text's intentions with classical themes; cf. Freer, 220.

8 **the Queene went to bedde to *Palmerin*** Munday leaves out that the Queen was "toute nuë" (S1r; *stark naked*).

9 ***Brangiena*, who endured these sweet skirmishes, because she should not manifest the Historie of *Yseul* her Mistresse, and *Tristram*** In the Arthurian tradition Brangiena is Isolde's handmaid, entrusted with the love potion Yseult and Tristram mistakenly drink. Brangiena takes Yseult's place on the wedding night in order that Mark may think he has married a virgin, as we read in *Le roman*

de Tristan en prose: "Brangain, dit Gorvenal, je vos dirai coment vos la porroiz aidier a sauver. Vos cocheroiz Yselt el lit, ensi com vos devez faire, et seront les chandoiles estaintes. Et quant li rois Mars voudra venir cochier, nos vos metrons el lit, et Yselt s'en istra. Et quant li rois Mars avra fait sa volenté de vos, vos vos retreroiz arrieres, et Yselt se metra en vostre leu. Et quant li rois vos avra trovee pucele, et les chandeles seront alumees, et il verra Yselt dejoste li, il cuidera qu'il ait despucelee," ed. Renée L. Curtis (Leiden: Brill, 1976), 2:92: "'Brangain,' said Gorvenal, 'I'll tell you how you can help to protect Iseut. You will see her to bed, as is your duty, and the candles will be extinguished. When King Mark is ready to lie down, we'll put you in the bed, and Iseut will slip out. And after King Mark has had his pleasure with you, you will withdraw and Iseut will take your place. Once King Mark has found you to be a virgin, the candles will be relit, and he'll see Iseut behind him and think he has taken her," trans. Renée L. Curtis, *The Romance of Tristan: The Thirteenth-Century Old French "Prose Tristan"* (Oxford: Oxford University Press, 1994), 93–94. Indeed Brangiena sacrifices her virginity to preserve the secret of Isolde's relationship with Tristram. We cannot say, however, that the circumstances of Brangiena and the Queen of Tharsus are equivalent; as Patchell states, "the only similarity between the two incidents is the magic potion; for Brangwain, by substituting in the marriage bed, sacrificed her own honor for Ysolt, whereas the Queen of Tharsus, far from making a sacrifice, was following her own pleasure" (88). Note that Brangiena's substitution is not included by Malory and might not have been entirely understandable to Munday's readers. More appropriate in this context seems a different Arthurian episode where Lancelot, with the magic intervention of Dame Brusen, is made to have sex with Elaine and as a result Galahad is begotten; see Malory, XI.ii.-iii.401–2. See Daniel Gutiérrez Trápaga, "El engaño del caballero y la concepción forzada e inconsciente: el caso de *Lanzarote del Lago* y *Palmerín de Olivia*," in *Palmerín: 500 años*, 427–47.

10 a fantasie appeared to *Palmerin*, resembling his Ladie *Polynarda* . . . brake foorth into these speeches By means of this dream Palmerin discovers his unfaithfulness, unknown to him until this point. The absolute fidelity that enables Palmerin to succeed in the test of the burning crown (see 361.41–362.5) is now in question. In the first part Palmerin's virtual infidelity with Laurana stirs up Polinarda's anger (see n. 7 to chap. I.xx), but this time the infidelity is consummated. In ordering Palmerin immediately to abandon the Queen of Tharsus, Polinarda is once again influencing Palmerin to choose the steps he has to follow. Cf. González, "Sueños," 242–44.

11 whome the mother caused to bee named *Palmendos* . . . from them deriuing his name While the Sp. original explains, "le puso nombre Polendus porque tomasse los nombres de Palmerín e de su abuelo Florendos, porque eran la flor de la cavalería del mundo" (195; *she named him Polendus so that he took the names of Palmerin and of his grandfather Florendos, because they were the flower of* *the world's chivalry*), the Fr. translator provides onomastic clarity in creating the portmanteau-word "Palmendos" (S1v), thus making self-evident how this character embodies the virtues of both Pal*me*rin and Flor*endos*, from whom his own name is derived. Cf. Carmen Marín Pina, *Páginas de sueños: Estudios sobre los libros de caballerías castellanos* (Saragossa: Institución Fernando el Católico, 2011), 230; and Purser, 432.

12 as you may at large perceyve in his Historie Fr. "ainsy qu'on lict en autre histoire" (S1v; *as can be read in a different* story). Munday subtly alters his source, maybe suggesting that the exploits of Palmendos make up the core of an independent story ("his Historie," i.e., Palmendos's), not just a part of a larger book ("en autre histoire"). Here Munday was probably pointing to the fact that, even while he was translating this section of *Palmerin d'Oliva* sometime in 1587, he had already committed himself to publish the story of Palmendos as a separate book, and not as an integral part of *L'Histoire de Primaleon de Grece* (FB 44731–36), the Fr. translation of the Sp. continuation to *Palmerín de Olivia*. In February 1589 appeared Munday's *The Honorable, Pleasant and Rare Conceited Historie of Palmendos* (STC 18064), comprising only the first thirty-two chapters of the Fr. *Primaleon*. For more information, see Hayes, "Romances," 61; Hamilton; 91–92; Thomas, 250; and Leticia Álvarez-Recio, "Chapters Translated by Anthony Munday in *The History of Palmendos* (1589): A Long-Standing Error," *Notes and Queries*, n.s., 62 (2015): 549–51.

Chapter 21

1 a Castell of pleasure It refers to a castle used for recreational purposes.

2 three times fell on their knees kissing the ground Fr. "jetterent leurs armes en terre, les ayans baisées par trois fois" (S2r; *they threw their arms to the ground after having kissed them three times*).

3 all the partes sensatiue I.e., all the sensory organs.

4 (hauing seene the fortune of theyr Brethren, and their owne badde successe in Armes) that they will serue you with continuall loyaltie Fr. "veu le traictement que leurs ferez, les fournissant d'armes, qu'ilz vous seruiront loyaument" (S2v; *in view of the treatment that you'll give them, supplying them with arms, [I think] they will serve you loyally*). Munday perhaps misunderstood the original and, instead of "ferez" (*you will give*), he read "frerez" (*brothers*).

5 the man so much inferiour to you Fr. "vn qui n'est centiesme de vous" (S3r; *one who is not worth one hundredth part as you*). Munday dispenses with the specific details in his source. Note that the second edition reads "mee" instead of "you" (see "Historical collation"). Although I have preferred the variant in the 1616 edition, i.e., "you," we cannot rule out the possibility that Munday knowingly changed his source in order to call attention to Alchidiana's haughtiness instead of Palmerin's unrivalled reputation.

Chapter 22

1 **had long time liued there in that thraldome** Fr. "qu'on vouloit faire Cheualiers de la chiorme, par l'accolée de la cadene" (S3v; *they wanted to turn them remigatory knights of the galleys by giving them the accolade of the chain*). Munday's text lacks the more specific information contained in his source.

2 **on the gouernment of *Neptune*** I.e., in the sea.

3 **this winde** Fr. "le Siroc . . . (vent qui leur estoit lors propre pour tirer à Pouge)" (S4r; *the scirocco, a wind which was suitable then for them to go to Pouge*). Munday perhaps has difficulties translating the name of the wind; note that the word *scirocco* is not attested in English until 1617 according to the *OED*. Although it may also be that Munday, who traveled little by boat, lacked knowledge about how his fellow countrymen described winds, since in 331.12 he also leaves the names of other winds untranslated; see n.8 to chap. I.lxiv.

4 **and they to prate no more** Note that a verb of speaking involving some command is implied: *he commanded that they should prate no more*. This kind of ellipsis was acceptable to Elizabethan writers and readers (cf. Abbott, *Grammar*, 280), but probably not to the compositor of the 1637 edition, which contains a variant reading: "bidding them to prate no more"; see "Historical collation."

5 ***Tolledo*** Fr. "Toleda" (S4v); Sp. "Taledo" (199). There is no German port of this name or similar, while the only city that can be associated with "Tolledo" is *Toledo* in inland Spain. This is certainly not the city intended by the author of the Sp. original.

6 **on my Knighthood** Fr. "par tous noz Dieux" (S4v; *by all our Gods*). Considering that Palmerin and Olorico apparently waver about their religious allegiance, Munday prefers to delete any possibility of misunderstanding.

7 **the next morning** Fr. "apres que Palmerin eut ouy la messe en la grande Eglise" (S5r; *after Palmerin had heard mass in the cathedral*). One more time, Munday suppresses a display of religious belief.

Chapter 23

1 ***fiue daies*** Fr. "quinze iours" (S5v; *fifteen days*); Sp. "quinze días" (201; *fifteen days*).

2 **after that I vnfortunately lost them** See chap. I.lxv.

3 **I leaue to the opinion of long absent friends** This clause is Munday's interpolation.

4 **the Gardein, where first his sweet Amours were sollicited** See 198.31–201.39.

5 **I hope will not now deny me** Munday omits a passage from the Fr. (S7v: "Adonc embrassant la Princesse . . . d'amourese mercy?") where Palmerin is unable to resist his desires, but is first met with Polinarda's resistance.

6 **not long since I was sollicited with a vision . . . acquainted her with his dreame that night likewise** The dream mentioned by Polinarda corresponds exactly to Palmerin's latest dream (see 406.4–13), since the two of them simultaneously have the same dream. This kind of oneiric experience may be described as a *double dream* in which, besides, "los dos sueños no se limitan a referir una misma realidad, sino que ambos se refieren mutuamente, ambos se incluyen recíprocamente" (González, "Sueños," 246). Moreover, Polinarda's revelation complements Palmerin's dream and provides sufficient evidence to confirm that the infidelity has indeed taken place. Palmerin is now able to reconstruct the circumstances surrounding his breach of loyalty, but he is not dreaming "his future infidelity to his lady" as mistakenly stated by Patchell, 38.

7 **they spent that night, and foure more afterward** Palmerin's visit to Polinarda in the Fr. (as well as in the Sp.) is not as chaste as Munday's translation suggests: "laschans tous deux la bride à leurs plus affectionnez desirs, receurent l'vn de l'autre le bien à quoy tendent tous ceux qui font profession d'amour" (S7v; *the two of them giving free rein to their most affectionate desires, they received from each other the blessing which all those who profess love are aiming for*); this kind of half-spoken sexual activity is repeated every night for a fortnight in the Fr., but for only five nights in the English as the chapter title announces.

Chapter 24

1 **The tempest which had thrown *Palmerin* on *Hercules* pillars** See 413.17–25; *Hercules* pillars refers to the Strait of Gibraltar.

2 ***Natolia*** Here it seems to refer not to the entire Anatolian peninsula (cf. n. 20 to chap. II.xli), but to a seaport on the Anatolian coast, namely, Antalya, in the south of present-day Turkey. This city is also referred to in Christopher Marlowe's *2 Tamburlaine the Great*: "Who meanes to gyrt *Natolias* walles with siege, / Fire the towne and overrun the land" (III.v.8–9, ed. David Fuller, *The Complete Works of Christopher Marlowe* 5 [Oxford: Clarendon Press, 1998], 119).

3 **the *Bosphor*** The Bosphorus.

4 **thy youth forbids thee to venture so soone** Munday departs from his Fr. source: "j'ay grand paour de ne vous reuoir jamais" (S8r; *I greatly fear I'll never see you again*).

5 **fiue thousand** Fr. "quinze mile" (S8v; *fifteen thousand*)

6 **that brake from the rest vpon sight of the pollicie** This clause is inserted by Munday.

7 *Pera* The name of a hill in the district of Galata in Constantinople. The name of Pera derives from the Greek word for "beyond," in this case meaning *beyond the Golden Horn, to the north*. See Mansel, 12, 115, and the map on xii–xiii.

8 **because we must now reuiue matter long expected, as concerning the noble Prince** *Florendos* **of** *Macedon* This passage is Munday's addition.

Chapter 25

1 **let vs nowe remember how after that** *Palmerin* **was departed from** *Macedon***, hauing recouered the health of the olde king** *Primaleon* See 156.24–157.40.

2 **appeasing his complaints for the Princesse** *Griana***, by the happie tidings of the ancient knight, that sent the sheeld to** *Palmerin* **at his knighting** See 149.32–37.

3 **the Spanishe Leather Cape, Shooes, Frocke** Fr. "la cape de marroquin, l'escharpe, le bourdon" (T1r; *the cape of Moroccan leather, the scrip, the staff*). The traditional pilgrim's attire is immediately recognizable in the Fr., not so in the English translation.

4 **Nowe did he not demaunde this time of his Subiects, for any desire he had to bee a Pilgrim . . . but for he longed to see his sweete mistresse** *Griana* **. . . as till death he would not marrie without her consent and licence** This episode develops a motif familiar to English audiences from medieval romance, namely, *disguise as palmer* (K1817.2; see Bordman, 55). In medieval romances it is not unusual to see a hero returning from exile and adopting a pilgrim's disguise in order to test the loyalty of their beloved. As happens in *Palmerin*, the pilgrim's attire does not imply any special piety on the part of the pilgrims, but instead it serves more pragmatic purposes, namely, gaining access unsuspectedly to the lady. For a discussion of the presence of this motif in insular romances, both Anglo-Norman and Middle English, see María Dumas, "The Use of the Pilgrim Disguise in the *Roman de Horn, Boeve de Haumtone* and Their Middle English Translations," *SELIM* 19 (2012): 81–110.

5 *Buda***, where as then the King kept his Court** When the Sp. original was written in 1511, Buda was the capital of Hungary, but had fallen under Ottoman rule by 1540.

6 **the holy voyage of** *Ierusalem* One of the great pilgrimage destinations of late medieval Christendom.

7 **will** Imperative form, in this context meaning "to pray, request, entreat" (*OED*, s.v. *will* v. 2, 4a).

8 **the holie Citie** I.e., Jerusalem.

9 **the fayth, which hee vowed to you at *Constantinople* in your fathers Pallace** See 122.12–20

10 **it is more then twentie yeeres since I promised thy death** Cf. 125.20–22 and 129.13–15.

11 ***Cardino* one of the Queenes Squires, her brother that caried yong *Palmerin* to the mountaine** While in chap. I.v (see 119.16–17) Munday substitutes the female character Cardina for the male Cardino of his source, now he creates a new male character, Cardina's brother, named Cardino, since it seems more natural for a man to carry arms. It is important to mention, not only that Munday takes the trouble to establish an identity for this character that consistently agrees with his narrative alterations, but also that he does not lose track of the change introduced more than eighty chapters before.

12 **the Queene and the Pilgrime ought presently to die** The events that ensue are based on a false accusation against the queen, a common romance motif since medieval times that in England lived on well into the Tudor period. The accusation is made by Tarisius, Griana's husband, one of the familiar situations reflected in other Elizabethan texts, as we see for instance in Robert Greene's *Pandosto* of 1588. For a discussion of this motif and its presence in contemporary works, see Helen Cooper, *The English Romance in Time: Transforming Motifs from Geoffrey of Monmouth to the Death of Shakespeare* (Oxford: Oxford University Press, 2004), 274–80.

Chapter 26

1 **how might I credite thy continuall mallice but by this strange and vnexpected accident** Munday departs from his Fr. source: "combien je craignois ton retour, qui trop à la mal'heure m'est suruenu" (T2v; *how much I feared your return, that came to me in such an evil hour*).

2 **committe it to the Combat** I.e., ordain a judicial combat to reach a decision about the accusation.

3 **shee was further out of pacience then shee was before . . ., then to come with this reproach before her Father** This fragment is Munday's insertion.

4 **if heeretofore against the *Turke Gamezio* thou didst me seruice** See 112.31–38

5 **you are the onely cause of my dishonour . . . and contrarie to her owne liking** See 117.16–20.

Chapter 27

1 **but hee whom now the question concerneth** Fr. "mesmes cestuy dont il est question" (T4r; *even the one we are talking about*).

2 **with what violence you enforced mee to match with the King** *Tarisius* See 131.28–37.

3 **Soft and fayre** "Gently, quietly, without haste or violence," *OED*, s.v. *fair*, adv. 7a; cf. *soft*, adv. 8b.

4 **putting such a Prince to death, without hearing how he can answere for himselfe** Earlier on the Sultan does not offer Palmerin the possibility of stating his case; see 354.12–17.

5 **twelue dayes** Fr. "dix jours" (T5r; *ten days*).

Chapter 28

1 **if shee shewe not some part of her desire, by lookes (the faithfull and secrete messengers)** See n. 6 to chap. I.ii.

2 **that (then which) nothing is more precious** Fr. "ce qui ne se peut forcer qu'vne fois" (T5v; *that which can be forced only once*). Munday entirely leaves to the imagination of the reader to guess what is most precious, whereas the Fr. more explicitly suggests a woman's maidenhood.

3 *Aurora, Phoebus* **his faire Porter** Aurora is the Roman goddess of the dawn; cf. Freer, 217.

4 **a feuer** *Quotidian* A fever occurring at twenty-four-hour intervals, referring particularly to malaria; see *OED*, s.v. *quotidian* adj. 1.

5 **a Woman can inuent a lie without studie** Tilley records a proverbial expression of a similar import dated 1589: "Women naturally deceive, weep, and spin" (W716).

6 **when I beholde you both aduisedly . . . it neuer came by the Fathers side** Another humorous remark involving Urbanillo; cf. 147.43–148.1. See Daniels, 29.

7 *Barbarie* The Saracen territory of northern Africa; this occurrence predates the earliest example in the *OED*, s.v. *Barbary*, n. 4a.

8 **I am the better contented to part with him** This sentence is Munday's interpolation.

9 **ambushed** The 1616 edition reads *in Embuscado*, meaning "an ambuscade"; this word is first attested in 1686 according to the *OED*, that is, seventy years after this occurrence.

10 If the Prince commended her beautie, when being ambushed hee sawe her passe by See 416.19–417.2.

11 I knowe not howe I shall dissemble my torments This sentence is Munday's insertion.

12 before the earth bee readie for mee, I shall bee forced to take vp my endlesse Hostage Munday changes the expression, not the meaning, of his Fr. source: "deuant que je soys en bas, vous me veriez rendre l'esperit" (T6v; *before I am down below, you would see me give up the ghost*).

Chapter 29

1 Heretofore I came to thee on another Mountaine, where I and my Sisters healed the woundes thou didst receiue by the Serpent See 152.19–35.

2 assuring thee that they whom thou seekest . . . thy best and dearest Freendes Once again the text includes a prophecy, couched in mysterious and enigmatic language, that foretells the development of the plot, since the prediction turns out to be true, as the text itself indicates: "he esteemed to bee true," (440.27). Thus, Trineus is freed in 524.41–525.8, Colmelio in 538.2–6, and Ptolome in 561.16–30. Besides, in this same chapter we read how Palmerin's arch enemy, Frisol, becomes his "vowed, true, and trustie Friend" (444.16–17). Cf. González, "Sistema," 68–69.

3 they espyed tenne Knights comming before them, the formost of them leading a Ladie . . . whereby they might express their comfort Rape is a common ingredient in chivalric romance and serves to emphasize one of the knights' social functions, namely, protecting women and their sexual integrity. Writing about contemporary romance and prose fiction, including other texts from the *Palmerin* cycle, Jocelyn Catty, *Writing Rape, Writing Women in Early Modern England: Unbridled Speech* (1999; repr., New York: Palgrave, 2011), 25, states, "the majority of the rape scenarios (roughly two-thirds of them) feature attempted rather than successful rape," and that is exactly what happens in this particular case, in which Palmerin and his friends prevent the lady from being raped; cf. the case of the giant Franarco's attempted rape of Agriola and her mother (chap. I.li). The episodes of rape follow a more or less predictable pattern (Catty, ibid., 26). The distressed damsel is weeping or screaming: "a Ladie, who made verie greeuous and pitifull lamentations" (440.37); the rescuers hear the damsel's screams while they witness the violent scene: "they espyed tenne Knights . . ." (440.36); the setting is usually a wood, and in this case we know they are in a mountain "passing through a great forrest" (440.7–8). Finally and after the damsel is freed from her oppressors, the next step is to show gratitude to her rescuers: "they knew not in what sort to entertain them, whereby they might express their comfort"

(441.42–43). Note that the clause **who when they had satisfied their villainous willes** (441.31) is added by Munday.

4 **But since it hath beene my good happe to prevent your ominous fortune, I must aduise yee heereafter to beware of like hazard** Fr. "Toutesfois, puis que vous l'auez sauue, il se faut garder de plus grand encombrier" (T8r; *nevertheless, since you have saved him, it is necessary to protect yourself against greater difficulty*).

5 **To put him from these cogitations,** *Olorico* **ashamed of his absence in such a needfull time, came to** *Palmerin* **with these words** Fr. "Olorique tant honteux que plus ne pouuoit, fit ses complaintes à Palmerin" (T8r; *Olorique, so ashamed that he couldn't be more so, made his complaints to Palmerin*).

6 *Leonarda* Note that Leonarda makes her first appearance in the story in 239.28–30.

7 **with the Sunne painted therein, which hee well remembred to be his deuise** This clause is introduced by Munday in order to help the reader identify this character.

8 **as you haue heard in the former part of this Historie** I.e., in the first part of the romance; see 230.8–40. The remainder of this chapter performs a recapitulatory function, linking the ensuing action with the point where the adventures of Agriola, Trineus, and Frisol himself are last described.

9 **the fight on my behalfe was so dangerous, as but by the fauour of a Lady and a Squire, I neuer had escaped with life** See 292.7–31.

10 **kissed** *Palmerin* **in the Bedde, to seale the perpetuall league of amitie betweene them** Fr. "le baisa en la bouche, comme son amy singulier" (T8v; *he kissed him on the mouth, as his best friend*; for "amy singulier," see Huguet, s.v. *singulier*); Sp. "E abraçáronse e besáronse en la boca en señal de mucho amor e paz" (220; *and they embraced and kissed each other on the mouth as a sign of great love and peace*). Munday censors this expression of homophilia, not at all unusual in the chivalric culture of medieval Iberia, for which see Roberto J. González-Casanovas, "Male Bonding as Cultural Construction in Alfonso X, Ramon Llull, and Juan Manuel: Homosocial Friendship in Medieval Iberia," in *Queer Iberia: Sexualities, Cultures, and Crossings from the Middle Ages to the Renaissance*, ed. Josiah Blackmore and Gregory S. Hutcheson (Durham, NC: Duke University Press, 1999), 157–92; González-Casanovas defines homophilia "as a predilection for same-sex friendships based on close intimacy, which can extend over the full range of emotional attractions and sentimental expressions that lie outside genital interaction; it is illustrated in notions of blood brothers and boon companions" (161). See also Nieves Baranda, "Gestos de la cortesía en tres libros de caballerías de principios del siglo XVI," in *Les traités de savoir–vivre en Espagne &*

au Portugal du Moyen Âge à nous jours (Clermont–Ferrand: Faculté de Lettres de Clermont–Ferraud, 1995), 65.

11 **the rape of** *Agriola* See 323.16–33.

12 **coueting in nothing to extoll himselfe** This clause is Munday's insertion.

13 **He forgot not likewise to report how that Lady cured him of a long and greeuous disease** See 240.3–6.

14 **there louingly togither** This clause is Munday's addition.

Chapter 30

1 **I thank you good Syr** Fr. "Louange soit au Seigneur" (V1r; *the Lord be praised*).

2 **and because it was too soone to take vp their lodging** Fr. "se voyans logez de grand Soleil" (V1r; *seeing that they had found lodging in the middle of the day*).

3 *Thrace* A region located in the area north of the Aegean Sea and west of the Black Sea.

4 **is this that** *Palmerin* **who kild the Serpent . . . in the Companie of Prince** *Adrian***, and** *Ptolome* This recapitulatory paragraph alludes to episodes from the first part of the romance. Palmerin kills the dragon in 152.1–5, brings the healing water to King Primaleon in 154.33–39, defeats the giants in 170.21 and 172.18–25, and fights against the Count of Ormeque and his cousins in 180.17–38.

5 **hauing the onelye Champion of the worlde on his side** This clause is Munday's insertion.

6 **Then carelesse what became of my selfe, being depriued of my loue and honour of my life** Munday departs from the Fr.: "Mais, ó dur helas! la cherchant je me suis jetté en vne fosse pleine de peines excedans toutes morts!" (V2r; *but, alas! looking for her I threw myself into a pit full of torments far exceeding all deaths*).

7 **but seeing thou art now so happilie come** This clause is Munday's addition.

8 **the mariage was not to be allowed, in that it was doone against her will: she beeing (as I haue said) my Wife, by solemne speeches before God married to me** See n. 19 to chap. I.vi, and n. 3 to chap. I.ix.

9 **falling on his knee** Fr. "hauçant les mains au Ciel" (V2r; *raising his hands to Heaven*).

10 **Now my gracious Lorde, I come to vnderstand your answer** Munday's insertion.

11 **I giue these false accusers such discipline, as their wicked and treacherous dealings deserue** This clause is an amplification of its Fr. source, "je monstre à ces faux accusateurs leur folie" (V2v; *I show these false accusers their folly*).

12 **place** Fr. "la grand' place" (V3r; *the main square*). In this context, we need to bear in mind that the word *place* in English was "[e]mployed in 16th c. to render F. *place* and its Italian, Spanish, and German cognates" (see *OED*, s.v. *place* 1b).

13 **practise it well thou art best** I.e., you had best practice it well. In the past the phrase *you had best do (something)* was expressed in impersonal construction: *thee were best*. As these impersonal constructions disappear, the indirect personal pronoun is replaced by a subject pronoun, as happens in our case, which represents an intermediate stage between the old impersonal form and the modern one (*you had best*). See *OED*, s.v. *better* 4b; and Mustanoja, 434–36.

14 **saying hee woulde see the ende thereof before he tooke any sustenaunce** The emperor decides to postpone the meal until the combat is finished. Here the emperor is imitating a traditional Arthurian custom, in which king Arthur on a feast day such as Pentecost may choose not to eat until something marvellous happened or a challenge was presented before his court. This custom was already part of the English literary tradition, as we can read in this illustrative excerpt from Malory: "Sire, sayd Sir Kay the Stewarde, yf ye goo now vnto your mete ye shalle breke your old customme of your courte, for ye haue not vsed on this day [i.e., Pentecost] to sytte at your mete or that ye haue sene som aduenture" (XIII. ii.428); cf. *Sir Gawain and the Green Knight*, lines 90–99. The Sp. text makes no reference to this motif, which is added by Maugin: "il vouloit voir la fin du combat deuant le disner" (V3r; *he wanted to see the outcome of the combat before eating*).

Chapter 31

1 **vnlesse some bodie for pittie carrie them out before** This clause is added by Munday.

2 **because hee was lothe his Brother should fall without companie** Munday inserts this clause with mocking intent in requital for and to parallel the fact that previously the two brothers address Palmerin and Frisol "in mockage" (451.14).

3 **Strange was it to beholde this violent fight** Munday summarizes the sense of the Fr.: "& tant se chamaillerent, qu'on s'esbahissoit comme ilz pouuoyent plus viure" (V3v; *and so much did they strike each other that one wondered how they could live any longer*).

4 **not one minute will I graunt thee to trauerse with mee** Fr. "n'aurez vne seule mynute de treues auec moy" (V3v; *you won't have a minute of truce with me*). Maugin's *truce* becomes a more nuanced action in Munday's translation; the verb *traverse* means "to dispute, discuss" (*OED*, s.v. *traverse* v. 13).

5 **the Father of thy villainie** Fr. "Lucifer" (V3v), Sp. "ynfierno" (225; *hell*).

6 **that her Mother was so graciouslie defended** This clause is Munday's insertion.

7 **I will not be vnmindfull of your gentlenesse** This clause is an amplification of the Fr. "je le recognoistray" (V4r; *I will recognize him on account of it*).

8 **shall my cheefest aduersaries stop their mouthes** Munday's insertion.

9 **remembring what the Queene of *Tharsus* had saide to him, howe hee should deliuer his Father from death, before he could know him, which was likewise confirmed by the apparition of the Ladie to him, vnder the name of his best and deerest of Freendes** In 405.16–17 the Queen of Tharsus foretells that Palmerin will set his father free. It is not so clear, however, what is meant in the second part of this statement. In the same chapter (406.4–13), after Palmerin is tricked into having sex with the Queen of Tharsus, Polinarda appears to him in an admonishing dream, but no explicit mention is made of his involvement in the exoneration of Florendos.

10 **the Fayries tolde mee on the Mountaine *Artifaeria*, that one daie I shoulde bee Lord of all *Greece*** See 152.23–25.

Chapter 32

1 **and so hath an honorable victorie declared** Munday departs from the Fr., "ains est le cas auenu par Fortune, qui l'a permis ainsi" (V4v; *instead Fortune has caused it to happen and allowed it this way*).

2 **it will bee counted a speciall point of courtesie, to visite them that ventured for you** Munday slightly alters his source: "ne sçauriez (ce me semble) moins faire, qu'en le voyant luy en rendre graces" (V4v; *it seems to me that the least you could do is to see him and thank him on account of that*).

3 **not forgetting howe the Traytours threatned me** They were hoping that the Princess Armida would be "declared not legitimate, and so disinherited of the Kingdome" (435.3–4).

4 **and the fauourable countenaunce of such a Ladie, is more then so meane a Knight as my selfe can merit** Munday expands his source: "tant s'en faut que de telle Dame je pretende recompense aucune" (V5r; *not in the least do I ask for a reward from such a lady*).

5 **I tooke such a religious vowe of bondage on mee** Munday introduces the religious dimension, which should be understood as courtly love in its most devoted expression; cf. Fr. "je deuins tellement vostre serf" (V5r; *I become entirely your servant*).

6 **shee behelde the mole on his face like a Crosse . . .when *Cardyna* tooke him from her and caried him to the Mountaine** See 133.41–42.

7 **was nowe in the midst of his onely desire, verilie perswading himselfe that the Queene was his mother** Munday departs from the Fr., "ores qu'il desirast sur tout

ce que pensoit ja la Royne sa Mere" (V5v; *now that he wished above all that which the Queen his mother was already thinking*).

8 **a Crucifixe of Golde, which was tied about my necke when I was founde, and hath of long time beene kept by the most perfect Lady in the world** See 134.1–2; "the most perfect Lady," in this context refers to Palmerin's foster-mother Marcella, who keeps the crucifix until Palmerin requests it (see 142.19–21).

9 **so soone as Nature had brought him into the world** Munday uses a euphemism to avoid referring to the act of giving birth: "estant encores bien à peine sorty de son ventre" (V5v; *being just come out of her womb*).

10 **that iewel on him, which she most of all esteemed** Munday prefers to use this periphrasis rather than directly translate the euphemistic expression in the Fr., "sa fleur virginale" (V5v; *her virginal flower*).

11 **he had first solemnly vowed marriage to mee** See 122.12–20.

12 **you honoured the Temple of Loue with so sweete an offering** Fr. "vous vous estes esbatuë par amours auec luy" (V6r; *out of love you had a very good time with him*). As happens throughout the scene, Munday feels more comfortable describing it with vague language.

13 **hee was so sicke, as euerie howre his death was expected?** See 129.13–29.

14 **in our last warres thou tookest away my Sonne *Caniano*** See 422.16–17.

15 **albeit thou hadst not shewen such probable arguments, yet doost thou so perfectlie resemble my Sonne *Caniano*, as easily may be coniectured whence thou art discended** A probable argument describes logical reasoning based not on factual evidence but on probability. When using this kind of deductive reasoning Aristotle offers the following advice: "we must not carry its reasoning too far back, or the length of our argument will cause obscurity; nor must we put in all the steps that lead to our conclusion, or we shall waste words in saying what is manifest. It is this simplicity that makes the uneducated more effective than the educated when addressing popular audiences . . .; uneducated men argue from common knowledge and draw obvious conclusions. We must not, therefore, start from any and every opinion, but only from those of definite groups of people — our judges or those whose authority they recognize," *Rhetoric*, II.22, trans. W. Rhys Roberts, *The Complete Works of Aristotle: The Revised Oxford Translation*, ed. Jonathan Barnes (Princeton: Princeton University Press, 1995), 2:2224. Since it is impossible to establish Palmerin's ancestry with certainty, the use of probable arguments becomes necessary. Palmerin's long-winded discourse, however, does not qualify as a *probable argument*. In contrast, Remicius constructs an enthymeme or syllogism based on probable premises that is simple, avoids presenting all the steps used in the reasoning process, and ultimately appeals to

the authority of a judge, in this case the emperor himself. This way Palmerin's descent is determined and leaves no room for discussion.

16 the teares trickled downe his milke-white Bearde Munday amplifies the Fr. "pleurant" (V6v; *weeping*).

17 I would not suffer thy Mother to enioy the Prince *Florendos.* See 131.9–13, 28–37.

18 by the Archbishop of *Constantinople* Fr. "par vn Archeuesque" (V7v; *by an archbishop*).

19 the Prince *Florendos* **and** *Griana* **were affianced together** An early commentator censoriously summarizes the course of events as follows: "after Palmerin has delivered the Prince [i.e., Florendos] and Griana, by slaying their accusers [i.e., Promptaleon and Oudin] in combat, the submissive widow [i.e., Griana] marries, to the great joy of all parties, the base assassin [i.e., Florendos] of her unoffending husband! [i.e., Tarisius]" (*British Bibliographer*, 147).

Chapter 33

1 the Law of iudgement and reason Fr. "le droit d'amytié" (V7v; *the law of friendship*).

2 of two euilles I choose to take the least Proverbial; see Tilley, E207.

3 to suffer open violence Here *open* means "declared or held in public or by public authority" (q.v. *OED*, adj. 25a); it is therefore a euphemistic formula to refer to *execution*. Cf. Fr. "estre mené au suplice" (V7v; *to be led to torture*).

4 *Netrides,* **whom long since his eldest Brother disinherited, and banished him his Countrey to a little Castle** See 234.37–40 and 235.30ff.

5 Then *Frisol* **rehearsed before them all, the three Combats hee had with** *Palmerin,* **and what great honour he woonne at the Tourney in** *France* Their first combat takes place in the so-called tournament in France (231.5–15); they next exchange blows after Myseres's death (292.2–31); and finally at the *pass d'armes* called by the Duke of Gaule (314.38–315.36). The great honor Frisol obtains in France consists in having come out undefeated by Palmerin, thus the Duke of Gaule "esteemed him [i.e., Frisol] for a hardy and valiant Knight, hauing so long endured against *Palmerin* vnuanquished" (243.3–4).

6 his conquest on the Mountaine *Artifaeria,* **with his Combats both in** *Bohemia* **and** *Durace* For the conquest on the Mountain Artifaeria, see 151.15–152.5; for his combat in Bohemia, see 180.17–39, and in Durazzo, see 158.33–159.27.

7 *Polynarda,* **daughter to the Emperour of** *Allemaigne,* **and his Wife by solemne vowes passed betweene them** See 250.19–25.

8 **because the winde and weather was not nauigable** Fr. "attendans l'equipage de leur nauire" (V8v; *waiting for the crew of their ship*).

9 **wherefore (meeting with this earnest Louer) hee thus laboured to please him** This clause is Munday's insertion.

Chapter 34

1 **The infant of whome you speake ... which none of mine owne Children durst at any time aduenture** This clause is Munday's interpolation. For the episodes Gerrard reminisces about, see 135.12–31 and 140.8–14.

2 **with the teares trickling downe his graie beard** Amplification of the Fr. "pleurant" (X1r; *weeping*).

3 **countrey fines** Clothes of the finest quality for traveling across the rural districts of the country.

4 **as sometime did the foster Father of *Paris Alexander*, his Wife, and their Daughter *Pegasis*, when they brought the Cradle and acoustrements of the infant royall, to the Cittie of *Troy*, after he was knowne by his Father King *Priam*, and Queene *Hecuba* his Mother** Paris Alexander was the second son Priam had with Hecuba, who, while pregnant with him, dreamt that he would be the cause of his country's destruction. Priam then resolved to take the newborn to Mount Ida for exposure, until the shepherd Aegalos found and adopted him as his son. Aegalos named him Paris, who later acquired the further name of Alexander (cf. Apollodorus, III.xii.5, 124–25). In his youth Paris rediscovered his parents when they were celebrating games in honor of Priam's lost son. For the occasion Priam's servants took Paris's favorite bull, which became the prize for the winner of the games. Paris won the games after defeating everyone, even his brothers: "In anger [his brother] Deiphobus drew his sword agaisnt him, but he [i.e., Paris] leaped to the altar of Zeus Herceus. When Cassandra prophetically declared he was her brother, Priam acknowledged him and received him into the palace," Hyginus, *The Myths*, 91, trans. Mary Grant (Lawrence, KS: University of Kansas Press, 1960), 82. The part describing the return of the belongings of the exposed child is not included in the mythological accounts I have consulted, thus suggesting that Maugin added it to parallel more exactly the circumstances attending on Palmerin's recognition; cf. Freer, 217.

5 **sauing my life in my yongest yeares, and nourishing me to the state of discretion** Amplification of Fr. "depuis mon berceau jusques à l'adolescence" (X1v; *from the cradle up until the adolescence*). Palmerin expresses his thanks to his foster parents, who are properly rewarded by the emperor, as happens also in Munday's *Palmerin of England*, I.xlvii; cf. Patchell, 74.

6 **but when they came to vnfold** *Palmerins* **little pack of cloathes ... when** *Cardyna* **carried him hence to the Mountaine** This is an example of *identification by cloth or clothing* (motif H110; see Bueno Serrano, "Índice," 737).

7 **as though a new world had bene to be conquered** Fr. "que chacun s'en esbahissoit" (X2r; *that everyone was amazed*).

Chapter 35

1 **hee by whose meanes your health was recouered** See 154.33–38.

2 **Sir** *Palmerin* **your Sonne** Palmerin is Primaleon's grandson; here Munday applies the word *Sonne* to "one who is regarded as a son, or takes the place of a son" (*OED*, s.v. *son*, n. 1, 3a).

3 **with which inwarde oppressing conceite ... taking the Knight by the hande, he sayde** This passage summarizes the information in the Fr.: "& ce peu qu'il auoit de foyble vie ... embrassant le Cheualier, luy dist" (X2r).

4 **as well might content a greater personage** Munday departs from his source: "que de là en auant luy & son lignage n'eurent aucun besoin" (X2v; *that henceforward he and his lineage had no need whatsoever*).

5 *Pontus* Ancient region in Asia Minor on the Black Sea coast.

6 **cautelous** *Vlisses* Roman sobriquet for Odysseus, the protagonist of the *Odyssey*, known for his wiliness.

7 **where the rest of their traine might be decently entertained** Munday changes his source: "pour heberger les cheuaux" (X2v; *for stabling the horses*).

8 **neuer did the Ring of** *Giges* **bring him more honour, then this will to mee: for this could not profite or aduantage him, but onely by beeing inuisible** In his *Republic* (II.358e–360d) Plato tells the story of a shepherd, "an ancestor of Gyges of Lydia," who came upon a magic ring that could make him invisible. The shepherd decided to make an ignoble use of the ring's special powers, so "he seduced the king's wife and with her help assaulted and killed the king, and so took possession of the throne," trans. Robin Waterfield (Oxford: Oxford University Press, 1993), 47. The ring did bring "honor" to the shepherd in that he became king and possessed the queen, though the means were dishonorable murder, but only through invisibility. Whereas Frisol has honor only when visibly in the presence of Armida. She it is that brings him honor, and nothing in himself or his deeds. I am grateful to Alastair Henderson for this reading.

Chapter 36

1 **the like** Fr. "durant son regne n'en auoit eu du Leuant" (X3r; *during all his reign he hadn't had any from the Levant*).

2 **your Sonne *Trineus* and the faire *Agriola* Daughter to the King of *England*, whom two yeeres since and more hee lost in the East Seas** See 332.4–15. They departed from England and intended to go to the Continent, but a heavy storm caused them to stray into the eastern Mediterranean, i.e., the East Seas.

3 **hee vnderstood that they were liuing and in health, also that himselfe should in the ende recouer them** See the prophecy in 440.21.

4 **hee thought it necessarie to acquaint you herewith, because he doubted of your extreame sorrow and heauinesse** This passage is Munday's interpolation.

5 **hee deliuered them with very great reverence** Amplification of the Fr. "luy presenta" (X3v; *he presented to him* [the letter]).

6 **If heeretofore my good Lorde, I excused my obeysance to your commandement, especially for taking a husband, it was onely for the promise I made to my Brother *Trineus*.** See 254.10–13.

7 **the Lord Almoner** Fr. "l'Ausmoiner" (X4v; *the almoner*). An *almoner* was "an official responsible for distributing alms on behalf of another individual, or of an institution," who in the case of the British royal household was designated as *Lord High Almoner* (see *OED*, s.v. *almoner* n.2 2a). Probably in imitation of the royal title, Munday calls him *Lord*. For a discussion of the roles of this office in contemporary times, see R. A. Houston, "What Did the Royal Almoner Do in Britain and Ireland, c.1450–1700?," *English Historical Review* 125 (2010): 279–313.

8 **as they iudged her rather an Angell then anie earthly creature** Amplification of "qu'on l'eust mile fois plustost jugée diuine qu'humaine" (X4v; *one would have judged her one thousand times more divine than human*).

9 **as neither to *Nero* or *Galba* were done the like, no not by *Constantine* himself to the Pope** Nero was a Roman emperor (AD 54–68) famous for his cruelty, as also was his successor Galba (AD 68–69). Constantine was the first emperor to convert to Christianity and declared it the official religion of the Roman Empire in AD 324, thus recognizing the authority of the Pope.

10 **what the Poets described of *Helena*, tearming her the Goddesse of beautie . . . *Paris* may not be equalled with *Palmerin*.** We read in Homer's *Iliad*, "wondrously like is she [i.e., Helen] to the immortal goddesses to look upon" (III.158), trans. A. T. Murray, The Loeb Classical Library (Cambridge, MA: Harvard University Press, 1971), 1:129; Helen turned down many suitors, including the Greek princes Theseus and Odysseus, in favor of Menelaus. While Menelaus was away, the outstandingly beautiful Paris visited Sparta and there seduced Helen and carried her away with him to Troy, bringing about the Trojan War.

Chapter 37

1 **speake of such things as are most needfull** Amplification of Fr. "diray seulement" (X5r; *I'll just say*).

2 **the Patriarche of *Constantinople*** As one of the chief sees of the ancient world, Constantinople's bishop bears the title of *Patriarch* (q.v. *OED*, n. 1a).

3 *That true loue neuer wanteth his reward* Proverb; cf. Tilley, L515: "Love is the reward of love."

4 **where necessitie ruleth, reason hath no place** Proverb; cf. Tilley, N61: "necessity is the mother of invention."

5 **for the Knightes haue doone as best beseemed them, not to aduenture on their Lord and Maister . . . Armed in such sorte as none shoulde knowe him** It is not unusual in chivalric literature to find fellow knights resorting to incognito, as they would be unwilling to fight otherwise. For instance, in Malory we read about the Knights of the Round Table how "ony of hem will be loth to haue adoo with other, but yf hit were ony knyght at his owne request wold fyghte dysguysed and vnknowen" (VIII.iv.203); cf. 253.37–38. See Patchell, 36.

6 **In breefe** Munday summarizes the descriptions of the tournament as they appear in the Fr. throughout the entire chapter.

7 **her Brother** I.e., Palmerin. Palmerin and Frisol have sworn compagnonage in 444.20–26.

8 **Some haue reported this Giant to be a Monster . . . let vs proceede as occasion doth lead** vs The Sp. original (245–47) at this point describes the appearance of a Sagittarius, itself a kind of centaur, that inspires sheer terror among a few knights who "eran salidos por la puerta, tan grande era el miedo que avían del sagetario" (246; *ran away through the door, so greatly did they fear the Sagittarius*). It is obviously Palmerin who manages to defeat this creature. Maugin, however, decided to omit this passage and instead introduced a mythological parallel duly translated by Munday; according to Freer (208), this is Maugin's only substantial omission (see also Freer, 220). The mythological episode mentioned now in the English text refers to the battle of the Lapiths and Centaurs: Pirithous, king of the Lapiths, married Hippodamia and invited the Centaurs to the wedding, who enebriated with wine attempted to abduct the bride; see Ovid, *Met.*, XII.210–535. This section of Ovid's text makes no explicit reference to Hercules' involvement, which is however confirmed in the following lines: "As Nestor all the processe of this battell did reherce / Betweene the valeant Lapithes and misshapen Centawres ferce, / Tlepolemus displeased sore that Hercules was past / With silence, could not hold his peace, but out theis woordes did cast: / My Lord, I muse you should forget my fathers [i.e., Hercules'] prayse so quyght. / For often unto mee himself was woonted to recite, / How that the clowdbred

folk by *him* were cheefly put to flyght" (Golding, XII.593–599, 315, corresponding to Ovid, *Met.* XII.536–41). For an analysis of Hercules' Centauromachies, see Ruth Parkes, "Hercules and the Centaurs: Reading Statius with Virgil and Ovid," *Classical Philology* 104 (2009): 476–94. For a discussion of the episode of the Sagittarius in the Sp., see Campos, 276–78, and Lidia Beatriz Ciapparelli, "La conquista de sí mismo. La lucha de Palmerín con el Sagitario," in *Studia Hispanica Medievalia IV. Actas de las V Jornadas Internacionales de Literatura Española Medieval*, ed. Azucena Adelina Fraboschi et al. (Buenos Aires: Universidad Católica Argentina, 1999), 100–3. Cf. also Shakespeare, *Midsummer Night's Dream*, V.i.44–47.

Chapter 38

1 **the disease hee had when hee departed from you** See 237.18–239.16

2 **hauing deliuered the Queene Griana . . . against the two Nephewes of King Tarisius** See 451.6–452.2.

3 **were ye not sometime of my Brothers Court? . . . your Father I serued as a Page in his Chamber** See 462.36–38.

4 **my cheefest Freendes** Fr. "mes enfans & neueux" (X8r; *my children and nephews*).

5 **the thought were base and abiect in me to make refusall** Amplification of Fr. "je ne refuseray la condition" (X8r; *I will not refuse the condition*).

6 **nor shee enioy a fitter Husbande, and so may the Realme lineallie discende, from *Netrides* nowe aged, to his noble sonne** Fr. "à fin aussy que le mariage consommé, Netrides soit de leur consentement creé gouuerneur & regent de leur Royaume" (X8r; *in order that, once the marriage is consumated, Netrides by their agreement be made governor and regent of their kingdom*). Munday fails to mention how it is decided that Netrides should become governor of Hungary, thus making his text less coherent when a few lines later Netrides is "instituted Gouernour" (483.1).

7 **whose secrete desires were now effectuallie requited** Munday summarizes the sense of the Fr. "ausquelz Amour estoit si aspre & cruël, que sans se voir l'vn l'autre, ilz enduroyent vne peine plus que mortelle" (X8r; *to whom Love was so rough and cruel that without seeing each other, they endured a more than mortal punishment*).

8 **who had not forgot their former loue to him: and the vnnatural dealing of their king his deceased brother** This passage is added by Munday.

Chapter 39

1 to depart the new maried couple Palmerin is loath "to put asunder, sunder, separate, part" (*OED*, s.v. *depart* v. 3) the newlyweds.

2 the desire which conquers all men Fr. "le desir voluptueux, & concupiscence" (X8v; *voluptuous desire and concupiscence*). Munday prefers a euphemistic paraphrase to substitute for the more explicit Fr.

3 determining to recompence his princelie kindnesse, if Fortune did not contrarie him in this enterprised iourney This passage is Munday's insertion.

4 for well he knewe, that if shee could any waie hinder his departure, his iourney should be soone preuented Fr. "car il sçauoit, s'il eust fait autrement, qu'il ne l'eust sçeu obtenir tant elle l'aymoit" (X8v; *for he knew, if he had done otherwise, he wouldn't have been able to obtain it, because she loved him so much*).

5 the vulgar sort iudge after their owne humours, not according to the quallitie and estimation of vertue Fr. "qui ne juge que du present, sans regarder au passé, ou futur" (Y1r; *who judge only about the present, without considering the past or the future*).

6 as thou tenderest my life and thine owne good This clause is added by Munday.

7 without anye occasion of iealouzie to the Princesse Fr. "taisant en tout les caresses & bon recueil que Palmerin auoit fait aux Dames Gregeoises" (Y1r; *being completely silent about all the caresses and good welcome that Palmerin had done to the Greek ladies*).

8 the Merchaunt... that was *Palmerins* Maister I.e., Estebon.

9 there is no remedie for troublesome age, but onelie death it selfe Cf. Tilley, R69: "There is a remedy for all things but death."

10 euen dried vp my vitall blood This clause is Munday's addition.

11 with the perfect discourse of thine owne fortunes This clause is introduced by Munday.

Chapter 40

1 because it was his will it should be so Munday alters his Fr. source: "pour viure en sa compagnie n'auoit encores voulu se marier" (Y1v; *in order to live in his company she hadn't wanted to marry yet*).

2 shee committed the whole affayres of the Realme to the Counte *Roldin* Fr. "donnant ordre auec le conte Roldin grand Maistre de Macedone, aux affaires du

Royaumé" (Y1v; *putting in order the affairs of the kingdom with the help of the Count Roldin, Great Master of Macedon*).

3 **one appointed for that office by generall good liking** This clause is Munday's interpolation.

4 **and if I stay (quoth hee) longer . . . the Queene my Mother** Palmerin's words appear in reported speech in the Fr. (Y2r).

Chapter 41

1 **sixe or seuen dayes** Fr. "deux jours" (Y2v; *two days*).

2 **The Moore *Olimaell*, as ye haue read in the former part of this Historie . . . entred into so great credit** See chap. II.i. The events referred to in the text are not placed in "the former part of this Historie," i.e., in the first part of the romance (cf. n. 8 to chap. II.xxix; I understand *former* as "the first of two," q.v. *OED*, adj. 2a). This inaccuracy suggests that Munday, while preparing the translation, was well aware that it would be published in two volumes, but the textual limits of each volume had not been determined when he wrote this passage or differed from those finally used. Since the Fr. has 139 chapters, it seems safe that the events referred to here, which occur in chap. 66 of the Fr. version, should have appeared in the first volume of the English translation, which however ends in chap. I.lxv.

3 **hee was made high Admirall of *Turkie*** See 344.16–18.

4 **because I can well speake the *Arabian* language** This clause is Munday's insertion, although later on the Fr. reads, "Palmerin entendant son langage" (Y3r; *Palmerin understanding their language*).

5 **they could skill of such affayres** I.e., they had practical knowledge of such kind of events; for the expression *could skill*, see *OED*, s.v. *skill*, n. 5.

6 **the faire Princesse *Laurana* . . . often solicited him in his dreames** See 161.40–42.

7 **this Cittie . . . not manie yeeres since, with the price of my blood I laboured to defende it** See 158.33–159.27; Palmerin defended this city (Durazzo, in Albania) from the attack of Count Passaco of Messina, referred to above.

8 **therefore no great maistrie to winne it quickly** I.e., it was not a great achievement to conquer it quickly; see *OED*, s.v. *mastery*, 5b.

9 **hauing endured a long and furious skirmish** This clause is introduced by Munday.

10 *Thessalie* Thessaly, in north-eastern Greece.

11 **the three Magical Sisters . . . *Artifaeria*, and one of them afterwarde in his going to *Buda*.** For their appearance on the Mountain Artifaeria, see 152.19–43; for the presence of one of them in Hungary, see 440.17–25.

12 **where the wofull Queene remained** This explanatory clause is Munday's insertion.

13 **The Damosell Enchauntresse aduertised . . . she should be maried to one of the best Knights of the world** This prophecy is repeated in chap. xx of Munday's *Palmendos*, the continuation to *Palmerin d'Oliva*: "*Francelina* alreadie had felte the flames of looue . . . because the Fairies (knowing the end of the enchauntment was at hand) told her that ere long shee should be conquered, and deliuered from that Castel by one of the best Knights in the world" (sig. Q4r). This knight is Palmendos, Palmerin's son, to whom Francelina offers herself as his "loyall spouse and Wife" (sig. Q4v). See González, "Sistema," 67; cf. n. 9 to chap. II.lxvii.

14 **wealth and welfare** Fr. "plaisirs & contentemens" (Y4r; *pleasures and contentments*).

15 **Ouer the gate stoode a huge Image of Copper, holding a mightie Mace of Steele, wrought by such cunning, as if anie Knight but he that was destenied to end the aduenture, should assay to enter, hardly might he escape to returne againe** Here we find the description of a human automaton that keeps guard of the tower. This is a motif familiar from Arthurian romances and, in fact, there is some similarity with the characteristics of another automaton presented in one version of the *Prose Tristan*: "Or dit li contes que, a celui point que li filz Don fu venuz au chastel Arès, que dit avoit esté Arès son aiol, il trova li chasteaux tot ploins d'enchantement. *Il est empêché par un chevalier* de coivre fait por grant soutiliece *d'entrer dans le château*," ed. E. Löseth, *Le roman en prose de Tristan, le roman de Palamède et la compilation de Rusticien de Pise: analyse critique d'après les manuscrits de Paris* (Paris: Émile Bouillon, 1891; the words in italics were provided by Löseth as a summary), 223: "*Now the tale says that at the moment when the son of Don came to the castle of Ares, which he said it had belonged to Ares his grandfather, he found the castle completely full of enchantment. He is prevented access by a copper knight made with great skill.*" The detail of the automaton in *Palmerin d'Oliva* is first introduced by Jean Maugin, who a few years afterwards got engaged in the publication of a modernized version of the *Tristan en prose* (Paris, 1554; FB 49894); see Renée L. Curtis, *Le roman de Tristan en prose* (Munich: Max Hueber, 1963), 1:17. This motif was not entirely foreign to English readers, who could have encountered it in *Huon of Burdeux* (ca. 1515): "at the entre of the gate there are .ii. men of brasse, eche of them holdynge in there handys a flayll of Iren, wher with without sesse daye and nyght they bete," 96.20–23; cf. Patchell, 48. For a survey of the presence of this kind of contraption in literary texts, see J. Douglas Bruce, "Human Automata in Classical Tradition and Mediaeval Romance," *MP* 10 (1913): 511–26.

16 **as though the greatest Monarch in the worlde had come to take landing** Fr. "si hautement qu'on n'eust pas ouy le dyable hurler" (Y4v; *as loudly as if one had never heard the devil howling*). Munday removes this reference to the devil.

17 **from the very meanest to the highest, shall humble themselues at your maiesties foote** Fr. "Lesquelz du plus petit jusques au plus grand' adorerent la grand' medalle de chair" (Y5r; *who from the least to the most important worshipped the great face of flesh*).

18 **vncircumcized Tirant as thou art** Fr. "Tyran inique que tu es" (Y5r; *iniquitous tyrant that you are*). In changing his source Munday introduces a fact-based historical remark, since it was traditional among Ottoman rulers to attract notice to their children's circumcision; cf. Mansel, 75–78.

19 **before I yeelde so much as in thought to thee** This clause is Munday's insertion.

20 *Natolia* I.e., the Anatolian peninsula.

21 **which before hee did not ... least crooked fortune should now againe preuent him** Although Munday condenses the sense of his Fr. source ("Lors s'esuanouyt la Princesse ... & par ce moyen eust esté perdu," Y5v), there is one significant detail he probably overlooks intentionally: "Palmerin fut ... triste en ce qu'il pensa que le Turc la tenoit pour femme" (Y5v; *Palmerin was sad thinking that the Turk had taken her [i.e., Agriola] as his wife*).

22 **seeing *Hippolyta* was not present** This clause is Munday's addition. Munday here refreshes the memory of his readers, who may not remember that Hippolita is the only character among the Ottomans that understands English (see 344.10). Now they certainly understand that Hippolita's absence makes this episode possible.

23 **knowing the Turks censures were very peremptorie** This clause is Munday's insertion.

24 **do not the thing in haste, for which afterwarde you will be sorrie** Proverbial; cf. Tilley, H191: "He that resolves in haste repents at leisure."

25 **I would haue you forsake the follie of your Christianitie, and yeeld your selfe to our Law** The Ottomans showed greater religious tolerance than the Christian nations of Western Europe. Different manifestations of the three monotheist religions coexisted in sixteenth-century Constantinople; cf. Mansel, 47–53.

26 **what became of *Trineus*, after that so vnhappily I departed from you** See 331.26–30.

Chapter 42

1 **you remember, without repetition ... *Trineus* bare the likenesse of a goodly Dogge** See 334.3–35.

2 **Hauing this dellicate flower in her hand ... as hardly could any abide to stand by her.** Although it may look like a fabulous disease, it has been described in modern medical literature. The worm-like infestation of the nose could be caused by maggots or screw-worms (known as myiasis of the nose) and produce "a foul fetor." For a recent review of medical knowledge about this disease, see A. Kalan and M. Tarik, "Foreign Bodies in the Nasal Cavities: A Comprehensive Review of the Aetiology, Diagnostic Pointers, and Therapeutic Measures," *Postgraduate Medical Journal* 76 (2000): 484–87. For a discussion of Zephira's disease and cure in the Sp. version, see Ivy A. Corfis, "The Representation of Illness in the Hispanic Chivalric Romance," *Courtly Arts and the Art of Courtliness*, ed. Keith Busby and Christopher Kleinhenz (Cambridge: D. S. Brewer, 2006), 331–47, at 341–45.

3 **shee behelde the Dogge which was the Prince *Trineus* ... and hauing obtained her request** The relationship between Zephira and the dog-shaped Trineus is analyzed in Campos, 283.

4 *Elain* Arab. *al-'Ayn*, meaning "the spring," is a common element in place names from Arab countries.

Chapter 43

1 **not contented with infinite number of Concubines** See 347.36–37 and n. 10 to chap. II.i.

2 **hath many times made loue to me** The expression *to make love to* in this context should be interpreted as "to pay amorous attention; to court, woo" (*OED*, s.v. *love* n. 7g).; Fr. "m'a ja priée par plusieurs fois d'amour" (Y7v; *has already begged me for love on many occasions*).

3 **to goe spoyle to Isle of *Rhodes*** This reference is already present in the Sp. (264), but it had different historical connotations for English readers. When the Sp. original was printed in 1511, the island of Rhodes was an object of desire and ambition of the Ottoman Empire, but also a symbol of Christian resistance. But when Munday's translation was published, the Ottomans had already gained the upper hand, since Suleyman took control of the island in 1523. Strictly speaking, however, this state of affairs should have no real bearing on the interpretation of the text, since the romance's narrative framework refers to a historical period prior to the Ottoman conquest of Constantinople of 1453.

4 **a beginning so good, must needes sort to a successiue ende** Proverbial; cf. Tilley, B259: "A good beginning makes a good ending"; B262: "Such beginning such end."

5 **when such waightie occasions commaundeth our diligence** Amplification of "qu'on nous y surprenne" (Y8r; *that one surprises us*).

6 **I will make you my Wife** The practice of polygyny, or of a man having several wives, is acceptable among Muslims.

7 **I feele my selfe not halfe currant** I.e., he feels below par; cf. Fr. "que je me trouue mal" (Y8r; *that I feel ill*).

8 **Ianizaries** A *janizary* was "one of a former body of Turkish infantry, constituting the Sultan's guard" (*OED*, s.v. *janizary* n. 1). See further in Mansel, 17.

9 **to vse drunken *Holofernes* as hee hath deserued** Equating the Grand Turk with Holofernes, the Assyrian general in the apocryphal book of Judith, invites us to interpret this episode in the romance vis-à-vis the biblical story. Just as in the Vulgate Bible Judith takes the initiative to free the city of Bethulia from the siege of Holofernes (Jth. 8:31–32), in *Palmerin d'Oliva* Laurana devises a ruse to break free from the Turk, "who holdes vs in this thrall and bondage" (501.7–8). Just as Judith uses her beauty to beguile Holofernes (Jth. 10:17), Laurana bases her stratagem on her feminine wiles. Finally, both Holofernes and the Great Turk are beheaded. While the former is killed by Judith herself (Jth. 13:10), the latter is killed by the Duke Pontus disguised as Laurana. Before his decapitation Holofernes is "exceedingly drunk" (Jth. 13:4), as is the Great Turk. Note that the Biblical analogy was not part of the original Sp.

10 **mustachoes** Contemporary images of Ottoman Sultans portray them sporting a moustache; cf. Mansel, fig. 1, showing Mehmed II in Constantinople in 1453.

11 *Phoebus* I.e., the sun.

12 **mine Vnckle of a poore Ianizarie made thee his cheefe Admirall** See 344.16–18.

13 **Basso** Fr. "Bascha" (Z1v). *Basso* is a variant spelling of *bashaw*, the earlier form of the Ottoman title *pasha*, used for "a Turkish officer of high rank, as a military commander or a provincial governor" (*OED*, s.v. *pasha*, n. 1).

Chapter 44

1 **In breefe** Indeed Munday is summarizing the naval attack in his source. From this chapter onward he changes his translation strategy. Munday is no longer closely following the Fr. source, but instead prefers to summarize passages which are not essential to the narrative development of the story. He normally prefers

to condense sections describing military activity. It may simply be that he was trying to meet a specific deadline set by the printer, or perhaps was getting bored with the verbose and prosy style of his source (see n. 3 to chap. II.xlviii). In the sections where Munday is summarizing it is no longer possible to make a direct verbal comparison with his source, in which case I will make reference only to narrative changes which significantly depart from the Fr.

2 **I wil sende thy soule after thy fellowes** Fr. "je feray de vostre teste quinze pieces" (Z1v; *I will divide your head in fifteen pieces*). Munday settles on a rather more sedate expression than his gory source.

3 *Estebon* . . . **who first gaue me horse and armour for knightly seruice** See 144.35–38.

4 **heeretofore thou didst deliuer me from the Lions throat** See 142.26–37.

5 **enemies** Fr. "compagnons" (Z2r; *companions*).

6 **a mightie winde at Northeast** Fr. "vn vent Mestral" (Z2r; *mistral*). Munday mistranslates the Fr., since the mistral is a north-westernly wind. The English word *Mistral* is first attested in 1604 according to the *OED*.

7 **as though the furies had stood to chase them** Fr. "qu'il sembloit que le Diable les chassast auec vn fouet" (Z2v; *that it seemed the Devil chased them with a whip*). Munday replaces the Fr. *Diable* with a reference to the classical Furies, sent to punish wrongdoing.

8 *Palmerin* **could not be enchaunted . . . of the three wise Sisters on the Mountaine** *Artifaeria* See 152.27–28. For an analysis of this scene in the Sp., see Marín Pina, "Maga", 80–81.

9 **Ah stepmother too cruell** By calling Fortune a stepmother, Munday implicitly alludes to the proverb "Fortune to one is mother, to another is step-mother" (Tilley, F609; note that this proverb is first attested in 1596; cf. *OED*, s.v. *stepmother* n. 1c, entry under year 1659).

10 **when I perswaded my Friendes to goe against their Christian Brethren** See 491.20–35.

11 **in the ende left not one to carrie reporte of this massacre** Munday omits a long passage in the Fr. (Z2v) where precise details of a bloodbath are provided.

12 **Neuer did** *Circes* **deale so cruelly with** *Grillus***, and other Souldiers to the wise** *Vlysses* When Ulysses, Roman name of Odysseus, reached the island of Aeaea where the enchantress Circe dwelt, he divided his men in two groups. Odysseus sent the first group, made up of twenty-three men, to visit Circes, who transformed them into pigs (see *Odyssey*, X.208–60; cf. n. 6 to chap. I.lxv). Plutarch used this episode to compose a dialogue between Odysseus and Gryl-

lus, one of those turned into pigs by Circe. In Plutarch's dialogue Odysseus tells Gryllus (meaning *grunter, swine*) that he has asked Circe to return the Greeks back to their human form. But much to his surprise, Gryllus declines the offer: "you are trying to persuade us, who live in an abundance of good things, to abandon them, and with them the lady who provides them," *Moralia*, 986D, trans. Harold Cherniss and William C. Helmbold, The Loeb Classical Library (Cambridge, MA: Harvard University Press, 1984), 12:499. It is therefore obvious that Circe gave generous treatment to her prisoners, as accurately suggested in Munday's translation.

13 **and therefore subiect to euerie inconuenience** This clause is Munday's insertion.

14 **from the Turks which cherished you ... to the cruell and mercilesse** *Malfada* Munday avoids reproducing the Christian antithesis in the Fr., which describes the situation of Agriola and Laurana in the Ottoman court as "Paradis du Turc" (*paradise of the Turk*) in contrast to "l'enfer de l'impitoyable Malfade" (Z3r; *the hell of the pitiless Malfada*).

15 **Wandering along in these mones ... where at the gate he sawe two Damoselles** Here Munday leaves out a lengthy passage corresponding to more than a column of text on sig. Z3r: "Helas mon cueur! ... deuant de luy deux jeunes Damoyselles."

16 **that shee might abuse him** This clause is Munday's interpolation. She would want to abuse him sexually, as happens to Dyardo; see 510.4–7.

17 **I will sende your soules after your Mistresse** Fr. "Fuyez d'ici, que je ne vous enuoye au sein de Lucifer auec vostre Maistresse" (Z3v; *get out of here so that I won't send you to the bosom of Lucifer with your mistress*). Munday avoids mentioning Lucifer.

18 *Dyardo*, **whose life you defended in the king of** *Bohemiaes* **Court** See 180.9–35.

19 *Dyardo* **gaue** *Palmerin* **a lustie Courser, and taking leaue of him, set forward on his iourney** Note that Palmerin is about to depart the Island of Malfada, but we are only told about his going on horseback, not making any sea-crossing.

Chapter 45

1 **So soone as** *Palmerin* **had thus left the Isle ... imaginations passed him concerning the Princesse** *Zephira* The beginning of this chapter condenses the action described in the Fr.: "Tant chemina Palmerin par l'isle de Malfade ... rauasser apres ceste Princesse Zerphire" (Z4r).

2 **as all knights errant are bound by dutie, to defende the iust quarrell of distressed Ladies** The influential *Llibre de l'Ordre de Cavalleria*, composed in Catalan by Ramon Llull between 1274 and 1276, already establishes a knight's obligation to defend women, as can be read in William Caxton's translation of 1484: "Thoffyce of a knyght is to mayntene and deffende wymmen / wydowes and orphanes," *The Book of the Ordre of Chyualry*, ed. Alfred T. P. Byles, EETS os 168 (London: Oxford University Press, 1926), 38.

3 **True it is, that I stayed with** *Malfada* ... **bring my troubles to anie good ende** See 499.27–41.

4 **A thousand thankes good Knight ... how his Armie was discomfited at** *Constantinople*. The final paragraph is actually a concise summary of chap. 111 in the Fr., which has the following title: "Comme la Princesse Zerphire sceut par vn Escuyer que son frere venoit assaillir Elain auec grosse armée: & de ce qui en auint" (Z5r; *How the princess Zephira learnt from a squire that her brother was coming to attack Elain with a large army and what came of it*). The narrative events contained in this chapter are of a military kind, in which Munday generally shows little interest.

Chapter 46

1 **The King of** *Balisarca*, **(as you haue heard before) ... his Galleys burnt before** *Constantinople*. See 422.12–40.

2 **one Galley** Fr. "deux galeaces" (Z7r; *two galleys*).

3 **The King of** *Balisarca* ... **hee called his Lorde Ambassadour** *Maucetto* **to him, saying** The opening paragraph corresponds to almost an entire page in the Fr.: "Le Roy de Balisarque occis ... fit appeller Maucette son Ambassadeur, & luy dist" (Z7r).

4 **farre worsse mishapen then was** *Thersites* **the** *Greek* The deformity of Thersites is described in the *Iliad*, II.216–19: "Evil-favoured was he beyond all men that came to Ilios: he was bandy-legged and lame in the one foot, and his two shoulders were rounded, stooping together over his chest, and above them his head was warpen, and a scant stubble grew thereon," trans. A. T. Murray, 1:67.

5 **who went to see his Falcon flie, when the Pirates came and vnhappilie tooke vs** See 331.22–332.14.

6 **if he bee of our Lawe, and hath beene dumbe of long** See 352.25–30.

7 **profession** It may refer to Palmerin's *profession of religion* (*OED*, s.v. *profession* n. 5a), but also to his *occupation* (*OED*, s.v. *profession* n. 6b).

8 **beside the continuall fauours of a Princesse** This clause is Munday's insertion.

9 **and till I returne let good hope perswade yee** These words are introduced by Munday.

Chapter 47

1 **After that** *Maulerino* **was crowned king of** *Nabor* **. . . a Basilisque, whome** *Palmerin* **with the helpe of the dog** *Tryneus* **valiantly ouercame** Once again this chapter opens with a summary of the narrative action in the Fr., this time centered on the fight that Palmerin, aided by dog-shaped Trineus, has with a basilisk (Z8v–Aa1r). For this episode in the Sp. version, see José Luis Moure, "El basilisco: mito, folclore y dialecto," *Revista de Filología Española* 79 (1999): 191–204, at 198.

2 **they are Christians, and extract of the greatest linage on the earth, in bountie and valour incomparable** Although this statement provides no valuable information, it has prophetic significance for its recipients. González describes the statment as an example of *present prophetic discourse* because the truth revealed in the prophecy does not refer to a future state but is already in place ("Sistema," 47).

3 *Sir Knight, in these pauillions . . . before the deede be doone* This quatrain (EV 20421) is written in iambic pentameters with a rhyming scheme abab.

Chapter 48

1 **not seeing the Piller** Fr. "Palmerin ayant leu ce qui estoit graué au Perron" (Aa2r; *Palmerin having read the inscription on the pillar*); Munday contradicts the Fr., but without narrative consequences. As happens in previous chapters, Munday continues summarizing his source.

2 **his successe** Although syntactically the possessive *his* seems to refer to Palmerin, from a purely narrative point of view it is more likely to refer to Drumino. Alternatively, it could be applied to Palmerin's *successe* if we interpret it as "the fortune (good or bad) befalling anyone in a particular situation or affair" (*OED*, s.v. *success*, n. 2), obviously here *bad fortune*.

3 **But not to hold you with tedious discourse considering which way the victorie is intended** Fr.: "Voulez vous que je m'amuse icy vn an à descrire la particularité des attaintes?" (Aa3r; *do you want me to busy myself for a year describing the details of the assaults?*). What Maugin sees as an opportunity to *amuse himself* ("m'amuse") becomes tedious for Munday; what Maugin considers an interesting *particularité* seems commonplace and trite to Munday. Munday's remarks offer a glimpse of his narrative and stylistic preferences and suggest that at times he felt his commission to translate the *Palmerin* romances was somewhat tedious; see the prefatory epistle in part II (339.17–18).

4 **whose meanes ere sixe Monethes be past, the greatest nobilitie in the world shall receyve incredible honour** This prophecy refers to Palmerin and predicts his coronation as emperor; see 577.26–27.

Chapter 49

1 **who by the meanes of noble *Palmerin*, will restore your health, and him will I acquaint with the manner how it must be compassed** Below, Muzabelino gives instructions to Palmerin, who restores Zephira's health in 527.13–528.9. As González argues, Muzabelino's statement is part of a complex prophecy: he reveals the outcome in his prediction, but gives not even a veiled hint about the means used to achieve such an outcome ("Sistema," 61).

2 **Your disease happened by smelling to a flower** See 499.18–24.

3 **more skilfull in all artes, then euer was the skilfull *Medea*** In mythology Medea is a sorceress who helped Jason obtain the Golden Fleece.

4 **ten Rocks of Marble without the Castell . . . and by these Rocks was the Castle named** The adventure at the Castle of the Ten Rocks is reminiscent of Lancelot's adventure of the Dolorous Guard: in order to defend the castle, "there were two sets of walls, and in each wall a gate; and at each gate the newcomer had to fight *ten knights*" (*Lancelot-Grail*, 3:143; my emphasis). In Fr. the rocks are described as "Perrons" (Aa4r), for which see n. 2 to chap. I.xxxii.

5 **this good Knight aduentured his life, in the daungerous battell when my Brother was slaine** See 513.11–12.

6 **hee that slewe *Malfada*, and her Seruaunts** See 508.22–28.

7 **they behelde a goodly Sworde, enclosed therein vp to the crosse . . . it is in vaine to striue any further** This is another occurrence of the motif of dislodging sword already used in 165.38–40, although now "the motif is debased by the substitution of tawdry magic for knightly strength and prowess" (Patchell, 51).

Chapter 50

1 **In breefe** The Fr. describes Palmerin's fight against only two of the ten knights, but Munday seems to see no point in translating even such piece of chivalric action. For a discussion of this episode in connection to the *Arabian Nights*, see Lidia B. Ciapparelli, "La relación intertextual entre *Las mil y una noches* y *El Palmerín de Olivia*," *II Coloquio Internacional de Literatura Comparada: "El Cuento," Homenaje a María Teresa Maiorana* (Buenos Aires: Universidad Católica Argentina, 1995), 2:35–38.

2 **bad successe** "failure, misaduenture, misfortune" (*OED*, s.v. *success*, n. 2a).

3 **when suddenly he vanished away, and was no more seene afterward** Fr. "ou si tost ne fut, qu'il deuint froid & royde, comme s'il eust esté mort" (Aa6r; *where very quickly he became cold and stiff, as if he were dead*). Munday decides to introduce some magic not present in his source.

4 *Agriola*, **who afterwarde was likewise enchaunted in the Isle of** *Malfada* See 507.38–39.

5 **two moneths** Fr. "six moys" (Aa6v; *six months*).

6 **such coniurations hath she charmed them withall, as they shall not stirre till you haue taken the Birde you aske for: at whose fearefull crie they shall all awake** This bird is already mentioned in Munday's *Palmerin of England*, II.lxiv, published sometime between 1581 and 1585. The reference in *Palmerin of England* suggests that well before his translation of *Palmerin d'Oliva* was published in 1588, Munday had become thoroughly familiar with the latter; for this suggestion and a transcription of the relevant passage, see Sánchez-Martí, "*Zelauto*'s Polinarda and the *Palmerin* Romances," 77–78. For more information on this bird, see n. 5 to chap. II.li.

Chapter 51

1 **the Princesse of** *Romata* **whom he woonne in the Ioust** See 519.28–520.11.

2 *Hercules* **of** *Libia*, **who ouercame Tyrants and Monsters at his pleasure** George Sandys's allegorical commentary added to his translation of Ovid's *Metamorphoses* reads, "*Hercules* better deserued a Deity then all the rest of the *Heroes:* who conquered nothing for himselfe; who ranged all over the world, not to oppresse it, but to free it from oppressors and by killing of Tyrants and Monsters preserued it in tranquility," *Ovid's Metamorphosis Englished, Mythologized, and Represented in Figures*, ed. Karl K. Hulley and Stanley T. Vandersall (Lincoln, NE: University of Nebraska Press, 1970), 439. Cf. *FQ*, V.i.2: Hercules, "Who all the West with equall conquest wonne, / And monstrous tyrants with his club subdewed" (7–8).

3 *Amphion* **or** *Orpheus* **of** *Thrace*, **who with theyr melodie tamed the Fishes, Beasts, and Birds.** Amphion, king of Thebes and musician, played the lyre much to his wife Niobe's pleasure. Orpheus, a Thracian musician, who with his singing and lyre playing could enchant wild beasts.

4 **the Prince** *Trineus*, **who saued my life when the Traytour would haue slaine mee in my bedde** See 500.19–29.

5 **take you no care for nourishing your Birde . . . then when the souereigne water fell from her beake, wherewih the Princesse** *Zephira* **was cured** In bestowing this bird on Palmerin, Muzabelino confers oracular powers on the bird, in addition to the curative properties already seen in the text. Here we find a case of

ornithomancy in which the sounds produced by the bird are endowed with divinatory value. This oracular activity was practiced in Europe since classical antiquity and throughout the Middle Ages. See what the influential Isidore of Seville has to say about ornithomancy in his encyclopedic *Etymologies*: "Augures autem dicunt et in gestu et in motu et in volatu et in voce avium signa esse constituta. Oscines aves vocant, quae ore cantuque auspicium facium; ut corvus, cornix, picus," *Etymologiarum sive Originum*, XII.vii.75–76, ed. W. M. Lindsay (Oxford: Clarendon Press, 1911; *Augurs say that omens are found in the gestures and movements and flights and calls of birds. Those birds are called "oscines" that produce auspices with their mouths and their song, such as the raven, the crow, and the woodpecker*; trans. Stephen A. Barney et al. [Cambridge: Cambridge University Press, 2010], 269). According to Isidore's classification, the bird in *Palmerin d'Oliva* belongs to the *oscines*. But in order for the bird's oracular sounds to be properly interpreted, Muzabelino instructs Palmerin with the necessary information. As Muzabelino masterminds, this bird will serve Palmerin until his death, which will coincide with the bird's own death, as can be read at the end of Munday's *Primaleon*, III.lii.239–40: "So soone as the Emperour [i.e., Palmerin d'Oliva] entred into the great Hall, the inchaunted Bird cast forth a dolorous crie, and therwith he remembring that *Mozabelin* tolde him, that the same should be one of the signes of his [i.e., Palmerin's] death ... As soone as he was dead, the inchaunted Bird dyed likewise, casting foorth so lamentable a cry, that it put all the Court into a great feare." For an analysis of Palmerin's death in the Sp., see A. C. Bueno Serrano, "La muerte de Palmerín de Olivia (*Primaleón*, II, ccxii, 535–537) interpretada con ayuda de los motivos folclóricos," *Memorabilia* 11 (2008): 31–46. Muzabelino even enchants the bird so that it needs no further nourishment to live ("I threw such a charme on her, as hencefoorth shee shall liue without taking any foode," 530.14–15). For a comprehensive discussion about the origin and nature of this bird, see Javier Roberto González, "El ave profeta en *Palmerín de Olivia y Primaleón*," *Exemplaria* 4 (2000): 73–107. This motif may have come to the knowledge of the Sp. romancer by means of either the Greco-Roman or the Arabian tradition. The latter had already left its mark on the ornithomancy found in Castilian epic literature; see Álvaro Galmés de Fuentes, *Épica árabe y épica castellana* (Barcelona: Ariel, 1978), 123–30. It is therefore not unlikely that ornithomancy of Arabian tradition could have indirectly influenced the Sp. author. Furthermore, in northern Europe existed the perception that ornithomancy was one of the augural practices of the Arabs in Spain; cf. William of Malmesbury, *Gesta Regum Anglorum*, ii.167.3, where he explains how Gerbert, the future pope Silvester II, traveled to Muslim Spain: "Ibi quid cantus et uolatus auium portendat didicit" (*There he learnt to interpret the song and flights of birds*), ed. and trans. by R. A. B. Mynors, completed by R. M. Thomson and M. Winterbottom (Oxford: Clarendon Press, 1998), 1:280–81.

Chapter 52

1 **which I passe ouer as matter altogether impertinent** With this clause Munday signals that he is leaving out a section in the Fr. (sig. Bb1 recto and verso), because in his opinion it is *impertinent*, i.e., irrelevant or unconnected to the main plot. In fact, the tendency to summarize Munday displays in previous chapters is reinforced in this one in a remarkable way, since chap. II.lii corresponds to chap. 118–123 in the Fr. There seems to be little doubt that Munday is rushing to meet a deadline and his priority for the remainder of the text is not to offer a faithful and accurate translation of his source, but one that explains strictly those aspects that are *pertinent* to the story. From this point onward in the text it becomes more difficult to establish a direct comparison between the English version and Maugin's text, so I desist from identifying how Munday alters or departs from his source.

2 **The Soldane angrie at his hard fortune ... was immediately so surprised with loue** Another example of the use of the *prisoner of love* motif; see Daniels, 7.

3 **Wisely sayd the Poet, *That badlie doo loue and Maiestie agree togither*** The poet is Ovid and the quote is copied from his *Metamorphoses*: "non bene conveniunt nec in una sede morantur / maiestas et amor" (II.846–47; *Betweene the state of Majestie and love is set such oddes, / As that they can not dwell in one*, trans. Golding, II.1057–58; 59).

Chapter 53

1 **report flieth quicklie far** It seems proverbial, although not included in Tilley; but cf. R83, "a false report rides post."

2 *Colmelio* **... whome *Maucetto* hadde bought** See 514.20–28.

3 **Arch-Flamin** "Archbishop" (OED, s.v. *arch-flamen*) "used by Geoffrey of Monmouth to denote the two grades of alleged sacerdotal functionaries in heathen Britain, whose place was taken on the conversion of the island by bishops and archbishops" (s.v. *flamen*); Fr. "le grand Mesen des Mahumetistes" (Cc2v; *the great leader of the Muslims*).

4 **there doth *Ptolome* finde great fauour ... the Soldanes Daughter, onely for your sake.** See 514.35–515.9.

5 **The soldane was crediblie enformed, that you and *Olorico* were drowned in the sea** See 514.12–14.

6 **little doo I delight in any such exercises** Fr. "Il est vray, Sire, respond Palmerin, non que je m'ennuye d'vn tel passetemps honneste" (Cc3r; *it is true, sir, answered Palmerin, not that I dislike such an honest pastime*). It seems that in the Fr. Palmerin is more inclined to dancing than in Munday's translation.

7 **I pray you tell mee the truth ... of which exploits remaine such fame through all** *Turkie?* See 381.30–382.24, and 397.9–43.

Chapter 54

1 *Galappa* The name bears clear similarity with Galata, the prosperous district of Constantinople north of the Golden Horn where Arabs from Granada migrated after 1502, building the Arab Mosque; see Mansel, 12–15, 123. While this identification is probable, it does not fit in the narrative, since Constantinople has not been conquered by the Ottomans in the romance.

2 *Donadell*, **who was slaine in the battaile against the King** *Abimar* See 531.21–23.

3 *Dieu Vous gard* Fr. "Dieu vous gard" (Cc4r; *may God protect you*).

4 **If the Poets had hetherto spared the discription of** *Cupid* **... to whom your gentle** *Ironia, Oronia,* **I should saye, dooth not deserue the name of her seruant** Throughout classical antiquity the image of Cupid was that of a naked, winged infant with bow and arrows (cf. Propertius, *Elegies*, II.12; Seneca, *Octavia*, I.557ff.; Apuleius, *Metam*. IV.30). In fact, the Italian humanist Mario Equicola (d. 1525) remarks in his *Di natura d'Amore* that classical authors seem to be ignorant of Cupid's blindness (IV.6); see *La redazioni manoscritta del "Libro de natura de amore" di Mario Equicola*, ed. Laura Ricci (Rome: Bulzoni, 1999), 440. Insofar as classical poets did not represent Cupid as blind, they precluded all the negative moral associations attributed to Cupid in the Middle Ages, thus explaining why Munday states that classical poets *spared* the description of Cupid, i.e., they abstained from damaging it. During the late medieval period we find poets arguing that Cupid is not blind but instead is endowed with eyesight; e.g., Chaucer, in his *Legend of Good Women*, comments, "And al be that men seyn that blynd is he [i.e., Cupid], / Algate me thoughte he myghte wel yse" (G.169–70). For Chaucer to make this defence of Cupid, there must have already existed the belief that Cupid was indeed blind. As stated by Trineus in his attempt to affront Orzadine, the confirmation of Cupid's blindness comes from Orzadine's being successful in love; for a less deprecating use of this motif, see Shakespeare, *A Midsummer Night's Dream*, "Love looks not with the eyes, but with the mind; / And therefore is wing'd Cupid painted blind" (I.i.234–35). Continuing with the same mocking attitude, Trineus makes a pun with the name of Oronia by intentionally calling her *irony* and thus ridiculing both her and her lover. Note, however, that Munday's translation does not exactly reproduce the sense of his Fr. source: "Vrayment si les Poëtes ont bandé jusques à present Cupido filz de la déesse d'Amours, ilz le peuuent bien paindre maintenant du tout aueugle" (Cc4r; *really if the Poets have until now blindfolded Cupid, son to the goddess of Love, they now can well take him to be blind*). Cupid had also been represented as blindfolded, as Maugin suggests in his version, and for instance, in his *Genealogia Deorum*, IX.4, Boccaccio

argues that rather than being just blind Cupid is blindfolded. For this note, I am indebted to Erwin Panofsky, *Studies in Iconology: Humanistic Themes in the Art of the Renaissance* (New York: Oxford University Press, 1939), 95–128.

5 **My selfe that slew the Brother to your Goddesse of beautie** For the first time we are told that Trineus has killed Donadel, although Munday seems unaware that this is news to us. This narrative inconsistency is caused by Munday's translating strategy. In chap. II.lii he decides to condense the descriptions of chivalric action in the Fr. (see n. 1 in II.lii), leaving out the information about Donadel's death as presented in his source: Trineus "luy mist la teste en deux parties" (Bb6r; *Trineus split Donadel's head in two*).

6 **as did *Achilles* against noble *Hector*** The text refers to the fight between these two heroes of the Trojan War where Achilles defeats Hector, the chief Trojan hero; see the *Iliad*, bk. XXII.

7 **The bodie of the dead King was giuen to them that came with him ... and so with great heauinesse they returned home againe** Fr. "Ausquelz il donna tant de richesses, & leur sçeut remonstrer de telle grace le tort de leur maistre, qu'eux & le Calife de Siconie s'en retournerent contens en leurs maisons" (Cc5v; *to whom he gave so many riches and he knew how to remonstrate with them with such grace for the wrong they have done to their master, that they and the Caliph of Siconie went back contented into their houses*).

8 **obiect** I.e., "placed before one's eyes" (*OED*, s.v. *object* adj. 1); cf. Fr. "subiet" (Cc6r; *subject*).

Chapter 55

1 **as might mooue the spirits of a verie staied Gentleman** This clause is Munday's insertion.

2 ***Iupiter* with his lightning, *Neptune* with his three forked Mace, and *Pluto* with his *Cerberus*.** This is a reference to the threatening combination of three gods with attributes respectively associated with them. As described by Apollodorus, "the Cyclopes then gave Zeus [i.e., Jupiter] thunder, lightning, and a thunderbolt ... and a trident to Poseidon [i.e., Neptune]" (I.ii.1, 28). Pluto is the god of the underworld whose entrance is guarded by Cerberus, a monstrous dog with three heads.

3 **a precious Carbunckle which supplied the office of *Venus* her fire–brand** The purpose of this jewel and of its location is to excite the passions related to Venus, goddess of love.

4 **The Dittie sung by Aurecinda to the Prince Trineus** The title of the poem (EV 22671) is provided by Munday, since the Fr. reads only "CHANSON" (Cc6v; *song*). The poem is made up by two sonnets, each containing three qua-

trains and a couplet (abbaabbacddcee / abbacddceffegg) in iambic pentameters. The poem is not in the Sp.; it was added by Maugin (see Freer, 209). This poem has been previously edited in the *British Bibliographer*, 147–48, where the text is reproduced as printed in the fourth edition of *Palmerin d'Oliva*, but with substantive errors introduced in the transcription by the editor.

5 *The God of warre, fierce, stearne, and rigorous . . . But suddainlie became full amorous* The story of the love between Venus and Mars, the god of war, first appears in Homer's *Odyssey*, VIII.266ff.; see also Ovid, *Ars Amatoria*, II.561ff., Ovid, *Met.*, IV.172–86.

6 **vnlesse you graunt me one request, before your face will I presentlye sleye my selfe** In view of Ardemia's suicide previously in the story (see 368.8–14), this cannot be taken as an idle threat.

7 **I am not woorthie to bee helde betweene thine armes** Fr. "je ne merite vous tenir nu entre mes bras?" (Cc7r; *Am I not worthy to hold you naked between my arms?*); Munday continues suppressing the expression of female desire.

8 **of a Maiden, he made her the fayrest woman in *Persia*** Once again Munday censors the description of the sexual encounter of Aurecinda and Trineus as shown in the Fr. (Cc7v).

9 **haue I so lately escaped by my freende, the cruell enchauntments of the hellish *Malfada*** See 524.41–525.8.

10 **who forsooke Parents, Freendes, and all for thee** See chap. I.lxi. This clause is Munday's interpolation, showing his bias in favor of Agriola and adding to the moral disapproval of Trineus's conduct.

11 **in reuenge of his wrong** Fr. "qu'elle [i.e., Trineus's death] ne soit vengée" (Cc8v; *rather than the death not be revenged*).

Chapter 56

1 **of that, which is the onelie sweete solace in loue** Fr. "de ce, pour lequel seulement on pourchasse l'amour des Dames" (Dd1v; *of that which is the sole reason for which one seeks the love of ladies*).

2 **to performe the debt we all owe to nature** Proverb; cf. Tilley, D168: "To pay one's debt to nature."

3 **By the Starres** Fr. "Par le grand' Dieu" (Dd1v; *by the great God*). Munday wants to avoid any possible confusion of the Christian God with the Muslim one.

4 **wringing her hands, and renting her comely locks of haire, shee brake forth into these pittifull speeches** Amplification of "se prit à pleurer disant" (Dd2r; *started to cry saying*).

5 **many sorrowfull farewels to *Agriola* and *Palmerin*** These *farewells*, voiced in direct speech in the Fr. (Dd2r), are not translated by Munday.

6 **While these strange mishappes were discoursing** I.e., while these extraordinary misadventures were being told. This is an instance of the use of an intransitive verb instead of a passive expression; cf. Mustanoja, 441.

Chapter 57

1 **Stoute *Hercules* . . . did not hee for the loue of *Iole*, weare feminine garments, and . . . *Achilles* the like . . . in the Courte of King *Lycomedes*, *Marke Anthonie* . . ., did not he follow *Cleopatra* before *Octauius*, although his armie on the Sea was twofolde . . .?** The text draws on the example of two classical heroes and a Roman emperor who fell short of behaving according to their honor and rank. While their ludicrous conduct is imputed to their love for a woman, in the case of Achilles he donned women's clothes not for love but as part of a strategem as described by Apollodorus: "When Achilles was nine years old, Calchas declared that Troy could not be taken without him, but Thetis—who knew in advance that he was fated to be killed if he joined the expedition—disguised him in women's clothing and entrusted him to Lycomedes in the semblance of a young girl. While he was growing up at his court, Achilles had intercourse with Deidameia, the daughter of Lycomedes" (III.xiii.8, 129). Hercules, despite being married to Deïanira, fell in love with Iole and started to act in a way perceived as unmanly: "do you not think that you [i.e., Hercules] brought disgrace upon yourself by wearing the Maeonian girdle like a wanton girl? . . . Ah, how often, while with dour finger you twisted the thread, have your too strong hands crushed the spindle!," Ovid, *Heroides*, IX.65–66, 79–80; trans. Grant Showerman, *Heroides and Amores*, 2nd ed. rev. G. P. Goold, The Loeb Classical Library (Cambridge, MA: Harvard University Press, 1977), 112–15; cf. Munday, *Amadis*, 981 n. to 343. Apropos of Mark Antony (ca. 83–30 BC), Plutarch's account is enlightening: "*Cæsar* [i.e., Octavian] sayde furthermore, that *Antonius* was not Maister of him selfe, but that *Cleopatra* had brought him beside him selfe, by her charmes and amorous poysons," (Plutarch, 6:370; cf. n. 6 to chap. I.xlvii). Indeed, Mark Antony's fleet was double the size of Octavian's, as Plutarch reports: "*Antonius* had no lesse then five hundred good ships of warre . . . Now for *Cæsar*, he had two hundred and fifty shippes of warre" (6:371).

2 **to continue them in remembrance** I.e., to retain them in his memory.

3 **the way you brought Madame *Zephira*** I.e., the way you were directed by Zephira; cf. Fr. "le chemin par ou vous amena ma Dame Zerphire" (Dd4r; *the way through which my lady Zerphire led you*). The inversion of the verb and the subject in Munday's translation is influenced by the order in the Fr. original. Having said that, we need to bear in mind that inversion of subject and verb occurred in the sixteenth century, particularly in the case of nominal subjects, as

in this case; see Rissanen, "Syntax" in *CHEL*, 264–65. Nevertheless, the resulting translation could have easily been misunderstood by contemporary readers.

4 **a yong Knight my brother** These two noun phrases are connected by apposition; see Sylvia Adamson, "Literary Language," *CHEL*, 568–70.

5 **the Brother to *Zephira*** I.e., Maulerino.

6 **the Ring he founde in the Cuppe at the Castle of the tenne Rocks** See 525.39–42.

7 **I haue it on my finger sir** Amplification of "Ouy, mon amy" (Dd4r; *yes, my friend*).

8 **they remaine prisoners to doo pennaunce for the hard speeches they gaue you** See 509.23–30.

9 **Then beeing fearefull of death, presently fell on their knees** The non-expression of the subject-pronoun of the third person plural was common in Middle English (Mustanoja, 138–44) and tolerable in early Modern English when the context allows for easy identification (Rissanen, "Syntax," in *CHEL*, 249), in this case the two women prisoners. Note, however, that this ellipsis was no longer tolerated in 1616 by the corrector of the third edition, which inserts the pronoun "they"; see "Historical Collation".

10 **by the reading of *Dulacco*, and the sounde of the Cornet, all that were enchaunted in the Islande came running thither** The enchantment is dissolved by reading the book of necromancy and sounding the idol's ivory horn; for other formulas for dispelling charms in the Iberian romances, see Patchell, 50–51.

11 **all that you haue heard alreadie ... as nowe they ioyntly reioyce in this happie successe** Munday omits a section from his source (Fr. Dd5r).

12 **the man not woorthie to taste the sweete, that cannot abide to feele the sower** Proverb; cf. Tilley, S1035: "He deserves not the sweet that will not taste of the sour."

13 **to discourse the pleasure on each side conceiued ... I referre it to your gentle consideration** Once again Munday decides to leave out part of the Fr. text (Dd5v–6r), in this case because he considers it superfluous.

14 **two, the most loyall Seruants that euer Loue had** The text seems to refer to Trineus and Agriola, who, in spite of their separation, remain loyally in love with each other. Though their loyalty is not without problems: Agriola is forced into marriage and shares her bed with the Sultan, while Trineus has an affair with Aurecinda, who as a result becomes pregnant.

Chapter 58

1 as *Phoebus* gan enter his Chariot, to display his golden beames on his Vncle *Neptunes* regions I.e., when the rays of the rising sun started touching the surface of the sea. Phoebus, epithet of Apollo to refer to the sun; Neptune, Apollo's uncle and Roman god of the sea. This periphrasis to describe the moment of daybreak is Maugin's creation; see Freer, 217–18. Here the *gan*-periphrasis is used to underscore the ingressive aspect of the action. While common in Middle English narrative discourse, this periphrastic construction disappeared in the early Modern English period. Note that it is the only occurrence of the *gan*-periphrasis in the whole romance and that Munday agrees with Chaucer (*The Parliament of Fowles*, 266: "Til that the hote sonne gan to weste") in using this archaic construction to describe the transition from day to night; see Mustanoja, 610–5.

2 Three dayes sayled our Knights without anie aduenture . . . and *Dyardo* in great perill of his life Munday summarizes this episode, as he does with the rest of the chapter.

3 the best limme on his bodie Fr. "la meilleure Prouince de Grece" (Dd7r; *the best province in Greece*).

4 *Colmelio* was ioyfull to behold Sir *Ptolome* . . . when they were ledde to be solde as slaues See 514.20–30.

5 ten Fr. "neuf" (Dd7r; *nine*)

6 our Mother I.e., Palmerin's mother, Griana.

7 bir Ladie Contraction of *by our Lady*.

Chapter 59

1 onelie to keepe my promise . . . to accomplish the marriage betweene you and Madame *Alchidiana* See 394.35–36.

2 reuenge for your deceassed brother *Gamezio* See 112.31–113.12.

3 when the Prince *Amarano* was slaine in your presence See 382.16–24.

4 I promised you my seruice, when I should returne from *Constantinople* See 387.3–37.

5 fiftie *Grecian* Knights Fr. "quatre cens jeunes Cheualiers de Grece" (Ee1v; *four hundred young knights from Greece*).

6 the number being supplied with other, in stead of them that were slaine This clause is Munday's interpolation. This chapter is translated without abridging the Fr. source.

7 remember our taking by the Admirall *Olimaell* See 491.3–19.

8 **the tenne knights went on shore, they that were left of the companie which the Princesse** *Alchidiana* **gaue to** *Ptolome* See 561.38–41. Fr. "les neuf Cheualiers qui restoient de ceux qu'Archidiane auoit donnez au Seigneur Ptolome" (Ee1v; *the nine knights that remained alive of those that Archidiana had given to Sir Ptolome*). Note that Munday emends his source in order to be coherent with the information provided previously.

9 **make you answere** Munday reproduces almost exactly the structure of his source: "je vous feray response" (Ee2r; *I will give you an answer*).

10 **with solemne protestations and irreuocable vowes** This clause is added by Munday.

11 **against all your enemies (Christendome excepted) you shall be assured of his succour and assistance** The text here fantasizes about a historically unlikely peace between the Byzantine and Ottoman Empires.

Chapter 60

1 **the time when you did cutte off the great Turks head** See 503.43–504.2.

2 **For the King of** *Fraunce* **... the King** *Recinde* **of** *Spaine* **... the King of** *England,* **haue leueyed such an Armie on the Sea, as neuer was the like seene to passe the** *Rheine* Munday's *Palmerin d'Oliva* appeared in a moment of political and religious conflict in Europe, involving particularly England, Spain, and France. Therefore, the supposed alliance of these three countries against the German Emperour would have been deemed unrealistic. For the events of 1588, the year of publication of our romance, see Robert Hutchinson, *The Spanish Armada* (New York: St. Martin's Press, 2014).

3 *Iuno,* **when shee stood to abide the arbitrement of** *Paris,* **or like** *Voluptas* **following her Mother** *Venus* For Paris's judgment of Juno, see n. 7 to chap. II.xii. Voluptas is actually the daughter of Cupid and Psyche, so she is Venus' granddaughter. Yet Venus may be figuratively understood as *mother* of Voluptas inasmuch as the former incites, gives rise to, and so in a sense gives birth to the kind of desire represented by the latter.

4 **her former courtesies to her friend** I.e., Polinarda's past sexual experiences with Palmerin, for which see 420.18–22.

5 **the rudest of the Gods, had it bene** *Vulcan* **or** *Neptune* **themselues** Vulcan and Neptune could be considered among the most impolite Roman deities, the former as the god of destructive fire, and the latter as god of the sea. Both of them are known for their rough, aggressive, and tempestuous character.

6 **are religiously married betweene themselues, let me intreate your highnesse to confirme it with open solemnization** Fr. "faites fiancer des maintenant mon

frere auec la Princesse Agriole" (Ee3v; *caused my brother to be engaged immediately to the Princess Agriole*). The Fr. text makes no reference to the fact that Trineus and Agriola are already married by mutual consent (see 330.31–331.5). Munday here departs from his source in order to endow his translation with greater narrative cohesion. About the love relationship between Trineus and Agriola and their marriage, it is worth quoting the remarks of an unidentified critic as an example of a romantic approach to chivalric literature: "Whether it be so in the original, or whether it be from partiality to this country in the translation, I know not, but the daughter of the King of England [i.e., Agriola] is almost the only woman of rank, throughout the history, who has patience to wait for the offices of the church, ere she makes her lover happy" (*British Bibliographer*, 147).

7 **So highly am I beholding vnto you my Lord ... then would I think no storme could wrong vs** Fr. "je le traiteray à mon possible, non tant que je voudrois pource qu'il me faudra coucher en la chambre de ma Dame Polinarde" (Ee3v; *I'll treat him as well as I can, but not as much as I would like to, since I will have to sleep in my lady Polinarda's chamber*). While in the Fr. Brionella openly makes known her wish to sleep with Ptolome, Munday has preferred to suppress this expression of female desire.

8 **with exceeding ioy and rare tryumphs, were *Palmerin* and *Polinarda* married togither, and thus was long and faithfull loue worthily requited** Munday alters his source (cf. Fr. Ee4r; Sp. 356) and decides that the wedding of Palmerin and Polinarda should coincide with that of his companions Trineus and Ptolome with Agriola and Brionella. Munday's decision has an anticlimactic effect, since Palmerin's union to Polinarda is not singled out as happens in the Fr.

Chapter 61

1 **Digeon** Dijon, formerly capital of Burgundy.

2 **who nowe was wedded to the Princesse *Polynarda*** Fr. "mesmes qu'il auoit fiancé Polinarde" (Ee4v; *even that he had become engaged to Polinarde*). Munday departs from the Fr. and decides to move forward the public ceremony to solemnize Palmerin's marriage to Polinarda. In doing so, however, Munday's text lacks all the glamor and jubilation expected for the long-awaited wedding of the romance's protagonist; cf. n. 4 to chap. II.lxii.

3 **in *Fraunce* he combatted for his Ladie *Polinarda*** See chap. I.xxxvi and xxxix.

4 **that** I.e., the thing that. Non-expression of the antecedent of *that* occurred in Middle English (Mustanoja, 190) and was common in the sixteenth century (*OED*, s.v. *that* relative pron. 3a).

5 **shee was sometime promised to mine eldest Sonne** See 326.4–10 and 327.40–329.37.

6 **both your Maister and the Prince** *Tryneus* **did me manifest dishonor** I.e., when Agriola joined them and fled from England without her father's permission; see chap. I.lxi.

7 **when against his Fathers will, he came with** *Palmerin* **to assist me** See 251.26–40.

8 **how amourous the great Turke was on the Princesse** *Agriola* See chap. II.ii. Note, however, that Munday perverts the meaning of the original Fr., which openly states that the king of England is not informed of the Great Turk's dealings with Agriola: "le Duc luy en fit le discours tel qu'il vous a esté recité cy deuant, sans dissimuler, ou celer aucune chose, que l'emprisonnement d'Agriole auec le grand Turc, qu'il ne vouloit declarer, pour ne causer vne suspicion d'impudicité en la Princesse" (Ee5r; *the Duke has made an accurate account exactly like the one that has been told to you, except for Agriola's imprisonment with the Great Turk, that he didn't want to retell in order not to cause any suspicion of indecency on the part of the Princess*).

Chapter 62

1 **take heede if you laie claime to her now as sometime yee did . . . let no such youthfull pranckes be nowe remembred** See 230.22–39.

2 **louelie** *Paris* **and faire** *Helena*, **or puissaunt** *Hector* **and wise** *Andromacha* Handsome Paris fell in love with the most beautiful of ladies, Helen, though it caused the start of the Trojan War. Valiant Hector, who was Paris's brother, married Andromache.

3 *Alba* Fr. "ville de Hongrie sur le Danube" (Ee5v; *town in Hungary on the Danube*). It refers to Alba Julia, in modern Romania, that for the best part of the sixteenth and seventeenth centuries was capital of the Eastern Hungarian Kingdom.

4 **who was a right welcome Ladie into** *Greece* Fr. "& trois jours apres espousa Polinarde" (E5v; *and three days later he married Polinarde*); cf. Sp. 362. Since Munday moves the wedding forward (see 573.18–19), he now has to make a slight alteration to the narrative in order to produce a coherent text. Note, however, that there is a sense of occasion to welcome the newly-wed couple that is lacking when they get married.

5 **whose death was signified three dayes before, by the enchaunted Bird** For more information on the enchanted bird, see n. 5 to chap. II.li.

6 **of the Emperour and Empresse** Fr. "de l'Empereur" (Ee6r; *of the Emperor*).

Chapter 63

1 **In one of the Chapters before you haue heard . . . to the Emperor** *Palmerins* **Court** See 569.13–17.

2 **within short time after that trouble was past** I.e., shortly after giving birth. Fr. "estant releuée de la couche de son filz" (Ee6r; *having got up from childbed*).

3 **wafting on a plancke for safegarde of her life** Fr. "Archidiane se voyant en tel danger, deuint si esperduë, que c'estoit pitié de la voir" (Ee6r; *Archidiane, seeing herself in such a danger, became so distraught that it was a pity to see her*). Munday sensationalizes Alchidiana's situation.

4 **into what want and pouertie shee was now brought** The English version here falls into an apparent contradiction, since the text previously mentions how Alchidiana is taken in by a wealthy merchant who provides her with all she might wish. The cause for this contradiction lies in an unfortunate intervention of the translator, who decides to present the merchant as rich when the Fr. calls her "vne marchande veuue" (Ee6v; *a merchant woman who is a widow*). Later on, to reinforce the idea that this lady is rich, Munday alludes to her servants: "and one of the Merchants Seruants" (579.41–42).

5 **after shee hadde walked in the coole shaddowe of the Trees** Fr. "apres auoir repris ses forces, par quelques douceurs que luy donnerent les filles de l'hostesse" (Ee7r; *after having regained her strength by means of certain sweets given to her by the hostess's daughters*).

6 **walked** Fr. "faisoit ses plaintes" (Ee7r; *made her laments*).

7 **departure** Meaning "the action of departing this life; decease, death" (*OED*, s.v. *departure* n. 2b); cf. Fr. "la sortie de l'ame de la miserable Archidiane" (Ee7r; *the departure of the miserable Archidiane's soul*).

8 **The loue of wedlocke faire Princesse, said** *Palmerin*, **cannot make me disclose her preiudice that honoured me so much** Fr. "j'aymerois mieux auoir perdu l'vn de mes membres" (Ee7v; *I would have rather lost one of my limbs*). Munday alters the sense of the Fr. in conveying the impression that the attentions Alchidiana offers Palmerin in chap. II.ix help him improve his self-esteem and increase his honor in spite of compromising his marriage, should these circumstances come to the knowledge of Polinarda. The Fr., on the contrary, is more categorical in denouncing Palmerin's past conduct as improper, though it considers it preferable to blot out all memory of the incident and keep it secret from Polinarda.

9 **when you found me in lyke place** Earlier in the book Alchidiana finds Palmerin by a fountain while she is hunting (see chap. II.iv), just as happens now but with both their roles reversed.

10 **when shee redeemed you from base seruitude** See 515.2–7.

11 **the Prince *Olorico*, that named himselfe my Dwarffes Brother when I was with you last at *Gaunt*** Olorico was actually presented as Urbanillo's cousin; see 437.31.

12 **and *Palmerin* taking her courteouslie in his armes** This clause is Munday's insertion, which allows us to guess Palmerin's special fondness for Alchidiana.

13 **I doubt not thereof . . . good or bad newes of the Prince *Olorico*** The final paragraph of this chapter amplifies the Fr. (Ee8r).

Chapter 64

1 **the Coast of *Propontida*** Propontis is a variant name of Marmara, the small sea connected to the Black Sea through the Bosphorus.

2 **it would demaunde a larger volume to set downe . . . as great honour as may be deuised** Munday summarizes the action and reduces it to its bare bones throughout this chapter.

3 **the Soldane confessing his iniurie to *Trineus*, while he was in his Court** See 552.19–553.4.

4 **his discourtesie to the gentle Knight *Tryneus*, when hee became enamoured on the Princesse *Aurecinda*** See previous note.

5 **if their loue then sorted to a philosophicall trope or figure** Munday's translation misrepresents the Fr., which makes no reference to "a philosophicall trope" but instead to someone who is "trop Philosophe," i.e., *very philosophical*: "Que si à quelqu'vn trop Philosophe, l'amour en semble peu pudique, si est ce qu'il en est sorty vn fruit, que mon Maistre tient plus cher que son grand tyare à trois degredz, ne le reuenu d'iceluy" (Ff2r; *For if to someone who is very philosophical the love doesn't seem very modest, nevertheless a fruit has come forth from it, a fruit which my master holds more dear than his great tiara with three crowns, nor than the income that comes from his rank*). This translation error is probably caused by the haste with which Munday was working, although it is not unlikely that he was trying to make a pun with these two words' similar pronunciation and spelling in Fr.

6 **the Son to the Prince *Tryneus*** I.e., Ryfarano the son Trineus begets on Aurecinda; see 547.12–15.

Chapter 65

1 **when hee finished the enchantments . . . as you haue heard.** See 558.32–559.4.

2 **the Admirall *Olimaell*, hee that at the taking of *Agriola*, had the Prince *Tryneus* for his prisoner** See 332.4–15.

3 **you haue not as yet reuenged the death . . . with many Knights of cheefe and especiall account** See 503.40–504.2, and 504.40–505.3.

4 *Zabulus, Orpheus, Hermes, Zoroastres, Circes, Medea, Alphonsus, Bacon, Apolonius*, **and all the rest that write of the blacke speculatiue** Zabulus is a name for the devil. Orpheus, because of the mysterious power of his songs (see n. 3 in chap. II.li), was considered well versed in eschatology and theogony. The Greek god Hermes, when associated with knowledge of magic and the occult, receives the epithet Trismegistus and is attributed the composition of works on Egyptian religion, astrology, and alchemy. Zoroaster, also known as Zarathustra, is believed to be the founder of Zoroastrianism, the pre-Islamic religion of ancient Persia, and erroneously credited with the composition of works on magic. For Circe, see n. 6 to chap. I.lxv. Medea shares with her aunt Circe her knowledge for concocting drugs and magic potions; see also n. 3 to chap. II.xlix. Petrus Alphonsus was a Spanish Jew, converted to Christianity in 1106, and author of *Disciplina Clericalis*, which considers necromancy as one of the three liberal arts forming the Latin *trivium*. Roger Bacon (ca. 1214–94) was an Oxford philosopher who acquired a reputation for sorcery in the sixteenth century: John Bale, in his *Illustrium Majoris Britanniae Scriptorum Summarium* (London, 1548; STC 1295), describes Bacon as "Magus necromanticus" (Ff2v; *a necromantic magician*); a prose romance, *The Famous Historie of Fryer Bacon*, probably dating from the middle of the sixteenth century, (although the earliest extant copy is from 1627; STC 1183), exploits the image of Bacon as a sorcerer and is the source of Robert Greene's comedy of *Friar Bacon and Friar Bungay* (ca. 1589); Christopher Marlowe presents "wise *Bacons* . . . workes" as pertaining to necromancy in his *Dr Faustus* (I.i.154, ed. Roma Gill [Oxford: Clarendon Press, 1990], 8). For more information, see Waldo F. McNeir, "Traditional Elements in the Character of Greene's Friar Bacon," *Studies in Philology* 45 (1948): 172–79, at 172–73 n. 2. The reference to *Apolonius* alludes to Apollonius of Tyana, a Neo-pythagorean holy man of the first century AD who, according to the biographical account *Life of Apollonius* written by Philostratus, was involved in thaumaturgic activities. For the classical references, see Daniel Ogden, *Greek and Roman Necromancy* (Princeton: Princeton University Press, 2001). About this list of both legendary and historical figures as presented in Munday's translation, McNeir states in his article, "This list, Professor Patchell informs me, is not found in Munday's original"; this information is inaccurate, since it already appears in Munday's source and is in fact attributable to Maugin (Fr. sig. Ff2v); cf. Freer, 223.

5 **you may be Registred for euer** I.e., that as a result of your actions and success you will go down in history; cf. OED s.v. *register* v. 1.

6 **therein shall you be assisted by a Christian Knight . . . landed there for the same cause** This knight is Nardides. Note that in the Sp. there is a more com-

plete prophecy, though inaccurate, mostly because it predicts the assassination of Palmerin; cf. González, "Sistema," 45.

7 **you remember the two Traytors *Promptaleon* and *Oudin* . . . whome *Palmerin* and *Frysoll* slew at *Constantinople*** See 451.22–452.2.

8 **as beseemes a cause so weightie . . . and I that can commaunde the winde and weather** These two clauses are inserted by Munday. Cf. the astronomer in Samuel Johnson's *Rasselas*: "I have possessed for five years the regulation of weather," *Rasselas and Other Tales*, edited by Gwin J. Kolb, *The Yale Edition of the Works of Samuel Johnson* 16 (New Haven: Yale University Press, 1990), 144. I bring in this reference because Johnson acknowledges his familiarity with and fondness for the Iberian chivalric romances; see *Boswell's Life of Johnson*, ed. George Birkbeck Hill, rev. L. F. Powell (Oxford: Clarendon Press, 1934), 1:48–49.

9 **there is a Bird pearched in the Hall . . . she bewrayes the same by her song or fearefull crie** For this bird, see n. 5 to chap. II.li.

10 **at the Port** Meaning at the gate or gateway (see *OED*, s.v. *port* n. 3, 1a); Fr. "à la porte" (Ff3r; *at the gateway*). Note that in the Fr., by contrast, the enchantment does not affect those leaving their houses, but those who go through this gateway.

11 **awarded it** I.e., he used the cup to ward off Nardides's blow; see *OED*, s.v. *award* v. 2, 2.

12 **as if *Ptolome* had not borne off the blowes with a great siluer plate** Fr. "que sans Ptolome qui luy saisit le bras c'estoit fait de la vie d'Olorique" (Ff3v; *which without Ptolome, who seized his arm, the life of Olorico would have been over*). In imitation of the defense Palmerin puts up using a golden cup, Munday depicts Ptolome protecting himself with a different piece of tableware, in his case made of silver.

Chapter 66

1 **calling his familiars together** Fr. "inuoqua ses gentilz Chahuans d'enfer" (Ff4r; *invoked his noble owls from hell*).

2 **in the selfe same maner as he was when he succoured the Prince *Tryneus*** See 554.3–15.

3 **as each one thought the world had beene ended** This clause is Munday's addition.

4 **in my guarde** I.e., in my keeping; see *OED*, s.v. *guard* n. 1.

5 ***Muzabelino* gaue him some of the water to drink, which before had healed the Princesse *Zephira*** See 527.13–528.7.

Notes to the Text: Part II 745

6 **On the morrow hee commaunded the bodies of** *Nardides* **and** *Menadeno* **to be burned** Munday is summarizing the description in the Fr., where Muzabelino does not actually command that the bodies of Nardides and Menadeno be burnt, but instead states, "faites des trahistres ce qu'il vous plaira" (Ff4v; *do with the traitors as you wish*); next, their bodies are cut in a thousand pieces and only then burnt.

7 *Alexander* **the great, and** *Iulius Cæsar,* **are examples thereof** Palmerin is compared with possibly the two greatest leaders of classical antiquity, namely, Alexander the Great (356–323 BC) and Julius Caesar (100–44 BC). According to the contemporary account in Thomas North's translation of Plutarch, Alexander and Julius Caesar respectively exemplify the two extremes, mentioned by Muzabelino, of being "loued of manie" and "hated likewise of a number": "And as for his death [i.e., Alexander's], as the countinuance and greatnes of his glory was pure and unspotted, free from envie, during the strength of his age whilest he lived in this world . . . Whereas *Cæsar* to the contrarie, having with so great labour and travell by many obscure and oblique waies, attained to the height of a shamefull glorie, and which wan him the hatred of the chiefest members of the commonwealth: was immediatly cast downe, litle lamented of those that loved good lawes and the good of the estate, the which he left turmoiled with civill warres" (Plutarch, 8:359). The lives of "great Alexander, [and] strong Julius Caesar" are also used as examples of power in Munday's *Amadis*, 228.

8 **the water in this viall, which will restore your former beautie, as sometime it did to the Princesse** *Zephira* See n. 5 above.

Chapter 67

1 **the Princesse** *Alchidiana* **was deliuered of a faire Daughter, who at the Emperor** *Palmerins* **request was baptized, and named** *Philocrista* Baptism is required as a guarantee that the baby is raised a Christian from the start; cf. the Sp.: "Alchidiana . . . parió una fija muy fermosa. El Emperador e la Emperatriz rogaron mucho que gela diesse e consintiesse que la tornassen cristiana . . . e la Infanta fue bautizada con gran fiesta e pusiéronle nombre Esquivella" (381; *Alchidiana gave birth to a very beautiful daughter. The emperour and empress begged to be entrusted with her and to be allowed to raise her a Christian . . . and the infanta was baptized with great celebration and named Esquivella*). Note that Maugin does not retain the original name "Esquivella," but replaces it with "Philocriste" (sig. Ff5v), of more obvious Christian connotations, since the etymological meaning of the name is "devoted to Christ." Munday, however, makes no reference to the fact that Palmerin and Polinarda asked to be entrusted with the baby and thus causes a bit of confusion when below we read that Philocrista's biological parents send presents to Palmerin and Polinarda from Babylon, "not forgetting somwhat to his [i.e., Olorico's] daughter *Philocrista*" (594.17–18).

2 *Frysoll* **the king of** *Hungaria* **. . . at the byrth of these children** This fragment is a summary of all the events in the Fr. In fact, the entire chap. II.lxvii condenses all the narration in chps. 138 and 139 in the Fr. The action corresponding to chap. 139 in the Fr. starts precisely at this point in the English text. This passage actually caused some confusion to Purser, who erroneously comments, "Policia is turned into Philocriste by the French translator of *Palmerin de Oliva* . . ., who gives her *proprio motu* a sister, whom he calls Bellizie" (425). In fact the Fr. *Philocriste*, as discussed in the previous note, corresponds to the Sp. *Esquivella*, while the Fr. *Bellicie* is not invented by Maugin but the name of Palmerin's daughter, who is called *Pulicia* in the Sp. With this name resembling *belleza*, the Sp. word for beauty, perhaps Maugin was trying to signify the superlative beauty of the hero's daughter.

3 remembring the death of his Father before that Citie See 422.12–40. Fr. "en la terre où auoyent autresfois esté desfaitz tant de ses parens" (Ff6r; *in the land where so many of his relatives had been foiled on another occasion*). A mistranslation probably caused by reading "parent" (*father*) instead of "parens" (*relatives*).

4 a day will come to abate thy pride and insolency On May 29, 1453, Mehmed II, Sultan of the Ottoman Empire, entered triumphantly the newly-conquered city of Constantinople.

5 and forget the folly that too much conquered her appetite This clause is Munday's interpolation.

6 the Pilot that saued the Princesse life See 578.33–38.

7 in King *Arthurs* **time, when he made the great Tourney before the Castell of Ladies.** It most probably refers to "the grete turnement that shold be att the Castel of Maydens" (Malory, IX.xxvii.271), to which came "many knyghtes rydynge" (IX.xxvii.272), and was presided by King Arthur "set on hyhe vpon a schaffold" (IX.xxix.274).

8 a time shal come, that the renowne of them and thee, shall be vtterly abolished by Strangers, chiefely by one, whose vertue and bountie shall be such, as thy selfe shalt account him the best that euer bare Armes This prophecy predicting the coming particularly of a knight who will surpass all others has a narrative reference outside *Palmerin d'Oliva*. It points to *Palmendos*, where this prophetic revelation is recalled by Palmerin: "Nowe call I to minde the Damosels wordes, that departed so suddainlie without aunswer: and verilie I am perswaded this Knight is the man shee spake of" (Munday, *Palmendos*, sig. K1r). The knight meant by the damsel is none other than Palmendos, about whom another prophecy is made previously in *Palmerin d'Oliva*; see n. 13 to chap. II.xli. For a discussion of this prophecy in the Sp., see González, "Sistema," 64–66.

Notes to the Text: Part II *747*

9 til time bring on the following booke of *Primaleon* and *Palmendos* The sequel to *Palmerin d'Oliva* is the book of *Primaleon*. Note, however, that the first thirty-two chapters in the Fr. *Primaleon*, concerning the adventures of Palmendos, were published in England as a separate book on 5 February 1589. Munday's allusion to the "booke of *Primaleon* and *Palmendos*" refers to *a book*, thus suggesting that probably he had not yet decided on publishing the adventures of Palmendos separately.

Postscript

1 My promise performed Munday wants us to know that he has fulfilled his promise of translating the entire *Palmerin d'Oliva* as stated in his dedication of part I to Edward de Vere; see 102.32–33, and cf. 339.13–17.

2 *Palmendos* will leaue his Mother the Queen of *Tharsus*, and *Primaleon* hasten his order of Knight-hood, that you may bee acquainted with their rare aduentures Munday refers to events occurring in the sequel to *Palmerin d'Oliva*.

3 *Palladine* of *England* is arriued, and to feede you with varietie of delights, his History by Easter tearme next will be with ye His translation of *Palladine of England* was published on 23 April 1588.

Appendix

This appendix contains the alternative version of the dedicatory epistle to the two parts that Munday prepared for the second edition of the romance, published in 1597 and reused in later reprints. The copy-text is always the earliest existing edition.

1. Part I: Epistle Dedicatory (1615/1616, 1637)

TO THE WORSHIPFVLL
Master Frances Yong, of Brent-Pelham, in the County of Hertfort, Esquire, and to Mistresse Susan Yong his wife, and my most kind Mistresse,
health, and their hearts contentment,
continually wished.

Being indebted to you both for your manifold kindnesses, I am bold to continue my labour begun, concerning the course of my promised Histories, this being the first part of Palmerin D'Oliua, *ring-leader to all the rest, and therefore the originall from whence they which follow haue bin deriued. Though in my translating they came last which should haue bin first, now I haue good hope, that by the reprinting of them ouer againe, at length they will come to a iust order, and each haue his place as their course describeth. The second part of this will shortly follow: then the third and last that I am now in hand withall, which concluding with* Palmerin *of* England, *and* Primalion *of* Greece, *their seuerall last part, will perfect the whole history, and make it complete in euery part. As the rest, so I commend this to your worshipfull protection, remaining alwayes yours with my vttermost endeuours, and praying that your prosperity may neuer faile.*

Your poore well-willer till death,

A. M.

2. Part II: epistle dedicatory (1597)

To the worshipfull Mai-
ster *Fraunces Young,* of *Brent Pelham,* in the Countie of Hertford, Esquire, and to Mistresse *Susan
Young,* his wife, and my most kind Mistresse:
*this worldes ioy and heauenly felicitie in-
tirely wished.*

Promise is debt (worshipfull Syr) as the Prouerbe auoucheth, and debt must needes be paide, as reason requireth: the one not arguing so much liberalitie in speech, as the other doth vertue in accomplishing. When I presented ye my first part of Palmerin of England, I promised to hasten these likewise that should preceede it.[1] because this Historie of Palmerin d'Oliua, is the beginning and inducement to all those that followe thereon. Wherfore hauing sent ye the first, so likewise doe I now the seconde, and will make what speede I can in translating the third and last,[2] if your kinde fauour spurre me on, as I doubt not but it will. So still remaining yours (euen to my vttermost,) I humbly take my leaue, this first of August.[3]

Your Worships euer to be commaunded,

Anthony Munday.

Notes to the Text of the Appendix

1 **Promise is debt (worshipfull Syr) ... I promised to hasten these likewise that should preceede it** Note that the opening section of the 1597 epistle follows closely the wording of the original one. For explanatory notes, see •••.

2 **will make what speede I can in translating the third and last** No third part of *Palmerin d'Oliva* was ever published in English. The continuation of the Sp. *Palmerín de Olivia* was *Primaleón: Libro segundo del emperador Palmerín*. But Munday could not be referring to this work, since by 1597 he had already printed *Palmendos*, corresponding to the first thirty-two chapters of *Primaleón*, and parts one and two of *Primaleon*, whose part three was printed also in 1597. It is possible that Munday was considering the possibility of translating the Italian continuation to *Palmerin d'Oliva* composed by Mambrino Roseo da Fabriano and published in 1560 as *Il secondo libro di Palmerino di Oliva*. The same allusion to a forthcoming third part to our romance was probably made in the now-lost dedication to the first part of *Palmerin d'Oliva* printed in 1597; for the text, see the textual collation on •••. For a more thorough discussion of the third part of *Palmerin d'Oliva*, see Sánchez-Martí, "The Publication History of Anthony Munday's *Palmerin d'Oliva*," *Gutenberg-Jahrbuch* 89 (2014), 199 n. 37; and Hayes, "Romances," 63–67.

3 **this first of August** This reference gives us the date for the publication of the second edition of the second part in 1597.

Historical Collation

NOTE: This section records all substantive variants from the edited text within the four editions of *Palmerin d'Oliva*.

749.2   *Pelham,*] ED; *Pelhan,,* 3; *Pellam,* 4
749.6   continually] connually 4
749.11 *haue*] 4; *hane* 3
750.3   Hertford,] ED; ~ ͕ 2

Editorial Principles

The present edition of *Palmerin d'Oliva* uses as copy-text the earliest surviving textual witnesses of the romance, trusting that they are the ones that most closely represent Anthony Munday's intentions. For the first part of the romance I follow the text in the Folger Shakespeare Library copy (call number STC 19157) of the *editio princeps*, which has been sight-collated against the other existing copy of this edition, now in the BL (C.56.d.6). The text of the second part is based on the BL copy of the second edition of 1597 (C.56.d.7), which has been collated against the other extant copy of this edition, now held at the Huntington Library (330331). Since the two extant copies of *Palmerin d'Oliva II*, both of them imperfect, lack the final leaves, I have used the BL copy of the third edition (C.56.d.8) to transcribe the missing text (two leaves: 593.22–596.11). In addition, as the examination of the publication history of the romance has revealed, the 1616 edition of the second part seems to reprint the prefatory material that supposedly appeared in the first edition of 1588. Therefore, I have chosen it for the present edition in place of the revised version that Munday prepared for the 1597 edition, which is also included in an appendix.[1]

In accordance with W. W. Greg's concept of copy-text, this critical edition preserves the accidentals of the selected texts,[2] thus the spelling, word-division, capitalization, and punctuation of the original have been retained with minor alterations, herein explained. As regards the spelling, it is kept unmodernized,[3] with the following exceptions. The long "s" ("ſ") is silently replaced by the modern letter "s", as is "VV" by "W". Contractions such as "qd", "&", "yt", and "Chap." are expanded without note. The tilde is also expanded, thus, the form *whō*, for instance, is spelled out as *whom*. Ligatures such as "æ" and "œ" are altered to their

---

[1] In the address "To the Friendly Readers" of the second part, I have edited the text of the 1597 edition, although giving greater authority to the substantive readings in the 1616 edition.

[2] "The Rationale of Copy-Text," *SB* 3 (1950-1951): 19–36; Greg introduces the term *accidentals* on page 21.

[3] For some of the advantages of this decision, see John Russell Brown, "The Rationale of Old-Spelling Editions of the Plays of Shakespeare and his Contemporaries," *SB* 13 (1960): 49–67, and more recently Paul Hammond, ed., *Shakespeare's Sonnets: An Original-Spelling Text* (Oxford: Oxford University Press, 2012), 89–97.

component letters.[4] The hyphen used to avoid the confusion between "ſ" and "f" in words such "satiſ-fie" and "miſ-fortune" has been deleted without note, because the modernization of long "s" renders such distinction unnecessary.[5] In the late sixteenth century printers used the letter "v" in initial position (e.g., *vnable*) and "u" in the middle of words (e.g., *haue*) regardless of their phonetic value as vowel or consonant, and both were printed as "V" in capital form (e.g., *Very, Vrbanillo*). This practice has been reproduced, as also the use of "i" and "I" in initial position (e.g., *iust, Ioyfull*), since no distinction was yet established with "j" and "J".[6] The spelling in the copy-text has been retained if verifiable in the *OED*, but wrong-fount letters and swash capitals have not been reproduced. The capitalization in the copy-text has been kept, except that ornamental initials that begin the first paragraph of each chapter have been replaced by plain ones, and the practice of capitalizing the first letter following the initial has not been followed.[7] I have silently substituted the form "IV" for "IIII" in the Roman numerals used in chapter headings and silently corrected wrong chapter numbers.[8] Finally, considering that Renaissance punctuation was founded on rhetorical principles and

---

[4] The form "ée", transcribed as "ee" in the present edition, may be described as a ligature too, for which, see McKerrow, *Introduction*, 313 n. 1. See also Vivian Salmon, "Orthography and Punctuation," in *CHEL*, 3:27.

[5] As suggested by McKerrow, *Introduction*, 314 n. 5, this "hyphen should perhaps not be retained in a reprint which does not use long ſ." This decision seems sensible, since the second edition, used as copy-text for the second part, makes no use of this kind of hyphen. Therefore, our edition makes a uniform presentation of these words in both the first and the second part. The occurrence of such a hyphen at the end of a line is not recorded in the "Word-division" section of this edition.

[6] The distinction of the forms i/j and u/v became common among English printers in the 1630s; see Salmon, "Orthography and Punctuation," 39. Fredson Bowers, "Readability and Regularization in Old-Spelling Texts of Shakespeare," *Huntington Library Quarterly* 50 (1987), 210, states, "the old u-v and i-j conventions . . . can be argued are orthographical only and just as much a convention that should be replaced as is the long s." But one difference needs to be mentioned in this respect: the long *s* is no longer part of modern typographical conventions and is therefore foreign to the readers of this edition, thus justifying the need for substitution. Strictly speaking, standardizing u/v and i/j implies a modernization not entirely justified in an original-spelling edition. By retaining the Elizabethan value of u/v and i/j I hope more closely to reproduce the original texture of Munday's translation; cf. McKerrow, *Prolegomena*, 78–79. I have made only one exception to this rule: when a word like "whereupon" is used at the end of a line it sometimes appears as "where- | vppon" (e.g., part 2, X3v; cf. "Here- | vpon", part 2, Z4r). The letter *v* is here used with the phonetic value of *u*, because it is printed at the beginning of a line. However, since this and similar words are not hyphenated unless they come at the end of a line, I have regularized them as "whereuppon", "Hereupon", etc.

[7] Cf. McKerrow, *Prolegomena*, 20 n. 4.

[8] For the occurrence of wrong chapter numbers, see the bibliographical description of each edition under the section "Typography."

was mostly aimed at facilitating the reading experience, I have chosen to keep it almost unaltered, excepting errors of omission or corruption.[9] By doing so I hope that modern readers might replicate or recover the same cadence and effects intended for sixteenth-century audiences, who even in private would prefer to read books out loud. Therefore, no effort has been made to standardize the original punctuation, but it has for the most part been retained with its own inconsistencies and idiosyncrasy. It has been emended when it is clearly mistaken according to early-modern punctuating conventions and occasionally when later editions improve or clarify the original punctuation. The only systematic alteration I have silently introduced corresponds to crotchets (square brackets), whose value in Elizabethan founts is equivalent to the round ones—"( )"—used in the present time.[10]

In all four early-modern editions of *Palmerin d'Oliva* the text of the romance is printed in black letter, while italic and roman types are used for providing typographical contrast. The 1588 edition prints foreign language terms, place names and chapter titles in italic, and personal names in roman. While the default type for the text is black letter, it is excluded from the paratexts, thus "The Epistle Dedicatorie" is printed in italic, and "To the Reader" and the postface at the end of volume I in roman. The 1597 edition, taken as copy text for the second part, also uses black letter for the text of the romance but chapter titles and all proper names, with only a handful of exceptions, are printed in roman, as well as the prefatory epistle. The choice of italic is reduced to foreign words and the lines of verse included in the work, in addition to the prefatory address to the readers. The postface, here transcribed from the 1616 edition, is printed in roman. In the present edition the black-letter portions of the text are printed in roman, whereas italic is used to represent words printed both in italic and in roman, following McKerrow's suggestion.[11] In the case of the paratext, I follow the choice

---

[9] Cf. McKerrow, *Prolegomena*, 40–41, and Bowers, "Old-Spelling Texts of Shakespeare," 213. In order to avoid confusion, I have silently removed the period that in early printed texts was conventionally placed after numerals, both Roman and Arabic. I have kept this period only after the chapter number, because there it can cause no confusion. When a chapter number is followed by a comma, I have silently replaced it with a period. For a brief but useful discussion of the value of punctuation marks seen in our edition, see Salmon, "Orthography and Punctuation," 21.

[10] See McKerrow, *Introduction*, 318. From a syntactical point of view the two types of parentheses fulfill the same "removability" criterion; see further in Colette Moore, *Quoting Speech in Early English* (Cambridge: Cambridge University Press, 2011), 73–76. Cf. Salmon, "Orthography and Punctuation," 22.

[11] *Introduction*, 298 n. 1; see also Bowers, "Old-Spelling Texts of Shakespeare," 211. The 1597 edition prints all personal names in roman, but shows less rigor for place names. For the use of roman in the text of the second part I have chosen to follow the 1616 edition, since we know it is also derived from the *editio princeps*. In a prose text printed with extremely long paragraphs the use of typographical contrast would make

of typeface in the copy-text and thus, for instance, I use italic for "The Epistle Dedicatorie" of part one, and roman for the postface. Taking into account that the printers of our copy-texts used roman and italic types differently, the distribution of types adopted for this critical edition makes possible the production of a homogeneous text with typefaces used uniformly in the two parts of the text. Only one exception has been made. By printing all chapter titles in italics, I have preferred to erase the discrimination of proper names in the 1588 edition, where they appear in roman, rather than to editorially replicate such kind of differentiation for the chapter headings of the 1597 edition, printed entirely in roman type.

The textual apparatus records all the significant textual irregularities in the editions taken as copy-text, including obvious misprints and turned letters. All alterations to the copy-text are included in the list of emendations with reference to the earliest authority used for the correction. As a general policy I have tried to keep alterations of the original to a minimum, making only those that "I suppose that a contemporary corrector would have made," as McKerrow suggests.[12] Consequently, the accidentals in the emended text do not necessarily reproduce those in the textual authority mentioned in the textual apparatus, even when it provides the textual evidence that supports the emendation.

In addition to presenting the most authoritative text possible, I have also wanted to document the textual alterations this romance suffered in the course of its fifty-year printed history, thereby exposing the degree of editorial intervention and, to some extent, textual degradation experienced by Munday's translation. Therefore, I have collated the transcription of the copy-text against all later textual witnesses, namely, the BL copy of the second edition (for the first part), the 1616 BL copy of the third edition (for the two parts, except for the final signature of the second part), and the University of Alicante Library copy of the fourth edition for the entire text of *Palmerin*. This information appears in the historical collation, where all substantive variants in the selected textual witnesses are recorded.[13] Variations in the accidentals have been ignored, as have been misprints in later editions when they represent obvious typographical

---

reading easier, as the readers of this edition can appreciate. For a recent edition that has also retained typographical contrast, see *Gulliver's Travels*, ed. David Womersley, The Cambridge Edition of the Works of Jonathan Swift (Cambridge: Cambridge University Press, 2012).

[12] *Prolegomena*, 77.

[13] For the concept of *substantive variant*, see Greg, "The Rationale of Copy-Text," 21. As a general rule, I have considered a spelling variation to be substantive when it has a separate entry in the *OED* (one not simply stating that it is an alternative form). However, I have made exceptions to this rule, since the historical collation does not record the following variations: *afterward(s)*, *among(st)*, *backward(s)*, *beside(s)*, *farther / further*, *forward(s)*, *toward(s)*.

errors, except if the error originated a variant reading in a later edition or if the typographical error results in a different word.[14]

Since Munday's *Palmerin d'Oliva* is not an original composition but a translation, consulting the aforementioned English textual witnesses does not suffice to produce the most authoritative text. We need also to compare the English version with its source, namely, Jean Maugin's French rendering. From a traductological point of view, a comparison of Munday's text and Maugin's version reveals Munday's competence as a translator as well as the degree of fidelity to and manipulation of his source.[15] But such a comparison also has textual implications, since the French translation is an antecedent document of authorial potential and can help us in recovering Munday's intention. When the English text presents incongruous or inconsistent readings, the French version has been consulted, first, to assess the cause for the possible error, and next, if necessary, to emend the English text and bring it into conformity with the French witness.[16] My purpose has been not to force the agreement of Munday's version with his source, but instead to use the latter to render the English text intelligible when deficient. The recourse to Maugin's text enables us to detect and rectify errors made in the translation process by Munday as well as those made in the printing process and thus attributable to the compositors and correctors. Consulting the French version has proved essential for the second part, since no copy of the *editio princeps* of this part is extant. However, since we have two editions independently descended from the first edition of 1588, I have used the French text when choosing between variant readings from the second and third editions. I have adopted the reading closest to Maugin's version in the belief that it is more likely to have been printed in 1588 and to represent Munday's translation.[17] Emendations not derived from the historical collation, like those based exclusively on the French text, are marked "ED" in the textual apparatus. Maugin's translation was published at least sixteen times before 1588 (FB 40395–40408, 40413–14), although I have been unable to determine exactly the edition used by Munday for his translation. The French edition chosen for comparison with and correction of Munday's text is the one printed by Jan Waesberghe (*fl.* 1555–1589) in Antwerp in 1572 (FB 40407), since it could have more easily been in circulation when Munday's interest in the *Palmerin* romances developed, probably some-

---

[14] Cf. McKerrow, *Prolegomena*, 67 and 79 n. 1.
[15] See the Introduction, 77–97.
[16] Cf. Bowers, "Old-Spelling Texts of Shakespeare," 222 n. 8.
[17] Note that, when the French reading is not unambiguous, I have usually preferred the variant in the copy-text. I have adopted this criterion because the compositors of the third edition are somewhat liberal and treat their exemplar with freedom, rephrasing it and supplying additional words. In contrast, the text of the second edition is more conservative and, hence, less likely to deliberately introduce substantive changes, although it is not necessarily free from error.

time before 1580.[18] There is yet one last layer of textual authority, namely the Spanish original, to which I resort when a deficiency in Munday's translation is directly attributable to the French version of the romance. The Castilian text can shed light on passages whose real meaning was inaccessible to Munday, since it is unlikely that he systematically used a copy of the original work. The Spanish text I have consulted is the scholarly edition of *Palmerín de Olivia* prepared by Giuseppe di Stefano in collaboration with Daniela Pierucci.

These are the principles that have informed my editorial decisions, included in the critical apparatus when not applied silently as explained in this section. The apparatus, based on the recommendations of G. Thomas Tanselle,[19] contains the following sections: textual notes, a list of emendations, a list of ambiguous line-end hyphenation, and the historical collation. Also following Tanselle,[20] I have chosen to present a "clear text" in order that the reader may peruse the text of Munday's translation without any editorial interference or distraction and freely decide when to consult the editorial apparatus and explanatory notes.

---

[18] As Freer states, "l'edizione stampata da Waesberghe... contribuì forse a dare alla traduzione una certa popolarità nell'Europa settentrionale" (184). For my convenience, I have consulted the copy of Waesberghe's *L'Histoire de Palmerin d'Olive* in the Biblioteca Nacional in Madrid (shelfmark R/36497). For information on Waesberghe, see Anne Rouzet, *Dictionnaire des imprimeurs, libraires et éditeurs des XVe et XVIe siècles dans les limites géographiques de la Belgique actuelle* (Nieuwkoop: B. de Graaf, 1975), 243–44. For dating Munday's interest in the *Palmerin* cycle of chivalric romances, see my article "*Zelauto*'s Polinarda and the *Palmerin* Romances," *Cahiers Élisabéthains* 89 (2016): 74–82.

[19] "Some Principles of Editorial Apparatus," *SB* 25 (1972): 63–88.

[20] Op. cit., 45.

Textual Notes

The notes below comment on textual issues affecting either the copy-text or subsequent editions. When the notes refer to a case of emendation of the copy-text, they provide the evidence or argument justifying the decision to emend. Here the bracket follows the reading in the present edition, known as the lemma, and a statement of variation precedes the commentary. The sigla for the texts are explained in the list below. When a reading not present in the texts collated is adopted for the first time in this edition it is marked with ED.

Sigla

Palmerin d'Oliva (1588), the first edition = *1*
    Folger Shakespeare Library copy = *1(a)*
    British Library copy = *1(b)*
Palmerin d'Oliva (1597), the second edition = *2*
    British Library copy = *2(a)*
    Huntington Library copy = *2(b)*
Palmerin d'Oliva (1615/1616), the third edition, 1st and 2nd states = *3*
Palmerin d'Oliva (1637), the fourth edition = *4*
Palmerin d'Olive (1572) = Fr.

Part I

124.22   her] his *3, 4*. The variant reading of the third and fourth editions is corrupt and incongruous, since Tarisius is in no position to make promises about Griana's marriage.

151.28   greene] *2*; sweete *1*. The choice of the adjective "greene" agrees with the Fr. "verde" (D2v; *green*).

151.32   who said] ED; saying *1+*. This emendation is necessary because the words following are uttered not by Palmerin, as the English text suggests, but by the Serpent. This error may have been caused by the possibly accidental omission of the passage "Si est ce qu'il le trouua à la fin . . . commança à se reprendre, disant à part soy" in the Fr. (D2v).

166.7   beholden] ED; am *1+* The English text makes poor sense due to a mistranslation of the Fr.: "pour la perte qui en auiendra à celle à qui je suis" (D8v; *on account of the loss that will affect her to whom I belong*); cf. the Sp. text: "que gran daño vendrá por ello a la señora que me crió" (p. 53; *on account of which great harm will come to the lady that raised me*).

169.31 wher] ED; when *1+*; Fr. "ou" (E2r; *where*). Palmerin commands Darmaco's squire to inform the giant of his arrival. Palmerin urges him to go to a place ("wher") now, not at any other particular time ("when"). The copy-text is here corrected to agree with the Fr. original.

174.18 him] ED; me *1+*; Fr. "le" (E4r; *him*). Palmerin here prays God for the protection not of himself but of the man who sent this damsel, namely, Prince Adrian.

177.23 vile] vild *2, 3, 4*. Note that the form *vild* adopted in the 1597 and subsequent editions is in fact a variant of *vile* that was "extremely common from *c*1580 to 1650" (*OED*, s.v. *vild* adj.).

178.6 his] ED; this *1+*; Fr. "son" (E5v; *his*). It is important to attribute this slander to Domarto, Count of Ormeque, thus the use of the possessive seems preferable as in the Fr.

183.17 deliuered to him] ED; reskewed *1+*; Fr. "si on ne luy deliure le prince Trineus, & la belle Polinarde" (E8r; *if one fails to hand Prince Trineus and the beautiful Polinarda over to him*). The Fr. *delivrer* (q.v. Huguet) in this context means "to hand somebody over." The verb chosen by Munday, *reskewe*, however, means "to set free (a hostage, a person captured by an enemy); to deliver a person out of the hands of enemies" (*OED*, s.v. *rescue* v. 1a); but Trineus and Polinarda have not yet fallen into the hands of the enemy and thus they do not need to be *reskewed*. A more accurate translation of the Fr. *delivrer* seems to be its English derivation *deliver*, one of whose senses corresponds to the meaning intended by Maugin: "to hand over, transfer, commit to another's possession or keeping" (*OED*, s.v. *deliver* 1, v. 8a).

190.16 my lady] ED; his Lady *1+*; Fr. "ma Dame" (F3r; *my Lady*). The purpose of this emendation is not only to further the agreement between the English text and its Fr. source, but more significantly to prevent a narrative inconsistency, since after listening to Urbanillo at first Polinarda does not identify with Palmerin's beloved (cf., "she thinking it was some other and not herselfe," 192.19). The use of the third person possessive would have given this information away.

190.23 he] ED; his *1+*; Fr. "que ses jours fussent aussy qu'il les desire" (F3r; *that his days were as short as he wants them to*).

207.9 holpe] ED; hope *1*; helpe *2, 3, 4*. Fr. "ayde" (G3r; *help*). The evidence from the Fr. and the other English editions suggests that the copy-text intended reading was *holpe*, a variant spelling commonly used in the rest of the Part I; cf. also Munday, *Roman Life*, 72.2004.

215.22 Lorde] most neerde *3, 4*. The reading in *3* and *4* is a misprint, probably for *most reueerde*. The compositor of *4* is unable to correct it and prefers instead to reproduce it, thus showing how closely he follows his copy-text.

221.7 conquerer] conquered *2, 3, 4*. The variant reading in *2* and all subsequent editions is mistaken because the person conquered is not the Duke of Gaule but Lewes, Prince of France.

242.33 were Nephewes] ED; was Nephewe *1+*. Both the King of Scotland and the King of Norway were nephews to the Holy Roman Emperour, not just the King of Norway; cf. Fr. "neueuz" (I5v; *nephews*).

246.41 loue] sake *4*; the catchword in *3* reads *sake*, hence the reading in *4*.

248.22 thy Maister beares me] ED; thou bearest thy Maister *1, 2, 3*; thou bearest my Master *4*; Fr. "L'asseurance que tu me donnes de l'amytié de ton Maistre" (I8r; *the assurance that you give me of your master's friendship/love*). Urbanillo's speech clearly emphasizes Palmerin's devotion to Polinarda, not Urbanillo's friendship with Palmerin.

266.22 as to such persons alloweth honor and good affection] *om. 3, 4*. This omission is caused by eye-skip from the first *as* to the next one.

278.5 not] ED; *om. 1+*; Fr. "ne trouvant ceux qu'il desiroit rencontrer" (L6r: *not finding those he desired to meet*). Franarco decides to abduct the Queen and Agriola because he does *not* find "him that slew his brother," i.e., Palmerin (278.3). Without this emendation the text is contradictory.

284.36 not] ED; *om. 1+*; Fr. "si ne l'auez fait" (M1r; *if you haue not done it*). The logic of the sentence demands the introduction of *not*.

293.5 not] ED; so *1+*; Fr. "Frisol ne fust encores sain" (M5r; *Frisol was not yet whole*). This emendation is necessary to avoid contradiction with the statement opening the following paragraph: "Frisol stayed there . . . till he had perfectlie recouered his health."

319.1 not] ED; *om. 1+*; Fr. "ne leur suffisoit" (O1r; *did not suffice them*). See the following textual note below.

319.2 to vaunt themselues] ED; *om. 1+*; Fr. "ains auoyent de coustume s'en venter à leurs compagnons" (O1r; *they were in the habit of boasting about it to their companions*). While Munday censors some of the content in his source, mostly episodes with erotic overtones, the behavior now omitted may not receive general approval but is not indecent or immoral. The syntactic structure of the sentence together with it semantic organization anticipates the sense conveyed by the Fr., which has served to propose this emendation. The omission was probably caused by a mechanical error.

320.6 the Lady of the Castell in the Lake] ED; she *1+*. This emendation is necessary because the text as it was printed fails to maintain the narrative coherence of the romance. It suggests that Polinarda gives a ring to Palmerin before he embarked to travel to England. At that point the text reads, "the Knights humbly tooke their leaue of their Ladies" (255.18), with no reference to a ring being made. The ring meant by the narrative is actually the one Palmerin received from the Lady of the Castle in the Lake (ch. I.lvi), where he was expressly commanded to "gyue this Ring to her whome aboue all other you moste esteem" (302.20–21), i.e., to Polinarda. The other ring is intended for "the Ladie your deere Freende [i.e. Trineus] beloueth" (302.25–26), and next Palmerin obeys this command saying, "I must giue you this ring, as I was commaunded by the Lady of the Castell in the Lake" (320.25–26; see explanatory note on p. 668, n. 2). Note that this error originates in the Fr. translation (see sig. O1v); cf. Sp. "el anillo que le dio la dueña" (p. 151; *the ring the lady gave him*).

323.21 Chamber] *2*; Camber *1* While the spelling *Camber* is recorded in the *OED*, I have chosen to change it because all other occurrences of this word spell it as *chamber*. It seems natural to think that *camber* is an unintended spelling.

334.29 sunk in] ED; *om. 1+*; Fr. "il sembloit qu'il fust fondu en abisme" (O8r; *it looked as if it had sunk into an abyss*). A verb is missing in the copy-text and the form *sunk* is supplied as suggested by the Fr.

334.36 had] *2*; *omit. 1*. The copy-text prints *had* only as the catchword on sig. Yy3v.

Part II

347.1 *Mofti*] ED; *Mosti 2*. A Mofti was "A Muslim cleric or expert in Islamic law empowered to give rulings on religious matters, *esp.* a legal scholar competent to deliver a fatwa. In the Ottoman Empire: the official head of religion within the state" (*OED*, s.v. *musti* n.1, 1). The mistake did not originate with Munday, since his Fr. source also reads "Mosti" (P2v).

357.21 bountie] *3*; beautie *2*; Fr. "vertu" (P6v; *virtue*). The contemporary meaning of *bountie* was "goodness in general, worth, *virtue*" (*OED*, s.v. *bounty* n. 1; my emphasis).

405.24 just like] ED; so well, as *2, 3, 4*; Fr. "aussy bien" (S1r; *just like*). This emendation is necessary for the English version to represent accurately the meaning of the reference to Ogier in fairyland and thus retain its narrative significance. Munday's translation suggests that while dancing Palmerin and the Queen of Tharsus are *so well as* Ogier en fairyland. However, the English text misconstrues the meaning of this reference as introduced by Maugin, who wants to highlight how Palmerin and the Queen find themselves in a position *just like* the one of Ogier in fairyland. Far from having a good time in fairyland, Ogier is known to have been starving, *just like* Palmerin and the Queen who are dancing supperless. See further in the explanatory note (698, n. 6).

413.29 eight hundred] ED; eight hundred thousand *2, 3*; eight thousand *4*; Fr. "plus de dixhuit cens mile" (S4v; *more than eighteen hundred miles*). Considering that a league is about three miles, the emendation produces a measure that approximates the one in the Fr. more closely than any of the variants in the three textual witnesses.

416.34 assistaunce] *3*; assurance *2*; Fr. "si Olorique ne l'eust retenu" (S6r; *had Olorique not held him*). The action as described in the Fr. is better encapsulated by the textual reading in *3*.

430.36 companie (such was her greefe to come before her Parents), shee] ED; companie, such was her greefe to come before her Parents, as shee *2, 3, 4*. Fr. "Et pour la consoler fut mise auec elle la Princesse Hermide sa fille, sans laquelle (tant auoit de deul de comparoistre deuant l'Empereur & l'Imperatrice) elle fust morte cent & cent fois par les chemins" (T3r; *And in order to soothe her, they placed with her her daughter the Princess Armida, without whom she would have died hundreds of times on the roads (because she was so afraid of appearing before the Emperor and Empress)*). Munday gets confused with the long and convoluted sentence in the Fr. and produces a syntactically problematic translation. The emendation reproduces the punctuation and structure of the French with minimal intervention on the English text.

451.15 I thinke you] These words start an unwarranted new paragraph in *2*, but not in *3*, a decision that I follow here.

463.3 Brother] *3*; Brethren *2*. We are only informed of her one brother Cardino. Here Munday intervenes in order to endow his translation with internal coherence.

481.9 not] ED; om. *2, 3, 4*; Fr. "il ne le recogneust" (X7v; *he didn't recognize him*). The fact that *2* and *3* agree against the reading in the Fr. version suggests that this textual omission was already present in the 1588 edition.

491.22 Fischermen] ED; Frenchmen *2, 3, 4*; Fr. "pescheurs" (Y3r; *fishermen*). There are no narrative reasons justifying the presence of Frenchmen on the coast of Albania, neither is it explained why French nationals could be interested in providing information to the Turks. Instead, it seems more likely that the text was corrupted.

503.1 faile] taile *4*; Fr. "faillir" (Y8v; *fail*); the *f* is misprinted in *3* and looks more like a *t*, thus the reading in *4*.

505.10 great] ED; and great *2, 3, 4*. The textual variants of the three editions offer a corrupt reading, most probably caused by the corruption of the reading in the *editio princeps*. The old Basso cannot be *declared* brother to the deceased Sultan and new Emperour. Instead, the old Basso is the one who designates a younger brother of the Sultan as the new Emperor, a reading confirmed by the Fr.: "il fit publier vn jeune frere du Sultan decedé, grand' Empereur de Turquie" (Z1v; *he had a young brother of the deceased Sultan proclaimed Grand Emperour of Turkey*).

533.9 loue] *3*; warre *2*. In this passage Munday is not translating directly from the Fr. (sig. Cc1r), but nonetheless the context allows us to surmise that indeed the Sultan discusses issues relating to the peace with Abimar and the love engagements that will ensue, as the reading in *3* states.

541.26 pessant] ED; peasant *2*; weighty *3, 4*. This reading is corrected to "puissant" by a contemporary hand in *2(b)*.

547.1 she] ED; he *2, 3, 4*; Fr. "celle" (Cc7r; *she*). One could argue that by using the masculine pronoun *he* Munday wants to highlight how the loyalty to his companion Palmerin takes precedence over that to his beloved. Munday seems to contradict this idea when below he singles out in an interpolation the preeminence of "the loyaltie of *Agriola*" (548.20–21), thus suggesting that in Munday's view Trineus's number-one commitment should be with Agriola and not with Palmerin. The emendation resolves this apparent conflict of loyalties implied in the textual readings of all existing editions.

557.31 shall] *2(a)*; shalc *2(b)*. The final letter as printed in *2(b)* is not exactly a *c* as printed in the font used in the edition. It has a foot, an ascender, and then a shoulder. It could have been intended to represent a *t*, although the ascender does not protrude over the shoulder or cross-bar.

578.34 Pylots] Pyrates *3, 4*; Fr. "Comites" (Ee6v), "chef des rameurs d'unes galère, spécialement, celui qui commande aux esclaves, aux forçats ramant sur une galère" (Huguet, s.v. *comite* 1).

581.18 of spirit] ED; despised *2, 3, 4*; "Pauure d'esprit" (Ee7v; *poor of spirit*). This translation error is caused by misreading the original; probably Munday read or understood the form "despité" (*despised*) instead of "d'esprit."

593.22 sonne] The British Library copy of *2* is mutilated from this point on; for the Huntington Library copy, see the bibliographical description. The remainder of the critical edition follows the text as presented in the British Library copy of *3*.

List of Emendations

Note: All alterations, whether substantive or accidental, to the copy-text are listed below, with their immediate source, except for those specified in the Editorial Principles as silently made. A few common conventions of notation are used here. The swung dash (~) appears when the lemma and the stemma present identical substantive readings and thus serves to call attention to the accidental variation, usually affecting punctuation. An inferior caret (ₐ) indicates where the stemmatic reading lacks punctuation found in the lemmatic reading. An asterisk (*) preceding the page-line reference indicates the presence of a Textual Note.

Part I

99.3	Anatomie] *3*; Anotamie *1*	138.42	irreuocablie] *2*; irreuocable *1*; cf. Fr. "irreuocablement" (C5v; *irrevocably*)
102.18	*discharge.*] ED; ~, *1*		
103.20	reading.] *3*; ~ₐ *1*		
104.34	*Tarisius,*] ED; ~ₐ *1+*	142.2	she] *2*; she she *1, 3*; he *4*
105.43	strongelie] *2*; strangelie *1*	143.15	exspected] *2*; erpected *1*
108.29	and] *2*; aud *1*	147.39	your] *2*; you *1*
110.16	in generall] *2*; ingenerall *1*	151.3	*Artifaeria*] ED; *Artaeferia 1, 2, 3, 4*
112.8	ordayning] *2*; doraynning *1*	*151.28	greene] *2*; sweete *1*
115.17	vnaduised] *2*; vnsaduised *1*	*151.32	who said] ED; saying *1+*
122.9	or] ED; of *1+*	154.14	roughlie] *2*; ronghlie *1*
122.27	(said] *2*; said (said *1*; said *3*; saith *4*	156.15	contents,] *2*; ~: *1*
123.25	(though] ED; ₐ~ *1+*	157.17	heare,] *2*; ~ₐ *1*
126.13	shewes:] *2*; ~ₐ *1*	*166.7	beholden] ED; am *1+*
127.13	before] *1(b)*; be-before *1(a)*	166.20	three] ED; two *1+*
128.2	it] *2*; om. *1*	168.42	acceptable] *2*; acceptaple *1*
131.35	inuiolablie] *2*; inuiolalablie *1*	*169.31	wher] ED; when *1+*; Fr. "ou" (E2r; *where*).
137.1	semblaunce of discontent took] ED; semblaunce to take *1, 2, 3*; shew of discontent tooke *4*; Fr. "sans faire vn seul semblant de partir à regret d'auec l'Empereur" (C4v; *without showing any sign of regret on leaving the Emperor*).	173.9	*Palmerin,*] *2*; ~ₐ *1*
		*174.18	him] ED; me *1+*; Fr. "le" (E4r; *him*).
		177.29	not] ED; *om. 1+*; cf. Fr. "vostre bon droict ne sera retardé" (E5r; *what is rightfully yours will not be delayed*).

*178.6 his] ED; this *1+*; Fr. "son" (E5v; *his*).
181.1 in generall] *2*; ingenerall *1*
*183.17 deliuered to him] ED; reskewed *1+*; Fr. "si on ne luy deliure le prince Trineus, & la belle Polinarde" (E8r: *if one fails to hand Prince Trineus and the beautiful Polinarda over to him*).
185.35 being] *2*; bein *1*
187.15 interest] *2*; interrest *1*
*190.16 my lady] ED; his Lady *1+*; Fr. "ma Dame" (F3r; *my Lady*).
*190.23 he] ED; his *1+*
191.23 mislike not] *2*; not mislike *1*; mislike not of *3, 4*
192.13 companie] *2*; comanie *1*
193.13 conuersing] *2*; conuerssing *1*
196.37 As I am,] *2*; ~∧ *1*
202.26 earnestlie] *2*; earnestle *1*
204.3 his] *2*; hys his *1*
*207.9 holpe] ED; hope *1*; helpe *2, 3, 4*. Fr. "ayde" (G3r; *help*).
207.22 beautie] *2*; beauties *1*; Fr. "beauté" (G3r; *beauty*)
207.30 rather] *2*; om. *1*
208.18 Fathers,] ED; ~∧ *1+*
213.36 lineaments] *2*; linaments *1*
214.30 Pantofle] *2*; Pantefle *1*
215.5 Kings] *2*; King *1*; Fr. "Roys d'armes" (G7v; *Kings of arms*)
215.32 Lords,] *2*; ~∧ *1*
216.18 But] *2*; Bnt *1*
218.10 happily] ED; vnhappily *1+*
218.37 *Phoebus*] *2*; *Phaebus 1*
220.13 me,] ED; ~∧ *1+*
222.37 deeds] *2*; dee[ ]ds *1*
224.4 fresh] *2*; frsh *1*
226.8 conferring] *3*; om. *1, 2*
230.8 the fielde] *3*; fielde *1, 2*
232.13 *English*] *2*; *Englih 1*
234.12 extinguished] *2*; extingushed *1*
235.20 die?] ED; ~, *1, 2*; ~: *3, 4*; Fr. "me conuiendra il mourir de faim?" (I2r: *should I starve to death?*)
236.40 He,] ED; ~∧ *1+*
237.35 a long] *2*; along *1*

240.35 freelie] *2*; feelie *1*
*242.33 were Nephewes] ED; was Nephewe *1+*
*248.22 thy Maister beares me] ED; thou bearest thy Maister *1, 2, 3*; thou bearest my Master *4*
251.42 to] *2*; to to *1*
254.3 *Ptolome*] *2*; *Ptoleme 1*
256.27 themselues] *2*; themselus *1*
257.19 animate] *2*; annimate *1*
258.4 Lordes] *2*; Lorde *1*; Fr. "Seigneurs" (K5v; *Lords*)
259.5 foure] *2*; 4 *1*
259.18 that] *2*; that that *1*
260.17 woulde,] *2*; ~∧ *1*
260.37 *Ptolome*] *2*; *Ptoleme 1*
262.3 vnderstoode] *2*; vnder-derstoode *1*
263.2 your] *2*; you *1*
263.37 *Scots*] *2*; *S[ ]ots 1*
264.8 cleft] *1(b)*; clest *1(a)*
265.40 assisted] *2*; asisted *1*
266.3 recouered] *2*; recoueced *1*
267.32 Daughter,] *2*; ~∧ *1*
267.40 sufficientlie] *2*; sufficienlie *1*
273.2 your] *2*; you *1*
275.18 so] *1(b)*; to *1(a)*
277.12 the King] *2*; King *1*
277.21 gone] *2*; goe *1*
*278.5 not] ED; om. *1+*
278.43 that] *2*; the *1*
279.6 thou] *2*; thon *1*
279.19 villanie] *2*; villaine *1*
279.25 they] *2*; thy *1*
*284.36 not] ED; om. *1+*
285.1 (in mine opinion)] *4*; in (mine opinion) *1, 2, 3*
286.37 named] *3*; name *1, 2*
289.26 you] *2*; your *1*
290.20 premeditate] *2*; premiditate *1*
291.26 your] *2*; you *1*
*293.5 not] ED; so *1+*
294.6 other waie] *2*; otherwaie *1*
296.10 neighboures] *2*; neighboues *1*
296.40 your] *2*; you *1*
297.31 your] *2*; you *1*
297.34 it] *2*; ti *1*
300.8 which] *2*; whieh *1*

List of Emendations

303.18 preuent] *2*; peruent *1*
305.12 extreamitie] *2*; extreamite *1*
306.4 Squires] *2*; Squirs *1*
309.5 comfortlesse place] *2*; comfortlesse, place *1*
312.14 Knightes] *2*; Kinghtes *1*
312.18 Tents] ED; Tent *1*+. Cf. 293.30.
312.38 he] *2*; be *1*
313.18 *Palmerin*)] *2*; ~∧ *1*
314.26 seeing] *2*; see- *1*
314.30 twelue] *4*; 12 *1, 2, 3*
315.4 these] *2*; thess *1*
315.21 your] *2*; you *1*
316.29 he (beyond] *2*; (he beyond *1*
318.21 your] *2*; you *1*
318.24 Chamber.] ED; ~, *1*+
*319.1 not] ED; *om.* *1*+
*319.2 to vaunt themselues] ED; *om.* *1*+; Fr. "ains auoyent de coustume s'en venter à leurs compagnons" (O1r; *they were in the habit of boasting about it to their companions*).
*320.6 the Lady of the Castell in the Lake] ED; she *1*+
321.37 the] *2*; the the *1*
322.8 of] ED; or *1*+. Cf. Fr. "qu'un tel Royame qu'est celuy de mon Pere" (O2v; *a kingdom like the one that belongs to my father*).
322.10 your] *2*; you *1*
322.22 *Agriola*] *2*; *Argiola 1*
322.41 beseemes] *2*; be seemes *1*

323.15 depart as] *2*; departas *1*
*323.21 Chamber] *2*; Camber *1*
323.27 Princes chamber] *2*; Princes-chamber *1*
324.13 surpassing] *2*; supassing *1*
324.17 Cittie,] *2*; ~. *1*
326.17 Emperour,] *2*; ~. *1*
326.18 presence] *2*; prsence *1*
326.40 be] *2*; he *1*
327.11 shorte returne] *2*; shortereturne *1*
328.3 mean while] ED; me any while *1*+
328.5 if] *2*; of *1*; Fr. "si" (O5r; *if*)
328.37 will] *2*; well *1*
329.1 secret] *2*; fecret *1*
329.41 *Palmerin*] *2*; *Paomerin 1*
330.22 imaginations. Perswade] ED; imaginations. perswade *1*; imaginations, perswade *2*; imaginations: perswade *3, 4*
330.30 preferment] *2*; perferment *1*
330.33 *Palmerin*,] *2*; ~∧ *1*
332.5 fiue] *2*; fine *1*
333.1 theefe] *2*; theese *1*
333.34 *Agriola*,] *2*; ~. *1*
334.4 parted] *2*; parting *1*
*334.29 sunk in] ED; *om.* *1*+; Fr. "il sembloit qu'il fust fondu en abisme" (O8r; *it looked as if it had sunk into an abyss*).
334.34 enchaunted] *2*; enchannted *1*
*334.36 had] *2*; *omit.* *1*
335.11 together in] *2*; togetherin *1*

Part II

340.3	Palmerin] *3*; *this second booke of Palmerin 2*	352.18	Soueraigne] *3*; Saueraigne *2*
340.3	and hauing] *3*; *and he hauing 2*	352.24	with] *3*; *om. 2*
340.16-19	Paladine *sonne to . . . at Cripplegate this ninth of March.*] *3*; *I will hasten on the translation of the third part of this most famous Historie, which beeing of some great quantitie, wil aske the longer time ere hee can enioy the benefit thereof: bee therefore kind to these two former Bookes, and that will be the better meanes of hastening the third. 2*	354.23	perceyue] *3*; peceyue *2*
		354.41	passe)] *3*; ~ˆ *2*
		355.2	*was*] *3*; *is 2*; Fr. "fut" (P5v; *was*)
		355.5	according] *3*; accoridng *2*
		355.6	Gentleman] *3*; Gentlman *2*
		355.29	crennels] ED; creuises *2*; Fr. "creneaux" (P5v; *crenels*)
		*357.21	bountie] *3*; beautie *2*; Fr. "vertu" (P6v; *virtue*).
		358.7	determined] *3*; determindd *2*
		358.24	so] *3*; *om. 2*; Fr. "si riche" (P7r; *so rich*)
340.20	1588.] *3*; *om*. *2*, *4*	359.1	his] *3*; *om. 2*; Fr. "sa" (P7r; *his*)
340.22	*Monday*] *3*; *Mundy 2*	359.3	vnworthie] *3*; worthie *2*; Fr. "indigne" (P7r; *unworthy*)
341.17	And] *3*; An[] *2*		
342.9	Mountainets] *3*; Mountaines *2*; Fr. "montaignettes" (O8v; *small mountains*)	359.13	especially] *3*; especiall *2*
		360.13	pleasure] *3*; pleasures *2*
		362.3	effect] *3*; effects *2*
343.12	and honor] *3*; an[] honor *2*	362.5	againe] *3*; agaiue *2*
343.36	presence] *3*; prsence *2*	362.7	and] *3*; *om. 2*; Fr. "& se tournant" (P8r; *and turning*)
344.6	cloth] *3*; bloth *2*		
344.16	of] *3*; *om. 2*	362.24	body bee] *3*; bodybee *2*
345.5	had so good knowledge in] *3*; could not so well speake *2*; Fr. "pource qu'elle sçauoit le langage des sa jeunesse" (P1v; *because she spoke the language since she was young*).	363.2	bashfull] *3*; lashfull *2*
		364.21	carelesse] *3*; earelesse *2*
		364.32	Princesse] *3*; Prineesse *2*
		364.36	the wood cow] ED; the wood *2*, *3*, *4*; Fr. "la Vache de boys" (Q1r; *the wooden cow*).
345.36	vertuous and] *3*; vertuousand *2*	364.37	countenaunce] *3*; countnnaunce *2*
346.41	beyonde] *3*; beyonde beyonde *2*	365.3	Oh] *3*; *om. 2*; Fr. "Las" (Q1r; *Alas*)
*347.1	*Mofti*] ED; *Mosti 2, 3, 4*	365.15	that] *3*; *om. 2*
347.1	the royall] *3*; thy royall *2*	365.20	*Zephira,*] ED; ~ˆ *2+*
347.20	loue passions] *3*; louepassions *2*	365.34	Ardemias] *3*; Ardemia, *2*
349.36	him] *3*; his *2*	367.8	*louely*] *3*; *lonely 2*
350.11	forward] *3*; forword *2*	367.19	*If*] *3*; *if 2*
351.28	shee] *3*; hee *2*	367.32	hell.] *3*; ~? *2*
351.34	princesses] *4*; princesse *2*, *3*	368.11	complainte] *3*; complaints *2*; Fr. "plaint" (Q2v; *complaint*)
351.37	for] *3*; of *2*		
352.1	the eare] *3*; t[]e eare *2*	368.18	next] *3*; nxet *2*
352.1	turne] *3*; holde *2*; Fr. "tourner" (P4r: *turn*)	368.29	to] *3*; lo *2*
		370.8	that] *3*; the *2*
352.3	quittance] *3*; quttance *2*	370.9	Armes] arm *3*
352.9	her] *3*; his *2*; Fr. "sa presence" (P4r; *her presence*)		

List of Emendations

371.17 pleasure?] ED; pleasure 2; pleasures? 3, 4
371.24 knewe not] ED; knewe 2; om. 3, 4; Fr. "ne sçauoit" (Q4r; *did not know*)
371.35 she] 3; wee 2; Fr. "elle" (Q4r; *she*)
373.4 dissembled not] 3; dissembled 2; Fr. "simuloit n'aymer Palmerin" (Q4v; *feigned not to love Palmerin*)
373.25 come in time] ED; come time 2; find time 3, 4; Fr. "je suis venu à temps pour venger vostre mort" (Q4v; *I have come in time to avenge your death*)
374.31 *Alchidiana*] 3, *Aldhidiana* 2
376.3 enterprised] 3; eaterprised 2
376.20 as were] 3; aswere 2
376.40 haue] 3; ~, 2
378.26 did not the feare of reproch] 3; did not feare and reproch 2; Fr. "n'eust esté que crainte de reproche" (Q6v; *had it not been for fear of reproach*).
378.30 miracle] 3; miracles 2; Fr. "miracle" (Q6v; *miracle*)
378.36 that] 3; as 2
378.37 But] 3; but 2
379.14 and] 3; aud 2
379.33 such] 3; rich 2
381.2 *Amarano*] 3; *Armarano* 2
381.25 be] 3; qe 2
383.41 onely] 3; onsly 2
384.5 (according] 3;)~ 2
384.8 *Alchidiana*] 3; *Alchidinia* 2
384.12 and] ED; om. 2 (word in cw, sig. E1r), 3, 4
384.19 Princes] 3; Princesse 2
385.6 fiftie] 4; fiue 2, 3; Fr. "cinquante mil" (R1v; *fifty thousand*)
386.35 and] 3; aud 2
387.7 Monarch or Prince] 3; Monarce or Princh 2
389.11 Taborlanes] 4; Toborlanes 2, 3
389.15 *Alchidiana*] 3; *Alchidinia* 2
391.21 endeuours] 3; endeouurs 2
391.30 deuise] 3; om. 2; Fr. "deuiserent" (R3v; *devised*)
393.10 and] 3; ond 2

393.29 detracted] 3; detract 2
394.4 young] 3; om. 2; Fr. "jeunes" (R4v; *young*)
395.6 sollicited] 3; solliced 2
395.25 of] 3; of of 2
396.2 *Amaranoes*] 3; ~, 2
396.3 killed.] 3; ~˰ 2
396.21 Forces] 3; men 2; Fr. "forses" (R5v; *forces*)
397.6 where in] 3; wherin 2
397.12 then] 3; Then 2
397.13 Wherefore] 3; Whereore 2
397.18 *Orinello*] 3; *Orinella* 2
397.24 *Palmerin*] 3; *Palmeriu* 2
397.25 them,] 3; ~. 2
397.36 body] 3; boyd 2
398.3 *Flaminius*] 3; *Elaminius* 2
398.6 manie] 3; manie *turned "e" in* 2
398.30 as you] 3; asyou 2
398.32 summoning] 3; smmoning 2
398.43 among] 3; a | mong 2
399.11 running] 3; runnning 2
399.14 enemie] 3; eneme 2
400.2 *of*] 3; *ef* 2
400.11 kinsman] 3; kiseman 2
400.20 resistaunce] 3; resistanuce 2
400.21 greeuouslye] 3; greeuonslye 2
400.26 by] 3; of 2
400.30 opened] 3; open 2
401.13 haue] 3; om. 2
401.28 holes] 3; wholes 2
402.17 raunsome] 3; *"r" printed upside down in* 2
403.5 Here] 3; Hhere 2
403.9 own] 3; onwn 2
403.40 not] 3; not not 2
404.12 commaundement] 3; commaundemente 2
404.28 Princes] 3; Princesse 2
405.9 Mother] 3; Motber 2
*405.24 just like] ED; so well, as 2, 3, 4; Fr. "aussy bien" (S1r; *just like*).
406.1 *Yseul*] 3; *Ysuel* 2
406.12 iniurie] 3; iuiurie 2
408.23 they] 3; thy 2
408.23 *Alchidiana*] 3; *Alchidinia* 2
408.42 *Alchidiana*] 3; *Alchidinia* 2

409.8 vertuous] *3*; vertuons *2*
409.13 feigning not to] *3*; feigning to *2*; Fr. "faignit n'entendre" (S2v; *faigned not to understand*)
409.21 *Alchidiana*] *3*; *Achidinia 2*
410.16 aboard] *3*; abroad *2*
410.33 you] *3*; mee *2*; Fr. "vous" (S3r; *you*); see explanatory note (700, n. 5)
411.4 to] *3*; of *2*
411.16 this] *3*; his *2*; Fr. "ceste" (S3r; *this*)
412.4 Quickly *Palmerin*] *3*; Quickly *Palmein 2*; *Palmerin* quickly *4*
412.4 desiring] *3*; desiriug *2*
412.20 aboard] *3*; abroad *2*
412.21 after] *3*; ofter *2*
412.30 then] *3*; my *2*; Fr. "doncq'" (S4r; *then*)
412.30 ioy] *3*; my ioy *2*; Fr. "en lieu de joyeuse" (S4r; *instead of joy*)
412.36 seeing] *3*; feeling *2*; Fr. "voyans" (S4r; *seeing*)
413.10 night] *3*; neght *2*
413.15 Christians] *3*; Christans *2*
413.24 strayed] *3*; strained *2*; Fr. "errerent" (S4r; *wandered about*)
*413.29 eight hundred] ED; eight hundred thousand *2, 3*; eight thousand *4*; Fr. "plus de dixhuit cens mile" (S4v; *more than eighteen hundred miles*).
413.38 things] *3*; ihings *2*
414.6 now] *3*; know *2*
414.36 or] *3*; and *2*; Fr. "ou bien" (S5r; *or else*)
414.37 *Palmerin* embracing] *3*; *Palemrin* embraicng *2*
414.39 Armes] *2(b)*; Armex *2(a)*
415.4 Merchants] ED; ~, *2, 3, 4*
415.10 Palmerin).] ED; *Palmerin*)∧ *2*; *Palmerin?*) ∧ *3, 4*
415.14 Emperour] *3*; Emperous *2*
415.20 losse] *3*; loue *2*; Fr. "perte" (S5r; *loss*)
416.27 fauours] *3*; fanours *2*
*416.34 assistaunce] *3*; assurance *2*
417.10 contentment.] *4*; ~? *2, 3*

417.15 of] *3*; *om. 2*
417.19 vnfortunately] *3*; vnfortunate *2*; Fr. "malheureusement" (S6r; *unfortunately*)
418.21 speeches] *3*; speeche *2*; Fr. "propoz" (S6v; *speeches*)
419.12 more)] ED; ~∧ *2*; ~,) *3, 4*
419.28 such] *3*; sueh *2*
420.8 his] *3*; *om. 2*
420.20 Princesse] ED; Prince *2, 3, 4*; Fr. "Princesse" (S7v; *Princess*).
421.16 thou] *3*; thon *2*
422.1 whose] *3*; whote *2*
422.6 Armie was] *3*; Armiewas *2*
422.16 Califfes] *3*; Cailiffes *2*
422.29 *Arabes*] *3*; *Arabies 2*
422.38 sight] *3*; fight *2*
423.6 *Griana*] *3*; *Oriana 2*
424.15 hee was] *3*; heewas *2*
424.21 without] *3*; with out *2*
424.34 the] *3*; *om. 2*
424.36 remembred] *3*; remembring *2*
425.3 *Frenato*] *3*; *Frenata 2*
427.10 him] *3*; htm *2*
427.33 I] *3*; I will *2*
427.36 deathes.] *3*; ~∧ *2*
430.18 *Constantinople*] *3*; *Constantiople 2*
*430.36 companie (such was her greefe to come before her Parents), shee] ED; companie, such was her greefe to come before her Parents, as shee *2, 3, 4*
431.3 Princes] *3*; Princesse *2*; Fr. "Princes" (T3r; *Princes*)
431.21 punishment] *3*; puuishment *2*
431.29 Princes] *3*; Prince *2*; Fr. "Princes" (T3v; *Princes*)
432.7 to be] *3*; tobe *2*
432.14 seeke] *3*; speake *2*
432.21 you] *3*; me *2*; Fr. "ostez de vous" (T4r; *remove from you*)
432.35 concerneth] *3*; cencerneth *2*
433.6 excuse] *3*; excnse *2*
433.9 enforced] *3*; enforce *2*
433.12 mee his] *3*; meehis *2*
433.18 honourable] *3*; hrnourable *2*
433.22 iealousie] *3*; iealousiie *2*

List of Emendations

434.5   impute] *3*; im pute *2*
434.16   such infamous] *3*; with infamons *2*
434.41   iniustice] *3*; iniurie *2*; Fr. "iniustice" (T4v; *injustice*)
435.13   defence] *3*; defende *2*
435.33   Challengers] *3*; Challenger *2*; Fr. "ennemys" (T5r; *enemies*)
437.19   *Aurora*,] *4*; *Aurora*ˆ *2, 3*
437.32   this] *3*; his *2*; Fr. "ce" (T6r; *this*)
438.27   faire] *3*; ~, *2*
441.26   my] *3*; mn *2*
441.31   villainous] *3*; vallainous *2*
442.38   saued] *3*; sauled *2*
443.37   Chamber] *3*; Chamer *2*
443.37   or] *3*; of *2*
443.42   he] *3*; be *2*
444.37   debonaire] *3*; debonarie *2*
444.42   sende] *3*; sennde *2*
446.6   *Frysol*] *3*; *Ffysol 2*
446.9   as] *3*; and *2*
446.14   companions.] *3*; ~, *2*
446.21   whereto] *4*; where to *2*; where too *3*
447.1   spake.] *3*; ~, *2*
447.4   (so] *3*; ˆ~ *2*
447.9   reuiued] *3*; receiued *2*; Fr. "resuscité" (V1v; *revived*)
447.15   enterprise] *3*; enrerprise *2*
448.26   *Tarisius*] *3*; *Tarsius 2*
449.7   *Frysoll*)] *3*; ~, *2*
449.13   come] *3*; ccme *2*
449.19   vertues] *3*; vertuous *2*
450.11   Prince.] ED; ~? *2, 3, 4*
450.27   two] *3*; tooo *2*
452.9   this] *3*; his *2, 4*; Fr. "leur victoire" (V3v; *their victory*)
452.21   Ladye.] *3*; ~ˆ *2*
453.17   aduersaries] *3*; adnersaries *2*
453.19   Duke] *3*; Dnke *2*
453.32   of] ED; *om. 2, 3, 4*; Fr. "du plus grand de ses amys" (V4r; *of the greatest of his friends*)
457.3   Notwithstanding] *3*; Norwithstanding *2*
457.25   violentlie] *3*; violatelie *2*
458.23   Chirurgions] *3*; Chirugions *2*

459.9   some hope of loue] *3*; such hope of her loue *2*; Fr. "quelque espoir d'amitié" (V6v; *some hope of love*)
459.28   occasioned] *4*; accasioned *2*; accustomed *3*
460.30   that] *3*; th[ ]at *2*
461.7   *Palmerins*] *3*; *Plamerins 2*
462.34   and] *3*; *om. 2*; Fr. "et" (V8r; *and*)
*463.3   Brother] *3*; Brethren *2*
464.7   happy] *3*; gracious *2*
466.33   *Gerrard*] *3*; *Cerrard 2*
466.39   will] *3*; well *2*
467.8   *Paris*] ED; ~, *2, 3, 4*; cf. Fr. "Paris Alexandre" (X1v)
468.10   likewise] *3*; iikewise *2*
468.16   *Frysoll*] *3*; *Erysoll 2*
468.19   Tryumphe] *3*; Tryumyhe *2*
469.3   fathers] *3*; ~, *2*; Fr. "les Princes & Cheualiers de son Pere" (X2r; *his father's princes and knights*)
471.15   this] *3*; his *2*; that *4*
472.16   aboord] *3*; abroade *2*
472.16   away] *3*; a way *2*
472.26   afterward] *3*; afterwrd *2*
472.41   to the King] *3*; *om. 2*
473.13   concerning] *3*; considering *2*
473.20   Nor] *3*; Now *2*
473.28   these] *3*; this *2*
474.9   Lordes] *3*; Lorde *2*; Fr. "Seigneurs" (X4r: *Lords*)
476.5   *Licena*] *3*; *Cicena 2*; Fr. "Lycene" (X4v)
477.16   Patriarche] *3*; Patriache *2*
477.28   consequently the] *3*; consequentlythe *2*
477.29   Marquesses] *3*; Marqusses *2*
478.42   with] *3*; wiih *2*
479.21   was] *3*; wss *2*
479.30   your] *3*; yonr *2*
479.33   my] *3*; me *2*
479.34   especially] *3*; especially *with* turned "a" in *2*
479.36   *Palmerin*] *3*; *Palmrin 2*
480.18   such] *3*; suih *2*
*481.9   not] ED; *om. 2, 3, 4*
481.21   *Netrydes*.] *3*; ~ˆ *2*
482.1   *Apolonio*] *3*; *Apolonia 2*

484.15	by] *3*; vy *2*; with *4*	497.27	meane] *3*; meame *2*
484.22	sinister] *3*; ssnister *2*	499.8	Isle] *3*; Islle *2*
484.33	exceeded] *3*; ~ - *2*	499.21	nose-thrilles] *3*; nose? | thrilles *2*
485.21	graciously] *3*; gracionsly *2*	499.22	poysone] *3*; poysome *2*
485.21	Emperour] *3*; Emperonr *2*	499.24	Father] *3*; Fa, | ther *2*
486.5	*Arismena*] *3*; *Arismenia 2*	500.4	strengths] *3*; strength *2*; Fr. "fortes places" (Y7r; *strongholds*)
486.12	I deuoted] *3*; Ideuoted *2*	500.7	*Maulerino*] *3*; *Mulerino 2*
486.15	a] *3*; om. *2*	500.17	fiftie] *3*; thirtie *2*; Fr. "cinquante mil" (Y7r; *fifty thousand*)
486.39	Subiects] *3*; Subiests *2*		
488.3	*Princesse Arismena*] *3*; *Piincesse Arismen 2*	500.25	throate] *3*; thraote *2*
488.4	*Florendos.*] *3*; ~, *2*	501.25	neuer] *3*; neeuer *2*
488.6	resigned] *3*; resined *2*	501.27	I] *3*; *om. 2*
488.6	celestiall] *3*; celistiall *2*	501.28	yeeldings] *3*; dealings *2*; Fr. "accordz" (Y7v; *consent*)
488.10	discontented] *3*; disconted *2*		
488.22	but] *3*; But *2*	501.28	and] *3*; aud *2*
488.34	were] *3*; where *2*	502.9	when] *3*; wheu *2*
488.39	Mother.] *3*; ~, *2*	502.37	one] *3*; man *2*; Fr. "quelqu'vn" (Y8r; *someone*)
489.1	ioyfully] *3*; ioyfnlly *2*		
490.3	*by Olimaell,*] *3*; *by, Olimaell*ˬ *2*	504.10	constantlie] *3*; constanlie *2*
490.3	*of*] *3*; *om. 2*; Fr. "des" (Y2v; *of*)	504.17	to] *3*; fo *2*
490.9	mercy] *3*; ~. *2*	504.42	abie] *3*; abide *2*
491.3	Christians?] *3*; ~¿ *2*	505.9	he proclaimed a yonger] ED; he was proclaimed yonger *2*; he was declared yonger *3*, *4*; see Textual note to 505.10
491.5	and] *3*; snd *2*		
*491.22	Fischermen] ED; Frenchmen *2*, *3*, *4*; Fr. "pescheurs" (Y3r; *fishermen*).		
		*505.10	great] ED; and great *2*, *3*, *4*
491.41	and] *3*; *om. 2*; Fr. "&" (Y3v; *and*)	506.17	thinking] *3*; thinkiny *2*
492.1	proclamation] *3*; protestation *2*; Fr. "fit crier" (Y3v; *proclaimed*)	506.23	necke] *3*; necks *2*; Fr. "col" (Z1v; *neck*)
		506.32	fetching] *3*; ~, *2*
493.29	wealth] *3*; health *2*	507.6	Seruants] *3*; Seruant *2*; Fr. "seruiteurs" (Z2r; *servants*)
493.30	the Damosell] *3*; che Damosell *2*		
494.1	denie] *4*; demaund *2*, *3*; Fr. "refuser" (Y4v; *refuse*)	507.8	deceiued,] *3*; ~ˬ *2*, *4*
		507.9	simple] *3*; simble *2*
494.28	reason, that to] *3*; reason that *2*	507.20	licence] *3*; lisence *2*
494.35	Tyrants] *3*; Traitours *2*; Fr. "Tyran" (Y5r; *Tyrant*)	507.24	returne] *3*; retuene *2*
		508.10	meanes] *3*; meaues *2*
495.12	departed] *3*; de parted *2*	508.11	pittie had power] *3*; power had pittie *2*; Fr. "si onques pitie vous sçeut esmouuoir" (Z2v; *if ever pity could move you*)
495.34	disloyally] *4*; dissloyally *2*; disloyall ye *3*		
496.6	executed] *3*; excuted *2*		
496.22	*Agriola*] *3*; *Agrola 2*	508.14	enchaunted,] *3*; ~. *2*
496.23	prisoner] *3*; prisoners *2*	508.15	incantations] ED; incontations *2*; incantatious *3*, *4*
496.27	courtesie] *3*; countesie *2*		
497.7	liberalitie] *3*; libertie *2*; Fr. "liberalité" (Y6r; *liberality*)		
497.27	I] *3*; we *2*; Fr. "je" (Y6v; *I*)		

List of Emendations

508.28 his lamentations] *3*; this lamentation *2*; Fr. "ses complaintes" (Z2v; *his complaints*)
508.41 kindnes] *3*; knidnes *2*
509.13 Castle] *3*; Castale *2*
509.15 Ladies] *3*; Ladys *2*
509.24 him] *3*; them *2*; Fr. "pensans qu'il vint" (Z3v; *thinking he comes*)
509.35 accursed] *3*; accur[ ]sed *2*
510.1 quoth] *3*; quothe *2*
511.12 hence] *3*; thence *2*; Fr. "d'icy" (Z4r; *hence*)
511.22 take] *3*; taste *2*; Fr. "surprendre" (Z4r; *take by surprise*)
511.22 auaunt-currers] *3*; auaunt,currers *2*
511.32 prisoner] *3*; prisonrr *2*
511.36 conducted] *3*; conducteth *2*; Fr. "l'auoit amené" (Z4r; *had conducted him*)
511.37 for that] *3*; *om.* *2*; Fr. "pource que" (Z4v; *because*)
511.42 his cries] *3*; cries *2*; Fr. "ses crieries" (Z4v; *his cries*)
512.14 honourablie] ED; honourablye *2*; Honourably *3, 4*
512.40 Countrey] *3*; Couutrey *2*
513.11 proceeded] *3*; proceededed *2*
515.3 Princesse.] *3*; ~? *2*; ~, *4*
515.37 expect] *3*; except *2*
516.2 (quoth she to *Ptolome*)] ED; (quoth she) to *Ptolome 2, 3, 4*
516.7 *Tryneus*] *3*; *Treneus 2*
517.8 bequeathed] *3*; bequeathing *2*
517.11 ouercame, at] *3*; ~. At *2*
517.20 aunswered] *3*; anuswered *2*
517.26 the] *3*; his *2*; Fr. "l'vn des deux" (Aa1v; *one of the two*)
517.35 Countrey] *3*; Conntrey *2*
517.41 selfe] *3*; slefe *2*
518.2 dare] *3*; daer *2*
518.11 whereupon] ED; wherenpon *2*; whereon *3, 4*
519.40 *Palmerin*] *3*; *Palmeiin 2*
520.32 be] *3*; bo *2*
520.32 mounted] *3*; mouuted *2*
521.3 *Romata*] *3*; *Romato 2*
521.20 most] *3*; must *2*

521.25 to] *3*; to to *2*
521.30 sorrowfully] *3*; scr[ ]owfully *2*
521.33 expected] *3*; expectted *2*
522.16 part with] *3*; par twith *2*
523.17 encountering] *3*; enconntering *2*
524.29 personage] *3*; personages *2*
525.10 long absent] *3*; longabsent *2*
525.10 especially] *3*; especally *2*
525.27 trampling] *3*; trambling *2*
525.32 where] *3*; were *2*
525.34 Pagan] *3*; Pagon *2*
526.2 knees] *3*; knee *2*
526.41 olde,] *3*; ~ˬ *2*
528.3 Rocke.] *3*; ~ˬ *2*
528.26 monuments] *3*; mounments *2*
528.42 brought] *3*; bronght *2*
529.12 thinke] *3*; thiuke *2*
529.26 Friend] *3*; Friendes *2*; Fr. "mon compagnon" (Aa8r; *my companion*)
529.31 *Abimar*] *3*; *Arbimar 2*
530.39 you. Vpon] ED; you, vpon *2, 3, 4*
530.40 chambers] *3*; cambers *2*
531.18 10000] *3*; 30000. *2*; Fr. "dix mile" (Bb2r; *ten thousand*)
531.20 *Sauata*] *3*; *Seuata 2*; Fr. "Sauat" (Bb2r)
531.39 passions,] *3*; ~. *2*
532.18 coloured] *3*; colourer *2*
532.36 *Belsina*] ED; *Belfina 2, 3, 4*
533.5 the Soldanes] *3*; to Soldanes *2*
*533.9 loue] *3*; warre *2*
533.14 our] *3*; out *2*
533.16 posted] *3*; passed *2*; Fr. "partit en poste" (Cc1r; *departed in haste*; cf. *OED*, s.v. *post* n.2 8d)
534.29 *Aurecinda*] *3*; *Arecinda 2*
534.42 to each] *3*; of *2*
535.4 beautie] *3*; beantie *2*
535.10 ende] *3*; eude *2*
536.1 Soldane] *3*; Soldame *2*
536.10 amorous] *3*; amarous *2*
536.14 messengers] *3*; mssengers *2*
536.16 foundation] *3*; fouudation *2*
537.3 *Colmelio*,] *3*; ~ˬ *2*
537.13 Arch-Flamin] *3*; Arch ˬ Flamin *2*
537.28 crediblie] *3*; credible *2*
537.43 much] *3*; mnch *2*

538.23   her?] *3*; ~, *2*
538.24   hee] *3*; shee *2*; Fr. "il" (Cc3r; *he*)
538.31   Aurecinda] *3*; Aerecinda *2*
539.2   Babylon] *3*; Balylon *2*
539.4   Orzodine] ED; Orzadine *2, 3, 4*
539.7   message] *3*; embssage *2*; Fr. "message" (Cc3v; *message*)
539.7   illustrious] *3*; illuous *2*
539.13   Ambassador] *3*; Ambassdor *2*
540.6   Orzodine] *4*; Orzadine *2, 3*
540.27   worthie] ED; worthilie *2*; moste worthie *3, 4*
540.35   slew] *3*; flew *2*; Fr. "occis" (Cc4r; *slew*)
540.40   Orzodine] *3*; Ozodine *2*
541.5   the] *3*; the the *2*
541.18   the two] *3*; the the two *2*
*541.26 pessant] ED; peasant *2*; weighty *3, 4*
541.34   Aurecinda] *3*; Aureeinda *2*
542.23   Soldane] *3*; Soldanen *2*
543.5   of] *3*; ot *2*
543.31   Cabinette,] *3*; ~) *2*
543.34   of] *3*; o- *2*
543.35   torments] *3*; tor | ments *2*
543.39   and there] *3*; amd there *2*
544.8   of] *3*; ot *2*
544.20   little] *3*; lttle *2*
544.26   resembling] *3*; resemblingng *2*
544.36   *Trineus*] *3*; *Trinens 2*
545.3   disloyalty] *3*; disloyalay *2*
545.18   And] *3*; Vnd *2*
545.19   God] *3*; Cod *2*; Fr. "DIEV" (Cc7r; *God*)
545.34   Aurecinda] *4*; Auredinda *2*; Auricinda *3*
*547.1   she] ED; he *2, 3, 4*; Fr. "celle" (Cc7r; *she*).
547.8   Loue] ED; loue *2, 3, 4*
548.36   as] *3*; *om. 2*; Fr. "autant ... que" (Cc8r; *as ... as*)
549.1   worthily] *3*; worthi[]y *2*
549.35   worthily] *3*; worthilye *2*
549.43   Courrier] ED; Courtier *2, 3, 4*; Fr. "courrier" (Cc8v; *courier*)
550.1   Palmerin,] *3*; ~₍ *2*
550.9   and] *3*; aud *2*

550.18   soldane] *3*; soldaine *2*
550.29   foole] *2(b)*; soole *2(a)*; Fr. "fol" (Dd1r; *fool*)
551.11   Palmerin] *3*; Parmerin *2*
552.28   withall] *3*; with | all *2*
552.41   will not exchaunge] ED; will exchaunge *2, 3, 4*; Fr. "l'autre, pour chose que je luy sçache dire, ne veult changer d'opinion" (Dd2r; *the other will not change his mind, no matter what I tell him*).
553.4   saide] *3*; saie *2*; Fr. "dist" (Dd2r; *said*)
553.7   Belsina] *4*; Bel-sina *2*; Belsino *3*
555.17   yet] *3*; yer *2*
556.8   the] *3*; the the *2*
556.27   concupiscence] *3*; coucupiscence *2*
557.13   and] *3*; aud *2*
557.34   *Muzabelino*] *3*; *Mnzabelino 2*
557.35   sooner] *3*; sonner *2*
557.37   founde] *3*; fonnde *2*
557.39   then] *3*; *om. 2*; Fr. "donques" (Dd4r; *then*)
558.24   enchauntments. My] *3*; ~, my *2*
558.28   he] *3*; they *2*
558.40   Aurecinda] *3*; Arecinda *2*
559.8   Princes] *3*; Prince *2*
560.8   two,] *3*; ~₍ *2*
561.10   on the Deck] *3*; *om. 2*; Fr. "sur le tillac" (Dd6v; *on the deck*)
562.5   Ptolome] *3*; Polome *2*
562.9   to] *3*; td *2*
562.16   Fortune] *3*; Fortnne *2*
562.19   what] *3*; that *2*; Fr. "ce que" (Dd7v; *that which*)
562.39   intreaties] *3*; intreattes *2*
563.22   and] *3*; aud *2*
563.27   Palfraies] *3*; Palfaies *2*
563.36   aunswered] ED; annswered *2*; answered *3, 4*
564.14   who] *3*; wha *2*
565.37   *Maucetto*] *3*; *Mucerto 2*
566.4   continually] *3*; continnally *2*
566.7   with credit] *3*; withcredit *2*
566.29   Brethren] *3*; Brother *2*; Fr. "freres" (Ee1v; *brothers*)
566.38   on] *3*; of *2*; Fr. "sur" (Ee1v; *on*)

List of Emendations

567.4	alliance,] *3*; ~. *2*	581.26	there] *3*; their *2*
567.6	but] *3*; not *2*	582.11	Empresse,] *3*; ~' *2*
567.7	your] *3*; my *2*; "vostre personne" (Ee1v; *your person*)	582.19	with] *3*; wirh *2*
		582.26	offend] *3*; affend *2*
567.9	to] *3*; to to *2*	583.14	with pittie] *3*; *om. 2*; Fr. "eut vne pitié" (Ee8v; *had pity*)
567.38	length] *3*; lengith *2*		
568.12	Ambassadours] *3*; Ambassadoures *2*	583.30	aware] *3*; beware *2*; a ware *4*
		584.9	said] *3*; sail *2*
568.15	Soldane] *3*; Soladne *2*	584.42	amitie] *3*; amititie *2*
569.13	of] *3*; os *2*	585.7	highnesse] *3*; highuesse *2*
569.18	referre] *3*; rcferre *2*	586.5	*Menadeno*] ED; *Meuadeno 2*; *Meuodeno 3*; *Menodeno 4*
569.37	Friend] *3*; Friendes *2*		
570.6	*Greece*] *3*; *Greeece 2*	586.31	our] *3*; the *2*; Fr. "nostre" (Ff2v; *our*)
570.10	his] *3*; their *2*		
570.10	came] *3*; hee came *2*	587.9	your] *3*; our *2*; Fr. "ses" (Ff2v; *your*)
570.22	Archbishop] *3*; Achbishop *2*		
571.2	good] *3*; so good *2*; Fr. "en bonne disposition" (Ee3r; *with a good attitude*)	587.10	*Apolonius*] ED; *Aponius 2*; *Apponius 3, 4*; Fr. "Apolonius" (Ff2v)
		587.13	*Constantinople*] *3*; *Constantinole 2*
571.22	since] ED; siuce *2*; *om. 3, 4*	587.33	yeeres] *3*; dayes *2*; Fr. "ans" (Ff3r; *years*)
571.36	in] *3*; *om. 2*		
572.19	*Cardonya*] ED; *Cordonya 2, 3, 4*	587.35	or] ED; for *2, 3, 4*; Fr. "par combat ou trahyson" (Ff3r; *by combat or treason*)
573.9	*Burgundie*] *3*; *Buroundie 2*; Fr. "Bourgongne" (Ee4v; *Burgundy*)		
		587.41	departed] *3*; depart *2*; Fr. "auez party" (Ff3r; *departed*)
573.29	their] *3*; there *2*		
577.4	fortune] *3*; fortnne *2*	588.32	presence.] *3*; ~, *2*
578.24	Emperours] *3*; Emperous *2*	588.37	of] *3*; *om. 2*
578.32	split] *3*; spilt *2, 4*	590.5	Books] *3*; Booke *2*
579.11	aduised] *3*; adnised *2*	593.5	so] *3*; *om. 2*
579.19	onely] *3*; ouely *2*	593.24	Hauen] *4*; Pauen *3*; Fr. "port" (Ff6r; *haven*)
579.22	hard] *3*; heard *2*		
580.1	remembraunce] *3*; remembrounce *2*	593.25	to *Alchidiana*] *4*; te *Alchidiana 3*
581.12	then] *3*; theen *2*	593.32	*Olorico*,] ED; ~∧ *3, 4*
581.18	Poore] *3*; Heere *2*; Fr. "Pauure" (Ee7v; *poor*)	594.1	as it] *4*; asit *3*
		594.4	her desire] *4*; herdesire *3*
*581.18	of spirit] ED; despised *2, 3, 4*; "Pauure d'esprit" (Ee7v; *poor of spirit*).	594.33	shewed] *4*; wewed *3*
		595.5	made such] *4*; madesuch *3*
581.20	or] *3*; of *2*; Fr. "de vostre rigueur, ou desdain" (*because of your rigor or disdain*)	595.9	following] *4*; follo[ ] *3 is damaged*
		595.10	fauourable] *4*; [ ]le *3 is damaged*

Historical Collation

Note: This section records all substantive variants from the edited text within the four editions of *Palmerin d'Oliva*.

Part I

99.3	Anatomie] *3*; Anotamie *1*	105.43	would] should *2*
102.18	*discharge.*] ED; ~, *1*	105.43	strongelie] *2*; strangelie *1*
103.1	To the courteous Readers.] To the Reader. *3, 4*	106.2	it] *om. 2*
		106.6	or] of *2*
103.14	as] *om. 3, 4*	106.13	vnfitting] vnbefitting *3, 4*
103.15	grutcheth] grutched *3, 4*	106.19	in] *om. 2, 3, 4*
103.20	reading.] *3*; ~ˬ *1*	106.23	her freende] a friend *3, 4*
103.25	applause] appliance *3, 4*	106.34	wishlie] wistlye *2, 3, 4*
103.28	Emperours] the Emperours *3, 4*	106.37	to] vnto *4*
103.36	The second parte . . . A. Munday.] *om. 3, 4*	107.3	but] but by consent of *3, 4*
		108.8	to] vnto *3, 4*
104.4	the King] *King 3, 4*	108.15	sure] *om. 3, 4*
104.7	etc] *om. 3, 4*	108.20	to be] too *3, 4*
104.10	which] that *3, 4*	108.24	yonger] young *2, 4*
104.11	at] of *3, 4*	108.29	and] *2*; aud *1*
104.13	eight] eighth *4*	108.33	immediatlie shee] shee immediately *4*
104.14	*Remicius*] *Remigius 4*		
104.19	receite] respect *4*	108.35	hearing] fearing *4*
104.21	his] the *3*	108.36	conceite] content *4*
104.26	as] as that *4*	109.4	she] he *3, 4*
104.27	verie] *om. 4*	109.9	time] times *3, 4*
104.34	*Tarisius,*] ED; ~ˬ *1+*	109.10	at that] til that *2, 3, 4*
105.13	when] whome *2*	109.14	discerned] discouered *2, 3, 4*
105.14	through] throughout *4*	109.14	But] and *2, 3, 4*
105.16	he] *om. 4*	109.19	you] *om. 2, 3, 4*
105.17	desire] desires *4*	109.27	or] and *4*
105.20	discourses] discourse *4*	109.28	so] *om. 2, 3, 4*
105.27	liued] sued *4*	109.30	you honour] your Honour *4*
105.27	meane] meanes *4*	110.2	ought] ought to *2, 3, 4*
105.34	nowe] *om. 4*	110.3	it I] it that I *3, 4*
105.38	extremitie] extremities *2, 3, 4*	110.16	in generall] *2*; ingenerall *1*

110.27	this good] this great good *3, 4*	117.22	as in her laie, hinder] as lay in her to hinder *3*; as in her lay, to hinder *4*
110.31	thus began] thus he beganne *3*; thus he began to speake *4*		
110.36	for] at *3, 4*	117.24	the] her *2, 3, 4*
111.5	of the Historie] *om. 4*	117.24	looke] lookes *3*
112.4	Immediatlie was] As soone as *4*	117.28	*Caniano*] *Caniano* his Sonne *4*
112.4	discouered] was discouered *4*	117.31	greatlie] highly *3*
112.5	Cittie] Citie of *Constantinople 4*	117.35	Yes certainlie] Yea certaine *2, 3, 4*
112.5	whereupon] *om. 4*	117.42	heauen] God *2, 3, 4*
112.8	of] at *4*	118.1	more] *om. 2, 3, 4*
112.8	ordayning] *2*; doraynning *1*	119.5	So soone as Griana hadde left] Griana thus leauing *4*
112.9	marche] marchde *2, 3, 4*		
112.15	within] with- *2 (hyphen at the end of line, with the second half forgotten)*; with *3*.	119.5	she] *om. 4*
		119.5	into] vnto *4*
		119.8	endaunger] endangers *4*
112.17	gaue the] putting *4*	119.16	named] *om. 4*
112.17	when] *om. 4*	119.17	began] began to speak *4*
112.17	not long] not very long *4*	119.19	long] a long *4*
112.24	disperse] dispose *3, 4*	119.29	other] any other *4*
113.2	of account] of chiefe accompt *4*	119.33	good] great *3*
113.20	recounted] did declare *4*	119.39	worthy your] worthy of your *2, 3, 4*
113.26	such] *om. 3, 4*	119.41	whereof] *omit. 4*
113.34	trauaile] trauell *3, 4*	120.3	went vp] got vp *3*
114.3	when] which when he had obtained, *4*	120.12	that] which *3*
		120.18	my Ladie] any Ladie *3*
115.4	the] his *4*	120.19	thereof] therefore *3*
115.6	My] Most *3, 4*	120.24	verie] *om. 3*
115.15	woorthie so] worthy of so *2, 3, 4*	120.26	past] ouer-past *3*
115.17	vnaduised] *2*; vnsaduised *1*	120.26	gracious] most gracious *3*
115.20	hether] thither *3*	121.7	she] *om. 3, 4*
115.22	vnspotted] *om. 4*	121.14	by] *om. 3, 4*
115.24	shoulde] would *2, 3, 4*	121.25	life] deerest life *3*
116.2	and] or *4*	121.29	recouered] well recouered *3*
116.11	meane] maine *3*; mane *4*	121.29	place] a place *3, 4*
116.13	the] *om. 3*	121.30	we] hee *2, 3, 4*
116.15	haue] *om. 3*	121.30	well] safely *3*
116.16	thy] my *4*	121.42	howre] *omit. 4*
116.18	date] hate *3, 4*	122.4	gotte] got to *2, 3, 4*
116.24	vnluckie] vnfortunate *3*	122.9	or] ED; of *1+*
116.26	or Fortune had been fauourable to me in choise] or else that Fortune had bin more fauourable to mee in my choyse *3*	122.11	that shee] in that shee *3*
		122.27	(said] *2*; said (said *1*; said *3*; saith *4*
		122.28	well] now *3*
		122.31	modesties] modesty *3, 4*
117.6	for] because *3*	122.32	supprized] surprized *2, 3, 4*
117.13	himselfe] him *3*	122.36	his] the *3*
117.15	perswading] and perswading *3*	122.42	thereto] therevnto *3, 4*
117.19	as] *om. 3*	123.7	deuise] aduise *3*

123.9	with great and reuerend honour] with great reuerence and Honour *4*	130.14	fell out not] fell not out *3, 4*
123.17	effected] affected *3*	130.14	fauour] fauours *2, 3, 4*
123.25	kissing] kissed *2, 3, 4*	130.20	her] *om. 3*
123.25	(though] ED; ∧~ *1+*	130.24	saying] thus saying *3*
123.43	of the] to his *2, 3, 4*	130.25	the only Princesse] the onely fayrest Princesse *3, 4*
124.5	cheefe] the chiefe *3*	130.25	for her sake] And (for her sweet sake *3*, (sweet *om. 4*)
124.5	in] of *2, 3, 4*	131.5	Letter] letters *3*
124.11	at this time] now at this time *3, 4*	131.6	albeit] although *3, 4*
124.14	so braue a Husbande] so braue and worthie a Husbande *3, 4*	131.18	One] Yet one *3*
124.22	her] his *3, 4*	131.19	the] as the *3*
124.33	be enforced at length] at length be inforced *3, 4*	131.35	inuiolablie] *2*; inuiolalablie *1*
125.20	cruell a stroake] great a blowe *3, 4*	132.5	hath] had *3, 4*
125.21	the ground] ground *3, 4*	132.15	anie] doe any *4*
125.27	what] well what *3, 4*	132.19	reuerend] reuerent *2, 3, 4*
125.28	into] in *4*	132.28	readie] *om. 2, 3, 4*
125.31	my] thy *4*	132.30	her] *om. 2, 3, 4*
125.42	trouble] troubles *3, 4*	132.39	meane] meanes *3, 4*
126.1	forth] out *3, 4*	133.7	giue] will giue *3, 4*
126.8	to] vnto *4*	133.9	If] *om. 4*
126.13	shewes:] *2*; ~∧ *1*	133.20	imminent] eminent *3, 4*
126.17	it is possible] it it possible *3*; it possible *4*	134.17	compassion] some compassion *2, 3, 4*
126.30	*Cardina*] *Garidian 3*; *Griana 4*	134.18	powers] powers aboue *2, 3, 4*
126.33	in] it in *4*	135.12	melanchollique] Melancholy *4*
126.35	as] as that *4*	135.36	this] the *4*
126.40	furious] *om. 4*	136.1	reioyced much] much reioyced *2, 3, 4*
127.13	before] *1(b)*; be-before *1(a)*	136.7	she] hee *2, 3, 4*
127.22	following] not following *4*	137.1	semblaunce of discontent took] ED; semblaunce to take *1, 2, 3*
127.24	you (carried] you (are caried *4*	137.6	the] her *3*
127.38	so] *om. 4*	137.6	such as shee brought] all such as she had brought *4*
127.40	he] *om. 4*	138.4	*would haue died*] *had like to haue dyed 4*
127.42	offende] ffend *3, 4*	138.27	swoune] sounde *2, 3*
128.2	it] *2*; *om. 1*	138.28	full] *om. 2, 3, 4*
128.23	he would] would *3*	138.36	vnprouided] vnprouded *2*
128.29	on] vpon *3, 4*	138.37	matter] a matter *2, 3, 4*
129.3	*Griana away*] *away Griana 3, 4*	138.42	irreuocablie] *2*; irreuocable *1*
129.9	too] vnto *3, 4*	139.15	Hermit] Father *4*
129.25	no] not *2, 3, 4*	139.16	this] his *4*
129.30	is all this] all this is *3, 4*	140.5	*Palmerin*] Young *Palmerin 4*
129.35	meane] meanes *4*	140.8	as well might] *om. 2*
130.7	Husbande] other Husband *3*	141.29	she] he *2, 3, 4*
130.8	to him] vnto him *3, 4*		

142.2	she] *2*; she she *1, 3*; he *4*	148.10	as] that *2, 3, 4*
142.21	on] vpon *4*	148.12	loyaltie] royalty *4*
142.29	and] *om. 2, 3, 4*	149.18	imploying] imployment *3, 4*
142.32	complaine] one complaine *4*	149.22	health] strength *3, 4*
142.33	he) had] hee) and had *2, 3, 4*	149.25	Azier] Azure *4*
142.41	trauaile] trauell *3, 4*	149.26	the Sheelde] his Shield *3, 4*
142.42	parted] departed *2, 3, 4*	149.26	hande] hands *3, 4*; Fr. "main" (D1v; *hand*)
143.1	misfortune] mischance *2, 3, 4*		
143.2	assistance] resistance *2, 3, 4*	149.31	saie] stay *4*
143.5	his] the *2, 3, 4*	149.36	heereof] thereof *3, 4*
143.5	come] to come *2, 3, 4*	149.37	seene you. Damosell] your Damosell *4*
143.14	of his] his *2, 3, 4*		
143.15	exspected] *2*; erpected *1*	150.3	to you] *om. 3, 4*
144.5	at] in *3, 4*	150.10	knee] knees *2, 3, 4*
144.12	amiable] nimble *3, 4*	150.23	the Sheelde] his sheeld *2, 3, 4*
144.29	shouldest] couldest *2, 3, 4*	150.31	maie] might *3, 4*
144.35	my] mine *2, 3, 4*	150.32	as] as that *4*
144.35	contented] content *2, 3, 4*	150.33	humour] honour *2, 3, 4*
144.36	to] *om. 2, 3, 4*	150.35	thy] the *2, 3, 4*
144.39	it] *om. 4*	150.35	so] soon *3, 4*
145.5	Such speede made *Palmerin* beeing departed from the Marchant, as] Being departed from the Merchant, *Palmerin* made such speed, that *4*	150.37	companie] his company *4*
		150.39	great] *om. 4*
		151.2	on] *of 3, 4*
		151.3	*Artifaeria*] ED; *Artaeferia 1, 2, 3, 4*
		151.5	Eight daies had *Palmerin* stayed] When the Eight dayes were fully expired which *Palmerin* had stayed *4*
145.6	Riuers] riuer *2, 3, 4*		
145.10	not] no *3*		
145.11	this] the *2, 3, 4*		
145.12	to] vnto *4*	151.10	resolute] resolued *2, 3, 4*
145.15	answered] sayde *2, 3, 4*	151.12	who] which *2, 3, 4*
145.24	will I] I will *2, 3, 4*	151.12	lend] send *4*
145.24	the] *om. 2, 3, 4*	151.21	at] to *2, 3, 4*
145.37	so] *om. 2, 3, 4*	151.28	greene] *2*; sweete *1*
145.41	foorth] out *4*	151.32	who said] ED; saying *1+*
146.5	haue] had *2, 3, 4*	151.38	had] hee *2, 3, 4*
146.7	againe] *om. 2, 3, 4*	152.6	so] as *2, 3, 4*
146.10	mellancholique] melancholie *2, 3, 4*	152.9	to] of *2, 3, 4*
146.25	trauaile] trauell *3, 4*	152.10	sciences] science *2, 3, 4*
146.35	doo] to doe *3, 4*	152.11	that] the *2, 3, 4*
147.6	or] nor *4*	152.17	there] *om. 2, 3, 4*
147.29	said] quoth *3, 4*	152.40	his] a *2, 3, 4*
147.34	so great daunger] a great daunger *2, 3*; so great a danger *4*	152.40	full] *om. 2, 3, 4*
		153.17	my] this *2, 3, 4*
147.39	your] *2*; you *1*	154.13	couching] touching *4*
147.43	called] named *2, 3, 4*	154.14	roughlie] *2*; ronghlie *1*
148.6	you neede] is needfull *4*	154.35	next] next to *3, 4*
148.7	so] *om. 4*	154.36	needes] *om. 3, 4*

154.38	me] *om.* 3, 4		162.5	should] could 2, 3, 4
156.5	*straight*] *om.* 3, 4		162.26	mellanchollie] melancholike 2, 3, 4
156.6	So farre was spread the fame of this victory] Fame of this victory was so farre spread 4		162.28	gracious] great 2, 3, 4
			162.43	climbes] climbe 2, 3, 4
			163.7	fonde] *om.* 2, 3, 4
156.7	Mountaine] Fountaine 4		163.9	all night were] were all night 2, 3, 4
156.15	contents,] 2; ~: 1			
156.17	and] who 2, 3, 4		163.11	admonished] aduertised 2, 3, 4
156.18	his] the 3, 4		163.14	that] *om.* 2, 3, 4
156.39	my] of my 3, 4		163.18	shall] will 3, 4
157.4	his] your 2, 3, 4		163.20	constraines] constraine 4
157.17	heare,] 2; ~ˆ 1		163.26	yee] you 2, 3, 4
157.19	Knighthoode] the Knighthood 2, 3, 4		163.29	resolute] resolued 2, 3, 4
			163.34	quieted] quited 2
157.22	so] *om.* 2, 3, 4		163.38	am I] I am 3, 4
158.9	outbraue] ouerbraue 3, 4		163.40	returne the] returne to the 3, 4
158.15	walking] walked 2, 3, 4		164.4	his] the 3, 4
158.15	the Duchesse] where the Duchesse 4		164.5	discoursed] discouered 2, 3, 4
			164.10	such] that such 3, 4
158.17	fixed] fixeing 2, 3, 4		164.16	the sorrowful] *om.* 3, 4
158.18	Duchesse] Duchesses 4		164.19	her] her selfe 2, 3, 4
158.20	Countie] Court 3, 4		164.21	all] all this 3, 4
158.23	and] *om.* 2, 3, 4		164.21	with] *om.* 3, 4
158.23	gone] were gone 2, 3, 4		165.5	*Durace*] *Duraco* 3, 4
158.24	the Duke] and the Duke 2, 3, 4		165.12	light] little 3, 4
158.25	as] *om.* 2, 3		165.16	sadnes] sicknes 3, 4
158.28	Duchesse] Duchesses 4		165.21	supprized] surprized 2, 3, 4
158.36	all] the 2, 3, 4		165.31	trauaile] trauell 3, 4
158.39	you] they 2, 3, 4		165.32	trauailed] trauelled 3, 4
158.42	liues] liue 3; life 4		165.33	met] met with 3, 4
159.4	betake] to betake 2, 3, 4		165.38	hope] hopes 3, 4
159.8	the] their 2, 3, 4		165.42	trauailed] trauelled 3, 4
159.9	forced] enforced 2, 3, 4		166.1	other, where] others, whereof 2, 3, 4
159.21	a quittaunce] a cquittance 2, 3; an acquittance 4			
			166.2	trauailing] trauelling 3, 4
159.22	of] for 2, 3, 4		166.4	trauaile] trauell 3, 4
159.34	as you shall] what you 2, 3, 4		166.6	so] so much 3, 4
159.36	the] this 3, 4		166.7	beholden] ED; am 1+
160.2	holpe] helpt 4		166.18	to] vnto 3, 4
160.4	the Duchesse] and the Duchesse 2, 3, 4		166.20	three] ED; two 1+
			166.26	seconde] other 2, 3, 4
160.11	demaunding] demaunded 3, 4		166.35	assist] haue assisted 3, 4
161.13	your] you 4		167.9	trauaile] trauell 3, 4
161.17	doo] to doe 3, 4		167.13	other] others 3, 4
161.36	their] Lauranaes 4		167.16	me] *om.* 3, 4
161.38	discoursed] discouered 2, 3, 4		167.17	hande] hands 3, 4
162.3	Sisters] three sisters 3, 4		167.25	the] *om.* 3, 4

167.26	trauaile] Trauell *3*		181.13	trauaile] trauell *3, 4*
167.29	found] found out *3, 4*		181.18	the] his *2, 3, 4*
167.30	Ladies] Deere Ladyes *3, 4*		181.20	noble] notable *2, 3, 4*
168.7	Lady] Ladyes *2, 3, 4*		181.26	it] him *3, 4*
168.28	soone] shortly *3, 4*		181.26	the Countie] Count *3*
168.32	the] his *2, 3, 4*		181.26	Countie and] Countand of *2*
168.34	violentlie] most violently *3, 4*		181.28	depart] haue departed *2, 3, 4*
168.36	him] them *2, 3, 4*		181.30	could] that could *3, 4*
168.37	the] this *2, 3, 4*		181.35	other] others *3, 4*
168.42	acceptable] *2*; acceptaple *1*		181.43	her] his *4*
169.4	ere] here *4*		182.6	taken] betaken *3, 4*
169.16	euening] morning *3, 4*		182.9	to] of *3, 4*
169.28	heade] heads *3, 4*		182.10	or] and *2, 3, 4*
169.31	wher] ED; when *1+*		182.17	regarde] carefull regard *3, 4*
170.12	the head] his head *4*		182.19	is] *om. 3, 4*
170.32	meane] the mean *3, 4*		182.29	daunger] a daungerous aduenture *3, 4*
171.4	learned alreadie to kill] alreadie killed *3, 4*		182.31	auayle] preuaile *3, 4*
171.7	Women] woman *3, 4*		182.31	to] *om. 3, 4*
171.8	them] they *4*		182.32	pleaseth] please *2, 3, 4*
172.2	*returning*] *running 3, 4*		182.33	him] his minde *3, 4*
172.9	as] at *4*		182.40	finished] solemnized *3, 4*
172.15	he] they *2, 3, 4*		182.40	their] the *3, 4*
172.19	the] this *2, 3, 4*		182.42	come] came *3*
173.9	*Palmerin,*] *2*; ~∧ *1*		183.15	all are] are all *3, 4*
174.1	Knights] Knight *2, 3, 4*		183.16	our] the *4*
174.18	him] ED; me *1+*		183.17	deliuered to him] ED; reskewed *1+*
175.27	this] that *2, 3, 4*		183.19	other] others *3, 4*
175.34	the] a *3, 4*		183.22	arrowes] poysoned Arrowes *3, 4*
175.42	I am] am I *2, 3, 4*		183.23	so fit] such *2, 3, i4*
176.6	to] of *2, 3, 4*		183.23	his] the *2, 3, 4*
176.18	doone] put *4*		183.27	sterne] both sterne *3, 4*
177.23	vile] vild *2, 3, 4*		183.39	Lordes] Nobles, Lords *3, 4*
177.29	not] ED; *om. 1+*		183.42	though] although *3, 4*
178.6	his] ED; this *1+*		184.1	mangled] mingled *3*
178.23	Kinges] Knightes *2*		184.6	reele] stagger, and reele *3, 4*
178.30	Lord] good Lord *2, 3, 4*		184.7	expence] effusion *3, 4*
178.32	quoth] saide *2, 3, 4*		184.12	crueltie. And to] mischieuous crueltie. And for to *3, 4*
180.7	commaunde] commandement *2, 3, 4*		184.15	Magicall] *om. 3, 4*
180.16	deuoire] endeuour *2, 3, 4*		184.18	let] set *3, 4*
180.33	knees] knee *2*		184.21	trauailed] trauelled *3, 4*
181.1	in generall] *2*; ingenerall *1*		185.15	entrance] extreame *3, 4*
181.5	it] *om. 2, 3, 4*		185.35	being] *2*; bein *1*
181.6	the] and *2, 3, 4*		186.17	scant she] she scant *2, 3, 4*
181.8	against] between *3, 4*		186.20	of] to *2, 3, 4*
181.11	hath] *om. 3, 4*		186.28	her] *om. 4*

186.40	affliction] affection *3, 4*		191.23	mislike not] *2;* not mislike *1;* mislike not of *3, 4*
187.2	the good] his good *4*		191.26	acquaint you] make you acquainted *3, 4*
187.15	interest] *2;* interrest *1*			
188.6	alteration] alterations *4*		191.34	So good newes] *om. 3, 4*
188.13	not you] you not *2, 3, 4*		192.3	prescience] presence *3, 4*
188.17	as] as that *4*		192.7	dailie haue her] haue her daylie *3, 4*
188.23	it] *om. 4*			
189.39	he came] his comming *3, 4*		192.9	yee] you *2, 3, 4*
189.40	Madame] good Madame *3, 4*		192.11	there to] there also, to *3, 4*
189.40	not] *om. 3, 4*		192.12	There] So that there *3, 4*
189.42	other] others *3, 4*		192.13	companie] *2;* comanie *1*
189.42	When] *om. 3, 4*		192.20	couller] her colour *3, 4*
190.3	no] not *2, 3, 4*		192.33	the purpose] that purpose *3, 4*
190.5	bee] tende *3, 4*		192.34	*Ganareno] Ganerino 3, 4*
190.7	make me hide what you] compell mee to hide whatsoeuer you shall *3, 4*		192.35	in] of *3, 4*
			192.38	in hope] hoping *3, 4*
190.9	thy] my *4*		192.38	the] that *3, 4*
190.9	well] deerely *3, 4*		192.42	he] be *2*
190.13	now] eyther *3, 4*		193.2	to] vnto *3, 4*
190.14	made] had made to *3, 4*		193.4	continued their amorous discourses] thus continued their louely amorous discourse *3, 4*
190.16	my lady] ED; his Lady *1+*			
190.18	as] that *3, 4*			
190.18	is it] it is *3, 4*		193.4	newlie] but newly *3, 4*
190.22	accounted] counted *2, 3, 4*		193.5	greatly] much *3, 4*
190.23	he] ED; his *1+*		193.11	oportunitie] good opportunity *3, 4*
190.25	perplexitie] a perplexitie *3, 4*		193.13	conuersing] *2;* conuerssing *1*
190.26	her] her minde *3, 4*		193.14	Mistresse] Ladie and Mistresse *3, 4*
190.27	opinions] varieties of opinion *3, 4*			
190.29	on] onward *3, 4*		193.15	supprised] surprised *2, 3, 4*
190.32	flower of all] onely flower of all true *3, 4*		193.25	speeches] wordes *2, 3, 4*
			193.26	as such] perhaps *3, 4*
190.33	if] *om. 3, 4*		193.26	in] giuen him in *3, 4*
190.35	Master] Lord and Maister *3, 4*		193.28	pleasure] good pleasure *3, 4*
190.41	desired] most desired *3, 4*		193.29	grace may fall] fauour and grace may happily fall *3, 4*
190.41	earnest] somewhat earnest *3, 4*			
191.6	supprized] surprised *2, 3, 4*		193.32	fauoured] Fauourite *3, 4*
191.6	yet] for *4*		193.36	commande] commaund mee, *3, 4*
191.8	well] *om. 3, 4*		193.40	trauaile] trauell *3, 4*
191.8	yee] you *2, 3, 4*		193.42	gaine] but gaine *3, 4*
191.8	long] a long *3, 4*		193.43	life] eyther life *3, 4*
191.11	of] with *3, 4*		194.4	afflictions] affections *2, 3, 4*
191.12	esteemed] in such estimation *3, 4*		194.4	breaking] then breaking *3, 4*
191.17	she] *om. 3, 4*		194.7	so] *om. 2, 3, 4*
191.17	promised] promise *2*		194.15	till] vntill *3, 4*
191.19	great] high and mighty *3, 4*		194.17	please] shall please *3, 4*
191.20	Lorde] Lord and Maister *3, 4*		194.18	ye] you *2, 3, 4*

194.21	talke] familiar talke *3, 4*	200.14	am I] I am *4*
195.6	that] as *2, 3, 4*	200.17	shoulde] would *3, 4*
195.8	nine] none *3*; *om. 4*	200.24	and] and now *3, 4*
195.11	carrires] carriers *2, 3, 4*	200.24	Heerehence proceedeth, that my] Heere hence then proceedeth, that these my *3, 4*
195.15	Sable fielde] field of Sable *2, 3, 4*		
195.18	conuenience] countenance *3, 4*		
195.19	right arme] arme *4*	200.25	able] once able *3, 4*
195.25	ended] tended *3, 4*	200.32	the] that the *3, 4*
195.28	that] who *2, 3, 4*	200.33	trauaile] trauell *3, 4*
195.32	Knights] thirty Knights *4*	200.35	attempt] present attempt *3, 4*
196.14	that] the *2, 3, 4*	200.36	time] the Time *3, 4*
196.15	thus spake] spake thus *2, 3, 4*	200.37	if] yet if *3, 4*
196.16	vnhappie] an vnhappie *4*	200.37	accuse] then accuse *3, 4*
196.17	so] *om. 2, 3, 4*	200.38	regarded] obserued *3, 4*
196.21	Thus] There *2, 3, 4*	200.40	speake] speake and conferre *3, 4*
196.27	now] new *2, 3, 4*	200.43	by] onely by *3, 4*
196.28	as] was *2, 3, 4*	201.5	put] put foorth *3, 4*
196.32	*Grecian*] the *Grecian 3, 4*	201.7	Ah Madame] Ah (sweet Madame *3, 4* (3: literally "lweet")
196.37	As I am,] *2*; ~∧ *1*		
196.40	one of her] one of the *2, 3*; and one of the *4*	201.8	liuing] this day liuing *3, 4*
		201.15	not] *om. 3, 4*
196.41	all] and *2, 3, 4*	201.15	that] in that *3, 4*
197.5	yee] you *2, 3, 4*	201.16	to] vnto *3, 4*
197.20	had] *om. 4*	201.19	supprised] surprised *2, 3, 4*
197.26	her] *om. 4*	201.21	bee] both be *3, 4*
198.2	*disclosed*] discoursed *2, 3, 4*	201.21	yet] and yet *3, 4*
198.9	discouer] to discouer *4*	201.23	the] her *3, 4*
198.15	did torment] had tormented *2, 3, 4*	201.24	locks] locke *3, 4*
198.19	these] this *2, 3, 4*	201.28	faile] faile each other *3, 4*
198.24	royall] a royall *4*	201.29	place] fittest place *3, 4*
198.30	chatte] that *3*; talk *4*	201.32	yee] you *2, 3, 4*
198.38	Lady] my Lady *2, 3, 4*	201.36	seeing] remembring *3, 4*
199.6	luckilie] luckie *2, 3, 4*	202.7	hauing] who had *3, 4*
199.8	howe] now *2*	202.15	his Realme] the Realme *2*; the whole Kingdome *3, 4*
199.10	charge] in charge *3, 4*		
199.17	surely] sure *2, 3, 4*	202.17	furnished] well furnished *3, 4*
199.20	had beene] should be *2, 3, 4*	202.26	earnestlie] *2*; earnestle *1*
199.21	thys] thus *4*	202.27	fairer] farre fairer *3, 4*
199.30	shewed] had shewed *2, 3, 4*	202.30	lodging] lodging which *3, 4*
199.32	they] shee *2, 3, 4*	202.35	trauailing] trauelling *3, 4*
199.36	destenies] destenie *2, 3, 4*	202.42	no] an *3, 4*
199.38	gorgious] glorious *2, 3, 4*	203.2	opinion] owne opinion *3, 4*
199.39	more bright] brighter *2, 3, 4*	203.3	accept] chaunce to accept *3, 4*
199.42	selfe] *om. 4*	203.4	thought] though *4*
200.3	fauour] fauours *3, 4*	203.13	reuiewing] renuing *4*
200.7	preordained] preordinate *3, 4*	203.16	of] by *4*
200.7	appointed] thus appointed *3, 4*	206.17	shoulde] woulde *2*

Historical Collation

203.18	by] of *3, 4*		211.15	seemed] seemeth *3, 4*
203.19	haue] that *4*		211.18	thus] he thus *3, 4*
203.23	me, seeing Fortune] my sute, seeing hard Fortune *3, 4*		211.19	woorthy] most woorthie *3, 4*
203.24	tender and] tender, fresh, and *3, 4*		211.19	good] *om. 4*
203.25	Atropos] *Antropos 3, 4*		211.20	to the] to see the *3, 4*
203.34	countenaunce] her countenance *4*		211.21	Courte] noble Court *3, 4*
203.37	ye] you *2, 3, 4*		211.23	In sooth *Palmerin*] In good sooth Syr *Palmerin 3, 4*
204.2	passionate] most passionate *3, 4*		211.34	ended] once ended *3, 4*
204.2	got] had gotten *3, 4*		211.34	will I] I intend my *3, 4*
204.3	his] *2*; hys his *1*		211.40	so] such *3, 4*
204.4	place] a place *4*		211.42	seeing] seeing that *3, 4*
204.9	though] although *3, 4*		212.1	vertues] the vertues *3, 4*
204.11	of] *om. 4*		212.2	seauenteene] seuenteenth *3, 4*
204.12	you] me *3, 4*		212.2	Prouided] Prouide *2, 3, 4*
204.13	pleased] liked *2, 3, 4*		212.2	you] your *4*
204.14	manifold thankes, sayd] againe manifolde thankes, he sayde *3, 4*		212.5	trauaile with] attend on *3, 4*
			212.8	expedition] all expedition *3, 4*
204.17	worthy] worthy of *4*		212.9	and] who *4*
205.22	Knight] Knights *3, 4*		212.17	they may] may they *4*
205.31	they shall there] there shall they *3, 4*		212.20	but] yet *2, 3, 4*
			212.38	this] his *4*
205.32	Starres] Starre *4*		212.43	well] all *2*; all well *3, 4*
205.36	portraitures] protraitures *3, 4*		213.3	leaue] to leaue *3, 4*
205.39	may] might *4*		213.4	but] but also *3, 4*
206.26	pleaseth] please *2, 3, 4*		213.4	is] is a thing *3, 4*
206.26	intelligencers] intelligences *4*		213.7	is it to] it is for *3, 4*
206.43	this] his *4*		213.8	vertue] worthy vertues *3, 4*
207.9	holpe] ED; hope *1*; helpe *2, 3, 4*		213.11	coniurations] coniuration *2, 3, 4*
207.22	beautie] *2*; beauties *1*		213.16	knowe] well know *3, 4*
207.26	may] can *4*		213.20	for] of *2, 3*
207.30	rather] *2*; *om. 1*		213.21	Ladies] faire Ladyes *3, 4*
207.40	trauaile] trauell *4*		213.22	trauaile] trauell *3*
207.40	shall] will *4*		213.26	arme] came *3, 4*
208.7	Father] a Father *4*		213.26	and] *om. 3*; to *4*
208.11	places] place *2, 3, 4*		213.28	with you] *om. 3, 4*
208.16	Cittizen] Citizens *3, 4*		213.30	trauaile] trauell *3, 4*
208.18	Fathers,] ED; ~ₐ *1+*		213.31	louinglie] most louingly *3, 4*
208.33	wold] should *4*		213.35	Golde] the purest *Arabian*-golde *3, 4*
208.40	care] a care *4*			
210.26	commande] to command *2, 3, 4*		213.35	hands] hande *3, 4*
210.27	Embassade] Embassage *2, 3, 4*		213.36	lineaments] *2*; linaments *1*
210.32	deedes] deede *3*		213.36	this portrait caused he] this portrait caused her *3*; this her portrait he caused *4*
210.42	honor] honours *4*			
210.42	These] The *3, 4*		213.37	couered] couered ouer *3, 4*
211.7	these] their *2, 3, 4*		214.5	order] direction *3, 4*
211.8	some] Some of them *3, 4*			

214.7	so tormented] did so torment 2, 3, 4	218.18	approoued] prooued 2, 3, 4
214.9	King,] King and 3, 4	218.18	Ladies counterfeite] Ladyes to counterfeite 3
214.12	afflictions] affections 2, 3, 4	218.36	rather] eyther 2, 3, 4
214.14	a] so 2, 3, 4	218.37	*Phoebus*] 2; *Phaebus* 1
214.20	doo] loue 2, 3, 4	218.39	abated] abate 2, 3
214.27	temptresse] Empresse 4	218.39	brauer] better 4
214.28	attende] so vainely attend 3, 4	219.3	not] got 3, 4
214.30	Pantofle] 2; *Pantefle* 1	219.3	his] the 3, 4
214.32	Duchesse] Duchesses 4	219.11	to] on 2, 3
214.34	Tent erected at] Pauilion erected neere 3, 4	219.20	declarest] declare 3, 4
		219.29	the Ladies] his Ladies 2, 3
214.38	Iasper] Iaspis 3, 4	219.35	thou] that I 3, 4
214.40	a seemelie place appointed] appoynted a seemely place 4	219.40	experience] experient 3, 4
		220.7	this] your 2, 3, 4
214.42	greatlie] highly 3, 4	220.8	these] those 4
214.42	time] Times 3, 4	220.13	me,] ED; ~∧ *1*+
215.2	Noble] for Noble 3, 4	220.23	with] and with 4
215.3	comes] comes in 3, 4	220.24	his] the 2, 3, 4
215.5	Kings] 2; *King 1*	220.26	was] were 4
215.5	the] *om.* 2, 3, 4	220.34	paines] painles 2
215.8	foorth with] foorth, and with 3, 4	221.2	*with*] *and of* 2, 3, 4
215.9	liuely] *om.* 3, 4	221.5	arriued at *Paris, Palmerin, Trineus,*] *om.* 4
215.10	gorgious] glorious 2; rich and glorious 3, 4		
		221.7	conquerer] conquered 2, 3, 4
215.11	in] of 3, 4	221.9	glory] honour 2, 3, 4
215.15	in] with 2, 3, 4	221.12	to] of 2, 3, 4
215.18	vnualuable stones] vnualuable rich stones 3, 4	221.20	one] man 4
		221.24	giue] gives 4
215.22	Lorde] most neerde 3, 4	221.25	assured] assuredly 3, 4
215.29	fayrest] most fairest 3, 4	221.27	loude] low 3
215.30	in] in all 3, 4	221.28	courage] (conge) 3, 4
215.30	doo] to do 2, 3, 4	221.32	thee] thee to verifie it 3, 4
215.31	reade, the] read, and the 4	221.33	see] soone see 3, 4
215.32	Lords,] 2; ~∧ *1*	221.34	they broke] both of them brake 3, 4
215.35	stature] statue 2, 3, 4		
216.3	yee] you 2, 3, 4	221.37	swords] good Swoords 3, 4
216.9	part] depart 2, 3, 4	222.4	due] to doo 4
216.9	I] he 3, 4	222.7	Prince] the Prince 3, 4
216.13	in] into 2, 3, 4	222.10	his present] the present 4
216.16	quicklie beginne] begin quickly 4	222.11	continued] so continued 3, 4
		222.15	*Frenchman*] *Frenchmen* 3, 4
216.18	But] 2; *Bnt 1*	222.32	sooth] good sooth 3, 4
216.34	his] the 2, 3, 4	222.33	but] *om.* 4
216.35	defiances] defiance 2, 3, 4	222.37	deeds] 2; dee[ ]ds *1*
217.4	of] for 2, 3, 4	222.39	were] we 3, 4
218.8	former] other 2, 3, 4	222.41	to] of 4
218.10	happily] ED; vnhappily *1*+		

223.6	other] others *4*	229.29	is] his *2*
223.7	put] puts *4*	229.42	not] got *3, 4*
223.10	manie] Inscriptions of many *3, 4*	230.8	the fielde] *3*; fielde *1, 2*
223.11	drawne] extracted *3, 4*	230.18	thou] you *4*
223.11	Greeke as Latin] in Greeke, as in Latine *3, 4*	230.31	desire rather] rather desire *2, 3, 4*
		230.43	it in] in it *4*
223.18	encouraged] much encouraged *3, 4*	231.7	forcibly] forcible *3*
223.20	Knights] Knights at Armes *3, 4*	231.25	this] the *4*
223.20	his] the *4*	231.26	importing] importeth *3, 4*
223.23	rare] great *4*	231.29	Lords] Ladyes *4*
223.26	sette] sate *4*	231.32	of] for *3, 4*
223.32	vndiscretion] indiscretion *3, 4*	231.37	of matter that] of that which *4*
223.35	their] both their *3, 4*	231.40	quieted] quiet *4*
223.38	flew foorth of] sparkled from *3, 4*	231.42	you again] him againe *2, 3*
223.40	valiantly] most valiantly *3, 4*	232.12	beautifull] beautifully *3, 4*
223.41	throughlie] (beeing throughly *3, 4*	232.13	*English*] *2*; *Englih 1*
224.4	fresh] *2*; frsh *1*	232.15	so] *om. 4*
224.6	vnder] with *3, 4*	232.19	helpe me God] God help me *4*
224.6	he] that he *3, 4*	232.36	will] would *4*
224.6	wearyed,] wearied, and bruised, *3, 4*	232.40	the] his *2, 3, 4*
		232.43	bidding] abidding *3, 4*
224.9	from] from off *3, 4*	233.2	had he] he had *4*
224.9	but] but onely *3, 4*	233.3	the] *om. 4*
224.15	hee made] he had made *3, 4*	233.8	become] be *4*
224.16	he] *om. 3, 4*	233.9	to] and *2, 3, 4*
224.18	but] but yet *3, 4*	234.4	had] bad *4*
225.10	*Polinarda*] *Polinarda* seemed to bee *3, 4*	234.6	yeere] yeeres *2, 3, 4*
		234.6	elder] *om. 4*
225.13	vnwoorthy] vnwoorthy of *4*	234.9	the] *om. 3, 4*
225.19	ought] might *3, 4*	234.12	extinguished] *2*; extingushed *1*
225.24	this] the *3, 4*	234.13	affection] Loue and affection *3, 4*
225.29	your] my *3, 4*	234.13	an] any *4*
225.32	as] *om. 2, 3, 4*	234.15	in his] in the *2, 3, 4*
225.36	destenied] Destinated *3, 4*	234.21	I may] may I *3, 4*
225.40	els] *om. 4*	234.24	intent] intent or meaning *3, 4*
225.42	doubt not] make no doubt *3, 4*	234.25	Maiestie] Highnesse *3, 4*
226.2	in] surely in *3, 4*	234.29	not] not once *3, 4*
226.3	passeth] surpasseth *3, 4*	234.34	hereof] thereof *4*
226.5	your] you *3*	234.35	paracide] paradice *2, 3, 4*
226.8	conferring] *3*; *om. 1, 2*	235.1	Horse] Steede *3, 4*
226.9	not foyled] foyled *2, 3, 4*	235.2	so closely] as closely *2*; away as close *3, 4*
226.10	maimed] mained *2*		
226.15	had] hee hadde *3, 4*	235.5	tooke] went *2, 3, 4*
226.19	constancie] inconstancie *3, 4*.	235.5	Hauing] Hauing not *4*
226.37	trickling] trinckling *3, 4*	235.6	trauailed] Trauelled *3, 4*
227.15	Sister] Mistresse *3, 4*	235.8	or] and *4*
229.15	come] to come *4*	235.9	sought] sought the meanes *3, 4*

235.9	shroude him] shrowd himselfe *4*	237.39	had] had before *3, 4*
235.11	this] that *2, 3, 4*	237.40	so] such *4*
235.11	place] place for him *3, 4*	239.7	to seeke] and to seeke *2, 3, 4*
235.12	turning] turned *4*	239.9	mellanchollie] melancholyke *2, 3, 4*
235.17	thou nowe] that now thou *3, 4*		
235.20	die?] ED; ~, *1, 2*; ~: *3, 4*	239.16	trauailing] trauelling *4*
235.21	supprised] surprised *2, 3, 4*	239.20	trauailed] trauelled *4*
235.24	or] or else *3, 4*	239.26	beside the] beside his *2, 3, 4*
235.24	could] might *3, 4*	239.37	happy] happier *2, 3, 4*
235.30	This] The *4*	239.39	Mayden] mayde *2, 3, 4*
235.33	hearing] heard *4*	239.40	heauens] heauen *4*
235.35	mones] meanes *4*	239.41	if] *om. 4*
235.37	therefore cherrish] wherefore cherish vp *3, 4*	239.41	perceiue] perceiues *4*
		240.1	that] of *2, 3, 4*
235.38	heauines] your heauinesse *3, 4*	240.3	arise] ryse *2, 3, 4*
235.43	aunswered] aunswered him thus *3, 4*	240.13	thence forward] henceforward *3, 4*
		240.19	a] in *2, 3, 4*
236.5	discoursed] discoursed all *3, 4*	240.26	trauaile] trauell *4*
236.12	he] we *2, 3, 4*	240.31	seeing] *om. 4*
236.12	glad] very glad *3, 4*	240.32	that] *om. 2, 3, 4*
236.12	companie] good companie *3, 4*	240.33	not to cast] cast not *4*
236.13	good] happie *3, 4*	240.34	anie thing to] any thing that may *3, 4*
236.17	well] so well *3, 4*		
236.22	other] many other *3, 4*	240.35	freelie] *2*; feelie *1*
236.23	Lorde] deere Lord *3, 4*	240.36	her] his *3, 4*
236.29	sorrowe] sorrowes *3, 4*	240.37	trauayled] trauelled *3, 4*
236.30	shoulde] would *3, 4*	240.39	he] *om. 4*
236.30	trauaile] Trauell *3, 4*	240.39	hearde] hearde (as it were) *3, 4*
236.34	resembled] somwhat resembled *3, 4*	240.43	strong] *om. 3, 4*
		241.1	saying] thus saying *3, 4*
236.40	He,] ED; ~∧ *1+*	241.2	who prouoked] what prouoketh *3, 4*
237.2	of her] of this her *3, 4*		
237.6	opinions] varieties of opinion *3, 4*	241.2	with which] wherewith *3, 4*
237.6	certaintye] pretended certaintie *3, 4*	241.3	soundlye] sodainely *2, 3, 4*
237.11	to beholde] in beholding *3, 4*	241.4	the] those *3, 4*
237.11	whereof] whereat *3, 4*	241.5	them] him *2*
237.18	one daie] on a day *3, 4*	241.7	embraced] embracing *3, 4*
237.21	trembled] trembled, shiuering *3, 4*	241.7	my] *om. 4*
237.23	Phisition] Physitions *3, 4*	241.20	aduenture] aduentures *2, 3, 4*
237.25	was] were *3, 4*	241.21	they] he *2, 3*
237.26	bee] to be *3, 4*	241.21	cause they entertained him] caused him to be entertained *4*
237.26	except] except onely of *3, 4*		
237.27	greefe] a griefe *3, 4*	241.26	to] in *4*
237.29	Realme] Kingdome *3, 4*	241.30	trauaile] travell *4*
237.34	vsed] had vsed *3, 4*	241.34	whereupon] whereon *2, 3, 4*
237.35	a long] *2*; along *1*	241.35	knowe] knowing *2, 3, 4*
237.38	pleaseth] it pleaseth *3*	241.43	hath] haue *2, 3, 4*

242.10	at Parris] of Paris 2, 3, 4		246.43	she recompence you not] make you not recompence 3; she make not recompence 4
242.25	hee] it 4			
242.26	hath] it hath 2, 3; hee hath 4			
242.33	Kings] King 2, 3, 4		247.5	deserues] winneth 3, 4
242.33	were Nephewes] ED; was Nephewe 1+		247.14	things] earthly things 3, 4
			247.17	qualitie] qualities 3, 4
242.42	their] the 2, 3, 4		247.18	beauty] beauties 4
243.3	hardy] woorthy 2, 3, 4		247.20	behalfe] behalfes 3, 4
243.16	warres] warre 2, 3, 4		247.21	some] some of them 3, 4
244.2	and] and to 3, 4		247.23	prowesse] valor and prowesse 3, 4
244.6	Prince] the Prince 3, 4		247.27	Realme] Empyre 3, 4
244.6	to whome] vnto whom 3, 4		247.27	ende] ende that 3, 4
244.8	these] those 4		247.28	both be] be both 3, 4
244.11	and that] and for that 2, 3, 4		247.32	was] seemed 3, 4
244.15	hee] both hee 3, 4		247.42	seeing] hearing 3, 4
244.23	into] to 4		248.4	rare wit] so rare a wit 3, 4
244.23	Pallace] stately Pallace 3, 4		248.6	her aunswere] the answer she made 3, 4
244.24	and] om. 3, 4			
244.24	their] the 4		248.7	the] all the 3, 4
244.25	by him] by 3, 4		248.11	meeting] next meeting 3, 4
244.36	Orleaunce] Orleaunces 3, 4		248.12	brought] had brought her 3, 4
244.41	discredite] disgrace 3, 4		248.13	therewith] therewithall 3, 4
244.41	spake] vttered 3, 4		248.17	Therefore] Wherefore 3, 4
245.12	Courte] Highnesse Courte 3, 4		248.22	thy Maister beares me] ED; thou bearest thy Maister 1, 2, 3; thou bearest my Master 4
245.13	Lord] deere Lord 3, 4			
245.17	nobilitie] Noblenesse 3, 4			
245.22	hide] hyde or conceale 3, 4		249.22	our present] and present 2, 3, 4
245.26	and] as 2		249.23	conceits] conceit 2, 3, 4
245.32	desire] great desire 3, 4		249.25	cause] a cause 3, 4
245.36	had] there 4		249.27	I depart] you depart 4
245.37	Princes] Knights 2, 3, 4		249.28	trauailes] travels 4
245.38	with] and 4		249.31	prize] prise you 3, 4
245.40	discourse] circumstance 3, 4		249.35	endeuours] endeuour 3, 4
245.43	she must] must shee 3, 4		249.37	faire] sweete 2, 3, 4
246.15	much] om. 3, 4		250.12	my] om. 2, 3, 4
246.16	sort] a pensiue sort 3, 4		250.13	nor] or 2, 3, 4
246.17	iudge him] iudge whether he were 3, 4		250.18	ouertrauailed] ouertrauelled 2, 3, 4
			250.24	trauailed] traueled 3, 4
246.19	immouable] vnmoueable 4		250.26	of] in 2, 3, 4
246.23	complaine] so complaine 3, 4		250.29	trauailes] travels 4
246.27	ende] successe 3, 4		250.43	now] om. 4
246.31	all] om. 4		251.5	of] to 2, 3, 4
246.33	deliuered] had deliuered 3, 4		251.20	possiblie] possible 2, 3, 4
246.41	to] vnto 3, 4		251.21	Kings] warres 3, 4
246.41	loue] sake 4		251.42	and] om. 4
246.42	trauailes] Trauells 3, 4		251.42	to] 2; to to 1
			252.13	you] we 2, 3, 4

253.15	a] *om. 3, 4*	258.7	sende] sent *3*
253.18	referre] deferre *3, 4*	258.8	yeelde] yeeld vp *3, 4*
253.31	by] for *4*	258.10	rested] resisted *2*; refreshed *3, 4*; Fr. "sejournerent" (K5v; *sojourned*)
253.33	wold] shuld *2, 3*		
254.3	Ptolome] *2*; Ptoleme *1*		
254.9	Kinsman] own Kins man *3, 4*	258.15	as his] as of his *3, 4*
254.15	thinges] things fit *3, 4*	259.2	Prince] Princes *3*
254.21	greene] great *3, 4*	259.5	foure] *2*; 4 *1*
254.23	which] that *4*	259.8	meant] went *3, 4*
254.28	into] to *2, 3, 4*	259.8	his] the *4*
254.30	the newe] this newe *3, 4*	259.8	that had so boldlie] for that hee had boidly *3*; for that hee had boldly *4*
254.36	maie] might *2, 3, 4*		
255.1	melanchollie] in Melancholie *3, 4*		
255.2	bewray] too soone bewray *3, 4*	259.12	trauaile] trauel *3, 4*
255.3	thinke] to thinke *3, 4*	259.14	come] came *4*
255.4	fought] haue fought *3, 4*	259.15	accept] except *2*
255.9	shall] shall then *3, 4*	259.18	that] *2*; that that *1*
255.12	spake] speake *3, 4*	259.19	Daughter] fayre Daughter *3, 4*
256.12	best] fittest *3, 4*	259.20	came where] they came where then *3, 4*
256.13	hearde] beard *3*		
256.15	of his] from his *3, 4*	259.24	faire] the fayre *3, 4*
256.16	gaue] he gaue *3, 4*	259.25	from] from off *3, 4*
256.21	well] will *2*	259.30	her] the *3, 4*
256.26	tooke] betooke *3, 4*	259.31	meruailous] a marvellous *4*
256.27	themselues] *2*; themselus *1*	259.41	that] not *3, 4*
256.28	Horse] Horse-men *3, 4*	260.2	rich] *om. 4*
256.36	perceiuing] perceiuing that *3, 4*	260.16	shall] wall *4*
256.38	entred they] they entred *3, 4*	260.17	woulde,] *2*; ~ˌ *1*
257.4	els had they] or else they had *3, 4*	260.19	perfections] affections *2, 3, 4*
257.6	thence] from thence *3, 4*	260.37	Ptolome] *2*; Ptoleme *1*
257.8	ones] others *3, 4*	260.37	great] very great *4*
257.19	animate] *2*; annimate *1*	261.1	Sir] *om. 4*
257.20	in our] in these our *3, 4*	261.5	but] *om. 4*
257.25	to the] to theyr *3, 4*	261.6	is] was *4*
257.25	the enemie] the Enemies *3*; our Enemies *4*	261.6	your] *om. 4*
		261.8	will] shall *4*
257.26	a] the *4*	261.8	fal] to fall *4*
257.26	Norwayes very] Norwayes being very *3, 4*	261.13	behinde] beyond *2, 3, 4*
		262.3	vnderstoode] *2*; vnder-derstoode *1*
257.34	stoutest was] stoutest of them were *3*,	262.24	our] the *4*
		262.32	dare to] *om. 4*
257.41	victory to] victory of *2, 3, 4*	262.34	ranged] empaled *3, 4*
257.43	the Armie] the whole Armie *3, 4*	262.34	for] in order of *3, 4*
		262.36	Magdalen] of Magdalen *2, 3, 4*
258.1	to] *om. 2*	262.39	vertue and valoure] valour and Prowesse *3, 4*
258.2	that] to the ende *3, 4*		
258.4	Lordes] *2*; Lorde *1*		
258.6	expected] exacted *2*	262.40	calling] which calleth *3, 4*

262.42	to] vnto *3, 4*		267.32	Daughter,] *2*; ~ˬ *1*
263.1	tirannous] most Tyrannous *3, 4*		267.34	you] your *2*
263.2	your] *2*; you *1*		267.36	answer] this answer *4*
263.3	reason] right and reason *3, 4*		267.40	sufficientlie] *2*; sufficienlie *1*
263.12	enemies] enemy *4*		267.41	giue] gaue *3, 4*
263.20	then] they *2*		268.3	so] *om. 2, 3, 4*
263.24	middest] the midst *3, 4*		268.4	words] wards *4*
263.37	*Scots*] *2*; *S[]ots 1*		268.8	sometime] sometimes *3, 4*
263.40	*Magdalen*] of *Magdalen 4*		268.9	hearde of] could heare of *3, 4*
264.1	*Magdalen*] of *Magdalen 4*		268.11	beene towards] beene done towards *3*; beene done to *4*
264.8	cleft] *1(b)*; clest *1(a)*			
264.9	sight] fight *4*		268.11	doone] *om. 3, 4*
264.11	*Magdalens*] of *Magdalens 4*		268.19	wordes] his words *3, 4*
264.13	such] their *2, 3, 4*		268.19	he] least he *3, 4*
264.16	had not] but that *4*		268.20	humblie intreated] humbly intreate *2*; most humbly haue intreated *3, 4*
264.21	they] then *4*			
264.21	other] other part *3, 4*			
264.23	meanes] helpe and means *3, 4*		268.21	whence] of whence *3, 4*
265.9	meane] the meane *2, 3, 4*		268.24	would] should *4*
265.13	Gentlemen] Gentleman *2, 3*		268.25	neere] neere vnto *3, 4*
265.29	hurts] hearts *2*		268.27	to] *om. 2, 3, 4*
265.35	his] the *2, 3, 4*		268.29	foure] about foure *3, 4*
265.36	such] of such *3, 4*		268.33	serue] seeme *3, 4*
265.39	Queene] Queene and the Noble Lords *3, 4*		268.34	founde] found out *3, 4*
			268.35	hope] good hope *3, 4*
265.40	assisted] *2*; asisted *1*		268.38	greefe] loue *2, 3, 4*
266.1	can] can doo *3, 4*		268.39	chaunce] shall chaunce *3, 4*
266.3	recouered] *2*; recoueced *1*		268.41	perceiue] well perceyue *3, 4*
266.14	feared] now feared *3, 4*		268.42	haue] haue now *3, 4*
266.15	deuise] well deuise *3, 4*		268.43	sighes] store of sighes *3, 4*
266.16	stande] so stand *3, 4*		269.1	exceeded] exceedeth *4*
266.17	at] as *3, 4*		269.3	*Agriola*] fayre *Agriola 3, 4*
266.20	trauailed] trauelled *3, 4*		269.5	not] not but *3, 4*
266.22	as to such persons alloweth honor and good affection] *om. 3, 4*		269.6	ingratefull] vngratefull *4*
			269.8	subtiltie] subtile *2, 3, 4*
266.25	serue you] doo you seruice *3, 4*		269.14	thy] my *2, 3, 4*
266.30	or] nor *2, 3, 4*		269.21	*Europe*] all *Europe 3, 4*
267.3	and] and of *4*		269.21	neuer was] was neuer *2, 3, 4*
267.4	After] When after *2, 3, 4*		269.23	little] *om. 4*
267.6	arriued at the Cittie] *om. 2*; came *3, 4*		269.30	then] *om. 3, 4*
			269.33	that shall] to *4*
267.9	preserued] presented *2*		270.34	by] *om. 3, 4*
267.10	as] and *3, 4*		270.34	Ladie] Ladyship *4*
267.13	such] *om. 3, 4*		270.39	father] Father is *4*
267.16	the] a *2, 3, 4*		271.3	commaunde] demaund *3, 4*
267.17	Knights] strange Knightes *3, 4*		271.21	talked] talke *3, 4*
267.19	he)] hee) who seemes *3, 4*		271.22	be easilie] easily be *4*

271.32	trauaile] trauell *4*		277.12	*Garbones*] *Carbones* 2, 3, 4
271.36	toyles] foyles *3, 4*		277.13	his Tents] the tents *4*
271.41	chase] chose *2*; choise *3, 4*		277.18	newes] bad newes *3, 4*
271.41	fallen] faken *3*; taken *4*		277.20	ye] you *3, 4*
272.15	Maisters] mistresse *2, 3, 4*		277.21	gone] *2*; goe *1*
272.29	mine] my *3, 4*		277.25	Gentlewomen] the Gentle- women *3, 4*
273.2	your] *2*; you *1*			
273.24	them] the rest *3, 4*		277.32	all *England*] *England* 2, 3, 4
273.25	in] into *2, 3, 4*		277.36	hearde)] heard before) *3, 4*
273.36	I renounce] Ile renounce *4*		277.38	borne allegeaunce] borne dutie and allegeance *3, 4*
273.37	haue] *om. 4*			
273.43	ill] well *2, 3, 4*		277.40	as] that *3, 4*
274.10	tel] till *2*		277.41	diuers] diuers other *3, 4*
274.14	impart] impute *4*		278.2	his victory] this victory *2*; his great Victorie *3, 4*
274.23	such] with *2, 3, 4*			
274.28	change] charge *4*		278.5	not] ED; *om. 1+*
274.34	he] *om. 2, 3, 4*		278.5	meete] weete *3*
274.35	shee] we *3, 4*		278.9	offended] very much offended *3*; was very much offended *4*
274.39	mee] *om. 4*			
275.4	passe the time] sporte *3, 4*		278.10	defended] defending *4*
275.5	perceiued] perceyued well *3, 4*		278.11	armed] well armed *3, 4*
275.6	for] for that *3, 4*		278.14	thence] from thence *3, 4*
275.7	too] *om. 3, 4*		278.17	maist] mayest *4*
275.10	endurest] hast endured *3, 4*		278.17	worthy] worthy of *4*
275.10	attending] in attending *3, 4*		278.22	who made] what maketh *3, 4*
275.10	howre] houres *3, 4*		278.25	but] *om. 4*
275.14	infortunate] vnfortunate *4*		278.28	*Palmerin*] But *Palmerin 3, 4*
275.17	toyles] foyles *3, 4*		278.32	hilts] hils *2*
275.18	so] *1(b)*; to *1(a)*		278.32	fell] *om. 3*
275.19	earelie] easily *4*		278.36	a] *om. 3, 4*
275.22	trusting] but trusting *3, 4*		278.39	all them] them all *3, 4*
275.27	her] the *4*		278.42	arriued] pursued *3, 4*
275.28	to] vnto *3, 4*		278.43	that] *2*; the *1*
275.33	not faithfull] vnfaithfull *3, 4*		279.4	all] *om. 3, 4*
275.34	shoulde] might *3, 4*		279.4	fortune] high Fortune *3, 4*
275.35	beene] beene plunged *3, 4*		279.4	such] *om. 3, 4*
275.37	but] then *3, 4*		279.5	company] good companie *3, 4*
275.39	take] *om. 3, 4*		279.6	thou] *2*; thon *1*
276.1	come] *om. 3, 4*		279.6	escape] safely escape *3, 4*
276.7	be amisse] be much amisse *3, 4*		279.10	well] *om. 4*
276.9	that] *om. 3, 4*		279.16	meane] meanes *3, 4*
276.10	goe] gor *3*; got *4*		279.17	kneeled] kneeling *2, 3, 4*
276.16	we] as we *3, 4*		279.19	villanie] *2*; villaine *1*
276.18	chase] Chafe *4*		279.25	they] *2*; thy *1*
277.6	infortunate] vnfortunate *3, 4*		279.26	honorable Sepulture] honourably Sepulture *3*; honourably Sepul- tured *4*
277.7	beheld] behold *3, 4*			
277.12	the King] *2*; King *1*			

279.32	so] such 3, 4		285.6	she bare] shee beare 3; she did beare 4
279.33	liue] liue and prosper 3, 4			
279.34	prosper in their] be most happy in all theyr 3, 4		285.10	Mistresse] Faire Mistresse 3, 4
			285.11	gaue] giue 3; gives 4
280.2	be easilie] easily be 2, 3, 4		285.12	needes] om. 3, 4
280.3	Targe] Target 3, 4		285.14	happen to so] haue befallen to such 3, 4
280.5	Gate] gates 2, 3, 4			
280.10	why] who 2		285.15	a] variable 3, 4
280.15	so] as 2, 3, 4		285.16	carrie] conuey 3, 4
281.5	on] om. 2, 3, 4		285.17	prouided Shippes] made prouision both of Shipping, 3, 4
281.10	the] om. 2, 3, 4			
281.10	made] kept 4		285.18	conueying] transporting 3, 4
281.13	for the] of the 2, 3, 4		285.18	aboorde] abroade 2
281.29	pleased] please 2, 3, 4		286.5	that] om. 4
281.34	bee] he 4		286.6	nothing] nothing else 3, 4
281.35	to] of 2, 3, 4		286.7	auncient] graue Auncient 3, 4
282.10	thereof] hereof 2, 3, 4		286.8	Squires] comely Squyres 3, 4
282.14	his Father] your father 2, 3, 4		286.9	on] vpon 3, 4
282.16	meane] meanes 4		286.12	reputed] pretendedly reputed 3, 4
282.16	displeasure] pleasure 2, 3, 4		286.15	but remember] doo but once remember 3, 4
282.23	not] dot 4			
282.23	on] no 3		286.19	Knowe] Knowe you 3, 4
282.25	that] which 2, 3, 4		286.21	too] two 2
282.26	till] to 2, 3, 4		286.21	thinking] and in a good opinion of him, thinking 3, 4
282.39	gladly woulde] would gladly 2, 3, 4			
283.3	soueraigne] sodaine 2, 3, 4		286.22	shewes and behauiour] fained shewes and counterfait behauiour 3, 4
283.4	them] them both 2, 3, 4			
283.7	my charge] the charge 2, 3, 4			
283.14	fortune] misfortune 2, 3, 4		286.23	to beguile and falselie] falsely to beguile 3, 4
283.17	so] om. 2, 3, 4			
283.30	him] vnto him 4		286.28	made] often made 3, 4
283.31	bare] beare 2, 3; beares 4		286.31	take] be pleased to take 3, 4
283.37	he] she 2, 3, 4		286.37	named] 3; name 1, 2
283.38	heereon] heerein 3, 4		286.37	if] if so bee 3, 4
284.14	meane] meanes 2, 3, 4		286.38	vntrueth] any vntruth 3, 4
284.21	equal your] equ al your 3; equall all your 4		286.42	his dumps] this dumpe 2, 3, 4
			287.4	well] once well 3, 4
284.26	happy] so happie 3, 4		287.5	first] the first 3, 4
284.30	imagined] and imagined 2, 3, 4		287.8	most] om. 3, 4
284.33	your] for your 3, 4		287.14	cause] onely cause 3, 4
284.35	faith] sooth 4		287.17	heard] had heard 3, 4
284.36	not] ED; om. 1+		287.19	knowne] and well known 3, 4
284.39	meane] meanes 4		287.21	bee] to be 3, 4
285.1	(in mine opinion)] 4; in (mine opinion) 1, 2, 3		287.21	right] right and Title 3, 4
			287.24	mouth] owne mouth 3, 4
285.3	behauiour] behauiours 3, 4		287.25	or] or else 3, 4
285.3	both fal] fall both 4		287.26	anger] choller 3, 4

287.28	in meruailous choller] as it were in a maruellous rage *3, 4*	289.22	Mightie] High and mightie *3, 4*
287.29	proofe thereof in Combatte] tryall therof in single Combatte *3, 4*	289.25	time] present time *3, 4*
		289.26	you] *2*; your *1*
287.30	King so] Kings Maiestie *3, 4*	289.28	please] pleaseth *3, 4*
287.31	lacke] want *3, 4*	289.31	shall I] I will *4*
287.33	tryed] decyded *3, 4*	289.32	so] such *3, 4*
287.33	thus spake] spake thus *2, 3, 4*	289.35	his] the *4*
287.35	is] it is *2, 3, 4*	289.39	or] nor *3, 4*
287.36	if] that if *3, 4*	289.40	his] the *2, 3, 4*
287.37	to deliuer it] for to bee surrendred *3, 4*	289.41	where] where as *3*
		289.43	there] then *3, 4*
287.39	the] this *3, 4*	290.1	*Tryneus*] the Prince *Trineus 3, 4*
287.40	required] requested *3, 4*	290.2	cause] vrgent occasion *3, 4*
287.43	till] vntill *3, 4*	290.3	paine] paines *3, 4*
288.2	what] who *3, 4*	290.6	charge] stricte charge *3, 4*
288.4	his] the *2, 3, 4*	290.7	paine] the paine *3, 4*
288.12	Knight] young Knight *3, 4*	290.7	cause] vse *4*
288.13	Combatte] Combatte performed *3, 4*	290.8	seeke] make syarch *3*; make search *4*
288.14	remayned] remainev *3*; remaineth *4*	290.9	his Dwarffe] the Dwarfe *3, 4*
		290.10	and] and then *3, 4*
288.16	to him] *om. 3, 4*	290.12	bewraie] not bewray *3, 4*
288.17	recouerie] the recouery *3, 4*	290.15	seeke] goe seeke *3, 4*
288.20	more] much more *3, 4*	290.16	King] King himselfe *3, 4*
288.21	especiallie] most specially *3, 4*	290.18	honour] to honour *2, 3, 4*
288.24	Iudges] as Iudges *3, 4*	290.20	premeditate] *2*; premiditate *1*
288.25	meane] means *4*	290.24	displeased] disquietted *3, 4*
288.26	determination] pretended determination *3, 4*	291.4	trauailed] trauelled *3, 4*
		291.12	finde] finde out *3, 4*
288.26	The time] Now the time *3, 4*	291.14	what] that *3, 4*
288.27	their] the *3, 4*	291.19	sight] the sight *2, 3, 4*
288.29	persons] Personages *3, 4*	291.25	whereof] wherefore *2, 3, 4*
288.31	deuoyre] best deuoyre *3, 4*	291.26	your] *2*; you *1*
288.33	through] quite through *3, 4*	291.34	correcte] contract *4*
288.34	Traytour to fall deade] false traytour to fall downe dead *3, 4*	291.39	doo] *om. 3, 4*
		292.2	multiply no more wordes,] would not multiplie any more words, but *3, 4*
288.35	sawe] and seeing *3, 4*		
288.37	if there yet remaine] So that now (I say) if there remaine yet *3, 4*	292.7	likest] likliest *3, 4*
		292.12	great] very great *3, 4*
288.41	so] *om. 2, 3, 4*	292.28	By God] In troth *4*
289.6	considering] concealing *2, 3, 4*	293.5	not] ED; so *1+*
289.13	that] that now *3, 4*	293.13	for] to *3, 4*
289.14	of] one of *3, 4*	293.14	in] of *2, 3, 4*
289.16	hee] that hee *3, 4*	293.19	trauayling] trauelling *4*
289.17	come to] to come to *2*; come hether to *3, 4*	293.40	yet] *om. 3,4*
		294.4	great] *om. 2, 3, 4*

Historical Collation

294.6   other waie] *2*; otherwaie *1*
294.13   you haue] I haue *4*
294.14   little] small *4*
295.2   to] *om. 2, 3, 4*
295.2   we] that we *3, 4*
295.4   holpe] helpt *4*
295.12   meant] meane *3*
295.23   verie] a very *3, 4*
295.25   come to] at *3, 4*
295.26   her] her to her great aduancement *3, 4*
295.30   Father loouing] good Father louing *3*; good Father loved *4*
295.30   matched] so as he matched *3, 4*
295.33   Husbande] good Husband *3, 4*
295.33   little] short *3, 4*
295.34   My] Now my *3, 4*
295.36   mee to] to my *3, 4*
295.39   Daughter] faire Daughter *3, 4*
295.42   howe] how that *3, 4*
295.43   vnwoorthy] vnwoorthy of *3, 4*
296.3   from] away from *3, 4*
296.4   sollicitings] solliciting *2, 3, 4*
296.5   freendlie meeting] friend meeting me *2, 3, 4*
296.6   long] not long *4*
296.8   the] a *2, 3, 4*
296.9   feared] feared that *3, 4*
296.10   neighboures] *2*; neighboues *1*
296.15   hath] had *3, 4*
296.16   did I] I did *4*
296.19   beside] besides *3, 4*
296.19   Traytour] false Traytour *3, 4*
296.20   (vnmanlie)] most (vnmanly,) *3, 4*
296.23   inuocations] inuocation *2, 3, 4*
296.24   villainie] Villain *3, 4*
296.25   firste his Mother] first of all, his owne Mother *3, 4*
296.25   disease] cruell disease *3, 4*
296.30   escaped] made an escape *3, 4*
296.32   wordes] good words *3, 4*
296.34   misfortune] misfortunes *3, 4*
296.36   enchauntments] forcible Enchauntments *3, 4*
296.39   vertue] Valour, Vertue *3, 4*
296.40   your] *2*; you *1*
296.41   this] the *2, 3, 4*

296.41   hardly] valiauntly *3, 4*
296.42   I] *om. 4*
296.43   a Sworde] an excellent good Sword *3, 4*
296.43   and] with *3, 4*
297.1   so] *om. 2, 3, 4*
297.2   matter] *om. 3, 4*
297.3   pittie] some pittie *3, 4*
297.3   Mother] distressed Mother *3, 4*
297.4   aduenture] boldely Aduenture *3, 4*
297.4   cause of honour] Honourable cause *3, 4*
297.4   thereto] hereto *2*; herevnto *3, 4*
297.7   wrong is] wrongs are *3, 4*
297.8   somewhat] sometimes *2*; in some sorte *3, 4*
297.9   villainie] cursed Villany *3, 4*
297.11   Ladie] deare Ladie *3, 4*
297.12   neuerthelesse] Yet neuerthelesse *3, 4*
297.13   I meruaile] I much maruell *3, 4*
297.17   ende] finish *3, 4*
297.18   the] this *3, 4*
297.19   as to] as once to *3*
297.20   for] of *2*; to *3, 4*
297.20   other] *om. 3, 4*
297.22   beeing] being layde *3, 4*
297.23   then] and then *3, 4*
297.24   morning] next Morning *4*
297.24   with] to *4*
297.24   to seruice] to heare diuine Seruice *3, 4*
297.26   abused] abased *3, 4*
297.31   your] *2*; you *1*
297.31   good] sound *3, 4*
297.34   to] *om. 4*
297.34   it] *2*; ti *1*
297.36   offer] courteous offer *3, 4*
297.37   wrought] written *3, 4*
297.39   *this*] *at this 3, 4*
297.42   the] his *2, 3, 4*
298.1   behelde] beholde *2*
298.2   noble] *om. 3, 4*
298.3   beeing curiouslie] beeing most curiously *3, 4*
298.4   engrauen] all engrauen *3, 4*
298.4   as] such as *3, 4*

298.9	for] for that *3, 4*	299.28	(of courtesie) allight] (of courtesie to alight) *3, 4*
298.11	leade] ledde *3*; led *4*		
298.14	vntie] vndoo *3, 4*	299.32	escaping] escaped *2, 3, 4*
298.16	assaulted] violently assalted *3, 4*	299.32	the Horsse] his Horse *2, 3, 4*
298.18	these] those *3, 4*	299.34	striue] grapple *3, 4*
298.19	as] as that *3, 4*	299.39	sore] shrewd *3*; cruell *4*
298.20	labour] valour *3, 4*	299.39	thigh] right Thigh *3, 4*
298.21	necessitie] great necessitie *3, 4*	299.40	of] that belonged to *3, 4*
298.24	he] him hee *3, 4*	299.41	apace] apace backe *3, 4*
298.25	the other after] his other fellow *3, 4*	299.42	Gate] Gates *3, 4*
		299.43	sware] swore, that *3, 4*
298.25	meruailous] extraordinarie *3, 4*	300.2	other] others *3, 4*
298.28	beganne] he beganne *3, 4*	300.6	witte] wittes *3, 4*
298.30	much a doo to keepe] very much a doo to saue and keep *3*; had very much to doo to save *4*	300.6	to] directly to *3, 4*
		300.8	which] *2*; whieh *1*
		300.12	meanes] best meanes *3, 4*
		300.12	but] but now *3, 4*
298.30	vpwarde] vpside downe *3, 4*	300.13	abye] abyde *4*
298.32	mischaunce] misfortune *3, 4*	300.20	trecherous] Trayterous *2, 3, 4*
298.32	a meruailous great and ouglie Monster suddainlie] suddenly a maruellous great, huge, and ouglie Monster *3, 4*	300.28	so] *om.* *2, 3, 4*
		300.36	haue you] you haue *4*
		300.41	care] are *2*
		301.5	parts] the parts *4*
298.33	meanes possible to ouerturne] the meanes he could to ouerwhelme *3, 4*	301.12	the] *om.* *3, 4*
		301.12	hautie] harty *4*
		301.18	woorthy] great *3, 4*
298.34	Nowe] So that now *3, 4*	301.20	his answers] his answere *3*; this answer *4*
298.36	rough] *om.* *3, 4*		
299.3	wherof] whereat *3, 4*	302.2	*trauayling] travelling 4*
299.4	God] the Highest *3, 4*	302.9	great] greater *4*
299.8	may] can *4*	302.18	trauailes] trauels *4*
299.10	called aloude] called with alowde *3*; called with a loud voice *4*	302.26	beloueth] beloued *3, 4*
		302.27	his] this *2, 3*
299.10	open] come open *3, 4*	302.30	came] come *3, 4*
299.11	that] that at last *3, 4*	302.30	so] *om. 4*
299.12	cammest] commest *3, 4*	302.40	on] vpon *3, 4*
299.13	meruaile] much maruell *3, 4*	302.40	trauailing] trauelling *4*
299.13	guyded] hath guyded *3, 4*	302.41	iudging] iudging for *3, 4*
299.15	haue] hath hitherto *3, 4*	303.1	Hearest thou] Heare a thou *3, 4*
299.16	at thy] at the *3, 4*	303.2	inhabited] vnhabited *3, 4*
299.17	let] make *3, 4*	303.3	two] to *3*
299.18	great] loftie *3, 4*	303.6	the] a *2, 3, 4*
299.19	proude] *om. 3, 4*	303.8	quaking] all quaking *3, 4*
299.20	villainously] like a Villaine *3, 4*	303.18	preuent] *2*; peruent *1*
299.26	of the Castell] at the Castle Gate *3, 4*	303.23	matter] a matter *4*
		303.26	altogether] all together *3, 4*
299.28	manhood] knigh[t]hoode *3, 4*	303.37	trauailed] troubled *3, 4*

303.39	so] *om. 2, 3, 4*	306.9	vnhonourablie] honourably *4*
303.42	a hart] even a heart *3, 4*	306.10	preferre] now to preferre *3, 4*
304.5	not] *om. 4*	306.12	so] *om. 3, 4*
304.9	And] And now *3, 4*	306.12	sayde] sayde thus *3, 4*
304.11	thinges] *om. 4*	306.12	the] a *2, 3, 4*
304.13	diuine] *om. 4*	306.12	wouldest forestall] wouldest forest all *2*; would forestall *3*; would forest all *4*
304.16	should] would *3, 4*		
304.18	or] and *3, 4*		
304.33	supprised] surprised *2, 3, 4*	306.13	Knight] Knights *2, 3, 4*
304.34	I] *om. 2, 3, 4*	306.13	By] Now by *3, 4*
304.40	Ladie] Lorde *3, 4*	306.14	gaue] lent *3, 4*
305.3	vnconstant] inconstant *4*	306.14	stroke] sound stroake *3, 4*
305.4	the Knight] this Knight *4*	306.16	Squires] two Squyres *3, 4*
305.11	my] any *4*	306.18	to the Ladie] where the Lady is *3, 4*
305.12	extreamitie] *2*; extreamite *1*		
305.15	drewe hee] then he drew *3, 4*	306.19	Squire durst doo no otherwise] Squyre by no meanes durst doo otherwise *3, 4*
305.15	offered] offered for *3, 4*		
305.16	reuiued] receiued *2, 3, 4*		
305.16	him] him fast *3, 4*	306.20	little Gate] Wicket *3, 4*
305.18	a] such a *3, 4*	306.21	opened] opening *3, 4*
305.19	to condemne] for to condemne *3, 4*	306.22	was] had bene *3, 4*
305.20	you will affoorde no pittie] that you will not affoorde any pittie *3, 4*	306.24	abashed] much abashed *3, 4*
		306.27	So] So that *3, 4*
305.21	yet let mee] let me now *3, 4*	306.28	mounting] presently mounted *3, 4*
305.21	humour] bad humour *3, 4*	306.28	caused] causing *3, 4*
305.22	reason] great reason *3, 4*	306.29	escape] make an escape *3, 4*
305.26	shame] open shame *3, 4*	306.30	ryding on] ryding away *3, 4*
305.28	selfe,] *om. 3, 4*	306.30	night] darke Night *3, 4*
305.29	suddaine] suddenly *3, 4*	306.31	place] fitte place *3*
305.30	where] when *3, 4*	306.33	turning] returning *2*; turning foorth *3, 4*
305.31	so] *om. 3, 4*		
305.31	feruentlie] frequently *4*	306.34	content] contented *3, 4*
305.33	prouidence] good Prouidence *3, 4*	306.36	deceiued] thus deceiued *3, 4*
305.37	and] and then *3, 4*	306.37	Freende] deere Friende *3, 4*
305.37	pittaunce] proportion of Pittance *3, 4*	306.38	Fortune] harde Fortune *3, 4*
		306.39	chaunge] exchaunge *3, 4*
305.38	refreshed] well refreshed *3, 4*	306.39	pleasures] pleasure *2*
305.39	meanes] good meanes *3, 4*	306.41	appointed] appoynted this contrarietie *3, 4*
305.41	to the] into the *3, 4*		
305.41	had] then had *3, 4*	307.1	the worlde] this Worlde *3, 4*
306.2	sollitarie] the poore solitary *3, 4*	307.1	If hee haue] And seeing he hath *3, 4*
306.2	Ryding] So ryding *3, 4*		
306.4	Squires] *2*; Squirs *1*	307.2	participate a little] in some sorte participate *3, 4*
306.5	if] if that *3, 4*		
306.5	returne] make thy return *3, 4*	307.3	speake] haue spoken *3, 4*
306.8	mooued] being mooued *3, 4*	307.4	and] and that *3, 4*
306.8	trecherie] false treacheryes *3, 4*	307.4	from] away from *3, 4*

307.5   grace] good fauour *3, 4*
307.8   to that] with that *3, 4*
307.9   let mee] me *2*; I had *3, 4*
307.16 Gods] God *3, 4*
307.19 bridling] bridling of *3, 4*
308.6   whom] one whom *3, 4*
308.8   the] *om. 3, 4*
308.17 my] the *2, 3*
308.17 ending the] to finish that *3, 4*
308.18 torments] torments which *3, 4*
308.19 such] many such *3, 4*
308.22 *Valerica*] faire *Valerica 3, 4*
308.24 fauour] fauours *3*
308.27 therof] whereof *4*
308.29 the] *om. 4*
308.39 want] the very want *3, 4*
308.41 speak] to speake *2, 3, 4*
308.42 rested] restored *4*
308.42 hearbs] fragrant Hearbes *3, 4*
309.5   comfortlesse place] *2*; comfort- lesse, place *1*
309.13 shold] would *3, 4*
309.15 it may] may it *3*
309.16 is comprised] consists *3, 4*
309.20 a] my *2, 3, 4*
309.20 so] so much *3, 4*
309.21 compelled] thus compelled *3, 4*
309.31 By God] In faith *4*
310.14 sad] said *3, 4*; Fr. "triste" (N5r; *sad*)
310.15 thereof] together *4*
311.12 sight] fight *3*
311.22 beene] practised to be *3, 4*
311.24 supprized] surprised *3, 4*
311.27 may] might *3, 4*
311.28 trauaile] trauell *3, 4*
311.29 stranger] meere straunger *3, 4*
311.31 conuay] transporte *3, 4*
311.32 one] to be one *4*
311.34 delightes] delights and delicates *3, 4*
311.39 little] small store of *3, 4*
311.40 to forgoe] so soone to forgoe *3, 4*
312.1   please] so please *3, 4*
312.1   forget] be vnmindefull of *3, 4*
312.2   vouchsafed] vouchsafe *3, 4*
312.8   note] uote *3*
312.11 how] *om. 3, 4*

312.14 Knightes] *2*; Kinghtes *1*
312.18 Tents] ED; Tent *1+*
312.24 if] whether *3, 4*
312.25 it] her *3, 4*
312.28 it] *om. 3, 4*
312.29 mee] *om. 4*
312.35 in] *om. 4*
312.38 he] *2*; be *1*
312.40 sayd] saying *2, 3, 4*
313.7   he] I *3*
313.9   or] nor *4*
313.15 serue] served *4*
313.18 *Palmerin*)] *2*; ~∧ *1*
313.25 trauaile] trauel *2, 3, 4*
314.7   his Castell] the Castle *4*
314.11 sometime I combated] I com- bated sometime *2, 3, 4*
314.12 so] such *2, 3, 4*
314.12 had] *om. 4*
314.13 verely] he verily *2, 3, 4*
314.14 he should] you should *4*
314.26 seeing] *2*; see- *1*
314.27 shall] can *2, 3, 4*
314.29 mounted] mounting *2, 3, 4*
314.30 twelue] *4*; 12 *1, 2, 3*
314.31 trauaile] travell *4*
314.33 supprized] surprised *2, 3, 4*
314.34 hether to] hither is to *2, 3*
314.35 the fight] that fight *3, 4*
314.37 fellowes] fellow *2, 3, 4*
315.4   these] *2*; thess *1*
315.7   horsse] Hose *2*
315.21 your] *2*; you *1*
315.22 trauaile] travell *4*
315.24 to him] to his *2*
315.27 trauailed] travelled *4*
315.35 with] *om. 4*
315.37 goes] shall goe *3, 4*
315.37 who was] being *3, 4*
315.43 wyll] *om. 4*
316.1   will I] I will make *3, 4*
316.4   thee not] not thee *2, 3*; it not thee *4*
316.4   rob] now robbe *3, 4*
316.6   very] *om. 3, 4*
316.7   to me] mee now *3*; now to me *4*
316.13 present] in presence *3, 4*

Historical Collation

316.14	that] onely that *3, 4*	320.3	*freend*] *friendes 2, 3, 4*
316.18	Chirurgions] best Chyrurgions *3, 4*	320.6	the Ring] a ring *2, 3, 4*
316.23	of] on *2, 3, 4*	320.6	the Lady of the Castell in the Lake] ED; she *1+*
316.29	he (beyond] *2*; (he beyond *1*	320.12	nowe] *om. 2, 3, 4*
316.30	other] others *3, 4*	320.12	noble] nobly *2, 3, 4*
316.31	iniured] iniuried *2, 3, 4*	320.14	Hauking] Hunting *2, 3, 4*
316.35	hereat] thereat *3, 4*	320.14	his] the *2, 3, 4*
316.36	my] *om. 3, 4*	320.28	accomplishe] performe *4*
316.36	the] his *2, 3, 4*	320.39	vertuous] vertuous and worthie *3, 4*
317.4	many] many and sundry *3, 4*		
317.6	lyttle] small *3, 4*	320.40	so] no *2, 3, 4*
317.9	any] that any *3, 4*	320.42	strang] solitary, strange *3, 4*
317.17	*Colmelio*] hee *3, 4*	321.3	rule] rule and gouernment *3, 4*
317.17	sought] made search and sought *3, 4*	321.8	regard] any regard *4*
		321.22	indiscreet] vndiscreet *4*
317.19	meane] meanes *3, 4*	321.29	recount] account *4*
317.19	brought] had restored *3, 4*	321.37	inwardly] now inwardly *4*
317.20	Afterward] And afterwardes *3, 4*	321.37	the] *2*; the the *1*
317.20	trauailing] trauelling *3, 4*	322.1	I] *om. 3, 4*
317.26	gentle] gentlest *3, 4*	322.2	as] *om. 2, 3, 4*
317.35	mounted presently] presently both mounted *3, 4*	322.8	of] ED; or *1+*
		322.10	your] *2*; you *1*
317.35	meete] meete with *3, 4*	322.16	meane] meanes *3, 4*
317.38	Lord] good Lord *3, 4*	322.18	worthie] most woorthy *3, 4*
317.38	Fortune] hard Fortune *3, 4*	322.21	carefull] most carefull *3, 4*
317.40	perswaded] perswade *4*	322.22	*Agriola*] *2*; *Argiola 1*
317.42	Lord] deere Lord *3, 4*	322.26	but] but that *3*
318.4	as] as that *3, 4*	322.33	obtayned] had obtained *3, 4*
318.4	till] vntill *3, 4*	322.34	gentle] sequele of the gentle *3, 4*
318.6	euer they] they ever *4*	322.34	These] Those *3, 4*
318.19	hath] haue *2, 3*; having *4*	322.37	true] a true *4*
318.21	your] *2*; you *1*	322.40	Lord] onely Lord *3, 4*
318.22	trauailes] trauells *3, 4*	322.41	beseemes] *2*; be seemes *1*
318.23	goe] should goe to *3, 4*	322.41	the] that *2, 3, 4*
318.24	Chamber.] ED; ~, *1+*	323.15	depart as] *2*; departas *1*
318.25	as] accordingly as *3, 4*	323.19	your] my *2, 3, 4*
318.27	depart] depart thence *3, 4*	323.21	Chamber] *2*; Camber *1*
318.28	his trauaile] all his Trauells *3, 4*	323.27	Princes chamber] *2*; Princes-chamber *1*
318.34	my] *om. 4*	324.6	absented] absenting *2, 3, 4*
318.40	trauayled] trauelled *3, 4*	324.13	surpassing] *2*; supassing *1*
319.1	in] into *3, 4*	324.17	Cittie,] *2*; ~. *1*
319.1	not] ED; *om. 1+*	324.30	ingrateful] vngratefull *2, 3, 4*
319.2	to vaunt themselues] ED; *om. 1+*	324.31	enorme] enforme *3, 4*
319.3	with] and *4*	324.37	these] those *2*
319.4	to] vnto *3, 4*	324.42	an] a *3, 4*
319.9	trauaile] trauell *4*		

325.2	he] *om.* 2, 3, 4	330.14	seruice] good Seruice 3, 4
326.4	In this place our history taketh this occasion] Our Historie in this place taketh occasion to speake 4	330.16	forbeare] to forbeare 3, 4
		330.17	these] your 2, 3, 4
		330.18	wursse] worser 2, 3, 4
		330.22	imaginations. Perswade] ED; imaginations. perswade 1; imaginations, perswade 2; imaginations: perswade 3, 4
326.8	embassade] embassage 2, 3, 4		
326.17	Emperour,] 2; ~. 1		
326.18	presence] 2; prsence 1		
326.18	so] *om.* 2, 3, 4	330.26	not though] not Madame, though 3, 4
326.29	by] *om.* 3, 4		
326.33	so soone as] soone so as 3	330.28	such] your 3, 4
326.40	be] 2; he 1	330.29	reputed] imputed 3, 4
327.11	shorte returne] 2; shortereturne 1	330.29	finde true] finde it true 3, 4
327.21	deliuering] deliuered 4	330.30	preferment] 2; perferment 1
327.23	possible] possibly 2, 3, 4	330.32	expell] excell 2, 3, 4
327.26	will pray] pray you 2, 3, 4	330.33	*Palmerin,*] 2; ~∧ 1
327.42	to the Courte] to Court 3, 4	330.33	country] Natiue Countrey 3, 4
328.3	mean while] ED; me any while 1+	330.40	sollemnized] duely Solemnized 3, 4
328.5	if] 2; of 1		
328.10	misliked] disliked 4	330.40	come] shall come 3, 4
328.13	went to] went vnto 3, 4	330.41	claime] claimes 2, 3, 4
328.23	of *Europe*] in *Europe* 2, 3, 4	330.41	reproche] any reproach 4
328.28	supprized] surprized 2, 3, 4	331.4	ther] *om.* 3, 4
328.30	sad] a sadde 3, 4	331.14	discerne] desire 3, 4
328.35	impeache] impeaching 3, 4	331.23	vp on] vpon 3, 4
328.37	will] 2; well 1	332.5	fiue] 2; fine 1
329.1	secret] 2; fecret 1	332.15	This] The 3, 4
329.4	and] as 2, 3, 4	332.24	meane] meanes 4
329.7	babled] doubled 3, 4	332.26	misse] mishap 2, 3, 4
329.9	pleasure, but] good pleasure: But yet 3, 4	332.27	vse] do 3, 4
		332.38	many] any 3, 4
329.11	my brother] vnto my deere Brother 3, 4	333.1	theefe] 2; theese 1
		333.6	phisnomie] phisiognomy 4
329.11	so] but once so 3, 4	333.17	no] *om.* 3
329.12	I were not woorthie] I should thinke my selfe vnwoorthie 3, 4	333.18	parted] departed 4
		333.33	these] those 3, 4
329.12	named] called 2, 3, 4	333.34	*Agriola,*] 2; ~. 1
329.16	other] *om.* 2, 3, 4	333.36	your selfe] her selfe 3
329.16	embassade] embassage 2, 3, 4	334.4	parted] 2; parting 1
329.17	greefes so] greefe as 2, 3; griefe so 4	334.8	the] *om.* 3, 4
		334.13	who] which 3, 4
329.31	to] so 2, 3, 4; Fr. *tant* (O5v)	334.17	practise] practised 3, 4
329.41	*Palmerin*] 2; *Paomerin* 1	334.18	of long time enchaunted] long time enchaunted 2; of a long time before Enchaunted 3, 4
330.6	*Agriola*] the Princesse *Agriola* 3, 4		
330.7	kisses] welcomes and kisses 3, 4		
330.9	that] *om.* 2, 3, 4	334.18	what Ships] what Shipping soeuer 3, 4
330.9	Mistresse] deere Mistresse 3, 4		

Historical Collation 801

334.19	entred] once entred *3, 4*	334.34	enchaunted] *2*; enchannted *1*
334.20	Isle] Island *3, 4*	334.35	sorte] *om. 3, 4*
334.21	Bores] Beares *3, 4*	334.36	had] *2*; *om. 1*
334.23	she had] he hadde *3*	335.11	together in] *2*; togetherin *1*
334.25	and the whole Isle] this Island was *3, 4*	335.13	perfourmes] is performed in *4*
334.28	her seruauntes to take] her trustyest Seruaunts to take away *3, 4*	335.13	which shall be published so soone as it can be printed] of this History *4*
334.29	sunk in] ED; *om. 1+*	335.15	FINIS] *om. 4*
334.30	in] into *3, 4*	335.16	Munday] *Mundy 2, 3, 4*
334.33	beast] Beast assume *3*; Beast to assume *4*		

Part II

340.3	*Though*] *Yhough 3, 4*	341.25	resisted] rested *3, 4*
340.3	*Palmerin*] *3*; *this second booke of Palmerin 2*	341.31	noting] and noting *3*; and nothing *4*
340.3	*and hauing*] *3*; *and he hauing 2*	341.32	the] thy *4*
340.11	*sporting*] *spurting 4*	341.32	deliuerance] happy deliuerance *3, 4*
340.16-19	Paladine *sonne to . . . at Cripplegate this ninth of March.*] *3*; *I will hasten on the translation of the third part of this most famous Historie, which beeing of some great quantitie, wil ask the longer time ere hee can enioy the benefit thereof: bee therefore kind to these two former Bookes, and that will be the better meanes of hastening the third. 2*	341.34	thankfull] a thankfull *3, 4*
		341.40	carefully] carefull *4*
		342.9	Mountainets] *3*; Mountaines *2*
		342.10	his] this *3, 4*
		342.15	tydings] tyding *3, 4*
		342.18	hee had] *om. 3, 4*
		342.24	the Pilot] theyr Pylot *3, 4*
		342.32	Realme] Dominion *3, 4*
		342.32	so supprised] surprized *3, 4*
		343.6	wreakfull] dreadfull *3, 4*
		343.9	hath] haue *3, 4*
340.20	1588.] *3*; *om. 2, 4*	343.12	and honor] *3*; an[ ] honor *2*
340.22	*Monday*] *3*; *Mundy 2*	343.18	offende] disquiet and offende *3, 4*
341.15	remember] cannot choose but call to your memorie *3, 4*	343.22	sure] well assured *3, 4*
		343.23	our] this our *3, 4*
341.15	part] rapt *4*	343.24	her,] hee, *4*
341.17	And] *3*; An[ ] *2*	343.24	in] within *3, 4*
341.18	all meanes] by all the best meanes *3, 4*	343.26	were come] came *3, 4*
		343.27	downe] downe before him *3, 4*
341.19	but] But yet *3, 4*	343.28	such] such a *3, 4*
341.19	were bestowed] were lost, and bestowed *3, 4*	343.31	and thou] that thou *3, 4*
		343.33	her] is *3, 4*
341.19	woulde receyue no] would not receyue any *3, 4*	343.36	presence] *3*; prsence *2*
		343.36	solemnized] solemnizes *4*
341.25	the Turke] this cursed Turk *3, 4*	343.43	her what] or what *4*

344.4	maruailous] most *3, 4*	347.40	twaine] two *4*
344.5	such] most *3, 4*	347.42	specially] deerely *4*
344.6	cloth] *3*; bloth *2*	349.15	regard] reward *3*
344.8	demaunding] demanding of *4*	349.20	haplesse] an haplesse *3, 4*
344.12	but] but that *3, 4*	349.22	iniurie] iniure *3, 4*
344.16	of] *3*; om. *2*	349.26	vnhappily] unhappy *4*
344.18	had] he had *3, 4*	349.31	occasions] afflictions *4*
345.5	daily conuersing] being daily conuersant *3*	349.35	creatures] creature *3, 4*
		349.35	meane] meanes *4*
345.5	*Agriola*] the Princesse *Agriola 3*	349.36	him] *3*; his *2*
345.5	had so good knowledge in] *3*; could not so well speake *2*	349.36	passe] trauaile *3, 4*
		350.11	forward] *3*; forword *2*
345.6	Emperor] Emperour himself *3, 4*	350.15	laying] he laying *3, 4*
345.6	because] to the ende *3, 4*	350.16	as] so *3, 4*
345.7	sate downe] sate him downe *3, 4*	351.12	the Gods] his Gods *3, 4*
345.8	her:] her, and beholding her excellent Beauty *3, 4*	351.13	the health] any health *3, 4*
		351.15	his iourney] this iourney *3*
345.13	this] it *3, 4*	351.17	infortunate] unfortunate *4*
345.13	infortunate] vnfortunate *3, 4*	351.23	of her time] in her time *3, 4*
345.17	riches] richnesse *3, 4*	351.28	shee] *3*; hee *2*
345.22	displeasure] his displeasure *3, 4*	351.29	should] would *4*
345.23	sundrie] diuers *3, 4*	351.33	withall] om. *4*
345.26	munificent] manificent *3, 4*	351.34	so] om. *4*
345.27	in] to *3, 4*	351.34	princesses] *4*; princesse *2, 3*
345.30	could] would *4*	351.37	the choyse] choyse *3, 4*
345.31	so] om. *3, 4*	351.37	for] *3*; of *2*
345.36	vertuous and] *3*; vertuousand *2*	352.1	the eare] *3*; t[ ]e eare *2*
346.5	their] the *4*	352.1	turne] *3*; holde *2*
346.6	take] talke *3*	352.3	the Moore] him *4*
346.9	sent he] he sent *4*	352.3	quittance] *3*; quttance *2*
346.17	thy] the *3, 4*	352.4	abashed] Ambushed *3, 4*; Fr. "esbahiz" (P4r; surprised)
346.18	thou] you *4*		
346.29	were] where *4*	352.9	was] might be, *3*
346.40	good] goe *4*	352.9	her] *3*; his *2*
346.41	beyonde] *3*; beyonde beyonde *2*	352.12	braue] braue and comely *3, 4*
347.1	*Mofti*] ED; *Mosti 2, 3, 4*	352.13	high birth] high and Noble byrth *3, 4*
347.1	the royall] *3*; thy royall *2*	352.17	wel pleased] glad *4*
347.18	apoplexie] apoplexies *4*	352.18	Soueraigne] *3*; Saueraigne *2*
347.20	loue passions] *3*; louepassions *2*	352.20	sayd] she said *4*
347.21	thus spake] uttered these speeches *4*	352.24	with] *3*; om. *2*
		352.28	of this world] in this world *4*
347.22	Ah,] O *4*	352.39	should] would *3*
347.24	heard of] ere suffered *4*	353.12	a Hare] the Hare *3, 4*
347.25	thou induced] be perswaded *4*	353.13	life] selfe *3, 4*
347.25	horrible] greevous *4*	353.19	trauayled] trauelled *3*
347.27	desires] desire *4*		
347.40	this] his *3, 4*		

353.29	Kings] Knights *3, 4*; Fr. "Roys" (P5r; *Kings*)	358.5	these] this *4*
353.31	so be] be so *3, 4*	358.6	with conceit] with very conceite *3, 4*
353.39	person] personage *4*	358.7	my] thy *3*
353.39	other] others *4*	358.7	determined] *3*; determindd *2*
354.1	had] *om. 4*	358.10	in] of *3, 4*
354.7	hardy] hardiest *4*	358.21	neuer shall] shall neuer *3, 4*
354.15	not heard or seene] not yet heard nor seene *4*	358.24	so] *3*; *om. 2*
354.16	yet] but *4*	358.24	on] vpon *3, 4*
354.23	perceyue] *3*; peceyue *2*	358.30	people] Subjects *4*
354.25	meane] meanes *3, 4*	358.30	that] *om. 4*
354.33	therefore to content her selfe] desiring her to rest contented *4*	358.33	endow] endowed *3*
		358.35	answered] she answered *4*
354.35	causing] caused *3*; who caused *4*	358.36	maister] Prince *4*
354.41	passe)] *3*; ~∧ *2*	358.42	is there] there *3*; there is *4*
355.2	was] *3*; is *2*	359.1	cease] ease *3, 4*; Fr. "mettra fin" (P7r; *will put an end to*)
355.5	according] *3*; accoridng *2*	359.1	paines] paine *4*
355.6	Gentleman] *3*; Gentlman *2*	359.1	his] *3*; *om. 2*
355.11	to returne] returne *4*	359.3	vnworthie] *3*; worthie *2*
355.20-22	God disposed of him, made fast the doore after him, and with his sworde drawne, and his Mantle wrapped about his arme, went to see how the beasts would deale with him] *om. 4*	359.9	trauailed] trauelled *3*
		359.9	realmes] Dominions *3, 4*; Fr. "Royaumes" (P7r; *realms*)
		359.13	especially] *3*; especiall *2*
		359.15	trie] to trie *3, 4*
		359.17	mine] my *4*
355.29	crennels] ED; creuises *2*	359.18	maruailous] most maruellous *3, 4*
356.9	their] the *4*	360.2	the] *om. 4*
356.14	no better equipped] not better furnished *4*	360.11	so] *om. 3, 4*
		360.11	broken] plighted *4*
356.16	benigne and full of courtesie] so courteous and benigne *4*	360.12	may wee] we may *4*
		360.13	pleasure] *3*; pleasures *2*
357.2	the] *om. 4*	360.14	hence to his owne content] to his content *3, 4*
357.4	dured] endured *3, 4*		
357.9	Moore] *Moorish 4*	360.16	hath] that *3, 4*
357.9	and] *om. 3*	360.31	mourning blacke] Black mourning *4*
357.12	sworne] *om. 4*		
357.12	of whole] to *3*; of *4*	360.32	he was] was he *3, 4*
357.17	King of *Pasmeria*] King *Pasmeria 3*	360.41	so] such *4*
357.21	bountie] *3*; beautie *2*	360.42	consumed hee] he consumed *4*
357.22	neighbour] the neighbouring *4*	360.42	as formall] so formall *3, 4*
357.23	Ambassadours to] Embassadours vnto *3, 4*	361.11	Court] the Court *3, 4*
		361.11	to] *om. 4*
357.28	of] in all *3, 4*	361.20	sate downe] sette downe *3, 4*; Fr. "s'alla seoir" (P8r; *went to sit*)
357.28	young Widdow and rich] yong and rich Widow *4*		
		361.23	deuoire] order *4*
357.38	presuming] she presuming *4*	361.32	greeuous] wretched *4*

361.35	to] as *3*; and *4*		365.6	by iournying] as to goe with me *4*
361.35	be] to be *3, 4*		365.6	with mee] *om. 4*
361.37	in] *om. 3*		365.7	any] any other *3, 4*
361.42	onely] my only *4*		365.9	loued] beloued *3, 4*
362.3	effect] *3*; effects *2*		365.9	these] my *4*
362.3	not be] not to be *4*		365.10	Ladie and vnmaried] unmarried Lady *4*
362.5	surprised] supprised *3*			
362.5	againe] *3;* agaiue *2*		365.10	loue] feruent Loue *3, 4*
362.7	and] *3*; *om. 2*		365.12	shamefaste] shamefac'd *4*
362.16	any] a *4*		365.15	that] *3*; *om. 2*
362.18	no one] none *3, 4*		365.18	*Palmerin*] *Polinarda 3*
362.24	body bee] *3*; bodybee *2*		365.19	that making] therefore made *4*
362.26	that is no iote] that it is not *4*		365.20	*Zephira,*] ED; ~ˏ *2+*
362.33	so] *om. 3, 4*; Fr. "si odoriferante" (P8v; *so odoriferous*)		365.21	and mooued] and being mooued *3, 4*
362.40	most noble] *om. 3, 4*		365.28	now] *om. 3, 4*
362.41	Knight] valiant knight *3, 4*		365.34	*Ardemias*] *3; Ardemia, 2*
363.2	bashfull] *3*; lashfull *2*		365.34	in vnfitte] in an vnfit *3, 4*
363.6	vp] *om. 4*		365.38	otherwise] or otherwise *3, 4*
363.11	will wee] we will *4*		365.42	agreeued] grieved *4*
363.14	and] *om. 4*		365.42	wrong] minde *4*
364.2	*fayre*] *om. 3, 4*		366.2	haue] gaue *3*
364.4	*despight*] *despaire 4*		366.7	any way] euer *3, 4*
364.6	Ladies] fayre Ladyes *3, 4*		366.8	abide in] contain thy selfe within *3, 4*
364.7	the man] the only man *3, 4*			
364.7	they] they both *3, 4*		366.9	of the] *om. 3, 4*; Fr. "quel-qu'vn" (Q1v; *some of the*)
364.7	to haue] aspyring to obtaine *3, 4*			
364.10	Hall] great Hall *3, 4*		366.10	the] such a *3, 4*
364.10	chambers] priuate Chambers *3, 4*		366.24	shee] we *3*
364.11	on] onwards *3, 4*		367.3	my] by *4*
364.14	aduenture] but aduenture *3, 4*		367.8	*louely*] *3; lonely 2*
364.19	Gentlemen] Gentleman *3, 4*; Fr. "Gentilz-hommes" (Q1r; *Gentlemen*)		367.9	recks] wrecks *4*
			367.19	*If*] *3; if 2*
			367.32	hell:] *3*; ~? *2*
364.21	carelesse] *3*; earelesse *2*		368.1	*to rest*] *to the rest 3*
364.27	hap] chance *4*		368.5	*destenied*] *destined 3*
364.32	was woont to visite] continually visited *4*		368.8	euils] *Ils 4*
			368.11	complainte] *3*; complaints *2*
364.32	Princesse] *3;* Prineesse *2*		368.18	next] *3*; nxet *2*
364.36	the wood cow] ED; the wood *2, 3, 4*		368.19	bedde side] Beddes side *3, 4*
			368.21	at] with *4*
364.37	countenaunce] *3*; countnnaunce *2*		368.21	to] into *3, 4*
364.39	of *Leo*] *Leo 4*		368.23	the] those *3, 4*
365.3	Oh] *3*; *om. 2*		368.25	other] others *3, 4*
365.4	you esteeme of mee] I esteeme of you *4*		368.29	to] *3;* lo *2*
			368.34	for] *om. 3, 4*
365.5	deigne] grant *4*			

368.37	cause] case *3*; Fr. "cause" (Q3r; *cause*)	373.4	dissembled not] *3*; dissembled *2*
369.5	for] or *3*; Fr. "car" (Q3r; *for*)	373.6	the meane] meane *3*
369.5	the Woman hath] Women have *4*	373.7	Ambassade] Embassage *3*; Ambassadour *4*
369.6	the effect of her] to effect their *4*	373.8	Ambassadours arriued] Ambassador being arrived *4*
369.8	her from her] them from their *4*	373.9	their] his *4*
369.16	so chaunced] happened so *4*	373.14	iniuried] injured *4*
370.8	that] *3*; the *2*	373.25	come in time] ED; come time *2*; find time *3, 4*
370.9	Armes] arm *3*	373.32	should] would *3*
370.11	commended beyond al other Ladies of the East, the faire *Ardemia* Daughter to the King of *Armenia*] the faire *Ardemia* daughter to the King of *Armenia* commended above all other Ladies of the East *4*	373.35	goodly] a goodly *4*
		373.38	and] but *4*
		373.39	fight] Warre *4*
		374.3	your] the
		374.28	then] thus *3, 4*; Fr. "Puis" (Q5r; *afterwards, then*)
		374.31	*Alchidiana*] *3*, *Aldhidiana 2*
370.13	the Trompe of] *om. 4*	374.37	such] which *3, 4*
370.14	her affecting] *affecting 4*	374.37	famous] infamous *4*
370.18	doubted] feared *4*	374.38	trauelling] trauailing *3, 4*
370.22	complaints] complaint *3, 4*; Fr. "complaintes" (Q3v; *complaints*)	374.40	of such weight] so such weighty *3*; so weighty *4*
370.26	causes] causers *3, 4*; Fr. "causes" (Q3v; *causes*)	375.6	as] according as *3, 4*
		376.3	enterprised] *3*; *eaterprised 2*
370.41	so] *om. 3, 4*; Fr. "tant faucement" (Q3v; *so falsely*)	376.3	*himself*] *himselfe in 3, 4*
		376.9	and] to *4*
371.3	made] had made *3, 4*	376.18	siely] sillie *4*
371.5	ouer] of *3, 4*	376.20	as were] *3*; aswere *2*
371.8	alliaunce] our Alliaunce *3, 4*	376.40	haue] *3*; ~, *2*
371.14	is] is only *3, 4*	377.12	pityed] pittying *3, 4*
371.17	pleasure?] ED; pleasure *2*; pleasures? *3, 4*	377.35	a frollicke] an audacious *4*
		378.4	you haue] haue you *3, 4*
371.24	these vnseemelye speeches ... to make for his aunswere] this aunswer *3, 4*	378.22	recompence] make recompence *3, 4*
		378.26	did not the feare of reproch] *3*; did not feare and reproch *2*
371.24	knewe not] ED; knewe *2*; *om. 3, 4*	378.30	miracle] *3*; miracles *2*
371.28	would let slip such effronted wordes and audacious] would let slip such effronted and audacious words] *3*; should harbour such unchaste imaginations *4*	378.30	haue] hath *4*
		378.32	sometime was fayre] sometimes was the faire *3, 4*
		378.36	that] *3*; as *2*
		378.37	But] *3*; but *2*
371.30	as] that *4*	378.41	selfe] selfe then *3, 4*
371.35	she] *3*; wee *2*	378.42	be] is *4*
372.1	perceiuing] soone perceiuing *3, 4*	379.2	Soldane,] Soldane of him, *3*; *Soldane*) of him *4*
372.8	all] *om. 3, 4*; Fr. "tout" (Q4r; *all*)		
372.13	thee] him *4*		
372.15	that] as *3, 4*		
372.20	couer] recover *4*		

379.5	handes] hand *3*	383.22	my Daughter and mee hee hath sheelded] he hath shielded my Daugther and me *4*
379.7	salutations] salutation *3, 4*		
379.8	had] of enuie had *3, 4*		
379.8	was likewise] likewise was *3, 4*	383.41	onely] *3*; onsly *2*
379.12	wouldest] *om. 3*	384.5	(according] *3*;)~ *2*
379.13	aduertise] aduise *3, 4*	384.5	thus] *om. 3, 4*
379.14	and] *3*; aud *2*	384.8	*Alchidiana*] *3*; *Alchidinia 2*
379.17	doth] also dooth *3, 4*	384.12	and] ED; *om. 2* (word in cw, sig. E1r), *3, 4*
379.28	seeing] seeing that *3, 4*		
379.33	such] *3*; rich *2*	384.15	commonly] publikely *4*
379.42	know this present seruice] have finished this Combat *4*	384.16	your good report] my good name *4*
		384.16	eyther to] *om. 4*
381.2	*Amarano*] *3*; *Armarano 2*	384.16	from your presence for euer] for ever from your presence *4*
381.3	*the great honors*] *of the great Honours which 3, 4*		
		384.17	with open] by their *4*
381.4	the words] of those reportes, *3, 4*	384.19	Princes] *3*; Princesse *2*
381.5	reported] made relation of *3, 4*	384.22	crueltie] cruelties *3, 4*; Fr. "cruauté" (R1r; *cruelty*)
381.5	glad] meruellous glad *3, 4*		
381.6	of so] descended of such *3, 4*	384.33	the cheefe cause of] nothing but *4*
381.6	noble] honourable *4*	384.33	discontent] griefe *4*
381.6	renowned] much renowned *3, 4*	384.34	sufferest me too importunate] art too too cruell *4*
381.20	appointed] appointing *3, 4*		
381.23	shewed] ewed *4*	385.2	grauen] engrauen *3, 4*
381.25	be] *3*; qe *2*	385.6	fiftie] *4*; fiue *2, 3*
381.26	great] high *3, 4*; Fr. "grand" (Q7v; *great*)	385.7	tooke] betooke *3, 4*
		386.4	Remembring] But remembring *4*
381.27	sightly] Knightly *4*	386.5	of] *om. 3*
381.38	the] his *3, 4*	386.8	better meane] more reason *4*
382.6	held] hold *4*	386.35	earst] *om. 4*
382.15	returne] return to *4*	386.35	and] *3*; aud *2*
382.16	ranne] came *3, 4*	386.36	of nature] hearted *4*
382.19	perceyued] perceiving *4*	387.2	ought] owed *4*
382.19	and] *om. 3, 4*	387.4	meane] meanes *4*
382.21	till] vntil *3, 4*	387.7	Monarch or Prince] *3*; Monarce or Princh *2*
382.28	conspyring head] Spring-head *3, 4*		
382.29	be any thing] bee any other thing *3*; is any other thing *4*	387.17	vngratefull] ingratefull *3, 4*
		387.17	pleasure] reason *3, 4*
382.34	this] euen this *3, 4*	387.21	these] those *3, 4*
382.41	and] *om. 3*	387.28	wished] good *4*
382.43	gate of the Pallace] Pallace Gate *4*	387.28	effect] *om. 3*
383.5	be] by *3, 4*	387.29	beautifie] Beauty *3*
383.9	your] thy *3, 4*	387.36	in the meane while] *om. 4*
383.11	holpe] help'd *4*	387.37	gracious] most gracious *3, 4*
383.16	forced] enforced *3, 4*	387.40	vnderstand more] haue more knowledge *3, 4*
383.17	hee] they *3, 4*; Fr. "il" (Q8v; *he*)		
383.20	so] *om. 3, 4*	387.41	gather] can gather *3, 4*
		387.41	knowledge] vnderstanding *3, 4*

388.2	shee] we *4*		394.32	so] as *4*
388.4	perceyuing] perceived *4*		394.38	a] *om.* *3, 4*
388.5	and in this sort] And so in this manner *3*; Ann so leaving her *4*		394.42	owe I] I owe *3, 4*
			395.6	sollicited] *3*; solliced *2*
388.7	his Chamber] his owne Chamber *4*		395.9	so] *om.* *4*
388.10	present, humblie] in presence, most humbly *3*; in presence, humbly *4*		395.18	that] the *3, 4*
			395.23	trauails] trauells *3, 4*
			395.25	of] *3*; of of *2*
388.11	requesting] requested *4*		395.29	as] and *4*
388.12	nor] neyther *3, 4*		396.2	*Amaranoes*] *3*; ~, *2*
388.16	euen] ever *4*		396.3	*killed.*] *3*; ~˄ *2*
389.5	Now] But now *4*		396.4	Following] But following *4*
389.7	that hee had] having *4*		396.4	historie, the] Historie of the *3*
389.11	Taborlanes] *4*; Toborlanes *2, 3*		396.4	*Balisarca*, Lieuetenant] *Balisarca*, who beeing Lieutenant *3, 4*
389.15	expected time] wished *4*			
389.15	*Alchidiana*] *3*; *Alchidinia 2*		396.5	of the] of all the *3, 4*
389.15	likewise] *om.* *4*		396.6	go] to goe *3, 4*
389.17	deuoutly] dearely *4*		396.7	Villages] Villages along the Countrey *3, 4*
389.22	to] for *3, 4*			
389.26	you] as you *4*		396.7	on the] vpon the *3, 4*
389.35	fauours and courtesies] curtesies and favours *4*		396.11	night] Night long *3, 4*
			396.12	making] digging and making *3, 4*
390.3	Thus speake] This spake *3*; This speake *4*		396.12	occasions] actions *4*
			396.20	reuenge] be reuenged of *3, 4*
390.9	this] the *3, 4*		396.21	Forces] *3*; men *2*
390.17	meane] meanes *4*		396.26	the] *om.* *3, 4*
390.19	his] the *3, 4*		396.37	their message beeing deliuered] they delivered their Message *4*
390.28	his] this *3, 4*			
390.31	these] the		396.37	who were] being *4*
390.36	to our] of our *3, 4*		396.40	euen] *om.* *4*
391.7	personages] personaged *4*		396.40	for that] Because *4*
391.21	endeuours] *3*; endeouurs *2*		397.6	his] well his *3, 4*
391.30	deuise] *3*; *om.* *2*		397.6	where in] *3*; wherin *2*
392.13	seruice] seruices *3, 4*		397.12	then] *3*; Then *2*
392.20	meane] meanes *4*		397.12	thy Brother had when] thy false Brother when *3, 4*
393.10	and] *3*; ond *2*			
393.22	your] you *4*		397.13	Wherefore] *3*; Whereore *2*
393.29	detracted] *3*; detract *2*		397.13	be] wilt prooue *3, 4*
393.29	though] although *3, 4*		397.14	thee] thee to bee *3, 4*
393.31	bad] did bid *4*		397.18	*Orinello*] *3*; *Orinella 2*
394.4	young] *3*; *om.* *2*		397.24	*Palmerin*] *3*; *Palmeriu 2*
394.4	conferring] conferred *3, 4*		397.25	them,] *3*; ~. *2*
394.5	greefe] great griefe *3, 4*		397.27	hee had brought with] following after *4*
394.20	it bee] shee bee *3, 4*			
394.21	albeit I died therefore] though it cost my life *4*		397.32	should] would *4*
			397.32	being] *om.* *4*
394.26	albeit] yet *4*			

397.33 which hee had] which had *3*; with *4*
397.34 would] it would *4*
397.36 body] *3*; boyd *2*
397.36 moouing] remoouing *3, 4*
398.1 other] others *4*
398.3 *Flaminius*] *3*; *Elaminius 2*
398.6 manie] *3*; manie *turned "e" in 2*
398.11 that] this *3, 4*
398.12 Brethrens] Brothers *3, 4*
398.13 in] into *4*
398.17 Brother] late Brother *3, 4*
398.28 Armour] Armours *3, 4*; Fr. "harnoys" (R6v; armor)
398.30 as you] *3*; asyou *2*
398.32 summoning] *3*; smmoning *2*
398.34 dislodge] dislodge from *4*
398.35 so] *om. 4*
398.35 departure] flight *4*
398.41 shamefull] most shamefull *3, 4*
398.42 chaunce] great chaunce *3, 4*
398.42 *Gramiell* came] was *Gramiell* come *3*
398.43 among] *3*; a | mong *2*
398.43 vnderstanding] vnderstanding how *3, 4*
399.1 alarme] Alarum *3, 4*
399.9 as] as that *3, 4*
399.9 *Gramiell*] When *Gramiell 3, 4*
399.11 running] *3*; runnning *2*
399.14 greatly] highly *3, 4*
399.14 enemie] *3*; eneme *2*
399.16 cutte] cut off *3, 4*
399.23 him they hemde] they hem'd him *4*
399.33 ouertrauailed] ouertrauelled *3*
400.2 *of*] *3*; *ef 2*
400.5 Immediatlie] Now suddainly *4*
400.11 kinsman] *3*; kiseman *2*
400.15 espiall] espials *3, 4*; Fr. "vn Espion" (R7r; *lookout*)
400.19 he ioyned the Kings power] the King joyned his power *4*
400.20 resistaunce] *3*; resistanuce *2*
400.21 greeuouslye] *3*; greeuonslye *2*
400.21 enquired] required *3*; demanded *4*; Fr. "s'enquist" (R7r; *inquired*)
400.23 The] This *3, 4*
400.25 the rest] all the rest *3, 4*
400.25 Townes] Cittyes and Townes *3, 4*
400.26 by] *3*; of *2*
400.30 opened] *3*; open *2*
400.31 read] hearing *4*
400.31 the Soldane] he *4*
400.33 the] *om. 4*
400.34 after] when *4*
400.36 rewarded the Messenger so well] so well rewarded the Messenger *3, 4*
401.1 forwarde next] forwards the nexte *3, 4*; the *a* in "forwarde" is printed upside down in *2*
401.2 in readines] in a readinesse *3, 4*
401.3 all] *om. 3, 4*
401.5 And] And when *3*; But when *4*
401.13 haue] *3*; *om. 2*
401.16 had doone] did *4*
401.18 which] who *4*
401.21 could passe but two] could passe two *3*; could not passe two *4*; Fr. "qu'on n'y pouuoit passer que deux à deux" (R7v; *that it could not be crossed but two at a time*)
401.22 they woulde] the should *4*
401.22 tops] top *4*
401.27 climbe] clime *3*
401.28 holes] *3*; wholes *2*
401.42 hast with thine owne hand] with thine owne hand hast *3, 4*
402.5 to thy] at thy *4*
402.6 to whom] vnto whom *3, 4*
402.10 them] him *4*
402.15 gaue hee] he gave *4*
402.16 losse] losses *3, 4*; Fr. "perte" (R8r; *loss*)
402.17 raunsome] *3*; "*r*" *printed upside down in 2*
402.18 all] *om. 4*
402.18 rest] repose *3, 4*
402.20 wearied] ouer-wearyed *3, 4*
402.21 trauaile] trauell *3*
402.21 prouided for] well prouided, both for *3, 4*
402.22 his Freende *Olorico*] his good Friend the Prince *Olorico 3, 4*

Historical Collation

403.3	*meane*] meanes *3, 4*		408.18	ground] Earth *3, 4*
403.5	Here] *3*; Hhere *2*		408.23	they] *3*; thy *2*
403.5	how] how that *3, 4*		408.23	*Alchidiana*] *3*; *Alchidinia 2*
403.6	rich] moste rich *3, 4*		408.31	noted] ere noted *3*
403.7	was] was made *3*; being made *4*		408.32	when] and straight *4*
403.8	caused] inforced *3, 4*		408.34	more] done *3*
403.9	and] and that *3, 4*		408.36	*Phrygian*] *Phrygians 3, 4*
403.9	own] *3*; onwn *2*		408.42	all] *om. 4*
403.24	so] was exceeding *4*		408.42	*Alchidiana*] *3*; *Alchidinia 2*
403.25	as could be deuised, in that] because *4*		409.3	so] as *4*
			409.7	faith] sooth *3, 4*; Fr. "foy" (S2v; *faith*)
403.25	meane] meanes *3, 4*			
403.26	the Prince] *om. 3, 4*		409.8	honest] curteous *4*
403.40	not] *3*; not not *2*		409.8	vertuous] *3*; vertuons *2*
404.12	commaundement] *3*; commaundemente *2*		409.11	other] others *3, 4*
			409.13	feigning not to] *3*; feigning to *2*
404.13	ioyned] enioyned *3, 4*		409.21	*Alchidiana*] *3*; *Achidinia 2*
404.14	paine] paines *4*		409.28	that] *om. 3, 4*
404.22	Cupboorde] faire Cupboord *3, 4*		409.30	indiscreetlie] vndiscreetly *3, 4*
404.26	dare say] dare well say *3, 4*		409.32	my] *om. 3, 4*
404.28	commaund] her command *4*		409.37	beares] beare *3*
404.28	Princes] *3*; Princesse *2*		409.41	they] then *3*
404.30	beganne] she beganne *3, 4*		410.14	your] this your *3, 4*
404.38	to] *om. 3, 4*		410.15	good] a good *3, 4*
405.4	in the meane] in meane *3, 4*		410.15	readie] being ready *4*
405.9	Mother] *3*; Motber *2*		410.16	aboard] *3*; abroad *2*
405.14	As] And *4*		410.20	should] would *3, 4*
405.24	just like] ED; so well, as *2, 3, 4*		410.33	you] *3*; mee *2*
405.40	bedde] bende *3*		410.34	so] *om. 3*; but *4*
405.43	should] would *3, 4*		410.34	would] wouldst *4*
406.1	*Yseul*] *3*; *Ysuel 2*		410.36	cause] reason *3, 4*
406.4	fantasie] fansie *3, 4*		410.36	for in] Because *4*
406.7	Doost] Doest *3, 4*		411.2	loued] beloued *3, 4*
406.12	iniurie] *3*; iuiurie *2*		411.4	to] *3*; of *2*
406.25	carriage] Carryages *3, 4*; Fr. "bagage" (S1v; *carriage*)		411.4	if I would] should I *4*
			411.7	make] cause *3, 4*
406.27	*Palmerin*] Syr *Palmerin 3, 4*		411.8	leaue the] forsake this *3, 4*
406.33	you so small a request] your small request *3, 4*		411.9	each one] him *4*
			411.10	dignities,] both Dignities˄ *3*
406.41	to] into *3*		411.11	do you] doo *3, 4*
406.41	Countrey] owne Citie *4*		411.11	all] *om. 4*
407.2	*Palmendos*] *Palmerendos 3, 4*		411.11	feare not] *om. 4*
407.8	his deeds as yet] as yet his deeds *4*		411.12	So well could *Palmerin* dissemble the matter] *Palmerin* dissembled the matter so well *4*
408.5	Greatlie] Now greatly *4*			
408.6	by] through *4*			
408.7	where] whence *4*		411.13	somewhat better] well *4*
408.9	of] to *3, 4*		411.13	of her] *om. 4*

411.15	libertie] theyr libertie *3*	414.11	to the] in the *3*
411.15	notwithstanding] *om. 4*	414.17	Soldane] Soldans *3*
411.16	this] *3*; his *2*	414.22	thence] from thence *3, 4*
411.17	commanded] gave *4*	414.33	then] but *4*
412.4	Quickly *Palmerin*] *3*; Quickly *Palmein 2*; *Palmerin* quickly *4*	414.34	worst] best *4*
		414.36	or] *3*; and *2*
412.4	to] for to *3, 4*	414.37	*Palmerin* embracing] *3*; *Palemrin* embraicng *2*
412.4	desiring] *3*; desiriug *2*		
412.5	to make] to the end they might make *3, 4*	414.39	Armes] *2(b)*; Armex *2(a)*
		415.4	Merchants] ED; ~, *2, 3, 4*
412.5	vessel] Vessells *3, 4*; Fr. "nauire" (S3v; *ship*)	415.10	*Palmerin*).] ED; *Palmerin*)ˬ *2*; *Palmerin*?) ˬ *3, 4*
412.7	which] who formerly *3, 4*	415.12	became] is become *4*
412.10	long] of a long *3*; of long *4*	415.14	Emperour] *3*; Emperous *2*
412.12	answered] thus answered *3, 4*	415.17	receiue] sustaine *3, 4*; Fr. "receüra" (S5r; *will receive*)
412.12	of] borne in *3, 4*		
412.17	other] others *3, 4*	415.20	losse] *3*; loue *2*
412.20	aboard] *3*; abroad *2*	415.21	meane] meanes *4*
412.21	after] *3*; ofter *2*	415.23	the search] search *3, 4*
412.24	great greefe] great griefe and sorrow *3*; griefe and sorrow *4*	415.26	Knight] Knightes *3, 4*; Fr. "Cheualier" (S5r; *Knight*)
412.26	soone] and soone *4*	415.32	for] onely for *3, 4*
412.26	lamentable] lamenting *3, 4*	415.37	kept] hee kept *3, 4*
412.30	then] *3*; my *2*	416.5	companions,] Companyons, and most woorthy Knightes, *3, 4*
412.30	ioy] *3*; my ioy *2*		
412.31	immediate] my *4*	416.6	castle] strong Castell *3, 4*
412.35	vnable was hee] he had bin unable *4*	416.6	foure leagues] about foure myles distante *3, 4*; Fr. "lieuës" (S5v; *leagues*)
412.36	seeing] *3*; feeling *2*		
413.10	night] *3*; neght *2*	416.7	to] for *4*
413.14	set] *om. 4*	416.8	melancholy] melancholie and sadnesse *3, 4*
413.15	meane] meanes *4*		
413.15	Christians] *3*; Christans *2*	416.8	sonne] beloued Sonne *3, 4*
413.24	strayed] *3*; strained *2*	416.9	shadowing] vnder pretence of shadowing *3, 4*
413.26	that] how that *3, 4*		
413.26	any] *om. 4*	416.11	tydings] certaine tydings *3, 4*
413.26	feare] there *3*; Fr. "paour" (S4r; *fear*)	416.11	had] *om. 3, 4*
		416.11	trauailed] trauelled *3*
413.29	eight hundred] ED; eight hundred thousand *2, 3*; eight thousand *4*	416.12	the] that the *3, 4*
		416.14	two] *om. 4*
		416.15	abide] Lodge *3, 4*
413.31	choler] anger *4*	416.15	little] homely *3, 4*
413.31	much] *om. 4*	416.16	that] which *3, 4*
413.32	and they] bidding them *4*	416.27	fauours] *3*; fanours *2*
413.38	things] *3*; ihings *2*	416.29	who] which *3, 4*
414.3	request of any] *om. 4*	416.34	assistaunce] *3*; assurance *2*
414.6	now] *3*; know *2*	416.34	his] off his *3, 4*

416.37	these] those *3, 4*		421.16	thou] *3*; thon *2*
416.38	which] who *3, 4*		421.20	sette] se- *4*
416.42	more then a] a good *4*		422.1	whose] *3*; whote *2*
416.42	affaires] like affaires *4*		422.6	Armie was] *3*; Armiewas *2*
417.5	you] *om. 4*		422.12	of] *om. 4*
417.5	this] with this *3*		422.16	Califfes] *3*; Cailiffes *2*
417.8	knowe] knew *3*		422.24	despight] in despight *3, 4*
417.9	if] it *3*		422.29	*Arabes*] *3*; *Arabies 2*
417.10	contentment.] *4*; ~? *2, 3*		422.37	sallie] saile *3, 4*
417.12	thy] my *4*		422.38	sight] *3*; fight *2*
417.15	of] *3*; *om. 2*		423.6	*Griana*] *3*; *Oriana 2*
417.15	meane] meanes *4*		423.14	now] not *4*
417.19	faire] the faire *3, 4*		424.2	his Cozin *Frenato*] *Frenato* his
417.19	vnfortunately] *3*; vnfortunate *2*			Cozen *4*
417.19	heard] I heard *4*		424.4	in] to *3, 4*
418.5	be] *om. 3*		424.15	hee was] *3*; heewas *2*
418.10	their] her *4*		424.21	without] *3*; with out *2*
418.18	can] shall *3, 4*		424.25	caped] scaped *3, 4*
418.21	speeches] *3*; speeche *2*		424.34	the] *3*; *om. 2*
418.22	the] all the *3, 4*		424.36	remembred] *3*; remembring *2*
418.25	the more] more *3, 4*		424.40	swoune] swound *4*
418.29	Mistresse] deere Mistresse *3, 4*		424.42	Tower of] Tower at *3, 4*
418.33	I] *om. 3, 4*		425.1	the] her *3, 4*
418.40	of] *om. 4*		425.3	*Frenato*] *3*; *Frenata 2*
419.2	comming] good comming hither *3, 4*		425.21	of] *om. 3, 4*
419.5	his desire, woulde trifle no further time, but entred] *om. 3, 4*		425.32	greefe] griefe of minde *3, 4*
			425.34	twentie yeeres] for twenty yeeres long *3, 4*
419.6	angerly] angrily *3*		425.41	doe] one *3, 4*
419.12	more)] ED; ~ˬ *2*; ~,) *3, 4*		426.1	to] now to *3, 4*
419.15	saide] thus saide *3, 4*		426.5	make] cause *3, 4*
419.18	seeke you foorth] haue sought you out *3, 4*		426.14	talked] were talking *3, 4*
			426.22	thy] shy *3*
419.18	haue] *om. 4*		426.25	swoune] swound *4*
419.18	trauaile] Trauell *3, 4*		426.31	attended] attending *3, 4*
419.21	sometime] Sometimes *3, 4*		426.40	quoth] said *3, 4*
419.22	bee] haue *3, 4*		426.41	vnfortunate] infortunate *3*
419.28	such] *3*; sueh *2*		426.42	it is] is it *3*
419.43	seemed] thought *4*		427.6	daunger] present danger *3, 4*
420.8	incessantly shee] she incessantly *4*		427.10	him] *3*; htm *2*
420.8	his] *3*; *om. 2*		427.23	is] yet *3*; shall *4*
420.20	Princesse] ED; Prince *2, 3, 4*		427.23	to] *om. 4*
421.6	The] Now the *4*		427.24	drawing] drawing out *3, 4*
421.11	that came, hee could heare no tidings of *Palmerins* Carrick:] *om. 4*		427.26	this] the *4*
			427.29	companie] whole companie *3, 4*
			427.32	and] and then *3, 4*
421.15	lucklesse] a lucklesse *4*		427.33	I] *3*; I will *2*

427.34	hazard] should hazard *3, 4*		433.6	excuse] *3*; excnse *2*
427.36	deathes.] *3*; ~∧ *2*		433.9	enforced] *3*; enforce *2*
427.38	nobilitie] Noblenesse *4*		433.12	mee his] *3*; meehis *2*
428.6	must you] you must *4*		433.18	honourable] *3*; hrnourable *2*
429.3	taken.] taken prisoner. *3, 4*		433.21	meane] means *4*
429.6	sorrowfull] sadde sorrowfull *3*; sad and sorrowfull *4*		433.22	iealousie] *3*; iealousiie *2*
			433.29	this] which *3, 4*
429.6	misfortunes] seuerall misfortunes *3*; severally misfortunes *4*		434.5	impute] *3*; im pute *2*
			434.11	impudencie] impudence *3, 4*
429.8	that] onely that *3, 4*		434.16	such infamous] *3*; with infamons *2*
429.9	Knights] worthy Knightes *3, 4*		434.20	caused] brought *3, 4*
429.10	while] whiles *3, 4*		434.27	innocence] innocencie *3, 4*
429.12	sake] fake *3*		434.32	occasions] occasion *4*
429.13	vnfortunate] infortunate *3, 4*		434.36	good] great *3, 4*
429.18	mine] my *3, 4*		434.41	iniustice] *3*; iniurie *2*
429.20	but] *om. 3, 4*		435.1	dares] dare *3, 4*
429.23	loyaltie] great loyaltie *3, 4*		435.3	ye] you *4*
429.24	sometime] sometimes *3, 4*		435.6	then] *om. 4*
429.25	note] iote *3, 4*; Fr. "note" (T2v; note)		435.9	ye] you *4*
			435.12	defence] defende *3, 4*
430.18	*Constantinople*] *3*; *Constantiople 2*		435.13	defence] *3*; defende *2*
430.20	strength] owne strength *3, 4*		435.33	Challengers] *3*; Challenger *2*
430.29	the Ambassade] commission of the same Embassage *3, 4*		435.34	these] those *4*
			436.3	his] *om. 3, 4*
430.36	companie (such was her greefe to come before her Parents), shee] ED; companie, such was her greefe to come before her Parents, as shee *2, 3, 4*		436.5	presume] willingly presume *3, 4*
			436.6	her] her owne *3, 4*
			436.6	faithfulnesse] trusty faithfulnesse *3, 4*
			436.6	shee would suffer] that shee would permit or suffer *3, 4*
430.41	yet] and yet *3, 4*		436.8	such trust] especiall charge *3, 4*
431.2	false and most shamefull] moste false and shamefull *3, 4*		436.11	talke] Familiar talke *3, 4*
			436.15	to] vnto *3, 4*
431.2	aduise] good aduise *3*		436.30	yee] you *4*
431.3	Princes] *3*; Princesse *2*		436.35	ye] you *4*
431.11	must] maist *4*		436.42	meane] meanes *3, 4*
431.21	punishment] *3*; puuishment *2*		437.10	mine] my *4*
431.29	Princes] *3*; Prince *2*		437.14	I perceiue] may I well perceyue *3, 4*
431.35	of] to *3, 4*		437.19	*Aurora,*] *4*; *Aurora*∧ *2, 3*
432.7	to be] *3*; tobe *2*		437.20	prouide] provided *4*
432.13	of them] to them *3, 4*		437.23	meane] means *4*
432.14	seeke] *3*; speake *2*		437.28	till] vntill *3, 4*
432.21	you] *3*; me *2*		437.29	you,] yee, and *3*; you, and *4*
432.31	out nowe] now out *3, 4*		437.30	yee] you *3, 4*
432.31	tribulation] tribulations *3, 4*		437.32	this] *3*; his *2*
432.35	concerneth] *3*; cencerneth *2*		437.34	leaue] leaves *4*
433.2	thou] thee *4*		437.43	trauaile] trauell *3, 4*
433.3	of] to *3, 4*; Fr. "de" (T4r; *of*)			

438.1	luckie] good lucky *3, 4*	442.37	clamours] clamour *3, 4*
438.13	for] to *4*	442.38	saued] *3*; sauled *2*
438.18	ambushed] in Embuscado *3, 4*	443.6	who] whom *4*
438.19	wee] he *4*	443.16	inconueniences] inconuenience *3, 4*
438.23	hee] *om. 3, 4*	443.21	two] the two *4*
438.27	faire] *3*; ~, *2*	443.24	will] *om. 3, 4*
438.35	Monarchie] whole Monarchie *3, 4*	443.29	holpe] helpe *3*; helped *4*
438.42	trauailed] trauelled *3, 4*	443.29	brought] she brought *3, 4*
438.43	greefe] griefes *3, 4*; Fr. "mal" (T6v; *pain*)	443.32	would] should *3, 4*
		443.33	trauaile] trauell *3, 4*
439.8	offendeth] much offendeth *3, 4*	443.34	many] manifolde *3, 4*
439.13	courtesies] louing Courtesies *3*; lossing Curtesies *4*	443.37	Chamber] *3*; Chamer *2*
		443.37	or] *3*; of *2*
439.14	each of other] of eache other *3, 4*	443.42	he] *3*; be *2*
439.15	Ladder] Ladders *3, 4*	444.22	happie] an happy *3, 4*
440.2	*departed*] *delivered 4*	444.28	*Crenus*] *Grenus 3, 4*
440.2	to] *unto 4*	444.35	there] then *4*
440.7	into] to *3, 4*	444.37	debonaire] *3*; debonarie *2*
440.9	suddainly] vpon a sudden *3, 4*	444.42	sende] *3*; sennde *2*
440.9	by manie darke] with many darksome *3, 4*	444.43	beeing] bee *3*
		445.6	yee] you *4*
440.10	and rayne beganne] *om. 3, 4*	446.6	*Frysol*] *3*; *Ffysol 2*
440.11	rested] sheltred *3, 4*; Fr. "arrestez" (T7r; *stopped*)	446.7	speedie] his speedy *3, 4*
		446.8	friendes] new Friends *3, 4*
440.14	desirous] being desirous *3, 4*	446.9	as] *3*; and *2*
440.19	At] And *4*	446.9	at] *om. 4*
440.23	thou] that thou *3, 4*	446.11	to the Cittie] to her Fathers Court, to the Cittie *3, 4*
440.30	made] had made *3, 4*		
440.32	then] more then *3, 4*	446.14	companions.] *3*; ~, *2*
440.36	comming] *om. 3, 4*	446.14	in] at *3, 4*
440.41	neerer] more neerer *3*; more neere *4*	446.21	whereto] *4*; where to *2*; where too *3*
		446.21	meane] means *4*
441.13	bide] abide *3, 4*	446.32	matter is] matters are *4*
441.26	the] this *3, 4*	447.1	spake.] *3*; ~, *2*
441.26	my] *3*; mn *2*	447.3	trauailed] trauelled *3, 4*
441.26	brethren] Brothers *4*	447.4	(so] *3*; ^~ *2*
441.31	the] his *3, 4*	447.9	reuiued] *3*; receiued *2*
441.31	villainous] *3*; vallainous *2*	447.15	enterprise] *3*; enrerprise *2*
441.41	these] the *3, 4*	447.19	then] *om. 3, 4*
442.1	very] vere *4*	447.33	see] *om. 3*; to *4*
442.4	this] that *3, 4*	447.37	may you] you may *3, 4*
442.11	Mountaines] Mountaine *3*	447.43	vsed] entertained *3, 4*
442.12	fiue] fine *3*; Fr. "cinq" (T7v; *five*)	448.7	thy] *om. 3*
		448.8	verye] carelesse *3, 4*
442.16	his] their *4*	448.15	thou art now] now thou art *4*
442.26	what] that *3, 4*	448.23	deserues] deserue *3*
442.35	tende] extend *3, 4*	448.24	if] it *4*
442.36	heard] hearing *4*		

448.26	*Tarisius*] *3*; *Tarsius 2*	457.25	violentlie] *3*; violatelie *2*
448.35	as] as that *3, 4*	458.1	Knight] Prince *3, 4*; Fr. "Cheual-ier" (V6r; *knight*)
448.38	*Florendos*] *Florendoes 3*		
449.2	ye] you *4*	458.3	minde] mindes *4*
449.7	*Frysoll*)] *3*; ~, *2*	458.4	hope] dare *3, 4*; Fr. "j'espere" (V6r; *I hope*)
449.13	come] *3*; ccme *2*		
449.18	through] throughout *3, 4*	458.23	Chirurgions] *3*; Chirugions *2*
449.19	vertues] *3*; vertuous *2*	458.26	this] his *4*
449.22	as] as so *3, 4*	458.29	breake] to breake *3, 4*
449.29	so] such *3, 4*	458.29	comeliest] goodlyest *4*
450.3	two] the two *3, 4*	458.29	sawe] beheld *4*
450.5	hath beene] bin *3, 4*	458.33	me] *om. 4*
450.11	Prince.] ED; ~? *2, 3, 4*	459.9	some hope of loue] *3*; such hope of her loue *2*
450.27	him to] him but to *3, 4*		
450.27	two] *3*; tooo *2*	459.28	occasioned] *4*; accasioned *2*; accustomed *3*
450.29	price] pride *4*		
450.32	hast learned] haue *3, 4*	460.10	through] throughout *3, 4*
450.38	assurance] the assurance *4*	460.30	that] *3*; th[ ]at *2*
451.4	*meane*] *meanes 3, 4*	460.33	double] doubly *4*
451.4	Queene] the Queene *4*	461.7	*Palmerins*] *3*; *Plamerins 2*
451.6	the Hall] the sumptous Hall *3, 4*	461.11	thy] the *4*
		461.11	wee my] with me *4*
451.8	themselues] themselues, for performance of the Action vndertaken *3, 4*	461.17	on horsebacke] to horsebacke *3, 4*
		462.6	*Olorico* and *Frysoll*] *Frisoll* and *Olorico 4*
451.13	eldest] eldest of them *3, 4*		
451.17	ye] you *4*	462.10	very] *om. 4*
451.17	ye] you *4*	462.18	eldest] elder *3, 4*
451.39	thy slaunder] the slander *4*	462.26	not] nor *3, 4*
452.9	this] *3*; his *2, 4*	462.30	forget] consent *4*
452.12	Duke of] *om. 3*; Duke *4*	462.34	and] *3*; *om. 2*
452.21	Ladye.] *3*; ~ˬ *2*	463.3	Brother] *3*; Brethren *2*
453.4	trauaile] trauell *3, 4*	463.10	discoursed] discouered *3, 4*
453.17	aduersaries] *3*; adnersaries *2*	463.15	trauailed] trauelled *3, 4*
453.19	Duke] *3*; Dnke *2*	463.32	trauaile] trauell *3, 4*
453.32	of] ED; *om. 2, 3, 4*	463.34	the] *om. 3, 4*
454.2	happens] happinesse *3*; happened *4*	463.36	the Court] our Court *3, 4*
		463.41	you] ye *3, 4*
455.12	in] into *3, 4*	464.7	happy] *3*; gracious *2*
455.18	we] on *4*	464.9	should] would *3, 4*
455.22	giue] to giue *3, 4*	464.13	sounded] founded *3*
455.23	trauailed] trauelled *3, 4*	464.40	that] as *3, 4*
456.13	wounds] wound *3*	465.6	his Realme] this Realme *4*
457.3	Notwithstanding] *3*; Norwithstanding *2*	466.18	of whom] whereof *3, 4*
		466.33	*Gerrard*] *3*; *Cerrard 2*
457.3	reuerent] reuerend *3, 4*	466.38	for] to *3, 4*
457.6	account] count *4*	466.39	will] *3*; well *2*
457.12	for her] of her *3, 4*	467.7	fines] tyres *4*
457.17	discourse] discouer *4*		

467.8	Paris] ED; ~, 2, 3, 4		476.16	Prince] Princes 3; Fr. "Prince" (X5r; Prince)
467.25	is it] it is 4		477.9	garments] vestures 3, 4
467.25	nurriture] nurture 3, 4		477.10	But] And 3, 4
467.32	requited] repaied 3, 4		477.16	Patriarche] 3; Patriache 2
468.1	intermedle] intermingle 4		477.24	sorts] sort 3, 4
468.10	likewise] 3; iikewise 2		477.28	consequently the] 3; consequent-lythe 2
468.16	Frysoll] 3; Erysoll 2		477.29	Marquesses] 3; Marqusses 2
468.19	Tryumphe] 3; Tryumyhe 2		478.23	to] vnto 3, 4
469.3	fathers] 3; ~, 2		478.31	Armed] to be Armed 3, 4
469.16	is] in 3		478.38	other] others 3, 4
469.22	oppressing] oppression 3, 4		478.42	with] 3; wiih 2
469.23	not able] vnable 3, 4		478.43	see] know 3, 4
470.7	Ambassade] Embassage 3, 4		479.1	in his companie] companie 3; afterward 4
470.23	his] hie 4		479.7	them] him 3, 4
470.42	my Lorde] my of Lord 3		479.7	cast] cast off 3, 4
471.9	a] om. 3, 4		479.8	spurres] the spurres 3, 4
471.15	this] 3; his 2; that 4		479.10	holde] fast holde 3, 4
472.2	at] in 3, 4		479.21	was] 3; wss 2
472.6	Ambassade] Embassage 3, 4		479.30	your] 3; yonr 2
472.8	came] they came 3, 4		479.31	this] his 4
472.13	you] ye 3, 4		479.33	my] 3; me 2
472.14	you] your 3, 4		479.34	especially] 3; especially with turned "a" in 2
472.16	aboord] 3; abroade 2		479.36	Palmerin] 3; Palmrin 2
472.16	away] 3; a way 2		479.39	yee] you 4
472.17	expected] suspected 3, 4		480.13	go] om. 4
472.26	afterward] 3; afterwrd 2		480.18	such] 3; suih 2
472.41	to the King] 3; om. 2		481.7	followed] he followed 4
473.1	trauaile] trauel 3, 4		481.9	beheld] seen 4
473.13	concerning] 3; considering 2		481.9	not] ED; om. 2, 3, 4
473.20	Nor] 3; Now 2		481.15	eyed] viewed 4
473.27	haue] hath 3, 4		481.21	Netrydes.] 3; ~ˬ 2
473.27	conuentions] conditions 4		482.1	Apolonio] 3; Apolonia 2
473.28	these] 3; this 2		482.21	imagination] imaginations 3, 4
473.32	But] And 4		484.15	by] 3; vy 2; with 4
473.33	requesteth] requested 3, 4		484.22	sinister] 3; ssnister 2
473.42	whereof] whereas 4		484.22	trauaile] trauell 3
474.9	Lordes] 3; Lorde 2		484.32	depart] part 3, 4
474.11	for] to 4		484.33	exceeded] 3; ~ - 2
474.22	beseemes] beseeming 3, 4		485.13	thine] thy 3, 4
475.19	ye] you 3, 4		485.21	graciously] 3; gracionsly 2
475.22	meane] meanes 4		485.21	Emperour] 3; Emperonr 2
475.24	to] om. 3; by 4		485.27	without] with 3, 4
475.25	though] om. 3, 4		486.5	Arismena] 3; Arismenia 2
476.5	Licena] 3; Cicena 2			
476.9	immortall] famous 4			
476.10	for] on 4			

486.7	the greatest] greatest *3, 4*	491.20	neare] neere to *3, 4*
486.8	I] *om. 3*	491.22	Fischermen] ED; Frenchmen *2, 3, 4*
486.12	I deuoted] *3*; Ideuoted *2*		
486.15	a] *3*; *om. 2*	491.26	of] at *3, 4*
486.30	trauaile] Trauell *3, 4*	491.28	was] thus *3, 4*
486.30	ye] you *4*	491.29	Turkes] Turke *3, 4*; Fr. "Turcz" (Y3v; *Turks*)
486.39	Subiects] *3*; Subiests *2*		
488.3	*Princesse Arismena*] *3*; *Piincesse Arismen 2*	491.31	sometime was] was sometimes *3, 4*
		491.37	so good] so worthy *3*; as worthy *4*
488.4	*the prince*] Prince *4*	491.38	selfe] selues *3, 4*
488.4	*Florendos.*] *3*; ~, *2*	491.38	her] both her *3, 4*
488.6	resigned] *3*; resined *2*	491.40	While] Whiles *3, 4*
488.6	celestiall] *3*; celistiall *2*	491.41	and] *3*; *om. 2*
488.10	discontented] *3*; disconted *2*	492.1	proclamation] *3*; protestation *2*
488.22	but] *3*; But *2*	492.1	could enter] Entred *3, 4*
488.25	meane] means *4*	492.1	haue anie boone of him] obtaine of him any Boone *3, 4*
488.29	trauaile] trauell *3, 4*		
488.34	were] *3*; where *2*	492.3	scaling Ladders] strong Scaling-Ladders *3, 4*
488.34	the Prince] Prince *4*		
488.39	Mother.] *3*; ~, *2*	492.3	sette] raised vp *3, 4*
489.1	ioyfully] *3*; ioyfnlly *2*	492.6	Gate] Gates *3, 4*; Fr. "porte" (Y3v; *gate*)
490.3	*by Olimaell,*] *3*; *by, Olimaell*˄ *2*		
490.3	*of*] *3*; *om. 2*; Fr. "des" (Y2v; *of*)	492.22	this] these *3, 4*
490.5	*Roldin* established] *Roldin* beeing established *3*; Now *Roldin* being established *4*	492.22	whereto] wherewith *3, 4*
		492.32	to returne] returne *3, 4*
		492.42	all] *om. 3, 4*
490.9	sworne the search] sworne theyr endeuors in the search *3, 4*; Fr. "ayans juré la queste de Trineus" (Y2v; *having sworn the search of Trineus*)	493.10	when shee] then he *3*
		493.11	trauell] traiuaile *3*; trauaile *4*
		493.25	Knights of] Knights in *3, 4*
		493.27	Husbande] deere Husband *3, 4*
		493.29	wealth] *3*; health *2*
490.9	mercy] *3*; ~. *2*	493.30	the Damosell] *3*; che Damosell *2*
490.9	winds] Winde *3, 4*	493.37	attended] attained *3*
490.12	went vp on the decke] climbed vp to the maine toppe, *3, 4*; Fr. "monterent sur le tillac" (Y2v; *they went up on the deck*); cf. emendation to 561.10	493.38	on] in *3, 4*
		493.41	with] by *3, 4*
		494.1	denie] *4*; demaund *2, 3*
		494.8	Monarch] Monarchie *3, 4*
		494.17	were] are *4*
490.13	espyed] esyed *4*	494.21	the] *om. 3*
490.16	ye] you *3, 4*	494.28	good] great *3, 4*
490.24	no way there was] no was there war *3*; no way was there *4*	494.28	reason, that to] *3*; reason that *2*
		494.30	these] their *3, 4*
490.25	hem them in] him *3, 4*	494.32	very many] every man *4*
490.33	with] to *3, 4*	494.33	handes] armes *3, 4*; Fr. "mains" (Y5r: *hands*)
490.35	prowesse] valour *4*		
491.3	Christians?] *3*; ~¿ *2*	494.35	Tyrants] *3*; Traitours *2*
491.5	and] *3*; snd *2*	495.4	thou] *om. 3*

495.5	captiue] captaine *3*; Fr. "captif" (Y5r; *captive*)	500.1	Melancholie] melancholike *3, 4*
		500.4	strengths] *3*; strength *2*
495.10	his] this *3, 4*	500.7	*Maulerino] 3; Mulerino 2*
495.12	departed] *3*; de parted *2*	500.10	quiet] good quiet *3, 4*
495.20	highnesse] highne *3*; high *4*	500.14	Realme] Kingdome *3, 4*
495.34	disloyally] *4*; dissloyally *2*; disloyall ye *3*	500.14	practised] cunningly practised *3, 4*
		500.15	purpose] mischieuous purpose *3, 4*
495.37	perfection] protection *3, 4*	500.16	Princesse] Princesses *3, 4*
496.6	executed] *3*; excuted *2*	500.16	woulde kill] would but condiscend to kill *3, 4*
496.9	I do] doo I *3, 4*		
496.13	conditionally] conditionall ye, *3, 4*	500.17	fiftie] *3*; thirtie *2*
496.15	moitie] mostie *3*; most *4*	500.25	throate] *3*; thraote *2*
496.15	dominions] my dominions *4*	500.35	pause] pursue *3, 4*
496.16	my] me *3*	501.5	meane] meanes *3, 4*
496.17	this] his *3, 4*	501.14	to conuay] conuaye *3, 4*
496.17	foote] *2(a)*; soote *2(b)*	501.25	neuer] *3*; neeuer *2*
496.17	entertainment] entreatance *3, 4*	501.27	I] *3*; *om. 2*
496.18	sad] said *4*	501.28	yeeldings] *3*; dealings *2*
496.22	*Agriola*] *3*; *Agrola 2*	501.28	and] *3*; aud *2*
496.23	prisoner] *3*; prisoners *2*	502.9	when] *3*; wheu *2*
496.24	thee] this *3, 4*; Fr. "vous" (Y6r; *you*)	502.10	should] would *4*
		502.22	in] into *3, 4*
496.27	courtesie] *3*; countesie *2*	502.31	imagining] imagined *4*
496.32	Turks] Dukes *3*; Fr. "du Turc" (Y6r; *the Turk's*)	502.37	one] *3*; man *2*
		503.1	faile] taile *4*
497.5	life] both Life *3, 4*	503.2	couertly] courtly *3, 4*
497.5	to] *om. 3*	503.7	her] *om. 3, 4*
497.24	meanes] good means *3, 4*	504.10	constantlie] *3*; constanlie *2*
497.26	will I therefore] therefore will I *3, 4*	504.17	to] *3*; fo *2*
		504.28	as] that *3, 4*
497.7	liberalitie] *3*; libertie *2*	504.33	they] she *4*
497.27	I] *3*; we *2*	504.37	with] in *3, 4*
497.27	meane] *3*; meame *2*	504.42	abie] *3*; abide *2*
499.6	repetition] repetitions *3, 4*	505.1	cheefe] chieft *3*; chiefest *4*
499.8	Isle] *3*; Islle *2*	505.8	this] the *4*
499.10	bare] had *4*	505.9	he proclaimed a yonger] ED; he was proclaimed yonger *2*; he was declared yonger *3, 4*; see Textual note to 505.10
499.15	waiting] wanting *3*		
499.21	nose-thrilles] *3*; nose? | thrilles *2*		
499.22	poysone] *3*; poysome *2*		
499.24	Father] *3*; Fa, | ther *2*	505.10	great] ED; and great *2, 3, 4*
499.25	see] know *3, 4*	506.4	*his*] *this 3, 4*
499.25	deuised] concluded vpon *3, 4*	506.6	ioyfull] ioyfully *3*
499.25	trauaile] trauell *3, 4*	506.17	thinking] *3*; thinkiny *2*
499.27	change] turne *4*	506.23	necke] *3*; necks *2*
499.27	incurable] vncurable *3, 4*	506.23	the poore slaues are] are the poore slaues *3, 4*
499.28	actions] things *4*		
499.37	represse] expresse *3, 4*		
499.42	Realme] Kingdome *4*	506.26	Keyes] bunch of Keyes *3, 4*

506.32	fetching] *3*; ~, *2*	510.13	Science] Magicall Science *3, 4*; Fr. "sa science" (Z3v; *her science*)
506.33	bounde] round *4*		
506.34	vp] *om. 3, 4*	510.14	am I] I am *3, 4*
506.37	*Palmerins*] his *4*	510.15	shoulde] would *3*
506.37	maruailing] and marvailing *4*	511.6	So soone as] Immediatly after *4*
506.39	the] these *3, 4*; Fr. "des" (Z2r; *of the*)	511.6	thus] *om. 4*
		511.6	Isle] Island *3, 4*
506.40	ye not me] you me not *3, 4*	511.6	and had that day] he *4*
507.3	the] this *3, 4*; Fr. "le" (Z2r; *the*)	511.6	likewise] *om. 3, 4*
507.4	happie] a happy *4*	511.7	passed] passed through *3, 4*
507.6	Seruants] *3*; Seruant *2*	511.7	very] *om. 4*
507.8	deceiued,] *3*; ~∧ *2, 4*	511.7	at] the same *3, 4*
507.9	simple] *3*; simble *2*	511.8	vp] vs *3*
507.18	in] of *4*	511.8	in talke] in talking *3*; a talking *4*
507.20	licence] *3*; lisence *2*	511.9	expert] expert and skilfull *4*
507.24	returne] *3*; retuene *2*	511.12	hence] *3*; thence *2*
507.37	followed] following *3, 4*; Fr. "furent" (Z2v; *went*)	511.13	her] her meanes *3, 4*
		511.17	to some man] by direction, vnto some other man, *3, 4*
507.38	The two] Both tho *4*		
508.10	meanes] *3*; meaues *2*	511.22	take] *3*; taste *2*
508.11	pittie had power] *3*; power had pittie *2*	511.22	auaunt-currers] *3*; auaunt,currers *2*
		511.30	or] *om. 3, 4*
508.14	enchaunted,] *3*; ~. *2*	511.32	prisoner] *3*; prisonrr *2*
508.15	incantations] ED; incontations *2*; incantatious *3, 4*	511.36	conducted] *3*; conducteth *2*
		511.37	for that] *3*; *om. 2*
508.23	they] the *3*	511.40	Princesse] Princesses *3, 4*
508.28	his lamentations] *3*; this lamentation *2*	511.42	his cries] *3*; cries *2*
		512.4	answered] answere *4*
508.41	Turks which] Turke that *3, 4*	512.6	hee] she *4*
508.41	kindnes] *3*; knidnes *2*	512.7	would he] he would *3, 4*
509.13	Castle] *3*; Castale *2*	512.11	Freende] great Friend *3, 4*
509.15	Ladies] *3*; Ladys *2*	512.14	honourablie] ED; honourablye *2*; Honourably *3, 4*
509.24	him] *3*; them *2*		
509.26	knowledge] Artificial skill *3, 4*; Fr. "sçauoir" (Z3v; *knowledge*)	512.15	may you] you may *3, 4*
		512.29	*Malfada*] *Malfado 3, 4*
509.31	strumpets] Trumpets *4*	512.34	my iniurious] by injurious *4*
509.31	or] or else *3, 4*	512.40	Countrey] *3*; Couutrey *2*
509.33	heauen] Heauens *3, 4*	513.7	is] be *3, 4*
509.35	fortune] crosse Fortune *3, 4*; Fr. "quelle fortune" (Z3v; *what fortune*)	513.10	meane] means *3, 4*
		513.11	proceeded] *3*; proceededed *2*
		513.13	Nabor] Nabar *3, 4*
509.35	accursed] *3*; accur[ ]sed *2*	514.4	bought] brought *3*; Fr. "*acheta*" (Z7r; *bought*)
509.43	fiue] the *3, 4*; Fr. "cinq" (Z3v; *five*)		
		514.22	why] wherefore *3, 4*
510.1	Moorish] the Moorish *3, 4*	514.26	who] *om. 3, 4*
510.1	quoth] *3*; quothe *2*	514.29	Embassade] Embassage *4*
510.8	meane] meanes *3, 4*	514.39	captiue] captaine *3*

515.3   Princesse.] *3*; ~? *2*; ~, *4*
515.5   Squires] Sisters *3, 4*; Fr. "Escuyers" (Z7v; *squires*)
515.9   began] be spake *3, 4*
515.35 neuer intend I] I neuer intend *3, 4*
515.36 our] *om. 3*; the *4*; Fr. "mes" (Z8r; *my*)
515.36 that] *om. 4*
515.37 expect] *3*; except *2*
516.2   (quoth she to *Ptolome*)] ED; (quoth she) to *Ptolome 2, 3, 4*
516.7   *Tryneus*] *3*; *Treneus 2*
516.14 trauaile] trauell *3*
516.23 shall] *om. 3, 4*
516.23 greatest] greater *3*
516.25 as that daie] that very day *4*
517.5   *Nabor*] *Mabor 3, 4*
517.8   bequeathed] *3*; bequeathing *2*
517.11 ouercame, at] *3*; ~. At *2*
517.16 commaund] commanded *3*
517.18 threatning] *om. 4*
517.18 Embassade] Embassage *3, 4*
517.20 aunswered] *3*; anuswered *2*
517.26 to] *om. 3, 4*
517.26 the] *3*; his *2*
517.35 Countrey] *3*; Conntrey *2*
517.41 selfe] *3*; slefe *2*
518.2   dare] *3*; daer *2*
518.7   be your Brother *Drumino*] your Brother *Drumino* be *4*
518.9   be your Sister] your Sister be *4*
518.11 whereupon] ED; wherenpon *2*; whereon *3, 4*
518.19 haue] hast *3*
519.6   were] are *4*
519.18 woulde] should *4*
519.22 all his] his Knights *4*
519.25 *Drumino*] *Crumino 3, 4*
519.40 *Palmerin*] *3*; *Palmeiin 2*
520.17 qualitie] qualitie and woorth *3, 4*
520.21 I see] see I *3, 4*
520.32 be] *3*; bo *2*
520.32 mounted] *3*; mouuted *2*
520.33 founde] they found *3, 4*
520.40 not his] not as his *3*
521.3   *Romata*] *3*; *Romato 2*
521.5   yet] as yet *3, 4*
521.6   them] them both *3, 4*
521.6   began] beganne her speeches *3, 4*
521.7   great] deepe knowledge and great *3, 4*
521.8   my] *om. 3*
521.8   comming] comming hither at this time *3, 4*
521.8   will] be pleased to *3, 4*
521.12 and] *om. 3, 4*
521.17 artes] Magicall Artes *3, 4*; Fr. "en tous artz" (Aa4r: *in all arts*)
521.18 deceassing] deceassed *4*
521.18 an] a *3, 4*
521.20 most] *3*; must *2*
521.22 enchauntment] Enchauntments *3, 4*
521.23 exorcise] Exercise *4*
521.23 passe] passe by *3, 4*
521.25 to] *3*; to to *2*
521.29 trauaile] trauell *3, 4*
521.30 sorrowfully] *3*; scr[]owfully *2*
521.31 suffiseth] ye suffiseth *4*
521.33 expected] *3*; expectted *2*
521.38 specially] highly and specially *3, 4*
522.6   Rockes] Rockes with safety *3, 4*
522.8   companions] companion *4*
522.12 will] shall *3*
522.16 part with] *3*; par twith *2*
522.18 trauaile] trauell *3*
522.24 assailed] assailed to *4*
523.10 these diuelries and enchauntments] this diuilish enchatment *3, 4*; Fr. "ces enchantemens & dyablerie" (Aa5r; *these enchantments and diablerie*)
523.17 encountering] *3*; enconntering *2*
523.20 stray] starte *3, 4*; Fr. "fuyr" (Aa5r; *escape*)
523.21 the] *om. 3*
523.30 abide] bide *3, 4*
523.34 breathing] breaking *4*
524.1   of] in *3, 4*
524.25 of] *om. 3*
524.29 personage] *3*; personages *2*
525.10 long absent] *3*; longabsent *2*
525.10 especially] *3*; especally *2*
525.23 there] they *3, 4*

525.27	trampling] *3*; trambling *2*	531.20	*Sauata*] *3*; *Seuata 2*
525.31	table] tables *4*	531.26	Princesse] Princesses *3, 4*
525.31	goodly] good *3, 4*	531.28	liked best] best liked *3, 4*
525.32	where] *3*; were *2*	531.30	mislike] dislike *3, 4*
525.34	Pagan] *3*; Pagon *2*	531.31	you] you hither *3, 4*
526.2	knees] *3*; knee *2*	531.35	Chirurgions] best Chyrurgions *3, 4*
526.10	into] to *3, 4*		
526.24	Arbour] Arbours *4*	531.39	waighting] weightie *3, 4*
526.26	selues] selfe *4*	531.39	passions,] *3*; ~. *2*
526.41	olde,] *3*; ~∧ *2*	531.40	hee thus] in this sort he *3, 4*
527.5	courteous] coueteous *3*	531.42	milde] kinde and milde *3, 4*
527.8	fares] faires *3, 4*	532.8	desire] desired content *3, 4*
528.2	*Trineus*] how *Tryneus 3, 4*	532.17	mine] my hatefull *3, 4*
528.3	Rocke.] *3*; ~∧ *2*	532.18	coloured] *3*; colourer *2*
528.10	and] as *3, 4*	532.20	last] lust *3*; just *4*
528.18	this] the *4*	532.20	of the] of all the *3, 4*
528.26	other] the other *3, 4*	532.25	while] whilest *3, 4*
528.26	monuments] *3*; mounments *2*	532.26	all] in all *3, 4*
528.42	brought] *3*; bronght *2*	532.36	*Belsina*] ED; *Belfina 2, 3, 4*
529.12	thinke] *3*; thiuke *2*	532.42	King *Abimar*] King of *Abimar 3, 4*
529.17	refuse] deny *4*	533.4	march] to martch *3, 4*
529.17	me] my *3*; Fr. "me refuser" (Aa8r; refuse me)	533.5	the Soldanes] *3*; to Soldanes *2*
		533.9	loue] *3*; warre *2*
529.18	the] *om. 3, 4*	533.14	our] *3*; out *2*
529.19	that] *om. 3, 4*	533.15	sixe] the sixe *3, 4*
529.26	Friend] *3*; Friendes *2*	533.16	posted] *3*; passed *2*
529.28	pardon] hasten *4*	533.19	to] *om. 3, 4*
529.29	come] came *3, 4*	534.9	*Belsina*] *Belfina 3, 4*
529.31	*Abimar*] *3*; *Arbimar 2*	534.12	done] *om. 4*
529.38	and] an *4*	534.21	matters] matter *3, 4*
530.9	waight] wait *3, 4*	534.24	rare] care *3, 4*
530.12	in] *om. 3, 4*	534.29	*Aurecinda*] *3*; *Arecinda 2*
530.21	the] that *3, 4*	534.33	meane] meanes *3, 4*
530.23	life] leaue *3*	534.37	desired] desire *3*
530.32	will I] I will *3, 4*	534.42	to each] *3*; of *2*
530.33	feare I] doe I feare *3, 4*	535.4	beautie] *3*; beantie *2*
530.34	cause] *om. 3*	535.7	on] one *3, 4*
530.37	till] vntil *3, 4*	535.10	ende] *3*; eude *2*
530.37	no] not *3, 4*	535.12	stature] statures *3, 4*
530.39	you. Vpon] ED; you, vpon *2, 3, 4*	535.33	like] likely *3, 4*
530.40	chambers] *3*; cambers *2*	535.40	beseemed me] beseemeth *3, 4*
531.4	*Abimar*] *of Abimar 4*	536.1	Soldane] *3*; Soldame *2*
531.9	determination] cruell determination *3, 4*	536.6	to her] the *3, 4*
		536.10	amorous] *3*; amarous *2*
531.9	his aduise] this good aduisement *3, 4*	536.10	furies] furie *3, 4*
		536.14	messengers] *3*; mssengers *2*
531.18	10000] *3*; 30000. *2*	536.16	foundation] *3*; fouudation *2*

537.3	Colmelio,] *3*; ~∧ *2*	541.34	*Aurecinda*] *3*; *Aureeinda 2*
537.10	Princesse] Prince *4*	542.2	of] *om.* *3, 4*
537.13	Arch-Flamin] *3*; Arch ∧ Flamin *2*	542.4	giuen] deliuered *3, 4*
537.14	thereof] thereat *3, 4*	542.5	audacious] most audacious *3, 4*
537.22	most specially] speciall *3, 4*	542.19	her] the *4*
537.26	in] into *4*	542.20	yet] *om.* *3*; but *4*
537.28	crediblie] *3*; credible *2*	542.20	dooth not he] he doth not *4*
537.43	much] *3*; mnch *2*	542.22	meane] meanes *4*
538.2	But] But yet *4*	542.23	Soldane] *3*; Soldanen *2*
538.9	this] the *4*	542.29	he] *om.* *3*
538.23	her?] *3*; ~, *2*	542.37	if] *om.* *3*; Fr. "si" (Cc5v; *if*)
538.24	hee] *3*; shee *2*	543.3	*thereon*] *om. 4*
538.31	*Aurecinda*] *3*; *Aerecinda 2*	543.5	of] *3*; ot *2*
539.2	*Babylon*] *3*; *Balylon 2*	543.11	the] to the *3*
539.4	*Orzodine*] ED; *Orzadine 2, 3, 4*	543.12	see I] I see *4*
539.7	message] *3*; embssage *2*	543.27	the frozen] his frozen *4*
539.7	Mighty] Most high, mighty, *4*	543.31	Cabinette,] *3*; ~) *2*
539.7	illustrious] *3*; illuous *2*	543.34	of] *3*; o- *2*
539.13	Ambassador] *3*; Ambassdor *2*	543.35	torments] *3*; tor | ments *2*
539.21	opinion] Religion *3, 4*	543.35	meane] means *4*
539.24	late] great *4*	543.37	that] *om. 3, 4*
539.26	the Soldane] if the Soldan *3, 4*	543.39	and there] *3*; amd there *2*
539.38	By God] Madam *4*	543.41	whome] *om. 4*
540.6	*Orzodine*] *4*; *Orzadine 2, 3*	544.5	thy] my *3*; Fr. "vostre" (Cc6v; *your*)
540.11	trauailed] trauelled *3, 4*	544.8	of] *3*; ot *2*
540.20	his] is *4*	544.9	he] *om. 3, 4*
540.27	worthie] ED; worthilie *2*; moste worthie *3, 4*	544.10	pittie] pittied *3, 4*; Fr. "vous meut à pitié" (Cc6v; *arouses pity in you*)
540.31	where] whereas *3, 4*	544.18	this] his *3, 4*
540.32	follie] great Folly *3, 4*	544.20	little] *3*; lttle *2*
540.33	canuazado] Camizado *3*; Canvizado *4*	545.21	liuely] lovely *4*
540.34	from] from off *3, 4*	544.26	resembling] *3*; resemblingng *2*
540.35	slew] *3*; flew *2*	544.36	*Trineus*] *3*; *Trinens 2*
540.40	*Orzodine*] *3*; *Ozodine 2*	545.3	disloyalty] *3*; *disloyalay 2*
541.1	contend] to contend *3*	545.18	And] *3*; *Vnd 2*
541.3	hither come] come hither *4*	545.19	God] *3*; *Cod 2*
541.5	the] *3*; the the *2*	545.32	as] and *3*
541.5	thy] that thy *3, 4*	545.32	forced] it forced *4*
541.6	shall] will *4*	545.34	*Aurecinda*] *4*; *Auredinda 2*; *Auricinda 3*
541.18	the two] *3*; the the two *2*	547.1	she] ED; he *2, 3, 4*
541.19	Princes] other Princes *3, 4*	547.8	Loue] ED; loue *2, 3, 4*
541.23	themselues] themselues againe *3, 4*	547.26	at] of *4*
541.26	pessant] ED; peasant *2*; weighty *3, 4*	548.6	Freendes] Friend *3, 4*
541.28	trauersing] trasuersing *3*	548.12	wherein] when *3, 4*; Fr. "ou" (Cc8r; *where*)
541.33	trauaile] trauell *3*		

548.36 as] *3*; *om. 2*
549.1 worthily] *3*; worthi[]y *2*
549.12 ire] fire *4*
549.35 worthily] *3*; worthilye *2*
549.43 Courrier] ED; Courtier *2, 3, 4*
550.1 *Palmerin*,] *3*; ~∧ *2*
550.9 and] *3*; aud *2*
550.18 soldane] *3*; soldaine *2*
550.19 from] from off *3, 4*
550.19 Then were] There *3*; Fr. "Adonc furent" (Dd1r; *Then were*)
550.24 vnaduisedly] most vnaduisedly *3, 4*
550.26 a man] the man *3, 4*
550.29 foole] *2(b)*; soole *2(a)*; Fr. "fol" (Dd1r; *fool*)
551.3 *followed*] *followe 4*
551.4 aduise] good counsell and aduisement *3, 4*
551.5 defence] the defence and safe-gard *3, 4*
551.5 all the meanes] by all the best meanes *3, 4*
551.5 coulde] possibly could *3, 4*
551.6 the Prince] Prince *3, 4*
551.11 *Palmerin*] *3*; *Parmerin 2*
551.14 as] as that *3, 4*
551.15 intreatie] great intreatie *3, 4*
551.17 so] so much *3, 4*
551.21 giue] to giue *3, 4*
551.29 haue sworne] sworne *3, 4*
551.30 but] but that *3, 4*
551.32 companion] company *3, 4*; Fr. "compagnon" (Dd1v; *companion*)
552.9 did I first] first did I *3, 4*
552.9 offer] proffer *3, 4*
552.12 induced] prouoked *3, 4*; Fr. "induit" (Dd1v; *induced*)
552.15 Verily] Very *3, 4*
552.28 withall] *3*; with | all *2*
552.39 woonder] to wonder *3, 4*
552.41 will not exchaunge] ED; will exchaunge *2, 3, 4*
552.41 soone] full soone *3*
553.4 saide] *3*; saie *2*
553.7 *Belsina*] *4*; *Bel-sina 2*; *Belsino 3*
553.38 summons] the summons *3, 4*
554.10 set] les *4*

554.11 who] *om. 3*; which *4*
555.2 beare] heare *3, 4*; Fr. "prenez en pacience" (Dd3r; *bear with patience*)
555.11 erecting] erected *4*
555.11 caused] causing *4*
555.14 remaining] remained *4*
555.17 yet] *3*; yer *2*
556.5 rode] did ride *4*
556.8 the] *3*; the the *2*
556.27 concupiscence] *3*; coucupiscence *2*
556.34 words at their gracious entertainment] gracious words at their entertainment *3, 4*
557.13 and] *3*; aud *2*
557.20 should] would *3, 4*
557.28 to] so to *3, 4*
557.31 shall] *2(a)*; shalc *2(b)*
557.34 *Muzabelino*] *3*; *Mnzabelino 2*
557.35 sooner] *3*; sonner *2*
557.37 founde] *3*; fonnde *2*
557.39 then] *3*; *om. 2*
558.16 Then] They *3, 4*; Fr. "lors" (Dd4r; *then*)
558.24 enchauntments. My] *3*; ~, my *2*
558.28 he] *3*; they *2*
558.40 *Aurecinda*] *3*; *Arecinda 2*
558.42 embracings] embrabings *3, 4*
559.8 Princes] *3*; Prince *2*
559.14 called] galled *3*
559.38 that] who *3, 4*
559.40 contents] content *3, 4*
560.6 the wicked] wicked *3, 4*
560.8 two,] *3*; ~∧ *2*
560.19 to] into *4*
560.19 his] the *3, 4*
560.19 of the Isle] *om. 3*; of the Island *4*
561.4 made] *om. 3*
561.5 aduenture] straunge Aduenture *3, 4*
561.6 golden] radiant golden *3, 4*
561.9 cried] cryed aloud *3, 4*
561.10 on the Deck] *3*; *om. 2*
561.14 King] Kings *3*
561.19 got] got to *3*
561.34 all] the discourse of all *3, 4*
561.36 all] *om. 3, 4*

Historical Collation 823

561.39	both] as well *3, 4*	566.29	Brethren] *3*; Brother *2*
561.39	and Lande] as by Land *3, 4*	566.38	on] *3*; of *2*
561.42	the] he *4*	566.39	the Daughter] Daughter *3, 4*
562.1	Ambassade] Embassage *4*	567.4	loue] lone *4*
562.5	*Ptolome*] *3*; *Polome 2*	567.4	alliance,] *3*; ~. *2*
562.8	that commaunded] who commanded *3, 4*	567.6	would] should *3, 4*
562.8	trauaile] trauell *3, 4*	567.6	but] *3*; not *2*
562.9	to] *3*; td *2*	567.7	your] *3*; my *2*
562.11	to] vnto *3, 4*	567.9	these] their *3, 4*
562.13	will] commaund *3, 4*	567.9	to] *3*; to to *2*
562.14	befall] haue befallen *3, 4*	567.10	their] there *4*
562.15	our] your *4*	567.14	matters] seuerall businesses *3, 4*
562.16	Fortune] *3*; Fortnne *2*	567.16	the] *om. 3, 4*
562.19	what] *3*; that *2*	567.18	Knights] other Knightes *3, 4*
562.24	to] *om. 3*	567.18	naturally] naturall *4*
562.26	vnderstoode] vnderstanding *3, 4*	567.19	as] *om. 3, 4*
562.27	thus] she thus *3, 4*	567.22	did] had *3, 4*
562.29	full charie] full of charitie *3, 4*	567.22	ouer-rule] ouer-ruled *3, 4*
562.34	My] Me *3*	567.22	call] cald *3, 4*
562.36	not] yet not *3, 4*	567.23	renounce] forsake *3, 4*
562.39	intreaties] *3*; intreattes *2*	567.26	doo] also doe *3, 4*
563.4	ioyfull] most ioyfull *3, 4*	567.26	conceiue] receive *4*
563.4	entered] entred into *3, 4*	567.38	length] *3*; lenigth *2*
563.9	exceeding] was exceeding *3, 4*	568.12	Ambassadours] *3*; Ambassadoures *2*
563.22	Princesses] Princes *3, 4*	568.15	Soldane] *3*; Soladne *2*
563.22	and] *3*; aud *2*	569.5	enioyed] entred *3, 4*
563.27	Palfraies] *3*; Palfaies *2*	569.13	of] *3*; os *2*
563.36	aunswered] ED; annswered *2*; answered *3, 4*	569.18	referre] *3*; rcferre *2*
564.10	bir] hir *4*	569.28	will] a will *3, 4*
564.14	courrier] Courtier *3, 4*	569.32	worthie] *om. 3, 4*
564.14	who] *3*; wha *2*	569.33	will] will not faile to *3, 4*
565.5	trauaile] travell *4*	569.33	to] vnto *3, 4*
565.19	you can] can you *3, 4*	569.34	promise faithfully] moste faithfully promise *3, 4*
565.25	made me] madame *4*	569.35	and] *om. 3, 4*
565.32	*Soldane*] *Sultane 3*	569.36	assurance] assistaunce *3, 4*; Fr. "asseurance" (Ee2v; *assurance*)
565.37	*Maucetto*] *3*; *Mucerto 2*	569.37	Friend] *3*; Friendes *2*
566.4	continually] *3*; continnally *2*	569.39	Prince] worthie Prince *3, 4*
566.6	can] am *3, 4*	570.6	Soone] Now soone *4*
566.7	with credit] *3*; withcredit *2*	570.6	*Greece*] *3*; *Greeece 2*
566.13	your] to your *3, 4*; Fr. "luy donnant ma Dame Archidiane" (Ee1r; *giving him my lady Archidiane*)	570.9	conducted] already conducted *3, 4*
		570.10	his] *3*; their *2*
		570.10	came] *3*; hee came *2*
566.17	Your] Yours *3, 4*	570.22	Archbishop] *3*; Achbishop *2*
566.19	Prince] *om. 3, 4*	570.41	daughter] onely Daughter *3, 4*

571.2	good] *3*; so good *2*		578.2	*trauaile*] *trauell 3, 4*
571.5	hope] haue *3, 4*		578.3	see] visit *3, 4*; Fr. "voir" (Ee6r; *to see*)
571.10	trauaile] trauel *3, 4*		578.4	Sea] Seas *3, 4*; Fr. "mer" (Ee6r; *sea*)
571.19	beheld] behold *4*		578.6	In] Before in *4*
571.22	since] ED; siuce *2*; om. *3, 4*		578.6	heard] heard mentioned *3, 4*
571.24	*Venus*] om. *3, 4*		578.8	imprinted] kept imprinted *3, 4*
571.36	in] *3*; om. *2*		578.10	trauaile] Trauell *3, 4*
572.2	and] end *4*		578.12	would not denie] not denyed *3, 4*
572.8	could] can *3, 4*		578.14	accompanie] guide me, and accompany *3, 4*
572.19	*Cardonya*] ED; Cordonya *2, 3, 4*		578.14	I desire] that I am desirous *3, 4*
572.19	of] any tydings of *3, 4*		578.16	trauaile] trauell *3, 4*
572.19	the time] om. *3, 4*		578.16	Sea] Seas *3, 4*; Fr. "Mer" (Ee6r; *sea*)
572.19	taken] first taken *3, 4*		578.20	Horses] great Horses *3, 4*
573.8	to onely] vnto onely *3, 4*		578.21	great] much *3, 4*
573.9	*Burgundie*] *3*; *Buroundie 2*		578.21	should] would *4*
573.10	Lordes] worthy Lordes *3, 4*		578.23	all] om. *3, 4*
573.11	acquainted] made acquainted *3, 4*		578.24	Emperours] *3*; Emperous *2*
573.13	sometime] sometimes *3, 4*		578.25	euer] euermore *3, 4*
573.16	trauaile] trauell *3, 4*		578.26	builded] building *3, 4*
573.26	the] these *3, 4*		578.29	suddaine] sudden storme *3, 4*
573.29	their] *3*; there *2*		578.32	split] *3*; spilt *2, 4*
574.6	shee] we *3, 4*; Fr. "elle" (Ee4v; *she*)		578.34	Pylots] Pyrates *3, 4*
574.12	but I woulde haue pursued the iniurie he did to me? yet did] om. *3, 4*		578.40	trauailing] trauelling *3, 4*
			578.42	Sea] Seas *3, 4*
			579.3	that] om. *3, 4*
576.14	husbande] Husband *3, 4*		579.7	so] om. *3, 4*
576.26	till] vntill *3, 4*		579.11	aduised] *3*; adnised *2*
576.26	Realme] Kingdome *3, 4*		579.12	an inordinate] in ordinate *3*; inordinate *4*
576.27	attended] attending *4*			
576.30	sometime] sometimes *3, 4*		579.19	onely] *3*; ouely *2*
576.30	for] because that *3, 4*		579.22	hard] *3*; heard *2*
576.31	whosoeuer] whomsoeuer *3, 4*		580.1	remembraunce] *3*; remembrounce *2*
576.31	Lorde] good Lord *3, 4*		580.22	was she] she was *3, 4*
576.36	to] vnto *3, 4*		581.12	then] *3*; theen *2*
576.38	courteously] most courteously *3, 4*		581.18	Poore] *3*; Heere *2*
576.42	deuises] rare Deuices *3, 4*		581.18	of spirit] ED; despised *2, 3, 4*
577.4	fortune] *3*; fortnne *2*		581.20	or] *3*; of *2*
577.4	fall to] befall *3, 4*		581.20	affabilitie] affabilities *3, 4*
577.8	the cause] that cause *3, 4*		581.22	Daughters] Daughter *3, 4*; Fr. "filles" (Ee7v; *daughters*)
577.12	mee] to me *3, 4*			
577.14	that] as that *3, 4*		581.24	come] come on and goe *3, 4*
577.27	same] next *3, 4*; Fr. "le jour mesmes" (Ee6r; *the same day*)		581.26	on] forward *3, 4*
			581.26	there] *3*; their *2*
577.29	to] vnto *3, 4*		581.29	trauaile] trauell *3, 4*
578.2	thinking] *pretending 3, 4*; Fr. "pensans" (Ee6r; *thinking*)		581.37	but] om. *3, 4*; Fr. "Mais" (Ee8r; *but*)
			582.2	Lords] good Lords *3, 4*

582.4	if you] it *3, 4*	587.13	*Constantinople*] *3*; *Constantinole 2*
582.8	with you last] last with you *3, 4*	587.24	As concerning] As concern *3*; To declare *4*
582.11	Empresse,] *3*; ~' *2*		
582.19	although] though *3, 4*	587.33	two] about some two *3, 4*
582.19	with] *3*; wirh *2*	587.33	yeeres] *3*; dayes *2*
582.20	vsed] attended *3, 4*	587.35	or] ED; for *2, 3, 4*
582.24	to] *om. 3, 4*	587.36	in] at *3, 4*
582.26	therof] whereof *3, 4*	587.39	one of the Cabins] the Maisters Cabin *3, 4*; Fr. "la chambre" (Ff3r; *the chamber*)
582.26	offend] *3*; affend *2*		
583.7	Gallies] greate Galleyes well appoyinted *3, 4*; Fr. "deux galions" (Ee8r: *two galleys*)		
		587.41	departed] *3*; depart *2*
		588.3	you haue] haue you *3, 4*
583.8	newly] but lately *3, 4*	588.7	*Alchidiana*] *Alchidianaes* Friends *3, 4*
583.8	hardie] hardy and valiant *3, 4*		
583.14	with pittie] *3*; *om. 2*	588.14	pearched] peatched *3, 4*
583.16	so] *om. 3, 4*	588.15	or] nor *4*
583.17	stuffed] well stuffed *3, 4*	588.17	so] and so *3, 4*
583.21	hast] *om. 3, 4*	588.18	houre] good houre *3, 4*
583.30	aware] *3*; beware *2*; a ware *4*	588.32	presence.] *3*; ~, *2*
583.31	greatly] very much *3, 4*	588.33	knew] well knew *3, 4*
583.36	as] that *3, 4*	588.37	of] *3*; *om. 2*
583.36	a] *om. 3, 4*	590.5	Books] *3*; Booke *2*
583.38	of] of this *3, 4*	590.32	they sawe] the saw *3*; he saw *4*
584.9	said] *3*; sail *2*	590.32	embrace] embraced *3, 4*
584.17	ioyes] toyes *4*	590.39	hee] she *4*
584.28	Pirate] Prince *3, 4*	591.6	necessitie] a necessitie *3*
584.39	Ambassade] Embassage *3, 4*	593.5	so] *3*; *om. 2*
584.42	amitie] *3*; amititie *2*	593.24	Hauen] *4*; Pauen *3*
585.7	highnesse] *3*; highuesse *2*	593.25	to *Alchidiana*] *4*; te *Alchidiana 3*
586.5	*Menadeno*] ED; *Meuadeno 2*; *Meuodeno 3*; *Menodeno 4*	593.32	*Olorico,*] ED; ~ ∧ *3, 4*
		594.1	as it] *4*; asit *3*
586.7	at] of *4*	594.4	her desire] *4*; herdesire *3*
586.30	a] *om. 3, 4*	594.8	she] we *4*
586.31	our] *3*; the *2*	594.32	*Tirendos*] *Florendos 4*
586.36	our] vs *4*	594.33	shewed] *4*; wewed *3*
586.36	presence] *om. 3, 4*	595.5	made such] *4*; madesuch *3*
586.42	trauaille] Trauell *3, 4*	595.9	following] *4*; follo[ ] *3 is damaged*
587.9	your] *3*; our *2*	595.10	fauourable] *4*; [ ]le *3 is damaged*
587.10	*Apolonius*] ED; *Aponius 2*; *Apponius 3, 4*	596.10	*Antonie Monday.*] *om. 4*
		596.11	Honos alit Artes.] *om. 4*
587.11	againe] ouer againe *3, 4*		

Word-Division

1. Line-End Hyphenation in the MRTS Edition

NOTE: The following compounds, hyphenated at the end of the line in the MRTS edition, are hyphenated within the line in the copy-text.

| 225.36 | ouer- \| bolde | 463.26 | fore- \| pointed |
| 292.28 | with- \| holding | 522.19 | gaine- \| say |

2. Line-End Hyphenation in the Copy-Text

NOTE: The following compounds, or possible compounds, are hyphenated at the end of the line in the copy-text. The form in which they have been given in the MRTS edition, as listed below, represents the usual practice of the copy-text as ascertained from other appearances or parallels.

104.26,		205.40,	
124.6,		214.4,	
463.3,		399.11	Horsemen
596.2	Gentlemen	231.18	withdrewe
104.32	workmanshippe	247.13	sometimes
110.40	counteruaile	248.17	hartfast
116.20	countermaundeth	263.37	withstand
116.21	outbraue	265.9	withdrew
129.37,		271.23	wythdrawne
156.35	Gentleman	271.40	Greyhoundes
134.9,		308.39	ouer-watched
553.10	Horsebacke	373.26	gaine-say
140.13,		382.10,	
427.3	oftentimes	576.17	ouercome
154.26	Sheepeheards	398.34	midnight
163.41	horseback	400.28	horseman
171.8,		405.35	good-night
276.18,		421.23	faint-harted
302.40	horsebacke	427.17	withdraw
189.22	pastime	444.18	friendshippe
192.27	pastimes	463.32,	
203.9	good-morrow	554.41	welfare

477.35	afternoone	524.8	ouer-spent
477.38	Bridgegroome	534.17	good-will
499.21	nose-thrilles	573.40	withstand
506.19	ouercame	581.32	shipwracke
508.31	ouerwhelmed	585.1	warlike
515.34	foresight	590.13	fire-brand

3. Special Cases

(A) Line-end word-division with hyphen omitted in the copy-text: The following compounds, or possible compounds, appear in the copy-text at a line-end without a hyphen, but have been transcribed in the MRTS text, listed below, in accordance with the general practice of the copy-text as ascertained by other appearances or by parallels.

283.20   with | drew (withdrew)
293.39   ouer | come (ouercome)

(B) Line-end hyphenation coinciding in the MRTS edition and the copy-text: The following compound is hyphenated at a line-end in both the MRTS edition and the copy text.

321.1   Ship- | wracke

Bibliographical Descriptions

1. The First Edition (1588)

Title-page: Palmerin D'Oliua>. | The Mirrour of nobili- | tie, Mappe of honor, Anotamie of rare | *fortunes, Heroycall preſident of Loue:* | VVonder for Chiualrie, and moſt accompliſhed | Knight in all perfections. | (∴ | *Preſenting to noble mindes, theyr Courtlie deſires, to Gentles,* | *theyr choiſe expectations, and to the inferiour ſorte, howe to imi-* | *tate theyr vertues: handled vvith modeſtie, to ſhun* | *offence, yet all delightfull, for re-* | *creation.* | Written in the Spaniſh, Italian and French, | and from them turned into Engliſh | by *A. M.* one of the Meſ- | ſengers of her Maieſties | Chamber. | Patere aut abſtine. | At London, | Printed by I. Charlewoode, for Willi- | am VVright, and are to bee ſolde at his Shoppe, adioy- | ning to S. Mildreds Church in the Poul- | trie, the middle Shoppe | in the rowe. | 1588. Stet Anotamie

Head-title: [orn: cat's head with horns at center, 17x85 mm.] | ✣ The firſt parte of the auncient | *and honorable Historie, of the valiant* | Prince *Palmerin D'Oliua,* Emperor of *Constantinople,* | Sonne to the King *Florendos* of *Macedon,* and the | fayre *Griana,* Daughter to *Remicius,* Emperour of | *Conſtantinople:* a Hiſtory full of ſinguler and | Courtlie recreation &c. | (∴)

Running-title: The famous Hiſtorie | of *Palmerin D'Oliua>.* [*D'Oliua>* A3[r], L3–4[r], N3–4[r], P3–4[r], R3[r], S1–4[r], V1–4[r], Y1–4[r], Bb1–4[r], Dd1–4[r], Ff1[r], Ff3[r], Gg1–4[r], Ii1–4[r], Ll1–4[r], Nn1–4[r], Pp1–4[r], Qq1–4[r], Rr1–4[r]; *D'Oliua* Vv3–4[r], Yy3–4[r]]

Collation: 4º : *⁴ A–Y⁴; Aa–Yy⁴ [$4 (–B3, E4, Gg4, Tt4, Yy4) signed except for the first gathering (*3 missigned as *2); Gg3 missigned as G3; Ss3 in ital.; Ss1, Tt1, Vv1, Xx1, Yy1 signature does not include numeral; Ss4, Vv4, Xx4 give Arabic not Roman numeral], 180 leaves, ff. [4] [1] 2–176 [*var*: misnumbering 26 as 28, 28 as 26]; plate [1]

Contents: *1[r]: title-page (verso blank). *2[r]: coat of arms of the Edward de Vere, seventeenth earl of Oxford (verso blank). *3[r] (missigned *2): '✣ To the right noble, learned, and | *worthie minded Lord,* Edward de Vere, *Earle of* Ox- | enford, Vifcount Bulbeck, Lord Sanford, and of Ba- | *delfmere, and Lord high Chamberlaine of England*: A. M. | wifheth continuall happines in this life, and | in the world to come.' ital. with 8-line initial (38 × 38 mm). *3ᵛ: dedication ending *'Sometime your Honours feruant,* | yet continuing in all humble duty. | *Anthonie Monday.'* *4ʳ: '✣ To the courteous Readers.' rom. with 9-line initial (38 × 38 mm). A1ʳ: HT and text. Yy4ʳ: *'FINIS.* A. Munday, | Honos alit Artes.' (verso blank).

Catchword variants: B4ᵛ mee [me] C3ᵛ hee [he] F1ᵛ angry [angrie] G4ʳ rehearfed [fhe rehearfed] H4ᵛ (Pal-)merin, [merin] I2ʳ fhoulde [fhould] I4ʳ heard [hearde] M1ʳ Sword, [Sworde,] Q2ʳ (Ma-)dame [dame,] Q4ʳ (at-)tend [tende] R3ᵛ feare, [feare] Aa1ʳ death [death,] Aa4ʳ Lord [Lorde] Dd1ᵛ Fréende, [Fréend,] Hh3ʳ felues [felues,] Ll2ᵛ (trou-)bled, [bled] Ll3ᵛ blow [blowe] Ll4ʳ hys [his] Mm3ʳ (be-)feech [feeche] Mm3ʳ royalty, [roylatie,] Nn1ʳ began [beganne] Nn2ᵛ he [hee] Oo2ʳ Combat [Combatte] Qq2ᵛ how [howe] Qq4ᵛ hys [his] Ss3ʳ *Howe* [CHAP.] Ss4ʳ (Neuerthe-)leffe, [leffe] Tt2ʳ howe [how] Vv3ᵛ not [not.] Xx2ᵛ (de-)termined [termined,] Yy3ʳ (dif-)perfed, [perfed] Yy3ᵛ had [*omit.*]; no cw on Dd2ʳ

Typography and plate: 36 ll., 147 (159) × 86 mm. (R4ʳ in Folger); text, black letter (and some roman and italic) 82 mm. for 20 ll.; dedication: italic 94mm. (*3ᵛ); 'To the Reader': roman 94 mm. (*4ᵛ); the plate with the earl of Oxford's arms measures 109 × 73 mm.

Copies examined: Folger Shakespeare Library (STC 19157), designated *1(a)* in the critical apparatus; British Library (C.56.d.6), designated *1(b).*

STC 19157

2. The Second Edition (1597)

Volume 1:

Imperfect. Title-page, prefatory material, and first leave of text (sig. A1) are lacking in British Library copy (C.56.d.7), but inferred in the collation below.

Running-title: The famous Hiftorie | of Palmerin D'Oliua. [faomus B8ᵛ; D'Oliua, P8ʳ; Hiftorie. S1ᵛ, S2ᵛ; D'Oliua: X6ʳ, Y2ʳ, Z3ʳ; D'Oliua, X7ʳ, Z1ʳ]

Collation: 4º: π⁴ A⁴, B–Y⁸, Z⁴ [$4 (–A4, Z4) signed], 180 leaves unnumbered

Contents: A2ʳ–Z4ʳ: text. Z4ʳ: 'FINIS. | *A. Mundy*. | Honos alit Artes.' (verso blank).

Catchword variants: B2ᵛ day [day,] B4ᵛ mée [me] B5ᵛ knew [knewe] D1ᵛ angry [angrie] D6ᵛ (nurtu-)red [he] D7ʳ (ef-)fect [fect:] D8ʳ rehearſed [ſhe rehearſed] E4ᵛ (Pal-)merin, [merin] E8ʳ heard [heard,] H2ʳ credibly [credible] H4v CHAP. [Chap.] H5ʳ to [ſo] I2ʳ (Ma-)dame [dame,] I4ʳ (at-)tend [tende] I7ᵛ feare, [feare] M5ʳ death [death,] M8ʳ Lord [Lorde] N2ᵛ where [where,] O1ᵛ Friend, [Frićend,] O7ᵛ knight, [Knight,] P3ʳ paines [paines,] P8ʳ Realme [Realme.] Q3ʳ ſelues [ſelues,] R3ᵛ loue [loue,] R4ʳ Madam, [Madame,] R6ᵛ (trou-)bled, [bled] R7ᵛ blow [blowe] S5ʳ began [beganne] S6ʳ iudgment [iudgement] T1ᵛ Truelie [Truely] T2ʳ Combat [Combatte] V1ʳ CHAP. [Chap.] V2ᵛ how [howe] V4ʳ euery [euerye] V8ᵛ CHAP. [Chap.] X1ʳ (Palme-)rin [merin] X5ᵛ CHAP. [Chap.] X6ʳ howe [how] Y2ᵛ (beha-)uiour [uior,] Y6ᵛ (de-)termined [termined,] Z3ʳ (diſ-)perſed, [pearſed]

Typography: 36 ll., 146 (160) × 87 mm. (P2ʳ in BL); text, black letter (and some roman) 81 mm. for 20 ll.

Volume 2:

Title-page: THE | Second Part of the | honourable Hiſtorie, | of *Palmerin d'Oliua:* | Continuing his rare fortunes, Knightly deeds | *of Chiualrie, happie ſucceſſe in loue: and how* | *he was Crowned Emperour of* | Conſtantinople. | *Herein is likewiſe concluded the variable troubles of the* | Prince TRINEVS, and faire AGRI- OLA, the | Kings daughter of ENGLAND: with | their fortunate Marriage. | *Tranſlated by* A. M. *one of the Meſſengers of* | her Maieſties Chamber. | *Patere aut abſtine.* | [orn. double row of two fleurons,Yamada 21] | LONDON | Printed by Thomas Creede. | 1597.

Head-title: [orn. Yamada 12] | ❧ The ſecond part of | the auncient and honou- | rable Hiſtorie of Palmerin | D'Oliua. | *Continuing his rare fortunes, Knightly deedes of Chiual-* | *rie, happie ſucceſſe in loue, and how he was crowned Em-* | *perour of Conſtantinople. Herein is likewiſe conclu-* | *ded the variable troubles of* Trineus, *and faire* | Agriola *of* England, *with their for-* | *tunate mariage, &c.*

Running-title: The famous Hiſtorie | of Palmerin D'Oliua. [famcus C7ᵛ, C8ᵛ; Hſtoriie K7ᵛ; Of, A2ʳ, A3ʳ, B1ʳ, B2ʳ, D2ʳ, D4ʳ, E1ʳ, E4ʳ, G1ʳ, G3ʳ, I1ʳ, I3ʳ, K3ʳ; D'Oliua: A4ʳ, B5ʳ, B6ʳ, D5ʳ, D7ʳ; D'Oliua‸ B3ʳ, B4ʳ, D1ʳ, D3ʳ, E2ʳ, E3ʳ, G2ʳ, G4ʳ, I2ʳ, I4ʳ, K1ʳ, K4ʳ]

Collation: 4º: πA⁴, A–Aa⁸, Bb⁴ [$4 (–πA2, πA4); missing Bb2-4], 200 unnumbered.

Contents: π A1 (blank except for sig. 'A'). π A2ʳ: title-page (verso blank). π A3ʳ: [*orn.* Yamada 12] | 'To the worshipfull Mai- | fter *Fraunces Young*, of *Brent Pelham*, in the Coun- | tie of Hertford Efquire, and to Miftreffe *Sufan* | *Young*, his wife, and my moft kind Miftreffe: | *this worldes ioy and heauenly felicitie in-* | *tirely wifhed.*' rom. with 6-line init. [Yamada P1] (28 × 26 mm.). π A3ᵛ: dedication ending 'Your VVorfhips euer to be commaunded, | Anthony Mundy.' π A4: [*orn. triple row of fleurons*, Yamada 21] '⚘ To the Freendlie | READERS.' ital. with 5-line init. [Yamada T3] (22 × 22 mm). A1ʳ–Bb3ᵛ: HT and text, chap. 1–67. Bb4 (blank?; missing)

Catchword variants: B4ᵛ CHAP. [Chap.] C1ᵛ CHAP. [Chap.] C6ᵛ nature [nature,] D2ʳ know [knowe] D7ᵛ promife [promife,] E1ʳ and [on] E7ᵛ hands, [hands] F2ᵛ body [bodie] F4ᵛ fiercely [fiercelie] F6ʳ (Pas-)meria [meria,] H3ᵛ Hée [He] I1ᵛ knewe [knew] I4ʳ truft [trufting] I5ʳ feeing [féeing] K1ʳ (tor-)ment [ments?] K3ʳ Polinarda, [Polinarda] L1ᵛ Count [Counte] L6ᵛ he [hée] L8ʳ mée [me] M4ᵛ highneffe [highnes] M5ᵛ Palmerin [Palmerin,] N2ʳ CHAP. [Chap.] N8ʳ CHAP. [Chap.] O6ᵛ note [note,] P8ᵛ it, [it:] Q3ᵛ carrie, [carrie] Q7ᵛ theyr [their] R4ᵛ queftions [queftions,] T4ᵛ honour, [honor,] T6ʳ fifter [Sifters] V6ᵛ (fe-)cretlie, [cretlye,] X6ʳ (after-)ward [warde]

Typography: 36 ll., 148 (162) × 87 mm. (P2ʳ in BL); text, black letter (and some roman and italic) 82 mm. for 20 ll. Chapter 23 misp. 20.

Copies examined: British Library (C.56.d.7), designated *2(a)* in the critical apparatus. Bound as one volume with the preceding item; the Henry E. Huntington Library copy (330331) of volume 2 only, designated *2(b)*.

Note: The copy in the Huntington Library is imperfect and lacks eight leaves: A1, A4, A5, K1 and the entire signature Bb. The text in those leaves is provided in interleaved manuscript pages, except for the text in sig. Bb1. When the transcript was made the sig. Bb1 was probably still extant, hence no transcription was required. Though extant, this leaf was possibly loose and got definitely lost before or at the time of binding. This loss would not have become immediately apparent, since the catchword at the bottom of both Aa8v and Bb1v is the same ("and"). The transcript is based on a copy of the fourth edition of 1637, with which it shares the same substantive textual variants. A note in the copy attributes the transcript to John Brand (1744–1806) and dates it ca. 1750, quite an unlikely possibility if we consider that Brand would be approximately six years old. It is also mentioned that Brand owned this copy before it was bought by Richard Heber. The book-sale catalogue of Brand's library, *Bibliotheca Brandiana: A Catalogue of the Unique, Scarce, Rare, Curious, and Numerous Collection of Works . . . being the entire Library of the late Rev. John Brand* (1807), p. 253, contains a lot, no. 6657, described as comprising the two volumes of the 1588 edition of *Palmerin d'Oliua*. It seems likely that the description was based on the first volume of the first edition, but that the second part was actually the Huntington copy of the 1597 edition and not of the original 1588 edition.

STC 19158

3. The Third Edition (1615–1616)

Volume 1:

Title-page: *Palmerin D'Oliua*. | [*rule*] | THE MIRROVR | OF NOBILITIE, THE MAPPE | of Honour, Anatomie of rare Fortunes, | *Heroycall prefident of Loue: Wonder* | for Chiualrie, and moſt accompli- | ſhed Knight in all perfections. | [*rule*] | *Prefenting to Noble mindes, their Courtly defires, to Gen-* | *tles their choyfe expectations, and to the inferiour fort,* | *how to imitate their vertues: handled with mode-* | *ftie, to fhunne offence, yet all delight-* | *full, for Recreation.* | [*rule*] | Written in Spaniſh, Italian, and French, | and from them turned into Engliſh, by | *A.M.* one of the Meſſengers | of his Maieſties Chamber. | [*rule*] | *Patere & Abftine* | [rule] | [*orn*. Yamada 22] | [rule] | LONDON | Printed by *Thomas Creede*. | 1615.

Cancellans title-page: Palmerin d'oliua | THE FIRST PART, | SHEWING THE MIRROVR | of *N*obilitie, the Mappe of *H*onor, A- | natomie of rare Fortunes, Heroycall pre- | ſidents of Loue, Wonder for Chiualrie, | and the moſt accompliſhed Knight | inall perfections. | [*rule*] | *Prefenting to Noble minds, their Courtly defire, to Gentiles* | *their expectations, and to the inferiour fort, how to imitate* | *their vertues: handled with modeftie, to fhun offence,* | *yet all delightfull for Recreation.* | [*rule*] | VVritten in Spaniſh, Italian, and French: and from | them turned into Engliſh, by *A.M.* one of | the Meſſengers of his Maieſties | Chamber. | [*rule*] | *Patere & Abftine.* | [*orn: double row of three fleurons*, Yamada 21] | *LONDON,* | Printed by *T. C.* and *B. A.* for *Richard Higgenbotham*, and | are to be ſold at his ſhop at the ſigne of the Cardinals | Hat without Newgate. 1616. *Stet* inall

Head-title: [*orn*. Yamada 13] | THE FIRST PART | OF THE ANCIENT AND HO- | nourable Hiſtorie of the valiant Prince *Pal-* | *merin D'Oliua*, Emperour of Conſtantinople, | *Sonne to King* Florendos *of Macedonia, and* | the Fayre *Griana*, Daughter to *Remici-* | *us*, Emperour of Conſtantinople: a | *Hiftory full offingular and* | *courtly recreation.*

Running-title: THE HISTORIE | OF PALMERIN D'OLIVA. [*HISTORY* G4ᵛ; *OFP ALMERIN* S6ʳ, T5ʳ, T6ʳ, V5ʳ, V8ʳ, Y5ʳ, Y7ʳ; *PALMERI* C5ʳ; *PALMERIND'OLIVA.* T1ʳ, T2ʳ, V1ʳ, V4ʳ, X2ʳ, Y4ʳ; *DOLIVA.* A6ʳ, A8ʳ, D6ʳ,

E2ʳ, E4ʳ, F1ʳ, F4ʳ, F5ʳ, F6ʳ, F7ʳ; *DOLIVA* C5ʳ, E6ʳ, E8ʳ; *DE'OLIVA*. B1ʳ, B2ʳ, B3ʳ, B4ʳ, C1ʳ, C2ʳ, G1ʳ, G2ʳ, G4ʳ, H2ʳ, H4ʳ, I2ʳ, I3ʳ; *D'OLIVE*. C3ʳ; *DOLIVE*. D7ᵛ; *D'OLIVIA* G5ʳ; on X2ᵛ, X3ᵛ, and Z3ᵛ the RT mistakenly prints '*OF PALMERIN D'OLIVA.*'; X4ᵛ–5ʳ invert the order of the two parts of RT; X6ʳ, Z1ʳ, and Z2ʳ mistakenly print '*THEHISTORIE*' and X7ʳ '*THE HISTORIE*']

Collation: 4°: A–Y⁸, Z⁴ [$4 (–A2, Z4), A1 blank?, missing; E3 missigned as C3], 180 leaves unnumbered.

Contents: A2ʳ: title-page (verso blank). A3ʳ: [*orn*. Yamada 12, upturned] 'TO THE WORSHIPFVLL | Mafter *Frances Yong*, of *Brent-Pelhan*, in the | County of *Hertfort, Efquire, and to* Miftreffe *Su- | fan Yong* his wife, and my moft kind Miftreffe, | *health, and their hearts contentment,* | continually wifhed.'; ital. with 6-line initial [Yamada B1] (26 × 26 mm). A3ᵛ–A4ʳ: [*orn*. Yamada 15] 'To the Reader'; rom. with 7-line initial [Yamada W1] (27 × 28 mm). A4ᵛ: blank. A5ʳ–Z4ʳ: HT and text, ch. 1–65. Z4ʳ: 'FINIS. | *A. Mundy* | Honos alit Artes,' (verso blank).

Catchword variants: A5ʳ very [came into his Court, without verie] B2ᵛ day [day,] B3ʳ not [Notwithftanding,] C2ᵛ bat [that] D1ʳ yongeft [youngeft] D8ʳ rehearfed [she rehearfed] E2ʳ (occafi-)on [on,] E4ᵛ (Pal-)merin, [merin] E8ᵛ heard [heard,] F2ᵛ Chap. [CHAP.] G2ᵛ(re-)turned [returned] I2ʳ (Ma-)dame [dame,] I7ʳ the [The] K6ᵛ head [heade] K8ᵛ loue. [loue] L7ᵛ honour [honor] M5ʳ death [death,] M7ʳ Scyci- [Scicilian] M8ʳ Lord [Lorde] N1ʳ (fay-)ing, [ing.] N2ᵛ where [where,] N5ᵛ Gen, [Gentlemen,] O5ʳ (pro-)céeding [céeding,] O6ʳ (Pal-)merin [merin,] O7ʳ fake [loue] O8ʳ birth, [Byrth] P3ʳ paines [paines,] P7ʳ con- [Conquere,] P8ʳ Realme, [Realme.] Q3ʳ felues [felues,] Q3ᵛ wil [will] Q6ᵛ (Fa-)hearts [thers] R1ʳ foftly [foftly,] R3ʳ refpect [refpect,] R3ᵛ loue [loue,] R4ʳ Madam, [Madame,] R6ᵛ (trou-)bled, [bled] R7ʳ defired, [defired] R7ᵛ blow [blowe] T1ᵛ Truly [Truely] T4ᵛ loue [Loue] T6ʳ fhe [fhee] T7ʳ pro- [Protection,] T8ᵛ to [fo] X1ʳ (Palme-)rin [merin] Y1ʳ he [hee] Y2ᵛ (beha-)uiour [uior,] Y6ᵛ (de-)termined [termined,] Y7ᵛ fhee [fhe] Y8ᵛ Hall, [hall.] Z3ʳ (dif-)perfed, [pearfed]; no cw on Y4ᵛ

Typography: 36 ll., 148 (156 / 158) × 88 mm. (D2ʳ and M3ʳ in Lambeth Palace copy); text, black letter (and some roman and italic) 81 / 82 mm. for 20 ll. Chapter 4 misp. 3, chap. 18 misp. 17, ch. 24 misp. 22, ch. 55 misp. 53, ch. 59 misp. 61, ch. 65 misp. 63.

Note: the first volume of the third edition is printed from two quite distinct founts of type. The first (fount x) was used from the beginning up to sig. F8ᵛ; the second (fount y) from sig. G1ʳ to the end of this part. For a facsimile reproduction of the two founts, see Jordi Sánchez-Martí, "The Publication History of Anthony Munday's *Palmerin d'Oliva*," *Gutenberg Jahrbuch* 89 (2014), 203, fig. 4.

In Lambeth Palace copy C8 is misbound between D3–4; E8 is lacking. In the BL copy A8 is lacking.

Copies examined: Lambeth Palace (ARC K73.3B P18), first issue; British Library (C.56.d.8), second issue. Both copies bound as one volume with the following item.

STC 19159, 19159a

Volume 2:

Title-page: THE | SECOND PART | OF THE HONOVRABLE | HISTORIE, OF *PALMERIN* | *D'OLIVA*. | Continuing his rare fortunes, Knightly deeds of | Chiualrie, happie fucceffe in loue: and how | he was crowned Emperour of | *Conftantinople*. | *Herein is likewife concluded the variable troubles* | *of the Prince* Trineus, *and faire* Agriola *the* | *Kings daughter of England: with their* | *fortunate Marriage.* | Tranflated by *A. M.* one of the Meffengers of | her Maiefties Chamber. | *Patere aut abftine.* | [*orn.* Yamada 3] | *LONDON,* | Printed by *T. C.* and *B. A.* for *Richard Higgenbotham* and | are to be folde at his fhop, at the figne of the Car- | dinals hat without Newgate, 1616.

Head-title: [*orn.* Yamada 14] | THE SECOND | PART OF THE AVN- | TIENT AND HONOVRA- | ble Hiftorie of *Palmerin D'Oliua*. | *Continuing his rare Fortunes, Knightly deedes of Chiual-* | *rie, happie fucceffe in Loue, and how hee was crow-* | *ned Emperour of* Conftantinople. *Herein* | *is likewife concluded the variable trou-* | *bles of* Trineus, *and faire* Agriola | *of England, with their for-* | *tunate Marriage. &c.* | [*rule*]

Running-title: THE HISTORIE | OF PALMERIN D'OLIVA. [*APLMERI ND'OLIVA.* L1ʳ, L5ʳ, L6ʳ; *APLMERIN* H3ʳ, I1ʳ, I3ʳ, K2ʳ, K3ʳ, M6ʳ, N3ʳ, O1ʳ; *PALMRIN* G1ʳ, G2ʳ, G4ʳ, H5ʳ, I5ʳ, I7ʳ, K5ʳ, K8ʳ, L3ʳ, L4ʳ, L7ʳ; *PALMERN* B5ʳ, C5ʳ, C7ʳ, D6ʳ, D7ʳ, E6ʳ, E7ʳ, F5ʳ, F6ʳ, O5ʳ, Q1ʳ, Q2ʳ, Q5ʳ, R6ʳ, S8ʳ, T6ʳ, T8ʳ, V8ʳ, X6ʳ, X7ʳ, Y4ʳ, Y8ʳ, Z1ʳ, Bb5ʳ; *D'OLVA.* M4ʳ, N5ʳ; B1ʳ and G7ʳ mistakenly read '*THE HISTORIE*'; B8ᵛ and G8ᵛ mistakenly read '*OF PALMERIN D'OLIVA*.' Letters in the running-title are unevenly spaced on many instances, but vary from copy to copy and thus are not recorded.

Collation: 4º: A–Bb⁸ [$4 (–A1, A2); R3 missigned K3; Bb2 missigned B2; Bb8 blank? missing], 200 leaves unnumbered.

Contents: A1 (blank). A2ʳ: title-page (verso blank). A3ʳ: [*orn. two rows of fleurons*, Yamada 23] | 'TO THE RIGHT | HONOVRABLE AND HIS | VERY GOOD LORD *EDWARD* | *DE VERE,* EARLE OXEN- | *ford,* Vifcount

Bulbecke, Lord San- | ford of Badelefmere, and Lord | high Chamberlaine of | England. | A. M. *wifheth the full iffue of his* | *noble defires.*' rom. with 6-line init. [Yamada P1] (26 × 28 mm.). A3ʳ: dedication ending '*Your Honours in all* | humilitie. A. M.' A4ʳ: [*orn. two rows of fleurons*, Yamada 23] | 'TO THE FRIEND- | LY READERS.' ital. with 6-line initial [Yamada Y1] (26 × 28 mm). A4ᵛ: epistle ending 'Yours to his vttermoſt | *Anthony Monday.*' A5ʳ–Bb7ʳ: HT and text, blackletter. Bb7ᵛ: translator's address to readers with announcement (roman), '*Antonie Monday.* | Honos alit Artes. | *FINIS.*'

Catchword variants: C1ᵛ Friend, [Friende,] C2ʳ fire. [fire.] C4ʳ cruell [cruel] D2ᵛ nature [nature,] D8ʳ with [without] D8ᵛ signes, [signes.] E3ʳ ſtrokes, [ſtrokes.] F2ᵛ Olorioco [Olorico] F5ʳ life, [life.] H1ᵛ turnde [turned] H3ᵛ Lorde [Lord] I1r CPAP. [*CHAP.*] I8ʳ truſt [truſting] K3ᵛ (con-)ſider, [conſider,] K5ʳ (tor-)ments [ments?] L6ʳ depri [depriued] M3ᵛ clothed [lothed] M8ʳ cheerfull [chéerefull] M8ᵛ High- [hignes] N1ᵛ Palmerin [Palmerin,] N5ᵛ ſhee [ſhe] N7ᵛ Ladie, [Lady,] O2ᵛ solem- [sollemnized] P2ᵛ note [note,] P5ʳ ally [olly] P6ᵛ Friends [Fiiends] Q1ᵛ Caſtells [Caſtels] Q2ᵛ perforce) [perforce(] Q7ᵛ carry [carrie] R2ᵛ giuen [giuen,] R6ᵛ Hagge [hagge] R7ᵛ CHAP [*CHAP.*] R8ᵛ queſtion [queſtions,] S1ᵛ glad [right gladſome] S6ʳ guiltie [guilty] S7ᵛ hap [happe] T4ᵛ honours [honors] T8ᵛ pompe [honor,] V2ʳ Sifter [Sifters] V8ᵛ (Cer-)berus [berus,] Y8ʳ find [finde] Z1ᵛ ſtead [ſteade] Z2ʳ delight [delight,] Z6ʳ CHP. [*CHAP.*] Aa1ᵛ wel [well] Aa2ʳ (hin-)dered, [dered] Aa3ʳ mourn [mourne] Aa5ʳ *Pal*- [(Palmerin] Bb1ᵛ ſonnes, [Sonnes,] Bb2ᵛ (Em-)perour, [perour]; no cw D6ᵛ, I3ᵛ. Note that all cw preceding a new chapter print the abbreviation "CHAP." in roman, but it is printed in italics at the chapter heading.

Typography: 36 ll., 149 (158) × 85 mm. (E1ʳ in British Library copy); text, black letter (and some roman) 83 mm. for 20 ll. Chapter 3 misp. 62, chap. 4 misp. 7, ch. 6 misp. 62, ch. 9 misp. 7, ch. 14 misp. 13, ch. 19 misp. 16, ch. 23 misp. 24, ch. 41 misp. 61, ch. 44 misp. 64,

Note: In the Lambeth Palace copy, signatures B8 recto and verso are reversed. The entire gathering G presents serious textual disruptions. Some leaves are misbound: the leaf bound right after G1 should in fact be K7; and sig. P2 is misbound between N6 and N7. There is a note by librarian J. M. O. on front fly-leaf dated 1982 stating. "Part 2 B8 (recto and verso reversed?). ? Leaf bound as G[2] (out of place in part 2?). G gathering has 9 leaves (!) – some are not in the correct order." In BL gathering G is properly printed for sig. G1–G6; G6v should be followed by G8v, next G8r, then G7v, and finally G7r. But the Huntington library copy contains a correct printing of gathering G. The Huntington copy wants signatures C1, P7, and Bb1, while sig. Bb7 is torn out with text missing, but completed by hand.

Copies examined: British Library (C.56.d.8), Henry E. Huntington Library (330330; part 2 only), and Lambeth Palace (ARC K73.3B P18). The two volumes of the third edition are designated *3* in the critical apparatus.

STC: 19159a

4. The Fourth Edition (1637)

Volume 1:

Title-page: Palmerin D'Oliva. | THE FIRST PART: | [*rule*] | SHEWING | THE MIRROVR OF NOBI- | litie, the Map of Honour, Anatomie of rare | Fortunes, Heroicall prefidents of Love, won- | der of Chivalrie, and the moft accomplifhed | Knight in all perfection. | [*rule*] | Prefenting to Noble minds, their Courtly defire, | to Gentiles their expectations, and to the inferiour | *fort, how to imitate their Vertues: Handled with* | modeftie to fhun offence, yet delightfull | for Recreation. | [*rule*] | *Written in* Spanifh, Italian, *and* French: *and from* | them turned into *Englifh,* by *A. M.* one of the | Meffengers of his Majefties | Chamber. | *Patere & Abftine>.* | [*orn. Yamada 15*] | LONDON, | Printed for B. ALSOP and T. FAVVCET, dwelling in | *Grub-ftreet* neere the lower Pumpe. | 1637.

Head-title: [*double rule*] | [*orn.*] | THE FIRST PART | OF THE ANCIENT | and honourable Hiftorie of the | valiant Prince *Palmerin D'Oliva,* | Emperour of *Conftantinople* ; | Sonne to King FLORENDOS of *Macedonia,* | and the Faire GRIANA, Daughter to *Re-* | *micius,* Emperour of *Conftantinople:* | a Hiftory full of fingular and | *Courtly recreation.* | [*rule*]

Running-title: || The Hiftorie of *Palmerin D'Oliva*, || | ||Emperour of *Conftantinople.* PART. I. || [Hiftory A5–8ᵛ, B1ᵛ, B3–4ᵛ, C1ᵛ, C3ᵛ, D2–3ᵛ, E1ᵛ, E3ᵛ, F2–3ᵛ, G2–3ᵛ, H3ᵛ, H7–8ᵛ, I6–7ᵛ, K6–7ᵛ, L5ᵛ, L8ᵛ, M5ᵛ, M7ᵛ, N7–8ᵛ, O6–7ᵛ, P5–6ᵛ, Q7–8ᵛ, S5ᵛ, S7ᵛ, T6ᵛ, T8ᵛ, V6–7ᵛ, X6ᵛ, X8ᵛ, Y7ᵛ; Y6ᵛ–7ʳ invert the two parts of the RT; Y8ᵛ–Z1ʳ print 'Emperour of *Conftantinople.* PART. I.' in both parts of RT]

Collation: 4º: A–Y⁸, Z⁴ [$4 (–A2, Z4) signed; missigning O3 as O4, S2 as S4], 180 leaves unnumbered

Contents: A1 (blank except for sig. 'A'). A2ʳ: title-page (verso blank). A3ʳ: [*double rule*] | [*orn.*] | 'TO | THE WORSHIPFVLL, | Mʳ. FRANCIS YONG, *of Brent-* | *Pellam* [stet], in the County of *Hertford* Efquire, | and to Miftreffe SVSAN YONG his wife, | *and my moft kind Miftreffe>, health, and* | their hearts contentment, con- | nually [*stet*] wifhed.' ital. with 6-line init. (26 × 26 mm.). A3ᵛ: dedication ending 'Your poore well-willer | till death, | *A. M.*' | [*rule*] | [*orn. Yamada 14*] A4: [*double rule*] | [*three rows of type orn.*] | '*To the Reader.*' rom. with 10-line init. (38 × 40 mm). A5ʳ–Z4ʳ: HT and text, black-letter. Z4ʳ: 'FINIS' followed by recapitulation and announcement by the translator, '*A. Mundy.* | Honos alit Artes.' (verso blank).

Catchwords: B2ᵛ day [day,] B4ᵛ here, [heere,] C2ʳ (se-)cretly [cretly,] C8ᵛ she [shee] D1ʳ yongest [youngest] E5ʳ faid [fayd] F6ᵛ lone [love] G2ᵛ fome [fomewhat] H5ᵛ folemnized [folemnized,] H6ᵛ (Ptolo-)mes [mies] I7ʳ (dif-)courfe, [difcourfe,] L1ʳ (him)felfe [felfe,] M5ʳ death [death,] M6ᵛ Staves [Staues] M8ʳ accom- [acoompany] M8ᵛ having [hauing] N1ʳ (of-)teu [ten] O3ʳ world. [world,] O4ᵛ Country [Countrey] O5ʳ (pro-)céeding [céeding,] O8ᵛ Chap. XLII. [Chap. XLIII.] P1ʳ happe [hap] P3ʳ paines [paines,] P6ʳ Citty [City,] P7ʳ con- [Conquer] Q1ᵛ (beau-)ty [tie] Q3ʳ loofe [lofe] Q8ᵛ Chap. XLVIII. [Chap. L.] R3ʳ refpect [refpect,] R5ʳ (vnhappi-)ly [lie] R5ᵛ fighes [fighes,] V2ᵛ Befides, [Befides] V8ʳ (afflicti-)ons [ons,] X1ʳ neuer [never] X4ᵛ (Pal-)merin [merin,] Y5ᵛ finger [finger,] Y8ʳ Believe [Beléeue] Z1ʳ (deter-)mined [determined] Z2ᵛ (afflicti-)ons? [afflictions?].

Typography: 35 ll., 144 (160) × 90 mm. (H1ᵛ); text, black letter (and some roman and italic) 82 mm. for 20 ll.; dedication: italic 94 mm. (A3ʳ); '*To the Reader.*': roman 82 mm. (A4ᵛ); headline roman and italic. Chapter 18 misp. 17, chap. 24 misp. 22, chap. 32 misp. 22, chap. 33 misp. 34, chap. 49 misp. 43, chap. 54 misp. 52, chap. 55 misp. 53, chap. 59 misp. 61, chap. 65 misp. 63.

Note: The Huntington copy wants sig. C3–6.

Volume 2:

Title-page: Palmerin D'oliva. | THE SECOND PART: | OF *T*HE HONOVRABLE | HISTORIE OF *PALMERIN* | *D'OLIVA.* | [*rule*] | Continuing his rare fortunes, Knightly | deeds of Chiualry, happy fucceffe in love, | and how he was crowned Emperour of | *Conftantinople.* | [*rule*] | *Herein is likewife concluded the variable troubles* | *of the Prince* Trineus, *and faire* Agriola *the* | *Kings daughter of England: with their* | *fortunate. Marriage.* | [*rule*] | Tranflated by *A. M.* one of the Meffengers of | her Majefties Chamber. | *Patere aut abftine:* | [*orn. Yamada 3*] | LONDON. | Printed for B.Alsop and T.Favvcet, dwelling in | *Grub-ftreet,* neere the lower Pumpe. | 1637.

Head-title: [*orn. Yamada 14 upturned*] | THE SECOND | PART OF THE AN- | *T*IENT AND HONORA- | ble Hiftory of *Palmerin D'Oliva.* | *Continuing his rare Fortunes, Knightly deedes of* | *Chiualry, happy fucceffe in Love, and how he was crow* | *ned Emperour of* Conftantinople. *Herein* | *is likewife concluded the variable* *trou-* | *bles of* Tryneus, *and faire* Agriola | *of* England, *with their for-* | *tunate Marriage. &c.* | [*rule*]

Running-title: || The Hiſtory of [Of NOSTYZAa1ᵛ, LMRX2ᵛ, MPQTV3ᵛ, ANOPQRSVXYZAaBb4ᵛ] *Palmerin D'Oliva.* [*D'Oliva*ₐ NOSTYZAa1ᵛ, LMRX2ᵛ, MPQTV3ᵛ, ANOPQRSVXYZAa4ᵛ; *DOliva.* K4ᵛ, L6ᵛ] || | || Emperour of *Conſtantinople*. PART. 2. [*Conantnople* K5ʳ, L3ʳ; 2 turned T6, 8ʳ; 2ₐ A5, 7ʳ, I1–2ʳ, K5–6, 8ʳ, L2–4ʳ, O2–3ʳ, S5–6ʳ, TVXYZAa5–8ʳ, Aa2ʳ, Bb5ʳ] || [*Oliva* with turned *a* A5ᵛ; F7ᵛ–F8ʳ invert the two parts of the RT; G6ᵛ–G7ʳ print 'The Hiſtory of *Palmerin D'Oliva.*' in both parts of RT; G8ᵛ–H1ʳ print 'Emperour of *Conſtantinople*. PART. 2.' in both parts of RT]

Collation: 4° A–Bb⁸ [$4 signed; misſigning G4 as G2, H4 as H2, I[1] as F[1], O3 as M3], 200 leaves unnumbered

Contents: A1ʳ: title-page (verso blank). A2: [*orn. Yamada 12*] | 'TO THE RIGHT HONO- | RABLE AND HIS VERY | GOOD LORD *EDWARD* | *DE VERE, EARLE OXEN-* | *ford*, Viſcount, Bulbecke, Lord San- | ford of Badeleſmere, and Lord | high Chamberlaine of | England. | [*rule*] | A. M. *Wiſheth the full iſſue of his* | *noble deſires.*' rom. with 7-line initial [Yamada P1] (27 × 27 mm.). A3ʳ: [*three rows of type orn.*] | 'TO THE FRIENDLY | READERS', ital. with 6-line initial. A3ᵛ: epiſtle ending, 'Yours to his vttermoſt | *Anthony Monday.*' A4ʳ–Bb6ᵛ: HT and text, black-letter. Bb6ᵛ: 'FINIS.' Bb7ʳ: translator's address to readers, announcement and '*FINIS.*' (verso blank).

Catchwords: A3ʳ ſonne [ſon] A5ʳ (Fa-)vour [vour,] A5ᵛ honor [honor,] A8ᵛ Aneas [Æneas] B2ᵛ CHAP. IV. [CHAP. III.] B6ᵛ God [The] B7ᵛ CHAP. VII. [CHAP. VI.] D5ᵛ ſignes, [ſignes.] E5ʳ CHAP. XIII. [CHAP. XIIII.] F2ʳ thinke [hinke] F2ᵛ colours [colours,] F3ʳ Madam [Madam,] G1ᵛ any [further] H4ᵛ hereof [hereof,] H6ʳ me, [me.] L2ʳ ekéef [féeke] L3ᵛ (apper-)tained, [taine,] L7ᵛ (perfor-)mance [manen] M2ᵛ thanks [thanks,] M4ᵛ Madame, [Madam,] M8ʳ CHAP. XXXIII. [CHAP. XXXII.] P2ʳ (boun-)den [den.] P4ᵛ (en-)tered [tred] P7ʳ (en-)chantment [chantment,] Q1ᵛ gréeved [gréeved,] Q2ʳ Beſide [Beſide,] Q4ʳ Citie [Citty] Q6ᵛ Hyppolita [Hypolita,] Q8ᵛ CHAP. XLIV. [CHAP. XLIIII.] R4ʳ Iſle [Iſle,] S4ʳ an [and] T1ʳ Palmeri [Palmerin] T2ᵛ (be-)fore [fore:] T3ᵛ honours [honors] T5ᵛ highnes [Highneſſe] T6ᵛ CHAP. LI. [CHAP. LIII.] V4ʳ (grea-)ter [ter,] V6ʳ Need- [Néedleſſe] X1ʳ (La-)dy, [die,] X2ʳ hitherto- [hitherto] Y2ᵛ Trineus [Tryneus] Z1ᵛ delight [delight,] Z3ʳ doth [do h] Z4ʳ ſaid [ſaid:] Z5ʳ meane [mean] Aa1ᵛ defence [defence,] Aa2ᵛ (pa-)tience [tience,] Aa3ʳ (Em-)perour [perour,] Aa6ʳ highly [hlghly,] Aa8ᵛ nor [not]

Typography: 35 ll. 143 (157) × 89 mm. (A5ᵛ); text, black letter (and some roman and italic) 82 mm. for 20 ll.; dedication: roman 82 mm. (A2ʳ); 'TO THE

FRIENDLY | READERS': italic 94 mm. (A3ʳ). Chapter 4 misp. 3, chap. 19 misp. 18, chap. 23 misp. 24, chap. 33 misp. 32, chap. 59 misp. 57.

Copy collated: University of Alicante Library (FA/012). *Other copies examined*: Folger Shakespeare Library (STC 19160) copies 1 and 2, Henry E. Huntington Library (62839); all copies examined are bound together as one volume with the preceding item. This edition is designated *4* in the critical apparatus.

Note: the University of Alicante copy wants sig. Bb7–8. For a bibliographical description with illustrations, see Jordi Sánchez-Martí, "The University of Alicante Library Copy of *Palmerin d'Oliva* (London, 1637): A Bibliographical Description," *Sederi* 23 (2013): 123–37.

STC 19160

Glossary

The glossary is selective and comprises only words and expressions that may cause difficulty to the modern reader. It records terms whose archaic spelling makes them hard to recognize, in which case only the modern spelling of the word is provided. Words and expressions are also glossed if they have become obsolete or if their meaning has changed since the sixteenth century. The definitions are based primarily on the printed edition of the *OED* (2nd ed., 1989), whose definition number is provided in parentheses where applicable. If a definition is taken from the 3rd edition (in progress, www.oed.com), it is noted in the entry. When an asterisk precedes the word to be defined, this occurrence predates the first recorded usage in the *OED*. When the usage in *Palmerin d'Oliva* provides the earliest example in the *OED*, a bullet precedes the entry in the glossary. In both cases the information has been confirmed against the 3rd edition of the *OED* [*OED*3] at the time of writing. Note, however, that I have dated the entire text to 1588, even if no copy of the second part of the first edition has been preserved, whereas the *OED* inconsistently dates this part to 1588 or 1597.

A

abide *v.*	(1) to remain in expectation, wait
	(8) to dwell, reside
abiding *n.*	(7) a place where one habitually remains or resides; abode, habitation, dwelling
abiect *n.*	a degraded or downtrodden person
aboad(e) *n. 1*	(2) a temporary remaining; a stay in a place, a sojourn
abroad *adv.*	(4) out of the home country; far away from home
abuse *v.*	(3) to show oneself in false colors, to make false pretensions
abye *v.*	(2) to pay the penalty for (an offence), to redeem, atone for, suffer for, make amends for, expiate
acceptation *n.*	(2) favorable reception, approval
accident *n.*	(1a) an occurrence, incident, event
accord *v.*	(6) to agree to (rule, course to be taken); to assent or consent to
account *n.*	(12) *to make ~ of* to hold in estimation, regard as important; to value, esteem
	(13) *to make ~ that, to do* to calculate, reckon, expect

accoustred *adj.*	accoutred
addicted *adj.*	(1d) committed (in a specified manner or to a specified thing); (also occas.) bound or orientated (in a specified direction) [*OED*3]
addresse *v.*	(14a) to direct one's course, to make one's way [*OED*3]
adiewe *n.*	adieu
adiuration *n.*	an earnest appeal
admirable *adj.*	(1) exciting wonder, to be marvelled at; wonderful, remarkable, astonishing, surprising [*OED*3]
aduantage *n.*	(3) a place of vantage
	(5b) *to take ~ of* (a thing): to use any favorable condition which it yields
	(5c) *to play upon ~* to cheat
	(8) *to ~* in addition; further, more
aduenture *n.*	(2) a chance occurrence; an event; an accident
aduenture *v.*	(2) to risk the loss of, to risk, stake
aduertise *v.*	(1d) with prepositional phrase or *that*-clause as complement. To apprise, notify, warn (a person) by some means, that something is the case, etc. [*OED*3]
	(2a) to take note of, attend to, notice, observe (a thing) [*OED*3]
aduertisement *n.*	(1b) the action or an act of calling the attention of someone; (an) admonition, warning, instruction [*OED*3]
affayre *n.*	(1b) a thing that concerns any one; a concern, a matter
	(2c) *pl.*: public business, transactions or matters concerning men or nations collectively
affect *v.* 1	(1a) to aim at, aspire to, or make for (something); to seek to obtain or attain
	(4a) to be drawn to, have affection or liking for (a person); to take to, be fond of, show preference for; to fancy, like, or love [*OED*3]
affected *adj.* 1	(2b) having a favourable affection or inclination; favorably disposed or inclined; attached, partial (*to*) [*OED*3]
affection *n.*	(5) state of the mind toward a thing; disposition toward, bent, inclination
affectionate *adj.*	(3) passionate, wilful, obstinate
afford *v.*	(5) to bestow, grant
affright *v.*	(1) to frighten, to terrify
against *prep.*	(5a) in a direction facing; towards, forward to, so as to meet
	(18) of time: close to
	(19) in anticipation of, in preparation for, in time for
agatha *n.*	agate
agreeue *v.*	(2) to afflict oneself, to grieve, to feel grief

Glossary

allay *v. 1*	(4a) to destroy or overcome (a principle, attribute, tendency, etc.). [*OED*3]
allow *v.*	(7a) to take into account or give credit for (a person's action or intention). [*OED*3]
allowable *adj.*	(1) worthy of praise; praiseworthy, laudable
alteration *n.*	(2b) a disordered state of the body; a disease, a disorder [*OED*3]
amaine *adv.*	(2a) at full speed
*amarous *adj.*	bitter, sharp, froward, hard to be appeased, spightful, sour
amaze *v.*	(3) to alarm
ambush *v.*	(1b) *refl.* to lay in wait
amend *v.*	(6a) to heal or recover
amiable *adj.*	(2) worthy to be loved, lovable, lovely
ancient *adj.*	(6) of living beings: old, aged
angerly *adv.*	(2) with anger or resentment
annihilate *v.*	(2) to make null and void, annul, cancel
anon *adv.*	(4) straightway, at once, forthwith, instantly
answerable *adj.*	(2) such as responds to demands, needs, wishes; suitable, fitting, proper, becoming
	(3) corresponding, correspondent, accordant
	(4) corresponding in quantity or amount; proportional, commensurate
antiquities *n. pl.*	(6) ancient records
apparrell *v.*	(7) to deck, adorn, embellish
appoint *v.*	(6) to determine, resolve, purpose
	(15) to equip completely, fit out, furnish; to accoutre
appointment *n.*	(2) an agreement, pact, contract
	(6) the action of ordaining what is to be done
approue *v. 1*	(1) to make good (a statement or position); to show to be true, prove, demonstrate
approued *adj.*	(1a) proved or established by experience, tried, tested
arbour *n.*	(2) a garden of herbs or flowers; a flower-garden
argue *v.*	(3) to prove
arise *v.*	(1) to stand up
	(11) to rise in rank or eminence
arm *v. 1*	(2e) to prepare (for resistance)
arrest *v.*	(6a) to cause to stop; to stop the course of a person or animal
	(10) to catch, capture, seize, lay hold upon
arrieregarde *n.*	rearguard
artificially *adv.*	(1b) with skill directed to hide or deceive [*OED*3]
	(2) with much art, skilfully
assaie *v.*	(16) to attempt, try to do (anything difficult)
*assaile *v. 1*	(10) to address with offers of love, to woo

assurance *n.*	(2) a marriage engagement, betrothal
	(7) security
assure *v.*	(1) to render safe or secure (from attack or danger)
astonied *adj.*	(1a) stunned, stupefied, deprived of sensation; primarily by a blow
attaine *v.*	(8) to come into the possession of, to gain by effort, acquire, obtain
attaint *v.*	(3) to convict, prove guilty
attainted *ppl. adj.*	(1) hit, struck
attempt *v.*	(5) to try with temptations, try to win over, seduce, or entice; to tempt
attend *v.*	(13) to look out for, wait for, await
	(13b) to wait for, await a future time, event, result
attendaunce *n.*	(1) the action or condition of applying one's mind or observant faculties to something
auail *n.*	(1) advantage, benefit, profit
auailable *adj.*	(1) capable of producing a desired result; of avail, effectual, efficacious
auaunce *v.*	(1b) *refl.* to move (oneself) forward
*auaunt courer, auaunt-currer *n.*	one who runs or rides before, a herald; esp. in pl. the scouts, skirmishers, advance-guard of an army
audacious *adj.*	(2) unrestrained by, or setting at defiance, the principles of decorum and morality
*auditrice *n.*	a female hearer or auditor (s.v. *auditress*)
auncient *n.*	*see* ancient
awarrant *v.*	to vouch for, warrant, guarantee
•aymer *n.*	a person who aims (in various senses of the verb)
ayre *n.*	air

B

bad *pa. t. of* bid *v.*	(10) to command, enjoin, order
bag *n.*	(20) ~ *and baggage* a military phrase denoting all the property of an army collectively
barriers *n. pl.*	(2a) the palisades enclosing the ground where a tournament or tilting was held; the lists. Also, a low railing or fence running down the center of the lists on opposite sides of which, and in opposite directions the combatants rode, reaching their lances accross.
	(2b) hence, the expression *to fight at* ~
base *adj.*	(3) occupying a low position, low-lying; of lower situation than neighboring parts
base court *n.*	(1) the lower or outer court of a castle or mansion, occupied by the servants

battaile *n.*	(8a) battalion (s.v. *battle* n.)
batterie *n.*	(3) a succession of heavy blows inflicted upon the walls of a city or fortress by means of artillery; bombardment
battle *n.*	(9) more fully called *great* or *main battle*: the main body of an army or naval force, as distinguished from the van and rear, or from the wings
beast *n.*	(3) a domesticated animal part of a farm's "stock" or cattle
bed *n.*	(6b) ~ *of honor* the grave of a soldier who has died on the field of battle
before time *adv.*	previously
begin *v.* 1	(1c) to begin a speech, to start speaking, to speak
begirt *ppl.* of **begird** *v.*	(3) to beset in hostile array, to besiege
beguile *v.*	(5) to charm away, wile away
beholding *ppl. adj.*	(1) under obligation, obliged, indebted
beleeue *v.*	to believe
belike *adv.*	in all likelihood, probably. Also in weaker sense: perhaps, possibly
*****benefitte** *n.*	(3b) a natural advantage or "gift"
benighted *ppl. adj.*	(1) overtaken by the darkness of the night
bequeath *v.*	(6) to deliver, bestow, give, yield, furnish
beseem *v.*	(3) to be becoming or fitting
besturre *v.*	(2) to stir up, to put into vigorous action (s.v. *bestir*)
bethink *v.*	(8) to occupy oneself in thought; to reflect, consider, think
betimes *adv.*	(2) at an early hour, early in the morning
betwixt *prep.*	between
bewray *v.*	(3) to divulge or reveal (secrets)
beyond *prep.*	(5a) outside the limit or sphere of
bide *v.*	(7) to await in resistance, to face, encounter, withstand
blubred *ppl. a.*	blubbered; flooded with tears
bold *adj.*	(3) *to make* ~ to take the liberty (*to do* a thing)
bootlesse *adj.* 1	(2) without help or remedy; incurable, remediless, helpless
*****boudged** *pa. t.*	(1a) to stir or move from one's place; s.v. *budge* v.1
bounden *adj.* 1	(4) under obligation on account of favors received; obliged, beholden, indebted (to)
brave *adj.*	(2) splendid, showy, grand, fine, handsome
brave *v.*	(7) to boast, glory, vaunt
braving *ppl. adj.*	(1) daring, defiant, boasting
break(e) with *v.*	(22b) to reveal what is in one's mind to a person
breathe *v.*	(5) to pause, take rest
briding *vbl. n.*	wedding

brooke *v.*	(1a) to enjoy the use of, make use of, profit by; to use, enjoy, possess, hold
	(3) to put up with, bear with, endure, tolerate
bruite *n.*	(2) report noised abroad, rumor, tidings
brunt *n. 1*	(2) an assault, charge, onset, violent attack
brute *n.*	see **bruite**
buckle *v.*	(3b) to close, come to close quarters; to grapple, engage
budget *n.*	(1a) a pouch, bag, wallet, usually of leather
buffell *n.*	(1) buffalo; s.v. *buffle*
build *v.*	(6b) to found one's confidence, establish an argument, etc. *on*; to rely confidently *on* a person or thing
bumbaste *v.*	to flog, beat soundly, thrash
buy *v.*	(3a) to pay the penalty of, suffer the consequences of, "pay for"
byllow *n.*	(2a) a great swelling wave; s.v. *billow*

C

cabbanet *n.*	(3) a small chamber or room; a private apartment, a boudoir (s.v. *cabinet* n.)
calling *vbl. n.*	(10) position, estate, or station in life; rank
camizado *n.*	(1) a night attack
canuaz *v.*	(2) to knock about, shake and shatter thoroughly; to buffet; to beat, batter (s.v. *canvass*)
*canuazado *n.*	(2) a night attack; a camisado
capacity *n.*	(5) active power or force of mind; mental ability
cap a pe *adv.*	from head to foot: in reference to arming or accoutring
carkasse *n.*	(1a) the dead body of a man or beast
carricke *n.*	carrack
carrire *n.*	(2a) of a horse: a short gallop at full speed; a charge, encounter (at a tournament or in a battle); s.v. *career*, n.
*carrire *v.*	(1) to take a short gallop, to "pass a career"; to charge (at a tournament); to turn this way and that in running (said of a horse); s.v. *career*, v.
cary *v.*	carry
casuall *adj.*	(5a) subject to chance or accident; frail, uncertain, precarious
catarre *n.*	(1) the profuse discharge from nose and eyes which generally accompanies a cold, and which was formerly supposed to run down from the brain
catife, caytife *n.*	(1) a captive, a prisoner
	(2) expressing commiseration: a wretched miserable person, a poor wretch, one in a piteous case

Glossary

cause *n.*	(10) a matter of concern, affair, business; the case as it concerns any one
censure *v.*	(1) to form or give a "censure" or opinion; to estimate, judge of, pass judgment on, criticize, judge
certifie *v.*	(1) to give certain information (of)
	(3a) to make a person certain or sure of a matter; to inform certainly
chair of state *n.*	(17b) costly and imposing chair as befits persons of rank and wealth; s.v. *state* n.
challenge *v.*	(1) to accuse, bring a charge against
	(5) to lay claim to, demand as a right, arrogate (to) oneself
	(6a) to demand, to claim
chamber *n.*	(1b) ~ *of presence*: the reception room in a palace
character *n.*	(2) a distinctive significant mark of any kind; a graphic sign or symbol
charge *n.*	(16b) *to lay to one's* ~ to impute to one as a fault, charge one with
*****charie** *adj.*	(3) dear, precious
	(8) charily; carefully; *quasi-adv.*
chased *ppl. adj. 2*	of plate, etc.: ornamented with embossed work, engraved in relief
check *v. 1*	(10) to reproach, taunt, revile
chirurgie *n.*	that part of medical science and art which is concerned with the cure of diseases or bodily injuries by manual operation
chirurgion *n.*	one whose profession it is to cure bodily diseases and injuries by manual operation
chiualrie *n.*	(4) a feat of knightly valor; a gallant deed
*****clamor** *n.*	(4) loud noise of musical instruments
cleane *adv.*	(4) properly, completely
closely *adv.*	(3) secretly, covertly, privately, privily
coast *v.*	(2a) to go or move by the side or border of (a place, etc.); to skirt
	(4) to sail by the sea-coast; to sail in sight of land
	(8) to approach, make one's way *to* or *towards* (a place or person)
coche *n.*	coach
coll *v. 1*	(1) to throw one's arms round the neck of; to embrace, hug
collombes *n. pl.*	columns
comfort *v.*	(4) to strengthen (the bodily faculties, organs, etc.); to invigorate, refresh
command *n.*	(4b) *at* ~ under one's control
command *v.*	(7) with ellipsis involving the sense of a verb of giving: to order to be given

*commaundresse *n.*   (1) a female commander
commoditie *n.*   (4) convenient juncture of events; opportunity, occasion
commonlie *adv.*   (4) openly, in public, publicly
commune *v.*   (6a) to talk together, converse
compact *v. 2*   (1) to make a compact
companie *n.*   (3c) *a great* ~ a great number
company *v.*   (1) to have society with; to keep company with
compasse *n. 1*   (1) measure
(3a) designing, skillful devising; subtilty, cunning
(11a) circular movement, course, or journey, circuit, round
compasse *v. 1*   (2) to contrive, devise, machinate (a purpose)
(11) to attain to or achieve (an end or object aimed at)
(13) to get over, surmount
complaire *v.*   to be complaisant to, to gratify
conceit(e) *n.*   (1) that which is conceived in the mind, a conception, notion, idea, thought
(4) opinion, judgment, consideration
(8b) a fanciful action; a trick
conceiued *ppl. adj.*   (1b) pregnant
conclude *v.*   (13) to come to a decision, make an arrangement, resolve, determine
condigne *adj.*   (1) equal in worth or dignity
(3a) worthily deserved, merited, fitting, appropriate; adequate
condiscende *v.*   (5) to give one's consent, to accede or agree to (a proposal, request, measure, etc.); to acquiesce
condition *n.*   (11b) *pl.* personal qualities, manners, morals, ways; behavior, temper
conditioned *ppl. a.*   (1a) of persons, having a (specified) disposition or temperament
confederate *n.*   (1) a person in league with another or others for mutual support or joint action
conference *n.*   (5) communication, converse, intercourse
*confident *adj.*   (6) trustworthy, trusty, to be depended on
confine *n. 2*   (2) *pl.* region, territory
confound *v.*   (1) to defeat utterly, bring to ruin, overthrow (an adversary)
coniuration *n.*   (1) a swearing together; a banding together against a superior power
(2) solemn appeal or entreaty, adjuration
coniure *v.*   (3) to constrain (a person to some action) by appealing to something sacred; to adjure
(4a) to appeal solemnly or earnestly to; to beseech, implore
*conqueringly *adv.*   in a conquering manner, victoriously

conscience *n.*	(8a) tenderness of conscience with regard to an act, scruple; also compunction, remorse
consist in *v.*	(6a) to be, reside in
consort *v.*	(6) to accord, agree, harmonize
construction *n.*	(8a) interpretation put upon conduct, action, facts, words
consumate *v.*	(1) to complete, finish
consume *v. 1*	(1b) to do away with by evaporation or the like, cause to disappear or vanish away
	(1c) to destroy (a living being), by disease or any wasting process
	(6b) ~ *awaie* to waste away with disease
	(6c) to burn away, become burned to ashes
contagious *adj.*	(6) injurious to human life or health otherwise than by breeding disease; pernicious, noxious
contemne *v.*	(1) to treat as of small value, treat or view with contempt; to despise, disdain, scorn, slight
content *n. 2*	(1) satisfaction, pleasure
content *v.*	(1b) to please, gratify; to delight
	(4) to satisfy (a person) by full payment; to compensate, remunerate
contentation *n.*	(1) the action of contenting or satisfying
continencie *n.*	(2) self-restraint in the matter of sexual appetite
continent *adj.*	(2) characterized by self-restraint in the matter of sexual indulgence; chaste
contract *v.*	(3b.b) *refl.* to enter into a matrimonial contract with
contracted *ppl. adj.*	(2) betrothed, affianced
contrarie *adj.*	(3a) of persons and their actions: actively opposed, antagonistic, hostile
contrarie *n.*	(6) an adversary, opponent
contrarie, contrary *v.*	(1) to oppose
	(2a) to contradict, gainsay a person
	(3) to do what is contrary to or the reverse of
conuenable *adj.*	(1) suitable, appropriate
conuenience *n.*	(1a) agreement, accordance
conuersant *adj.*	(2a) having regular or frequent intercourse *together*
conueyaunce *n.*	(9b) form of expression, style
*copartner *n.*	(3) a fellow; an equal; a match
cope *v. 2*	(3) to contend, fight with
cornet *n. 1*	(1a) in early times a wind-instrument made of a horn or resembling a horn; a horn
coronet *n.*	(1a) a small or inferior crown
correction *n.*	(1b) *under* ~ subject to correction; a formula expressing deference to superior information or critical authority

correspondent *adj.*	(2) agreeing with something else in the way of analogy
couller *n.*	color; *pl.* (7d) *to dreade no* ~ to fear no foe, to have no fear (12d) *under* ~ *of* under pretext or pretence of (13) *pl.* rhetorical modes, ornaments
couller *v.*	to color; (3) to represent in fair colors (what is of the opposite character); to disguise, excuse
coullorable *adj.*	(1b) ornamental
countenance *n.*	(1b) *to make or set (a)* ~: to assume or have a certain demeanor or attitude; to comport oneself (2) appearance, aspect, look
*****countenance** *v.*	(5b) to encourage a thing (action, practice, opinion, etc.)
counterfeite *n.*	(3) an image, likeness, portrait
counterfeite *v.*	(3) to put on a false or deceiving appearance; to disguise, falsify
countermaundeth *v.*	countermand
counteruaile *v.*	(2b) to make an equivalent return for; to reciprocate
countie *n.* 2	count
course *n.*	(3) a race (5) the rush together of two combatants in battle or tournament; charge, onset; a passage at arms (7a) the action or practice of coursing, or pursuing game with hounds (7b) beast being coursed or pursued in hunting with hounds (12a) the direction in which a ship sails (22a) a line of personal action, way of acting, method of proceeding
courtelace *n.*	a kind of short cutting sword; a cutlass
courtelax *n.*	a short broad cutting sword, a cutlass; any heavy slashing sword
coutch *v.* 1	(7) to lower (a spear, lance, etc.) to the position of attack, grasping it in the right hand with the point directed forward
cozin *adj.*	cousin
crazed *ppl. a.*	(4) broken down in health; diseased; infirm
credit *n.*	(2c) *letter of* ~ a document recommending the bearer to confidence
crosse *n.*	(14b) the cross-piece dividing the blade of a sword, etc. from the hilt, and serving as a guard to the hand; the cross-guard
*****crosse** *v.*	(14a) to thwart, oppose, go counter to (14c) to contradict, contravene, traverse (a sentence, statement, etc.)
culpable *adj.*	(1) guilty, criminal; deserving punishment

cupboorde *n.*	(1) a "board" or table to place cups and other vessels, etc. on; a piece of furniture for the display of plate; a sideboard, buffet
curious *adj.*	(7a) made with care or art
curiouslie *adv.*	(5) finely, excellently, beautifully
*****currant** *adj.*	(8) *for* ~ generally related, reported, or accepted (s.v. *current*)
*****curre** *n.*	(1b) as a term of contempt: a surly, ill-bred, low, or cowardly fellow; s.v. *cur*
currying *vbl. n.*	(1) the action of rubbing down with a curry-comb

D

daintie *adj.*	(1) pleasant, delightful
	(5b) with *of*: particular or scrupulous about (anything); careful, chary, or sparing *of*
	(5c) disinclined or reluctant
dalliance *n.*	(4) waste of time in trifling, idle delay
dally *v.*	(3) to trifle *with* a person or thing under the guise of serious action
deal *v.*	(19) to act towards people generally (in some specified way); to conduct oneself, behave, act
decipher *v.*	(3) to make out the meaning of (anything obscure or difficult to understand or trace)
	(5) of actions, outward signs, etc.: to reveal, make known, indicate; to give the key to (a person's character, etc.)
declare *v.*	(1) to make clear or plain (anything that is obscure or imperfectly understood)
	(2) to unfold, set forth (facts, circumstances); to recount, relate
deerelie *adv.*	dearly
defamed *ppl. adj.*	(1a) brought to disgrace, dishonored, of ill fame
defend *v.*	(1) to repel or avert
defie *v.* 1	(5) to set at nought; to reject, renounce
degree *n.*	(4b) a rank or class of persons
deign *v.*	(3) to treat (a person) as worthy of; to dignify (him) with
*****deintie** *n.*	(5b) as a term of endearment
delicate *n.*	(2b) a choice viand; a delicacy
deliuer *v.* 1	(2d) to get rid of, dispel (pain, disease); to relieve
deliueraunce	(2) the being delivered of offspring; the bringing forth of offspring; delivery
delude *v.*	(2) to deride, mock, laugh at
demaund *v.*	(4) to make a demand for (a thing) to (a person)
depart *v.*	(12a) ~ *with* to take leave of; to go away from
depriue *v.*	(5) remove

descry *v. 1*	(2) to disclose, reveal
	(6) to catch sight of
desert(e), desart *n. 1*(1b)	meritoriousness, excellence, worth
	(3) a due reward or recompense, whether good or evil
desire *v.*	(6) to request, pray, entreat
despayre *v.*	(1) to lose or give up hope *of*
despight *prep.*	despite
detain *v.*	(2) to keep back, withhold; esp. to keep back what is claimed
detain *v.*	(3b) to hold, hold down
detect *v.*	(2a) to inform against, accuse
detection *n.*	(1) exposure, revelation of what is concealed; criminal information, accusation
detraction *n.*	(2) the utterance of what is depreciatory or injurious to a person's reputation
deuine *v.*	divine
deuise *n.*	device
	(4) opinion, notion; what one thinks about something
	(11) something devised or fancifully invented for dramatic representation
deuise *v.*	(14) to confer, discourse, converse
deuoire *n.*	(1) that which one ought to do
	(2) that which one can do, (one's) utmost or best; chiefly in phrase *to do one's ~, to put oneself in ~* to do what one can
direct *v.*	(2a) to address (spoken words) to any one
discharge *v.*	(11) to fulfill, execute, perform (a charge, duty, trust)
discipline *n.*	(7a) correction, chastisement, punishment
discomfit *v.*	(1) to undo in battle; to defeat or overthrow completely; to beat, to rout
	(2a) to defeat or overthrow
discourse, dyscourse *n.*	(4) narration; a narrative, tale, account
discourse *v.*	(5) to tell, narrate, relate
discretion *n.*	(3) discernment
discrye *v.*	descry
dislodge *v.*	(1b) to shift the position (of a force); *refl.* to shift one's quarters
	(2b) to leave a place of encampment
dismaid *ppl. adj.*	overwhelmed with fear
disparage *v.*	(1) to match unequally; to dishonor by marrying to an inferior
dispatch *v.*	(8) to start promptly for a place, get away quickly
	(9) to make haste (*to do something*), hasten, be quick
displeasant *adj.*	(2) displeased, angry, grieved

Glossary

displeasantlie *adv.*	(2) in a displeased or offended manner
displeasure *n.*	(2) the opposite of pleasure; discomfort, uneasiness, unhappiness; grief, sorrow, trouble
	(3) that which causes or occasions offence or trouble; a wrong, an offence
dissemble *v. 1*	(5) to put on a feigned or false appearance of; to feign, pretend, simulate
distain *v.*	(2) to defile; to bring a blot or stain upon; to sully, dishonor
distempered *ppl. adj. 1*	(2) disturbed in humor, temper, or feelings; troubled
distraught *ppl. adj.*	(2b) ~ *of* (wits, senses): driven to madness, mentally deranged, crazy
diuerlry *n.*	devilry
doctor *n.*	(2b) one who is eminently skilled in a particular art or craft
dolor *n.*	(1) physical suffering, pain
domageable *adj.*	(1) causing loss or injury; hurtful, injurious
dote *v. 1*	(1) to talk foolishly or stupidly
double *adj.*	(5) characterized by duplicity, false, deceitful
doubt *n. 1*	(2) a matter or point involved in uncertainty; a doubtful question; a difficulty
	(3a) apprehension, dread, fear
	(4a.a) *to make* ~ to hesitate, to scruple
doubt *v.*	(5) to dread, fear, be afraid of
doubtfull *adj.*	(5) full of fear or apprehension
dread *ppl. adj.*	(2) held in awe; revered
drift *n.*	(5) a scheme, plot, design, device
dump *n. 1*	(1) a fit of abstraction or musing, a reverie; a dazed or puzzled state, a maze; perplexity, amazement; abscence of mind (*often in pl.*)
	(2) a fit of melancholy or depression
dure *v.*	(4) to sustain, undergo, bear
durst *pa. t.*	dared

E

earnest *n. 2*	(1) a foretaste, pledge, of anything afterwards to be received in greater abundance
earst *adv.*	(5b) referring to a recent past: not long ago, a little while since
effect *n.*	(2a) a contemplated result, a purpose; esp. in phrases, *to this* or *that* ~, *to the* ~ *that*
effectuallie *adv.*	(2) earnestly, ardently
	(5) in effect; in fact, in reality
efficacie *n.*	(3a) effect

*effronted *ppl.*	shameless, barefaced, unblushingly insolent
*effuse *n.*	a pouring out, effusion
embassage *n.*	(2) the message conveyed by an ambassador; the business entrusted to him
encurre *v*	to incur
endamage *v.*	(2) to damage physically, inflict material injury upon (a person or thing)
endure *v.*	(2) to last, continue in existence
enforce *v.*	(2) to strengthen in a moral sense; to impart resolution or fortitude to (a person); to encourage (5b) *refl.* to exert onesefl, strive (7a) to drive by force a person from a place
enorme *adj.*	(2) of sins and crimes (rarely of persons): abnormally wicked, monstrous, outrageous
entend *v.*	to intend
enterprise *n.*	(1) a design of which the execution is attempted
enterprise *v.*	(1) to attempt or undertake (a war, an expedition, etc.), run the risk of or adventure upon (danger)
enterprised *ppl. adj.*	that has been undertaken, ventured upon
entertain *v.*	(9c) to give occupation to (an enemy's forces); to engage (12) to give reception to; to receive (a person) (14) to give reception (to something); to receive in a certain manner
*entertainment *n.*	(5) treatment (of persons) (11a) the action of treating as a guest, of providing for the wants of a guest
entire *adj.*	(9) of persons and their actions: characterized by integrity; incorruptible, honest, upright
enuiron *v.*	(2b) to surround with hostile intention
equall *adj.*	(5) fair, equitable, just, impartial
equipage *n.*	(9) the appurtenances of rank or social position: ceremonious display (14) *in ~* in military array
ere *adv.*	(4) before
escuyrie *n.*	(2b) an officer in the service of a royal or other exalted personage, charged with the care of the horses (s.v. *equerry*)
espiall *n.*	(2) a body of spies; hence (chiefly in *pl.*) a spy, a scout
espousall *n.*	(1a) the celebration of a marriage; nuptials, wedding
espouse *v.*	(2) to marry
espy *v.*	(2b) to perceive by chance or unexpectedly (2c) to observe, perceive
estate *n.*	(1a) state or condition in general; *see also* **state**
estimation *n.*	(2b) the condition of being esteemed; repute

euen *adv.*	(6) exactly, precisely, "just"
except *conj.*	(2) unless
exception *n.*	(6) objection
exclaim *n.*	exclamation, outcry
exclaim *v.*	(2b) *to ~ on* to cry out loudly and suddenly against, accuse loudly, blame (persons, their actions and attributes)
executor *n.*	(2) executioner
exempt *v.*	(1) to take out or away; to put far away, remove, cut off
exigent *n. 1*	(1) an extremity, strait
expect *v.*	(2a) to wait for, await
expectation *n.*	(1) the action or state of waiting for or awaiting (something)
expedition *n.*	(1) speedy performance or prompt execution (of justice, a journey)
expence *n.*	(1b) expenditure (of substance, strength, labor, time, etc.); loss (of blood, etc. of men in battle, etc.)
experience *n.*	(1a) *to make ~ of* to make trial of
expulse *v.*	(a) to drive or thrust out from a place; to eject, evict from a possession or holding
extract *ppl. adj.*	(1b) descended (from an ancestry)
extremitie *n.*	(4) extreme or inordinate intensity of passion, suffering, labor, etc.
	(6) extreme severity or rigor
eye *n.*	(8) manner or way of looking at a thing; opinion, judgement; *one ~ of pittie* judging with pity

F

fable *v.*	(3) to speak falsely, lie
fagot *n.*	(1b) a bundle of sticks, twigs and branches for use in fascines
fall *v.*	(67e) *~ to* begin to
familiar *n.*	(3) a familiar spirit, a demon or evil spirit supposed to attend at a call
fantasie *n.*	(2) a spectral apparition, phantom; an illusory appearance
	(7) inclination, liking, desire
farre *adj.*	far
fatall *adj.*	(1) allotted or decreed by fate or destiny; destined, fated
faune *v.*	fawn
*****fauour** *n.*	(3a) *by the ~ of* leave, permission, pardon
	(7a) something given as a mark of favor; a gift given to a lover, or in medieval chivalry by a lady to her knight to be worn conspicuously as a token of affection
fayne *adj.*	(1) glad, rejoiced
feare *v.*	(3) *refl. I ~ me* I am afraid

feared *ppl. a.*	(1) affected with fear, frightened, afraid
feast *v.*	(3) to entertain hospitably and sumptuously
feign *v.*	(3) to relate or represent in fiction; to fable
***feminine** *adj.*	(3b) designating an item, esp. clothing, designed for women; adapted for use by women or girls [*OED*3]
fetch *n. 1*	(2) a contrivance, stratagem, trick
fie *int.*	(1) an exclamation expressing disgust or indignant reproach
figure *n.*	(10) an artificial representation of the human form
finish *v.*	(4a) to perfect finally or in detail
***fitlie** *adv.*	(1b) at the fitting time or season
floute *n. 1*	(1) a mocking speech or action; a piece of mockery, jeer, scoff
foile, foyle *n. 2*	(2) a repulse, defeat in an onset or enterprise
foile, foyle *v. 1*	(1) to tread under foot, trample down
foolish hardie *a.*	foolhardy
footcloth *n.*	(1) a large richly-ornamented cloth laid over the back of a horse and hanging down to the ground on each side. It was considered as a mark of dignity and state
footing *vbl. n.*	(1a) the act of walking, stepping; *to get* ~ to enter, set foot (*in a place*)
force *v. 1*	(14b) chiefly in negative sentences: to trouble oneself, be concerned, care
fore-pass *v.*	(1) to go beyond, surpass, excel
fore-point *v.*	(1a) to appoint or determine beforehand; to predestine *to* or *unto*
forfait *v.*	(1) to do amiss, sin, transgress
***forget** *v.*	(5b) *to* ~ *oneself* to lose remembrance of one's own station, position, character
formall *adj.*	(4b) of feature, stature, etc.: regular, shapely
***formatrix** *n.*	formative faculty
forraine *adj.*	foreign
fortefie *v.*	(3a) to provide (an army, etc.) with necessaries
forwardnesse *n.*	(3) proneness or inclination *to*
foyst *n. 1*	(1) a light galley; a vessel propeled both by sails and oars
frankely *adv.*	(1) freely; unrestrictedly, without restraint or constraint
freende *n.*	(4) a lover or paramour
fretting *vbl. n. 1*	(4) vexation, worrying
froward *adj.*	(2b) perverse, ill-humored
fruition *n.*	(1) enjoyment
frustrate *ppl. a.*	(2) failing of effect; ineffectual, fruitless
full *adv.*	(1) very, exceedingly
funeralles *n. pl.*	(1b) pl. with sing. sense; s.v. *funeral*
furnish *v.*	(1) to accomplish, complete, fulfill

Glossary 857

furniture *n.*	(4b) armor, suit of armor
	(4c) trappings of a horse

G
gadge *n.*	gage
gallant *n.*	(1a) a man of fashion and pleasure; a fine gentleman
gardant *n.*	guardant: a keeper, guardian, protector
garde *n.*	guard
garde *v.*	to guard
generall *adj.*	(11c.b) *in* ~ in all respects
generally *adv.*	(2) with few or no exceptions; with respect to every (or almost every) individual or case concerned
giue ouer *v.*	(63a) *to giue* ~ to give up, abandon (an attempt, a habit, a mode of life)
glad *v.*	(2) to make glad, to cause to rejoice
glory *v. 1*	(1) to exult with triumph, rejoice proudly
goodly *adj.*	(1) of good appearance
*gore blood *n.*	(2b) quasi-*adj.* gory with blood, besmeared with gore
gouernment, gouernement *n.*	(2b) in moral sense: conduct, behavior; becoming conduct, discretion
grace *n.*	(19) *pl. to do* ~ to give thanks; thanksgiving
gramercies *n. pl.*	(1) thanks; thank you
gratefy *v.*	(1) to show gratitude to (a person) in return for benefits received, esp. in a practical manner; to reward, requite
gratulation *n.*	(2) manifestation or expression of joy; esp. with adj. and pl., an instance of this; a rejoicing
graund *adj.*	grand
graundsire *n.*	(1) grandfather
great *adj.*	(3a) ~ *with child* pregnant, far davanced in pregnancy
greeue *v.*	(7) to feel annoyance or anger
greeuous *adj.*	(3a) of a disease, wound or pain: causing great suffering or danger; acute, severe
grosse *adj.*	(1a) massive, big
guarde *n.*	(1a) keeping, guardianship, custody, ward
guarderobe *n.*	a private room, a bedchamber; s.v. *garderobe*

H
habillment *n.*	(5) anything worn as an ornament
habit *n.*	(1c) *pl.* clothes, garments
hale *v. 1*	(1b) to draw or pull along, or from one place to another, esp. with force or violence
*hammer *v.*	(4a) to debate or deliberate earnestly (*upon, on, at, of*)
handfast *adj.*	(1) contracted by the joining of hands; espoused

handkercher *n.*	handkerchief
happilie *adv.*	(1) by chance, perchance
hardie *adj.*	hardy
hardly *adv.*	(2) boldly, daringly, hardily
	(4) harshly
hart(e) *n.*	heart
harten *v.*	to hearten
hartie *adj.*	hearty
hartilie *adv.*	heartily
hatch *n. 1*	(3a) a movable planking forming a kind of deck in ships; hence, also, the permanent deck (normally plural)
heapes *n. pl.*	(5a) *on ~* in crowds, in great numbers
heart *n.*	(49) *take ~* to pluck up courage
heerehence *adv.*	(1) from this fact or circumstance; as a result of this
heerewithall *adv.*	herewith: (2) at the same time with this; upon this; with these words
helhound *n.*	(2) a fiendish person, as a term of execration
•hell *n.*	(3c) an infernal or devilish assembly; a hellful. Freq. with *of.* Also *fig.* and in figurative contexts [*OED*3]
helpes *n. pl.*	(1b) acts of helping; aids
hether *adv.*	hither
holpe *pa. t. of* **help** *v.*	helped
holpen *pa. ppl. of* **help** *v.*	helped; (9) to relieve or cure of a disease, or of some evil condition
hostage *n. 2*	a hostel, hostelry, inn
hot house *n.*	(1) a bathing-house with hot baths, vapor-baths, etc.
house *n. 1*	(6) a family including ancestors and descendants; a lineage, esp. one having continuity of residence, of exalted rank
howbeit *conj.*	although
hower *n.*	hour
humanitie *n.*	(3a) civility, courtesy, good behavior
humour *n.*	(4) a mental disposition (orig. as determined by the proportion of the bodily "humours"); constitutional or habitual tendency; temperament
	(6) a particular disposition, inclination, or liking, esp. one having no apparent ground or reason

I

illuding *adj.*	deceiving

imagination *n.*	(1) a mental image or idea (often with implication that the conception does not correspond to the reality of things); e.g. *extreame imaginations* (416.12)
	(2a) scheming or devising; a device, contrivance, plan, scheme, plot
	(2b) impression as to what is likely; expectation, anticipation
	(5) thought
imbolden *v.*	to embolden
impeach *n.*	(1) hindrance, impediment, prevention
	(2) injury, damage, detriment
impeache *v.*	(1) to impede, hinder, prevent
	(2) to affect detrimentally or prejudicially; to hurt, harm, injure, endamage, impair
impeachment *n.*	(1) hindrance, obstacle
imperialist *n.*	(1) an adherent of the (or an) emperor; one of the emperor's party
•import *n.*	(2) that which is implied or signified, esp. by a document, phrase, word, etc.; purport, significance, meaning [*OED3*]
import *v.*	(4) to bring about, cause, occasion; to carry with it or involve as a consequence or result
importunate *adj.*	(3) pressing, urgent; busy
impudency *n.*	(1) shamelessness, immodesty
impudent *adj.*	(1) wanting in shame or modesty
incident *adj. 1*	(3) relating or pertinent to
incontinent *adj.*	(1) wanting in self-restraint: chiefly with reference to sexual appetite
incontinent *adv.*	straightway, at once, immediately
indifferent *adj. 1*	(1b) of a thing or action, esp. ~ *justice* impartial or even-handed justice
indifferent *adv.*	indifferently; to some extent, in some degree; moderately, tolerably, fairly
inducement *n.*	(2b) any reason which leads one to a course of action; a moving cause
indure *v.*	to endure
inexplicable *adj.*	(2) that cannot be "unfolded" or expressed in words; inexpressible, indescribable
infortune *n.*	(1b) an instance of lack of good fortune; a misfortune, an unfortunate event [*OED3*]
ingratefull *adj.*	(2) unfriendly, harsh
	(3) not feeling or showing gratitude
*inhabited *adj.*	not dwelt in, uninhabithed

iniuried *ppl. of* **iniury** *v.*	(2) to abuse with words, revile (3) to hurt, harm, damage
iniury *n.*	(2) intentionally hurtful or offensive speech or words; reviling, insult, calumny; a taunt, an affront
instant *adj.*	(2a) now present, or present at the time defined; now (or then) existing or happening
instaunce *n.*	(7) a proof, evidence; a sign, token, mark
insufficiencie *n.*	(1) of a person, inability to fulfill requirements; unfitness, incapacity, incompetence
intelligence *n.*	(7a) information, news, tidings
intelligencer *n.*	(a) an informer, a spy
intent *n.*	(1) intention, purpose (3) intent or assiduous effort, endeavor (4) what is in the mind, notion, opinion or thought of any kind
intercept *v.*	(1c) to interrupt, break in upon (esp. a narrative or a person speaking)
***intercepting** *ppl. adj.*	(2) that cuts off or stops (a person or thing) from accomplishing some purpose; that prevents, stops, hinders
intermedle *v.*	(1) to "meddle" or mix together; to intermingle; to intermix
intire *adj.*	entire; (10) of feelings: unfeigned, sincere, genuine
intirely *adv.*	(4a) heartily, sincerely
intollerable *adj.*	(1b) that cannot be tolerated or put up with, mentally or morally
intreat *v.*	(1) to treat, deal with, act towards (a person) in a (specified manner) (7) to sue, plead *for*
intreataunce *n.*	(1) treatment; dealing with, or behavior toward, a person
***intreating** *vbl. n.*	(2) beseeching
inueigle *v.*	(1) to blind in mind or judgement
inuenter *n.*	(2) one who devises or contrives; contriver, designer
inuention *n.*	(6) design, plan, scheme
inuocate *v.*	(2) to make invocation; to call in prayer
iote *n.*	a very little part or amount
iourney *n.*	(2a) an ordinary day's travel, the distance usually traveled in a day
ioyn *v.* 2	(1) to enjoin or impose (penance, a task) upon a person
***irreuocablie**	irrevocably
ise *n.*	ice
issue *n.*	(5a) a place or means of egress; way out; outlet; *place of* ~
iudgement *n.*	(8b) good sense, understanding, wisdom
iuggle *v.*	(3) to practice artifice or deceit *with*

iustifie *v.*	(5) to confirm or support by attestation or evidence; to corroborate, prove, verify

K
ken *v. 1*	(11) to know (a thing)
kenning *vbl. n. 1*	(3) visual cognition; sight or view
knit *ppl. adj.*	(1a) knotted, tied, fastened together; contracted together
knowledge *n.*	(2) the fact of recognizing as something known, or known about, before; recognition

L
labour *v.*	(6) to work for or with a view to (a result)
	(7a) to endeavor to influence or persuade; to urge or entreat
	(13) to exert one's influence in urging a suit or to obtain something desired
laie *v. 1*	(32e) ~ *about* to deal violent and repeated blows on all sides
lamentable *adj.*	(1) full of or expressing sorrow or grief; mournful, doleful
langourous *adj.*	(1) distressful, sorrowful, mournful
large *n.*	(5c) of speech or writing: at length, in full
late *adj. 1*	(5b) of a person: that was recently (what is implied by the n.) but is not now
	(6) recent in date; that has recently happened
launce *v.*	(3a) to launch (a boat)
league *n. 2*	(2) a covenant, compact, alliance
learn *v.*	(4) to teach
leasing *n.*	(1) lying, falsehood
leaue *v. 1*	(4a) to neglect or omit to perform (some action)
lecture *n.*	(1) the action of reading, perusal. Also, that which is read or perused
leude *adj.*	lewd
leuie *v.*	(4) to enlist (armed men), bring into the field (army)
licence *v.*	(1) to give permission
lien *ppl. of* lie *v.*	
ligne *n.*	line, lineage
like *adv.*	(8) likely, probably
liking *vbl. n. 1*	(4b) *good* ~ approval, good-will
limit *v.*	(1c) to lot or plot out; to allot, apportion
linament *n.*	(2) a portion of the body, considered with respect to its contour or outline, a distinctive feature
list, lyst *v. 1*	(2b) to wish, desire, like, choose
	(3) to desire or wish for (something)
load *n.*	(7a) *to lay on* ~ to deal heavy blows

Lord Chamberlaine *n.*	(1b) an officer charged with the management of the private chambers of a sovereign or nobleman
lothe *adj.*	loath
lustie *adj.*	(2) pleasing, pleasant
luxurious *adj.*	(1) lascivious, lecherous, unchaste
lystes *n. pl.*	lists

M

madame *n.*	(2a) as a title prefixed to a first or sole name
Mahumetiste *n.*	a Muslim
maist *v.*	may, *2nd p. sg.*
maistry *n.*	(5b) *it is no ~* it is no achievement, it is easy (to do something); s.v. *mastery*
mallice *v.*	(1) to regard with malice; to seek or desire to injure
man *v.*	(5) to escort (a person, esp. a woman)
mannerlie *adv.*	(1) in a seemly manner, decently, becomingly, properly
*mappe *n. 1*	(5b) an embodiment or incarnation of a quality, characteristic; the very picture or image or something [*OED3*]
martered *adj.*	martyred, expressive of martyrdom
martin *n.*	marten
mastiue *n.*	mastiff
match *v. 1*	(1c) to ally oneself in marriage (with)
mauger *adv.*	(1) in spite of, notwithstanding; notwithstanding the power of
maunde *n. 1*	(1) a wicker or other woven basket having a handle or handles
maydenhead *n. 1*	(2) the first stage or first-fruits of anything
meane *adj. 1*	(2a) of persons, their rank or station: undistinguished in position; of low degree (3b) petty, unimportant, inconsiderable
meaning *vbl. n. 1*	(1) intention, purpose
meaning *vbl. n. 2*	moaning, lamentation
meate *v.*	(2) to feed, partake of food
meete *adj.*	(3) suitable, fit, proper (for some purpose or occasion)
meetlie *adv.*	(1) moderately, fairly, tolerably
mellancholique *n.*	(2) depression of spirits, melancholy
mellanchollie *adj.*	(2) irascible, angry; sullen
merchandise *n.*	(1) the action or business of buying and selling goods or commodities for profit
merely *adv.*²	(3) without any other reason, quality, purpose
meruaile, meruayle *v.*	marvel
meruailous *adv.*	marvelously
me thinkes *impers. v.*	it seems to me

middest *n.*	midst
mind *v.*	(6a) to have in view, have a mind to (an action, plan); to intend, aim at doing something; sometimes with clause as object
	(6b) with *inf.* as object: to have a mind *to do* something; to wish, be inclined, purpose, intend
mirrour *n.*	(5b) of persons: a model of excellence; a paragon
miscarry *v.*	(1) to come to harm, misfortune, or destruction; to perish; (of a person) to meet with one's death
misconceit *n.*	misconception
misconceiue *v.*	(1) to have a false conception or entertain wrong notions (*of*)
miscontent *v.*	to dissatisfy, displease
misdeem *v.*	(2) to form an unfavorable judgement
misdo *v.*	(3) to do evil or wrong (to a person); to harm, injure
misdoubt *v.*	(4) to fear or suspect the existence or occurrence of (something undesirable or evil)
misgouerned *ppl. adj*	(1) characterized by misconduct; ill-conducted, immoral
misprise *v. 1*	(1a) to despise, contemn, scorn
misse *n. 1*	(1a) the fact or condition of missing, having lost, or being without a person or thing
misuse *v.*	(2b) to violate, ravish, or debauch
misusing *vbl. n.*	(3) maltreatment
modestie *n.*	(1) moderation; freedom from excess or exaggeration; self-control
moitie *n.*	(1) a half, one of two equal parts
molde *n.*	mould
mollify *v.*	(1a) to render soft or supple; to make tender; to reduce the hardness of
monarchie *n.*	(4) the territory of a monarch
mooue *v.*	(9b) to provoke to anger, to make angry
morisco *n.*	(4) a morris dance
mot *n. 1*	(1) a motto
motion *n.*	(4) excitement, agitation (of the mind or feelings)
	(7a) the action of moving, prompting, or urging (a person to do something, or that something be done); a proposal, suggestion; an instigation, prompting, or bidding
mountainet *n.*	a small mountain
mouth *n.*	(3k) *to stop (a person's)* ~ to keep (him/her) from talking
multiply *v.*	(1b) to use or utter a multiplicity of (words); *to ~ words* to be loquacious
muse *v.*	(3a) to be affected with astonishment or surprise; to wonder, marvel

N

name *n.*	(7b) *of* ~ noted, distinguished, famous
narrowly *adv.*	(5) closely, straitly
necessarie *adj.*	(1c) pleasant; commodious, comfortable
needfull *adj.*	(2a) of occasions: characterized by need, necessity, or straits
needs *adv.*	of necessity, necessarily
neere *adv.*	near, nearly
neerelie *adv.*	nearly
nie, nigh *adv.*	nearly, almost
*notoriously *adv.*	(2) manifestly, evidently, obviously [*OED*3]
nouels *n. pl.*	(2a) news, tidings
nourish *v.*	(1) to bring up, rear, nurture (a child, or young person)
nouriture,	(1) nourishment, food
nurriture *n.*	(2) nurture, upbringing
nye *adv.*	nearly, almost
nypt, nipt *ppl. of* nip *v.*	(3a) *to* ~ *in the head*: to reduce to a state of helplessness

O

obeysance *n.*	(1) the action or fact of obeying
obseruation *n.*	(2) that which is observed or practiced
occasion *n.* 1	(3d) the action of causing or occasioning
	(7a) a casual occurrence; an event, incident
offend *v.*	(5) to attack, assault, assail
	(7b) *to be offended (with)* to be displeased, vexed, or annoyed
office *n.*	(2c) the performance of, or an act of performing a duty, function, service, attendance, etc.
officious *adj.*	(2) dutiful: active or zealous in doing one's duty
ofspring *n.*	(4) the fact of springing or descending from some ancestor or source; descent, origination, derivation, origin
often *adj.*	done, made, happening, or occurring many times; frequent
onelie, onely *adj.*	only: (5) unique in quality, character, rank, etc.; peerless, preeminent
onsette *n.* 1	(2a) *to give the* ~ to make a beginning, to start
open *v.*	(9a) to reveal, disclose, declare, make known
opinion *n.*	(2a) belief, view, notion
	(7) the thought of what is likely to happen; expectation; apprehension
oppression *n*	(2a) the action of weighing down or bearing heavily on a person, the mind, feelings, etc.; pressure of outward circumstances, or of grief, pain, or trouble; the condition of being pressed hard by misfortune, distress.
oratour *n.*	(4) one sent to plead or speak for another; an ambassador, envoy, or messenger

oratrix *n.*	(1) a female plaintiff or petitioner
order *n.*	(14) *to take* ~ to take measures or steps, to make arrangements
order *v.*	(3) to put in order or readiness (for a purpose); to make ready, prepare
originall *n.*	(2a) the thing (or person) from which something else arises or proceeds; a source, cause; an originator, author
orison *n.*	(1) prayer
osterie *n.*	hostelry
ouerlaboured *pa. ppl.*	fatigued
ouerlate *adv.*	too late
ouer-maistre *v.*	(2) to be master over; to dominate; to hold in one's power or possession
*****ouer-spent** *adj.*	completely spent, exhausted [OED3]
ouertane *pa. ppl.*	to overtake
ouertrauail *v.*	to work too much, oppress or harass with toil; to overwork
ouer-watched *ppl. adj.*	wearied with too much watching (all through a night)
ought *n.*	anything
ought *pa. t. of* **owe** *v.*	(2a) had to pay; owed
ounce *n. 2*	(1) small or moderate-sized feline beast
*****outbraue** *v.*	(3) to outdo or surpass in bravery or daring [OED3]
out place *n.*	an out-lying, out-of-the-way place
outrage *n.*	(3a) *to make or offer* ~ to exercise violence, to do grievous injury or wrong to any one
outreach *v. 1*	(2) to overreach; to deceive; to outwit

P

pacify *v.*	(2d) to calm, appease
packet *n.*	(1a) a parcel of letters or dispatches
pageant *n.*	(1b) *to play one's* ~: to act one's part; the part acted or played by any one in an affair, or in the drama of life
paillardise *n.*	lewdness, fornication, lechery (s.v. *palliardise*)
pallet *n. 2*	(1) a straw bed; a mattress
pantofle *n.*	any type of indoor shoe, esp. applied to high-heeled cork-soled Spanish or Italian chopins
paracide *n.*	parricide
parasite *n.*	(1a) a person who lives at the expense of another, or of society in general [OED3]
parle *v.*	(1) to speak; to talk in conference
parragon *v.*	(1) to parallel, compare
part *n.*	(12) *pl.* abilities, capacities, talents
	(26b) *in good* ~: favorably or without offence

particular *n.*	(4a) a single thing among a number, considered by itself; each one of a number or group of things; an individual thing or article
passenger *n.*	(1a) a passer by or through
passion *n.*	(3) suffering or affliction generally
	(6a) any kind of feeling by which the mind is powerfully affected or moved
	(8a) *pl.* amorous feelings or desires
passionate *adj.*	(5) moved with sorrow; grieved, sad, sorrowful
pate *n. 1*	(1) the head, the skull; applied to that part which is usually covered with hair
peirced *pa. t.*	to pierce
pelfe *n.*	(1) spoil, booty
pel mel *adv.*	(1b) in a confused medley; said of pursuers and pursued
peremptorie *adj.*	(6) deadly, destructive
perfection *n.*	(1) the action, process, or fact of making perfect or bringing to completion; completing, finishing, accomplishing
	(2) the fact or condition of being perfected or completed; completion; completed state, completeness
perforce *adv.*	(1a) by violence, forcibly
	(1b) by constraint of circumstances
perpetuall *adj.*	(2a) constant, continuous, unfailing
perplexitie *n.*	(1b) trouble, distress
personage *n.*	(1) a representation or figure of a person; an image or effigy; a statue or portrait
	(2) the body of a person; chiefly with reference to appearance, stature, etc.; bodily frame, figure; personal appearance
perswade *v.*	(4) to induce belief of (a fact, statement, opinion); to lead one to think or believe
perswasion *n.*	(1b) somenthing tending or intended to induce belief or action; an argument or inducement
pertinacie *n.*	pertinacity; very common in the 17th c. mostly in an evil sense
pessant *adj.*	(a) having great weight; heavy, massive (s.v. *peisant*)
	(b) forcible, as a blow given with a heavy body
pestre, pester *v. 1*	(2) to obstruct or encumber (a place) by crowding; to crowd to excess, overcrowd
phife *n.*	fife
philosophie *n.*	(3b) magical or occult science
phisicke *n.*	(5b) mental, moral, or spiritual remedy
phisition *n.*	physician

pittaunce *n.*	(2) a small allowance or portion of food and drink; a scanty meal
plaine *adj. 2*	(3) *in ~ combat* in regular open combat
platforme *n.*	(4a) a plan of action; a scheme, design, device
pleasure *n.*	(2) with possessive pronoun, one's will, desire, choice
point *n. 1*	(C.1) a feat; esp. a feat of arms, a deed of valor, an exploit; also, an encounter, skirmish
	(D.1.d) *at a ~* decided, determined, resolved
pollicie *n. 1*	(4b) a device, a contrivance, an expedient; a stratagem, a trick
pollitique *adj.*	(2) judicious, expedient, shrewd
pollitiquelie *adv.*	shredwfully, artfully, craftily
porphire *n.*	porphyry
post *v.* 1	(2) to ride, run, or travel with speed or haste; to make haste, hasten, hurry
pot *n. 1*	(13f) *to the ~* to be cut in pieces like meat for the pot
power *n. 1*	(9) a body of armed men; a fighting force, a host, an army
practise *n.*	(1b) an action, a deed
	(3) the practical acquaintance with or experience in a subject or process, so gained
practise *v.*	(8) to bring about, compass, effect, accomplish
	(8b) to devise means to bring about (a result); to plan, scheme, intend (something to be done)
	(8c) to exert oneself in order to effect (something); to attempt, try
preferment *n.*	(1) furtherance, promotion
	(2) that which is done or given toward the advancement of the children of a family or the promotion of the marriage of a daughter
preiudicate *ppl. adj.*	(3) affected by a preconceived opinion; prejudiced, prepossessed, biased
preiudice *n.*	(1b) injury, damage, hurt, loss
prescription *n.*	(1) the action of prescribing or appointing beforehand; that which is prescribed or appointed
presence *n.*	(2c) a place prepared for ceremonial presence or attendance; a presence-chamber
	(2d) *chamber of ~* same sense as 2c above; see under *chamber*
present *adj.*	(9a) occurring or used at the very time, without delay; immediate, instant
	(9b) of a remedy: taking immediate effect
present *n. 1*	(4b) *at this ~* at the present time, now
president *n.*	(1b) a presiding deity, patron or guardian

presume *v.*	(6) to advance or make one's way over-confidently into an unwarranted position or place; to presume to go
presuming *ppl. adj.*	that presumes; presumptuous, arrogant
pretended *ppl. adj.*	(4) intended, designed, purposed, proposed
priuie *adj.*	(5) kept secret or concealed; hidden; secluded
procure *v.*	(3) to endeavor to cause or bring about (mostly something evil)
	(4) to bring about, cause, effect, produce
procurer *n.*	(2) a promoter, prime mover, instigator, contriver
prolong *v.*	(3) to delay, postpone, put off (an action or event)
prompt *adj.*	(2b) ready in mind; inclined, disposed [*OED*3]
prosecute *v.*	(2) to carry on, engage in, follow, exercise
prospect *n.*	(4) the appearance presented by anything; aspect
prosper *v.*	(2) to cause to flourish; to promote the prosperity or success of; to be propitious to
protest *v.*	(4) to promise or undertake solemnly
protestation *n.*	(2a) in pleading, an affirmation or denial, introduced in form of a protest, of some allegation
prouide *v.*	(4) to prepare, make preparation, get ready
prouision *n.*	(2b) the providing or supplying of necessaries for a household, an expedition, etc.
publique *adj.*	(5a) existing, done or made in public; manifest, not concealed
puissaunce *n.*	(1a) power, strength, might, force
pull *n. 1*	(6b) a stab or tug of the heart, as caused by sudden fear, alarm, etc. [*OED*3]
purchase *v.*	(2) to exert oneself for the attainment of some object; to endeavor; to strive
	(4a) to procure for oneself, acquire, obtain
	(4b) to obtain from a constituted authority
	(6b) to acquire (something immaterial) at the cost or as the result of something figured as the price paid
purpose *n.*	(10a) *of* ~ purposely, designedly
pyke *n. 5*	(2a) *to pass through the pykes* to pass through difficulties or dangers, esp. to come through successfully
pyoner *n.*	pioneer

Q
quaint *adj.*	(6) of speech, language, modes of expression, etc.: carefully or ingeniously elaborated; highly elegant or refined; full of fancies or conceits
qualify, quallifie *v.*	(9) to appease, calm, pacify
quality *n.*	(4a) nobility, high birth, good social position; *of* ~

Glossary

quarrel *n. 3*   (2b) with possessive pronoun or genitive: one's cause, side, or party in a complaint or contest; one's claim to a thing
question *v.*   (2) *to ~ with* to ask questions of; to hold discourse or conversation with; to dispute with
quicke *n. 1*   (3a) any part of a wound, an ulcer, the body, etc., that is sensitive or painful (now *rare*). Freq. in *to the ~* [OED3]
quiet *v.*   (2c) to reduce to quietness a disturbance, dissension, etc.
quite *v.*   (1b) to free, clear
quittance *n.*   (3) recompense or requital; repayment, reprisal
    (4) *to cry ~* to declare oneself clear or even *with* another; hence, to make full repayment or retaliation
quoth *pa. t. of* **quethe** said

R

race *n. 2*   (2a) a limited group of persons descended from a common ancestor; a house, family
race *v. 3*   (3) to scrape out, erase (a word, etc.); to remove by scraping
rake *v. 1*   (6a) to go over with a rake
rape *n. 2*   (2) the act of carrying away a person, esp. a woman by force
rapt *ppl. adj.*   (6a) carried or removed from one place, position or situation to another; chiefly said of persons
rare *adj. 1*   (6a) unusual in respect of some good quality; of uncommon excellence or merit; remarkably good or fine
raunge *v. 1*   (1a) to draw, arrange an army in ranks
rayl *v. 4*   (1b) *to ~ on* to utter abusive language against
rebated *ppl. adj. 1*   blunted, dull
receite *n.*   (7a) the act of receiving a person to a place
reck *v.*   (1a) to take care, heed, or thought *of* some thing (or person), with inclination, desire or favor toward it, interest in it
reckon *v.*   (4b) to estimate, value
reclaimed *ppl. a.*   tamed, reformed
recorde *n.*   (10) a musical note
recouer *v. 1*   (6a) to get or obtain; to get hold of
recreate *v. 1*   (4a) to refresh or enliven (the mind, the spirits, a person) by some pastime, amusement, occupation
    (4b) *refl.* to refresh (oneself) with some agreeable occupation or pastime
redeeme *v.*   (3) to ransom, free a person from captivity
redoubted *ppl. adj.*   reverenced, respected; noted, distinguished. Common in 15th–17th c. in addressing sovereigns
refer, referre *v.*   (7a) to defer, postpone, put off (something) *to, unto, till, until* another time or season

regard *n.*	(5a) repute, account, or estimation, in which anything is held
	(7a) *to have* ~ *to* to give protective attention or heed to, to take care of
regiment *n.*	(1) rule or government over a person, people or country; esp. royal or magisterial authority
	(2a) the office or function of a ruler; common *ca.* 1550–1610 with verbs of receiving, accepting
*regratiate *v.*	to gratify in return [*OED*3]
*religion *n.*	(7) strict fidelity or faithfulness; conscientiousness; devotion or fidelity to some principle [*OED*3]
religious *adj.*	(4a) scrupulous, strict, conscientious
remembrance *n.*	(1b) *to put* (one) *in* ~ *of* to remind
remorse *n.*	(3a) sorrow, pity, compassion
remunerate *v.*	(2) to reward (a person); to pay (one) for services rendered
renown, renowme *v.*	(1) to make famous, spread the fame of; to celebrate
repent *v.*	(1) *refl.* to affect oneself for something done
report *n.*	(1a) rumor, common talk
	(1c) repute, fame, reputation
reproch *n.*	(2) shame, disgrace, opprobrium or blame, incurred by or falling upon a person
reprooue *v. 1*	(3) to reprehend, rebuke, blame or find fault with (a person); const. with *of*
	(5) to prove (an idea, statement, etc.) to be false or erroneous
repugne *v.*	(3b) to oppose, resist or contend against (something); to repel or reject
repute *v.*	(2a) to take (one) *for* something
•requitall *n.*	phrase: *in* ~ (b) in revenge, by way of retaliation [*OED*3]
reserue *v. 1*	(10a) to keep in one's possession
resign *v. 1*	(1) to relinquish, surrender, hand over (something)
resist *n.*	(1) resistance
resolue *v.*	(15a) to free (one) from doubt or perplexity; to bring to certainty or clear understanding
	(16a) to convince one of something
	(19a) *refl.* to make up one's mind
	(19d) to assure, satisfy, or convince (oneself) on some point
resolued *ppl. adj.*	(2) convinced, satisfied
resort *n.*	(5b) an assemblage, gathering, throng, crowd
resort *v. 1*	(7) to proceed or go to (or toward) a place
rest *n. 2*	(8b) *to set down one's* ~ to make up one's mind; to determine
retrait *n. 1*	(2) the signal for retiring
•return *v. 1*	(1d) *refl.* to come or go back to a place [*OED*3]

	(16a) to provide or bring back in exchange for effort or investment or as a result of ownership; to yield as a return [OED3]
retyre *n.*	(3) the act of drawing back or yielding ground in warfare; retreat
•reuiew *v.*	(5a) to look at or over [OED3]
reward *v.*	(7a) to requite or repay (one) for evil-doing; to punish, chastise
right *adv.*	(9) with intensive force: very
ring *v.* 2	(12a) to utter sonorously; to proclaim aloud; to re-echo
roome *n.* 1	(6a) a particular place or spot, without reference to its area
rouer *n.* 2	(1) a sea-robber, pirate
	(1b) a pirate ship
•rough *adj.*	(10c) of a voyage: undertaken in turbulent weather [OED3]
royaltie *n.*	(2a) pomp, splendor
ruinate *v.*	(2) to bring destruction or ruin upon, to overthrow, destroy
	(4a) to demolish or destroy; to lay waste
rumour *n.*	(6) uproar, tumult, disturbance

S

saucie *adj.* 1	(2a) of persons, their dispositions, actions, or language: insolent toward superiors, presumptuous
sauegard *n.*	(1b) *for ~ of* for the defence or protection of
*scandall *n.*	(2a) damage to reputation; rumor or general comment injurious to reputation
*scandalous *adj.*	(2) of the nature of a scandal: grossly disgraceful
*scanning *ppl. adj.*	(1) that scans or examines closely; critical
school *v.* 1	(3b) to reprimand, scold, admonish [OED3]
scourge *n.*	(2) a thing or person that is an instrument of divine chastisement
*scuffle *v.* 1	(1) to struggle confusedly *together* or *with* another or others; to fight at close quarters in a disorderly manner
search *v.*	(8) to probe (a wound)
seauen *num.*	seven
secrecie *n.*	(4) the condition of being entrusted with a person's secrets
secret(e) *adj.*	(1c) of a person: secluded from observation
	(2a) not given to indiscreet talking or the revelation of secrets
seelie *adj.*	(6) deserving of pity or sympathy; miserable; helpless
semblable *adj.*	(1a) similar
semitary *n.*	scimitar
sennight *n.*	a period of seven (days and) nights; a week
sent *n.*	scent

sentence *n.*	(1) opinion
senternell *n.*	sentinel
seraph *n.* 2	a Turkish gold coin
serue *v.* 1	(24b) of the wind, weather, tide: to be favorable or suitable
seruiceable *adj.*	(3b) capable of being applied to an appropriate purpose, or to the performance of a proper function
set down *v.*	see under *rest*, n.
shaddow *v.*	(3b) to screen from blame or punishment, or from wrong (6a) to screen from view or knowledge
shalbe *v.*	shall be
shamefaste *adj.*	(1) bashful, modest
sheelde *v.*	to shield
shewe *n./v.*	show
shift *v.*	(7a) *to ~ for oneself*: to provide for one's own safety, interests, or livelihood (implying either absence of aid, or, sometimes, want of concern for others); to depend on one's own efforts
shoare *n.*	shore
shrewd *adj.*	(6a) as an intensive, qualifying a word denotig something in itself bad; applied to injury, loss, disease, etc.
shrike *n.* 1	shriek
siely *adj.*	(5) innocent, harmless; often as an expression of compassion for persons or animals suffering undeservedly
signorie *n.*	(2) a domain, territory, esp. one held by a feudal lord
*simpathie *n.*	(1) a (real or supposed) affinity between certain things, by virtue of which they are similarly or correspondingly affected by the same influence, affect or influence one another (3c) the quality or state of being affected by the suffering or sorrow of another; rarely with *of*
sithence *adv.*	(3) at some or any time since; s.v. *sith*
skill *v.* 1	(1c) to make free or quit *of*
sleight *n.* 1	(6) a cunning trick; an artifice, ruse, stratagem or wile
slender *adj.*	(7b) insignificant, trifling, of persons in respect of station or capacity
smart *n.* 1	(2) grief, sorrow, affliction
*smoother *v.*	smother: (2c) to repress, retain from displaying, (feeling, etc.) by the exercise of self-control
solicit, sollicit *v.*	(1) to disturb, disquiet, trouble (9a) to urge or plead (one's suit or cause)
*sollicitour *n.*	(4) a suitor (to a woman); s.v. *soliciter*
sooth *n.*	(1) truth
*sooth *v.*	(2b) to maintain or put forward (a lie or untruth) as being true

Glossary

sore *adv.*	(6) to a grievous or serious extent; greatly
sort(e) *n. 2*	(11a) a particular class, order, or rank of persons
	(21) manner, way
sort(e) *v. 1*	(5) to arrive at, attain to, result in or reach (an effect, end, etc.)
	(7a) to come or attain *to* an end, conclusion, effect
	(7b) to end in coming or leading *to* a specified result
	(10a) to place in a class or sort; to give a place to; to classify (used with *together*)
	(14b) to choose (a thing or person) from others
soueraigne *adj.*	(3) of remedies, etc.: efficacious or potent in a superlative degree
sought *pa. t. of* **seek**	(9) To entreat, beseech (a person) *to do* something; also *of* (the thing asked for)
space *n. 1*	(3c) *in the meane* ~ meantime, meanwhile
speede *v.*	(1a) to succeed or prosper
	(1b) to succeed in getting, obtaining or accomplishing
	(6a) to cause to succeed or prosper
spight *n.*	spite; (1) action arising from or displaying hostile feeling
splendant *adj.*	splendent
spoyle *v. 1*	(3a) to pillage or plunder (a country, city, house, ship, etc.); to clear of goods or valuables by the exercise of superior force; to ravage or sack
*****squiffe** *n. 1*	skiff
stale *adj. 1*	(3a) that has lost its novelty
standing *vbl. n.*	(4a) a standing place, station: the place in or upon which a person stands
state *n.*	(15a) a person's condition or position in life; a person's natural, social or legal status, profession or calling, rank or degree
	(21) class, rank, order, sort or body of persons
	(24) a person of standing, importance or high rank; a great man, personage, dignitary; a noble, lord, prince
stature *n.*	(3) an effigy, statue
staues *n. pl.*	(3b) a spear, lance, or similar armed weapon; s.v. *staff*, n. 1
stay, staie *n. 3*	(1) the fact of being brought to a stand or delayed
	(3) *to make a* ~ to make a stop
	(4) delay, postponement, waiting
stay *v. 1*	(19) to wait for, await (a person, his coming, an event, etc.)
	(20) to detain, hold back, stop (a person or thing); to check or arrest the progress of, bring to a halt
sted, stedde *n.*	stead; (13a) advantage, avail, profit, service, support, esp. in *to stand in (good)* ~

	to stand in ~ to take the place of, represent, do duty for (49; s.v. *stand*)
sticke *v. 1*	(15) to hesitate, scruple, be reluctant or unwilling: ~ *to* (do something); only with negative.
stomach *n.*	(5a) appetite or relish for food
	(6a) used (like "heart," "breast") to designate the inward seat of passion, emotion, secret thoughts, affections, feelings
	(7a) temper, disposition; state of feeling with regard to a person
	(8a) spirit, courage, bravery
store *n.*	(3) a body of persons
straight *n.*	strait
straite *n.*	(4) a narrow pass or gorge between mountains; a defile, ravine
strange *adj.*	(1a) of or belonging to another country; foreign, alien
	(8) of a kind that is unfamiliar or rare; unusual, uncommon, exceptional, singular, out of the way
stratageme *n.*	(3) a violent act, esp. a murder [OED3]
stream *n.*	(3) used vaguely for water, sea
strength *n.*	(10a) a stronghold, fortress
	(11a) troops, forces
strout *v.*	(5a) to behave proudly or vaingloriously; to flaunt, triumph, swagger (s.v. *strut* v. 1)
studie *n.*	(3a) a state of mental perplexity or anxious thought
	(4a) thought or meditation directed to the accomplishment of a purpose; studied or deliberate effort or contrivance
•suborning *adj.*	that suborns a person or thing, also *fig.* [OED3]
substance *n.*	(16a) possessions, goods, estate; means, wealth
subtill *adj.*	(8) cleverly devised; ingeniously contrived, ingenious
subtiltie *n.*	(1b) a cunning or crafty scheme; a trick; a clever stratagem
successe *n.*	(1a) the termination (favorable or otherwise) of affairs
successiue *adj.*	(4) attended or fraught with success; successful
suffer *v.*	(18a) to allow a certain thing to be done
sufferaunce *n.*	(6c) *by the* ~ *of God* by divine permission
sum, summe *n. 1*	(9a) an abridged statement containing the substance of a matter; a summary, epitome
	(13a) the ultimate end or goal; the highest attainable point
sumpter *n.*	(2) ~ *horse* a pack or baggage horse
superficiallie *adv.*	(3) as to outward appearance or form
superintendaunce *n.*	(1) the function of superintendent
superstitious *adj.*	(4) regarded or observed in the way of superstition
supplie *n.*	(5) an additional body of persons, esp. reinforcements of troops

supprize *v.*	(2) of a feeling, etc.: to come upon suddenly and forcibly, seize, overtake, affect violently
suretie *n.*	(1) safety, security from danger, an enemy, etc.
surfette *v.*	(3b) to indulge in something to excess; to take one's fill, "feast," "revel"
surplusage *n.*	(1) superabundance
surprise *v.*	(1a) to be seized *with* (or *of*) a desire, emotion, etc., a disease or illness
suspecte *n. 1*	(1b) *in* ~ to be suspicious of, suspect
suspence *n.*	(3c) *in* ~ undecided, doubtful
sustenance *n.*	(3) the action of upholding or giving one's support to an argument, a cause, etc.; an instance of this [*OED*3]
sute, suit *n.*	(5a) pursuit, chase; also a pursuit
	(11a.a) petition, supplication, or entreaty; esp. a petition made to a prince or other high personage
	(11c) earnest search for or endeavor to obtain something

T

taffata *n.*	(a) in early times apparently a plain-wove glossy silk
talent *n.*	(1b) the value of a talent weight (of gold, silver, etc.): a money of account (used by the Assyrians, Babylonians, Greeks, Romans, and other ancient nations)
tallants *n. pl.*	(2a) the powerful claws of a bird of prey, or of a dragon, griffin, etc.; s.v. *talon*
tardie *adj.*	(2a) *to take* a person ~ to detect, catch in a crime, fault, error
targe *n. 1*	(1) a shield, esp. a light shield or buckler
taster *n. 1*	(2) a domestic officer whose duty it is to taste food and drink about to be served to his master, in order to ascertain their quality, or to detect poison
tearmes, termes *n. pl.*	(14b) *in* ~ in express words, expressly, plainly
tell *prep., conj.*	till
tenure *n.*	tenor
then *conj.*	than
thether *adv.*	thither
think *v.*	(11a) ~ *on* to value or esteem something
throughlie *adv.*	thoroughly
*thwart *n. 1*	a check, hindrance, obstruction, frustration
time *n.*	(46c.c) *in good* ~ at the right or seasonable moment; luckily
timorous *adj.*	(1b) modest, reverential
toyles *n. 2*	(1) nets set so as to enclose a space into which the quarry is driven
traffique *n.*	(2a) the buying and selling or exchange of goods for profit; bargaining; trade

traitourly *adj.*	having the character of a traitor; traitorous
trauaile *n. 1*	(1) bodily or mental labour or toil; exertion; trouble; hardship; suffering
trauaile *v.*	(5) to journey
trauel *n.*	(1) labour, toil; suffering, trouble; labor of child-birth
trauerse *v.*	(15) to move from side to side
tread *v.*	(5b) *to ~ under foot* to step with pressure so as to crush
trickt vp *ppl. adj.*	(b) artfully decked or adorned; dressed up
trifle *v. 1*	(5) to pass or spend (time) frivolously or idly; to waste (time)
triumphe, tryumphe *n.*	(4) a public festivity or joyful celebration; a spectacle or pageant; esp. a tournament
tromperesse *n.* (not in *OED*)	*fem.* of *tromper*: a deceiver, impostor, cheat
trothlesse *adj.*	(2) destitute of truth; false, mendacious; untrustworthy
troublesome *adj.*	(4) toilsome, laborious, difficult; tiresome, oppressive
troupe *n.*	(1b) a number of persons collected together; a party, a company, a band; s.v. *troop*
trunchion *n.*	(1b) a fragment of a spear or lance; a piece broken off from a spear
truth *n.*	(1a) the character of being true to a person, principle, cause, etc.; faithfulness, loyalty, constancy
tryed *ppl. adj.*	(2a) chosen, select, choice; excellent
tryumphe *v.*	(3) to be in a state of pomp or magnificence
***tune** *n.*	(5) frame of mind, temper, mood, disposition, humour
twaine *num.*	two, in two (parts)
twit *v.*	(1) to cast an imputation on

V

valewe *n.*	value
varlet *n.*	(2) a knave, rogue, rascal
vassaile *n.*	vassal
vauntage *n.*	(4b) an opportunity; a chance
verely *adv.*	(1) in truth, truly, really, actually
vertue *n.*	(6a) physical strength, force, or energy
villaynie *n.*	(2) treatment of a degrading or shameful nature as suffered or received by a person
visit *v.*	(9c) to examine medically
***vituperous** *adj.*	(2) shameful, discreditable, disgraceful, ignominious
vnconstant *adj.*	inconstant
vnderstand *v.*	(11) to have knowledge or information, to learn, *of* something
vndiscreete *adj.*	indiscreet
vndiscretion *n.*	indiscretion

vndoone *ppl. adj. 2*	(1) ruined, destroyed
vnfained *adj.*	unfeigned
vngentlenesse *n.*	(1) lack of good manners; discourtesy
vnhappilie *adv.*	(3) mischievously, maliciously
vnmanlike *adj.*	(1) below the level of manly conduct toward others; brutally harsh or cruel; inhuman
vnpartiall *adj.*	(1a) impartial, unbiassed, fair
vnpossible *adj.*	impossible
vnprouided *ppl. adj.*	(1) not furnished or equipped (with something) (2) unprepared (to resist attack, make reply)
vnshamefastnesse *n.*	immodesty
vnweldie *adj.*	(1b) of age, etc.: characterized or attended by infirmity, weakness, or impotence
***voltage** *n. 1*	the action of causing a horse to move in voltes
vse *v.*	(18a) to treat or deal with a person in a specified manner
vttermost *adj.*	(7) *to the* ~ to the extreme degree, extent, capacity or limit; to death

W

waft *v. 1*	(2) to convey safely by water
wagge *n. 2*	(1) a mischievous boy (often as a mother's term of endearment to a baby boy); in wider application, a youth, young man, a "fellow," "chap"
waie *n.*	way
waight *n.*	weight
want *n. 2*	(2a) lack of something desirable or necessary
warder *n. 1*	(1) a soldier set to guard an entrance
weede *n. 2*	(2) clothing, raiment, dress, apparel (5) a garment, or garb, distinctive of a person's profession, state of life; e.g. *Pylgrims weede* (433.25–26)
weene *v.*	(1) to think, surmise, suppose, conceive, believe, consider
well-willer *n.*	one who wishes well to another
were *v.*	wear: (8b) to possess and enjoy as one's own; it may refer to a favor won in the tilt, or to a king's crown
whether *adv.*	whither
will, wyll *v. 1*	(1) to desire, wish for
wing *n.*	(7a) either of the two divisions on each side of the main body of an army
wish *v.*	(4b) to desire, or express a desire for, the welfare or misfortune of (a person)
wishly *adv.*	steadfastly, fixedly, intently
without *adv.*	(2a) outside (or out of) the place mentioned or implied; outdoors

withstand *v.*	(2d) to stand in the way of; to oppose or hinder the performance, operation, or progress of
witnesse *v.*	(1d) to give evidence of by one's behavior; to make evident
wont, woont *ppl.*	(1) used to, accustomed
woodman *n.* 1	(1) one who hunts game in a wood or forest; a huntsman
worke *v.*	(1) to do, perform
working *vbl. n.*	(4a) *in* ~: being worked upon, in operation, in use
worth *n.* 1	(P2) *to take in* ~: to take (something) at its true or proper value [*OED*3]
wot *pres. t. of* **wit** *v.*	(1) to have cognizance or knowledge of; to be aware of; to know
would *pa. t. of* **will** *v.*	to desire, wish for
wrack *n.* 1	(2) damage, disaster, or injury to a person, state, etc., by reason of force, outrage, or violence; devastation, destruction
writhen *ppl. adj.*	(1b) twisted out of regular shaper or form, of persons, their features, etc.
wunted *ppl. adj.*	accustomed, customary, usual

Y
yeelde *v.*	to yield

Index of Personal Names

Note: This index serves a double purpose. First and foremost, it provides quick identification of the characters in the romance, thus allowing readers to better follow the development of the narrative plot while avoiding frustrating confusions. Moreover, the index also includes the form of each of the names as given in the three versions Munday mentions on the title page of his translation, namely, French, Italian, and Spanish.[1] This latter information enables us to understand how Munday went about fixing the English names of the characters. The striking similarities between some English names and their Italian counterpart, as for instance *Urbanillo*, point to the following conclusion: while we have no doubt that Munday's translation follows closely Maugin's text, he must have been consulting simultaneously a copy of the Italian translation to accomplish efficiently such onomastic imitation. The numbers in parenthesis make reference to the chapter in which the name of a character is mentioned for the first time. Characters exclusively designated by alluding to their titles or place of origin (e.g., the Duke of Gaule) are not included in this list.

Abimar: king of Romata and Grisca (II.47); Fr. *Abimar*; It. *Abimarro*; Sp. *Abimar*

Adrian: prince, father of Dyardo, uncle of the king of Bohemia, of the empress of the Holy Roman Empire of the German Nation, and of Polinarda (I.24); Fr. *Adrian*; It. *Adriano*; Sp. *Adrián*

Agariell: King of France, Lewes's father (I.31); Fr. *Agariel*; It. *Agriello*; Sp. *Agriel*

Agriola: daughter to the king of England (I.35); Fr. *Agriole*; It. *Agriola*; Sp. *Agriola*

Alchidiana: Maulicus's daughter (II.4); Fr. *Archidiane*; It. *Alchidiana*; Sp. *Alchidiana*

Alfarano: admiral of Tharsus (II.19); Fr. *Alfaran*; It. *Alifarano*; Sp. *Alí Farán*

Alibarbanco: moorish pirate (II.64); Fr. *Alibarbanco*; It. *Alibarvanco*; Sp. *Alí Barbancho*

Amarano: son to the king of Phrygia (II.9); Fr. *Amaran*; It. *Amarano*; Sp. *Amarán*

Amenada: sister to Urbanillo (II.67); Fr. *Amenade*; Sp. *Menedala*; not in It.

Apolonio: an old knight from Hungary (II.33); Fr. *Apolon*; It. *Polo*; Sp. *Apolón*

---

[1] I copy the forms as they appear in the following editions: *Palmerin d'Olive* (Antwerp, 1572), *Palmerino d'Oliva* (Venice, 1544), and Claudia Demattè, *Palmerín de Olivia: Guía de Lectura,* Guías de Lectura Caballeresca 6 (Alcalá de Henares: Centro de Estudios Ceervantinos, 2004), 59–82.

ARDEMIA: Guilharan's sister and niece to the king of Armenia (II.4); Fr. *Ardemire*; It. *Ardemia*; Sp. *Ardemia*

ARISMENA: Florendos's sister (I.14); Fr. *Arismene*; It. *Arismena*; Sp. *Arismena*

ARMIDA: Griana's and Tarisius's daughter (II.26); Fr. *Hermide*; It. *Armida*; Sp. *Armida*

ASTOR: Duke of Durazzo (I.19); Fr. *Astor*; Sp. *Astor*; not in It.

AURECINDA: the Sultan of Persia's younger sister (II.53); Fr. *Aurencide*; It. *Aurecinda*; Sp. *Aurencida*

BELCAR: Frisol's and Armida's son (II.58); Fr. *Belcar*; It. *Belcarro*; Sp. *Belcar*

BELLECHINO: Muzabelino's son (II.52); Fr. *Bellequin*; It. *Bellichino*; Sp. *Belequín*

BELLIZA: daughter to Palmerin and Polinarda (II.67); Fr. *Bellicie*; Sp. *Pulicia*; not in It.

BELSINA: daughter to the sultan of Persia (II.52); Fr. *Belsine*; It. *Belsima*; Sp. *Belsima*

BRIONELLA: the Duke of Saxony's daughter and Polinarda's maid (I.27); Fr. *Brionnelle*; It. *Brionella*; Sp. *Brionela*

CALAMENO: king of Alexandria (I.2); Fr. *Calameno*; It. *Salameno*; Sp. *Çalameno*

CANIANO: Remicius' son (I.1); Fr. *Caniam*; It. *Caniano*; Sp. *Caniano*

CARDINA: Griana's maid and confidante (I.5); male counterpart: Fr. *Cardin*; It. *Cardino*; Sp. *Cardín*; cf. CARDINO

CARDINO: Cardina's brother (II.25); not in Fr., It., Sp.; cf. CARDINA

CARDONIA/CARDONYA: the Duke of Lorraine's sister and Dyardo's wife (I.24); Fr. *Cardoyne*; It. *Cardonia*; Sp. *Cardonia*

CARITEOS: Caniano's son (II.24); Fr. *Cariteos*; not in It. and Sp.

CERIDES: the king of England's nephew (I.48); Fr. *Cerides*; It. *Cerido*; Sp. *Cerides*

COLMELIO: Gerrard's and Marcella's son (I.10); Fr. *Colmelie*; It. *Colmelio*; Sp. *Colmelio*

CORAX: Tomano's nephew (II.55); Fr. *Corax*; It. *Gorace*; not in Sp.

CORMEDES: a German knight (I.29); Fr. *Cormedes*; It. *Cormede*; Sp. *Cormedes*

CRENUS: duke of Gaule (I.35); Fr. *Crenus*; It. *Ereno*; Sp. *Erenes*

CRISPINO: Esmerinda's fiancé (I.23); Fr. *Crespin*; It. *Crispano*; Sp. *Crispano*

DARMACO: giant, father of Mordano (I.22); Fr. *Darmaque*; It. *Damarco*; Sp. *Darmaco*

DENISA: Griana and Florendos's daughter (II.58); Fr. *Denise*; Sp. *Dionisea / Dionisia*; not in It.

DOMARTO: Count of Ormeque (I.24); It. *Dommarto*; Sp. *Domarco*

DONADEL: Prince of Siconia and allied of the Sultan of Persia (II.52); Fr. *Donadiel*; It. *Donadiello*; Sp. *Donadiel*

DRUMINO: son to King Abimar (II.47); Fr. *Drumin*; It. *Dormino*; Sp. *Dormín*

DULACCO: Muzabelino's brother (II.57); Fr. *Dulaque*; It. *Dulacco*; Sp. *Dulaque*

DURCELL: Count of Aragon (I.34); Fr. *Durcel*; It. *Rosello*; Sp. *Conde de Urxel*

DYARDO: Adrian's son (I.24); Fr. *Dyart*; It. *Diardo*; Sp. *Diardo*

DYOFENA: daughter to Gerrard and Marcella (I.12); Fr. *Dyofëne*; It. *Diofena*; Sp. *Diofena*

DYTRIUS: Frisol and Armida's son (II.58); Fr. *Ditreus*; Sp. *Ditreo*; not in It.

EDRON: one of Domarto's cousins (I.24); Fr. *Edron*; It. *Esdrone*; Sp. *Edrón*

EDWARD: one of Domarto's cousins (I.24); Fr. *Edouard*; not in It. and Sp.

ESMERINDA: girl kidnapped by Darmaco (I.22); Fr. *Esmerinde*; It. *Smerinda*; Sp. *Esmerinda*

ESTEBON: merchant from Macedonia saved from a lion by Palmerin (I.13); Fr. *Estebon*; It. *Estebono*; Sp. *Estebon*

EUFEMIA: daughter to the Duke of Norgalles (I.50); Fr. *Eufemye*; It. *Eufemia*; Sp. *Femia*

Index of Names

EUSTACE: son to the duke of Mecæna (II.40); Fr. *Eustrace*; It. *Estocchio*; Sp. *Estochio*
FLORENDOS: the king of Macedon's son (I.1); Fr. *Florendos*; It. *Florendo*; Sp. *Florendos*
FRANARCO: a giant (I.51); Fr. *Franarque*; It. *Franarco*; Sp. *Franarque*
FRANCELINA: the king of Thessaly's daughter (II.41); Fr. *Franceline*; It. *Francellina*; Sp. *Francelina*
FREDERICK: the king of England's son (I.50); Fr. *Falerique*; It. *Fedrigo*; Sp. *Fadrique*
FRENATO: Florendos's cousin (I.4); Fr. *Fresne*; It. *Frinatto*; Sp. *Frinato*
FRYSOL: Netrydes' son (I.40); Fr. *Frisol*; It. *Frisolo*; Sp. *Frisol*
GAMEZIO: the sultan of Babylon's son (I.2); Fr. *Gamezio*; It. *Guamizziro*; Sp. *Guamezir*
GANARENO: nephew to the German emperor (I.28); Fr. *Gauaran*; It. *Ganareno*; Sp. *Ganarén*
GERRARD: Palmerin's foster father (I.10); Fr. *Gerard*; It. *Geraldo*; Sp. *Geraldo*
GRAMIEL: one of Amarano's brothers (II.13); Fr. *Gramiel*; It. *Gravuello*; Sp. *Gravuel*
GRIANA: Remicius' daughter (I.1); Fr. *Griane*; It. *Griana*; Sp. *Griana*
GUERESIN: son to the king of Balisarca (II.18); Fr. *Gueresin*; It. *Guerisino*; Sp. *Gueresín*
GUILHARAN: Alchidiana's cousin and nephew to the king of Armenia (II.4); Fr. *Guilharan*; Sp. *Guilarán*
HERMES: commissioner for the king of England (I.54); Fr. *Hermes*; It. *Hermes*; Sp. *Ermes*
HIPPOLITA: daughter of a Sicilian merchant and captive of the Great Turk (II.1); Fr. *Ypolite*; It. *Hippolita*; Sp. *Ipólita / Pólita*
LAURANA: Duke Astor's daughter (I.19); Fr. *Laurene*; It. *Laurena*; Sp. *Laurena*
LEONARDA: daughter of a rich man from Hungary (I.41); Fr. *Leonarde*; It. *Leonarda*; Sp. *Leonarda*
LERINA: Cardina's sister (I.6); Fr. *Lerine*; It. *Lerina*; Sp. *Lerina*
LETHEA: the Soldan's wife (II.7); Fr. *Lethea*; not in It. and Sp.
LEWES: son to the King of France (I.31); Fr. *Loys*; It. *Luimane*; Sp. *Luymanes*
LINUS: servant to the Soldan of Babilone (II.5); Fr. *Linus*; It. *Livaello*; Sp. *Livael*
LOMBARDO: Netrides's father-in-law (I.40); Fr. *Lombard*; It. *Lombardo*; Sp. *Lombardo*
LUCEMANIA: Lewes's sister (I.32); Fr. *Lucque*; It. *Lucemania*; Sp. *Lucemana*
LYCADO: nephew to Olimael (II.65); Fr. *Libcade*; It. *Liccado*; Sp. *Lidcate*
LYCOMEDES: father of Maurice's wife (II.6); Fr. *Olicomed*; It. *Licomede*; Sp. *Olicomed*
LYOMENUS: one of Florendos's squires (I.11); Fr. *Lyomenus*; It. *Liomene*; Sp. *Liomeno*
LYZANDA: the Sultan of Persia's elder sister (II.53); Fr. *Lizande*; It. *Leggiadra*; Sp. *Liçadra*
MALFADA: enchantress who dwells in the magic island of Malfada (I.65); Fr. *Malfade*; It. *Malfato*; Sp. *Malfada*
MARCELLA: Palmerin's foster mother (I.10); Fr. *Marcelle*; It. *Marcella*; Sp. *Marcela*
MAUCETTO: ambassador of the Sultan of Babilone (II.46); Fr. *Maucette*; It. *Maucetto*; Sp. *Maucete*
MAULERINO: Zephira's younger brother (II.42); Fr. *Maulerin*; It. *Maulerino*; Sp. *Maulerín*
MAULICUS: Gamezio's brother and Soldan of Babilone (II.4); Fr. *Maulicus*; It. *Maulecco*; Sp. *Maulequí*
MAURICE: prince of Pasmeria (II.6); Fr. *Mauorix*; It. *Manarisso*; Sp. *Manarix*

MELICIA: daughter to Frisol and Armida (II.67); Fr. *Melicie*; Sp. *Melisa*; not in It.
MENADENO: Lycado's brother (II.65); Fr. *Menaden*; It. *Menadeno*; Sp. *Menadén*
MENADUS: a knight from the German Emperor's court (I.29); Fr. *Menadus*; Sp. *Mesnades*; not in It.
MISERES, MYSERES: a knight of the king of England's court (I.53); Fr. *Miseres*; It. *Misero*; Sp. *Miseres, Misseres*
MISOS: Gamezio's father (II.4); Fr. *Misos*; not in It. and Sp.
MORDANO: giant, son of Darmaco (I.22); Fr. *Mardane*; It. *Mordaneo*; Sp. *Murdaneo*
MUZABELINO: wiseman from the court of Romata and Grisca in Persia (II.42); Fr. *Mussabelin*; It. *Muçabelino*; Sp. *Muça Belín*
MYSOS: Soldan of Babilone (II.4); Fr. *Misos*; not in It. and Sp.
NARDIDES: son to the Duchess of Ormeda and nephew to Tarisius (II.65); Fr. *Nardides*; It. *Nardito*; Sp. *Nardides*
NETRIDES: Tarisius' brother (I.40); Fr. *Netrides*; It. *Netrido*; Sp. *Netrido*
OLIMAEL: Turkish pirate (I.65); Fr. *Olimael*; It. *Olimaello*; Sp. *Olimael*
OLORICO: eldest son to the king of Arabia (II.16); Fr. *Olorique*; It. *Olorico*; Sp. *Olorique*
ORINELLO: one of Amaran's brothers (II.18); Fr. *Orinel*; It. *Orinello*; Sp. *Orinel*
ORONIA: daughter to the calif of Siconia and Donadell's sister (II.54); Fr. *Oronie*; Sp. *Oredina*
ORZODINE: king of Galappa (II.54); Fr. *Orzodin*; It. *Orodino*; Sp. *Orozdín*
OUDIN: son to the Duchess of Ormeda and nephew to Tarisius (II.24); Fr. *Oudin*; It. *Ordino*; Sp. *Ordín*
PALMENDOS: son to Palmerin and the queen of Tharsus (II.20); Fr. *Palmendos*; It. *Polendo*; Sp. *Polendus*

PALMERIN: son to Griana and Florendos (I.10); Fr. *Palmerin*; It. *Palmerino*; Sp. *Palmerín*
PASSACO: Count of Messina, Sicily (I.19); Fr. *Passaco*; It. *Passaccarro*; Sp. *Passacar*
PHILOCRISTA: daughter to Olorico and Alchidiana (II.67); Fr. *Philocriste*; Sp. *Esquivella*; not in It.
POLIDIA: daughter to the king of Armenia and Alchidiana's aunt (II.4); Fr. *Polidia*; not in It. and Sp.
POLINARDA/POLYNARDA: daughter to the German emperor, Adrian's niece, Trineus' sister (I.16); Fr. *Polinarde*; It. *Polinarda*; Sp. *Polinarda*
PRIMALEON: king of Macedon and father of Florendos (I.14); Fr. *Primaleon*; It. *Pigmaleone*; Sp. *Primaleón*
PROMPTALEON: son to the Duchess of Ormeda and nephew to Tarisius (II.24); Fr. *Promptaleon*; It. *Prontaleone*; Sp. *Prontaleo* or *Ponteleo*
PTOLOME: Frenato's son (I.19); Fr. *Ptolome*; It. *Tolomeo*; Sp. *Tolomé*
RECINDE: king of Spain (II.60); Fr. *Rescinde* (the king of Spain's daughter); Sp. *Recindos*; not in It.
REMICIUS: eighth emperor of Constatinople, father of Caniano and Griana (I.1); Fr. *Remycius*; It. *Remigio*; Sp. *Reymicio*
RISDENO: son to Urbanillo (II.67); Fr. *Risdene*; It. *Rideno*; Sp. *Risdeno*
ROLDIN: a count that becomes lieutenant of Macedon after the death of Primaleon (II.40); Fr. *Roldin*; It. *Roldino*; Sp. *Roldín*
RYFARANO: Trineus's son with Aurecinda (II.56); Fr. *Rifaran*; Sp. *Rifarán*; not in It.
SABINDA: niece to the queen of England and the Duke of Mecæna's wife (II.61); Fr. *Sabinde*; Sp. *Sabrinda*; not in It.
SCLOTO: enchanted, evil knight who kidnaps a maiden (I.55); Fr. *Sclote*,

Index of Names 883

Esclote; It. *Escloto*; Sp. *Esclote* or *Eclotre*.
S<small>ERGILLO</small>: son to Cardino (II.64); Fr. *Sergil*; It. *Sergino*; Sp. *Seregín*
T<small>ARISIUS</small>: the king of Hungary's son (I.1); Fr. *Tarisius*; It. *Tarisio*; Sp. *Tarisio*
T<small>IRENDOS</small>: son to the Duke Eustace (II.67); Fr. *Tirendus*; It. *Tirendo*; Sp. *Tirendo*
T<small>OLANO</small>: general of the emperor's army (I.44); Fr. *Conte de Tolan*; It. *Tolano*; Sp. *Conde de Tolanque*
T<small>OLOMESTRA</small>: gentlewoman in charge of Griana while she is imprisoned in tower (I.7); Fr. *Ptolomestre*; It. *Tolomestra*; Sp. *Tolomestra*
T<small>OMANO</small>: son to King Abimar (II.47); Fr. *Toman*; It. *Tomano*; Sp. *Tomán*
T<small>RINEUS</small>: son to the German emperor and Polinarda's brother (I.25); Fr. *Trineus*; It. *Trineo*; Sp. *Trineo*

T<small>YRENO</small>, T<small>IRENO</small>: Zephira's older brother (II.42); Fr. *Tirene*; It. *Tireno*; Sp. *Tireno*
V<small>ALERICA</small>: damsel from England who rejects Varnan's love (I.56); Fr. *Valerique*; It. *Valerica*; Sp. *Valerica*
V<small>ARNAN</small>: knight from England found in a cave by Palmerin (I.56); Fr. *Varnan*; It. *Varuano*; Sp. *Varván* or *Barván*
V<small>RBANILLO</small>: dwarff attending on Palmerin as his squier (I.14); Fr. *Urbande*; It. *Vrbanillo*; Sp. *Urbanil*
Z<small>EPHIRA</small>: daughter to Onodius, king of Nabor and wife of the Soldan of Persia (II.42); Fr. *Zerphire*; It. *Zerfira*; Sp. *Zerfira*

Addendum

Late in 2017, when the present critical edition was already in production, it came to my notice that fragments belonging to a copy of *Palmerin d'Oliva* had been identified in the special collections library of Christ Church, Oxford. The fragments, shelfmarked P.163*, are from two leaves corresponding to signatures B1 and B8 of *Palmerin d'Oliva I* and were used as endleaves in a copy of volume two of Cicero's *Orationes* (London: Richard Field, 1618; STC 5310.5) held in the same library (shelfmark P.163).

I have been unable to consult these fragments directly, but have instead obtained photographic reproductions from which the following textual information derives. The text contained and recoverable from these fragments corresponds to the following sections in the present critical edition: 109.14–15; 109.22–23; 110.2–3; 110.9–11; 119.42–120.10; 120.12–17; 120.18–27; 120.28–121.3; 121.8–15. The textual variants found (see below) indicate that these textual remnants come from a separate edition, heretofore unknown to us, that must have been produced after 1597 and before 1615. The ESTC (citation no. S506036) tentatively dates it to ca. 1600 and assigns it to the printers Thomas Creede and Bernard Alsop, though it is unlikely that the latter was involved in printing this edition in 1600, since his printing career did not get started until 1615.[1]

Here below I provide the substantive variants contained in the newly found fragments. The lemmatic reading is that of the critical edition, whereas the stemmatic one refers to the Christ Church fragments.

109.14 discerned] discouered
109.14 But] and
110.2 ought] ought to
110.3 it I] it that I
120.19 thereof] therefore
121.14 by] *om.*

---

[1] See Jordi Sánchez-Martí, "The Publication History of Anthony Munday's *Palmerin d'Oliva*," *Gutenberg-Jahrbuch* 89 (2014): 201 n. 42. I want to acknowledge the contribution of Elizabeth Ward Ramos, a former research assistant, who alerted me to the discovery of these fragments. For a full description and discussion of these fragments, see my note "A Newly Discovered Edition of the English *Palmerin d'Oliva*," *The Library*, forthcoming in 2020.